Ontario Public Service Employment & Labour Law

SECOND EDITION

Ontario Public Service Employment & Labour Law

SECOND EDITION

Timothy Hadwen & David Strang

IRWIN LAW

Ontario Public Service Employment and Labour Law, second edition

Published in 2024 by
Irwin Law Inc
Suite 206, 14 Duncan Street
Toronto, Ontario M5H 3G8
www.irwinlaw.com

Cover image: Adobe Stock (vejaa)

ISBN 978-1-55221-693-4 (print) | 978-1-55221-694-1 (PDF)

Library and Archives Canada Cataloguing in Publication

Title: Ontario public service employment & labour law / Timothy Hadwen & David Strang.
Names: Hadwen, Timothy. author. | Strang, David (Retired lawyer), author.
Description: Second edition. | Includes bibliographical references and index.
Identifiers: Canadiana (print) 20230548687 | Canadiana (ebook) 20230548725 | ISBN 9781552216934 (softcover) | ISBN 9781552216941 (PDF)
Subjects: LCSH: Employee-management relations in government—Law and legislation—Ontario. | LCSH: Collective labor agreements—Government employees—Ontario. | LCSH: Civil service—Ontario. | LCSH: Labor laws and legislation—Ontario.
Classification: LCC KEO647.P4 H33 2023 | DDC 342.713/068—dc23

Canada

ONTARIO CREATES | ONTARIO CRÉATIF

Printed and bound by CPI Group (UK) Ltd, Croydon, CR0 4YY

1 2 3 4 5 28 27 26 25 24

To my family: my wife, Alison Colvin; my sons, David and Jacob; my daughter-in-law, Mina Lee; and my grandson, Calvin. They have unstintingly given me the precious gifts of encouragement and time, for which I am very grateful. I hope my grandchild always lives in a jurisdiction with a strong public service committed to the public interest.

—TIM HADWEN

To my wife Patricia Galloway, who has tolerated my fixation with labour law all these many years with a smile; my son, Ian; and daughter, Caroline; all three of whom are or have been active in their unions.

—DAVID STRANG

Summary Table of Contents

Detailed Table of Contents

CHAPTER TWO

CHAPTER TEN

Key Aspects of the OPSEU/MBC Collective Agreements, as Interpreted by the GSB 635

CHAPTER TWELVE

Acknowledgments

There is a community of dedicated and thoughtful people concerned with the employment and labour law governing Ontario's public service and designated Crown agencies. It is our hope that this book will be useful to them. Quite a few members of this community have contributed in one way or another, and the authors are very grateful to them.

This is a second edition. While it has been substantially rewritten, there is still a huge debt owed to the legion of people previously acknowledged. We thank all of them again.

In this edition, several people were prepared to invest some of their considerable expertise in much appreciated written contributions on particular topics: Cynthia Crysler of Cavalluzzo LLP (OPS pensions); Katherine Ferreria of Koskie Minsky LLP (occupational health and safety); Ian Roland of Paliare Roland Rosenberg Rothstein LLP (Ontario Provincial Police); and Cameron Walker, retired Senior Negotiator, Ontario Public Service Employees Union (job security under the OPSEU/MBC collective agreements).

Among others, the following people helped in other valuable ways, including, in some cases, providing very helpful comments on part of the manuscript:

- Kevin Banks
- Tim Bartkiw
- Sara Blake
- Paul Cavalluzzo
- Ian Colvin

- Peter Dailleboust
- Don Eady
- Sandra Girard
- Murray Gold
- Robin Gordon
- Sandra Harper
- Len Hatzis
- Bram Herlich
- Henry Huang
- Sarah Kraicer
- Howard Law
- Legislative Assembly Library staff
- Archana Mathew
- Eric O'Brien
- Lisa Park
- Amanda Pask
- Frank Rooney
- Joel Schwartz
- Susan Stewart, former Chair of the Grievance Settlement Board
- The Office of the Integrity Commissioner

We are grateful to Brian Smeenk, Chair of the Public Service Grievance Board (PSGB) and Matt Wilson, Chair of the Grievance Settlement Board (GSB), for graciously providing comments.

John Wilkinson, a student at the Queen's University Faculty of Law, did a really good literature search for us.

Many thanks to Christine Callier, Registrar, and the staff of the Public Service Appeal Boards (GSB and PSGB) for their ongoing support, including answering numerous inquiries and retrieving material from their records. The reference librarians and staff of the Great Library, Osgoode Hall have been helpful.

We wish to thank Lesley Steeve, Jeff Miller, and the team at Irwin Law, in addition to our editors Laura Ellyson and Leanne Rancourt, for all their support, attention, and care.

The authors engaged in a good deal of debate about some of the content of this book, and the result is a joint effort to accurately state the Ontario law as of 31 December 2022. Tim Hadwen was the originator and project manager. He had primary responsibility for chapters 1, 4 (other than Pay Equity), 5, 6, 7, 8, 10, 11, and sections D2 to end of Chapter 2. David Strang had primary responsibility for chapters 3, 4 (on Pay Equity), 9, 12, 13, and sections A to D1 of Chapter 2.

Any errors or omissions are the responsibility of the authors, not the contributors or commentators. The views expressed in this book are ultimately those of the authors only.

Introduction

To regulate and structure public service employment, the Ontario government has enacted two particular employment and labour statutes, the *Public Service of Ontario Act, 2006* (*PSOA*)[1] and the *Crown Employees Collective Bargaining Act, 1993* (*CECBA*),[2] and modified how other acts apply.

Chapter 1 reviews the rationale for and history of the special regulation of public service employment in Ontario. There is some discussion of public administration literature.

Chapter 2 sets out the structure and application of the *PSOA*, reviews managerial authority over the public service, including the role of the Management Board of Cabinet (MBC), and then describes the *PSOA* employment provisions applying to government employees appointed under *PSOA* Part III.

Chapter 3 sets out the *PSOA* ethical framework—the oaths, duty of loyalty, conflict of interest provisions, political activity rules, and disclosure of wrongdoing provisions—that is applicable to all public servants: those employed in government as well as those at designated agencies.

Chapter 4 deals with special classes of government public servants: employee office holders, professionals (doctors, dentists, and lawyers), the Ontario Provincial Police, and a small anomalous group, Provincial Schools Authority teachers.

---

1 SO 2006, c 35, Sch A.

2 SO 1993, c 38.

Chapter 5 considers individuals with legislatively or constitutionally mandated roles who are not employed as public servants: the Lieutenant Governor, members of the Legislative Assembly, employees of the Legislative Assembly and its offices, provincial judges and justices of the peace, and order-in-council appointees. Their special regimes, including ethical frameworks, are examined.

Chapter 6 deals with general employment-related legislation applicable to the Crown. The chapter reviews the unique treatment of the Crown under the provincial *Employment Standards Act, 2000*,[3] *Freedom of Information and Protection of Privacy Act*,[4] *Human Rights Code* (*HRC*),[5] *Occupational Health and Safety Act* (*OHSA*),[6] *Pay Equity Act*,[7] *Workplace Safety and Insurance Act, 1997*,[8] and pension legislation, as well as federal benefits legislation. (The *HRC* and *OHSA* sections include discussion of caselaw from all the tribunals involved.) The chapter also references the *Canadian Charter of Rights and Freedoms*.[9]

Chapter 7 sets out the structure of the *CECBA* and its scope, including specific exclusions from its coverage. The *CECBA*'s government bargaining parties and their representational jurisdictions, along with some of their history, are described, including the jurisdictional disputes between unions. The unusual Ontario Public Service Employees Union (OPSEU) "carriage rights" policy is also discussed.

Chapter 8 reviews *CECBA* interest dispute resolution (that is, the negotiation and settlement of the terms and conditions of employment not prescribed by statute or regulation), focusing on strikes by government employees. While the *CECBA* makes the *Labour Relations Act, 1995*[10] strike/lockout regime generally applicable, an extensive essential services requirement is added. The only other Ontario essential services strike/lockout regime, the *Ambulance Services Collective Bargaining Act, 2001*,[11] is also described. Picketing of government premises, return to work protocols, and illegal strikes are covered. The exceptional case

3 SO 2000, c 41.
4 RSO 1990, c F.31.
5 RSO 1990, c H.19.
6 RSO 1990, c O.1.
7 RSO 1990, c P.7.
8 SO 1997, c 16, Sched A.
9 *Constitution Act, 1982*, being Schedule B to the *Canada Act 1982* (UK), 1982, c 11.
10 SO 1995, c 1, Sch A.
11 SO 2001, c 10.

of interest arbitration for the government's corrections bargaining unit is explained. There is a section on return to work and wage restraint legislation.

Chapter 9 deals with the legal framework governing the transformation of government employment through transfers and downsizing. This includes the non-applicability of related employer provisions, the application of the *Public Sector Labour Relations Transition Act, 1997 (PSLRTA)*,[12] and statutory successorship under special purpose statutes. Negotiated transfer agreements are also described. Finally, there is a review of the OPSEU/MBC collective agreement provisions:

1) requiring the employer to make "reasonable efforts" to obtain similar employment for divested employees; and
2) establishing job security entitlements for transferred and laid off employees.

Chapter 10 sets out key aspects of the OPSEU/MBC collective agreements, as interpreted by the Grievance Settlement Board (GSB), that are not covered elsewhere: reasonable exercise of management rights, "contracting in," job competitions, conversion of fixed-term to regular employment, the rights of seasonal employees, and just cause for discipline and dismissal relating to general conduct expectations.

Where a legal dispute arises concerning individual employment in government or a designated Crown agency, the dispute resolution mechanism depends on the status of the employee. Presumptively, disputes proceed as follows:

- unionized employees → union files grievance → GSB
- non-unionized public servants → individual files grievance → Public Service Grievance Board (PSGB)
- employees of the government who are not public servants (including order-in-council appointments), and non-unionized employees of designated Crown agencies → individual seeks redress from Ontario courts (by lawsuit or judicial review)

Each mechanism is subject to exceptions and exclusions. The unique jurisprudence that has developed through their use is discussed in the remaining chapters of the book. Chapter 11 reviews the jurisdiction, administration, procedure, and remedial authority of the GSB. The

12 SO 1997, c 21, Sch B.

PSGB's jurisdiction, complaint process, caselaw, and practice and procedure are addressed in Chapter 12. Chapter 13 reviews direct access to the courts for employment claims through lawsuits and judicial review.

CHAPTER ONE

Context for the *PSOA* and *CECBA*

A. INTRODUCTION: DIFFERENCES AND THE PUBLIC INTEREST JUSTIFICATION

The context for the *Public Service of Ontario Act, 2006* (*PSOA*)[1] and the *Crown Employees Collective Bargaining Act, 1993* (*CECBA*)[2] needs to be approached with a note of caution and a sense of inquiry.

Some caution is needed because, until relatively recently, there was a presumption of the validity of the exercise of Crown employer authority or executive sovereignty, counterbalanced by judicial striving to articulate checks on that sovereignty. Now, many of the prerogatives and immunities of the Crown that used to dominate the government's legal relationship with its citizens and employees have, by statutory change or the evolution of the common law, disappeared.[3] The common law of employment largely now applies to government as it does to other employers.[4]

---

1 SO 2006, c 35, Sch A [*PSOA*].

2 SO 1993, c 38 [*CECBA*].

3 See, generally, *Ross River Dena Council Band v Canada*, 2002 SCC 54 at para 54 and, in the employment context, *Dunsmuir v New Brunswick*, 2008 SCC 9, as discussed in Chapter 13.

4 *OPSEU (DeFreitas) and Ministry of Environment and Energy*, PSGB#0007/94, 28 May 1998 (Lynk) at 56–57. See also *Thomson v Canada (Minister of Agriculture)*, [1992] 1 SCR 385 at para 19.

Turning to inquiry, Ontario, like all other Canadian provinces and the federal government,[5] has tailored legislation in place for employment in its public service and for collective bargaining with Crown employees. How did this legislation come to be in its current form? Tradition, aspirational political leadership, employee and union voice, "deal making" through the political process, and collective bargaining, as well as expediency, have all played their part, as outlined below and referenced in the subsequent chapters of this book.

How is this legislation to be evaluated? Ontario's private sector employment and labour law—mainly set out in the common law, the *Employment Standards Act, 2000*,[6] and the *Labour Relations Act, 1995 (LRA)*[7]—establishes the generic benchmark for how the province regulates employment and labour relations. It has been usefully suggested that

> [t]he individual employment and collective bargaining regimes governing the public service should be the same regime in effect for other employees unless the difference is justifiable in the public interest.[8]

The leading justifications for the differences found in Ontario Crown employment and labour law are:

- the maintenance of a non-partisan and impartial public service
- ensuring that government and designated Crown agency collective bargaining does not unduly disrupt the public service or the provision of public services

Those justifications and their history are reviewed in this chapter.

---

5 Saskatchewan was the last province to adopt this approach. Since 1944, it had included its own employees under the general labour legislation: *The Trade Union Act*, RSS 1978, c T-17, s 2(g). In 2008, the *Public Service Essential Services Act*, SS 2008, c P-42.2 introduced an essential services regime for the Saskatchewan public sector, including government employees. For other provinces, see John E. Hodgetts & Onkar I. Dwivedi, *Provincial Governments as Employers: A Survey of Public Personnel Administration in Canada's Provinces* (Toronto: Institute of Public Administration of Canada, 1974). For the federal experience, see Advisory Committee on Labour Management Relations in the Federal Public Service, *Identifying the Issues: First Report* (Ottawa: The Committee, 2000), online: www.fryercommittee.com at 17–30.

6 SO 2000, c 41.

7 SO 1995, c 1, Sch A.

8 Donald Carter, "Legal Regulation of Collective Bargaining in the Ontario Public Sector" (1974) 29:4 *Relations Industrielles/Industrial Relations* 776 at 778 [Carter].

Over time, there have been varying views on whether special employment and labour legislation for Crown employees can be justified. At a time of greater commonality of view, in 1962, it was said:

> There is, to be sure, substantial agreement that public employment differs from private employment; and this in turn suggests there should be differences in their procedures of staff relations.[9]

More recently, a different view has been expressed:

> The special statutes that segregate provincial employees and make them easy targets for discriminatory treatment need to be repealed. Their historical relevance is just that—historical.[10]

The view of the authors of this book is that, while Ontario's public service employment and labour law framework does not always meet the standards it claims to promote, it is justified in the public interest because it effectively serves valuable public purposes.

B. *PUBLIC SERVICE OF ONTARIO ACT*

The *PSOA*'s core stated purposes are to ensure that the public service of Ontario is effective, "non-partisan, professional, ethical, and competent," and to set out roles and responsibilities in its administration.[11]

The Act addresses these topics directly in its parts. Positive attributes are addressed through sections on oaths of office and allegiance (sections 5–7), and parts on rules for ethical conduct, political activity, and processes for disclosing wrongdoing (Parts IV, V, and VI). Governance

---

9 Saul J. Frankel, *Staff Relations in the Civil Service: The Canadian Experience* (Montreal: McGill University Press, 1962) at 318.

10 John L. Fryer, "Provincial Public Service Labour Relations" in Gene Swimmer & Mark Thompson, eds, *Public Sector Collective Bargaining in Canada* (Kingston: IRC Press, 1995) at 341.

11 *PSOA*, above note 1, s 1, 1–3. These subsume the remaining purposes listed in s 1, 4–7, which are to provide a framework for leadership and management, to set out rights and duties concerning ethical conduct and political activity, and to establish procedures for disclosure of wrongdoing and whistleblowing. On introduction of the bill, the Minister of Government Services, the Honourable Gerry Phillips said "[t]he legislation includes a new statement of purpose, which I frankly think is important. I think it will foster a greater common understanding of the role of this fundamental democratic institution that we call our public service.": Ontario Legislative Assembly, *Hansard*, 15 November 2006 at 1610.

and management are addressed through a part on roles and responsibilities in administration (Part II). However, the Act has one additional substantive part, not directly referenced in the stated purposes, which establishes terms and conditions of employment by the Crown. Part III is specific and detailed (for example, dealing with the maximum length of a probationary period[12]). It is important to understand why this part is present in the Act.

The positive attributes of the public service intended to be fostered by the Act are more likely to be realized when public servants are individually employed on terms that support personal adoption and maintenance of those attributes. Furthermore, fostering staff adherence to public service standards is a central role and responsibility of public servants engaged in management. The legislative history makes it clear it has always been intended that the core values of Ontario's public service are to be nurtured by supportive terms of employment and by a management structure that will ensure the public service is both directed by the elected executive and seized with the responsibility to uphold the Act's ethical and human resources standards.

1) Constitutional Context

The preamble of the *Constitution Act, 1867* expresses the desire to give Canada "a Constitution similar in Principle to that of the United Kingdom."[13] Canada and its provinces are Westminster-model parliamentary democracies:[14]

> Our political system is based on the Westminster model of parliament, a cabinet government with its accompanying constitutional conventions of ministerial responsibility, political neutrality, and public service anonymity. These conventions provide the basis for relations between politicians and public servants and between government officials and the public.[15]

---

12 See the discussion in Chapter 2.

13 *Constitution Act, 1867* (UK), 30 & 31 Vict, c 3, Preamble reprinted in RSC 1985, App III, No. 5 [*Constitution Act*].

14 *Figueroa v Canada (Attorney General)*, 2003 SCC 37 at para 82; *Chagnon v Syndicat de la fonction publique et parapublique du Québec*, 2018 SCC 39 at para 1.

15 *Valcourt v Tyler*, 1996 CanLII 18644 (NB QB) at para 3.

In particular, the constitutional convention of "an impartial and effective public service" is "one of the most honourable traditions of our public life."[16]

The legislative origin of Ontario's public service is found in section 134 of the *Constitution Act*, which states in part:

> Until the Legislature of Ontario or of Quebec otherwise provides, the Lieutenant Governors of Ontario and Quebec may each appoint under the Great Seal of the Province the following Officers, to hold office during pleasure, that is to say,—the Attorney General, the Secretary and Registrar of the Province, the Treasurer of the Province, the Commissioner of Crown Lands, and the Commissioner of Agriculture and Public Works, … and may, by Order of the Lieutenant Governor in Council, from Time to Time prescribe the Duties of those Officers, and of the several Departments over which they shall preside or to which they shall belong, and of the Officers and Clerks thereof, and may also appoint other and additional Officers to hold Office during Pleasure, and may from Time to Time prescribe the Duties of those Officers, and of the several Departments over which they shall preside or to which they shall belong, and of the Officers and Clerks thereof.

Section 92 of the Act grants the following powers to the provinces:

> In each Province the Legislature may exclusively make Laws in relation to Matters coming within the Classes of Subject next herein-after enumerated that is to say,—
>
> 1. The Amendment from Time to Time, notwithstanding anything in this Act, of the Constitution of the Province, except as regards the Office of Lieutenant Governor. …
> 4. The Establishment and Tenure of Provincial Offices and the Appointment and Payment of Provincial Officers. …
> 13. Property and Civil Rights in the Province.

In *Ontario (Attorney General) v OPSEU*,[17] the Supreme Court addressed how section 92 empowers Ontario government oversight of its public service. Section 92(4), dealing with the establishment of

---

16 *Fraser v PSSRB*, [1985] 2 SCR 455 at 470 & 471, Dickson J quoting the MacDonnell Committee [*Fraser*]. For interest concerning the United States, see *United Public Workers of America v Mitchell*, 67 S Ct 556 (1947) at 580, Douglas J.

17 [1987] 2 SCR 2 [*Ontario v OPSEU*].

"provincial offices," authorizes the regulation of the structure of the public service. The section 92(13) power over "Property and Civil Rights in the Province," which includes regulation of employment in the private sector, also includes regulation of employment within the public service.

In the same decision, the public service was found to be an "organ of government," required to function in accordance with the principle of impartiality.[18] The majority held that an Act dealing with this core value of the public service amends the "constitution of Ontario" and as such can only do so in accordance with the requirements of that constitution. The Supreme Court has since commented that "constitutional conventions" are "not enforceable in a court of law unless they are incorporated into legislation,"[19] and certainly can be subject to both statutory amendments and review under the *Canadian Charter of Rights and Freedoms* (the *Charter*).[20]

In any case, the *OPSEU* decision and later cases have consistently recognized "the existence of a convention of political neutrality, central to the principle of responsible government":[21]

> Clearly there was a convention of political neutrality of Crown servants at the time of Confederation and the reasoning in support of such convention has been consistent throughout the subsequent years.[22]

Cabinet solidarity, ministerial responsibility, and unwritten constitutional conventions, including the impartiality of the public service, are a major part of Canada's and Ontario's machinery of government. The conventions have been defined as "a binding rule, a rule of behaviour accepted as obligatory by those concerned in the working of the

---

18 *Ibid* at para 93.

19 See *Osborne v Canada (Treasury Board)*, [1991] 2 SCR 69 at 87 [*Osborne*]; *Toronto (City) v Ontario (Attorney General)*, 2021 SCC 34 at para 56 [*Toronto (City)*]. See also *Martin v Ontario*, [2004] OJ No 2247 (SCJ) at paras 27–29 concerning an allegation that a constitutional convention was violated by the location of the budget speech.

20 *Canadian Charter of Rights and Freedoms*, Part I of the *Constitution Act, 1982*, being Schedule B to the *Canada Act 1982* (UK), 1982, c 11. See also *Osborne*, above note 19 at 88.

21 *Osborne*, above note 19 at 86.

22 *Ontario v OPSEU*, above note 17 at 44, citing MacKinnon ACJO.

constitution."[23] They form the legitimate basis for criticism of legislation or management actions that violate those conventions.

The current *PSOA* reinforces the convention of impartiality of the public service through its stated purposes[24] and three specific provisions:

1. Deputy ministers are to promote effective, non-partisan, professional, ethical, and competent public service by public servants.[25]
2. The Public Service Commission shall "ensure by directive that the recruitment and employment of public servants appointed by it are non-partisan."[26]
3. The Management Board of Cabinet (MBC) shall not set a policy or issue a directive "that would be inconsistent with the non-partisan nature of the public service of Ontario."[27]

It seems this incorporation of the convention of impartiality into the legislation also now makes this convention judicially enforceable, although to what extent is yet to be determined.

2) Intended Functions and Positive Attributes

In public administration terms:[28]

---

23 Sir Kenneth Wheare, *Modern Constitutions* (Oxford: Oxford University Press, 1951) at 179, as cited in Donald J. Savoie, "The Canadian Public Service Has a Personality" 2006 49:3 *Canadian Public Administration* 261. See also Geoffrey Marshall, *Constitutional Conventions: The Rules and Forms of Political Accountability* (Oxford: Clarendon Press, 2001); Andrea Heard, *Canadian Constitutional Conventions: The Marriage of Law and Politics* (Toronto: Oxford University Press, 1991); Lorne Sossin, "Defining Boundaries: The Constitutional Argument for Bureaucratic Independence and Its Implications for the Accountability of the Public Service" in *Research Studies*, Vol 2 (Ottawa: Commission of Inquiry into the Sponsorship Program and Advertising Activities [*Gomery Inquiry*], 2006), online: http//ssrn.com/abstract=1911245, at 27, 65, and 43. See also *Toronto (City)*, above note 19 at para 56.

24 *PSOA*, above note 1, s 1.

25 *Ibid*, s 29(3).

26 *Ibid*, s 43(2).

27 *Ibid*, s 43(4).

28 The discussion in the public service section of this chapter is indebted to the extensive Canadian public administration literature on the public service, highlights of which are listed in the bibliography. See especially Canada, Task Force on Public Service Values and Ethics (John Tait, Chair), *A Strong Foundation: Report of the Task Force on Public Service Values and Ethics* (Ottawa: Canadian Centre for Management Development, February 2000) [Tait] and Joseph Heath,

> The Ontario government is not a business. It is the embodiment of the collective will of the Ontario people, with responsibility for such public goods as justice, equity, order, prosperity, health and social well-being. In order to achieve these goals, the OPS [Ontario Public Service] must not only function effectively as an organization, its staff must be imbued with uncommon dedication and commitment not just to customer service but to public service.[29]

In Ontario's political system, as in the rest of Canada, the elected government is a small group of politicians. Those politicians and their aides have a very limited ability to administer the province on their own. To be truly effective, they need a "standing army" of public servants ready to take direction. But the "government" needs assistance of another kind as well. Politicians need assistance making decisions. By themselves, they have a finite decision-making capacity in a number of ways: a finite range of consideration, there being only so many topics that the "government" can productively turn its mind to; a finite capacity to think decisions through, there being little time to conduct the in-depth review needed to arrive at optimal solutions; and a finite capacity of knowledge, there being within any political group only so much background expertise about the matters at hand. They are also at risk of being politically partisan and not always governing on behalf of the entire province.

The government's public service has a special responsibility to support the elected government, and democracy, by performing four functions: enabling, informing, amplifying, and caretaking.

The first function of the public service is the enabling of political will, which is most clearly seen after a change in government. The newly elected government can directly command the public service to carry out its policies. It does not need to pass statutes or regulations or negotiate contracts to begin to govern. The machinery is already in place. The new government can start to give orders to the public service, including

---

The Machinery of Government: Public Administration and the Liberal State (Oxford University Press, 2020) [Heath]. For a discursive review of public service ethics in practice, see Kenneth Kernaghan & John Langford, *The Responsible Public Servant*, 2d ed (Institute of Public Administration, 2014).

29 Graham White, "Revolutionary Change in the Ontario Public Service" in Evert A. Lindquist, ed, *Government Restructuring and Career Public Service* (Toronto: IPAC, 2000) at 341.

directions to produce new statutes and regulations or amendments to old ones. The public service can be told to adopt new approaches for the services it delivers directly. When the public service carries out these tasks, it is carrying out its primary function of enabling democracy.

The second function of the public service is one of informing. In order to assist the government of the day to arrive at good decisions on many complicated issues, the public service is obligated to bring its accumulated expertise and knowledge to bear and to provide frank, direct advice. The public service must be able to tell the politicians what they need to hear, not just what they want to hear. Public servants are to take a broad perspective and include points politicians may prefer to downplay. Once a decision is made by the politicians, democracy requires the public service to carry it out; but while decisions are being contemplated, it is the duty of the public service to enrich those decisions with dispassionate and expert advice. This is the function of informing democracy.

The third function is that of amplifying. While government will specify its intentions, it will not be able to do so with sufficient detail to cover all eventualities. In order for a policy or law to have its full effect, those who carry it out must ensure that the specifics are in accordance with the government's general intent. By the amplification of general policies, the democratically determined wishes of a society are brought to fruition.

Finally, there is the caretaking function. While a government is expected to set direction, myriad issues will arise in many areas, and they cannot all be subject to immediate or close attention. Some of those issues may eventually come to the detailed attention of the government, and on some issues there will be little or no governmental direction. Nonetheless, all issues must be addressed in some fashion, and it is the public service that deals with them, including during election campaigns and the transition to a new government. The public service is relied upon by society to be the caretaker for government.

The importance of the public service was the subject of insightful comment in the 1986 Ontario Law Reform Commission's *Report on Political Activity, Public Comment and Disclosure by Crown Employees*:

> It is now widely recognized that public servants, as a result of their responsibilities to provide policy advice to political superiors and to make discretionary decisions in the course of policy implementation,

> are major actors in the political system.... Thus, public servants are involved in "politics" in the broad sense of the word: the authoritative allocation of social values.
>
> Despite these considerations, the notion that politics and policy can and should be separated from administration has endured. This can be largely explained by the practical appeal that this artificial separation has for both elected and appointed officials. It enables governments to claim that they have removed certain functions—for example regulation of rent levels, or the granting of liquor licences—from the sphere of "politics" by transferring these functions to semi-independent agencies, boards, and commissions. In addition, the fiction that public servants simply execute decisions made by elected officials permits public servants to exercise power while retaining their anonymity and protection from public criticism.
>
> Thus, while politicians formally make the major policy decisions, public servants influence these decisions and make decisions of their own under authority delegated to them by the legislation and the Cabinet. Political involvement in this broad sense can be distinguished from the narrower concept of partisan politics, which implies identification with a political party, and which can more easily be separated from administration.[30]

It has been pointed out that this important role is performed at all levels:

> The exercise of discretionary powers is also pervasive in that these powers are dispersed to various levels of the hierarchy. Both the scope and importance of discretionary powers increase, however, as one moves up the administrative pyramid into the upper echelons of the bureaucracy. It is therefore among senior public servants that value problems and priorities are most crucial for the determination of public policy and the state of administrative responsibility. It is important, however, not to overestimate the value problems of the most senior bureaucrats and thereby to minimize the substantial, sometimes critical, significance of value choices made by professional, technical, and administrative personnel at lower levels of the hierarchy. The

---

30 Ontario Law Reform Commission, *Report on Political Activity, Public Comment and Disclosure by Crown Employees* (Toronto: Ministry of the Attorney General, 1986) [*OLRC Report*] at 16–17. The authors of this book wish to acknowledge the debt they owe to the authors of the report and, in particular, to Research Consultant Kenneth Swan, also one of Ontario's leading arbitrators.

> failure of such officials to act responsibly, particularly by making decisions that are efficient, effective, and responsive, may seriously jeopardize policies and programs determined at the top executive levels of the organization.[31]

Indeed, the average Ontarian is most likely to engage with the public service through interactions with, and decisions made by, front-line staff.

There is an ongoing public administration debate about whether a modern public service receives sufficient direction from politicians to guide its actions or whether public servants need to supplement political direction with their own normative principles and, if so, what those would be. The traditional view is that "faithful execution of democratic decisions is what a public service is for, not to substitute for them some other definitions of the public good"[32] and that it is not the prerogative of unelected officials to "define the public interest."[33] The contrary argument is that this traditional formulation "dramatically understates the amount of raw power that is directly exercised by the public service" and does not permit a full discussion of the normative principles that actually guide the exercise of that power.[34] It is further argued that the right normative principles are revealed in the existing best practices of liberal democracies, including administrative law, the professional ethics found in the institutional culture of the public service, and, as necessary, the principles of efficiency, equality, and liberty that form "the normative core of modern liberal theories of justice."[35] Regardless, there are underlying attributes that support both "faithful execution" of political will and the responsible exercise of "raw power."

---

31 Kenneth Kernaghan, "Power, Politics and Bureaucracy" in Ron S. Blair & Jack T. McLeod, eds, *The Canadian Political Tradition, Basic Readings*, 2d ed (Scarborough: Nelson Canada, 1993), excerpts at 454 and 455 [Kernaghan and Blair]. To the same effect see Heath, above note 28, Chapter 6: Administrative Discretion and the Rule of Law, and in particular Chapter 6.1 on discretion, and citing Martin Lipsky, *Street-Level Bureaucracy* (New York: Russell Sage, 1980) and Bernardo Zacka, *When the State Meets the Street* (Cambridge: Harvard University Press, 2017). For a discussion of the exercise of discretion by municipal case workers administering the provincial Ontario Works social assistance program, see Stephanie B. Collins, "The Space in the Rules: Bureaucratic Discretion in the Administration of Ontario Works" (2016) 15:2 *Social Policy and Society* 221.

32 Tait, above note 28 at 16.

33 *Ibid* at 17.

34 Heath, above note 28 at 607–8.

35 *Ibid* at 97–98.

At the core of the capability and commitment of the public service to carry out these functions must be the attribute of "impartiality" or "neutrality," which ensures the public service serves every government with the same dispassion and is trusted by all of them and by the public. As stressed by the Supreme Court, the loyalty of the public service is owed to the government and "not the political party in power at any one time."[36] A neutral public service does not take sides in the partisan debate between political parties, but rather provides balanced information and advice. Neutrality also helps to ensure that Ontarians who did not vote for the incumbent government will accept that there is no partisan bias influencing the implementation of government decisions affecting them.

Impartiality in a public service is supported when that impartiality is championed and modelled by management through statements and actions. Under the *PSOA*, deputy ministers do have the obligation to "promote effective, non-partisan, professional, ethical and competent public service by public servants."[37] However, the regulation of employment also has a central and not always recognized role. That is why the *PSOA* sets out certain terms of employment statutorily and why the remaining terms are set by directives that must ensure "the recruitment and employment of public servants [employed in the government] are non-partisan."[38] Terms and conditions of employment can hearten employees to be impartial public servants or can discourage them. Fair and stable terms and conditions of employment, including security of tenure, can give public servants the resolve to be impartial even in the face of immediate political pressure.

Well-known federal commentary on the public service describes the traditional bargain reached between politicians and public servants:

> [P]ublic servants exchanged overt partisanship, some political rights, and a public profile in return for permanent careers, or at least indefinite tenure, anonymity, selection by merit, a regular work week, and the promise of being looked after at the end of a career that did not require

---

36 *Fraser*, above note 16 at 470.

37 *PSOA*, above note 1, s 29(3).

38 *Ibid*, s 43(2). This section sets out Public Service Commission responsibility, augmented by the requirement in s 43(4) that directives set by the Management Board of Cabinet "cannot be inconsistent with the non-partisan nature of the public service."

> paying close attention to their own material self-interest. Politicians meanwhile exchanged the ability to appoint or dismiss public servants and change their working conditions at will for professional competence and non-partisan obedience to the government of the day. . . .
>
> Thus, the architects of the political order sought to establish distinct spaces for politicians and bureaucrats. Ministers would decide policy; career officials would provide fearless advice on policy matters but then implement whatever policy decision ministers would make and administer programs in an apolitical manner.[39]

Much of this "bargain" exists in Ontario and is reflected in the *PSOA* and the directives it has empowered. It should also be mentioned that public service pensions have received special attention since 1920.[40]

A note of caution is warranted. Crown employees are an ever more privileged component of Ontario's workforce due to the increasing comparative scarcity of full-time, unionized jobs with defined benefit pension plans.[41] Fair and stable terms of employment for public servants should be designed and bargained to support effective government and not to unduly favour the private interests of public servants.

The Treasury Board Secretariat, then Management Board Secretariat (MBS), issued a 2000 discussion paper on reform of the predecessor *Public Service Act* (*PSA*)[42] suggesting the following as a priori principles for the efficacious functioning of the public service:

> 1. The [Ontario Public Service] OPS is independent, impartial, and apolitical.
> 2. The recruitment, management, and advancement of OPS employees are based on merit and equal opportunity.[43]

These principles previously received more detailed and sophisticated treatment in the 1986 Law Reform Commission Report as follows:

---

39 Donald J. Savoie, *Breaking the Bargain: Public Servants, Ministers and Parliament* (Toronto: University of Toronto Press, 2003) at 5–6 [Savoie].

40 See the discussion of public service pensions in Chapter 6, Section G.

41 See the discussion in Claire Mummé, "Unifying the Field: Mapping the Relationship Between Work Law Regimes in Ontario" (2020) 43:2 *Dalhousie Law Journal* 544.

42 SO 1961–1962, c 121 [*PSA*].

43 Management Board Secretariat, *The Ontario Public Service Act in the 21st Century: Discussion Paper on the Public Service Act* (March 2000). For discussion of the MBC and the role of Treasury Board Secretariat, see Chapter 2.

1. Public servants are appointed and promoted on the basis of merit rather than on the basis of party affiliation.
2. Public servants do not engage in partisan political activities while at work, and must otherwise limit such activity so as to maintain impartiality.
3. Public servants do not, except as required by their jobs, express publicly their personal views on government policies or administration.
4. Public servants provide forthright and objective advice to their political masters, and do so in confidence.
5. Public servants execute policy decisions loyally and zealously irrespective of the philosophy and programmes of the party in power and regardless of their personal opinions. As a result, public servants enjoy security of tenure unless there is cause to dismiss them or they are laid off.[44]

The Law Reform Commission formulations are updated and discussed in more detail below.

a) Public Service Employment Is Managed on the Basis of Merit and Equal Opportunity

According to the merit principle, everyone should have a reasonable opportunity to be considered for appointment to the public service, and all appointments should be based on merit in the sense of fitness for the job.[45]

The intention of this principle is threefold. First, adherence to the merit principle has the effect of preventing victorious political parties from installing and promoting their loyalists in the public service in preference to the supporters of other political parties. Hiring, promotion, and firing based on political affiliation or partisanship can give rise to several problems. Policy advice and implementation can be motivated by the desire to curry favour with politicians rather than on the basis of giving the best advice or doing what the current policy or law prescribes. There would be a high turnover of staff as successive

44 *OLRC Report*, above note 30 at 13–25.

45 *Ibid* at 17. What constitutes merit is complex. It has been argued that part of demonstrated merit for public service is "public service motivation," which consists of such elements as commitment to the public interest, compassion, and self-sacrifice: Kenneth Kernaghan, "Getting Engaged: Public-Service Merit and Motivation Revisited" (2011) 54:1 *Canadian Public Administration* 1.

governments "cleaned house." A particular concern has been that politicians will seek direct political control of staffing and operations, resulting in a form of "politicization" of the public service that runs counter to the tradition of impartial and non-partisan management.[46]

Second, there is a need to avoid "bureaucratic patronage" in the form of unwarranted favouritism in hiring and promotions by public service managers.[47] Third, merit is not just the best protection against political and bureaucratic patronage, it is also a positive virtue devised to ensure that the public service is staffed by effective and ethical people.[48] All of the functions of the public service are best advanced by independent, non-partisan, high-quality staff.

On the introduction in the early 1960s of major *PSA* amendments, the provincial treasurer stated that

> [t]he province of Ontario is a fine, proud land with responsible energetic citizens. It is therefore appropriate that Ontario's employees are of a sufficiently high caliber to win and hold the respect of the 6 million residents of the province.[49]

The 1960s amendments fixed processes for hiring to avoid the permanent hiring of unfit employees and to ensure tenure could not be obtained through temporary contracts. A one-year probationary period was enacted, allowing for release of a public servant "for failure to meet the requirements of his position." Temporary appointments were term limited and "a person who is appointed to a position in the public service

---

46 Peter Aucoin, "New Political Governance in Westminster Systems: Impartial Public Administration and Management Performance at Risk" (2012) 25:2 *Governance* 177. See also Dennis Grube, "Responsibility to Be Enthusiastic? Public Servants and the Public Face of 'Promiscuous Partisanship'" (2014) 28:3 *Governance* 305 discussing trends in partisanship among senior public servants across Commonwealth countries; Luc Juillet & Ken Rasmussen, *Defending a Contested Ideal: Merit and the PSC of Canada 1908–2008* (Ottawa: University of Ottawa Press, 2008), Conclusion, para 17 [Juillet and Rasmussen] citing B. Guy Peters & Jon Pierre, eds, *Politicization of the Civil Service in Comparative Perspective* (London: Routledge, 2004); Ezra Suleiman, *Dismantling Democratic States* (Princeton: Princeton University Press, 2003), especially at 191–278; Richard Mulgan, "Truth in Government and the Politicization of Public Service Advice" (2007) 85:3 *Public Administration* 569.

47 See Savoie, above note 39 at 242–43.

48 Juillet and Rasmussen, above note 46, Conclusion at para 18.

49 Ontario Legislative Assembly, *Hansard*, 9 April 1962, No 63 at 2119 (J.N. Allan, Provincial Treasurer).

for a specified period ceases to be a public servant at the expiration of that period." These statutory requirements have continued to the present.

More important in practice is the degree of management commitment to merit-based recruitment, retention, and promotion practices. There has been continuing attention to the improvement of management oversight and practices in the OPS.[50] The current Public Service Commission *Employment Policy* establishes practices for recruitment, development, deployment, and retention that are to apply the principles of "merit, inclusion and accessibility" and are intended to be "fair, objective, reasonable and transparent."[51] Commitment to this policy is reinforced by the ability of public servants to challenge the outcome of job competitions through grievances by non-unionized public servants at the Public Service Grievance Board (PSGB) and by unionized public servants at the Grievance Settlement Board (GSB).[52]

Unions representing government employees have commonly bargained to ensure collective agreements contain significant seniority-based entitlements:

> [T]he preservation of job security through seniority has been preferred, in part because of the fairness implicit in the notion that the length of an employee's service should give rise to a corresponding equity in his or her job security and in part because seniority offers a system of work allocation that is objective, easily administered and avoids the risk of disputes that would arise under a more discretionary system.[53]

For example, government collective agreement provisions provide that, in job competitions where the candidates' qualifications and ability are

---

50 See the "Public Service Management" section below.

51 Public Service Commission, *Employment Policy*, 6 November 2020, provided to the authors, Art 6.2 [*PSC, Employment Policy*].

52 See the discussion in Chapter 12 of the Public Service Grievance Board jurisprudence on job competitions. The Grievance Settlement Board is discussed in Chapter 11.

53 *Re Northern Telecom Canada Ltd and United Automobile Workers, Local 1525*, 1983 CanLII 4850 (ON LA) at 229, building on the classic statement of the centrality of seniority in collective agreement interpretation found in *Re United Electrical Workers, Local 512, and Tung-Sol of Canada Ltd*, 1964 CanLII 1021 (ON LA) [*Tung-Sol*]. The *Tung-Sol* principle has been adopted by the GSB in interpreting OPS collective agreements: *Ontario Public Service Employees Union (Union) v Ontario (Natural Resources and Forestry)*, 2019 CanLII 97253 (ON GSB) (Dissanayake) at para 25.

relatively equal, seniority is the deciding factor and that, in the event of layoffs, senior employees will have more job security.[54] Seniority can protect against favouritism and support the security of tenure that is an attribute of public service employment, as further discussed below. Whether giving effect to seniority ultimately promotes merit will continue to be debated.

The goal of equal opportunity, or inclusion, warrants separate mention. The *Human Rights Code* (*HRC*)[55] is applicable to the Ontario government as an employer,[56] and the Supreme Court has stressed the obligation of all employers to "build conceptions of equality into workplace standards."[57] Public servants, and those aspiring to be public servants, should have equal access, free of barriers, to full participation in all aspects of public service employment. The public service should be reflective of the diversity of Ontario's population. This is supported by an OPS commitment, under the MBC *Respectful Workplace Policy*, to fostering and sustaining workplaces that are "inclusive, diverse, equitable, accessible and free from workplace harassment and discrimination."[58] That commitment is reinforced by the enforceability of the *HRC* through the PSGB and GSB grievance mechanisms.

b) Public Servants Are to Keep Separate Their Public Positions and Their Partisan Political Activities

Public servants would not be able to fulfill their duties if their own political activities caused politicians and the public to doubt their "on the job" impartiality. Confidence in the public service would be diminished by concern that public servants were making decisions to undercut the political party in power or, alternately, to further that party's electoral

54 Collective agreement provisions applying seniority to job competitions are discussed in Chapter 10, and its application to selection of employees for layoff is discussed in the Chapter 9.

55 RSO 1990, c H.19.

56 See the discussion of human rights in Chapter 6.

57 *British Columbia (Public Service Employee Relations Commission) v BCGSEU*, [1999] 3 SCR 3 at para 68.

58 Management Board of Cabinet, *Respectful Workplace Policy (Policy to Support a Respectful Workplace and Prevent Workplace Harassment and Discrimination)*, 1 October 2017, copy made available to authors, Art 4.1.

interests. Restrictions on the political activity of public servants help maintain the confidence of politicians and the public.[59]

In Ontario in the late nineteenth century, there was broad consensus that the public service should not participate in political activity. An 1895 report commissioned by the Legislative Assembly suggested that "whilst public servants should not be debarred from exercising their voting franchise, they should not be strenuously partisan."[60] It was felt that there was no need for special legislation or the imposition of penalties. The Legislature passed a non-binding resolution that staff should not participate in federal or provincial election campaigns or be municipal candidates.[61] By the 1960s, opinions had changed. An early version of the present political activity provisions was enacted that permitted public servants, except the highest ranking, to engage in a range of political activity, including participating in party politics away from public service work, as well as to take leaves of absence to be candidates. As well, the previous complete prohibition on outside employment was replaced with a more subtle prohibition on any conflict of interest and other full-time employment.[62]

It was noted by the Law Reform Commission that reduced restrictions on political activity would increase the vulnerability of public servants to improper treatment and that a properly maintained merit system would help ensure employees could exercise their allowable freedom of expression without suffering employment consequences.[63]

The advent of the *Charter*, including the right to freedom of expression, resulted in sustained fine tuning of the scope of restrictions on public servant's political activity rights, which is now reflected in the current *PSOA* provisions, discussed in Chapter 3.

---

59 *Fraser*, above note 16 at 470, Dickson J, endorsing the United Kingdom's *Royal Commission on the Civil Service Report* (MacDonnell Committee), c 11, paras 10–11.

60 "Report of The Commissioners Appointed to Inquire Concerning the Mode Of Appointing And Remunerating Certain Provincial Officials Now Paid By Fees And The Extent Of The Remuneration They Should Receive," *Ontario Sessional Papers*, 1895, No 081/032 (Toronto: Warwick Bros & Rutter, 1895) at 35.

61 *Legislative Journals*, 17 March 1897. Moved by Mr. Garrow and passed without debate. This was the only statement on political activity of public servants until the passage of the 1962–63 *PSA* amending legislation. The legislative history is discussed in more detail in Chapter 3.

62 Ontario Legislative Assembly, *Hansard*, 6 February 1963, No 22 at 715–18 (J.N. Allan, Treasurer).

63 *OLRC Report*, above note 30 at 271.

c) Public Servants Do Not Express Publicly Their Personal Views on Government Policies or Administration

The public should not be caused to doubt whether personal views possessed by public servants will interfere with their employment obligations. This justifies some restriction on public comment by public servants. Attitudes about this restriction have changed over time. The ideal of circumspect refraining from public comment has given way, through litigation about the defensibility of employer discipline, particularly under the *Charter*, to the acceptance that "a public servant may actively and publicly express opposition to the policies of a government," provided that "the public servant's criticism has no impact on his or her ability to perform effectively the duties of a public servant or on the public perception of that ability."[64]

This value has been challenged from another source, collective bargaining. In the course of collective bargaining and grievance representation, criticism of the government and the public service by union representatives is virtually routine. This has been claimed to erode the respect paid to the public service. It has been asserted in relation to the federal civil service that

> [t]he aura of being a "civil servant" that characterized the liberal democratic state in the first half of the twentieth century no longer exists. In the second half of the last century, the regulations governing the behaviour of the employees working for the state were contested and modified, both through militant action of employees working within the state and in the courts. Civil servants at the beginning of the twenty-first century have indeed become "uncivil," and the discourse of civil service has been transformed into one of public employees who are regulated in much the same way as those in the private sector. . . . The social category of "'civil servant," with all its accompanying characteristics, including loyalty to the state and privileged status within society, is a discourse that for the moment has disintegrated.[65]

---

64 *Fraser*, above note 16 at 470.

65 Rosemary Warskett, "Law, Regulation, and Becoming 'Uncivil': Contestation and Reconstruction within the Federal Administrative State" in Michael MacNeil et al, eds, *Law, Regulation and Governance* (New York: Oxford University Press, 2002) at 199.

This is overstated and fails to account for the distinction developed in labour law jurisprudence between comments made in one's capacity as a public servant and one's role as a union representative.[66]

d) Public Servants Provide Forthright and Objective Advice to Politicians in Confidence

Providing forthright and objective advice to politicians has been described as telling politicians "things they do not necessarily wish to hear."[67] It has been noted that

> [s]peaking truth to power—as long as it is accompanied by a duty of faithful execution once decisions have been taken—is not something important for deputies and ministers alone. It is just as relevant or precious between employees and supervisors, at the level of middle managers, directors, directors general, and [assistant deputy ministers]. Public servants owe their supervisors not just their loyalty but their best professional judgement. Where this is discouraged or inhibited, the professionalism and the values of the public service suffer. So does good government.[68]

In order to foster candour, the *Freedom of Information and Protection of Privacy Act* does contain a discretionary exclusion for confidential advice, which has been broadly interpreted by the Supreme Court in order to avoid the risk of "advice or recommendations that are less candid and complete, and the public service no longer being perceived as neutral."[69]

In addition, the convention is that ministers take responsibility for large decisions and public servants stay anonymous. It has been noted that this part of the "bargain" has declined and cannot always be relied on.[70] The advice given is more likely to become public. What is to remain is that the advice be forthright and objective. That forthrightness is fuelled by ensuring civil servants "remain sufficiently independent

---

66 See the discussion of union speech in Chapter 3.

67 Tait, above note 28 at 47.

68 *Ibid* at 48.

69 *Freedom of Information and Protection of Privacy Act*, RSO 1990, c F.31, s 70 discussed in *John Doe v Ontario (Finance)*, 2014 SCC 36, Rothstein J at paras 43–46, as further discussed in Chapter 6.

70 See Savoie, above note 39, Chapter 9, especially 239–44, and *OLRC Report*, above note 30 at 22–23.

of the political executive to exercise impartial judgment in the public interest."[71]

e) Public Servants Are Loyal and, in Return, Have Security of Tenure

Stability of terms of employment and security of tenure provide protection against partisan or unmeritorious reprisal and dismissal. In 1962, when introducing the updated *PSA*, the treasurer of Ontario said that

> [p]rotection against interrupted employment, sickness, and improper dismissal must be accorded if the independence of the civil service is to be established and if each employee may feel free to follow the dictates of his conscience without fear or favour.[72]

The amendments included limitations on management's authority to suspend, dismiss, or accept resignations, resulting in a real increase of security of tenure. These provisions have been carried through into the present Part III of the *PSOA* dealing with employment by the Crown.

Security of tenure ensures continuity of acquired knowledge and expertise[73] and fosters institutional loyalty. Valuable and dispassionate advice can inform each successive government. The presence of permanent officials in senior roles supports:

- "keeping the show on the road"
- engaging in long-term planning
- maintaining consistency over time
- using better information
- focusing on the general interest
- resisting democratic pandering
- maintaining constitutionality[74]

Security of tenure should not be absolute. It is not a guarantee of a job until retirement. Governments reserve the right to change the size of the public service:

---

71 See Lorne Sossin, "Speaking Truth to Power? The Search for Bureaucratic Independence in Canada" (2005) 55:1 *University of Toronto Law Journal* 1 at 24.

72 Ontario, Legislative Assembly, *Hansard*, 9 April 1962, No 63 at 2119 (J.N. Allan, Provincial Treasurer).

73 Kernaghan and Blair, above note 31, excerpts at 465.

74 Heath, above note 28 at 70–74.

> Security of tenure covers two potential notions that are often collapsed but need to be distinguished. The first is protection from partisan dismissal. The second is permanent or lifetime employment. The first is fundamental to the employment regime and values of the public service. The second is not. Indeed, public service employment has always been based on the principle that employment continues only as long as, in the eyes of the government, there is work to be done.[75]

As mentioned above, for unionized employees, seniority provisions in collective agreements can support the security of tenure of individual employees, even when their position is abolished. Under OPS collective agreements, laid off employees may have a right of redeployment within the public service or, if their work is divested, to "follow their job" to the new employer.[76]

Whether unionized or not, it remains a traditional core attribute of the public service that a public servant should not be dismissed from employment except for cause, for incompetence, or for job redundancy. This is reflected in Part III of the *PSOA*.

This attribute has been contentious, as it has been seen as producing insufficient management control over the staff in the public service. The leading Ontario example occurred in 1995 with the Progressive Conservative amendment to the *PSOA* empowering dismissal of certain senior public servants without cause, but with reasonable notice, which was described as appropriate "to harmonize with notice provisions in the private sector."[77] That rationale is suspect. There has been much debate about the extent to which the traditional principles of the public service need modification. The stability, expertise, public interest focus, and measured political accountability of the public service have been contrasted with a claimed need to assert more effective political and democratic control over bureaucracy and to have a focus of real benefit for the "customer" or citizen.[78] However, continued consideration about whether and how to increase the responsiveness of the public

---

75 Tait, above note 28 at 21.

76 See Chapter 9 for a discussion of rights under successorship legislation and the collective agreement.

77 Ontario Legislative Assembly, *Hansard*, 4 October 1995, No 6 at 100 (David Johnson, Chair of Management Board of Cabinet). See the fuller discussion in Chapter 2.

78 See, for example, Charles Goodsell, *The New Case for Bureaucracy* (New York: Sage Publications, 2015); and David Osborne & Ted Gaebler, *Reinventing*

service should be dealt with as a matter of adjustment within the *PSOA* scheme and not by ending the justified distinctiveness of the approach to security of tenure under public service employment legislation.

For some people who work in governmental functions, there is a crucial qualification needed regarding their loyalty and security of tenure. Their roles require that they be loyal not to the government but to another institution or calling. The examples discussed in this book are (1) the Lieutenant Governor; (2) members of provincial Parliament; (3) legislative staff and officers, who are loyal to the Legislative Assembly or related statutory responsibilities; (4) provincial judges and justices of the peace, who are loyal to the Constitution and the rule of law; and (5) order-in-council appointees or office holders who are loyal to a specific statutory mandate that has been established to fulfill an aspect of the public interest.[79] In each case, there are also tailored security of tenure provisions in place that contrast with those for the public service.

3) Public Service Management

Upholding the ethical and human resources standards of the OPS requires supportive governance and management. This has been understood since the origin of the *PSA*. However, the size and complexity of Ontario's society and economy have grown enormously, and the role of government has greatly expanded. While the essential features of the Westminster model have remained fixed, it has been necessary for public service administration to evolve. There have been three sets of changes since Confederation. This historical context assists in understanding the governance and management structure presently set out in the *PSOA*.

The first phase of change in public service governance and oversight was the assertion of control by the legislature and Cabinet. The initial 1878 *PSA* established the "departmental staff of the civil service of Ontario."[80] The statute determined that every appointment was to be "during pleasure." The statute also fixed classifications and salaries.[81]

Government: How the Entrepreneurial Spirit Is Transforming the Public Sector (Reading, MA: Addison-Wesley, 1992).

79 See Chapter 5 on legislative, judicial, and order-in-council roles.

80 *An Act Respecting the Public Service of Ontario*, 1878, 41 Vict, c 2, assented to 7 March 1878, s 1.

81 The highest rate of pay, for a "first class clerk," was fixed at $1,400 per year: *ibid*, s 4.

Civil servants were not to receive any allowance or compensation for "any extra services whatsoever." Civil servants took an oath of loyalty and promised not to receive any payments other than their salary. These provisions were intended to deny managers the ability to individually grant or remove tenure and to adjust rates of pay or related perquisites. During the reading of the Bill leading to the *PSA*, the goal of depoliticizing the civil service was highlighted:

> One of the chief objects of the Bill was that the position of clerks must be fixed by statute, and that they may not be affected by the whim, caprice, and good or bad will of the party for the time being in power.[82]

Management was put under the direct administrative authority of the Lieutenant Governor in Council or Cabinet. The Lieutenant Governor's authority was delegable in varying degrees to deputy ministers. The Act's limitation on the power of individual ministers was explained as follows:

> The Bill, instead of providing for the heads of the departments [ministers] making changes, provided for an order in council, so that all the members of the government should know of, and take part in, the changes. This was in order to increase safety, and to make sure that every appointment made should be done deliberately, and not be the act merely of one member of the government but of all members.[83]

As the range of Cabinet responsibilities and the size of the OPS both grew, Cabinet's self-appointed task of directly managing the public service was not seen as sustainable. In 1918, through *An Act to Provide for the Better Regulation of Public Service*,[84] Cabinet appointed a Civil Service Commissioner, and then Commission, which over the following decades was given increasing responsibility for ensuring the integrity of public service appointments through oversight of appointments, classifications, and salaries. This was complemented by an ever more detailed regulation setting out the details of and responsibility for working conditions. This reached the point that the 1970 regulation[85] gave the Commission control over the authorization of overtime pay for

---

82 *The Globe*, "Report on Ontario Legislature," 3d Parliament, 3d Sess, 7 February 1878, column 5.

83 *Ibid*, column 7.

84 *The Globe*, 19 February 1918 at 1.

85 RRO 1970, Reg 749, s 27.

many public servants, and responsibility to provide training programs, schedules, and educational grants.

An important check and balance for employees was introduced during this period. In 1960, the *PSA* was amended[86] to make provision for the establishment of a "grievance board," the PSGB. A public servant was entitled to present a grievance personally or to be represented by an employee representative, who could be a member of an employee association. The PSGB's creation was at least in part a response to demands for more "voice" by the pre-union employee representative organization, the Civil Service Association of Ontario.[87] The existence of an effective enforcement mechanism provided a vehicle for further monitoring and controlling the exercise of management discretion at a time of rapid growth in the size of the public service.[88]

The second phase of governance and management was more organized executive oversight and better internal public service administration. The rapid and accelerating growth of the public service during the 1950s and 1960s produced growing concern about the size and cost of the bureaucracy,[89] and it was recognized that this needed to be addressed, at least in part, both by increasing the capacity of the executive to oversee the OPS, and the capacity of the public service to manage itself. The influential Committee on Government Productivity recommended more integrated human resources management and less reliance on a structure of positions classified and regulated centrally by an independent commission.[90]

In 1971–72, a standing Cabinet committee, the MBC, was created and given statutory authority for "the efficient and effective operation

---

86 *Public Service Amendment Act, 1960*, SO 1960, c 97.

87 Wayne Roberts, *Don't Call Me Servant—Government Work and Unions in Ontario 1911–1984* (Toronto: OPSEU, 1994) at 72 [Roberts].

88 *Ibid* at 162.

89 George G. Bell & Andrew D. Pascoe, *The Ontario Government—Structure and Functions* (Toronto: Wall and Thompson, 1988) at 360.

90 Ontario, Committee on Government Productivity (COGP), *Interim Report No 1* (Toronto: Queen's Printer, 1970), as discussed in Ontario, Public Service Restructuring Secretariat, *Transforming Public Service for the 21st Century: An Ontario Perspective* (Toronto: Queen's Printer, 2000). See the discussion of the implementation of COGP by successive secretaries of Cabinet in Bryan Evans, "Capacity, Complexity, and Leadership: Secretaries to Cabinet and Ontario's Project of Modernization at the Centre" in Patrice A. Dutil, *Searching for Leadership: Secretaries to Cabinet in Canada* (Toronto: University of Toronto Press, 2008) at 125–29.

of the public service generally."[91] A specific responsibility was oversight of an ever more detailed regulation setting out guaranteed terms and conditions of employment, intended to provide minimum employment standards. At the same time, the Civil Service Commission lost its unique status as a department, and the commissioner became a deputy minister like the others.[92] Over time this had some of the desired effect of leading to the MBC providing oversight through regulation, while the OPS internally improved its management.[93]

From 1972 on, the scope of the *PSA* regulation expanded to address the growing complexities of an increasing range of guaranteed terms and conditions of employment, motivated in part by the need to respond to a range of rights, including collective bargaining and human rights. This form of oversight became increasingly cumbersome. At the same time, the public service continued to be asked to demonstrate the ability to reorganize itself and implement alternate forms of service delivery, including divestment of operational services.

There also continued to be a decline in ministerial capacity to oversee the public service. A major study by Britain's Institute for Public Policy Research concluded that, in the twenty-first century, British ministers could not effectively hold civil servants to account.[94] The *Gomery Report*,[95] following an inquiry into the "sponsorship scandal" that had

---

91 *Management Board of Cabinet Act, 1971*, SO 1972, c 12, s 2.

92 *Public Service Amendment Act, 1972*, SO 1972, c 96, s 2, amending s 2(3). The chairman of the commission was clarified to "rank as and have all the [same] powers and duties of a deputy minister of a ministry."

93 In the mid-1980s, recommendations of the *Moher Report* (W.P. Moher, *Managing Human Resources in the Ontario Public Service* (Toronto: Queen's Printer, 1986)) were implemented to give responsibility for improvement of executive recruitment, career development, and succession planning to the secretary of Cabinet and the new Executive Development Committee composed of deputy ministers, while responsibility for junior management and for bargaining unit staff was vested within the ministry structure at the Management Board Secretariat.

94 Guy Lodge & Ben M. Rogers, *Whitehall's Black Box—Accountability and Performance in the Senior Civil Service* (London: Institute for Public Policy Research, 2006) at 3.

95 John H. Gomery, Commissioner, Commission of Inquiry into the Sponsorship Program & Advertising Activities, *Who Is Responsible? Vol 1* (Ottawa: Privy Council, 2005). During second reading debate on the *PSOA*, members of the opposition took advantage of the opportunity to remind the then Liberal government of their federal cousins' difficulties with the "sponsorship scandal": Ontario Legislative Assembly, *Hansard*, 15 November 2006.

engulfed the federal Liberal administration and dominated political discussion in Canada in 2004 and 2005, arrived at a similar conclusion. The report noted that ministers "must deal with their constituencies; attend Cabinet and Cabinet committee meetings; prepare for Question Period and parliamentary committees; deal with the requirements of their political party, the media and their Cabinet colleagues; and act as members of the government caucus."[96] The evidence suggested ministers work between seventy and eighty hours a week but have only three hours a week to meet with their deputy ministers. The report concluded it was ever more difficult for ministers to assume full responsibility for management of their departments.

A third phase of improving public service human resources management, through strengthened and streamlined MBC management of general terms and conditions of employment and a more centralized and directly accountable public service led by the Public Service Commission (PSC), was ushered in by the *PSOA* in 2006. On introduction of the Bill, the Minister of Government Services, the Honourable Gerry Phillips, said

> [t]his act, in my mind, sets the framework for how our public service manages the affairs of the public service. If passed, the legislation will strengthen human resource management and administration by establishing clear accountability, introducing modern language.
>
> Responsibilities related to human resource matters will be clarified for the two prime responsibilities, Management Board of Cabinet and the Public Service Commission. The Public Service Commission will be given all human resource management authorities, with the power to delegate, and will have responsibility for approving government-wide—or enterprise-wide, to use the jargon—and also cluster-specific human resource policies. Cabinet will continue to be responsible for all fiscal decisions.[97]

The responsibility for setting of wages and terms and conditions of employment was removed from the regulatory responsibility of Cabinet, and the *PSA* regulation that had been a fixture of public service

96 John H. Gomery, Commissioner; Commission of Inquiry into the Sponsorship Program & Advertising Activities, *Restoring Accountability*, *Vol 2* (Ottawa: Privy Council, 2006) at 134.

97 Ontario Legislative Assembly, *Hansard*, 15 November 2006 at 1610 (Gerry Phillips, Minister of Government Services).

administration for decades was repealed. As described in Chapter 2, the MBC was given the power to set general terms and conditions of employment by directive, and the PSC, functionally a committee of deputy ministers,[98] was empowered to issue directives for the effective administration of human resources,[99] which, upon delegation by the MBC, can include all classification, remuneration, and other terms and conditions of employment.[100]

Many crucial matters are now addressed by MBC directive set without full Cabinet involvement. Compensation is set by an MBC *Compensation Directive*.[101] The overall approach to human resources management is set by the MBC *Human Resources Management Directive*.[102] The PSC *Employment Policy*[103] deals with:

- recruitment and selection
- appointment, assignment, and transfer
- workforce adjustment
- suspension and termination

A consequence of the repeal of the regulation is a reduction in the transparency of public service terms and conditions of employment, as not all directives are publicly available. As of date of publication of this volume, the MBC *Compensation Directive* and the PSC *Employment Policy* are not posted on the government's website, although other less important directives are posted.[104]

Many checks and balances continue. The PSGB retains its authority to review the application of directives to non-unionized employees.

98 They are appointed to the Public Service Commission by the Lieutenant Governor in Council.

99 *PSOA*, above note 1, s 43.

100 Under the *PSOA*, MBC powers over classification, remuneration, and other terms and conditions of employment under s 33 are fully delegable to the PSC under s 45(1).

101 MBC, *Compensation Directive*, 20 August 2007, provided to the authors, s 28. Directives are discussed in Chapter 2.

102 MBC, *Human Resources Management Directive*, 17 May 2017, online: http://www.ontario.ca/page/human-resources-management-directive.

103 *PSC, Employment Policy*, above note 51.

104 See online: www.ontario.ca/page/sharing-government-directives-policies. An archive of all directives is to be kept, indicating when they applied: *PSOA*, above note 1, s 33(7).

And, since the introduction of the predecessor *CECBA 1972*,[105] the mechanisms of collective bargaining, including union representation, an enforceable collective agreement between each union and the MBC, and rights arbitration at the GSB, have determined terms and conditions of employment for unionized staff that are not explicitly set out in the *PSOA*.

The collective bargaining parties have agreed to treat the repeal of the regulation as not affecting unionized employee entitlements. The *Association of Management, Administrative and Professional Crown Employees of Ontario (AMAPCEO/MBC) Collective Agreement* states:

> The parties agree that there will be no diminution of entitlements provided for under the previous collective agreement as a result of changing the description of entitlements from the former Public Service Act and the regulations under that Act, to the Public Service of Ontario Act and any applicable Management Board of Cabinet Compensation Directives made under that Act.[106]

4) Ethical Framework's Application Outside Government

The 2006 *PSOA* extended the Act's ethical framework—oaths, prohibition of conflict of interest, limitations on political activity, and the protected right to disclose wrongdoing—to Crown agencies outside government that are designated as "public bodies." For this purpose, the employees of public bodies are made "public servants." However, they are not appointed to Crown employment under the *PSOA* Part III and so do not have the same terms of employment of the OPS.

While not substantively commented upon in the legislative debates, this is a major expansion in the coverage of part of the *PSOA*, for understandable reasons. The legislature's extension of the ethical framework to Crown agencies that are engaged in public services funded by the government provides a layer of assurance of good public administration and an added layer of protection against poor administration and scandal.

It is also understandable that the application of the *PSOA* Part III was not extended to those agencies. Part III makes the government

---

105 *An Act to Provide for Collective Bargaining for Crown Employees*, SO 1972, c 67 [*CECBA 1972*].

106 *AMAPCEO/MBC Collective Agreement, 2018–2022*, Letter of Understanding dated 27 April 2009, online: https://amapceo.on.ca/ops.

responsible for appointments, and mandates terms and conditions of employment that result in a degree of security of tenure. Such provisions are appropriate to support the impartiality of those public servants who have the direct responsibility for supporting the elected government. If made applicable outside of government, these provisions would greatly reduce the agencies' intended managerial autonomy and staffing flexibility, attributes that led to the establishment of those agencies outside government in the first place.

C. *CROWN EMPLOYEES COLLECTIVE BARGAINING ACT*

CECBA collective bargaining, as with the whole Canadian public sector, has evolved through increasing accommodation of the collective interests of employees. There has been a substantial, although gradual, expansion of the rights of unions, and shrinking of areas or topics reserved to management.

Yet, there is still general acceptance in Ontario that government is not an employer like others, due to its public service role. In addition to normal private sector and public sector management rights, the Crown must also always retain the capacity to act effectively in support of Ontario's democracy and population. Government must always be able to function and to step in when other institutions fail.

There has been much academic discussion[107] and much political debate about the needed extent of reserved state capacity under labour legislation. A principled attempt to determine the appropriate amount of reserved jurisdiction states:

> Government, as government, must retain authority to carry on the business of government. Broadly speaking, it cannot surrender to the representative of employees authority that would prevent it from performing the duties and discharging the functions that have been vested in it by parliament unless it first obtains the consent of such representatives.[108]

It has been suggested that the sovereign rights that must be retained include not only the enacting of legislation but also the reorganization

---

107 See Saul J. Frankel, "Staff Relations in the Public Service: The Ghost of Sovereignty" (1959) 2 *Canadian Public Administration* 65 and articles by Arthurs, Carter, and Swan in the bibliography.

108 Jacob Finkelman, QC, "Public Sector Bargaining: Some Basic Considerations" (1976) 16 *Queen's Law Journal* 17 at 24–25.

of any service or activity provided by government, while only permitting bargaining about the impact of these changes on government employees.[109] However, this formulation does not really clarify the extent to which the implementation of a reorganization should be bargainable, let alone how.[110]

As outlined in the next section, concerns about executive sovereignty delayed the introduction of labour legislation to the OPS until 1972. When the first version of *CECBA* was then introduced, it contained three main alterations to the *LRA* scheme, which have been retained, in changing ways, to this day:

- required stability of large government-wide bargaining units and their collective bargaining
- maintenance of essential services
- reservation of particular management rights[111]

There is a fourth area of labour law exceptionality that is always present in government even though it is not referenced in the *CECBA*. That is the capacity of government, unique among employers, to "change the rules of the game" by altering the law governing collective bargaining. The use of this power is discussed in Chapter 8 when reviewing "return to work" and wage restraint legislation.

1) Evolution of Collective Bargaining for Government Employment in Ontario

In 1944, a joint employer/employee advisory council was introduced to the OPS.[112] The council was the forum for discussion of terms and conditions of employment for front-line staff across the government until into the 1960s. The seven members, which included an appointed chair, three Civil Service Commission employer representatives, and

---

109 *Ibid* at 24.

110 For example, consider interim relief decisions by the GSB that halted the divestment of government services until there had been compliance with collective agreement provisions dealing with the rights of displaced employees. See Chapter 9.

111 Thanks is owed to David Doorey, *The Law of Work*, 2d ed (Toronto: Emond Publishing, 2020), ch 38, Public Sector Labour Relations, which discusses the key differences in public sector labour relations more generally.

112 The British civil service council system was launched in 1919 by J.H. Whitley, Deputy Speaker of the British House of Commons. See Frankel, above note 9 at 54–102 and, concerning its use in Ontario at 259–79.

three persons from the Civil Service Association of Ontario (CSAO), the precursor of the Ontario Public Service Employees Union (OPSEU), were to "make such recommendations to the Executive Council as may be deemed proper and advisable."[113] The preamble to the regulation refers to "the advisability of gaining the fullest benefit from the experience and opinions of the members of the Civil Service in matters pertaining to their employment and welfare."

Over time, regulations[114] established procedures for negotiations between the Commission and the CSAO. It was thought that the more informal system had become ineffective because it failed to produce any organized pattern of negotiations.[115] The actual sharing of power began in 1963 when interest dispute resolution was added with the determination of certain wages and benefits by the Civil Service Arbitration Board (although express limitations were placed on the range of arbitrable issues). The staff relations branch of the Treasury Board, later Management Board Secretariat and now Treasury Board Secretariat was established to represent the government in the negotiations and at arbitration. The director of the staff relations branch and the general manager of the CSAO acted as the chief negotiators for the parties.[116]

In 1969, an appointed special advisor, His Honour Judge Walter Little, recommended a statutory collective bargaining regime largely modelled on the Ontario *LRA*, but with some key differences. Rather than the right to strike, compulsory interest arbitration was viewed as more appropriate for government, combined with a list of matters reserved exclusively for determination by management. The stated purpose of the *CECBA 1972* was to implement those recommendations.[117] However, a real reason for the legislation may have been a rising tide of "militancy" among public servants, spurred by moves toward collective bargaining regimes both federally and in other provinces, as well as

113 O Reg 340/44. Specific power to pass a regulation setting up such a council was included in the 1947 Act: *The Public Service Act, 1947*, SO 1947, c 89, s 9(j).

114 *PSA*, above note 42, s 20(1)(r).

115 Ontario Legislative Assembly, *Hansard*, 7 March 1963, No 48 at 1511 (J.N. Allan, Treasurer).

116 Referenced in Ontario, His Honour Judge Walter Little, *Report of the Special Advisor on Collective Bargaining in the Ontario Government Service* (Toronto: Queen's Printer, 1969) [*Little Report*] at 4.

117 Ontario Legislative Assembly, *Hansard*, 9 May 1972, No 57 at 2246 (Charles McNaughton, Chair, Management Board of Cabinet).

inflation and the possibility of layoffs.[118] It has been said that the Act appeared to be an attempt to respond to those pressures by creating collective bargaining that still left control of many important issues firmly in the hands of the employer.[119]

Relatively standard *LRA* collective agreement negotiation provisions were a substantial change for the public service. Previously, negotiations had taken place in three separate bargaining cycles dealing with salaries, fringe benefits, and other matters relating to working conditions and terms of employment. Agreements were implemented by amendment to various Ontario regulations, orders-in-council, directives issued by the Treasury Board, the Civil Service Commission, or the relevant departments. Further, none of the settlements were reflected in a collective agreement. This meant that the parties did not negotiate on a regular basis for a single package of economic benefits and working conditions, and were, in theory, free to reopen any issue at any time. One benefit of the *CECBA* for the government was that negotiations became consolidated and took place at regular intervals, with more organized and centralized internal government control of the issues.

Judge Little was satisfied that the existing bargaining agents represented a substantial majority of the employees involved and there was no rational justification for interfering with existing representation rights.[120] It seems that he was persuaded by the CSAO having achieved 56 percent voluntary dues deduction within the approved bargaining unit. Judge Little gave some effect to employee freedom of choice in the selection of bargaining agents by recommending decertification and representation application provisions paralleling the private sec-

---

118 See Harry W. Arthurs, *Collective Bargaining by Public Employees in Canada: 5 Models* (Ann Arbour: Institute of Labour and Industrial Relations, University of Michigan, 1971), especially Chapter V, "The Informal Public Sector Model: Collective Bargaining in the Public Service of Ontario" at 104–30; Morley Gunderson, ed, *Collective Bargaining in the Essential and Public Service Sectors* (Toronto: University of Toronto Press, 1975), particularly Jean Boivin, "Collective Bargaining in the Public Sector: Some Propositions on the Cause of Public Employee Unrest" at 3–36. For the perspective of OPSEU, see Roberts, above note 87 at 130–34.

119 Carter, above note 8 at 779.

120 The public service exception was the representation of the Don Jail guards and Metropolitan Toronto court clerks by the Canadian Union of Public Employees Locals 878 and 79. Judge Little recommended that they be swept into the larger unit, which was done by the all-encompassing scope of the regulation designating the public service unit.

tor. The subsequent *CECBA* included an initial designation of existing bargaining agents by regulation, as well as standard provisions for certification, decertification, and termination proceedings. Under the regulation,[121] OPSEU was designated as the employee organization with representation rights for the public service.

Judge Little felt that the public interest would be best served if the public service was not fragmented by the introduction of new units, which could give rise to multiple bargaining. He recommended that existing province-wide bargaining units be maintained for the OPS, the Ontario Provincial Police, the Liquor Control Board of Ontario (LCBO) and Liquor Licence Board, and the other Crown agencies. The government supported Judge Little's recommendation on this point, and the Act removed any determination of the appropriate bargaining unit from the purview of the tribunal by providing in the *CECBA* that "the bargaining units designated in the Regulations are appropriate units for collective bargaining purposes under this Act." Bargaining units were designated for the OPS, the LCBO and Liquor Licence Board, Niagara Parks Commission, and Ontario Housing Corporation.[122]

In opposing the right to strike, Judge Little produced a spirited defence of the principle of executive sovereignty over the delivery of government services:[123]

> Governments are elected to formulate policies and make decisions for the benefit of the whole community. No individuals in the community, and particularly those who are employed to ensure, and are actively engaged in, the effective implementation of such policies and decisions, should be able by concerted action, to impede or frustrate such implementation, in order to enforce their will on the citizens as a whole.
>
> Those who favour extending the same rights to employees in the public sector as prevail in the private sector usually support their contention by the argument that some independent tribunal, or the government itself, should have the right to impose compulsory arbitration on an ad hoc basis if the welfare of the community is seriously

121 O Reg 577/72.

122 *Ibid.*

123 He adopted the view of Rand J that public service strikes were "the harbinger of social disintegration." See Ontario, Royal Commission of Inquiry into Labour Disputes (Commissioner Ivan C. Rand), *Report of the Royal Commission of Inquiry into Labour Disputes* (Toronto: Queen's Printer, 1968) at 111.

affected by a strike. In my view this is manifestly wrong in principle. Rights should not be granted to our citizens if, at the same time, it is contemplated that when they are legally exercised by them, they may be taken away. Such a "right" can only be characterized as a fiction and a mockery under such circumstances. It is therefore more prudent, and certainly more honest, to recognize initially, without equivocation, that the welfare of the community must prevail, and simply not grant a "right" which may prove completely abortive.

Furthermore, the principle of free collective bargaining is predicated upon the reciprocal rights of the employees to strike and the employer to enforce a lockout. It is inconceivable to me that public opinion would condone a lockout of public servants under any circumstances. Consequently, the right to strike cannot be justified and should likewise not prevail.

In view of the observations I have made and the conclusions I've reached, I must add in fairness that there undoubtedly have been situations, both federally and provincially, where public servants, had they been faced with the same working conditions and employer attitudes as have occurred in some situations in the private sector, could reasonably have decided to strike to enforce greater consideration of their demands. However, governments are demonstrating by their conduct their increasing realization that their employees are entitled to be remunerated for their services on a scale comparable to that in effect in the private sector.

It is therefore implicit in the conclusions I have reached against the right to strike in the public service that governments have a duty to ensure that those [who] are not accorded the right to strike are rewarded for their services on a basis at least as favorable as those who have such right. In addition, governments have a responsibility to see that this is accomplished in an expeditious and orderly manner. Justice delayed is justice denied, and this does not apply only to procedures in our courts.[124]

Judge Little also noted that the CSAO and the government were reasonably satisfied with the resolution of interest disputes by final and binding arbitration. The government justified its adoption of this recommendation on the basis that the public paid taxes to receive

124 *Little Report*, above note 116 at 42–43.

uninterrupted services and that public servants voluntarily accepted that they could not withdraw those services.[125]

A wide range of rights was recommended to not be bargainable, including departmental organization, complement (including whether to layoff), classification, job evaluation, the merit system, and superannuation or pensions. This recommendation was accepted by the government, which explained in the legislature that "there obviously must be limits to what may be so handed over [to the judgments of a third party], if the government of the day is to remain responsible for managing public programs in the public interest."[126] This distinction was difficult to administer in practice as the reserved items overlapped with bargainable items. For example, there was an obvious overlap between the bargainable matters of methods of promotion, demotion, transfer, layoff, and reappointment, and the non-bargainable matters of the principles and standards governing promotion, demotion, transfer, layoff, and reappointment.[127]

CECBA 1972, section 13, was clear that neither a collective agreement nor a decision of a board was to contain any term that would require, either directly or indirectly, the enactment or amendment of legislation for the implementation of such a term, except for the purpose of appropriating moneys for its implementation. The government stated that, as long as it was the guarantor of the pension fund, it was not prepared to add pensions to the list of arbitrable items.[128]

It was twenty years later, in 1993, that the legislation governing collective bargaining in the OPS was thoroughly revised. The reason for the change was the election of the NDP, which brought forward the current

---

125 Ontario, Legislative Assembly, *Hansard*, 4 May 1972, No 51 at 1994, and 9 May 1972, No 57 at 2247 (Charles McNaughton, Chair, Management Board of Cabinet).

126 Ontario Legislative Assembly, *Hansard*, 4 May 1972, No 51 at 1994–95 (Charles McNaughton, Chair, Management Board of Cabinet).

127 *CECBA 1972*, above note 105, ss 6 and 17. For a discussion of the leading cases on bargainability at the time, see Robert Hebdon, "The Freezing Effect of Public Sector Bargaining: The Case of Ontario Crown Employees" (1995) 24:3 *Journal of Collective Negotiations in the Public Sector* 233 at 244–49. See also *Re Liquor Control Board of Ontario et al and Ontario Liquor Board Employees Union* (1980), 29 OR (2d) 705 (Div Ct).

128 Ontario Legislative Assembly, *Hansard*, 11 February 1975, No 180 at 7546 (Eric Winkler, Chair, Management Board of Cabinet).

CECBA,[129] to introduce the right to strike. This shift was explained as being in the best interests of labour relations for the OPS and desired by both the government and the CSAO's greatly evolved successor, OPSEU. The government intended to make government labour relations fairer, less cumbersome, and less expensive, and, through replacing interest arbitration with the right to strike, to place the responsibility for resolution of workplace disputes on the two parties and not on arbitrators.[130]

Further, in what was stated to be "an especially welcome, long-awaited" development, most management rights were made the subject of collective bargaining.[131] It is worth noting that this contrasts with the federal public service regime where there are limits on bargaining over pensions, appointments, job classifications, assignment of duties, and layoff selection and processing.[132]

In speaking to the new *CECBA*, Frances Lankin, chair of the MBC, noted that, prior to her election, she had been an OPSEU executive board member and staff member and that the union and its chief negotiator, Andy Todd, had been working to reform the *CECBA* for twenty years.[133] Her critique of the labour relations aspects of the predecessor *CECBA 1972* was as follows:

> It was a regime which really relegated public servants, public service workers, to second-class citizens with respect to labour relations rights, a law which said there are certain issues that can't be negotiated, on which the employer has the complete right to determine all conditions, as the union has no ability to address this in the realm of collective bargaining, a law that dictated that the parties, if they had issues in dispute, would resolve them by reference to binding arbitration, a system which doesn't place pressures on the parties to deal seriously with their issues, a system which doesn't allow for the maturation of labour relations within the Ontario public service.

---

129 *CECBA*, above note 2, introduced through the *Public Service and Labour Relations Statute Law Amendment Act*, SO 1993, c 38. The bill also amended the *PSA* to increase political activity rights, as discussed in Chapter 4.

130 Ontario Legislative Assembly, *Hansard*, 18 November 1993, No 84 at 4145 (Mike Cooper, Parliamentary Assistant to the Minister of Labour) [Cooper].

131 *Ibid.*

132 *Federal Public Service Labour Relations Act*, SC 2003, c 22, s 2, s 113.

133 Ontario Legislative Assembly, *Hansard*, 14 December 1993, No 98A at 5020 (Francis Lankin, Chair, Management Board of Cabinet).

Further context was provided by testimony years later from a then MBS policy advisor and former OPSEU local president, Kevin Wilson:

> The Federal government's experience with compulsory arbitration had been of a negative nature. The government seemed to always be in bargaining, and there was no appetite or willingness to come to an agreement. Wage freezes lasted for lengthy periods and one unit or another was in arbitration, resulting in a lack of labour relations stability. Mr. Wilson testified that there was no desire for the Provincial government to model its legislation on this approach.[134]

While the creation of the right to strike made the *CECBA* more similar to the *LRA* regime, large differences were maintained. First was the inclusion of an essential services requirement. The right to strike was made contingent on ensuring that essential services would not be "threatened" by any strike or lockout.[135] Second was the retention of the requirement for large, stable bargaining units. As put by Mr. Wilson:

> The government had no desire to allow for smaller bargaining units because they lacked the bargaining strength to operate independently. These smaller units were viewed by the government as disadvantageous to both the employer and employee. Their preference was for larger units, which possessed positive traits such as more power and authority from which a more stable and efficient environment for collective bargaining would be present.[136]

Third, while most of the pre-existing restrictions on the negotiation of management rights were removed, one was retained and one was added. There was continuation of the pre-existing *CECBA* proviso that when making a decision, an interest arbitrator or board of arbitration should not include any term that would require, either directly or indirectly, the enactment or amendment of legislation for its

134 *Public Service Alliance of Canada v The Crown in Right of Ontario*, 2016 CanLII 5565 (ON LRB) at paras 14–18 [*PSAC v The Crown*]. Wilson was called as a witness in a case about a certification that attempted to create or "carve out" separate bargaining units for correctional front-line management.

135 Cooper, above note 130 at 4145.

136 *PSAC v The Crown*, above note 134 at paras 14–18. Large bargaining units also facilitated the inclusion of more employees in collective bargaining without needing to create new bargaining units. See the history of the creation of the AMAPCEO in Chapter 7.

implementation, except when the appropriation of money was required for its implementation.[137] The addition was a ban on the arbitrating of classification grievances.[138] The rationale was that classification grievances had resulted in frequent orders to reclassify employees, which had been costly and detracted from the capacity of the bargaining parties to negotiate bargaining classification adjustments.

Over the following thirty years, *CECBA 1993* was the subject of some amendment, particularly to increase the essential services requirement, but the scheme of the Act has remained generally intact. The major change was in 2016 to reintroduce interest arbitration for the OPS correctional bargaining unit. This development is reviewed in the Chapter 8 section on current *CECBA* collective bargaining.

137 *CECBA*, above note 2, s 4 (11).

138 *Ibid*, ss 51 & 52, as discussed in Chapter 11.

CHAPTER TWO

PSOA Employment

The *Public Service of Ontario Act 2006* (*PSOA*), proclaimed in 2007, replacing the *Public Service Act (PSA)*, addresses two primary concerns.[1] The first is to modernize the legal structure of the public service to align with the more centralized nature of modern government and a whole government approach to human resources while preserving its impartial, non-partisan nature. The second is to strengthen the ethical standards expected of public servants and expand the coverage to agencies. The beginning of this chapter addresses how the *PSOA* structures the public service. The remainder of the chapter reviews terms and conditions of employment established under Part III of the Act. The ethical framework, including the oaths of loyalty and office and Parts IV, V, and VI, of the *PSOA* dealing with conflict of interest, political activity, and disclosure of wrongdoing, are addressed in the next chapter.

A. LEGAL AND POLITICAL CONTEXT

In accordance with the *Constitution Act, 1867* and constitutional conventions, Ontario is a Westminster-model parliamentary democracy.[2] The executive branch of government is divided into ministries, each of

---

1 *Public Service of Ontario Act, 2006*, SO 2006, c 35, Sch A [*PSOA*], replacing *Public Service Act*, RSO 1990, c P.47 [*PSA*].

2 *Constitution Act, 1867* (UK), 30 & 31 Vict, c 3, s 134, reprinted in RSC 1985, App II, No 5 [*Constitution Act, 1867*]. See Chapter 1 for a discussion of the constitutional context.

which is headed by a minister who is answerable to the legislature for the conduct of their ministry. Executive authority resides with the elected executive council, or Cabinet, composed of the premier and their ministers.[3] The Cabinet is responsible for and has authority to direct the operations of government, including the public service. This includes the authority to create ministries (though key ministries are created by statute) or alter the assignment of responsibilities among ministers.[4]

A permanent politically neutral public service able to provide advice and implement political direction impartially and effectively is essential to the functioning of a parliamentary democracy.[5] New administrations must have a loyal, experienced, efficient, effective public service to allow the new administration to govern successfully and begin to implement their policy agenda when they take office. While the public service must be non-partisan, it must also be effectively directed and managed by the elected executive.

With the growth in the size and complexity of government, the former *PSA* became inconsistent with the increasingly centralized nature of modern government and the effective supervision of the public service by the elected executive.

The *PSOA* formalized a fundamental change in the structure of the public service from one that had separate ministries reporting to a deputy minister who reported to their minister, to a whole government structure where the management of the public service was centralized. The role of the secretary of the Cabinet as head of the public service was strengthened and formalized, with deputy ministers having a reporting relationship to the secretary. The role of the Management Board of Cabinet (MBC) was also strengthened. With the exception of hiring and dismissal, which are central to ensuring the non-partisan nature of the public service, the MBC retains authority over all aspects of the management and direction of the public service. In practice, responsibility for management of the public service is delegated to the Public Service Commission (PSC) and then to deputy ministers and their management teams, but the authority of the elected executive to direct or limit the exercise of delegated authority is clear so long as its directions do not compromise the non-partisan nature of the public service.

---

3 *Ibid*, ss 63, 65 & 66; *Executive Council Act*, RSO 1990, c E.25.

4 *Executive Council Act*, *ibid*, ss 2 and 5.

5 See Chapter 1 for a discussion of the role and attributes of the public service, and the history of its oversight.

The *PSOA* preserves the fundamental nature of the Westminster model while addressing the practical issues of maintaining an effective, democratically controlled, large, complex, and non-partisan public service.

B. APPLICATION OF THE ACT

1) Definitions and Terminology

The *PSOA* defines the "public service of Ontario" broadly to encompass both ministries, including ministers' offices, and public bodies. "Public bodies" are agencies prescribed by regulation for the purpose of making those bodies subject to the *PSOA*'s ethical framework.[6] "Public servants" are defined for the same purpose to be employees in ministries or public bodies, deputy ministers including the secretary of the Cabinet, and appointees to public bodies (except judicial appointees and officers of the legislature).[7] In practice, entities that are agencies of the government of Ontario are prescribed as public bodies.[8] Those provisions of the *PSOA* that apply to "public servants" apply to both ministry staff and appointees to and employees of public bodies.

The term "Ontario Public Service" (OPS) has been traditionally, but not statutorily, applied to the direct employees of the Ontario government. The OPS includes employees in ministries and in agencies of the Ontario government that do not have authority to hire their own employees that are prescribed as commission public bodies.[9] Under Part III of the Act, members of the OPS are appointed under the authority of the Public Service Commission to employment in ministries or commission public bodies under section 32, or by a person delegated by the premier or a minister to employment in a minister's office under section 47.

Appointments by the PSC may be "for a fixed term or otherwise."[10] In practice, "regular" appointments are for an indefinite period to a position established and classified within a ministry or commission public body. "Fixed- term" appointments are for a specific period and cease

6 *PSOA*, above note 1, s 2(1).
7 *Ibid*, s 2(2)d–(3).
8 O Reg 147/10.
9 *Ibid.*
10 *PSOA*, above note 1, s 32.

when the period ends.[11] Appointments by the PSC, either directly or with authority delegated by it, must be in writing. In the absence of an appointment under sections 32 or 47 in writing, an individual cannot be an employee in a ministry or in a commission public body.[12] Such status cannot be inferred from the workplace or role. This avoids the risk that a board or tribunal may find or deem an individual to be a member of the OPS.[13]

2) Interrelationship of the *PSOA* and Collective Agreements

The vast majority of public servants employed in the OPS are unionized. For most, their terms and conditions of employment are determined by collective agreements negotiated under the *Crown Employees Collective Bargaining Act (CECBA)*;[14] for provincial police officers, the *Ontario Provincial Police Collective Bargaining Act*;[15] or for professionals, voluntary agreements with their associations.[16] Where a provision of a collective agreement conflicts with a regulation or directive made under the *PSOA*, the collective agreement prevails.[17] This provision applies to the non-OPS public bodies whether they bargain collectively under the *CECBA* or the *Labour Relations Act*.[18]

Where no conflict arises between a collective agreement and a regulation or directive under the *PSOA*, the regulation or directive will apply to bargaining unit members. The provisions of the *PSOA* itself prevail over collective agreement terms in the event of a conflict. For bargaining unit employees in the OPS, this means the terms concerning hiring, discipline, and termination in Part III apply. The ethical obligations implied in the oaths, and the conflict of interest, political activity, and whistleblowing provisions of Parts IV, V, and VI also apply to all unionized public servants. The application of those provisions to

---

11 *Ibid*, s 54.

12 *Ibid*, s 52.

13 This also prevents a board or tribunal from determining the related scope of the *Crown Employees Collective Bargaining Act, 1993*, SO 1993, c 38 [*CECBA*]. See the discussion of determining employee status under both statutes in Chapter 7.

14 *Ibid*. Discussed in Chapter 7.

15 SO 2006, c 35, Sch B. Discussed in Chapter 4.

16 Framework agreements with lawyers, doctors, and dentists are discussed in Chapter 4.

17 *PSOA*, above note 1, s 152.

18 *Labour Relations Act, 1995*, SO 1995, c 1, Sch A.

members of a bargaining unit, including matters involving the discipline or termination of a bargaining unit member's employment or alleged reprisal for relying on the political activity or disclosure of wrongdoing provisions, are subject to grievance and arbitration by the union representing the public servant concerned.

The *CECBA* applies to employees in the ministries of government and commission public bodies. It also applies to other agencies prescribed (largely for historic reasons) under the *CECBA*. Prescribing an agency under the *CECBA* does not affect the application of the *PSOA* to the agency, and prescribing an agency as a public body under the *PSOA* does not affect the application of *CECBA* to the agency.

C. PSOA PART II: ROLES AND RESPONSIBILITIES IN THE ADMINISTRATION OF THE PUBLIC SERVICE OF ONTARIO

Under *PSOA* Part II, roles and responsibilities are specifically assigned to interconnected individuals and institutions.

1) Ministers

Each ministry is headed by a minister who is also a member of Cabinet and answerable in the legislature for their ministry. Ministries may be created by statute or by order in council (OIC). Each ministry has a deputy minister who is responsible for managing the ministry's staff. Ministers have no role in the management of the staff of their ministry. They may be involved in staffing their office, though this is normally delegated to an official in the premier's office or the minister's executive assistant.

2) Management Board of Cabinet

The MBC is the Cabinet committee that deals with matters relating to the administration of the OPS. It is established by the *Management Board of Cabinet Act (MBCA)*.[19] The actions of the MBC are subject to the directions of Cabinet which, under the *MBCA*, can revoke or amend its actions.[20]

---

19 RSO 1990, c M.1 [*MBCA*]. The MBC now sits as part of a joint subcommittee of Cabinet called Treasury Board/Management Board of Cabinet (TB/MBC).

20 *Ibid*, s 3(5).

The MBC is given broad responsibility under the *PSOA* for setting the terms and conditions of employment in the OPS.[21] The MBC has separate statutory authority under the *MBCA* in respect of the public service, defined to mean "every ministry, every Crown agency, every corporation, with or without share capital, that is not a Crown agency but is owned, operated, or controlled by the Crown, and every other board, commission, authority or unincorporated body of the Crown,"[22] which in practice includes all of the public service defined in the *PSOA*. The authority includes approval of organization and staffing of the public service, establishment of necessary policies and procedures, and the supervision of management practices and systems.[23]

The MBC is the vehicle that permits Cabinet to control and manage the public service. However, the MBC is not permitted to issue a directive or set a policy or procedure under either the *PSOA* or the *MBCA* that would be "inconsistent with the non-partisan nature of the public service."[24]

3) Public Service Commission

The *PSOA* continues the Civil Service Commission,[25] originally created under the *PSA*, as the PSC. The members of the PSC are appointed by OIC,[26] and in practice the PSC is a committee of deputy ministers.

The statutory responsibilities of the PSC are set out in *PSOA* Part III. The role of the PSC is to ensure the hiring, promotion, discipline, and dismissal of public servants employed directly by the government (excluding ministers' office staff) is non-partisan. It is also responsible for protecting the merit principle in the management of the OPS. The PSC delegates its responsibility for hiring, discipline, and termination to deputy ministers but has retained authority to appoint assistant or associate deputy ministers and equivalent levels of executive, as well

---

21 *PSOA*, above note 1, s 33.

22 *Ibid*, s 1(1).

23 *MBCA*, above note 19, s 3(1).

24 *PSOA*, above note 1, s 43(4).

25 *Ibid*, s 9(1).

26 *Ibid*, s 9(2).

as its authority over dismissals of public servants in all executive class positions.[27]

The Cabinet may assign additional responsibilities to the PSC by regulation, and the MBC may and has delegated many of its responsibilities to the PSC.[28]

4) The Secretary of the Cabinet

The secretary of the Cabinet is clerk of the executive council and the head of the Public Service of Ontario, with the authority to appoint public servants to act for absent deputy ministers.[29] Cabinet office is the premier's ministry, and the secretary of the Cabinet is the premier's deputy minister.[30] The secretary of the Cabinet's tenure is that of a deputy minister, as discussed below. The position of the secretary of the Cabinet and head of the public service predates the *PSOA*, but the *PSOA* has enhanced the formal authority of the position. The authority to appoint acting deputy ministers rested with the minister under the former *PSA*.[31] The MBC *Human Resource Management Directive* now provides that the secretary of the Cabinet will manage the performance of deputy ministers and communicate Cabinet's decisions to them.[32]

The secretary is appointed to the PSC. Significantly, the secretary also chairs the internal Executive Development Committee, composed of senior deputy ministers, which has existed since the late 1980s. It is concerned with corporate organization, executive recruitment, the size of the OPS executive group, and executive development. The chair of the PSC also sits on the Executive Development Committee.

---

27 Public Service Commission (PSC), *Business Plan for 2021–2024*, online: www.ontario.ca/page/public-service-commission-business-plan-202122-202324 [*PSC Business Plan*].

28 *PSOA*, above note 1, s 31(1)g and s 45, respectively.

29 *Ibid*, ss 28 and 30. The power to appoint a public servant to act for a deputy can also be delegated to the deputy minister with conditions or restrictions.

30 *Ibid*, s 4.

31 *PSA*, above note 1, s 21(2).

32 MBC, *Human Resources Management Directive*, 12 May 2017, online: www.ontario.ca/page/human-resources-management-directive, ss 10.52–10.53 [*MBC Directive*].

5) Deputy Ministers

A deputy minister is responsible for the operation of their ministry to fulfill the agenda of the minister.[33] At the same time, deputy ministers are public servants under the *PSOA* and consequently are to be non-partisan and adhere to the Act's ethical framework in carrying out their duties.[34] They are to "promote effective, non-partisan, professional, ethical and competent public service by public servants."[35]

Deputy ministers are not appointed under *PSOA* Part III, and the terms of deputy minister appointments are not prescribed by statute. Their terms of employment are normally established in an individual contract of employment in accordance with standards set for deputy minister compensation. The deputies are appointed by OIC, on recommendation by the premier and, subject to any contractual termination benefits, are subject to removal by OIC without cause.[36]

The *PSOA* reflects a significant change in the deputy minister position over time. Deputy ministers once sat at the apex of the permanent public service in answering to their ministers, with full managerial authority derived from their statutory responsibility for the operation of their ministry.[37] They now answer to the secretary of the Cabinet as head of the public service.[38] From the point of view of ministry staff, the deputy minister is the person in charge of the ministry, much as deputies have always been. However, under the *PSOA*, authority over human resource matters is now centralized under the MBC and the

---

33 *PSOA*, above note 1, s 29(1).

34 *Ibid*, s 2(2)3.

35 *Ibid*, s 29(3).

36 Ministries are usually created by statute, which may often create the position of deputy minister to be appointed by OIC (e.g., see *Ministry of Community Safety and Correctional Services Act, 2018*, SO 2018, c 6, Sch 1, s 5) or may just define the role of the deputy minister (e.g., see *Ministry of Health and Long-Term Care Act*, RSO 1990, c M.26, s 4).

37 The principle of the deputy minister's wide managerial authority under the former *PSA* was affirmed in *Legris and Department of Lands and Forests*, PSGB#386/71, 13–14 July 1967 (Presgrave) through an attached opinion of the attorney general, as adopted in *Douglas*, PSGB#596/71, 14 October 1971 (Presgrave) at 3–4, where the Public Service Grievance Board stated "[t]he Board is in full agreement with this statement of principle and sees nothing to be gained by further debating it."

38 Under the *PSA*, above note 1, s 8, authority to hire unclassified staff (fixed-term under the *PSOA*) was delegated to deputy ministers from their minister.

PSC and exercised through mandatory directives, policies, or guidelines and delegation of authority to deputy ministers who may delegate authority within their ministry. Deputies are to establish mechanisms for employee "awareness, instruction and compliance" with the *PSOA* and all directives and policies.[39] While deputies answer to their minister in respect of the conduct of the ministry, ministries are now part of an OPS that "functions as a single employer" with an enterprise-wide human resources system.[40] Treasury Board Secretariat (TBS), formerly Management Board Secretariat (MBS), provides central advice, support, and monitoring, and sets performance measures, answering to the MBC and the PSC.[41]

6) Integrity Commissioner

The integrity commissioner is established under the *Members Integrity Act, 1994*[42] and is authorized in Part III of the *PSOA* to fulfill the roles assigned to that office under the conflict of interest, political activity, and disclosure of wrongdoing parts of the *PSOA*. The commissioner is an officer of the legislature who reports directly to the legislature regarding matters assigned to them.[43] This circumvents the traditional reporting relationship to the legislature through the ministers and provides a new avenue for supervision of aspects of conduct of the public service of particular concern to the legislature. The MBC and the minister can require matters to be included in the commissioner's annual report, preserving the executive's right to ensure the report to the legislature is, in its view, complete.[44]

The integrity commissioner and employees in the commission's office are protected from personal liability when acting in good faith in the performance of their duties.[45] The integrity commissioner and the

39 *MBC Directive*, above note 32, s 10.21.

40 *Ibid*, s 8.1.

41 *Ibid*, ss 10.24–10.30. TBS is also responsible for representing the MBC in OPS collective bargaining, as discussed in Chapter 7.

42 SO 1994, c 38.

43 *Ibid*, ss 23 and 25; *PSOA*, above note 1, s 18.

44 *PSOA*, above note 1, s 18.

45 *Ibid*, s 19.

staff of their office are neither competent nor compellable witnesses regarding anything done under the Act.[46]

7) Public Service Grievance Board

The *PSOA* continues the Public Service Grievance Board (PSGB),[47] which was originally created by regulation under the *PSA*. The PSGB is an adjudicative board, and its members are appointed by OIC for a fixed term.[48] The PSGB provides a process for a group of non-unionized public servants defined by the Cabinet in regulation to seek specific performance of the terms and conditions of their employment, including the right to grieve for reinstatement if unjustly dismissed for cause. The scope and limitations on complaints to the PSGB are prescribed by regulation under authority provided in Part II of the *PSOA*. The PSGB is also given statutory authority over reprisal complaints under the political activity and disclosure of wrongdoing parts of the Act.[49] Unlike common law employment remedies available in the courts, which do not include specific performance, the PSGB in effect holds the management of the OPS to the rule of law by providing specific enforcement of the terms of employment determined by the MBC or made under its authority. The PSGB and its functions are addressed at length in Chapter 12.

For unionized employees under the *CECBA*, a similar enforcement function is carried out by the Grievance Settlement Board, described in Chapter 11.

D. *PSOA* PART III: EMPLOYMENT BY THE CROWN

1) Authority

Part III of the *PSOA* establishes the line of authority over public servants employed in the ministries and agencies prescribed as commission public bodies, including employment in ministers' offices. These arrangements address three key issues: appropriate political control over the public service, maintenance of the non-partisan nature of the

46 *Ibid*, s 19.

47 *Ibid*, s 21(1).

48 *Ibid*, s 21(2).

49 *Ibid*, ss 104(3) and 140(3), respectively.

OPS, and managing the inherently partisan nature of public service employment in ministers' offices.

a) Employment in Ministries and Commission Public Bodies

The PSC is responsible for ensuring the OPS is non-partisan.[50] It is given express exclusive statutory authority to appoint persons to employment[51] in the OPS, impose discipline, and end such employment,[52] except with respect to employment in ministers' offices. The PSC is given authority to issue directives governing the management and administration of human resources of the public servants appointed by it or under its delegated authority.[53] Unlike its authority over hiring and termination, the PSC's directive-making authority is subordinate to MBC directives.[54] However, the MBC may not issue directives or policies that are inconsistent with the non-partisan nature of the public service.[55]

Until the 1990s, the PSC's authority to involuntarily terminate the employment of public servants was limited to circumstances of misconduct by the public servant, shortage of work or funds, or elimination/reorganization of the public servant's position. Then, as discussed below, authority was provided to dismiss without cause on reasonable notice. The original requirement that involuntary termination had to be justified against a business requirement or disciplinary cause protected against partisan interference and provided public servants with a significant level of security in exchange for their commitment to the public service. The use of not-for-cause termination has been restrained, and since it is exercised by the PSC it will presumably not be subject to partisan abuse. The potential impact on long-term commitment to the OPS is harder to assess.

The MBC is responsible for determining the terms and conditions of employment in the OPS, including in ministers' offices. It may, by directive, create classes of positions, the duties of and qualifications for the positions, wage ranges, other remuneration (including benefits), and establish other terms and conditions of employment for public servants

---

50 *Ibid*, s 43(2)
51 *Ibid*, s 32.
52 *Ibid*, ss 34–42.
53 *Ibid*, s 43(1).
54 *Ibid*, s 43(3).
55 *Ibid*, s 43(4).

in ministries and commission public bodies.[56] The MBC is required to maintain an archive of all such directives indicating the period during which each directive applies.[57] These directives form part of public servants' contracts of employment and are administratively binding on OPS management,[58] but they are not subject to Part III (regulations) of the *Legislation Act, 2006*.[59] The *PSOA* expressly distinguishes between directives and regulations: MBC directives impose administrative and contractual obligations but do not have the force of regulations.

The terms and conditions of unionized employees are determined by their collective agreements, which are negotiated with the MBC. Where MBC or PSC directives or policies conflict with a collective agreement, the collective agreement term will prevail.[60]

The MBC may delegate its authority to create positions and set wage ranges and other terms and conditions of employment of public servants appointed by the PSC to the OPS,[61] and in practice it does.[62] The PSC has authority to delegate both its authority over the appointment and termination of public servants, and any authority delegated to it by the MBC, to deputy ministers who are authorized to subdelegate this authority to public servants in their ministry.[63] With the approval of the PSC, a deputy minister may subdelegate their authority, with the exception of authority to dismiss or declare a position abandoned, to an individual other than a *PSOA* Part III public servant.[64]

The delegation of authority from the MBC and then the PSC establishes a chain of authority and supervision. Both bodies have the responsibility to communicate their plans, directives, and policies.[65] Deputy ministers are then responsible for the management of their ministries and in that regard answer through the secretary of the Cabinet to the premier, and through the premier to the Cabinet and the legislature. Deputies are also responsible for supporting their minister, who is responsible for the

---

56 *Ibid*, s 33(1) to (4).
57 *Ibid*, s 33(7).
58 *Lee et al v Ontario (Ministry of Community Safety and Correctional Services)*, 2013 CanLII 4672 (ON PSGB) at para 50.
59 *PSOA*, above note 1, s 33(6); *Legislation Act, 2006*, SO 2006, c 21, Sch F.
60 *PSOA*, above note 1, s 152.
61 *Ibid*, s 45.
62 *PSC Business Plan*, above note 27.
63 *PSOA*, above note 1, s 44(1)(2).
64 *Ibid*, s 44(3).
65 *MBC Directive*, above note 32, "Mandatory Requirements," s 9.1.

conduct of the ministry and answers to the legislature for the ministry. Managers and employees are expected to uphold the directives and policies, and employees are expected to comply with them.[66]

The legislative scheme provides for a number of structures to ensure compliance. Collective agreements are policed by the unions, and alleged non-compliance is addressed through grievance and arbitration. Non-union public servants, with the exception of senior managers, are entitled to grieve to the PSGB about failures to comply with certain terms and conditions established by the MBC. Dismissals for cause are reviewable by the PSGB on complaint by non-union public servants. As will be noted in the Chapter 3 discussion of the conflict of interest, political activity, and disclosure of wrongdoing provisions, the integrity commissioner, an officer of the legislature, has a role in seeing that those key standards are subject to non-partisan review and, at an individual level, serious wrongdoing can be reported and addressed outside the normal line of authority.

b) Employment in a Minister's Office

The *PSOA* recognizes minister's offices as distinct entities that, while part of the OPS supporting ministers in their public function, do have an inherently partisan character. The staff of ministers' offices are appointed for a fixed term under section 47 of the *PSOA* by a person designated by the premier, or if no person is designated by the premier then the minister. The premier's designee or the minister may delegate responsibility for appointing the minister's office staff to the minister's executive assistant. The authority to discipline or dismiss any minister's office staff rests with the person with authority to appoint and may be similarly delegated. A prudent minister will leave the hiring and management of their staff to their executive assistant and the premier's office.

The rules regarding employment in a minister's office are similar to those for PSC appointees. The MBC has the same authority to establish the terms and conditions of employment by directive.[67] The disciplinary provisions, and those dealing with layoff, resignation, and abandonment, that are applicable to PSC appointees also apply to ministers' staff with necessary modifications to reflect that the person who appoints

66 *Ibid*, s 10.11 discusses the responsibility of managers to establish clear responsibilities for employees, including compliance with directives and policies, and ss 10.1 and 10.4 discuss the responsibility for employees to comply, at risk of discipline.

67 *PSOA*, above note 1, s 48.

a minister's office staff acts in the place of the PSC in respect of those provisions.[68] Since the ministers' office staff are all fixed-term appointees, they are not subject to probation periods. Ministers' office staff can be dismissed on reasonable notice by the person designated to appoint them under section 47.[69]

2) Terms and Conditions of Employment

This section briefly sets out how the MBC's and PSC's directive and policy authority has been exercised.

a) Human Resources Policy

The current PSC directive, *Employment Policy*, establishes practices for recruitment, development, deployment, and retention that are to apply the principles of "merit, inclusion and accessibility" and be "fair, objective, reasonable and transparent."[70] A range of employment practices are covered, and only highlights are discussed below.

Competitions are to be used to fill vacancies "unless other selection methods better meet business or operational goals."[71] Those other methods are competition waivers, talent pools, and talent management.[72] The selection criteria are to be qualifications that "reflect the relative importance of each aspect of the work."[73] "Employee selection must be based on a thorough assessment of the candidate's ability to demonstrate the qualifications required for effective performance."[74] Seniority does not form part of the selection criteria. The application of this policy by the PSGB is discussed at length in Chapter 12. That application contrasts with the OPS collective agreement job competition provisions giving effect to seniority, which are discussed in Chapter 10. In any event, the policy has processes for eligibility to apply, screening, and rating.

When "workforce adjustment" occurs either through the transfer of work out of the OPS or downsizing, the policy's mandatory

---

68 *Ibid*, s 49.

69 *Ibid*, s 50.

70 Public Service Commission, *Employment Policy*, 6 November 2020, provided to the authors, s 6.2 [*PSC Employment Policy*].

71 *Ibid*, "Recruitment and Selection, Preamble" at 5.

72 *Ibid*, "Other Recruitment and Selection Methods" at 12.

73 *Ibid*, "Selection Criteria" at 5.

74 *Ibid*, s 8.29.

requirements include six months' notice of layoff; enhanced severance and exit options, including immediate payout on notice; or remaining employed with the opportunity to be redeployed.[75] There is some similarity to the collectively bargained provisions, which are discussed at length in Chapter 9, with two major differences.

First, for transfers there is no requirement for the employer to make "reasonable efforts" to have the new employer make a comparable job offer on divestment. This contrasts with the collective agreement "reasonable efforts" provisions discussed in Chapter 9. For non-unionized employees, where the employer does negotiate a job offer or offers with the new employer, and an employee refuses a comparable (or better) job offer from the new employer, the employee is not eligible to receive enhanced severance.[76] Under the policy, comparability is determined by the PSC. For unionized employees, the issue of comparability can be brought to arbitration before the Grievance Settlement Board (GSB).

Second, with respect to entitlements on layoff, or "job security," under the policy, seniority is not a factor in determining who is laid off. When making layoff decisions, within the part of the public service not covered by a collective agreement, the determination of the employees to be laid off in a downsizing of multi-incumbent positions is determined by competition among incumbents for the remaining positions.[77] The most qualified employees are to be retained based on assessed merit, and "[l]ayoff decisions must not be based on the length of an employee's continuous service." This contrasts with the collective agreement seniority-based "job security" entitlements discussed at length in Chapter 9.

b) Human Rights Commitment

The OPS is committed, under the MBC *Respectful Workplace Policy (Policy to Support a Respectful Workplace and Prevent Workplace Harassment and Discrimination)*, to fostering and sustaining workplaces that are "inclusive, diverse, equitable, accessible and free from workplace harassment and discrimination."[78] The legal implications of this

75 *Ibid*, s 8.29.

76 *Ibid*, ss 10.9 & 10.10.

77 *Ibid*, s 10.6.

78 *Respectful Workplace Policy (Policy to Support a Respectful Workplace and Prevent Workplace Harassment and Discrimination)*, 1 October 2017, copy made available to authors, Art 4.1.

commitment are discussed at length in Chapter 6. There are also policies on preventing barriers to employment, disability accommodation, and workplace violence prevention.

c) Setting of Terms and Conditions for Categories of Employees

The MBC creates classes of positions for public servants appointed by the PSC and determines:

- the duties of and qualifications for the positions
- salary or wage ranges
- other remuneration, including benefits
- other terms and conditions of employment for public servants[79]

These powers extend to the terms and conditions of employment for public servants appointed to work in ministers' offices.[80] MBC directives may be general or particular, but are usually fairly general.

Collective agreements made in accordance with legislative bargaining procedures are to be implemented.[81] Where a provision in a collective agreement conflicts with a provision in a directive, the provision in the collective agreement prevails,[82] and where there is no conflicting collective agreement provision, the directive provision will apply.

d) Classification

Similar job duties are bundled together into classifications. Those classifications are then used as the basis for determining standard rates of pay and benefits appropriate to those bundled duties. The intent is "consistency of practice throughout the public service, and equitable treatment of individual employees. It follows that it is an abuse of the system and unfair to employees if the positions of employees who are performing substantially similar work are placed in different classifications."[83]

---

79 *PSOA*, above note 1, s 33. The responsibilities of the MBC and PSC are set out in the *MBC Directive*, above note 32.

80 *PSOA*, above note 1, s 47.

81 *Ibid*, s 153. This includes decisions of the OPP Negotiating Committee and any OPP interest arbitration board: *PSOA*, s 154.

82 *Ibid*, s 152.

83 *OPSEU (Beals and Cain) and Ministry of Community and Social Services*, GSB#29/79, 20 May 1981 (Draper) at 11.

The public service is divided into six classifications:

- *Deputy ministers:* Terms of employment are normally set in an individual employment contract negotiated in accordance with the terms of the compensation plan for deputy ministers.
- *Senior management group (SMG):* This group includes the classifications that apply to the senior management level of the public service, typically associate deputy ministers, assistant deputy ministers, executive directors, directors, and some other senior staff.
- *Management compensation plan (MCP)/excluded employees:*[84] The MCP covers managers below the rank of SMG, non-managerial administrative staff of matching "rank," and professional staff excluded from the *CECBA*. The plan also covers all technical, clerical, operational, and administrative staff as well as staff employed in confidential capacities who are excluded from bargaining units under the *CECBA*. Where the entire group is being referred to, they are often called the "management and excluded group." Excluded non-managerial employees will be treated separately for some purposes.
- *Unionized employees under the* CECBA: This group includes those employed in the bargaining units of the Ontario Public Service Employees Union (OPSEU), Association of Management, Administrative and Professional Crown Employees of Ontario (AMAPCEO), and Professional Engineers of the Government of Ontario.
- *Ontario Provincial Police (OPP) members*: this includes those who are uniform and civilian.
- *Practising lawyers and medical professionals.*

The OPP and members of the legal and medical professions are further discussed in Chapter 4.

The current classifications are largely the product of the MBC *Continuation of Existing Classes and Salaries Directive*,[85] under which all classifications, salaries, and salary ranges (including adjustments and pay for performance) that were put in effect under the now repealed *PSA* and its detailed regulation on terms and conditions of employment

---

84 For a discussion of bargaining unit exclusions, see Chapter 7.

85 MBC, *Continuation of Existing Classes and Salaries Directive*, 12 May 2017, online: www.ontario.ca/page/continuation-existing-classes-and-salaries-directive.

(O Reg 977) are continued until amended or replaced by a further MBC directive. Under the PSC *Classification and Position Administration Directive*,[86] individual position specifications must be revised and positions re-evaluated when there are significant changes to the organization or job duties.

While classification can be collectively bargained, it is not arbitrable. The PSGB does not have jurisdiction over the assignment of a public servant to a particular "class of position";[87] and the *CECBA* prohibits the GSB from requiring the creation of a new classification or the alteration of an existing classification, or from requiring a change to be made in the classification of an employee, although the GSB will enforce agreements concerning the process of classification and any agreed adjustments to classifications.[88] This returns the focus to the status quo of management-established classifications and any collective bargaining adjustments. The OPSEU/MBC and AMAPCEO/MBC collective agreements prohibit reclassification to another bargaining unit.[89]

Under the MBC *Compensation Directive*,[90] the effect on an employee of position reclassifications and reassignments to lower classifications is ameliorated by transitional provisions.

e) Salaries

Under the *Salary Rates/Ranges Directive*, all salary rates must be the approved ones or those negotiated with approved bargaining units,

---

86 PSC, *Classification and Position Administration Directive*, 1 November 2012, provided to the authors.

87 O Reg 378/07, s 4(2)2, as discussed in Chapter 12.

88 *CECBA*, above note 13, s 52, discussed in Chapter 11. For examples of a process agreement, see *OPSEU/MBC Unified Bargaining Unit Collective Agreement, 2022–2024* and *OPSEU/MBC Correctional Bargaining Unit Collective Agreement, 2018–2021*, Appendix 34, Classification System, online: https://opseu.org/information/general/find-your-collective-agreement [*OPSEU/MBC Unified and Correctional Collective Agreements*]; *AMAPCEO/MBC Collective Agreement, 2018–2022*, Memorandum of Agreement re Implementation of New Job Evaluation System, 18 October 2012, online: https://amapceo.on.ca/ops.

89 *OPSEU/MBC Unified and Correctional Collective Agreements*, above note 88, Art 1.6; *AMAPCEO/MBC Collective Agreement, 2018–2022*, above note 88, Art 48.

90 MBC, *Compensation Directive*, 20 August 2007, provided to the authors, s 28 [*Compensation Directive*].

and in both cases will relate to classifications, except that individual arrangements are allowed for the SMG and deputy ministers.[91]

Employees are to have an anniversary date for their position and, "provided their work is satisfactory," receive at least annual or semi-annual increases until they progress to the maximum of the salary range of their class.[92]

f) Benefits and Perquisites

Under the *Compensation Directive*, regular full-time employees are generally entitled to a fairly standard set of benefits—holidays and vacation, sick leave, and special and compassionate leave.[93] All benefits are subject to collective bargaining.

The Crown enters into agreements with insurance underwriters for provision of benefit plans: life insurance, long-term disability, critical illness, and supplementary health, dental, accidental death, and dismemberment coverage.[94] The levels of benefits provided to employees are set by the terms of the agreements with the insurance companies, except as specifically provided in the *Compensation Directive*. All benefits are subject to variation through collective bargaining, and collective agreements commonly contain enhanced benefits provisions.[95]

Fixed-term employees are generally excluded from coverage under the common benefit provisions and then separately provided reduced benefits, notably 6 percent of wages, in lieu of the group insured benefits.

Under the *Perquisites Directive*, no perks are permitted, thus banning any "privilege that is provided to an individual or to a group of individuals [that] provides a personal benefit, is not generally available to others, and is not a business-related requirement," like club memberships and sport seasons tickets.[96] This helps avoid arrangements that

---

91 MBC, *Salary Rates/Ranges Directive*, 12 May 2017, online: www.ontario.ca/page/salary-rates-ranges-directive. The directive does not apply to the SMG or deputy ministers.

92 MBC, *Merit Increases Directive*, 12 May 2017, online: www.ontario.ca/page/merit-increases-directive. The directive does not apply to the SMG or deputy ministers.

93 *Compensation Directive*, above note 90, ss 30–84.

94 *Ibid*, s 49.

95 For example, see the benefits provisions in the *OPSEU/MBC Unified and Correctional Collective Agreements*, above note 88; and the *AMAPCEO/MBC Collective Agreement 2018–2022*, above note 88.

96 MBC, *Perquisites Directive*, 12 May 2017, online: www.ontario.ca/page/perquisites-directive. Special consideration for individual business-related

would circumvent the intended consistency of compensation administration and that can lead to conflicts of interest.[97]

g) Hours of Work

The *Hours of Work Directive* sets out the principle that "hours of work shall be arranged to facilitate the achievement of organizational objectives and serve the convenience of the public, while accommodating employee needs wherever possible" and that employees are to be assigned the hours prescribed for their position's classification.[98] Each class is listed in a schedule of a group of classes contained in the "Hours of Work" section of the *Compensation Directive*, and each schedule has common hours of work, all to ensure that individuals in positions with certain shared characteristics receive similar hours of work.

Virtually all the classifications in the OPS, including all positions that are found in *CECBA* bargaining units, have been listed in schedules. Schedule 3, mainly office employees, has a maximum of 36 ¼ hours per week; Schedule 4, mainly operational staff, has a maximum of 40 hours per week; Schedule 5, mainly lead hands, has variable hours with a minimum of 36 ¼ hours and a maximum of 40 hours per week; Schedule 6 has variable hours, with a minimum of 36 ¼ hours per week but no maximum.[99]

The lack of maximum hours in Schedule 6 is to address the varying demands of professional or managerial work, where employees are expected to manage their own time and workload.[100] As this may not adequately recognize the link between compensation and the demands placed on an employee's time, the directive also creates management compensation option (MCO) credits, commonly known as MCO days.[101] They are similar to vacation credits but do not have a cash value on termination of employment. MCO credits compensate Schedule 6 regular management employees and professionals (that is, archi-

---

requirements must be "well documented" and publicly available. See also the *Travel, Meal, and Hospitality Directive*, November 2004, online: www.ontario.ca/page/travel-meal-and-hospitality-expenses-directive-2020.

97 See conflict of interest requirements discussed in Chapter 3.

98 MBC, *Hours of Work Directive*, 12 May 2017, online: www.ontario.ca/page/hours-work-directive. The directive does not apply to the SMG and deputy ministers.

99 *Compensation Directive*, above note 90, s 3.1.

100 *Employment Standards Act, 2000*, SO 2000, c 41 [*ESA*], including the hours of work provisions in ss 17–19, does apply to the Crown. See Chapter 6.

101 *Compensation Directive*, above note 90, s 4.

tects, engineers, dentists, doctors, and lawyers) for the otherwise unpaid overtime they are expected to work from time to time. Term employees do not receive MCO days and neither do regular employees in *CECBA* units or non-managerial employees excluded from those units.

Based on the schedules, specific hours of work are set.[102] A deputy minister may set shorter or longer hours for any position in a classification listed in Schedules 3 or 4, and shorter hours for any position in Schedules 5 or 6. The salary is pro-rated accordingly. A minimum of fourteen hours per week or nine full days in four consecutive weeks must be maintained.

The classification schedules deal only with regular employees, which means that fixed-term employees are implicitly excluded. However, fixed-term staff will normally work the hours set for the position, because this will be the requirement under their contract or collective agreement, and not because of a directive requirement.

The employer's power to unilaterally prescribe the hours of work can only be limited by a specifically negotiated restriction. If the collective agreement lacks such a specific limitation, the employer is free to unilaterally allocate classifications to hours of work schedules,[103] subject only to the possible limitation that the employer's discretionary power must not be used in an arbitrary or discriminatory way. The current OPSEU/MBC collective agreement[104] provisions state that where the employer intends to transfer employees or an employee between schedules, the employer will, before the transfer, discuss the transfer with the union, and, when the transfer takes place, the employee's weekly salary, based on their basic hourly rate, will be adjusted. The current AMAPCEO/MBC collective agreement establishes that the hours of work for the AMAPCEO unit are set out in Schedule 6.[105]

3) Discipline, Suspension, and Termination

PSOA sections 34 to 42 structure and limit the power of OPS management to discipline, suspend, and terminate OPS employees. The history

102 *Compensation Directive*, above note 90, s 3(2)–(6).

103 *OPSEU (Gillespie, Costello, Legouffe) and Ministry of Natural Resources*, GSB#1711/96, 16 December 1999 (Brown) at 5 and cases cited therein.

104 *OPSEU/MBC Unified and Correctional Collective Agreements*, above note 88, UN 2.6, Corr 2.6.

105 *AMAPCEO/MBC Collective Agreement*, above note 88, Art 46.1.

of the legislation makes it clear that statutory security of tenure protections were viewed as important to support the impartiality and permanence of the public service.[106]

The power to discipline and dismiss employees is vested in the PSC and its delegates.[107] It is subject to extensive limitations in the *PSOA* and the PSC's *Employment Policy* (except that the policy has very limited application for fixed-term employees in short-term roles).[108] Disciplinary and dismissal powers may be delegated by the PSC to a deputy minister, who may delegate those powers to public servants in their ministry.[109] With the approval of the PSC, a deputy may delegate to a non-public servant the power to engage in a disciplinary suspension, investigative suspension, and approve the withdrawal of resignation, but not the power to dismiss a public servant or to declare abandonment.[110]

There is no specific legislative or directive treatment of disciplinary warnings, but they are regularly used. Disciplinary demotions are rarely if ever used and seem incompatible with the detailed scheme of discipline discussed below. The PSC's *Employment Policy* treats demotion as primarily non-disciplinary and to be used when the employee demonstrates an inability to perform the essential duties of the position.[111]

In all cases of suspension and dismissal, an employee must be issued a written notice citing the relevant authority for the suspension or dismissal.[112] (This entitlement does not apply to fixed-term employees in Group 1.)

Employees will typically have access to some form of adjudication of any discipline or dismissal. Unionized employees have access to the grievance process under their collective agreements and to arbitration at the GSB.[113] Grievances of members of lawyers' bargaining units and the OPP may proceed to private arbitration or statutory tribunals.[114]

---

106 See the Chapter 1 discussion of security of tenure.

107 *PSOA*, above note 1, s 34.

108 *PSC Employment Policy*, above note 70 at 34. The only substantive section of the policy that applies to fixed-term employees in Group 1, those in short-term roles, is "Termination of Fixed-Term Non-Represented Employees."

109 *PSOA*, above note 1, s 44(1) and (2).

110 *Ibid*, s 44(3).

111 *PSC Employment Policy*, above note 70 at 22, setting out when a demotion may occur, and non-statutory procedural requirements.

112 *Ibid*, s 11, "Mandatory Requirements."

113 See the discussion of the GSB in Chapter 11.

114 See the discussion of special categories of employees in Chapter 4.

Non-unionized employees will be able to proceed to the PSGB[115] or to the courts.[116]

The discussion below deals only with those largely procedural aspects of discipline and dismissal addressed in *PSOA* Part III. Standards of conduct established by the public service ethical framework are addressed in Chapter 3. The only other systemic effort by the PSC to set standards for discipline is the general statement in the MBC *Human Resources Management Directive* that employees are to "understand that employees found to have violated any HR directive or policy may be subject to discipline up to and including dismissal, in accordance with the principles of progressive discipline"[117] and that managers are to establish "clear and specific accountabilities, duties and responsibilities for every employee including the importance and implications of employee compliance" with human resources directives and policies.[118]

a) Disciplinary Suspension

A disciplinary suspension is to be without pay and cannot be longer than one month,[119] which has been interpreted as being twenty working days.[120]

Where a grievor has been discharged and then reinstated on the basis that the discharge is not warranted, it seems that the record can then only reflect a suspension of twenty days.[121] It has been asserted that it is only in "rare cases," where the grievor's record was exceptionally poor, that compensation for the remaining period off work can be denied.[122] However, GSB vice-chairs have not hesitated to replace discharge penalties with lengthy suspensions,[123] and in effect the

---

115 See Chapter 12.

116 See Chapter 13.

117 *MBC Directive*, above note 32, s 10(4).

118 *Ibid*, s 10.11.

119 *PSOA*, above note 1, s 35.

120 *Rimmer and Ministry of Government Services*, PSGB#865/75, 18 November 1975 (Presgrave) at 7; *OPSEU (Antle) and Ministry of Correctional Services*, GSB#66/76, 24 November 1976 (Beatty) at 2.

121 *Ontario Public Service Employees Union (Rodriques) v Ontario (Labour)*, 2007 CanLII 14614 (ON GSB) at 7.

122 *Ibid*.

123 For example, see *Ontario Public Service Employees Union (Girardi) v Ontario (Community Safety and Correctional Services)*, 2009 CanLII 59465 (ON GSB) at 21–22; *Ontario Public Service Employees Union (Fraser) v Ontario (Community Safety and Correctional Services)*, 2012 CanLII 24024 (ON GSB).

twenty-day limit has been routinely ignored by the GSB. It may be that the appropriate disposition for conduct that does not warrant discharge but does warrant consequences more serious than a twenty-day suspension is for the formal discipline to be for twenty days and for the remaining period of absence post-discharge to be without compensation.[124]

Under the *Employment Policy*, the employee must be issued a written notice of suspension stating the effective date and duration of the suspension, the reason for the suspension, the authority for the suspension,[125] and the employee's right to submit a grievance to the appropriate grievance board, as applicable.[126]

b) Suspension Pending Investigation

Investigations may be conducted to determine if there is cause for discipline or dismissal.[127] Under the *PSOA*, a public servant can be suspended during the investigation for up to two years.[128] Under the *Employment Policy*, the initial and any subsequent period of suspension must not exceed twenty working days, and the employer is to ensure the investigation proceeds in "an expeditious manner."[129] The suspension should only be for the length of time that is reasonably needed to investigate, and each twenty-day suspension is a separate act.[130] The employee is to be issued a written notice of the suspension stating the effective date and duration, reason, and authority.[131]

Salary or other remuneration may be withheld during the suspension if the employer considers it appropriate, and reimbursement may occur at the end of the investigation if considered appropriate.[132] The use of this statutory authority to suspend is not dependent on the employer proving just cause to discipline.[133] Rather, the employer need only establish the need for and existence of an ongoing investigation.

---

124 *Association of Management, Administrative and Professional Crown Employees of Ontario v Ontario (Finance)*, 2013 CanLII 87767 (ON GSB) at 41.

125 *PSOA*, above note 1, s 34(a).

126 *PSC Employment Policy*, above note 70, s 11.4.

127 *PSOA*, above note 1, s 36(1).

128 *Ibid*, ss 36(2) and s 55(1) and O Reg 379/07.

129 *PSC Employment Policy*, above note 70, ss 11.1–11.2.

130 *OPSEU (Miller) and Ministry of Correctional Services*, GSB#2613/87, 14 February 1989 (Samuels) at 9 [*Miller*].

131 *PSC Employment Policy*, above note 70, s 11.3.

132 *PSOA*, above note 1, s 36(3).

133 *Miller*, above note 130 at 9.

This provision recognizes that the employee's presence in the workplace during an investigation may have a negative impact on the operation of the workplace or may hinder the employer's investigation.[134]

The legislation does not authorize a suspension where no investigation is intended or carried out. The decision to conduct the investigation may perhaps be subject to a bad faith assessment.[135] Waiting for the disposition of criminal charges is not an investigation.[136]

The investigation is to be undertaken by the employer, not by any other person or organization.[137] The following are not investigations covered by the section: an investigation by the Canada Revenue Agency of an employee's tax declaration,[138] an investigation by the College of Nurses into the professional conduct of a nurse employed in the OPS,[139] and an employer-requested review by the Ontario College of Dental Surgeons of the fitness to practise as an employed dentist.[140] A police investigation into the alleged criminal conduct of the grievor is not an investigation by the employer (even if the ministry offers ongoing active assistance to the police investigation).[141] The OPP acts independently when engaged in police investigations. Therefore, an OPP investigation cannot be relied on by the ministry to justify a suspension pending investigation.[142]

The permissible period of investigation under the section comes to an end after the employer has had a reasonable period of time to consider the findings.[143]

---

134 *OPSEU (Reale) and Ministry of Solicitor General and Correctional Services*, GSB#99/96, 21 January 1997 (Dissanayake) at 8 [*Reale*].

135 Similar to that which may apply to a probationary termination, see "Probationary Termination" later in this chapter.

136 *Miller*, above note 130 at 11; *OPSEU (Mailloux) and Ministry of Correctional Services*, GSB#1064/90, 8 June 1995 (Kirkwood) at 76–77.

137 *Reale*, above note 134 at 8–9.

138 *Ibid* at 8.

139 *Ibid.*

140 *Hough and Ministry of Community and Social Services*, PSGB#927/84, 11 December 1984 (Simmons) at 30.

141 *Reale*, above note 134 at 10.

142 *Ibid* at 10.

143 *OPSEU (Group Grievance, Sammy) and Ministry of Correctional Services*, GSB#0224/01, 9 October 2001 (Harris) at 9, where the employer was ordered to pay the salaries of suspended employees for the period of time following employer receipt of the investigation report.

c) Termination of Employment

Under the *PSOA*, the methods of terminating the employment of regular and fixed-term employees by the PSC or its delegates are as follows:

- dismissal for cause
- dismissal without cause on reasonable notice
- probationary termination (not applicable to fixed-term employees)
- dismissal due to surplussing

and the following methods of termination by means other than dismissal or release:

- abandonment of position
- resignation and retirement
- end of a fixed-term appointment

When a regular employee is dismissed, consideration must be given to whether the employee should be restricted in writing from seeking future OPS employment.[144]

The PSC itself retains decision making over the "potentially high risk matter" of dismissals of employees in executive classes of positions (or equivalent) within the SMG.[145] The PSC has directed that the power to dismiss a public servant or to declare that a public servant has abandoned their position cannot be delegated by a deputy minister to any person outside a deputy minister's ministry.[146]

If no termination occurs under the *PSOA*, the regular employee remains a public servant, though they may be on unpaid and unauthorized leave.[147] When the dismissal of a public servant takes effect, they cease to be employed by the Crown.[148]

The requirements of these various methods of terminating employment, combined with any internal limitations on delegated authority, supplemented by any rights of released employees to be redeployed to

---

144 *PSC Employment Policy*, above note 70, s 11.5.

145 *PSC Business Plan*, above note 27.

146 PSC, *Human Resources Management Delegation of Authority Directive*, 12 May 2017, online: www.ontario.ca/page/human-resources-management-delegation-authority-directive, s 9.6.

147 *Shorthill and Ministry of Health*, PSGB#P/0929/84, 14 December 1984 (Simmons) [*Shorthill*].

148 *PSOA*, above note 1, s 40.

other positions[149] together constitute the security of tenure of public servants. In brief, non-unionized public servants have significantly more security of tenure than normally enjoyed by non-unionized staff in other employment by virtue of legislative provisions that establish:

- the ability to grieve dismissal for cause and potentially be reinstated
- the limit of probation to one year
- the ability to withdraw a resignation before its effective date

In addition, there may also be enhanced security stemming from any augmented internal review of dismissal without cause on reasonable notice. Unionized public servants have only marginally more security of tenure than their unionized counterparts with other employers as both can grieve their dismissals and both will have access to arbitral standards for the use of probation and the deeming of abandonment.

Regular employees can be entitled to a termination payment made up of two benefits. The first, under the *Compensation Directive*, is a severance benefit of one week's wages per year of service to a maximum of half a year's wages, commonly referred to as "legislated severance,"[150] which may only be paid once for each period of service. The second benefit, paid only to management and excluded staff, also calculated as one week's wages per year of service and commonly called "enhanced severance," is paid only in the event a regular employee is released as a result of layoff due to reorganization or lack of work or funding for their position.[151]

"Legislated severance" is payable to most employees who have completed one year of continuous service and cease to be an employee because of death, permanent total disability, or dismissal due to surplussing; or where the employee has completed five years of continuous service and ceases to be employed as an employee for any reason other than dismissal for cause or abandonment of position or, for service after 31 December 2011, resignation. Therefore, an employee employed for between one and five years obtains severance in certain limited circumstances, whereas an employee who has completed more than five years of continuous service is entitled to severance on termination of

149 Most notable are the rights to redeployment under the *PSC Employment Policy*, above note 70, "Workforce Adjustment" at 24–32, and, in the case of unionized civil servants, negotiated redeployment rights, as discussed in Chapter 9.

150 *Compensation Directive*, above note 90, ss 60–68.

151 *PSC Employment Policy*, above note 70, Art 10.21.

employment, including retirement, other than dismissal for cause or abandonment of position or voluntary resignation. This "legislated severance" entitlement is not payable to probationers or to fixed-term employees, and it is convertible, in whole or in part, into leave with pay.

The "legislated severance" entitlement appears to have been introduced to compensate civil servants for the loss of the opportunity to accumulate sick credits under a sick leave plan that was replaced in the early 1970s. The "enhanced severance" was introduced to provide management and excluded employees with a benefit equivalent to that negotiated by OPSEU in the 1996 round of bargaining.

In addition, where the PSC is of the opinion that "special circumstances exist," an additional termination allowance can be paid to a regular employee.[152]

i) Dismissal for Cause

The PSC and its delegates may, for cause, dismiss a public servant.[153] Under the *Employment Policy*, there must be sufficient documentation to substantiate the decision and "the employee's incompetence, offence or other conduct must warrant dismissal without notice or pay in lieu of notice."[154] The employee must be issued a notice stating the following:

- the effective date of the dismissal
- the reason for the dismissal
- the authority for the dismissal (which is *PSOA* s 34(b))
- the employee's right to submit a grievance to the appropriate grievance board (for eligible employees only)[155]

Dismissal for cause is not subject to further specific treatment under the *PSOA* or the government's directives and policies. Instead, general common law and arbitral principles are relied upon—some of which are discussed in Chapter 10.

ii) Dismissal Without Cause on Reasonable Notice

Under *PSOA* section 38, a non-unionized public servant employed in the SMG or MCP may be dismissed without cause by giving the public

---

152 *Compensation Directive*, above note 90, s 68.

153 *PSOA*, above note 1, s 34(b).

154 *PSC Employment Policy*, above note 70, ss 11.12–11.13.

155 *Ibid*, s 11.14.

servant reasonable notice or compensation in lieu of notice.[156] A public servant dismissed under section 38 cannot be ordered reinstated.[157] Individuals appointed to a minister's office by the premier or a minister may be dismissed without cause by giving reasonable notice or compensation in lieu of notice, and also cannot be ordered reinstated.[158]

Under the PSC *Employment Policy*, the employee must be provided with the reasons for the dismissal, and reasonable notice or compensation in lieu of reasonable notice.[159] The employee will be entitled to compensation in lieu of notice in accordance with common law standards. In a contested case, it will be up to the courts to determine whether to adjust the amount of deemed notice to provide adequate redress for the loss of a reasonably permanent senior public service position.

This statutory provision was introduced in the 1990s to "harmonize" public service employment release provisions with the private sector and to make it possible to terminate public servants for any reason on adequate notice or payment of compensation.[160] Such a dismissal may be motivated by considerations that would normally be characterized as disciplinary, but the legislation does allow a termination of employment without an administrative appeal against the adequacy of the cause.[161]

Such a dismissal is not a decision of the elected executive, and so the independence of senior public servants from political interference by the elected executive should not be compromised by the operation of the section. Furthermore, if the matter is dealt with by the PSC itself,[162] the decision would require the actual consideration of the deputy minister of the given ministry and a number of deputies from other ministries, which should help ensure that the release without cause is justified. PSC review is not a statutory or formal policy requirement, although

---

156 *PSOA*, above note 1, ss 38 and 55, and O Reg 380/07 "Dismissal without Cause" (Part III of the Act).

157 *Ibid*, s 38(2).

158 *Ibid*, s 50.

159 *PSC Employment Policy*, above note 70, s 11.8.

160 Ontario, Legislative Assembly, *Hansard*, 4 October 1995, No 6 at 100 (Dave Johnson, Chair of Management Board of Cabinet).

161 Judicial review is not an option. See Chapter 13 for a discussion of *Dunsmuir v New Brunswick*, 2008 SCC 9.

162 Under the repealed *PSA* O Reg 977, s 14.1(2), the Civil Service Commission was required to provide prior written approval of this method of dismissal.

in practice the PSC does require it for dismissals of executives. Given the negative impact on job security of such a release, it seems that PSC review should be a requirement for all dismissals without cause.

The justification for this section is debatable. There is a public service policy rationale for maintaining a greater degree of security of tenure for government employees than provided to private sector employees. In *Spinks and Threader and Treasury Board*,[163] a federal public service labour relations tribunal case, the argument was made that, even though there was no just cause for dismissal, the grievors should nonetheless receive damages in lieu of reinstatement. The Public Service Staff Relations Board held that appointments should be made on the basis of merit and that terminations be made only for good reasons, to ensure fair treatment of public servants and to satisfy the public that there is a politically neutral public service. Further, the Federal Court held that remedying an unjustified termination by monetary compensation would, in effect, mean that the government had a new power to terminate without just cause simply upon payment of compensation, which would destroy the underlying principles of public servant's tenure, and ordered the grievors' reinstatement.[164]

The counterargument relates to the need for good public service management. The proper functioning of government and implementation of the policies of the elected executive are frustrated if a manager is unable to cause a unit, branch, or division to meet its objectives. The PSGB has made the obvious point that "[g]ood management is not something that can be ordered or bad management something that can be corrected by discipline."[165] Disciplinary dismissal is not necessarily an available or appropriate response to management failure. Ongoing litigation about who should occupy a management position must invariably leave both the person filling the position and the employees reporting to the position in a state of uncertainty. Indeed, members of the public may also be left unsure about the direction of the program or institution with which they must deal. Neither of these situations is consistent with the effective operation of the public service.

A stronger case may be made for the need for the power to dismiss without cause in the case of senior executives where the uncertainty of

163 [1986] CPSSRB No 339 at 31.

164 *Threader v Canada (Treasury Board)*, [1987] 1 FC 41 (CA).

165 *McDade and Ministry of Community and Social Services*, PSGB#P/0832/75, 5 February 1975 (Pringle) at 8–9.

having a senior position be the subject of protracted litigation may be very damaging, and executives have some scope for negotiating termination packages in their employment contracts. There is much less justification for this power in the case of lower-level positions, and there are significant risks. Accepting a promotion into a first-level management position means bargaining unit employees lose their job security, discouraging more senior and experienced employees from seeking promotion. The existence of the potential for arbitrary dismissal, thus ending a career in the public service, undermines both commitment to the public service and the rule of law within the OPS. There seems to be little justification for a manager or executive to be delegated authority to use public money to dismiss a public servant with potential loss of valuable knowledge and experience without being required to show reasonable cause.

iii) Probationary Termination

Under *PSOA* section 37, a regular employee may be put on probation, which cannot be for longer than one year, and, while on probation, that employee may be dismissed "for failure to meet the requirements of the position."[166]

A probationary period is neither compulsory nor automatic; it is entirely a matter of discretion for the employer to decide whether any appointment should have a probation period and, if so, what the length will be, provided it is less than a year. [167]

During the probationary period, the employer may dismiss the employee "for failure to meet the requirements of the position" but may also dismiss the employee for cause or without cause on reasonable notice provided there is compliance with the requirements of those methods. As discussed below, it may be that the probationary status of the employee will lower the threshold of justification for cause or reduce the amount of notice to which the individual is entitled.

The probationary year is a year of work, not a calendar year, and approved absences from work do not count as part of the probationary period.[168] This ensures that the employer has the benefit of a full year of active work for employee assessment purposes. It is also a year of

166 *PSOA*, above note 1, s 37(1)–(2).

167 *OPSEU (Black) and Ministry of Housing*, GSB#2248/91, 13 February 1995 (Dissanayake) at 16.

168 *OPSEU (Walker) and Ministry of Correctional Services*, GSB#1272/88, 30 January 1990 (Fisher) at 4.

employment under the employee's current contract of employment. An employee who has worked under prior contracts of employment, even in consecutive periods of employment, is still treated as being in the first year of employment for purposes of probation.[169] Any period of employment as a fixed-term employee is not relevant to the determination of the one-year probationary period of a regular employee.

The requirements for dismissal of a probationary employee for failure to meet the requirements of the position have only been addressed by the GSB, because they have limited application to non-unionized employees. The PSGB cannot deal with any termination purported to be a probationary release under any circumstances.[170] There is no court decision on the matter, and in any case the issue will be whether the employer had cause to terminate without notice and, if not, the amount of the notice entitlement.

The discussion immediately below reviews the GSB's interpretation of the requirements of probationary releases in three parts: the timeliness of the dismissal, the permitted substantive reasons, and the probationer's fairness entitlements. This is followed by a discussion of the employer's alternative of dismissal for cause or on reasonable notice. Finally, the effect of the collective agreement, including the GSB's procedure and remedial approach, is discussed.

A probationary dismissal must be done during the affected employee's probation period. Notice of dismissal is effective on the date the employee receives it. If the employee receives the notice after the expiration of the probationary year, the dismissal is not effective.[171]

A probationary dismissal must be non-disciplinary. In the leading case of *Re Leslie and the Crown in Right of Ontario (Ministry of Community and Social Services)*,[172] the GSB noted that the employer retains the general right to dismiss all employees, including probationary employees, for cause and reasoned that then section 22(5) must therefore provide a different entitlement. In the view of the GSB, "the employer cannot camouflage either discipline or the termination of an employee for a reason other than employee's failure to meet the requirements of his position … by the guise of a 'release' under section 22(5)

169 *Re Ontario Public Service Employees Union and The Queen in Right of Ontario et al* (1983), 42 OR (2d) 139 (HC).

170 See Chapter 12.

171 *OPSEU (Muir) and Ministry of Labour*, GSB#3166/92, 12 January 1994 (Gray).

172 1978 CanLII 3504 (ON LA) at 134 [*Leslie*].

of the *Public Service Act*," which was the predecessor provision to the current *PSOA* section 37(2). The only change in wording is that *PSOA* section 37(2) uses the word "dismissed" rather than "release," but this does not seem material, as in both cases the action is permitted to be taken "for failure to meet the requirements of the position." To rely on the section, the employer must demonstrate that in good faith they released (now dismissed) the employee specifically for a failure to meet the requirements of their position.

Another leading case, *OPSEU (Haladay) and Ministry of Industry and Tourism*,[173] assists in distinguishing between release for failure to meet the requirements of the position and dismissal for cause. The GSB took the view that dismissal is "punishment for voluntary malfeasance" and held that, if punishment for specific incidents of blameworthy conduct is the real basis for the release, then the release is really a disguised dismissal for cause. A dismissal for cause cannot take place under the probationary release section and must instead meet the relevant just cause test. At the same time, "failure to meet the requirements of his or her position" can include voluntary deficiencies, such as attitude and capacity, and such deficiencies can form the basis of a release even though the grievor may have been able to improve their attitude or behaviour.[174] Furthermore, where the employer does have grounds that justify a release, and acted in good faith on that basis, it can find additional (including disciplinary) fault with the grievor.[175] In one more recent case under the PSOA, the GSB has invited reconsideration of this distinction between probationary release and termination for cause.[176]

A release must relate to the requirements of the probationer's particular position. There has been a difference in the GSB's jurisprudence about whether "requirements of his or her position" mean the suitability of a probationary employee should be examined on broad grounds, which include character, attitude, compatibility, absenteeism, quality of

173 GSB#94/78, 5 June 1979 (Swan) [*Haladay*]. A case where the purported release of an unsatisfactory employee is found to be disguised discipline is *OPSEU (Leblanc) and Ministry of Consumer and Commercial Relations*, GSB#630/81, 8 June 1982 (Verity).

174 *Re Bartello and the Crown in right of Ontario (Ministry of Transportation and Communications)*, 1982 CanLII 5133 (ON LA), followed in *OPSEU (Lau) and Ministry of Municipal Affairs*, GSB#143/89, 12 June 1990 (Brandt) at 33.

175 *Haladay*, above note 173 at 7.

176 *OPSEU (Caza) v Ontario (Labour)*, 2015 CanLII 89918 (ON GSB) (Anderson) at 5–6 [*Caza*].

work, as well as the ability of the employee to meet the requirements of the employer;[177] or whether suitability is to be determined with reference to the requirements of the particular position, as set out in the formal position description.[178] The specific wording of the section seems to indicate that the section should be read narrowly. It has been found that the "requirements of the position" do not include standards that are generic expectations, such as the usual obligations to report for work on time, avoid abusing sick leave, or avoid engaging in acts of insolence to supervision.[179]

The reasons for release must be reasonable. In *OPSEU (Sheppard) and Ministry of Government Services*,[180] the GSB held that it is not entitled to substitute its assessment of the probationer's performance for that of the deputy minister, but it may review the release for (1) presence/absence of good faith, (2) reasonableness, and (3) presence/absence of a rational relationship between the facts and the release.

An evaluation undertaken with apparent *animus* toward the employee will be in bad faith.[181] Relevant to the issue of good faith is whether the employer's treatment of the grievor is consistent with its treatment of other employees performing the same duties.

The reasonableness inquiry requires an objective assessment of whether the release flows "logically or rationally from the facts."[182] If there was an absence of evidence that a probationary employee had not fulfilled or could not fulfill the job requirements, then the release would

---

177 *OPSEU (Blundell) and Ministry of Consumer and Commercial Relations*, GSB#685/81, 15 April 1982 (Verity) at 10.

178 *OPSEU (Keane) and Ministry of Consumer and Commercial Relations*, GSB#596/81, 18 March 1982 (Roberts) at 11–12 [*Keane*].

179 *Ibid* at 11–12.

180 GSB#2492/86, 10 March 1988 (Slone) [*Sheppard*] and cases cited therein. See also *OPSEU (Shaw) and Ministry of Community and Social Services*, GSB#410/88, 30 October 1990 (Barrett); *OPSEU (Fox) and Ministry of Correctional Services*, GSB#739/91, 19 November 1992 (Dissanayake) [*Fox*]; *OPSEU (Syed) and Ministry of Community and Social Services*, GSB#1329/92, 14 October 1994 (Fisher); *Ontario Public Service Employees Union (Blanchette) v Ontario (Natural Resources)*, 2007 CanLII 11297 (ON GSB) (Dissanayake) [*Blanchette*]; *Ontario Public Service Employees Union (Niyonkuru) v Ontario (Ministry of Transportation)*, 2013 CanLII 88092 (ON GSB) (Devins) at 10 [*Niyonkuru*]; and *Caza*, above note 176.

181 *OPSEU (Agboka) and Ministry of Revenue*, GSB#729/90, 15 January 1993 (Fisher) at 8–11 [*Agboka*].

182 *Sheppard*, above note 180.

be an unreasonable exercise of authority. The "rational relationship" inquiry is similar to the reasonableness inquiry, although it looks into the facts upon which the release was based and whether they rationally justify the release "on any half-intelligent view."[183] That the employer was wrong in its assessment is not "sufficient in itself" to overturn the decision and the employer is not required to prove the facts supporting its assessment.[184]

Where the employer's actions do not meet these tests, the GSB has set the release aside even where satisfied that the grievor was not capable of fulfilling the requirements of the position.[185]

The employer must conduct a systematic review and evaluation of the employee's job performance in order to determine whether they have met the requirements.[186] A decision to release will not be reasonable if based upon inaccurate performance (or attendance) reports or subordinates' opinions that have no basis in fact.[187]

The treatment of absenteeism indicates how the good faith/reasonableness standard has been applied to a particular issue. Absenteeism has been found to be a valid basis for a probationary release,[188] provided it is reasonable to conclude that there is a likelihood of excessive future absenteeism. A failure to take into account more recent, improved attendance suggests bad faith on the part of the employer.[189] Authorized absences cannot be used to support a conclusion that an employee will be unreliable in their attendance.[190]

Under the PSC *Employment Policy*, the employer must have provided the employee with

- the opportunity to understand the position's requirements and to demonstrate compliance with those requirements

183 *Ibid* at 15. There is a great deal of similarity between the standard to be applied under s 22(5) and to other probationary terminations. See *OPSEU (Mitchell) and Ministry of Energy*, GSB#1610/89, 6 June 1991 (Emrich) at 4–5.

184 *Caza*, above note 176 at 5.

185 *Agboka*, above note 181 at 14.

186 *OPSEU (Crooks) and Ministry of Correctional Services*, GSB#1562/87, 11 October 1988 (Draper) at 6 [*Crooks*].

187 *OPSEU (Collins) and Ministry of Consumer and Commercial Relations*, GSB#518/92, 20 December 1993 (Gray) at 19 [*Collins*].

188 *OPSEU (O'Connor) and Ministry of Health*, GSB#1173/85, 25 May 1988 (Swan) at 4.

189 *Sheppard*, above note 180 at 16; *Collins*, above note 187 at 17.

190 *Collins*, above note 187 at 15.

- performance feedback, reasonable support, and periodic assessment of where they failed to meet the position's requirements
- an opportunity to identify other issues (such as health or family concerns) that may influence work performance[191]

Prior to this policy, probationary release cases[192] established a fairly broad fairness entitlement: that the employee is entitled to a fair assessment, which gives the employee time to prove themselves in circumstances where they have had their duties clearly explained to them and where the employer has instructed the employee throughout the probationary period. On the other hand, deficiencies in training, supervision, and direction will only give rise to remedies when it can be shown that those deficiencies seriously affected the employee's ability to meet the job requirements.[193]

Performance standards should be objective, measurable, and reasonably related to the work and responsibilities.[194] A probationary employee is entitled to have supervision that affords an adequate opportunity to demonstrate that performance standards can be met. Where the employer has guidelines for the evaluation and release of probationary employees, it must ensure the employee receives the benefit of the procedural protections contained in those guidelines.[195]

As well as monitoring the employee's job performance, the employer must make the employee aware if their poor performance is jeopardizing successful completion of the probationary period.[196] If the employer consciously adopts and conspicuously applies a very tolerant standard

---

191 *PSC Employment Policy*, above note 70, s 11.6. This has some similarity to the *AMAPCEO/MBC Collective Agreement 2018–2022*, above note 88, Art 17.2, which requires that, within the first month of the probationary period, performance standards will be reviewed with the employee and the employee will be advised if they are meeting the standards.

192 *OPSEU (Ericksen) and Ministry of Correctional Services*, GSB#12/75, 19 January 1976 (Beatty) at 23, as followed in *OPSEU (Joyce) and Ministry of Attorney General*, GSB#21/76, 13 August 1976 (Beatty) at 34–35, and later in *OPSEU (Ferraro) and Ministry of Correctional Services*, GSB#373/84, 30 October 1984 (Delisle) at 6–7.

193 *OPSEU (Jelinek) and Ministry of Community and Social Services*, GSB#1938/90, 20 December 1993 (Emrich) at 9–11 [*Jelinek*] and cases cited therein.

194 *Ibid*.

195 *OPSEU (Dadula) and Ministry of Transportation*, GSB#1089/92, 20 September 1993 (Kaplan) at 49.

196 *Crooks*, above note 186 at 4.

during the first few months of employment, it cannot rely on pre-employment instructions to justify a shift, without warning, to a more demanding standard.[197]

While normally it is reasonable to expect that an employer will carry through a remedial program to completion, it will be reasonable to release the employee early if the employer reasonably concludes from the first phases of the program that the entire program will not cure the employee's deficiency.[198]

A probationer, like any other employee, may be dismissed for cause, or, if a non-unionized employee, without cause on reasonable notice, if authorized.[199] A termination may have been framed as a dismissal for cause from the start. In the alternative, it may be that a tribunal or court will find that a purported release under section 22(5) is actually a dismissal for cause. In either case, the same issue will then arise, and that is how the probationary status of the employee affects the just cause standard. In recognition of the purpose of the probationary period, which is to provide an opportunity for the assessment of the suitability of employee for ongoing employment,[200] the standard of just cause for probationers is substantially lower than that for regular employees. On this point, the jurisprudence of the GSB is no different from that of the private sector.

The GSB will give effect to any collective agreement provision related to the probationary period provided that, where the provision imposes a probationary period, then the period must in fairness be brought to the attention of the grievor, unless explicit language authorizes leaving the grievor unknowing about their probationary status.[201]

The GSB has dealt with an OPSEU/MBC collective agreement provision that limited the probationary period to not more than nine months.[202] The reference to nine months has been interpreted to be

197 *Collins*, above note 187 at 18.

198 *Fox*, above note 180 at 29.

199 See the discussion of dismissal without cause on reasonable notice above.

200 *Keane*, above note 178 at 20–21 and *OPSEU (Von Buchstab) and Ministry of Attorney General*, GSB#1358/85 17 June 1987 (Gorsky) at 5–6. In support of this approach, see *Caza*, above note 176 at 5.

201 *Association of Management, Administrative and Professional Crown Employees of Ontario (Reveendra) v Ontario (Training, Colleges, and Universities)*, 2010 CanLII 64232 (ON GSB) (Dissanayake).

202 *OPSEU/MBC Collective Agreement, 2005–2008*, Art 18.1, now *OPSEU/MBC Unified and Correctional Collective Agreements*, above note 88, Art 18.1.1.

calendar months.[203] Therefore, a probationer's absence from work due to approved leaves or sickness did not permit the employer to lengthen the probationary period accordingly, at least in cases where the probationer is covered by an OPSEU/MBC collective agreement.

There is a jurisdictional issue about the GSB's jurisdiction over probationary releases occurring under the OPSEU/MBC collective agreements. That agreement gives employees the right to grieve discipline and dismissal, but also provides that a probationary employee who is dismissed or released is not entitled to file a grievance.[204] Notwithstanding this "apparent bar" to grieving, these provisions have been reconciled on the basis that there is no right to apply a just cause standard to a bona fide probationary release. It has been said that this produces, for bona fide probationary releases, the "very narrow" basis of review set out in *Sheppard* discussed above, coupled with the ability to apply the just cause standard to disguised discharges,[205] but not to a bona fide release.[206]

Given that a probationary termination case often involves a dispute about whether the employer action is a release or discharge, the GSB has suggested that it might be practical for the parties to each case to adduce all their evidence and for the board to reserve its decision until the end of the hearing on the preliminary question of whether or not the termination of the probationer in the case is a disciplinary dismissal or a non-disciplinary release.[207]

The burden of proof is on the employer. The GSB can require the employer to proceed first with its entire case.[208]

A finding that a release was in fact a dismissal does not immediately result in a finding that the release was void and the employee should be reinstated. Instead, the board has proceeded to deal with the merits of the dismissal for cause.[209]

---

203 *OPSEU (Sparks) and Ministry of Transportation*, GSB#2408/95, 24 November 1997 (Mikus).

204 *OPSEU/MBC Unified and Correctional Collective Agreements*, above note 88, Arts 21.1, 21.2, and 22.8.1.

205 *Niyonkuru*, above note 180 at 10.

206 *Caza*, above note 176 at para 7.

207 *OPSEU (Turcotte) and Ministry of Solicitor General and Correctional Services*, GSB#2196/97, 11 August 1999 (Marszewski) at 24.

208 *Agboka*, above note 181 at 1–2; *Blanchette*, above note 180; *Niyonkuru*, above note 180 at 13–14.

209 *Keane*, above note 178 at 19–20.

The GSB's normal manner of remedying the improper release of a probationer is reinstatement to probation with the balance of the probationary period to run, plus, on a more discretionary basis, compensation for the period between termination and reinstatement.[210] Entitlement to that compensation should actually be made conditional on the subsequent successful completion of the probationary period. The rationale is that the damages should only put the employee in the position they would have been in, but for the breach, and they would only have received ongoing wages in the normal course of employment if they had passed their probation.[211]

iv) Dismissal Due to Surplussing

Under *PSOA* section 39, a public servant may be dismissed due to

- a shortage of work
- a shortage of funds
- the elimination of the public servant's position
- a material change in the ministry or commission public body in which the public servant works

This is the public service equivalent of non-disciplinary layoff and brings with it the right to recall. The rights set out below are supplemented, in the case of unionized public servants, by the extensive layoff entitlements found in the respective collective agreements, including "reasonable efforts" to obtain employment for staff when work is divested outside the public service.[212]

The GSB and the PSGB, have stated that they do not have jurisdiction to review the merits of a release under section 39[213] but have engaged in a more limited review. The GSB has considered whether the termination of a public servant is a bona fide release within the requirements of the section, or whether it is, in fact, a disguised dismissal

210 *Agboka*, above note 181 at 17 and cases cited therein.

211 *Ibid* at 15, followed in *Jelinek*, above note 193 at 44–45.

212 See the discussion in Chapter 9. The *AMAPCEO/MBC Collective Agreement, 2018–2022*, above note 88, Art 27.18.2 also contains "reasonable efforts" language that has not been the subject of reported cases.

213 *OPSEU (Giannou) and MBS*, GSB#570/96, 8 May 1997 (Leighton) at 4, citing *Leslie*, above note 172; *Handlarski and MOF*, PSGB#P/0027/92, 12 November 1996 (Leighton) at 6 [*Handlarski*]; *Tyynela and MOL*, PSGB#P/0016/93, 17 December 1993 (Leighton) at 3.

for other reasons.[214] It is open to the GSB to ensure that the release was in good faith and not arbitrary[215] and, pursuant to the collective agreement, that the identification of the surplus employee to be laid off was made according to seniority. The PSGB will undertake a review to ensure that the release and the selection of employees to be released are decided upon in good faith and without discrimination,[216] and that any notice provisions are complied with.[217]

There has been some dispute about who bears the onus of establishing whether the circumstances are in compliance with the reasons permitted under the Act. The GSB has held that the onus is first on the union to establish that the termination was not what it purported to be,[218] and also that the onus is on a ministry to show how it arrived at the decision to release, and that a ministry must show that the power was exercised bona fide.[219]

The requirements of the section cannot be abrogated by contract. In *Dafoe*,[220] the GSB held that, regardless of a collective agreement provision, and a term in an unclassified, now term, contract, that both allowed only one week's notice in the event of premature termination, the statute continued to apply, meaning that the release had to be for one of the reasons listed in the section.

In deciding whether one of the listed reasons in the section is present, a good faith or reasonableness test will be applied. In *Dafoe*, the employer was found not to have complied with the requirements of the section. The employer claimed a lack of funds, due to an unexplained decrease in the work unit's budget that occurred after the employee had been hired. The GSB found that the employer did not establish

---

214 *OPSEU (Doyle-Marshall) and Ministry of Industry and Trade*, GSB#460/83, 20 October 1983 (Samuels) at 4; *OPSEU (Bliss) and Ministry of Health*, GSB#80/93, 13 March 1995 (Finley) at 31–33 [*Bliss*]; *Handlarski*, above note 213 and cases cited therein.

215 *OPSEU (Dafoe et al) and Ministry of Natural Resources*, GSB#1868/87, 23 June 1989 (Wilson) at 19 [*Dafoe*].

216 *Roy and Ministry of Labour*, PSGB#P/0022 and 0038/93, 30 September 1996 (Leighton); *Handlarski*, above note 213; *McGrath and Ministry of Labour*, PSGB#P/0020/93, 27 July 1995 (Leighton) at 12–13.

217 *Callaghan and Ministry of Agriculture and Food*, PSGB#P/0009/89, 10 January 1991 (Willes).

218 *OPSEU (Varin) and Ministry of Correctional Services*, GSB#496/82, 19 April 1983 (Jolliffe) at 30.

219 *Dafoe* above note 215 at 22.

220 *Ibid.*

that it actually lacked the funds. By contrast, in *Bliss*,[221] a review of budgetary and staffing decisions showed that the employer reached a "reasonable conclusion" about funding and availability of work. The GSB has also addressed the claimed necessity for layoffs according to a good faith test.[222]

Employees may benefit when a situation is characterized as a release. Where an employer sought to characterize a refusal by employees to relocate to a new work site in a different city as abandonment, the GSB found instead that the employees had been released within the meaning of the predecessor to section 39 of the *PSOA*.[223] The employees were thus entitled to the benefits of the layoff provisions of the collective agreement.

OPSEU has sought to characterize the transfer of employees to broader public sector employers as a "release" under the predecessor provision so as to entitle those employees to severance pay under the collective agreement. The transfer agreements between MBS and the union provided that employees who have transferred to a new employer (or failed to accept a good offer from the new employer) are *deemed to have resigned*. Having resigned, the employees cannot then be said to have been released.[224]

The remedy for improper release under the section is normally reversal of the release, combined with wages and benefits for the period between the improper release and the reinstatement or delivery of a proper release.[225]

Non-unionized MCP/excluded regular employees' specific entitlements on dismissal due to surplus are set out in the PSC *Employment Policy*.[226]

---

221 *Bliss*, above note 214 at 34.

222 See *OPSEU (Union) and Ministry of Natural Resources*, GSB#613/89, 13 August 1990 (Gorsky) at 22–23.

223 *OPSEU (Union) and Ministry of Health*, GSB#665/81, 16 February 1982 (Kennedy) [*Union (Kennedy)*].

224 *OPSEU (Policy Grievance) and Ministry of Health and Long-Term Care*, GSB#1723/99, 9 November 2000 (Brown) [*Health (Brown)*]; *OPSEU (Valentine et al/Union Grievance) and Ministry of Finance*, GSB#2105/96, 23 March 1999 (Leighton) [*Valentine*]; *OPSEU (Union) and Ministry of Consumer and Commercial Relations*, GSB#201/97, 30 May 1997 (Fisher) [*Union (Fisher)*].

225 For PSGB jurisprudence, see Chapter 12.

226 *PSC Employment Policy*, above note 70, "Workforce Adjustment" at 24–32 and "Voluntary Exit Registry" at 37.

PSOA-related entitlements on layoff are not available to executives/SMG employees, unionized staff, or lawyers.[227]

In determining which positions and employees will be laid off by the given "change initiative," an organizational unit is defined based on the job functions to be reduced, and an assessment is done of the type of work and the positions to be affected. If less than all of the affected complement in that unit is to be reduced, the most qualified, not the most senior, employees must be retained according to assessed merit.

Individually affected employees are to be issued a written notice of layoff six months in advance, which needs to state the notice period, reason for their surplussing, options, and entitlements.[228]

Non-unionized employees who receive a surplus notice have two options:

1. Exit with pay in lieu of notice, termination pay, and enhanced severance, as well as the right to apply to restricted competitions for 24 months after layoff (enhanced severance is not payable if, on divestment of work, a job offer with the new employer is negotiated and then an employee refuses a comparable or better job [comparability is to be determined by the PSC, not the ministry]); or
2. Continue to work during the notice period and access any targeted direct assignment opportunity for the period of notice (meaning a right to apply for posted vacancies with a maximum salary no more than 5 percent above that of the employee's home position and to receive priority consideration over applicants not in receipt of a notice of layoff), access support services, and, if not successful in securing a new permanent job, receive termination pay and enhanced severance, but not pay in lieu of notice.[229]

Under either option, employees also receive the right for 24 months after any layoff to apply to restricted competitions.[230]

Other employees in the same organizational unit can volunteer to be surplussed at the employer's discretion[231] and receive the same package as exiting laid-off employees. In addition, any MCP/excluded

227 Lawyers can access the Lawyers Transition Support Program. For a discussion of the special treatment of lawyers, see Chapter 4.

228 *PSC Employment Policy*, above note 70, Art 10.11.

229 *Ibid*, Art 10.

230 *Ibid*, Art 10.36.

231 *Ibid*, Art 10.2.

employee can register their position for the Voluntary Exit Registry and, if a laid-off employee is assigned to their position, the displaced registered employee receives pay in lieu of notice, termination pay, and enhanced severance pay.[232]

The PSC can approve exceptions to the operation of the workforce adjustment portion of the *Employment Policy*. However, in accordance with the MBC delegation to the PSC, the PSC may not make any broader amendments to those provisions that would necessitate resources beyond approved allocations.[233]

The entitlements of fixed-term employees and SMGs are limited. Under the PSC *Employment Policy*, fixed-term employees are only eligible to apply to restricted OPS job competitions for 24 months.[234] They do not have any other layoff right under *PSOA* related entitlements.

No notice requirement is specified in the *Employment Policy* for fixed-term employees. These employees are entitled to the greater of any notice period in their contract of employment or the minimum notice required under the *Employment Standards Act*.[235] Given the size of the OPS, it is not unusual for the mass termination provisions of the *ESA* to apply, which entitle fixed-term staff to as much as sixteen weeks' notice.

Members of the excluded SMG group are provided termination benefits in accordance with an executive redundancy plan currently called the Executive Transition Support Program.

v) Abandonment

In response to an absence of two weeks or more without approved leave, the employer may declare in writing that a public servant has abandoned their position and their employment is terminated.[236] The result is that the position becomes vacant, and the person ceases to be a public servant.

This section serves two purposes. It is the mechanism by which public servants who leave their position without providing a resignation can be formally removed from their position. The section also allows the employer to terminate the employment of public servants who, though

---

232 *Ibid*, "Voluntary Exit Registry" at 37.

233 *Ibid* at 24.

234 *Ibid* at 37.

235 *ESA*, above note 100, and O Reg 288/01.

236 *PSOA*, above note 1, s 42.

they have no intention to quit, choose to absent themselves from their workplace without authorization for two weeks or longer.

Under the *Employment Policy*, before the dismissal for abandonment, "reasonable efforts" must first be made to:

- contact the employee to determine the reasons for being absent without approved leave
- notify the employee of the consequences of the unapproved absence[237]

The employee must also be issued a written notice stating the effective date, reason, and authority for the dismissal.[238]

The *Employment Policy* seems to supersede the earlier caselaw that held there is no need to consider the employee's intention[239] or to warn an employee about the possibility of a declaration of abandonment.[240]

Since the authority to issue a declaration of abandonment is found in the *PSOA*, and no appeal of such a declaration is contemplated in the statute, the merits of the decision to issue a declaration are not subject to review by either the GSB or the PSGB. Neither board has the power to mitigate the resulting termination.[241] There is no requirement for management to be reasonable in invoking the decision.[242] However, like all discretionary decisions under the Act, a declaration of abandonment can be scrutinized for whether it was issued in bad faith, constituted a disguised dismissal, or was discriminatory, although no such allegation has ever been successful.

---

237 *PSC Employment Policy*, above note 70, s 11.10. This parallels the *AMAPCEO/MBC Collective Agreement, 2018–2022*, above note 88, Art 22, which also requires that reasonable efforts be made to determine the cause of the absence and to advise the employee of the consequences of the absence.

238 *PSC Employment Policy*, above note 70, s 11.11.

239 *OPSEU (Baldeo) and Management Board Secretariat*, GSB#1270/93, 5 June 1996 (Finley) at 19 [*Baldeo*]; *OPSEU (Tam) and Ministry of Revenue*, GSB#1/76, 31 March 1976 (Beatty) at 8 [*Tam*]; *OPSEU (Szabo) and Ministry of the Attorney General*, GSB#292/91, 21 July 1992 (Saltman) at 13 [*Szabo*].

240 *Szabo*, above note 239 at 12.

241 *Tam*, above note 239 at 18.

242 *Baldeo*, above note 239, followed in *Ontario Public Service Employees Union (Botosh) v Ontario (Attorney General)*, 2018 CanLII 45308 (ON GSB) (Abramsky) at paras 86–88.

The employer bears the onus of proving that the statutory prerequisites have been complied with.[243] The requirement that the public servant be "absent from duty without official leave" means the absence cannot be a period for which the requisite authorization actually was, would have been, or should have been granted.[244]

The boards will also review whether the employee actually applied for leave[245] and whether or not official leave was "unreasonably, discriminatorily or arbitrarily withheld"[246] before determining the validity of a declaration of abandonment. Where a grievor can demonstrate a reasonable justification for the absence, it will not suffice for the employer to claim that leave would inevitably have been denied. Two inquiries need to be made: (1) whether the grievor had a valid and legitimate reason for failing to return to work when scheduled to do so, and (2) whether the employer has given tacit permission for the grievor to remain off work. The intention of the employee to retain their position or return to work is not a factor in determining whether the declaration of abandonment is bona fide.[247]

Reasonable notice of the termination of a leave period must be provided to an employee before the employer relies on the date of revocation of a leave of absence as the starting point for the two-week period. In the absence of such notice, the employer cannot assert that the employee was absent from duty without official leave for the requisite period. In such cases, the official leave ends (and the two-week clock starts) on the date the employee receives notice that the leave is at an end.[248]

---

243 *OPSEU (Tran) and Ministry of Consumer and Commercial Relations*, GSB#711/93, 10 April 1995 (Gorsky) at 88.

244 *Tam*, above note 239 at 9; *OPSEU (LeGallais) and Ministry of Government Services*, GSB#107/79, 29 February 1980 (Brunner) [*LeGallais*].

245 *Ontario Public Service Employees Union (Grant) v Ontario (Community Safety and Correctional Services)*, 2014 CanLII 40107 (ON GSB) (Harris) at 22, stating "the onus was on the grievor to provide his request, in writing, laying out, in detail, the circumstances that supported his request."

246 *Tam*, above note 239 at 10; *Baldeo*, above note 239 at 20; *Edwards and Ministry of Correctional Services*, PSGB#P/0049/01, 4 February 2003 (Leighton), judicial review denied, [2004] OJ No 168 (SCJ); *Ontario Public Service Employees Union (Sookdeosingh) v Ontario (Solicitor General)*, 2022 CanLII 31338 (ON GSB) (Petryshen) at para 24.

247 *Tam*, above note 239 at 7–8; *Szabo*, above note 239 at 12–13; *Baldeo*, above note 239 at 19.

248 *LeGallais*, above note 244 at 10–11.

A letter from a deputy minister indicating that they are declaring, pursuant to the relevant section, that the employee has abandoned their position is sufficient written notice.[249] An employer cannot dismiss an employee for cause and then later attempt to rely on the abandonment section when the employer failed to make a formal declaration of abandonment at the time of the dismissal.[250] Where the employer seeks to terminate the employment of a public servant without making a formally correct declaration of abandonment, the termination will be reviewed as a dismissal for cause. The employer may argue that an extended absence without leave was cause for dismissal.[251]

Where a public servant is transferred, the failure to take up the transfer will not expose the public servant to a declaration of abandonment if the relocation entitles them to be declared surplus.[252] In that case, they must be considered as having been released within the meaning of *PSOA* section 39. However, refusing to undertake a reassignment pending the outcome of a grievance will give grounds for a declaration of abandonment because an employee must work and grieve.[253]

Where an employee took a vacation after approval had been denied based on business need, a declaration of abandonment was upheld.[254] An extension to a leave period may be denied where the public servant could reasonably be expected to return. Failure to return in such circumstances exposes the public servant to the risk of a declaration of abandonment.[255] A declaration of abandonment will also be permitted where a public servant remains off work claiming illness but fails to provide the required medical reports.[256]

The section provides discretion to issue a declaration. A public servant on an unauthorized leave remains a public servant until a declaration is made. Where such an employee returns before a declaration is

---

249 *OPSEU (Roy) and Ministry of Education*, GSB#6/78, 15 August 1978 (Brunner) at 8 [*Roy*]; *LeGallais*, above note 244 at 4.

250 *OPSEU (Zaidi) and Ministry of Community & Social Services*, GSB#2078/95, 19 May 1998 (Finley) at 63–64.

251 *Ibid.*

252 *Union (Kennedy)*, above note 223.

253 *Roy*, above note 249; *Tejura v Ministry of Housing*, P/0890/79, 15 March 1979 (Presgrave).

254 *Szabo*, above note 239.

255 *OPSEU (Jones) and Ministry of Government Services*, GSB#1098/87, 13 April 1989 (Emrich).

256 *Shorthill*, above note 147 at 7–8.

made, they are no longer absent without leave and the right to make a declaration under the section ceases.

vi) Resignation and Retirement

Under *PSOA* section 41, a public servant can resign by giving two weeks' written notice of the intention to resign, but may, by notice in writing and with management approval, withdraw the notice to resign at any time before its effective date, provided no person has been appointed or selected for appointment to the position that would become vacant because of the resignation. This provides a structured means for public servants to voluntarily and clearly end their appointment to the public service.[257] (This seems to cover retirement as well, although there is no case or policy on point.)

A resignation cannot be implied[258] because to resign, a public servant must communicate that intention in writing. Unlike in the private sector, an accumulation of actions inconsistent with an intention to continue in employment will not allow the employer to infer that a resignation has occurred. However, a deemed resignation provision in a collective agreement, contingent on a specific event, will be effective.[259]

Although a public servant may voluntarily leave the public service by resigning with two weeks' notice, a public servant can provide a longer period of notice. During a notice period the public servant continues to enjoy the same protections against termination as they did prior to giving notice. The requirement for consent to withdraw a resignation implies that consent is required to change the effective date of a resignation.[260] Once a resignation is effective, the person is no longer a public servant and their rights as a public servant cease. Any attempt to withdraw a resignation after the effective date of the resignation or after a successor is named is statute barred.

A decision to refuse to allow a timely request to withdraw a resignation is not subject to review in the absence of evidence of bad faith

---

257 *OPSEU (Rao) and Ministry of Community and Social Services*, GSB#1542, 1544, and 1545/85, 21 August 1989 (Fisher) at 4–5 [*Rao*].

258 *OPSEU (Schoular) and Ministry of Education*, GSB#1203/00 and 1531/00, 18 July 2002 (Gray) at para 51.

259 *Union (Fisher)*, above note 224; *Valentine*, above note 224 at 16; *Health (Brown)*, above note 224 at 6.

260 *Baxter and Ministry of Housing*, PSGB#P/0003/90, 18 December 1990 (Springate) [*Baxter*].

or discrimination. In *Rao*,[261] the union submitted that resignations were conditional on not being revoked prior to the effective date and, that if no other person was selected to fill the vacancy, an employee had a right to withdraw their resignation. The GSB rejected the argument and distinguished the deputy minister's decision-making process from disciplinary decisions. It is strictly a management function to decide whether or not to accept a withdrawal of a resignation, and that management decision is not open to arbitral review unless the collective agreement clearly provides for it. In *OPSEU (Zahniser) and Ministry of Community and Social Services*,[262] the GSB did not find the employer's decision to refuse to allow withdrawal of a resignation to be improper or unreasonable where it was apparent that the resignation had merely been a tactic by which the grievor sought to express his disagreement with management decisions and his discontent with other aspects of his employment. The grievor had been allowed to withdraw a prior resignation, but was advised that if he submitted another resignation, he would not be allowed to withdraw it. The grievor could not reasonably expect his employer to allow him to withdraw the resignation when the employer's reason is that the employee conducted himself in the same way that the employer had previously stated would not be tolerated.

Neither the GSB nor the PSGB has jurisdiction to reverse a resignation. However, both boards will review whether a voluntary resignation has occurred. In determining whether the grievor has voluntarily resigned, the GSB will apply the normal arbitral jurisprudence and assess whether the grievor intended to resign as shown by actions reviewed objectively and by subjective state of mind.[263]

The objective aspect of the test is met by a written resignation and, in the absence of contrary evidence, the subjective intention of the grievor may also be inferred from a letter of resignation.[264] The public

---

261 *Rao*, above note 257, followed in *OPSEU (Witherow) and Ministry of Labour*, GSB#0912/98, 4 December 2000 (Herlich).

262 GSB#0974/88, 29 March 1988 (Dissanayake).

263 *Ontario Public Service Employees Union (Cusack) v Ontario (Community Safety and Correctional Services)*, 2016 CanLII 7452 (ON GSB) (Petryshen); *Ontario Public Service Employees Union (Sinclair) v Ontario (Northern Development and Mines)*, 2007 CanLII 14610 (ON GSB) (Mikus); and *Ontario Public Service Employees Union (Knox) v Ontario (Ministry of Attorney General)*, 2010 CanLII 72680 (ON GSB) (Abramsky).

264 *OPSEU (Kolmann) and Ministry of the Solicitor General and Correctional Services*, GSB#1372/92, 21 October 1997 (Mikus) at 17; and see *OPSEU (Goossen)*

servant's motivation for deciding to resign is not relevant to determining whether a resignation is valid. However, a resignation will only be effective if it is voluntary. A resignation obtained by coercion or which was given by a public servant who was not competent by reason of illness to resign is not an effective resignation.[265] On this point, the general private sector arbitral jurisprudence on whether an employee has validly quit is applicable.

A valid resignation terminates a public servant's seniority even where they are re-employed shortly thereafter.[266]

vii) Termination of Fixed-Term Employees

A fixed-term employee has no statutory right to renewal of their contract,[267] and there is no such right contained in any of the individual contracts signed by unclassified employees.[268] More importantly, the *PSOA* deems that a public servant whose employment is for a fixed term ceases to be employed by the government when that period expires.[269] The effect of this provision has been summarized as follows:

> In the non-renewal cases, the employment relationship is not severed by reason of any action of the Employer. It is severed by operation of [now *PSOA* s 54] or by the terms of the contract itself. If the Employer were to do nothing the contract would come to an end upon the expiry of its terms. There is, therefore, no "action" by the Employer the motivation for which requires investigation. Nor do we regard the giving of notice that the Employer does not intend to re-new the contract as constituting "action" which brings about the severance of

---

and Ministry of Community and Social Services, GSB#1898/93, 12 November 1998 (Roberts) at 64, which held out the unresolved possibility that even where the grievor intended to resign, the resignation may still be subject to being set aside if the grievor "formed a well-founded belief that there was no alternative."

265 *Baxter*, above note 260.

266 *OPSEU (Union Grievance) and Ministry of Public Safety and Security*, GSB#2095/02, 17 July 2003 (Briggs) at 5.

267 *OPSEU (Milks) and Ministry of Attorney General*, GSB#1000/92, 11 March 1993 (Low) [*Milks*] and cases cited therein.

268 For a discussion of the contents of an unclassified "contract," see *OPSEU (Gallagher) and Ministry of Solicitor General and Correctional Services*, GSB#152/94, 24 October 1996 (Gray) at 2–3 [*Gallagher*].

269 *PSOA*, above note 1, s 54.

> the relationship. It is more of a courtesy which permits the employee to seek other employment.[270]

Because an unclassified employee has no contractual right to contract renewal,[271] even "bad faith" in the non-renewal itself will not make that non-renewal reviewable. The GSB has held, "Why would it matter if the failure to renew was 'tainted by bad faith' (whatever that would mean in the circumstances)? This Board simply has no jurisdiction over non-contractual problems."[272] However, the board has been prepared to inquire whether a non-renewal was either (1) a component part of a course of conduct which violated the grievor's entitlements under the collective agreement, or (2) in violation of a specific right under the other acts or the collective agreement.[273]

Under exception (1), the union may not be able to rest its case solely on the non-renewal, but neither has the GSB required a great deal more. An implied collective agreement requirement that management rights not be exercised in bad faith has supported jurisdiction over a grievance challenging a non-renewal.[274] The employer acted inappropriately by counselling the grievor that they needed to demonstrate improvement in their availability and then only giving them five days to do so before giving them notice of non-renewal of their contract. Where another grievor was denied the opportunity to compete, but the contracts of similarly situated unclassified, now term, employees were renewed, jurisdiction was taken to examine whether the non-renewal was in bad faith.[275] The GSB ultimately found that management's actions were not in bad faith because they were motivated by legitimate business and financial considerations.

---

270 *OPSEU (Cascagnette) and Ministry of Health*, GSB#1246/85, 2 September 1986 at 7–8.

271 *Milks*, above note 267, and cases cited.

272 *OPSEU (Shipley) and Ministry of Correctional Services*, GSB#0223/86, 10 November 1987 (Samuels) at 8.

273 *Public Service Employees Union v Ontario (Ministry of Consumer and Business Services)*, 2003 CanLII 52899 (ON GSB) (Herlich).

274 *OPSEU (Gagnon) and Ministry of the Solicitor General and Correctional Services*, GSB#1067/96, 2 June 1997 (Roberts).

275 *OPSEU (Mistry) and Ontario Human Rights Commission*, GSB#569/96, 15 October 1999 (Verity) at 35.

Under exception (2), incorporation of the *Human Rights Code* into all collective agreements,[276] let alone the anti-discrimination clause of a collective agreement, supports the GSB's jurisdiction where the non-renewal was allegedly discriminatory,[277] although an employer is not required to renew an incapacitated employee simply to preserve the possibility of future accommodation.[278] A clause protecting employees from discrimination for union activity gives jurisdiction where the non-renewal was influenced in part by the employee exercising their grievance rights.[279] Jurisdiction over alleged discrimination was declined when the decision not to renew was taken *after* the pre-existing contract had expired, as the collective agreement no longer applied at that point.[280]

Where there is a finding of wrongful non-renewal, the issue of remedy has been complicated by the lack of certainty about whether there would have been subsequent renewals. In seeking to put grievors in the position they would have been in, but for the employer's actions, by compensating them for the lost opportunity to demonstrate suitability for reappointment, the GSB has awarded compensation for all renewals missed between the non-renewal and the issuance of the GSB's award.[281]

---

276 *Human Rights Code*, RSO 1990, c H.19. See the discussion of the applicability of the *Human Rights Code* in Chapter 6.

277 *Ontario Public Service Employees Union (Howells) v Ontario (Ontario Clean Water Agency)*, 2006 CanLII 17520 (ON GSB) (Dissanayake) [*Howells*]; *OPSEU (Merson) and Ministry of Correctional Services*, GSB#16/93, 23 March 1994 (Gray), citing *OPSEU (Pitirri) and Ministry of Correctional Services*, GSB#1685/92, 3 May 1993 (Kaplan) at 16.

278 *Howells*, above note 277.

279 *OPSEU (Merson) and Ministry of Correctional Services*, GSB#299/93, 26 July 1996 (Gray) [*Merson, 1996*], where the grievor was found to have a protected right to forcefully advocate his position at a Step II meeting, and to have involved the union in a prior attempt to advance his employment interests. To the same effect concerning the GSB's jurisdiction, see *OPSEU (Jafri) and Ministry of Correctional Services*, GSB#933/91, 23 May 1995 (Dissanayake) and *OPSEU (Ghiandoni) and Ministry of Solicitor General and Correctional Services*, GSB#0518/94, 8 June 1998 (Mikus) [*Ghiandoni*], and cases cited.

280 *Gallagher*, above note 268 at 17, and *OPSEU (Daley) and Ministry of Solicitor General and Correctional Services*, GSB#151/94, 24 October 1996 (Gray) at 16–17: both affirmed on judicial review in *Ontario Public Service Employees Union v Ontario (Ministry of the Solicitor General and Correctional Services)*, [1999] OJ No 47 at 75 (Div Ct); and *OPSEU (Hannant-Steffler) and Ministry of Correctional Services*, GSB#1597/93, 28 September 1995 (Barrett).

281 *Ghiandoni*, above note 279 at 2; *Merson, 1996*, above note 279 at 17.

If the employer can demonstrate that there would not have been any ongoing work available, the board has only awarded compensation equal to a single renewal.[282] There are no cases where a non-renewed unclassified, now term, employee has been given a classified position. Presumably it might be an available remedy if it could be proven that the employee would have eventually received such a position, but for the wrongful non-renewal.

Under the *Employment Policy*, a fixed-term employee who has been employed in the OPS continuously for at least twelve months has been given the right to apply to restricted competitions for twelve months after termination of their contract.[283]

Mid-contract termination may not be provided for in fixed-term contracts themselves,[284] but current OPS collective agreements provide that the employment of a term employee "may be terminated by the Employer at any time with two (2) weeks' notice, or pay in lieu thereof."[285] Yet, the just cause provision of the collective agreements also apply, and so the GSB has had to harmonize the application of both provisions. Where the termination is an employer response to the conduct of the employee, the just cause provision applies to permit review of the discharge.[286] This is so regardless of whether the conduct in question is culpable or accidental. It is only where the reasons for the termination are unrelated to the conduct of the employee that the employer can rely on the two weeks' notice provision.[287] This harmonizes the two provisions by providing just cause protection while still permitting terminations that arise because of workplace staffing changes.

The employer has argued that the remedy for wrongful mid-term termination should be capped at compensation for the length of time remaining in the grievor's contract, which may be only a few weeks. In

---

282 *Ghiandoni*, above note 279.

283 *PSC Employment Policy*, above note 70, "Termination of Fixed-Term Non-Represented Employees" at 37.

284 See the unclassified contract as discussed in *Gallagher*, above note 268.

285 *OPSEU/MBC Unified and Correctional Collective Agreements*, above note 88, Art 31A.12.1; *AMAPCEO/MBC Collective Agreement 2018–2022*, above note 88, Art FXT 11.1.

286 *AMAPCEO (Stewart) and Ministry of Municipal Affairs and Housing*, GSB#0942/99, 14 February 2000 (Abramsky) [*Stewart*] applying *OPSEU (Ambrey) and Ministry of Attorney General*, GSB#429/84, 15 January 1985 (Knopf).

287 *Stewart*, above note 286 at 12.

OPSEU (Miller and MacPhail) and Ministry of Correctional Services,[288] the GSB determined it can exercise its remedial authority to "put the grievors in the position they would have been in but for the employer's actions, and compensate them for the lost opportunity to demonstrate suitability for reappointment."[289] This has resulted in reinstatement for the grievor for the balance of the contract[290] *and* full retroactivity for the entire period between the initial termination of the contract and the post-hearing reinstatement.[291] The board has opined that reinstatement should not occur routinely, but only in special circumstances,[292] and found the need to restore the grievor's reputation was a special circumstance, but has also held that such a standard is "a dubious proposition" and each case should be decided on its facts.[293] In one case, the GSB also ordered that the grievor should be able to "pick up exactly where [they] left off" by receiving any retraining or refresher courses prior to their actual reinstatement and, on expiry of the new contract period, that the grievor be assessed for further renewals as if the unjustified dismissal had not occurred.[294]

In any event, a term employee who is terminated mid-contract may be eligible for *ESA* termination and severance pay.

---

288 GSB#532/82, 2 March 1987 (Verity) [*Miller and MacPhail*], ordering the remedy; and 3 January 1990, summarizing all the litigation relating to the remedy.

289 *Ghiandoni*, above note 279 at 2, summarizing the effect of *Miller and MacPhail*, above note 288.

290 For an example of reinstatement to the balance of the contract, but denial of other compensation, see *OPSEU (Seguin) and Ministry of Community Safety and Correctional Services*, GSB#2004/0009, 13 January 2005 (Brown) at 16–17.

291 For example, see *OPSEU (Inkumsah) and Ministry of Correctional Services*, GSB#968/91, 14 October 1992 (Stewart) at 25–26; but see *OPSEU (Garrie) and Ministry of Correctional Services*, GSB#2039/93, 12 April 1995 (Finley), capping retroactive compensation at twenty days prior to the filing of the grievance.

292 *OPSEU (Auger-Beaulieu) and Ministry of Attorney General*, GSB#469/92, 15 October 1993 (Finley) at 46.

293 *OPSEU (Pickett) v Ontario (Ministry of Solicitor General and Correctional Services)*, GSB#2251/93, 15 January 1996 (Kaplan) at 33.

294 *Ibid* at 34.

CHAPTER THREE

PSOA Ethical Framework

A. INTRODUCTION

A central purpose of the *Public Service of Ontario Act, 2006* (*PSOA*)[1] is to ensure that the public service is "non-partisan, professional, ethical and competent," in accordance with constitutional convention, given the need to relax the strict prohibitions of the past.[2]

By defining public servant to include public servants appointed by the Public Service Commission (PSC) under *PSOA* Part III (employees in ministries) and also appointees and employees in "public bodies," the requirement to take the oaths and the obligations imposed by the ethical framework is extended to agencies prescribed as public bodies.[3]

Public servants are entrusted with public authority solely for the purpose of implementing the policies of the elected executive subject to the laws passed by the legislature and the provisions and democratic conventions of the Constitution.[4] Every elected executive is owed equal diligence regardless of the public servant's personal view of the wisdom of a particular instruction or policy. However, in the event an

---

1 SO 2006, c 35, Sch A [*PSOA*].

2 *Ibid*, s 1, as further discussed in Chapter 1.

3 O Reg 147/10, as amended, which includes agencies typically seen as agencies of the provincial government.

4 Lorne Sossin, "Defining Boundaries: The Constitutional Argument for Bureaucratic Independence and Its Implication for the Accountability of the Public Service" in *Research Studies*, Vol 2 (Ottawa: Commission of Inquiry into the Sponsorship Program and Advertising Activities (*Gomery Inquiry*), 2006) at 37.

instruction is contrary to law, or the requirements of the democratic conventions of the Constitution, the public servant may have a legal right and certainly has an ethical obligation to object.[5]

Historically, public servants' ethical obligations were grounded in the tradition of non-participation in partisan politics, faithful service to the elected executive, and complete discretion and anonymity. These values were reflected in the oaths of allegiance and office and supplemented by regulations governing conflict of interest.

The expansion in the size, complexity, and role of government made adherence by every public servant to the strict tradition of complete non-participation in politics or making any public comment increasingly untenable. The prohibitions on political activity did not survive *Charter*[6] challenge, resulting in amendments to the former *Public Service Act (PSA)*[7] to permit a degree of political activity while ensuring the public service remained, and appeared to remain, a non-partisan organization.

The *PSOA* includes Parts IV (Conflict of Interest), V (Political Activity), and Part VI (Disclosure of Wrongdoing).[8] These are commonly referred to as the ethical framework, though only Part IV is actually titled "Ethical Conduct," and all three impose strict legal, not merely ethical, obligations. This chapter begins with the oaths since they and constitutional convention still form the basis for public servants' ethical obligations.

The *PSOA* did not make significant changes to the rules regarding conflict of interest and political activity. It did formalize and improve the process for dealing with these matters. Deputy ministers and the executive head of each agency are made "ethics executives" for their ministry or agency. Employees that suspect that they may fall afoul of a conflict or political activity rule must ask for and be given an authoritative ruling including measures that will address the concern, allowing violations to be avoided. The integrity commissioner is the ethics executive for employees in ministers' offices and may be referred cases where other ethics executives think it advisable.

---

5 *Ibid* at 30; *Fraser v PSSRB*, [1985] 2 SCR 455 at para 41 [*Fraser*].

6 *Canadian Charter of Rights and Freedoms*, Part I of the *Constitution Act, 1982*, being Schedule B to the *Canada Act 1982* (UK), 1982, c 11 [*Charter*].

7 SO 1993, c 38, replaced by the *PSOA*.

8 For discussion of the structure and application of the *PSOA*, see Chapter 2.

The disclosure of wrongdoing provisions was first introduced in the *PSOA*. While public servants were always free—indeed, may have been under an ethical duty—to disclose serious wrongdoing, there was no process that assured that the disclosure would be investigated or that the public servant would not face reprisal.

The Act was strengthened by an amendment transferring the role of the order-in-council appointed conflict of interest commissioner to the integrity commissioner, an officer of the legislature. This consolidated the roles of the two offices into a single office headed by a commissioner with the greater security of tenure and who reports directly to the legislature. The processes for dealing with conflicts, political activity, and disclosure of wrongdoing are intended to allow matters to be addressed in a professional non-political manner. The integrity commissioner's ability to report directly to the legislature on any failing in these processes allowed the legislature a new avenue to discover and address such a failure.

B. DUTY OF LOYALTY AND DISCRETION

1) Oaths

Ontario public servants are required to swear or affirm two oaths the wording of which are prescribed in regulation.[9]

The first is a traditional oath of allegiance to the monarch.[10] Swearing an oath of allegiance to the person who sits on the throne of another country has the appearance of a troubling anachronism, but the English sovereign is still the constitutional head of the Canadian government and will remain so until the Canadian Constitution is amended. The members of the legislature are required by section 128 of the *Constitution Act, 1867*[11] to swear the same oath of allegiance prescribed for public servants.

The oath of allegiance is not in the context of the Canadian Constitution in its current form an oath of allegiance to a physical person. By swearing allegiance to the Queen [now King] of Canada, the public servant is swearing to a symbol of Ontario's form of democratic

9 *PSOA*, above note 1, ss 5–6.

10 O Reg 373/07, s 1.

11 *Constitution Act, 1867* (UK), 30 & 31 Vict, c 3, s 134, reprinted in RSC 1985, App III, No 5.

government. "Similarly, in today's context, the reference in the oath to the Queen [now King] of Canada's 'heirs and successors' is a reference to the continuity of our form of government extending into the future."[12]

The concept of loyalty to the Constitution, as symbolically recognized as the Crown and separate from the elected executive, is fundamental to a public service in Canada's democratic system.[13] The concept of the Crown as representative of the state is similarly important in that it reflects the legal continuity of the Constitution from the period of Canada's creation as a unit in the British Empire to its full independence as a democratic country. This is exemplified by the recent addition to the oath of office prescribed under the *PSOA* of "the recognition and affirmation of the aboriginal and treaty rights of Indigenous peoples," which date in some cases to the pre-Confederation period.[14]

There are two exceptions to the requirement to take the oath of allegiance: non-Canadian citizens that would lose their foreign citizenship (and presumably become stateless) by taking the oath and Indigenous persons who find the oath inconsistent with their view of the relationship between the Crown and Indigenous peoples.[15]

There are no exceptions to the taking of the oath of office. The oath of office requires faithful discharge of the public servant's duty and maintaining the confidentiality of information and documents that comes to their knowledge or possession as a public servant.[16]

The taking of the oaths is mandatory and does not appear to be open to challenge.[17] With the exception of the obligation of confidentiality, the legal impact does not seem to extend beyond highlighting responsibilities otherwise inherent in employment in government.[18] In

---

12 *McAteer v Canada (Attorney General)*, 2014 ONCA 578 at para 54 [*McAteer*].

13 *Fraser*, above note 5 at para 41.

14 O Reg 373/07, s 3.

15 *Ibid*, s 2.

16 *Ibid*, s 3.

17 *Ontario (Attorney General) v OPSEU*, [1987] 2 SCR 2, Dickson J at para 75; *McAteer*, above note 12.

18 Ontario Law Reform Commission, "Political Activity, Public Comment and Disclosure by Crown Employees" (Toronto: Ministry of the Attorney General, 1986) [*OLRC Report, 1986*] at 157. The use of oaths and other statements of values as general urgings is a choice. It would be possible to make them enforceable by specific conduct expectations. This has been done in Australia as part of reforms of federal public service employment law. See Phillipa Weeks, "The Reshaping of

Serco Facilities Management and PSAC (Baggs), for example, it was specifically argued that a non-public servant working in a federal public service environment did not owe a duty of loyalty to his employer because he had not taken an oath of allegiance. The argument was rejected, and the employee was found to have been bound and violated the general common law employment obligation of loyalty and fidelity to their employer.[19] However, the oaths do highlight the ethical standards required in a democratic public service. The Ontario Law Reform Commission noted that "[t]he oath, both in terms of its form and substance, has a cautionary effect on employees, reminding them, in solemn terms, of their general common law duties of loyalty, good faith, and confidentiality."[20]

The portion of the oath requiring public servants to maintain confidentiality is essentially unchanged from the oath in the former *PSA*—"except as I may be legally authorized or required, I will not disclose or give to any person any information or document that comes to my knowledge or possession by reason of my being a civil servant [now public servant]"—that was ruled on in the case of *George v Harris*.[21] The plaintiffs sought to interview public servants about their involvement with the events (an Indigenous man was killed by the Ontario Provincial Police [OPP] during the contentious occupation of Indigenous land taken during the Second World War and not returned), and asked the court to declare that the oath of secrecy was unconstitutional to the extent that it prevented the public servants from being able to choose to talk to the plaintiff's lawyers. The court dismissed the motion, holding that the oath

> is essential to the functioning of the public service in serving the elected government. This is because democratic government requires that ministers have effective control of the civil service and be responsible for holding civil servants accountable. Civil servants are properly bound by oaths of secrecy that reflect the importance of a trusting

---

Australian Public Service Employment Law" in Marilyn Pittard & Phillipa Weeks, eds, *Public Sector Employment in the Twenty First Century* (Australian National University Press, 2007).

19 *Serco Facilities Management Inc and PSAC (Baggs) (Re)*, 2000 CanLII 50265 (CA LA) (Oakley) at 299.

20 *OLRC Report, 1986*, above note 18 at 308.

21 2003 CanLII 48416 (ON SC), leave to appeal denied, [2003] OJ No 1900 (Div Ct).

> relationship between ministers and officials. Abolition of the oath of secrecy would open the way for civil servants to disclose matters—beyond those governed by freedom of information legislation—without the authorization of ministers. This would be detrimental to ministerial responsibility and the political neutrality of the civil service, which would have far-reaching consequences for the viability of our system of democratic government. This system depends on a close working relationship between ministers, who have the constitutional duty to decide, and civil servants, on whom ministers rely for confidential advice and loyal administration, and whose discretion is essential to the proper working of responsible government.
>
> In addition to the requirements for confidential advice to ministers, the public expects its servants to keep secret a wide range of personal, commercially confidential, and security-related information, as well as information the release of which could prejudice the public interest.[22]

The court concluded that the authorization to disclose can only be given by the government employer. Such authorization may be explicit, or it may be implied.[23] The court further found that, where a court or tribunal determines that it requires confidential information for a proceeding before it, then the public servant can be ordered to produce the information and is, to the extent of complying with that order, not limited by the oath. A court's determination that it requires confidential information in the possession of a public servant will not be made without balancing the value of confidentiality to the administration of the government.[24] In any event, it remains the function of the court, not the individual public servant, to determine when to require the disclosure of clearly confidential information. Hence, the oath does have the effect of requiring a public servant to not release a range of confidential advice and information without the express permission of the government employer or a court order.[25]

---

22 *Ibid* at paras 29–30.

23 See Section C(2)(f) "Disclosing Confidential Information" later in this chapter.

24 *Carey v Ontario*, [1986] 2 SCR 637.

25 For a case reiterating the seriousness of the unauthorized release of confidential information, see *Alberta and AUPE, Loc 6 (Smith), Re* (1996), 57 LAC (4th) 400 (Moreau) at 415 [*AUPE-Smith*].

An exception is found in the *Public Inquiries Act, 2009*,[26] which provides that the oath of office of a Crown employee is not breached where information is disclosed in good faith to a public inquiry.

2) Loyalty, Discretion, and Freedom of Expression

The seminal common law decision regarding the balance between public servants' duties of loyalty and discretion and their right to freedom of expression is Dickson CJ's judgment in *Fraser*.[27] A Revenue Canada supervisor engaged in a very public, sustained, nasty attack against the federal government's introduction of metric measurement and the *Charter*, and eventually made derogatory personal comments about the prime minister. They were dismissed. Their dismissal was upheld by the Supreme Court of Canada, which ruled that "although there is not an absolute prohibition against public servants criticizing government policies, Mr. Fraser in this case went much too far."[28] Chief Justice Dickson balanced a public servant's right to speak out in a free and democratic society with the importance of an impartial and effective public service with loyal employees. The case arose before the advent of the *Charter*, but the balancing was adopted in *Osborne v Canada (Treasury Board)*, as generally being the appropriate balancing of interests under section 1 of the *Charter* as well.[29]

Chief Justice Dickson started by accepting that public servants could not be prohibited entirely from expressing their views. Then they went on to note "a public servant may actively and publicly express opposition to the policies of a government" if government was engaged in illegal acts or a policy "jeopardized the life, health or safety of the public servant or others" or if the criticisms did not affect their ability to perform the duties of a public servant or the public perception of that ability.[30] However, no value, including free speech, is absolute, requiring that the right to speak must be balanced against the requirements of public service, loyalty, impartiality, and effectiveness.

The elected government is entitled to the loyal support of the public service. This does not require public servants to support the incumbent

26 SO 2009, c 33, Sch 6, s 18(2).

27 Above note 5.

28 *Ibid* at para 50.

29 *Osborne v Canada (Treasury Board)*, [1991] 2 SCR 69 at paras 43–44 [*Osborne*].

30 *Fraser*, above note 5 at para 41.

government's party or espouse the government's policies, but it does require public servants to serve the government loyally and to refrain from comment that suggests they are not loyal to the government. "A person entering the public service, or one already employed there must know, or at least be deemed to know, that employment in the public service involves acceptance of certain restraints. One of the most important of those restraints is to exercise caution when it comes to making criticisms of the Government."[31] Public, sustained attacks on major government policies evidence disloyalty to the government inconsistent with the duties of a public servant.[32] Public attacks on the premier or the administration as opposed to temperately criticizing a policy would similarly be inconsistent with government employment.

A public servant must also refrain from public speech that either brings into question their ability to perform the duties of their job or to meet the general public service standards of impartiality and effectiveness. This may, as in the *Fraser* case, include comments by an employee in an important and sensitive job that "placed [their] impartiality and judiciousness in doubt" and consequently their ability to perform both their job and more broadly to undertake any comparable public service position.[33]

It has been pointed out that the *Fraser* case recognizes exceptions to the duty of loyalty but does not claim to set out a complete list.[34] In *Chopra and Treasury Board (Health Canada)*, a federal public servant, who was a member of a visible minority group, publicly criticized their department's claimed failure to adequately implement an earlier human rights tribunal decision concerning their own employment that required departmental remedial action. They were disciplined, but the discipline was voided, even though the critical comments made by the public servant were extremely forceful. It was noted that the public servant would have the right to make this criticism at a public human rights hearing and that it would be a "strange result indeed" if comments to the same effect at a press conference were held to be a violation of loyalty.

The more that the criticism relates directly to the employee's job duties, the more there will be concern about adverse impact on perceptions

31 *Ibid* at para 43.
32 *Ibid* at para 41.
33 *Ibid* at para 46.
34 *Chopra and Treasury Board (Health Canada)*, 2001 PSSRB 23, 12 March 2001 (Galipeau) at para 91.

of their ability to carry out those functions. For example, in the federal public service, a parole officer was found to have engaged in unacceptable public speech when, during the course of running for municipal office, they criticized the decision of the Parole Board concerning a particular case.[35] The conflict with the grievor's ability to perform their duties arose from their work responsibilities to make representations to the Parole Board about particular cases and to carry out the terms of supervision of paroled offenders in accordance with specific directives from the Parole Board. Their criticism raised a concern about their ability to accept and implement Parole Board determinations.

Alberta Union of Provincial Employees v Alberta[36] concerned a public servant serving as a child protection social worker, employed by the Alberta Department of Family and Social Services, who wrote a letter in which they expressed their concerns about the planned redesign of social services to a member of the Opposition and sent copies to their own member of the legislative assembly, their department's minister, and the regional board responsible for social services in the area. The public servant was subject to an oath very similar to that under the *PSOA* in Ontario.[37] As a result of their letter of concern, which was the second time they had engaged in such conduct, the employee received a letter of reprimand. The Alberta Court of Appeal reviewed the *Fraser* case and commented that it required a review, in part, of the level of employment of the speaker and the type and degree of visibility of the publicity.[38] The court found, in brief reasons, that this letter by a front-line public servant was not a general attack, nor was it "clearly opposite in interest to" the government. The public comments related to a concern shared by all, namely the ability of social workers to safeguard children. The court also noted that the government's evidence did not show that the employee's criticism damaged the employee's impartiality or the public perception of that impartiality. The court concluded

35 *Nowoselsky v Treasury Board (Solicitor General Canada—Correctional Service)*, [2001] CPSSRB No 12, application for judicial review dismissed on procedural basis, [2004] FCJ No 2077 (CA). The political nature of the speech was not the issue, as the employer had approved the employee running for office. This was not a "whistleblowing" case as there was no allegation that the public was being saved from serious harm.

36 2002 ABCA 202 [*AUPE*].

37 *Public Service Act*, RSA 2000, c P-42, s 20(1).

38 *AUPE*, above note 36 at para 31.

that the letter did not breach the duty of fidelity, but rather that the employer's action violated the public servant's freedom of expression. It is notable that the employee was commenting on matters that were directly concerned with their area of employment and doing so in quite a critical and public fashion. It appears that the crucial factors were that the criticism was constructive and non-disruptive, and that it did not raise a question about the grievor's ability to do their job.

The right to freedom of speech does not protect the making of derogatory or disrespectful comments about individual public officials.[39] Making "allegations that there was abuse of power, that the merit principle is dead in selection processes and that the ethics commissioner, the Treasury Board president and the auditor general dropped the ball, without a factual basis, provable on a balance of probabilities" is similarly not protected.[40] A lower-level federal clerk placed an advertorial in a national paper venting about their failure to obtain promotion. While it did little harm and did not, given their low-level position, bring their ability to do their job into question, it warranted a short disciplinary suspension.[41]

In *Mullins v Deputy Head (Department of the Environment)*,[42] a federal policy analyst was given a five-day suspension for speaking at an anti-Olympics protest rally. He was responsible for providing advice about land claim negotiations. The basis for his opposition to the Olympics was his assertion that they were being held on stolen Indigenous land. The board held that any restriction on public servants' freedom of speech "must be rationally linked to the employee's job and must not exceed what is required to achieve the objective of an impartial and effective public service."[43] While opposition to initiatives or organizations that get government funding cannot be seen as criticism of the employer or its policies, the basis for Mullins's objection, that the land was stolen, was inconsistent with him being an impartial advisor on land claims matters and discipline was upheld.[44]

---

39 *Alberta v Alberta Union of Provincial Employees*, 2021 CanLII 56919 (AB GAA).

40 *MacLean v Treasury Board (Department of Public Works and Government Services)*, 2011 PSLRB 40 (CanLII) at para 139.

41 *Ibid*.

42 2013 PSLRB 21.

43 *Ibid* at para 65.

44 *Ibid* at paras 66–67.

The *Fraser* decision was about the balance between freedom of speech and the duty of loyalty. The obiter comments about disclosure of illegality or threats to life, health, or safety, while they may involve speech, are fundamentally about exceptions to the duty of confidentiality for disclosure of wrongdoing and give rise to the defence of whistleblowing.

3) Union Speech

The *Fraser* line of cases delineating the range of freedom of speech of public servants does not address the status of a speaker as union spokesperson.[45] However, there is no reason why the usual labour law rules regarding the greater latitude to criticize the employer given to members of bargaining units holding union positions and speaking for the union would not apply to public servants.[46] Where a union spokesperson is a public servant, the obligation to maintain the necessary impartiality of a public servant does continue, but the employee is entitled to put forward the views of union members.[47]

4) Whistleblowing

OPSEU (MacAlpine) v Ministry of Natural Resources illustrates the potential difficulties the requirement for confidentiality may create.[48] Mr. MacAlpine was dismissed for breaching their oath of confidentiality by taking ministry documents to their member of Parliament that they believed suggested bias by the ministry in favouring one forestry company over the other. The union was successful at arbitration where the Grievance Settlement Board (GSB) found that whether a public servant's duty was to maintain confidentiality or disclose apparent impropriety was at least ambiguous. The case illustrates one of the problems *PSOA* Part VI disclosure of wrongdoing provisions are intended to address.

Disclosure of documents to a member of provincial Parliament (MPP) is inherently partisan. It will facilitate a partisan attack on the

---

45 *King v Treasury Board (Canada Border Services Agency)*, 2008 PSLRB 64 at paras 224–29.

46 *King v Deputy Head (Canada Border Services Agency)*, 2010 PSLRB 31 at para 234.

47 *AUPE-Smith*, above note 25.

48 *OPSEU (MacAlpine) v Ministry of Natural Resources*, GSB#241/82, 18 November 1982 (Jolliffe) [*MacAlpine*].

minister in the legislature. However, it is the duty of the legislature to hold ministers to account for the conduct of their ministries. In the absence of a legislated disclosure of wrongdoing process, a public servant with a reasonable belief that illegality is occurring must decide either to ignore the illegality or disclose not only the allegation but, to be effective, confidential documents supporting the allegation compromising both their obligation of confidentiality and their duty of loyalty.

There is a common law defence for whistleblowers facing discipline.[49] The defence is not easy to establish and requires four elements:

1) The purpose must be to expose, in exceptional circumstances, government wrongdoing, for example, illegality, or jeopardizing life, health, or safety.[50]
2) The issue must be more than a difference of opinion.[51]
3) Absent exceptional circumstances an employee must have taken all reasonable steps to address the matter internally before "going public."[52]
4) The concerns must be accurate.[53]

The whistleblower defence has recently been addressed by the Ontario Divisional Court.[54] An Ontario Provincial Police (OPP) officer was disciplined for public criticism of a decision by the OPP to relocate some helicopter operations, in a letter to a newspaper. The officer's whistleblower defence was rejected on the basis that the matter had to be raised internally before public disclosure could be justified. The common law test was found to be a reasonable limit on speech under section 1 of the *Charter*.[55] The decision approved comments by arbitrator J.M. Weiler that, before going public, an employee:

---

49 The defence dates at least to *Gartside v Outram* (1856), 26 LJ Ch 113 [*Gartside*].

50 *Read v Canada (Attorney General) (FCA)*, 2006 FCA 283 at para 119 [*Read*]; *Mulligan v Ontario Civilian Police Commission*, 2020 ONSC 2031 [*Mulligan*].

51 *Stenhouse v Canada (Attorney General) (FC)*, 2004 FC 375 at para 39.

52 *Mulligan*, above note 50.

53 *Read*, above note 50.

54 *Mulligan*, above note 50.

55 *Fraser*, above note 5, did not deal with the *Charter*, but in *Haydon v Canada*, [2001] 2 FC 82, the court concluded that the balancing of the duty of loyalty and freedom of speech in *Fraser* was a reasonable limit within the meaning of s 1 of the *Charter*, a conclusion quoted with approval by the Federal Court of Appeal in *Haydon v Canada (Treasury Board) (FCA)*, 2005 FCA 249 at para 33.

> should attempt to get all the facts and give his employer an opportunity to explain or correct the problem. Most employers have a variety of mechanisms, formal or informal, under which an employee may lodge a complaint about the manner in which the enterprise should be operated. Only if no satisfaction results from those channels, then and only then, may an employee "go public."[56]

However, the court noted that "[t]here may be a situation where the issues raised are so pressing and urgent and the chain of command so obviously dysfunctional or corrupt that going public first is the only reasonable option."[57]

In *Stencell and Ontario Provincial Auditor*,[58] the whistleblower defence was found by the Public Service Grievance Board (PSGB) to be unavailable to an employee because there was no factual basis for the allegations of fraud or impropriety and available internal channels were not exhausted.

The Ontario case of *Attorney General of Ontario v Gowling and Henderson*[59] considered whether to order a law firm to disclose the identity of an anonymous public servant who had provided confidential Cabinet documents to the plaintiffs in a lawsuit. If the disclosure of the documents was protected, then the whistleblower's anonymity could be preserved. The disclosure of confidential matters was a flagrant breach of the duty of loyalty and confidentiality. The whistleblower defence was found not to apply because the allegation against the government was of "an error in judgment or in priorities" and not wrongdoing in the form of "fraud or corruption."[60]

The whistleblower defence is a remedy of last resort. Due to the obligation to seek an internal remedy before going public it is unlikely that a whistleblowing defence would now be possible given the option of disclosure under the disclosure of wrongdoing provisions in Part VI of the *PSOA* discussed below.

Where a public disclosure does not meet the requirements of the common law whistleblower defence, with the result that discipline is

---

56 *Mulligan*, above note 50 at para 54, quoting *Haydon v Canada (Treasury Board) (FC)*, 2004 FC 749 at para 47.

57 *Mulligan*, above note 50 at para 57.

58 PSGB#P/0043/95, 19 August 1996 (Lynk) at 69.

59 (1984), 47 OR (2d) 449 (HCJ) at 463.

60 *Ibid.*

warranted, there will still be the issue of determining the appropriate level of penalty. Five relevant factors have been identified:

1) What was the content of the criticism disclosed by the employee? (That is, how strong and how justified.)
2) How confidential or sensitive was the information? (That is, whether the material was correspondence of a not particularly confidential nature or whether it was more sensitive documentation.)
3) What was the manner in which the criticism was made public? (Which includes whether the employee attempted first to address the matters internally with their superiors.)
4) Were the employee's statements true or false?
5) To what extent was the employer's reputation damaged or jeopardized?[61]

The Grievance Settlement Board (GSB) has also attached significant importance to whether the employee acted in good faith and without hope of personal gain.[62]

C. *PSOA* PART IV: CONFLICT OF INTEREST

The purpose of the *PSOA* Part IV conflict of interest provisions is to avoid conflicts or potential conflicts of interest by requiring public servants to report "any personal or pecuniary interests that could raise an issue under the conflict of interest rules"[63] to their ethics executive who is then required to determine if there is a potential conflict and, if so, issue directions to address it. Both public servants and their supervisors are entitled to request and receive a determination by their ethics executive of a question about the application of the conflict of interest rules to the public servant.[64] Where an inquiry reveals an existing violation of the conflict of interest rules, then there may of course be a disciplinary response by the employer.

---

61 *MacAlpine*, above note 48.

62 *Ibid* at 85. In finding that the grievor was acting in good faith, the board noted, "He did not (as others have done) make his disclosures in a 'brown paper envelope.'"

63 *PSOA*, above note 1, ss 65(3) and 69(3).

64 *Ibid*, ss 65(1), (2), and (5) and 69(1), (2), and (5).

The statute provides that conflict of interest standards are to be set by regulation[65] and that each public servant must comply with the conflict of interest rules applicable to them.[66]

The conflict of interest rules are established in two substantively identical regulations, one applicable to public servants in ministries appointed by the PSC and the other to public servants employed in ministers' offices.[67] The first regulation also applies to public bodies unless they develop rules approved by the integrity commissioner as providing an ethical standard at least equal to the regulation.[68] Approved rules only come into force when they are posted on the integrity commissioner's website.[69] The Act provides for revising approved rules in the event the rules established in regulation are amended to require a higher standard of ethical conduct.[70] However, the rules have not been changed substantively since they were established in 2007.

The rules include provisions covering both current public servants and former public servants, meaning public servants who have ceased to be public servants since the *PSOA* came into force.[71]

1) Ethics Executives

The integrity commissioner is the ethics executive for the secretary of the Cabinet, the ethics executives prescribed for public servants in each public body, chairs of public bodies, former deputy ministers, former public servants in ministers' offices, and former public servants who worked in public bodies.[72] In addition, the integrity commissioner has responsibility to educate and train ethics executives. The commissioner is given an advisory role to, upon request, provide advice regarding conflict of interest to the PSC in respect of appointments to the public service, consultants or independent contractors providing service to a ministry or a public body, and secondees from outside the public service

---

65 *Ibid*, ss 57 and 66.
66 *Ibid*, ss 57, 58, and 66.
67 O Reg 381/07 and O Reg 382/07.
68 *PSOA*, above note 1, s 59(1) & (2).
69 *Ibid*, s 59(3) & (4).
70 *Ibid*, ss 61 & 62.
71 *Ibid*, s 3.
72 *Ibid*, ss 62(1)4, 63(2)–(3), and 68.

of Ontario. The commissioner also advises the Public Appointments Secretariat regarding proposed appointments to public bodies.[73]

The integrity commissioner receives the declarations of financial interest required of public servants who routinely work on matters involving the private sector[74] and provides advice to the public servant's ethics executive regarding the actions to be taken to avoid a conflict including advice concerning the transfer of assets to a neutral third party.[75]

The integrity commissioner's role is central but not supervisory. The individual ethics executives are responsible for making determinations and directions under the rules in the context of their organizations. There is no appeal to the integrity commissioner from an ethics executive's determination or direction.

The secretary of the Cabinet is the ethics executive for deputy ministers.[76] The ethics executive for employees in a ministry, but not in a minister's office, is their deputy minister.[77] The ethics executive for public servants in public bodies is the person prescribed by regulation, normally the most senior executive or managerial official or the chair of the public body.[78] The PSC is the ethics executive for former public servants in ministries, except public servants that worked in minister's offices.[79]

Ethics executives for public servants, except those in ministers' offices, are required to both ensure the public servants who are responsible for are aware of their obligations under the conflict of interest rules and to promote ethical conduct.[80] Ethics executives are required to investigate and make a determination with respect to questions raised by a public servant or supervisor and notifications by public servants of a possible issue under the conflict of interest rules. If necessary, the ethics executive may provide advice to the employer and give the public servant binding directions to resolve a conflict or potential conflict.[81]

---

73 O Reg 384/07.
74 O Reg 381/07, s 11 and O Reg 382/07, s 11.
75 O Reg 384/07, s 1(5).
76 *PSOA*, above note 1, s 62(1)2.
77 *Ibid*, s 62(1)1.
78 *Ibid*, s 62(1)3 and O Reg 147/10.
79 *PSOA*, above note 1, s 63(1).
80 *Ibid*, s 64.
81 *Ibid*, s 65(4) & (5) and O Reg 383/07, s 1.

The directions may include a requirement to transfer property to a neutral third party.[82] In the case of ethics executives who are the head of the public servant's agency or the deputy minister of their ministry, they are giving advice to themselves, so will presumably act on their findings.

The integrity commissioner may be consulted by other ethics executives for advice or be referred matters by other ethics executives for the integrity commissioner to address as ethics executive.[83] Except for the authority given to the deputy minister of Community Safety and Correctional Services to delegate their powers, duties, and functions as ethics executive in respect of the OPP to the commissioner of the OPP, and the referral of a matter to the integrity commissioner, the responsibilities of an ethics executive may not be delegated though the functions necessary to meet those responsibilities may be carried out at the direction of the ethics executive.

An ethics executive is given authority to make inquiries in respect of notifications of potential conflicts by public servants or questions by supervisors but is given no authority to require the production of documents or to compel a person to provide evidence. An ethics executive is authorized to collect personal information necessary to the inquiry and is required to maintain it in confidence except as disclosure is permitted by the regulation. In summary, the regulation provides that disclosure can be made with the public servant's consent, as is required for the inquiry into the potential conflict, for purposes of law enforcement and as required by law.[84] The integrity commissioner has the same authority to collect personal information and similar limits on its disclosure in conducting the commissioner's duties when a matter is referred to the commissioner by another ethics executive.[85]

Where the ethics executive has managerial responsibility over the public servant, the ethics executive will have the authority and the resources of the employer to make inquiries[86] and implement any resulting determination, recommendations, and directions. Where a

---

82 O Reg 383/07, s 1.

83 *PSOA*, above note 1, ss 62(1)4 and 65(6).

84 O Reg 383/07, s 2.

85 O Reg 384/07, s 2.

86 *Ontario Public Service Employees Union (Norsworthy) v Ontario (Transportation)*, 2015 CanLII 60420 (ON GSB) at para 56, finding refusal to respond to a reasonable request for information in connection with a conflict of interest investigation is disciplinable misconduct.

direction is given to a public servant by their ethics executive or the integrity commissioner, the statute requires the public servant to comply.[87] The statute also makes the failure to follow the conflict of interest rules or a direction from the public servant's ethics executive subject to discipline including suspension and dismissal.[88]

Within a ministry, authority over the operation of the ministry and responsibility for compliance with the conflict of interest rules rests with the deputy minister. In a minister's office, responsibility is divided. The integrity commissioner is the ethics executive for a minister's staff but does not have managerial authority within a minister's office. The minister is required to ensure that public servants in the minister's office are familiar with the conflict of interest rules and promote ethical conduct, responsibilities normally imposed on the ethics executive,[89] but again the minister does not have direct managerial responsibility over their office staff. When the integrity commissioner, as ethics executive for public servants in a minister's office, makes a determination or gives directions, the commissioner must notify the minister.[90] The minister will presumably ensure the cooperation of the person responsible for managing the staff in the minister's office with both any inquiry and the addressing of any determinations and directions.

A similar issue arises with inquiries into potential contraventions of the conflict rules by appointees to public bodies. As order-in-council appointees, responsibility for enforcing compliance with a directive rests with the appointing authority, the minister, or the Cabinet. Any determinations with respect to appointees or former appointees are reported to the responsible minister.[91] The minister or the Cabinet would need to consider what action if any is required.

Since there is a clear statutory provision requiring public servants and former public servants to comply with the conflict rules and directions of their ethics executive one would expect voluntary compliance, but there will be occasions where public servants disagree with a determination or choose not to comply with advice or directions.

---

87 *PSOA*, above note 1, ss 65(8) and 69(6).

88 *Ibid*, s 70.

89 *Ibid*, s 67.

90 *Ibid*, s 69(7).

91 *Ibid*, s 65(9) & (10).

2) Review and Enforcement of Ethics Executive Determinations and Directives

The ethics executive for most public servants, including all those in a bargaining unit, are the public servant's deputy minister or the executive in their agency responsible for managing the agency (typically the chief executive officer or executive director). Consequently, any conflict of interest determination or direction will be by management unless the ethics executive elects to refer a matter to the integrity commissioner. The *PSOA* provides authority for ethics executives to recommend discipline or transfers, but this is only necessary in respect of the integrity commissioner since other ethics executives have the managerial authority to make such decisions.

A determination by an ethics executive may be retrospective and potentially form the basis for discipline. However, even an entirely prospective determination may lead to mandatory directions that may have a significant impact on the public servant's employment or their off-duty activities. An employee may, for example, be directed to end their involvement with an entity or divest themselves of an ownership interest in an asset. A public servant may have as strong an interest in reviewing non-disciplinary directions as disciplinary ones.

a) Review of Conflict of Interest Rules for Reasonableness

The legal status of the conflict of interest rules is somewhat ambiguous, particularly with respect to approved rules developed by public bodies. Normally standards set by regulation such as the conflict of interest rules under the *PSOA* would not be open to review. However, *PSOA* section 152 provides that where a collective agreement provision conflicts with a regulation made under the Act, the collective agreement prevails. Management rights clauses in collective agreements in the sector permit the making of only "reasonable rules."[92] Agencies are bound by the rules governing employees in ministries but may develop their own rules subject to the approval of the integrity commissioner.

---

92 *OPSEU/MBC Unified Bargaining Unit Collective Agreement, 2022–2024* and *OPSEU/MBC Correctional Bargaining Unit Collective Agreement, 2018–2021*, online: https://opseu.org/information/general/find-your-collective-agreement, Art 2.1; *AMAPCEO/MBC Collective Agreement, 2018–2022*, online: https://amapceo.on.ca/ops, Art 3.1; *PEGO/MBC Collective Agreement, 2019–2022*, online: https://pego.on.ca/pego-collective-agreements, Art 3.

The process for developing and approving agency rules is statutory and therefore binding on arbitrators, so review of a rule must wait until it is approved by the integrity commissioner.[93] Rules submitted to the integrity commissioner "shall" be approved by the commissioner if they "establish a degree of ethical conduct that is at least equal" to the prescribed rules having regard for the "powers, duties and functions of the public body." The commissioner is not empowered to address the appropriateness of the rules to the extent that they seek to set a higher standard or may impose unnecessary restrictions.[94]

Arbitrator Burkett in *Ontario (Alcohol and Gaming Commission) v OPSEU, Local 565* found that, where the reasonableness of an agency's rules is subject to challenge under a collective agreement, "the minimum statutorily mandated rules must be construed as, per se, reasonable. It cannot be that what is approved by the Conflict of Interest Commissioner [now the integrity commissioner] under the statute . . . is somehow unreasonable under the collective agreement."[95] The passage of fifteen years without a substantive change or challenge to these rules must strengthen that view. However, to the extent that an agency's approved rules go beyond the minimum established by regulation, they are subject to review for reasonableness.[96]

Arbitrator Burkett's approach is appropriate. Unlike regulations or directives that establish terms of employment that may conflict with collective agreement terms, the obligation to comply with the conflict of interest rules in the regulations is found expressly in the statute and is not subject to section 152. Allowing collective agreement terms to prevail over the conflict of interest rules would lead to the absurd result that public servants from different bargaining units in a ministry working on the same matter dealing with the same members of the public could be subject to different conflict of interest rules.

Ministry rules going beyond or clarifying the prescribed rules are like other employer rules subject to review by the GSB for reasonableness.[97]

---

93 *Ontario (Alcohol and Gaming Commission) v OPSEU, Local 565* (2008), 171 LAC (4th) 382 (Burkett).

94 *Ibid* at para 15.

95 *Ibid* at para 14.

96 *Ibid* at para 19.

97 *Association of Management, Administrative and Professional Crown Employees of Ontario (Braun et al) v Ontario (Attorney General)*, 2017 CanLII 52715 (ON GSB) at paras 7 and 12.

b) Review of Conflict Determinations and Directions

In *Doyle v Ontario (Ministry of Municipal Affairs)*,[98] the PSGB found that a deputy minister's conflict determination and associated transfer of an employee may be disciplinary, giving the PSGB jurisdiction. The legislated conflict of interest provisions were part of the employee's terms of employment and their application was subject to review by the PSGB regardless of whether discipline resulted from a determination. In a subsequent decision the employer was unsuccessful in arguing mootness based on the complainant no longer being employed. The board held that the reputational damage to the grievor continued after the end of his employment by the ministry. The PSGB addressed the merits of the complaints by reviewing both the fairness of the deputy's process in finding a conflict and reviewing the substantive finding that a conflict existed. The complainant was successful on both counts.[99]

Labour arbitrators and the GSB are given express statutory authority to interpret and apply employment-related statutes, which includes the *PSOA* and regulations.[100] Bargaining unit members would appear to have the right to grieve that a finding of conflict of interest or a subsequent direction under the *PSOA* were incorrect or not authorized.

The GSB has been seen as ruling in *Ontario Public Service Employees Union (Halsall) v Ontario (Agriculture, Food, and Rural Affairs)*[101] that it does not have jurisdiction to review conflict of interest determinations made by management unless they gave rise to discipline or some other action such as a transfer that was grievable.[102] The *Halsall* case was argued on the basis that the threat of discipline could be viewed as discipline giving the GSB jurisdiction. A warning that discipline may be imposed if an employee continues to refuse to follow a management direction is not discipline. It was not disputed that there had to be a breach of the collective agreement alleged for the GSB to take jurisdiction if no discipline had been issued. No other violation being alleged,

98 2017 CanLII 52705 (ON PSGB) [*Doyle*, 2017].

99 2018 CanLII 109219 (ON PSGB) [*Doyle*, 2018].

100 *Labour Relations Act, 1995*, SO 1995, c 1, Sch A [*LRA*], s 48(12)j, incorporated into the *Crown Employees Collective Bargaining Act, 1993*, SO 1993, c 38 [*CECBA*]. See Chapter 7 for a discussion of the interrelationship between the *CECBA* and the *LRA*.

101 2009 CanLII 15420 (ON GSB) (Briggs) at para 39 [*Halsall*].

102 *Ontario Public Service Employees Union (Finn) v Ontario (Agriculture, Food and Rural Affairs)*, 2019 CanLII 35308 (ON GSB) at para 4.

the grievance was dismissed. The authority to apply labour relations statutes was not raised.

A second GSB panel[103] was expressly skeptical of the suggestion in *Halsall* that an employee had to refuse to comply with a direction and be disciplined to grieve. *Halsall* would also seem to be at odds with the comments of Dickson J in *Kelso v R* that

> [a]t common law, employees were under a duty to obey all reasonable orders.... This rule has been preserved in the collective bargaining context, where the employee must "obey now, grieve later" except where the order involves the performance of an illegal act or will endanger the safety of the worker.... It would be intolerable if employees were forced to risk disciplinary action in order to preserve legal rights. Rights are not extinguished by obeying the employer's instruction while at the same time contesting his decision.[104]

Failing to comply with a deputy minister's direction regarding a conflict of interest is insubordination that may lead to a disciplinary response.[105] The work/comply now and grieve later rule applies to conflict of interest directions.[106]

c) Review of Integrity Commissioner Determinations and Directions

In *Doyle* the issue was a determination and direction by a deputy minister, not the integrity commissioner. The PSGB has authority to review employment decisions of deputy ministers. Had the matter been referred to the integrity commissioner and the commissioner determined that a conflict existed, the PSGB's authority to overrule or review is doubtful. While the PSGB could address the appropriateness of any resulting discipline or other actions by the employer, the Integrity Commissioner is an independent legislative officer given specific statutory authority to make determinations and issue directions. The commissioner enjoys a greater level of independence than the PSGB and would be acting within

---

103 *Ontario Public Service Employees Union (Rouatt) v Ontario (Ministry of Labour)*, 2013 CanLII 26531 (ON GSB) (Herlich) at para 19.

104 [1981] 1 SCR 199 at 209, cited in *Metropolitan Toronto (Municipality) v CUPE (CA)*, 1990 CanLII 6974 (ON CA).

105 *Association of Management, Administrative and Professional Crown Employees of Ontario v Ontario (Ministry of Health and Long-Term Care)*, 2006 CanLII 30727 (ON GSB) [*AMAPCEO v Ministry of Health*].

106 *Ibid.*

the core of its expertise. The legislation distinguishes between matters of conflict of interest, where the commissioner makes determinations and directions, and employment matters of discipline and transfers, where the commissioner only makes recommendations. Similar concerns would arise before the GSB.

The statutory scheme gives the integrity commissioner responsibility for ensuring the conflict of interest rules are enforced at a consistent appropriate standard. One would assume that in dealing with the interpretation of the conflict of interest rules the GSB would be guided by the commissioner's decisions and advice. Since the commissioner does not have the power to compel disclosure and sworn testimony there may be scope for distinguishing a commissioner's determination and directions. However, there remains the fact that the authority of the GSB comes from the collective agreement. The integrity commissioner's determinations and directions are under statutory authority as is the obligation to comply. The integrity commissioner is not party to public servants' collective agreement or the contracts of employment of unrepresented public servants. There does not seem to be any basis for the GSB or PSGB to take appellate jurisdiction over actions by the commissioner.

The appropriate avenue to review a decision of the integrity commissioner would appear to be judicial review. The integrity commissioner is an independent officer of the assembly[107] required by statute to make determinations when they are requested and to issue directions that are binding on public servants.[108] The integrity commissioner is exercising a statutory power subject to judicial review.[109] There is no administrative appeal process provided, so judicial review is the only remedy available.

The only judicial comment on the subject comes in obiter comments by the Divisional Court in *Democracy Watch v Ontario Integrity Commissioner*,[110] and it is incorrect. The court easily concluded that Democracy Watch had no standing to judicially review decisions of the integrity commissioner under the *PSOA* and could and should have stopped there.[111] The court correctly recognized that the integrity

---

107 *Members' Integrity Act, 1994*, SO 1994, c 38, s 23.

108 *PSOA*, above note 1, s 65(5) and (8).

109 See *Judicial Review Procedure Act*, RSO 1990, c J.1 for definitions of "statutory power" and "statutory power of decision."

110 2020 ONSC 6081 at paras 62–75.

111 *Ibid* at paras 42 & 43.

commissioner was a legislative officer independent from the Crown, but then without explanation concluded that it operated within the "contractual relationship between employer and employee." The suggestion that a non-party that does not represent a party to a contract operates within the contractual relationship is extraordinary and untenable. The Supreme Court has indicated that where the government, not an independent officer of the legislature, is acting under a contract of employment, not separate statutory authority, the law of contract applies.[112] The court's statement that the commissioner's "function is limited to conducting the inquiry and to providing recommendations to the ethics executive" is clearly wrong. The integrity commissioner is the ethics executive for certain employees and former employees, and when a matter is referred to the commissioner by another ethics executive the commissioner acts as the ethics executive in the matter.[113] The court seems to have mistaken the additional powers to recommend discipline in the regulations for a statement of the extent of the commissioner's authority.[114] The resultant obiter comments about judicial review of a commissioner's determination and binding directions must be disregarded.

3) Conflict of Interest Rules

a) History

The prohibition against conflicts of interest is a long-standing component of the special responsibilities of public servants. The current conflict of interest rules are established by regulation and have remained substantially unchanged since they were enacted in 2007.[115] Those rules are largely reflective of the rules in place under the *PSA* that were in turn reflective of the development of standards through legislative changes and administrative decisions over the prior half century.

---

112 *Dunsmuir v New Brunswick*, 2008 SCC 9 at para 106.

113 *PSOA*, above note 1, ss 62(1)4, 63(2) & 3, and 68.

114 O Reg 384/07, s 2(2)4. The regulation also authorizes the commissioner acting under s 65(6) to require a public servant to take or refrain from taking certain actions including "to transfer ownership or control of an asset to a neutral third party"; ethics executives, including the commissioner, are given similar powers under O Reg 383/07, s 1(2) and (5).

115 O Reg 381/07 and O Reg 382/07.

The leading early statement of the essence of conflict of interest is found in the 1973 federal public service case of *McKendry and the Treasury Board*:

> The essential requirements are that the public servant should serve only one master and should never place himself in a position where he could be even tempted to prefer his own interests or the interests of another over the interests of the public he is employed to serve. Those requirements constitute the rationale of the doctrine that he should avoid a position of *apparent* bias as well as actual bias, and that he should never place himself in a position where . . . "two interests clash or *appear to clash.*"[116]

The Federal Court of Appeal considered the appearance of conflict so serious that the public service would not be effective if apparent conflicts between the private interest and the public duties of public servants were tolerated.[117]

In Ontario jurisprudence, the leading GSB case of case *OPSEU (Edwards) and Ministry of Health* holds

> [t]he nature of conflict of interest legislation and policy respecting public servants in the Province of Ontario is preventive in direction and is very broad in concept. It puts the onus on the employee to make known to the Deputy Minister an actual, perceived, or potentially actual or perceived conflict in order that the Deputy Minister may provide "advice" on the matter and see that the matter is promptly resolved. The penalty for failure to notify can be severe; it can go so far as dismissal. The Deputy Minister has wide discretion in providing that advice and resolving the issue or in removing the conflict . . . It is not necessary for any financial advantage to come to a public servant for a conflict of interest to exist.[118]

In 1948, the first conflict of interest provision[119] appeared prohibiting a civil servant from engaging in any profession, trade, or business

---

116 *McKendry and the Treasury Board*, 31 May 1973 (EB Jolliffe), unreported, quoted in *OPSEU (Hannan) and Ministry of Economic Development, Trade and Tourism*, GSB#0008/96, 7 January 1998 (Gray) at 32–33.

117 *Threader v Treasury Board*, [1987] 1 FC 41 (CA) at 53–57.

118 *OPSEU (Edwards) and Ministry of Health*, GSB#2216/94, 9 January 1996 (Finley) at 25–26.

119 O Reg 36/48, s 12.

undertakings for personal gain unless they had the consent of their minister. In 1962, the complete prohibition on outside employment was replaced with a prohibition on involvement in any work or business undertaking if it interfered with the performance of the employee's duties, conflicted with the best interests of the Crown, enabled the taking of an advantage from employment as a public servant, or otherwise constituted full-time employment for another person.[120] The changes expanded the scope beyond activities for gain but were intended to remove restrictions on responsible civil servants and permit reasonable outside activities, which corresponded with the right and freedom of other citizens to engage in any legal activity.[121] While the rules have been clarified on a number of occasions since then, the basic principles have not changed.

There are several themes consistently articulated in the Ontario cases and integrity commissioner summaries of determinations and directions. First, the conflict need not be actual, it is sufficient for the conflict to be potential or perceived. (This contrasts with the more limited requirement for members of the Legislative Assembly that they avoid actual conflicts.) Second, the conflict need not be one that could personally benefit the grievor. Third, the perception of conflict can be found in the perspective of the employer, third parties, and even the other party involved in the conflict, although that perspective needs to be reasonable. Fourth, there is a positive obligation to advise the ethics executive of possible conflicts.

b) Duty to Report

Public servants or former public servants are required to notify their ethics executive of any "personal or pecuniary interests that could raise an issue under the conflict of interest rules" applicable to them.[122] The ethics executive, not the public servant, determines if a conflict exists or what must be done to avoid, minimize, or mitigate it.

The integrity commissioner's website provides summaries of determinations and directions and advice, which are limited in specific personal details by the need to protect the confidentiality of individual

120 O Reg 190/62, s 15.

121 Ontario, Legislative Assembly, *Hansard*, 9 April 1963, at 2121 (J.N .Allan, Treasurer).

122 *PSOA*, above note 1, ss 65(3) and 69(3).

disclosures, but do provide useful clarification of the scope of the duty to disclose, the factors considered, and the type of directions issued.

"Personal or pecuniary interest" is very broad, including outside undertakings of a business, voluntary, or professional nature, and personal relationships within the workplace. For example, two employees in a relationship only occasionally working on the same file, not in a supervisory relationship, does not create a conflict of interest, though the "prudent course would be to make a disclosure to the ethics executive."[123] By contrast, having supervisory responsibility for an employee you are in a long-term personal relationship with is a conflict of interest.[124] Where extended family members are in a direct or indirect reporting relationship there is a potential for conflict.[125]

c) Transfer to the Private Sector

Additional disclosure, limitations, and obligations are placed upon public servants in both ministries and ministers' offices that routinely work on the review or implementation of a proposal for a private sector entity to provide all or part of a service or the funding of a service provided by the Crown, a public body, another agency of the Crown, or a corporation controlled by the Crown.[126] When a public servant begins work on such a matter they must disclose to their ethics executive their investment assets with limited exceptions for pension, publicly traded mutual funds, fixed value securities, guaranteed investment certificates, family residences, and recreational properties.[127] Any changes in assets subject to disclosure must be disclosed while working on a transfer. Employees working on a transfer are also required to declare the assets of their spouse and children that they are reasonably aware of that might create a conflict, and are prohibited from investing in an entity that is or is about to take over the provision or financing of a service

---

123 *Ontario Public Service Employees Union (Chabanova) v Ontario (Community and Social Services)*, 2011 CanLII 23159 (ON GSB) (Devins) at paras 133–34.

124 Case Summary M25-16/17 (case summaries of conflict of interest commissioner and integrity commissioner cases are published on the integrity commissioner's website; the conflict of interest commissioner's responsibilities were transferred to the integrity commissioner on 1 May 2019. Beginning in 2020–2021 the commissioner's site numbers Conflict of Interest and Political Activity summaries separately).

125 Case Summary C04-13/14.

126 O Reg 381/07, ss 10–13; O Reg 382/07, ss 10–13.

127 O Reg 381/07, s 11; O Reg 382/07, s 11.

until six months after the transfer is completed or work on a proposed transfer ceases.[128]

d) Benefiting Self, Spouse, or Children; Hiring Family Members; Participating in Decision Making

"Spouse" means a spouse as defined in the *Family Law Act*[129] or either of two persons living together in a conjugal relationship outside of marriage.[130] A public servant shall not use or attempt to use their position to benefit themself, their spouse, or their children.[131] A public servant shall not hire or contract (directly or indirectly) with their spouse, a parent, their children, or their siblings on behalf of the Crown.[132] A person should not be hired into a position where they supervise or are supervised by a parent, spouse, sibling, or child.[133] The prohibition covers direct reporting relationships, but its application to indirect reporting relationships depends on the circumstances.[134] In the event a public servant is placed in a position where they supervise a family member it should be reported to their ethics executive. Potential conflicts periodically arise where a spouse has or obtains a senior position, or volunteers with a stakeholder organization, or is employed by a business dealing with the public servant's ministry or public body. The public servant will need to recuse themselves from decisions concerning their spouse's organization and may need to be screened from matters related to the organization.[135] A declaration of the relationship may be sufficient if the organization is only one among many organizations affected by a decision.[136] A public servant will be screened from files that contain their spouse's personal information.[137]

A public servant shall not participate in decision making in respect of a matter that the public servant could, in the course of their duties, influence if the public servant could benefit from the decision, unless

128 O Reg 381/07, s 12; O Reg 382/07, s 12.
129 RSO 1990, c F.3.
130 O Reg 381/07, s 1; O Reg 382/07, s 1.
131 O Reg 381/07, s 3; O Reg 382/07, s 3.
132 O Reg 381/07 s 7; O Reg 382/07, s 7.
133 O Reg 381/07, s 7(3); O Reg 382/07, s 7(3).
134 Case Summaries C11-08/09, C15-11/12.
135 Case Summaries C01-07/08, C05-08/09, C08-09/10, C14-11/12, C05-14/15.
136 Case Summary C08-12/13.
137 Case Summary C15-11/12.

the public servant has the prior approval of their ethics executive.[138] An exception to the prohibition is rarely made. Where a public servant's role requires participation in decision making that might affect them, the questions in each case will be how much influence the public servant would have and how likely is the public servant to benefit from the decision.[139]

e) Accepting Gifts

Public servants shall not accept gifts from people, groups, or entities that have dealings with the Crown, seek to do business with the Crown, or to whom the public servant provides services in the course of their duties, with the exception of a gift of nominal value as a courtesy or hospitality if it is reasonable in the circumstances. If a gift of more than nominal value is received it must be declared to the public servant's ethics executive.[140]

Where a public servant receives a token of appreciation for speaking on behalf of the Crown of more than nominal value it must be accepted as a gift to the Crown or public body;[141] payment for speaking on behalf of the Crown other than for expenses not reimbursed by the Crown must be declined.[142] However, a prize won by chance while attending a function for the Crown may be kept.[143] Tickets to events or dinners should normally not be accepted.[144]

f) Disclosing Confidential Information

Public servants are precluded from disclosing information that comes to their attention in the course of their duties that is not available to the public, that if disclosed could harm the Crown or give a person receiving disclosure an advantage, except as authorized by law or the Crown.[145] A public servant is precluded from using such information for their own advantage or receiving a gift in exchange for such information.[146] The

---

138 O Reg 381/07, s 9; O Reg 382/07, s 9.

139 Case Summary C05-13/14.

140 O Reg 381/07, s 4; O Reg 382/07, s 4; Case Summary C14-09/10.

141 Case Summary C05-12/13.

142 Case Summary C14-09/10.

143 Case Summary C04-12/13.

144 Case Summaries C17-11/2, M01-17/18, C02-12/13.

145 O Reg 381/07, ss 1 and 5; O Reg 382, ss 1 and 5.

146 O Reg 381/07, s 5(2) & (3); O Reg 382, s 5(2) & (3); *OPSEU (DeFreitas) and Ministry of Environment and Energy*, PSGB#0007/94, 28 May 1998 (Lynk) at 54.

restriction on disclosing or using confidential information applies regardless of the activity a public servant may be undertaking. A public servant sitting as a representative of the Crown on a board or engaging in outside academic or professional duties within the scope of their employment is still required to ensure they do not disclose government information that is not otherwise public without obtaining authorization.[147]

g) Giving Preferential Treatment

A public servant is not to give any person or entity, including family or friends, preferential treatment and shall not offer any person or entity dealing with the Crown more assistance than is given in the ordinary course of business.[148] The regulation provides that public servants must also avoid, when performing their duties, creating the appearance that preferential treatment is being given. The integrity commissioner has found that engaging in activities they regulate (such as purchasing licences they enforce)[149] may suggest they are getting preferential treatment or are benefiting themselves. A potential conflict or perception of preferential treatment will arise where an appointee to a public body or other public servant has a relationship with persons or entities dealing with or regulated by their public body or ministry. In some cases, the potential conflict can be addressed by recusing the public servant from certain matters.[150] In the case of an executive joining an agency from a position in an entity having dealings with the agency, the executive may need to recuse themselves from matters related to the entity for a limited period.[151] Where the public servant's role is broader or the ongoing affiliation raises a larger concern, the public servant will need to end their relationship with the outside person or entity.[152] A public servant must be cautious that their appearance at an event does not suggest that the sponsor or organizer will be seen as getting or likely to get preferential treatment.[153]

---

147 Case Summaries C11-11/12, M11-16/17, M12-16/17, M13-16/17.

148 O Reg 382/07, s 6; O Reg 382/07, s 6.

149 Case Summary C12-12/13.

150 Case Summaries C17-09/10, C01-07/08, C01-16/17, C02-16/17, M04-16/17, Conflict of Interest I02-20/21

151 Case Summary Conflict of Interest I01-20/21.

152 Case Summaries C08-11/12, C11-09/10, C13-09/10, C18-09/10, C07-08/09, I01-19/20.

153 Case Summary M04-17/18.

h) Engaging in Business or Outside Undertaking

A public servant may not become engaged in a business or undertaking that could conflict with their duties, would interfere with their ability to perform their duties, is likely to influence or detrimentally affect the performance of their professional duties, could cause any person to derive an advantage from their employment as a public servant, or involves the use of government premises, equipment, or supplies. The prohibition applies to employment,[154] operation of a business,[155] participation in a spouse's business,[156] sitting on a board/committee/municipal office,[157] volunteer activities,[158] professional[159] or academic activities,[160] and participation in organizing sporting events,[161] whether for profit or charitable purposes.[162] In reviewing potential conflicts, ethics executives will focus on the nexus between the public servant's duties and the outside activity.[163] The standard for assessing whether an actual, perceived, or potential conflict exists is the "test of a reasonable well-informed person."[164]

A full-time public servant may not take an outside position that would be a full-time position for someone else unless they are on a leave of absence.[165] A public servant on a leave of absence is still subject to the other conflict of interest rules. This prohibition is not related to the particular duties of the public servant.

Sometimes outside activity is part of the public servant's ministerial duties (for example, serving on the board of a public body); if this is the case, the strict rules applicable to outside activities under section 8

---

154 Case Summary M16-16/17.

155 Case Summary N06-16/17.

156 Case Summary M03-17/18.

157 Case Summaries M04-16/17, M05-17/18, P01-17/18, M02-16/17; *OPSEU (Schoular) and Ministry of Education*, GSB#1203/00, 18 July 2002 (Gray) at 24–25 [*Schoular*]; *OPSEU (Hallborg) and Ministry of Revenue*, 1979 CanLII 4005 (ON LA) (Weatherill).

158 Case Summary C02-09/10; *AMAPCEO v Ministry of Health*, above note 105.

159 Case Summary M05-16/17.

160 Case Summaries M11-16/17, C02-16/17.

161 Case Summary C01-16/17.

162 Case Summary M01-16/17; using ministry letterhead to seek charitable donations is not permitted.

163 Case Summary M02-17/18.

164 *AMAPCEO v Ministry of Health*, above note 105.

165 O Reg 381/07, s 8(4) and O Reg 382/07, s 8(4).

of Regulation 381/07 do not apply.[166] This does not relieve the public servant from the obligation to avoid conflicts and particularly the rules regarding confidential information, participating in a decision that may benefit the public servant, and the appearance of giving or receiving preferential treatment under sections 5, 6, and 9.

Measures can often be taken to allow a public servant to participate in a business or other outside activity. Public servants can use skills learned in public service in other employment or a business so long as they do not use confidential information; solicit ministry-funded clients; use their ministry position to market, promote, or solicit business; or otherwise violate the conflict rules.[167] A business with other public servants as customers will require strict measures to avoid any suggestion of undue influence.[168]

A helpful example involved a new public servant whose public service role included dealing with farm stakeholders and overseeing some transfer payment agreements with agricultural organizations.[169] The public servant disclosed they were involved with a family farm and a voluntary member of an economic development and local food organization that might seek public project funding, and also had immediate and extended family members involved in rural organizations that would receive public funding. The integrity commissioner sought to separate the public servant's public and private activities. Personal activities were to be conducted on personal time without the use of government resources. Public duties were to take precedence and leaves were required for private activities done during a normal workday. The public servant was not to provide advice to family members about public matters. While participating with external organizations, the employee was not to give the impression of representing the ministry or the Crown. The employee was directed not to participate in the development of applications, be signatory to applications, and to recuse themself from discussions in relation to applications to the government of Ontario (including agencies) for funding. Further, the employee was directed to advise the chairs of the organizations of their conflict of interest obligations as a public servant and their inability to participate in discussions about public funding for the organization.

---

166 Case Summary M12-16/17.

167 Case Summary M06-16/17, Conflict of Interest I02-21/22.

168 Case Summary M06-17/18.

169 Case Summary M07-16/17.

Some outside activities may be incompatible with a particular public servant's role, such as engaging a vendor to their agency privately, and must be avoided or terminated.[170] The closer or more frequent the intersections between the interests of the outside business/undertaking and the ministry, and the intersections between the stakeholders of the outside business/undertaking and the ministry, the more the public servant's responsibilities involve them, the more likely that engaging in the outside business/undertaking would contravene the rules.[171]

i) Rules for Public Servants on Leave and Former Public Servants

Public servants[172] on leaves of absence, salary continuation, or secondments[173] are still public servants and are bound by the regular conflict of interest rules though their absence from the workplace may make the avoidance of conflict of interest easier. A public servant on salary continuation is considered to be on a leave of absence and consequently entitled to take full-time employment outside the public service.[174]

All former public servants are bound by the obligation not to disclose or use in a business undertaking information gained while in the public service but not available to the public that could, if disclosed, result in harm to the Crown or confer an advantage on the person receiving the confidential information.[175] Former public servants are also bound not to seek preferential treatment by or privileged access to public servants.[176] A public servant who advised the Crown about a proceeding, negotiation, or transaction cannot as a former public servant advise another party about the matter until the Crown ceases to be involved.[177]

Senior former public servants who occupied the designated positions of the secretary of the Cabinet, deputy minister, associate deputy minister, assistant deputy minister, Senior Management Group SMG 2, Executive—Ontario Financing Authority XOFA 1 and 2, and Information

170 Case Summary C07-08/09, Conflict of Interest I01-19/20 and I01-21/22.

171 Case Summary C01-10/11.

172 This refers to public servants that left the public service after August 2007 when the *PSOA* came into force; O Reg 381/07, s 15; O Reg 382/07, s 15.

173 Case Summary C01-10/11.

174 Case Summary M14-16/17.

175 O Reg 381/07, s 17; O Reg 382/07, s 17.

176 O Reg 381/07, s 16; O Reg 382/07, s 16.

177 O Reg 381/07, s 20; O Reg 382/07, s 20.

Technology Executive ITX 2, 3, and 4 classifications are restricted from lobbying their former ministry or minister for twelve months, or taking a job with a public body or another entity for twelve months if they had substantial involvement with it and had access to confidential information that if disclosed to the public body or other entity could harm the Crown.

D. *PSOA* PART V: POLITICAL ACTIVITY

1) Nature and Significance of Political Neutrality

There has been a long-standing social consensus on the need for the Ontario Public Service (OPS) to be politically neutral.[178] As early as 1854 there was a consensus among British politicians that a politically neutral permanent public service staffed by career public servants was essential.[179] While hiring in the nineteenth-century OPS was partisan, regular public servants served subsequent governments as permanent non-partisan employees of the Crown. As Ontario's society has become more developed, the role of government has necessarily expanded, and the necessity of a neutral public service has become ever more apparent.[180] The impartiality of the public service is recognized as a constitutional convention.[181]

In a democracy, where governments are expected to change, a permanent public service must necessarily be politically neutral both to be trusted by the changing political executives and to ensure incumbents cannot compromise the fairness of elections by using the public service to gain a partisan advantage.[182] The Supreme Court has noted that

> if restrictions on the political activities of public servants were withdrawn two results would probably follow. The public might cease to believe, as we think they do now with reason believe, in the impartiality of the permanent Civil Service; and Ministers might cease to feel the wellmerited confidence which they possess at present in the loyal

178 See the discussion in Chapter 1.

179 Northcote-Trevelyan, *Report on the Organization of the Permanent Civil Service*, House of Commons, London 1854.

180 Joseph Heath, *The Machinery of Government—Public Administration and the Liberal State* (Oxford: Oxford University Press 2020) at 176–80 [Heath].

181 See the discussion in Chapter 1.

182 Heath, above note 180 at 33.

> and faithful support of their official subordinates; indeed they might be led to scrutinise the utterances or writings of such subordinates, and to select for positions of confidence only those whose sentiments were known to be in political sympathy with their own.
>
> If this were so, . . . the Civil Service would cease to be in fact an impartial, nonpolitical body, capable of loyal service to all Ministers and parties alike; the change would soon affect the public estimation of the Service, and the result would be destructive of what undoubtedly is at present one of the greatest advantages of our administrative system, and one of the most honourable traditions of our public life.[183]

Neutrality is also necessary to assure the public will be provided services fairly in a non-partisan manner. Access to public service positions must be open to all based on qualifications, not party affiliation.[184]

In reviewing the legislated limits on political activity, it is important to remember that they reflect minimum requirements. Legislation can bar manifestations of disloyalty and partisanship, but this is insufficient to create an effective neutral public service. The necessary ethic of neutrality of the public service "requires much more than just prescinding from partisan political activity."[185] The public and the elected government's "usual expectation is that the civil service will exhibit loyalty to the government of the day and be vigorous in advancing its agenda."[186] However, the expansion of government has meant that most public servants fill administrative, professional, or technical roles that have little or no contact with the elected executive. They have no direct influence on policy and their performance is not perceived as likely to be influenced by any partisan affiliation that would justify precluding the public servant from participating in and enriching the political life of the community.

Initially, political neutrality focused on the neutrality of individual public servants—both in preventing them from choosing to engage in political activity and preventing them being required to engage in partisan activity. In the case of senior public servants that deal directly with the elected executive or provide policy advice to the elected executive, it remains essential for them to maintain the trust of successive elected

---

183 *Fraser*, above note 5 at para 42, Dickson J.

184 *OLRC Report, 1986*, above note 18 at 257–58.

185 Heath, above note 180 at 34.

186 *Ibid.*

executives from differing partisan backgrounds. With respect to the larger public service the concern is more appropriately on the neutrality of the institution.[187] A public service that hires and promotes based on ability and performance will reflect the diversity of the population in any number of respects including political views so long as those views are consistent with the non-partisan functioning and appearance of the public service.

The common law context for the current Ontario legislation is Supreme Court jurisprudence establishing that public servants' right to freedom of political expression is subject only to the minimal restraint needed to ensure that the civil service operates and is seen to operate in a loyal, impartial, and non-partisan fashion.[188] A greater degree of restraint is justified for the most senior staff because of the visibility of their position, the amount of discretion exercised and the degree of their involvement in policymaking, and a much reduced degree of restraint is appropriate for those whose jobs involving tasks that are not really susceptible to partisan political influence. One matter that has not been the subject of any litigation is whether the current political activity provisions of the *PSOA* accord with the test established in the Supreme Court cases.[189]

2) Ontario Context

In the 1895 legislative "Report of The Commissioners Appointed To Inquire Concerning The Mode Of Appointing And Remunerating Certain Provincial Officials Now Paid By Fees And The Extent Of The

---

187 *OLRC Report, 1986*, above note 18 at 261.

188 *Fraser*, above at note 5 at paras 33–36; *Osborne*, above note 29 at paras 43–44.

189 Since political activity restrictions usually involve restrictions on expression, s 2(b) of the *Charter* will be engaged, though it does not necessarily protect access to a particular platform for expression such as the right to run in municipal elections. See *Baier v Alberta*, 2007 SCC 31; *Toronto (City) v Ontario (Attorney General)*, 2021 SCC 34. Section 3 of the *Charter*, "which protects not only the right of each citizen to have and to vote for an elected representative in Parliament or a legislative assembly, but also to the right of each citizen to play a meaningful role in the electoral process," clearly places some limits on restrictions of certain political activity by public servants: *Figueroa v Canada (Attorney General)*, 2003 SCC 37 at para 58.

Remuneration They Should Receive,"[190] it was suggested that "whilst public servants should not be debarred from exercising their voting franchise, they should not be strenuously partisan." It was felt that there was no need for special legislation or the imposition of penalties and that a circular letter to the civil servants would be adequate. The view was that any breach of strict neutrality should be dealt with as misconduct, warranting dismissal from office. The legislature passed the following non-statutory resolution, which was the only provision dealing with political activity until 1963:

> Resolved, That this House is of the opinion that officers or clerks of the civil or public service of the province, or permanent employees, who solely or for the most part obtain their livelihood in the public service, should not actively participate in provincial or Dominion election campaigns, and that officers or clerks of the civil service should not become candidates for municipal councillors.[191]

In 1963, when political activity rights were finally codified in the *PSA*,[192] the provincial treasurer, J.N. Allan stated:

> This legislation underlines our belief that employees of the government have the right, and indeed the duty, to play a full part in our political and democratic institutions ... It is important that the higher public service be impartial and objective to provide continuity of government administration, thus respecting the professionalism and high standards of conduct that have been everywhere identified with the Ontario public service. It is not our intention to take the restrictions provided for deputy ministers and other Crown employees below the level of branch heads or operating heads of major institutions, so that there remains available to participate in our local government institutions, provincial and federal party activities, persons of high technical and professional competence and administrative ability.[193]

190 Ontario Sessional Papers, 1895, No 081/032 (Toronto: Warwick Bros and Rutter, 1895) at 35.

191 Legislative Journals, 17 March 1897. It was passed without debate.

192 SO 1962–63, c 118, s 3 [*PSA 1962–63*].

193 Ontario, Legislative Assembly, *Hansard*, 6 February 1963, No 22 at 715–18 (J.N. Allan, Treasurer).

The 1963 *PSA* amending Act dealt with the regulation of political activity by introducing the broad concept of "Crown employee,"[194] which included both direct employees of the Crown and employees of certain Crown agencies. All Crown employees were not, during working hours, to engage in activity for a provincial or federal political party. Most Crown employees were able to be municipal political candidates or work in support of one, provided the activity did not interfere with the performance of duties as a Crown employee or conflict with interests of the Crown, or if the activity was not "in affiliation with or sponsored by a provincial or federal political party." Most Crown employees were entitled to a leave of absence that allowed them to be a candidate, to solicit funds, or to "associate his position in the service of the Crown" with that political activity. The Act barred deputy ministers and other senior designated employees from being municipal, provincial, or federal candidates, working for such candidates, or obtaining political activity leave. Direct regular employees of the Crown were also prohibited from canvassing during provincial or federal elections but, except for deputy ministers and senior designated employees, could canvass at other times. Except while on a political activity leave, a regular direct employee of the Crown could not speak in public or express views in writing for distribution to the public on any matter that "forms part of the platform of a provincial or federal political party." A contravention of any of these restrictions was deemed to be sufficient cause for dismissal.

In a 1987 decision, *Ontario (Attorney General) v OPSEU*,[195] the Supreme Court concluded that restrictions on political activity by provincial Crown employees in connection with federal elections could be validly enacted by a provincial legislature and reiterated the importance of upholding the constitutional convention of the impartiality of the public service.

Then, the 1991 Supreme Court decision in *Osborne v Canada (Treasury Board)*[196] found a federal prohibition on public servants from engaging in work for or against a candidate or a political party infringed public servants' right to freedom of expression under section 2(b) of the *Charter* and was not a "reasonable limit" under section 1 of the *Charter*

194 *PSA 1962–63*, above note 192, s 1.

195 *Ontario (Attorney General) v OPSEU*, above note 17.

196 *Osborne*, above note 29.

because it banned all partisan-related work by all public servants, without distinction either as to the type of work or their relative role, level, or importance in the public service hierarchy. Protecting the neutrality of the public service was a valid objective. The broad prohibition on political activity by all public servants failed the minimal impairment test under section 1 having regard for the importance of broad participation in the discussion of public affairs, the number of people now employed by government, and the prohibition of activity that, when engaged in by many public servants, could not reasonably be seen as undermining the neutrality of the public service. While the broad prohibitions were justified for "deputy heads" (deputy ministers), their application to other public servants was beyond what was required to protect the neutrality of the public service. The court did not suggest that restrictions on political activity by public servants were not permissible. However, they needed to reflect what was necessary to protect neutrality given the role and responsibilities of the level of the public servant.

The complete prohibition on engaging in political activity protected public servants from being required to aid the incumbent elected government in its partisan activities. The relaxation of rules prohibiting political activity requires the introduction of a prohibition on requiring public servants to engage in political activity to prevent "political enslavement."[197] This does not of course prevent a public servant inappropriately engaging in political activity in the hope or at the suggestion that it may advance or protect their career. A complete prohibition is seen as a limitation on political activity by a person protected by a collective agreement but to a senior public servant terminable on reasonable notice it is a protective barrier against political machinations.

In light of *Osborne*, the attorney general for Ontario conceded before the Ontario Court of Appeal that certain provisions in the *PSA* and the *Crown Employees Collective Bargaining Act (CECBA)* were unconstitutional restrictions on freedom of expression and entered into an Ontario Court of Appeal consent order that struck down certain sections of the *PSA* and *CECBA*, removing some restrictions on political activity.[198] The order maintained all the prohibitions against political activity on deputy ministers and certain classes of restricted employees. Subject to avoiding

197 *OLRC Report, 1986*, above note 18 at 289.

198 *Ontario Public Service Employees Union v Ontario (Attorney General)*, 1993 CanLII 8619 (ON CA).

activities that interfered with the performance of the person's duties or would be a conflict of interest, other Crown employees were no longer prohibited from being, or supporting, a municipal candidate affiliated with a provincial or federal provincial party, or canvassing during a provincial or federal election. The requirement to be on leave to solicit funds for a federal or provincial party or candidate or engage in political speech was ended. The *CECBA* limitations on trade unions supporting political parties or collecting and remitting donations to those parties was removed. The court noted that without the agreement of the parties it would not have engaged in such extensive redrafting.[199]

In 1993 the *PSA* was amended to include political activity provisions that are substantively similar to those that are now in the *PSOA*. The *PSA* retained restrictive provisions for designated senior public servants but significantly reduced the restrictions applicable to other public servants in line with the *Charter* decisions and expressly prohibited any public servant being required to engage in political activity. The *PSOA* expanded the definition of political activity to include public comments related to the public servant's duties on positions expressed by municipal as well as federal or provincial candidates. The secretary of the Cabinet and deputy ministers were excluded from the right to join or contribute to a political party. Political activity of public servants in a minister's office was specifically addressed, recognizing that some aspects of their duties involve what would be prohibited political activity for other public servants. However, the primary reforms introduced in the *PSOA* are procedural. The integrity commissioner, a politically neutral person, was appointed to give advice and, when requested, make determinations about the application of the political activity provisions in individual cases.

3) Role of the Ethics Executive

Public servants' ethics executives for political activity purposes are the same as for conflict of interest purposes.[200] Ethics executives may refer matters to the integrity commissioner who will then deal with the matter as the ethics executive.[201] Ethics executives must respond to

---

199 *Ibid.*

200 *PSOA*, above note 1, s 73.

201 *Ibid*, ss 84(5) and 93(5).

questions about the political activity rights of a public servant from the public servant or their supervisor, including applications to engage in otherwise restricted political activity and applications for unpaid leaves to engage in political activity.[202] In the event a public servant is elected to municipal office, their ethics executive must determine whether they must resign.[203]

Ethics executives may also make inquiries when they are concerned a public servant has engaged in or is about to engage in political activity in contravention of the Act or regulations.[204] However, the ethics executives have no powers to compel testimony or the production of documents, so must rely on their management authority.

Public servants are required to notify their ethics executive of potential conflicts between their political activity and the interests of the government or the agency where the public servant is employed.[205]

Public servants are required to comply with the directions of their ethics executive and the integrity commissioner.[206] Since the Act gives a public servant access to their ethics executive and mandates the ethics executive to decide questions regarding political activity rights, a public servant cannot rely on advice from their supervisor or another management official.[207]

Enforcement of the political activity provisions is by employee discipline. The provisions are statutory and so they prevail over the provisions of a collective agreement.[208] The *PSOA* provides that the violation of the political activity provisions is subject to discipline including suspension and dismissal.[209] In the case of government appointees, directions are reported to the responsible minister. In respect of other public servants any action is left to the employer. Whether a violation has occurred, and the discipline imposed, are consequently subject to arbitration under the applicable collective agreement, or to adjudication at the PSGB or in court. An ethics executive's factual determinations are not protected by a privative or finality clause. In the context of a discipline arbitration, an

---

202 *Ibid*, ss 84(1), (3), 93(1), (3), and 98(1), (3).

203 *Ibid*, s 101.

204 *Ibid*, ss 84(3), 93(3), and 98(3).

205 *Ibid*, ss 84(2), 93(2), and 98(2).

206 *Ibid*, ss 84(7), 93(7), and 98(5).

207 *Schoular*, above note 157 at para 59.

208 For discussion of interaction of the *PSOA* and a collective agreement, see Chapter 2.

209 *PSOA*, above note 1, s 99.

arbitrator may find a direction was based on a mistaken understanding of the facts and deal with the matter on the facts the arbitrator finds.

Compliance with an ethics executive's direction about political activity is mandatory, so arguably the requirement to comply with a direction is not reviewable by an arbitrator. There has been no litigation on the matter, but the PSGB has taken jurisdiction to review a conflict of interest determination and direction made by a deputy minister as ethics executive, and the GSB would likely take jurisdiction similarly if asked.[210] The conflict of interest sections are similar to the political activity sections, so one would expect a similar result. The arbitral jurisdiction to review directions by the integrity commissioner is more speculative. The Office of the Integrity Commissioner is an independent agency, not party to or bound by the collective agreement, acting at the core of its statutory jurisdiction. Judicial review would seem to be the more appropriate recourse.

4) *PSOA* Definition of Political Activity

A public servant engages in political activity when they do anything in support of or in opposition to a federal or provincial political party or a candidate in a federal, provincial, or municipal election; seek to become a candidate in a federal, provincial, or municipal election; or comment publicly and outside the scope of their duties on matters directly related to those duties and that are dealt with in the positions or policies of a federal or provincial political party or a candidate in a federal, provincial, or municipal election.[211]

Attending a public meeting where an MPP is the speaker is not political activity unless there is a fundraising or overtly partisan aspect to the meeting[212] or it was sponsored by a political party.[213]

The term "candidate" is not defined in the Act, so it would be reasonable to adopt the definition in the *Elections Act*, which states that an individual only becomes a candidate once the election writ is issued.[214] Supporting an individual before they are officially nominated

---

210 See the detailed discussion in the conflict of interest section above.

211 *PSOA*, above note 1, s 72.

212 Case Summary P02-16/17.

213 Case Summary C02-08/09.

214 *Ibid* discussing the *Elections Act*, RSO 1990, c E. 6, s 27.1 .

as a candidate would not necessarily be political activity. However, supporting an individual who has publicly announced an intention to become a candidate and is clearly identified with a federal or provincial political party may be action in support of a political party.[215]

The term "municipal election" includes elections for a school board trustee as these are governed by the *Municipal Elections Act, 1996*.[216] A band council election is not held under that Act, so seeking election to a band council is not "political activity" for *PSOA* purposes.[217]

An article by a public servant that is critical of a policy of a political party will be political activity within the *PSOA* definition if "the content of the article overlapped with the area of work in which the public servant was engaged."[218] Whether comments deal with the position or policies of a party or candidate is determined with reference to the impact on a "reasonably well informed member of the public."[219] Not mentioning a party or candidate's name or focusing on the language used rather than substance may but will not necessarily exclude the comment from the definition of political activity.[220] Similarly, speaking at a function designed to encourage interaction with politicians aligned with a particular political philosophy but not sponsored by a political party may be political activity.[221]

Lobbying an MPP is political activity,[222] as is commenting on a candidate,[223] membership in a riding association,[224] attending a political fundraiser even as a guest,[225] posting an election sign at one's residence,[226] door-to-door canvassing, speaking to voters on the telephone, fundraising, working on administrative matters in a campaign office,[227]

---

215 *Ibid.*

216 SO 1996, c 32 Sch, s 3(1)(iii) applies to elections to local boards defined in section 1 as defined in the *Municipal Affairs Act*, RSO 1990, c M.46; "local board" means a school board; Case Summary C03-09/10.

217 Case Summary C01-18/19.

218 Case Summary C01-15/16.

219 Case Summaries C03-11/12 and C07-11/12.

220 *Ibid.*

221 Case Summary C02-10/11.

222 Case Summary C03-12/13.

223 Case Summary C01-09/10.

224 Case Summary C07-09/10.

225 Case Summary C04-08/09.

226 Case Summary C02-07/08.

227 Case Summary C01-11/12.

organizing fundraising or other political events, or managing riding association activities.[228]

5) Rules for Different Categories of Public Servants

To ensure that political activity restrictions are tailored to differing roles and responsibilities of levels of public servants, political activity restrictions vary according to categories.

a) Public Servants Not Specially Restricted or Employed in a Minister's Office

Public servants who are not specially restricted or employed in a minister's office may engage in political activity subject to restrictions set out in the *PSOA* Part V. They are also entitled to decline to engage in political activity.[229]

A public servant may not engage in political activity in the workplace; while wearing their uniform; using government premises, equipment, or supplies; or if the activity interferes with the performing of their duties or associates their position with the political activity.[230] These activities are prohibited without exception even while on an unpaid leave of absence. However, a public servant seeking to become a candidate in a federal, provincial, or municipal election may associate their position with this activity, but only to the extent necessary to identify the public servant's position and work experience.[231]

Public servants are generally prohibited, unless they are on an unpaid leave, from seeking to become a candidate in a federal or provincial election; commenting publicly on matters that are directly related to their duties that are addressed in the policies of a federal or provincial party or in the policies of a candidate in a federal, provincial, or municipal election; or engaging in political activity that could interfere with the performance of their duties or conflict with the interests of the Crown or, if they work in a public body, that public body.[232] Public

---

228 Integrity Commissioner, *Guidance on Political Activity for Ministers' Office Staff*, online: http://oico.on.ca [*Guidance on Political Activity*].

229 *PSOA*, above note 1, s 76.

230 *Ibid*, s 77.

231 *Ibid*, s 77(d).

232 *Ibid*, s 79.

servants in a supervisory position or who deal directly with the public in a position of real or perceived authority must take an unpaid leave to fundraise for federal or provincial parties or candidates in federal, provincial, or municipal elections.[233]

During an election period, from the date of the writ to election day in the case of federal and provincial elections and the sixty days prior to a municipal election,[234] public servants are entitled to a leave of absence to engage in political activity on application to their ethics executive.[235] Outside an election period, an ethics executive may grant a leave of absence to engage in political activity. In the event a public servant seeks to be or becomes a candidate in a federal or provincial election outside the election period, their ethics executive will grant an unpaid leave if it is necessary or determine that a leave is not necessary and authorize the public servant to be or seek to become a candidate without being on an unpaid leave.[236]

While public servants are not required to take an unpaid leave to run in a municipal election, they remain subject to the general limitations on political activity in the workplace, or that interferes with their duties, or creates a conflict with the Crown or their public body. Similarly, a public servant may hold municipal office provided the office does not place the public servant in a conflict requiring resignation. In addressing these issues their ethics executive will consider the extent and nature of the interaction between the public servant's ministry and the municipality, whether the public servant's duties involve decisions affecting the municipality, and the time commitment the municipal position requires.[237] An ethics executive may impose restrictions to minimize the potential for conflict.[238] A candidate for municipal office may be moved from a public facing role to avoid the need for a leave.[239] Where a manager with supervisory authority will be fundraising while campaigning for municipal office they will be required to take an unpaid leave.[240]

233 *Ibid*, s 79(1)b.
234 *Ibid*, s 78.
235 *Ibid*, ss 80(1), (2) and 81(1), (2)a.
236 *Ibid*, ss 80(1), (2)b and 81(1), (2)b.
237 Case Summaries M02-16/17, M03-16/17, and C02-18/19.
238 Case Summary C01-13/14.
239 Case Summary C02-14/15.
240 Case Summary M19-16/17.

A public servant running for provincial or federal office is required to be on unpaid leave during the election period.[241] Both the time commitment and the nature of political campaigning are inconsistent with performing the duties of a public service position and maintaining the appearance of public service neutrality.[242] A public servant who is running for office outside the election period is not required to be on an unpaid leave unless their ethics executive determines that in the circumstances it is necessary, in which case a leave will be granted.[243]

Public servants who wish to engage in other political activity that requires a leave or is not restricted are entitled to be granted an unpaid leave of absence for that purpose during an election period.[244] Outside an election period an ethics executive may grant a public servant's request for a leave to undertake political activity that requires a leave or is not restricted.[245] This discretion will be exercised having regard for the purpose of the legislation to maintain the fact and appearance of a non-partisan public service. Short leaves to satisfy the letter but not the purpose of the political activity restriction are unlikely to be approved.

b) Specially Restricted Public Servants

The Act establishes a class of senior public servants that are under the greatest political activity restrictions.[246] The specially restricted public servants are the secretary of the Cabinet, deputy ministers, associate deputy ministers, assistant deputy ministers, directors and deputy directors of legal branches, Crown attorneys, commissioned officers and detachment commanders in the OPP, members of adjudicative tribunals, and other appointees prescribed by regulation.[247]

Specially restricted public servants are entitled to decline to engage in political activity[248] and are limited to political activity that is expressly permitted by the Act.[249] Most specially restricted public servants are

---

241 *PSOA*, above note 1, ss 79(1) and 81(2)a.

242 *Cambrian College v OPSEU*, 2007 CanLII 7390 (ON LA) at 11 [*Cambrian College*], quoting *OPSEU v Ontario (Attorney General) (Ont HCJ)*, 1988 CanLII 4679 (ON SC).

243 *PSOA*, above note 1, ss 79(2) and 80(3).

244 *Ibid*, s 81.

245 *Ibid*.

246 *Ibid*, s 85.

247 O Reg 377/07.

248 *PSOA*, above note 1, s 87.

249 *Ibid*, s 86.

limited to voting, contributing money to political parties or candidates, being a member of a political party, and attending all-candidates meetings.[250] The secretary of the Cabinet and deputy ministers are further restricted and may only vote and attend all-candidates meetings.[251] The right to membership in a political party does not mean a person is entitled to participate in the activities of the party.[252]

Upon request a specially restricted public servant's ethics executive may authorize the public servant to seek municipal office or campaign for a candidate for municipal office if the ethics executive concludes to do so would not interfere with the performance of their duties or create a conflict with the interests of the Crown or, if the public servant works for a public body, the interests of the public body.[253] The concern when a specially restricted public servant campaigns for municipal office is whether they are affiliating themselves with a partisan interest.[254] Putting up a municipal election sign will be permitted if it does not show a party affiliation.[255] An authorization may be subject to conditions, including taking an unpaid leave.[256]

If the public servant is or is seeking to become a candidate in a municipal election, they may associate their position with this activity, but only to the extent necessary to identify the public servant's position and work experience.[257]

There are, of course, no exceptions to the rules that a public servant will not engage in political activity in the workplace; while wearing their uniform; using government premises, equipment, or supplies; or if the activity interferes with the performing of their duties.[258]

Part-time government appointees who are specially restricted may apply to the integrity commissioner to be permitted to engage in political activity subject to the limitations noted above.[259] The integrity commissioner must determine if the proposed activity would interfere with the performance of the public servant's duties or create a conflict of

250 *Ibid*, s 89(1).
251 *Ibid*, s 89(2).
252 Case Summaries C12-07/08 and 14-07/08.
253 *PSOA*, above note 1, s 90.
254 *Cambrian College*, above note 242.
255 Case Summary C03-18/19.
256 *PSOA*, above note 1, s 90(5).
257 *Ibid*, s 88(d).
258 *Ibid*, s 88.
259 *PSOA* above note 1, s 92.

interest with the public body to which they are appointed. In doing so, the commissioner considers the nature of the political activity specified in the request, the scope of the public servant's discretion, whether it could be reasonably seen as affected by political considerations, the visibility of the position, and other factors the integrity commissioner views as relevant in the circumstances. In granting authority to engage in political activity, the commissioner may impose conditions including requiring the public servant to be on unpaid leave. The integrity commissioner views the determination as balancing the need for neutrality of the public service with the public servant's interest in engaging in political activity.[260]

The integrity commissioner does not authorize activity that visibly identifies a part-time specially restricted public servant appointee as a partisan, such as door-to-door canvassing or distribution of flyers, fundraising, acting as a scrutineer, or putting up a lawn sign, but will authorize work in a campaign office and making calls where the public servant does not identify themselves.[261] Having regard for the role of a part-time appointee's role at their agency the integrity commissioner approved the appointee's request for permission to manage a municipal candidate's election campaign.[262] The supervised exception for part-time appointees reflects the fact that a part-time appointee is not making a full-time commitment and should not be restricted in their other activities when it can be avoided.

A specially restricted public servant may join a political party or contribute money but the integrity commissioner will not authorize attending fundraisers, endorsing a candidate, or taking riding or national executive positions in a party.[263] In one instance the integrity commissioner authorized working on a transition team since there was no reasonable perception it would have an impact on the public servant's decisions at their public body.[264]

A chair of a public body asked about being invited to a $500-a-ticket political fundraiser. Since the *PSOA* expressly permits specially restricted public servants to belong to and contribute to a political party but not engage in other political activity, the integrity commissioner found that

---

260 Case Summary C01-11/12.

261 Case Summaries C02-07/08, C06-07/08, and C01-11/12.

262 Case Summary Political Activity I01-21/22.

263 Case Summaries C04-08/09, C10-07/08, and C12-07/08.

264 Case Summary C03-14/15.

under the *PSOA* the chair could purchase a ticket, thereby making a donation, but could not attend a public party function.[265] Since the records of donations to Ontario political parties are now publicly available online, in practice, specially restricted public servants may consider the wisdom of exercising the right to make political donations. Traditionally, senior public servants have avoided overt participation in partisan politics for practical and ethical reasons.[266]

c) Public Servants Employed in a Minister's Office

Separate rules apply to ministers' staff, reflecting the unique position of ministers. They are responsible as senior public officials for the implementation of the partisan policy agenda of the elected government. Ministers are also partisan politicians with an interest in the successful re-election of their party to government. Ministers are expected to explain, implement, monitor, and defend the government's initiatives and must have public service staff to support them. Ministers are also entitled to have staff who share their partisan belief in the government's initiatives to assist them in their role as a public official implementing government policy. However, government resources are not to be used for partisan purposes not necessary to the exercise of a ministerial power, duty, or function.

Public servants employed in ministers' offices are entitled to engage in political activity except as restricted by the Act.[267] They can decline to engage in political activity "unless the political activity is related to the performance of a ministerial power, duty or function."[268]

While at work or using government resources ministers' staff can only engage in political activity that is related to the performance of a ministerial power, duty, or function and does not conflict with the interests of the Crown.[269] They can assess the consistency of the ministry's activities with a party's position, prepare responses to the positions of the political opposition to the minister's actions, and communicate the elected government's position. By contrast, during their usual working hours, they cannot conduct riding or party business or fundraising. They cannot publicly endorse or oppose a political party or candidate

265 Case Summary Political Activity I02-21/22.
266 Heath, above note 180 at 33–34.
267 *PSOA*, above note 1, s 95.
268 *Ibid*, s 96.
269 *Ibid*, s 97.

or mix political campaign activity with ministry business meetings or activities.[270]

Public servants in ministers' offices remain subject to the conflict of interest rules and confidentiality restrictions on public servants when engaging in political activity. Seeking contributions from ministry stakeholders, registered lobbyists for their ministry, or using their connection to the minister's office to fundraise would contravene these provisions.[271] The integrity commissioner has noted that, like ministers, their staff, especially those in the most senior roles, always carry ministerial authority with them "regardless of whether they mean to employ it," and so they must constantly be aware of the need to ensure that there is "a distinct line" between their governmental staff and party worker roles.[272] Solicitation of funds from stakeholders "by a minister's chief of staff or senior advisor may create an appearance that some form of preferential treatment will flow from the donation regardless of the time of day the solicitation was made or even if a government resource was not used to make the contact."[273] "Cash for access" (the appearance that ministers and staff are providing preferential access to political donors) is inappropriate[274] and, while not a breach of the minister's responsibilities under the different standards of the *Members' Integrity Act*,[275] may very well be a breach of the *PSOA*.

However, the only provision in the *PSOA* directly imposing a responsibility on ministers requires they ensure their staff are familiar with the conflict of interest rules that apply in respect of a minister's office and that they promote ethical conduct by their staff.[276] There is no enforcement provision in the *PSOA* if a minister fails to live up to these requirements.

---

270 *Guidance on Political Activity*, above note 228.

271 *Ibid*; Integrity Commissioner, *Report re: The Honourable Bob Chiarelli, The Honourable Charles Sousa and the Honourable Yasir Naqvi*, 8 December 2016 at paras 74–77.

272 *Ibid* at para 75, quoting from Commissioner Morrison, *Minister's Staff Report*.

273 *Ibid* at para 74.

274 *Ibid* at para 77.

275 See the discussion of members responsibilities in Chapter 5.

276 *PSOA*, above note 1, s 67.

6) Leaves of Absence and Election to Office

Leaves of absence to engage in political activity are unpaid. They do not break the public servant's continuous service, but the period of the leave is excluded in calculating length of service.[277] The length of a leave will be determined by the public servant's ethics executive when granting a leave outside an election period. A leave requested with respect to activity during an election period will fall entirely within the election period.

Election to the provincial assembly or federal Parliament terminates a public servant's employment.[278] Public servants, other than fixed-term employees and government appointees, have a right to reinstatement if they cease to be a member of the assembly or Parliament within five years and seek reinstatement within twelve months and there is a vacant position for which they are qualified.[279] This right to reinstatement in a vacant position does not prevail over a right under a collective agreement or a redeployment directive.[280] In the event of reinstatement, the public servant's employment is considered continuous, but the period from termination to reinstatement is not counted when calculating length of service.[281]

Whether campaigning raises a conflict or interferes with the public servant's duties is a different question than whether the holding of a municipal office raises a conflict requiring a choice between the municipal office and remaining in the public service. Holding municipal office raises broader issues of conflict of interest.[282] In the event the public servant's ethics executive determines the municipal office conflicts with the interests of the Crown or interferes with the performance of their duties, their employment will be terminated. A public servant can seek an advance ruling on the matter from their ethics executive.[283]

A public servant, excluding fixed-term employees and government appointees, elected to municipal office, and terminated because of a finding by their ethics executive or the integrity commissioner that holding

277 *Ibid*, s 91.

278 *Ibid*, s 100.

279 *Ibid*, s 102.

280 *Ibid*, s 102(9).

281 *Ibid*, s 102(10).

282 *Schoular*, above note 157 at para 63; *ibid*, s 101(3), similar to O Reg 381/07, s 8; Case Summary C02-18/19.

283 *PSOA*, above note 1, s 101(2).

the municipal office conflicts with their position has the same right to reinstatement if they cease to hold municipal office after four years.[284]

7) Reprisal

The Act prohibits reprisals against public servants for engaging in political activity in accordance with the Act or declining to engage in political activity. Reprisal is defined as "any measure taken against a public servant that adversely affects his or her employment or appointment."[285] Public servants are entitled to take a complaint to an arbitrator under their collective agreement, or if they are appointed under *PSOA* Part III and are not subject to a collective agreement, the PSGB, or otherwise to the Ontario Labour Relations Board (OLRB).[286] On a complaint of reprisal, the respective boards have authority, if they find a reprisal has occurred, to provide remedies including reinstatement and damages[287] but not punitive damages or costs.[288]

There has been no discussion of these provisions by a tribunal. A complainant would need to plead an act or acts of political activity within the meaning of that term as defined in the *PSOA* and an adverse employment consequence imposed as a result of the activity. The reprisal provisions do not contain a reverse onus provision, in contrast to the reprisal provision in Part VI,[289] so the complainant would have the onus of proving their political activity, the act of reprisal and that the adverse employment action was motivated, at least in part, by the political activity.

E. *PSOA* PART VI: DISCLOSURE OF WRONGDOING

1) Background

The concept of whistleblowing—that an employee can lawfully breach the duty of confidentiality to release evidence of employer wrongdoing or recklessness to the proper authorities or the public—is an

284 *Ibid*, s 102(3).
285 *Ibid*, s 104(1).
286 *Ibid*, s 104(2), (3) & (4).
287 *Ibid*, s 104(8) & (9).
288 *Ibid*, s 104(10).
289 *Ibid*, s 140(13).

employment issue of general concern.[290] The common law recognized the issue as early as the mid-nineteenth century when in *Gartside v Outram*[291] the court held that there exists "no confidence as to the disclosure of iniquity." The Organisation for Economic Co-operation and Development promotes whistleblowing legislation to its members as an anti-corruption vehicle.[292] The Supreme Court said the purpose of public sector whistleblowing provisions "is to avoid the waste of public funds or other abuse of state-conferred privileges or authority."[293]

The original impetus for inclusion of whistleblower protection for Ontario's public servants was the 1986 Ontario Law Reform Commission, *Report on Political Activity, Public Comment and Disclosure by Crown Employees*.[294] The report reflected the view that whistleblowing should lead to public disclosure of otherwise confidential material. The resulting amendments of the *PSA* (Part IV—Whistleblowers' Protection) in 1993 created a complex process for releasing confidential material from a public service that already had freedom of information legislation. The provisions, though passed and given royal assent, were not proclaimed by three successive administrations by each of the three major parties.[295]

---

290 There are two forms of statutory whistleblowing provisions in various Ontario statutes. Anti-reprisal provisions such as in the *Environmental Protection Act*, RSO 1990, c E.19, s 174 provide employees civil remedies against reprisal for seeking enforcement or providing information to an enforcement agency, and express whistleblower provisions such as in the *Long-Term Care Homes Act, 2007*, SO 2007, c 8, ss 26–27 that provide protection to both employee and non-employee whistleblowers with both civil remedies for employees who are subject to reprisal and potential prosecution for seeking to frustrate or punish whistleblowers.

291 *Gartside*, above note 49.

292 Organisation for Economic Co-operation and Development, *Committing to Effective Whistleblower Protection* (Paris: OECD Publishing, 2016) [*Whistleblower Protection*]. The majority of OECD members have whistleblower protection legislation at the national level, including the United States, Britain, Germany, France, Japan, New Zealand, and Australia.

293 *Merk v International Association of Bridge, Structural, Ornamental and Reinforcing Iron Workers, Local 771*, 2005 SCC 70 at para 14.

294 *OLRC Report, 1986*, above note 18.

295 *PSA*, above note 7, s 28.43 stated that "Sections 28.11 to 28.42 come into force on a day to be named by proclamation of the Lieutenant Governor." The lack of proclamation of these provisions was the subject of comment in the *Report of the Review into the Meat Regulatory and Inspection Regimes in Ontario* (The Honourable Roland J. Haines, Reviewer) (Toronto: Queen's Printer for Ontario, 2004) at 475–76, which recommended that the government consider enacting whistleblower protection for public servants.

The impetus for disclosure of wrongdoing provisions was renewed by the focus on a major scandal at the federal level.[296] Political pressure, auditors' reports of the inappropriate use of public funds, and a commission of inquiry led to the passage of the federal *Public Servants Disclosure Protection Act*[297] in 2005. When the *PSOA* was passed in 2006, it contained the current disclosure of wrongdoing provisions that are focused on confidential disclosure of an allegation, investigation, and correction of the alleged wrongdoing, but not necessarily public disclosure, resulting in a very different process than the never-proclaimed whistleblowing provisions of the *PSA*.

2) Scope of the Disclosure Provisions

The *PSOA* Part VI deals with the disclosure by a public servant or former public servant[298] of "wrongdoing" in relation to the public service of Ontario,[299] defined to mean acts or omissions by a public servant, a minister, or parliamentary assistant that (1) contravene a federal or provincial Act or regulation; (2) create a grave danger to the life, health, or safety of persons or to the environment, where the danger is unreasonable having regard to their duties, powers, and functions and any other relevant circumstance; (3) gross mismanagement; or (4) directing or counselling such wrongdoing.[300] Wrongdoing by a person before they left their public service or ministerial or parliamentary assistant position continues to be subject to disclosure.[301]

The right to make disclosures in accordance with Part VI prevails over any other law limiting disclosure except that disclosure of anything that (1) would reveal the substance of the Cabinet or Cabinet committee deliberations; (2) is subject to solicitor–client privilege; or (3) is prepared by or for counsel for a ministry or a public body for use in giving legal advice or in contemplation of or for use in litigation is not

296 *Whistleblower Protection*, above note 292 at 150, referencing the federal sponsorship scandal and related auditor general reports and the Gomery Inquiry.
297 SC 2005, c 46.
298 *PSOA*, above note 1, s 114.
299 *Ibid*, s 110.
300 *Ibid*, s 108(1).
301 *Ibid*, s 108(2).

authorized.[302] Nothing in Part VI limits a right to disclose wrongdoing under any other law.[303]

3) Disclosure Processes

A public servant has two options for making a disclosure. The PSC for ministries and the Management Board of Cabinet for public bodies are authorized to issue directives and have issued similar directives setting out procedures for making disclosures of wrongdoing to the responsible ethics executive.[304] Where the public servant believes disclosure to their ethics executive (in ministries their deputy minister) is inappropriate or is unsatisfied with the response to a disclosure to their ethics executive, they may disclose to the integrity commissioner.[305] The integrity commissioner must address the disclosure in accordance with the process set out in Part VI.

a) Disclosure Under a Directive

A public servant can contact the integrity commissioner in confidence for advice about making a disclosure.[306] The commissioner is not compelled to act on a disclosure if the public servant chooses not to make a formal disclosure. A public servant may also seek advice from offices within their ministry/public body. Whether or not a disclosure is made, managers are obligated to act on information that they consider serious and are similarly required to protect the identity of the employee.[307] A disclosure that is made to a manager must be referred to the ethics executive for review.

A disclosure must provide sufficient detail to allow the disclosure to be properly evaluated and investigated but has no formal requirements.

---

302 *Ibid*, s 113.

303 *Ibid*, s 113(3).

304 Management Board of Cabinet, *Disclosure of Wrongdoing Directive Employees/Appointees of Public Bodies (i.e., Agencies)*, 12 May 2017, online: www.ontario.ca/page/disclosure-wrong-doing-directive-employees-appointees-public-bodies-ie-agencies; PSC, *Disclosure of Wrongdoing Directive — Employees in Ministries/Ministers' Offices*, 12 May 2017, online: www.ontario.ca/page/disclosure-wrongdoing-directive-employees-ministries-ministers-offices [*Disclosure Directives*].

305 *Disclosure Directives*, above note 304, s 7.2.

306 *Ibid*, s 7.1.

307 *Ibid*.

However, a disclosure should not contain anything that would reveal Cabinet or Cabinet committee deliberations, solicitor–client privileged information, or anything prepared by or for counsel for use in giving legal advice.[308] It is an offence to make a knowingly false statement in a disclosure of wrongdoing.[309]

Ethics executives assess each disclosure to determine whether there is enough information to address the issue. A disclosure filed anonymously with insufficient information will not proceed. Disclosures that are or should be dealt with by another process, that are solely related to a public policy decision, that relate to an adjudicative decision or prosecutorial discretion, are frivolous, or are subject to a lengthy delay so that the process will serve no useful purpose and will not proceed under the disclosure of wrongdoing process.[310] A deputy minister or ethics executive for an agency may address the issue under another applicable process or refer the matter or the disclosing employee to a more appropriate process.[311] An ethics executive has wide discretion to decline to deal with a matter or refer it to a more appropriate process. An ethics executive may transfer a matter to a more appropriate ethics executive if the disclosure relates to another ministry, for example.

Ethics executives are required to investigate disclosures in a fair, timely way maintaining the confidentiality of the discloser, witnesses, and alleged wrongdoers to the extent consistent with a fair and effective investigation. Those accused of wrongdoing must be given the particulars of the allegations and a fair chance to respond. Those involved in an investigation of a disclosure are entitled to the support of a union representative or co-worker/friend. Public servants are required to follow the directions of the ethics executive conducting an investigation.[312] Public servants are also subject to the obligations under the Act not to tamper with or conceal documents or make false or misleading statements or cause another person to do so in relation to a disclosure.[313]

In the course of investigating, an ethics executive cannot require information that could jeopardize a criminal proceeding, breach Cabinet privilege, compromise an investigation into a criminal matter, is

308 *Ibid*, s 7.2.

309 *PSOA*, above note 1, s 144(2).

310 *Disclosure Directives*, above note 304, s 7.3.

311 *Ibid*, s 7.3, e.g., the *Workplace Discrimination and Harassment Policy*.

312 *Ibid*, s 7.4.

313 *PSOA*, above note 1, s 144(2), (3) & (4).

subject to solicitor–client privilege, or is prepared by a lawyer for a ministry or public body in connection to litigation.[314]

After investigating, an ethics executive may find that no wrongdoing occurred, that wrongdoing occurred and that corrective action is required, or that another forum would be more appropriate to address the matter. At the conclusion of the investigation, the ethics executive will report the result to the discloser.[315]

b) Disclosure to the Integrity Commissioner

The process followed by the integrity commissioner is governed by detailed statutory provisions and is more formal than under the directives. The commissioner must refuse to deal with a disclosure that

- is being dealt with as a matter of law enforcement or in accordance with a procedure under another Act
- is a matter that could be dealt with through an employment or labour relations dispute resolution mechanism established under an act, a collective agreement, or an agreement of another kind
- could be dealt with under Part V of the *Police Services Act*[316]
- concerns a decision or deliberations of a court or other statutory tribunal
- concerns an exercise of prosecutorial discretion
- relates solely to a public policy decision
- is not sufficiently important or frivolous, vexatious, or made in bad faith
- because of substantial delay would serve no useful purpose
- another "valid reason"[317]

When the commissioner refuses to deal with a disclosure they will inform the discloser and may advise them of the reason.[318]

Upon accepting a disclosure, the commissioner must refer the disclosure for investigation by the deputy minister, ethics executive prescribed by regulation,[319] chair of a public body, the secretary of the Cabinet, or a person designated by the premier who is responsible for

314 *Disclosure Directives*, above note 304, s 7.4.
315 *Ibid*, s 7.5.
316 RSO 1990, c P.15.
317 *PSOA*, above note 1, s 117.
318 *Ibid*, s 134.
319 *Ibid*, s 118 and O Reg 147/10.

the area that is the subject of the disclosure.[320] The person receiving the referral may decline to investigate in the event of an actual or perceived conflict of interest, lack of resources, or other reason.[321]

Subject to the integrity commissioner's authority to shorten or lengthen a time period or reporting requirement, the person receiving a referral of a disclosure is required to investigate the matter and provide the commissioner with a detailed report including findings and corrective action taken or proposed in thirty days.[322] Upon receipt of the report the commissioner may require further information, make recommendations, and require a report respecting implementation of the recommendations.[323] If the commissioner finds the report satisfactory, the discloser must be informed and provided such information as the commissioner deems appropriate, subject to the statutory limits on the commissioner's authority to disclose information collected in an investigation.[324]

If the report is not satisfactory to the commissioner, or the person declines to investigate, the commissioner may refer the disclosure to another appropriate person for investigation or may initiate their own investigation.[325]

During an investigation, the commissioner may refer a matter to a law enforcement agency or a process established under another Act and may or may not suspend the commissioner's investigation.[326] If the commissioner becomes aware during an investigation that one of the other circumstances mentioned above for the commissioner not to deal with a disclosure applies, the commissioner must end the investigation.[327]

If it appears to the integrity commissioner during their investigation that grounds may exist to make a report that might adversely affect a person or body, the commissioner shall take reasonable measures to provide that person or body with an opportunity to be heard on the relevant matters. In these circumstances the person or body is entitled to be represented by counsel.[328]

---

320 *PSOA*, above note 1, s 118(1)–(4); the minister responsible for the OPP may refer an investigation to the OPP commissioner.

321 *Ibid*, s 119.

322 *Ibid*, ss 118(5), (6), (7), and 120.

323 *Ibid*, s 121.

324 *Ibid*, s 135.

325 *Ibid*, s 122.

326 *Ibid*, s 123.

327 *Ibid*, s 124.

328 *Ibid*, s 125.

The commissioner's extensive investigative authority[329] includes the power to require any public servant or former public servant to provide any information, documents, or things that they may have that in the opinion of the commissioner may be relevant to the investigation. Any public servant or former public servant who, in the commissioner's opinion, can give relevant evidence may be examined under oath or affirmation. The commissioner may enter and inspect any premises of the public service of Ontario. It is an offence to wilfully obstruct or make false or misleading statements to the commissioner or destroy, alter, falsify, or conceal documents relevant to an investigation.[330] The commissioner cannot require the production of information, documents, or answers that might interfere with law enforcement investigations or prosecutions, reveal the substance of Cabinet or Cabinet committee deliberations, or disclose information that is subject to solicitor–client privilege.[331]

Unless required by law, the commissioner and persons working for the commissioner are prohibited from disclosing information that comes to their attention in the course of their duties.[332] Persons compelled to produce documents, information, things, or answer questions in an investigation by the commissioner have the same protections as witnesses in any court proceeding. Except in a trial for perjury, answers and statements given to the commissioner in an investigation are not admissible as evidence in any other proceeding against the person giving the statement or answer.[333]

c) Integrity Commissioner's Reporting Obligations

At the conclusion of an investigation by the commissioner, a report of the findings of wrongdoing, if any, the reason for the findings, and the recommendations made must be provided to the person the matter was originally referred to for investigation, or an alternate in the event such disclosure would create a conflict, and the responsible minister. Where recommendations have been made the commissioner may require a report explaining the response to the recommendations and provide that report to the responsible minister.[334]

---

329 *Ibid*, s 126.
330 *Ibid*, s 144.
331 *Ibid*, s 127.
332 *Ibid*, s 127(4).
333 *Ibid*, s 128.
334 *Ibid*, s 129.

When the commissioner determines it is in the public interest that there be a public report, the commissioner makes a report, delivers it to the speaker of the assembly, and makes it available to the public.[335]

The public report shall not contain information exempt from disclosure under the *Freedom of Information and Protection of Privacy Act (FIPPA)*,[336] or employment and labour relations information excluded from that Act, or information exempted from disclosure by other statutes.[337] With the agreement of the deputy ministry or chair of the public body or ethics executive or premier's appointee responsible, certain matters[338] excluded from *FIPPA* or employment and labour relations information may be disclosed. Where such information is necessary to explain the commissioner's findings or there is a compelling public interest in disclosure the commissioner may include the information without agreement after hearing the reasons for refusing to agree and where appropriate from persons to whom information relates.[339]

The commissioner must inform the discloser that the investigation has been concluded and provide them with a copy of a public report if one is made.[340] The commissioner may provide additional information, subject to the limitations on disclosure applicable to a public report, though the commissioner may exercise the authority of a head under *FIPPA* to authorize disclosure of information.[341]

4) Protection from Reprisal

The Act contains a detailed prohibition against reprisals for not only making a disclosure but also seeking advice about making a disclosure or seeking enforcement, acting in compliance with or cooperating in an investigation or process under the disclosure of wrongdoing provisions, and seeking enforcement of the reprisal protections.[342] Reprisal is broadly defined as "any measure taken against a public servant that

335 *Ibid*, s 130.
336 RSO 1990, c F.31, ss 12-21.1 [*FIPPA*].
337 *PSOA*, above note 1, s 131(1).
338 *FIPPA*, above note 336, ss 13, 17, 18, 20, 21, and 21-1.
339 *PSOA*, above note 1, ss 131(3) and 132.
340 *Ibid*, s 138.
341 *Ibid*, ss 136 & 137.
342 *Ibid*, s 139(1).

adversely affects his or her employment or appointment."[343] This would include a change of assignment without loss of wages.[344]

The reprisal provision applies to "a disclosure about wrongdoing in accordance with" Part VI. In *Ois v Ontario (Community Safety and Correctional Services)*,[345] the PSGB discussed the meaning of these words in connection with a report of alleged wrongdoing made in an occurrence report. The board found that while the report alleged something was wrong, it did not "allege breach of statute, the creation of grave danger, or gross mismanagement" and so did not qualify as a disclosure of wrongdoing under the Act. Further, the employee had made no effort to bring the alleged wrongdoing to the attention of his ethics executive or the integrity commissioner or given any indication that his occurrence report was intended as a disclosure of wrongdoing. The complaint was dismissed.

While there may be situations where strict compliance with the disclosure process is not necessary for the triggering of the reprisal provision, disclosure in a public forum is not disclosure "in accordance with" Part VI.[346] Where the alleged act of reprisal occurs before the alleged disclosure there cannot be a reprisal.[347] A complaint of bullying to senior managers does not fall within the scope of the disclosure of wrongdoing provisions and was not made in accordance with those provisions.[348] Similarly, complaints of mistreatment by fellow workers to management is not protected by the reprisal provisions.[349] A complaint alleging disclosure of violations of employment-related statutes that could be dealt with through a dispute resolution mechanism under other acts, and consequently not a disclosure the integrity commissioner could deal with, is still a disclosure that is protected by the reprisal provisions.[350]

Public servants subject to a collective agreement are entitled to take a reprisal complaint to an arbitrator under their collective agreement or the OLRB.[351] Public servants appointed under the *PSOA* Part III and not

---

343 *Ibid*, s 139(2).

344 *Doyle*, 2018, above note 99 at para 138.

345 2014 CanLII 76835 (ON PSGB).

346 *Doyle*, 2017, above note 98 at para 55.

347 *Ibid* at para 57.

348 *Barker v Ontario (Natural Resources and Forestry)*, 2021 CanLII 16291 (ON PSGB) at paras 76–79.

349 *Polanski v Ontario (Solicitor General)*, 2021 CanLII 95125 (ON PSGB).

350 *Binda v Ontario (Environment)*, 2011 CanLII 93306 (ON PSGB) at para 22.

351 *PSOA*, above note 1, s 140(2).

subject to a collective agreement may take a complaint to the PSGB.[352] Public servants in a public body may take a complaint to the OLRB.[353] A person subject to a rule or code of discipline under the *Police Services Act* shall have their complaint dealt with under that Act.[354] On a complaint of reprisal, the respective boards have broad remedial authority, including orders to cease or rectify acts complained of, damages for lost wages reinstatement, or damages in lieu of reinstatement[355] but not punitive damages or costs.[356]

In determining whether an alleged reprisal has occurred, the boards will have regard to the substantial jurisprudence regarding allegations of reprisal under other employment-related statutes.[357] The reverse onus provision in Part VI puts the burden of proof on the employer to prove that the reason for the alleged reprisal was not a response to a protected activity under the reprisal provision:

> Nonetheless, the issue is not whether there was 'just cause' for the action taken, or whether the complainant agreed with the choices made by the employer. The burden of proof remains that of the balance of probabilities, rather than the criminal standard of 'beyond a reasonable doubt.' Mere possibility of an intent to punish a complainant for engaging in protected activity is not enough to base a finding that there has been reprisal.[358]

A lengthy delay in the alleged reprisal may prevent a finding the events are connected.[359]

---

352 *Ibid*, s 140(3).
353 *Ibid*, s 140(4).
354 *Ibid*, s 140(7).
355 *Ibid*, s 140 (8)–(10).
356 *Ibid*, s 140(11).
357 *Ronkai v Ontario (Community Safety and Correctional Services)*, 2017 CanLII 77179 (ON PSGB) at paras 33 & 34, cited in *Doyle*, 2018, above note 99.
358 *Ibid* at para 34.
359 *Doyle*, 2018, above note 99 at para 142.

CHAPTER FOUR

Special Classes of Government Public Servants

A. INTRODUCTION

In recognition of a real or perceived uniqueness, some public servants appointed under the *Public Service of Ontario Act, 2006* (*PSOA*)[1] Part III are subject to additional employment frameworks.

Employees who perform inspection roles that require additional independence have been made employee office holders. Ontario Public Service (OPS) doctors, dentists, and lawyers, who have been excluded from labour relations statutes, including the *Crown Employees Collective Bargaining Act, 1993* (*CECBA*),[2] are subject to non-statutory negotiated labour relations framework agreements.

The Ontario Provincial Police (OPP) are subject to the *PSOA*, and to the *Police Services Act*,[3] which covers all the province's police officers and provides the employment mechanism through which policing standards are upheld. Rather than the *CECBA*, the OPP are covered by a special labour relations statute, the *Ontario Provincial Police Collective Bargaining Act, 2006* (*OPPCBA*),[4] designed in part to provide an interest arbitration regime.

Finally, this chapter deals with an anomalous group, teachers in ministry-run schools for students with special needs. By operation of

1 SO 2006, c 35, Sch A [*PSOA*].
2 SO 1993, c 38 [*CECBA*].
3 RSO 1990, c P.15.
4 SO 2006, c 35, Sch B [*OPPCBA*].

the *Provincial Schools Authority Act*,[5] these teachers are not *PSOA* Part III employees. Instead, their terms and conditions of employment are set through provincial teacher collective bargaining.

B. EMPLOYEE OFFICE HOLDERS

Certain public servants hold additional statutory offices. Examples include employment standards officers under the *Employment Standards Act, 2000* (*ESA*)[6] and occupational health and safety inspectors under the *Occupational Health and Safety Act* (*OHSA*).[7] The performance of those particular offices involves independent decision making, and that requirement is enforceable by the affected interest.

The degree of independence mandated by a statute needs to be determined on a case-by-case basis. The Supreme Court has stated that, absent the application of the *Canadian Charter of Rights and Freedoms* (the *Charter*),[8] the legislature is empowered to determine the degree of regulatory independence enjoyed by adjudicators and, by implication, other office holders.[9] However, affected individuals will have an enforceable right to have decisions about them made as independently as contemplated by the statute in question. In a case concerning employment standards officers under a former version of the *ESA*, prior to an amendment giving binding policy authority to their director,[10] the Ontario Court of Appeal stated that

> [e]mployment standards officers . . . have broad powers under the Act and are charged with the obligation of determining the legal rights and liabilities of employees and employers. Employment standard officers must make findings of fact and apply the law as they understand those findings of fact. They are given broad investigative powers to assist in performing these important tasks. When adjudicating claims

---

5 RSO 1990, c P.35 [*PSAA*].

6 SO 2000, c 41, s 86 [*ESA*].

7 RSO 1990, c O.1, s 6 [*OHSA*].

8 Part I of the *Constitution Act, 1982*, being Schedule B to the *Canada Act 1982* (UK), 1982, c 11 [*Charter*].

9 *Ocean Port Hotel Ltd v British Columbia (General Manager, Liquor Control and Licensing Branch)*, 2001 SCC 52; *Bell Canada v Canadian Telephone Employees Association*, 2003 SCC 36.

10 For the director's authority to issue binding policies, see *ESA*, above note 6, ss 88(2) and 89(2).

> as between employers and employees, employment standards officers are obliged to act independently of the Ministry and the parties. They must arrive at their own factual findings, make their own legal interpretations, and arrive at their own conclusions.[11]

The Court of Appeal determined that the employment standards officer had not been able to act in the independent fashion required under the statute, but instead had been inappropriately dictated to by their superiors in the ministry. As a result, the regulatory decision was set aside. This enforceable right to the statutorily mandated degree of independence does not seem specific to employment standards officers, but rather would seem to apply, depending on the statute, to all regulatory office holders.

The further issue is how the requirement of independence affects the administration of the employment relationship between the office holder and management. A logical implication is the placing of some limit on the degree to which an employee can be disciplined for acting contrary to instructions from management. The appropriate balance does not appear to have been litigated in Ontario and, indeed, not much litigated in Canada. In *Burchill v Yukon (Commissioner)*,[12] the reasons for dismissal of a public servant related to the signing authority for the several regulatory offices held by the employee. It was alleged that they failed to deal properly with the delegation of that signing authority during their absence. The court ruled as follows:

> The plaintiff seems to believe that he had an unfettered discretion with respect to the delegation of signing authority. That is clearly not the case. It was not open to him to decide unilaterally to add to the workload of junior staff within the unit. It was not open to him to insist that someone outside of his office be appointed to the unit in order to take on additional duties. Such a scenario is inconsistent with the realities of a government bureaucracy governed by a collective agreement. The plaintiff could have brought his proposals to his superior; instead, he presented them as fait accompli.[13]

---

11 *Libbey Canada Inc v Ontario (Ministry of Labour)* (1999), 42 OR (3d) 417 (CA) at para 68 [*Libbey*], citing *Downing v Graydon* (1978), 21 OR (2d) 292 at 305–7.

12 [2000] YJ No 117 (YTSC), appeal to Court of Appeal dismissed on other grounds, [2002] YJ No 19 (CA), application for leave to appeal to the Supreme Court of Canada dismissed, [2002] SCCA No 233.

13 *Ibid* (YTSC) at para 46.

Employee office holders are required to conduct their official duties in accordance with lawful direction. As an example, officers must accept direction on which cases they are to take on, regardless of the degree of independence, required by the statutory framework, in making decisions about those cases. At the same time, it is unacceptable for management to issue a direction or order that compromises what is required to be an independent decision.

The Grievance Settlement Board (GSB) has found that the employee right to refuse to obey illegal orders applies where the illegality of the order is "clear and unambiguous."[14] In *Ontario Public Service Employees Union (Gray et al) v Ontario (Transportation)*, transportation enforcement officers (TEOs) were directed to stop or redirect commercial drivers for the purposes of asking them to participate in a survey conducted by a third party, using the *Highway Traffic Act*[15] authority given to TEOs to pull commercial drivers over and redirect them for the purposes of doing an inspection. The union asserted that "survey stops" are arguably contrary to section 9 of the *Charter*, which grants everyone the right not to be arbitrarily detained. The board found the matter to be reviewable, as "an employee ought not to be forced, by threat of discipline, to perform a task they know will violate the rights of another."[16] However, if the state of the law is unclear, as will be fairly common for employers and employees engaged in active regulation, it is up to the employer as regulator to provide direction, and it is only where it is "clear and unambiguous" that the employer's direction would result in an illegality that the employee is entitled to refuse the order.[17]

Health and safety inspectors are subject to standards and directions from their employer. However, they cannot be disciplined for the refusal to issue an order that they believe, after their inspection or investigation, is unwarranted.[18] Discipline for inspectors exercising their authority in good faith may support an allegation of reprisal for exercising their role in seeking enforcement of the *OHSA*, though it may not give rise

14 *Ontario Public Service Employees Union (Gray et al) v Ontario (Transportation)*, 2021 CanLII 17449 (ON GSB) (Gee) [*Gray*].

15 RSO 1990, c H.8.

16 *Ibid* at para 72.

17 *Ibid* at para 78.

18 *Libbey*, above note 11.

to any different remedy than would be available at arbitration.[19] While the issue has not been the subject of a binding decision, an inspector would appear to be required to follow a legal direction to not proceed with an order that is against ministry policy.[20] Once an order is issued, it is the director who becomes a party to any appeal—not the inspector.[21] There are express provisions for mediation of appeals, which would be inconsistent with inspectors issuing orders the director was not prepared to defend.[22] Similarly, while the *OHSA* makes inspectors non-compellable witnesses, it also contemplates inspectors giving testimony in connection with litigation related to their work. The privilege to waive the immunity against being summoned as a witness and the obligation to maintain confidentiality rests with the ministry.[23] An *OHSA* director is required to be an inspector and as a matter of practice, managers of inspectors are also inspectors.[24] Inspectors may rescind orders so a director would appear to be able to rescind an order made contrary to policy or their direction without an appeal being filed.

C. PROFESSIONALS: DOCTORS AND LAWYERS

1) Overview

The employment relationship between the government of Ontario and doctors, dentists, and lawyers employed in their professional capacities rests on the *PSOA* and the framework and collective agreements voluntarily entered into between the government and the respective professional associations, all of which are supplemented by the common law.

Although the vast majority of non-managerial OPS employees have had an entitlement, since 1972, to bargain with the government over salaries, benefits, and working conditions, the first version of *CECBA*[25] excluded from its coverage anyone who was "a member of the

---

19 *Ontario Public Service Employees Union (Betsch) v Ontario (Labour)*, 2012 CanLII 34668 (ON GSB) (Gray), a non-precedential mediation/arbitration decision.

20 *Ibid*; *Gray*, above note 14.

21 *OHSA*, above note 7, s 61(2).

22 *Ibid*, s 61(3.1).

23 *Ontario Public Service Employees Union (Rouatt) v Ontario (Ministry of Labour)*, 2013 CanLII 26531 (ON GSB) (Herlich), a non-precedential med/arb decision.

24 *OHSA*, above note 7, s 6.

25 *The Crown Employees Collective Bargaining Act, 1972*, SO 1972, c 67.

architectural, dental, engineering, legal and medical professions entitled to practice in Ontario and employed in a professional category."[26] This exclusion seems grounded on two concerns about collective professional action: (1) that salary determination on a collective basis would mean the opportunity to reward individual merit (an important trait for highly skilled and trained professionals) would be lost, and (2) collective bargaining would "create some risk to their professional calling and to the welfare of the people whom they were obliged to serve."[27] This exclusion from collective bargaining created difficulties, including perceived government delays in addressing compensation issues. A government commissioned report, the *Weiler Report*, recommended an interest arbitration regime.

The lack of statutory entitlement to collective bargaining for doctors, dentists, and lawyers employed by the Crown in their professional capacity has since remained in place. During the *CECBA 1993* reforms, the decision was made for dispute resolution with professionals to "continue undisturbed."[28] The one exception was that for a brief period in 1994–1995[29] lawyers had a statutory entitlement to collective bargaining under the *CECBA*.

Furthermore, the *Labour Relations Act, 1995 (LRA)* deems doctors, dentists, and lawyers, among others, not to be employees for the purposes of that Act,[30] and in any event the *LRA* does not apply to the Crown.[31] Accordingly, doctors, dentists, and lawyers employed by

---

26 *Ibid*, s 1(1)(f)(iv).

27 Paul C. Weiler, *The Professional Employee in Government: A Report to the Honourable Murray Elston, Chairman, Management Board of Cabinet, Government of Ontario on the Appropriate Methods for Establishing Conditions for Professional Employees of the Government of Ontario*," January 1988 at 39 [*Weiler Report*].

28 Testimony of Management Board Secretariat Policy Advisor Kevin Wilson in *Public Service Alliance of Canada v The Crown in Right of Ontario*, 2016 CanLII 5565 (ON LRB) at para 20.

29 *CECBA 1993* extended these rights, and the 1995 amendments removed them: *CECBA*, above note 2, s 1.1(3), (4), (5) & (6). See *Workers' Compensation Board*, [1995] OLRD No 875 [*Workers' Comp, 1995*], where the board found the Association of Law Officers of the Crown to be a "trade union" within the meaning of the Act and certified it as a bargaining agent for a bargaining unit of civil lawyers.

30 SO 1995, c 1, Sch A, s 1(3)(a) [*LRA*], and see *Ontario*, [1999] OLRD No 1396 at para 33.

31 *Ibid*, s 4(2), and see *Ontario (Premier)*, [2001] OLRD No 3040 at paras 152–53.

the Crown in their professional capacities are excluded from collective bargaining pursuant to both statutory schemes.

Engineers were included under the *CECBA* collective bargaining regime in 1993, and, since then, have been represented under the Act by a trade union, the Professional Engineers of the Government of Ontario.[32]

The Supreme Court has stated, at least in respect of Royal Canadian Mounted Police members,[33] "it is not apparent how an exclusion from a statutorily protected collective bargaining process ensures neutrality, stability or even reliability" and struck down such an exclusion in federal legislation as an unjustified violation of the section 2(d) *Charter* right to freedom of association, stating "the evidence suggests that respecting associational rights has the potential to ensure, rather than undermine, a positive working relationship and therefore enhance labour stability." While the implications for OPP officers are most clear, and it is to be noted that there is a statutory regime for their collective bargaining, discussed below, there are also clear implications for other professionals.[34] Yet, there is no decision ruling on the exclusion of physicians or lawyers from the *CECBA* or the *LRA*, and it seems this is because those concerned have been able to negotiate acceptable solutions.

The lack of an ongoing statutory framework for collective bargaining has not stopped the government and the associations representing lawyers, doctors, and dentists from bargaining on a voluntary basis. In the 1980s, lawyers, as well as doctors and dentists, each collectively entered into compensation agreements with the government.[35] These early negotiations have evolved into the current extensive agreements that cover the process and content of negotiations and the terms

---

32 See Chapter 7.

33 *Mounted Police Association of Ontario v Canada (Attorney General)*, 2015 SCC 1 at para 146.

34 See David Doorey, "The Stubborn Persistence of the Lawyer Exemption in Canadian Collective Bargaining Legislation" (2022) 45:1 *Dalhousie Law Journal* 65. The lawyers at Legal Aid Ontario unionized through voluntary recognition in settlement of a *Charter* application: see *Legal Aid Ontario v The Society of Energy Professionals, IFPTE Local 160*, 2017 CanLII 26673 (ON LA).

35 John F. Hanbidge, "The History of Labour Relations between the Ontario Crown Attorneys and the Government of Ontario" (1996) *Ontario Crown Attorneys' Association Newsletter* at 10 [Hanbidge].

and conditions of employment for the doctors, dentists, and lawyers who are members of their respective associations.[36]

In addition to those professionals covered by agreements between their respective associations and the government, there are excluded professionals occupying senior positions whose terms and conditions of employment are not covered by the framework agreements, since the recognition clauses set out in the agreements specifically exclude them.[37] The *PSOA*, Management Board of Cabinet (MBC) directives and policies, and the common law determine the parameters for the excluded professionals' employment relationship with the government.

2) Association of Ontario Physicians and Dentists in Public Service

In 1973, the doctors and dentists working in the province's psychiatric hospitals and "mental retardation" facilities (as they were then known) organized themselves into a Psychiatric Hospitals Medical Staff Association that dealt informally with the ministries operating the facilities. By 1980, a formal agreement was adopted, creating a joint negotiating committee that negotiated salaries and benefits and made recommendations.[38] This agreement broke down due to the non-binding nature of the recommendations and the fact that the OPS doctors and dentists' salaries were significantly lower than in the private sector. Limited job action was begun in early 1986, and a "full-scale" walk out was averted by an agreement to establish a tripartite board of conciliation, which recommended a defined bargaining unit, use of an independent body to

---

36 *Memorandum of Agreement between the Government of Ontario and Ontario Psychiatric Hospitals and Hospital Schools Medical Staff Association*, 8 December 1988 [*1988 Agreement*], as amended, including *Memorandum of Agreement between the Government of Ontario and Association of Ontario Physicians and Dentists in Public Service*, 8 October 2002; *Public Sector Compensation Framework Agreement between ALOC and OCAA and the Crown*, 18 August 2010, online: http://docplayer.net/60426897-Public-sector-compensation-framework-agreement-association-of-law-officers-of-the-crown-aloc-and-ontario-crown-attorney-s-association-ocaa-and.html [*Public Sector Compensation Framework Agreement*].

37 See *ibid*, in the Association of Ontario Physicians and Dentists in Public Service (AOPDPS) agreement, Art 2 and the ALOC and OCAAA agreement, Art 1.0 (iv).

38 *Weiler Report*, above note 27 at 8.

determine whether the association was an appropriate representative, stipulated negotiable items, and binding arbitration.[39]

In 1988, the Ontario Psychiatric Hospitals and Hospital Schools Medical Staff Association, since renamed the Association of Ontario Physicians and Dentists in Public Service (AOPDPS), entered into a *Memorandum of Agreement* with the Government of Ontario,[40] which recognized the AOPDPS as the bargaining agent for full-time, part-time, and sessional staff; established a requirement to bargain in good faith to reach a collective agreement with respect to salaries and benefits; and set parameters for mediation and ultimately for binding interest arbitration. The 1988 agreement was amended in 1993,[41] with amendments to the definition of the unit and the provision for association dues, and is now referred to as the *Framework Agreement*.

Pursuant to the *Framework Agreement*, which focuses on compensation, the parties have agreed to collective agreements that provide for salary increases, increased allowances, and sessional rates; and the arbitrator retaining jurisdiction to settle disputes concerning the implementation of the agreement. In 2007, the one available interest arbitration award between the parties ordered the elimination of pay for performance for clinical classifications and the redirection of the savings into revised salaries.[42]

The AOPDPS *Framework Agreement* does not deal with a variety of other working terms and conditions, such as leaves, job security, and mobility, to name but a few. The working terms and conditions not covered by the *Framework Agreement* are regulated by the *PSOA*, its regulations, and MBC policies and procedures.

Where the parties are unable to negotiate a renewal collective agreement, then either party may refer the issues remaining in dispute to a board of interest arbitration that will make a final and binding award

---

39 *Award re: Bargaining Relationship and Process, between The Government of Ontario and The Ontario Psychiatric Hospitals and Hospital Schools Medical Staff Association*, 27 November 1986 (Burkett, Burnet, and Paliare).

40 *1988 Agreement*, above note 36.

41 *Supplementary Framework Agreement between the Government of Ontario and Association of Ontario Physicians and Dentists in Public Service*, 4 May 1993 [*Supplementary Framework Agreement, 1993*].

42 *Association of Ontario Physicians and Dentists in Public Service v Ontario (Government Services)*, 2007 CanLII 8675 (ON LA) (Kaplan).

under the *Arbitration Act*.[43] Where the matter in dispute is an allegation of non-compliance with the *Framework Agreement*,[44] a party may refer the dispute to a referee, appointed under the agreement, who appoints an umpire to make a final and binding decision. Where the matter in dispute relates to the implementation of the collective agreement elements, the parties have agreed that the mediator has the jurisdiction to settle any difficulties.[45]

Disputes about employment may also be pursued through the *PSOA* grievance procedure for non-unionized employees before the Public Service Grievance Board (PSGB), except that hospital administrators are excluded from filing complaints about working conditions or terms of employment.[46] Whether the PSGB would take jurisdiction over a matter within the jurisdiction of one of the dispute resolution mechanisms agreed between the parties is unclear. The *PSOA* states that a provision in a collective agreement "prevails" over a provision in a regulation or directive under the Act,[47] but the AOPDPS *Framework Agreement* is not a collective agreement under any labour relations legislation. The courts are an alternative forum for addressing wrongful dismissal.

3) Lawyers (Ontario Crown Attorneys' Association and Association of Law Officers of the Crown)

Most government lawyers, including those placed in the various ministries, are directly responsible to the attorney general, assisting in fulfilling the attorney general's mandate to ensure "that the administration of public affairs is in accordance with the law."[48] It can be challenging to balance the loyalty expected of public servants with the commitment to the rule of law,[49] although the answer lies in the realization

43 The *1988 Agreement*, above note 36, Art 6, sets out a procedure for selecting the interest arbitration panel, its jurisdiction (salaries, rates of pay, and issues relating to salaries and rates of pay), and procedures.

44 *Supplementary Framework Agreement, 1993*, above note 41, Arts 11 and 14.

45 *Ibid*, Art 10.

46 O Reg 378/07, s 7, and see the discussion of the PSGB in Chapter 12.

47 *PSOA*, above note 1, s 152.

48 *Ministry of the Attorney General Act*, RSO 1990, c M.17, s 5(b), as discussed in Mark J. Freiman, "Convergence of Law and Policy and the Role of the Attorney General" (2002) 16:1 *Supreme Court Law Review* (2d) 335.

49 See John M. Keyes, "Loyalty, Legality and Public Sector Lawyers" (2019) 97:1 *Canadian Bar Review* 129; Andrew F. Martin, "Where Are We Going? The Past

that government lawyers are asked to fulfill their loyalty by advising government to uphold the rule of law.

Turning to the professional obligations of lawyers, it has been held that "[a]ll lawyers in Ontario are subject to the same single high standard of professional conduct. It is not flattering to the lawyers of Ontario to say that most of them are held to a lower standard of professional conduct than government lawyers."[50] The *Law Society Act*[51] and its professional regulatory provisions apply, by necessary implication, to the Crown.[52]

Government lawyers' associations assert that without their representation of government lawyers, "which sought to ensure a degree of independence and security for lawyers in the discharge of their roles, the confidence that we have, as citizens, in the administration of public affairs would greatly be diminished."[53]

The Ontario Crown Attorneys' Association (OCAA) represents more than 700 assistant Crown attorneys and Crown law officers.[54] The Crown attorneys formed an informal association in 1946 and a more formal association in the 1960s. In its early days, it had mainly social and professional goals. By the 1980s, however, it commissioned studies on compensation;[55] reached agreement with the government on salary improvements, benefits, and pensions; and sought the payment of Law Society fees. The OCAA has also intervened in court proceedings that may affect a Crown counsel, dealing with the appropriate notice to be given to Crown counsel where an allegation of wilful non-disclosure is made[56] and the extent of liability for the handling of police wrongdoing allegations that arise during a prosecution.[57]

The Association of Law Officers of the Crown (ALOC) represents the remaining lawyers employed by the Ontario government, including

---

and Future of Canadian Scholarship on Legal Ethics for Government Lawyers" (2021) 99:2 *Canadian Bar Review* 322.

50 *Everingham v Ontario*, 1992 CanLII 7681 (ON SC).

51 RSO 1990, c L.8.

52 *LSUC v OPSEU et al*, 2014 ONSC 270.

53 See Tom Marshall, QC, quoted on the ALOC website, online: www.aloc.ca.

54 See OCAA website, online: www.ocaa.ca; Hanbidge, above note 35; Kate Matthews, "Neither Fish nor Fowl: The Evolution of the Ontario Crown Attorneys' Association" (2017) 8 *Crown's Newsletter* 3.

55 *Peat Marwick Report*, 1981; *Sibson Report*, 1986. No longer available.

56 *R v Leduc*, 2003 CanLII 52161 (ON CA).

57 *Ontario (Attorney General) v Clark*, 2021 SCC 18.

certain lawyers employed in Crown agencies.[58] The civil lawyers did not form an association as early as the Crown attorneys did. ALOC was initially set up in 1987 as a voluntary organization to address the *Weiler Report*.

Following the release of the *Weiler Report* in 1988, the OCAA and ALOC formed an alliance to deal directly with the government, resulting in a *Framework Agreement* on collective bargaining. Collective agreements followed, providing for salary increases and employer responsibility for Law Society fees.

The *CECBA, 1993* removed the exclusion of Crown lawyers from collective bargaining under the statute and, for the first and only time, gave Crown lawyers the statutory eligibility to bargain collectively. Lawyers were to be in bargaining units separate and apart from other Crown employees. At the time, the Law Society of Upper Canada (now Law Society of Ontario) took the position that it was acceptable to extend collective bargaining and interest arbitration to lawyers, but that they should not be given the right to strike.[59] The position of the Law Society was that lawyers did not want the right to strike and that a strike by lawyers would be an unacceptable burden on the court system and the public. The position of the government was that unionized lawyers could choose whether to strike.[60]

Both the OCAA and ALOC applied for certification as trade unions and then, in advance of a scheduled labour board application for certification by the OCAA, both associations entered into voluntary recognition agreements with the Crown.[61] ALOC was also certified to represent a bargaining unit of lawyers employed in their professional capacity by the Workers' Compensation Board, and so attained recognized status as a trade union under the *LRA*.[62] The right of lawyers to collectively bargain under the *CECBA* lasted approximately eighteen months. The *CECBA, 1995* amendments excluded lawyers from the operation of the Act and terminated the *Framework Agreement*, interim

58 See ALOC website, online: http://www.aloc.ca.

59 Letter, 13 February 1993, from Law Society of Upper Canada to Ministry of Labour, as quoted in Ontario Legislative Assembly, *Hansard*, 13 December 1993, No 97 at 4923 (Mike Cooper, Parliamentary Assistant to Minister of Labour).

60 *Ibid*.

61 *The Government of Ontario*, [1995] OLRD No 383; *Crown in Right of Ontario*, [1995] OLRD No 3797.

62 *Workers' Comp, 1995*, above note 29.

agreements, and the associations' status as unions. In 1999, the Ontario Labour Relations Board (OLRB) found that ALOC was no longer a trade union within the meaning of the *LRA* because of the above-noted 1995 amendments.[63]

Nonetheless, both the OCAA and ALOC continued to bargain terms and conditions of employment on behalf of their members. The Ontario government, as the employer, recognized a council composed of the OCAA and ALOC as the exclusive bargaining agent representing lawyers employed in their professional capacity.

For both associations, the lawyers classification structure consists of four classifications: CC1 (entry level), CC2 (working level), CC3 (senior working level), and CC4 (expert counsel), plus one management level (CC5).[64] Initially there were also population controls that limited the number of lawyers who could be classified in the CC3 classification to 20 percent of the bargaining unit and the number of lawyers who could be classified in the CC4 classification to 2 percent of the bargaining unit. Through the bargaining process, the CC2 and CC3 classifications were merged effective 1 January 2003, and the population control limiting entry to the CC3 classification was eliminated. The 2 percent population control for the CC4 classification was retained and continues to this day. Upon being hired following their call to the bar, the typical bargaining unit lawyer takes approximately four years to reach the maximum of the CC1 salary classification, and approximately seventeen years to reach the top of the CC3 salary classification. There is no arbitral jurisdiction over merit pay or "pay for performance," the classification structure, progression through the salary grids, or the population controls the parties have negotiated.

Salary increases for lawyers have been particularly contentious. Against a background of no salary increases for seven years, the associations and government were unable to resolve their differences on salary increases for 1999 and 2000. The dispute was referred to an interest arbitration panel chaired by William Kaplan, which awarded

63 *Association of Law Officers of the Crown v The Crown in Right of Ontario*, 1999 CanLII 19978 (ON LRB).

64 See discussion in *The Association of Law Officers of the Crown (ALOC) v Ontario (Management Board of Cabinet)*, 2014 CanLII 87074 (ON LA) (Davie) [*ALOC v Ontario, 2014*].

a 30 percent salary increase for 1999 and 2000.[65] At least some of the justification for the increase was as follows:

> Crown attorneys are clearly unique in their employment relationship with the government. They must be appointed by order-in-council, and this appointment process reflects the critical role they play in society. On the one hand, they must be neutral and impartial, on the other, they must be fearless and vigorous advocates. Their contribution to the administration of justice is indispensable, and they exercise tremendous power in their prosecutorial functions, functions which place upon them a huge responsibility to act properly, fairly, and dispassionately.
>
> Likewise, it is clear that government lawyers on the civil side discharge significant public duties and responsibilities and, in doing so, also exercise considerable discretion. They represent the government, and by extension the people of Ontario, at all levels of the legal system in the most critical and important matters.[66]

A majority of the panel further reasoned that the increase was justified on the following grounds: a lengthy period of no increase while the cost of living had been rising, restoring and maintaining parity with provincial court judges (for the top 2 percent of Crown counsel), reducing the growing salary disparity between Crown counsel and their private sector counterparts, and bringing the salaries into their previous relationships with other comparators (agency heads, assistant deputy ministers, etc.).

In June 2002, the OCAA and ALOC entered into a further *Framework Agreement* with the government, a comprehensive twelve-year agreement.[67] The terms of the *Framework Agreement* recognized the associations as exclusive bargaining agents for the lawyers, defined the scope of bargaining,[68] set negotiation parameters, defined the scope

---

65 *ALOC and OCAA and The Crown in Right of Ontario (Management Board of Cabinet)*, 26 October 2000 (Kaplan).

66 *Ibid* at 4–5.

67 *2002–2013 Framework Agreement between Her Majesty the Queen as represented by Management Board of Cabinet and the Ontario Crown Attorneys' Association (OCAA) and the Association of Law Officers of the Crown (ALOC)*, 6 June 2002 [*2002–2013 Framework Agreement*].

68 Retirement entitlements, while not dealt with explicitly in the agreement, were found to be "benefits" under the agreement and within the jurisdiction of a rights

of neutral third-party assistance, set out a mediation process and a final-offer mechanism, set up a Central Provincial Joint Committee and the Professional Excellence Committee, determined a referee, defined the agreement's duration, and included an enforcement clause.

Additionally, the *Framework Agreement* used a formula — the annual change of the Ontario Industrial Aggregate Index (IAI) — to set the general salary adjustments for all years of the *Framework Agreement*, except the years when the collective agreements are to be renegotiated.

In 2010, as part of a government wage restraint initiative,[69] the parties departed on a one-time basis from their four-year bargaining cycle to agree to two years of zero salary adjustment and a forty-seven-year *Framework Agreement* setting out a process for the negotiation and resolution of disputes with respect to terms and conditions of employment for lawyers represented by the associations.[70] It is to be noted that absent a voluntary *Framework Agreement*, the lawyers have no legal status to bargain, and so "the Associations achieved a measure of security and certainty which they had not experienced in the past."[71]

The agreement contained special treatment of implementation, allowing the government to reject salary determinations of the interest arbitration panel for certain periods and for the Ontario Industrial Aggregate to apply. From 2025 to 2057, the government can reject a decision made by an interest board of arbitration in any of the four-year cycles, but if it does that, the salary adjustments for the first two years of the four-year cycle will be based on the IAI and the determination of the interest board of arbitration for the next two four-year cycles will be final and binding on all issues.[72]

The 2014 award provided for modest wage increases.[73] The factors that influenced the award to be more modest than the 2000 Kaplan award were as follows:

---

arbitration panel because benefits were included in the items that could be arbitrated as set out in the *Framework Agreement*: *Ontario v Ontario Crown Attorneys' Association (OCAA)*, 2015 CanLII 94983 (ON LA) (Burkett), which also deals with the Association of Law Officers of the Crown.

69 See the wage restraint section in Chapter 8.

70 *Public Sector Compensation Framework Agreement*, above note 36.

71 *ALOC v Ontario, 2014*, above note 64.

72 *Public Sector Compensation Framework Agreement*, above note 36, Art 6, "Dispute Resolution Mechanism."

73 *ALOC v Ontario, 2014*, above note 64.

- The judicial comparator was not as strong because the bargaining unit had grown by more than 50 percent and not all government lawyers exercise a quasi-judicial function.
- The private sector comparator was not overriding because the compensation for private sector lawyers is different.

As the panel noted,

> [t]he private sector lawyers comparable to senior CC3 and CC4 government lawyers at maximum salaries referred to by the Associations are equity partners who have contributed capital. The manner in which they earn and receive compensation is different than the salary method of government lawyers. As part of their compensation model the government lawyers enjoy advantages such as benefits, pension and job security which differ significantly from their private sector counterparts.

Another factor was the absence of recruitment or retention concerns.

In addition to the *Framework Agreement*, the parties have negotiated extensive four-year "collective agreements"[74] addressing such issues as discharge and discipline (including a "just cause" clause), the grievance and arbitration process, alternative work arrangements, travel, conversion of unclassified (now term) employees, filling vacancies (including by merit-based competition), an internal transfer policy, vacation and benefit entitlements, job security, bumping rights, and salary and merit/pay for performance. These are more comprehensive in their breadth of coverage than the agreement between the doctors and dentists, which was specifically limited to compensation-related terms. There is no "reasonable efforts" provision as found in the OPSEU and AMAPCEO agreements, although there is a nine-month notice of layoff provision.

In addition to the *Framework Agreement* and the collective agreement, the MBC *Compensation Directive* applies to association lawyers. The directive contains a detailed set of hours of work and benefits provisions that apply to them in a specific way and that must be read in

74 See *Collective Agreement between Her Majesty the Queen as represented by Management Board of Cabinet and the Ontario Crown Attorneys' Association (OCAA) and the Association of Law Officers of the Crown (ALOC), January 1, 2001, to December 31, 2004*, and *2013–2017 Collective Agreement between the Crown and OCAA and ALOC*, online: http://www.ocaa.ca/wp-content/uploads/2016/12/2013-2017-Collective-Agreement-FINAL-Signed-November-30-2016.pdf [*OCAA, ALOC and Crown Collective Agreement, 2013–2017*].

tandem with the agreements to determine association lawyers' working terms and conditions.

Articling students are now represented by the ALOC and the OCAA. In 1995, ALOC applied under the *CECBA* to represent articling students employed by the Crown. The OLRB found that OPSEU already held bargaining rights for articling students and therefore the application was untimely.[75] ALOC's second attempt to represent articling students occurred in 1999, which the OLRB dismissed on the basis that the *CECBA* exclusion of "a member of the legal profession entitled to practice in Ontario and employed in a professional capacity" applied.[76] As of 2005–08, the OPSEU/MBC collective agreement has contained a letter of understanding voluntarily transferring jurisdiction over articling students from OPSEU's bargaining unit to the ALOC/OCAA *Framework Agreement*.[77]

Agreements between the Ministry of the Attorney General and individuals clerking at the Superior Court that they will not be called to the bar during their clerkship have been found void as contrary to the requirement that fundamental terms and conditions of employment must be negotiated with the bargaining agent.[78] The agreements appeared to be about avoiding paying clerks, who became lawyers by being called to the bar, at the rate of a lawyer under the ALOC agreement.

Where a dispute arises under the *Framework Agreement*, it goes to a "dispute resolution subcommittee" of the Central Provincial Joint Committee, and, if there is no resolution, the matter proceeds to an arbitration panel pursuant to the *Arbitration Act, 1991*[79] (subject to certain restrictions on the panel's jurisdiction) for final and binding arbitration.[80] Where a rights dispute arises under the collective agreement, the matter may be grieved under that contract. In contrast to the doctors and dentists, the lawyers have no right to proceed to the PSGB

75 *Crown in Right of Ontario as represented by Management Board of Cabinet*, [1995] OLRD No 5342 at para 28.

76 *Ontario*, [1999] OLRD No 1396 at paras 5–8.

77 *OPSEU/MBC Unified Bargaining Unit Collective Agreement, 2022–2024* and *OPSEU/MBC Correctional Bargaining Unit Collective Agreement, 2018–2021*, online: https://opseu.org/information/general/find-your-collective-agreement, Appendix 31.

78 *Management Board of Cabinet v Association of Law Officers of the Crown*, 2012 CanLII 49233 (ON LA) (Kaplan).

79 SO 1991, c 17.

80 *Public Sector Compensation Framework Agreement*, above note 36, Art 11.

on breaches of working terms and conditions.[81] Accordingly, the only forum for lawyers to address alleged breaches of working terms and conditions not covered by their agreements is the courts.

The collective agreement, after clarifying that certain issues are outside the arbitrator's jurisdiction, and clarifying that the parties may attempt to resolve such an issue before the Central Provincial Joint Committee, makes it clear that any rights the associations, or individual lawyers, may have to enforce such issues in the courts is not affected by the collective agreement.[82] On the other hand, where a dispute can be dealt with by the arbitrator, it is unlikely that a court will take jurisdiction.[83]

It is not clear why doctors and dentists may grieve to the PSGB, but lawyers cannot.

4) "Excluded Professionals" or Management (Non-association) Doctors, Dentists, and Lawyers

In addition to those doctors, dentists, and lawyers covered by their respective framework and collective agreements, there are doctors, dentists, and lawyers who are excluded from coverage pursuant to the recognition clauses in the respective framework agreements entered into by the associations. Certain managerial professionals are by position (for example, psychiatrists in chief or medical directors, or equivalent if unclassified) excluded under the AOPDPS *Framework Agreement*.[84] In contrast, the recognition clause in the lawyers' framework and collective agreements uses more general wording to exclude those engaged in managerial or labour relations confidential capacities.[85] The working terms and conditions of employment of all these excluded professionals are therefore covered solely by the *PSOA*, MBC directives, and the common law.

---

81 O Reg 378/07, s 5(2)1.

82 *OCAA, ALOC and Crown Collective Agreement, 2013–2017*, above note 74, Art 6.9.4, under which differences over filling vacancies and redeployment and other matters are not arbitrable.

83 See Chapter 13.

84 See amendment 1(a) to the *Supplementary Framework Agreement, 1993*, above note 41, which includes "geographic full-time appointments and sessional dentists" within section 1(c).

85 *2002–2013 Framework Agreement*, above note 67, Art 1.0(iv); *LRA*, above note 30, s 1(3)(b).

When setting the compensation of excluded professional doctors, dentists, and lawyers, it is the government's practice to track the salary increases, and changes to salary structures, set for the professionals represented by the associations. As far back as the 1986 OCAA negotiations, it was informally understood that the employer would make similar compensation adjustments for excluded lawyers.[86] This practice continues.

The dispute resolution mechanisms available to excluded professionals to deal with disputes over working terms and conditions with the employer are the courts[87] and, to some extent, the PSGB. The right to complain to the PSGB is dependent on whether the excluded professional is a doctor or a dentist or a lawyer, as discussed above.

D. ONTARIO PROVINCIAL POLICE

1) Introduction

OPP employment is governed by an interwoven combination of the *Police Services Act*, the *PSOA*, and the *OPPCBA*.

The *Police Services Act* applies the same code of conduct and discipline process to OPP officers as it applies to all municipal police officers in the province.[88] The rationale is based on the nature of a police officer's position, summarized as follows:

> there is a fundamental difference between the domestic relation of servant and master and that of the holder of a public office and the State which he is said to serve. The constable falls within the latter category. His authority is original, not delegated, and is exercised at his own discretion by virtue of his office: he is a ministerial officer exercising statutory rights independently of contract.[89]

---

86 Hanbidge, above note 35 at 18.

87 See Chapter 13.

88 The *Police Services Act*, above note 3, defines a "police force" to include the OPP or a municipal police force in s 2(1). Some of the legislative history of the *Police Services Act* is reviewed in *Hutton v Ontario (Attorney General)* (1987), 62 OR (2d) 676 (HCJ) [*Hutton*].

89 *Re A Reference Under the Constitutional Questions Act*, [1957] OR 28 (CA) at 31–32 [*Reference*] quoting Viscount Simonds in *Attorney-General for New South Wales v Perpetual Trustee Co (LD)*, [1955] AC 457 at 489.

The *Police Services Act* provides that "[a] police officer has authority to act as such throughout Ontario,"[90] and so there is a need for the police code of conduct to have universal application to all forces.[91]

At the same time, the Act establishes a unique provincial governance structure and mandate for the OPP. Also, in respect to terms and conditions of employment, other than conduct and discipline, the OPP is treated quite differently from other police forces. Section 42(2) of the *Police Services Act* requires all OPP police officers[92] to be public servants appointed under Part III of the *PSOA*,[93] with its provisions applying to OPP officers as they do to any other public servant appointed under the *PSOA* Part III, subject only to expressly stated variations. The application of the *PSOA* results in OPP officers being both police officers and *PSOA* Part III public servants. Civilian employees of the OPP are also appointed as PSOA Part III public servants.[94]

OPP collective bargaining is covered by the *OPPCBA*, which applies to those non-managerial police officers and civilian employees represented by the Ontario Provincial Police Association (OPPA). Other labour relations statutes do not generally apply to the OPP. The *CECBA* does not apply to the OPP, as it specifically states it does not apply to persons to whom the *OPPCBA* applies.[95] The *LRA* does not apply to the Crown, which includes the entire OPP, or to "members of a police force,"[96] which includes OPP officers. Under the *OPPCBA*, the OLRB does decide whether or not a particular OPP civilian employee is in the OPPA bargaining unit and it resolves any jurisdictional dispute concerning OPPA civilian bargaining unit work.[97]

The legal regime governing employment in the OPP can be generally summarized to consist of

- a unique governance structure and mandate established by the *Police Services Act*
- a standard *Police Services Act* code of conduct and discipline process for all police officers in Ontario, including the OPP officers

90 *Police Services Act*, above note 3, s 42(2).
91 *Reference*, above note 89 at 32.
92 Other than the commissioner.
93 See Chapter 2 on *PSOA* Part III employment.
94 *Police Services Act*, above note 3, s 18(1)(c).
95 *CECBA*, above note 2, s 1.1(3)1.
96 *LRA*, above note 30, s 3(d).
97 *OPPCBA*, above note 4, ss 2(4) and 9.

- the employment status of public servant appointed under the *PSOA* Part III (with certain statutory employment rights)
- a distinct collective bargaining regime under the *OPPCBA* for OPP members who are in the OPPA uniform and civilian bargaining units

2) Governance Structure and Mandate

a) Relationship Between the Solicitor General and the Commissioner of the OPP

The OPP has been described as "a department of the Ontario government."[98] The head of the OPP is the commissioner, who is somewhat similar to a municipal chief of police. The commissioner is appointed by the Lieutenant Governor in Council[99] and is subject to the direction of the solicitor general. The commissioner has the general control and administration of the OPP.[100]

It has been recommended by the integrity commissioner, in light of the "sensitivity of the relationship" between the OPP and the OPS and the executive, in part because the OPP may have to investigate them, that instead of an ad hoc appointment process, there should be "an established process that is independent, transparent and readily activated with predetermined criteria and membership on a selection committee."[101] Their report found that a competition for the position of commissioner was flawed due to a lack of fair process for the candidates who were not favoured by the premier's chief of staff.[102]

By comparison, municipal police chiefs are subject to appointment by and the direction of a municipal police services board. This relationship is subject to the proviso that the board shall not direct the chief of police with respect to specific operational decisions.

---

98 *McNabb v Ontario (Attorney General)* (2000), 50 OR (3d) 402 at 411 (SCJ), determining that the OPP is not a separate legal entity for purposes of civil liability, but rather part of the Crown in Right of Ontario.

99 *Police Services Act*, above note 3, s 17(1).

100 *Ibid*, s 17(2).

101 See the integrity commissioner's report into the consideration of Ron Travener for OPP commissioner; Integrity Commissioner, *Re the Honourable Doug Ford Premier of Ontario*, 20 March 2019, online: www.oico.on.ca/en/mpp-integrity-commissioner%27s-reports, at paras 98, 340, and 384–91.

102 *Ibid* at para 272.

The common law principles of police independence mean that "[i]t would seem safe to conclude that the Minister could not direct the Commissioner in respect to 'operational' policing matters."[103]

b) Administration of the OPP

The OPP force consists of the commissioner and police officers and civilian employees appointed under the *PSOA*.[104] At time of writing, there are more that 5,500 officers and 2,500 civilians employed with the OPP. The commissioner determines the officer ranks within the OPP and determines the rank of each officer.[105] By contrast, available ranks for municipal officers are established by regulation[106] and assigned by each municipal police services board for their respective municipality. Members of the OPP of the rank of inspector or higher are titled "commissioned officers" because they receive a commission.[107] Municipal officers of equivalent rank are titled "senior officer"[108] and are not "commissioned."

c) Mandate of the OPP

Under the *Police Services Act*, the OPP is specifically charged with providing police services for the parts of Ontario that do not have municipal police forces, as well as for navigable water and highways.[109] The OPP also provides municipal policing. Each municipality has the obligation to "provide adequate and effective police services in accordance with its needs."[110] Municipalities may fulfill this obligation by establishing police forces, or by entering into an agreement to have all or part

---

103 Paul Ceyssens & Scott Childs, *Ontario Police Services Act, Fully Annotated*, 2017 edition (Toronto: Earlscourt Legal Press, 2017) at 38 [Ceyssens, *Annotated 2017*]. The issue of political direction of police is also discussed in Paul Ceyssens, *Legal Aspects of Policing* (Toronto: Earlscourt Legal Press, 1994) at 1.3 [Ceyssens, *Legal*] and the authorities referred to therein. See also Kent Roach, *Four Models of Police-Government Relationships* (Ipperwash Inquiry/Osgoode Hall Law School Symposium on Police and Government Relations, 28–29 June 2004), online: www.attorneygeneral.jus.gov.on.ca/inquiries/ipperwash/report/vol_3/index.html.

104 *Police Services Act*, above note 3, s 18(1).

105 *Ibid*, s 18(2), Ceyssens, *Annotated 2017*, above note 103 at 42.

106 O Reg 268/10, s 8.

107 *Police Services Act*, above note 3, s 18(3).

108 *Ibid*, s 114.

109 *Ibid*, s 19(1).

110 *Ibid*, s 4.

of their police services provided by the OPP.[111] If a municipality fails to provide for police services, then those services will be provided by the OPP and the funding deducted from provincial funds normally payable to the municipality.[112] The funding of OPP police services for municipalities is set out in a detailed and extensive formula set by regulation.[113]

If municipal police services are "absent or inadequate,"[114] the OPP, through its commissioner, can be asked to provide assistance to or to assume all or part of the policing function of an existing municipal police force. For example, the Ontario Civilian Police Commission (OCPC), formerly called the Ontario Civilian Commission on Police Services,[115] which provides a supervisory or review mechanism for all Ontario police forces, may find that a municipal police force is not providing "adequate and effective police services"[116] and may direct the board of the police force to take remedial action. If that direction is not complied with, the OCPC "may request that the OPP Commissioner have the OPP give assistance"[117] at the municipality's expense. The powers of the OCPC are extensive. The OCPC may also impose an administrator and, ultimately, disband the municipal police force and transfer its responsibilities to the OPP.[118]

d) Transfer of Officers and Employees from a Municipal Police Force to the OPP

The transfer of a municipality's policing from a municipal force to the OPP occurs in accordance with an agreement entered into between the solicitor general and the municipal council.[119] The content of the agreement tends to be the result of negotiations involving the ministry, the OPP, the municipal police force, and the municipality.

Terms have included an OPP commitment to hire all suitable serving municipal police officers who are not charged criminally, hire all municipal force civilians required to meet the servicing contract, set new

---

111 *Ibid*, s 10.

112 *Ibid*, s 5.1.

113 O Reg 267/14.

114 *Police Services Act*, above note 3, s 9.

115 *Ibid*, s 21. OCPC staff members are appointed under the *PSOA* Part III: *Police Services Act*, s 21(4).

116 *Ibid*, s 9(2).

117 *Ibid*, s 9(3).

118 *Ibid*, s 23(1).

119 *Ibid*, s 10.

probationary periods, bridge seniority rankings, decide on rank determination through a Rank Level Determination Board recommendation to the OPP commissioner, and impose restrictions on the involuntary relocation of police officers.[120] Such agreements need to comply with the collective agreements between the OPP and the OPPA. The OPP will not assume a municipality's police services if, in the solicitor general's opinion, the municipality's intention is to defeat the collective bargaining rights of the municipal police officers.[121]

A transfer of police services from a municipal force to the OPP will also trigger a review by the OCPC. A municipal police services board may only terminate the employment of a member of that municipality's police force for the purpose of abolishing the police force or reducing its size if the OCPC consents. The consent of the OCPC is conditional on two matters.[122] First, the abolition or reduction cannot result in less than "adequate and effective police services." The OCPC engages in assessing whether the officers terminated by one police force are adequately replaced by the new police force. This may result in the OCPC making specific orders requiring the OPP to employ members of the former municipal force.

Second, the OCPC will only consent to the termination of employment of a member of a municipal police service if the severance pay entitlement of the terminated member is settled or submitted to arbitration between the municipality and the member.[123] This power to require arbitration does not extend to requiring the OPP to assume the employment of a member of a municipal police service that it judges unsuitable, as the power is only to order arbitration of the severance entitlement and does not extend to making the OPP a party to the required arbitration.[124]

The rights of civilian employees of the OPP have been supplemented in the OPPA civilian collective agreement by a provision that, where an employee of a municipal police service is hired by the OPP, and the police service from which the employee is hired amalgamates with the OPP any time within five years from the date of hire, the OPP will

120 Ministry guidelines have been developed to address this recurring situation.

121 *Police Services Act*, above note 3, s 10(5).

122 *Ibid*, s 40. See, for example, OCCOPS Decision #03-04, *Quinte West Police Services*.

123 *Ibid*, s 40(2) & (3).

124 *Prescott v Ontario Provincial Police*, [2003] OJ No 4288 (SC).

recognize prior full-time unbroken service with the amalgamating police organization for the purposes of vacation and continuous service, as well as full credit for pensionable service with the amalgamated police service for amalgamations occurring on or after 1 January 2009.[125]

3) *Police Services Act* Code of Conduct and Discipline Process

OPP officers are to comply with duties and responsibilities applicable to all Ontario police officers. Those standards are enforceable through the discipline/complaint procedures under Part V of the *Police Services Act*.

a) Code of Conduct

All Ontario police officers, including OPP officers, are required to comply with a code of conduct that prohibits misconduct, including discreditable conduct, insubordination, neglect of duty, deceit, breach of confidence, corrupt practice, unlawful or unnecessary exercise of authority, damage to clothing or equipment, and consuming drugs or alcohol in a manner prejudicial to duty.[126]

i) Avoidance of Conflict of Interest or Unacceptable "Secondary Activity"

A member of a police force must not engage in any "secondary activity" that is likely to adversely affect the performance of their duties, that places them in a conflict of interest, that amounts to other full-time employment, or that allows them to benefit from being a police officer.[127] A chief of police, including the commissioner of the OPP, may not impose more onerous conflict of interest provisions on police officers than those set out in the *Police Services Act*.[128]

The police officer is required to disclose any activity that might be considered to be a conflict of interest to the chief of police, including the commissioner of the OPP, who will decide whether the member is permitted to engage in the activity.[129]

---

125 Management Board of Cabinet and Ontario Provincial Police Association, *Civilian Memorandum of Understanding*, 2019–22, Art 33.

126 O Reg 268/10, Sched, "Code of Conduct."

127 *Police Services Act*, above note 3, s 49.

128 *Toronto (City) Police Services Board v Toronto Police Association*, [2004] OJ No 988 (Div Ct).

129 *Police Services Act*, above note 3, s 49 (3).

These provisions are not substantively different from the restrictions on engaging in a business or undertaking outside employment by the Crown under *PSOA* O Reg 381/07 that apply in any event to the members of the OPP.[130]

One additional specific provision for the OPP is that no uniform member is to contract debts that the member is "unwilling or unable to discharge" and that may interfere with the performance of their duties.[131]

ii) Political Activity

All employees of the OPP, both uniform and civilian, have limitations on their rights to engage in political activity. O Reg 268/10 under the *Police Services Act* restricts the political activity of OPPA uniform and civilian members to those political activities as set out in the *PSOA* Part V.[132] Similarly, O Reg 268/10 under the *Police Services Act* restricts political activities of uniform and civilian municipal police force members.[133] The two codes of political activity conduct are somewhat differently organized but not significantly different in substance. OPP commissioned officers and detachment commanders are in a "restricted" category of public servants to whom certain political activity restrictions apply.[134] The commissioner of the OPP is the decision maker for determining whether to approve unpaid political leaves.

For uniform members, the discipline/complaints procedure under Part V of the *Police Services Act* governs discipline for improper political activities, even though the obligation that is being enforced is found in the *PSOA*, and even though the *PSOA* provisions provide for an alternative method of contesting any such discipline. Since the *Police Services Act* code of conduct requires officers to abide by all regulatory provisions,[135] failure to abide by the imported *PSOA* political activity provisions may be the basis for a complaint or "charge" of discreditable conduct to be dealt with under Part V of the *Police Services Act*.

---

130 *PSOA*, above note 1, O Reg 381/07, s 8.

131 *Police Services Act*, above note 3, O Reg 268/10, s 24.

132 *Ibid*, s 23. Those provisions apply automatically to the OPP by virtue of the application of the *PSOA*, including Part III—Political Activity Rights, ss 28.1–28.10.

133 *Ibid*, ss 11–17.

134 *PSOA*, above note 1, s 29.3(3)iv.

135 *Police Services Act*, above note 3, O Reg 268/10, Sched "Code of Conduct," s 2(1)(a)(x).

As the provisions of the *PSOA* are already directly binding on uniform members of the OPP, by virtue of the members of the OPP also being public servants, the only real purpose for including reference to the *PSOA* political activity provisions in a *Police Services Act* regulation appears to be to provide for enforcement under the *Police Services Act*.

While the means of addressing formal discipline for breaching political activity restrictions for uniform members is through the *Police Services Act*, it is less clear how an individual uniform employee who wishes to enforce their rights to engage in political activity, or claims to have suffered adverse employment consequences other than formal discipline, is to enforce those rights or contest those consequences. These issues are addressed below, under the section dealing with the statutory employment entitlements of OPP officers.

Civilian members of the OPP covered by the OPP civilian collective agreement may be disciplined by management for improper political activities, subject to the civilian member's right to grieve and arbitrate the issue pursuant to the applicable provisions of the OPPA civilian collective agreement. Likewise, OPPA civilian bargaining unit members may grieve to enforce their rights to engage in political activities that are permitted by Part V of the *PSOA*.

b) Other Prohibited Misconduct

The *Police Services Act* supplements the code of conduct with other provisions, applying to all police officers, that specifically prohibit additional listed activities, including resigning during an emergency, inducing the misconduct of a fellow officer, withholding services,[136] joining a trade union,[137] dealing inappropriately with money or firearms, and contravening regulations concerning equipment, using force, standards of dress, and police pursuits or records. In addition, uniform members of the OPP are to give two weeks' notice of their resignation.[138]

Unlike discipline sanctions for other public servants or civilian members, police officers may forfeit pay or time off and hence be required to work without pay.[139]

---

136 *Ibid*, s 81(2).

137 *Ibid*, s 117.

138 *Ibid*, O Reg 268/10, s 26.

139 *Ibid*, s 85(1)(e) & (f).

c) Complaints, Investigations, Hearings, and Sanctions

The duties of all chiefs of police, including the OPP commissioner, include "ensuring . . . that discipline is maintained in the police force" and "administering the complaints system" under Part V of the *Police Services Act*.[140] The discipline process applicable to all police officers, including OPP uniform members, differs fundamentally in two ways from the process applicable to the civilian members of the OPP and other public servants. First, discipline cannot be imposed on an officer until a complaint or charge under the *Police Services Act* has been heard and there is a finding of misconduct. Second, the hearing is conducted by an OPP commissioned officer (subject to appeal), while the discipline of OPPA civilian bargaining unit members is imposed by management. This discipline may then be challenged by the civilian member by way of grievance and arbitration under the OPPA civilian collective agreement.

Generally speaking, Part V of the *Police Services Act* requires that, where a concern is raised about the conduct of an OPP officer, the commissioner or, in the case of a complaint by a member of the public, the independent police review director (IPRD) is to investigate.[141] If, at the conclusion of the investigation, the commissioner or IPRD is of the opinion the complaint is unsubstantiated, then no action will be taken. If the commissioner or IPRD is of the opinion that there was misconduct or unsatisfactory work performance, but that it was "not of a serious nature," the commissioner may resolve the matter informally without holding a hearing, provided the parties involved consent.[142] If the commissioner or IPRD is of the opinion that the police officer's conduct constitutes serious "misconduct"[143] or "unsatisfactory work performance," a formal complaint against the officer is referred to a hearing into that complaint.[144] The commissioner designates a prosecutor and may conduct the hearing directly or through a designee.[145] In practice, hearings are normally conducted by designated commissioned officers.

---

140 *Ibid*, s 41(1)(b) and (d). See Ceyssens, *Annotated 2017*, above note 103, Part V, Complaints and Disciplinary Process, at 160–432 and Ceyssens, *Legal*, above note 103, Chapter 5, The Police Discipline Process.

141 *Ibid*, ss 63–78.

142 *Ibid*, s 69(7) re public complaints, s 76(10) re internal complaints.

143 "Misconduct," is defined in *ibid*, s 80.

144 *Ibid*, ss 73(1) and 76(9).

145 *Ibid*, s 82.

The hearing must be conducted in accordance with the *Statutory Powers Procedure Act*.[146]

Following a finding of misconduct, the designated commissioned officer decides the penalty. The police officer may appeal the decision to the OCPC and from there to the Divisional Court.[147] A hearing conducted by the OCPC is an appeal on the record, although new evidence into allegations of misconduct may be heard. On an appeal, some deference is paid to the findings of the original designated hearings officer.

All complaints about the conduct of the OPP commissioner or a deputy OPP commissioner must be referred to the solicitor general to be dealt with as they see fit. There is no appeal from any decision or action taken by the solicitor general.[148]

i) Unsatisfactory Work Performance

If the concern is "unsatisfactory work performance" of an officer, the commissioner is to comply with a series of prerequisites *before* making a formal complaint of unsatisfactory work performance.[149] Those prerequisites include the following:

> (a) the police officer's work performance shall have been assessed in accordance with . . . established procedures
> (b) the Commissioner shall advise the police officer of how he or she may improve his or her work performance
> (c) the Commissioner shall accommodate the police officer's needs . . . if the police officer has a disability
> (d) the Commissioner shall recommend that the police officer seek [needed] remedial assistance . . .; and
> (e) the Commissioner shall give the police officer a reasonable opportunity to improve their work performance.

ii) Public Complaints and Investigations

The discipline/complaint provisions of Part V of the *Police Services Act* also provide for complaints by affected members of the public about an OPP police officer's conduct. Such complaints may be made to the OPP or to the IPRD. Also, the OCPC can launch its own investigation

---

146 *Ibid*, s 83.
147 *Ibid*, ss 87–88.
148 *Ibid*, ss 61(9) and 70.
149 *Ibid*, O Reg 268/10, s 29(3).

of police matters. These mechanisms for external scrutiny are subject to two significant modifications in the case of the OPP. First, the commissioner of the OPP is the only chief of police not subject to an OCPC investigation.[150] Second, a decision by the OPP commissioner to take no action on a public complaint about OPP policies and services (other than where the municipality has contracted for OPP services) is not subject to review by a dissatisfied complainant.[151] By contrast, a public complaint about the policies and services of a municipal police force, or the OPP in respect of municipal contract policing, can be taken before the local police services board by the complainant.

iii) Administrative Suspension

If a police officer is suspected of an offence or misconduct and is awaiting the completion of the discipline process, the chief, including the OPP commissioner, may suspend them with pay[152] and may do so repeatedly. "Although the rule that suspended police officers should be paid has been criticized on public policy grounds, especially where serious misconduct or criminal activity is alleged or found, the rule nonetheless remains."[153] The rule is grounded in the concept that the officer continues to hold the position of constable even if the duties are not being performed. The officer may only be suspended without pay if convicted of an offence and sentenced to a term of imprisonment.[154]

d) Penalties for Misconduct

In an apparent attempt to formally recognize that police officers have some private life out of reach of discipline, a police officer will not be found guilty of misconduct if "there is no connection between the conduct and either the occupational requirements for a police officer or the reputation of the police force."[155]

The jurisprudence on misconduct penalties for police officers is beyond the scope of this book. While many principles common in employment law govern the determination, including that corrective

---

150 *Ibid*, s 25(1).

151 *Ibid*, s 65.

152 *Ibid*, s 89.

153 Paul Ceyssens, Susan Dunn & Scott Childs, *Ontario Police Services Act, Fully Annotated, 2008–2009 Edition* at 166.

154 *Police Services Act*, above note 3, s 89(6).

155 *Ibid*, s 80(2).

dispositions should prevail where possible, there is a higher standard applicable to police. They have discretionary power to affect fundamental rights in order to uphold the law. This is a position of public trust and, in the words of the Supreme Court, "exemplary probity is an essential qualification for employment as a police officer."[156]

e) Exclusive Jurisdiction of the *Police Services Act* over all Discipline, Unsatisfactory Work Performance, and Complaints Issues Concerning Police Officers

Generally, the mechanisms set out under the *Police Services Act*, Part V, are to be exclusively used to litigate misconduct and unsatisfactory work performance issues. In *Regina Police Association v Regina (City) Board of Police Commissioners*,[157] the Supreme Court examined a similar scheme in Saskatchewan, consisting of a *Police Act, 1990*[158] disciplinary scheme that cohabited with a collective bargaining regime. The Court found that those *Police Act* provisions created a "complete code" for police discipline matters. This was seen as reflective of the public policy that police forces should have "exclusive responsibility for disciplining their own members."[159] As a consequence, collective agreement arbitration could not be used for discipline matters. By similar reasoning, a civil action cannot be brought either,[160] although the courts will maintain the capacity to judicially review decisions made under the *Police Services Act*.

Where the employer action was allegedly punishment for "misconduct," but the action was undertaken without following the proper procedures under Part V of the *Police Services Act*—that is, where the employer, for example, had simply engaged in an allegedly "disciplinary" transfer or reassignment without Part V due process—the Ontario Court of Appeal, in *Abbott v Collins* found that a civil lawsuit could still not be brought because the available avenues of redress formed a

156 *Montréal (City) v Quebec (Commission des droits de la personne et des droits de la jeunesse)*, 2008 SCC 48 at para 33; *Lévis (City) v Fraternité des policiers de Lévis Inc*, 2007 SCC 14. See the discussion in Ceyssens, *Legal*, above note 103 at 5-339–5-340.

157 2000 SCC 14 [*Regina Police*].

158 SS 1990–91, c P-15.01.

159 *Regina Police*, above note 157 at para 31.

160 *Abbott v Collins* (2003), 64 OR (3d) 789 (CA) [*Abbott*].

"complete code."[161] The employer action may be amenable to review through the appeal processes provided to officers under Part V of the *Police Services Act*. In addition, there could be an application for judicial review to require the police force to comply with the terms of Part V. The court concluded that reassignment of several detectives to different duties, when considering the essential nature of this management action in its factual context, amounted to disguised discipline and therefore had to be dealt with under the Part V discipline process.

A 2022 decision of the Alberta Court of Appeal[162] reviewed the Supreme Court's decision in *Regina Police* and subsequent cases, including *Abbott v Collins*.[163] The court found that it is not helpful to characterize a police human resources decision as being based on "discipline" or "disguised discipline." The court stated:

> [W]hether a human resources dispute falls under the grievance procedure in the collective agreement or under Part V of the *Police Services Act* does not depend on that distinction. If the Chief of Police generates a "complaint", then the matter proceeds under Part V of the *Police Services Act*. If the police service responds to the conduct of a police officer through the exercise of the general authority to manage the human resources of the police service, then the remedy of the dissatisfied police officers is through filing a grievance. It does not matter if the conduct was culpable or non-culpable.[164]

This continues to be an area of controversy.

4) *Ontario Provincial Police Collective Bargaining Act*

Apart from discipline matters and police complaints made about the conduct of OPP officers, their working conditions and terms of employment are governed by the collective bargaining regime between the Crown in the Right of Ontario (the Crown) and the Ontario Provincial Police Association (the OPPA) under the *OPPCBA*.[165]

---

161 *Ibid* at para 33.
162 *Edmonton (Police Service) v Deluca*, 2022 ABCA 86 [*Deluca*].
163 *Abbott*, above note 160.
164 *Deluca*, above note 162 at para 75.
165 The labour relations of municipal police forces is covered by the *Police Services Act*, Part VIII—Labour Relations.

The *OPPCBA* establishes two employee bargaining units:

(a) a police officer bargaining unit consisting of "cadets, recruit constables, probationary constables, constables, sergeants, staff sergeants, and sergeants major"; and
(b) a civilian bargaining unit consisting of "public servants who are employed at an OPP headquarters, at the Ontario Police College or at the OPP Academy or who worked under the supervision of the Commissioner of the OPP or the Chief Firearms Officer of Ontario and who . . . do not have duties or responsibilities that, in the opinion of the Ontario Labour Relations Board, constitute a conflict of interest with their being members of this bargaining unit."[166]

The OPPA is the exclusive statutory bargaining agent for both the uniform and civilian bargaining units. It bargains with the Crown with respect to the terms and conditions of employment "except as to matters that are exclusively the function of the employer."[167]

The matters excluded from collective bargaining are leaves of absence for elective public office; political activities; training and development;[168] police officer discipline, pensions, apart from prescribed supplementary pension benefits; and the creation of a new classification, the alteration of an existing classification, or a change to be made in the classification of an employee.[169] This leaves a wide scope for collective bargaining that expressly includes:

- rates of remuneration
- hours of work
- overtime and other premium allowance for work performed
- mileage rate payable to employee for miles travelled when the employee is required to use their automobile on the employer's business
- benefits pertaining to time not worked by employees
- paid holidays
- paid vacations
- group life insurance
- health insurance and long-term income protection insurance

---

166 *OPPCBA*, above note 4, s 2(1).
167 *Ibid*, s 2(2).
168 *Ibid*.
169 *Ibid*, ss 4(1) and 7.

- the procedures applicable to the processing of grievances
- the methods of affecting promotions, demotions, transfers, lay-offs, or reappointments
- the conditions applicable to leaves of absence other than any elective public office, political activity, or training and development

In the event a uniform or civilian collective agreement is not arrived at through negotiations between the OPPA and the Crown, either party may have the outstanding matters in dispute resolved by way of interest mediation and arbitration.[170]

The consequence of this collective bargaining regime is detailed, comprehensive, and sophisticated collective agreements that, apart from the discipline of police officers, are comparable to private and public sector collective agreements and, in particular, comparable to collective agreements for uniform and civilian members of municipal police services in Ontario. This includes grievance and arbitration provisions to resolve alleged breaches of the collective agreements.[171] In the case of civilian members, employer-imposed discipline, including dismissal, may be challenged through the grievance and arbitration process.

5) Other Employment-Related Statutes

All OPP employees appointed to the *PSOA* Part III public service have employment entitlements under that Act.[172]

All OPP employees, including special constables, also have individual employment entitlements under other statutes such as the *Human Rights Code* and the *Workplace Safety and Insurance Act*.[173] Members

---

170 *Ibid*, s 6.

171 *Ontario Provincial Police Association (OPPA)/Crown Uniform Collective Agreement, 2019–2022* and *OPPA/Crown Civilian Collective Agreement, 2019–2022*, Art 4. The 2019–2022 collective agreements are not available online as of the time of writing, but the identical provisions are found in the 2015–2018 collective agreements, online: https://sp.ltc.gov.on.ca/sites/mol/drs/ca/Public%20Administration/912-2052-18%20(931-0001).pdf; and the *OPPA/Crown Civilian Collective Agreement*, online: https://sp.ltc.gov.on.ca/sites/mol/drs/ca/Public%20Administration/912-2880-18%20(931-0029).pdf.

172 See Chapter 3.

173 Under one arrangement for the employment of First Nations constables, the OPP was found to be the employer for purposes of workers' compensation: *Parties not Published*, [2001] OWSIATD No 3491. See the *Human Rights Code*, RSO 1990, c H.19; *Workplace Safety and Insurance Act, 1997*, SO 1997, c 16.

of police forces, including the OPP, have an explicitly stated statutory right to accommodation in accordance with the *Human Rights Code.*[174] A uniform member of the OPP may be discharged or retired if the commissioner, or designee, concludes that the member cannot be accommodated without undue hardship, subject to appeal to the OCPC.

6) Means of Enforcement of Employment Rights

The means by which OPP employees enforce their employment entitlements (other than the right under the *Police Services Act* to contest discipline) is best addressed by separate reference to two different classes of OPP employees: police officers, cadets, and civilian members, represented by the OPPA; and civilian managerial employees and "commissioned officers," who are not represented by the OPPA.

a) Officers, Cadets, and Civilian Members Represented by the OPPA

For the non-commissioned police officers represented by the OPP, cadets, and OPP civilian members who are also represented by the OPPA, the grievance procedure in the OPPA uniform and civilian collective agreements provide the primary avenue for the enforcement of employment entitlements, other than the police officer discipline issues covered by the *Police Services Act*.

The application of grievance rights under the OPPA collective agreements covers all terms and conditions of employment, apart from police officer discipline under Part V of the *Police Services Act*. Exclusive management rights may be challenged if "exercised in a discriminatory manner" or if they are exercised inconsistent with the provisions of the collective agreements.[175]

Probationary constables must serve a twelve-month probationary period before they are confirmed as constables.[176] They do not have the right to grieve their dismissal or release from employment,[177] but they do have the right to be provided with reasonable information about their failure to meet the requirements of their position and the "opportunity

174 *Police Services Act*, above note 3, s 47.

175 *OPPA/Crown Uniform Collective Agreement, 2019–2022* and *OPPA/Crown Civilian Collective Agreement, 2019–2022*, above note 171, Art 1.01.01.

176 *OPPA/Crown Uniform Collective Agreement, 2019–2022*, above note 171, Art 28.03.

177 *Ibid*, Art 4.00(c).

to reply orally or in writing and to have their reply considered by the employer."[178] This implies that the employer is required to answer the assertions made by the probationary officer.

These collective agreement provisions mean that probationary officers may grieve any failure on the part of the employer to provide "reasonable information" or to provide an opportunity for the officer to respond to the "reasonable information" provided to the officer to justify the decision to terminate the officer's employment.

In light of the Supreme Court's decision in *Parry Sound (District) Social Services Administration Board v OPSEU*,[179] confirming the broad authority of arbitrators to apply employment-related statutes, and the very broad definition of "grievance" in both the OPPA uniform and civilian collective agreements to include a dispute concerning the working conditions or terms of employment covered by the collective agreements, as well as disputes concerning the "Regulations and Directives under the *Public Service Act in Ontario, 2006*, the *Police Services Act*, the *Ontario Human Rights Code*, the Management Board of Cabinet or Public Service Commission *Directives* and Guidelines, or any other employment related statutes," there are few working conditions that are beyond the jurisdiction of a rights arbitrator.[180]

Like all unionized employees, OPPA members may only pursue rights arising from the uniform and civilian collective agreements through their exclusive collective bargaining agent, the OPPA. They do not have the individual right to enforce the provisions of the collective agreements.

Unionized employees who are covered by the *CECBA* or the *LRA* have the right to complain to the OLRB that their union has not fairly represented them and to obtain from the board a meaningful remedy if the complaint is sustained. There is no comparable statutory provision for the enforcement of rights of an OPPA member to be fairly represented by the OPPA. As a consequence, OPPA members who assert that they have not been fairly represented by the OPPA are forced to commence court proceedings to seek enforcement of the common law right to fair representation.[181]

---

178 *Ibid*, Art 28.04.

179 2003 SCC 42.

180 *OPPA/Crown Uniform Collective Agreement, 2019–2022* and *OPPA/Crown Civilian Collective Agreement, 2019–2022*, above note 171, Art 4.00(b).

181 *Gagnon v Canadian Merchant Service Guild et al*, [1984] 9 DLR (4th) 641.

b) Commissioned Officers and Civilian Members of the OPP Excluded from the OPPA Collective Bargaining Units

Commissioned officers and excluded civilian members do not have a statutory right to collectively bargain. Commissioned officers are OPP officers in the ranks of inspector, superintendent, and staff superintendent. They serve in approximately 205 approved positions. Excluded civilian members are those who exercise management functions or who are employed in a confidential capacity in relation to labour relations. Excluded civilian members have approximately 100 positions within the OPP. Unlike municipal senior officers and senior civilian employees employed in managerial and confidential positions in relation to labour relations who are entitled to be members of a police association, whether an all-employee association or a senior officers' association,[182] OPPA commissioned officers and excluded senior civilian employees have been consistently denied the statutory or legal right to collective bargain terms and conditions of their employment.

The differential treatment of OPP commissioned officers, as compared with municipal senior police officers, was the subject of a *Charter* challenge under the equality provisions in section 15 of the *Charter*. In *Hutton v Ontario (Attorney General)*,[183] the Ontario Provincial Police Commissioned Officers' Association (OPPCOA) brought a court challenge because the ministry of the solicitor general had declined to collectively bargain with the OPPCOA. The Ontario court found no organizational or public justification for the differential treatment and ordered that the OPP commissioned officers be able to bargain collectively. This ruling was never implemented because a government appeal was allowed, on consent, with the OPPCOA *Charter* challenge being discontinued. The discontinuance occurred as a result of changes to the jurisprudence under section 15 of the *Charter*. The Supreme Court clarified that, to be actionable, the differential treatment must be related to a personal ground of discrimination, like race or gender, and cannot be simply based upon differential legislative treatment.[184]

More recently, in a 2015 decision, *Saskatchewan Federation of Labour v Saskatchewan*,[185] the Supreme Court found that not only did the right of association in section 2(d) of the *Charter* entitle employees

182 *Police Services Act*, above note 3, s 118.

183 *Hutton*, above note 88.

184 *Andrews v Law Society of British Columbia*, [1989] 1 SCR 143.

185 2015 SCC 4.

to meaningful collective bargaining, but also that such a right included the right to strike or, in the case of essential services, "access to a meaningful alternative mechanism for resolving bargaining impasses, such as arbitration."

The OPP commissioned officers continue to be represented by the OPPCOA. It is a voluntary organization comprising all commissioned officers. It is not a statutory bargaining unit, but it informally bargains memoranda of agreement of salary, benefits, and working conditions with the Crown in Right of Ontario. The OPPCOA does not have the statutory right to enforce provisions of the memoranda of agreement or to resort to interest arbitration in the event the parties are unable to reach agreement. However, in light of the *Saskatchewan Federation of Labour v Saskatchewan* case and the fact that municipal senior officers in Ontario have the statutory right to collectively bargain, and access to interest and rights arbitration, there is and should continue to be a significant degree of cooperation between the OPPCOA and the employer, the Crown in Right of Ontario, to resolve employment issues. Generally, the OPPCOA awaits the results of collective bargaining between the OPPA and the Crown, and then negotiates comparable provisions, as well as additional matters and benefits that are particular to the commissioned officers.

Much of the same observations apply to excluded civilian members of the OPP. Approximately 100 OPP civilian employees fall within this group, represented by the OPP Civilian Association of Managers and Specialists (CAMS). Although not able to arbitrate rights disputes under the collective bargaining regime, the *PSOA* permits individual OPPCOA and CAMS members to complain about a working condition or term of employment[186] other than an assignment to a particular class of positions or a performance evaluation and the resulting compensation,[187] and to have the complaint resolved through the hearing process of the PSGB. For excluded civilian members, this includes discipline, including dismissal for cause.[188]

---

186 *PSOA*, above note 1, O Reg 378/07, ss 4(1), 5(1), and 5(2)1.

187 O Reg 378/07, s 4(2).

188 O Reg 278/07, ss 3 & 4. Under s 4(2)3, there is no right to challenge a dismissal without cause under *PSOA* s 38(1). See the discussion of *PSOA*, above note 1, s 38(1) in Chapter 2.

c) Complaints Concerning Political Activities or Disclosure of Wrongdoing

Grievances concerning reprisals or discipline for alleged contravention of Parts V and VI of the *PSOA* that deal with political activities and disclosure of wrongdoing may be determined by arbitration for OPPA civilian members who are subject to the terms of the OPPA civilian collective agreement. The challenge of discipline by OPPA uniform members is dealt with under the discipline provisions of Part V of the *Police Services Act*.

In addition, OPPA members appear to have an individual right to file a complaint to the PSGB concerning reprisals or discipline for alleged contravention of Parts V and VI of the *PSOA*.[189] This right also appears to extend to commissioned officers and excluded civilian members.

7) Special Constables, First Nation Constables, and Auxiliary Members

The *Police Services Act* defines "police officer" to be a person "appointed as a police officer . . . but *does not include* a Special Constable, a First Nation Constable, a municipal law enforcement officer or an auxiliary member of a police force."[190]

"With the Solicitor General's approval, the Commissioner may appoint a Special Constable to act for the period, area and purpose that the Commissioner considers expedient."[191] The appointment will provide the Special Constable with the powers of a police officer to the extent set out in the appointment.[192] The taking of oaths of office and confidentiality is required.[193]

Special constables are employed by the OPP, municipal police services, ministries and agencies, conservation authorities, universities, colleges, Crown corporations, public transit, and community housing.

OPP special constables are OPP civilian employees covered by the OPPA civilian collective agreement. They have limited police officer powers granted by the commissioner for specific jobs or tasks. These include the positions of offender transportation officers, security officers, court officers, and forensic identification analysts. They are generally

189 O Reg 378/07, s 5(3).
190 *Police Services Act*, above note 3, s 2(1).
191 *Ibid*, s 53(2).
192 *Ibid*, s 53(3).
193 *Ibid*, s 53(9).

not armed with firearms, except for security officers deployed at Queen's Park. Since OPP special constables are civilian employees covered by the OPPA civilian collective agreement, they have all the rights of civilian bargaining unit members, including job security.

With the approval of the OCPC, First Nations constables are appointed by the OPP commissioner to perform specified duties.[194] There are a number of First Nations police services in Ontario. First Nations constables' duties relate to land reserved for "Indians" by the federal *Indian Act*.[195] Their appointment requires the approval of the reserve's police governing authority or band council, and any suspension or termination of that appointment by the OPP commissioner cannot be carried out without first consulting with the police governing authority or band council that approved the appointment.[196] Whether the employment of a First Nations constable is subject to federal or provincial labour legislation has been the subject of lengthy litigation.[197] However, First Nations constables are normally employed by a reserve's police governing authority or the band. In either case, they are not employees of the OPP and are not members of the public service of Ontario subject to the *PSOA*, meaning the governance of their employment is outside the scope of this book.

Municipal police services board and the commissioner of the OPP may appoint auxiliary members to their respective police forces.[198]Auxiliary members are civilian volunteers. They are not employed by their police forces and, consequently, they are not paid for their services, which are part-time or occasional, and are described as police duties performed "only in special circumstances, including in emergency, that the police officers of the police force are not sufficiently numerous to deal with."[199] An auxiliary member "has the authority of a police officer if he or she is accompanied or supervised by a police officer."[200] OPP auxiliary members have their own uniform, distinct from the uniform

194 *Ibid*, s 54(1).
195 RSC 1985, c I-5.
196 *Ibid*, s 54(4).
197 *Nishnawbe-Aski Police Service Board v Public Service Alliance of Canada*, 2015 FCA 211; *Quebec (Attorney General) v Picard*, 2020 FCA 74.
198 *Police Services Act*, above note 3, s 52(1) and (3). Municipal forces need the approval of the solicitor general.
199 *Ibid*, s 52(5).
200 *Ibid*, s 52(4).

of police officers. In the OPP, their duties include patrols with regular members and assisting with community events, seatbelt clinics, drunk driving initiatives, safety displays, presentations, victim assistance, and ceremonial duties. As volunteers, auxiliary members must commit to ten hours on patrol and six hours of training per month. There are approximately 600 OPP auxiliary members.

E. PROVINCIAL SCHOOLS AUTHORITY—TEACHERS

Under the *Provincial Schools Authority Act (PSAA)*, teachers, principals, and vice-principals who are members of the Ontario College of Teachers and are employed by three ministries—Correctional Services, Education, and Health and Long-Term Care—in their educational capacities in the schools operated by those ministries are deemed employed by the Provincial Schools Authority (PSA). As such, they are not public servants under the *PSOA* or Crown employees under the *CECBA*. They are treated in substantially the same manner as staff employed by a single school board, and the teachers are represented in bargaining by the Ontario Secondary Schools Teachers Federation (OSSTF).[201] While in law they are employed by the PSA, it is the government that bargains with the teachers' union. The ministries that operate schools employing teachers administer, and view themselves as bound by, the collective agreement negotiated on behalf of the PSA, and for some labour relations purposes may be treated as an employer along with the PSA.[202] The effect of this legal structure is to include the teachers working in schools operated by the government directly in the collective bargaining, employment, and regulatory scheme applicable to teachers in the province generally.

The PSA was created in 1975 so that a single, consolidated, collective bargaining unit structure[203] would replace a fractious labour relations scheme under which teachers employed in provincial schools

201 *School Boards Collective Bargaining Act, 2014*, SO 2014, c 5, s 10 (4) [*SBCBA*]. Section 8 excludes principals and vice-principals from bargaining units.

202 *Ontario Secondary School Teachers' Federation, District 57/PSAT and Federation of Provincial Schools Authority Teachers v The Provincial Schools Authority*, 2001 CanLII 6655 (ON LRB) at para 8 [*FOPSAT & OPSEU*]. FOPSAT was the predecessor of the OSSTF as negotiator for the teachers at the provincial schools.

203 *Ibid.*

were represented by three employee organizations under a variety of contractual arrangements.[204]

The legislation respecting collective bargaining by teachers in the province was significantly amended in 2014 by the introduction of the *School Boards Collective Bargaining Act*, under which the PSA bargains.[205] Ontario teacher collective bargaining is now conducted in accordance with that Act,[206] and the *LRA*, under which the PSA bargains centrally jointly with the OSSTF employer bargaining agency. That framework includes the Education Relations Commission, which advises the Cabinet when a strike or lockout of teachers, including the PSA's teachers, will place a school year in jeopardy.[207]

OSSTF represents, at the time of writing, approximately 250 teachers who work in provincial schools for the blind, deaf, and deaf-blind in adult and youth correctional facilities across the province. The Ministry of Education is responsible for the administration of five sites with provincial schools:[208] Sir James Whitney in Belleville, Robarts in London, EC Drury in Milton, Centre Jules Legere in Ottawa/Sudbury, and W Ross Macdonald in Brantford. The Ministry of Community Safety and Correctional Services operates schools within a number of its correctional facilities (although municipal school boards are now generally contracted to provide schooling to those detained in young offender facilities). The PSA is the employer of the teachers in the unit and has the powers and duties of a public school board under the *Education Act*.[209] Part X of the *Education Act* applies to the PSA and its teachers. However, all matters relating to administration in respect of teachers are the responsibility of the deputy minister of the ministry running a school. To deal with the *Teachers' Pension Act*,[210] the teachers employed by the PSA are deemed by the *PSAA* to be employed by a

204 *Federation of Provincial Schools Authority Teachers v Ontario (Provincial Schools Authority)* (1993), 12 OR (3d) 296 (CA).

205 *Education Quality Improvement Act, 1997*, SO 1997, c 31, s 122, adding Part X.1 to the *Education Act*, RSO 1990, c E.2.

206 *SBCBA*, above note 201, s 23(6) and O Reg 50/18, Column 1, Item 6.

207 *Ibid*, s 50. While no legal requirement exists to respond to this advice, it will usually trigger a decision to introduce return to work legislation.

208 Four for deaf students and one for blind and deaf-blind students.

209 *PSAA*, above note 5, s 4.

210 RSO 1990, c T.1.

minister of a ministry of the Ontario government.[211] The non-teaching staff of the schools are public servants.

The OLRB reviewed the teachers' bargaining scheme in a dispute regarding jurisdiction over the teaching of basic literacy and numeracy programs to incarcerated male offenders at a correctional facility operated by the Ministry of Correctional Services.[212] The disputed work also included assisting inmates to prepare for the test leading to the High School Equivalency Diploma (GED). It was recognized that the usual tests applicable in a jurisdictional dispute would only apply after it was determined that the statutory scheme did not require the allocation of the work to a teacher. The board found that while the provision of assistance to those studying for a GED did not require a teacher's certificate, and adult literacy programs need not be provided in a day school, where, as in the case before it, a day school program is offered on instructional days in the school year, the *Education Act* does require that a teacher be employed. There is no statutory exception that would allow a direct employee of the government, other than a teacher, to instruct in these day school program courses. As a consequence, such duties must be assigned to a teacher union member, except when provided by a community organization, school board, or volunteer. It should be noted that given the nature of the instruction at correctional facilities, the ministry is not required to operate day schools at most adult facilities.

Where the ministries named in the *PSAA* choose to operate a day school or to employ qualified teachers as teachers, they must employ the teachers under the PSA collective agreement. Given that the term "teacher" in the *PSAA* is defined in terms of "school," which is restricted by the Act's definition to the three named ministries, a teacher employed by another ministry would appear to fall outside the scope of the PSA collective agreement.

211 *PSAA*, above note 5, s 4(4).

212 *FOPSAT & OPSEU*, above note 202.

CHAPTER FIVE

Legislative, Judicial, and Order-in-Council Roles

A. INTRODUCTION

Certain roles essential to the functioning of the government of Ontario are not created and managed through normal public service employment practices and are not covered by the *Public Service of Ontario Act, 2006* (*PSOA*).[1] Instead, special status and arrangements support the independence required for these exceptional positions.

The Canadian Constitution provides "There shall be a Legislature for Ontario consisting of the Lieutenant Governor and of One House, styled the Legislative Assembly of Ontario"[2] and that certain Ontario judges shall be federally appointed.[3] Other judges that are provincially appointed are treated similarly to their federal counterparts. All these constitutionally delineated roles require such a substantial degree of independence that they are not to be viewed as "employees." Unique terms and conditions of recruitment, retention, oversight, and compensation have been established for these positions—Lieutenant Governor, members of provincial Parliament (MPPs), and judges—and for those who directly support MPPs in particular, the Office of the Legislative Assembly, and the officers of the legislature. Judges are supported on special terms by court staff who are public servants.

---

1 *Public Service of Ontario Act, 2006*, SO 2006, c 35, Sch A [*PSOA*].

2 *Constitution Act, 1867* (UK), 30 & 31 Vict, c 3, s 134, reprinted in RSC 1985, App III, No 5, s 69 [*Constitution Act, 1867*].

3 *Ibid*, s 96.

Order-in-council appointments, which are non-constitutional, are created and governed solely by the standards set through special provisions in provincial statutes. Although much less protection is accorded to them by the terms of their appointment and employment, they are still expected to make decisions independent of specific government direction.

B. LIEUTENANT GOVERNOR

The Lieutenant Governor is the personal representative of the Crown and is formally the chief executive officer of the province with responsibility to exercise the powers of the Crown, including ensuring there is always a premier able to command the confidence of the legislature,[4] and to "summon and call together" the legislature.[5] The Lieutenant Governor endorses Cabinet decisions, which gives them the force of law and brings an end to the governmental approval process. Where an Act refers to the Lieutenant Governor in Council, it is referring to the Lieutenant Governor acting on the advice of Cabinet.

The Canadian Constitution establishes the position of provincial Lieutenant Governor is to be appointed by the Governor General in Council, meaning acting on the advice of the federal Cabinet.[6] The nature of Cabinet's advice is not justiciable unless there is a possibility that the action has violated rights under the *Canadian Charter of Rights and Freedoms* (the *Charter*).[7]

Prior to taking office, the Lieutenant Governor takes oaths of allegiance and office.[8] Once appointed, the Lieutenant Governor is not an agent of the federal government but is obliged by constitutional convention to act on the advice of the provincial Cabinet.

---

4 Lieutenant Governor's website, online: http://www.lgontario.ca.

5 *Constitution Act, 1867*, above note 2, s 82.

6 *Ibid*, ss 58 and 13. An administrator can be appointed to fulfill the role during the Lieutenant Governor's absence, illness, or other "inability"; *ibid*, s 67.

7 *Canadian Charter of Rights and Freedoms*, Part I of the *Constitution Act, 1982*, being Schedule B to the *Canada Act 1982* (UK), 1982, c 11 [*Charter*]. See *Operation Dismantle v The Queen*, [1985] 1 SCR 441 as discussed in *Acadian Society of New Brunswick v Right Honourable Prime Minister of Canada*, 2022 NBQB 85, dealing with the appointment of a unilingual Lieutenant Governor in Canada's only officially bilingual province.

8 *Constitution Act, 1867*, above note 2, s 61.

The Lieutenant Governor is appointed "during the Pleasure of the Governor General."[9] During the first five years of their tenure, the Lieutenant Governor can only be removed for cause. The appointment can be for longer than five years, but it has been agreed that a longer appointment, with the resultant loss of the "for cause" protection, results in a loss of security of tenure that is incompatible with the desired independence of the office.[10] Ontario practice has been five-year terms.

The Lieutenant Governor's salary is to be set and paid by the federal Parliament,[11] done through the federal *Salaries Act*, which provides for statutory adjustments in accordance with a wage index.[12] All other costs of the office are paid provincially.

C. MEMBERS OF PROVINCIAL PARLIAMENT

MPPs are governed by the *Legislative Assembly Act*.[13] Conflict of interest requirements are set out in the *Members' Integrity Act, 1994*.[14] Pensions are governed by the *MPPs Pension Act, 1996*.[15] Members of the Legislative Assembly have unique employment related obligations and rights in part because they are a form of self-governing collective.[16] The speaker has a leading role as "the guardian of the rights, immunities, privileges and powers of the Assembly, its committees and its members."[17]

---

9 *Ibid*, s 59.

10 W. Laurier, Canada, *House of Commons, Debates*, 31 January 1893, Vol XXXVI at 84, as discussed in John T. Saywell, *The Office of the Lieutenant-Governor: A Study in Canadian Government and Politics* (Toronto: University of Toronto Press, 1957) at 229.

11 *Constitution Act, 1867*, above note 2, s 60.

12 *Salaries Act*, RSC 1985, c S-3, s 3.

13 RSO 1990, c L.10 [*Legislative Assembly Act*]. Provincial legislation now covers what was previously addressed by the *Constitution Act, 1867*, above note 2, ss 82–89.

14 SO 1994, c 38 [*Members' Integrity Act*].

15 SO 1996, c 6, Sch A [*MPPs Pension Act*].

16 The seminal case on parliamentary operations is *Canada (House of Commons) v Vaid*, 2005 SCC 30 [*Vaid*]. For a discussion of the obligations of members of the federal Parliament, see Lindsay Aagaard, "Fiduciary Duty and Members of Parliament" (2008) 31:2 *Canadian Parliamentary Review* 31.

17 *Legislative Assembly Act*, above note 13, s 28.1.

1) Eligibility to Serve as an MPP

An MPP must be at least eighteen years of age and a Canadian citizen residing in Ontario.[18] Members of the federal Senate or the House of Commons at the time of being nominated to run for election are ineligible. Once elected, MPPs may not hold office as municipal councillors or as members of local municipal boards.[19] Persons who hold an "office, commission or employment" in the service of either the federal or provincial government for which they receive some form of remuneration are ineligible, with some exceptions, including ministers, parliamentary assistants, coroners, and members of boards, committees, or commissions, although order-in-council appointees to certain boards, including the Ontario Labour Relations Board (OLRB) and the Civil Service Commission, remain ineligible to be members of the legislature.[20] Where a person who is ineligible is nevertheless elected, the election is void.[21] A sitting MPP who becomes disqualified may continue to sit until that disqualification is confirmed by an election court.

MPPs are "returned" as elected in accordance with the *Election Act*, which includes provision for resolving contested elections, including recounts.[22]

Before "taking their seat" in the Legislative Assembly, each member is to take an oath of allegiance[23] to the reigning monarch.

---

18 *Ibid*, s 6.

19 *Ibid*, s 9(1).

20 *Ibid*, s 8(2).

21 *Ibid*, ss 13–17.

22 RSO 1990, c E.6, ss 69–80 [*Election Act*].

23 *Constitution Act, IX.128*, Westminster: Parliament of the United Kingdom, and Fifth Schedule. The oath of allegiance is to the sitting English monarch. There has been a bill before the Ontario Legislative Assembly to make the oath an Ontario legislative requirement and to add Canada to the oath, but it has not passed first reading: *Members' Oath of Allegiance Act, 2000*, Bill 167, introduced 14 December 2000, 37th Parliament, 1st Session. The oath was also questioned but not changed, due to it being in the federal Constitution, when the provisions for the administration of the oath of allegiance to Legislative Assembly employees, as discussed below, were recently altered: Ontario Legislative Assembly, *Hansard*, 18 February 2020 at 900 (Gilles Bisson, New Democratic Party), during debate of the *Legislative Assembly Amendment Act, 2020*, Bill 167. For further discussion of the oath of allegiance and other oaths, particularly as they apply to public servants, see Chapter 2.

2) Rights, Privileges, and Restrictions Under the *Legislative Assembly Act*

MPPs have "absolute privilege" and personal immunity for their statements in the legislature, and their legislative choices,[24] as exercised through their democratic rights under the Standing Orders of the Legislative Assembly.[25] MPPs cannot be held civilly or criminally liable for anything they bring before the legislature.[26] They are also protected, during a session and during the twenty days preceding or following a session, from arrest or detention for any civil matter (except where the matter involves the Legislative Assembly addressing a contravention of the *Legislative Assembly Act*). Members cannot be called as jurors during the same periods.

Under the *Legislative Assembly Act*, the assembly has the right to inquire into and punish, as breaches of privilege or as contemptuous, enumerated matters affecting an MPP or the Legislative Assembly as a whole, including the following:[27]

- assaulting, insulting, or libelling of a member; or assault upon or interference with an officer of the Legislative Assembly
- obstructing, threatening, or attempting to force or intimidate a member
- offering a bribe to, or the acceptance by, a member in respect of a legislative matter
- taking any civil proceeding against, or effecting the arrest or imprisonment of, a member because of a legislative matter

---

24 For a discussion of the absolute privilege for statements made in the legislature, as contrasted with a lesser privilege for statements made at municipal council meetings, see *Gutowski v Clayton*, 2014 ONCA 921. See also *Ontario (Speaker of the Legislative Assembly) v Ontario (Human Rights Commission)*, 2001 CanLII 8549 (ON CA) on the non-reviewability of standing orders calling for daily recital of the Lord's Prayer. For a detailed discussion of the immunity of the attorney general from Law Society discipline, see Andrew F. Martin, "The Immunity of the Attorney General to Law Society Discipline" (2016) 94:2 *Canadian Bar Review* 413.

25 *Standing Orders of the Legislative Assembly of Ontario*, online: www.ola.org/en/legislative-business/standing-orders, which provide that all contingencies not provided for in those orders are to be decided by the speaker, who shall have regard for "any applicable usages and precedents of the Legislature and Parliamentary tradition." Those precedents and traditions are beyond the scope of this book.

26 *Legislative Assembly Act*, above note 13, s 37.

27 *Ibid*, s 46.

- effecting the arrest or detention of a member for any civil matter during a session of the legislature or during the twenty days preceding or twenty days following a session
- tampering with a witness in a legislative matter
- forging or falsifying documents and records related to the legislature
- serving civil proceedings upon a person in the legislative precinct—Legislative Building and a room or office used for legislative proceedings—except for a constituency office[28]

In addition to any penalty or punishment to which they might be subject by law, a person or member who is found guilty by the Legislative Assembly of committing any of these acts may be subject to a fine, imprisonment, or other penalty.[29] The decision of the legislature on any proceeding under the Act is final,[30] and the doctrine of legislative privilege—the common law privilege of legislative assemblies giving them the "necessary immunity in order for these legislators to do their legislative work"[31]—will likely mean that all such decisions are not subject to judicial review. To emphasize the point, the Act provides that, except in respect of being bribed for legislation, any rights, immunities, privileges, or powers that are inherent to members of the legislature (and to the legislature itself) are protected against the operation of the provisions of the Act itself.[32]

3) Salary

MPPs' salary entitlements are set out in the Act, which provides an annual base salary of 75 percent of the salary of federal MPs, except that MPP salaries have been frozen since 2009 and are to remain frozen

---

28 *Ibid*, s 39.

29 *Ibid*, s 47.

30 *Ibid*, s 49.

31 *New Brunswick Broadcasting Co v Nova Scotia (Speaker of the House of Assembly)*, [1993] 1 SCR 319; *Vaid*, above note 16 at para 29. Legislative privilege applies to both the process for, and resolution of, discipline of a member: *Saunders v Nunatsiavut Assembly*, 2022 NLSC 142. Note that legislative privilege does not automatically extend to management of Legislative Assembly employees, as discussed below in Section D.

32 *Legislative Assembly Act*, above note 13, ss 53 and 41.

until there is a balanced budget.[33] This is a rare example in the public sector of salary tied to a specific outcome.[34]

Members in a number of roles are entitled to an additional percentage of the base salary.[35] Recipients in legislative roles include the speaker (31.2 percent additional entitlement), leader of the Opposition (55.2 percent additional entitlement), and committee chairs (14 percent additional entitlement). A member who holds more than one such position is entitled to be paid only for the additional position with the higher salary. In addition to these salaries set by the *Legislative Assembly Act*, there are additional salaries payable under the *Executive Council Act* for the ministers (42.3 percent additional entitlement) and premier (minister entitlement plus 37 percent).[36] For the purpose of computing salaries, members are deemed to have been members from the polling day on which they are elected to the day before the next polling day (following the dissolution of the legislature) or the day of their death, whichever occurs first.[37]

4) Pensions and Severance Pay

MPPs' pension entitlements were effectively eliminated in 1996.[38] While the *MPPs Pension Act* is still in effect, there are no contributions and no service credit after June 1995.[39] This is highly unusual in comparison with the pension plans in effect for the public service.[40]

Members who resign, or seek re-election but are not elected, or die in office are entitled to severance pay based on years of service as follows:

---

33 *Ibid*, s 61.

34 For a discussion, see "MPPs Are Marking 10 Years Without a Pay Raise" *Toronto Star* (13 December 2019), online: www.thestar.com/politics/provincial/2019/12/13/mpps-are-marking-10-years-without-a-pay-raise.html.

35 *Legislative Assembly Act*, above note 13, s 62.

36 *Executive Council Act*, RSO 1990, c E.25, s 3.

37 *Legislative Assembly Act*, above note 13, s 61(2).

38 See the comments of the longest serving speaker of the legislature, Dave Levac, in "The Surprising Reason You Shouldn't Complain About MPPs' Pension Plans" *TVO* (19 March 2019), online: www.tvo.org/article/the-surprising-reason-you-shouldnt-complain-about-mpps-pension-plans.

39 For discussion of issues arising out of the vesting of prior pensions, see Integrity Commissioner, *Re Ernie Eves, Former Member of the Legislative Assembly with respect to the MPPs Pension Act, 1996 and the Income Tax Act*, 6 May 2002 [*Eves, 2002*].

40 For a discussion of public service pension plans, see Chapter 6.

- four years or less: one-half annual salary
- four years up to eight years: one year
- more than eight years: one-and-a-half years

based on salary as a member and, if applicable, as a minister.[41]

5) Personal Expenses and Allowances

Personal expenses of members are overseen by the Board of Internal Economy and, for the expenses of ministers (including parliamentary assistants) and opposition leaders incurred in the performance of their additional duties, by the integrity commissioner.

The Board of Internal Economy is an all-party committee of MPPs, chaired by the Speaker, that sets and controls financial and operating policies applicable to the legislature,[42] and whose proceedings are deemed to be "proceedings in Parliament." (The roles of the Speaker and the board in overseeing Legislative Assembly staff are discussed below.) The speaker has the duty to post the rules set by the Board of Internal Economy governing expenses of members for travel, accommodation, meals, and hospitality expenses; and to post information online respecting payment of expenses.[43] Each expense is to be posted along with its purpose. Information may be excluded if posting it would likely "constitute an unjustified invasion of privacy"[44] or jeopardize security. There are some specific statutory provisions for accommodation payments, particularly for MPPs whose principal residence is more than fifty kilometres from the legislature, and for car mileage allowance or other transportation expense reimbursement to and from the legislature and within the member's riding.

MPPs are not allowed to be paid a tax-free allowance for expenses related to the discharge of their duties.[45]

---

41 *Legislative Assembly Act*, above note 13, s 69.

42 *Ibid*, ss 87–90.

43 *Ibid*, ss 67–68, resulting from the *Public Sector and MPP Accountability and Transparency Act, 2014*, SO 2014, c 13, Sch 7. Expense rules and disclosures are on the Legislative Assembly website: Expense Disclosure, online: www.ola.org/en/members/expense-disclosure.

44 This language is similar to language under the *Freedom of Information and Protection of Privacy Act*, RSO 1990, c F.31 [*FIPPA*], as discussed in Chapter 6.

45 *Legislative Assembly Act*, above note 13, s 63.1(1).

Under the *Cabinet Ministers' and Opposition Leaders' Expenses Review and Accountability Act, 2002*[46] various expenses for travel, meals, and hospitality are reviewed and reported on by the integrity commissioner.[47] The expenses need to be "reasonable and appropriate in the circumstances" and allowable under the rules established by the Management Board of Cabinet (MBC). The commissioner can require unallowable expenses be reimbursed, and, if that does not occur, may include details in the annual report to the Speaker.[48] Reviewed expenses are to be posted online within ninety days of the commissioner reporting that the review is complete. The responsibility for posting expenses is with the Speaker for Opposition leaders and the president of the Treasury Board Secretariat for ministers and parliamentary assistants.

6) Staff

For purposes of understanding staffing in support of MPPs, it is important to distinguish between legislative and executive roles:[49]

- Members are part of the legislative branch of government responsible for making laws. In support of this role, the legislature gives every MPP a budget for a constituency office:

> The constituency office is part of the legislative branch of government. Constituency offices help constituents with issues related to the provincial government. Staff in these offices are not public servants, but rather are employees of the MPP through the budget provided by the Legislative Assembly.[50]

- The Legislative Assembly is in part responsible for holding the executive branch of government accountable.

---

46 SO 2002, c 34, Sch A.

47 See Office of the Integrity Commissioner, *Expenses Review, Ministers and Opposition Leaders Expenses*, online: www.oico.on.ca/home/expenses-review---ministers-and-opposition-leaders/overview.

48 *Cabinet Ministers' and Opposition Leaders' Expenses Review and Accountability Act*, above note 46, s 9(7).

49 For further discussion of this distinction see Chapter 2. The below description is adapted from Integrity Commissioner, *Re the Honourable Peter Bethlenfalvy*, 21 October 2020 at paras 20–22 [*Bethlenfalvy*].

50 *Ibid* at para 25.

- The executive consists of ministers and parliamentary assistants, supported by ministers' staff. Its role is to administer the law and set policy. Executive branch resources are to be used only for that purpose and cannot be used to support constituency work or MPP work. Ministers' staff are employed under the *PSOA* Part III.[51]

These arrangements support the separation of the legislative from the executive branch.

For legislative purposes, each member is provided with a global budget for staff, constituency office rental, and the costs of providing staff with phones and laptops. They are also furnished legislative email accounts. As discussed further below concerning the *Members' Integrity Act*, "[t]hese publicly-funded resources are provided to assist the members in their duties to respond to the requests from all of their constituents and not for participation in partisan activities."[52]

While a member's staff are employees of the member, they work on employment terms prescribed by the Board of Internal Economy.[53] The OLRB dismissed an application for certification of "all employees in all NDP constituency offices in the Province of Ontario" naming the Board of Internal Economy as employer, with the rationale that the board was not the real employer of the employees, being "little more than a paymaster," and the real employer of MPP staff is the MPP, as follows:

> Constituency office workers are interviewed and hired by each individual Member. A standard form contract is provided by the Office of the Legislative Assembly, but it is signed by the Member and the employee. The form lists "conditions of employment" which the employee and Member agree to have apply to the contract or alternatively agree not to have apply to the contract. The Member determines the number of employees, their hours of work, and vacations; he directs, disciplines, evaluates, assigns work, and fires the employees. The Member also sets the rate of pay of the employees. Although his spending from the fund is limited to the maximum amount allocated by the Board for salaries, there is no prohibition on the Member supplementing this amount from his own pocket or other sources. The Member directs the Office of the Legislative Assembly to pay his

51 See the discussion in Chapter 2.

52 Integrity Commissioner, *Report re Stan Cho, September 14, 2021*, at para 83 [*Cho*].

53 *Legislative Assembly Act*, above note 13, s 74.

employees and the money is withdrawn from the Member's budget and a cheque is issued by the office.[54]

Under the *PSOA*, special provision has been made for ministers' staff supporting the executive function, who are appointed as public servants with terms and conditions of employment similar to term public servants.[55] They are subject to tailored political activity restrictions.[56]

7) Obligations Under the *Members' Integrity Act*

Under the *Members' Integrity Act*, it is recognized that MPPs can best represent the people of Ontario if they can continue to be active in their own communities, whether in business, in the practice of a profession, or otherwise, if they "arrange their private affairs in a manner that promotes public confidence in the integrity of each member."[57]

a) Specific Requirements

Members have the ability to engage in businesses and professions provided they avoid conflicts of interest,[58] do not benefit from a contract with the government,[59] and do not become members of the executive. Cabinet members have additional restrictions. They cannot:

- engage in employment or a profession or hold a company office or directorship[60]

---

54 *Association of Commercial and Technical Employees, Local 1704 CLC v Province of Ontario Board of Internal Economy*, 1980 CanLII 826 (ON LRB) at para 5. There was no discussion of legislative privilege.

55 See Chapter 2.

56 See Chapter 3.

57 *Members' Integrity Act*, above note 14, Preamble.

58 An MPP dealing with an Act that also governs matters in which they represent clients as lawyer is not in conflict as long as the Act is a matter of general application, especially if there is no evidence that the MPP received any personal benefits from any client to pursue amendments to the legislation: Integrity Commissioner, *Re Joseph Tascona*, 15 January 1998.

59 *Members' Integrity Act*, above note 14, s 7. The prohibition applies to personal contracts and contracts of a partnership or company in which the member has an interest. Exceptions exist for contracts in existence prior to the member's election, for company interests if the commissioner is of the opinion that there is no conflict, and for interests in commissioner approved trusts.

60 *Ibid*, s 10.

- hold investments or trade in the financial market, absent a blind trust approved by the commissioner[61]
- manage a business,[62] unless approved by the integrity commissioner[63]
- buy land, other than for residential or recreational use[64]

There is also a restriction on former Cabinet ministers entering into government contracts within the first year of leaving office.[65] This two-tier structure with greater restrictions for Cabinet members has some similarity to the differences in ethical requirements between public service regular employees and senior managers.[66]

All members, including Cabinet ministers, are to file a private disclosure statement on being elected, and annually, setting out the income, assets, and liabilities of the member, their spouse, and children under eighteen years of age; all significant involvement in any business; any benefits that any of those persons have received from a government contract; and any gifts over $200.[67] After filing, the member and spouse, if available, are to meet with the integrity commissioner each year to review the disclosure and obtain advice on the member's obligations under the Act. A statement of any material change must be filed within thirty days of the change.

For each member, the commissioner shall issue a public disclosure statement annually that sets out the "nature and source" of the member's income, assets, and interests, but not the value, with exceptions from posting for such items as personal property, cash, retirement savings, and pension plans.[68] These statements are all posted on the commissioner's website.[69]

---

61 *Ibid*, s 11. See the discussion of breach of the blind trust requirements discussed in Integrity Commissioner, *Re the Honourable Harinder Takhar*, 4 January 2006 [*Takhar*].

62 *Ibid*, s 12.

63 *Ibid*, s 13.

64 *Ibid*, s 15 unless inherited, through the operation of a mortgage, or adding to a farm.

65 *Ibid*, ss 17–18.

66 See Chapter 3.

67 *Members' Integrity Act*, above note 14, s 20. Gifts are further discussed below.

68 *Ibid*, s 21.

69 Office of the Integrity Commissioner, *Public Disclosure Statements*, online: http://pds.oico.on.ca/Pages/Public/PublicDisclosures.aspx#.

b) Rules of Conduct

The *Members' Integrity Act* sets out rules for members on:

- Avoidance of actual personal conflict of interest (including not receiving gifts, fees, or benefits that raise a conflict)
- Adherence to "Ontario parliamentary convention," including the prohibition on use of government resources for partisan purposes (there is specific statutory treatment of personal social media accounts)

i) Conflict of Interest

A member is not to use their office to further their own private interests or improperly further another person's private interests[70] and is not to "make a decision or participate in one if there is such an opportunity."[71] A member is not to put "insider information" to personal use or to share it if it may be so used.[72] If a member has reasonable grounds to think they have a conflict of interest in a matter before the Legislative Assembly or Cabinet, they need to disclose the conflict and withdraw from the matter.[73]

A member's own "private interest" includes pecuniary and purely personal interests but does not include the broader political interest of the member's party or the government of the day.[74] Also excluded from the definition of "private interest" is a matter that is of general application or affects a member of the legislature as one of a broad class of persons.[75] This means that members can, for example, participate in making decisions about provincial taxation despite being taxpayers.[76] It also means that they can participate in voting and debate on bills of general application even though their private investment or business interests are

70 *Members' Integrity Act*, above note 14, s 4.

71 *Ibid*, s 2. Although "decision" is not a defined term, it has been interpreted to mean a decision in the legislature, Cabinet, or perhaps a committee: Integrity Commissioner, *Re David Levac, with respect to his attendance at the Toronto Don Jail*, 23 July 2003 at para 25 [*Levac*].

72 *Ibid*, s 3.

73 *Ibid*, s 8.

74 Integrity Commissioner, *Re The Honourable Doug Ford*, 20 March 2019 at para 290 [*Ford, March 2019*].

75 *Members' Integrity Act*, above note 14, s 1.

76 *Eves, 2002*, above note 39 at para 42.

affected.[77] However, they must be careful to not engage in the debate in a way that forwards their private business or investment interests.

For there to be a private interest "there must be a direct and personal benefit accruing to the member, rather than an indirect and political one."[78] General party fundraising produces "a wide political benefit" that is not equated with a personal benefit. Where contributions are made to a political party and the member does not get possession or control of the money, there is no "conflict of interest" under the terms of the *Members' Integrity Act* because there is no "private interest."[79] Even "cash for access" to a member, if it results only in money paid to a political party, while inappropriate, is not a violation of the Act.[80] On the other hand, a political donation directly to an individual candidate may give rise to a conflict of interest where there is "a sense of obligation" created, as would be the case if the arrangement was "cash for questions" asked in the legislature.[81] Note that political contributions are also governed by the *Election Finances Act*,[82] which is outside the scope of this book.

It is not a breach of the *Members' Integrity Act* for members or ministers to use their office to forward their political interest. For example, a minister pressuring a stakeholder for a favourable media response to a policy initiative is the forwarding of a political not a private interest and not a violation of the Act.[83]

Even though it is a matter of personal interest, members are specifically permitted by the Act to participate in decisions about their own remuneration and benefits,[84] including their own pensions.[85]

---

77 Integrity Commissioner, *Re Stephen Crawford*, 17 February 2022.

78 Integrity Commissioner, *Re The Honourable Bob Chiarelli, The Honourable Michael Coteau and The Honourable Yasir Naqvi*, 8 December 2016 at para 49 [*Chiarelli et al*].

79 Integrity Commissioner, *Re The Honourable Doug Ford*, 9 December 2021 at paras 13–14 [*Ford, December 2021*].

80 *Chiarelli et al*, above note 78 at paras 77–80. The inappropriateness of the arrangement may make it a breach of ministers' staff obligations under the *PSOA*, as discussed in Chapter 4.

81 *Chiarelli et al*, above note 78 at paras 50–51.

82 RSO 1990, c E.7.

83 Integrity Commissioner, *Re the Honourable Lisa Macleod*, 23 May 2019 at para 14 [*MacLeod, 2019*].

84 *Members' Integrity Act*, above note 14, s 1.

85 *Eves, 2002*, above note 39.

Turning to a member advancing the interests of other persons, the prohibition on "improperly furthering" another person's interests prohibits conduct that is objectionable, unsuitable, or wrong.[86] There are five factors that the integrity commissioner takes into account in reaching that conclusion, none of which is decisive on its own:

1) The relationship between the member and the other person: close friendship by itself is insufficient to establish impropriety
2) The degree of the member's involvement in the decision at issue, or the process leading to it
3) Whether the member acted for an improper purpose: the principle in *Roncarelli v Duplessis*[87] establishes that the person needs to act in good faith for a proper purpose
4) The process used for the decision in question: whether it was fair and open, and did not provide for preferential treatment for a member's preferred outcome
5) Whether there was an objective basis for the decision.[88]

For example, "[a]ppointing a friend with no qualifications for the job would certainly strengthen a conclusion that the appointment was made to further the interests of the friend improperly."[89] To avoid breaching the Act when the government awards contracts, it is best for politicians to be separated and insulated from request for proposal processes. They can be involved in setting priorities such as whether to build hospitals (the "what" question) and in the selection of the method such as public private partnerships (the "how" question), but they should be insulated from the selection of the winning proponent (the "who" question).[90] Similarly, individual companies should not be given special opportunities to partner with government that are not over time made generally available.[91]

---

86 *Ford, March 2019*, above note 74 at paras 298–99.

87 *Roncarelli v Duplessis*, [1959] SCR 121 at para 140.

88 *Ibid* at paras 303–20 and cases cited.

89 *Ford, March 2019*, above note 74, addressing the allegation that the premier improperly furthered his friend's application for OPP commissioner. The integrity commissioner found (at paras 321–58) that the individual was qualified and there was no evidence that the premier improperly furthered his friend's application.

90 Integrity Commissioner, *Re the Honourable Ernie Eves, and The Honourable Tony Clement with respect to the government's decision to use private sector financing agreements to construct and operate two hospitals*, 13 August 2013.

91 Integrity Commissioner, *Re The Honourable James M. Flaherty with Respect to a One-Time Tax-Free Payment of $100 per Child under Age Seven*, 8 February

It is also improper for ministers to seek to further a constituent's private interest by publicly opposing the implementation of a government policy, such as by indicating dissatisfaction with the decision of a government established commission due to the effects in their constituency.[92]

Letters of reference for individuals should only be provided where the MPP actually knows the individual and they should be specific to the matter.[93] References for people and organizations concerning a court appearance should be avoided, absent a subpoena, as any involvement could be interpreted as an attempt to influence the legal process.

All these conflict of interest prohibitions apply only to actual conflict of interest and not to a perceived conflict of interest or the appearance of conflict of interest.[94] For example, "[i]t is conceivable that a reasonably well-informed person could have reasonable concerns about a $7,500 per person fundraising event, held one month after the conclusion of a transaction" attended by private parties involved in the transaction, but that is the appearance of conflict and not proof of actual conflict.[95] The use of this actual conflict standard is quite different from the appearance of conflict of interest standard under the *PSOA*. The actual conflict standard has been defended on the basis that few people are ready to be sufficiently dispassionate in assessing the conduct of legislators and so an appearance or "perception" of conflict standard would be overly subject to "distortion by false rumours, media manipulation and public relations hyperbole."[96]

To address the conflict of interest concern raised by the receipt of gifts, fees, or benefits, MPPs are prohibited from accepting a gift, fee, or benefit that is connected with their office.[97] (They are not prohibited

---

2002, which concerned partnering with a single private company to launch a program of matching government funding.

92 Integrity Commissioner, *Re The Honourable Allan Leach*, 25 June 1997.

93 Integrity Commissioner, *Guidance on Letters of Reference*, online: www.oico.on.ca/home/mpp-integrity/guidance-on-letters-of-reference.

94 *Ford, March 2019*, above note 74; *Report re: The Honourable Bob Chiarelli and The Honourable Charles Sousa*, 9 August 2016.

95 Integrity Commissioner, *Report re: The Honourable Bob Chiarelli and The Honourable Charles Sousa*, 9 August 2016 at paras 65 and 69. The integrity commissioner did encourage the legislature to review the Act to consider including the appearance of conflict.

96 Integrity Commissioner, *Re The Honourable Frances Lankin*, 2 May 1991 at 4.

97 *Members' Integrity Act*, above note 14, s 6(2).

from receiving gifts that are entirely personal.[98])Then, there are three exceptions to the prohibition:[99]

- gifts received in instances of protocol, customs, or social obligation
- if the integrity commissioner is of the opinion it is unlikely the gift or benefit was given in order to influence the MPP[100]
- gifts given to a member by a political party or constituency association[101]

The specifically listed exemptions from the "no gift" rule must meet certain criteria.[102] "Protocol" refers to a gift offered on behalf of a level of government (Canada or international) during a meeting, conference, or official visit. "Customs" refers to a gift or benefit, usually of nominal value, that is customarily offered as a way to express gratitude or commemoration for participation in an event. "Social obligation" refers to a benefit, usually a meal or refreshment, offered as a matter of courtesy when attending an event in an official capacity.

The integrity commissioner notes that some lobbyists "persist in the belief" that buying a meal for an MPP or a public office holder is not a gift but "relationship building," even though the commissioner has consistently advised that the practice amounts to the giving of a gift and is only acceptable if it falls under one of the statutory exceptions.[103]

---

98 Integrity Commissioner, *Re Patrick Brown, MPP for Simcoe North*, 26 April 2018 at para 215 [*Brown, 2018*] dealing with a gift of admission and accommodation at his friend Wayne Gretzky's hockey camp; *Re The Honourable Michael Harris and the Honourable Charles Harnick*, 20 January 1999 dealing with Premier Harris and a minister being hosted by friends whose business was the Stratford Festival.

99 *Members' Integrity Act*, above note 14, s 6(1).

100 "The test is not a subjective one but rather an objective one—it is the Commissioner's call, not that of the member or staff": Office of the Integrity Commissioner of Ontario, *Annual Report 2017–2018*, Commissioner's Message.

101 Gifts from the member's own party have long been out of scope for declaring. See gifts to then Premier Harris of a housing upgrade and a golf club membership being found to be out of scope: Integrity Commissioner, *Re Michael Harris*, 9 May 1996.

102 Integrity Commissioner, *Gift Guide for MPPs*, online: www.oico.on.ca/home/mpp-integrity/guidance-on-the-gift-rule [*Gift Guide*].

103 Office of the Integrity Commissioner of Ontario, *Annual Report 2017–2018*, Commissioner's Message.

The integrity commissioner has provided advice that it is not generally allowable to be the keynote speaker at an event in another city if airfare and accommodation is offered by the organizers, to have a meal paid for by a stakeholder during which official matters are discussed, to accept paid "fact finding" tours, or tickets to an event where the MPP does not have an official role, including tickets to sporting events,[104] or for an MPP to accept donations for a community event.[105]

In any case, all gifts received valued over $200, other than from political party sources, are to be disclosed to the integrity commissioner.[106]

ii) Compliance with Parliamentary Convention

The *Members' Integrity Act* further states it "does not prohibit actions done in accordance with Ontario parliamentary convention."[107] This is a curiously worded provision that has been interpreted, in the course of the commissioner dealing with inquiries under the Act, to mean that actions which do not accord with Ontario parliamentary convention are prohibited.

"Ontario parliamentary convention" is a set of rules or practices that members accept as governing their ethical conduct. Guidance is found in the preamble to the Act and its references to "promoting public confidence," maintaining "the Assembly's dignity," justifying society's respect for the legislature, and to "acting with integrity and impartiality." But "Ontario parliamentary convention" is not a statutorily defined term and lacks certainty in comparison with the Act's more specific conflict of interest provisions.[108] A body of jurisprudence developed by integrity commissioners on a case-by-case basis has generated guidance for members and their staff.[109] The parliamentary conventions are expected to continue to evolve while needing to be grounded in the views of legislators rather than being based only on the discretion of

---

104 It is not acceptable to seek to exempt them on the basis that attendance by the politician is a favour to their host: *Brown, 2018*, above note 98 at paras 235–37.

105 *Gift Guide*, above note 102.

106 *Members' Integrity Act*, above note 14, s 6(3).

107 *Ibid*, s 5.

108 *Levac*, above note 71 at para 29; *Macleod, 2019*, above note 83 at para 14.

109 *Macleod, 2019*, above note 83 at paras 20–26 quoting Senator Eugene Forsey and the Honourable Coulter A.A. Osborne; Integrity Commissioner, *Re The Honourable Brad Duguid*, 11 July 2013 at para 84 [*Duguid, 2013*].

the commissioner.[110] The commissioner has stated that caution should be exercised by the commissioner in declaring a particular activity to be contrary to parliamentary convention for the first time, although conduct can be so egregious that a breach of parliamentary convention can be presumed.[111]

Presently, there is a general obligation not to mix government and political party activity, for example, making it unacceptable to be on ministerial business and make a partisan comment.[112] There are six more specific categories of activity that have been identified as being contrary to convention:[113]

- *Advocacy:* Ministers and parliamentary assistants are prohibited from appearing before, or having communication on behalf of a private party, with any agency, board, or commission that falls under the jurisdiction of the minister. (And ministers should refrain from intervening for a private interest before such bodies that are under the jurisdiction of another minister.[114])
- *Judicial interference:* Members are not permitted to interfere in judicial processes in any way. The prohibition includes not interfering with police activities, advocating to the judiciary, or publicly commenting on matters before the judiciary.
- *Interference with the public service:* Ministers and their offices do not advocate directly to public servants from other ministries about constituent issues but must go through the responsible minister.

---

110 *Macleod, 2019*, above note 83 at paras 33–35, in part discussing the difficulty of setting standards for the use of social media, including dealing with "hyper partisan" tweets and posts.

111 Integrity Commissioner, *Re Randy Hillier No 2*, 13 April 2022 at paras 23–24 [*Hillier No 2*].

112 Integrity Commissioner, *Re The Honourable Ernie Eves, the Honourable Tony Clement, The Honourable James Flaherty, and Brian Coburn with Respect to Partisan Political Conduct while Engaged in Ministry Business*, 28 November 2003.

113 Integrity Commissioner, *Re Patrick Brown*, 14 July 2016 at para 3 [*Brown, 2016*]. See the cases and annual reports cited.

114 Integrity Commissioner, *Re The Honourable Allan Leach*, 25 June 1997, in which the commissioner also advises that the entire executive council needs to collectively respect adjudicative processes.

- *Management of trust account:* Ministers granted permission to hold certain assets in trust accounts must do so in a manner that promotes public confidence.[115]
- *Assisting others in a manner that interferes with public duties:* Members must ensure that constituent representation and support activities members normally engage in are not done in a manner that undermines the member's public duty.[116]
- *Using government resources for partisan purposes:* Government resources, including constituency offices, telephones, computers, and the salaried time of staff, should be used to assist constituents and not for matters related to partisan politics.

A seventh category of highly objectionable speech that is unanimously viewed as such was effectively created in *Hillier No 2* where the commissioner penalized an MPP for posting the names and faces of persons they asserted were killed by COVID-19 vaccinations without consulting with their families.[117] The commissioner found a breach of parliamentary convention due to the clearly objectionable nature of the conduct, the unanimous censure by the legislature, and the MPP's apologies.

The convention most often considered by the integrity commissioner is that members are not to use legislative resources for partisan purposes, but only for legislative and constituency purposes. This convention is consistent with the *Members' Integrity Act* preamble provision that members must "broadly represent . . . their constituents' interests"[118] and not act for the benefit of specific groups such as their political supporters.[119]

---

115 *Takhar*, above note 61 at para 94. The relationship with the trustee must be arm's length and that is not the case where the trustee is also the treasurer of the minister's riding association and CFO for the minister under the *Election Finances Act*. The result was a recommended reprimand of the minister and a requirement that the trustee be removed.

116 Integrity Commissioner, *Re Sandra Pupatello*, 12 December 2002 at paras 30–35 [*Pupatello*] regarding using the government courier service not to ship the member's personal goods, which was allowable as long as the member paid the bill, but to ship a friend's goods; *Levac*, above note 71 at paras 29–34, where the MPP used his statutory right to visit a jail to get access for a member of the media.

117 *Hillier No 2*, above note 111.

118 *Bethlenfalvy*, above note 49 at para 40.

119 *Duguid, 2013*, above note 109 at para 84.

This means that the Legislative Assembly itself, or access to it or any particular part of it, such as a lounge or gallery, should not be used for party fundraising by members.[120]

This also applies to government resources provided individually to MPPs: offices (both constituency and legislative), human resources (for example, legislative and constituency office staff), and information technology (for example, MPP legislative and constituency websites).[121] The constituency office is to serve all constituents in the riding without regard for political affiliation.[122] Constituency staff can only work on partisan activities from a location other than the constituency office, on their own time, and with resources not funded by the legislature.[123] Fundraising and organizing a partisan rally are not to be carried out as part of constituency office activities.[124] It is partisan and unacceptable to use legislative and constituency resources to organize a public town hall event at which only one party's MPPs are invited to speak, along with a candidate of that party.[125] It is a breach to use government resources, including salaried staff time, to develop a partisan ad strategy targeted to likely political supporters.[126]

In contrast to constituency and legislative staff, ministers' staff may have periods during regular business hours when they are involved in partisan work, but only to a limited extent.[127] Such work needs to relate to the ministerial function and can include:

- assessing how materials prepared by a ministry align with a political party's position on an issue
- preparing responses to opposition party positions on ministerial activities

---

120 *Brown, 2016*, above note 113.

121 *MacLeod, 2019*, above note 83 at para 32; *Cho*, above note 52 at para 82; Integrity Commissioner, *Re Jessica Bell*, 31 March 2022 [*Bell*].

122 Integrity Commissioner, *Re Jagmeet Singh*, 26 June 2015 at 15–16 [*Singh*], quoted in *Cho*, above note 52 at para 84.

123 Integrity Commissioner, *Re Randy Hillier No 1*, 13 April 2022 at paras 128 and 130.

124 *Singh*, above note 122.

125 Integrity Commissioner, *Re Vijay Thanigasalam*, 21 December 2021.

126 *Bethlenfalvy*, above note 49 at para 40.

127 Integrity Commissioner, *Minister's Staff, Guidance on Political Activity*, online: http://5157144009.saas.quicksilk.com/en/ministers-staff-guidance-on-political-activity. See also *Singh*, above note 122 at 16. For further discussion of the *PSOA* treatment of political activity of minister's staff, see Chapter 3.

- communicating positions that reflect the elected government's perspective
- liaising with other ministers' offices

Partisan work cannot conflict with the interests of the Crown. It cannot include endorsing a party or candidate, engaging stakeholders on campaigning, or organizing political events or riding association activities. On their own time, ministers' staff may participate in political activity provided they do not use government resources and there is no conflict with the interests of the Crown.

Concerning websites, "visitors to constituency [and legislative] websites are entitled to access MPPs without being subjected to partisan messaging in the same way that visitors to physical constituency offices are assured of a neutral environment."[128] Constituency sites should be non-partisan and not display party logos, reference riding associations, provide information about riding association activities, or provide information on how to make donations,[129] and they should not link to partisan sites. It is a breach of parliamentary convention to link constituency sites to partisan sites, to seek feedback from a legislative account that linked to a partisan page, and to post partisan messages on social media accounts linked from constituency websites.[130] Constituency and partisan sites should not be blended.[131] (At the same time, and as discussed below, social media accounts in the member's own name are allowable provided conflict of interest is avoided and further to specific provisions in the Act discussed in the social media section below.)

Concerning staff conflicts, members are normally responsible for them as it is their responsibility to provide adequate supervision, direction, and training.[132] They will not be held responsible if it was not reasonable for them to anticipate the breach[133] or to expect the member to supervise the activity.[134]

---

128 Integrity Commissioner, *Re Daiene Vernile, Member for Kitchener-Centre, and Jeff Leal, Minister of Agriculture, Food and Rural Affairs*, 22 December 2015 at 4, referencing guidelines from the *2012–2013 Integrity Commissioner's Report*.

129 Integrity Commissioner, *Re Ted Chudleigh*, 11 December 2008.

130 Integrity Commissioner, *Re Catherine Fife*, 14 September 2021 [*Fife*].

131 *Singh*, above note 122 at 16.

132 *Cho*, above note 52 at para 98.

133 Integrity Commissioner, *Re Andrea Horvath*, 27 April 2022.

134 *Duguid, 2013*, above note 109 at para 78.

According to the integrity commissioner, the Queen's Park and constituency staff of MPPs, who are employees of the member, can be a source of ethical concern because, unlike ministers' staff, they are not subject to the *PSOA* confidentiality, gift, and political activity restrictions; they do not have an ethics code; and they "must rely on their own moral compass."[135] In the commissioner's view, it would be much less problematic if the same ethics rules applied to all staff who support a member, whether as MPP, minister, or a parliamentary assistant. This would enhance accountability for MPPs' staff members.

A member who is a minister or parliamentary assistant cannot use the resources of their ministerial office to support the work of their constituency office.[136] Except for the coordination of logistical issues like scheduling, there must be a "bright line" between the work of a minister's or parliamentary assistant's staff and the work of that person's Queen's Park or constituency staff supporting them as MPP.[137] This convention flows from the separation of powers between the legislative and executive branches of government.[138]

As ministers' staff members are subject to the *PSOA* regime, there is an additional responsibility on them to avoid the appearance of conflict, as opposed to (just) avoiding the actual conflict that must be avoided by MPPs. The *PSOA* ethical obligations of public servants employed in a minister's office are discussed in Chapter 3.

The only provision in the *PSOA* relating to ministers is section 67, which requires that they ensure their staff are familiar with the conflict of interest rules that apply in respect of a minister's office and that they promote ethical conduct by their staff.[139] There is no enforcement provision in the *PSOA* if a minister fails to live up to these requirements.

Turning to social media, MPPs can have accounts "in their own name" and can post partisan content on their accounts, but must follow the Act's conflict of interest requirements.[140] Partisan material is defined as material supporting a particular candidate, party, or issue not related to government work for the public at large, or a member's constituency work at large.

---

135 *Cho*, above note 52 at para 105.

136 *Duguid, 2013*, above note 109 at para 84.

137 *Cho*, above note 52 at para 104.

138 *Bethlenfalvy*, above note 49 at para 41; *Cho*, above note 52 at paras 82–83.

139 *PSOA*, above note 1, s 67.

140 *Members' Integrity Act*, above note 14, s 9.1(6).

In order to maintain the non-partisan nature of constituency websites, those sites should not contain links to social media accounts that contain partisan messaging.[141] However, linking from the partisan social media account to the constituency website does not, by itself, contravene parliamentary convention. While everyone should, by convention, "encounter a partisan-free zone in the constituency office" and with its staff employed with use of public funds, the convention does not apply to a link to the constituency office website that is "made available in a partisan environment."

c) Process of Complaint and Potential Consequences

Only MPPs may complain about MPP integrity breaches to the commissioner, supported by an affidavit filed with the speaker along with a copy of the complaint.[142] The speaker shall inform the assembly of the complaint. Note that the legislature cannot conduct an inquiry into a matter referred to the commissioner.

A complaint need not be specific about which parliamentary convention has been breached.[143] There will be insufficient grounds to launch an inquiry if the affidavit in support does not provide information about how the member complained against was actually involved in the incident, since to commence an inquiry without that information would be "tantamount to embarking on a fishing expedition."[144]

The complaint is to be based on "reasonable and probable grounds to believe" there has been a contravention.[145] This requires an honest belief there has been a contravention and objective reason for that belief.[146]

While media reports are hearsay and not evidence for an inquiry, they can provide "reasonable and probable grounds" for a member to believe another member has contravened the Act and be sufficient for the integrity commissioner to commence an inquiry.[147] Media

141 Integrity Commissioner, *Guidance on Using Social Media*, online: www.oico.on.ca/en/mpp-integrity-guidance-on-social-media.

142 *Members' Integrity Act*, above note 14, s 30.

143 *Macleod, 2019*, above note 83 at para 33, following *Pupatello*, above note 116 at 10–11.

144 Integrity Commissioner, *Re The Honourable Doug Ford*, 7 May 2019 at para 12.

145 *Members' Integrity Act*, above note 14, s 30(1).

146 *Ford, December 2021*, above note 79 at paras 9–10.

147 *Ford, March 2019*, above note 74 at para 9; *Brown, 2018*, above note 98 at para 228.

reports will not substitute for the reliable evidence needed to make determinations.[148]

The integrity commissioner has the power to hold a public hearing[149] but has never done so as it has not proven necessary to gather the facts, could lead to time-consuming requests for standing and funding for same, is unpredictable in focus and length, and is more suitable to a post-mortem rather than live issues such as the conduct of a member of the House, while a full report is capable of being transparent.[150]

The commissioner's inquiry into a matter referred by a member is halted by either a resignation or an election.[151] If there are reasonable grounds to believe there is a contravention of any other Act or the *Criminal Code*, the commissioner shall refer a matter to the appropriate authority and suspend the inquiry.[152]

After reasonable notice to the member complained against[153] and due inquiry, the commissioner may issue an opinion and a recommendation to the members complaining and complained against, the leaders of the parties, and the speaker (so that the opinion and recommendation may be laid before the Legislative Assembly) that

- the complaint is frivolous, not in good faith, or without sufficient grounds[154]
- a contravention occurred but no penalty is recommended as the member or former member took all reasonable measures to prevent it, or a contravention occurred that was trivial or committed through inadvertence or an error of judgment made in good faith[155]
- a contravention occurred and the recommended consequence is no penalty, a reprimand, suspension (perhaps on condition), or declaring the seat vacant[156]

---

148 *Chiarelli et al*, above note 78 at paras 62–63.

149 *Members' Integrity Act*, above note 14, s 31(2).

150 *Ford, March 2019*, above note 74 at paras 14–17.

151 *Members' Integrity Act*, above note 14, s 31(4.1), but it can be restarted at the request of the member complained against.

152 *Ibid*, s 33.

153 *Ibid*, 31(1).

154 *Ibid*, s 31(5).

155 *Ibid*, s 31(6).

156 *Ibid*, s 34.

Breaches may not lead to the recommendation of a penalty where they are inadvertent and where the post-revelation response was appropriate,[157] including an acknowledgement of error and corrective steps and perhaps an apology.[158]

Breaches of disclosure requirements will lead to a recommended penalty if they are deliberate and not corrected.[159] In *Brown, 2018*, a case of multiple non-disclosures over a long period of time, a reprimand was seen as appropriate rather than suspension or declaring the seat vacant because Parliament was almost at an end and the member was not running again (so a more serious penalty was almost moot), the member was cooperative with the inquiry, had not been the subject of a previous negative finding, and the inquiry had "extracted a political price" on the member.[160]

In *Hillier No 2*, a reprimand was recommended where there were multiple breaches of parliamentary convention mitigated by an apology and stated intention not to seek re-election in a pending election.[161]

The Legislative Assembly has thirty days to consider and respond to the commissioner's report[162] by either accepting or rejecting any recommendation. The legislature's decision is "final and conclusive."[163] However, by virtue of the Act,[164] the Legislative Assembly does not have power to inquire into a matter referred by a member to the commissioner, to inquire further into a contravention after it has been the subject of a report by the commissioner, to impose a penalty if the commissioner recommended that none be imposed, or to impose a penalty other than the one recommended.

157 *Fife*, above note 130 at para 73.

158 Integrity Commissioner, *Re Laurie Scott, Member for Haliburton-Kawartha Lakes-Brock*, 1 October 2013 at paras 15–16; *Bell*, above note 121.

159 *Brown, 2018*, above note 98 at paras 259–62: "When the leader of a political party is substantially indebted to a candidate for election as an MPP for that party, the interests of transparency require that the indebtedness be made known so that people have an appropriate context to assess the relationship between the leader and the candidate."

160 *Ibid* at paras 269–76.

161 *Hillier No 2*, above note 111.

162 *Members' Integrity Act*, above note 14, s 34(2).

163 *Ibid*, s 34(5).

164 *Ibid*, s 34(4).

Declaring a seat vacant for breach of parliamentary convention can only happen after the legislature receives the recommendation of the commissioner and accepts it.[165]

The mechanism of a public report and recommendation from an external entity before a final decision by one's peers is unique in Ontario public service conflict of interest regimes and contrasts with the unpublished reports and decisions by internal ethics executives used in the public service.[166] That seems inevitable due to legislative privilege.

The commissioner's duties in respect of MPPs are not reviewable by the courts.[167] It is notable that the Act does limit what the legislature can do in response to a commissioner's report. It seems an open question whether any violation of those limitations, as unlikely as it may be, would also be privileged from judicial review.

The Cabinet may also ask for an opinion on whether a Cabinet member has contravened the Act or an "Ontario parliamentary convention,"[168] and then the commissioner reports their opinion to Cabinet.[169] This process is halted if the Cabinet member resigns from Cabinet.[170] At no point in this Cabinet-initiated process is the Legislative Assembly prevented from addressing the matter.[171]

D. THE LEGISLATIVE ASSEMBLY AND ITS OFFICES

1) Employment in the Office of the Assembly

Many Legislative Assembly employees were public servants from the commencement of the *Public Service Act*.[172] It was only in 1974 that amendments to the *Legislative Assembly Act* transferred employment

---

165 *Ibid*, ss 30 and 34, discussed in *Hillier No 2*, above note 111 at para 35.

166 See the *PSOA* conflict of interest process discussed in Chapter 3.

167 *Tafler v British Columbia* (1998), 161 DLR (4th) 511 (BCCA) at 17; *Canada (Board of Internal Economy) v Boulerice*, 2019 FCA 33; *Kirby v Chaulk*, 2021 NLSC 86.

168 *Members' Integrity Act*, above note 14, s 30(5).

169 *Ibid*, s 31(4).

170 *Ibid*, s 31(4.6).

171 *Ibid*, s 30(6).

172 The 1878 *PSA*, s 41 stated that it would apply to the permanent staff of the legislative assembly, "saving always all legal rights and privileges of the House as respects the appointment or removal of its officers and servants or any of them." Such an explicit provision existed until the *PSA, 1947*, SO 1947, c 89.

authority to the Office of the Legislative Assembly.[173] Those amendments have been found to show a clear intention by the legislature to be an employer separate from the executive branch.[174]

Under the *Legislative Assembly Act*, the "Office of the Assembly" is made up of "the Speaker, the Deputy Speaker, the Clerk of the Legislative Assembly, the Sergeant-at-Arms," and other employees.[175] The speaker—by election—and deputy speaker are, of course, appointed by and from among their fellow members of the assembly.[176] While the *Members' Integrity Act* applies to the conduct of the Speaker as member, it does not apply to the Speaker as Speaker.[177] The Speaker is only answerable to the Legislative Assembly. A reason is that if a complaint is made by a member under the *Members' Integrity Act*, then the House cannot consider the matter and to have that apply to a complaint about the conduct of the Speaker would be damaging to maintaining the confidence of the House in the Speaker.

Similar to legislative officers, as discussed below, the legislature appoints the clerk following selection by an all-party committee on which the speaker sits as a non-voting member.[178] The clerk may be

173 The *Legislative Assembly Act, 1974 (No 2)*, SO 1974, c 116, s 91, as amended 20 December 1974, provided that legislative staff would cease to be employed in the public service. The circumstances of the transfer are discussed in a decision of the Ontario Public Service Labour Relations Tribunal (OPSLRT) dismissing a subsequent attempt by the Ontario Public Service Employees Union (OPSEU) to obtain certification under the *Crown Employees Collective Bargaining Act*: *OPSEU and Ministry of Government Services*, OPSLRT#T/0002/75, 1 March 1976.

174 *Craib and Management Board Secretariat*, OPSLRT#T/0054/93, 12 January 1994 (Mole) at 3–4 [*Craib*].

175 *Legislative Assembly Act*, above note 13, s 76.

176 *Ibid*, s 28.

177 See Integrity Commissioner, *Re Michael A. Brown, with Respect to Whether as Speaker He Breached Parliamentary Convention Contrary to the Act by Attending a Post-Election Dinner for Liberal Caucus Members and Their Spouses*, 14 February 2008.

178 *Legislative Assembly Act*, above note 13, ss 77 and 77.1. The appointment of the clerk by the Legislative Assembly, rather than the Lieutenant Governor in Council, was introduced at the same time as similar changes were introduced for Officers of the Assembly: *Restoring Trust, Transparency and Accountability Act, 2018*, c 17, Sch 23. For an interjurisdictional comparative discussion featuring the prior Ontario regime, see Deborah Deller, "Selection and Appointment of Clerks in Canadian Jurisdictions" (2018) 41:3 *Canadian Parliamentary Review* 2. The tenure of legislative officers is discussed below.

removed by two-thirds vote of the legislature. There is power to suspend the clerk for a maximum of twenty sessional days into the next sitting.[179]

All other employees of the Office of the Assembly are appointed by the Speaker "as may be required for the proper conduct of the business of the Office of the Assembly," and the Speaker can discipline and dismiss employees, other than the clerk.[180]

There is special treatment of those members of the branch of the Office of the Assembly that is the Legislative Protective Service, charged with the security of the legislative precinct.[181] The sergeant-at-arms and other selected employees are "peace officers" while on active duty, can be authorized to have and use firearms, and are subject to some police oversight processes.[182]

The Board of Internal Economy (BIE), an all-party committee of members of the legislature,[183] approves the organization and staff establishment of the Office of the Assembly.[184] Subject to the BIE's approval, the Speaker manages the Office of the Assembly staff and sets their terms and conditions of employment, including job classifications, salary ranges, vacation, and benefits.[185] The Speaker may delegate any employment powers, including the power of appointment, to the deputy speaker, or any employee of the Office of the Assembly.[186]

Benefits for permanent and full-time Legislative Assembly employees are to be the same as public servants (unless the Speaker puts a

---

179 The twenty-day maximum for suspension is similar to the limit of suspension of regular employees under *PSOA*, as discussed in Chapter 2.

180 *Legislative Assembly Act*, above note 13, s 76. Included in the staff of the Office of the Assembly are employees of the integrity commissioner: *Members' Integrity Act*, above note 14, s 23(10).

181 *Legislative Assembly Act*, above note 13, s 102.2.

182 They are subject to Special Investigations Unit investigations per the *Special Investigations Unit Act, 2019*, SO 2019, c 1, s 1(1), and the public complaints provisions in the unproclaimed *Community Safety and Policing Act, 2019*, SO 2019, c 1, Sch 1.

183 *Legislative Assembly Act*, above note 13, s 87. The proceedings of the Board of Internal Economy are deemed to be proceedings of Parliament for purposes of privilege: s 88.1.

184 *Ibid*, s 90.

185 *Ibid*, s 92; *Soth v Ontario (Speaker of the Legislative Assembly)*, 1997 CanLII 16228 (ON SC) [*Soth*].

186 *Ibid*, s 107. This is similar to the delegation power of deputy ministers discussed in Chapter 2.

different plan into place).[187] Full-time employees are covered under the Public Service Pension Plan,[188] and the Speaker is an employer for purposes of the *Workplace Safety and Insurance Act*.[189] Other employment policies have been noted to be virtually identical to the OPS.[190]

Every employee of the Office of the Assembly takes an oath of office and an oath of allegiance to the reigning sovereign.[191] The oaths of office and allegiance are the same as that of MPPs, but there are now also exemptions from taking the oath of allegiance[192] if an employee is a citizen of another country and asserts that making the oath could result in loss of that citizenship, or if an employee identifies as Indigenous and asserts that "making the oath or affirmation would be inconsistent with his or her views regarding the relationship between the Crown and Indigenous peoples." In addition, the oath of office has been altered so that, instead of the employee swearing or affirming that they "will observe and comply with the laws of Canada and Ontario,"[193] they now swear or affirm that "I will respect the laws of Canada and Ontario, including the recognition and affirmation of the aboriginal and treaty rights of Indigenous peoples in the Constitution."[194]

In one case, where a researcher employed at the Legislative Assembly deliberately misled the employer during her hiring interview about their past affiliation with the NDP, it would have reasonably raised concerns in the employer's mind about their ability to do research in an unbiased and non-partisan manner.[195]

The speaker's authority to discipline and dismiss employees is not subject to any specific statutory qualification. Previously the *Legislative*

---

187 *Ibid*, s 92(2).

188 *Ibid*, s 93.

189 *Ibid*, s 102; *Workplace Safety and Insurance Act, 1997*, SO 1997, c 16, Sch A [*WSIA*].

190 *Wight v Ontario (No 2)*, 1998 CanLII 29885 (ON HRT) at para 271 [*Wight HRT*]. The case was a human rights complaint that proceeded without the possible objection of the Speaker. See the discussion later in this section.

191 *Legislative Assembly Act*, above note 13, s 101.

192 This has been explained as allowing the few employees in this category to be able to progress in their employment: Ontario Legislative Assembly, *Hansard*, 18 February 2020 at 900 (Paul Calandra, Government House Leader) [*Hansard, Calandra*] during debate on the 2020 *Legislative Assembly Amendment Act*, Bill 167.

193 *Legislative Assembly Act*, above note 13, s 101(1), repealed 2020, c 15, s 15.

194 *Ibid*, s 101(1) & (2).

195 *Wight HRT*, above note 190 at para 309.

Assembly Act provided for prior notice and binding arbitration concerning discipline of employees for misconduct.[196] It is notable that binding arbitration in front of the Public Service Grievance Board (PSGB) is available to some employees of the Offices of the Assembly, as discussed below, but now not to employees of the legislature. The removal of those provisions[197] for employees of the legislature has been explained as bringing in a "modern relations code."[198] The content of this "code" is unclear, as it is not certain what statutory employment provisions are part of it, how much of this regime is subject to the jurisdiction of tribunals or the courts, and how much is subject to legislative privilege.[199]

Turning to the public service employment statutes, the *Crown Employees Collective Bargaining Act* (*CECBA*) and the *PSOA* only apply to the government and specifically listed types of employees and so do not generally apply to the Legislative Assembly and its employees.[200]

---

196 *Legislative Assembly Act*, above note 13, ss 95–99, repealed 2020, c 15, s 14.

197 Under the former provisions, the employee alleged to have engaged in misconduct was entitled to "written notice of the proposed action" and had the right to a hearing before a tripartite board composed of a chair (appointed by the Speaker, who was to seek and consider the views of the chair of the PSGB), one member representing the Office of the Assembly, and one member representing the employee who required the hearing. The tripartite board determined whether or not the employee was "guilty" and, if guilty, recommended the penalty to be imposed. The Speaker had to carry out the recommendation. From 1974 until 1983, employees of the Office of the Legislative Assembly could grieve against dismissals or suspensions to the PSGB itself, which heard several such cases: *King and Hansard Reporting Service*, PSGB#901/80, 6 August 1980 (Pringle); *Madisso and the Office of the Legislative Assembly*, PSGB#918/83, 24 June 1983 (Simmons); *Chortyk and the Office of the Legislative Assembly*, GSB#913/82, 23 August 1982 (Simmons). The right to a PSGB hearing was introduced by the *Legislative Assembly Amendment Act, 1974 (No 2)*, s 89(1)–(4) and removed by SO 1983, c 50, s 91.

198 *Hansard, Calandra*, above note 192, during debate on the *Legislative Assembly Amendment Act, 2020*, c 15, Bill 167, with the debate showing all-party consent.

199 As an example of inconclusive litigation see *Thompson v McLean*, [1998] OJ No 2070 (Gen Div) at paras 51–56 [*Thompson*], refusing to strike the claim of a dismissed employee on the grounds that the extent of the privilege was not clear, in which earlier cases are reviewed.

200 See the discussions of the applicability of the *Crown Employees Collective Bargaining Act, 1993*, SO 1993, c 38 [*CECBA*] in Chapter 7, and the *PSOA* in Chapter 2. See also *Craib*, above note 174 at 3–4 dealing with the former *PSA* but not distinguishable on that basis.

It is worth noting that the federal *Parliamentary Employment and Staff Relations Act*[201] establishes a collective bargaining regime, administered by the Public Service Staff Relations Board, which includes interest arbitration; a right to grieve breaches of the collective agreement, termination (excluding that of probationers), suspensions, financial penalties, and demotion; and job competitions and classification. Federal Parliament employees are also given employment standards and occupational health and safety rights. The federal view was that a collective bargaining regime, specially fitted to the needs of parliamentary institutions, was required for the process of building constructive labour–management relations.[202] An example of the operation of this regime is that during a grievance hearing contesting the termination of a Senate employee, the adjudicator upheld parliamentary privilege over the internal discussion of the Senate's Internal Economy Committee.[203]

The application of the general Ontario labour relations statutory framework to the Ontario Legislative Assembly is not resolved. Given its independence from the Crown as employer, it is unlikely that the Legislative Assembly is exempt by virtue of the Crown not being bound under the *Labour Relations Act* (*LRA*).[204] In *MGEA v Manitoba (Legislative Assembly Management Commission)*,[205] the court found that a legislative assembly act, fairly similar to the *Legislative Assembly Act* in establishing employment separate from the public service, also had the effect of ensuring that the legislative employer was not the Crown for purposes of that province's *LRA*. Another issue is whether the Legislative Assembly is within the general definition of an employer set out in the *LRA*.[206] It is notable that the Ontario *LRA* does not require, by statutory definition, that an employer be any particular form of entity. Rather, the statutory focus is on whether the union has applied for a bargaining unit that is determined to be appropriate for collective

201 RSC 1985, c 33 (2nd Supp) discussed in *Vaid*, above note 16.

202 Ray Hnatyshyn, House of Commons, *Minutes of Proceedings and Evidence of the Legislative Committee* on Bill C-45, 13 May 1986 at 1:50, and see 1:74 and 1:75.

203 *Routliffe v Senate of Canada*, 2009 PSLRB 5.

204 *Labour Relations Act, 1995*, SO 1995, c 1, Sch A, s 4(1) [*LRA*].

205 [1990] MJ No 72 (QB) [*MGEA*].

206 This was an issue in other jurisdictions: *Re House of Commons and Canada (Labour Relations Board)* (1986), 27 DLR (4th) 481 (FCA); *MGEA*, above note 205.

bargaining.[207] Therefore, a central consideration in Ontario would be whether a unit composed of certain types of employees working for the legislature would be appropriate, given the scope of legislative privilege.

Would the existence of legislative privilege by itself result in the dismissal of an application for certification of some or all Legislative Assembly staff under the *LRA?* The common law legislative privilege to establish and regulate the legislature's internal affairs without any interference from the other two branches of the government, the executive and the judiciary, covers those categories of matters which are "necessary to the functioning" to the Legislative Assembly's constitutional role.[208] The application of this "standard of necessity" to employment matters at the Legislative Assembly has not been resolved in Ontario. The Supreme Court case of *Vaid* endorses a joint report of the British House of Lords and the House of Commons on parliamentary privilege, which itself stated, in relation to privilege for the "internal affairs" of a legislature, that

> "[i]nternal affairs" and equivalent phrases are loose and potentially extremely wide in their scope. On one interpretation they embrace, at one edge of the spectrum, the arrangement of parliamentary business and also, at the other extreme, the provision of basic supplies and services such as stationery and cleaning. This latter extreme would be going too far if it were to mean, for example, that a dispute over the supply of photocopy paper or dismissal of a cleaner could not be decided by a court or industrial tribunal in the ordinary way. Here, as elsewhere, the purpose of parliamentary privilege is to ensure that Parliament can discharge its functions as a legislative and deliberative assembly without let or hindrance. This heading of privilege best serves Parliament if not carried to extreme lengths.[209]

In other words, the Supreme Court views "all aspects of management of all employees" as an overly broad category of legislative privilege. In *Chagnon v Syndicat de la fonction publique et parapublique du Québec*, the Supreme Court has also rejected "all aspects of the management of

207 *LRA*, above note 204, s 7.
208 *Vaid*, above note 16 at para 29.
209 House of Lords and the House of Commons *Report on Parliamentary Privilege*, 30 March 1999, Chapter 5: "Control by Parliament over Its Affairs" at para 241, quoted in *Vaid*, above note 16 at para 72.

security guards" as an appropriate scope of privileged activity.[210] When considering if unionized security guards at the Quebec National Assembly should be able to have their dismissals arbitrated, the Supreme Court held that there may need to be privilege over certain functions exercised by that, or any other group, but the enforcement of "basic employment and labour protections" would not undermine the independence truly needed by the National Assembly.[211]

The question then is whether a given bargaining unit exercising the full range of union rights under the *LRA* would undermine the legislature's independence. The British Columbia Labour Relations Board has found that the Legislative Assembly Protective Services Association could unionize without impeding the BC legislature from carrying out its constitutional functions,[212] centrally because the BC legislation contains provisions allowing the setting of essential service levels in a manner that "ensures that the public interest is protected during labour disputes."[213] The *LRA* contains no such generally applicable essential services provisions. There are essential services provisions under the *CECBA*[214] but that statute does not apply to the Legislative Assembly. The question then becomes whether the exercise of all or some bargaining unit rights by any proposed bargaining unit would impede the core functions of the legislature, and, if so, whether some lesser set of rights would be acceptable and/or whether it would be within the jurisdiction of the OLRB to balance interests by giving effect to the *Charter* right of freedom of association.

For non-unionized employees, the question is what recourse would be available from the courts. The *Vaid* type of approach was applied in the one Ontario case that has discussed the application of legislative privilege to general employment matters, *Thompson v McLean*,[215] which dealt with an employee's claim for damages arising out of alleged sexual harassment by the Speaker of the Legislative Assembly. The court was asked to strike out the claim on the basis that employment

210 2018 SCC 39.

211 *Ibid* at paras 44–45.

212 *Illi v Legislative Assembly of British Columbia*, 2021 BCLRB 176.

213 *Labour Relations Code*, RSBC 1996, c 244, s 2(g) and Part 6—Essential Services.

214 See Chapter 8.

215 *Thompson*, above note 199 at para 39. The other court case dealing with employment at the Legislative Assembly is *Soth*, above note 185, which focuses on the wording of the *Legislative Assembly Act* and not on legislative privilege.

of staff was a matter of legislative privilege, but refused to do so, on the following grounds:

> As a practical matter the speaker is the chief administrative officer of a large branch of the public service with many employees, some of whom perform no political or legislative or parliamentary duties. It is not consistent with modern ideas of employment to say that they are all automatically stripped of the normal protection enjoyed by employees, including access to the courts, without examining the claim of parliamentary privilege carefully in those cases where it may not clearly apply.

In relation to the *Human Rights Code*,[216] it is notable that a human rights complaint concerning certain employment practices in the Office of the Assembly has proceeded on the merits without objection from the Speaker.[217] There is no apparent reason why the *Employment Standards Act (ESA)* would not apply.[218]

There is no judicial review remedy enforcing a fairness requirement. In *Soth*, a judicial review of the Speaker's dismissal of an employee,[219] the Ontario Divisional Court found that the Speaker's statutory right to set the terms and conditions of employment included the right to enter into contracts of employment, which in turn included the right to establish the standard common law implied term of employer entitlement to terminate the employment of the applicant upon notice or upon payment of compensation in lieu of notice. Employees in the legislature were found to be simply employees and not office holders, and so there was no free-standing common law duty to act fairly.[220]

2) Employment in the Offices of the Legislative Assembly

The following Offices of the Legislative Assembly serve the members of the legislature and the public:

---

216 RSO 1990, c H.19.

217 Jurisdiction under the *Human Rights Code* was not made an issue in *Wight v Office of the Legislative Assembly*, [1998] OHRBID 385.

218 *Employment Standards Act, 2000*, SO 2000, c 41 [*ESA*].

219 *Soth*, above note 185.

220 For more discussion of the history of the common law duty to act fairly in employment matters, see Chapter 13.

- Auditor General (including, as an employee and not an officer, the commissioner of the environment)
- Chief Electoral Officer
- Financial Accountability Officer
- Information and Privacy Commissioner
- Integrity Commissioner
- Ombudsman (including, as an employee and not an officer, the French language services commissioner)

Each office "requires a high degree of public trust for its work to be both accepted and effective. Accordingly, it operates by design and by statute as a body independent from the provincial government and its administration."[221]

a) Employment of the Officers

The *Restoring Trust, Transparency and Accountability Act, 2018*[222] ended the appointment of officers as order-in-council appointments and made them all direct appointees of the legislature with a standard process:

- unless decided otherwise by a unanimous vote of the legislature, the person to be appointed is selected by unanimous agreement of a panel composed of one member of the legislature from each recognized party, chaired by the Speaker who is a non-voting member[223]

---

221 *Stencell and Office of the Provincial Auditor*, PSGB#0043/95, 19 August 1996, at 3–4, and 25 March 1997 (Lynk) [*Stencell*]. For one of many papers on the officers of the assembly, see Jocelyn McCauley, *Officers of the Assembly and the Ontario Legislature: Reconsidering the Relationship*, Master's Research Paper, York University, July 2020, online: yorkspace.library.yorku.ca/xmlui/bitstream/handle/10315/37805/Jocelyn%20McCauley%20-MRP.pdf.

222 SO 2018, c 17.

223 *Auditor General Act*, RSO 1990, c A.35, s 2 [*Auditor General Act*], under which the chair of the standing Public Accounts Committee must be consulted; *Election Act*, above note 22, s 3.1; *Financial Accountability Officer Act, 2013*, SO 2013, c 4, s 2 [*Financial Accountability Officer Act*]; *FIPPA*, above note 44, s 4; *Members' Integrity Act*, above note 14, s 23; *Ombudsman Act*, RSO 1990, c O.6, s 2 [*Ombudsman Act*]. The acts also deal with temporary officers in the event that the officer is unable to fulfill the duties.

- the Legislative Assembly by two-thirds vote may remove or suspend the officer for cause, with any suspension not continuing past the twentieth sessional day of the next sitting of the legislature[224]

This process was supported by all parties on the basis that the appointment process entrenched the long-standing practice of a unanimous all-party panel of members selecting the officers.[225] The suspension and removal power was introduced in the bill as only requiring a majority vote. This resulted in a point of legislative privilege being raised and then rejected by the Speaker on the basis that "Ultimately, it's for the House to decide if the proposed measures need to be amended in order to guarantee the independence of its parliamentary officers."[226] The majority vote provision permitting a majority government to "fire" an officer was described as "dangerous because it takes away from the independence of the officer. If they think they may get fired, they may not do the type of work that they should be doing, holding whatever department they've got to account,"[227] and all parties supported amendments to require a two-thirds vote for suspension or removal.[228]

The auditor general holds office for a non-renewable ten-year term,[229] while the chief electoral officer's term of office is not fixed in statute. The four remaining officers of the assembly are appointed for five-year terms, with the option of reappointment for one further term of five years.[230] It has been the practice of the House to hold an open process for selecting the appointees and any re-appointees.[231] In keeping

224 *Auditor General Act*, above note 223, s 5; *Election Act*, above note 22, s 3.3; *Financial Accountability Officer Act*, above note 223, s 4; *FIPPA*, above note 44, s 6; *Members' Integrity Act*, above note 14, s 23.2; *Ombudsman Act*, above note 223, s 3.

225 Ontario Legislative Assembly, *Hansard*, 26 November 2018 at 1440 (Gilles Bisson, NDP).

226 *Ibid* at 1140.

227 *Ibid* at 1440.

228 Ontario Legislative Assembly, Standing Committee on Finance and Economic Affairs, 4 December 2018.

229 *Auditor General Act*, above note 223, ss 4 and 5.7.

230 *Financial Accountability Officer Act*, above note 223, s 3; *FIPPA*, above note 44, s 5; *Members' Integrity Act*, above note 14, s 23.1; *Ombudsman Act*, above note 223, s 3.

231 See the discussion in "Ombudsman Andre Marin, Other Watchdogs Must Reapply When Contracts Expire," *Toronto Star*, 25 February 2015, online: www.thestar.com/news/queenspark/2015/02/25/ombudsman-andr-marin-other-watchdogs-must-reapply-when-contracts-expire.html.

with *Vaid*, discussed above, it is highly likely that a vote of the Legislative Assembly to suspend or remove an officer for cause is an exercise of legislative privilege that is not reviewable by the courts.[232]

The BIE is to determine the salary and benefits of officers, with each officer being a member of the Public Service Pension Plan unless they elect not to be.[233] Each officer shall not be a member of the legislature and shall not, without prior approval by the legislature, hold any other office or employment.[234]

Each officer shall take an oath to "faithfully and impartially exercise the functions of the office."[235] Although all officers will have some implicit or explicit duty or responsibility of confidentiality,[236] the ombudsman's oath uniquely also says they will not disclose any information received as ombudsman except as ought to be disclosed to establish grounds for their conclusions and recommendations. Officers do not appear to take an oath of allegiance to the reigning monarch, presumably because their allegiance is only to the performance of their particular office.

When the Office of the Environmental Commissioner was discontinued in 2018, the functions of that office under the *Environmental*

---

232 See the discussion about *Vaid*, above note 16, and its application in *Newfoundland and Labrador (Child and Youth Advocate) v Newfoundland and Labrador (House of Assembly)*, 2009 NLTD 189, finding a legislative vote, held in accordance with the relevant legislation, to remove an officer is an absolutely privileged act.

233 *Auditor General Act*, above note 223, s 5.1 under which the salary and benefits of the auditor general shall be "within the highest range of salaries paid to deputy ministers in the public service of Ontario, and the Auditor General is entitled to the privileges of office of a senior deputy minister"; *Election Act*, above note 22, s 3.4; *Financial Accountability Officer Act*, above note 223, s 4.1; *FIPPA*, above note 44, s 7; *Members' Integrity Act*, above note 14, s 23.3; *Ombudsman Act*, above note 223.

234 *Auditor General Act*, above note 223, s 5.5; *Election Act*, above note 22, s 3.10; *Financial Accountability Officer Act*, above note 223, s 4.5; *FIPPA*, above note 44, s 7.4; *Members' Integrity Act*, above note 14, s 23.7; *Ombudsman Act*, above note 223, s 7.2.

235 *Auditor General Act*, above note 223, s 5.6; *Election Act*, above note 22, s 3.11; *Financial Accountability Officer Act*, above note 223, s 4.6; *FIPPA*, above note 44, s 7.5; *Members' Integrity Act*, above note 14, s 23.8; *Ombudsman Act*, above note 223, s 7.3.

236 For example, the auditor general and staff under the *Auditor General Act*, above note 223, s 27.1 and the integrity commissioner under *Members' Integrity Act*, above note 14, s 29. The *Ombudsman Act*, above note 223, s 7.3 also has a confidentiality provision, reinforced concerning information about children to whom an investigation may relate.

Bill of Rights were transferred to an employee of the auditor general with no special status but called the commissioner of the environment.[237] When the Office of the French Language Services Commissioner was discontinued at the same time, the functions of that office were transferred to the ombudsman who must appoint an employee as a "deputy ombudsman" to be known as the French language services commissioner, who is required to be "proficient in French."[238] The ombudsman is to ensure there is an annual report to the Speaker known as the *Annual Report of the French Language Services Commissioner*.[239]

b) Employment of Staff

Subject to the approval of the BIE, the auditor general, chief electoral officer, and financial accountability officer are given the power to employ staff, and determine their classifications, salaries, and conditions of employment, with the stated requirement that salaries are to be "comparable" to that for similar positions in the public service.[240] At the Offices of the Information and Privacy Commissioner and Ombudsman, the salaries need not be comparable.[241]

The integrity commissioner can hire staff,[242] but they are part of the Office of the Assembly.[243]

The acts governing these officers provide that the employee benefits for non-unionized public servants under the *PSOA* Part III will apply to employees of the officers.[244] Most staff are in the Public Service Pension

237 *Environmental Bill of Rights, 1993*, SO 1993, c 28, s 50 [*EBR*]. The staff of the environmental commissioner who joined the employment of the auditor general were deemed not to be terminated by the transfer: *EBR*, s 52.

238 *Ombudsman Act*, above note 223, s 12.9. The staff of the French language services commissioner who joined the employment of the ombudsman were deemed not to be terminated by the transfer: *Ombudsman Act*, s 12.7.

239 *Ibid*, s 12.5.

240 *Auditor General Act*, above note 223, s 20; *Election Act*, above note 22, s 114(1); *Financial Accountability Officer Act*, above note 223, s 8.

241 *FIPPA*, above note 44, s 8(1); *Ombudsman Act*, above note 223, s 8(1).

242 *PSOA*, above note 1, s 15.

243 *Members' Integrity Act*, above note 14, s 23.11.

244 *Auditor General Act*, above note 223, s 22(1); *Election Act*, above note 22, s 116(1); *Financial Accountability Officer Act*, above note 223, s 8(3); *FIPPA*, above note 44, s 8(2); *Ombudsman Act*, above note 223, s 8(2).

Plan (PSPP) due either to an explicit statutory provision to that effect,[245] or due to the application of *PSOA* Part III benefits.[246]

Since the employees of these offices are not expressly appointed to be Crown employees, and indeed are intended to be independent from the Crown, the *CECBA* does not apply. The *PSOA* is also generally inapplicable for the same reason, save those certain specific provisions deemed applicable as set out in this section. The partial or complete exemption for the Crown that appears in any other applicable employment legislation would appear not to apply to these offices for the same reason that it does not apply to the Legislative Assembly itself, namely that these offices are not part of the Crown.

There is no apparent extension of common law "legislative privilege" to the internal functioning of these offices, with the exception of the Office of the Integrity Commissioner by virtue of the inclusion of its staff in the Office of the Assembly. The other offices serve the Legislative Assembly, but are not part of it, and so there does not seem to be any basis for privilege from other employment legislation for these offices when engaged in employing staff. For example, the employees of the Office of the Ombudsman were found to be a bargaining unit of employees appropriate for collective bargaining under the *LRA*.[247]

i) *Staff Rights in the Event of Discipline*

The legislation concerning the financial accountability officer, information and privacy commissioner, and ombudsman contain no special provision for the employer's right to discipline or an employee's right to grieve.

The auditor general and chief electoral officer, "after a hearing," may discipline, including suspension or dismissal, any employee, with the terms of any suspensions to comply with those under *PSOA* for public servants,[248] and the auditor general is explicitly authorized to

---

245 *Election Act*, above note 22, s 116(2) & (3); *Financial Accountability Officer Act*, above note 223, s 8(5); *FIPPA*, above note 44, s 8(3); *Ombudsman Act*, above note 223, s 8(3).

246 See *Office of the Auditor General of Ontario Operations Report*, November 2022 at 26.

247 *Office and Professional Employees International Union, Applicant v Ombudsman Ontario, Responding Party*, [1993] OLRB Rep February 147.

248 *Auditor General Act*, above note 223, s 26; *Election Act*, above note 22, s 117. For discussion of suspensions under the *PSOA*, see Chapter 2.

dismiss an employee for other than cause. An employee has the right to appeal discipline to the PSGB, which makes a binding decision.

ii) Oaths, Confidentiality, and Political Activity

The legislation concerning the financial accountability officer, information and privacy commissioner, and ombudsman contains no particular treatment of staff oaths, confidentiality, or political activity.

The *Auditor General Act* and *Election Act* require that every employee of the relevant offices, before assuming employment, take oaths of office and secrecy and, absent an exemption, of allegiance that are very similar in form to the *PSOA* oaths with the addition that the *Auditor General* and *Election Acts* specifically state that

> [t]he failure of an employee ... to take and to subscribe or to adhere to either of the oaths ... may be considered as cause for dismissal.[249]

Furthermore, under the *Auditor General Act*, every employee of that office is to preserve as confidential those matters that come to their attention in the course of their employment duties and "shall not communicate any such matters to any person, except as may be required in connection with the administration of this *Act* or any proceedings under this *Act* or under the *Criminal Code (Canada)*."[250] These provisions have been found to impose a particularly binding obligation of confidentiality. Where an employee of the provincial auditor wrote a letter to the premier in breach of these requirements, and was discharged for doing so, the PSGB did not reinstate him.[251] Instead, the seven-year employee was given two months' salary and a letter of reference. His claimed defence of "whistleblowing," or exposing government wrongdoing, was not accepted.

The political activity rights of the auditor general's staff are circumscribed closely by the *Auditor General Act*. In contrast to the *PSOA*, the limitations do not vary depending on the nature of individual employment. Employees of the auditor general are not to be candidates in provincial, federal, or municipal elections, or fundraise or associate their position with any political activity[252] and any contravention "may

249 *Auditor General Act*, above note 223, s 21(4); *Election Act*, above note 22, s 115.

250 *Auditor General Act*, above note 223, s 27.1(2).

251 *Stencell*, above note 221.

252 *Auditor General Act*, above note 223, s 25(1).

be considered as cause for dismissal."[253] It appears they are only free to make personal donations or work in the campaigns of others.

E. PROVINCIAL COURT JUDGES AND JUSTICES OF THE PEACE

1) Introduction

The role of the provincial judiciary is shaped by the terms of the Constitution, and constitutional conventions. (This contrasts with other provincial office holders, whose relationship with the state remains largely contractual.[254]) Judicial independence is required by the entitlement of every person charged with an offence to a "hearing by an independent and impartial tribunal" under section 11(d) of the *Charter* and by an unwritten constitutional norm of judicial independence, recognized and affirmed by the reference in the *Constitution Act, 1867* preamble to "a Constitution similar in Principle to that of the United Kingdom." "Superior courts, by virtue of their role as courts of inherent jurisdiction, are constitutionally required to possess objective guarantees of both individual and institutional independence."[255] The status of federally appointed Superior Court judges is expressly addressed in sections 96 and following of the *Constitution Act, 1867* and is not dealt with in this volume.[256] It is now established that the constitutional imperatives apply to the provincial courts.[257] Ontario justices of the peace, who perform judicial functions, are also guaranteed similar independence to

253 *Ibid*, s 25(2).

254 *Wells v Newfoundland*, [1999] 3 SCR 199 at paras 30–31 [*Wells*].

255 *Reference re Remuneration of Judges of the Provincial Court of Prince Edward Island, Reference re Independence and Impartiality of Judges of the Provincial Court of Prince Edward Island*, [1997] 3 SCR 3 [*PEI Reference*]; *Ocean Port Hotel Ltd v British Columbia (General Manager, Liquor Control and Licensing Branch)*, 2001 SCC 52 at para 23 [*Ocean Port*].

256 *Constitution Act, 1867*, above note 2, ss 96–100.

257 *Valente v The Queen*, [1985] 2 SCR 673 [*Valente*]; *PEI Reference*, above note 255; *Moreau-Bérubé v New Brunswick (Judicial Council)*, 2002 SCC 11; *Provincial Court Judges' Association of New Brunswick v New Brunswick (Minister of Justice), Ontario Judges' Association v Ontario (Management Board); Conférence des juges du Québec v Quebec (Attorney General), Minc v Quebec (Attorney General)*, 2005 SCC 44 [*New Brunswick Provincial Court Judges*].

judges.[258] There are other judicial offices in Ontario—associate judges (formerly case management masters) and deputy judges—which are not discussed in detail below. The requirements of judicial independence do vary between the different offices.

The importance of judicial independence has been reiterated by the Judicial Council of Canada. Judges need to be

> free from fear or favour, and independent of any and all forms of coercion, threat, or harassment direct or indirect whether from government, politicians, persons in authority, relatives, neighbours, interested parties, fellow judges, chief justices, judicial bodies or organizations or any other source of improper influence whatsoever. By insisting upon such barriers, both in perception and in fact, we seek to protect the judge, as the decision maker, from any improper influence. Why? So that the decision will be based and only based upon the law as it applies to the evidence presented and properly admitted so as to do justice between the parties.[259]

At the same time, judges intend to hold themselves to high ethical standards,[260] including avoidance of conflict of interest, where their impartiality may be questioned, and avoidance of conduct that may undermine public confidence in their impartiality, with the goal of "virtually irreproachable conduct" that shows respect for the rule of law in public and private life.[261]

For Ontario provincial court judges, standards of conduct are established by the chief justice of the Ontario Court of Justice,[262] along with a plan for continuing education with the goals of maintaining and developing professional competence and "social awareness" and

---

258 *Ontario Federation of Justices of the Peace Associations et al v Ontario (Attorney General)* (1999), 43 OR (3d) 541 (Div Ct) [*Ontario Federation*].

259 Canadian Judicial Council, *Why is Judicial Independence Important to You?* 2016 CanLIIDocs 4688 at 5.

260 Canadian Judicial Council, *Ethical Principles for Judges (2021)*, 2021 CanLIIDocs 2336 [*CJC, Ethical Principles*].

261 *Ibid* at 21, quoting from *Therrien (Re)*, 2001 SCC 35 at para 111 [*Therrien*].

262 *Courts of Justice Act*, RSO 1990, c C.43, ss 51.9–51.11 [*Courts of Justice Act*]. See *Principles of Judicial Office for Judges*, online: www.ontariocourts.ca/ocj/ocj/principles-of-judicial-office. *CJC, Ethical Principles*, above note 260, also form part of the ethical standards for provincial court judges; see Judicial Conduct, online: www.ontariocourts.ca/ocj/conduct.

"encouraging personal growth." The chief justice may establish a program of confidential performance evaluation that shall not consider any decision made in a particular case. For justices of the peace, the associate chief justice coordinator may set standards of conduct and establish a plan for continuing education.[263]

Ontario judges and justices of the peace take an oath of office to "faithfully, impartially and to the best of my skill and knowledge" carry out their duties,[264] and appropriately do not take an oath of allegiance to the reigning monarch.

In *Valente*,[265] the Supreme Court set out the essential elements of judicial independence applicable to provincial judges. The first requirement is security of tenure in that a judge can only be removed for cause related to the capacity to perform the judicial function. The second requirement is financial security, elaborated upon by the Supreme Court in *PEI Reference*[266] and *New Brunswick Provincial Court Judges*,[267] which has been found to mean that the determination of judicial compensation levels must comply with a minimum standard of adequacy and is only to be made after the Crown receives and considers the recommendations of an independent commission. Third, courts are to be accorded institutional independence with respect to administrative matters directly related to the judicial function,[268] although the Supreme Court clarified that this does not normally permit judges to "enter the field of political matters such as the allocation of public funds."[269]

This section will now deal with the implementation of the judicial independence requirements for Ontario judges and justices of the peace in the following order: non-employment status, recruitment, security of tenure, remuneration, and administrative independence.

---

263 *Justices of the Peace Act*, RSO 1990, c J.4, ss 13 & 14 [*Justices of the Peace Act*]. See *Principles of Judicial Office for Justices of the Peace*, online: www.ontariocourts.ca/ocj/ocj/principles-of-judicial-office.

264 *Courts of Justice Act*, above note 262, s 80; *Justices of the Peace Act*, above note 263, s 3.

265 *Valente*, above note 257.

266 *PEI Reference*, above note 255.

267 *New Brunswick Provincial Court Judges*, above note 257.

268 *Valente*, above note 257. See *PEI Reference*, above note 255 at para 251.

269 *Ontario v Criminal Lawyers' Association of Ontario*, 2013 SCC 43 at para 41 [*Ontario*].

2) Non-employment Status of Ontario Judges

While provincially appointed judges and justices of the peace are appointed by order in council and paid from public monies, they cannot be employees of the executive branch of government[270] and they are not public servants.[271] Judicial administrative independence, which requires that judicial officers be "completely separate in authority and function"[272] from the executive, is probably not consistent with any form of employee status.

Judges and justices of the peace are not covered by the *ESA*, which explicitly excludes "judicial officers."[273] That exclusion has been found to apply to justices of the peace, even though most of the common tests of employment status indicated that a justice of the peace (JP) ought to be considered to be an employee.[274] The *LRA* explicitly excludes "a provincial judge"[275] and does not reference justices of the peace.

The *Workplace Safety and Insurance Act* requires employment for coverage,[276] and judicial administrative independence is probably not consistent with employee status even for this purpose. On the other hand, the *Occupational Health and Safety Act*[277] applies to "workers," and there is no apparent reason to exclude judges from coverage.

Somewhat at odds with non-employment status is the decision of the information and privacy commissioner that certain records dealing with deputy judges are covered by the *Freedom of Information and Protection of Privacy Act (FIPPA)* "labour relations and employment" exclusion due to their collective action through the Ontario Deputy Judges Association to negotiate with the government.[278] The

---

270 *R v Solloway* (1930), 65 OLR 303 (CA) at 307.

271 *PEI Reference*, above note 255 at para 143: The constitutional requirements of judicial independence "provide a range of protections to members of the judiciary to which civil servants are not constitutionally entitled . . . Civil servants are part of the executive; judges, by definition, are not part of the executive."

272 *The Queen v Beauregard*, [1986] 2 SCR 56 at para 30 [*Beauregard*].

273 *ESA*, above note 218, s 3(5)7.

274 *Re Devine*, [1996] OESAD No 41 (Muir).

275 *LRA*, above note 204, s 3(i).

276 *WSIA*, above note 189, s 11(1).

277 RSO 1990, c O.1, s 1(1), definition of "worker."

278 *FIPPA*, above note 44, ss 65(6) & (7), as discussed in *Order PO-2501, Ontario (Attorney General) (Re)*, 2006 CanLII 50844 (ON IPC). The independence of deputy judges is adequately guaranteed by an independent remuneration commission: *Ontario Deputy Judges Association v Ontario*, 2005 CanLII 42263

information and privacy commissioner explained that the exclusion of these records from being produced does not in any way reduce the deputy judges' unquestioned judicial independence.

3) Jurisdiction and Responsibilities of Provincial Court Judges and Justices of the Peace

Provincial court judges deal with a range of family, child, criminal law, and provincial offence matters.[279] They may hear *Provincial Offences Act (POA)* trials (although virtually all of those trials are conducted by justices of the peace), and they do hear all provincial offence appeals from decisions of justices of the peace.

There are also associate judges who deal with certain procedural matters in civil cases and have other specific jurisdiction for matters such as construction liens. There are specific provisions in the *Courts of Justice Act*[280] addressing the terms of independence of associate judges, which are a simplified version of those applicable to provincial court judges. Appointments are by the Lieutenant Governor in Council on recommendation of the attorney general. Complaints are resolved by the chief justice unless a hearing is warranted, in which case a three-person panel holds the hearing and recommends a disposition to the chief justice. The chief justice's decision may be appealed to the Court of Appeal.

The modern office of the justice of the peace was created by reforms culminating with the passage of the *POA* in 1979. Justices of the peace hear provincial offence trials and bail applications; issue criminal processes, such as search warrants, informations, and summonses; and perform many other judicial and administrative functions.[281] The office

---

(ON SC), aff'd *Ontario Deputy Judges Association v Ontario (Attorney General)*, 2006 CanLII 17250 (ON CA), as discussed below.

279 *Courts of Justice Act*, above note 262, s 38. The relevant statutes that assign functions to the Ontario Court of Justice include the *Provincial Offences Act*, RSO 1990, c P.33 [*POA*]; *Family Law Act*, RSO 1990, c F.3; *Children's Law Reform Act*, RSO 1990, c C.12; *Child and Family Services Act*, RSO 1990, c C.11; and the *Criminal Code*, RSC 1985, c C-46.

280 *Courts of Justice Act*, above note 262, s 86.1. For litigation that resulted in increasing the similarity of the terms of independence between provincial judges and associate judges, see *Masters' Association of Ontario v Ontario (Attorney General)*, 2010 ONSC 3714.

281 The various statutes cited above in note 279 also assign functions to justices of the peace.

is largely governed by sections 42 to 44 of the *Justices of the Peace Act*. Justices of the peace need not be lawyers, as discussed below.

Small claims courts are typically staffed by deputy judges who are part-time senior lawyers with fixed terms of appointment and without as much procedural security of tenure as provincial court judges, although the power of re-appointment and revocation is exercised by a judicial officer.[282] This has been found to provide sufficient independence for judicial officers who exercise the more limited jurisdiction of the small claims court.[283] Following a twenty-four-year remuneration freeze, deputy judges were subject to a court-ordered remuneration commission process[284] that was a modification of the version for provincial court judges and justices of the peace, discussed below, and which gave rise to the current regulation setting out their per diem pay rate.[285]

4) Recruitment

a) Provincial Court Judges

Pursuant to the *Courts of Justice Act*,[286] provincial court appointees must have practised law for at least ten years. The Judicial Appointments Advisory Committee makes recommendations to the attorney general for the appointment of provincial court judges. The committee is composed of two provincial court judges, three lawyers, seven laypersons appointed by the attorney general, and a member of the Judicial Council. The committee advertises a judicial vacancy and reviews the candidates according to set criteria that assess merit and recognize "the desirability of reflecting the diversity of Ontario society."[287]

---

282 Following a full hearing, and if there are grounds for a sanction, the regional senior judge may discipline or dismiss a deputy judge: *Courts of Justice Act*, above note 262, s 33.1.

283 *Ontario Deputy Judges Association v The Attorney General of Ontario*, 2011 ONSC 6956, aff'd *Ontario Deputy Judges' Association v Ontario (Attorney General)*, 2012 ONCA 437.

284 *Ontario Deputy Judges Association v Ontario (Attorney General)*, above note 278, finding that the prior process of remuneration being entirely set by Cabinet through an order in council was "purely political" as evidenced by the government's refusal to provide any rationale for the lengthy remuneration freeze.

285 *Courts of Justice Act*, above note 262; O Reg 161/08.

286 *Courts of Justice Act*, above note 262, ss 42–43.

287 *Ibid*, s 43.1.

The committee is to provide the attorney general with a ranked list of at least six candidates whom it recommends, with brief supporting reasons. The attorney general may only recommend a candidate on the ranked list for appointment by the Lieutenant Governor in Council to fill a judicial vacancy. The attorney general may reject the committee's recommendations and require it to provide a fresh list. Records related to the appointment process are exempt from *FIPPA*.[288]

There cannot be a contractually enforceable promise of appointment because it is contrary to the unconditional exercise of discretion by Cabinet, acting in the interests of the public, as supported by the appointments process, and because it would create a loyalty or a perception of loyalty by the judge to the government promisor, lacking in the appearance of independence.[289]

b) Justices of the Peace

Pursuant to the *Justices of the Peace Act*, appointees must have ten years' work experience and a secondary degree or diploma but need not have practised law.[290] Although some lawyers have been appointed to the office of justice of the peace, it is generally intended to be a position open to otherwise qualified members of the public.[291]

The Act requires an Appointments Advisory Committee[292] to make recommendations to the attorney general. The committee is to be composed of a judge, two justices of the peace (one being the regional senior justice of the peace), up to four persons appointed by the attorney general, and a practising lawyer or paralegal.[293] Justices of the peace are to be recruited through an open process where vacancies are advertised, and candidates assessed against criteria that assess merit and recognize "the desirability of reflecting the diversity of Ontario society."[294]

---

288 *Ibid*, s 42(11)–(12).

289 *Donald Frederick Angevine v Her Majesty the Queen, in Right of Ontario*, 2011 ONSC 4523, where the plaintiff claimed to have been personally promised an appointment by the attorney general.

290 *Justices of the Peace Act*, above note 263, s 2(1.1)–(1.3). There can be a requirement for "training in the justice system."

291 Ontario, *Justices of the Peace Remuneration Commission [April 1, 1996 to March 31, 2002]: Submissions of the Government of Ontario* (Toronto: Queen's Printer, 30 May 2000) at 5.

292 *Justices of the Peace Act*, above note 263, s 2(1).

293 *Ibid*, s 2.1.

294 *Ibid*, s 2.2.

Candidates are to be classified as "Not Recommended," "Recommended," or "Highly Recommended" and provided to the attorney general for review. The attorney general shall only seek an appointment from the Lieutenant Governor in Council for those "Recommended" or "Highly Recommended." Records related to the appointment process are exempt from disclosure under *FIPPA*.[295]

5) Retirement

The *Courts of Justice Act* stipulates that every provincial court judge must retire at the age of sixty-five years but has tenure until then. Individual judges may apply to continue working until seventy-five years of age, subject to the annual approval of the chief justice of the Ontario Court of Justice.[296]

This arrangement is different from the mandatory retirement age of seventy-five for Superior Court justices under the *Constitution Act*.[297] In *Valente*, this less secure arrangement was found "by no means ideal" but acceptable.[298] The "standard of judicial independence cannot be a standard of uniform provisions" but need only reflect what is "at the heart of . . . the essential conditions of judicial independence in Canada,"[299] which is to be "secure against interference by the Executive."[300]

Most of the comments with respect to re-appointment and retirement of provincial court judges also now apply to justices of the peace under the *Justices of the Peace Act*.

6) Misconduct

a) Provincial Court Judges

Alleged misconduct by a provincial court judge must be addressed by a complaint to the Ontario Judicial Council, a body comprised of lawyers, judges, Law Society benchers, and Cabinet appointees.[301] A complaint can be made by any person and so the complaint need not be by the

---

295 *Ibid*, s 2(6).
296 *Courts of Justice Act*, above note 262, s 47.
297 *Constitution Act, 1867*, above note 2, s 99(2).
298 *Valente*, above note 257 at para 39.
299 *Ibid* at para 27.
300 *Ibid* at para 31.
301 *Courts of Justice Act*, above note 262, s 49.

"victim" but can be made by officials of the Ministry of the Attorney General.[302] A subcommittee reviews and investigates the complaint in private[303] and may in the interim recommend the suspension with pay of the judge who is the subject of the complaint or their assignment to a different location.[304] The subcommittee may dismiss the complaint, refer the complaint to the chief justice, refer it to mediation prior to hearing, or refer the complaint to the Judicial Council with or without recommending it hold a hearing. The Judicial Council shall consider, in private, every complaint referred to it by the subcommittee and may dismiss the complaint, refer it to the chief justice, refer it to mediation, or hold a hearing.

Mediation is not to be used if there is "a significant power imbalance between the complainant and the judge" or there is such a disparity in the versions of events that mediation would be "unworkable," or the complaint involves an allegation of sexual misconduct or discrimination or harassment, or the public interest requires the hearing of a complaint.[305]

The screening prior to the holding of a hearing is to maintain public confidence by both protecting judges from "routine vulnerability to public opprobrium when the complaints are spurious" and ensuring genuine issues about fitness or capacity are publicly addressed.[306]

If a complaint ultimately makes its way to hearing, the Judicial Council has a range of disciplinary options at its disposal, including warnings, reprimands, ordering an apology, other specified actions such as education or treatment, suspension, or a recommendation to the attorney general that the judge in question be removed. The hearings will be public, except in "exceptional circumstances."[307] A recommendation for removal may only occur if the Judicial Council concludes, upon completion of a hearing, that the judge has become incapacitated or disabled from the due execution of their office by reason of an inability to perform the essential duties of their office, conduct that is

302 Dealing with identical wording, see *Massiah v Justices of the Peace Review Council*, 2014 ONSC 3415 at para 7.

303 There are reduced natural justice entitlements at this non-hearing stage: *ibid.*

304 *Courts of Justice Act*, above note 262, s 51.4.

305 *Ibid*, s 51.5.

306 *Hryciuk v Ontario (Legislative Assembly)*, 1996 CanLII 4013 (ON CA); *Kipiniak v The Ontario Judicial Council*, 2012 ONSC 5866.

307 *Courts of Justice Act*, above note 262, s 51.6.

incompatible with due execution of the office, or a failure to perform the duties of that office.[308]

A removal order shall be tabled by the attorney general in the legislature if it is in session or, if not, within fifteen days after the commencement of the next session. There is no provision for the attorney general to hear an appeal from the hearing panel recommendation or to make a separate recommendation to Cabinet, as such a process would undermine the independence of the process from the political arm of government.[309] Ultimately, a removal is effectuated by the Lieutenant Governor "on the address" (with the approval) of the legislature. The requirement for legislative approval for provincial court judges goes beyond the constitutional requirement of security of tenure:

> It may be that the requirement of an address of the legislature makes removal of a judge more difficult in practice because of the solemn, cumbersome, and publicly visible nature of the process, but the requirement of cause, as defined by statute, together with a provision for judicial inquiry at which the judge affected is given a full opportunity to be heard, is in my opinion a sufficient restraint upon the power of removal.[310]

In any event, this process is intended to maintain the independence of judges by making them largely responsible for their own discipline. According to the Canadian Judicial Council, "[g]iven the independence accorded judges, they share a collective responsibility to promote high standards of conduct."[311] "[T]he vulnerability of judges is clearly greater than that of the mass of humanity or of 'elites' in general: it is rather as if his or her function, which is to judge others, imposed a requirement that he or she remain beyond the judgment of others."[312]

308 *Ibid*, s 51.8.

309 *Barriolhet v Justices of the Peace Review Council*, 2011 ONSC 3246 at para 51 [*Barriolhet*].

310 *Therrien*, above note 261 at para 67 quoting LeDain J, from *Valente*, above note 257 at 697.

311 *CJC*, *Ethical Principles*, above note 260, Judicial Independence, heading 5.

312 *Therrien*, above note 261 at para 111, quoting Yves-Marie Morissette in "Figure actuelle du juge dans la cité" (1999) 30 *Revue de Droit de l'Université de Sherbrooke* 1 at 11–12.

The judiciary must "project and strive to maintain impartiality, independence and integrity."[313] The purpose of judicial misconduct proceedings is "essentially remedial" and "not to punish the judge, but rather to ensure that public confidence of reasonable people in the judge, judiciary and the administration of justice is maintained."[314] The test for judicial misconduct consists of (1) an impact on public confidence that (2) implicates the integrity, impartiality, or independence of the judiciary.[315] Public confidence should be viewed from the perspective of the "reasonable, fair-minded, informed member of the public."[316] Evidence of bad faith, ulterior motives, or deliberate misconduct is not required for a finding of judicial misconduct.[317] In determining what disposition is required the council is to consider "the least serious—a warning—and move sequentially to the most serious—a recommendation for removal—and order only what is necessary to restore" public confidence.[318] Factors to consider include whether the conduct is isolated or part of a pattern, occurred in an official capacity or in private life, whether there has been rehabilitation, the record of service of the judge, and the effect on the integrity and respect for the judiciary.[319]

Findings of misconduct against provincial court judges are not frequent. Positive participation in advocacy in a worthy general cause, when combined with attempts to comply with judicial obligations, does not diminish public confidence even if it does result in the judge being inappropriately involved in public affairs.[320] Taking an argumentative position on a legal issue such as encouraging an appeal in a related case, targeting professional witnesses and criticizing other judges' decisions is "close to the line" but not judicial misconduct if the judge is sincere and repentant in acknowledging their inappropriate conduct.[321]

---

313 *Therrien*, above note 261 at para 107.

314 *Re McLeod* (OJC, 2 June 2021) at para 67 [*McLeod, OJC, June 2021*], quoting from *Re McLeod* (OJC, 20 December 2018) at para 70 and taken from *Ruffo v Conseil de la magistrature*, [1995] 4 SCR 267 at para 68.

315 *Re Chisvin* (OJC, 26 November 2012) at para 37 [*Chisvin*].

316 *Re Baldwin* (OJC, 10 May 2002) [*Baldwin*].

317 Re *Welsh* (JPRC, 2018).

318 *Baldwin*, above note 316.

319 *Chisvin*, above note 315 at para 38, as incorporated in *Ontario Judicial Council Procedures Document*, updated December 2021, Rule of Procedure 23.3, online: www.ontariocourts.ca/ocj/jprc/policies-and-procedures.

320 *McLeod, OJC, June 2021*, above note 314 at paras 574–76.

321 *Re Douglas* (OJC, 6 March 2006) at paras 42–45.

An isolated incident of misconduct in the courtroom accompanied by regret, an apology, and rehabilitation to address stress because of personal problems warrants a reprimand.[322]

A single pattern of conduct involving well-intentioned but inappropriate involvement in a child protection matter including criticizing the Children's Aid Society and gaining access to confidential information followed by full contrition resulted in a reprimand, requirement to apologize, and a thirty-day suspension.[323]

Presiding in court wearing a red "Make America Great Again" baseball hat the day after Donald Trump was elected president of the United States would cause a reasonable person to think the judge endorsed Trump's campaign and that could give rise to concerns about impartiality.[324] Evidence that the judge did not hold any of the polarized, misogynistic, racist, or homophobic views that many of the complainants attributed to Trump was found to mean that members of the public need not fear the treatment they would receive in the judge's court in the future. Due to long years of impeccable service, the penalty imposed was "the most serious sanction permitted by law short of removal," namely a thirty-day suspension.

A case of multiple incidents of sexual misconduct, along with a finding that the judge's testimony lacked credibility, resulted in a finding of misconduct, including condemnation of his behaviour, leading to the resignation of the judge before disposition.[325]

The hearing panel has discretion to award legal costs to the judge complained against. The starting point is to be that costs ought usually to be borne by the taxpayer because it is in the best interests of the process that the judicial officer complained against have legal representation. Factors considered in deciding whether there should be compensation for all, some, or no legal costs include whether the conduct was directly related to the judicial function, was clearly inappropriate, was repeated, and whether the judge's position in the litigation lengthened the hearing.[326]

---

322 *Chisvin*, above note 315 at paras 41–51.

323 *Re Keast* (OJC, 15 December 2017).

324 *Re Zabel* (OJC, 11 September 2017).

325 *Re Evans* (OJC, 23 September 2004) and see *Law Society of Upper Canada v Kerry Patrick Evans*, 2007 ONLSAP 5.

326 See *Massiah v Justices of the Peace Review Council*, 2016 ONSC 6191, discussed in the compensation for legal costs decision in *Re Keast* (OJC, 6 February 2018); *Re Bisson* (JPRC, 10 July 2018) at paras 54–62 [*Bisson*]; *Re Macleod* (OJC, 29 July 2021).

b) Justices of the Peace

The complaints procedure for justices of the peace[327] is similar to that for provincial judges. A Justices of the Peace Review Council consisting of judges, justices of the peace, and government appointees deals privately with complaints against a justice of the peace.[328] A complaints committee is established to investigate the complaint. The committee may dismiss the complaint, counsel the justice of the peace, refer the complaint to the chief justice or order a formal hearing. A hearing panel may impose warnings, reprimands, ordering of apologies, and other specified measures such as education or treatment, and suspensions, and recommend to the attorney general that the justice of the peace be removed from office. A removal can only occur by order of Cabinet after there is a complaint, hearing, and recommendation to the attorney general that the justice of the peace is incapacitated, has engaged in conduct incompatible with their office, or failed to perform their duties. The order is to be "laid before" (provided for the information of) but not approved by the Legislative Assembly.[329]

All the judicial principles of conduct apply equally to justices of the peace because "for the vast majority of society who have contact with the court system, their first and only contact would be to appear before a justice of the peace."[330] The different environments in which judges and justices of the peace perform their duties may be relevant to finding misconduct "but the test to be applied must be the same. To do otherwise would be wrong in principle and diminish the important work done by those subject to [a] lesser standard."[331] The factors governing the disposition of cases involving findings of misconduct are virtually identical to those for provincial judges.[332]

---

327 *Justices of the Peace Act*, above note 263, ss 10.2–11.2.

328 *Ibid*, s 8.

329 *Ibid*, s 11.2.

330 *Re Phillips* (JPRC, 17 January 2013) at para 14 quoting from *Report of a Judicial Inquiry Re: His Worship Benjamin Sinai*, released 7 March 2008.

331 *Report of a Judicial Inquiry Re: His Worship Quon*, released 9 August 2006 at 12–13.

332 *Justices of the Peace Review Council Procedures Document* revised September 2021, online: www.ontariocourts.ca/ocj/jprc/policies-and-procedures, Rule 17, discussed in *Re Phillips* (JPRC, 24 October 2013) [*Phillips*, Oct 2013] and *Lauzon v Justices of the Peace Review Council*, 2021 ONSC 6174 at para 38 [*Lauzon*].

Persistent failure to know or apply the relevant law resulted in a reprimand and education.[333]

An isolated incident of procedural misconduct by a reputable justice of the peace followed by contrition warrants a warning,[334] except that failure to understand the seriousness of the mistake will warrant a suspension.[335]

Repeated procedural impropriety including an arrogant attitude to a self-represented defendant and peremptory dismissal of an entire list of sixty-three charges after five minutes delay, all with no timely remorse, resulted in a seven-day suspension without pay and an ordered apology.[336] Repeated instances of procedural misconduct "indicating a lack of respect for proper court processes"[337] resulted in a ten-day suspension. In another case, repeated instances of procedural impropriety demonstrating a lack of respect for the rule of law were mitigated by active rehabilitation, leaving the panel of the view that confidence could be restored by a reprimand, letters of apology, a year-long training program, and the warning that "any further findings of misconduct may put [the justice of the peace] beyond any possibility for redemption."[338]

Repeatedly acting as an advocate in court without a license, and without insurance, while making misleading statements is conduct that compromises a judicial officer's "core personal and professional integrity" and, when combined with a failure to understand the misconduct, means that no disposition other than removal will be sufficient to restore public confidence.[339]

Interfering with an official inspection of a friend's restaurant warranted a seven-day suspension even though the justice was contrite and apologized.[340] A further incident by the same justice of the peace of personally intervening in a criminal prosecution warranted a recommendation for removal.[341] Interfering with and attempting to influence the

333 *Re Romagnoli* (JPRC, 29 August 2018).

334 *Ibid*.

335 *Re Winchester* (JPRC, 24 July 2020).

336 *Re Johnston* (JPRC, 19 August 2014).

337 *Re Welsh, Third Hearing* (JPRC, 15 February 2018) at para 73.

338 *Re McLeod* (JPRC, 20 April 2021).

339 *Re Ballam* (JRPC, 20 June 2022).

340 *Re Foulds* (JPRC, 24 July 2013).

341 *Re Foulds* (JPRC, 27 April 2018).

conduct of a prosecution against one's child, while lacking testimonial credibility, and showing no real insight or remorse, warrants removal.[342]

Repeated and serious procedural breaches revealing serious deficiencies in the necessary knowledge, combined with lack of contrition and insight, warrant removal from office.[343] Justices of the peace have also been recommended to be removed from office for speaking publicly "conveying disdain for the justice system in which she is an integral participant," repeated irrational and arbitrary behaviour that denied defendants fair process, or repeated conflict of interest, as well as lack of appreciation of the impact of their actions on public confidence, and failure to show timely remorse.[344]

Lying to a police officer engaged in an investigation warrants removal because the public would in the future wonder if the justice of the peace was biased for or against police officers.[345]

A "short incident" of sexual comments to a court clerk that were the subject of contrition and the justice of the peace volunteering to have his assignment changed to avoid contact resulted in a reprimand.[346] Two incidents of sexual assault of a fellow justice of the peace while intoxicated, and after a conference, followed by contrition, warranted a thirty-day suspension.[347] Repeated gross and disgusting comments to young persons in the course of duty warrant removal even if the justice is contrite.[348] Repeated sexual harassment of women, combined with "a refusal or inability to accept that sexually inappropriate conduct by a justice of the peace towards women in the workplace is not acceptable, is so manifestly and profoundly destructive of the judicial role and integrity in the judiciary that public confidence requires" removal from office.[349]

---

342 *Re Gibbon* (JPRC, 7 February 2022 and 25 August 2022).

343 *Bisson*, above note 326.

344 See the following judicial reviews of Justices of the Peace Review Council decisions: *Lauzon*, above note 332 at para 22; *Romain v Lieutenant Governor in Council*, 2005 CanLII 31588 (ON SCDC); *Barriolhet*, above note 309; *Sinai v Ontario (Commissioner)*, 2010 ONSC 8025.

345 *Phillips*, Oct 2013, above note 333.

346 *Re Kowarsky* (JPRC, 30 May 2011).

347 *Report of a Judicial Inquiry Re: Obokata*, released 6 November 2003.

348 *Report of a Judicial Inquiry Re: Blackburn*, released 21 January 1994.

349 *Re Massiah* (JPRC, Decision on Disposition, 28 April 2015) at para 65. This was the second decision on sexual harassment by Justice of the Peace Massiah. In *Re Massiah* (JPRC, 12 April 2012), the panel found the justice of the peace had made a series of sexually harassing comments, but, following that hearing

7) Remuneration

The principle of judicial independence requires a minimum level of pay and a commission process.[350] In the *PEI Reference*, where a *Public Sector Pay Reduction Act* reduced the salary of that province's provincial court judges in order to address a provincial deficit, many defendants in criminal trials argued that the court had lost its status as an independent and impartial tribunal under section 11(d) of the *Charter*.[351] The majority of the Supreme Court confirmed that section 11(d) of the *Charter* does not necessarily provide the same level of protection to provincial court judges as that afforded under the *Constitution Act, 1867* to federally appointed Superior Court judges, but that it does require that an appropriate guarantee of financial security be provided to provincial court judges.

Several principles must be adhered to. First, it is not permissible for the judiciary to either collectively or individually engage in direct negotiations over remuneration with the executive or representatives of the legislature. The "expectations of give and take, and of threat and counter-threat," typical of salary negotiations are inconsistent with judicial independence.[352] Second, any reductions to judicial remuneration, including de facto reductions through the erosion of judicial salaries by inflation, cannot take those salaries below a basic minimum level of remuneration that is required for the office of a judge. Third, provincial court judge salaries can be adjusted due to economic policy if the policy affects the salaries of all or some employees who are remunerated with public funds, or if it is a measure that is directed at provincial court judges as a class, although the salaries of individual judges must be secured by law and not be subject to arbitrary interference. If the measure directed at judges as a class is a pay reduction, the burden of justification will be substantial.

---

process, stated their confidence that he would not engage in such conduct again and decided on a reprimand, professional training, and a suspension.

350 The seminal cases are *Valente*, above note 257, and *Beauregard*, above note 272. More recently, see *Conférence des juges de paix magistrats du Québec v Quebec (Attorney General)*, 2016 SCC 39 [*Conférence des juges*], and Josh Hunter & Sarah Kraicer, "Keeping the Scales of Justice Balanced—Québec Justices of the Peace and Judicial Independence" (2017) 81 *Supreme Court Law Review: Osgoode's Annual Constitutional Cases Conference* 149.

351 *PEI Reference*, above note 255 at paras 23–24.

352 *Ibid* at para 246.

Furthermore, any changes to or freezes in judicial remuneration require prior recourse to an independent body to avoid the possibility of, or the appearance of, political interference through economic manipulation. The Supreme Court has held that subsequent retroactively applicable commission review is acceptable for sitting judges reappointed to a newly created office, so as to avoid delaying judicial reforms.[353]

Although governments are constitutionally bound to go through the commission process, the recommendations of the commissions are not constitutionally required to be binding on the executive or the legislature.[354] When deciding whether to accept or reject the commission's recommendations, the legislature must have legitimate reasons with a reasonable factual foundation based on a good faith consideration of the commission's reasons.[355] Putting it another way, the standard of justification for not following a commission recommendation is "simple rationality [which] requires that the government articulate a legitimate reason" why it has chosen to depart from the recommendation of the commission.[356] The Ontario Court of Appeal[357] has applied this test to find the government's response needs to be justified by reasons that relate to the public interest and are not purely political, discriminatory, or lacking a rational basis. The courts' review of government reasons is to be "a cautious and modest review."[358] Further it cannot be that the guarantee of a minimum acceptable level of judicial remuneration will operate to exempt the courts from deficit reduction:

> Nothing would be more damaging to the reputation of the judiciary and the administration of justice than a perception that judges were not shouldering their share of the burden in difficult economic times. . . . In particular, courts should not misuse the introduction of a constitutional process for determining judicial compensation as a vehicle to shield the judiciary from government decisions that treat them as well as, or even better than, others paid from the public purse. To do this would trivialize the great principle of judicial independence.[359]

---

353 *Conférence des juges*, above note 350 at paras 57–63.
354 *Ibid* at para 133.
355 *New Brunswick Provincial Court Judges*, above note 257 at para 39.
356 *PEI Reference*, above note 255 at 110.
357 *Ontario Judges' Assn v Ontario*, 2003 CanLII 50088 (ON CA).
358 *Ibid* at para 65.
359 *Ibid* at paras 101 and 116.

a) Provincial Court Judges

i) Framework Agreement and Judicial Remuneration Commissions

The remuneration of provincial court judges is determined through a Provincial Judges Remuneration Commission operating under a *Framework Agreement*,[360] which governs the jurisdiction and terms of reference for Triennial Commissions. These commissions make recommendations about judicial salaries, benefits and allowances, and pensions. The commissions are tripartite bodies composed of an appointee of the Lieutenant Governor in Council, an appointee representing provincial court judges, and a mutually agreed upon third member. Each commission serves a term of three years. Commissions are established as public inquiries (with the powers of a commission under the *Public Inquiries Act, 2009*),[361] but in practice function much in the same manner as interest arbitrations. Commissions generally make a public call for submissions and receive written submissions from interested individuals or groups, but the focus of their activity is a hearing where the Crown and an association representing judges[362] file written submissions and then present their views at an oral hearing.

The commission's recommendations concerning salary, benefits, and allowances, but not pension, are binding on the government, but any pension recommendations are not binding.[363] By binding itself to aspects of the commission process, the Ontario government has exhibited stronger deference to the commission process than the minimum constitutional requirement of full consideration.[364] The recommendations of the commission, except those related to pensions, come into effect on the first day of April in the year following the year the commission began its inquiry (except in the case of salary recommendations, which come into effect on the first of April in the year in which

---

360 *Courts of Justice Act*, above note 262, s 51.13 and Schedule A *Framework Agreement On Judges' Remuneration, between Her Majesty the Queen in Right of the Province of Ontario, represented by the Chair of Management Board, and the Judges of the Ontario Court (Provincial Division) and the former Provincial Court (Civil Division), represented by the respective Presidents of The Ontario Judges Association, The Ontario Family Law Judges Association and the Ontario Provincial Court (Civil Division) Judges' Association*, dated 18 November 1992.

361 SO 2009, c 33, Sch 6.

362 *Ontario Conference of Judges v Ontario (Chair of Management Board)* (2005), 71 OR (3d) 528 (Ont Sup Ct) [*Conference of Judges v Ontario*].

363 *Courts of Justice Act*, above note 262, Reg 407/93, Sch A, s 27.

364 See the discussion of the *PEI Reference* above note 255.

the commission began its inquiry). The recommendations, except those related to pensions, have the same force and effect as if enacted by the legislature and must be implemented by order in council within sixty days of the delivery of the commission's report.[365] The decision of the commission is not legislation until implemented by order in council and can be the subject of judicial review.[366]

A non-exhaustive list of criteria to be used by commissions for determining recommendations is enumerated in the *Framework Agreement*, and includes the laws of Ontario; the need to provide fair and reasonable compensation for judges in light of prevailing economic conditions in the province and the overall state of the provincial economy; the growth or decline in real per capita income; the parameters set by any joint working committees established by the parties; the fact that the government may not reduce the salaries, pensions, or benefits of judges, individually or collectively, without infringing the principle of judicial independence; and any other factor that the commission considers relevant to the matters in issue.[367]

ii) Salary Determinations

The salary differential between provincial court judges and federally appointed judges has been substantial and increased in the 1980s and 1990s.[368] In 1988, the First Triennial Commission rejected parity between provincial and federal judges, but did recommend substantial increases. The provincial government partially implemented the recommendations. Then, the fiscal restraint of the early 1990s, including the *Social Contract Act, 1993*,[369] resulted in no increase in any compensation between 1991 and 1 April 1996.

The Fourth Triennial Commission of 1998–2001 recognized an increase in the workload of provincial judges, after an expansion of their criminal law jurisdiction, as well as a buoyant provincial economy following a period of restraint, as grounds for providing a 28 percent salary increase. The commission also considered the need to attract

365 *Courts of Justice Act*, above note 262, Reg 407/93, Sch A, s 27.

366 *Conference of Judges v Ontario*, above note 362.

367 *Courts of Justice Act*, above note 262, Reg 407/93, Sch A, s 25.

368 Ontario, *Provincial Judges Remuneration Commission, Fourth Triennial Report* (Toronto: The Commission, 1998) at 5–15.

369 SO 1993, c 5.

high-quality applicants, and a "significant inequity" between the salaries of federally and provincially appointed judges.

After the release of the Report of the Fifth Triennial Provincial Judges Remuneration Commission, the Ontario government attempted to judicially review the commission's award of a 21 percent salary increase over three years.[370] The government argued that the commission erred in allowing its "desire to avoid the creation of, or perception of, a two-tiered court system" to be the determinative factor in concluding that provincial judges' salaries should be based on those of Superior Court judges. The court dismissed the government's application, holding that the government should have sought reconsideration through the commission first, as envisaged by the *Framework Agreement*.[371]

There have since been several more provincial judges remuneration commissions. The salaries and benefits of provincial court judges are set out in a regulation to the *Courts of Justice Act*.[372]

iii) Pensions

Pension issues are exempted from the provisions of the *Framework Agreement* that give salary recommendations of the commission the same force and effect as legislation.[373] The agreement stipulates that recommendations with respect to pensions, or any reconsideration of initial findings relating to pensions, shall be presented to the MBC for consideration which, while bound to "make every effort to implement them at the earliest possible date," may also vary the recommendations in consultation with Cabinet.

The majority of the Fourth Triennial Commission was of the view that the pension scheme for provincial court judges should be substantively equal to, or at least closer to, the pension for federally appointed judges.[374] The government chose not to implement the recommendations regarding pensions, stating that the existing pension entitlements were adequate and had been increased in value by the salary adjustment.

---

370 *Ontario Conference of Judges v Ontario (Management Board)*, [2004] OJ No 2643 (Div Ct) at para 1. The government's procedural delay occasioned an interim costs order: [2004] OJ No 1297 (Div Ct).

371 *Ibid* at para 60.

372 *Courts of Justice Act*, above note 262, O Reg 67/92 as amended.

373 *Ibid*, Sch A, ss 27–29 and 33.

374 As recounted in *New Brunswick Provincial Court Judges*, above note 257 at paras 4–9 and 89–90.

The government further justified its position on the basis of the favourable comparison between the Ontario judicial pension and that of other provinces, as well as the province's continued commitment to financial restraint.[375] The Supreme Court held that these reasons were acceptable.

The Supreme Court has also held that judicial officers can be members of the broader civil service pension plan provided any changes to the plan as it applies to judges are put before a commission before being implemented.[376] The Court has also rejected the argument that the lack of reflection of the shorter average length of a judicial career compared to a civil service career was unconstitutional, provided the plan remained generally adequate.

The pensions of provincial court judges are set out in a regulation to the *Courts of Justice Act*[377] and administered by the Provincial Judges Pension Board.

b) Justices of the Peace

i) Remuneration Commissions

Remuneration commissions are also used to set the compensation levels of justices of the peace. The legislation governing justices of the peace commissions is different in some respects from that governing the provincial judges' commissions.

The Lieutenant Governor in Council determines the remuneration, and is empowered to make regulations that specify the criteria to be used by the Justices of the Peace Remuneration Commission when developing recommendations.[378] The commission is tripartite with one person selected by the justices of the peace representatives, one person selected by the chair of the MBC, and one selected jointly, with terms of four years.[379] The commission is to conduct an inquiry every four years and report to the chair of the MBC.

The non-exhaustive list of criteria to be used by commissions for determining recommendations is enumerated in the *Framework Agreement* and includes items similar to those for provincial judges but rather than referencing that there may be no reduction in compensation

---

375 *Ibid* at paras 95–102.

376 *Conférence des juges*, above note 350 at paras 86–95.

377 *Courts of Justice Act*, above note 262, O Reg 290/13.

378 *Justices of the Peace Act*, above note 263, s 21.1.

379 *Ibid*, O Reg 319/00.

without infringing on judicial independence, the criteria reference "the principles of compensation theory and practice in Canada."[380]

The Lieutenant Governor in Council is not bound by, but must give full consideration to, the reports of the commission submitted to Cabinet by the chair of the MBC.[381] The Crown is under a constitutional obligation to provide a rational reason for not accepting the commission's recommendations.[382]

Remuneration commissions are also used to set salaries for associate judges and deputy judges.

ii) Salary and Pension Determinations

The history of justice of the peace compensation begins with the seminal 1981 *Mewett Report*,[383] which raised concern over the use of fees for particular judicial acts as a method of payment and led to the codification of the wages and benefits.[384] In 1993, the government and representatives of the justices of the peace agreed to a non-statutory Justices of the Peace Remuneration Commission to make recommendations concerning such compensation.[385]

The 1995 report of the first commission called for substantial wage increases and was rejected by the government. The justices of the peace subsequently brought an application for judicial review of the government's actions to the Divisional Court. In the 1999 *Ontario Federation of Justices of the Peace* decision,[386] the court held that the principles of judicial independence should apply to justices of the peace in the same way as to the provincial court judges and that justices of the peace should be afforded the constitutional guarantees enjoyed by provincial court judges. The court recognized the level of compensation for justices of the peace as inadequate and directed that justices of the peace

---

380 *Ibid*, s 7.

381 *Ibid*, s 10(1).

382 *Ontario Federation*, above note 258.

383 Alan W. Mewett, *Report to the Attorney General of Ontario on the Office and Function of the Justices of the Peace in Ontario* (Toronto: Ministry of Attorney General, 1981).

384 As discussed in Ontario, *Justices of the Peace Remuneration Commission (April 1, 1996 to March 31, 2002): Submissions of the Government of Ontario* (Toronto: Queen's Printer, 30 May 2000) at 26.

385 Ontario, *Justices of the Peace Remuneration Commission: Submissions of the Association of Justices of the Peace of Ontario* (29 May 2000) at 74–76.

386 *Ontario Federation*, above note 258.

were to receive increases at least equal to the average industrial wage for the years 1996 forward, until the government considered the second commission's recommendations. That order, and Ontario's constitutional obligations, led to an amendment to the *Justices of the Peace Act*[387] to provide for the statutory establishment of a Justices of the Peace Remuneration Commission.

The recommendations of the second and third justices of the peace remuneration commissions were ultimately implemented by the government, and remuneration provisions evolved to include automatic indexed increases. The sixth commission found that the ongoing evolution in the complexity of the work of justices of the peace meant that the automatic salary rise in accordance with indexing was not adequate and recommended a further "significant" in year increase. The government was of the view that the work was not much more complex, and that the proposed increases would generate a per capita income well above comparators. On review, this was found to be rational.[388]

The salaries and benefits, including pensions, of justices of the peace are set out in a regulation under the *Justices of the Peace Act*.[389] Until the recommendations of the Second Commission were accepted, benefits for justices of the peace were designated as being the same as those provided to management under the *Public Service Act* regulation.[390] This was objected to on the grounds that it did not meet the requirements of judicial independence. Pursuant to the recommendations of the Second Commission, a separate regulation was passed to deal exclusively, and comprehensively, with benefits provided to justices of the peace. Their pensions are still under the PSPP, which applies to most non-unionized public servants, but are specifically supplemented. The lack of a separate pension plan has been the subject of objection by the Association of

387 *Justices of the Peace Act*, above note 263, s 211, as amended by the *Red Tape Reduction Act*, SO 1999, c 12, s 12, O Reg 139/00.

388 *The Association of Justices of the Peace of Ontario/L'Association des juges de paix de l'Ontario v Ontario*, 2016 ONSC 6001.

389 *Justices of the Peace Act*, above note 263, O Reg 247/94, Salaries and Benefits of Justices of the Peace.

390 *Public Service Act*, Reg 977, Part VI.

Justices of the Peace[391] on the ground that an independent pension is an aspect of constitutionally required financial security.[392]

8) Administrative Independence

Institutional independence also involves judges having the administrative autonomy to administer their courts, which entails some degree of direction over the administrative staff who perform courtroom functions.[393] This has been codified in the *Courts of Justice Act* with provisions that establish the attorney general shall "superintend" court administration "other than matters that are assigned by law to the judiciary, including authority to direct and supervise the sittings and the assignment of the judicial duties of the court."[394] It is further confirmed that court staff can be provincial public servants,[395] but that "in matters assigned by law to the judiciary" court staff shall "act at the direction" of the judiciary.[396]

Judges are not vested with control over the personnel aspects of court administration, because it is not thought essential to their ability to control the administration of justice. Court administration that does not infringe on judicial independence is a provincial government responsibility,[397] and the Supreme Court has said that normally includes staffing of the courts.[398] The mandatory removal of Manitoba court staff on "Filmon Fridays," days of unpaid leave for provincial government employees, was an unacceptable incursion on judicial administrative independence, as it effectively shut down the Manitoba Provincial Court on those days.[399] The Ontario Court of Appeal has found that there is

---

391 *Ontario Submission of Association of Justices of the Peace to the Third Triennial Justices of the Peace Commission*, 10 February 2003 (Toronto: The Commission, 2003) at paras 480–84.

392 *Valente*, above note 257 at para 40, LeDain J: "In the case of pension, the essential distinction is between a right to a pension and a pension that depends on the grace or favour of the Executive."

393 *PEI Reference*, above note 255 at para 251.

394 *Courts of Justice Act*, above note 262, s 72.

395 *Ibid*, s 73(1).

396 *Ibid*, s 75.

397 *Constitution Act, 1867*, above note 2, s 92(14); *Administration of Justice Act*, RSO 1990, c A.6, s 1(a); *Beauregard*, above note 272 at para 43.

398 *Ontario*, above note 269 at para 41.

399 *PEI Reference*, above note 255 at para 270.

no necessary conflict between judicial independence and the membership of federally appointed judges' secretaries in the OPSEU-represented public service bargaining unit.[400] Where the 2002 OPSEU strike activities of those bargaining unit members resulted in actual or apprehended disruption of courtroom administration, the Ontario Superior Court of Justice considered whether such matters should be directly addressed by judicial order or by the OLRB and, generally, left those matters to be addressed by the OLRB.[401]

F. ORDER-IN-COUNCIL APPOINTMENTS

1) Background

Under various statutes, the government of Ontario is responsible for making about 4,800 specified appointments to more than 600 agencies.[402] Appointees, and the agencies they participate in and direct, are usually charged with fairly independent authority to undertake a certain statutory mandate. A significant number of broader public sector agencies are supervised by boards of directors that are wholly or partly composed of government appointees. Ontario's administrative justice system is composed of a host of adjudicative boards and tribunals staffed by a combination of full- and part-time appointees. While the appointment process allows the elected government to ensure key positions are filled by persons who will be committed to implementing its policy agenda, the appointment process is fundamentally a hiring process intended to effectively fill a large number of important positions.

2) Appointment Process

a) Cabinet

Appointments may be made by order in council (OIC), meaning an order of Cabinet, or by direct ministerial appointment, sometimes known as a

400 *Ontario (Attorney General) v Ontario Public Service Employees Union* (2000), 52 OR (3d) 77 (CA) at para 16.

401 See the discussion in Chapter 8.

402 The Public Appointments Secretariat site, online: www.pas.gov.on.ca/scripts/en/homeasp, describes the agencies to which appointments are made, and details of the appointments.

minister's letter, depending on the authority for the appointment, which will be set out in the statute establishing the organization.[403]

Potential OIC appointees are presented to Cabinet either by a minister or the premier. Those presented to Cabinet by ministers are called ministers' prerogative appointments and those presented by the premier are correspondingly called premier's prerogative appointments.

The government of Ontario has established a Public Appointments Secretariat (PAS) reporting to Cabinet Office to administer the appointment process, including receiving, reviewing, and recommending applications to Cabinet.[404] The PAS's stated responsibility is to make sure that appointees are representative of Ontario society and have "the personal and professional integrity to serve the public." The process for vetting a candidate for an appointment varies depending on the circumstances but will include a personal and conflict of interest disclosure statement and a police record check. The PAS solicits applications through its website, but recommendations may arise from other processes including an executive search or a consultation with the ministry and/or agency chair concerned.

There are few statutory requirements for appointments. The *Adjudicative Tribunals Accountability, Governance and Appointments Act, 2009*[405] requires that the selection process for appointment of members to an adjudicative tribunal be public, "competitive," and "merit-based"; that the criteria include expertise in the relevant subject matter and "aptitude for impartial adjudication"; and that the chair of the tribunal recommends the person for the appointment.

b) Review by the Legislature's Standing Committee on Government Agencies

The only global regulatory provision relating to OIC appointments is found in the Standing Orders of the Legislative Assembly of Ontario. Initial appointments for more than a year by OIC to an agency, board, commission, or to the board of directors of a corporation of which the government of Ontario is a majority shareholder, are subject to review

---

403 As but one example, under the *CECBA*, the Lieutenant Governor in Council appoints the chair of the GSB and, unusually, is to appoint the person selected for the position by agreement of the Crown and the trade unions representing Crown employees: *CECBA*, above note 200, s 47(2).

404 See Public Appointments Secretariat site, above note 402.

405 SO 2009, c 33, Sch 5, s 14.

by the Legislature's Standing Committee on Government Agencies.[406] Appointments by minister's letter or renewals of prior appointments are not subject to any review.

All proposed appointments subject to review by the standing committee are laid before the committee in the form of a certificate provided by Cabinet Office with a copy of the position description and a summary of the proposed appointee's qualifications. The committee may, and does, select a limited number of proposed appointees for review. Those selected are required to attend for a half-hour appearance before the committee and are subject to questioning by members. Following the appearance, the committee reports whether or not it concurs in the intended appointment and the report is deemed to be adopted by the House. The committee operates under strict time limits. Failure to act within the required time is effectively deemed to be approval of the proposed appointment. However, the process requires that the appointees' qualifications be a matter of public record in advance of appointment. While it is rare, on occasion the committee's questioning does result in an adverse report in spite of the government's majority control of the committee. Where a proposed appointment fails to obtain the committee's approval, the appointment is not made. Proposed appointees may also withdraw their names to avoid an adverse report. The review process provides a limited, but significant, check on OIC appointments.[407]

c) Right to Make "Political" Appointments

The filling of many public offices involves a legitimate political judgment. The fact that an appointment is left to Cabinet suggests a legislative intent that the appointment act as "a vehicle for the expression of government policy."[408] In commenting on the filling of public offices, the Ontario Court of Appeal has noted that "it would be intellectually naive not to recognize that elected governments must have room to

406 Ontario Legislative Assembly, *Standing Orders of the Legislative Assembly of Ontario*, October 2021, Chapter XX. Committees, para 106(e); first introduced in 1990.

407 See David Pond, "Legislative Control of Cabinet Appointments to the Public Service: A Canadian Case-Study in the Political Limits to Parliamentary Reform" (2008) 61:1 *Parliamentary Affairs* at 52–72.

408 *Oberlander v Canada (Attorney General)*, 2004 FCA 213 at para 51. See also *Suresh v Canada (Minister of Citizenship and Immigration)*, 2002 SCC 1 at para 31; *Baker v Canada (Minister of Citizenship and Immigration)*, [1999] 2 SCR 817 at para 59.

make political decisions and to conduct themselves in a manner to assure that their political policies are implemented."[409] In *Muscillo Transport v Ontario (Licence Suspension Appeal Board)*, a decision rejecting an allegation of bias based on the appointment of a close political associate of a minister to an adjudicative board before which the minister's officials appeared, an Ontario court recognized the legitimate role of political appointments to the public service:[410]

> Order-in-Council appointments to the public service frequently are politically motivated. The members of political parties who are elected to govern this province face an enormous task. To aid them in this task they must rely upon persons within the public service whose employment falls within the purview of the Public Service Commission. However, in addition to the permanent, non-political, professional staff of the civil service, elected representatives frequently must also rely upon a small group of persons who share their political views and who in a broad way wish to mold our society in particular fashion. The views of this group of persons of necessity must coincide with those of their political masters, since if they do not, the will of the electors as expressed by those representatives may be thwarted.[411]

The court decided that "bias, expressly permitted by legislation, cannot form the subject of legal complaint." Indeed, even continued participation in the political process to the extent of contributing to a political party is permissible as it cannot be assumed to detract from the integrity needed to perform the duties of an office.[412]

Whether an appointment is made by OIC, or minister's letter, does depend solely upon which legislation grants authority for the appointment. In *Muscillo Transport*,[413] the court concluded that a perception of bias did not arise from an appointee's political connection to the minister who was responsible both for recommending her appointment

409 *Hewat v Ontario*, 1998 CanLII 3393 (ON CA). See also *Saskatchewan Federation of Labour v Saskatchewan*, 2010 SKCA 27 at para 72.

410 *Muscillo Transport v Ontario (Licence Suspension Appeal Board)*, 1997 CanLII 12317 (Ont SC) at 561–62 [*Muscillo Transport*], leave to appeal refused (1997), 32 MVR (3d) 27 (Ont CA).

411 *Ken Neil v Government of Saskatchewan and George McLean*, unreported, 13 April 1984 (SKQB), as approved in *Muscillo Transport*, above note 410.

412 *Fletcher v Manitoba Public Insurance Corp*, [2004] MJ No 443 (CA) at para 29.

413 *Muscillo Transport*, above note 410 at 571.

and for the officials appearing before the board. However, the judge also noted that it had been long recognized that OIC appointments to adjudicative boards were preferable to ministers' letter appointments. It was noted that there is "a built-in structural bias or perception of unfairness" by virtue of the fact that ministers can nominate persons to quasi-judicial bodies relating to their own ministry. As a policy consideration this may be correct, but once the appointment authority is exercised in accordance with the statute, such decisions are not subject to judicial review on that ground.[414] While it is now general practice for the premier, not the minister, to recommend appointees to major adjudicative tribunals, this is not a legal requirement.

d) Prior Consultation

There can be statutory provisions requiring consultation before an appointment, although none seem to exist in Ontario. The interpretation of any such consultation requirement would be guided by the context and scheme of the Act, with care taken not to confuse the statutory duty to consult with a common law entitlement.[415]

The courts have left open the possibility that, in certain limited circumstances, a legitimate expectation may be created that might allow a common law entitlement to prior consultation about an appointment. No such claim has been successfully advanced. In *Wells v Newfoundland*,[416] an unsuccessful applicant could not challenge a failure to be granted an appointment, but the Supreme Court added the comment that the applicant "did not show any basis on which he could have formed a reasonable expectation to be consulted in the process." In *Canadian Union of Public Employees v Ontario (Minister of Labour)*,[417] the Supreme Court referred to the possibility of a claim of "legitimate expectation" of being consulted before an adverse decision. There is an

414 See *Ocean Port*, above note 255.

415 *Democracy Watch v Canada (Attorney General)*, 2018 FC 1290 [*Democracy Watch 1290*], dealing with the federal statutory requirement for the government to consult with all parties before appointing the conflict of interest and ethics commissioner; *Democracy Watch v Canada (Attorney General)*, 2018 FC 1291 [*Democracy Watch 1291*], dealing with the requirement to consult before appointing the commissioner for lobbying.

416 *Wells*, above note 254 at para 62. See also *Democracy Watch 1290*, *ibid* at paras 132–33, and *Democracy Watch 1291*, *ibid* at paras 141–42.

417 2003 SCC 29 at paras 128–33 [*CUPE*].

obvious difficulty in giving effective relief based on a right to consultation once an office is filed by an otherwise valid appointment.

e) Judicial Review of Appointment Process

Public appointments are matters of broad public policy[418] and are generally not subject to judicial review. No person has a right to a public appointment and consequently there is no vested interest that supports seeking review of an appointment.[419] A minister's recommendation to Cabinet of persons for appointment is not subject to review unless, possibly, there is evidence of bad faith.[420]

However, there is "no absolute and untrammeled discretion"[421] in the matter of appointments. Statutes include few, if any, express, or even reasonably implied, limitations on the individuals who can be selected for an appointment. However, where such limitations do exist, and it can be established that an appointment did not comply with them, the appointment can be challenged. In addition, it may be that "unbridled cases of clear abuse can be reined in by the courts."[422] The appropriate procedure for such a challenge would normally be to seek judicial review of a specific appointment. However, where the alleged defect can be established, and is systemic in nature, a challenge may be brought by application for a general declaration.[423] It should be noted that there appears to be only one such case in Canadian jurisprudence.

Under the Ontario *Hospital Labour Disputes Arbitration Act*, the minister of labour appoints, as chairs of ad hoc boards of interest arbitration, persons who are "in the opinion of the Minister, qualified to act."[424] In *Canadian Union of Public Employees v Ontario (Minister*

---

418 *AG (NSW) v Quinn* (1990), 93 ALR 1 (HCA).

419 *Wells*, above note 254 at para 62.

420 *Griffin v Canada*, [1997] FCJ No 322 (TD) at para 15.

421 *CUPE*, above note 417 at para 91, Binnie J, who refers to Rand J's statement in *Roncarelli v Duplessis*, above note 87 at 140, that "there is always a perspective within which a statute is intended to operate."

422 *Ford, March, 2019*, above note 74 at paras 379–81 commenting on *Roncarelli v Duplessis*, *ibid*, noting that there is no power other than the courts to address such an issue, as the integrity commissioner only has the authority to make recommendations, and pointing out that "in a legislature where the government has a large majority of the members any recommendation [by the integrity commissioner] under the Act that is critical of the conduct of a minister in exercising an appointment power and recommending a penalty would likely be voted down."

423 *CUPE*, above note 417 at para 79.

424 RSO 1990, c H.14, s 6(5).

of Labour), the Supreme Court held that the minister's obligation to exercise his power of appointment in accordance with the statute meant that he was required "to select arbitrators from candidates who were qualified not only by their impartiality, but by their expertise and general acceptance in the labour relations community."[425] Normally no reasons would be provided to explain appointments and consequently the reasons could not be tested against appointment criteria. In this case, the minister indicated that he would choose only retired judges and thereby expressly excluded full consideration of the relevant factors. The applicant unions were successful in obtaining declaratory relief.

The standard of review of an exercise of discretion in making an appointment is presumptively reasonableness and an appointment is most unlikely to fit into one of the narrow exceptions to that presumption.[426] If an appointment violated an express requirement, such as appointing a medical officer of health who was not a physician, as required,[427] the appointment would be unreasonable. Given the wide degree of latitude inherent in a statutory appointment power, successful review will be otherwise unlikely.

3) Terms and Conditions of Appointments

Subject to express legislative provisions to the contrary, and excluding "judges, ministers of the Crown and others who fulfill constitutionally defined state roles" whose relationship to the Crown is dictated by the terms and conventions of the Constitution, the relationship between the government and appointees serving in paid positions is governed by either an express or implied contract of employment.[428] Their contract of employment will be made up of the applicable legislative provisions, the written and verbal "manifestations" of the terms of employment, and the common law.[429]

Section 76 of the *Legislation Act, 2006*[430] governs the appointment of officeholders. Appointments may be for a fixed term, with contrac-

---

425 *CUPE*, above note 417 at para 49.

426 *Canada (Minister of Citizenship and Immigration) v Vavilov*, 2019 SCC 65.

427 *Health Protection and Promotion Act*, RSO 1990, c H.7, s 64.

428 *Wells*, above note 254, quoted in *Dunsmuir v New Brunswick*, 2008 SCC 9 at para 115. See the full discussion of these cases in Chapter 13.

429 *Wells*, above note 254 at para 33.

430 SO 2006, c 21, Sch F.

tual terms governing mid-term dismissal, or "at pleasure," meaning dismissal can be without cause or notice.[431] The legislation establishing a particular position may also provide for terms of the appointment.[432] Any entitlements of OIC appointees are enforceable through the courts, as discussed in Chapter 13.

a) Usual Terms

OIC appointments are governed by the MBC's *Agencies and Appointments Directive*.[433] The directive deals with three classes of appointees, short-term advisory appointments, all other appointments that are not adjudicative, and appointments to positions that are adjudicative. The application of the directive is subject to any statutory requirements in the legislation establishing a position.

Short-term advisory appointments are at pleasure for no more than three years and may or may not be paid positions.[434] Non-adjudicative government appointments are usually made at pleasure for a period not to exceed three years and may be renewed.[435] Adjudicative appointments and appointments to regulatory agencies are normally made for fixed periods not at pleasure, totaling no more than ten years. The initial appointment will normally be for two years followed by three and five-year appointments. There is no right to reappointment when an appointment of any length ends. The initial two-year appointment may be waived in favour of a longer initial appointment and in exceptional circumstances reappointment after ten years may be made.[436]

The *Agencies and Appointments Directive* includes provisions governing the remuneration of appointees including benefits and a schedule of rates for appointments to adjudicative and regulatory tribunals and agencies. The directive includes an ethical framework,[437] further reviewed in Chapter 3. Appointees to an agency prescribed as a public

---

431 *Ibid*, s 76(1) authorizes such appointments.

432 *Ombudsman Act*, above note 223, ss 3 & 4, for example, specifies a term of five years and requires a two-thirds vote of the legislature to end a term early.

433 Management Board of Cabinet (MBC), *Agencies and Appointments Directive*, 9 February 2018, online: www.ontario.ca/page/agencies-and-appointments-directive.

434 *Ibid*, s 2.5.

435 *Ibid*, ss 3.2 & 3.2.1.

436 *Ibid*, s 3.2.2.

437 *Ibid*, s 3.3.

body under the *PSOA* are public servants subject to the ethical framework in that Act.[438] Appointees to provincial agencies are also subject to a separate MBC directive covering reimbursement of expenses.[439]

MBC directives regarding OIC appointees are made pursuant to a general power to make directives for the efficient and effective management of the public service under the *Management Board of Cabinet Act*.[440] Those directives will form part of the employment contract of appointees who are engaged in paid employment, unless the effect of the directives is altered by provisions in their appointment.[441] A change in these directives that is adverse to the appointee's interest will only be applicable once the appointee is informed of the change.[442] The Act provides authority to both make directives or regulations, implying that directives are intended to be administrative actions enforced through contract, and are not subordinate legislation in the nature of regulations.[443] By contrast the provisions of the MBC *Perquisites Directive* under the *Broader Public Sector Accountability Act, 2010*[444] are made mandatory by that Act.

b) End of Appointments

Where an appointment is for a fixed term or a specific task, it expires on the date fixed or at the conclusion of the task without any further action being taken. On non-renewal of a fixed-term appointment, employment simply ceases, and the incumbent has no ongoing claim in contract,[445] nor does the person have a claim to reappointment.[446]

438 *PSOA*, above note 1, s 2(2)5.

439 MBC, *Travel, Meal and Hospitality Expenses Directive*, November 2004, online: www.ontario.ca/page/travel-meal-and-hospitality-expenses-directive-2020, Accountability Rules.

440 RSO 1990, c M.1.

441 *Wells*, above note 254.

442 *Appleby-Ostroff v Canada (Attorney General)*, 2011 FCA 84; *Plumadore v Canada (Attorney General)*, 2016 FC 553.

443 René Dussault & Louis Borgeat, *Administrative Law*, 2d ed (Toronto: Carswell, 1985), Vol 1 at 338–39, as quoted with approval in *Friends of the Oldman River Society v Canada (Minister of Transport)*, [1992] 1 SCR 3.

444 SO 2010, c 25, Part IV.I.

445 *Chambly (City) v Gagnon*, [1999] 1 SCR 8; *Gibson v Alberta*, 2013 ABQB 695.

446 *Wells*, above note 254 at para 62.

A public employer is not obliged to justify a decision not to extend an employment agreement that has expired.[447]

An appointment will also be ended by the death of the appointee or acceptance of their resignation.[448] However, in the absence of expiry, resignation, or death, an appointment will continue unless it is ended by a revocation of the appointment.[449]

c) Mid-term Termination of Appointments

Section 77(a) of the *Legislation Act, 2006* provides that the power to appoint a person to public office includes the power to remove an appointee. In the absence of a legislative process (for example, judges are subject to a statutory process where cause for removal is asserted),[450] Cabinet or the minister responsible for making an appointment is also responsible for removing an appointee. In the event the appointment is on good behaviour, Cabinet or the minister must examine the conduct of the appointee and determine whether it is inconsistent with the standard of good behaviour they determine is appropriate.[451]

The *Legislation Act* also gives the Crown authority to appoint at pleasure meaning that such an appointment may be terminated without notice or compensation.

An appointment that is not made expressly at pleasure may be terminated subject to the terms of the appointment and the underlying contract of employment in accordance with the general law applicable to employment contracts. For further discussion of the legal entitlements of dismissed appointees appointed on good behaviour, or with some express or implied fairness entitlements, either in contract or on judicial

---

447 *Rossmo v Vancouver (City) Police Board*, [2001] BCJ No 2698 (SC) at para 120, upheld on appeal, [2003] BCJ No 2761 (CA). There is the possibility that a legitimate expectation of consideration for renewal could give rise to some form of claim in damages for breach of an employment contract if damages could be proven: *Wells*, above note 254 at para 62. A claim for negligent misrepresentation may also be possible: *Matkowski v Saskatchewan*, 2007 SKQB 46.

448 *Wells*, above note 254 at para 63.

449 *Re Nicholson and Haldimand-Norfolk Regional Board of Commissioners of Police*, 1980 CanLII 1660 (Ont CA), leave to appeal to SCC refused, [1981] 1 SCR 92.

450 *Courts of Justice Act*, above note 262, as discussed above.

451 *Wedge v Canada (Attorney General)*, [1997] FCJ No 872 (FCTD) at paras 30 and 32.

review, see Chapter 13. There are particular complexities attaching to the termination of appointees to adjudicative or regulatory boards.

Good policy reasons exist for government to give up the comparative convenience of dismissing appointees at pleasure without compensation.[452] There is the human resource benefit of the ability to offer secure employment to good candidates for important positions. More importantly this security would serve to ensure officeholders feel confident to advise elected officials, based on their own opinion, rather than what elected officials may wish to hear; and ensure public officeholders carry out their duties without fear of reprisals from elected officials.[453] This choice is the legislature's.

---

452 *Ouellette v Saint-André, an Incorporated Rural Community*, 2013 NBCA 21 at para 17.

453 *Ibid.*

CHAPTER SIX

General Employment-Related Legislation Applicable to the Crown

The Ontario *Employment Standards Act, 2000 (ESA)*, *Freedom of Information and Protection of Privacy Act* (*FIPPA*), *Human Rights Code* (*HRC*), *Occupational Health and Safety Act (OHSA)*, *Pay Equity Act (PEA)*, *Pension Benefits Act (PBA)*, and *Workplace Safety and Insurance Act, 1997 (WSIA)*, as well as the federal employment insurance and Canada Pension Plan legislation and the *Canadian Charter of Rights and Freedoms* (the *Charter*), are the main employment-related statutes of general application that apply to the Crown in Right of Ontario.[1] This chapter deals with: (1) how these statutes apply to the Crown and (2) the caselaw about their application in the Ontario public service. The collective agreement provisions that closely relate to these statutes are also discussed. Labour relations statutes are discussed in later chapters.

Concerning the application of Ontario legislation to the Crown, the starting point is that it does not apply. The *Legislation Act, 2006*[2] provides that "No Act or regulation binds Her Majesty or affects Her Majesty's rights or prerogatives unless it expressly states an intention to do so." However, six Ontario employment-related statutes, the *ESA*,

1 *Employment Standards Act, 2000*, SO 2000, c 41 [*ESA*]; *Freedom of Information and Protection of Privacy Act*, RSO 1990, c F.31 [*FIPPA*]; *Human Rights Code*, RSO 1990, c H.19 [*HRC*]; *Occupational Health and Safety Act*, RSO 1990, c O.1 [*OHSA*]; *Pay Equity Act*, RSO 1990, c P.7 [*PEA*]; *Pension Benefits Act*, RSO 1990, c P.8 [*PBA*]; *Workplace Safety and Insurance Act, 1997*, SO 1997, c 16, Sch A, [*WSIA*]; *Canadian Charter of Rights and Freedoms*, Part I of the *Constitution Act, 1982*, being Schedule B to the *Canada Act 1982* (UK), 1982, c 11 [*Charter*].

2 SO 2006 c 21 Sch F, s 71.

FIPPA, *HRC*, *OHSA*, *PEA*, and the *WSIA*, state they apply to or bind the Crown[3] (although *FIPPA* is only concerned with public institutions in any event.)

Three other pieces of legislation, the provincial *PBA*, and the federal *Employment Insurance Act* (*EIA*)[4] and *Canada Pension Plan Act*[5] are applied to the Crown in a modified or idiosyncratic fashion. Public service pensions have had separate statutory treatment since their introduction.

There is a brief discussion of the Canadian residency requirement in the *Public Officers Act*.[6]

This chapter gives special attention to:

- the *FIPPA* treatment of labour relations and employment documents
- the upholding of the *HRC* through human rights complaints or grievances, including systemic remedies
- the *OHSA* right to health and safety committees, the duty of the employer to take "reasonable precautions," the right to refuse unsafe work, particularly as limited for certain occupations, and the right to not be subject to harassment
- the unique arrangements for the two separate public service pension plans

The Grievance Settlement Board (GSB) and Public Service Grievance Board (PSGB), like all employment arbitrators, have a general obligation to apply employment-related statutes.[7]

A. EMPLOYMENT STANDARDS ACT

The *Employment Standards Act, 2000* contains minimum employment standards applicable to certain classes of employees in Ontario.

---

3 *ESA*, s 3.1; *FIPPA*, s 70; *HRC*, s 47; *OHSA*, s 2(1); *PEA*, s 38; *WSIA* s 67; all above note 1.

4 SC 1996, c 23 [*EIA*].

5 RSC 1985, c C-8.

6 RSO 1990, c P.45.

7 For example, see the discussion in *R v Ontario Public Service Employees Union (Grievor)*, 2015 CanLII 19325 (ON GSB) (Briggs).

1) Application to the Crown

Some of the provisions in the *ESA* apply to the Crown and some do not. This selective application is accomplished by use of the regulatory authority in the *ESA* to exempt any class of employer from all or part of the Act.[8] Statutory language made significant parts of the *ESA* inapplicable to the Crown until 2017 when the statutory partial exemption was ended and replaced with a virtually equivalent regulatory exemption by a new government the following year.[9] There has never been any justification provided for the selective applicability of the ESA to the Crown.[10]

Further to the regulatory exemption power, only the following substantive provisions of the ESA apply to the Crown:[11]

- Continuity of Employment (Part IV)
- Records (Part VI)
- Minimum Wage (Part IX)
- Vacation with Pay (Part XI)
- Equal Pay for Equal Work (Part XII)
- Benefit Plans (Part XIII)
- Leaves of Absence (Part XIV)
- Termination and Severance of Employment (Part XV)
- Lie Detectors (Part XVI)
- Reprisal (Part XVII, except for section 74(1)(a)(vii) and section 74(1)(b))
- Building Services Providers (Part XIX)

General, non-substantive provisions also apply to the Crown.

The main provisions of the Act that are generally inapplicable to the Crown (and Crown agencies, authorities, boards and commissions

---

8 *ESA*, above note 1, s 141(1)3.

9 *The Fair Workplaces, Better Jobs Act, 2017*, SO 2017, c 22, was preceded by the government commissioned Changing Workplaces Review: Ontario Legislative Assembly, *Hansard*, 12 September 2017, 1540 (Kevin Flynn, Minister of Labour). The Review, s 9.2, recommended ending the partial exemption of the Crown, without reasons other than noting there were no submissions supporting its continuance.

10 A review of *Hansard* since the first *ESA* was debated in the legislature in 1968 records no comment on the degree of applicability of the Act to the Crown. The *ESA*, SO 1968, c 35, s 19(5) made only the Equal Pay for Equal Work provisions applicable to the Crown. The 1974 amending Act, SO 1974, c 112, added Benefit Plans, Pregnancy Leave, and Termination of Employment to the list.

11 *ESA*, above note 1, Reg 285/01, s 2.1.

all of whose members were appointed by the Crown) are Payment of Wages (Part V), Tips and Other Gratuities (Part V.I), Hours of Work and Eating Periods (Parts VII, VII.I), Overtime (Part VIII), Public Holidays (Part X), and Vacation with Pay (Part XI), as well as the related employer provision.[12]

The Act does not apply to inmates of correctional facilities; offenders performing work under sentencing order; holders of political, religious, or judicial office; members of quasi-judicial tribunals; or police officers.[13] A justice of the peace was found to be an "office holder" and accordingly not an employee, even though aspects of their employment indicated that they ought to be considered to be an employee.[14] While the *ESA* does not define a "quasi-judicial tribunal," most of the order-in-council appointees to the various adjudicative tribunals constituted under provincial legislation are likely to be exempted.

Where the *ESA* exempts prescribed employees from specific provisions of the Act—and not because these employees are Crown employees—the exemptions apply to the Crown as well. For example, severance pay provisions, which apply to the Crown, exempt employees in certain industries, including road maintenance, from receiving severance pay.[15] Accordingly, once the GSB found that government snowplow operators[16] and zone painters[17] were engaged in the maintenance of roads, they were excluded by the *ESA* and not entitled to severance pay.

2) Interrelationship with the *PSOA*

The *Public Service of Ontario Act, 2006 (PSOA)*[18] and government directives, combined with collective agreement entitlements, commonly provide the same or better employment standards for public servants

12 *Ibid*, s 4(4.1).

13 *Ibid*, ss 3(5) 4, 5, 7, 8, and 10. Police officers are subject to the Lie Detector (Part XVI) provisions and, under s 141(2.1)(c), can have access to emergency leave for infectious disease emergencies.

14 *Re Devine*, [1996] OESAD No 41 (Ont Adj Muir).

15 Reg 288/01, s 9(1)8.

16 *OPSEU (Group Grievance) and The Crown in Right of Ontario (Ministry of Transportation)*, GSB#2588/96, 6 May 1998 (Fisher).

17 *OPSEU (Blais) and The Ministry of Transportation*, GSB#2170/96, 4 May 1999 (Petryshen).

18 SO 2006, c 35, Sch A [*PSOA*].

than are contained in the *ESA*. For example, the *PSOA* provisions supporting security of tenure, and the directive and collective agreement provisions for benefits and job security entitlements for regular employees, are not in any way matched under the *ESA*. However, the *PSOA* regime sometimes provides lesser coverage, particularly in the areas of hours of overtime, vacation, and leaves. A leading example is that the Ontario Public Service (OPS) has no maximum hours of work for employees in Schedule 6, while the *ESA* (Part VIII, Overtime) requires overtime after a certain number of hours.

Where the provisions of the ESA are applicable to the Crown, and there are similar but not the same entitlements available to an OPS employee, it will be necessary to determine the applicability of section 5(2) of the *ESA*, which states that if other entitlements that directly relate to the same subject matter as an employment standard provide a greater benefit, then those provisions apply, and the employment standard does not apply. The greater benefit is determined taking into account the benefit for the bargaining unit as a whole, rather than the effect on an individual grievor.[19] Where the collective agreement provided for a wider range of relatives for whom bereavement leave could be taken than the Act, this did not cause the leave provisions to supersede the Act entitlement to a total of ten bereavement and emergency days.[20]

Where provisions in the *ESA* are not applicable to the Crown, the relevant parties may negotiate for terms of employment less than the *ESA* minimum. In other words, the "no contracting out" protection in section 5 of the *ESA* only applies to those provisions that apply to the Crown. For example, the GSB noted that Part X (Public Holidays) of the *ESA* did not apply to the Crown, and, since the collective agreement was silent on the issue of regular part-time workers being compensated for holidays that fell on their scheduled days off, the grievors were not entitled to compensation and their grievances were dismissed.[21] Under Part X of the *ESA*, these regular part-time workers would receive holiday pay for a pro-rated amount, assuming they met certain criteria.

---

19 *Ontario Public Service Employees Union v Ontario (Ministry of Community Safety and Correctional Services)*, 2013 CanLII 18496 (ON GSB) (Briggs).

20 *Ontario Public Service Employees Union (Van Zeggelaar) v Ontario (Community Safety and Correctional Services)*, 2017 CanLII 65617 (ON GSB) (Williamson).

21 *OPSEU (Derochie et al) v the Crown (Ministry of Community, Family and Children's Services)*, [2003] OGSBA No 44 (Hunter).

While termination and severance pay are an area of generally superior benefits for OPS regular employees, *ESA* entitlements have been important for employees who are not otherwise eligible to receive full collective agreement-based severance. The GSB has confirmed the *ESA* severance entitlements of public servants.[22] Temporary employees on short-term assignments were entitled to credit for all employment when severance pay entitlement was being determined.[23] Seasonal employees, who retain recall rights during the off-season, have been found entitled to severance pay based on cumulative service, despite section 9 of the *Public Service Act* (*PSA*), which stated that a person appointed for a specified period ceases to be a public servant at the expiration of that period.[24] The provisions of the collective agreement and the practices of the parties have been found to indicate a clear intention to structure and protect an ongoing relationship. The same rationale will likely apply under the virtually identical section 54 in the *PSOA*. In another case, the employee was not entitled to severance under the *ESA*, but the amount provided under that Act was used as a "yardstick" for the appropriate damages.[25]

B. *FREEDOM OF INFORMATION AND PROTECTION OF PRIVACY ACT*

The *Freedom of Information and Protection of Privacy Act* regulates access to the records of the government of Ontario, as well as designated agencies and service provider organizations, and protects the privacy of individuals' personal information held by those institutions.[26] The *FIPPA* treats each ministry as a separate institution, and any decisions made under the Act by a "head" of the institution may be appealed

---

22 *OPSEU v Ontario (Ministry of Health and Long-Term Care) (Severance Pay Grievance)*, [2003] OGSBA No 40 (Brown).

23 *OPSEU (Union Grievance) v The Crown in Right of Ontario (Management Board Secretariat)*, GSB#73/97, 17 November 1997 (Roberts) at 7.

24 *Re Ontario Ministry of Natural Resources*, [1992] OESAD No 218 (Ont Adj Randall) at 18.

25 *OPSEU (Maxwell) and The Crown in Right of Ontario (Ministry of Citizenship, Culture and Recreation)*, GSB#951/96, 25 July 1996 (Roberts).

26 *FIPPA*, above note 1, Purpose, s 1, definition of "institution," s 2(1), list of agencies: RRO 1990, Reg 460, Schedule. The *Personal Information Protection and Electronic Documents Act*, SC 2000, c 5 [*PIPEDA*] is federal legislation that applies to provincially regulated commercial activity but not the Ontario government.

to the information and privacy commissioner (IPC). The *FIPPA* binds the Crown.[27]

Two aspects of the *FIPPA* are particularly relevant to the employment of public servants:

1) The discretionary exclusion from disclosure of their advice
2) The non-application of FIPPA to records about employment and labour relations matters.

1) Exemption of Advice or Recommendations of a Public Servant

Under section 13 of the *FIPPA*, a head "may refuse to disclose a record where the disclosure would reveal advice or recommendations of a public servant." The head shall not refuse to disclose a record that contains factual material, surveys, an environmental impact statement, a test on a product, various reports, a feasibility study, a final plan, or proposal to change or establish a program, or reasons for a decision. A head shall not refuse to disclose a record where the record is more than twenty years old or where the head has publicly cited the record as the basis for making a decision or formulating a policy.

The reason for the discretion to not disclose advice and recommendations was stated by Rothstein J of the Supreme Court as being:

> to preserve an effective and neutral public service so as to permit public servants to provide full, free, and frank advice. . . . Failing to exempt such material risks having advice or recommendations that are less candid and complete, and the public service no longer being perceived as neutral. . . .
>
> In my opinion, Evans J. (as he then was) in *Canadian Council of Christian Charities v. Canada (Minister of Finance)*[[28]] persuasively explained the rationale for the exemption for advice given by public servants. . . . :
>
>> It would be an intolerable burden to force ministers and their advisors to disclose to public scrutiny the internal evolution of the policies ultimately adopted. Disclosure of such material would often reveal that the policy-making process included

27 *FIPPA*, above note 1, s 70.

28 *Canadian Council of Christian Charities v Canada (Minister of Finance)*, 1999 CanLII 8293 (FC) at paras 30–31.

> false starts, blind alleys, wrong turns, changes of mind, the solicitation and rejection of advice, and the re-evaluation of priorities and the re-weighing of the relative importance of the relevant factors as a problem is studied more closely. In the hands of journalists or political opponents this is combustible material liable to fuel a fire that could quickly destroy governmental credibility and effectiveness.
>
> Political neutrality, both actual and perceived, is an essential feature of the civil service in Canada (*Osborne v. Canada (Treasury Board))*[[29]]; *OPSEU v. Ontario (Attorney General)*[[30]]. The advice and recommendations provided by a public servant who knows that his work might one day be subject to public scrutiny is less likely to be full, free, and frank, and is more likely to suffer from self-censorship. Similarly, a decision maker might hesitate to even request advice or recommendations in writing concerning a controversial matter if he knows the resulting information might be disclosed. Requiring that such advice or recommendations be disclosed risks introducing actual or perceived partisan considerations into public servants' participation in the decision-making process.
>
> Interpreting "advice" in s. 13(1) as including opinions of a public servant as to the range of alternative policy options accords with the balance struck by the legislature between the goal of preserving an effective public service capable of producing full, free, and frank advice and the goal of providing a meaningful right of access.[31]

The protection applies to the advice whether or not it is communicated.[32] Public servants may engage in writing drafts until they are satisfied that the information is ready to communicate. In order for there to be "full, free, and frank participation" in the development process, the exemption must apply throughout.

It is only the disclosure of advice, and "not other kinds of information such as factual, background, analytical or evaluative material,

---

29 *Osborne v Canada (Treasury Board)*, [1991] 2 SCR 69 at 86, discussed in Chapter 3.

30 *Ontario (Attorney General) v OPSEU*, [1987] 2 SCR 2 at 44–45.

31 *John Doe v Ontario (Finance)*, 2014 SCC 36 at paras 43–46 [*John Doe*], discussed in *Ontario (Finance) (Re)*, 2015 CanLII 15989 (ON IPC); *Wilfrid Laurier University (Re)*, 2018 CanLII 49118 (ON IPC).

32 *John Doe, ibid* at paras 50–51.

which could reasonably be expected to inhibit the free flow of expertise and professional assistance within the deliberative process of government."[33] Neither of the terms "advice" or "recommendations" extend to "objective information" or factual material.[34] "To qualify as 'advice' or 'recommendations,' the information contained in the records must relate to a course or courses of action, which may ultimately be accepted or rejected by its recipient during the deliberative process."

Examples of the types of information that have been found *not* to qualify as advice or recommendations include:

- factual or background information
- analytical information
- evaluative information
- notifications or cautions
- views
- a supervisor's direction to staff on how to conduct an investigation[35]

The section 13 discretionary exemption is subject to review by the IPC for whether the institution was unreasonable in the exercise of that discretion.[36] In addition, the exemption can be overridden by the "compelling public interest" override of exemptions in section 23, under which the exemption does not apply if there is a compelling public interest

---

33 *Order PO-2028, Ontario (Northern Development and Mines) (Re)*, 2002 CanLII 46430 (ON IPC), upheld on judicial review in *Ontario (Ministry of Northern Development and Mines) v Ontario (Assistant Information and Privacy Commissioner)*, 2004 CanLII 15009 (ON SCDC) at para 18, aff'd 2005 CanLII 34229 (ON CA), leave to appeal refused [2005] SCCA No 564. See also *Ontario (Northern Development and Mines) (Re)*, 2016 CanLII 94023 (ON IPC) at paras 41–47.

34 Information and privacy commissioner, quoted with approval by Court of Appeal in *Ontario (Ministry of Transportation) v Consulting Engineers of Ontario*, 2005 CanLII 34228 (ON CA) at para 20 [*Consulting Engineers*], in deciding that "advice" does not extend to scores of bidders in a request for proposal.

35 *Order PO-2626, York University (Re)*, 2007 CanLII 54658 (ON IPC) at 10. The list in the case includes draft documents, but this is now too broad given the later decision in *John Doe*, above note 31. Where factual information and advice are "inextricably intertwined," disclosure will not be ordered: *Ontario (Health) (Re)*, 2022 CanLII 76330 (ON IPC) at para 80.

36 *Ontario (Labour) (Re)*, 2015 CanLII 31652 (ON IPC) at paras 45–49 [*Ontario (Labour)*] and *London Health Sciences Centre (Re)*, 2022 CanLII 61408 (ON IPC). See also the discussion of the exercise of this discretion in the labour and employment records discussion below.

that clearly outweighs the purpose of the exemption.[37] The IPC has found there is more likely to be a compelling public interest in learning about important facts, operational information, policies, and decisions, than in learning about bureaucratic advice.[38] Advice concerning how to keep drinking water safe was ordered to be disclosed because it could contribute to addressing gaps in regulatory protection.[39]At the same time, there is a public interest in "full, free, and frank" advice protected by confidentiality,[40] and disclosure may not be ordered because it may inhibit "the free flow of advice" about ongoing situations.[41]

2) Labour and Employment Records

The *FIPPA* is not applicable to a broad range of labour and employment records. Where the *FIPPA* does apply, those records, along with other personal information falling under the Act (for example, medical records), can still only be produced or disclosed in accordance with the Act. Applicability of the Act entails consideration of exemptions.

a) Non-application of *FIPPA* to Many Records Related to Employment and Labour Relations

Section 65(6) of the *FIPPA* establishes the non-application of the Act to, or records "in relation to," the following:

- Proceedings or anticipated proceedings before a court, tribunal, or other entity relating to labour relations or to the employment of a person by the institution
- Negotiations or anticipated negotiations relating to labour relations or to the employment of a person by the institution between the institution and a person, bargaining agent, or party to a proceeding or an anticipated proceeding

---

37 This override provision is also discussed in more detail concerning labour and employment records below.

38 *Ontario (Environment, Conservation and Parks) (Re)*, 2020 CanLII 92584 (ON IPC) at para 138; *Workplace Safety and Insurance Board (Re)*, 2021 CanLII 103987 (ON IPC) at para 70.

39 *Ontario (Environment, Conservation and Parks) (Re)*, 2022 CanLII 40810 (ON IPC) at para 85.

40 *Ontario (Labour)*, above note 36 at para 44.

41 *Ontario (Environment) (Re)*, 2014 CanLII 55702 (ON IPC) at para 119.

- Meetings, consultations, discussions, or communications about labour relations or employment-related matters in which the institution has an interest

The section only applies to employment records of the employer, and not to another institution's employment records.[42]

This exclusion makes the rest of the Act inapplicable, and so prevents access requests by third parties. It also precludes public sector employees from obtaining access to employment-related records about themselves and from proceeding with a privacy complaint under the *FIPPA* regarding disclosure or use of their personal information. The public interest override of exemptions from disclosure[43] does not apply to the records excluded from the scope of the Act under section 65(6).[44] Judicial review of a decision by the IPC regarding whether section 65(6) applies is on the standard of reasonableness unless the issues raised bring the matter within the exceptions to that standard articulated by the Supreme Court.[45]

The subsection has been broadly applied in accordance with the legislative intent. It was added to the *FIPPA* as part of sweeping labour law reforms asserted to be "designed to restore a much-needed balance to labour-management relations."[46] The included amendments to the provincial, and municipal, freedom of information legislation were

---

42 *Office of the Independent Police Review Director*, 2021 CanLII 113546 (ON IPC), finding that the Office could not rely on the section to deny access to investigation records related to the requestor's employment with the York Regional Police.

43 *FIPPA*, above note 1, s 23 is discussed below.

44 *Order MO-1806, Toronto Housing Authority*, 2004 CanLII 56247 (ON IPC) at 12 [*Order MO-1806*]; *Ontario (Solicitor General) v Mitchinson*, 2001 CanLII 8582 (ON CA) at para 21, leave to appeal to SCC refused, [2001] SCCA No 509 [*Ontario (Solicitor General)*].

45 *Ontario (Attorney General) v Ontario (Information and Privacy Commissioner)*, 2022 ONCA 74 (CanLII), leave to appeal granted 2022 CanLII 40784 (SCC); *Brockville (City) v Information and Privacy Commissioner, Ontario*, 2020 ONSC 4413 [*Brockville*]. *Canada (Minister of Citizenship and Immigration) v Vavilov*, 2019 SCC 65, has established a presumption that the standard of review of administrative tribunal decisions is reasonableness unless a different standard is determined by the legislature or is required by the rule of law (e.g., constitutional questions, matters affecting the legal system generally or the jurisdictional boundaries between administrative bodies).

46 Elizabeth Witmer, Minister of Labour, introducing the *Labour Relations and Employment Statute Law Amendment Act*, SO 1995, c 1, s 82: Ontario Legislative Assembly, *Hansard*, 4 October 1995, at 1350.

intended "to ensure the confidentiality of labour relations information."[47] (Section 65(7) creates a specific exception to the exclusion for certain agreements—collective agreements, settlements of grievances or other litigation, contracts of employment, and expense claims. These exceptions are discussed later in this chapter.)

The Court of Appeal has held that the words "in which an institution has an interest" should be read to refer to all matters involving the government's own workforce.[48] The word "interest" does require more than mere curiosity or concern but does not mean "legal interest." If the section 65(6) exclusion applied to the record at any time the record was being "collected, prepared, maintained or used" then the exclusion is permanently applicable, and the Act never applies.

If the preparation (or collection, maintenance, or use) of a record was for the purpose of, as a result of, or substantially connected to, labour or employment relations, it will be found to be "in relation to" that activity.[49]

The excluded records are "documents related to matters in which the institution is acting as employer, and terms and conditions of employment or human resources questions are at issue. Employment-related matters are separate and distinct from matters related to employees' actions."[50] The exclusion does not make the *FIPPA* non-applicable to records concerning the actions or inactions of an employee simply because that conduct may give rise to a civil action in which the Crown may be held vicariously liable for torts caused by its employees.[51]

It is the record as a whole that is examined, and the record as a whole must be "sufficiently connected" to an excluded purpose to remove the entire record from the scope of the Act.[52] If it is sufficiently

---

47 *Ibid*, David Johnson, Chair, Management Board of Cabinet.

48 *Ontario (Solicitor General)*, above note 44 at para 35.

49 *Order P-1223, Ontario (Agriculture, Food and Rural Affairs) (Re)*, 1996 CanLII 7647 (ON IPC) [*Order P-1223*]; *Order PO-2211, Ontario (Environment) (Re)*, 2003 CanLII 53961 (ON IPC) [*Order PO-2211*]; *Record PC-020052-1, Ministry of Public Safety and Security*, 2003 CanLII 53839 (ON IPC) [*Record PC-020052-1*].

50 *Order PO-4149, Workplace Safety and Insurance Board (Re)*, 2021 CanLII 49628 (ON IPC) at para 29.

51 *Ontario (Correctional Services) v Goodis*, 2008 CanLII 2603 (ON SCDC) [*Goodis*]. See also the discussion below about the notes and files of investigators.

52 *Order PO-3642, Ontario (Community Safety and Correctional Services) (Re)*, 2016 CanLII 55939 (ON IPC) 5–6 at paras 18–21. This is consistent with the lack

connected, the whole record is excluded as there is no provision for severance of such records.

The labour relations exclusion has three component sub-exclusions, but in practice it is the third—"meetings, consultations, discussions or communications about labour relations or employment related matters in which the institution has an interest"—that has the most application. In a case seeking disclosure of the Ministry of Government Services job evaluation system (JES), a database of job positions, job descriptions, classification standards, and job evaluations (a written rationale as to why a particular position was assigned to a particular classification level), the IPC held that, while parts of the JES were used in respect of grievance proceedings and labour negotiations, that was not the purpose of creating the entire record, so the first and second of the listed sub-exclusions did not apply.[53] However, the system was used in meetings and consultations, as it was created to assist the ministry in managing its workforce, and so the third sub-exclusion applied.

Under the third sub-exclusion, the focus shifts from "employment of a person" to "employment-related matters" more generally, but still should be taken to relate to the institution's own workforce.[54] The change in wording does not extend the reach of the provision to cover a ministry's interest in provincial agencies not designated as subject to the *FIPPA*, unless there is an employment relationship between the ministry and that agency's employees, or a labour relations relationship between the ministry and that agency.[55]

Grievances under a collective agreement between a union and the Ontario government are, by their very nature, about labour relations matters.[56] A ministry has an interest in records that relate to its own workforce. It also has an inherent interest in working with bargaining agents to resolve grievances filed pursuant to collective agreements

---

of severance of portions of excluded records, in contrast with the severability of records subject to the exemptions. See also *Order PO-3926, Ontario Power Generation (Re)*, 2019 CanLII 12445 (ON IPC); *Ontario (Finance) (Re)*, 2021 CanLII 93066 (ON IPC) at paras 39–41; *Windsor (City) (Re)*, 2022 CanLII 122358 (ON IPC).

53 *Order PO-2613, Ontario (Government Services) (Re)*, 2007 CanLII 42221 (ON IPC).

54 *Ontario (Solicitor General)*, above note 44.

55 *Order PO- 3982, Ontario (Finance) (Re)*, 2019 CanLII 82865 (ON IPC).

56 *Order P-1223*, above note 49; *Order P-1255, Ministry of Transportation (Re)*, 1996 CanLII 7679 (ON IPC).

involving the ministry's workforce. It therefore "has an interest" in all these matters, satisfying the requirements of section 65(6).[57]

The term "labour relations" refers to both a collective bargaining relationship governed by collective bargaining legislation, and to analogous relationships.[58] Records relating to negotiations with associations of professionals excluded from the coverage of the *Crown Employees Collective Bargaining Act, 1993* (*CECBA*)[59] are covered by the exclusion. The relationship between the government and physicians, and the work of the Physician Services Committee, which negotiates remuneration for physicians, are included as labour relations even though doctors are not employees. Records dealing with deputy judges are similarly covered by the exclusion due to their collective action through the Ontario Deputy Judges Association to negotiate with the government, which involves them in labour relations.[60]

The term "employment-related" does not limit the relationship in question to "employees" but can include relationships that have the "trappings" of employment.[61] Records dealing with auxiliary members of the Ontario Provincial Police (OPP) are included because, although they do not get a salary, they are hired, have performance standards, and are subject to termination.

Records dealing with order-in-council appointees to boards are covered by the exclusion because, while they have adjudicative independence, and are appointed through a political appointments process for

57 *Record PC-020052-1*, above note 49; *Amalgamated Transit Union—Local 1587 (Keaney) v Ontario (Greater Toronto Transit Authority—GO Transit)*, 2010 CanLII 45247 (ON GSB) (Harris).

58 *Order P-1257, Liquor Control Board of Ontario (Re)*, 1996 CanLII 7681 (ON IPC); *Ontario (Minister of Health and Long Term Care) v Mitchinson*, 2003 CanLII 16894 (ON CA). The adjudicator in *Order MO-1806*, above note 44, comes to a contrary opinion not realizing that the Court of Appeal had reversed the Divisional Court and quashed the decision on this point on 27 October 2003.

59 SO 1993, c 38 [*CECBA*].

60 *Ontario (Attorney General) (Re)*, 2006 CanLII 50844 (ON IPC). The principle of judicial independence is not impeded by a finding that excludes records on this basis from the scope of an access to information scheme, even though this includes deputy judges in a group with others to whom a constitutional guarantee of independence does not apply. As discussed in Chapter 5, their independence is supported by an independent remuneration commission.

61 *Order MO-3010* referred to in *Ontario (Community Safety and Correctional Services) (Re)*, 2017 CanLII 21092 (ON IPC).

a specified duration of time, and are not employed in the traditional sense, they are subject to a code of conduct to be applied by the chair in reviewing their performance, recommending re-appointment, and so on.[62]

Just as a wide range of relationships have been found to be within scope, so have a wide range of records. One IPC decision notes that "recording of information about overtime worked for scheduling and payment purposes is so clearly a part of standard personnel-management practices that it hardly requires any more specific an explanation of why such information" is excluded.[63]

Appointments, promotions, transfers, job competitions, resignations, dismissals, a "voluntary exit" program, and indeed any transactions that are significant to the employment relationship are employment-related matters and therefore excluded from the Act's coverage.[64] The complete hiring process, recruitment, screening, and interviewing satisfy the requirements of the term "employment-related" matter, regardless of the fact that a requester may not ultimately be the successful candidate and "employed."[65] Where records are kept about the hiring or potential hiring of employees by a security services contractor, they are subject to the exemption even though only some of those employees became employees of the institution itself.[66]

Minutes of meetings between employer and union representatives,[67] records collected in connection with occupational health and safety issues,[68] and material collected in an investigation under the employer's *Workplace Discrimination and Harassment Policy* (*WDHP*) are

---

62 *Landlord and Tenant Board (Re)*, 2011 CanLII 9755 (ON IPC).

63 *Order PO-2248, Ministry of Public Safety and Security (Re)*, 2004 CanLII 56366.

64 *Order PO-2106, Archives of Ontario (Re)*, 2003 CanLII 53857 (ON IPC); *Order M-830, City of Hamilton (Re)*, 1996 CanLII 7535 (ON IPC); *Order PO-1950, Ministry of the Attorney General (Re)*, 2001 CanLII 26148 (ON IPC); *Order P-1223*, above note 49; *Ontario (Consumer Services) (Re)*, 2011 CanLII 20308 (ON IPC); *Ontario Power Generation (Re)*, 2021 CanLII 27062 (ON IPC).

65 *Order P-1627, Ministry of the Attorney General (Re)*, 1998 CanLII 14324 (ON IPC); *Order PO-1685-F, Ministry of the Attorney General (Re)*, 1999 CanLII 14364 (ON IPC); *Order MO-1291, Durham Regional Police Services Board (Re)*, 2000 CanLII 21045 (ON IPC).

66 *Order MO-1806*, above note 44.

67 *Ibid.*

68 *Order P-1250, Ministry of the Attorney General (Re)*, 1996 CanLII 7674 (ON IPC).

subject to the exclusion,[69] even if the investigation is conducted by an external investigator.[70] The exclusion applies where the allegedly violent behaviour was by a member of the public against staff, as workplace violence is an employment-related matter.[71] A video surveillance tape of a picket line falls within the exclusion, even though the video captured individuals other than striking ministry staff.[72] An audit about use of external funds was excluded where employees were expected to comply with employer policy about funding.[73]

Retiree insurance policies and related documents are also excluded.[74] As the reimbursement of malpractice insurance fees is a form of compensation to physicians, records describing formal arrangements for government reimbursement of physicians' professional liability insurance premiums are within scope.[75]

The notes of investigators including OPP officers, need to be examined individually to determine if they are employment-related.[76] Where the request is essentially directed to the content of a police investigation, rather than the conduct of an officer, then the records will likely be found not to be covered by the exclusion, as a broad application of the exclusion "would have the effect of permanently removing certain information maintained by the Police with respect to their basic mandate (i.e., protection of the peace and investigation of possible criminal behaviour which comes to their attention) from the scope of the Act."[77] The original incident sheet and general occurrence report has been ordered disclosed where there is no direct relation to subsequent complaints or proceedings.[78] By contrast, where the investigation itself is generated by

---

69 *Order P-1223*, above note 49; *Order P-1242, Ministry of Community and Social Services (Re)*, 1996 CanLII 7666 (ON IPC).

70 *Order PO-2819, Northern College of Applied Arts and Technology (Re)*, 2009 CanLII 45428 (ON IPC).

71 *Order MO-3760, Thunder Bay (City) (Re)*, 2019 CanLII 144770 (ON IPC).

72 *Record PC-020052-1*, above note 49.

73 *Order PO-3320, McMaster University (Re)*, 2014 CanLII 14101 (ON IPC).

74 *Order PO-2212, Management Board Secretariat (Re)*, 2003 CanLII 53962 (ON IPC).

75 *Order PO-2497, Ontario (Health and Long-Term Care) (Re)*, 2006 CanLII 50840 (ON IPC) [*Order PO-2497*].

76 *Goodis*, above note 51 at para 29.

77 *Order PO-2809, Ontario (Community Safety and Correctional Services) (Re)*, 2009 CanLII 41336 (ON IPC) at 11, quoting *Order M-927, Toronto (Police Services Board) (Re)*, 2010 CanLII 13633 (ON IPC).

78 *Order MO-2556, London Police Services Board (Re)*, 2010 CanLII 61907 (ON IPC).

a complaint, disciplinary hearing, or where a verbal inquiry to the OPP led to an investigation into the conduct of an officer, the records of that investigation were found to be covered by the exclusion.[79]

Where a fire truck was stolen while the responsible firefighters were in a shopping plaza, there was a record-by-record analysis of whether each record related to employment matters, and the records regarding damage to the truck and negotiations with the insurance company were found to not "in essence" be about employment-related matters.[80] A combined spreadsheet used by OC Transpo to track bus collisions, containing fields setting out investigators notes, the city's determinations about driver fault, and recommendations and determinations about driver sanctions and retraining, was found to be an excluded employment record.[81]

Records about a complaint that relate to the existence of the complaint itself, how to gather information, and how to respond, but not to the actions of the employee, will not be excluded.[82]

The exclusion does not extend to general training materials about operational procedures although it does apply to communications about the employment-related training or qualifications of a particular individual.[83]

The broad scope of the exclusion is mitigated by the requirement that a "fairly substantial connection" to a labour relations or employment-related matter is required in order for section 65(6) to apply.[84] Recognizing that "government institutions necessarily act through their employees" and that the exclusion of large numbers of records can

---

79 *Order PO-2211*, above note 49; *Order PO-2931*, *Ontario (Community Safety and Correctional Services) (Re)*, 2010 CanLII 70804 (ON IPC); *Order MO-4029*, *Waterloo Regional Police Services Board (Re)*, 2021 CanLII 25301 (ON IPC).

80 *Order MO-2337*, *Toronto (City) (Re)*, 2008 CanLII 46556 (ON IPC) [*Order MO-2337*].

81 *Order MO-4080*, *Ottawa (City) (Re)*, 2021 CanLII 59459 (ON IPC).

82 *Ontario (Labour, Training and Skills Development) (Re)*, 2021 CanLII 93064 (ON IPC) at paras 30–36.

83 *Order PO-2928*, *Ontario (Community Safety and Correctional Services) (Re)*, 2010 CanLII 68842 (ON IPC) at 6–7.

84 *Order P-1223*, above note 49; *Order P-1369*, *Ministry of Consumer and Commercial Relations (Re)*, 1997 CanLII 11886 (ON IPC) [*Order P-1369*]; *Brockville*, above note 45, finding that it is reasonable for the IPC to conclude legal invoices for collective bargaining representation do not have sufficient connection to the substantive labour relations between the parties.

"undermine the public accountability purpose of the Act,"[85] the exclusion should not apply to routine operational records that only have the potential to be connected to an employment-related concern, such as routine recordings of telephone calls with customers.[86]

Information on the number of employees in different categories of employment is not excluded because it is not enough that the information is descriptive of the workforce, as the records need to "address matters in which the [employer] is acting as an employer, and the terms and conditions of employment or human resources questions are at issue."[87]

The exclusion does not apply to a broad operational review even though organizational structure is included,[88] and even though such a review contains information that may have an impact on future labour negotiations or may contain suggestions about the creation or elimination of certain positions in an organization.[89] However, an operational review will be excluded if it is focused on the working environment and human resources processes,[90] such as a review of the operation of a facility during a labour dispute that related conditions at the facility to the effects of the strike.[91] Records containing information about plans for staff reductions or redeployment, documents regarding ministry staffing levels and anticipated reduction in those levels, and briefing

---

85 *Consulting Engineers*, above note 34 at para 28, as discussed in *Workplace Safety and Insurance Board (Re)*, 2021 CanLII 134156 (ON IPC).

86 *Workplace Safety and Insurance Board (Re)*, *ibid*, discussing *Ministry of Community and Social Services v Doe*, 2014 ONSC 239, upheld in *Ontario (Community and Social Services) v John Doe*, 2015 ONCA 107 [*Doe, 2014 and 2015*].

87 *University of Ontario Institute of Technology (Re)*, 2022 CanLII 26220 (ON IPC) at para 90.

88 *Interim Order PO-3029-I, Ontario (Alcohol and Gaming Commission) (Re)*, 2011 CanLII 83521 (ON IPC) at para 49. Similarly, a report advising on the transfer of police services to First Nations communities was not excluded, even though it touched on employment matters, because it was not created to address employment matters: *Order PO-4095, Ontario (Solicitor General) (Re)*, 2020 CanLII 103774 (ON IPC).

89 *Order P-1369*, above note 84; *Order M-941, The Corporation of the Town of Oakville (Re)*, 1997 CanLII 11676 (ON IPC); *Order MO-1654-I, City of Hamilton (Re)*, 2003 CanLII 53752 (ON IPC).

90 *Order PO-3194, Algonquin College (Re)*, 2013 CanLII 24007 (ON IPC).

91 *Order PO-2157, Ministry of Public Safety and Security (Re)*, 2003 CanLII 53908 (ON IPC).

notes regarding planned reorganizations that involve declaring employees surplus are communications within the exclusion.[92]

Records collected or prepared in relation to a ministry's regulatory and policymaking responsibilities, such as consideration of a regulation governing political activity by police officers, may not be excluded, though they were "collected, prepared, maintained or used" by the ministry in relation to "meetings, consultations, discussions or communications," because the records were not "about employment-related matters" of the ministry.[93]

Note that the exclusion of employment and labour relations information from the application of the *FIPPA* does not imply that the employer's discretion with respect to such information is unfettered. The government is subject to restrictions that may be created expressly or by implication in public servants' employment contracts, collective agreements, or applicable legislation. Personal health information is to be safeguarded from inadvertent disclosure, and the employer is liable for not taking reasonable steps to prevent unauthorized access.[94]

The GSB has found that the employer was under an obligation to keep the addresses of staff at the Oak Ridge psychiatric facility confidential for health and safety purposes.[95]

Health professionals employed by government remain subject to professional obligations to ensure the confidentiality of health records in their custody or knowledge. These professionals are employed subject to their professional obligations and consequently the employer can only require disclosure of medical records in their custody where consent or express authority is provided.[96] This is reinforced by the

---

92 *Order P-1516, Ministry of Community and Social Services (Re)*, 1998 CanLII 14205 (ON IPC); *Order PO-2318, Ministry of Natural Resources (Re)*, 2004 CanLII 56436 (ON IPC).

93 *Interim Order PO-2093-I, Ministry of the Solicitor General (Re)*, 2002 CanLII 46494 (ON IPC).

94 *Ontario Public Service Employees Union (Myciak et al) v Ontario (Community Safety and Correctional Services)*, 2015 CanLII 90137 (ON GSB) (Briggs) at 16–17.

95 *OPSEU (MacLean, More and Union Grievance) and Ministry of Health*, GSB#1134/88, 9 January 1990 (Barrett); and *OHSA* section below.

96 See physician's confidentiality obligation to patient under *Medicine Act, 1991*, SO 1991, c 30, O Reg 856/93, s 1(1) 10; *Quebec (AG) v Canada (AG)*, [1979] 1 SCR 218, Pigeon J at 250: "[A]n employee's duty of obedience towards his employer does not mean that the latter has any power to compel his employee to act in breach of a duty of confidentiality The medical director of a hospital cannot release a doctor from his obligation of confidentiality towards his patient, only

OHSA[97] provision which states that "[n]o employer shall seek to gain access, except by an order of the court or other tribunal or in order to comply with another statute, to a health record concerning a worker without the worker's written consent," which has been interpreted to apply not just to requests from third parties but to the employer's own records.[98] In the absence of the patient's consent, the government will normally require an order or summons from the GSB or PSGB in order to obtain health information records in the custody of a health professional on its own staff.

Personal health information in the custody of health information custodians, which would normally include health care professionals in the employ of the government, is not subject to the *FIPPA* but is subject to the *Personal Health Information Protection Act, 2004* (*PHIPA*).[99] There is an exemption under the *PHIPA* if a record is "maintained primarily for a purpose other than the provision of health care or assistance in the provision of health care to employees or other agents."[100] Labour arbitrators and the Divisional Court have taken the view that an expansive view of "health care" includes determining if an employee can be accommodated without risk of further injury, with resultant limitations on the sharing of that information even for employment purposes.[101] The determination of the IPC, which seems more practical, is that the exemption does apply if the record is maintained primarily for employment purposes, such as capacity to work, entitlement to sick pay, and workplace accommodation needs.[102]

b) Application of *FIPPA* to Certain Labour Relations/Employment Records

Section 65(7) of the *FIPPA* establishes application of the Act through an exemption from the labour and employment record exclusion for a subset of labour relations and employment records, namely "[a]n agreement

the latter may release him from his duty"; *R v Worth*, [1989] OJ No 1301 (HCJ), and cases cited therein.

97 Above note 1, s 63(2).

98 *Orillia Soldiers' Memorial Hospital v Ontario Public Service Employees' Union, Local 383*, 2020 CanLII 91949 (ON LA) at para 41 [*Orillia*].

99 SO 2004, c 3, Sch A, s 8 [*PHIPA*].

100 *Ibid*, s 4(4)(b).

101 *Orillia*, above note 98; *Re Hooper v College of Nurses of Ontario*, 2006 CanLII 22656 (ON SCDC).

102 *PHIPA Decision 154, Sunnybrook Health Sciences Centre (Re)*, 2021 CanLII 70452 (ON IPC).

between an institution and a trade union," an agreement between an institution and an employee about employment-related matters, and expense claims. This obviously includes collective agreements, settlements of grievances or other litigation, and contracts of employment.

The term "[a]n agreement between an institution and a trade union" includes only an agreement itself, not minutes of meetings between employer and union representatives recording that a matter was agreed to at a meeting.[103] The term "trade union" applies to not only unions within the legal framework of collective bargaining but also voluntary unincorporated associations of professionals.[104] A contract between the employer and a third party, even a record used in labour relations, and hence excluded under section 65(6), is not within section 65(7) as it is not an agreement between the employer and an employee or union.[105]

The application of the *FIPPA* to the records listed in section 65(7) does not necessarily mean that these records, or any part of them,[106] are subject to disclosure. The information contained in such records must be reviewed against the general requirements and exemptions in the Act, of which the ones most applicable to employment records are discussed immediately below.

i) Mandatory Personal Information Exemption Applicable to Third-Party Request[107]

Under section 21(1), personal information is only to be disclosed to the person to whom it relates but will be disclosable to a third party "if the disclosure does not constitute an unjustified invasion of privacy."[108] In other words, a requestor will only receive the disclosure of the personal

---

103 *Order MO-1806*, above note 44; *Order P-1302*, *Ministry of Transportation (Re)*, 1996 CanLII 7726 (ON IPC).

104 *Order PO-2497*, above note 75. Further to records dealing with the labour relations between the government and the Ontario Medical Association being within scope of *FIPPA* s 65(6), the Ontario Medical Association is a trade union for purposes of the application of s 65(7).

105 *Order PO-2520*, *St Lawrence College of Applied Arts and Technology (Re)*, 2006 CanLII 50863 (ON IPC) [*Order PO-2520*]; *Order PO-2632*, *Ontario Power Generation (Re)*, 2008 CanLII 1826 (ON IPC).

106 Severance of information for purposes of allowing partial disclosure is an approach available under exemptions, whereas the exclusion applies to entire records.

107 The main points of this summary are detailed below.

108 *FIPPA*, above note 1, s 21(1)(f).

information of someone else if it would not constitute an unjustified invasion of that other person's personal privacy.

The first issue is whether the information is "personal information."

An unjustified invasion of privacy is conclusively presumed where personal information relates to medical or psychological history, employment or educational history, finances, personal evaluations, and other listed topics.[109]

This conclusive presumption is rebutted, meaning simply that the disclosure is not presumed to constitute an invasion of personal privacy, if the information discloses "the classification, salary range and benefits" of an employee.[110]

Where the presumption does not apply, or is rebutted, the head then still needs to make a discretionary decision whether disclosure of the personal information to a third party would constitute an unjustified invasion of personal privacy, and, in so doing, the head shall consider all the relevant circumstances including, but not limited to, those specifically listed,[111] which include "whether disclosure is desirable for the purpose of subjecting the activities of government and agencies to public scrutiny."[112]

As with other exemptions, this complicated but carefully scoped personal information protection scheme can be overridden under section 23 where "a compelling public interest in disclosure clearly outweighs the purpose of the exemption."[113]

a. Definition of Personal Information

Personal information is defined as recorded information about an identifiable individual.[114] To qualify as personal information, it must be reasonable to expect that an individual may be identified if the information is disclosed.[115]

---

109 *Ibid*, s 21(3). See the particularly detailed discussion in *Order PO-2536, Energy Board Ontario (Re)*, 2006 CanLII 50875 (ON IPC) [*Order PO-2536*].

110 *FIPPA*, above note 1, s 21(4).

111 *Ibid*, s 21(2).

112 *Ibid*, s 21(2)(a).

113 *Ibid*, s 23.

114 *Ibid*, s 2(1) The definition lists items that are included.

115 *Order PO-1880, Ontario (Health and Long-Term Care) (Re)*, 2001 CanLII 26053 (ON IPC), upheld on judicial review in *Ontario (Attorney General) v Pascoe*, [2002] OJ No 4300 (CA); *Order PO-2536*, above note 109 at 2.

Information about individuals of the kind commonly found in employment agreements has been found to relate to individuals in their personal capacity and so qualifies as personal information.[116]

A distinction is to be drawn between personal information and information relating to a person's professional, employment, or official government capacity.[117] Information associated with individuals that relates to their capacity as officials of the organization that employs them is not personal to them but rather relates to their employment by or association with the employer. This information is more appropriately described as related to the employment or professional responsibilities of the individuals than as personal information. However, even if information relates to an individual in a professional, official, or business capacity, it may still qualify as personal information if the information reveals something of a personal nature about the individual.[118]

Doctors' Ontario Health Insurance Plan billings are not personal information as they do not reveal anything that is "inherently personal in nature" because they represent gross billings, from which allowable business expenses have not been deducted, and are not an accurate reflection of personal income.[119]

Personal information in a settlement is accorded the same exemption from disclosure as other personal information under the *FIPPA*.[120]

---

116 *Order PO-2519, Loyalist College of Applied Arts and Technology (Re)*, 2006 CanLII 50862 (ON IPC) [*Order PO-2519*]. Some information about the discipline of unidentifiable employees may not involve personal information: *Order MO-2337*, above note 80.

117 *Order PO-1663, Pension Commission of Ontario (Re)*, 1999 CanLII 14343 (ON IPC); *Order R-980015, Ministry of the Attorney General (Re)*, 1998 CanLII 14229 (ON IPC).

118 *Orders P-1409, R-980015, PO-2225*, and *MO-2344*, summarized in *PO-3617, Ontario (Health and Long-Term Care) (Re)*, 2016 CanLII 32641 (ON IPC) [*Order PO-3617*].

119 *PO-3617*, above at note 118 at para 78, upheld on judicial review: *Ontario Medical Association v Ontario (Information and Privacy Commissioner)*, 2017 ONSC 4090 and 2018 ONCA 673.

120 *Order MO-1184, City of Hamilton (Re)*, 1999 CanLII 14419 (ON IPC) [*Order MO-1184*]; *FIPPA*, above note 1, s 2(1); *Interim Order PO-2924-I, York University (Re)*, 2010 CanLII 63576 (ON IPC) at 10.

b. Presumed Unjustified Invasion of Privacy

Section 21(3) lists personal information which if disclosed is presumed to be an unjustified invasion of personal privacy, including medical history, employment history, individual finances, and personal recommendations or evaluations.[121] This includes those terms of a settlement or amounts that disclose individual rates of pay or salary,[122] start and finish dates of salary, retirement eligibility, sick day entitlements and last day worked, contributions to the pension plan,[123] a letter of reference which contains an evaluation of work, and personal recommendations or evaluations attached to a settlement,[124] as well as other personal details like social insurance number and benefits beneficiary.[125]

Concerning expense claims, menu selections are personal information.[126] However, the names of the individuals for whom meals were purchased is not, as the entertainment was on public business, and accountability is appropriate. Telephone numbers called where an expense claim is made are also public.

A presumed unjustified invasion of personal privacy cannot be rebutted by the discretionary factors favouring disclosure under section 21(2),[127] discussed below.

The only ways in which a section 21(3) presumption can be overcome is if the personal information at issue falls under section 21(4) of the Act setting out information which is not to be presumed to constitute an unjustified invasion of personal privacy *or* where a finding is made under section 23 of the Act that a compelling public interest exists in the disclosure which outweighs the purpose of the section 21 exemption.

c. No Presumed Unjustified Invasion of Privacy

The list of items presumed under section 21(3) to be an unjustified invasion of privacy does not incorporate the following one-time amounts: the amount of a one-time monetary settlement of an individual's human

---

121 *FIPPA*, above note 1, s 21(3)(a), (d), (f), and (g). See *Interim Order PO-2924-I*, *ibid*.

122 *Order PO-2050*, *Northland Transportation Commission*, 2002 CanLII 46452 (ON IPC).

123 *PO-2519*, above note 116.

124 *Order MO-1184*, above note 120 at para 53.

125 *Order PO-2536*, above note 109 at 29.

126 *Ibid*.

127 *Order MO-1184*, above note 120 at para 61; *John Doe v Ontario (Information and Privacy Commissioner)*, 1993 CanLII 3388 (ON SCDC).

rights complaint,[128] settlement of a claim of wrongful dismissal,[129] one-time monetary amounts in a severance agreement,[130] a breakdown of settlement amounts detailing legal costs, and out-placement counselling.[131]

In addition, section 21(4)(a) of the Act sets out a range of types of information, the disclosure of which is not presumed to constitute an unjustified invasion of personal privacy.[132] This includes, for an individual who is or was an officer or employee of an institution or a member of the staff of a minister, the following: employment responsibilities, classification, salary *range* (as opposed to actual salary), and benefits. The meaning of "benefits" is the entitlements received because of being employed,[133] and includes all entitlements provided as part of employment or upon conclusion of employment,[134] including:

- severance entitlements
- pay-for-performance amounts
- insurance-related benefits
- sick leave and vacation
- leaves of absence
- termination allowance
- death and pension benefits
- business expense entitlements, car, and parking allowances
- right to reimbursement for moving expenses
- incentives and assistance given as inducements to enter into a contract of employment[135]

---

128 *Order M-1160, Regional Municipality of Haldimand Norfolk (Re)*, 1998 CanLII 14374 (ON IPC).

129 *Order MO-1184*, above note 120; *FIPPA*, above note 1, s 14(3)(f) does not apply to one-time amounts.

130 *Order MO-1405, Niagara Regional Police Services Board (Re)*, 2001 CanLII 26297 (ON IPC) [*Order MO-1405*]; *Order M-173, City of Ottawa (Re)*, 1993 CanLII 4992 (ON IPC) [*Order M-173*]; *Order MO-1676, Cobourg Police Services Board (Re)*, 2003 CanLII 53774 (ON IPC) [*Order MO-1676*]; *Order PO-3051, Ministry of Community and Social Services (Re)*, 2012 CanLII 7134 (ON IPC).

131 *Order MO-1405*, *ibid*; *Order MO-1676*, *ibid*.

132 *Order M-23, Town of Gravenhurst (Re)*, 1992 CanLII 4255 (ON IPC); *Order P-1212, Algonquin College of Applied Arts and Technology (Re)*, 1996 CanLII 7433 (ON IPC).

133 *Order M-23, Town of Gravenhurst (Re)*, 1992 CanLII 4255 (ON IPC), and as followed in *Order PO-2536*, above note 109.

134 *Order PO-2519*; above note 116.

135 *Order PO-1885, Royal Ontario Museum (Re)*, 2001 CanLII 26085 (ON IPC).

Note that section 21(4)(a) does not apply to entitlements that have been negotiated as part of a retirement or termination package,[136] except where the information reflects benefits to which the individual was entitled because of being employed[137] that are continuing post-employment.[138] Benefits received for the first time because of a settlement are not covered by section 21(4)(a).

To reiterate, settlement amounts that do not reveal actual salary, and benefits received for the first time as part of a settlement, are neither covered by the presumption nor the non-presumption of an unjustified invasion of privacy, and the issue of whether there is an unjustified invasion of privacy remains to be decided by a consideration of all the relevant circumstances.

d. Consideration of All the Relevant Circumstances

If the statutory presumption of unjustified invasion of privacy does not resolve the issue, then, under section 21(2), in determining whether there is such an invasion, the head shall consider all relevant circumstances—including unlisted ones and those listed under section 21(2) of which the most relevant to labour relations are:

> (a) the disclosure is desirable for the purpose of subjecting the activities of the Government of Ontario and its agencies to public scrutiny . . .
>
> (f) the personal information is highly sensitive, meaning that there is a reasonable expectation of significant personal distress if the information is disclosed . . .[139]
>
> (h) the information has been supplied in confidence . . .
>
> (i) the disclosure may unfairly damage the reputation of any person referred to in the record.

Monetary entitlements under severance agreements or settlements that do not fall under the presumption in section 21(3) may be subject

136 See, for example, *Order M-173*, above note 130; *Order M-204*, *Gananoque (Town) (Re)*, 1993 CanLII 5022 (ON IPC); *MO-1332*, *Hamilton (City) (Re)*, 2000 CanLII 20971 (ON IPC).

137 *Order MO-1749*, *Haldimand County (Re)*, 2004 CanLII 56190 (ON IPC); *Order PO-2050*, *Ontario Northland Transportation Commission (Re)*, 2002 CanLII 46452 (ON IPC).

138 *Order MO-1970* as quoted in *Order PO-2519*, above note 116.

139 *Order PO-3630*, *Ontario (Community Safety and Correctional Services) (Re)*, 2016 CanLII 46209 (ON IPC) at para 76.

to disclosure where the factors favouring disclosure suggest that to do so would not be an unjustified invasion of an individual's privacy.[140] Agreements between institutions and senior employees are records for which a high degree of public scrutiny is warranted,[141] especially where there is a significant expenditure of public funds.[142] The details of such settlements are highly sensitive, favouring privacy protection, but the weight given to this factor will be reduced in the absence of corroboration of the sensitivity by the named individual, or where the circumstances are generally known and were reported in the media.[143] A confidentiality clause in the settlement agreement is a factor favouring privacy protection,[144] but a settlement clause "contracting out" of the *FIPPA* does not affect the jurisdiction of the IPC and is only enforceable through other legal channels.[145]

Disclosure of expense claims is desirable for ensuring public confidence in the institution:

> In submitting expense claims for reimbursement, government employees should do so on the basis that they may be called upon to substantiate each and every expenditure, both internally to the management staff of the institution, and externally to the general public.[146]

And:

> The role of access to information legislation in ensuring openness and transparency is even more compelling when the taxpayer's funds are being used for expenditures in the nature of gifts, entertainment, food, and beverage. In my view the level of accountability must be very high on the part of those that have been entertained and those that have done the entertaining. Simply disclosing the amount of the claim is not enough to ensure accountability and transparency in relation to an expenditure.[147]

---

140 *Order MO-1405*, above note 130; *Order M-173*, above note 130; *Order MO-1676*, above note 130.
141 *Order M-173*, above note 130.
142 *Order PO-2519*, above note 116.
143 *Order MO-1184*, above note 120.
144 *Ibid.*
145 *Order PO-2520*, above note 105.
146 *Order PO-2519*, above note 116 and cases cited therein.
147 *Order P-256*, quoted in *Order PO-2536*, above note 109 at 31–32.

Where the requester originally supplied the information, or the appellant is otherwise aware of it, the information may be found not to be exempt under section 21(1) because to withhold their own information from the requester on grounds of privacy would be absurd and inconsistent with the purpose of the exemption.[148]

ii) Discretionary Exemptions

Under section 49, the head can exercise discretion to refuse to disclose information under several headings (in addition to the conclusion that the disclosure would be an unjustified invasion of personal privacy). The main ones related to employment records—legal privilege, commercial information in confidence, economic interest, threat to health and safety—are discussed below. As the exemption is discretionary, the IPC will consider[149] whether the institution exercised its discretion, or failed to do so, and, in addition

> the Commissioner may find that the institution erred in exercising its discretion where, for example, it does so in bad faith or for an improper purpose; where it took into account irrelevant considerations; or where it failed to take into account relevant considerations. In either case, [the IPC] may send the matter back for an exercise of discretion based on proper considerations. [The IPC] may not, however, substitute its own discretion for that of the institution.

Litigation and solicitor and client privilege are commonly asserted, under *FIPPA* section 19.[150] This discretionary exemption has been found to be extendable to settlement agreements, provided the institution weighs the interest in settling litigation against the public interest in transparency.[151]

---

148 *Wilfrid Laurier University (Re)*, 2021 CanLII 134202 (ON IPC) at paras 128–30.

149 *Order PO-3302, University of Ottawa (Re)*, 2014 CanLII 5255 (ON IPC) at para 93; *Order PO-4069, York University (Re)*, 2020 CanLII 72816 (ON IPC).

150 As an example, see *Order PO-3338, Ontario (Community Safety and Correctional Services) (Re)*, 2014 CanLII 24476 (ON IPC) at 34–39.

151 *Order MO-4006, Greater Sudbury (City) (Re)*, 2021 CanLII 8871 (ON IPC) and *Order PO-3627, Peterborough Regional Health Centre (Re)*, 2016 CanLII 41802 (ON IPC). Those cases rely on *Liquor Control Board of Ontario v Magnotta Winery Corporation*, 2010 ONCA 681, where the Ontario Court of Appeal found that the statutory litigation privilege in section 19 of *FIPPA* can protect end products, such as settlement agreements and minutes of settlement, and further opined, in a non-employment case, that "the public interest in transparency is trumped by the

Commercial information supplied to a ministry in confidence[152] can be exempt if there is a reasonable expectation of prejudicing negotiations and causing similar information to no longer be supplied or resulting in undue loss. A government and Ontario Medical Association agreement about malpractice insurance was not found to meet this test, in part because previous versions had been made public.[153]

To protect economic interest, a head may refuse to disclose a record that contains plans relating to the management of personnel or the administration of an institution that have not yet been put into operation or made public.[154]

Where there is a "reasonable basis" for believing a person's safety will be endangered, the record can be withheld.[155]

iii) Compelling Public Interest Override of Exemptions

A range of exemptions, including those discussed above *other than* legal privilege, can be overridden in the public interest. Under *FIPPA*, section 23, two requirements must be met: (1) a compelling public interest in disclosure and (2) this interest must outweigh the purpose of the personal interest exemption.

Compelling has been found to mean "rousing strong interest or attention" and is not established simply by the requester being a journalist,[156] although the fact of public debate will favour the application of this factor.[157]

The existence of another public process or forum for addressing the public interest does not satisfy the public interest in transparency.

---

more compelling public interest in encouraging the settlement of litigation" (para 36). See an earlier case where the privilege was upheld for the negotiations but not the final agreement that ended the employment of senior officials: *Order P-1348, Management Board Secretariat (Re)*, 1997 CanLII 11866 (ON IPC).

152 *FIPPA*, above note 1, s 17(1).

153 *Order PO-2497*, above note 75.

154 *FIPPA*, above note 1, s 18(1)(f) applied in *Order PO-2536*, above note 109 at 18. Details of an in effect compensation package are not general plans for management of personnel.

155 *Ibid*, s 20 applied in *Ontario (Information and Privacy Commissioner, Inquiry Officer) v Ontario (Minister of Labour, Office of the Worker Advisor)*, 1999 CanLII 19925 (ONCA); and *Order PO-3297, York University (Re)*, 2014 CanLII 4473 (ON IPC). See also *Doe, 2014 and 2015*, above note 86.

156 *Order PO-3617*, above note 118 at paras 163–64.

157 *Order PO- 3213 Algonquin College (Re)*, 2013 CanLII 34786 (ON IPC).

"Satisfying this interest requires that members of the public be able to independently understand and make political choices about government spending."[158] The fact that the information may be inaccurate or unreliable or lack context does not justify withholding it. As stated by the Supreme Court:

> If taken too far, refusing to disclose for fear of public misunderstanding would undermine the fundamental purpose of access to information legislation. The point is to give the public access to information so that they can evaluate it for themselves, not to protect them from having it.[159]

Concerning compensation, the IPC has said:

> In terms of the compensation packages given to senior government employees and senior employees of government agencies, the public interest demands that complete disclosure be made. It is disingenuous to take the position that the base salary of such executives is subject to public disclosure, but that other benefits and arrangements that supplement the base salary are private. In my view, the public interest in disclosing this type of information would, in most cases, be very compelling. These types of benefits and supplemental arrangements are of significant value to the employees that receive them and are a significant cost to the government. In determining whether the compensation paid to a particular individual is appropriate, the entire package is relevant and must be disclosed.
>
> Similarly, the expense accounts of these employees, paid by the public purse, must be made available, except to the extent that credit card or banking information may be disclosed. Without full disclosure, the ability to hold employees accountable for their expenditures will be impeded.[160]

And it has been further stated that this rationale would be sufficient to outweigh the personal interest exemption when the information "sheds any light" on the operations of the entity, including the compensation packages of senior executives and their expense accounts.

---

158 *Order PO-3617*, above note 118 at paras 163–64.

159 *Merck Frosst Canada Ltd v Canada (Health)*, 2012 SCC 3 at para 224, as applied in *PO-3617*, above note 118 at paras 176–77.

160 *Order PO-2536*, above note 109 at 32.

There is a compelling public interest in disclosure even where the *Public Sector Salary Disclosure Act, 1996* (*PSSDA*)[161] deals with some of the income in question. Where the *PSSDA* required the disclosure of total income, the IPC has ordered the disclosure of the base salary and the pay-for-performance components on the following rationale:

> The public has a right to know to the fullest extent possible how taxpayer dollars have been allocated to public servants' salaries, and this has particular force with respect to public servants at senior levels who earn significant amounts of money paid out of the public purse. Certainly, the PSSDA is one important tool for ensuring such openness and transparency. However, in my view, to limit disclosure to only those amounts that are disclosed under the PSSDA seems incongruent with the government's commitment to openness and transparency and, in turn, accountability for the allocation of public resources. In my view, when an individual enters the public service, he/she accepts that his/her salary may be exposed to public scrutiny.[162]

Concerning discipline, the human resources response of the employer to a high-profile incident can be of compelling public interest and some disclosure about a discipline settlement may be warranted to ensure transparency and accountability, although the names of the affected employee(s) may not need to be disclosed to ensure "sufficient public scrutiny."[163]

3) Institutional Use of Personal Information

As the *FIPPA* does not apply to a range of personal information contained in labour and employment records, the institution needs other policies to provide institutional guidance on how to safeguard such information to protect employee privacy. The Management Board of Cabinet (MBC) *Human Resources Management Directive* states that the OPS "adheres to sound privacy principles" in its approach to this

---

161 SO 1996, c 1, Sched A.

162 *Order MO-2563, York Police Services Board (Regional Municipality) (Re)*, 2010 CanLII 65788 (ON IPC) at 15–16, upheld by the Divisional Court in *York (Police Services Board) v (Ontario) Information and Privacy Commissioner*, 2012 ONSC 6175.

163 *Order MO-2337*, above note 80 at 34.

information and that it is a management responsibility to maintain records in accordance with "confidentiality rules."[164]

This section has no legal relevance to most labour and employment-related records due to their exclusion from the *FIPPA*, as described above. However, jurisprudence from the period prior to the introduction of that exclusion does contain some informative rulings on the appropriate internal institutional use of personal information.

Information should be shared internally on a need to know basis, not involving staff beyond those required to address the matter,[165] not having a witness's concerns about a harassment complaint shared before formal investigation,[166] and not revealing details of a medical condition when not needed to be shared.[167] There can be a need to share and know when disclosure of personal information is made to individuals charged with conducting a harassment investigation[168] and when disclosure is made to co-workers about an employee's suspension in order to support preventing the suspended employee having access to the employer's premises, files, or systems during the suspension period.[169]

It should go without saying that the availability of disclosure through *FIPPA* processes does not excuse employees from their employment obligation to maintain the confidentiality of information.[170]

There is also personal information not contained in labour and employment records. Under *FIPPA* section 42(1) an institution shall not disclose personal information in its custody except in accordance with listed exemptions, one of which is "where disclosure is made to an officer, employee, consultant or agent of the institution who needs the record in the performance of their duties and where disclosure is necessary

---

164 Management Board of Cabinet (MBC), *Human Resources Management Directive*, 12 May 2017, online: www.ontario.ca/page/human-resources-management-directive, ss 8.7 and 10.12 [*MBC Directive*].

165 *Investigation I95-099P, Ministry of Community and Social Services*, 31 May 1996.

166 *Investigation I94-084P, Ministry of Housing*, 8 June 1995.

167 *Investigation I93-043P, Ministry of Health*, 23 November 1993.

168 *Investigation I93-039P, Management Board Secretariat*, 8 June 1994.

169 *Investigation I94-101P, Ministry of Housing*, 4 April 1995.

170 *Ontario Public Service Employees Union (Fortin) v Ontario*, 2017 CanLII 16719 (ON GSB) (Luborsky) at 10 [*Fortin*], where the arbitrator rules that a grievor taking such information for purposes of advancing their case is misappropriation, that the information should be inadmissible, and that the union should disclose and remedy the matter.

and proper in the discharge of the institution's functions."[171] Where the IPC found there had been a disclosure of personal information in violation of section 42(1), it recommended improvements to policies, training, and auditing of access to personal information, as well as disclosure of the disciplinary measures imposed on the discloser.[172]

C. *HUMAN RIGHTS CODE*

The *Human Rights Code* is fully applicable to the Crown and every Crown agency. Human rights obligations apply to the government employer in the same manner that they apply to any other employer. Yet there are arguably unique aspects of human rights jurisprudence in the OPS resulting from it being one of the provinces most scrutinized and largest employers, with the particular challenge of continuously improving the culture in correctional institutions, resulting in use of systemic remedies.

The *HRC* establishes a "right to equal treatment in respect of employment without discrimination" because of listed grounds.[173] The MBC has sought to reinforce this obligation through the *Human Resources Management Directive* by requiring[174] Ontario public servants to "contribute to,"[175] managers to "foster,"[176] and deputy ministers to provide ministry leadership in "fostering and sustaining"[177] "an inclusive and accessible workplace free from discrimination and harassment."

Human rights decisions about the OPS are made by the Ontario Human Rights Tribunal of Ontario (HRTO), the GSB, and the PSGB. While each tribunal has its own statutory jurisdiction, there is no apparent reason why the rulings within those jurisdictions should be dissimilar as the effective vindication of human rights should not depend on the forum. This section begins with a discussion of human rights jurisprudence in the OPS drawing from all three forums. The OPS employer policy dealing specifically with human rights—the *Respectful Workplace Policy*—is then reviewed. This is followed by a discussion of

171 *FIPPA*, above note 1, s 42(1)(d).
172 *Ontario (Solicitor General) (Re)*, 2021 CanLII 116212 (ON IPC).
173 *HRC*, above note 1, s 5(1).
174 *MBC Directive*, above note 164.
175 *Ibid*, s 10.2.
176 *Ibid*, s 10.13.
177 *Ibid*, s 10.21.

particularly relevant aspects of the jurisdiction and procedure of each forum, including deferral between the HRTO and the other forums.

1) Establishing Discrimination and Harassment

Establishing discrimination is done by meeting the well-known test set out by the Ontario Court of Appeal in *Peel Law Association v Pieters*.[178] An applicant must be able to show that they are a member of an *HRC*-protected group, that they were subject to adverse treatment, and that the *HRC*-protected ground in question was a factor in that adverse treatment. As discussed in *Pieters*:

> In discrimination cases . . . the law, while maintaining the burden of proof on the applicant, provides respondents with good reason to call evidence. Relatively "little affirmative evidence" is required before the inference of discrimination is permitted. And the standard of proof requires only that the inference be more probable than not. Once there is evidence to support a prima facie case, the respondent faces the tactical choice: explain or risk losing.[179]

The events complained of must demonstrate some form of disadvantage, and "subjective perceptions of disadvantage alone are insufficient to establish discrimination."[180]

In a hiring case, statistical information will not likely be determinative, but a case of ethnic discrimination will be assisted if there is a "significant disequilibrium" between the percentage of minority candidates hired and in the general population.[181]

The HRTO has noted that, in assessing whether a pattern of discrimination has been demonstrated, "one must be cautious not to parse out individual allegations" where the applicant is asking for inferences

178 2013 ONCA 396, discussed in *Ontario Public Service Employees Union (Brydges et al) v Ontario (Transportation)*, 2014 CanLII 74778 (ON GSB) and *Jack v Ontario (Community Safety and Correctional Services)*, 2018 HRTO 144 [*Jack*].

179 *Pieters*, *ibid* at para 73.

180 *Klonowski v Ontario (Community Safety and Correctional Services)*, 2012 HRTO 1568 at para 29, rejecting the claim that the standard application of an attendance management program featuring a non-disciplinary meeting with the employer had a reasonable prospect of success.

181 *Lasani v Ontario (Ministry of Community and Social Services) (No 2)*, 1993 CanLII 16433 (ON HRT) at para 105.

to be drawn from a course of "perhaps subtle" differential treatment.[182] The GSB has accepted that there is racism in the OPS and that, as with the rest of the public sector, implicit racist stereotyping can subconsciously affect how White persons interact with Black persons.[183] Still, to resolve litigation, individual factual determinations need to be made. This cannot be done on the basis simply that a White person is interacting with a Black person. "There must be words or conduct which, on a balance of probabilities, lead to the conclusion that such bias was present and affected conduct."[184]

These issues are often addressed at an early stage of a GSB case through disputes about whether sufficient particulars have been provided and whether a *prima facie* case has been established.[185]

Workplace harassment is to be found and only is to be found if there is objective evidence to support there has been abusive conduct that detrimentally affects the work environment or has adverse employment consequences for the victim:[186]

> [H]arassment normally involves an element of persistent conduct or a course of activities that involves hostility, importuning, badgering, intimidation or bullying that causes a person distress that is inimical to a safe and positive work environment. The exercise of

---

182 *Jack*, above note 178 at para 77, citing *Lewis v Toronto Transit Commission*, 2015 HRTO 256 at para 43.

183 *Association of Management, Administrative and Professional Crown Employees of Ontario v Ontario (Attorney General)*, 2021 CanLII 58440 (ON GSB) (McLean) [*AMAPCEO v AG*], referencing at para 220, Arlene Huggins, *Independent External Review of Complex WDHP Cases*, 23 November 2018, online: www.ontario.ca/page/independent-external-review-complex-wdhp-cases#section-2 [*Huggins Report*] and on general prevalence, at para 214, several authorities from the Court of Appeal.

184 *Ibid* at para 221.

185 See Chapter 11 for discussion of GSB procedure.

186 *Ontario Public Service Employees Union (Grievor) v Ontario*, 2015 CanLII 20923 (ON GSB) (Briggs) at 26–27; *Ontario Public Service Employees Union (Barker) v Ontario (Solicitor General)*, 2020 CanLII 20374 (ON GSB) (Gee) at 31 [*Barker*]; *Ontario Public Service Employees Union (Solomon Smith et al) v Ontario (Children, Community and Social Services)*, 2019 CanLII 126475 (ON GSB) (Anderson) at para 10, quoting *Janzen v Platy Enterprises Ltd*, [1989] 1 SCR 1252 at 375; *Ontario Public Service Employees Union (Plouffe) v Ontario (Solicitor General)*, 2021 CanLII 127097 (ON GSB) (Harris) [*Plouffe*]; *Ontario Public Service Employees Union (Mohamed) v Ontario (Attorney General)*, 2021 CanLII 127098 (ON GSB) (Petryshen).

> normal management rights does not excuse harassment, and giving directions, evaluating performance, and disciplining employees should not be considered harassment in the normal course of events provided that such activities are not carried out in a manner that is abusive, demeaning, or hostile, and has a legitimate workplace purpose. Not every "employment bruise" should be treated as harassment, and . . . it would be unfortunate if a harassment process was "used to vent feelings of minor discontent or general unhappiness with life in the workplace, so as to trivialize those cases where substantial workplace abuses have occurred."[187]

It can be difficult to decide whether the supervisor "crossed the line" and went "beyond the reasonable norm" during an interaction that caused stress to the grievor.[188] Reasonable performance management is not harassment.[189] Individual fairly bruising managerial interactions may not constitute harassment, particularly if they are not part of a persistent course of conduct.[190] Harassment includes an aggressive and threatening meeting, including the suggestion of dishonesty, designed to cause an employee to abandon their accommodation claim, especially in the face of clear medical support for the accommodation.[191] Remote oversight can be harassing when it includes frequent inquiries about whether an employee is at their desk and short response time expectations that were not clearly communicated to the grievor, causing the grievor to think management thought they were untrustworthy.[192]

---

187 *Ontario Public Service Employees Union (Cross et al) v Ontario (Community Safety and Correctional Services)*, 2015 CanLII 60421 (ON GSB) (Misra) at 11, quoting from *UFCW Local 1518 v 55369 BC Ltd*, 2007 Carswell BC 3880 (Larson).

188 *Ontario Public Service Employees Union (Palmer) v Ontario (Community Safety and Correctional Services)*, 2018 CanLII 14321 (ON GSB) (Sheehan). See also *Ontario Public Service Employees Union (Ceresato) v Ontario (Liquor Control Board)*, 2018 CanLII 77316 (ON GSB) (Petryshen) at para 39 [*Ceresato*].

189 *Ontario Public Service Employees Union (Chung) v Ontario (Government and Consumer Services)*, 2022 CanLII 31334 (ON GSB) (Johnston) at para 96.

190 *Ontario Public Service Employees Union (Yousif et al) Ontario (Attorney General)*, 2021 CanLII 95698 (ON GSB) (Dissanayake) [*Yousif*].

191 *Ontario Public Service Employees Union v Ontario (Solicitor General)*, 2022 CanLII 31321 (ON GSB) (Dissanayake) at para 176 [*Solicitor General*, 2022].

192 *Ontario Public Service Employees Union (Del Casale) v Ontario (Government and Consumer Services)*, 2022 CanLII 31331 (ON GSB) (Hewat) [*Del Casale*].

Proving harassment is a violation of the *HRC* of course requires that discrimination is established to be a factor. Note that harassment not involving discrimination is still a violation of the OPSEU/MBC collective agreements,[193] in two ways (and, to a limited extent, of *OHSA*).[194] First, Article 3.3 commits the parties to a workplace free from workplace harassment without specifying the motivation. The agreement defines workplace harassment as "engaging in a course of vexatious comment or conduct against an employee in the workplace that is known or ought reasonably to be known to be unwelcome," which means that proving harassment involves meeting essentially the same standards as under the *HRC*, absent the requirement to prove discrimination is a factor.[195] Second, the collective agreement Article 9.1 obligation to "make reasonable provisions for the safety and health of its employees" results in an obligation to address harassment.[196]

Management's liability is not strict liability, but it does include responsibility for taking reasonable steps to ensure that employees are free from discrimination by management and other employees, including investigating allegations beyond "perfunctory inquiry."[197] In a case

---

193 *OPSEU/MBC Unified Bargaining Unit Collective Agreement, 2022–2024* and *OPSEU/MBC Correctional Bargaining Unit Collective Agreement, 2018–2021*, online: https://opseu.org/information/general/find-your-collective-agreement, Art 3.3 and 9.1 [*OPSEU/MBC Unified and Correctional Collective Agreements*].

194 *OHSA* prohibits workplace harassment but provides limited recourse, as discussed in the *OHSA* section below.

195 *Ontario Public Service Employees Union (Grievor) v Ontario (Solicitor General)*, 2020 CanLII 74251 (ON GSB) (Harris) at paras 86 and 88 [*Solicitor General, 2020, Harris*]; *Ontario Public Service Employees Union (Asztemborski et al) v Ontario (Treasury Board Secretariat)*, 2017 CanLII 92686 (ON GSB) (Briggs) at 21. To be actionable under Art 3, the objectionable conduct needs to go beyond just being "hurtful and disrespectful": *Yousif*, above note 190.

196 See the discussion of Art 9.1 below.

197 *Ontario Public Service Employees Union (St Amand et al) v Ontario (Solicitor General)*, 2022 CanLII 70866 (ON GSB) (Wacyk) at para 188 [*St Amand*] and cases cited; *Solicitor General, 2020, Harris*, above note 195; *Plouffe*, above note 186 at para 283; *Ontario Public Service Employees Union (Groves) v Ontario (Community Safety and Correctional Services)*, 2014 CanLII 70079 (ON GSB) (Mikus) at paras 95–96; *Ontario Public Service Employees Union (Ranger) v Ontario (Community Safety and Correctional Services)*, 2010 CanLII 7275 (ON GSB) (Leighton) at 40–44; *Ontario Public Service Employees Union (Tardiel) v Ontario (Community Safety and Correctional Services)*, 2010 CanLII 81917 (ON GSB) (Albertyn) [*Tardiel*]; *OPSEU (Simon) and Ministry of Correctional Services*, GSB#2568/96, 18 September 1998 (Dissanayake) at 13.

where the employer was found liable for permitting the workplace to deteriorate by not getting to the bottom of a "vendetta" by staff against the racialized grievor that occurred after she justifiably complained about discrimination against her, the GSB held:

> There is no strict liability on the employer, in that merely because an employee racially harassed or put another employee at a health or safety risk, the employer is not thereby exposed to liability. . . . The employer's liability depends on its knowledge of the offensive conduct and its response to it. However, in considering the employer's knowledge the test is not purely subjective. If the employer lacked knowledge because it showed a lack of interest or did not have a reasonable system for detecting and monitoring of offensive conduct, this does not exonerate it. To hold otherwise would be to make the obligation imposed on the employer by the collective agreement provisions meaningless. The employer would be able to circumvent that obligation by merely closing its eyes and ears. The parties could not have intended that.[198]

In systemic remedy cases, discussed below, there has been continued highlighting of the need to investigate individual incidents and respond promptly to address the grievor's interest.

Concerning consequences for perpetrators of harassment, there have been various cases where the GSB and PSGB have found that the grievor did engage in harassment as alleged, and that it was appropriate to discipline.[199]

The employer's obligation to accommodate an employee with a disability, and the employee's obligation to cooperate in the accommodation

---

198 *Solicitor General, 2020, Harris*, above note 195 at para 95, quoting cases cited; *St Amand*, above note 197 at paras 191–99. See also *AMAPCEO v AG*, above note 183 at para 190.

199 For example, *Ceresato*, above note 188, where the discharge was upheld due to threats of violence by the grievor against the supervisor, and *OPSEU (Hoffman) and Ministry of Correctional Services*, GSB#2552/91, 25 November 1993 (Gray) where the discipline was reduced due to the grievor's apology and the inconsistency of discipline of other perpetrators. See also PSGB cases upholding the discipline of managers who engaged in sexual harassment: *Canning and Ministry of Government Services*, PSGB#P/0008/92, 13 October 1993 (Springate); *Hardy and Ministry of Health*, PSGB#P/0034/93, 18 June 1997 (Leighton). For an OPP case before a private arbitrator addressing discipline for a harasser, see *Ontario Provincial Police v Ontario Provincial Police Association*, 2022 CanLII 50619 (ON LA) (Albertyn).

process, applies in the public service as it applies in any other workplace.[200] The disabilities to be accommodated certainly include mental disorders. As to be expected with a large "white collar" workforce, the GSB has dealt with a number of mental stress claims and worked to clarify how they are to be evaluated:

> [T]he Board accepts that an employee who has genuine symptoms of debilitating anxiety or experiences extreme stress reactions to work impeding the employee's ability to function may be suffering from a disability. But the determination of whether a disability in such circumstances exists is a matter of degree. Human beings are emotional creatures to greater or lesser extent, and there is a range of stress reactions to working situations that employees can reasonably be expected to bear, notwithstanding that the experience may be uncomfortable. Temporary periods of distress or apprehension, sleepless nights, loss of appetite, and the like, are common realities of the workplace that many employees must endure in the course of their careers; sometimes more often than not. Rushing to meet deadlines; making a presentation; surviving "office politics"; facing criticisms for deficient work or poor performance appraisals with the looming prospect of termination from employment; are among the multitude of situations that can reasonably result in the kind of general symptoms described by the Grievor. Some thrive in that environment while others falter; many are able to cope. The mere fact that an employee may be faltering because he or she can't handle the stress of the workplace does not in itself constitute a disability.[201]

---

200 *OPSEU (Kerna) and Ontario Human Rights Commission*, GSB#2002-0944, 10 February 2005 (Briggs) [*Kerna*]; *OPSEU (Balog) and Ministry of Community, Family and Children's Services*, GSB#1972/98, 12 November 1998 (Roberts) [*Balog*]; *OPSEU (Vasallo) and Ministry of Solicitor General and Correctional Services*, GSB#3402/92, 20 May 1997 (Kaufman); *Ontario Liquor Boards Employees' Union (Fenech) and Liquor Control Board of Ontario*, GSB#2152/95, 17 May 2002 (Marszewski); *Ontario Public Service Employees Union (Hart-Day) v Ontario (Ministry of Community Safety and Correctional Services)*, 2011 CanLII 49508 (ON GSB) (Dissanayake); *Ontario Public Service Employees Union v Ontario (Treasury Board Secretariat)*, 2017 CanLII 30341 (ON GSB) (Dissanayake). See also *Morrison and Ontario Human Rights Commission*, PSGB#37/94, 8 December 1995 (Lynk) at para 141 [*Morrison, 1995*].

201 *Fortin*, above note 170 at 69–70.

A grievor's mental stress disability can be made worse by the employer's harassing requests for more medical information, and threats to job security.[202]

Concerning physical accommodation, the GSB has approved of a ministry's practice of searching for alternative positions for employees only after it is clear that an employee cannot be accommodated in their home position.[203] The range of search to accommodate an individual should be incrementally broadened, extending to other positions in the employee's division, then ministry, then bargaining unit, and then "as a last resort" beyond the bargaining unit.[204] The employer is the Crown in Right of Ontario (aka the government), "a vast organization,"[205] and the government, with full knowledge of any available suitable positions throughout the public service, must comprehensively determine whether any suitable positions exist.[206] Currently, an employee with a disability who is permanently incapable of performing the essential duties of their home position can access the OPS health reassignment program as a means to achieve employment accommodation. The *MGS Reassignment Program Guide* (revised 2019) developed with the input of the Union sets out the program used by the parties. The process involves the reassignment to a vacant position either in the home ministry or elsewhere in the OPS.

A government-wide attendance management policy has been evaluated according to the general caselaw applicable to such policies, and shortcomings have been ordered to be corrected.[207] In particular, the employer was required to clarify that the Attendance Support Program

---

202 *Ontario Public Service Employees Union (Grievor) v Ontario (Community Safety and Correctional Services)*, 2017 CanLII 52722 (ON GSB) (Misra), also addressing human rights damages by referencing HRTO jurisprudence.

203 *Balog*, above note 200 at 108.

204 *Re Di Caro*, 2003-3162 (Dissanayake) at 50–51, quoted in *Solicitor General*, 2022, above note 191 at para 186.

205 *Solicitor General*, 2022, above note 191 at para 197.

206 *OPSEU (McInnis) and Ministry of Community and Social Services*, GSB#2967/92, 5 October 1993 (Kaplan) at 19. An interim-relief application was granted to require a grievor whose long-term disability benefits were about to expire be returned to the payroll even if suitable employment was not found for them: *OPSEU (Ranger) and Ministry of Community Safety and Correctional Services*, GSB#2002-2375, 6 October 2004 (Leighton).

207 *Ontario Public Service Employees Union (Union Grievance) v Ontario (Ministry of the Solicitor General and Correctional Services/Management Board Secretariat)*, GSB#1925/96, 31 May 1999 (Abramsky) at 75–76.

should be administered with flexibility to accommodate individual circumstances.

Occupational standards have been ordered changed if they are not bona fide occupational qualifications. The HRTO has found a specific eyesight acuity standard was not reasonably necessary to ensure a police officer is able to perform their work safely, and that the OPP could accommodate more individual capabilities and differences without incurring undue hardship.[208]

Time off from work to engage in religious observance is to be accommodated by the employer,[209] although, like other employers, the OPS can fulfill its duty to accommodate by providing appropriate scheduling changes without having to first demonstrate that additional leave with pay will result in undue economic or other hardship for the employer.[210] In the course of addressing accommodation of religious observance, the GSB has had occasion to comment on the need for public service uniformity. It was found to be "intolerable" for the extent of an employee's human rights, in the form of leave entitlement, to vary depending only on the ministry in which they happened to work.[211]

In a decision related to staffing, the GSB has held that a requirement for a minimum percentage of female, classified correctional officers was acceptable in light of the legitimate need that female inmates have for supervision by correctional officers of the same gender, and that, when identifying positions to be laid off, the gender mix could be taken into account.[212]

---

208 *Lauzon v Ontario Provincial Police*, 2011 HRTO 1404 [*Lauzon*]. See also *Kurpel v Ontario (Ministry of Community Safety and Correctional Services)*, 2021 HRTO 83 [*Kurpel*], where the OPP failed to clarify the abilities of an officer returning from medical treatment and so unreasonably denied their ability to use use-of-force equipment.

209 See the leading cases of *OPSEU (Kimmel/Leaf) and Ministry of Government Services*, GSB#1391/90, 7 October 1991 (Kaplan) [*Kimmel*]; *OPSEU (Tratnyek) and Ministry of Community and Social Services*, GSB#1301/95, 28 August 1997 (Gorsky), rev'd *Ontario (Ministry of Community and Social Services) v OPSEU* (2000), 50 OR (3d) 560 (CA) [*Tratnyek*].

210 *Ontario (Ministry of Community and Social Services) v OPSEU*, *ibid* at para 45.

211 *Kimmel*, above note 209 at 59.

212 *OPSEU (O'Toole) and Ministry of Correctional Services*, GSB#1790/00, 26 March 2003 (Briggs) at 12–13.

2) Systemic Remedies

In the words of the Supreme Court:

> [I]t is readily apparent that, in attempting to combat systemic discrimination, it is essential to look to the past patterns of discrimination and to destroy those patterns in order to prevent the same type of discrimination in the future.[213]

Adjudicative decisions can help "penetrate known institutional barriers to change."[214] In particular, government can be prone to systemic inertia so that a meaningful remedy for an individual may require broad based measures including specific accountabilities and responsiveness expectations.[215] The purpose of systemic remedies has been put more colloquially: "Lessons need to be learned from what happened . . . and changes must be made to ensure that this very unfortunate saga does not repeat itself."[216]

The GSB and HRTO have evidenced a willingness to address discrimination by ordering wide-ranging systemic remedies. The three leading cases, *O'Brien*, *McKinnon*, and *Tardiel*, are reviewed below.

In *O'Brien*,[217] an unclassified female correctional officer at the Windsor Jail was discriminated against and, after a lengthy hearing, the GSB issued a consent award in which the employer acknowledged that it had discriminated against the grievor by managing the workplace so as to create an environment poisoned through the actions of managers and through management condonation of discriminatory employee and inmate behaviour. The parties agreed that eliminating the sexual harassment and discrimination required a systemic approach to change the

---

213 *CN v Canada (Canadian Human Rights Commission)*, [1987] 1 SCR 1114 at 1145.

214 Gwen Brodsky, Shelagh Day & Frances M. Kelly, "The Authority of Human Rights Tribunals to Grant Systemic Remedies" (2017) 6:1 *Canadian Journal of Human Rights* 1 at 4 [Brodsky].

215 *Ibid* at 34 and 42.

216 *Ontario Provincial Police Association v Ontario (Provincial Police)*, 2018 CanLII 82193 (ON LA) (Abramsky) at para 329 [*OPPA, 2018*], dealing with reintegration of a person with mental health disabilities into the OPP workplace through systemic remedies including, at paras 329–40 and 351, requiring the existing Joint Employment Accommodation Committee to develop a protocol for addressing mental health issues, including return to work, and training on disability and the duty to accommodate for all OPP employees, supervisors, and management.

217 *OPSEU (O'Brien) and Ministry of Correctional Services*, GSB#1948/93, 1 August 1995 (Finley).

culture, policies, and practices of the ministry that allowed discrimination to exist. A range of personal remedies for O'Brien were agreed to; some specific remedies were agreed to for the Windsor Jail; and, in addition, the ministry agreed to work with the Ontario Public Service Employees Union (OPSEU) to develop and implement a systemic change program of measures to promote the equality of women correctional officers, including accommodating staff with family responsibilities, increasing the participation rate of women in the correctional officer workforce and in supervisory positions, and fostering the quick, effective resolution of discrimination complaints. The development and implementation of the systemic change program led to a series of supplementary awards[218] ordering a range of measures, including:

- establishment of a systemic change steering committee and site-specific committees
- integration of the systemic change policy into training courses, and specialized training
- numerical goals for gender balance[219]
- encouragement to hire women
- encouragement to retain women by lengthening unclassified contracts from a standard six months to a standard twelve months for second and subsequent contracts, and by bridging employment through reorganizations with the use of temporary classified assignments, lateral transfers, and job trades
- rotation of assignments through the list of qualified staff to increase female access to developmental opportunities
- establishment of a protocol to accommodate employees with family responsibilities (including provision for leaves and scheduling flexibility)
- establishment of exit interviews, especially to determine why female staff leave

The leading Human Rights Commission case concerning racial discrimination in the OPS, illustrative of the full range of potential

218 *OPSEU (O'Brien) and Ministry of Correctional Services*, GSB#1948/93, 27 July 2000, 13 October 2000, 14 November 2000, 7 December 2000, 6 June 2001, 24 December 2001, 10 May 2002, 24 September 2003 (Leighton) [*O'Brien*]. See also *OPSEU (Howe/Dalton/Loach) and Ministry of Solicitor General and Correctional Services*, GSB#3155/92, 5 November 1997 (Dissanayake) at 86–88.

219 *O'Brien*, *ibid*, 24 September 2003 at 3–4.

remedies, is *McKinnon v Ontario (Ministry of Correctional Services)*. A correctional officer of Indigenous ancestry was subject to a "poisoned atmosphere" at the Metro East Detention Centre in which racist slurs were the norm. No grievance was filed and instead a human rights complaint was commenced. In 1998, as part of the initial remedy, the complainant and his wife were ordered promoted to a first-line management, or OM 16, position, and the Ministry of Correctional Services was ordered to conduct a human rights training program approved by the Human Rights Commission within six months, in addition to the payment of damages and compensation, relocation of certain offending co-workers, editing of personnel files, and publication of the board's orders.[220] In 2002, where discrimination and retaliation had continued and where the initial decision was not properly implemented, the tribunal found the ministry liable for the acts of its managers and so fully responsible for failures to implement the prior decision, resulting in a presumptive continuation of a poisoned atmosphere at the workplace (unless proven otherwise, which it was not).[221]

The 2002 decision was judicially reviewed by the ministry resulting in a 2003 Divisional Court decision upholding the commission's finding and stating:

> there has been a ten-year history of resistance by this Ministry to the change of mind-set necessary to free the workplace from racism. . . . [The 1998 and 2002 decisions] indicate the existence of a shameful situation that is totally unacceptable in a civilized country.[222]

In the 2002 decision, the tribunal found that the continued discrimination and retaliation needed to be seen from the perspective of the "reasonable human rights complainant":

> In assessing the reasonableness of the complainant's fears and perceptions, boards of inquiry must be sensitive to the particular difficulties that confront complainants, many of whom experience great fear and anxiety surrounding the lodging and pursuit of a human rights

---

220 *McKinnon v Ontario (Ministry of Correctional Services) (No 3)*, 1998 CanLII 29849 (ON HRT).

221 *Ontario Human Rights Commission v Ontario (Correctional Services)*, 2002 CanLII 46519 (ON HRT) at 17–18 [*OHRC v Correctional Services, 2002*].

222 *Ontario v McKinnon*, unreported, 23 December 2003 (Ont Div Ct), upheld on appeal [2004] OJ No 5051 (CA).

> complaint. This is exacerbated where the complainant continues in an ongoing relationship with the respondent, especially where that relationship is complicated by a differential in power, such as is undeniably the case in the employer-employee setting.[223]

In considering its remedial approach, the tribunal took into account that the ministry had received many reports about various systemic discrimination problems and that its failure to respond had fostered systemic discrimination. The tribunal adjudicator reasoned that he needed to reshape the remedial orders to focus on addressing the "root causes," centrally "the indifference, ineptitude and bad faith of management at all levels" and that doing so required issuing more prescriptive and comprehensive ministry-wide orders on dealing with race-based complaints and *WDHP* matters generally, because, until that "larger dysfunction" is fixed, the board is "never going to be able to fix Metro East."[224]

A much wider ranging set of orders was then made, building on what was found to be the inadequate implementation of the systemic change training program that resulted from the *O'Brien* grievance, discussed above, and its expansion to have an anti-racism component. The remedies ordered included managerial training, human resources advisors, use of external investigators,[225] especially at the institution,[226] making *WDHP* compliance part of performance measures for managers, a compliance committee at the institution, regular reporting. and use of consultants to monitor progress.

In 2005, there was a hearing to clarify the role of the consultants, and the following observation was made:

> The "point" at which this [remedial] process is to end is not the implementation of each of the specific orders on a one-by-one basis until the last of them is impatiently checked off. The process will be complete when "the complainant's remedial right to full compliance with the Code in respect of future practices has been satisfied" by the

223 *OHRC v Correctional Services, 2002*, above note 221 at 147, quoting from other HRT jurisprudence.

224 *Ibid* at 162–67.

225 For decisions dealing on the selection of external investigators and the role of the third-party consultants, see *McKinnon v Ontario (Correctional Services)*, 2005 HRTO 23 and *McKinnon v Ontario (Correctional Services)*, 2005 HRTO 44.

226 As set out in *McKinnon v Ontario (Correctional Services)*, 2006 HRTO 20 at para 25.

> elimination of racism from the Ministry's workplaces. Despite protestations to the contrary, it seems to me that the Ministry is not truly focussed on that end as a positive institutional good to be desired by all affected thereby, from the top down, but views the orders as an unavoidable imposition that it wants both to limit and to have over with as soon as possible.[227]

The remedial orders were clarified to include the following:

- The consultants were to design and implement the needed programs.
- Racism toward inmates was in scope, on the grounds that "[s]urely the interactions of staff and inmates contribute as much to the atmosphere of the workplace as do staff-to-staff relations. Clearly, if the inmates are racially abused, that would poison the atmosphere for everyone, staff members included."[228]
- The deputy minister of the Ministry of Correctional Services was to bear the ultimate responsibility for the implementation of these orders and "what he does to promote or impede the change process is to be monitored and reported."[229]

Then, in 2007, a further hearing identified continued non-compliance by the ministry,[230] leading to wide-ranging orders, including orders that prior remedies be implemented, the ministry clarify that the complainant was not the source of problems, a province-wide complaint tracking system, and further compulsory training as well as personal remedies for the complainant and his wife.

Further litigation included disputed documentary disclosure, followed by a motion for the Tribunal to state a case for contempt to the Divisional Court, which was granted.[231] The whole case was ultimately settled confidentially between the parties.[232]

It is notable that *McKinnon* was a decade long proceeding brought by an individual complainant and driven by the orders of the tribunal,

---

227 *McKinnon v Ontario (Correctional Services)*, 2005 HRTO 15 at para 89.

228 *Ibid* at para 63.

229 *Ibid* at para 83.

230 *McKinnon v Ontario (Correctional Services)*, 2007 HRTO 4.

231 *McKinnon v Ontario (Correctional Services)*, 2010 HRTO 1521 and *McKinnon v Ontario (Correctional Services)*, 2011 HRTO 263.

232 As noted in *McKinnon v Ontario (Correctional Services)*, 2011 HRTO 591.

with a significant oversight role for external consultants.[233] This may have been necessary to produce needed change. On the other hand, it has been said that the creation of a more "dialogic" approach allows the parties to participate in finding solutions, to be better informed, to "own" the process, and results in a more effective remedy over time.[234]

The *Tardiel* case before the GSB stemmed from a long series of poisonous, racist, and threatening anonymous letters sent over multiple years to particular racialized individuals working at the Toronto Jail.[235]

> The effect of the letters was destructive of relationships within the jail. Thinly drawn divisions between individuals and groups became severe rents; former friends became suspicious of one another; rumour assumed the ring of truth; widespread doubt, fear, and recrimination became rampant. The management of the jail had little experience of dealing with so divisive and destructive an intrusion into workplace relationships.[236]

Numerous individual grievances, and a union policy grievance, were filed. The union and ministry agreed to consolidate all of them. The parties agreed on a process to handle suspicious mail, and a mediation-arbitration process to address all grievances and claims.

There were four broad parts to the mediation-arbitration process. The first was private hearings, with small attendance, for some of the individual grievors. The second consisted of hearings attended by representatives of all of the relevant constituencies in the jail at which the grievors and the employer had a representative opportunity to inform all present of the grievances, and the circumstances giving rise to them, and of actions taken to remedy the situation to that point. The third part involved the institutional parties in an organizational initiative designed to agree upon values, to reconstitute relationships within the jail and to address systemic remedies sought by the parties. A range

---

233 See the union's application for intervention in *McKinnon*, discussed below in the jurisdiction and procedure section.

234 Brodsky, above note 214 at 45.

235 *Ontario Public Service Employees Union v Ontario (Community and Correctional Services)*, 2008 CanLII 70513 (ON GSB); *Tardiel*, above note 197; *Ontario Public Service Employees Union (Tardiel et al) v Ontario (Community Safety and Correctional Services)*, 2011 CanLII 36560 (ON GSB) at 7–8, and 2011 CanLII 49519 (ON SGB).

236 *Ibid*, 2011 CanLII 36560 at 7–8.

of steps were taken, including establishing a local joint anti-racism committee that formulated a plan of action with the guidance of the mediator-arbitrator, training and orientation for staff and management, coaching and mentoring, joint statements condemning racism, clear expectations for management and staff conduct, new and active management, hospitable workplace improvements, improved processes for recruitment and promotion, and clearer processes for conflicts, complaints, investigations, and discipline in all cases. The fourth part was an expedited mediation-arbitration of the claims of each of the grievors which resulted in minutes of settlement for directly affected grievors and then, under a union policy grievance, a finding that, while management had "acted in good faith and with good intentions, it did so inadequately and incomprehensively," leading to damages for many staff solely because they had worked in a poisoned work environment for an extended period.

Ongoing grievances about whether the *WDHP* policy had been adhered to at the Toronto Jail continued to highlight the need for the employer to investigate individual incidents and respond promptly to a grievor's wish to obtain an outcome. Remedies included further clarification of process requirements and a damage award.[237]

In other cases, where the failure to accommodate a grievor's disability has systemic causes, the GSB has ordered the training and instruction of management,[238] including the establishment of detailed training programs about the symptoms of emotional instability and severe anxiety, where the attendees receive written material about the content of the program in which they are instructed that behaviour which aggravates or exacerbates emotional instability or anxiety may constitute a disciplinary offence; and ordered that the employer provide the union with a detailed written statement indicating the priorities, principles, and policies that management must follow when scheduling casual employees.[239]

Where it was asserted that granting time off for religious observance produced an excessive expense when applied to the entire OPS, the GSB stated it would be necessary for the employer to lay an evidentiary

---

237 *Ontario Public Service Employees Union (Williams) v Ontario (Community Safety and Correctional Services)*, 2015 CanLII 9001 (ON GSB) (Albertyn).

238 *OPSEU (Watts) and Ministry of Community and Social Services*, GSB#0524/94, 6 November 1997 (Mikus) at 108–9; *OPSEU (Latimer) and Ministry of Correctional Services*, GSB#131/95, 24 May 2001 (Kaufman) [*Latimer*].

239 *Latimer*, *ibid* at 217.

foundation for the argument by providing some projection of the cost it would bear when it set a public service-wide accommodation precedent.[240]

The employer's attempts to engage in systemic remedies that have had a negative impact on bargaining unit employee entitlements have been closely scrutinized. Job competition qualifications must be reasonable, and the GSB will review whether the employer has proven the reasonableness of a bilingualism requirement.[241] An employer affirmative-action program that was not part of the collective agreement approved equity program was found to breach the anti-discrimination language of the agreement.[242]

3) Damage Awards

Damage awards in the OPS accord with standard arbitral and human rights jurisprudence, hence focusing on the objective seriousness of the conduct and the effect on the particular applicant who experienced discrimination.[243] In an egregious accommodation case, the GSB demonstrated willingness to award compensatory, and not punitive, damages "to compensate for the intrinsic value of the loss of the right to be free from discrimination."[244] In an egregious case of discrimination by management against a correctional officer due to their sexual orientation, compensatory damages "to attempt, so far as is possible, to restore the dignitary interest of the grievor" were awarded in the amount of

---

240 *Tratnyek*, above note 209.

241 *OPSEU (Booth) and Ministry of the Solicitor General*, GSB#0386/91, 4 December 1992 (Gorsky); *OPSEU (Wilson) and Ministry of Natural Resources*, GSB#2488/92, 18 May 1994 (Gorsky) at paras 17–18.

242 *OPSEU (Kinsella) and Ministry of Correctional Services*, GSB#2293/92, 29 September 1995 (Finley) at 36–37.

243 *Ontario Public Service Employees Union (Grievor) v Ontario (Solicitor General)*, 2022 CanLII 31320 (ON GSB) (Harris) [*OPSEU (Grievor), 2022*]; *Deane v Ontario (Community Safety and Correctional Services)*, 2012 HRTO 1753; *Lauzon*, above note 208; and *Kurpel*, above note 208. For an example at the lower end of the damages scale, see *Del Casale*, above note 192.

244 *Association of Management, Administrative and Professional Crown Employees of Ontario (Bokhari) v Ontario (Economic Development, Employment, and Infrastructure)*, 2016 CanLII 51073 (ON GSB) (Dissanayake) at para 45 and paras 42–65.

$45,000, then the largest amount ever rewarded by the GSB.[245] Punitive damages were not awarded as the employer's conduct was not found to be "so malicious and outrageous."[246] The same total compensatory amount has been awarded in another very lengthy case where the ministry's repeated failure to properly accommodate an asthmatic grievor with cigarette sensitivity was humiliating, lasted for years, and resulted in significant psychological damages.[247] More modest amounts have been awarded for less severe cases.[248] Note that damages that would be compensable by the Workplace Safety and Insurance Board (WSIB) may not be awardable by any other tribunal.[249]

Where the *HRC* has been violated, the PSGB has indicated it may be less likely to defer to management's discretion when making remedial orders in cases of harassment or other serious violations.[250] The PSGB

---

245 *Ontario Public Service Employees Union (Ranger) v Ontario (Community Safety and Correctional Services)*, 2013 CanLII 50479 (ON GSB) (Leighton) at para 54.

246 *Ibid* at para 72.

247 *Ontario Public Service Employees Union (Hyland) v Ontario (Solicitor General)*, 2021 CanLII 26637 (ON GSB) (Petryshen) at paras 80–81, where the grievor's assignments were overly limited, narrow, and resulted in the unwarranted perception that he was not "pulling his weight." See the predecessor cases detailing the prior litany of failure of accommodation: *OPSEU (Hyland) and Ministry of Correctional Services*, GSB#1470/91, 13 May 2002, and 17 March 2003 (Petryshen); *Ontario Public Service Employees Union (Hyland) v Ontario (Children and Youth Services*, 2007 CanLII 40534 (ON GSB) (Petryshen); *Ontario Public Service Employees Union (Hyland) v Ontario (Children and Youth Services)*, 2009 CanLII 59463 (ON GSB) (Petryshen); *Ontario Public Service Employees Union (Hyland) v Ontario (Community Safety and Correctional Services)*, 2014 CanLII 8297 (ON GSB) (Petryshen).

248 As canvassed in *Ontario Public Service Employees Union (Grievor) v Ontario (Community Safety and Correctional Services)*, 2019 CanLII 12506 (ON GSB) (Misra). For a discussion of the relevant factors including the grievor's partial responsibility for her lack of income, see *Association of Management, Administrative and Professional Crown Employees of Ontario (GAM) v Ontario (Health)*, 2019 CanLII 118346 (ON GSB) (Herlich).

249 See the discussion of *Ontario Public Service Employees Union (Monk et al) v Ontario (Community Safety and Correctional Services and Ministry of Children and Youth Services)*, 2010 CanLII 28621 (ON GSB) (Gray) [*Monk*] in the health and safety section.

250 *Girling and MSGCS*, PSGB#P0013/98, 8 May 2002 (Leighton).

has also acknowledged its authority to award damages for injury to dignity or for mental distress[251] and has done so.[252]

4) OPS Employer Policy on Human Rights and Harassment

Under the *Respectful Workplace Policy (RWP)*,

> [t]he Ontario Public Service (OPS) is committed to fostering and sustaining a respectful workplace. A respectful workplace is one that values diversity and inclusion, dignity, courteous conduct, fairness, positive communication, and professional working relationships. A respectful workplace is inclusive, diverse, equitable, accessible, and free from workplace harassment and discrimination.[253]

The *RWP* is clearly intended in part to respond to the history of systemic remedies, to comply with the *OHSA* requirement[254] that the employer shall "prepare a policy with respect to workplace harassment," "develop and maintain a program to implement the policy," and to establish that employees cannot be the subject of reprisal for utilizing the policy.[255]

---

251 *Morrison, 1995*, above note 200 at 13, but see the discussion in *Monk*, below, about the extent of the WSIB's jurisdiction over mental distress claims.

252 *Charlton v Ontario (Community Safety and Correctional Services)*, 2007 CanLII 24192 (ON PSGB) (Carter).

253 Management Board of Cabinet, *Respectful Workplace Policy (Policy to Support a Respectful Workplace and Prevent Workplace Harassment and Discrimination)*, 1 October 2017, copy made available to authors [*RWP*]. The predecessor *Workplace Discrimination and Harassment Policy* contained more specific procedural requirements. There is also an *OPS Anti-Racism Policy*, effective 2 April 2018, online: www.ontario.ca/page/ontario-public-service-anti-racism-policy#antiracismpolicy, setting out systemic measures to address racism, including collection of data, anti-racism training, engagement, and an action plan led by an Anti-Racism Directorate, as well as a *Policy on Preventing Barriers in Employment*, and policies on disability accommodation and workplace violence prevention. A thoughtful union perspective on such policies is found in Administrative, Management and Professional Crown Employees of Ontario (AMAPCEO), *OPS Inclusive Workplace Policy and Program Review*, November 2020, online: http://amapceo.on.ca/publications.

254 *OHSA*, above note 1, ss 32.0.1 and 32.0.6. See the *OHSA* section below.

255 For a discussion of the enforceability of the *RWP*, above note 253, in the context of determining whether the employer has fulfilled their substantive obligations under the collective agreement, see the discussion below, and particularly *Ontario Public Service Employees Union (Grievor) v Ontario (Community Safety and*

The *RWP* states that prevention of harassment and discrimination is a shared responsibility between the employer, employees and, where applicable, bargaining agents. Managers, "with the assistance of human resource advisors," are to take "timely action" to resolve situations "contrary to respectful workplaces." Policy violations include:

- workplace harassment or discrimination in any aspect of employment
- failure of management, in keeping with its authority, to respond appropriately and expeditiously to workplace harassment or discrimination
- interference with a workplace harassment or discrimination investigation, including but not limited to intimidating a complainant, respondent, or witness, or influencing a person to give false or misleading information
- reprisal, including threatening or retaliating against an employee or other worker for exercising a right under this policy, or participating in the process (for example, an investigation) against any other person who is performing a legitimate role under this policy
- bad faith allegations, complaints, or accusations (e.g., submitting a *WDHP* complaint knowing there has been no policy violation)

Complaints are to be filed within six months of the most recent alleged incident of discrimination or harassment, although later complaints may be considered in extenuating circumstances. Consequences for violating the policy include discipline, and potential dismissal, "in accordance with the principles of progressive discipline."

Staff are encouraged to tell the alleged offender "to stop" and to rapidly notify management. When alleged discrimination and harassment are being investigated, "respondents and complainants must have access to sufficient information about the allegations to allow effective participation in the process." Management must notify the *WDHP* office of the Ministry of Government and Consumer Services upon receipt of a complaint or potential violation. The *WDHP* advisor is to conduct a preliminary assessment within fifteen working days of receipt. There are time limits for the completion of each of direct management

---

Correctional Services), 2017 CanLII 65618 (ON GSB) (Tims) at 102–5 [*Grievor, 2017*].

action, alternate dispute resolution, and investigation. Complainants and respondents are to be kept appraised of status. Complainants are to be informed in writing of the disposition. Managers must "take appropriate steps to improve and/or restore work environments and work relationships affected by allegations or incidents of workplace harassment or discrimination." Deputy ministers and chairs are to act upon reports arising from external investigations within thirty days.

The *RWP* references but does not explicitly require external investigations.[256] While external investigations may be necessary for some time period, or for some situations, due to shortcomings in the OPS, they do not result in building capacity in the OPS. While the policy says that reports from external investigations are to be acted upon, it does not say how, and there is no stated requirement to act on internal investigations.

Note that it is OPS practice to not issue internal reports to the complainants, but rather to use those reports to inform corrective action. In litigation, it is appropriate to have particulars provided by the grievor first before disclosure by the employer, in order to limit the case to the grievor's concerns, rather than having the case expand in response to statements revealed in the disclosure.[257] Once particulars are provided, all documentation generated during a *WDHP/RWP* proceeding will be ordered to be disclosed to all the parties, on the basis that the introduction of that material into evidence will be subject to the normal admissibility rules.[258]

---

256 The use of external investigations appears to be the result of the HRTO order in the *McKinnon* case discussed above and a recommendation from the *Huggins Report*, above note 183, Recommendation 11:

> Given that there appears to be no written or other criteria to determine when and why an internal investigation is appropriate or evidence that the Internal Investigators are trained on workplace investigations or have received anti-racism/anti-Black racism, unconscious bias/anti-Black bias, intersectionality, and cultural sensitivity training, it is recommended that the WDHP process dispense with internal investigations.

257 See the discussion about disclosure before the GSB in Chapter 11.

258 *OPSEU (Fournier) and Ministry of Transportation*, GSB#1530/93, 3 November 1994 (Kaplan) at 2.

a) Enforceability of Employer Human Rights Policy

i) GSB

Grievances by victims tend to be resolved by the direct application of the *HRC*.[259] The *WDHP*, now the *RWP*, is not part of the collective agreement, nor is it incorporated by collective agreement requirements of reasonable provision for health and safety or as an unreasonable exercise of management rights. In other words, the issue will remain whether alleged employer procedural flaws are established and constitute breaches of the employer's contractual or statutory obligations.[260] The additional effect of the *WDHP*, now the *RWP*, for unionized employees is to provide a benchmark to assist the board in determining whether the employer has acted with appropriate diligence in remedying the situation of victims and with appropriate procedural fairness in disciplining perpetrators.[261]

As context, the *HRC* jurisprudence establishes a duty to investigate complaints of discrimination.[262] Indicia of reasonable steps are:

(i) the response must be prompt;
(ii) there must be corporate awareness that the conduct complained of is prohibited;
(iii) the matter must be dealt with seriously;
(iv) there must be a complaint mechanism in place;
(v) the respondent must act so as to provide a healthy environment;
(vi) the respondent must communicate its actions to the complainant.[263]

The *RWP* is an attempt to ensure fulfillment of this obligation.

Workplaces with unresolved human rights issues are challenged to operate effectively and respectfully. Caution has been expressed about excessive scrutiny by arbitrators of investigators, reports as this can produce a tendency for investigators to "write for the arbitrator" rather

259 See for example *OPSEU (Koh) and Ministry of Health*, GSB#889/92, 14 February 1994 (Kaplan) at 95–96, where the arbitrator notes that both the *HRC* (as incorporated into the collective agreement) and the *WDHP* require the investigation of certain particularized allegations.

260 *Grievor, 2017*, above note 255 at 102–5.

261 *OPSEU (Wickett et al) and Ministry of Natural Resources*, GSB#0542/01, 12 August 2005 (Petryshen) [*Wickett*].

262 *Laskowska v Marineland of Canada Ltd*, 2005 HRTO 30 at para 53, as discussed in *Deane v Ontario (Community Safety and Correctional Services)*, 2011 HRTO 1863 at 30–31.

263 *Abdallah v Thames Valley District School Board*, 2008 HRTO 230 at para 87.

that conduct a "speedy" investigation.[264] It is important for investigators' reports to be prompt and persuasive so that they can foster timely resolution of the matter.

In discipline cases, an employee violation of the *WDHP* is a factor that can be taken into account when assessing the seriousness of the employee's misconduct. Concerning the emailing of pornography in the workplace, the GSB commented that it poisons the workplace and violates the *WDHP*.[265] Condonation may be a significant mitigating factor in discipline of an employee.[266]

ii) PSGB

The PSGB will likely enforce the *WDHP/RWP* procedure, by treating it as part of the grievor's terms and conditions of employment.[267] Where a respondent is not treated fairly under the policy, the PSGB will hear that grievance and provide a remedy. However, failure to comply with the requirements of the policy will not void subsequent disciplinary action against the grievor. Prior to amendments in 1996, the regulations to the *PSA* contained a pre-dismissal hearing process. The courts and the PSGB held that procedural failure under the provision was fully remedied by the right to a de novo hearing before the PSGB.[268] Consequently, on the same reasoning, the right to a de novo hearing before the PSGB will remedy a procedural failure or unfairness in a *WDHP* investigation. In any case, if a manager grieves about the outcome of a *WDHP* investigation, the employer's response must be justified by the evidence placed before the PSGB.[269]

---

264 *AMAPCEO v AG*, above note 183 at para 180.

265 *OPSEU (Hastie et al) and Ministry of Natural Resources*, GSB#0542/01, 23 January 2003 (Petryshen) at 44; *Wickett* above note 261; *Ontario Public Service Employees Union (Aboutaeib/Carletti) v Ontario (Community and Social Services)*, 2011 CanLII 83707 (ON GSB) (Johnston). For a systemic approach by the parties, see *Ontario Public Service Employees Union v Ontario (Community Safety and Correctional Services)*, 2009 CanLII 66589 (ON GSB) (Keller).

266 *Wickett*, above note 261 at 34.

267 *Paul v Ontario (Solicitor General)*, 2021 CanLII 26625 (ON PSGB) at para 27; *Di Gaetano and Ministry of Municipal Affairs and Housing*, PSGB#P/0061/95 and 0015/96, 26 October 2000 (Walters); *DaSilva and Ministry of Health*, PSGB#P/0070/93, 23 December 1997 (Leighton).

268 *Re Lochhead* (1978), 22 OR (2d) 673 (Div Ct); *Hardy*, PSGB#/0034/93, 18 May 1995 (Leighton).

269 *Morrison, 1995*, above note 200 at 153.

5) Jurisdiction, Deferral, and Procedure

a) Jurisdiction and Intervenor Status

i) HRTO

The jurisdiction of the HRTO is OPS-wide and is not limited to collective agreements. The work done by independent contractors may be employment subject to the right to equal treatment in respect of employment under section 5 of the *HRC*, and section 5 has been found to extend to an order-in-council appointment even though the appointee also signed a "consulting agreement" to provide consulting services, which stated "nothing in the agreement shall have the effect of creating an employment relationship between the Ministry and the consultant."[270]

Recognizing that a union will have an interest in a human rights application brought by an employee in a bargaining unit it represents when the application alleges discrimination in employment, the HRTO's established practice is to grant intervenor status when requested by the union, absent exceptional circumstances.[271] The union has a clear interest in any systemic remedies ordered by the tribunal and its access on an ongoing basis to the entire range of ministry operations give it a useful perspective that can be of assistance to the adjudicative process.[272]

ii) GSB and PSGB

A human rights matter does need to be characterizable as a "difference" between the parties arising in the course of the administration of management rights under the collective agreement for it to be within the jurisdiction of the GSB.[273] The alleged violation of the human rights of an unclassified employee that occurs *after* the expiry of the unclassified employee's contract of employment is not remediable at the GSB,[274] and

---

270 *Davey v Ontario (Health and Long-Term Care)*, 2013 HRTO 419, citing *Garofalo v Cavalier Hair Stylists Shop Inc*, 2013 HRTO 170 at para 169.

271 *Williams v Ontario (Community Safety and Correctional Services)*, 2012 HRTO 1413, following *Boyce v Toronto Community Housing Corporation*, 2009 HRTO 131 at para 13.

272 *McKinnon v Ontario (Correctional Services)*, 2005 HRTO 15 at 7–8.

273 See *Parry Sound (District) Social Services Administration Board v OPSEU Local 324*, 2003 SCC 42 [*Parry Sound*].

274 See discussion about term employees in Chapter 2.

neither is an allegedly discriminatory denial of a promotion to management,[275] or a grievance under one collective agreement about the proper application of another collective agreement.[276]

The GSB has addressed efforts to rely on the facts underlying settled grievances in support of ongoing harassment claims by consistently re-enforcing the principle of "sanctity of settlements."[277]

A manager accused of discrimination and harassment has been granted third-party status, where the employer indicated that it had a potential conflict of interest when defending the manager's actions.[278] An alleged harasser may also have the right to participate in a hearing where the remedy may deprive them of collective agreement benefits.[279] The right to participate will be limited to the "incident" involving the alleged harasser and any remedy that might affect them.

The GSB has stated that it is prepared to remove a discriminatory manager from the workplace, and perhaps from employment, if necessary to address discrimination, although it has never done so. In the leading case of *OPSEU (Naumenko) and Ministry of Solicitor General and Correctional Services*,[280] the GSB determined that its power to order that a non-bargaining unit member be transferred or discharged was not to be used as punishment, but only if no other order would ensure that the workplace was free of discrimination. If this power is ever exercised, it would directly affect the employment of a manager with

275 *Ontario Public Service Employees Union (Walji) v Ontario (Solicitor General)*, 2021 CanLII 71639 (ON GSB) (Banks) at para 12, citing *OPSEU (Schnoflak) and Ontario (Ministry of Community Safety and Correctional Services)*, 2017-3409 (19-11-19 Decision) (Petryshen) at para 9; *OPSEU (Dias) and Ministry of Revenue*, GSB#3479/92, 3 March 1995 (Gorsky).

276 *Ontario Public Service Employees Union (Ahmed) v Ontario (Transportation)*, 2014 CanLII 63513 (ON GSB) (Nairn).

277 *Ontario Public Service Employees Union (Kyba et al) v Ontario (Environment, Conservation and Parks)*, 2018 CanLII 119561 (ON GSB) (Dissanayake) at para 30 and cases cited.

278 *OPSEU (Fournier) and Ministry of Transportation*, GSB#1530/93, 28 December 1994 (Kaplan).

279 *Association of Management, Administrative and Professional Crown Employees of Ontario (Grievor) v Ontario (Attorney General)*, 2019 CanLII 97290 (ON GSB) (McLean).

280 GSB#613/94, 21 October 1997 (Mikus) at 31, and other cases cited therein; *OPSEU (Smith and McKinnon) and Ministry of Solicitor General and Correctional Services*, GSB#0545/94, 11 April 1997 (Finley) at 138; *OPSEU (Pinazza) v MCSCS*, [2004] OGSBA No 125 (Herlich).

the right to process a grievance to the PSGB. It is not clear how the procedural entitlements of that manager would be addressed.

The PSGB's jurisdiction over human rights complaints by managers and excluded staff is addressed in Chapter 12. The jurisdiction of the PSGB would be more limited than the GSB when addressing a grievance by a manager that a bargaining unit employee needs to be transferred or discharged to ensure a discrimination-free workplace. The PSGB has jurisdiction to make orders against the Crown, but no jurisdiction to grant remedies that directly impact collective agreement rights, unions, or bargaining unit employees.[281] An order affecting collective agreement rights, including those of a bargaining unit member, would require the union to be a party. If the grievor was inclined to seek this type of remedy, the HRTO seems to be the more effective forum.

Before both the GSB and the PSGB, where the interests of an individual involved in a grievance alleging discrimination will not be represented by one of the parties to the grievance (those being the union and employer before the GSB, and the employee and employer before the PSGB), the third party's participation, if they are given standing and chose to participate, might raise an estoppel in a hearing on the same matter before the other board. However, a third party who receives notice and declines to participate also does so at some risk. They are not bound by the tribunal's decision, but their employer will be both bound and required to implement orders that may affect the employee.

b) Deferral

i) By the GSB to the HRTO

Where the subject matter of a grievance is also the subject matter of a complaint before the Human Rights Commission, the GSB will need to decide whether to adjourn the grievance pending resolution of the complaint. The GSB has stated that, so far as it is concerned, a grievor is normally entitled to proceed with both the grievance and the human

---

281 *Burt v MCS*, PSGB#P0015/92, 6 April 1993 (Willes). The PSGB can order the employer to consider an excluded employee for bargaining unit position, but a placement requirement falls exclusively within the GSB's jurisdiction.

rights complaint simultaneously[282] and it applies contextual discretion to whether to adjourn the grievance.[283]

ii) By the HRTO to the GSB and PSGB

Unions, even though charged with representing the collective interest of the members of their bargaining units, have the responsibility to vindicate the individual human rights of those members. Those individual human rights are incorporated into the collective agreement[284] and the union is at risk of co-liability with the employer for any failure to uphold those rights.[285] It has been further confirmed by the Supreme Court in *Northern Regional Health Authority v Horrocks* that, since "labour arbitration is the primary forum for the enforcement of human rights in unionized workplaces,"[286] the exclusive jurisdiction of a labour arbitrator over all differences, including human rights, is to be given full effect unless there is clearly expressed legislative intent that competing tribunals, such as a Human Rights Commission or Tribunal, may "carve into that sphere of exclusivity."[287] As of the date of writing, the HRTO has found that the *HRC* demonstrates "a clear legislative intent to expressly displace the labour arbitrator's exclusive jurisdiction."[288] This conclusion is based on the *HRC*'s legislative history of intended concurrent jurisdiction and its mechanisms for sorting out which adjudicative body should hear the matter and when.

---

282 *OPSEU (Bertrand) and Ministry of Health*, GSB#1998/93, 24 July 1995 (Mikus) at 14; *Ontario Public Service Employees Union (Barillari) v Ontario (Community and Social Services)*, 2008 CanLII 19771 (ON GSB) (Carrier).

283 *Ontario Public Service Employees Union (Therrien) v Ontario (Community Safety and Correctional Services)*, 2008 CanLII 32795 (ON GSB) (Lynk) at 1–13.

284 *Parry Sound*, above note 273.

285 *Central Okanagan School District No 23 v Renaud*, [1992] 2 SCR 970 [*Renaud*].

286 *Northern Regional Health Authority v Horrocks*, 2021 SCC 42 at para 13 [*Horrocks*], citing Elizabeth Shilton, "'Everybody's Business': Human Rights Enforcement and the Union's Duty To Accommodate" (2014) 18 *Canadian Labour and Employment Law Journal* 209 at 235 and Peter A. Gall, Andrea L. Zwack & Kate Bayne, "Determining Human Rights Issues in the Unionized Workplace: The Case for Exclusive Arbitral Jurisdiction" (2005) 12 *Canadian Labour and Employment Law Journal* 381 at 397.

287 *Horrocks*, *ibid* at para 5.

288 *Weilgosh v London District Catholic School Board*, 2022 HRTO 1194.

In the exercise of its concurrent jurisdiction, the HRTO's policy is to usually initially defer to the GSB,[289] pending completion of GSB proceedings dealing with the same matter, where the proceedings deal with overlapping facts or issues within the authority of both tribunals. This is done due to *Parry Sound (District) Social Services Administration Board v OPSEU*,[290] where the Supreme Court confirmed that grievance arbitrators have the power and duty to enforce human rights and other employment statutes as if they were part of the collective agreement.[291] The HRTO has said "[t]he GSB is also an independent and unbiased body, who is able to address the issues as thoroughly and fairly as the Tribunal."[292] There will also be deferral to the pre-GSB grievance process even if there is some delay there.[293] Similarly, where a PSGB complaint is based on the same facts and issues as the tribunal complaint, the tribunal will defer to the PSGB pending the outcome of the grievance.[294] Deferral will occur where there is "substantial overlap" in the subject matter of the HRTO and the other proceeding,[295] but not where the subject matters are related but truly different.[296]

---

289 Ontario Human Rights Tribunal, *Rules of Procedure*, Rule 14—Deferral of an Application by the Tribunal.

290 *Parry Sound*, above note 273.

291 *Williams v Ontario (Community Safety and Correctional Services)*, 2012 HRTO 1749 at 9–12. To the same effect, see *Ng v Ontario (Ministry of Government Services)*, 2011 HRTO 1487; *Cox v Ontario (Community Safety and Correctional Services)*, 2009 HRTO 2046; *Strang v Ontario (Community and Social Services)*, 2016 HRTO 834; *Wainman v Ontario (Community Safety and Correctional Services)*, 2017 HRTO 316; *McNaughton v Ontario (Environment, Conservation and Parks)*, 2020 HRTO 461.

292 *Lupiani v Ontario (Ministry of Transportation)*, 2016 HRTO 1631 at para 9.

293 *Melville v Ontario Public Service Employees Union*, 2011 HRTO 419.

294 *Lipke v Ontario (Community Safety and Correctional Services)*, 2008 HRTO 285; *Muldoon v Ontario (Community Safety and Correctional Services)*, 2011 HRTO 735; *Achampong v Ontario (Government Services)*, 2011 HRTO 1417; *Jones v Ontario (Community Safety and Correctional Services)*, 2015 HRTO 834.

295 *Gallina v Ontario (Minister of Child and Youth Services)*, 2012 HRTO 1784; *Petrunti v Ontario (Community and Social Services)*, 2016 HRTO 108.

296 In *Lessard v Ontario (Attorney General)*, 2012 HRTO 1881 at para 9, the tribunal did not defer because, while the concurrent proceedings before the tribunal and the GSB flowed from the same event—the end of the applicant's employment—the subject matter before the GSB (the respondent's alleged failure to follow proper protocols for pre-notice and severance entitlements) and the subject matter before the tribunal (the respondent's alleged acts of discrimination based on disability and age) were different.

Where the GSB has concluded a grievance that addresses the issues in the human rights complaint, the issue will then be whether the tribunal should exercise its authority under the *HRC* section 45.1 to dismiss the application before it on the basis that the tribunal "is of the opinion that another proceeding[297] has appropriately dealt with the substance of the application."[298] A "proceeding" includes the settlement of that proceeding.[299] The main issue for the HRTO is not whether the adjudicator in the other proceeding has correctly decided the human rights issues raised in the application, but whether the applicant has had the opportunity to have their human rights issues considered by an adjudicator with jurisdiction to interpret and apply the *HRC*, as "the Tribunal may not evaluate the procedural or substantive correctness of the other proceeding."[300] A party will not be permitted to engage in "splitting one's case" by restricting *HRC* arguments in the labour arbitration so that they can be pursued later before the tribunal.[301]

The HRTO will consider whether it would be unfair to apply the doctrine of issue estoppel due to the unfairness of the prior proceedings or if it would nonetheless be unfair to use the results of the arbitral process to preclude the human rights complaint.[302]

Where the GSB upholds a termination, and deals implicitly with the allegation of reprisal under the *HRC*, the tribunal can still conclude that the substance of the matter has been appropriately dealt with because even if the human rights issues were not explicitly argued at the arbitration, the upholding of the termination implicitly includes a finding

297 A hearing before the Grievance Settlement Board is a "proceeding" within the meaning of s 45.1: *Warling v Ontario (Community Safety and Correctional Services)*, 2010 HRTO 826 [*Warling*], as is a hearing before the PSGB: *Taylor v Ontario (Community Safety and Correctional Services)*, 2016 HRTO 1306 [*Taylor*].

298 *HRC*, above note 1, s 45.1.

299 *Lessard v Ontario (Attorney General)*, 2013 HRTO 1902 adopting *Dunn v Sault Ste Marie (City)*, 2008 HRTO 149, where the tribunal determined that a GSB settlement allowing a tribunal application to continue did exclude facts and circumstances within the scope of the GSB matter.

300 *Belsky v Ontario (Government and Consumer Services)*, 2016 HRTO 272 at para 19, citing the leading Supreme Court cases of *British Columbia (Worker's Compensation Board) v Figliola*, 2011 SCC 52 at paras 37–38 and *Penner v Niagara (Regional Police Services Board)*, 2013 SCC 19 [*Penner*]. And see *Paterno v Salvation Army*, 2011 HRTO 2298 at para 24 [*Paterno*]; *Warling*, above note 297.

301 *Taylor*, above note 297 at para 22.

302 *Williams v Ontario Public Service Employees' Union*, 2021 HRTO 114 at paras 26–27, applying *Penner*, above note 300.

there was no violation of the Code, as the arbitrator had the duty to give effect to the *HRC*.[303] Similarly, it may be that to proceed with a tribunal application will be an abuse of process where all the facts of the case, and an assertion of employer unreasonableness, were before the GSB but, inexplicably, the grievor did not raise the alleged *HRC* violation.[304]

If it is truly unclear what was before the GSB or how it was dealt with, then it would be unfair to apply section 45.1 to preclude the application,[305] although clarity can be found in the circumstances of the matter, such as an expedited mediation-arbitration of the grievance, understandably involving no substantive reasons, where it was clear that the grievance dealt with the same issues as those at stake in the application.[306]

The circumstances of a unionized environment, including that the union has carriage and control of the grievance and of whether to pursue judicial review of the GSB final decision, certainly do not justify re-litigation of the same matter before the HRTO. The suggestion that, if unionized employees believe their opportunity to seek redress at the tribunal is compromised when they file human rights–based grievances, they may forgo using the grievance-arbitration process, is viewed as "speculative," and it is expected that "employees in a unionized environment would for the most part see advantages in having all of their issues determined in one forum."[307]

Where there was a settlement between the union and the employer, and the applicant employee did not sign a release, the tribunal will consider whether the applicant has explicitly or implicitly consented to the settlement and will defer to the GSB's determination of that issue.[308] While it has been found that an individual's agreement is required because *HRC* rights are individual rights,[309] it has also been noted that the union is entitled to resolve grievances about individuals and so the HRTO will consider both whether the applicant benefited from the settlement and

303 *Paterno* above note 300 at paras 26–29, quoted in *Gill v Ontario (Children and Youth Services)*, 2014 HRTO 640.

304 *Blanchette v Ontario (Natural Resources)*, 2010 HRTO 2280.

305 *Beausoleil v Ontario (Community Safety and Correctional Services)*, 2013 HRTO 1553.

306 *Marshall-Wilkinson v Ontario (Community Safety and Correctional Services)*, 2014 HRTO 1154 [*Marshall-Wilkinson*].

307 *Hussain v Ontario (Community and Social Services)*, 2014 HRTO 1788 at para 59. It is noted that an applicant can ask their union to withdraw their grievance.

308 *Holder v Ontario (Ministry of the Attorney General)*, 2022 HRTO 790.

309 *Ibid.*

the Ontario Labour Relations Board (OLRB) disposition of any duty of fair representation complaint filed by the applicant against the union.[310]

The tribunal has found on a number of occasions that filing a human rights application after executing a full and final release can amount to an abuse of process and has dismissed the application in question. The tribunal has considered factors such as whether the applicant understood the release, whether the applicant received consideration for it, and whether there is evidence of duress.[311]

Concerning an alleged lack of consideration, settlements will only be set aside if they are unconscionable, which is a high threshold.[312] Duress could void a settlement agreement but duress sufficient to have that consequence must involve "pressure the law regards as illegitimate" and it must be applied to such a degree as to amount to "a coercion of the will" of the party relying on the concept.[313] Finding the settlement process to be long and exhausting and being dissatisfied with a settlement is not sufficient duress to set the settlement aside.[314]

Non-compliance with a GSB settlement is to be pursued by asking the union to raise such concerns with the GSB, not by taking the matter before the HRTO.[315]

Where no grievance addresses the matter at issue, the HRTO will hear the matter and not defer, even if a grievance could have been filed.[316] This means an applicant has the ability under the current human rights system

---

310 *Bhandari v Ontario (Education)*, 2010 HRTO 1676 [*Bhandari*].

311 *Gallina v Ontario (Child and Youth Services)*, 2014 HRTO 390; *Karambetsos v Ontario (Community Safety and Correctional Services)*, 2014 HRTO 882.

312 *Abdul-Rahman v Ontario (Natural Resources and Forestry)*, 2016 HRTO 1151 at para 23, adopting the test of the Ontario Court of Appeal in *Titus v William F Cooke Enterprises Inc*, 2007 ONCA 573 at para 38.

313 *Taber v Paris Boutique & Bridal Inc (Paris Boutique)*, 2010 ONCA 157 at paras 8–9, cited in *Chapman v Ontario (Attorney General)*, 2014 HRTO 134 at para 18. See also *Abdul-Rahman*, *ibid* at para 18 adopting *Dai v Zuo*, 2015 ONSC 3008.

314 *Marshall-Wilkinson*, above note 306 at para 19; *Whitlow v Ontario (Environment and Climate Change)*, 2016 HRTO 184.

315 *Marshall-Wilkinson*, above note 306 at para 20.

316 *McKinnon v Ontario (Ministry of Correctional Services) (No 3)*, 1998 CanLII 29849 (ON HRT) at paras 11–13, and *Cox v Ontario (Community Safety and Correctional Services)*, 2012 HRTO 1607 where the grievor was a racialized correctional officer who was the subject of grievances for an earlier period and for systemic remedies in the *Tardiel* matter but not the subject of a grievance for the relevant period dealing with individual remedies.

to choose the forum for the determination of human rights issues.[317] Similarly, a union and grievor can withdraw a grievance mid-hearing and then the grievor can reactivate a tribunal application.[318] While a grievor/applicant has a choice of forum, an applicant "does not have the option to require an employer to litigate the same issues twice."[319]

This jurisprudence does not deal with the real possibility of a union bringing a grievance or continuing with a grievance against the wishes of the grievor. That would seem best addressed as a potential breach of the union's duty of fair representation under the *Labour Relations Act, 1995* (*LRA*).[320] It is notable, as discussed above, that, in the converse situation, where there was a settlement of a grievance between the union and the employer, and the applicant employee did not sign a release, the tribunal in considering the disposition of the applicant's human rights application, decided to dismiss the application under section 45.1 of the *HRC*, noting that the union is entitled to resolve grievances about individuals.[321]

c) Procedure

i) HRTO Procedure

To be timely under the *HRC*, an incident of discrimination must have occurred within one year before the issues were first raised[322] although older incidents may be timely if they are part of a "series of incidents."[323] The continuing effects of an act of alleged discrimination do not in themselves constitute further acts of discrimination or a series of incidents.[324] Consideration will be given to whether delay beyond one year was for a "good faith" reason.[325] If allegations are raised before the PSGB,

317 *Crowley v Liquor Control Board of Ontario*, 2010 HRTO 2407.

318 *Amurao v Ontario (Community and Social Services)*, 2012 HRTO 1903 [*Amurao*].

319 *Paterno*, above note 300 at para 33, cited in *Taylor*, above note 297 at para 24.

320 SO 1995, c 1, Sch A.

321 See discussion in *Bhandari*, above note 310.

322 *HRC*, above note 1, s 34(1) as discussed in *Kilpatrick v Ontario (Attorney General)*, 2016 HRTO 1142 at 9.

323 See the application of the standard to a sequence of events involving the Organizational Effectiveness Division of the Ministry of Correctional Services: *Robinson v Ontario (Community Safety and Correctional Services)*, 2013 HRTO 287.

324 *Mafinezam v University of Toronto*, 2010 HRTO 1495, cited in *Jones v Ontario (Community Safety and Correctional Services)*, 2011 HRTO 624 at para 12.

325 See the discussion of the "no good faith reason" in *Robins v Ontario (Community and Social Services)*, 2019 HRTO 873 at paras 10–40.

or presumably the GSB, then it is necessary, for purposes of assessing timeliness, to raise them at the same time in an HRTO application.[326]

The HRTO may hold a summary hearing "on its own initiative or at the request of a party, on the question of whether an Application should be dismissed in whole or in part on the basis that there is no reasonable prospect that the Application or part of the Application will succeed."[327] The tribunal may determine that some of the allegations have no reasonable prospect of success, but others may be allowed to proceed to a full hearing.[328] "Bald assertions" of discrimination will not suffice and the applicant must be able to identify evidence which would, if proven, establish a connection between the respondents' alleged actions and the grounds they have cited.[329] There are two main types of issues: (1) assuming the facts to be true, would they prove an *HRC* violation, and (2) whether the applicant can show a factual "link" between an event and the alleged prohibited ground.[330]

Similarly, the tribunal will consider, during a hearing, whether there is a prima facie case, meaning assessing whether there is a reasonable prospect of success.[331] The applicant's version of the facts, but not their assumptions about why they were unfairly treated, is assumed to be true unless there is clear evidence to the contrary, and the following test is applied:

> The mere fact that a person identified by a prohibited ground of discrimination experiences some kind of disagreeable or unfair treatment is not generally sufficient to support an inference of discrimination. The question that the Tribunal must decide at a summary hearing is whether there is likely to be sufficient direct or indirect evidence available to connect the unfair treatment experienced by the applicant with the applicant's personal characteristics.[332]

---

326 *Jones v Ontario (Community Safety and Correctional Services)*, 2011 HRTO 624 at paras 6–14.

327 Ontario Human Rights Tribunal, *Rules of Civil Procedure*, r 19A, s 19.1A.

328 *Stewart v Ontario (Government Services)*, 2013 HRTO 1635.

329 *Bangura v Ontario (Community and Social Services)*, 2014 HRTO 1353 at para 55, applying the test to dismiss an application alleging discrimination in the OPS not granting the applicant job interviews.

330 *Bangura, ibid*, at para 52, citing *Dabic v Windsor Police Service*, 2010 HRTO 1994 at paras 8–9.

331 *Finch v Ontario (Ministry of Community Safety and Correctional Services)*, 2020 HRTO 340.

332 *Morden v Ontario (Education)*, 2020 HRTO 202 at para 8.

The HRTO will consider whether to add or remove a party and, in refusing a request to name individual senior public servants as individual parties, noted that adding unnecessary individual respondents is "a practice to be discouraged, as this serves to unnecessarily add to the complexity of proceedings and can often operate as a roadblock to resolution."[333] Where there is no issue about the responsiveness of the corporate respondent, and no issue raised about that respondent's vicarious liability for individual managers in its employ, then the individuals should not be made parties in the absence of "some compelling juridical reason," such as their individual conduct being a central issue, or the real possibility of a remedy against them personally.

ii) GSB Procedure

The GSB has tended as a rule of thumb to allow evidence of events up to three years prior to the filing of the grievance to establish a pattern of harassment, so as to avoid the need for an employee to allege harassment every time there is employer conduct that seems unacceptable.[334] This is intended to balance the union's ability to establish a course of conduct with the employer's ability to defend itself against stale dated allegations.

Three-year rule is simply a point of departure and is not an inflexible rule to be mechanically applied in all cases.[335] The rule has been used in connection with requirements for particulars, to delineate the evidence to be called.[336] Where the three-year rule is applied, it does

333 *Amurao*, above note 318 at para 19, quoting *Sigrist and Carson v London District Catholic School Board*, 2008 HRTO 14 at para 42. See also *Persaud v Toronto District School Board*, 2008 HRTO 31 at para 5.

334 *Ontario Public Service Employees Union (Ramsook-Lall) v Ontario (Labour, Training and Skills Development)*, 2016 CanLII 156526 (ON GSB) (Williamson); *Ontario Public Service Employees Union (Akintunde) v Ontario (Community Safety and Correctional Services)*, 2018 CanLII 55850 (ON GSB) (Watters) [*Akintunde*]; *Ontario Public Service Employees Union (Bilardo) v Ontario (Labour)*, 2014 CanLII 74774 (ON GSB) (Herlich) at 6–8; *Ontario Public Service Employees Union (Lunan) v Ontario (Labour)*, 2015 CanLII 36166 (ON GSB) (Leighton) and cases cited therein.

335 *Akintunde*, *ibid* at paras 7–8. Also see the application of the rule in *Ontario Public Service Employees Union (Fletcher) v Ontario (Natural Resources and Forestry)*, 2018 CanLII 102772 (ON GSB) (Petryshen); *Ontario Public Service Employees Union (O'Flaherty) v Ontario (Community Safety and Correctional Services)*, 2018 CanLII 109253 (ON GSB) (Luborsky) at paras 15–22.

336 *Ontario Public Service Employees Union (Cooper) v Ontario (Clean Water Agency)*, 2019 CanLII 42398 (ON GSB) (Anderson).

not expand the grievance, and evidence is not admissible only by being within the three years. That evidence must be relevant to proving the facts on which the grievance is based.[337]

D. *OCCUPATIONAL HEALTH AND SAFETY ACT* AND RELATED COLLECTIVE AGREEMENT PROVISIONS

1) Introduction

The rights and obligations set out in the *OHSA* are applicable to public servants. This means that the management rights exercised by the government, and government employees' obligations, including the obligation to provide essential services during a lockout or strike, need to be considered in light of the rights and duties contained in the *OHSA*.

This section is focused on:

- proceedings before the OLRB under the *OHSA* that involve government employment
- GSB decisions about Article 9.1 of the OPSEU/MBC collective agreements, which addresses health and safety obligations and supplements the health and safety protections provided under *OHSA*

The government employer and the unions have a fairly advanced joint health and safety committee system through which they have demonstrated a real interest in promoting a safe and healthy workplace. As discussed later in this section, the right to refuse unsafe work has proven to be a more contentious area between these parties. On the one hand, there is a recognition that the government employer does not have the right to require government employees to unduly endanger themselves. On the other hand, there is concern that the right to refuse work only be exercised where there is such an urgent need to protect the employee's safety that it warrants the interruption of the provision of the needed service. Further, certain government employees have a limited right to refuse unsafe work under the *OHSA*.

337 *Barker*, above note 186 at para 56 and cases cited therein.

2) Application of the *Occupational Health and Safety Act* to Public Servants

The *OHSA* has been recognized as "the main legislative vehicle for maintaining and promoting workplace health and safety standards in Ontario."[338] Further, the *OHSA* has been recognized as a "remedial public welfare statute" which should be broadly interpreted. Narrow or technical interpretations of the Act are to be avoided.[339] However, interpretation of public welfare statutes "does not call for a limitless interpretation of their provisions."[340] That said, in a departure from its past jurisprudence, the OLRB has relied upon the purpose of the *OHSA* and its critical importance as a piece of public welfare legislation to find that the thirty-day time limit for filing an appeal under section 61 is not mandatory and the OLRB has the discretion to extend the time limit.[341]

Under section 2(1) of the *OHSA*, the Act is binding on the Crown, all persons in its employ, and "an agency, board, commission or corporation that exercises any function assigned or delegated to it by the Crown." This means that the Crown can be prosecuted for health and safety violations. Some judicial authority suggests that the government should be seen as a role model for other industries in health and safety matters and thus may face higher sanctions upon prosecution.[342]

It is significant that under section 2(1) of the *OHSA*, the Act is specifically applicable to "an employee in the service of the Crown." This provision allows public servants to exercise the rights of workers under the *OHSA*. It also means that individuals acting on behalf of the Crown, such as supervisors, are also covered by the rights and prohibitions under the *OHSA*. Notwithstanding that a supervisor may be excluded from the definition of an employee under the *LRA* for exercising supervisory or managerial functions, a supervisor does fall within the broad definition of a worker found under section 1(1), and

---

338 *R v Ellis Don Ltd* (1990), 1 OR (3d) 193 (CA) at 210. See also *R v Timminco Ltd*, 2001 CanLII 3493 (ON CA) at para 22.

339 *Ontario (Ministry of Labour) v Hamilton (City)*, 2002 CanLII 16893 (ON CA) at 43.

340 *Blue Mountain Resorts Limited v Ontario (Labour)*, 2013 ONCA 75 at paras 25–27 [*Blue Mountain*].

341 *OPSEU Local 234 v Ministry of Community Safety Correctional Services Vanier Centre for Women*, 2019 CanLII 14451 (ON LRB) [*Vanier, 2019*].

342 *R v Ontario (Ministry of Natural Resources)*, unreported, 7 March 2002 (Ont Ct J, Switzer JP) [*R v Ontario, 2002*].

consequently is likely able to exercise the right to refuse unsafe work under the Act. A supervisor is still likely to be treated as management under the *OHSA* for the purpose of determining the management and employee composition of a joint health and safety committee.

The breadth of the *OHSA* is also significant in the context of section 50, which provides that "no employer or person acting on behalf of an employer" shall *inter alia* discipline or impose a penalty upon a worker because the worker has sought the enforcement of the *OHSA*. This means that supervisors and others acting on behalf of the Crown can be subject to direct liability in the event of a reprisal complaint under section 50.[343]

Under section 50(2) of the *OHSA*, a Crown employee may elect to take a complaint of reprisal by the Crown employer to the OLRB or proceed to the GSB to enforce their occupational health and safety rights pursuant to the collective agreement. Once a grievance has moved past the grievance process to arbitration, even if the arbitration hearing has not yet commenced, the OLRB will generally find that an election has been made to proceed to arbitration and decline to hear a reprisal complaint.[344] Section 50(6) explicitly provides that the OLRB has jurisdiction over complaints made by a worker "who is a public servant within the meaning of the *Public Service of Ontario Act, 2006*." This clarification seems unnecessary given the clear general application of the *OHSA* to the Crown.[345]

A "workplace" is also broadly defined under section 1(1) of the *OHSA* as "any land, premises, location or thing at, upon, in or near which a worker works." This broad definition is especially relevant for those employed in the OPS given the wide variety of settings and situations in which public servants perform their work. For example, an air ambulance, which crashed, was found to come within the definition.[346]

343 *Ontario (Management Board of Cabinet)*, [2002] OLRB Rep March/April 176 at para 5. The case concerned the claim that it was a reprisal to refuse to pay nurses who were refusing to work during the 2002 OPSEU strike. The OLRB found that an individual manager could be named as respondent to the complaint.

344 *OPSEU v Kennedy House Youth Services Inc*, 2018 CanLII 97747 (ON LRB).

345 *OHSA* s 50(6) originated prior to 1993 at a time when the Ontario Public Service Labour Relations Tribunal (OPSLRT) operated as a public service labour-relations board. *OHSA* arguably had to specify whether the OPSLRT or the OLRB would have jurisdiction over section 50 complaints for public servants that were not referred to arbitration before the GSB.

346 *R v Ontario, 2002*, above note 342.

However, an ambulance has been ruled not to fall within the definition of an "industrial establishment," and so was not subject to the standards applicable to such premises.[347]

Notwithstanding the breadth of the *OHSA*, it remains focused on the worker. Its purpose is not to protect non-workers, even when they are present in a workplace. This was reflected in a case where the Ontario Court of Appeal found that the obligation to report critical injuries under the Act did not extend to critical injuries and fatalities suffered by non-workers like a guest who was found dead in a swimming pool at a resort.[348]

Section 2(2) confirms the legislative paramountcy of the *OHSA* over other legislation. In certain circumstances, however, proceedings under the *OHSA* may not prevail over other statutory regimes or competing or conflicting common law principles. Where an adjudicator under the *OHSA*, relying on section 2(2), ordered the employer to disclose information purportedly covered by the common law doctrine of police-informer privilege, this was quashed on judicial review, with the court taking the position that other policy concerns associated with police-informer privilege took precedence over the statutory obligations of a supervisor under section 27(2) of the *OHSA* to advise a worker of the existence of any potential or actual danger to the health or safety of the worker.[349]

3) Internal Responsibility System Within Government

The internal responsibility system is central to workplace health and safety in Ontario. Indeed, it has been recognized by the OLRB as the basis for the *OHSA*.[350] Although not defined under the *Act*, it is generally understood as founded on a shared responsibility for health and safety by all participants in the workplace, including employers, supervisors, and workers. This reflects that it is very often the workplace parties who can best assess hazards within the workplace and develop effective solutions. One of the prime ways in which workers, including

---

347 *OPSEU, Local 207 and Ontario (Ministry of Labour)*, [1990] OOHSA D No 8 (Dir App Blair) at para 6 [*Labour, 1990*].

348 *Blue Mountain*, above note 340.

349 *Ontario v OPSEU*, [1995] OOHSAD No 30 (Ont Adj Muir); application for judicial review allowed: *Ontario v Ontario Public Service Employees Union* (1996), 92 OAC 116 (Div Ct), leave to appeal refused (1996), 66 ACWS (3d) 11 (ON CA).

350 *Vanier, 2019*, above note 341 at para 31.

public servants, participate in the internal responsibility system is through joint occupational health and safety committees.[351]

The government has some well-developed ministry-wide committee structures. For instance, in corrections, OPSEU and management have two provincial joint occupational health and safety committees—one committee addresses safety throughout the Correctional Services Division and the other addresses safety in the Youth Justice Division. A letter of understanding appended to the collective agreement sets out the terms of reference for the committees.[352]

The purpose of the committees is to review health and safety issues that have ministry-wide application, and to act as a forum for discussing potential areas of concern and making recommendations for action. The terms of reference identify the following functions and matters for consideration by the committee:

- Receive and review accident occupational illness statistics
- Discuss issues which have ministry-wide application and have been identified by the union or the employer
- Review ministry and/or union health and safety training initiatives
- Review occupational health and safety and WSIB investigation reports of all fatal work-related accidents and critical injuries. The employer will notify the union provincial health and safety co-chair as soon as reasonably possible when a critical injury occurs and shall provide report(s) directly related to the critical injury for review
- Receive and review all newly issued health and safety directives and procedures issued by the employer at the ministry/divisional level
- Act as a resource to local workplace committees/representatives
- Review unresolved issues from the local level that have been referred to the ministry-level committee. The issues will be

---

351 *Musty and Meridian Magnesium Products Ltd*, [1996] OLRB Rep Nov/Dec 964 at 981. See also *Central North Correctional Centre*, [2004] OOHSAD No 132.

352 The Letter of Understanding, revised 26 May 2016, is Appendix COR20 to the *OPSEU/MBC Correctional Bargaining Unit Collective Agreement*, *2018–2021*, above note 193. The Committees also function per the provisions of guidelines originally established pursuant to the Memorandum of Settlement signed between the parties on 21 September 1990 (MCS), the Ministry of Labour Order dated 13 November 1990 (MCS), the Agreement of the parties dated 7 March 1991 (MCS), the *Right to Refuse Unsafe Work Protocol* dated 4 October 1991 (MCS), and the Agreement dated 19 October 2006 (MCYS).

reviewed by a worker representative selected by and from the worker representatives of the ministry-level committee and an employer representative of the ministry-level committee, with the objective of resolving the issue. This joint review will be undertaken prior to the unresolved issue being placed on the agenda for subsequent ministry-level committee meetings, or in the alternative the resolution of the issue will be reflected in the subsequent set of minutes.

- Promote conducting safety inspections on a regular basis through consultation with local occupational health and safety committees or worker representatives
- Review issues and minutes of local health and safety committees/representatives that have been raised at the local level and have been jointly referred to joint health and safety committees
- Inspect specific sites when there is appropriate justification for doing so as agreed upon by the committee(s) for matters raised in accordance with the previous item

The terms of reference restrict what can be discussed and resolved within the occupational health and safety committee structure and specifically exclude issues related to staffing (including complement, deployment, scheduling, assignments, posts, and so on), overcapacity, and security (both static and dynamic).

The terms of reference also encourage the resolution of all occupational health and safety complaints in accordance with its provisions and recommend that workers and supervisors jointly resolve occupational health and safety issues within their own workplaces through the local joint committee process. In addition, the terms of reference cite an expectation to resolve outstanding issues and complaints jointly before initiating grievances under the collective agreement. However, the terms of reference also clarify that they are not intended to abridge the union or workers' rights to inform the Ministry of Labour when they believe that a health and safety complaint has not been satisfactorily resolved.

The internal responsibility system should first be utilized to resolve health and safety concerns and failure to do so may create unnecessary litigation.[353] The OLRB has also recognized that joint health and safety

353 *Ontario Public Service Employees' Union and Ministry of Solicitor General and Correctional Services—Elgin Middlesex Detention Centre*, [1997] OOHSAD No 23 (Ont Adj Muir) at para 66 [*Elgin Middlesex, 1997*].

committee discussions can give rise to privacy concerns.[354] A requirement to inform the committee of the number of workers on accommodation gave rise to an unacceptable potential for loss of medical confidentiality.[355]

a) Composition of Joint Health and Safety Committees in Multi-union Workplaces

In many workplaces within the OPS, workers are represented in labour relations matters by more than one bargaining agent. This can lead to disputes over whether such workplaces' joint health and safety committees should be composed of members who are only selected by the largest union or, in the alternative, whether there should be a joint committee for each union. Section 9(8) of the *OHSA* contains this ambiguous wording: "The members of a committee who represent workers shall be selected by the workers they are to represent or, if a trade union or unions represent the workers, by the trade union or unions." The OLRB has addressed a claim by OPSEU, the union representing the most employees in a government workplace, about committee composition.[356] OPSEU asserted that the Ministry of Labour should have issued an order compelling the Ministry of Community and Social Services to either allow OPSEU to select all the workplace committee's worker members or to create two committees separately selected by OPSEU and the Association of Management and Administrative Professional Crown Employees of Ontario (AMAPCEO), respectively. The OLRB determined that the employer choice to only have one committee complied with the Act and that OPSEU needed to compromise on the selection of representatives.

4) Exclusive Representation in Health and Safety Matters

In the internal responsibility system, and health and safety matters generally, there is to be an arm's-length relationship between those persons who are representatives of workers, and those who are representative of the employer. The selection of a health and safety representative is a trade union function, which neither the employer nor the Ministry of

---

354 *Community Living Wallaceburg*, [2005] OOHSAD No 41.

355 *Ontario (Ministry of Community Safety and Correctional Services) v Ontario Public Service Employees Union, Local 517*, 2005 CanLII 13923 (ON LRB).

356 *Ontario Public Service Employees' Union and Ministry of Community and Social Services*, [2005] OOHSAD No 4.

Labour is to perform.[357] Accordingly, the employer was found to be in breach of the Act when it purported to deal with an untrained steward as the worker representative during the investigation of a work refusal.[358] An arbitrator also found that an employer could not impose term limits on a worker co-chair of a joint health and safety committee, noting that an employer could not unilaterally place restrictions on workers' right to choose their representative that were not found in the *OHSA*.[359]

5) Obligations of Employers

Several of the employer duties contained in section 25 of the *OHSA* have been invoked for workers in the public service, through either inspector's orders or appeals of inspector's decisions not to issue orders pursuant to section 61. Orders have at times required significant and costly changes to the way in which the work is carried out. In the private sector, the cost of a safety improvement that reduces the profitability below acceptable levels could lead to a decision to discontinue the work. In the OPS, the employer may not have the option to discontinue the work because it has a public duty to deliver the services and programs under its mandate. Yet budgets dictated by legislative appropriations may constrain the ability of managers to make health and safety related changes. This may in part explain why the OPS is apparently more litigious in respect of health and safety matters than the private sector.

Pursuant to section 25(2)(a) of the *OHSA*, which requires the employer to provide "information, instruction and supervision to a worker to protect the health or safety of the worker," particular types of additional training have been ordered for public servants.[360] A Ministry of Labour inspector required the Ministry of Correctional Services to train all the unclassified staff in a jail,[361] an order that in turn led to the unclassified staff in the entire ministry being trained over the following two years. The OLRB found that the Ministry of Health and

357 *Whitby Jail*, [1998] OOHSAD No 201 (Ont Adj Randall) at para 161 [*Whitby Jail, 1998*].

358 *Adult Occupational Centre (Re)*, [1989] OOHSAD No 20 (Dir App Smith).

359 *Fanshawe College v OPSEU, Local 110 (Union Grievance)*, [2013] OLAA No 408.

360 *OPSEU and Ontario (Ministry of the Solicitor General and Correctional Services)*, [1998] OOHSAD No 199 (Ont Adj Wacyk) [*Solicitor General, 1998*].

361 Ministry of Labour Inspector Order, Ministry of Correctional Services-Whitby Jail, 15 June 1994.

Long-Term Care was obligated to provide information, instruction, and supervision to paramedics regarding the "technological limitations of the communications system which they are required to use."[362] The paramedics were employed by a municipality. The employer obligation under section 25(2)(c) to appoint a competent person as supervisor has been relied upon to critically assess the training provided to acting managers in correctional facilities.[363]

a) Reasonable Precautions

The most frequently litigated provision in section 25 is section 25(2)(h), which requires an employer to take "every precaution reasonable in the circumstances for the protection of a worker." In assessing this requirement, it is necessary to take into account "the economic, social or physical realities which may have an impact on the nature of a particular workplace."[364]

The obligation is very similar to the obligation under Article 9.1 of the OPSEU/MBC collective agreements to take "every reasonable precaution." Indeed, the GSB caselaw under that Article, discussed below, has most fully set out the obligation of the employer to take health and safety precautions. However, under section 25(2)(h) of the *OHSA*, adjudicators have issued more orders requiring a range of corrective measures. This has especially occurred in the context of section 61 appeals before the OLRB from an order of an inspector.

i) Adequate Staffing Levels

Notwithstanding the presumptive right of the employer to manage the workplace, including the determination of staff levels and assignments, it has been held that adequate staffing is one element of reasonable

---

362 *Ontario (Health and Long-Term Care, Land Ambulance Programs) v CUPE, Local 29741*, 2010 CanLII 11302 (ON LRB) at para 172, request for reconsideration denied 2010 CanLII 23989 (ON LRB).

363 *OPSEU, Local 359 and Ontario (Ministry of the Solicitor General and Correctional Services-Whitby Jail)*, [1998] OOHSAD No 163 (Ont Adj Bradbury). See also *Ontario (Ministry of Correctional Services)*, [2002] OOHSAD No 74, where the OLRB allowed a work refusal by nurses who were concerned about the training provided to managers who were to escort them during their rounds during a strike.

364 *Ontario (Ministry of Solicitor General) and OPSEU*, [1996] OOHSAD No 18 (Ont Adj Blair) at para 47.

precautions.[365] Reduction of staffing levels in a correctional facility below a "red line" of minimum staffing, while insisting that regular activities for inmates be maintained, was found to be a breach of the obligation to take all reasonable precautions,[366] as it would produce an increased likelihood of endangerment to officers or inmates if inmate violence occurred. Where correctional officers refused to participate in a search for a handgun, partly on the basis that the search could not be conducted safely due to reduced staffing levels, new search procedures were agreed to.[367]

Although declaring it would be "an uncalled for foray ... into the labour relations arena" to interfere with staffing levels set by an essential services agreement during a public service strike, an adjudicator ordered that the level of activity in correctional facilities be reduced so that the activity could be safely carried out with reduced staffing.[368]

Many of these decisions about staffing levels arose from the former Office of the Adjudication, and it is unclear if the OLRB would make a similar order as its more recent jurisprudence has generally been more respectful of employer staffing decisions and exercises of management rights within the workplace.

---

365 *St Thomas Psychiatric Hospital and Ontario (Ministry of Health)*, [1998] OOHSAD No 16 (Ont Adj Randall).

366 *OPSEU Local 608 and Ontario (Ministry of the Solicitor General and Correctional Service- Sault Ste Marie)*, [1997] OOHSAD No 97 (Ont Adj Wacyk) [*Sault Ste Marie Jail (1)*].

367 *Ontario Public Service Employees Union v Ottawa Carleton Detention Centre and Ministry of Labour*, [1999] OOHSAD No 290 [*Ottawa Carleton*].

368 *OPSEU and Ontario (Ministry of the Solicitor General and Correctional Services)*, [1996] OOHSAD No 16 (Ont Adj Randall) at para 11. Adjudicator Randall made numerous subsequent decisions in this case concerning the amount of time that could be spent by prisoners outside of their cells during a public service strike that included correctional officers. Partly as a consequence of the strike, the decisions were not issued in the usual Office of Adjudication format. See interim orders: *OPSEU and Ontario (Ministry of the Solicitor General and Correctional Services) (Re)* (unreported, 15 March 1996, OHS 96-15A); *OPSEU and Ontario (Ministry of the Solicitor General and Correctional Services) (Re)* (unreported, 9 March 1996, OHS 96-15C); *OPSEU and Ontario (Ministry of the Solicitor General and Correctional Services) (Re)* (unreported, 9 March 1996, OHS 96-15D); OPSEU and *Ontario (Ministry of the Solicitor General and Correctional Services) (Re)* (unreported, 21 March 1996, OHS 96-15D); *OPSEU and Ontario (Ministry of the Solicitor General and Correctional Services) (Re)* (unreported, 28 March 1996, OHS 96-15A, B, C, D).

ii) Other Precautions

A range of other precautions has been required:

- Hard hats were to be disinfected prior to being worn by another worker, and a disinfected stethoscope was to be available for each ambulance paramedic.[369]
- An ambulance employer was to install stretchers that substantially reduce the back strain suffered when lifting a loaded stretcher into the ambulance, and provide additional training on the proper use of stretchers to ambulance paramedics.[370]
- Driver examiners employed by the Ministry of Transportation were to be informed about defects in applicants' cars, as well as an applicant's previous test experience, and were to receive instruction on how to safely monitor both traffic and applicants' driving behaviour during an examination.[371]
- For community escort duties, two correctional officers were to be used rather than one, and each was to be provided with protective vests, batons, and pepper spray.[372]
- As there were too many demands to have just one officer in a jail's control module, an employer was to have a second correctional officer in a control module to constantly monitor the correctional officers escorting inmates throughout the institution.[373]
- An unsecured access point to the exercise yard in a jail was to be enclosed.[374]
- Correctional officers were to be given a means of exiting the exercise yard in a moment of need,[375] and later, there was to

---

369 *Labour, 1990*, above note 347.

370 *District of Halton & Mississauga Ambulance Services (Re)*, [1994] OOHSAD No 24 (Ont Adj Muir).

371 *Ontario (Ministry of Transportation)*, [2001] OOHSAD No 119.

372 *Solicitor General, 1998*, above note 360; Special precautions may be required to escort an inmate with exceptional strength and a history of violence; *Treasury Board (Solicitor General Canada—Correctional Service), Hovey, and Gayger (Re)* (2002), 108 LAC (4th) 1 (Can PSSRB) [*Hovey and Gayger*].

373 *OPSEU and Ontario (Ministry of the Solicitor General and Correctional Service-Sault Ste Marie)*, [1997] OOHSAD No 2 (Ont Adj Muir) at para 67.

374 *Ontario (Ministry of Correctional Services)*, [2003] OOHSAD No 15.

375 *Elgin Middlesex Detention Centre*, [1992] OOHSAD No 27 (Ont Adj Alter).

be an independent observation of correctional officers escorting inmates into an exercise yard.[376]

- A protocol was to be developed and implemented that limited the use of an interlock bypass system (a system that permitted only one door or slider to be opened at one time unless the system was overridden by a correctional officer in the sub control room), as there was evidence that overriding the system had become somewhat routine, and the protocol was meant to make this exceptional rather than routine; provided for training and supervision to correctional officers once the protocol was developed; required removal or securing (by fastening to walls or the floor) of all objects, furniture or other items in areas that could function as sallyports (a double door system where only one door is unlocked at a time, that is, the first door is unlocked, then locked, and the second door is only unlocked after a person has passed through the first door); ensured that the software and hardware used to control doors and sliders in certain areas could allow for the opening of more than one access point when inmates were not in their cells without triggering the interlock bypass system; and treated the windows in inmate dayrooms so that they were opaque for those on the inside but transparent for those on the outside.[377]

A correctional facility failed to take reasonable precautions when it dealt inadequately with missing radios used for staff communication purposes, resulting in insufficient numbers of radios for those who needed them.[378] It was also found unreasonable to require correctional officers to use matches to light inmate's cigarettes through a hatch in the inmate's cell door.[379]

---

376 *OPSEU and Ontario (Ministry of the Solicitor General and Correctional Service—Hamilton Wentworth Detention Centre)*, [1998] OOHSAD No 3 (Ont Adj Novick) [*Hamilton Wentworth, 1998*]; *Maplehurst Detention Centre and OPSEU Local 234*, [1994] OOHSAD No 21 (Ont Adj Blair) [*Maplehurst, 1994*].

377 *OPSEU v Ministry of Correctional Services Maplehurst Correctional Complex*, 2010 CanLII 72088 (ON LRB).

378 *OPSEU Local 359 and Local 608 and Ontario (Ministry of the Solicitor General and Correctional Services—Sault Ste Marie Jail)*, [1997] OOHSAD No 319 (Ont Adj Cummings) [*Sault Ste Marie Jail (2)*].

379 *OPSEU, Local 252 and Ontario (Ministry of the Solicitor General and Correctional Services—Niagara Detention Centre) (Re)*, [1997] OOHSAD No 268 (Ont Adj Bradbury) [*Niagara*].

An employer has been ordered not to direct a public servant or other worker to perform a task which the worker's doctor says they are not fit to do.[380]

An order required the development, in consultation with a joint health and safety committee, of written procedures (to address staffing levels, and availability of back-up and regular relief) for the protection of workers when one-on-one monitoring is necessary for potentially aggressive clients.[381]

Conversely, the OLRB held that the provision of fire protective clothing to correctional officers was not a reasonable precaution under section 25(2)(h) of the *OHSA*.[382] In reaching this conclusion, the OLRB relied upon changes within the workplace to reduce the risk of fires, including the replacement of old mattresses with fire retardant mattresses, the installation of more fire alarms, and a directive to correctional officers that they were not supposed to fight large fires. The OLRB also found that it was not a reasonable precaution to provide pepper spray to transportation enforcement officers, finding that the degree of risk that could be reduced through the provision of pepper spray was minimal.[383]

Complaints and work refusals have also been settled on the basis of employer agreement to take certain precautions. Currently, the *OHSA* contains no apparent mechanism allowing the OLRB to enforce settlements of *OHSA* appeals under section 61. Adjournments *sine die* and consent OLRB orders tend to be used to ensure parties comply with settlements.[384] Sometimes the parties also address this apparent gap in the Act by agreeing that the settlement is enforceable as an order of the OLRB just like settlements under the *LRA*.

---

380 *OPSEU and Slack and Ontario (Ministry of the Solicitor General and Correctional Services)*, [1998] OOHSAD No 1 (Ont Adj Muir) [*Slack*].

381 *Ontario Public Service Employees' Union, Local 321 (Re)*, [1992] OOHSAD No 9 (Ont Adj Blair) [*Local 321, 1992*].

382 *Boychuk v Hamilton-Wentworth Detention Centre*, 2009 CanLII 37631 (ON LRB).

383 *OPSEU v Ontario (Ministry of Transportation)*, 2006 CanLII 10956 (ON LRB). However, the OLRB did note significant concerns with the employer's policy of disengagement in the face of threatening behaviour and found that the policy needed to be amended to disclose the circumstances under which a transportation enforcement officer could disengage and how that was to occur.

384 The OLRB enforced a consent order in *Ontario (Ministry of Correctional Services)*, [2005] OOHSAD No 218.

6) Right to Refuse Work

The right to refuse unsafe work, without reprisal, is a recognized exemption from the well-established labour relations principle of "work now and grieve later," and is supported both by the statutory provision in section 43 that a worker "may refuse to work or do particular work" and by the arbitral jurisprudence.[385] The right to refuse unsafe work is to be given a liberal and purposive interpretation.[386] The presence of the prerequisite substantial risk to health and safety is to be measured by considering both the probability of occurrence and the potential seriousness of the consequent injury.[387]

At the same time, the right to refuse work should not be used to circumvent the internal responsibility system. In a 1997 decision arising from a work refusal at the Sault Ste Marie Jail, Adjudicator Cummings wrote:

> Section 43 work refusals are, of course, not the only, nor in my view, the primary means to have workplace health and safety issues resolved. In fact, the core of the Act is the internal responsibility system whereby joint health and safety committees have roles and obligations to raise health and safety issues, and employers and others in control of a workplace (such as constructors) have a duty to ensure that health and safety concerns, and particularly, the health and safety standards of the Act and its regulations are met. In addition to the internal responsibility system, the Ministry of Labour has inspectors who assist workplace parties to meet their obligations under the Act. Inspectors

---

385 A worker is under no obligation to perform unsafe work: "Where the conditions set out in the Act have been met, an employee is not under an obligation to obey now and grieve later": *Zizek and Wilco Canada Inc (Re)*, [1983] OLRB Rep Oct 1759 at 1766. See also *Dominion Chain Co and IAM, Local 1927 (Re)* (1980), 29 LAC (2d) 263 (Ont Arb Bd) at 266; *OPSEU and Ontario (Ministry of the Solicitor General and Correctional Services) (Re)*, [1998] OLRB Rep May/June 382 at 396; *Lennox Industries (Canada) Ltd and USWA, Local 7235 (Re)*, [1999] OLAA No 158 (Arb Bd); *Battle Mountain Canada Ltd v USWA, Local 9364 (Wheadon Grievance)*, [2001] OLAA No 722 (RL Levinson) at para 60.

386 *Pharand and Inco Metals*, [1980] OLRB Rep July 981 [*Pharand*].

387 See the discussion of *Kut-Kwik Mower*, 10 May 1985 (Glasberg) in *Whitby Jail, 1998*, above note 357 at paras 175–76. See also *Domtar Inc*, [1988] OLRB Rep August 780 [*Domtar Inc*], where the OLRB held that miners did not need to wait until a fire broke out before they were entitled to refuse to work due to the employer's changes to emergency procedures.

> also have the power to issue orders when they believe there has been a breach of the Act.
>
> While inspectors make their own routine inspections of workplaces, they also investigate complaints. In my view, the right to refuse provisions of the Act were not intended to be a substitute for the internal responsibility system and recourse to an Inspector with a complaint.[388]

A work refusal is to be used only in urgent circumstances and not simply because one wants a quick answer to a health and safety concern;[389] that is, a refusal should be reserved for circumstances akin to an imminent danger.[390]

The statutory provision governing the right to refuse imposes a mandatory procedure on both the refusing worker and their supervisors. The procedural requirements have three main components: the worker's right to stop performing unsafe work, the worker's right to knowledgeable representation, and the supervisor's obligation to conduct an investigation of the worker's refusal forthwith.

The threshold degree of risk that warrants a work refusal is that continuation of the work is likely to endanger the refusing worker or another worker. This is applied in two stages.[391]

In order to be eligible for the protection offered by the *OHSA* at the initial or "first stage" work refusal, the worker must have a subjective "reason to believe" that the working conditions are "likely to endanger" the health or safety of the worker or another worker. The worker must immediately report the refusal to a supervisor and is then entitled to go to a safe place near the workstation to await the investigation of the refusal. The supervisor is required to conduct an investigation of the refusal with the worker and a worker member of the health and safety committee. Stage 1 of the work refusal must be addressed promptly and the OLRB has stated that a worker could not wait two hours to commence stage 1 of the work refusal process so that their preferred representative was available.[392] Under section 43(13) of the *OHSA*, workers who are involved in a work refusal are to be paid at their regular or premium rate of pay

---

388 *Sault Ste Marie Jail (2)*, above note 378.

389 *Ibid* at paras 37 and 69.

390 *Whitby Jail, 1998*, above note 357 at para 166.

391 Norman A. Keith, *Ontario Health and Safety Law* (Aurora, ON: Canada Law Book, 2004) at 7:3100, "Basis for Work Refusal."

392 *Lynda Kathleen Gough v Elgin-Middlesex Detention Centre*, 2016 CanLII 74661 (ON LRB).

as may be proper. However, the GSB found that the employer was not required to pay correctional officers where they continued to refuse work after an inspector had determined that the work refusal provisions were not applicable to their situation.[393]

After the first stage of the investigation has been completed, and the supervisor has made whatever adjustments they deem necessary, the refusing worker may either agree to return to work or continue to refuse to perform the work. If the refusal continues into a "second stage," the test under the *OHSA* changes from subjective "reason to believe" to "reasonable grounds to believe" that the work is likely to endanger. The OLRB has adopted the following formulation of reason able grounds:

> [I]n considering whether an employee had reasonable cause to refuse to work in a given situation, this Board must ask itself whether the average employee at the workplace, having regard to his general training and experience, would, exercising normal and honest judgement, have reason to believe that the circumstances presented an unacceptable degree of hazard to himself or to another employee.[394]

The work refusal must be objectively reasonable, although not necessarily correct, when all of the information available to the worker at the time is considered.[395] A refusing worker who meets this test is entitled to the continued protection of the *OHSA* and cannot be reassigned the unsafe work. The employee may either be assigned alternative work or given other instructions pending the investigation of the Ministry of Labour inspector. Either the supervisor or the refusing worker must report the continued refusal to work to a Ministry of Labour inspector who must investigate the refusal to work in consultation with the employer, the refusing worker, and the worker's health and safety representative. The inspector must render a written decision as to whether the circumstances at the time of the refusal were likely to endanger

---

393 *OPSEU (Aitken et al) v Ontario (Community Safety and Correctional Services)*, 2017 CanLII 52706 (ON GSB) (Petryshen) [*Aitken*].

394 *Pharand*, above note 386 at para 59. See also *Domtar Inc*, above note 387; *Boeing/DeHavilland Division*, [1990] OLRB Rep Dec 1213.

395 *Rooke v Stelco Inc (Hilton Works)*, 2004 CanLII 24928 (ON LRB) at para 92, request for reconsideration was dismissed *Rooke v Stelco Inc*, 2004 CanLII 28684 (ON LRB), application for judicial review was dismissed *Rooke v Ontario Labour Relations Board*, 2006 CanLII 23945 (ON SCDC).

the refusing worker or another worker. Pending the investigation and decision, other employees may be requested to perform the refused work, provided they are advised of the work refusal in the presence of a worker health and safety representative.

In case of both the "first stage" and "second stage" refusal, the standard of "likely to endanger" has been defined as one where the worker "would probably be placed in a situation with a substantial risk of injury"[396] or that "something is more likely than not" to result in endangerment to the worker.[397] There is also some need to balance the degree of likelihood and seriousness of risk so that, for example, the standard may be met by somewhat less likelihood coupled with a more serious risk.[398]

A worker may continue to refuse even after the inspector has found the workplace to have been not likely to endanger at the time of the work refusal *if* the quality of the inspector's investigation casts substantial doubt on the conclusion or the worker can still meet the onus to demonstrate reasonable grounds for believing the work is likely to endanger.[399]

There are certain limitations within the *OHSA* that affect the scope of the right to refuse for certain categories of workers. These limitations are discussed immediately below. Notwithstanding that these workers do not have the right to refuse work in particular situations, they always have the right to ensure that all reasonable precautions have been taken.[400] It has been recognized that the necessary corollary to a limited right to refuse unsafe work is employer and ministry vigilance in ensuring reasonable precautions and full access to all of the other investigative and enforcement procedures under the *OHSA*.[401] In particular, where an investigation of a work refusal determines that section 43

396 For a further discussion, see *Sault Ste Marie Jail (2)*, above note 378 at para 43.

397 *Sault Ste Marie Jail (1)*, above note 366 at para 251.

398 *Whitby Jail, 1998*, above note 357 at para 176.

399 *Domtar Inc*, note 387 at para 31; *Auto Jobbers Warehouse Ltd*, [1981] OLRB Rep Dec 1715; *Canadian Gypsum Construction*, [1978] OLRB Rep Oct 897.

400 *Maplehurst, 1994*, above note 376 at para 11.

401 *Local 321, 1992*, above note 381; see also *OPSEU, Local 608 and Ministry of Labour (Re)*, [1995] OOHSAD No 25 (Ont Adj Wacyk); *OPSEU and Ontario (Ministry of the Solicitor General and Correctional Services—Vanier Centre for Women) (Re)*, [1996] OOHSAD No 42 (Ont Adj Wacyk) [*Vanier*]; *Sault Ste Marie Jail (2)*, above note 378 at para 22; *Hamilton Wentworth, 1998*, above note 376 at para 25; *Dowling v Hamilton-Wentworth Detention Centre*, 2012

does not apply, the investigation still needs to consider whether all reasonable precautions have been taken to protect the worker under section 25(2)(h).[402]

a) Occupations with Limits on the Right to Refuse

Until 1990, police officers, firefighters, and correctional employees were expressly excluded from the right to refuse unsafe work. Health care workers had their right to refuse limited if the refusal would endanger another person. The purpose behind this legislative exemption was described by the OLRB as follows:

> Risking one's health and safety is one of the primary requirements of these occupations and if one were to allow individuals in these occupations to refuse work which involved a risk of injury, the important functions which they are obliged to perform would remain unfulfilled.[403]

In 1990, the legislation was amended to provide certain occupations with a limited right to refuse unsafe work. This was explained as providing a balanced assurance that emergency services and correctional officers will fulfill their fundamental responsibilities, but that they will not be placed in unnecessary danger.[404] Those occupations listed in section 43(2) of the *OHSA* are now permitted to exercise the right to refuse unsafe work *unless*, pursuant to section 43(1), the situation is one which is inherent in the worker's job, or a normal condition of the worker's employment, or the consequences of the refusal would directly endanger the life, health, or safety of another person.

The occupations that are now listed in section 43(2) are police force members, firefighters, persons employed in corrections, and persons

---

CanLII 81181 (ON LRB) at para 84, request for reconsideration dismissed, *Dowling v Hamilton-Wentworth Detention Centre*, 2014 CanLII 6664 (ON LRB) [*Dowling*].

402 *Maplehurst, 1994*, above note 376 at para 8.

403 *Lloyd v Ontario (Ministry of Community and Social Services)*, [1988] OLRB Rep Jan 50 at 58, application for judicial review dismissed, [1989] OLRB Rep Mar 316 (Div Ct). The Divisional Court found that this exclusion of certain occupations did not violate the equality provisions of the *Charter*, leave to appeal to Ontario Court of Appeal ref'd [1989] OLRB Rep June 698.

404 Ontario, Legislative Assembly, *Hansard*, 19 June 1990, No 49 at 1857 (Gerald Phillips, Minister of Labour).

employed in certain other critical services. These occupations are by no means staffed exclusively by public servants, but much of the jurisprudence concerning this section concerns employment within the OPS—particularly at correctional facilities.

b) Risks Inherent in the Worker's Employment

A worker engaged in one of the occupational categories listed in section 43(2) and who is facing a circumstance that is inherent in the worker's job, or is a normal condition of the worker's employment, cannot refuse to work simply because of subjective concerns.[405] In particular, the worker is not to use the work refusal procedure to question the existing and established practices of the institution.[406] A correctional officer could not refuse to be locked in a yard with potentially violent inmates, because yard duty was a "normal condition" of their employment. Similarly, it was a normal condition of employment for a correctional officer to assume the risk of escorting dangerous inmates.[407] Searching inmate living areas and cells where there is the prospect of homemade weapons, even a zip gun or a homemade gun, was found to be a normal part of a correctional officer's job.[408] Similarly, where metal plates had gone missing in a correctional institution and an inmate had provided intelligence to the effect that the metal plates were being weaponized, the GSB found that the correctional officers did not have the right to refuse work, noting that the potential for weapons was inherent to their work.[409]

However, workers may have the right to refuse when there is a dangerous deviation or departure from the established and prevailing practice—that is, a deviation from the normal conditions.[410] Such

---

405 *Maplehurst, 1994*, above note 376 at para 10, where it is also stated "[i]t is clear from the use of the word 'or' in section 43(1)(a) that the 'normal condition of employment' test is distinct from the 'inherent' test."

406 *Maplehurst, 1994*, above note 376 at para 16.

407 *Hamilton Wentworth, 1998*, above note 376 at para 65.

408 *Dowling*, above note 401 at paras 74–78.

409 *Aitken*, above note 393.

410 *Maplehurst, 1994*, above note 376. Contrast this with cases under the *Canada Labour Code*, RSC 1985, c L-2, where, until the inmate acts in a threatening manner toward the correctional officer, there is no danger, and the correctional officer is effectively barred from relying on the work refusal provisions. In the federal decisions, it has been suggested that some other process is necessary to deal with the unique circumstances of correctional facilities where "the source of the danger, the inmate, has intelligence and free will." See, for example, *Canada*

deviations could involve additional tasks or duties (lighting an inmate's cigarette with matches, which was not an inherent or normal part of the job of a correctional officer),[411] absent or malfunctioning safety equipment (missing radios were not a normal condition of employment),[412] or, as further examples, absence of procedures to address changed circumstances, or absence of assigned staff.

Workers in a correctional facility may be entitled to refuse work in circumstances where the employer is allowing the institution to function with below minimum staffing levels, particularly where this is found to be a violation of section 25(2)(h).[413] An adjudicator has found that these staffing levels were likely to endanger the workers and also were not an inherent or normal condition. Reduced staffing levels during a public service strike are neither inherent in the work nor a normal condition of employment of correctional officers.[414]

A worker who is medically unfit to perform certain duties is entitled to refuse to perform them, because a requirement to perform work beyond one's medical capacity is not inherent or a normal condition of one's employment.[415]

It has been held in one case that established practices may still trigger a valid work refusal when the worker can establish objectively that the established practice, in the circumstances, raises the prospect of unnecessary imminent danger or risk.[416] That same case suggested that an exercise of the right to refuse could eventually be used in normal conditions when workers and their union called problematic existing practices into question through the internal responsibility system, but their concerns remained unresolved and the Ministry of Labour was contacted but did not use its powers to issue necessary orders. However, the OLRB has found that a work refusal could not be used to challenge

---

(Attorney General) v Lavoie (1998), 153 FTR 297 (TD) at para 17 and *Hovey and Gayger*, above note 372 at para 214.

411 *Niagara*, above note 379.

412 *Sault Ste Marie Jail (2)*, above note 378. See also *Maplehurst, 1994*, above note 376.

413 *Sault Ste Marie Jail (1)*, above note 366.

414 *OPSEU (Metcalf/Mercer) and Ministry of Solicitor General and Correctional Services*, GSB#926/96, 7 July 1997 (Dissanayake) [*Metcalf*].

415 *Slack*, above note 380.

416 *Whitby Jail, 1998*, above note 357 at para 187, and also paras 170 and 180–81. Although, as discussed below, in *Dowling*, above note 401, the OLRB raised concerns about whether this decision was decided correctly in light of correctional officers' limited right to refuse unsafe work under s 43.

the application of a weapons search policy and management's decision regarding which level of search to apply in a correctional institution.[417]

The employer, or another party such as the Ministry of Labour seeking to rely on the exemption, has the onus to provide evidence that a hazard is inherent in the work or a normal condition of employment.[418] To hold otherwise, and to place the onus on the worker to show that the hazard is not inherent or a normal condition, was found to be incorrect.[419] In appeal proceedings, the party relying on the exception—for example, the Ministry of Labour—has been directed to provide particulars of the material facts upon which it was determined that the matter fell within the section 43(1) exception.[420] Furthermore, the Ministry of Labour has been found by certain adjudicators to be obliged to consider the evidence that a hazard is inherent before determining that the right to refuse does not apply.[421]

c) Directly Endangering the Life, Health, or Safety of Another Person

Workers in the occupational categories listed in section 43(2) do not have the right to refuse work where the work refusal would directly endanger the life, health, or safety of another person. Although there is little adjudicative interpretation of "directly endanger," there are certain obvious qualifications within it:

- the work refusal has to "directly" endanger—an indirect or speculative endangerment would arguably not be sufficient to disentitle the worker from the work refusal
- although a particular individual might not have to be specifically endangered by the work refusal, a defined group or class of person may well, at a minimum, have to be identified

---

417 *Dowling*, above note 401.

418 *Canadian Union of Public Employees, Local 1605 and Mohawk Hospital*, [1993] OOHSAD No 20 (Ont Adj Muir) [*Mohawk Hospital*]; *Niagara*, above note 379; *Sault Ste Marie Jail (1)*, above note 366; *Sault Ste Marie Jail (2)*, above note 378 at paras 21–24.

419 *Whitby Jail, 1998*, above note 357 at para 146.

420 *OPSEU and Ontario (Ministry of the Solicitor General and Correctional Services)*, [1997] OOHSAD No 126 (Ont Adj Petryshen).

421 *Mohawk Hospital*, above note 418; *Whitby Jail, 1998*, above note 357.

Further, the onus of demonstrating direct endangerment will be on the party seeking to invoke the exemption.[422]

Absence from assigned duties during a work refusal may not necessarily endanger the life, health, or safety of another person. In one case, the employer's counsel argued that correctional officers engaged in a work refusal made themselves unavailable for duties and thereby endangered the life, health, or safety of others. The adjudicator held that accepting that submission would remove the right to refuse work as every refusal removes a worker from work for a period of time.[423]

In a practical sense, the manner in which a particular work refusal occurs may be relevant in determining whether another person would be directly endangered. For example, a refusal to search an inmate for concealed weapons would be more likely to endanger the life, health, or safety of another person if the inmate was in an exercise yard with other inmates than if the inmate was locked in their own cell.

Notably, in *Dowling v Hamilton-Wentworth Detention Centre*, the OLRB extensively reviewed the right to refuse unsafe work in the context of a correctional institution. The decision arose where correctional officers engaged in a work refusal regarding the appropriate level of search to be conducted after the institution received a phone call suggesting that there was a zip gun (a type of homemade gun) in the institution. The OLRB found that the correctional officers did not have the right to refuse unsafe work in the circumstances. In reaching its decision, the OLRB questioned whether previous decisions regarding correctional officers' right to refuse unsafe work were correctly decided in the context of the limited right of refusal for certain workers under section 43.[424] The OLRB emphasized that the exemptions under section 43(1) and (2)

---

422 *Niagara*, above note 379; *Sault Ste Marie Jail (1)*, above note 366; *Sault Ste Marie Jail (2)*, above note 378 at para 34.

423 *Sault Ste Marie Jail (2)*, above note 378 at para 26.

424 The OLRB questioned whether *Re Venier*, [1998] OOHSAD No 2 (Muir) [*Venier*] and *Whitby Jail, 1998*, above note 357, were correctly decided. In *Venier*, the adjudicator found that correctional officers could refuse work where there was a dispute about the scope of the search to be conducted when a hiding place containing contraband (specifically a shank) was found in an inmate occupied area. In *Whitby Jail*, drugs were routinely being thrown to inmates in the yard and there was a concern that weapons could be thrown over the fence in the same manner. The adjudicator found that s 43(1)(a) of the *OHSA* could not deny correctional officers the right to refuse work in circumstances where the existing and established practices of the institution were likely to endanger a worker, provided that s 43(1)(b) was not applicable.

are narrow and that the public must be protected. Arguably in doing so, the OLRB outlined a narrower scope for the exceptions to refuse unsafe work under section 43(1) and (2) than had previously existed under the former Office of Adjudication. The decision arguably makes it less clear in what circumstances employees under section 43(2) of the Act can exercise their limited right to refuse unsafe work. The OLRB emphasized these workers obligations to protect the public and their correspondingly limited right to refuse unsafe work as follows:

> The result of the exemptions contained in section 43(1) and (2) for those workers described therein is a stark one. Those employees described in section 43(2) are subject to a limited right to refuse to work even if the work is dangerous, and even if the employer is violating the Act and its regulations. There is no doubt that the health and safety of workers in these jobs is given less protection than workers in other jobs. The reason for this is that the workers in these jobs have dangerous jobs and/or the protection of other people (members of the public, other workers, etc.) is dependent on these jobs being done despite the risks. The reason for the Legislature's choice in this regard is quite obvious. It does not make sense that a police officer or a fire fighter could engage in a work refusal where the dangerous situation is an inherent part of the job. Moreover, it does not make sense that such a worker could engage in a work refusal even where the situation is not an inherent part of the job if the effect is to endanger the life, health, and safety of someone else. Finally, it hardly seems possible that firefighters or other enumerated workers found within a dangerous situation could refuse work while the parties waited for a Ministry of Labour Inspector to conduct a section 43 investigation in order to declare if the risk is relevant in the firefighters' duty. It appears much more likely employees in those special categories of employees are more or less on their own in deciding whether to refuse work. They may refuse, but if the dangerous circumstances were inherent in their work, then they may suffer employment consequences. On the other hand, if they were right, then they will not. I do not mince words: the Legislature would rather a worker in this special category of professions have different health and safety rights than have a member of the public or someone under their care be hurt.[425]

425 *Dowling*, above note 401.

The GSB subsequently agreed with and adopted the OLRB's reasoning regarding correctional officers' limited right to refuse work under section 43 of the *OHSA* in another case involving a search for a potential weapon in a correctional institution.[426]

d) Decisions Regarding the Right of Public Servants to Refuse Work

Adjudicators have issued many decisions under the *OHSA* on the circumstances in which a public servant can refuse work. It has been found that, even in circumstances where the public servant cannot lawfully refuse work, it may be appropriate to order additional precautions pursuant to section 25(2)(h) of the *OHSA* to address the concerns that may have motivated the work refusal.

i) Where the Right to Refuse Under Section 43 Was Upheld

The right to refuse to work under section 43 was upheld in the following circumstances:

- lighting, with matches, the cigarettes of inmates was not an inherent or normal part of the job of a correctional officer[427]
- keeping of "end doors" open (a change to long-standing policy) created dangers of contraband-passing and difficulties in communication—the OLRB declared that these conditions were likely to endanger the officer and directed the joint health and safety committee to develop a protocol for the exercise of discretion to close "end doors"[428]
- when a concealed weapon was found, a correctional officer was allowed to refuse work when concerned about a danger imposed by hiding places at the jail where contraband could be stored and where the employer failed to take the reasonable precautions of locking-down inmates in a correctional facility and conducting a search for that contraband[429]
- short staffing made it dangerous for correctional officers to perform yard duties where inmates were outside of their cells engaged in exercise[430]

426 *Aitken*, above note 393 at para 62.
427 *Niagara*, above note 379.
428 *Elgin Middlesex, 1997*, above note 353.
429 *Venier*, above note 424.
430 *Sault Ste Marie Jail (1)*, above note 366.

- when a hospital employee, who experienced allergic and physical reactions to substances in the laundry facility where they were employed, exercised their right to refuse that was based on their good faith and reasonable belief that the level of dust in the laundry room workplace was a danger to them[431]

ii) Where the Right to Refuse Under Section 43 Was Not Upheld

The right to refuse to work under section 43 was not upheld in the following circumstances:

- the danger of being shot if a gun was thrown to inmates in the "yard" was a normal or inherent risk for a correctional officer[432]
- lock changes, lack of staffing, lack of training, and failure to order a search by correctional officers at the Vanier Centre for Women did not warrant a work refusal, because inmates did not have access to the area in question[433]
- concerns about the adequacy of gloves to be used by correctional officers during searches and the failure to have furniture in a correctional facility bolted to the building did not give rise to "such imminent jeopardy" that work refusals by correctional officers were warranted[434]
- where an external employee had not conducted a search when arriving on the premises, but a manager subsequently did, a work refusal was not warranted—the employer was ordered, under section 61(4), to conduct a thorough search of the premises and have regular search protocol put in place[435]
- the potential for exposure to the violent behaviour of a supervisor did not give rise to the right to refuse—although the employer did not contravene the Act, the Ministry of Labour inspector should have investigated, decided whether the behaviour would endanger the employee, and provided written decisions[436]

---

431 *Mohawk Hospital*, above note 418.

432 *Whitby Jail, 1998*, above note 357.

433 *Ontario (Ministry of Correctional Services)*, [2002] OOHSAD No 44.

434 *Ontario Public Service Employees Union v Ministry of Correctional Services (Brookside Youth Centre)*, [2002] OOHSAD No 43 at para 20 [*Brookside*]. This case arose during the 2002 OPSEU strike.

435 *Ontario (Ministry of Correctional Services)*, [2002] OOHSAD No 42.

436 *Ontario Public Service Employees' Union (Guelph Correctional Centre)*, [1997] OOHSAD No 352 (Ont Adj Novick).

- clerical workers at Old City Hall in Toronto did not have the right to refuse on the basis of workplace hazards such as carbon dioxide and ozone exposure, radiation exposure, PCB emissions from video display terminals, and nitropyrene exposure from toner replacement cartridges[437]
- when a call about a potential zip gun was made to a correctional institution, correctional officers did not have the right to refuse even though they felt that the institution was not taking the threat seriously enough and using the appropriate search level under the weapons search protocol[438]
- when there were missing metal plates in a correctional institution and a search of certain units had not uncovered them, correctional officers did not have the right to refuse because they wanted a higher level of search under the weapons search protocol: a search of the entire institution and the ability for all correctional officers to wear Kevlar vests (which provide protection against stabbing type weapons)[439]

7) Suspension of Orders

A common aspect of litigation about inspector's orders is a request by one party for a suspension of the order, pending a full hearing of the appeal. Section 61(7) of the *OHSA* allows the OLRB to suspend the operation of an order that is the subject of an appeal under section 61 pending the disposition of the appeal. Deference should generally be shown to the inspector.[440] They are intended to be the initial decision maker and have "the singular advantage" of attending at the workplace.[441] The OLRB has stated that there is a rebuttable presumption that an inspector's order is authorized under the *OHSA* and is correct.[442] The factors commonly considered in deciding whether to suspend an

437 *Ontario Public Service Employees' Union (Re)*, [1982] OOHSAD No 4 (Ont Adj Melinyshyn).

438 *Dowling*, above note 401.

439 *Aitken*, above note 393.

440 *Ontario (Ministry of Health and Long-Term Care)*, [2003] OOHSAD No 11 at para 21, but see *Toronto (City)*, [2004] OLRB Rep May/June 531.

441 *General Motors of Canada v CAW Local 199*, [1997] OOHSAD No 62 (Ont Adj Herman) at para 14 [*CAW*].

442 *RJ Dungey & Sons Ltd*, [1999] OLRB Rep Jan/Feb 82 at para 19.

order are (1) whether the suspension would endanger worker safety, (2) the degree of prejudice to the employer, and (3) whether there is a strong *prima facie* case for a successful appeal.[443]

The onus is on the party seeking the suspension to establish that the suspension should be granted.[444]

An order is more likely to be suspended where there is no real ongoing risk of harm to employees, for example, in the following circumstances:

- After an incident of potential violence from a manager, an inspector issued an order requiring the employer to develop a health and safety plan that would include a policy on workplace violence.[445] There was found to be an absence of any real risk of harm to employees, and the order was suspended.
- After a correctional officer was assaulted by three young offenders, an order was issued addressing the immediate risk by requiring another officer to have a "full view." A further order requiring the employer to conduct a hazard analysis and risk assessment of the young offenders unit was suspended.[446]
- Correctional officers refused work where only one officer was assigned at each sallyport of a maximum/medium security institution. OPSEU relied on an industry standard of assigning two officers at such locations to ensure officer safety. The inspector's order called for additional officers and the employer's appeal to suspend this order was denied.[447]
- The OLRB suspended an order requiring custom-made vests for nurses in correctional institutions who were required to administer medications to inmates in areas of the institution that had not yet been searched while a search for weapons was ongoing, where an interim order ensured that the nurses would be accompanied by a correctional officer, and have access to a vest that was not custom fit.[448]

---

443 *CAW*, above note 441 at para 10.

444 *Ontario (Community Safety and Correctional Services) v OPSEU*, 2008 CanLII 37474 (ON LRB) at para 8 [*Ontario v OPSEU, 2008*].

445 *Ontario (Ministry of Correctional Services)*, [2002] OOHSAD No 72.

446 *Ministry of Correctional Services, Thunder Bay Correctional Centre v Ontario Public Service Employees Union and Ministry of Labour*, [2000] OOHSAD 113.

447 *Ontario (Ministry of Public Safety and Security)*, [2003] OOHSAD No 105.

448 *Central North Correctional Centre v OPSEU*, 2007 CanLII 48630 (ON LRB).

The OLRB suspended an order and found that it did not need to determine the merits of the appeal where the inspector did not oppose the suspension of the order.[449] Similarly, the OLRB suspended an order regarding the appointment of health and safety representatives where both the ministry and the union consented to the suspension.[450]

The OLRB has also declined to suspend orders where the health and safety concern outweighed any prejudice[451] to the employer, in the following circumstances:

- An order to prevent the mixing of certain groups of inmates in a correctional facility, as the order of the inspector was reasoned and any economic or administrative prejudice to the employer was to be weighed against the health and safety concern.[452]
- After a complaint by the co-chair of the joint health and safety committee (JHSC) at the Windsor Courthouse, an order requiring better record-keeping, a better response to panic alarms, a comprehensive metal-detector system, an annual review of a court security plan, and consultation with the JHSC.[453]
- An order effectively requiring a third correctional officer to be present at the sallyport to provide assistance during a patrol of cell units.[454]
- An order requiring the employer to ensure that correctional officers working at a particular range were able to approach each cell with a full view of the inmate and without the inmate being able to make physical contact with the correctional officer. This required removing and/or moving a table located in the range.[455]
- An order requiring that the entirety of a large correctional facility be inspected at least once a month.[456]

---

449 *Ontario (Ministry of Labour)*, [2007] OOHSAD No 34.

450 *Liquor Control Board of Ontario v OPSEU*, 2019 CanLII 109451 (ON LRB).

451 *Ontario (Ministry of Transportation)*, [2005] OOHSAD No 68.

452 *Ontario (Ministry of Correctional Services)*, [2004] OOHSAD No 94.

453 *Ontario (Ministry of Attorney General)*, [2004] OOHSAD No 92.

454 *Toronto West Detention Centre*, [2008] OOHSAD No 1.

455 *Ontario v OPSEU, 2008*, above note 444.

456 *Ontario (Community Safety and Correctional Services) v Sullivan*, 2006 CanLII 43085 (ON LRB).

- An order requiring additional precautions in a lunchroom where the inspector had observed unmasked workers within six feet of each other during the COVID-19 pandemic.[457]

The OLRB has exercised its discretion to suspend an order in part. In one case, an inspector had issued an order at a correctional institution requiring the employer to advise the JHSC of the number of correctional officers on accommodation at the beginning of each shift and to ensure that a correctional officer on accommodation not be assigned to a position that would contradict the terms of their accommodation. The OLRB suspended the first part of the order requiring the disclosure of workers on accommodation but declined to suspend the second part of the order.[458]

Where the effect of an order is spent, there is nothing left to suspend.[459]

The OLRB has found that where an inspector issued and then rescinded an order, it could suspend the rescission of the order under section 61(7) of the *OHSA* thereby reviving the original order. In doing so, the OLRB noted that the rescission of the order raised a risk to workers' health and safety.[460] However, in a subsequent decision the OLRB found that it could not suspend an inspector's rescission of an order.[461]

A corollary to the power to suspend orders is the power to issue interim orders while hearing an appeal.[462] The OLRB's power to issue an interim order under the Act is "extremely broad."[463] The OLRB has rejected arguments that its jurisdiction to issue interim orders is limited to orders that an inspector had refused to issue, matters specifically

---

457 *Ontario (Liquor Control Board) v OPSEU*, 2021 CanLII 15607 (ON LRB).

458 *Ontario (Ministry of Community Safety and Correctional Services)*, [2005] OOHSAD No 114.

459 *Ontario (Ministry of Community Safety and Correctional Services)*, [2004] OOHSAD No 95.

460 *OPSEU v Toronto West Detention Centre*, 2008 CanLII 44403 (ON LRB).

461 *OPSEU v Ontario (Ministry of Youth and Children Services)*, 2014 CanLII 75073 (ON LRB), request for reconsideration dismissed *OPSEU v Ontario (Children and Youth Services)*, 2015 CanLII 36135 (ON LRB).

462 *OHSA*, above note 1, s 61(34).

463 *OPSEU v Central North Correctional Centre*, 2006 CanLII 34110 (ON LRB) at para 13.

identified in the Act, or matters that had been considered by a workplace's JHSC.[464]

Where a hearing will be lengthy and evidence is heard that the employer may have suspended efforts to improve conditions pending the OLRB's determination, the OLRB has encouraged parties to enter into interim minutes of settlement.[465]

8) Joint Health and Safety Committee Work Stoppage

A joint decision of one certified management member and one certified union member of the joint occupational health and safety committee can require the employer to stop its operation pending an investigation by the Ministry of Labour inspector.[466] The joint decision to stop dangerous work can be made where:

- the Act or the regulations are being contravened
- the contravention poses a danger or hazard to a worker
- any delay in controlling the danger or hazard may seriously endanger a worker

Both a management and a union committee member must agree that dangerous circumstances exist before a stop-work direction can be issued. If they do not agree, a Ministry of Labour inspector can be contacted, and an investigation will be conducted into the circumstances. A major difference between this provision and the right to refuse work is that there is no requirement that the health and safety committee members themselves be in danger before work can be halted.

The exercise of the right to stop dangerous work is restricted depending on the nature of the employment of the public servant exercising the right, the nature of their workplace, or the possible consequences for others of a work stoppage. The right to stop dangerous work does not apply to police, firefighters, or those employed in correctional institutions.

---

464 *Royal Ottawa Health Care Group v ONA*, 2015 CanLII 24413 (ON LRB), application for judicial review dismissed 2015 ONSC 6714.

465 *Ontario (Ministry of Public Safety and Security)*, [2005] OOHSAD No 22.

466 *OHSA*, above note 1, ss 44–48.

9) Declarations Against the Ministry of Labour (Including Whether Inspectors Are Required to Attend at the Workplace)

In the past, there were conflicting decisions on whether the manner in which an investigation by the Ministry of Labour was conducted could be challenged on appeal. Some adjudicators did issue orders against, or in respect of, the actions of inspectors and the Ministry of Labour itself.[467] The premise of such orders was that the *OHSA* binds the Crown, and that inspectors have positive obligations under the Act that can be enforced by the OLRB pursuant to its broad remedial powers under the *OHSA*.[468] However, subsequently the OLRB has held that, on appeal, it should not issue such declarations,[469] and has stated that

> [t]he scheme of the Act is not concerned with policing the actions or non-actions of inspectors and the Ministry. While the conduct of the inspector will often be an issue in an appeal under section 61, the inspector is relevant only to the extent necessary to illuminate the adjudication of the workplace dispute . . . The focus of an appeal under section 61 is always the substantive workplace health and safety concern, not how the inspector investigated (or failed to investigate).

The appropriate way for a party aggrieved by the form or manner of the Ministry of Labour's investigation is to seek an order through an application for judicial review.[470]

More recently, the OLRB has consistently stated that it does not review an inspector's conduct and/or how an investigation was conducted in the course of determining an appeal under section 61.[471]

---

467 *Newmarket (Town) and Ontario (Ministry of Labour)* (1992), 8 COHSC 85 (ON Adj); *Elgin Middlesex, 1997*, above note 353; *Sudbury Mine, Mill and Smelter Workers' Union, Local 598 (CAW) v Ministry of Labour, Falconbridge Ltd—Frasier Mine*, [1996] OOHSAD No 49 (Ont Adj Randall) [*Local 598*]; *Venier*, above note 424.

468 *Local 598*, above note 467 at para 32; *Venier*, above note 424 at para 162. However, see *CAW Local 222 and General Motors of Canada*, [1996] OOHSAD No 15 (Ont Adj Palumbo) [*Local 222*].

469 *Ottawa Carleton*, above note 367 at paras 16 and 19–20.

470 Although an application for judicial review was brought by OPSEU in respect of this decision, it was dismissed as moot in light of the 2001 legislative changes: *Ontario Public Service Employees Union v Ontario (Ministry of Labour)*, [2002] OLRB Rep Jan/Feb 96, [2002] OJ No 643 (ON CA).

471 *KE Electrical Services Ltd*, 2005 CanLII 35125 (ON LRB); *Spectra Aluminum Products Ltd v An Inspector under the Occupational Health and Safety Act*,

Rather, the appeal process is treated as a *de novo* hearing.[472] The OLRB has further stated that it has no jurisdiction regarding the conduct of inspectors and that allegations of improper behaviour by inspectors should be raised with the Ministry of Labour.[473]

The investigation will normally involve contact with the worker.[474] The ministry's obligation to inspect is not ended by employer suspensions of workers from work and the subsequent complaints of reprisal under section 50 of the *OHSA*. Instead, it has been held to be "clearly wrong" for the inspector to wait until those suspensions have been served before investigating a work refusal.[475]

A specific issue has been whether the OLRB could or should require an inspector to attend at the workplace to conduct an investigation. Prior to June 2001, section 43(7) of the *OHSA* stated that an inspector must investigate the refusal to work in the presence of the affected parties. Some adjudicators, other than the OLRB, found that this phrasing required the inspector to personally attend at the workplace.[476] Section 43(7) was amended to provide that "[a]n inspector shall investigate the refusal to work in consultation with the employer or a person representing the employer, the worker."[477] This been interpreted as providing an inspector with wide discretion concerning the manner of their investigation. In a decision arising from a work refusal in a youth detention centre during the OPSEU public service strike in 2002, the OLRB held that the decision about whether to attend at the workplace was for the inspector to decide in the exercise of their judgment and experience.[478] More recently, in addressing a work refusal in a correctional institution, telephone inquiries made by the inspector (as opposed to in person

---

2019 CanLII 7985 (ON LRB) at para 23, where the OLRB declined to look into how an inspector conducted themself.

472 *Vanier, 2019*, above note 341 at para 13.

473 *Blue Mountain Resorts Limited v Ontario (Labour)*, 2009 CanLII 13609 (ON LRB) at para 7, application for judicial review dismissed, 2011 ONSC 3057, rev'd on other grounds 2013 ONCA 75.

474 *Vanier*, above note 401 at 47.

475 *Whitby Jail, 1998*, above note 357 at para 151.

476 *Venier*, above note 424 at para 3; *Local* 222, above note 468 at para 50; *Local 598*, above note 467 at para 28; *Whitby Jail, 1998*, above note 357 at para 139; *Metcalf*, above note 414 at 26.

477 *OHSA*, 2001, c 9, Sched I, s 3(11).

478 *Brookside*, above note 434 at para 6.

attendance) were found to be sufficient and it was not necessary for the inspector to attend at the workplace.[479]

10) Workplace Violence and Harassment

In 2010, following the murder of a nurse at a Windsor hospital, the *OHSA* was amended to add Part III.0.1 Violence and Harassment. The *OHSA* section 1(1) was also amended to include definitions of "workplace violence" and "workplace harassment." Under the amendments employers are required to

- prepare policies regarding workplace violence and harassment and review those policies at least annually[480]
- have a program to implement the workplace violence policy, including measures for summoning immediate assistance when workplace violence occurs or is likely to occur, measures for reporting incidents of workplace violence to an employer or supervisor, and procedures for investigating and addressing incidents or complaints of workplace violence[481]
- conduct workplace violence risk assessments and reassessments[482]
- take every reasonable precaution for the protection of a worker if the employer is aware or ought reasonably to be aware that domestic violence that would likely expose a worker to physical injury may occur in the workplace[483]

The amendments also clarified that the employer duties, supervisor duties, and worker duties at sections 25, 27, and 28, respectively, apply with respect to workplace violence.[484] Further, the amendments[485] specifically provide that an employer's section 25(2)(a) duty to provide information to a worker and a supervisor's section 27(2)(a) duty to advise a worker include a duty to provide information related to a risk of workplace violence from a person with a history of violent behaviour if "the worker can be expected to encounter that person in the course of

---

479 *Dowling*, above note 401.
480 *OHSA*, above note 1, s 32.0.1.
481 *Ibid*, s 32.0.2.
482 *Ibid*, s 32.0.3.
483 *Ibid*, s 32.0.4.
484 *Ibid*, s 32.0.5.
485 *Ibid*, s 32.0.5(3).

his or her work" and "the risk of workplace violence is likely to expose the worker to physical injury."

In 2016 the *OHSA* Part III.0.1 was amended to include a definition of "workplace sexual harassment" in section 1(1), and, further, to require the employer to

- develop a written program in consultation with the JHSC or health and safety representative to implement the workplace harassment policy[486]
- ensure that the workplace harassment program includes measures and procedures for reporting incidents of workplace harassment to the employer or supervisor or to a person other than the employer or supervisor if they are the alleged harasser; sets out how incidents or complaints of workplace harassment will be addressed; sets out how to prevent the unnecessary disclosure of information obtained about an incident or complaint of workplace harassment; and sets out how a worker who experienced workplace harassment and the alleged harasser will be advised of the results of any investigation and corrective action or results of the investigation[487]
- ensure that an investigation appropriate in the circumstances is conducted into incidents and complaints of workplace harassment[488]
- provide a worker with information and instruction regarding the workplace harassment policy and program[489]

Further, the *OHSA* was amended to provide an inspector with the power to issue an order for a workplace harassment investigation to be conducted, at the employer's expense, "by an impartial person possessing such knowledge, experience or qualifications as are specified by the inspector."[490]

Previously the OLRB had contrasted the workplace violence provisions with the workplace harassment provisions and concluded that the *OHSA* does not provide workers with the right to a harassment-free

486 *Ibid*, s 32.0.6.
487 *Ibid*, s 32.0.6(2).
488 *Ibid*, s 32.0.7.
489 *Ibid*, s 32.0.8.
490 *Ibid*, s 55.3.

workplace and that the harassment provisions were procedural.[491] Even with the amendments the OLRB has maintained that the *OHSA* "does not expressly require employers to identify risks of workplace harassment, eradicate or prevent workplace harassment, or provide a harassment-free workplace."[492] Further, the OLRB has stated that a worker does not have any express statutory protection to engage in a work refusal due to workplace harassment.

To date, there has been very little OLRB caselaw interpreting the workplace violence and harassment provisions, both in the public sector and more broadly. For instance, while there is an obligation to conduct an investigation that is appropriate in the circumstances, there is little definition or clarity as to what the obligation entails.[493] Similarly, there is little direction as to when a workplace violence risk reassessment is required. Many of the decisions involving the workplace violence and harassment provisions have arisen at arbitration, and OPS arbitration cases are dealt with in the next section.

Notably following an incident of workplace violence where a nurse was stabbed in the neck by a patient using a contraband pen at a hospital, the OLRB issued an interim order requiring the hospital to place "an adequate number of properly trained security professionals" on the unit where the incident occurred on a twenty-four-hour basis "to accompany nurses when they provide nursing care or escort violent patients."[494] Under the interim order, the security professionals were "authorized to place their hands on a patient and detain them for the purposes of protecting themselves and the staff from injury."

As addressed in other sections, the OLRB is not the only adjudicative body that addresses workplace harassment. Workplace harassment issues may also be addressed by the GSB and the HRTO. Of those three

---

491 *Ljuboja v Aim Group Inc*, 2013 CanLII 76529 (ON LRB) at paras 35–36 [*Ljuboja*]; *Jennifer Ford v Anne Anderson*, 2015 CanLII 27353 (ON LRB) at para 19; *Chris Raby v St Marys Cement Bowmanville*, 2022 CanLII 119976 (ON LRB) at para 66.

492 *Wal-Mart Canada Logistics ULC v Gail Stewart*, 2020 CanLII 2070 (ON LRB) at para 22.

493 *ES Fox Limited v A Director under the Occupational Health and Safety Act*, 2020 CanLII 75931 (ON LRB) at para 77.

494 *Ontario Nurses' Association v Royal Ottawa Health Care Group—Brockville Mental Health Centre*, 2014 CanLII 75060 (ON LRB) at para 59. The interim order was clarified in a subsequent decision: *Ontario Nurses' Association v Royal Ottawa Health Care Group—Brockville Mental Health Centre*, 2015 CanLII 85528 (ON LRB).

bodies, only the GSB has full authority over the substance of workplace harassment as well as how to remedy it. As the OLRB has observed:[495]

- The HRTO can deal fully with harassment only to the extent that it involves a prohibited ground of discrimination;
- The OLRB can act on all harassment situations but only to the extent of enforcing the need for a policy and ensuring the compliance with that process. The OLRB cannot address the substance of harassment save that, where a harassment complaint was made, the OLRB can assess whether the worker experienced reprisal, including harassment, due to the making of the complaint.[496]

11) Health and Safety Provisions in OPSEU/MBC Collective Agreement Article 9.1

a) General Principles

Article 9.1 of the OPSEU/MBC collective agreement supplements the rights and obligations set out in the *OHSA*.[497]

Article 9.1 applies only to the employees who are covered by the collective agreement. The person whose safety is in question must therefore be a member of the bargaining unit. Non-members who perform tasks in the workplace, such as a chaplain or a social worker in a correctional facility, do not enjoy the protection of the collective agreement.[498]

The GSB will take jurisdiction over a matter properly before it unless there is specific statutory language reserving jurisdiction over that matter to another forum. The *OHSA* does not limit jurisdiction over most complaints to a particular tribunal, which leaves open the GSB's jurisdiction over health and safety matters. "Where the parties

---

495 *Melissa Art v Score Promotional Marketing Inc*, 2019 CanLII 97935 (ON LRB) at paras 11–12.

496 *Ljuboja*, above note 491 at para 63; *Jennifer Umlauf v Scarborough Rouge Hospital*, 2017 CanLII 51539 (ON LRB); *Nermine Youssef v University of Ottawa*, 2021 CanLII 69422 (ON LRB); *Simranpreet Kaur v ASP Incorporated*, 2022 CanLII 85176 (ON LRB) at para 6; *Rosario Galuego v Workplace Safety and Insurance Board*, 2022 CanLII 63839 (ON LRB) at para 8

497 The *AMAPCEO/MBC Collective Agreement, 2018–2022*, online: https://amapceo.on.ca/ops, Art 25.1 contains virtually identical language but there is no jurisprudence under it.

498 *OPSEU (Riendeau) and Ministry of the Solicitor General and Correctional Services*, GSB#1365/94, 9 August 1995 (Dissanayake).

have agreed on a process through which grievances and complaints can be addressed and, if necessary, rectified, it should require very clear language to convince a tribunal to deny that right to an aggrieved employee."[499]

In Article 9.1 of the collective agreement, the first stated principle places an onus on the employer to continue to "make reasonable provisions for the safety and health of its employees," while the second requires both parties to "co-operate to the fullest extent" to prevent accidents and to promote the safety and health of employees. The provisions of Article 9.1 have been found to require compliance with the *OHSA*, although compliance with that Act may not be sufficient if there is something more that needs to be done to make reasonable provision for health and safety.[500]

Of course, unsafe conditions will also trigger rights under the *OHSA*.[501] The legality of staff work refusals in response to allegedly unsafe conditions is assessed in accordance with the relevant provisions of the *OHSA*. The arbitral principle that employees need not obey an illegal order does not apply.[502]

i) *The First Principle: "The Employer Shall Make Reasonable Provisions for the Safety and Health of Its Employees During the Hours of Their Employment"*

The employer duty to make "reasonable" provision for health and safety is a requirement that can be "very wide and onerous."[503]

The onus is initially on the union to demonstrate "some degree of risk,"[504] sufficient "to call into question whether the employer is making

---

499 *Ontario Public Service Employees Union (Greenbank et al) v Ontario (Ministry of Finance)*, 2005 CanLII 55198 (ON GSB) (Mikus) at 7, which also notes that the OLRB can defer to arbitration. The one area under *OHSA* where the employee must elect either the GSB or the OLRB is a complaint about reprisal for filing a complaint: *OHSA*, above note 1, s 50(2).

500 *OPSEU (Davidson et al) and Ministry of Natural Resources*, GSB#595/80, 22 December 1982 (Samuels) at 10; *OPSEU (Gillies) and Ministry of Correctional Services*, GSB#339/82, 11 July 1984 (Saltman) at 5–6.

501 *Metcalf*, above note 414.

502 *Aitken*, above note 393 at 45.

503 *OPSEU (Union) and Ministry of Health*, GSB#581/84, 22 January 1985 (Kennedy) at 8.

504 *OPSEU (Watts/King) and Ministry of Correctional Services*, GSB#1367/90, 12 April 1991 (Kaplan) at 27 [*Watts/King, 1991*]. Where the employer had prohibited horseplay that posed a risk of injury but had allowed consensual and normally harmless physical interaction, an injury unexpectedly resulting

reasonable provisions to address or avoid that risk."[505] The existence, and severity, of the risk is to be objectively assessed as a subjective belief in the risk does not, by itself, trigger the application of the section.[506] The GSB dismissed a grievance by several helicopter paramedics seeking to have the employer make optional helmets available for use according to individual preference. The language of "reasonable provisions" was found to establish an objective standard that did not vary with the subjective preference of employees, but instead required steps to be taken for all employees.[507]

Determining what is reasonable requires assessing the degree of risk to employees. In the leading 1984 *Union* case, the GSB held that there was no obligation on the employer to protect against every possible risk, but rather to engage in "reasonable precaution."[508] What constitutes a reasonable precaution will be determined by a fact-specific analysis of the circumstances, involving a balancing of the safety interest of the individual and the operational interest of the employer.[509] The employer is required to take reasonable steps, but not "every" possible step,[510] and is to ensure reasonable safety, but need not ensure "optimum safety"[511]

---

from a casual exchange was not a breach of the employer's obligation to make reasonable provision for health and safety: *Ontario Public Service Employees Union (Lariviere) v Ontario (Community Safety and Correctional Services)*, 2006 CanLII 42759 (ON GSB) (Dissanayake).

505 *OPSEU (Andrews et al) and Ministry of Health*, GSB#1815/89, 15 May 1992 (Goldenberg) at 15 [*Andrews*].

506 *OPSEU (Danbrook) and Ministry of Transportation*, GSB#1494/89, 2 January 1992 (Stewart) at 18 [*Danbrook*]; *Ontario Public Service Employees Union (Anger et al) v Ontario (Community and Social Services)*, 2008 CanLII 70515 (ON GSB) (Watters) at 18 [*Anger, 2008*].

507 *Andrews*, above note 505 at 18.

508 *OPSEU (Union) and Ministry of Correctional Services*, GSB#69/84, 24 August 1984 (Samuels) at 6–7.

509 *Watts/King, 1991* above note 504 at 28. For a case finding that the employer's practices balanced "therapeutic objectives" with safety, see *OPSEU (Union) and Ministry of Health*, GSB#1933/89, 14 September 1995 (McCamus) at 40, dealing with escorting patients on temporary leaves of absence from the Oak Ridge Division of the Penetanguishene Mental Health Centre. See further cases below on balancing between employee rights and management interest in accommodating particularly vulnerable populations, namely prisoners with HIV and persons with disabilities.

510 *Watts/King, 1991*, above note 504 at 26; *St Amand*, above note 197.

511 *OPSEU (Taylor-Baptiste) and Ministry of Correctional Services*, GSB#469/88, 15 April 1992 (Dissanayake) at 24 [*Taylor-Baptiste*].

or eliminate all risks,[512] or provide the safest option.[513] While the balance is to be struck in favour of safety,[514] the union retains the onus of demonstrating that the balance has been inappropriately struck by exposure to real and unnecessary risk.[515] The union does not need to demonstrate actual or real harm, but can meet the onus by showing that the conditions "will more likely than not result in the possibility of unnecessary risk" to the health and safety of its members.[516]

The cost and effectiveness of a safety precaution is balanced against the likelihood and seriousness of the risk. Whether the precaution improves safety is by itself not relevant as "employees are not entitled to optimum or the best" precautions but reasonable ones.[517] For example, a causal connection must be shown between any alleged lack of training and a health and safety risk, as it is always possible to increase safety with training.[518]

When the employer increases the risk to employees, "the necessity and reasonableness" of the new, higher, level of risk must be justified.[519]

---

512 *OPSEU (Briek et al) and Ministry of Correctional Services*, GSB#1466/87, 21 October 1988 (Dissanayake) at 25; see also *Andrews*, above note 505 at 18.

513 *OPSEU (Willis) and Ministry of Correctional Services*, GSB#2755/91, 16 March 1995 (Stewart): although assigning male correctional officers to the female area of the facility may expose the male officers to a greater risk of sexual assault allegations, it is not an "unreasonable" provision of health and safety, given the excessive cost of alternatives and the limited degree of actual risk involved.

514 *OPSEU (Stockwell) and Ministry of Correctional Services*, GSB#1764/87, 10 February 1989 (Wilson) at 14–15 [*Stockwell, 1989*].

515 *Taylor-Baptiste*, above note 511 at 20; see also *OPSEU (Union) and Ministry of Correctional Services*, GSB#1929/91, 24 August 1994 (Barrett) at 7–10.

516 *Ontario Public Service Employees Union v Ontario (Community Safety and Correctional Services)*, 2016 CanLII 48159 (ON GSB) (Harris) at 8–9, citing *OPSEU (Ferrill et al) and The Crown in Right of Ontario (Ministry of Health)*, GSB#1665/90, 9 January 1992 (Kaplan), and noting this evidence need not be given by medical or scientific "experts," but what evidence is brought forward must be compelling. See also *Re OPSEU (Pereira et al) and Ministry of Community Safety & Correctional Services*, 2015 CanLII 60437 (ON GSB) (Harris) and *OPPA, 2018*, above note 216 at paras 306–7.

517 *Ontario Public Service Employees Union (Tomlinson et al) v Ontario (Environment, Conservation and Parks)*, 2020 CanLII 32558 (ON GSB) (Dissanayake) at 104–5, para 269 [*Tomlinson*]; *Anger, 2008*, above note 506.

518 *OPSEU (Union) and Ministry of Correctional Services*, GSB#311/88, 11 July 1991 (Watters): rejecting a claim that less training for unclassified correctional officers was a safety risk. For an example of training being found inadequate, see *Danbrook*, above note 506.

519 *Watts/King, 1991*, above note 504 at 27.

For example, an employer must provide sufficient evidence that the increased night-time inspection rounds in a prison facility improve the security of the inmates without unreasonably increasing the risk to correctional officers.[520] Similarly, the employer will have to justify a departure from generally accepted safety techniques.[521]

Some work involves inherent risks that the employer cannot remove. The employer must make reasonable efforts to mitigate them.[522] "To be sure, risk is part of the job. However, unnecessary risk is not."[523] It is unacceptably risky for correctional officers to be in direct contact with inmates in the following circumstances:

- requiring a correctional officer to ride in the secure portion of a transport van taking prisoners to and from court[524]
- touring prisoner dormitories after lights out[525]
- placing someone in the day room without being accompanied[526]
- without having another officer watching at the grille[527]

It is unacceptable to fail to contact the police when there is a real threat from an inmate to the safety of a correctional officer (and their family) outside the institution; it being understood that verbal threats inside the institution are more inherent to the occupation.[528]

---

520 *Ibid.* For a case where the employer "assessed a potential increased risk and then took adequate and appropriate steps to address the situation," see *OPSEU (Howard) and Ministry of Correctional Services*, GSB#1552/95, 26 September 1996 (Briggs) at 8.

521 *OPSEU (Storey) and Ministry of Community and Social Services*, GSB#1250/89, 3 July 1991 (Wilson) at 19 [*Storey*].

522 *Stockwell, 1989*, above note 514 at 14, finding that there is no good reason and significant risk involved in requiring a correctional officer to ride in the secure portion of a transport van taking prisoners to and from court.

523 *Watts/King, 1991*, above note 504 at 26.

524 *Stockwell, 1989*, above note 514 at 14.

525 *Watts/King 1991*, above note 504 at 26–27.

526 *OPSEU (Union) and Ministry of Correctional Services*, GSB#1252/85, 25 April 1987 (Jolliffe) [*Union, 1987*].

527 *OPSEU (Rowe) and Ministry of Correctional Services*, GSB#350/88, 18 September 1989 (Samuels).

528 Ontario *Public Service Employees Union (Bondy) v Ontario (Community Safety and Correctional Services)*, 2017 CanLII 25457 (ON GSB) (Sheehan); *St Amand*, above note 197.

Other examples of failure to make reasonable provision for safety include:

- not ensuring adequate air quality[529]
- exposing transportation enforcement officers to real risk of assault without proper training[530]
- failure to train management where staff was put at risk because a manager had failed to keep up to date in self-defence training and failed to follow the proper ministry procedures for dealing with crisis intervention at a residential school for the developmentally handicapped[531]
- allowing maintenance of a memorial to persons who died at a detention centre, which was located so that employees must drive by it to and from work, resulting in a constant reminder of traumatic circumstances that is injurious to the mental health of employees[532]

Normally, where a breach is found, the GSB will declare that a certain practice or situation is unsafe and remit the matter to the parties.[533] A specific order will be made if needed to resolve the matter.[534] To the extent possible, the order will correct the unsafe situation without creating new costs or obligations.[535]

---

529 *OPSEU (Rigglesworth) and Ministry of Transportation*, GSB#637/90, 20 August 1997 (Fisher) [*Rigglesworth*].

530 *Danbrook*, above note 506 at 23–24, although the grievors' request to be supplied with batons was denied.

531 *Storey*, above note 521, where the GSB ordered the manager to attend the prescribed courses and training required of all employees, despite the fact that the manager was outside the bargaining unit.

532 *Ontario Public Service Employees Union v Ontario (Solicitor General)*, 2021 CanLII 48171 (ON GSB) (Albertyn).

533 *Union, 1987*, above note 526, where a cease-and-desist order was not granted.

534 *OPSEU (Watts/King) and Ministry of Correctional Services*, GSB#1367/90, 12 April 1991 (Kaplan) and 24 May 1994; re plexiglass barriers: *Anger, 2008*, above note 506; re frisk searches: *OPSEU (Union) and Ministry of Correctional Services*, GSB#335/85, 28 November 1986 (Roberts) at 11–12; re specifying work obligations: *OPSEU (Baron et al) and Ministry of Community and Social Services*, GSB#2968/95, 28 June 1995 (Kaplan) at 53 [*Baron*].

535 *OPSEU (Sim) and Ministry of Correctional Services*, GSB#256/88, 7 February 1990 (Watters) at 11, where the danger of fatigue from too many midnight shifts was met not by pay for time off, but by granting a lieu day. See also *OPSEU (Stockwell) and Ministry of Correctional Services*, GSB#584/88, 1 March 1994 (Stewart).

Safety standards need not be as high if the employees can disengage from the unsafe conditions. It was not found too risky for agricultural investigators to be without firearms and pepper spray when enforcing food safety legislation, including standards for slaughterhouses, where potentially hostile workers had knives.[536] The evidence was that no one threatened physical harm to the investigators and that the investigators were instructed to disengage if anyone was agitated or angry. Similarly, senior environmental officers were not exposed to undue risk in dealing with unhappy property owners, even without soft body armour, because the employer prioritized disengagement and the "mantra" was, "If uncomfortable do not go. If already there and you feel unsafe or are told to leave, just leave. It is alright if the work does not get done." Whether or not one agrees with that approach, it is a decision the employer was legally entitled to make.[537]

A claim that an unacceptable level of unhealthy stress resulted from an increased workload was dismissed because there were other potential causes of stress in the lives of the grievors, and the union failed to show the link between the symptoms and conditions at work.[538]

A pattern of conduct over time may be relied on to establish failure to take reasonable precautions. The GSB has applied the three-year limitation for events before the date of the grievance that is used commonly to balance interests in relying on and proving facts over time in harassment and racial discrimination cases.[539]

Addressing safety risks can involve balancing between employee rights and employer obligations to the broader community. Concerning HIV positive inmates, the employer was required to take sufficient precautions to deal with the risk of employees contracting HIV, including the adoption of a comprehensive policy on communicable diseases that properly balanced the rights of the inmates with the health and safety concerns of the employees, but the employer was not required to warn of specific inmates with communicable disease or to develop

536 *Ontario Public Service Employees Union (Martin) v Ontario (Natural Resources and Forestry)*, 2019 CanLII 97224 (ON GSB) (Dissanayake).

537 *Tomlinson*, above note 517 at para 297.

538 *Baron*, above note 534 at 50.

539 *Ontario Public Service Employees Union (Lavoie et al) v Ontario (Community Safety and Correctional Services)*, 2015 CanLII 60426 (ON GSB) (Sheehan) at paras 33–42. The three-year rule is further discussed in the human rights section above.

criteria that would govern placing such persons in a segregation unit.[540] Concerning protective measures in Ontario Disability Support Program premises that serve mentally and physically disabled clients, the risk for employees of dealing with upset and unpredictable members of the public could be adequately addressed by counter design rather than a plexiglass barrier.[541]

As "being a CO [correctional officer] is a dangerous job and each CO is entitled to work with a partner they can rely on and trust," the employer may be justified in imposing discipline on employees who reduce the security of the institution.[542]

Where a health and safety grievance is about an individual grievor, the union must demonstrate that the particular employee's rights were infringed.[543] An example is failing to promptly inform a correctional officer cut by an inmate's weapon that they have the right to have the inmate provide a blood sample.[544] Where personal harm is claimed, the union must normally establish direct causation, supported by medical evidence, between the employee's symptoms and the employer's practices.[545] Failure to accommodate a physical disability, resulting in a risk of injury, will be a failure to make reasonable provision for health and safety, and, of course, is also a violation of the *HRC*.[546]

---

540 *OPSEU (Arnold/Zozzolotto) and Ministry of Correctional Services*, GSB#859/89, 27 March 1991 (Verity).

541 *Anger, 2008*, above note 506.

542 *Ontario Public Service Employees Union (Ataw) v Ontario (Community Safety and Correctional Services)*, 2019 CanLII 65164 (ON GSB) (Gee) at para 149 [*Ataw*].

543 *Taylor-Baptiste*, above note 511 at 13.

544 *Ontario Public Service Employees Union (Nichols) v Ontario (Community Safety and Correctional Services)*, 2014 CanLII 26453 (ON GSB) (Sheehan), referencing the right under the *Mandatory Blood Testing Act, 2006*, SO 2006, c 26.

545 *OPSEU (Alaksa, Polfer (Brown)) and Ministry of the Solicitor General*, GSB#1130/84, 27 September 1985 (Brent) at 10.

546 Accommodating physical disability in the OPS has been addressed primarily as a human rights issue, and those cases are referenced above starting with *Kerna*, above note 200. See also *OPSEU (MacKinnon) and Ministry of Health*, GSB#1378/92, 25 October 1994 (Verity); *OPSEU (Joynes) and Ministry of Correctional Services*, GSB#755/94, 14 February 1997 (Finley), where the grievor's disability arose out of a workplace injury and she was unable to perform repetitive wrist and elbow actions. The GSB held that the employer violated both the *HRC* and the health and safety article of the collective agreement by abdicating responsibility for accommodation to the Workers' Compensation Board and

Harassment affecting an employee's mental and physical health has been grieved as an occupational health and safety matter. As discussed in the *HRC* section above, it is also a violation of the harassment article of the OPSEU/MBC collective agreements and, when a prohibited ground of discrimination is a factor, a violation of the *HRC*. Indeed, the employer's failure to ensure employees have a workplace free of discrimination can violate Article 9.1. The discussion below focuses first on the specifics of an Article 9.1 claim, and then reviews the GSB's treatment of the relatively recent *OHSA* harassment provisions.

Under general arbitral caselaw, adopted by the GSB, workplace harassment is inconsistent with the employer's obligation to provide a safe working environment.[547] The employer will be liable for an abusive manager causing the reasonable probability of serious illness.[548] At the same time, the *OHSA* holds that reasonable management action is not harassment.[549] A grievor's health and safety rights are not violated by legitimate investigation of disciplinary allegations against a grievor, including a suspension with pay.[550]

---

by continuing to place the grievor in positions that were indicated as medically inappropriate for their condition. The employer was ordered to properly accommodate the employee, including ergonomic adaptation, possible occupational therapy, and the adjustment of duties. Because the employer had in fact acted in good faith, however, the GSB declined to order either damages or an apology.

547 As a leading example of the arbitral caselaw, see *Toronto Transit Commission v Amalgamated Transit Union (Stina)*, 2004 CanLII 55086 (ON LA) (Shime); *Toronto Transit Commission and ATU, Local 113 (Merolle), Re*, 2013 Carswell Ont 18432 (Shime) adopted by the GSB in *Plouffe*, above note 186 at paras 279–90.

548 *Ontario Public Service Employees Union v Ontario (Labour)*, 2009 CanLII 15421 (ON GSB) (Watters) at 53; *Ontario Public Service Employees Union (Lefkowitz) v Ontario (Community Safety and Correctional Services)*, 2015 CanLII 14070 (ON GSB) (Briggs).

549 *OHSA*, above note 1, s 1(4).

550 *Ontario Public Service Employees Union (Press) v Ontario (Health and Long-Term Care)*, 2007 CanLII 46151 (ON GSB) (Mikus) at 51–52.

In addition to the proof of harassment,[551] the evidence must show that the harassment directly caused illness.[552] That illness must be serious and more than "tension, stress, irritation or unhappiness."[553]

As discussed earlier, employer liability for harassment does normally depend on knowledge of the conduct. However, a "reasonable system of detecting and monitoring offensive conduct" needs to be in place.[554] Where an employer learns of harassment and then fails to properly investigate it, as it is required under Article 9.1 and the *OHSA* to do, liability can attach to the employer for subsequent harassment.[555]

The GSB has considered both the *OHSA* amendments[556] that establish specific substantive as well as program and policy obligations to address harassment, and the lesser requirements about workplace violence. The board has found that, for harassment, an investigation "appropriate in the circumstances"[557] always needs to be conducted unless the complaint is vexatious.[558] The *Respectful Workplace Policy*, discussed above in the human rights section, is an effort to fulfill the *OHSA* requirement to prepare a policy and program addressing harassment. In respect of workplace violence, about which the *OHSA* does not set a standard for the investigation of complaints, the GSB has held that some form of investigation is necessary to fulfill the general

551 *OPSEU (Welsh) and Ministry of Correctional Services*, GSB#1277/89, 6 July 1990 (Watters), where the union's claim that the assignment of the grievor was a wilfully applied stressor and discriminatory practice was rejected because discrimination was not established, and the medical evidence was insufficient to establish a breach of Article 9.

552 *OPSEU (Keeso) and Ministry of Correctional Services*, GSB#0009/88, 27 January 1989 (Watters). This proof would normally, but not necessarily, be medical. For a case where a racialized grievor, skeptical of the Canadian medical model for addressing stress, proved mental stress without medical evidence, see *Tardiel*, above note 197 at paras 140–43.

553 *OPSEU (Sager, Shelley) and Ministry of Transportation*, GSB#0377/00, 6 October 2004 (Mikus) at 7.

554 *Solicitor General, 2020, Harris*, above note 195 at para 95 quoting *Chan* 1990/90 (GSB); *AMAPCEO v AG*, above note 183 at para 190.

555 *Solicitor General, 2020, Harris*, above note 195.

556 *OHSA*, above note 1, Part 111.0.1 discussed above.

557 An investigation "appropriate in the circumstances" is required under *OHSA*, *ibid*, s 32.0.7(1)(a).

558 *Ataw*, above note 542 at paras 158–59.

obligation to take every reasonable precaution.[559] That investigation needs to be fair to properly support taking precautions going forward.

ii) The Second Principle: "Employer and Union Shall Co-operate to the Fullest Extent Possible in the Prevention of Accidents and in the Reasonable Promotion of Safety and Health of All Employees"

While the first principle of Article 9.1 contains substantive employer obligations, the second principle contains the procedural obligations of both parties. Both the "letter and the spirit" of all of Article 9.1 must be followed, and even well-intentioned compliance with the substantive provision will not be enough if the employer fails to consult with the union as required by the procedural component of the Article.[560]

The onus is on *both* the employer and the union to cooperate in the promotion of health and safety. The union need not first establish risk of harm before the employer is obligated to cooperate, but only that there is a health and safety concern that warrants investigation.[561] The GSB rejected the employer's argument that the union must first establish harm before the employer was obliged to cooperate with the testing of the video display terminal emissions. The obligation to make "reasonable provisions" for the health and safety of the workplace required the employer to allow the union to test one of the computers offsite. Because harm could only be identified after the fact, it was unreasonable for the employer to insist on proof before Article 9.1 could be invoked. Reasonable cooperation requires assisting with reasonable inquiries by the other party's experts[562] and may require cooperating in the conduct of reasonable evaluations or trials of safety equipment.[563] Where there was evidence that, due to an adversarial approach, the parties had failed to fulfill their "mutual obligation" of cooperative discussion, the issues

---

559 *AMAPCEO v AG*, above note 183 at para 194, where the report was found to be unfair as the grievor was not given a chance to respond and there was a failure to consider important evidence.

560 *OPSEU (Leeanan) and Ministry of Correctional Services*, GSB#1268/88, 22 August 1990 (Roberts), where the GSB found that although consultation would likely have resulted in the same conclusion, the procedural aspect of Article 9.1 is equally important as the substantive requirements. No remedial order was granted because there was good faith observance of the substantive requirement.

561 *OPSEU (Ethier) and the Ministry of Health*, GSB#959/87, 2 June 1989 (Wright) at 17–21.

562 *Ibid* at 22.

563 *Andrews*, above note 505 at 20.

were remitted to a committee of the parties for further discussion prior to any adjudication.[564]

b) Personal Damages and Property Damage

i) Personal Damages

An employer may be liable to pay damages that an employee suffers because of a breach of Article 9.1.[565] However, that liability is limited when any injury is compensable under worker's compensation legislation. In *Monk*, the GSB found that the *WSIA* should decide on worker's compensation entitlement and resulting benefits, and that the GSB does not have the jurisdiction to award additional damages for compensable accidents.[566] This ousts the GSB's ability to order "repayment of lost wages, including any lost opportunity for overtime; repayment of credits and benefits; special and general damages including damages for pain and suffering," all resulting from a compensable injury.[567] The GSB is also precluded from providing other compensatory relief based on the same facts.[568]

---

564 *OPSEU (Union) and Ministry of Correctional Services*, GSB#546/86, 3 February 1988 (Kennedy) at 8.

565 *Rigglesworth*, above note 529: failure to ensure adequate air quality resulted in payment of damages for directly caused income shortfall.

566 *Monk*, above note 249 at para 111, upheld in *OPSEU v Ontario et al*, 2012 ONSC 2348 and by the Court of Appeal in 2013 ONCA 406; *Ontario Public Service Employees Union (Grievor) v Ontario (Solicitor General)*, 2021 CanLII 71640 (ON GSB) (Carrier) [*OPSEU (Grievor), 2021*] at paras 63–69. The GSB will decide entitlement in the absence of a definitive WSIB ruling. *Monk* resolved divergent cases by overruling *Ontario Public Service Employees Union (Lariviere) v Ontario (Ministry of Community Safety and Correctional Services)*, 2005 CanLII 55163 (ON GSB) (Dissanayake). *Monk* has been followed in *Ontario Public Service Employees Union (Harrison) v Ontario (Community Safety and Correctional Services)*, 2015 CanLII 76837 (ON GSB) (Sheehan) and *OPPA, 2018*, above note 216 at paras 310–18. The *Monk* rationale also applies to compensation for second-hand smoke inhalation: *Ontario Public Service Employees Union (Yole) v Ontario (Community Safety and Correctional Services)*, 2017 CanLII 25449 (ON GSB) (Briggs).

567 *Ontario Public Service Employees Union (Mohamed) v Ontario (Attorney General)*, 2017 CanLII 47186 (ON GSB) (Gee) at 14 [*Mohamed, 2017*].

568 *Ontario Public Service Employees Union (Samuels et al) v Ontario (Community Safety and Correctional Services)*, 2017 CanLII 71793 (ON GSB) (Dissanayake); *Ontario Public Service Employees Union (Adams) v Ontario (Health)*, 2021 CanLII 95708 (ON GSB) (Lynk) [*Adams*], stating it needs to be possible to "see daylight" between other monetary claims and remedial jurisdiction under the *WSIA*.

This foreclosing of the GSB's jurisdiction extends to compensation for mental distress as a result of bullying or the reation of a toxic work environment because mental distress, including chronic mental stress, can be compensable by the WSIB.[569] However, the inclusion of mental distress under the *Monk* ruling is subject to two possible exceptions, the scope of which are not fully resolved at time of writing.

First, the *WSIA* provision entitling workers to benefits for chronic or traumatic mental stress arising out of and in the course of the worker's employment is subject to the exception that the worker is not entitled to *WSIA* benefits for mental stress caused by "decisions or actions of the worker's employer relating to the worker's employment, including a decision to change the work to be performed or the working conditions, to discipline the worker, or to terminate the employment."[570] In other words, there is no *WSIA* mental stress entitlement arising out of commonplace interactions with management. Interactions not compensable under the *WSIA* do include rude, disrespectful, and inappropriate behaviour toward a worker by a supervisor, management threats to a worker of suspension, and/or job loss and wrongful termination.[571] (This may leave such interactions within the GSB's remedial jurisdiction, but the mental stress produced by commonplace interactions is unlikely to be found to be a breach of the collective agreement in any event.) What has been found by the GSB to be included at the WSIB for consideration as a compensable cause of mental distress (and so outside the GSB's jurisdiction) is non-commonplace "objective harassment" and malicious or improper motives and egregious behaviour, including threats of violence.[572] Regardless of the exact scope of the exception for

569 *Ontario Public Service Employees Union (Patterson) v Ontario (Community Safety and Correctional Services)*, 2017 CanLII 25459 (ON GSB) (Briggs), upheld on judicial review in *OPSEU v The Crown in Right of Ontario*, 2019 ONSC 1077; *Association of Management, Administrative and Professional Crown Employees of Ontario (Wilson) v Ontario (Natural Resources and Forestry)*, 2017 CanLII 71789 (ON GSB) (Dissanayake); *Ontario Public Service Employees Union (Rosati) v Ontario (Community Safety and Correctional Services)*, 2018 CanLII 7264 (ON GSB) (Anderson).

570 *WSIA, 2017*, c 8, Sch 33, s 1 establishing *WSIA*, above note 1, s 13(5).

571 *OPSEU v The Crown (Ministry of Community Safety and Correctional Services)*, 2019 ONSC 2952, overturning *Ontario Public Service Employees Union (Grievor) v Ontario (Community Safety and Correctional Services)*, 2017 CanLII 92683 (ON GSB) (Carrier) at para 39.

572 *OPSEU (Grievor), 2021*, above note 566 at paras 63–69.

employer actions, this exclusion is limited to mental distress caused by employer decisions or actions relating to the worker's employment and does not extend to distress caused by the actions of a co-worker and the employer's failure to protect the grievor.[573]

The second possible exception to the *Monk* ruling may be human rights-based damages, such as damages for a victim of discrimination for injury to dignity, hurt feelings, and self-respect.[574] There has not yet been a ruling on whether a breach of the *HRC* that results in damages normally compensable by the WSIB would be an exception.[575] The GSB has awarded damages for failure to maintain a non-discriminatory culture in the workplace, which resulted in treatment that violated the human rights of a grievor.[576] In that case there was no claim for injury compensable under the *WSIA*.

Matters clearly not foreclosed by the *Monk* ruling include damage to personal property, or expenses or losses incurred to avoid or mitigate a risk to safety or health caused by the breach.[577] Also not included within the WSIB's jurisdiction is a declaration of breach of Articles 3 or 9 of the collective agreement, and requirements for the employer to take measures to improve health and safety.[578]

ii) Property Damage

Property damage flowing directly from the employer's failure to make reasonable provision for the grievor's safety is compensable.[579] Where the grievor had a car accident exiting the employer's premises because the employer did not remove ice and snow, and then the grievor claimed for car repairs, the employer's workplace obligation was found to apply

---

573 *Ontario Public Service Employees Union (Khan) v Ontario (Attorney General)*, 2020 CanLII 32582 (ON GSB) (Hewat) [*Khan*].

574 *Ontario Public Service Employees Union (Schultheis) v Ontario (Community Safety and Correctional Services)*, 2018 CanLII 33081 (ON GSB) (Wayck) at para 28.

575 That possibility has been raised in *ibid*.

576 *OPSEU (Grievor), 2022*, above note 243 at para 20.

577 *Ontario Public Service Employees Union (Foley et al) v Ontario (Community Safety and Correctional Services)*, 2018 CanLII 119566 (ON GSB) (Williamson) at para 29, following *Monk*, above note 249 at para 19; *Khan*, above note 573.

578 *Mohamed, 2017*, above note 567 at 14; *OPPA, 2018*, above note 216, referenced in *Adams*, above note 568.

579 *OPSEU (Gonneau) and Ministry of Attorney General*, GSB#227/81, 1 February 1982 (Teplitsky) at 7.

to the entire grounds and the employer was required to pay for the damage to the car. However, where there is no risk to the employee personally, damage to the employee's property is not compensable. Vandalism or other damage of employees' cars, even on the employer's property, which occurs when the employee is not present, will not be compensated under Article 9.1, because the employee owner of the car was not personally at risk at the time the vandalism occurred.[580]

The employer is not required to pay for all property losses suffered by employees in the course of their employment.[581] Provided reasonable steps are taken, the employer will not become a strict liability insurer against employee accidents with their personal property.[582]

E. *PAY EQUITY ACT*

The *Pay Equity Act* was the product of the assessment in the 1980s that discrimination in employment compensation due to gender was so pervasive that it could not be addressed by the complaint-based system under the *HRC*. There was a widespread practice of paying women doing work that was viewed as "women's work" less than men doing work of equal value. The OPS was a prominent beneficiary of lower cost female labour. Its clerical staff were almost entirely underpaid women, and the government also funded a vast number of agencies and suppliers of childcare, community health care, and long-term care homes staffed by underpaid female workers. The *PEA* was intended to address this form of discrimination[583] and is "quasi-constitutional human rights legislation directed at redressing systemic gender discrimination."[584]

---

580 *OPSEU (Group Grievance, Andersen et al) and Ministry of Correctional Services*, GSB#1093/01, 27 June 2002 (Brown); *Ontario Public Service Employees Union (McCafferty) v Ontario (Community Safety and Correctional Services)*, 2017 CanLII 47139 (ON GSB) (Sheehan), finding no possible liability for damage to an unoccupied car caused by a stone discharged from a lawnmower.

581 *OPSEU (Changoor) and Ministry of Transportation and Communications*, GSB#495/84, 7 February 1985 (Palmer), where the grievor was not reimbursed when he dropped his prescription glasses while crossing the highway in the course of employment duties.

582 *OPSEU (Myszko) and Ministry of Health*, GSB#2511/87, 12 September 1988 (Verity) at 16.

583 *PEA*, above note 1, s 4.

584 *Ontario Nurses' Association v 10 Community Care Access Centres*, 2021 ONSC 5348 at para 44 [*10 CCACs*].

The actual implementation of the Act is more about job classification than law.[585] The scheme of the Act is to identify male and female dominated job classes[586] (gender-neutral job classes are ignored) and rate them using a gender-neutral comparison system[587] based on skill, effort, responsibility, and working conditions[588] then move the job rate for female job classes to the level of the job rate for an equivalent male job class (the job-to-job approach).[589] Where direct comparison between male and female job classes is not possible, a scale is developed based on the relationship of the ratings of male job classes to their job rates, and then the job rates of female job classes are moved up to the scale of the male job classes based on the rating of the female job classes. In the simplest case of a female job class rated halfway between two male jobs classes, one higher and one lower, the female equity job rate would be halfway between the job rates of the two male job classes (the proportional value approach).[590] Certain public sector employers that have female job classes but no male classes to compare to may use the equity job rates of comparable female job classes in a proxy employer chosen from among eligible employers specified in regulation as a basis for setting equity job rates for their female job classes (proxy comparison).

The *PEA* achieves a singular level of confusion in remarkably few sections. Much of the confusion in the statute comes from the provisions dealing with the initial introduction of pay equity that required public sector (and large private sector) employers to adjust the wages of employees in female job classes to equity at the time the *PEA* came into effect. This required each employer to determine the required adjustment by identifying male and female job classes, determining the relevant characteristics of the work of each class, rating each class using a gender-neutral comparison system, and determining the equity rate for each female job class. The result in many cases required substantial

---

585 Job classifications and ratings are reviewed for application of the statutory criteria on a standard of reasonableness; see *Kristine Kiviaho, and Cynthia Farquhar v Huron Lodge Community Service Board Inc*, 2021 CanLII 115304 (ON PEHT) at para 28.

586 *PEA*, above note 1, s 1(1) "female job class" and "male job class."

587 *Ibid*, ss 12, 21.3(4), and 21.15(3).

588 *Ibid*, s 5.

589 *Ibid*, s 6.

590 *Ibid*, s 5.1(1) still in effect per the *Charter* decision in *Service Employees International Union, Local 204 v Ontario (Attorney General)*, 1997 CanLII 12286 (ON SC) [*SEIU*].

increases in wage costs; for the OPS, the necessary adjustments in wages of $96 million equalled about 2.5 percent of total payroll.[591] The total impact on the provincial budget was projected to be $1 billion.[592]

To mitigate the impact of these changes on employers the required adjustments could be phased in at the rate of 1 percent of total payroll per year. This required pay equity plans that provided for annual increases in addition to normal pay adjustments. OPS bargaining unit pay equity plans had to be negotiated with OPSEU, the only OPS union at the time.[593] Provisions governing pay equity plans were set out in Parts II, III.1, and III.2 of the Act that created exceptions to the general provision in Part I that employers subject to the Act were required to achieve and maintain equity following the Act coming into force. The process was complicated by the limiting of parties to job-to-job comparisons when the Act was first made effective on 1 January 1988. The *PEA* was amended in 1993 to add proportional value and proxy provisions, Parts III.1 and III.2, resulting in pay equity plans with phased in adjustments applicable to public sector employers with employees on 1 July 1993 in addition to those with employees on 1 January 1988.

The situation was further confused by the repeal of the proxy provisions[594] in 1996 and their restoration in 1997 by a decision that found the legislation repealing the proxy provisions was contrary to the *Charter*.[595] The *PEA* has never been amended to bring it into conformity with the *Charter* declaration, so it appears in the e-laws consolidation without the still binding Part III.2 proxy provisions. They must be found in a separate document.[596]

Public sector employers that employed staff when the *PEA* came into effect, and their successor employers, were required to make and implement pay equity plans and have long since reached equity. Their only continuing obligation under the Act is to maintain equity.

591 Elaine M. Todres, "Women's Work in Ontario: Pay Equity and the Wage Gap," (1990) 22:3 *Ottawa Law Review* 555 at 566 [Todres].

592 *1991 Ontario Budget*, Pay Equity at 15.

593 The OPSEU negotiations and plan are described in *Group of Employees v Ontario (Management Board Secretariat)*, 1999 CanLII 14827 (ON PEHT) and Todres, above note 591.

594 *PEA*, above note 1, Part III.2.

595 *SEIU*, above note 590.

596 Available on the Pay Equity Commission website: www.payequity.gov.on.ca.

While public sector employers that are established after 1 July 1993, (and are not a successor employer) are not required to post a pay equity plan as defined in the *PEA*, they must establish their workforce at equity and maintain it at equity.[597] Even though a new employer does not have to post a plan, they must in practice have one so they can effectively achieve and maintain equity and prove they have done so if a complaint is made to the Pay Equity Commission.[598]

While maintenance of pay equity was clearly always required, the implications and difficulties involved in maintenance can be understood largely by inference. The Act requires a gender-neutral job comparison system based on job-related criteria for certain job classes within an employer's workforce. While the *PEA* did not outlaw employers' existing discriminatory job comparison/rating system, it does force employers to test their job evaluation systems against the standard required by the Act. The requirement for job-related criteria, if adopted for all job ratings, potentially addresses other issues of fairness and possibly discrimination in workplaces. It also requires employers wanting to have a single job comparison system to choose one that meets the higher standard under the *PEA*.

Collective bargaining adjustments or general wage increases did not count toward pay equity adjustments under a pay equity plan. Pay equity adjustments are in addition to normal wage increases. Pay equity plans prevail over collective agreements, and unions and employers are not permitted to bargain collective agreement terms that cause a contravention of the employer's obligation to maintain pay equity.[599]

1) The Public Sector and Crown as Employer

The *PEA* defines "public sector" in the schedule to the Act. The definition includes what is often called the broader public sector: the Ontario government and its agencies, municipalities and their agencies, universities, hospitals, school boards, and government-funded entities such as long-term care homes and day cares, for example. The *PEA* applies to

597 *Oakwood Retirement Communities Inc v SEIU Local 1 Canada*, 2010 CanLII 76245 (ON PEHT) at paras 53 and 69 [*Oakwood*].

598 *Ibid* at para 54.

599 *PEA*, above note 1, ss 7(2) and 13(10).

the public sector without regard to the size of the employer.[600] It applies to the private sector except for employers that have not employed ten employees at one time.[601]

The Act requires employers to achieve equity among all their employees within an establishment. The non-union staff and each bargaining unit have a separate pay equity plan.[602] An employer that has employees in more than one municipality may have separate establishments with separate pay equity plans for different "territorial divisions" in accordance with the definition of "establishment" in the Act.[603]

For purposes of the *PEA*, the Crown is defined to be the employer of public servants appointed under Part III of the *PSOA* (employees in ministries and commission public bodies),[604] and employees of specific agencies prescribed by regulation[605] or that were found by the Pay Equity Hearings Tribunal to be part of the Crown in deciding an application made prior to 18 December 1991.[606] As a consequence, many employers funded by government delivering a government program and some public bodies[607] subject to the *PSOA* are part of the public sector under the *PEA* but all are separate employers from the Crown for purposes of implementing pay equity.

2) Pay Equity Commission

The Pay Equity Commission is the entity responsible for administering and enforcing the *PEA*. It has two parts: the Pay Equity Office and the Ontario Pay Equity Hearings Tribunal. The Pay Equity Office employs review officers authorized by the *PEA* to investigate and address allegations of non-compliance or disputes under the *PEA* and may make

600 *Ibid*, s 3(1).

601 *Ibid*, s 3(1) & (2).

602 *Ibid*, s 14(1).

603 *Ibid*, s 1, definitions of establishment and territorial division.

604 *Ibid*, s 1.1(1). See the discussion in Chapter 2 about the *PSOA* Part III.

605 *Ibid*, O Reg 387/07.

606 *Ibid*, s 1.1(4); the Children's Aid Society of the City of Kingston and the County of Frontenac seems to be the only agency found to be part of the Crown by the tribunal: *Canadian Union of Public Employees, Local 2175 v Ontario (Community and Social Services)*, 1992 CanLII 4693 (ON PEHT).

607 *PSOA*, above note 18, O Reg 146/10 defines both "public bodies" and "commission public bodies." See the discussion in Chapter 2.

orders enforcing the *PEA*.[608] Orders may be appealed to the Pay Equity Tribunal.[609]

3) Maintenance

Responsibility for maintaining pay equity in an employer's establishment rests with the employer.[610] Maintaining "pay equity will normally mean that, absent an exception under the Act, the actual wages that employees in female job classes receive must either remain constant or must increase in order to avoid the re-emergence of a wage gap."[611] Maintenance need not be negotiated with the union in the case of a bargaining unit plan.[612] However, the employer must advise the union of any actions taken to maintain equity.[613] Both the employer and union are required to ensure their collective bargaining is consistent with the maintenance of equity.[614] A union or an individual employee subject to a pay equity plan may complain to the Pay Equity Commission that equity has not been maintained.[615] The commission will investigate and may issue an order to remedy any failure to maintain equity binding on the employer subject to appeal to the Pay Equity Tribunal.[616] The tribunal will only hear matters that have been the subject of an investigation by a review officer.[617]

The *PEA* does not contain a time limit on pay equity claims nor does it specify how long records must be kept.[618] A 2019 Divisional

608 *PEA*, above note 1, ss 23 & 24.

609 *Ibid*, ss 23(4), 24(5)–(6), and 25.

610 *Ibid*, s 7(1).

611 *Corporation of the City of Windsor v Shirley D Moor*, 2017 CanLII 22919 (ON PEHT) at para 42. The *PEA*, above note 1, s 8 permits some exceptions but the definition of job rate in s 1(1) as top rate for a class does not permit reduction in other rates for the class.

612 *Ontario Nurses' Association v Central Community Care Access Centre*, 2019 CanLII 86314 (ON PEHT) at para 71 [*Central CCAC*], aff'd *10 CCACs*, above note 584.

613 *PEA*, above note 1, s 7(2); *10 CCACs*, above note 584 at para 73.

614 *Ibid*, s 7(2).

615 *Ibid*, s 22.

616 *Ibid*, s 24(3) and (6).

617 *Ontario Public Service Employees Union v Ontario (Government Services)*, 2009 CanLII 37958 (ON PEHT) at para 21.

618 *Glen Hill Terrace Christian Homes Inc v Canadian Union of Public Employees (CUPE) Locals 2225-06/12 and 5110*, 2021 CanLII 126444 (ON PEHT) at para 19 [*Glen Hill*].

Court decision[619] finding that maintenance of pay equity under proxy plans requires ongoing reference to the proxy comparators, reversing the long-held view that the comparison was a one-time event, will likely spark claims dating back to at least 2005. In a recent decision the tribunal limited retroactive damages in such a claim to the date the current employer purchased the business in 2011 on the basis that, in those circumstances, the employer could not reasonably be expected to have access to the records for the earlier period but the tribunal also cautioned that in other circumstances the absence of records could support an adverse inference.[620] While the Crown is not subject to proxy claims, it is the funder of proxy employers. It is also, at time of writing, negotiating a revised pay equity plan for OPSEU's OPS unified bargaining unit. Should a change in an OPS female job class duty, for example, put the OPS out of equity, liability would accrue until equity is restored.

Employers are expected to regularly review their pay equity plans to ensure that equity is being maintained in accordance with the Act. To meet its onus to prove that equity has been maintained an employer will need documentary evidence to show it adequately determined the facts necessary to assess each male and female job class against the statutory criteria using a gender-neutral comparison system,[621] and then took measures to identify changes in the job classes and reassess them in light of those changes.

There is no clear rule determining when changes in the workplace require a new pay equity plan to be created or negotiated. So long as an employer can make adjustments that keep it at equity, the plan can continue.

4) Sale of Business

The sale of business section is included in Part II of the Act and only applies to public sector employers that had employees on 1 January 1988, or 1 July 1993 and their successors.[622] It was intended to allow successors to employers that were phasing in pay equity adjustments to continue to phase them in rather than requiring them to reach

619 *Ontario Nurses' Association v Participating Nursing Homes*, 2019 ONSC 2168, aff'd 2021 ONCA 148, leave refused 2021 CanLII 98079 (SCC).

620 *Glen Hill*, above note 618 at paras 23 & 24.

621 *Oakwood*, above note 597 at para 57.

622 *PEA*, above note 1, s 11(2) & (3).

equity immediately upon taking over the business. In *Ontario Nurses' Association v Central Community Care Access Centre*,[623] the tribunal suggested, but did not decide, that the sale of business provisions applied to employers that first employed employees after 1 July 1993. This is clearly not a reasonable interpretation of the words of section 11(2) of the Act: "[t]his Part does not apply to an employer who does not have employees on the effective date" or section 11(3): "[d]espite subsection (2), sections 13.1 [successor rights], 14.1 and 14.2 apply to public sector employers that did not have employees on the effective date but that had employees on July 1, 1993." A successor employer of a business that only employed people after 1 July 1993 is an employer required to achieve and maintain equity within its business immediately on taking over like all employers subject to the *PEA*. However, it is not responsible for compensating for the failure of its predecessor employer to pay wages at equity.

The sale of business provisions in the *PEA* are similarly worded to the analogous provisions in the *CECBA* and the *LRA* so may be expected to apply to the same transactions. However, the purpose of the *PEA* and consequently the significance of the sale of business clause is different. The sale of business provision means the successor employer takes responsibility for any outstanding failures of the predecessor to pay wages at equity. This obligation applies to both bargaining unit and non-bargaining unit employees. In the event a predecessor's pay equity plan achieves and maintains equity it may remain in place whether or not the successor rights provision applies.[624] If the post-transfer circumstances mean the plan does not maintain equity, it must be modified or, if it is no longer appropriate, replaced. In any event the pay equity plan and changes to it must be disclosed to a union with members subject to the plan and subject to complaint to the Pay Equity Commission. The replacement of a bargaining unit plan transferred subject to the sale of business provisions must be bargained with the union and, failing agreement, referred to the Pay Equity Commission for resolution.[625]

---

623 *Central CCAC*, above note 612 at para 70.

624 *10 CCACs*, above note 584 at paras 77–79.

625 *PEA*, above note 1, s 13.1(2).

5) Changed Circumstances

Changed circumstances may render a pay equity plan inappropriate requiring replacement of the plan. Replacement of bargaining unit plans must be negotiated with the union and, failing agreement, referred to the Pay Equity Commission for resolution.[626] Like the sale of business provision, the changed circumstances sections[627] are in Part II of the *PEA*, which only applies to employers with employees on 1 January 1988 or 1 July 1993 or a successor to such an employer.[628] However, since an employer is required to maintain equity, the employer must modify or replace the measures it has adopted if they are inappropriate and advise the union. Any changes to a bargaining unit plan may be the subject of a complaint by the union so negotiation with the union in respect of a changed bargaining unit plan is likely to be required in some context whether or not the changed circumstances section applies. A failure to agree will lead to an investigation and decision by a review officer about what terms are required to maintain equity.[629]

Whether a plan is inappropriate is a matter of subjective determination.[630] So long as an employer is prepared to maintain equity under a plan there are no objective criteria for determining a plan is inappropriate. While the changed circumstances section[631] applicable to bargaining unit plans contemplates either the employer or union seeking replacement of a plan, in the event of a changed circumstance the employer has the obligation to maintain equity.[632] If the employer can address changes within the context of the existing plan and maintain equity, a direction to negotiate a new plan is unlikely.[633]

6) Ontario Public Service OPSEU and AMAPCEO Pay Equity Plans

The OPS bargaining units present significant challenges in managing job classification and pay equity. The province-wide OPSEU and AMAPCEO bargaining units are very large and complex covering

626 *Ibid*, ss 14.1 & 14.2.
627 *Ibid*.
628 *Ibid*, s 11(1) and (3).
629 *10 CCACs*, above note 584 at paras 81 and 91.
630 *Ibid*, at para 66.
631 *PEA*, above note 1, s 14.1(1).
632 *10 CCACs*, above note 584 at para 92.
633 *Ibid* at paras 77–79.

multiple ministries operating in various capacities in every sector in every part of the province. The operations of government and consequently the jobs in ministries are subject to significant change or evolution.

Pay equity is concerned with establishing equity between female job classes and equivalent male job classes. It is not concerned with other forms of equity within the workplace. Implementation of pay equity may even exacerbate inequities between different female wage classes that may find different male comparator classes.[634] An effective classification system should be gender neutral in assigning and updating job classifications to consistently reflect the value of each position. Introducing a new gender-neutral classification system to bargaining units of the size and complexity of the OPSEU and AMAPCEO units involves both difficult negotiations, given the impact on the collective agreements and the individual employees' vital interest in their income, and the large commitment of resources to develop and implement a plan involving the description and assessment of thousands of positions.

A new gender-neutral pay equity compliant job classification system was negotiated with AMAPCEO effective in 2013.[635] In 2005, OPSEU and the MBC negotiated a number of specific pay equity adjustments to maintain equity and committed to the negotiation of a new classification system.[636] In 2013, OPSEU and the MBC acknowledged prior efforts at revising the classification system had failed in the face of the complexity of the task and entered into a new process.[637] The new process expressly recognized that pay equity had to be maintained and that the process would value jobs based on the four criteria set out in the *PEA*. A joint working group was established to, among other roles, identify male and female job classes as defined in the *PEA*. The process has advanced but was not yet completed at the time of writing.

7) Individual Settlements

An employer cannot contract out of its obligations under the *PEA*. However, pay equity claims by an individual can be foreclosed by a

634 *Munro v Ottawa Heart Institute*, 2004 CanLII 60148 (ON PEHT) at para 11.
635 *AMAPCEO/MBC Collective Agreement*, above note 497 at 180 and 187.
636 *OPSEU/MBC Unified and Correctional Collective Agreements*, above note 193, Appendix 37.
637 *Ibid*, Appendix 34.

general release clause in a settlement of a dismissal grievance or an analogous settlement of employment-related claims on termination of employment.[638]

F. *WORKPLACE SAFETY AND INSURANCE ACT*

The *Workplace Safety and Insurance Act* applies to the Crown as it does to any other similar employer, and there is no unique treatment of the provincial government or Crown agencies under that Act. The Crown is deemed to be the employer, for workers' compensation purposes, of any person who assists in a search and rescue operation at the request of, and under the direction of, a member of the OPP, and who assists in connection with an emergency declared by the premier of Ontario.[639]

The Act establishes two schedules for purposes of determining employers' payment obligations. The provincial government is a Schedule 2 employer. Most employers are listed in Schedule 1, which establishes a system of collective liability. Schedule 1 employers are divided into groups according to type of business. Schedule 1 employers, by group, pay annual premiums set by the board that will approximate the costs of accidents to their workers. By contrast, Schedule 2 employers, who are, generally, large quasi-public or public institutions, including the provincial government, are each separately responsible for the payment of all compensation benefits awarded to their own employees. Schedule 2 employers directly pay those compensation benefit costs and an associated administration fee.

Where it was claimed that government ministries should be treated as separate employers, an appeals resolution officer ruled the provincial government is one entity and each ministry is not independent.[640] The employer had claimed that the employee had switched employers by moving from one ministry to another. A worker can lose entitlement to a future economic loss award when voluntarily accepting lower-paid employment with a different employer. The WSIB ruled that the worker had not changed employers, but rather had taken another job "within the Ontario Government service."

---

638 *Better Beef Ltd v MacLean*, 2006 CanLII 17930 (ON SCDC); *Bucyrus Blades of Canada Ltd v McKinley*, 2005 CanLII 1491 (ON SCDC).

639 *WSIA*, above note 1, s 71(2) & (3).

640 *Appeals Resolution Officer Decision, Claim 20068715*, 24 May 2001 at 3.

The extent of the GSB's jurisdiction over compensation for workplace injuries is discussed under the relevant OPSEU/MBC collective agreement provision, Article 9.1, Occupational Health and Safety, above. The PSGB's lack of jurisdiction is discussed in connection with other PSGB jurisdictional issues in Chapter 13.

G. PENSIONS

Government employee pensions have received special legislative treatment for more than 100 years, including significant support for joint trusteeship.

In 1920, the government passed *An Act Respecting Superannuation and Retiring Allowances of Civil Servants*,[641] which established fixed pensions for civil servants. The government had been keeping on employees who were no longer useful rather than dismiss them from employment and leave them impecunious. The purposes of the bill were to make room for younger employees, and to ensure the dependants of public servants would be looked after.[642]

In 1989, the long-standing *Public Service Superannuation Act* was repealed and replaced with the *Public Service Pension Act* (*PSPA*) and its *Schedule 1*.[643] The intention was to allow for greater administrative flexibility, indexation of the public service pensions, and to provide for increases in some benefits.[644] The amendments were also intended to reflect the design of Ontario's *Pension Benefits Act*, so the continuing Public Service Pension Plan (PSPP) was made largely subject to the *PBA* provisions applicable to other pension plans.

Then, in 1994, the New Democratic Party government and OPSEU agreed to a separate plan for OPSEU-represented members. The result was public service pensions were split into two plans:

- the continuing PSPP, covering all employees not in the OPSEU Pension Plan (including both non-unionized employees and those

---

641 SO 1920, c 4.

642 Premier Drury, *The Globe*, 7 and 20 May 1920.

643 *Public Service Pension Act*, RSO 1990, c P.48, Sch I [*PSPA*], as amended (Unofficial Consolidation, amended to 1 February 2022, online: www.opb.ca/about-opb/pspp-plan-text) [*Schedule 1*].

644 Ontario, Legislative Assembly, *Hansard*, 20 June 1989, No 28 at 1435 (Murray Elston, Chair, MBC).

represented by certain bargaining agents including AMAPCEO, the OPPA, and PEGO)
- the OPSEU Pension Plan (OPSEU Plan), covering public servants represented by OPSEU, and certain other designated Crown agency bargaining units

The OPSEU Plan gave OPSEU and the Government of Ontario an equal voice in administration of the benefits and management of plan assets through joint trusteeship.

The *PBA* applies to both plans,[645] but its effect is modified by two plan-specific Acts: the *PSPA* and the *Ontario Public Service Employees' Union Pension Act, 1994* (*OPA*).[646] The PSPP is administered by the Ontario Pension Board (OPB) and has a membership specified by regulation. The joint trusteeship of the OPSEU Plan is done through a separate entity, the OPSEU Pension Trust (OPTrust). The OPTrust has a broader evolving membership determined by the trustees, although it was initiated by legislation.

Neither plan is fully incorporated into the Crown's various collective agreements, though both the OPSEU and AMAPCEO agreements refer to certain pension benefits. Employees and unions can challenge pension plan administration decisions through the plans themselves, subject to review and supervision of the Financial Services Regulatory Authority of Ontario (FSRA)[647] and related appeal mechanisms. Benefits expressly provided in the collective agreements can be the subject of grievances.

The pension benefits provided by the OPSEU Plan and the PSPP are very similar although not the same. For example, both plans provide defined benefits based on the best five-year average salary, on the same general formula (2 percent of average salary multiplied by the years of service, which is intended to provide about 70 percent of salary in retirement, assuming thirty-five years of service), including bridge benefits, as well as early retirement subsidies (for example, factors which allow an unreduced pension to be started before age sixty-five). Over time,

---

645 *PBA*, above note 1, Reg 909, ss 47.2 & 47.3 exempt each plan respectively from specific provisions of the *PBA*; the exemption for the OPTrust is limited to s 69 of the *PBA*, while there are several exemptions for the OPB.

646 *Ontario Public Service Employees' Union Pension Act, 1994*, SO 1994, c 17, s 143, Sch [*OPA*].

647 The FSRA was previously the Financial Services Commission of Ontario (FSCO).

minor differences in benefits have emerged, as well as the differences in the plans' governance models, financial position, and contributions.

1) Public Service Pension Plan

Following the split of the OPSEU Plan from the PSPP, the PSPP retained members not represented by OPSEU as well as existing pensioners, beneficiaries, and deferred pensioners. The PSPP continues to be a contributory defined benefit plan that defines the pension benefit according to the employee's salary and years of service for pension accrual purposes.[648] It is considered a single employer pension plan under the *PBA*, although it is an unusual single employer given its constituent elements include many commissions, agencies, boards, and ministries, which all operate separately. Under the *PSPA*, the Lieutenant Governor in Council may amend the PSPP although only in accordance with any agreement between the Crown and representatives of the members.[649]

As of the end of 2020, the PSPP fund amounted to approximately $31 billion. At the time of writing, the PSPP has about 90,000 members, including active, deferred, and retired members. About half the total are active.[650] The current contribution rates for members accruing the regular level of benefits are 7.4 percent on income up to the year's maximum pensionable earnings (YMPE) and 10.5 percent over the YMPE.[651] As of 31 December 2020, the PSPP was 90 percent funded on a going-concern basis.[652]

a) Who Is Covered

Membership in the PSPP is mandatory for persons under age sixty-five years and generally for those who are appointed as a public servant by the Public Service Commission under the *PSOA* section 32 (other than those appointed for a fixed term or those employed by a commission public body, which is covered by another pension plan according to legislation); members of a designated class employed by an Ontario

648 *Schedule 1*, above note 643, especially s 15.
649 *PSPA*, above note 643, s 6.
650 See online: www.opb.ca/about-opb/history.
651 *Schedule 1*, above note 643.
652 For much of the information noted in this paragraph, see the OPB *2020 Annual Report*, online: http://reports.opb.ca/2020/assets/pdf/OPB-2020-Annual-Report.pdf at 6, 47, and 63.

agency, board, commission, corporation, foundation, organization, or public body established by provincial legislation; and employees of the Office of the Auditor General or employees who are required by an Act of the legislature or an order in council to be a member.[653]

In addition, membership is optional for those who are not covered by the mandatory membership requirements and appointed as a public servant by the Crown under the *PSOA*; employed by an agency, board, commission, corporation, foundation, organization, or public body that has a designated class of employees or permanent and full-time probationary employees who are required to be members; deputy ministers; and persons designated by the Lieutenant Governor in Council.[654]

In any case, employees who are eligible or required to join the OPSEU Plan are excluded from the PSPP.[655]

b) Administration and Governance

The OPB administers the PSPP and monitors investment of the assets in the pension fund.[656] The OPB is responsible for ensuring that the PSPP

---

653 *Schedule 1*, above note 643, s 2(1). More specifically, membership is mandatory for public servants appointed under s 32 of the *PSOA*, except those who are appointed for a fixed term, unless another Act provides for membership in another plan; members of a class employed by an Ontario agency, board, commission, corporation, foundation, organization, or public body as designated by order of the Lieutenant Governor in Council; employees of the Office of the Auditor General of Ontario; employees required by an Act of the legislature or an order in council to be a member; and persons, other than deputy ministers, who, on or before 19 August 2007, were required to be members of the pension plan in accordance with the provisions of the plan as it read on that date. Under s 2(2) & (3), membership is optional for those to whom the mandatory membership provisions do not apply and who are employed as public servants in a minister's office; employed by an agency, board, commission, corporation, foundation, organization, or public body designated by order of the Lieutenant Governor in Council as one whose employees in a designated class are members of the plan; employed by an agency, board, commission, foundation, organization, or public body that has permanent and full-time probationary employees who are required to be members; effective 20 August 2007, deputy ministers; persons who, on or before 19 August 2007, were eligible to be members of the pension plan in accordance with the provisions of the plan as it read on that date; and persons designated by the Lieutenant Governor in Council.

654 *Ibid.*

655 *Ibid*, s 2(4).

656 Under *Schedule 1*, *ibid*, the province created the Public Service Pension Board, which became known as the Ontario Pension Board (OPB) effective 1 January 1992.

is administered in accordance with the plan terms, the *PBA*, the *Income Tax Act* (*ITA*),[657] and other applicable legislation.[658]

The OPB board of directors is to be composed of at least four members appointed by the Lieutenant Governor in Council, at least one of whom is a representative of the members of the plan who are also members of a bargaining agent with whom the employer has a collective agreement.[659] As of January 2023, the OPB board of directors is composed of nine members, each appointed by the plan sponsor (the Government of Ontario) and at least three of whom are nominees of bargaining agents representing PSPP members.[660] Although the PSPP has these member representatives, it remains an employer pension plan, which means the employer is ultimately responsible for any funding shortfalls.

The board of directors is authorized to have committees and has struck six (the governance, investment, audit, pensions, human resources, and managed plans committees).

The assets of the PSPP are invested through the Investment Management Corporation of Ontario, which was created by the province in 2016 to manage funds like those of the OPB.

As a government agency, the OPB has a particular obligation to manage costs and liabilities.[661]

As a large public sector plan that is also a government agency with heightened transparency requirements, the PSPP provides a wide range of information on its website, although there are elements that remain confidential. The OPB reports on an annual basis on its activities through an annual report that is tabled in the legislature.[662]

c) Collective Bargaining

Review of the *PSPA*'s *Schedule 1* provides insight into the nature of collective bargaining about pensions and how it has related to the PSPP. Most terms of the plan are constant for all members, which allows it

---

657 RSC 1985, c 1 (5th Supp) [*ITA*].

658 See, for example, *McHayle v Ontario (CEO of FSRA)*, 2021 ONFST 2 at para 12 [*McHayle*].

659 *Schedule 1*, above note 643, s 29(3).

660 See OPB, online: www.opb.ca/about-opb/board-of-directors.

661 See the OPB, *2020 Annual Report*, online: http://reports.opb.ca/2020/assets/pdf/OPB-2020-Annual-Report.pdf at 10 [*OPB, 2020 Annual Report*].

662 *Schedule 1*, above note 643, s 37. See, for example, *OPB, 2020 Annual Report*, *ibid*.

to be efficient in the provision of benefits. However, different groups of members who negotiate separately, including AMAPCEO-represented members, have slightly modified provisions related to contributions and benefits. For example, there have been various time-limited early retirement windows (incentives) related to specific groups of members.

There are several pension provisions referenced in the AMAPCEO collective agreement.[663]

2) OPSEU Pension Plan

In 1994, OPSEU negotiated with the Crown to split the PSPP into two pension plans. The negotiated agreement between OPSEU and Ontario was set out in a *Sponsorship Agreement*.[664] The new OPSEU Pension Plan became the pension plan for those members of the former PSPP who were in a bargaining unit represented by OPSEU. The OPSEU Pension Trust began operating on 1 January 1995. The OPSEU Plan is a jointly sponsored pension plan under the *PBA*, which is based on the joint governance model and affords the plan with funding flexibility compared to a single employer pension plan like the PSPP.

As of the end of 2021, the OPSEU pension fund amounted to approximately $26 billion with about 100,000 members, including active, deferred, and retired members. Less than half of the total are active. The current contribution rates for members accruing the regular level of benefits are 9.4 percent on income under the YMPE and 11 percent over the YMPE.[665] As of 2021, the OPSEU Plan was 100 percent funded on a going-concern basis.

Enrolment in OPTrust Select, a new part of the OPSEU Plan, began in early 2019. OPTrust Select targets Ontario workplaces in the broader

---

663 See for example: Articles 27.5.4, 27.9.3.9, 27.21, and 36.4 in the *AMAPCEO/MBC Collective Agreement*, above note 497.

664 *Sponsorship Agreement made as of the 18th day of April 1994 between Her Majesty in Right of the Province of Ontario as represented by the Chair of the Management Board of Cabinet and the Ontario Public Service Employees' Union* [*Sponsorship Agreement*], which was amended in 2013 and 2018 to allow for additional employers to join the plan. The *Sponsorship Agreement* is referenced in the introduction of the OPSEU Plan and was required under the *OPA*, above note 646, s 4(3) to be tabled in the legislature, although the tabling of the agreement did not occur.

665 The OPTrust's 2021 Funded Status Report, online: https://optrust.com/FundedStatusReport/2021/OPTrust-2021-FSR.pdf.

public sector, as well as charitable, and not-for-profit groups, that do not have a defined pension plan—a majority of whose employees are women.[666] An advantage of OPTrust Select to members is its ability to allocate risk and operational costs over a broader membership base and rely on the larger-scale administration and investment capacities of the OPTrust.[667]

Key features of OPTrust Select are that members can contribute 3 percent of earnings, which is matched by employers; an annual pension accrual rate of 0.6 percent of earnings; and earnings upgrades and cost of living increases, subject to annual board approval.[668] By 2021, the total number of organizations that had joined across Ontario grew to fifty, with roughly 1,700 members.[669] Those who have joined OPTrust Select work in industries including health care, community support, and environmental advocacy.

a) Who Is Covered Under the OPSEU Pension Plan, and OPTrust Select?

Membership in the OPSEU Plan is mandatory or optional depending on the nature of employment. In general, membership in the OPSEU Plan mirrors the terms for the PSPP for members of OPSEU employed by the same employers, with some notable additions. These additional members of the OPSEU Plan include all employees of the OPTrust, employees who have been divested to another employer as a group and were previously OPSEU represented, and employees as set out in a participation agreement with a post-2012 employer (as of that date, the sponsors agreed that the OPTrust would accept a broader group of employers).[670]

---

666 See OPTrust, online: www.optrust.com/AboutOPTrust/News/OPTrust-Select-continues-growth-50-employers-enroled.asp#.

667 See OPTrust, online: www.optrust.com/AboutOPTrust/News/OPTrust-Launches-New-Plan-Expansion-Offering-OPTrust-Select.asp.

668 *Ibid.*

669 See OPTrust, online: www.optrust.com/AboutOPTrust/News/OPTrust-surpasses-100000-member-milestone.asp.

670 See Art 3 of the OPSEU Plan text, online: www.optrust.com/documents/Plan-Text.pdf [*OPSEU Plan text*]. Employers at the time of writing include the Province of Ontario (civil servants and Crown employees), Alcohol and Gaming Commission of Ontario, Centre for Addition and Mental Health, Legislative Assembly of Ontario, Liquor Control Board of Ontario (LCBO), Niagara Parks Commission, North Bay Regional Health Centre (Northeast Mental Health Centre), Ontario Agency for Health Protection and Promotion, Ontario College of Trades, Ontario Lottery and Gaming Corporation, Ontario Pension Board, Ontario Public Service

OPTrust Select covers employees in Ontario workplaces in the broader public sector, charitable, and not-for-profit groups that do not have a workplace defined benefit pension plan. Employers are accepted if they had a defined contribution plan, a group RRSP, or no retirement savings at all. OPTrust Select is available to management, bargaining unit, and non-bargaining unit staff in participating employers.[671] In order for an employee to join, their employer must participate in OPTrust Select and the employee must be eligible under the employer's participation agreement.

Membership in OPTrust Select[672] is mandatory for employees of an eligible group in a participating employer who are under sixty-five years of age and working on a full-time basis. Membership is optional for employees who are under age sixty-five and working on a less than full-time continuous basis or who are between the ages of sixty-five and seventy-one when they enroll. Membership is not available to those who are participating in the primary schedule of benefits under the OPSEU Plan, are receiving a pension from the OPTrust, are over age seventy-one, or are not part of an eligible group from their employer's participation agreement.

b) Administration and Governance

The OPTrust is responsible for investing and managing the OPSEU Pension Plan. As with the OPB, the OPTrust is also responsible for ensuring that the OPSEU Plan is administered in accordance with the plan terms, the *PBA*, the *ITA*, and other applicable legislation.[673]

The *Trust Agreement* governing the OPTrust creates the OPSEU Pension Plan Trust Fund (the OPSEU Pension Fund) and defines the duties, powers, and responsibilities of the trustees who are responsible

---

Employees Union (seconded or acting employees), Ontario Shores Centre for Mental Health Sciences, Ontario Teachers' Pension Plan Board, OPSEU Pension Plan Trust Fund (bargaining and non-bargaining unit employees), Providence Continuing Care Centre, St Joseph's Care Group—Lakehead Psychiatric Hospital, Waypoint Centre for Mental Health Care, and Workplace Safety and Insurance Appeals Tribunal.

671 See OPSEU, online: http://opseu500.ca/2018/04/24/optrust-launches-new-retirement-income-offering-optrust-select.

672 See OPTrust, online: www.optrustselect.com/members/index.html.

673 See, for example, *McHayle*, above note 658 at para 12.

for its administration and management of the assets.[674] Like all pension trustees, the trustees of the OPTrust are required to act in a fiduciary capacity, setting aside their own interests and making decisions exclusively in the best interests of the pension fund and its beneficiaries.

The OPTrust is governed by a board of ten trustees. Five trustees are appointed by the Crown and five are appointed by OPSEU.[675] Many of the trustees appointed have pension, risk, and other related experience. There do not appear to be term limits for the trustees.[676]

The board has a chair and a vice-chair, one of whom is a trustee appointed by OPSEU and the other of whom is a trustee appointed by Ontario. The positions of chair and vice-chair rotate between OPSEU and Ontario appointed trustees every two years.[677]

The powers, duties, and responsibilities of the trustees are broadly defined but do not extend to amending or terminating the plan. The power to amend and terminate is exclusively with the plan's sponsors, Ontario, and OPSEU,[678] which means any party (for example, a local bargaining agent or agency that is an employer) that wishes to change the benefits or other terms must obtain agreement of the sponsors.

While the board of trustees does not make decisions in regard to the plan's benefit levels or its normal contribution rates, it does have important responsibilities in relation to both. For example, the board of trustees provides important information about funding and how contribution rates connect to the current and expected funding needs of the plan, and this would inform any negotiations about contribution rates and benefits at the sponsor level. In addition, as the administrator of the OPSEU Plan, the board of trustees is responsible for its interpretation and application. Any ambiguities in the plan text fall to be interpreted and applied by the board of trustees, whose decisions are subject to review by the chief executive officer of the FSRA, and then the Financial Services Tribunal, both pursuant to the *PBA*.

---

674 Like the *Sponsorship Agreement*, above note 664, the *Trust Agreement* is not publicly accessible, although referenced in the *OPSEU Plan text*, above note 670 and on the OPTrust website. It was established in 1994 alongside the *Sponsorship Agreement*.

675 See OPTrust, online:www.optrust.com/abutters'/default.asp.

676 The lack of term limits is implied by the length of the appointment of some board members, given the lack of accessibility to the *Trust Agreement*.

677 See the OPTrust's board of trustees, online: www.optrust.com/aboutoptrust/Board-of-Trustees.asp [*OPTrust, board of trustees*].

678 Article 18.1 of the *OPSEU Plan text*, above note 670.

In addition to a number of standing committees, the board has established an ad hoc governance committee to provide recommendations on governance issues outside those covered by the standing committees. The Adjudication Panel provides plan members with a review process in the event of certain types of disputes, and the Concern Assessment Panel provides a forum for addressing complaints pursuant to the OPTrust's whistleblowing policy.[679]

c) Collective Bargaining

Any jointly trusteed pension arrangement must address the relationship between pension administration and collective bargaining. The role of a pension plan administrator is to implement the pension plan terms subject to legislative requirements and exercise their fiduciary responsibilities within the parameters of the documents that have created and established the pension arrangement. Pension standards require pension plans to be administered according to the documents in a consistent manner; however, the nature of those benefits can be changed by the sponsor, or in the care of a jointly sponsored pension plan like the OPSEU Plan, by the sponsors according to the process upon which they have agreed.

Pension benefits, including the contributions to the plan, form part of the pension plan members' broader compensation arrangements so they can be bargained subject to any applicable legislation, including that specific to the OPSEU Plan. Any potential change to the plan terms as a result of bargaining is subject to the agreement of the sponsors of the plan, Ontario, and OPSEU, as set out in the OPSEU Plan terms. Any employer or employer unit that agrees to join the OPSEU Plan is bound by the term that says they cannot change their pension benefits unless the sponsors agree.

The OPSEU Plan, like most public sector pension plans, is contributory, meaning that it is funded by both employee and employer contributions. As a jointly sponsored pension plan, employees and employers fully share the funding risks, and the sponsors of this plan (Ontario and OPSEU) have agreed to execute this shared funding responsibility via matched contributions. This means the sponsors have no arrangement for the employer to make top up or additional payments to the OPSEU Plan. Consistent with the *PBA* guarantee for accrued pension benefits, and as long as the OPSEU Plan remains an ongoing plan, the plan

679 See *OPTrust, board of trustees*, above note 677.

sponsors cannot bargain a reduction in benefits already accrued. Future benefits, contributions, and any other terms can be negotiated, subject to legislation and the terms of the plan itself. In the case of the OPSEU Plan, both the normal contribution rate and the benefits provided are subject to agreement and negotiation between the sponsors and, once agreed, are set out in the OPSEU Plan text.[680]

The OPSEU Plan includes unions other than OPSEU that have bargaining rights for Crown employees. Like any OPSEU-represented group, these unions, and their respective employers, cannot agree on changes to plan terms unless the plan sponsors agree to them. It is assumed that the sponsors will avoid a significant number of unique terms for groups of members in the plan, given the impact on administration efficiency.

3) Dispute Resolution for Pension Disputes

a) Appeal Process Within Pension Plans

i) Public Service Pension Plan

The OPB has established a complaints resolution process[681] for dealing with claims or issues raised by interested parties. The available process has changed over time and may change in future. While the FSRA's policies for pension plan administrators, and principles of good governance, both recommend a process, the specifics of the process are to be tailored to the circumstances of the plan, which may change. This process is available to anyone with a benefit entitlement issue.

The internal complaints resolution process at the OPB currently consists of three steps, culminating in a senior management review.[682] If the party is not satisfied by the resolution proposed after all three steps, then they may either appeal the decision to the FSRA or file a claim through the courts, as explained below.

ii) OPSEU Pension Plan

The OPTrust has established a two-step dispute resolution and appeals process, which also may change over time.[683]

---

680 *OPSEU Plan text*, above note 670, Arts 4 and 10.

681 See OPB, online: www.opb.ca/about-opb/reporting-transparency/complaints-resolution/complaints-resolution-process.

682 *Ibid.*

683 See OPTrust, online: www.optrust.com/aboutoptrust/Dispute-Resolution-Appeals-Process.asp.

Any plan member or beneficiary/alleged beneficiary who has a concern or disagrees with a decision made by the OPTrust, the OPTrust's administration, or their pension entitlement, may escalate their complaint through the member experience team to request a review. This involves a formal review by senior staff of the complaint or concern.

A dissatisfied party may request that their matter be escalated further. If the OPTrust's general counsel determines that the matter is within the scope of the process, then it can proceed to the Adjudication Panel. In order for a dispute to be heard by the Adjudication Panel, it must involve an administrative matter which affects the party's rights, entitlements, or benefits under the plan, and the party must have exhausted other avenues for resolution.

The Adjudication Panel is composed of four members of the OPTrust's board of trustees, two members appointed by OPSEU, and two members appointed by the Government of Ontario. The panel is responsible for acting as an impartial adjudicator in overseeing the adjudication process and may seek assistance from independent legal counsel in its deliberations. After deliberating, the Adjudication Panel will issue a written decision, which is final, although it may be appealed through the FSRA.

b) Jurisdiction of Grievance Settlement Board

The GSB[684] does not have equitable remedial powers to address pension issues other than the pension entitlements that arise out of the collective agreement directly through its provisions or through legislation.[685]

The OPSEU/MBC collective agreements refer to plan-related entitlements and include a general agreement for the parties to negotiate regarding the OPSEU Plan.[686] The *AMAPCEO/MBC Collective Agreement* contains similar provisions referring to plan provisions.[687] The specific plan-related entitlements set out in these provisions appear to be enforceable under the collective agreement, although they focus on the employment obligations that are interconnected to pension benefits.

---

684 Note the PSGB's specific statutory jurisdiction does not include pension matters. See Chapter 12.

685 See *Ontario Public Service Employees Union (Varcoe) v Ontario (Attorney General)*, 2019 CanLII 56388 (ON GSB) at para 8 and cases referenced.

686 *OPSEU/MBC Unified and Correctional Collective Agreements*, above note 193, Appendix 11.

687 See *AMAPCEO/MBC Collective Agreement, 2018–2022*, above note 497.

Given the legislative basis and independent documents which create and support both plans, as well as the complaint/remedy mechanisms for pension disputes noted below, the collective agreement processes are less frequently used for pension disputes. There was a period of some uncertainty about whether the OPSEU Plan was generally incorporated into the collective agreement, but this was settled when the OPSEU and the MBC negotiated a new appendix to their collective agreement,[688] stating that, while pension issues are bargainable, the pension plan does not form part of the collective agreement.

More recently, the GSB addressed a pension plan-related entitlement matter. The OPSEU/MBC collective agreements provided that while the employer would continue to pay the employee pension contributions for employees on long-term disability, employees with a minimum of thirty years credit in the OPSEU Pension Plan, or eligibility to retire now, had to pay their employee share. An employee on long-term disability required to resume such contributions challenged the provision. The GSB struck down the requirement of the collective agreement as contrary to the *HRC* and the *Charter* equality provision.[689]

c) Supervision by the Financial Services Regulatory Authority of Ontario and by the Courts

As both the PSPP and the OPSEU plan are pension plans under the *PBA*, the administration of those plans is subject to the same supervisory provisions as any other Ontario provincial pension plan. An individual who has exhausted the appeal process with the OPB or the OPTrust has three additional ways to seek recourse. First, the individual may pursue the claim through the FSRA, after which a decision issued by the tribunal may be subject to judicial review.[690] Second, the individual may attempt to bypass the adjudication and appeal processes of the FSRA and seek a judicial review of the plan's decision. Third, the individual may sue in tort, alleging breach of trust and/or negligence.

An affected individual may seek an order from the CEO of the FSRA. The FSRA was created under the *Financial Services Regulatory Authority*

688 *OPSEU/MBC Unified and Correctional Collective Agreements*, above note 193, Appendix 20 (introduced in the 2001–2004 OPSEU/MBC agreement).

689 *Ontario Public Service Employees Union v Ontario (Government & Consumer Services)*, 2021 CanLII 19542 (ON GSB) (Dissanayake) [*Government & Consumer Services*]. Note this case is discussed later in relation to the *Charter*.

690 For a recent example related to the OPTrust, see *McHayle*, above note 658.

of Ontario Act, 2016 (*FSRA Act*).[691] The CEO of the FSRA has general supervisory responsibility for pensions and several other regulated sectors, as well as for the management and administration of the FSRA. The powers and duties of the CEO with respect to pensions are further set out in the *PBA*. The *PBA* permits the CEO to issue an order requiring the administrator or any other person to take, or refrain from taking, any action in respect of a pension plan or fund.[692] The CEO may issue such orders only if they, on reasonable and probable grounds, believe that (1) the pension plan or pension fund is not being administered in accordance with the *PBA* or regulations, FSRA rules, or the pension plan itself; (2) the plan does not comply with the *PBA*, regulations, or FSRA rules; or (3) the administrator of the pension plan, the employer, or other person is contravening the *PBA*, regulations, or FSRA rules.

The FSRA's responsibilities relating to pension plans include responding to complaints from pension plan members, investigating breaches of the *PBA*, and issuing notices of intended decisions (NOIDs). If the FSRA issues a NOID, the party has thirty days to request a hearing before the tribunal or, if the NOID includes a proposed administrative monetary penalty, the party has fifteen days to request a hearing.[693]

Requests for hearings are considered by the tribunal, and the tribunal decides if the CEO should make or refrain from making the proposed NOID. Decisions of the tribunal may be appealed to the Ontario Divisional Court.[694]

As an alternative to the adjudication and appeal processes of the FSRA, an individual may seek a judicial review of the OPB or OPTrust decision itself. However, the decision to hear a judicial review is discretionary, and the court may defer in the matter to the FSRA.

In *Burns v Ontario (Pension Board)*,[695] an individual who had unsuccessfully proceeded through the OPB's review process, then applied to the Divisional Court for a judicial review of the OPB decision. The individual argued that nothing in the *PSPA* or the *PBA* limits

691 SO 2016, c 37, Sch 8.

692 *PBA*, above note 1, s 87(1).

693 *Ibid*, ss 87–89. For explanation of the general process, see FSCO and FSRAO, online: www.fsco.gov.on.ca/en/pensions/pension-plan-guide/pages/How-FSCO-Regulates-Pensions.html and www.fsrao.ca/enforcement-and-monitoring/enforcement-and-monitoring.

694 *Ibid*, s 91.

695 [1999] OJ No 3306 (SCJ).

the authority of the court to set aside the decision of the OPB. The Divisional Court accepted that a final decision of the OPB may be subject to judicial review but noted that judicial review is discretionary and found that the then Financial Services Commission of Ontario was the better forum for determining the matter.

Concerning an action in tort, it is well-established in caselaw that the relationship between pension administrators and members of a pension plan is sufficiently proximate as to give rise to a duty of care. The failure by the pension plan administrator to inform a plan member about their pension rights or a failure to otherwise act according to the standard of care could form the basis of a court claim alleging negligent misrepresentation or breach of fiduciary duty.[696] Such an action may be met by the defence that the issue should be addressed by the FSRA.

As in judicial review, there are often arguments about whether the court is the appropriate forum for the dispute. There have been a number of other cases in which the court has found it is the better forum for a pension dispute, despite the arguments of the FSCO/FSRA to the contrary.[697]

H. FEDERAL EMPLOYMENT INSURANCE/CANADA PENSION PLAN

Public servants and persons employed by an agency of the provincial government are engaged in insurable employment for purposes of the federal *Employment Insurance Act (EIA)*. As such, they are normally required to pay employment insurance premiums and are entitled to benefits in the event of unemployment. However, persons employed directly by the province outside the scope of the *PSOA*, either under a contract or under another statute, are not engaged in insurable

696 *Queen v Cognos Inc* (1993), 99 DLR (4th) 626 (SCC) at 643, relied on in *Spinks v Canada* (1996), 134 DLR (4th) 223 (FCA), which is the leading Canadian case finding liability for negligent misrepresentation relating the failure to inform a pension plan member about a buy-back opportunity. To the same effect, see *Deraps v Labourer's Pension Fund of Central and Eastern Canada*, [1999] OJ No 3281 (CA); *Hembruff v Ontario Municipal Employees Retirement Board*, [2004] OJ No 1355 (SC); *Canada (Attorney General) v Jost*, 2020 FCA 212.

697 See, for example, *Anova Inc Employee Retirement Pension Plan (Administrator of) v Manufacturers Life Insurance Co*, 1994 CanLII 7519 (ON SC); *Brewers Retail v Campbell*, 2022 ONSC 850.

employment, are not subject to the payment of premiums, and are not entitled to benefits on account of their employment by the province.

Insurable employment is defined in the *EIA* to be employment in Canada subject to exclusions. One of the excluded types of employment is "employment in Canada by Her Majesty in right of a province" (which reflects the constitutional distribution to the provinces of the power to regulate the terms of employment by a provincial government).[698] However, the *EIA* provides authority for the Employment Insurance Commission, with the approval of the federal Cabinet, to make regulations to include in insurable employment, "employment in Canada by Her Majesty in right of a province if the government of the province waives the exclusion and agrees to insure all its employees engaged in that employment."[699] The regulations[700] to the *EIA* allow a provincial government to waive exclusion and insure their employees. However, only employees who are "appointed and remunerated under an Act governing a specific province's public service" or who are employed by a provincial agent are thereby included. This maintains the exclusion of persons employed by the government outside the public service legislation. The Federal Court of Appeal has upheld this exclusion.[701] Given the express appointment provisions in the Ontario *PSOA*, it is clear that only Ontario government employees who are expressly appointed under the *PSOA* fall within the scope of the *EIA*.

The employment of emergency staff under the authority of the Ontario *Forest Fires Prevention Act*[702] has been found to be excluded employment by the Canada Revenue Agency,[703] though the basis of the decision was not made clear. Employment under the *Forest Fires Prevention Act* is not employment under the *PSOA*, which would explain the result. Ontario has not taken advantage of the federal government's offer (made in correspondence between federal and provincial ministers

---

698 *EIA*, above note 4, s 5(2)(c). See Chapter 1 regarding the constitutional context of the *PSOA*.

699 *Ibid*, s 5(4)(d).

700 *Employment Insurance Regulations*, approved SOR/96-332, PC 1996-1056, 28 June 1996, s 2.

701 *Re Meherally v Minister of National Revenue*, 1987 CanLII 5364 (FCA); *Bergeron v Canada (MNR)*, [1988] FCJ No 219 (CA). See also *Lybbert v Canada (MN)*, [1995] TCJ No 236 (TD).

702 RSO 1990, c F.24.

703 *Administrative Appeal*, unreported ref #CE00229 7111 6479, 5 June 2003.

in August 1985) to allow it, by order in council, to declare such employees to be provincial employees.

The provincial government is, from time to time, required to take control of a business in the public interest. Where that business retains its independent status, or becomes a Crown agent, the entity will be subject to the *EIA*, and premiums will be required. Where the government assumes direct control of an operation and employs the staff directly (for example, the Ministry of Health may take over direct operation of a health facility under the *Health Facilities Special Orders Act*[704] to prevent harm to a resident and may employ staff to accomplish this goal), the resulting employment will be excluded employment unless the staff are expressly employed under the *PSOA*. Where the Ontario government uses a third party to pay wages to persons not employed under the *PSOA*, the deemed employer provisions[705] will not apply to the third party.[706]

All employment by the provincial government and its agencies, with the exception of the employment of federally appointed judges, is pensionable employment for purposes of the Canada Pension Plan. Pensionable employment is defined in the *Canada Pension Plan Act*[707] to include all employment in Canada that is not "excepted" and all employment included by regulation. Employment by a province is excepted employment, but may be included as pensionable employment by regulation with the agreement of the province. Employment by the Province of Ontario and its agents has been included by regulation, with the limited exceptions for certain non-salaried individuals, and federally appointed judges.[708] Subject to the general exemptions in the Act (for example, certain casual employees), where the government funds the retention of a person to perform work, the common law test of whether or not the person is an employee will be applied to determine whether they are engaged in pensionable employment.[709]

704 RSO 1990, c H.5, s 7.

705 *Insurance Earnings and Collection of Premiums Regulation*, SOR/97-33, PC 1996–1932, 19 December 1996, s 10.

706 *Family Services London v MNR*, [2001] TCJ No 821 (TCC) at para 30 [*Family Services London*].

707 RSC 1985, c C-8, as amended, ss 6–7.

708 *Canada Pension Plan Regulations*, CRC c 385, s 24 (Sch III & IV).

709 *Castonguay v MNR*, [2002] TCJ No 352 (TCC). Note that the obiter comments in *Family Services London*, above note 706 at para 29 fail to recognize that excepted employment by Ontario is made pensionable by regulation.

I. *PUBLIC OFFICERS ACT* RE CANADIAN RESIDENCY

Under the Ontario *Public Officers Act*,[710] persons "employed in any public office" are to be a citizen or permanent resident of Canada. There is no requirement to renounce other allegiances, such as foreign citizenship. The term "public officer" is not a defined term under the Act, but it is used extensively in Canadian jurisprudence.[711] Offices are positions defined in legislation or that exercise a public duty or function. These would seem to include order-in-council appointments, and also perhaps public servants appointed under *PSOA* Part III and other government employees filling positions defined in legislation or charged with a specific public function.

By partial contrast, the federal public service has a Canadian citizenship preference within open competitions for public service positions.[712] In *Lavoie v Canada*,[713] the Supreme Court upheld that citizenship preference, on the basis that it enhances the value of citizenship,[714] and noted that citizenship preference is a feature of many nations' public service employment regimes.[715] The Court also observed, it seems favourably, that, in the United States, citizenship requirements at the state level have been found unconstitutional. The Court does not deal directly with requirements in provincial public service legislation in Canada.[716]

J. *CANADIAN CHARTER OF RIGHTS AND FREEDOMS*

The Supreme Court has ruled that an exercise of government power, whether carried out directly or through the negotiation or administration of a collective agreement, will be invalid if exercised in a manner contrary to the *Charter*, and that the relevant administrative tribunal

---

710 RSO 1990, c P.45.

711 *McLaughlin v Halifax-Dartmouth Bridge Commission*, [1993] NSJ No 420 (CA) at paras 27–28 and cases cited; *Comeau's Sea Foods Ltd v Canada (Minister of Fisheries and Oceans)*, [1995] 2 FC 467 at para 116.

712 *Public Service Employment Act*, RSC 1985, c P-33, s 16(4)(c).

713 2002 SCC 23 at para 22 [*Lavoie*].

714 The restriction was found to violate the *Charter* s 15 equality right of non-citizens but also to be a justifiable infringement of that right under s 1 of the *Charter* because it forwarded the valid federal government objective of enhancing the value and importance of citizenship.

715 *Lavoie*, above note 713 at para 101.

716 *Ibid* at para 56.

can and should give effect to the *Charter*.[717] This makes the government as employer subject to the *Charter*, and both the GSB[718] and PSGB[719] have taken jurisdiction to apply it.

Where the OPSEU/MBC collective agreements were amended to add that while the employer would continue to pay the employee pension contributions for employees on long-term disability, employees with a minimum of thirty years' credit in the OPSEU Pension Plan or eligible to retire now had to pay their employee share, the GSB struck down the provisions of the collective agreement as contrary to the *HRC* and the *Charter* equality provision.[720] This was done despite the fact that both parties had agreed to the clause:

> The law is clear and long accepted that the unions and employers cannot contract out of obligations under either the Charter or the Code. See, *Central Okanagan School District No 2B v Renaud*.[[721]] If provisions in a collective agreement are discriminatory, both the employer and the union are party to that.[722]

---

717 See *Lavigne v Ontario Public Service Employees Union*, [1991] 2 SCR 211 at 312–13, where La Forest J, for the majority, held:

> For reasons discussed in *McKinney v University of Guelph*, [(1990), 78 DLR 4th 545] I am of the view that the collective agreement is law. It was entered into by a government agency pursuant to powers granted to that agency by statute in furtherance of government policy. The fact that the collective agreement was agreed to by the [union] does not alter the fact that the agreement was entered into by government pursuant to statutory power and so constituted government action. To permit government to pursue policies violating Charter rights by means of contracts and agreements with other persons or bodies cannot be tolerated.

To the same effect, see *Douglas/Kwantlen Faculty Assn v Douglas College*, [1990] 3 SCR 570. See also Supreme Court in *Nova Scotia (Workers' Compensation Board) v Martin, Nova Scotia (Worker' Compensation Board) v Laseur*, 2003 SCC 54 for additional affirmation of the jurisdiction of a tribunal to deal with the *Charter*.

718 *OPSEU (Union) and Management Board Secretariat*, GSB#0001/03, 17 April 2003 (Stewart), where the GSB granted an application for interim relief partly on the basis that the union had asserted a plausible claim of violation of *Charter* rights.

719 *Morrison v Ontario (Human Rights Commission)*, PSGB#P/0037/94 and P0037/95, 8 December 1998 (Lynk) at 15–17.

720 *Government & Consumer Services*, above note 689.

721 *Renaud*, above note 285 at 985–86.

722 *Government & Consumer Services*, above note 689 at para 52.

CHAPTER SEVEN

CECBA Application, Structure, Scope/Exclusions, and Parties

A. SUMMARY

The *Crown Employees Collective Bargaining Act, 1993* (*CECBA*)[1] is significantly different in several areas from the standard labour relations regime set out in the *Labour Relations Act, 1995* (*LRA*).[2] Those differences increase labour relations stability and government control in the Ontario Public Service (OPS) and specified agencies.

Under the *CECBA*'s generally applicable provisions:

- The statute applies to the government itself, and to other employers specifically designated by regulation[3] (as discussed in Section B below).
- Fewer types of employees are included in bargaining units than under the *LRA*, due to an expanded list of exclusions (as discussed in Section D below).
- Employers remain separate from other employers due to the non-applicability of *LRA*-related employer provisions (as discussed further in Chapter 9).
- Essential services must be maintained during any strike or lockout (as discussed further in Chapter 8).
- Rights arbitrations are to be conducted by members of a single tribunal, the Grievance Settlement Board (GSB), with accompanying

1 SO 1993, c 38 as amended [*CECBA*].
2 SO 1995, c 1, Sch A [*LRA*].
3 O Reg 386/07, Prescribed Agencies, Crown as Employer.

expectations for consistency in procedure and jurisprudence, and some common remedial limitations, such as non-grievability of classifications (as discussed further in Chapter 11).

For the government itself, there are additional stability measures designed to support the *Public Service of Ontario Act, 2006* (*PSOA*)[4] regulation of employment and produce more orderly bargaining:

- Only employees formally appointed to employment by the employer are considered employees, meaning there can be no finding that dependent contractors are employees (as discussed in Section D below).
- Bargaining units are tailored and stabilized, and proliferation is avoided, through the requirement for a unique set of fixed bargaining units (as discussed in Section E below).
- In corrections uniquely, strikes are prohibited, and interest arbitration is required (as discussed in Chapter 8).

The present degree of balance between standard collective bargaining rights versus enhanced stability is the result of decades of gradual loosening of the legislative control of collective bargaining in the *CECBA*, and of greatly increased conformity with the *LRA*.[5] Particular aspects of that history concerning the government bargaining agent and the three government unions covered by the *CECBA*—the Ontario Public Service Employees Union (OPSEU), the Association of Management, Administrative and Professional Crown Employees of Ontario (AMAPCEO), and the Professional Engineers Government of Ontario (PEGO)—are set out in Section E below.

B. APPLICATION

The *CECBA* applies to

1) government in its labour relations with persons employed under Part III of the *PSOA*, who are those formally appointed employees working in ministries and in very closely associated entities that do not have separate human resources[6]

---

4 SO 2006, c 35, Sch A [*PSOA*].

5 For more detail about that history, see Chapter 1.

6 See Chapter 2 for discussion of *PSOA* Part III employment.

2) certain agencies prescribed by regulation, listed below along with their current union bargaining agent if any:
   - Algonquin Forestry Authority: no unionized employees
   - Liquor Control Board of Ontario: OPSEU (formerly the Ontario Liquor Board Employees Union)
   - McMichael Canadian Art Collection: no unionized employees
   - Metrolinx: Amalgamated Transit Union, Local 1587
   - Metropolitan Toronto Convention Centre Corporation: Labourers International Union of North America, Local 506
   - The Niagara Parks Commission: OPSEU, and Workers United Canada Council (an affiliate of the Service Employees International Union)
   - Ontario Cannabis Retail Corporation: OPSEU
   - Ontario Public Service Pension Board: OPSEU
   - Ottawa Convention Centre Corporation: United Steelworkers
   - Science North: no unionized employees
   - Workplace Safety and Insurance Appeals Tribunal: OPSEU
   - Workplace Safety and Insurance Board: Canadian Union of Public Employees, Local 1750[7]

The Act applies "with respect to the Crown, Crown employees and bargaining agents of Crown employees."[8] The term "Crown" is deemed to include the agencies prescribed by regulation,[9] and the term "Crown employee" is specifically defined to mean (1) a public servant employed under Part III of the *PSOA* and (2) a person employed by an agency of the Crown prescribed by regulation.[10] The rationale for the selection of the prescribed Crown agencies is not evident and seems based on historical proximity to the government itself[11] rather than any logical or consistent assessment of the consequences of the *CECBA* applying.[12]

The *LRA* does not directly apply to *CECBA* employers, their employees, and their unions in their capacity of *CECBA* employee representatives.[13] They are only subject to the individual provisions of the

7 O Reg 386/07, Prescribed Agencies, Crown As Employer.

8 *CECBA*, above note 1, s 1.1(1).

9 *Ibid*, s 1(1.1).

10 *Ibid*, s 1(1).

11 See discussion about the history of *CECBA* prescribed employers in Chapter 1.

12 For a discussion of the rationale for inclusion in the *CECBA* essential services regime, see Chapter 8.

13 *LRA*, above note 2, s 4(2).

LRA that have been incorporated into the *CECBA*[14] and only to the extent and in the manner that they have been incorporated into the *CECBA*. Non-*CECBA* employers, unions, and employees are not subject to the *CECBA* and cannot claim rights under the *CECBA*.[15]

C. STRUCTURE AND INCORPORATION OF *LABOUR RELATIONS ACT, 1995* PROVISIONS

The *CECBA* contains five main parts. Four of those parts establish unique requirements:

- Part III—Collective Bargaining (for government)
- Part III.1—Interest Arbitration—Correctional Bargaining Unit
- Part IV—Essential Services
- Part V—Grievance Settlement Board

Under Part II—Application of *Labour Relations Act*, the *LRA* is deemed to form part of the *CECBA*, but with modifications.[16] The incorporation of most *LRA* provisions ensures protection of collective bargaining freedoms, establishment of bargaining rights by certification, notice to bargain and access to voluntary and first contract arbitration, standard contents of collective agreements, mechanisms for displacement and termination of bargaining rights, and access to unfair labour practices. The major alterations are:

- non-application of *LRA* employee exclusions[17] as the *CECBA* has its own

---

14 *Federated Contractors Inc v Ontario*, 2003 CanLII 15957 (ON LRB) at para 2 [*Federated Contractors*] states:

> The Crown is not subject to the *LRA*. *CECBA* incorporates the *LRA*. The *LRA* is "deemed to form part of" *CECBA*. That is, the applicant, in order to obtain relief against the responding parties must seek its remedy under *CECBA*, but it cannot do so. Simply put, *CECBA* does not apply to the applicant. It is neither the Crown nor an agency of the Crown. Thus the applicant cannot apply for a remedy under *CECBA*, which it must do in order to establish that the responding parties violated provisions of the *LRA*.

Followed in *R v Ontario Secondary School Teachers' Federation*, 2012 CanLII 80016 (ON LRB) at paras 31–32 [*R v OSSTF*].

15 See *Federated Contractors*, above note 14 and *R v OSSTF*, *ibid*.

16 *CECBA*, above note 1, s 2.

17 *Ibid*, ss 3(1) and 3.1.

- non-inclusion of related employer provisions,[18] and modifications to the application of the successor rights provision[19]
- requiring an essential services agreement before a strike, lockout, or alteration of working conditions[20]
- alterations to the rights grievance arbitration provisions[21]

and some secondary alterations:

- changes to the voluntary and first contract interest arbitration provisions,[22] as discussed in Chapter 8
- removal of the authority of the Ontario Labour Relations Board (OLRB) in an unfair labour practice complaint to order "any term that would require either directly or indirectly for its implementation the enactment or amendment of legislation except for the purpose of appropriating money for its implementation"[23]
- requiring a claim for illegal strike or lockout damages to be arbitrated by the GSB rather than an arbitration board[24]
- removing the Lieutenant Governor in Council's power to regulate tribunal administration[25]

D. EMPLOYEE STATUS AND EXCLUSIONS

Individuals working at a *CECBA* employer are only to be included in a *CECBA* bargaining unit if they meet a twofold requirement. First, they must be a "Crown employee." Second, the person must not be excluded by any of the express exclusions in the *CECBA*.

1) Employee Status

The effect of the requirement to be a "Crown employee" varies considerably depending on whether the employer is the government or one

18 *Ibid*, s 3(1) & (2).

19 *Ibid*, s 10.

20 *Ibid*, ss 13, 15, and non-application of essential services to corrections due to its interest arbitration regime, s 15.1.

21 *Ibid*, ss 7 and 9.

22 *Ibid*, ss 4 & 5.

23 *Ibid*, s 16(2).

24 *Ibid*, s 17.

25 *Ibid*, s 20.

of the designated agencies. If the employer is the government, a worker must be formally appointed by the employer as a direct employee; while, if the employer is a designated Crown agency, the normal *LRA* tests apply, including assessing whether a nominally independent contractor is actually a dependent contractor, and so an employee.[26] For government, the *CECBA* only applies to a public servant employed under the terms of Part III of the *PSOA*.[27] The *PSOA* states "[a] person's status as an employee of the Crown in a ministry or a Commission public body is established only by appointment in writing"[28] and "for greater certainty a person's status as an employee of the Crown in a ministry or in a Commission public body cannot be inferred from his or her workplace or workplace activities."[29] Under the *CECBA*, the OLRB is given the jurisdiction to determine employee status, but subject to the explicit limitation that "no person shall be found to be a Crown employee unless he or she is a Crown employee" under the *CECBA*.[30] In the context of a complaint from an individual employed through a hiring agency alleging that they should be represented as an employee of the Crown, the OLRB denied the complaint and reiterated that "some positive act of appointment must be undertaken in order to achieve the status of a Crown employee."[31]

The effect of formal appointment is not only to establish "Crown employee" status under *CECBA*, unless one of the exclusions discussed below applies, but also to place the employee in one of the "designated bargaining units" within the unique collective bargaining structure for direct employees of government,[32] discussed in Chapter 8.

2) Exclusions

The *CECBA* only applies to persons who are not excluded by four categories of exclusions:[33]

---

26 See the incorporated *LRA*, above note 2, s 1(1) definitions of "dependent contractor" and "employee."

27 *CECBA*, above note 1, s 1(1).

28 *PSOA*, above note 4, s 52(1).

29 *Ibid*, s 52(2).

30 *CECBA*, above note 1, s 19(2).

31 *Anna Carroca v Ontario Public Service Employees Union*, 2016 CanLII 47182 (ON LRB) (McKee) at para 24.

32 *CECBA*, above note 1, s 23(1).

33 *Ibid*, s 1.1(3).

- Occupationally specific:[34] persons to whom the *Ontario Provincial Police Collective Bargaining Act, 2006* applies;[35] persons employed in their professional capacity—architects,[36] dentists,[37] lawyers,[38] physicians/doctors[39]—as well as provincial judges[40] and persons employed as a labour mediator or labour conciliator[41]
- Managerial/confidential to labour relations[42]
- Government functions
- Conflict of interest

The last two categories—government functions and conflict of interest—are unique in Ontario and are a variant of even broader historical special exclusions.[43]

a) General Approach

Since a purpose of the statute is to make collective bargaining available to Crown employees, the burden of proof is on the party seeking to apply an exclusion: "The serious consequences of exclusion merit acting only on clear evidence, but the basic standard is still the balance of probabilities."[44]

The scope[45] of the occupationally specific and some of the government function exclusions are relatively clear—for example, members of

34 *Ibid*, s 1.1(3)1–8.

35 SO 2006, c 35, Sch B. See the discussion of the OPP in Chapter 4.

36 See the discussion of the Professional Engineers of the Government of Ontario union below.

37 See the discussion re the Association of Physicians and Dentists in Public Service (AOPDPS) in Chapter 4.

38 See the discussion about lawyers, including members of the Association of Law Officers of the Crown and Ontario Crown Attorneys' Association in Chapter 4.

39 See the discussion re the AOPDPS in Chapter 4.

40 See the discussion re provincial judges and justices of the peace in Chapter 5, including that judicial officers are not normally considered employees.

41 For an analogous category of employee, see the discussion in the conflict of interest exclusion section below about occupational health and safety advisors.

42 *CECBA*, above note 1, s 1.1(3)9. The exclusion, "Employees exercising managerial functions or employed in a confidential capacity in relation to labour relations" is virtually identical to that found in the *LRA*, above note 2, s 1(3).

43 See *An Act to Provide for Collective Bargaining for Crown Employees*, SO 1972, c 67 [*CECBA 1972*], as discussed in Chapter 1.

44 *Ontario (Management Board of Cabinet)*, [1998] OLRB Rep Mar/April 180, [1998] OLRD No 1682 at para 45 [*Province of Ontario Savings Office and Ontario Financing Authority*].

45 *CECBA*, above note 1, s 1.1(3).

the Ontario Provincial Police or "persons employed in the Office of the Premier or in Cabinet Office"—but in other cases the wording of the exclusion—for example, "persons who provide advice to Cabinet" and the managerial/confidential exclusion—indicates an intention to make determinations about the performance of specific duties.[46] Persons in the same classification—for example, a large cadre of identically classified front line managers—should normally be subject to a common exclusion determination. That common determination allows collective agreement bargaining and administration to occur "on a class basis without the difficulties inherent in focusing on separate individuals for bargaining purposes."[47] However, there may be truly significant differences in how individuals perform that job. The GSB is, of course, open to the possibility that such differences exist. In one case to date, a common supervisory position with incumbents responsible for varying numbers of subordinates located throughout the province did show sufficiently significant differences that an incumbent-by-incumbent determination was ordered even though it would be "administratively inconvenient."[48] Litigation about whether "Sergeants"/"Operational Managers" in correctional institutions exercised true managerial functions was expected to be lengthy as the parties have acknowledged the roles of the sergeants could materially differ from institution to institution.[49]

Jurisdiction under the *CECBA* to determine whether the exclusions apply exists for, and has been taken by, both the OLRB[50] and the GSB.[51] Even when an OLRB application has been filed on the issue, the GSB

---

46 *Province of Ontario Savings Office and Ontario Financing Authority*, above note 44 at para 56.

47 *OPSEU (Bethel) and Ministry of Correctional Services, Crown in Right of Ontario*, OPSLRT#T/9/76, 6 April 1977 at 14 (Chair Shime) [*Bethel*].

48 *OPSEU (Vott, Harwood, et al) and Crown in Right of Ontario (Ministry of Revenue)*, OPSLRT#T/13/86, 8 September 1988 at 27 [*Vott, Harwood*], dealing with thirty-one managers of mapping services in regional assessment offices.

49 *Association of Management, Administrative and Professional Crown Employees of Ontario (Association) and the Crown (Ministry of the Solicitor General)*, GSB#2013-4247, 24 February 2022 (McLean) at 3 [*AMAPCEO 2013*].

50 Pursuant to its jurisdiction to determine employee status under *LRA*, above note 2, s 114(2), in *Province of Ontario Savings Office and Ontario Financing Authority*, above note 44.

51 The GSB has taken jurisdiction to determine an issue of employee status that has not been referred to the OLRB: *AMAPCEO (Union) and Management Board Secretariat*, GSB#2003-2754, 23 August 2004 (Brown) at 8 [*AMAPCEO and MBS, 2004*]. See also *Canadian Union of Public Employees, Local 1750 and (Ontario*

has elected not to defer its decision, noting that "the choice is between a specialized tribunal exercising its expertise under the terms of its constituent statute and an expert tribunal exercising a more general labour relations and employment mandate."[52] It was noted the GSB's extensive experience with public sector labour relations gives it a good grasp of the context and the GSB provides the parties with an opportunity to be involved in the governance of the GSB and to tailor their own procedures. By reason of these factors, deferral by the GSB to the OLRB was found not to be warranted.

b) Managerial/Confidential Exclusion

As the *CECBA* managerial/confidential exclusion is worded virtually identically to the *LRA* exclusion, the OLRB jurisprudence applies.[53] There are no cases in which the OLRB has applied that jurisprudence to the public service itself. The *CECBA*'s unique conflict of interest exclusion, discussed below, also needs to be considered because it covers similar employment and its application has overlapped with labour relations confidentiality.[54]

The cases decided under the pre-1993 *CECBA* by the Ontario Public Service Labour Relations Tribunal (OPSLRT), prior to its jurisdiction being transferred to the OLRB, remain useful but have to be approached with caution because managerial/confidential exclusion language broader than the current wording was in place at that time. The predecessor Act contained a very broad exclusion of a "person employed in a managerial or confidential capacity," which gave the government authority to unilaterally determine exclusions by deeming the position to be managerial or confidential. As of 1993, the *CECBA* adopted the *LRA* definition that bases exclusion on a person exercising managerial functions, or being employed in a confidential capacity in matters relating to labour relations. Persons were now only excluded

---

Workplace Safety and Insurance Board), GSB#0950/03, 2 September 2003 (Nairn) [*CUPE, Local 1750, 2003*] where jurisdiction was taken on consent.

52 *Ontario Public Service Employees Union (Union) v Ontario (Revenue)*, 2008 CanLII 70536 (ON GSB) (Herlich) at 14.

53 See *CUPE, Local 1750, 2003,* above note 51, where the GSB applied the standard OLRB jurisprudence to a position covered by the *CECBA*, that of a privacy officer at the Workplace Safety and Insurance Board.

54 For discussion of both the managerial/confidential and conflict of interest exclusions, see *Ontario Public Service Employees Union (Union) v Ontario (Revenue)*, 2010 CanLII 52645 (ON GSB) (Herlich) [*OPSEU v Revenue*].

if they actually performed managerial functions or if their confidential work related to labour relations. However, the following early observations of Owen Shime, the chair of the former OPSLRT, about government managers have continuing relevance:

> The result of all of these regulatory forces has, by and large, stripped first line management of its traditional roles. A first line supervisor no longer hires or fires. He has little if any input into the collective bargaining process, promotions are governed by the provision of the collective agreement as are rates of compensation and fringe benefits.
>
> ... On the other hand, and despite all these considerations which tend to confine and limit the scope of a front line supervisor, there is an area of decision making and authority which may be required. Generally speaking, management needs people to direct the work force. Not every aspect of the work environment can be reduced to a predetermined policy or be governed by regulation or by a collective agreement. Nor can all the problems, difficulties, needs, and requirements be anticipated in advance. In the result, there usually remains a circumscribed area where individual initiative and independent decision making may be required. It is in that shadowy area that the quality and quantity of the independent decision making or its absence must be assessed. Often it is very difficult to determine on which side of the managerial line an individual falls.[55]

It has also been noted that it is common for employees in higher classifications to provide technical or professional supervision to employees in lower classifications and yet continue to be members of the bargaining unit. It is only managerial supervision affecting the terms and conditions of employment of subordinates that warrants managerial exclusion.[56]

Some of the following determinations about managerial inclusions and exclusions were made under the pre-1993 *CECBA*.

i) Managerial

The following employees have been found to be managerial and not covered by the Act: a senior municipal supervisor whose decision-making

---

55 *Bethel*, above note 47 at 7–8, 11–12, as adopted in *Ontario Association of Correctional Managers and the Ministry of Correctional Services*, OPSLRT#T/25/91, 23 January 1992.

56 *Vott, Harwood*, above note 48 at 21–22.

latitude was narrow and subject to approval, yet the extent of his supervision, control, and independent decision-making power over government employees together with his total responsibilities placed him within the supervisory exclusion;[57] a senior correctional officer with full onsite responsibility for an entire institution after 5:00 p.m.;[58] a ward supervisor with additional responsibilities on the weekend;[59] a regional manager who had complete control of the operation in his geographic area and exercised independent decision-making authority with effective control over the workplace;[60] a food-service supervisor who participated in the hiring and training of new employees and gave performance appraisals and verbal and written warnings to employees without higher approval;[61] an assistant tenant-placement manager who was involved in imposing discipline, authorizing leaves, interviewing prospective employees, and dealing with grievances;[62] and a supervisor in rehabilitation and employment programs.[63]

ii) Bargaining Unit

The following persons have been found to be in the bargaining unit and not to be covered by the managerial exclusion: a person who made entries into inmate records, managed minor financial matters, deposited revenue received by inmates, and supervised the weekly purchases of supplies, along with other general office duties;[64] "managers" doing technical and professional supervision rather than managerial supervision;[65] unit supervisors whose only area of control was in the selection of staff;[66]

---

57 *OPSEU v The Crown in Right of Ontario (Ministry of Transportation and Communication)*, OPSLRT#T/0007/76, 18 April 1977.

58 *Bethel*, above note 47.

59 *OPSEU (James Atwood et al) v The Crown in Right of Ontario*, OPSLRT#T/57/84, 21 September 1987.

60 *Bethel*, above note 47 at 6–7.

61 *OPSEU v The Crown in Right of Ontario (Management Board of Cabinet*, OPSLRT#T/7/79, 26 March 1980.

62 *CUPE Local 3096 v The Crown in Right of Ontario (Ontario Housing Authority)*, OPSLRT#T/27/86, 24 July 1987.

63 *OPSEU (Lasani) and The Crown in Right of Ontario*, OPSLRT#T14/87, 2 May 1989.

64 *OPSEU v the Crown in Right of Ontario*, OPSLRT#T/4/76, 18 April 1977.

65 *Vott, Harwood*, above note 48.

66 *OPSEU (Neely and Stewart) v The Crown in Right of Ontario (Ministry of Transportation)*, OPSLRT#T/67/89, 9 December 1991.

and shift supervisors who did not routinely exercise any supervisory powers.[67]

c) Exclusions Related to the Functioning of Government

i) "Provide Advice" Exclusion

Persons who "provide advice" at a senior level on certain issues are covered by certain exclusions.[68] There are no cases on these exclusions, but a pre-1993 case dealing with earlier sections provides some guidance on how these provisions might be interpreted. Where a research economist provided input into policy initiatives, there was an issue of whether they were excluded by the former managerial exclusion for persons who were "involved in the formulation of organization objectives and policy." The OPSLRT held that the section did not intend to exclude suppliers of information or suggestions, but only those who "play a vital and decisive role in the decision-making process."[69]

ii) Finance Exclusion

The finance exclusion[70] for employees who borrow, invest, and manage money, has been applied. Retail customer service representatives at the Ministry of Finance's then Province of Ontario Savings Office (POSO), who acted like bank tellers, were found not to be persons engaged in borrowing, investing, or management of the province's assets,[71] nor were they engaged in providing the related support services. There was no evidence that anyone employed to manage the assets and liabilities of the Consolidated Revenue Fund (CRF) required those customer service representatives' services to carry out the activities that are the focus of the exclusion.[72] The coordinator, branch services, who supervised the financial operations of retail POSO branches, was also not excluded[73] as the bulk of their duties were not engaged in managing the CRF, nor in supporting any excluded employee's cash-tracking functions.

67 *OPSEU Re The Crown in Right of Ontario (Ministry of Health/Thames Valley Ambulance)*, OPSLRT#T/79/91, 17 September 1997.

68 *CECBA*, above note 1, ss 11(3)12 & 13.

69 *OPSEU v The Crown in Right of Ontario*, OPSLRT#T/3/76, 6 April 1977 at 14.

70 *CECBA*, above note 1, s 11(3)14.

71 *Province of Ontario Savings Office and Ontario Financing Authority*, above note 44 at para 91.

72 *Ibid* at para 95.

73 *Ontario (Management Board of Cabinet)*, [2002] OLRD No 432 at para 43 [*MBC, 2002*].

Positions that involved making management or trading decisions about provincial treasury monies were excluded.[74] A revenue control analyst, who made screening decisions about cheques being deposited into the CRF,[75] did not exercise any actual meaningful, independent decision-making authority, but was excluded because they did provide technical, specialized, or clerical "services" necessary to support the activities of excluded persons who managed the CRF. The OLRB found that if the revenue control analysts went on strike, the government would lose an average of $54 million per day in revenue because nobody would be available to process cheques.

d) Conflict of Interest Exclusion

The *CECBA* contains a conflict of interest exclusion for persons with duties or responsibilities that, in the OLRB's opinion, constitute a conflict of interest with their status as members of a bargaining unit.[76] There is no equivalent in the *LRA*. The exclusion is limited in scope, referring only to membership in the bargaining unit, and so there must be clear evidence that the membership itself has produced conflicting loyalties that jeopardize the employee's ability to perform the assigned duties.[77] The exclusion should only be used in exceptional circumstances, particularly if the employee in question has been a member of the bargaining unit for some time "without any impairment of his functions."[78] The claim that it is onerous for the collective agreement to apply to a position should not be accepted as justifying exclusion because "[t]o go down that road is to conclude that only when the terms of the agreement are advantageous to the employer is there no conflict of interest."[79]

Bargaining unit membership is generally compatible with the performance of sensitive and confidential positions, provided only that the

---

74 *Province of Ontario Savings Office and Ontario Financing Authority*, above note 44 at para 26.

75 *MBC, 2002* above note 73 at paras 20–22.

76 *CECBA*, above note 1, s 11(3)15.

77 *CUPE, Local 1750, 2004* above note 51 at para 38. Another formulation of the standard is that "it must be demonstrated that there exists the real likelihood" of conflict of interest: *OPSEU v The Crown in Right of Ontario (Ministry of Labour)*, OPSLRT#T/53/87, 8 May 2008 at 17 [*OPSEU v Labour*].

78 *The Crown in Right of Ontario v OPSEU*, OPSLRT#T/10/76, 23 December 1977 at 6 [*Crown v OPSEU, December 1977*].

79 *OPSEU and Ontario*, [1998] OLRB Rep May/June 400 at para 26, rev'd *Ontario (AG) v OPSEU* (1999), 180 DLR (4th) 549 (Ont Div Ct), upheld (2000), 52 OR (3d) 77 (CA) [*OPSEU and Ontario, 1998*].

positions are not concerned with labour relations and human resources management, which proviso has resulted in excluding both the assistant to an assistant deputy minister responsible for a large division, whose duties included supporting human resources negotiations and conflict of interest determinations,[80] and a position known as "category lead" responsible for considering alternative service delivery options that may result in outsourcing bargaining unit work should be excluded:

> In order to perform their job appropriately, the Category Lead must be free, and be seen to be free, to assess all of the options openly and fully, and without regard to any potential impact that one option might create for their coworkers. They are otherwise put in the position of having divided loyalties. The exclusion is designed to protect such individuals from being put in such a position. The exclusion recognizes that they ought not to have to bear that responsibility.[81]

In contrast, a privacy officer at the Workplace Safety and Insurance Board may deal with information of substantial confidentiality and sensitivity, but this is not information that generates a conflict between employment and union obligations, as "being a member of a bargaining unit does not diminish the trust and loyalty of employees in their performance of the work of the employer."[82]

The secretaries of federally appointed judges can be in a bargaining unit without compromising judicial independence.[83] The Court of Appeal has held that the concept of judicial independence does not automatically deprive employees who work with judges of the right to union membership.[84] Since those secretaries did not report to the judge that they worked with, but reported to a Ministry of the Attorney General management official, unionization of the secretaries does not deprive judges of any pre-existing independent authority.[85] If unilateral government management is not a threat to judicial independence, then neither is unionization. The Court of Appeal determined that the most serious potential for interference with judicial independence was in the

---

80 *OPSEU v Revenue*, above note 54.

81 *Canadian Union of Public Employees, Local 1750 v Ontario (Workplace Safety and Insurance Board)*, 2007 CanLII 51781 (ON GSB) (Nairn) at 11.

82 *CUPE, Local 1750, 2003*, above note 51 at para 53.

83 *OPSEU and Ontario, 1998*, above note 79.

84 *Ibid* at para 21.

85 *Ibid* at para 20.

event of a strike or lockout, but noted that the OLRB had declared that judges' secretaries were essential and therefore required to work in the event of a strike or lockout.[86]

Several conflict of interest cases from the pre-1993 *CECBA* appear to have ongoing relevance. The former Act excluded persons "employed in a managerial or confidential capacity" by enumerating the specific managerial duties that would warrant exclusion. The last enumerated managerial exclusion was for persons who "in the opinion of the Tribunal should not be included in a bargaining unit by reason of his duties and responsibilities to the employer."[87] Pursuant to that subsection, the employer sought to exclude certain positions for reasons other than the exercise of managerial and confidential functions.

Where an industrial development officer 3, employed in the Ministry of Industry and Tourism, consulted with companies about manufacturing problems, including, on occasion, the possibility of the company closing because of "union problems," the mere fact that somebody outside the government might object to a public servant's own union involvement was not sufficient to justify exclusion. The OPSLRT was reluctant to accept that "there is a natural antipathy between union and management"[88] and preferred "to operate from the philosophical stance that greater cooperation between union and management will have a positive impact on the enterprise that both are involved in with a real benefit for all."[89] If an employee's active involvement in a union posed a real concern, then the employee could be transferred or the tribunal could reassess the situation.[90] A similar result was arrived at concerning provincial prosecutors.[91] They were not lawyers, but they exercised discretion with respect to the initiation of proceedings, the calling of cases, the withdrawal of charges, plea bargaining, disclosure, and recommendations for appeals. Any case involving the union (or its members) as a defendant could be dealt with by Crown attorneys.

---

86 *Ibid.* See the comment by Cameron J dissenting on legislative intent and the essential-services agreement at para 45.

87 *CECBA 1972*, above note 43, s 1(1)(m)(viii).

88 *Crown v OPSEU, December 1977*, above note 78 at 7.

89 *Ibid* at 6–8.

90 *Ibid* at 9–10.

91 *OPSEU (Collins et al) and The Crown in Right of Ontario*, OPSLRT#T/66/84, 14 April 1988, aff'd by Divisional Court, 12 October 1989 (unreported) and by the Court of Appeal, 16 July 1990 (unreported).

A different result was arrived at concerning occupational health and safety advisors. They assisted workplace parties in mediating disputes in the labour relations/health and safety fields. The OPSLRT found that mediation services must be provided neutrally and "[a]lthough [union] affiliation may not, in fact, compromise neutrality, it could be seen to have this effect and thereby impair the confidence of the parties and the service being provided."[92]

E. GOVERNMENT BARGAINING PARTIES AND THEIR JURISDICTIONS

1) Government Employer: Management Board of Cabinet, as Represented by Treasury Board Secretariat

The government's collective bargaining is overseen by the Management Board of Cabinet (MBC), a Cabinet committee,[93] and carried out by the Treasury Board Secretariat (TBS), formerly Management Board Secretariat (MBS), the ministry responsible for overseeing labour relations between the government and the public service and broader public sector. The TBS and the three *CECBA* unions representing government employees outside corrections—OPSEU, AMAPCEO, and PEGO—each have their own joint government-wide Central Employee Relations Committee and, separately for the Correctional Bargaining Unit, the TBS and OPSEU have a Bi-Ministry Employee Relations Committee.[94] Under the *Confidential Disclosure to Bargaining Agents Directive*,[95] and "[i]n recognition of the principle that positive labour relations needs to be based on a foundation of the timely sharing of appropriate and relevant information," the government is to make confidential disclosure two weeks in advance to bargaining agents both centrally, and at the ministry level,

---

92 *OPSEU v Labour*, above note 77.

93 *Management Board of Cabinet Act*, RSO 1990, c M.1, s 3(1). See the discussion of the MBC and Treasury Board Secretariat in Chapter 2.

94 See the *OPSEU/MBC Unified Bargaining Unit Collective Agreement, 2022–2024* and *OPSEU/MBC Correctional Bargaining Unit Collective Agreement, 2018–2021*, online: https://opseu.org/information/general/find-your-collective-agreement, Art 16; *AMAPCEO/MBC Collective Agreement, 2018–2022*, online: https://amapceo.on.ca/ops, Art 12: *PEGO/MBC Collective Agreement, 2019–2022*, online: https://pego.on.ca/pego-collective-agreements, Art 27.

95 MBC, *Confidential Disclosure to Bargaining Agents Directive*, 12 May 2017, online: www.ontario.ca/page/confidential-disclosure-bargaining-agents.

of business decisions that will "materially and substantially" affect the working terms and conditions of unionized employees. The examples of corporate initiatives to be disclosed include relevant legislative policy initiatives, divestments, layoffs, and relocations. The information to be disclosed is to include reasons for the decision, the names of affected employees, and the effects on them. The bargaining agents are to keep the disclosed information confidential until the employer's announcement. The directive does not apply in listed circumstances including throne speeches, budgets, "where there has been a breach of the confidentiality undertaking," and within ninety days of the transition to a new government.

2) Trade Unions

a) Statutory Treatment of Representation

Under the *CECBA*, outside the government there is no legislative determination of union representation or bargaining units.[96] Inside government, the legislation[97] "continues" three unions as bargaining agents for the employees in specific "designated" bargaining units:

- OPSEU continues as representing the "Unified Bargaining Unit" and the separate "Correctional Bargaining Unit"
- PEGO continues as representing the employees in the "Engineer Bargaining Unit"
- AMAPCEO continues as representing the employees in the "Fourth Bargaining Unit"

and the legislation establishes these units as the only possible bargaining units for government Crown employees.

The continued bargaining agents are subject to the displacement or termination of bargaining rights provisions in the *LRA*[98] with the following three adjustments:[99]

96 This has not always been the case as, under prior versions of the *CECBA*, the government authorized unions to represent the bargaining units of designated agencies. See Chapter 1 re the *CECBA*.

97 *CECBA*, above note 1, ss 23 & 24.

98 *Ibid*, s 24(4).

99 There are other time limited transitional provisions in the *CECBA*, contained in ss 24(5) and 26, that no longer apply.

1) The provision in the *LRA* allowing early termination of a bargaining agent that has not been certified by the OLRB does not apply.[100] This provision addresses the fact that OPSEU was never certified by the OLRB, as discussed below in the history of the union.
2) Any displacing union must be certified for the entire bargaining unit, and not a part,[101] as all Crown employees in government must be in one of the four units. The effect of this provision has been addressed by the OLRB in dismissing another union's application to represent correctional employees with the job titles of "sergeant" and "youth service manager."[102] The OLRB found that

   > the legislature has clearly mandated . . . that all public servants in Ontario not specifically excluded by the legislation be employed in one of four bargaining units—the two units represented by OPSEU, the unit represented by AMAPCEO, or the unit represented by PEGO. [The *CECBA*] anticipates that the bargaining agent identified by *CECBA* as representing the employees in these bargaining units may be displaced by a third party bargaining agent

   and that any displacing union must apply for certification of the entire unit as *CECBA* "does not provide a third party bargaining agent . . . with the opportunity to apply for certification to represent certain employees included within the bargaining units identified by the legislation," and there is no allowance for a fifth unit.[103] This is in keeping with the long-standing statutory intention to avoid "fragmentation and balkanization" of bargaining units within government.[104]

---

100 *Ibid*, s 24(6); *LRA*, above note 2, s 66.

101 *CECBA*, above note 1, s 23(1).

102 *Public Service Alliance of Canada v The Crown in Right of Ontario*, 2017 CanLII 51086 (ON LRB) (Shouldice) [*PSAC, 2017*], confirming dismissal of a long-standing application by PSAC to represent front-line corrections supervisors after an extensive litigation history referring to a prior version of the *CECBA*, including *R v Public Service Alliance of Canada*, 2014 CanLII 9886 (ON LRB) [*PSAC, 2014*] and *Public Service Alliance of Canada v The Crown In Right of Ontario*, 2016 CanLII 5565 (ON LRB) [*PSAC, 2016*].

103 *PSAC, 2017*, *ibid* at paras 23–24.

104 Statement about the intent of the *CECBA 1993*, from the testimony of MBS Policy Advisor Kevin Wilson in *PSAC, 2016*, above note 102 at para 20.

3) The Unified Bargaining Unit and the Correctional Bargaining Unit are to be represented by the same bargaining agent.[105] The two units have bargained separately, since the *CECBA* amendments in 2016, and this raises the question of why it is required that they both be represented by the same union. It stems from the prior history, discussed below, of both units always being represented by OPSEU and having interconnected terms and conditions of employment.[106] The two OPSEU units still share the same pension plan and health benefits administration. There is also agreement that seniority in one unit will be recognized in the other and that "employment mobility" between units will be maintained for many collective agreement purposes.[107] It remains to be decided whether this complex interconnection does sufficiently justifiy the requirement of common representation to withstand any constitutional challenge alleging a lack of freedom of choice of collective bargaining representative.[108]

As between OPSEU and AMAPCEO, there has been a lengthy jurisdictional dispute over classifications that are "on the border" between the recognition clauses of the collective agreements for their government units.[109]

b) Ontario Public Service Employees Union

The Civil Service Association of Ontario (CSAO) was formed in the spring of 1911 when 200 government workers met at Queen's Park to discuss "improving the [civil] service, promoting social togetherness, urging healthy athletics, and co-operating with one another in the purchasing of supplies."[110] In 1927, the CSAO incorporated itself, apparently to limit liability for debts arising out of the association's cooperative purchasing.[111] OPSEU remains a corporation under the

---

105 *CECBA*, above note 1, s 24(7).

106 For further historical context, see Chapter 1.

107 See the discussion in Chapter 8 on corrections interest arbitration.

108 See *Mounted Police Association of Ontario v Canada (Attorney General)*, 2015 SCC 1.

109 See the jurisdictional disputes section below.

110 Wayne Roberts, *Don't Call Me Servant* (Toronto: Ontario Public Service Employees Union, 1994) at 12–13.

111 *Ibid* at 28–29.

Corporations Act.[112] The mid-twentieth century history of the CSAO and its relationship with government can be traced through accommodating amendments to the early *Public Service Act* (*PSA*).[113] Then, in the late 1960s, the government began to consider introducing modernized and customized collective bargaining legislation, and commissioned a judicial report. Judge Little described the CSAO as evolving from "socially-oriented organization" into a "duly constituted, independent and progressive bargaining agent," that was effective in "representing on a voluntary basis the interests of all those for whom it bargain[ed]."[114] Judge Little opined that the public interest would be best served if employment relations in the public service was not fragmentable by the introduction of new units. Under the *CECBA 1972*,[115] OPSEU was designated by regulation as the employee organization with representation rights for the public service.[116]

Following the enactment of the *CECBA 1972* , there was a growing desire in the CSAO membership for a more formal union structure and approach.[117] At a 1975 special general meeting, the delegates approved the change of name from the CSAO to OPSEU.[118] Shortly thereafter, OPSEU accepted chartered membership in the Canadian Labour Congress.[119] That year, OPSEU also passed a new constitution that forms the basis of OPSEU's current constitution.[120] The constitution establishes a centralized model with union locals and shop stewards, offset by a regional political structure where seven geographical regions elect board members in their own area before elections for president and vice-president/treasurer are held.

---

112 RSO 1990, c C.38.

113 For a brief history of the evolution of collective bargaining in the Ontario Public Service, see Chapter 1.

114 *Report of the Special Advisor, Hon Judge Walter Little, on Collective Bargaining in the Ontario Government Service* (Toronto: Queen's Printer, May 1969) at 7.

115 *An Act to Provide for Collective Bargaining for Crown Employees*, SO 1972, c 67.

116 O Reg 577/72.

117 Speech by President C.J. Darrow, CSAO, *Minutes of Annual General Meeting*, November 1974, Section M at 7; *Reorganization Committee Report* (Director Ron Haggett, Chairman), passed in principle at CSAO Special General Meeting, June 13 and 14, 1975: Report in Minutes at 1–15, and motion at Minutes at 18.

118 Special General Meeting, *ibid* at 20; supplementary letters patent formally changed the name of the corporation in October 1975.

119 OPSEU Annual General Meeting, 29 October–2 November 1975, Minutes at 26.

120 *Ibid* at 51. The OPSEU constitution is on the OPSEU website, online: www.opseu.org.

Under the *CECBA 1972*, OPSEU and the government continued a pre-existing pattern of separate bargaining negotiations, largely on wages, for different categories of employees within the single public service bargaining unit. In 1979–80, a correctional officer category was added following an illegal strike by correctional officers, and a related interest arbitration award advising that a separate category would provide the needed forum for focused attention to correctional workplace issues.[121]

In 1993, the *CECBA* was substantially modernized to, in part, reduce the large number of excluded staff, establish a statutory structure for bargaining that built on OPS practice, and create the right to strike.[122] The bargaining structure is discussed below, while the right to strike is discussed in Chapter 8.

The government wanted to retain a structure of large stable bargaining units.[123] Smaller units were seen as lacking the strength and authority to operate effectively. Larger units were viewed as having the capacity and authority needed for "stable and efficient" bargaining. The Lieutenant Governor in Council exercised authority under the Act to designate seven bargaining units.[124]

Six of those bargaining units were based on the pre-existing categories—administrative, correctional, institutional and health care, office administration, operational and maintenance, and technical—and were designated to be represented by OPSEU.[125] This was done within a newly designed and unique structure that involved collective bargaining and collective agreements in each of these six designated units on many issues, including wages and, simultaneously, in a combined "central" unit, collective bargaining, and a central collective agreement on issues

---

121 *Management Board of Cabinet and Ontario Public Service Employees Union: Dispute Re Correctional Employees*, 21 December 1979 (Arthurs) at 6–7 and 10. For discussion of present interest dispute resolution in corrections, see Chapter 8.

122 *CECBA*, above note 1, introduced through the *Public Service and Labour Relations Statute Law Amendment Act*, SO 1993, c 38 [Bill 117].

123 See the discussion about bargaining unit structure in Chapter 1.

124 Order-in-Council No 234/94, 3 February 1994.

125 Bill 117, above note 122, s 24, and Order-in-Council No 127/94, 19 January 1994. The description of these units was subject to discussion between OPSEU as the principal bargaining agent and the government prior to their designation. See Ontario Legislative Assembly, *Hansard*, 18 November 1993, No 84 at 4145 (Mike Cooper, Parliamentary Assistant to the Minister of Labour), where the government spokesperson refers to "a process of consensus between all parties."

deemed by statute to be common across all the OPSEU represented units. The central issues included employment security and mobility, pensions, long-term disability insurance plans, and common benefits. As this hybrid bargaining continued over multiple rounds, the issues for all the non-correctional units became more and more common, while the correctional issues remained distinct.[126] In 2001, OPSEU and the government agreed to the consolidation of the six designated units into two: the Unified Bargaining Unit and the Correctional Bargaining Unit.[127] However, both those designated units also remained within a common central agreement until 2016.

In 2016, *CECBA* amendments[128] implemented an OPSEU and MBC agreement[129] to establish the following:

- entire separation of the collective bargaining and collective agreements for the Unified Bargaining Unit and the Correctional Bargaining Unit
- the Unified Bargaining Unit remaining in the strike/essential services regime common to *CECBA* employers
- the Correctional Bargaining Unit uniquely coming under an interest arbitration regime

This included expanding the Correctional Bargaining Unit to include all members of the Unified Unit headquartered at correctional

---

126 For example, OPSEU brought an application to the OLRB seeking greater corrections autonomy on a wider range of issues: *Ontario Public Service Employees Union v Management Board Secretariat*, 2002 CanLII 19374 (ON LRB) (Chair Whitaker).

127 *Memorandum of Agreement between Management Board of Cabinet and OPSEU*, 18 December 2001 at para 2. And see the treatment of recognition clauses in *OPSEU/MBC Unified and Correctional Collective Agreements*, above note 94, Appendix 2, UN 1.1 and COR 1.1.

128 *Building Ontario Up for Everyone Act (Budget Measures), 2016*, SO 2016, c 37, Sch 6, Bill 70, *An Act to implement Budget measures and to enact and amend various statutes*; Sch 6—*Crown Employees Collective Bargaining Act, 1993*.

129 These amendments were the result of the *Memorandum of Agreement between the Crown and OPSEU in the matter of Development of a Standalone Collective Agreement for the Correctional Bargaining Unit*, 23 November 2015, further discussed in Chapter 8, that was supported by secret ballot votes of the Correctional Bargaining Unit membership and of the Unified Bargaining Unit staff that worked in correctional work locations and who were to become members of the Correctional Bargaining Unit: *OPSEU Newsletter*, 17 November 2015, 18 December 2015, and 27 January 2016.

institutions, such as administrative staff, nurses, social workers, chaplains, and library technicians,[130] as well as the previously included correctional staff and probation and parole staff.

The two separate collective agreements, in place since 2018, and the two *CECBA* interest dispute resolution regimes—strike/essential services and corrections interest arbitration—are discussed in Chapter 8.

The seventh designated bargaining unit created in 1993 comprised all Crown employees who were public servants and not included in the other six bargaining units, other than excluded, engineers, and lawyers. The seventh bargaining unit was initially without a bargaining agent.

c) Association of Management, Administrative, and Professional Crown Employees of Ontario

Under the *CECBA 1972*, there were a large number of non-unionized but also non-managerial employees across the Ontario government. An informal coalition of various ministerial and regional associations had represented those employees. These associations were not trade unions or employee organizations and did not have any formal collective bargaining status, although they may have been consulted from time to time by the government or the particular ministry on issues affecting their members. AMAPCEO was formed out of these groups in 1992.[131]

The pending *CECBA 1993*[132] amendments made it clear that a large number of the non-unionized non-managerial employees were to be brought into the collective bargaining regime.[133] As mentioned in the managerial exclusion section above, the predecessor 1972 Act contained the expansive exclusion of a "person employed in a managerial or confidential capacity," which gave the government authority to unilaterally determine exclusions by deeming the positions to be managerial or confidential. The *CECBA 1993* adopted the *LRA* definition that a person is not an "employee" if that person exercises managerial functions or is employed in a confidential capacity in matters relating to labour relations. Persons were now only to be excluded if they actually

---

130 OPSEU/MBC *Memorandum of Understanding*, 23 January 2018.

131 The AMAPCEO website is found at www.amapceo.on.ca.

132 Bill 117, above note 122.

133 The estimate in 1993 was 9,000 additional previously excluded public servants were placed into bargaining units, with 2,000 joining OPSEU units and 7,000 in the seventh unit; see Ontario Legislative Assembly, *Hansard*, 18 November 1993, No 84 at 4145 (Mike Cooper, Parliamentary Assistant to the Minister of Labour).

performed managerial functions or if their confidential work related to labour relations.

After consulting with its membership, OPSEU's position was that any formerly-excluded employees should be moved into the bargaining units represented by OPSEU, but with comparatively limited seniority rights.[134] The formative AMAPCEO's response was that this would result in a significant disadvantage to previously excluded employees, leaving them as "second class" members in OPSEU.[135] It was claimed by AMAPCEO that, by making this distinction, OPSEU was giving up its claim to be the rightful bargaining agent for these excluded employees. AMAPCEO sought the establishment of a separate bargaining unit for employees previously excluded from the *CECBA*.[136]

In the meantime, AMAPCEO was designated as a bargaining agent pursuant to the *Social Contract Act, 1993* and negotiated a social contract local agreement with the provincial government on behalf of thousands of excluded employees.[137] The designation of AMAPCEO as a bargaining agent for the purposes of the *Social Contract Act, 1993* did not mean that AMAPCEO was accorded trade union status generally, but the local agreement did bind the Crown employees covered by the agreement.[138]

In 1995, AMAPCEO applied for certification of the seventh unit and, in response, AMAPCEO and the Crown entered into a voluntary recognition agreement[139] that also set out a process for resolving the placement of a number of contested positions. The agreement required AMAPCEO to establish it had majority support of the employees within the bargaining unit. Subsequently, the OLRB determined that

134 OPSEU, "It's Time for Change: Report on Talks for a New Law to Govern Public Service Bargaining," April 1992 at 6, as quoted in Evert A. Lindquist & Graham White, "Streams, Springs, and Stones: Ontario Public Service Reform in the 1980s and the 1990s" (1994) 37:2 *Canadian Public Administration* 267 at 288–90.

135 AMAPCEO, *Concerns of Currently Excluded Employees*, 15 September 1992 at 4.

136 See AMAPCEO, *Reform of the Crown Employees Collective Bargaining Act—A Response to the Employer's Report—Submission to the Ministry of Labour prepared by the Association of Management, Administrative and Professional Crown Employees of Ontario*, February 1993.

137 *Social Contract Act, 1993*, SO 1993, c 5, s 5.

138 *G Hughes and the Government in Right of Ontario (Ministry of the Environment and Energy)*, Public Service Classification Ratings Committee #C/0033/93, 14 August 1995 at 9.

139 Crown in Right of Ontario and AMAPCEO, *Voluntary Recognition Agreement*, 23 March 1995.

AMAPCEO did enjoy majority support and found that it was a trade union within the meaning of the *LRA*.[140]

From its start in 1993, AMAPCEO bargained entirely separately from OPSEU and was not part of the OPSEU oriented central agreement structure. This was done in a "pragmatic manner" by the parties despite the *CECBA* continuing to reference the seventh designated bargaining unit as being part of the central collective agreement along with the OPSEU designated bargaining units.[141] This oddity was not clarified until the 2016 *CECBA* amendments set out the entire separateness of the bargaining for the AMAPCEO agreement.

In 2008, it was proposed by the TBS (then called Management Board Secretariat) that a majority of AMAPCEO members be transferred, by a new *CECBA* amendment, into OPSEU; and a unit for all staff in correctional facilities, including any AMAPCEO members working in those facilities, be created and represented by OPSEU.[142] In explaining this, the MBC stated that it was now seeking greater flexibility of staff resourcing and harmonization of labour relations structures. Following contentious negotiations about the proposed change, the MBC decided not to proceed with the amendment, although AMAPCEO did agree to exit corrections.[143]

AMAPCEO now represents a bargaining unit composed of specifically listed classifications and any new classifications that are agreed or determined to be "materially similar" to classifications in the unit.[144] Following the reduction in the number of the OPSEU units to two, and treating the "Engineers Unit" as the third unit, the AMAPCEO unit is

---

140 *The Crown in Right of Ontario as represented by the Management Board of Cabinet*, [1995] OLRD No 3753.

141 See the discussion in *PSAC, 2014*, above note 102 at paras 25–26, decided prior to the curative 2016 amendments.

142 See the description in *AMAPCEO and AG, 2013*, above note 49 at para 8. For a less dispassionate account, see AMAPCEO, *Two Steps Forward, One Step Back: Legislating Labour Relations in the Ontario Public Service*, 2009 staff paper, online: www.cpsa-acsp.ca/papers-2009/Carson.pdf at 16–17.

143 *AMAPCEO and AG, 2013*, above note 49 at paras 21–24. This case dealt with a claim by AMAPCEO to positions in corrections management called "Sergeants" or "Operations Managers" and found that, under the 2008 agreement, AMAPCEO relinquished any bargaining rights it might have for all correctional employees, not only those previously in a bargaining unit, and that OPSEU was now the bargaining agent for all unionized employees employed at correctional institutions.

144 *AMAPCEO/MBC Collective Agreement*, above note 94, Art 1.1, Sch 1, 2.

known as the Fourth Bargaining Unit.[145] Further to the 2008 negotiations, the recognition clause for the fourth unit specifically excludes persons employed in the Correctional Bargaining Unit. It does not specifically exclude persons in the Unified Bargaining Unit. The possible overlap between the scope of the AMAPCEO unit and the OPSEU Unified Bargaining Unit is the subject of ongoing jurisdictional disputes between the two unions, as discussed below.

d) Professional Engineers of the Government of Ontario

In the 1980s, a loose association of professional engineers, mostly employed within the Ministry of Transportation, attempted to gain recognition and status for professional engineers employed by the Ontario government. In February 1989, the founding meeting of PEGO was held in Toronto. In 1990, a constitution was ratified, and architects were included in the association.[146]

PEGO then entered into a voluntary framework agreement with the Crown, which covered 700 engineers and thirty architects and, following an interest arbitration award,[147] entered into its first contract for salaries. These agreements were not collective agreements as PEGO had no formal recognition as an employee organization under the *CECBA* at the time. The framework agreement was terminated at the end of 1994 by virtue of the introduction of the *CECBA 1993*.[148] PEGO was also authorized under the *Social Contract Act, 1993* to negotiate a local agreement under the Ontario Public Service Sectoral Agreement.

Following the passage of the *CECBA 1993*, which allowed engineers and architects to unionize (separately from OPSEU and the "seventh unit"), PEGO applied for certification of a bargaining unit consisting of "all professional engineers and architects, engineers-in-training and architects-in-training employed in their professional capacity." In 1995, the OLRB found PEGO to be a trade union within the meaning of the *LRA* and certified PEGO as the bargaining agent for the above-noted bargaining unit.[149] The 1995 *CECBA* amendments excluded "architects

145 *CECBA*, above note 1, s 42(2).

146 See PEGO's website, online: http://www.pego.on.ca.

147 *Management Board Secretariat and Professional Engineers of the Government of Ontario*, 26 August 1991 (Dissanayake).

148 *CECBA 1993*, s 61.

149 *The Crown in Right of Ontario*, [1995] OLRD No 171 at para 4.

employed in their professional capacity,"[150] and PEGO lost the right to represent architects in collective bargaining.

PEGO represents a bargaining unit consisting of all professional engineers and Ontario land surveyors, and engineers-in-training who are employed in their professional capacity *except for* (1) persons at and above the classification Senior Management Group 3 (SMG3), (2) persons below SMG3 who exercise managerial authority, and (3) employees in bargaining units for which any trade union held bargaining rights as of *CECBA 1993*.[151] This unit is known as the Engineer Bargaining Unit[152] and bargains independently.

3) Duty to Bargain in Good Faith

Of course, under the *CECBA*, the duty to bargain in good faith applies to the government bargaining parties.[153] There have been hardly any decided cases.[154] *AMAPCEO v Ontario* illustrates the tensions that can arise in a collective bargaining environment like that of the four *CECBA* government bargaining units, where every unit's bargaining is with the same employer and is strongly influenced by other units' bargaining outcomes. Prior to the 2011 round of AMAPCEO/MBC bargaining, OPSEU and the Crown entered into their collective agreement, and a supplementary confidential agreement that the "across the board" increases in the final year of the OPSEU agreement would be 1 percent higher than reflected in the text of the OPSEU collective agreement. When AMAPCEO alleged that the government misled AMAPCEO about the terms of the recently concluded OPSEU/MBC collective agreement by not informing AMAPCEO of the "secret 1 percent," the government and OPSEU argued for the confidentiality of the supplementary arrangement on the basis that confidential agreements are instrumental to settlement of collective agreements. The OLRB ruled

150 *CECBA 1993*, s 11(3) as amended *Labour Relations and Employment Statute Law Amendment Act, 1995*, SO 1995, c 1, s 13; now *CECBA*, above note 1, s 11(3)3.

151 *PEGO/MBC Collective Agreement*, above note 94, Art 2.1.

152 *CECBA*, above note 1, s 24(3).

153 *LRA*, above note 2, ss 17 and 59, applies pursuant to *CECBA*, above note 1, s 2(2).

154 See *OPSEU v The Crown in Right of Ontario (Management Board Secretariat)*, [2005] OLRB Rep March/April 245, where the MBS was found to have breached the duty to bargain in good faith by requiring the union to sign a confidentiality clause limiting the dissemination of certain plans to only some members of the union's bargaining team.

the open hearing principle needed to be upheld as a guard against impropriety and that the documents at issue unusually themselves established a *prima facie* case of a breach of the duty to bargain in good faith.[155] On the merits, the OLRB found that the additional 1 percent increase was kept secret so that the public elements of the settlement would set the pattern for other OPS settlements, and concluded that the employer breached the duty to bargain in good faith when

> the employer deliberately created a construct whereby AMAPCEO, and others, would come into possession of incorrect information as to the terms of the OPSEU unified settlement in order that the OPSEU settlement would be perceived as being less costly than it in fact was with the intent of causing AMAPCEO to lower its expectations and demands at the bargaining table.[156]

F. JURISDICTIONAL DISPUTES

Outside of government, at the various designated Crown agencies, bargaining agents have tended to represent all employee units, meaning there have been no jurisdictional disputes as between competing unions certified to represent employees of the same employer. Within government, there have only been two jurisdictional disputes that have led to reported litigation. The contained dispute was whether the Ministry of Correctional Services erred in assigning the teaching of basic literacy and numeracy in correctional facilities to a member of the OPSEU bargaining unit that contained teacher's aides rather than to a teacher in the bargaining unit represented by the Ontario Secondary School Teachers Federation.[157]

The larger and ongoing jurisdictional dispute, which involves many different positions, concerns the boundary within government between

---

155 *Association of Management, Administrative and Professional Crown Employees of Ontario v Crown in Right of Ontario*, 2011 CanLII 24623 (ON LRB) at para 44.

156 *Association of Management, Administrative and Professional Crown Employees of Ontario v Ontario (Government Services)*, 2012 CanLII 3597 (ON LRB) at para 73.

157 *Ontario Secondary School Teachers' Federation, District 57/PSAT and Federation of Provincial Schools Authority Teachers ("FOPSAT"), Applicant v The Provincial Schools Authority, Ontario Ministry of Correctional Services, Responding Parties v Ontario Public Service Employees Union ("OPSEU"), Intervenor*, [2001] OLRD No 786 [*FOPSAT and OPSEU*], further discussed in Chapter 5.

the Unified Bargaining Unit represented by OPSEU and the Fourth Bargaining Unit represented by AMAPCEO. The dispute originates in the designation of bargaining units in 1993. Prior to the 2016 amendments, the *CECBA* stated that the seven bargaining units originally established in 1993 were "continued."[158] That earlier version of the *CECBA* also stated that all government employees who are not included in the other six bargaining units, were members of the seventh bargaining unit.

In addition, there was a 1994 order in council[159] that described the work done by all the bargaining units. Each of the OPSEU bargaining units were described as "composed of Crown employees who are public servants employed in positions responsible for [broadly stated functional areas] and includes employees falling under the following classes [with specific listed classifications] and such other classes as may be established within the above description." The seventh unit, which came to be represented by AMAPCEO in 1995, included Crown employees whose positions "are not included in the other six units," and then non-exhaustively listed such positions. This left arguable ambiguity about the proper bargaining unit for positions whose classifications were not specifically listed and whose functional duties were of a type claimed by both AMAPCEO and OPSEU.

Then, in 1995, as a result of OPSEU's intervention in AMAPCEO's application for certification as bargaining agent for the seventh unit, AMAPCEO, OPSEU, and the government entered into an agreement known as the Tripartite Agreement (TPA) dealing with various jurisdictional issues between the parties.[160] This agreement provided for the transfer of certain positions from the seventh bargaining unit into one of the six OPSEU bargaining units.[161] The union parties to the TPA also agreed that "all the employees in existing positions and classifications" set out in the order in council were located in the proper bargaining unit.[162] In other words, if a position was listed as being in an OPSEU bargaining unit, then AMAPCEO agreed not to assert that that position

158 *CECBA*, prior to the 2016 amendments, s 23(1) and (3).

159 Order-in-Council 243/94, reproduced in *OPSEU/MBC Unified and Correctional Collective Agreements*, above note 94, Appendix 2.

160 *Tripartite Agreement* between the Crown in Right of Ontario as represented by MBC and OPSEU and AMAPCEO, 23 March 1995 [*Tripartite Agreement*].

161 *Ibid* at para 1. See the discussion in *Association of Law Officers of the Crown v MBC*, [1995] OLRB Rep December 1424 [*ALOC v MBC*].

162 *Tripartite Agreement*, above note 160 at para 3.

should have been included in the AMAPCEO unit. Conversely, if a position was listed in the seventh bargaining unit, OPSEU agreed not to challenge that inclusion. The parties further agreed that, after the date of the agreement, jurisdictional dispute claims between the unions would only be filed following a change in work assignment or the creation of a new position.[163] This still left some arguable ambiguity about newly created positions, the classifications of which were not specifically listed.

The lack of precision in the separation of the two unions' units was first dealt with in a 1995 OLRB case about the question of the proper bargaining unit location for articling students.[164] The seventh unit was found to be "in essence, a 'tag end' unit," one that included positions not included in other units.[165] However, the OLRB found it necessary to first consider whether the positions in question did come within the functional description of the other six units. Lack of an explicit listing of a classification does not resolve the issue because the lists of classifications in both the OPSEU and AMAPCEO agreements are not exhaustive lists.

The ongoing dispute was the subject of an AMAPCEO policy grievance filed in 2000.[166] AMAPCEO's position in the grievance was that the employees it represented were not limited or restricted to those employees in positions listed in the seventh unit by the order in council, but that its bargaining unit was a "tag end" bargaining unit, meaning that it included all employees within the meaning of the Act who were not included in the other bargaining units.[167] The government took the position that the AMAPCEO bargaining unit was restricted to those positions listed in the order in council, any positions that the parties had agreed to be included in the bargaining unit, and any newly created positions that were similar to the positions already represented by AMAPCEO. OPSEU sought to intervene in the grievance because it asserted that its bargaining rights could be affected by the decision of the GSB. In a preliminary decision, the GSB found that OPSEU was entitled to intervene because "the issue of whether AMAPCEO's bargaining unit

---

163 *Ibid* at para 6.

164 *ALOC v MBC*, above note 161.

165 *Ibid* at 1427.

166 As discussed in *AMAPCEO (Policy) and Management Board Secretariat*, GSB#1357/00, 22 April 2002 (Knopf) [*AMAPCEO (Policy)*].

167 AMAPCEO also asserted that the Crown could not create positions that contained employees who did not fall within one of the bargaining units contemplated by the Act. That issue has since been resolved by the 2016 *CECBA* amendment establishing that all Crown employees must be in one of the current four units.

is a tag end unit may have an impact on the scope of the six other bargaining units."[168] The grievance was subsequently settled between AMAPCEO and the government on the basis that the AMAPCEO unit was a tag end unit,[169] but OPSEU was not a party to that settlement.[170]

In 2008, the AMAPCEO scope clause was significantly amended as part of the negotiations dealing with AMAPCEO exiting correctional institutions, described above.[171] The clause now recognizes AMAPCEO as representing existing bargaining unit classifications and "all employees in any newly established classification or position that is subsequently agreed, or determined by the OLRB, to be materially similar to a classification or position in the unit." It was further agreed that this agreement replaced all prior agreements between the parties concerning AMAPCEO as a tag end unit. The 2008 language seems to end AMAPCEO's status as a "tag end unit," although there is no GSB ruling to that effect.

Jurisdictional disputes between OPSEU and AMAPCEO still remain a real possibility because of disputes over (1) the assignment of positions to existing classifications and (2) whether new classifications are "materially similar" to pre-existing classifications in both unions' units.

Both the GSB and the OLRB appear to be available forums for contesting such jurisdictional disputes. The OLRB has the specific statutory authority to hear jurisdictional disputes.[172] Where a jurisdictional dispute has been filed with the OLRB, it will be the preferred forum because the GSB, like private arbitration boards, can only determine the jurisdictional issue under the particular collective agreement at issue, which leaves open the possibility of different determinations under the other collective agreements.[173]

---

168 *AMAPCEO (Policy)*, above note 166 at 16.

169 *Memorandum of Settlement* between AMAPCEO and MBC, 8 September 2004.

170 The meaning of the "tag end" clause was also an issue in ongoing litigation about AMAPCEO's claim to the "Sergeants" or "Operational Managers" in correctional institutions: *Association of Management, Administrative and Professional Crown Employees of Ontario v Ontario (Solicitor General)*, 2021 CanLII 7237 (ON GSB) (McLean) [*AMAPCEO v Solicitor General, 2021*], but that claim has now been rejected by the GSB on other grounds: *AMAPCEO, 2013*, above note 49

171 Set out in *AMAPCEO v Solicitor General, 2021*, *ibid* at paras 21 & 22.

172 *LRA*, above note 2, s 99. See for example, *FOPSAT and OPSEU*, above note 157, further discussed in Chapter 5.

173 *OPSEU (Union) and Ministry of Community and Social Services*, GSB#2004-0911, 22 February 2005 (Stephens) at 6, followed in *Ontario Public Service Employees Union (Union) v Ontario (Community and Correctional Services)*, 2010 CanLII 45251 (ON GSB) (Stewart).

However, the OLRB, in deciding those disputes, will have regard for whether the union asserting that a position was assigned to the wrong bargaining unit had filed a timely grievance. Where OPSEU filed such grievances on a regular basis, the employer then filed jurisdictional dispute applications.[174] On further consideration, the OLRB decided as follows:

> I am of the view that the point of time from which OPSEU ought to have put the employer on notice of its claim for the work in dispute for the purpose of these proceedings (and for the purpose of those proceedings held in abeyance pending the determination of the delay arguments in these proceedings) is to be calculated from the date of the initial posting of the position to which the work in dispute relates, or from the date that notice is given to OPSEU of the creation of a new position or new classification in accordance with Article 1.4 of the collective agreement, whichever occurs first.[175]

This is viewed as reasonable despite the breadth of the OPS in part because a job posting includes a Job Specification containing a full description of duties, and all jobs are posted electronically. It is not viewed as necessary for the applicant union to have the opportunity to observe the person performing the job as the likelihood that the new incumbent will undertake the full responsibilities of the job in the first month is very low. In any case, jobs will not uncommonly be posted well before an incumbent is actually put in the role.

In the absence of notice or a formal posting, e.g., where an individual simply fills an opening or new role without any formal notice, then the time limit does not start to run until a posting or notice.

The posting of a position that is additional complement for an already established position does not cause an extension of time, as to do so would mean that the employer adding complement to previously unchallenged positions would allow jurisdictional litigation and "to reach a result that would permit for that type of collateral attack on long-service employees creates unstable labour relations for all of these parties, and ought to be avoided."[176]

---

174 *Ontario (Government Services) v Ontario Public Service Employees Union*, 2011 CanLII 77708 (ON LRB).

175 *Ontario (Government Services) v Ontario Public Service Employees Union*, 2012 CanLII 32755 (ON LRB) at 9, para 34.

176 *Ibid* at para 88.

After these principles were clarified, the parties were to sort out which cases were to be discontinued due to delay and which were to be advanced for a hearing in the form of work assignment disputes. Years of delay ensued, and a large backlog accumulated. As a result, the OLRB ruled that OPSEU should have responsibility for moving any work assignment case forward and that the cases would be dealt with largely in writing.[177]

In the absence of an OLRB jurisdictional dispute application, the GSB will likely deal with the matter as best it can.[178] The reasons for taking secondary jurisdiction would be the same as those causing the GSB to take primary jurisdiction in an exclusions matter: the GSB's public sector experience, promptness of dispute resolution, and the parties' ability to tailor the method of dispute resolution.

G. OPSEU CARRIAGE RIGHTS

A unique aspect of OPS labour relations is that some grievors represented by OPSEU assert that they have "carriage rights" — the individual right to take a grievance to arbitration accompanied by a trade union obligation to provide supportive representation at the hearing.[179] This is incompatible with collective bargaining, which includes a union's duty to evaluate grievances on the basis of its duty to the entire bargaining unit, while taking into account a union's obligation to give effect to individual employment rights and the ability of the individual grievor to file a fair representation complaint with the OLRB. "Individual carriage rights" have been consistently and repeatedly rejected by the OLRB and the GSB[180] and appear not to be legally sustainable in any forum. Yet OPSEU hesitates at times to assert control of grievances including clearly unmeritorious grievances. Proceeding with significant numbers of losing grievances is, in the understated words of the GSB: "neither a viable labour relations strategy nor an efficient use of this board's limited resources. No matter how high the pile of such grievances becomes,

---

177 *The Crown in Right of Ontario as represented by the Ministry of the Attorney General v Ontario Public Service Employees Union*, 2016 CanLII 18412 (ON LRB).

178 See an exclusions case, *AMAPCEO and MBS, 2004*, above note 51 at 8–10.

179 *Ontario (Management Board of Cabinet)*, [1996] OLRD No 2097 at para 18 [*McLaughlin*].

180 *Ontario Public Service Employees Union (Therrien) v Ontario (Community Safety and Correctional Services)*, 2008 CanLII 32795 (ON GSB) (Lynk) at 8.

a mountain they do not make."[181] One consultant who interviewed a number of human resources staff in the OPS noted[182] that the carriage rights approach means OPSEU does not feel able to prevent "trivial and vexatious" grievances[183] from proceeding, with the result that time and money of the employer and union are wasted. In the absence of a willingness to control whether a matter will proceed to a hearing, the parties may be more reluctant to make their best offers to settle during the grievance procedure.

1) History

Commencing in the 1940s, the *PSA* gave individual public servants, then non-unionized, the right to individually grieve, first about their dismissals, and then in 1959 about a broad range of issues.[184]

CECBA 1972 introduced collective bargaining, and the individual statutory entitlement of the now-unionized Crown employees was both incorporated and significantly altered. Individuals did retain a personal right to grieve three issues—classification, appraisals, and discipline—but all other matters were to be grieved in accordance with the provisions of the collective agreement. Then, in 1993, the present *CECBA* removed all statutory reference to any individual right to grieve.

Meanwhile,OPSEU decided to continue to give some kind of recognition to the concept of carriage rights. In 1973, OPSEU's predecessor, the CSAO, put a provision in its constitution stating that "no grievor will be denied representation at any time," and that provision remains in the OPSEU constitution.[185] In 1975, OPSEU's executive board passed a still in effect policy resolution stating the interpretation of the provision was that

181 *Ontario Public Service Employees Union (Daley) v Ontario (Health and Long-Term Care)*, 2017 CanLII 7051 (ON GSB) (Herlich) at para 59.

182 Leslie Macleod, *Grievance Administration Project, Final Report* (Management Board Secretariat, 2000) at 42.

183 *OPSEU (Wilson) and Ministry of Correctional Services*, GSB#768/89, 8 February 1990 (Samuels).

184 See Chapter 1 for history of the *PSA* and the *CECBA*.

185 *OPSEU Constitution*, Art 25.2, previously 24.1.2, originally enacted at 1973 Convention of the CSAO. In 2002, the provision was altered so that the words "the union's policy is that" were deleted.

> [n]o one except the grievor can withdraw his/her grievance. If a member wishes to pursue his/her grievance to arbitration, Head Office will advise the grievor regarding the advisability of taking his/her grievance to arbitration. In the event that the grievor declines to accept this advice, Head Office is bound to represent the grievor at the arbitration hearing, if the grievor so wishes.[186]

The concept of individual carriage rights also receives some apparent support from the wording of the OPSEU/MBC collective agreement. Prior to 1998, the language for processing grievances included: "If a grievor is not satisfied with the [final answer of the employer], the grievor may apply to the Grievance Settlement Board for a hearing of the grievance."[187] However, the GSB never agreed that this language gave a grievor any personal right to arbitrate a grievance, and indeed held that there was no individual right to arbitration.[188] In other words, the purpose of referring to the grievor was understood to be clarification of the procedural means for referring a grievance to arbitration. Such clarification did not affect the union's control of whether or not the matter could be referred. Although the change is legally redundant, the OPSEU/MBC collective agreement was changed in 1998 to read that the "grievor may apply, *through the Union*, to the Grievance Settlement Board."[189]

2) GSB and OLRB Rulings

In the 1988 decision of *Blake et al and Amalgamated Transit Union and Toronto Area Transit Operating Authority*,[190] the GSB clarified that, even under the pre-1993 *CECBA*, the union was to decide whether any grievance proceeded to arbitration. Union carriage rights were necessary

---

186 *OPSEU Policy Manual*, s 12.1, which notes that the resolution was passed by the Board in July 1975.

187 *OPSEU/MBC Collective Agreement, 1994–1998*, Art 22.4 and functionally identical language in predecessor agreements.

188 Then Art 27.4 of the *OPSEU/MBC Collective Agreement*, as addressed in *OPSEU (Ally) and Ministry of Labour*, GSB#1036/90, 22 January 1991 (Kaplan) at 17. See also *OPSEU (Ethier) and Ministry of Community and Social Services*, GSB#2536/91, 1 September 1992 (Knopf) at 6.

189 *OPSEU/MBC Unified and Correctional Collective Agreements*, above note 94, Art 22.6.1 [emphasis added].

190 GSB#1276/87, 3 May 1988 at 9 [*Blake*]. This ruling was made under the pre-1993 *CECBA*, and despite the statutory provision that three issues were individually grievable.

because, in administering the agreement, the union has to consider the needs of all of the members of the bargaining unit and sometimes the individual interest must be subordinated. "Thus it is important that the union which is responsible for the collective interests of the members of the bargaining unit control access to arbitration."[191] While *Blake* happened to be a case involving a union other than OPSEU, at a designated Crown agency, the same rationale was found to be applicable to OPSEU, in the public service, for the same reasons.[192]

Where OPSEU has proceeded to arbitration only to agree with the employer that there is no dispute between the parties about any of the issues raised by the grievance, any contrary wishes of the grievor have not prevailed because the GSB has inevitably ruled, pursuant to *Blake*, that the grievance must be dismissed.[193] The practice of proceeding to arbitration only to tell the arbitrator that there is no dispute to arbitrate has been labelled a "charade" by the OLRB.[194] Nonetheless, the practice continues to some degree.[195]

---

191 *Ibid* at 5–6, quoting from *Amalgamated Transit Union (Francis) and The Crown*, GSB#1528/86 (Brandt).

192 *OPSEU (Glenny) and Ministry of Government Services*, GSB#0756/86, 11 January 1989 (Springate) at 9.

193 Examples under the pre-1993 *CECBA*: *OPSEU (Harrison/Leach) and Ministry of Correctional Services*, GSB#2551/91, 19 August 1992 (Watters) at 7; *OPSEU (Stewart) and Ministry of Correctional Services*, GSB#3843/92, 22 June 1995 (Briggs) at 6. For post-1993 examples, see *OPSEU (Outman) and Ministry of Health and Long Term Care*, GSB#2447/93, 12 October 2000 (Lee); *OPSEU (Low) and Ministry of Finance*, GSB#0707/00, 2 February 2001 (Petryshen); *OPSEU (Vairo) and Ontario Realty Corporation*, GSB#1593/98, 10 April 2001 (Johnston); *Ontario Public Service Employees Union (Ross) v Ontario (Municipal Affairs and Housing)*, 2009 CanLII 15413 (ON GSB) (Gray); *Ontario Public Service Employees Union (Tardiel) v Ontario (Community Safety and Correctional Services)*, 2010 CanLII 81913 (ON GSB) (Albertyn). This approach has been upheld by the Divisional Court : *Jamal v Crown Employees Grievance Settlement Board*, 2006 CanLII 45942 (ON SCDC) [*Jamal*].

194 *Price et al v Ontario Public Service Employees' Union*, [1996] OLRD No 3065 at paras 35–36.

195 *Ontario Public Service Employees Union (Prestage) v Ontario (Community Safety and Correctional Services)*, 2014 CanLII 70083 (ON GSB) (Briggs); *Ontario Public Service Employees Union (Bowman et al-Union) v Ontario (Treasury Board Secretariat)*, 2020 CanLII 32556 (ON GSB) (Devins), where the union acknowledged that there was nothing that distinguished these cases from the earlier matters that have already been decided and dismissed.

Where OPSEU was of the view that failure to settle a case before arbitration would have a serious negative impact on the grievor or the membership, the union has settled grievances before arbitration without obtaining the consent of the individual grievors.[196] A notable example is the monetary settlement, in 1993, of 7,000 outstanding classification grievances as part of concluding *Social Contract Act, 1993* negotiations. The settlement was subject to the collective ratification of the bargaining unit, but not to individual grievor consent.[197]

The courts have confirmed that, before the GSB, "a member of the bargaining unit represented by OPSEU does not have standing in his or her own right to process a grievance respecting employment. Only the union may do so."[198]

Where grievors have filed duty of fair representation complaints objecting to OPSEU's disposition of their grievances and have asserted a legally enforceable individual "carriage right" over the grievances, the OLRB has consistently rejected that assertion, holding that individual "carriage rights" are not good labour relations policy. Although a "trade union must give each grievance its honest consideration," the financial and collective bargaining reality is that "a trade union is not only entitled to settle grievances, in many cases it should."[199] Furthermore, any individual "carriage rights" policy will not be enforced by the OLRB, as it is an internal matter and the OLRB concerns itself

---

196 For examples that are recorded in jurisprudence, see *Ontario (Ministry of the Solicitor General)*, [2001] OLRD No 2475 [*Dehart*] and *Benny Ram v OPSEU*, [2004] OLRD No 704, where OPSEU settled the grievances against the wishes of the individuals.

197 See circumstances outlined in *OPSEU v David E Smith*, [1995] OLRD No 220, dismissing the complaint of a grievor on the basis that the OLRB was without jurisdiction, as the matter should have proceeded earlier before the OPSLRT, but finding that there was no violation of the Act in any event.

198 *Smith v Ontario Public Service Employees Union*, [2003] OJ No 2139 (Div Ct) at para 9 cited in *Jamal*, above note 193.

199 In *Syme and Graphic Arts International Union Local No 28-B*, [1983] OLRB Rep May 775 at para 20, as quoted in *Hamilton-Wentworth Detention Centre*, [1997] OLRD No 1455 at paras 17–19 [*Detention Centre*]. See *Anna Wilson*, [1990] OLRB Rep November 1167 at paras 83–85 [*Wilson*]; *McDermott v Wysocki (Ontario Public Service Employees Union)*, [1997] OLRD No 3663 at para 14 [*McDermott v Wysocki*]; *McLaughlin*, above note 179 at para 19; *Douglas v Ontario Public Service Employees Union*, 2006 CanLII 16943 (ON LRB) at para 10; *Beausoleil v Ontario Public Service Employees Union (OPSEU)*, 2007 CanLII 4727 (ON LRB) at para 15.

only with the actions of the trade union in relation to the employer.[200] To quote the OLRB, "[t]he Board's jurisprudence is clear that OPSEU employees do not have carriage rights. OPSEU retains that right to decide whether to pursue a matter to arbitration."[201] This extends to determining whether a grievance will be heard through expedited mediation/arbitration,[202] should be settled or withdrawn,[203] and telling the GSB that there is no dispute between the parties.[204] The OLRB has also upheld a system of prioritizing cases, even though the system results in some cases being left adjourned indefinitely against the wishes of the grievors.[205] A claim for individual carriage rights over a human rights–based claim has been rejected with the OLRB reminding the parties that "nothing in [the duty of fair representation] permits negligent treatment of human rights or the truncation of human rights."[206] OPSEU also has the authority to decide whether or not to judicially review an arbitration decision.[207] What the OLRB has done in every case is move past the assertion of "carriage rights" to focus directly on whether OPSEU actually breached the duty of fair representation when representing the employee in the grievance.

200 *McLaughlin*, above note 179 at para 22, followed in *Dehart*, above note 196 at paras 9–10; *Laderoute v Ontario Public Service Employees Union*, 2015 CanLII 34053 (ON LRB) (Nyman) at para 10.

201 *Cartier v Ontario Public Service Employees Union Local 636*, 2008 CanLII 20804 (ON LRB) at paras 26–27, citing *McLaughlin*, above note 179.

202 *McLaughlin*, *ibid.*

203 *Hazelton v Ontario Public Service Employees Union (OPSEU)*, 2011 CanLII 4926 (ON LRB).

204 *Glenny v Ontario Public Service Employees Union*, [2001] OLRD No 2281 at para 25.

205 *McDermott v Wysocki*, above note 199. To the same effect, see *Detention Centre*, above note 199 at para 17, where the then-head of the OPSEU grievance department testified that a priority system was essential because the union's budgetary restrictions, combined with its "policy" that grievances could not be settled without the consent of the grievor, made it impossible to process all grievances.

206 *Morsi v Ontario Public Service Employees Union*, 2011 CanLII 17935 (ON LRB) at para 18, and see also *Morsi v Ontario Public Service Employees Union*, 2011 CanLII 34938 (OLRB).

207 *Russell Best, Paul Spitzig, Laura Brandon and Shirley-Anne Lair v Ontario Public Service Employees Union (OPSEU)*, 2015 CanLII 43592 (ON LRB).

3) Potential Enforcement by the Courts

Union constitutions are legally enforceable to some extent through the courts[208] and, although no such case has been brought, the potential parameters of a court action about OPSEU individual "carriage rights" policy warrant discussion.

The first issue that might arise is whether the appropriate forum is the court or the internal political process of OPSEU. Courts asked to enforce a constitution will defer to the internal remedies of the union as contemplated by the constitution.[209] Any claim that the OPSEU constitution guarantees individual carriage rights over a grievance would likely be a disputed constitutional interpretation. The OPSEU constitution contains mechanisms for resolving such disputes,[210] and those may be the "other forums" that a court would think appropriate for dealing with the union's decision to resolve a grievance other than in accordance with the wishes of the grievor.

Second, courts have refused to give effect to a constitutional provision if it defeats or varies the rights or duties imposed by a statute.[211] OPSEU owes the statutory duty of fair representation to all of its membership, not just the grievor, which duty is enforceable at the OLRB. As indicated by the OLRB, the proper fulfillment of this duty may require it to settle grievances, even against the wishes of the particular member in question. It would seem inappropriate for a court to enforce any interpretation of the OPSEU constitution that would prevent OPSEU from properly fulfilling its duty of fair representation[212] and would prevent the OLRB from assessing whether the union had breached that duty.

---

208 Michael MacNeil, Michael Lynk & Peter Engelmann, *Trade Union Law in Canada* (Toronto: Canada Law Book, Thomson Reuters Canada, 2017), ch 4 [MacNeil et al].

209 *Ibid*, s 4.370, and Chapter 9, ss 9.320–9.390; George Adams, *Canadian Labour Law*, 2d ed (Aurora, ON: Canada Law Book, 2004), ch 14, §§ 14.26.

210 *OPSEU Constitution*, Art 18.1.3.

211 *Quale v Saskatchewan Registered Nurses' Association* (1970), 16 DLR (3d) 550 (Sask CA) at 555 and cases discussed therein.

212 For an example of the OLRB holding, on different facts, that the constitution and bylaws of the union "do not take precedence over the Act," see *Centro Mechanical Inc*, [1996] OLRB Rep September/October 762 at para 50. Arbitrators have ruled that a union constitution cannot take precedence over a collective agreement obligation; see *Int'l Association of Machinists and Orenda Engines Ltd* (1958), 8 LAC 116 (Laskin) at 123 and *Labatt Brewing Co Ltd and Brewery, Winery and Distillery Workers, Local 300* (1982), 2 LAC (3d) 373 at 382 (Getz).

Third, the constitutional provision itself (as opposed to the policy) may be unenforceably ambiguous. It has been noted by the OLRB that "it is difficult to construe 'representation' [as set out in the OPSEU constitution] as conferring on the . . . grievors an absolute right."[213] Indeed, representation of the members of the bargaining unit, including the representation of any individual grievor, is often carried out by the settlement or withdrawal of a grievance. In other words, the settlement or withdrawal of a grievance is not the withdrawal of representation, but an act of representation.

As for the effect of the OPSEU executive board policy interpreting the constitution, it is by no means clear that such a policy is enforceable as if it were part of the constitution. Policy statements may not have contractual effect and may instead be statements of political intent. Even if the policy was to some extent enforceable, it would be necessary to determine its actual substantive content, and it appears to be ambiguous in at least two respects. First, on a literal reading of the policy, the only proscribed conduct appears to be the unilateral outright withdrawal of grievances. The policy may not address the settlement of grievances. The second area of ambiguity is constitutional provisions will be interpreted in light of the custom or practice of the union.[214] It is clear that the custom or practice of OPSEU concerning the executive board policy on carriage rights is that OPSEU reserves the right to make considered exceptions to the policy in fulfillment of its duty of fair representation. As long as any union exception to individual carriage rights is made advisedly, it does not seem to be a violation of the constitutional practice of OPSEU.

---

213 *Wilson*, above note 199 at para 82.

214 See MacNeil et al, above note 208, Chapter 4.

CHAPTER EIGHT

CECBA Essential Services, Strikes, and Interest Arbitration

A. INTRODUCTION

The *Crown Employees Collective Bargaining Act, 1993* (*CECBA*)[1] incorporates essential services requirements into a strike/lockout regime. This is compared and contrasted with the only other essential services legislation in Ontario—the *Ambulance Services Collective Bargaining Act, 2001* (*ASCBA*).[2] The *CECBA* exceptionally requires interest arbitration for the Correctional Bargaining Unit.

CECBA Part IV—Essential Services and Part III.1—Interest Arbitration—Correctional Bargaining contain the main provisions of the *CECBA*'s unique interest dispute resolution scheme. Those provisions do operate in the context of the *Labour Relations Act, 1995* (*LRA*),[3] since the *CECBA* incorporates the interest dispute resolution provisions of the *LRA* in their entirety, subject only to the explicit modifications and additions contained in *CECBA* Part II—Application of *Labour Relations Act, 1995*.

For completeness, this chapter also reviews lived experience with:

- picketing issues unique to Ontario government employees on strike
- "return to work" protocols

1 SO 1993, c 38 [*CECBA*].
2 SO 2001, c 10 [*ASCBA*].
3 SO 1995, c 1, Sch A [*LRA*].

- illegal strikes
- possible ad hoc legislation restricting collective bargaining

Under the *CECBA* regime, there have been two strikes by direct employees of government, the OPSEU strikes of 1996 and 2002. The 1996 strike lasted five weeks and the 2002 strike lasted seven weeks. Each involved widespread strike and picketing activity across the Ontario Public Service (OPS) in Toronto and throughout the province.[4] The 1996 picketing of the Legislative Assembly and the resultant Ontario Provincial Police (OPP) response were the subject of a judicial inquiry. Lengthy essential services agreement negotiations preceded both strikes. Significant levels of essential services were required and performed during the strikes. Substantial litigation occurred in various forums as discussed below. The degree of disruption was a factor in the 2016 *CECBA* amendment, introducing interest arbitration for corrections. Both strikes were settled without legislation or interest arbitration. In the 1996 strike, a key issue was job security, with the settlement ending the contractual job offer guarantee that had been required for employees to be laid off due to divestment of work, and introducing enhanced severance and a requirement for the employer to make "reasonable efforts" to secure offers of employment for divested employees.[5] In the 2002 strike, key issues were conversion of fixed-term employees doing ongoing work to regular employment status[6] and employer-desired reorganization of insured health benefits administration.

B. *CECBA* ESSENTIAL SERVICES

1) Context

a) Legislative Models for Strikes/Lockouts and Essential Services

The three basic models of legislation dealing with strikes/lockouts and essential services are:

- the "unfettered strike" model: the standard strike/lockout regime

4 See D. Rapaport, *No Justice, No Peace: The 1996 Ontario Public Service Employees Union Strike against the Harris Government in Ontario* (Montreal: McGill-Queen's University Press, 1999) [Rapaport].

5 See history of OPSEU/MBS "reasonable efforts" and job security provisions in Chapter 9.

6 See discussion in Chapter 10 of conversion of fixed-term to regular employment.

- the "no strike" model: strikes and lockouts are illegal, and interest arbitration is used to finalize collective agreements
- the "designation" or "controlled strike" or "essential services" model: strikes and lockouts are legal, but some services are designated as essential by agreement of the parties and/or board order with the consequence that those services must be maintained during any strike or lockout[7]

Versions of all these schemes are used for different provincial and federal public sector workforces in Canada, and the strengths and weaknesses of the various models have long been the subject of debate.[8]

The "unfettered strike" model has been favoured because the negative impact of a strike or lockout, or the threat of same, motivates both parties to reach a compromise and leaves the nature of that compromise in the hands of those who know the issues best—the parties themselves. The concern raised by the model is that public services are provided on a monopoly basis, without alternate sources of supply, so strikes or lockouts will pose a threat to public welfare and give disproportionate bargaining power to public sector unions.

Where the social impact of any strike or lockout is seen as unacceptable, then the "no strike" model puts the resolution of the dispute in the hands of expert interest arbitrators. This model has its own risks. Conflict can be redirected away from strikes to higher grievance arbitration rates.[9] In bargaining, the "no strike" model has a "narcotic

---

7 For a review of the Canadian experience and evaluative commentary, see Bernard Adell, Michel Grant & Allen Ponak, *Strikes in Essential Services* (Kingston, ON: IRC Press, Queen's University, 2001), especially Chapter 2 [Adell et al]; Eric Tucker, "Regulating Strikes in Essential Services: Canada," in Moti Mironi & Monika Schlachter, eds, *Regulating Strikes in Essential Services: A Comparative "Law in Action" Perspective* (The Netherlands: Wolter-Kluwers, 2019); electronic copy online: ssrn.com/abstract=3277648 [Tucker]; Joseph B. Rose, "Regulating and Resolving Public Sector in Disputes in Canada" (2008) 50:4 *Journal of Industrial Relations* [Rose, 2008].

8 Harry W. Arthurs, *Labour Disputes in Essential Industries* (Ottawa: Privy Council Office, 1968); Mark Thompson & Sara Slinn, "Public Sector Industrial Relations in Canada: Does It Threaten or Sustain Democracy?" (2013) 34 *Comparative Labor Law and Policy Journal* 393 [Thompson & Slinn].

9 Robert Hebdon & Robert Stern, "Tradeoffs Among Expressions of Industrial Conflict: Public Sector Strike Bans and Grievance Arbitrations" (1998) 51:2 *Industrial and Labor Relations Review* 204.

effect"[10] on the parties as they will tend to avoid accountability for the difficult compromises inherent in free collective bargaining by leaving matters to be concluded through the interest arbitration process. The result can be prolonged bargaining, which was viewed as undesirable by the government of Ontario when designing *CECBA 1993*.[11] While interest arbitration jurisprudence stresses the importance of arbitrating outcomes that "replicate free collective bargaining" and avoid public sector worker subsidization of the public purse through foregone wages,[12] there is concern that interest arbitrators will focus on the interests of the immediate parties, not give enough weight to the public interest in cost containment,[13] and award a "wage premium" above what the parties would settle for under a strike regime.[14]

---

10 Michele Campolieti & Chris Riddell, "Interest Arbitration and the Narcotic Effect: Evidence from Three Decades of Collective Bargaining in Ontario" 2019 57:3 *British Journal of Industrial Relations* 421; Rose, 2008, above note 7 citing studies at 550.

11 See the discussion of the introduction of *CECBA 1993* in Chapter 1.

12 Jeffrey Sack, "Ability to Pay in the Public Sector: A Critical Appraisal" (1991) *Labour Arbitration Yearbook* 277 and articles cited.

13 See Richard Chaykowski, "Time to Tweak or Re-boot? Assessing the Interest Arbitration Process in Canadian Industrial Relations" CD Howe Institute (2019) Commentary 539 at 20, especially fn 39, online: www.cdhowe.org/sites/default/files/attachments/research_papers/mixed/Commentary_539pdf; Richard Chaykowski & Robert Hickey, "Reform of the Conduct and Structure of Labour Relations in the Ontario Broader Public Service" Report to the Commission on the Reform of Ontario's Public Service (Kingston, ON: Queen's University, School of Policy Studies, 2012).

14 In support of the existence of an interest arbitration wage premium, see Michele Campolieti, Robert Hebdon, & Benjamin Dachis, "Collective Bargaining in the Canadian Public Sector, 1978–2008: The Consequences of Restraint and Structural Change" (2016) 54:1 *British Journal of Industrial Relations* 192. This is contentious. For example, in one study of an American jurisdiction, little evidence was found that interest arbitration leads to higher wage outcomes; see Thomas Kochan, David B. Lipsky, Mary Newhart & Alan Benson, "The Long Haul Effects of Interest Arbitration: The Case of New York State's Taylor Law" (2010) 63:4 *Industrial and Labour Relations Review* 565. See also Thompson & Slinn, above note 8 at 403. In addition to the contention about interest arbitration wage premiums, there continues to be a lack of clarity about comparisons of public and private sector compensation generally. See Thompson & Slinn, above note 8 at 408–10, referencing the lack of good studies, including the difficulty of calculating total compensation that factors in the pensions, benefits, and deferred compensation that are more prevalent in the public sector. This lack of clarity is also discussed in *Ontario English Catholic Teachers Assoc v His Majesty*, 2022

A designated model is intended to have the main benefits of the other two models—the pressure to settle on, and problem solving of, the parties under the unfettered model combined with the continuity of needed services produced by the "no strike model."[15] Obviously, a designation model reduces the union's bargaining power, reducing the pressure to settle and potentially prolonging the strike or lockout. However, the model will still be supported by at least some unions to get access to the right to strike, so long as bargaining power is not unduly undermined. The designation model allows the parties to take ownership of and have accountability for the bargaining in a public service setting where interest arbitration would otherwise be imposed. This is indeed the stated legislative rationale for *CECBA 1993*,[16] which was designed to put the responsibility for settlements in the hands of the parties while simultaneously employing a designation model to ensure the continuity of essential services. A risk of the designated model is that the parties and tribunals can "tend to err on the side of safety" through excessive designation of services as essential, and resultant unwarranted weakening of union bargaining power.[17]

It is notable that there is a diversity of opinion between AMAPCEO and OPSEU, and within OPSEU, rooted in their different bargaining unit composition and history.[18] For the Unified Unit, OPSEU favours the right to strike and generally seeks to limit essential services. For the Correctional Unit, OPSEU has agreed to interest arbitration, as discussed below. For the Fourth Unit, AMAPCEO advocates independent binding interest arbitration for the resolution of its collective bargaining disputes with the government employer.[19]

One commentator has argued that governments can prefer the "essential services" or "designation" strike model because it avoids the possibility of unfavourable interest arbitration decisions, maintains essential services, and has an additional advantage of being a political

ONSC 6658 at paras 341–45 [*OECTA*], which references the effect of the public sector being much more unionized than the private sector.

15 Joseph B. Rose, "Regulating Essential Service Disputes in Canada: The Designation Model" (2018) 69:4 *Labour Law Journal* 194.

16 See the discussion of the introduction of *CECBA 1993* in Chapter 1.

17 *Rose, 2008*, above note 7 at 553.

18 See Chapter 7 for a discussion of the history of each union.

19 AMAPCEO, *Independent Binding Interest Arbitration Brief*, 2 March 2004, online: www.amapceo.on.ca.

"win–win" for the government, which can "always restrict the [strike] right to make it ineffective."[20] The appropriate response to this criticism is, of course, for government to implement an essential services scheme that restricts the right to strike to the minimum extent necessary to ensure essential services. If that leaves the impact of a strike so reduced as to make an "essential services strike" ineffective in motivating both parties to enter into a collective agreement, then consideration would need to be given to the "no strike" models.[21]

b) Relevance of *Saskatchewan Federation of Labour v Saskatchewan* (SCC)

In *Saskatchewan Federation of Labour v Saskatchewan*,[22] where a provincial government's essential services legislation gave the government unilateral authority to determine whether and how essential services were to be maintained during a work stoppage, with no adequate review mechanism, coupled with the absence of a meaningful dispute resolution mechanism to resolve bargaining impasses, the Supreme Court found the constitutionally protected right to strike had been violated and that the provincial legislation was not a justifiable limit. This raises the question of whether the *CECBA* or *ASCBA* essential services regimes would withstand a challenge under the *Canadian Charter of Rights and Freedoms* (the *Charter*)[23] based on this decision.[24]

The *CECBA* scheme does not appear vulnerable in the two most contested areas. Concerning the process of determining of essential services levels, unlike the unilateral government decision making under the impugned Saskatchewan legislation, the *CECBA* and *ASCBA* require negotiation of an essential services agreement subject to third-party adjudication by the Ontario Labour Relations Board (OLRB).

---

20 Paul J.J. Cavalluzzo, "Strikes in the Public Sector in the Second Millenium—Employee Right or Government Policy?" *Cambridge Lecture 1999*, unpublished at 23–24. The same point is made in Tucker, above note 7 at 140.

21 The legislative debate on the introduction of the *ASCBA*, discussed below, is instructive.

22 2015 SCC 4.

23 Part I of the *Constitution Act, 1982*, being Schedule B to the *Canada Act 1982* (UK), 1982, c 11 [*Charter*].

24 See Richard Chaykowski, "Labour Relations Policy and Practice, and Regulation of the Right to Strike in the Broader Public Sector: The Implications of Saskatchewan Federation of Labour" (2016) 19:2 *Canadian Labour and Employment Law Journal* 483, which has a section on *Charter* requirements for an essential services regime.

Concerning the absence of a meaningful interest dispute resolution mechanism to resolve impasses, while the board does not have the power to award interest arbitration as remedy for an ineffective strike under the *CECBA*, there is a history of meaningful strikes under the *CECBA*,[25] and the OLRB does have the power to adjust the essential services agreement to address "levels that are greater or less than required to provide the essential services."[26] By contrast, in the ambulance sector, where there is a greater concern about the ineffectiveness of strikes due to high levels of essentiality,[27] the *ASCBA* provides that, in the event an essential services agreement "has the effect of depriving" employees or the employer of a "meaningful" strike or lockout, the OLRB can order interest arbitration.[28]

It is quite possible to criticize other specific aspects of both the *CECBA* and *ASCBA* essential services regimes, including provisions that arguably unreasonably reduce the effectiveness of a strike or lockout. An example is *CECBA* section 32(2) under which "the number of employees in the bargaining unit that are necessary to provide the essential services shall be determined without regard to the availability of other persons [e.g., management staff] to provide essential services."[29] It cannot be assumed that such an issue will support a successful *Charter* application. The OLRB has rejected a *Charter* challenge to the *ASCBA* that argued the statute was unacceptably imbalanced by virtue of the non-inclusion of qualified supervisors in the count of essential services workers.[30] This non-inclusion does weaken any essential services strike by leaving the employer able to call on essential services workers *and* those supervisors. In rejecting this challenge, the board stated that critique of specific aspects of an essential services scheme are criticisms

25 The OPSEU government units struck in 1996 and 2002, with real effect, as evidenced by the legal issues covered in this chapter. While much of that jurisprudence concerns the operations of correctional facilities, which is now under interest arbitration, as discussed below, the strikes of the largely administrative workforce in what is now the Unified Unit also had some effect.

26 *CECBA*, above note 1, ss 38(2)(b) and 42, all discussed below.

27 See discussion in the *ASCBA* section below.

28 *ASCBA*, above note 2, s 18.

29 See the discussion below on "Number of Employees Necessary to Provide Essential Services."

30 See *ASCBA*, above note 2, s 4(2), which is substantively similar to *CECBA*, above note 1, s 32(2), and is discussed below.

at the "micro level"[31] and noted that the Supreme Court has held that the right to meaningful collective bargaining does not guarantee any particular system so long as fundamental requirements are met.[32] At the same time, the Supreme Court has noted that the legislated collective bargaining process is not to be one that "substantially interferes with a meaningful process of collective bargaining by reducing employees' negotiating power."[33]

c) Ontario Context

It has been noted that "[m]ost jurisdictions offer little in the way of [a] consistent policy rationale for their choice of public sector dispute resolution methods," and Ontario is no exception.[34] There is no consistency concerning which type of interest dispute resolution scheme is used for which type of public service. Many of the public services provided by *CECBA* employers cannot be said to be more or less essential than other public sector services, or more or less essential than the same services provided by non-*CECBA* employers. The government workforce includes administrative and policy workers, covered by the "essential services" model, whose work is similar to that of administrative and policy staff in non-designated agencies and in municipalities under the "unfettered strike" model. Correctional staff at the government run correctional facilities are (since 2016) subject to interest arbitration, while correctional staff at secure facilities operated by agencies are under the "unfettered strike" model. Further to designation of their employers as *CECBA* agencies, operational staff at convention centres, Science North, and transportation staff at MetroLinx are under the "essential services" model, while operational staff at municipalities are not. Similarly, just outside of the *CECBA*, firefighters and police are under "no strike"

---

31 *The Corporation of the City of Sault Ste Marie v Unifor Local 1359*, 2018 CanLII 56434 (ON LRB) at para 34 [*Sault Ste Marie*].

32 *Labourers' International Union of North America, Ontario Provincial District Council v Govan Brown & Associates Limited*, 2018 CanLII 27199 (ON LRB) at para 70, citing *Mounted Police Association of Ontario v Canada (Attorney General)*, 2015 SCC 1.

33 *Ibid* at para 71.

34 Jon Peirce & Karen J. Bentham, *Canadian Industrial Relations*, 3d ed (Toronto: Pearson, 2006) at 228, as quoted in Rose, 2008, above note 7 at 546.

regimes,[35] while ambulance paramedics are under an "essential services" regime established by the *ASCBA*.

Given this inconsistency of functional application, it is evident that the explanation for the existence of the "essential services" regimes under the *CECBA* and the *ASCBA* is found in history and, more specifically, in the political evolution of public service collective bargaining legislation from interest arbitration to permitting strikes and lockouts while ensuring the continued provision of essential services. Organizations historically closely associated with the government of Ontario, those designated under the *CECBA*, have remained under the *CECBA* regime while it has evolved. For example, the *ASCBA* was introduced when ambulance services were transferred from the province to municipalities, as discussed in more detail below.[36]

Maintaining essential services has been found by the OLRB to be the overriding statutory objective of the essential services part of the *CECBA*.[37] There is also some balancing to be done between the right to strike and the preservation of essential services. In the first of the cases under the *CECBA* essential services regime, the chair made the following general observations about the nature of the scheme that had been created:

> It is evident that the legislation reflects some of the philosophical tensions often identified with respect to public sector bargaining. On the one hand, there is no doubt that its intent is to provide government employees with a form of collective bargaining that more closely matches the traditional model. This is consistent with the view that the original objections to collective bargaining by public employees have been largely eroded by a combination of analysis and experience. The trend to move government functions to the private sector, often coupled with comprehensive regulation of those functions, has also had the effect of blurring both the lines between the private and public

---

35 In Ontario, the labour relations of those two public sector services are dealt with by interest arbitration legislation: *Fire Protection and Prevention Act, 1997*, SO 1997, c 4, Part IX—Firefighters: Employment and Labour Relations; *Police Services Act*, RSO 1990, c P15, Part VIII—Labour Relations. Note that the one police force composed of direct employees of the government, the OPP, is also under "no strike" legislation: *Ontario Provincial Police Collective Bargaining Act, 2006*, SO 2006, c 35, Sch B, as discussed in Chapter 6.

36 See Section C below.

37 *Ontario (Management Board Secretariat)*, [1998] OLRD No 3050 [*Misra*].

spheres, and the rationale for differential bargaining regimes. In addition, there is increasing recognition that there is a public interest in an equitable workplace and the harmonious labour relations which can be the product of collective bargaining.

At the same time, it is still undeniable that many functions performed by public employees play a unique role in the social fabric, especially those associated with more vulnerable citizens who may depend on government assistance for the most basic and critical of human needs. Moreover, increasing awareness of health, safety and environmental issues highlights the fact that there are areas in which all citizens are susceptible to harm. This is brought into even sharper focus in circumstances where the use of economic sanctions may have a greater impact on the public than either bargaining opponent, and where that third-party impact may largely capture both the spotlight and the attention of the parties.[38]

2) Bargaining an Essential Services Agreement

The *CECBA* incorporates section 79 of the *LRA*, under which prerequisites for a strike or lockout are the so-called no board report that completes the conciliation process and a mandatory strike vote.[39] The *CECBA* then adds the requirement of the finalization of an essential

---

38 *The Crown in Right of Ontario Represented by Management Board of Cabinet—Essential and Emergency Services*, [1995] OLRD No 2240 (Chair McCormack) at paras 4–6 and 9–10 [*McCormack*]. Note that the *CECBA* essential services regime introduced in 1993 by the then-NDP government, and commented upon in this 1995 OLRB case, was significantly amended in 1995 by the then-Conservative government to shift the balance more in the direction of preserving essential services, as referenced in the 1998 OLRB case above.

39 In the public service units represented by OPSEU, the strike vote is a large logistical task, involving tens of thousands of employees working at thousands of locations. OPSEU has held its strike votes at centralized polling stations. In advance of the 1996 strike, an application was brought by an employee alleging a violation of the *LRA*, s 79(9) requirement that the vote be conducted in a manner that provides "ample opportunity" to cast the ballot at a time and place that is "reasonably convenient." In *The Crown in the Right of Ontario as represented by Management Board of Cabinet*, [1996] OLRD No 1126 (Surdykowski) at para 1, the OLRB held that, considering the challenge faced by the union in conducting the vote, it was acceptable to require the voter to drive from their home in Oshawa to Toronto on a Saturday to vote. The Act did not give an employee any right to have a vote conducted during working hours or at a particular location.

services agreement between the employer and union,[40] providing for the use of bargaining unit employees during a strike or lockout. The parties must have such an agreement in place prior to any strike or lockout or alteration of terms and conditions of employment.[41] The OLRB has stressed that the level of essential services to be provided is determined by the essential services agreement and is "not a floating assessment of what services are or are not essential, to be ascertained as the strike or lockout unfolds."[42]

a) Requirement to Negotiate, and Do So in Good Faith

The collective bargaining parties are to "bargain in good faith and make every reasonable effort to make an essential services agreement."[43] Where there is no essential services agreement, the obligation to negotiate one begins fifteen days after giving notice to bargain a first contract[44] or at least 180 days before the expiry of an existing collective agreement.[45] The parties are given the statutory authorization to begin negotiations at a later time if they agree to do so.[46] Once in place, an essential services agreement need not be renegotiated for each round of collective negotiations. Any essential services agreement continues after the conclusion of collective bargaining and until one of the parties terminates it, by written notice given at least 190 days prior to the expiry of the collective agreement.[47] A conciliation officer will be appointed at the request of either party. The parties do not need to ratify essential services agreements, as is required for collective agreements.[48]

The ability of the parties to delay essential services negotiations has been used by parties to first attempt to reach a collective agreement. This is arguably not in keeping with the *CECBA*, which states that parties negotiating a collective agreement "shall" make an essential services

---

40 *CECBA*, above note 1, ss 30–42.

41 *Ibid*, ss 13 and 15.

42 *Ontario (Management Board of Cabinet) v OPSEU*, [2002] OLRD No 634 (McKee) at para 7 [*Psychiatric Hospitals No 1*].

43 *CECBA*, above note 1, s 31(2).

44 *Ibid*, s 33(1)(b).

45 *Ibid*, s 33(1)(a).

46 *Ibid*, s 33(2).

47 *Ibid*, s 37.

48 *OPSEU v Management Board of Cabinet*, [1995] OLRD No 2604 (Chair McCormack) at paras 5–6.

agreement.[49] The consequence of delay is that, if collective agreement negotiations break down, the parties cannot then proceed directly to a strike or lockout but must go back to the process of reaching an essential services agreement. The most recent negotiations for an essential services agreement between OPSEU and Management Board Secretariat (MBS), now Treasury Board Secretariat, representing the Management Board of Cabinet (MBC) were in 2014–15 for the 2015–17 rounds of collective bargaining. Since then, and to date of writing, those parties have agreed to conduct issues bargaining first and only negotiate essential services if they reached impasse, which has not occurred. Since the 2015–2017 round, the essential services regime has only applied to the Unified Bargaining Unit, due to the interest arbitration regime taking effect for the Correctional Bargaining Unit.

The OLRB has directed the parties to make every effort to bargain essential services agreements in good faith.[50] The board's jurisprudence on the duty to bargain does seem to apply to the negotiation of essential services agreements, but it is necessary to query its practical relevance. Any party experiencing frustration with the progress of essential services bargaining will consider simply asking the board to exercise its power to determine the matters to be included in the agreement,[51] rather than filing a complaint alleging a breach of the duty to bargain in good faith. Where the government brought an application requesting that the OLRB order the content of an essential services agreement, and OPSEU responded by noting that the employer had made little effort to bargain its position, the board indicated that the existence of an unresolved issue was by itself sufficient to invoke the OLRB's power to establish the terms of an essential services agreement.[52] The lack of employer disclosure during bargaining was addressed by requiring the employer to tender a statement of the material facts it intended to rely on.

---

49 *CECBA*, above note 1, s 31(1).

50 *The Crown in Right of Ontario v OPSEU*, OLRB File 2697-04-M, 26 November 2004 (Chair Whitaker) at para 27 [*Crown v OPSEU, 2004*].

51 *CECBA*, above note 1, s 36.

52 *The Crown in Right of Ontario v OPSEU*, [2005] OLRD No 384 (Freedman).

b) Conduct of Negotiations

The *CECBA* states that the parties are to negotiate the essential services part (as opposed to the emergency services part[53]) of an essential services agreement in the following prescribed order:

- what types of services are essential
- what levels of such services are necessary to prevent the specified dangers
- what employee positions are necessary
- how many employees are necessary
- which employees will be required[54]

Some parties have not adhered to this prescription in two main respects. First, they have engaged in the sensible practice of starting by negotiating general principles covering all these areas and then applying those principles to more specific situations. Second, they have expanded essential services agreements to include a number of additional, closely related topics. The leading example of these two variations is found in the OPSEU/MBS agreements governing negotiations for an essential services agreement. For example, in 2004, the central bargaining teams first negotiated the "Conditions for the 2004–2005 OPS–OPSEU Essential Services and Collective Agreement Negotiations,"[55] which contained a series of generally applicable provisions organizing the bargaining. Then sub teams negotiated many subsidiary worksite and service specific essential services agreements. The Corrections Bargaining Unit team negotiated a *Corrections Table Master Agreement for Essential Services*[56] and subsidiary agreements for the probation and parole service and individual jails. All these agreements set out both the staffing levels of different classifications of essential services workers and the specific work that was to be performed by that staff. That work was variously described by reference to entire positions of work or entire positions of work performing certain specified duties only or just the performance

53 *CECBA*, above note 1, s 30(b). Emergency services are discussed below.

54 *Ibid*, s 34.

55 *Conditions for the 2004–2005 OPS–OPSEU Essential Services and Collective Agreement Negotiations*, 1 December 2004 at B1 [*Conditions for Essential Services*], as ordered in *The Crown in Right of Ontario and OPSEU*, OLRB File 2697-04-M, 21 December 2004 (Chair Whitaker).

56 *Corrections Table Master Agreement for Essential Services*, as ordered by *The Crown in Right of Ontario and OPSEU*, OLRB File 2697-04-M, 7 March 2005 (Freedman).

of certain specified duties. In addition, the essential service agreement documentation covered such topics as the terms and conditions of employment of essential services workers, worksite visits, occupational health and safety, and so on. The agreements even contained two items dealing with non-essential workers. First, it was agreed that unclassified contracts would not be terminated solely because affected employees engaged in a strike or lockout. Second, it was agreed that any employee acting outside of the OPSEU bargaining unit would return to their home bargaining unit during the strike, with exact location to be determined.[57]

Determining essential services employees and functions requires a full cataloguing of the existing work and employees. The disclosure needs of the essential services bargaining process were last addressed in 2015 by the OPSEU/MBS parties agreeing to the provision of information that would produce the needed transparency about which employees were performing what work,[58] as follows:

- The employer would confirm if the regularly provided union dues list for employees was accurate for each worksite, including
  i. information about whether employees are actively working or not;
  ii. where employees are not actively working, the employer making reasonable efforts to determine the duration of their leave of absence; and
  iii. information about seasonal employees or students.
- The employer would provide
  i. current worksite organizational charts and current job specifications;
  ii. other non-listed worksites "where the Employer may reasonably anticipate that proposed essential services workers will be expected to work";
  iii. information about telework arrangements;
  iv. office case load statistics;
  v. existing scheduling information where the employer proposes work be scheduled outside of core business hours; and
  vi. all fixed-term bargaining unit members.

---

57 See *Ontario (Management Board of Cabinet)*, [2002] OLRD No 1065 (McKellar) at paras 17–18 [*Superior Court Registrar*].

58 OPSEU and the Crown, *Memorandum of Settlement*, 22 June 2015.

- All compressed workweek arrangements would be suspended, and there would be no remote computer (VPN) access, unless specifically negotiated.

Although the OLRB has the jurisdiction for the adjudication of essential services agreements, OPSEU and the MBS have also fashioned their own protocols for adjudication of those agreements.

In 2014–15 for the 2015–17 collective bargaining round, the parties entered into a negotiation protocol[59] under which they agreed to terminate the prior essential services agreement. However, in an approach quite similar to that to be expected from the OLRB, as discussed below under "Burden of Proof," the parties agreed that their prior essential services agreement was to "form the basis for negotiation" of the new essential services agreement. Where a service had been previously identified as an essential or an emergency service, it would stay so identified unless explicitly changed. The parties reserved the right to remove, amend, and add essential services. Any party proposing a change had to "show it is necessary because of a significant change since [the last round of essential services bargaining], which renders inappropriate that portion of the essential services agreement for which the change is proposed." In addition, either party could request a new service, not previously addressed, be added.

The OPSEU/MBS parties have also agreed to a mediation/arbitration protocol[60] that gives authority to finalize essential services agreements to specific private mediator/arbitrators. Those neutrals were given the same jurisdiction possessed by the OLRB under the *CECBA* to finalize the essential services agreement, except for the power of reconsideration. The mediator/arbitrators were to use "the most expeditious and informal procedure possible." The decision of a mediator/arbitrator was agreed to be final and binding, and their decisions were to be made board orders. Each party retained the right to request any dispute be formally litigated in accordance with OLRB rules of practice and procedure.

---

59 OPSEU/MBS, *Protocol for Negotiation of an Essential Services Agreement*, 12 February 2014.

60 *Memorandum of Agreement between The Crown in Right of Ontario and Ontario Public Service Employees Union: Mediation/Arbitration Protocol During the Negotiation of the Essential Services Agreements*, 14 February 2014.

The substantive decisions issued by mediators/arbitrators to assist the parties in finalizing essential services agreements have included dealing with the process and timetable,[61] determining that essential service levels were to be established based on the status quo of staffing organization (whether or not it involved extensive use of part-time and contract employees),[62] and staff location.[63]

c) Necessity of an Essential Services Agreement as a Prerequisite to Strike or Lockout

Under the *CECBA*, an essential services agreement must be in place before a legal strike or lockout.[64] As a consequence, the OLRB has ruled that the jurisdiction of any private arbitrator who had assisted in finalizing an essential services agreement terminates upon commencement of the work stoppage.[65] This helps ensure timely completion of the entire agreement.

At the same time, there is a possibility that comparatively small, unresolved, details might unduly prevent a strike or lockout from occurring. The OLRB will not allow the inclusion of provisions in an essential services agreement that permit a strike or lockout before the completion of the agreement.[66] However, the board is prepared to allow the parties to decide when an essential services agreement exists. In other words, the parties can deem a fixed point in the readiness process to be the formal point of completion, even if there is some more to do afterwards. In the OPSEU/MBS *Conditions for Essential Services* document, the finalization of the lists of selected employees was deemed to complete the agreement.[67]

The timing of the finalization of the lists of selected employees has been linked to the *LRA* required strike vote. A yes vote has triggered the selection process.[68] The method of finalization of the list is discussed below under "Pre-strike Selection of Essential Services Workers."

---

61 *OPSEU and MBS*, 21 February 2002 (O'Neil).

62 *OPSEU and MBS*, 6 March 2002 (O'Neil); *OPSEU and MBS*, 6 March 2002 (O'Neil).

63 *OPSEU and MBS*, 6 March 2002 (O'Neil).

64 *CECBA*, above note 1, ss 13 and 15, made non-applicable to Corrections in s 151.

65 *Ontario (Management Board of Cabinet)*, [2002] OLRD No 1088 (Chair Whitaker) at paras 17–21 [*Johnston Deferral*].

66 *McCormack*, above note 38 at paras 56–58.

67 *Conditions for Essential Services*, above note 55, Appendix B, Stage 2, Step 7.

68 *Ibid*, Appendix C.

d) Role of Ontario Labour Relations Board in Finalizing Essential Services Agreements

The *CECBA* mandates that the parties will make the essential services determinations.[69] It is only when either party applies to the OLRB for a determination of unresolved matters that the board has the power to determine any matters, specify the contents of an essential services agreement, deem the parties to have entered into an essential services agreement, or "give any other such directions as the Board considers appropriate."[70]

The OLRB has been candid about its ability to substitute its opinion for the agreement of the parties, acknowledging that its decisions can only be approximate and that the legislation's emphasis on the parties reaching agreement is appropriate because, as the employers and employees are in the workplaces, they are in the best position to make the necessary assessments and craft the necessary solutions.[71] It was noted that both parties have a "sincere commitment to the well-being of the very vulnerable people" who are dependent on the services provided.[72] Similar comments were made by the leading academic commentary:

> We have also come away with a sense of admiration for the ingenuity and seriousness of purpose of the men and women we interviewed. Repeatedly we observed the determination on their part to protect the public, whatever their personal misgivings about the fairness or legitimacy of particular dispute resolution procedures and notwithstanding the intense feelings often engendered at the bargaining table or on the picket line.[73]

Hence, it can be expected that the board's approach on any application to finalize an essential services agreement will be designed to first encourage the parties to complete the process, rather than to substitute its own opinion.

The OLRB has said it will not fine-tune its decisions according to the effect that they would have on either party's strike power.[74] It is

69 *Misra*, above note 37 at para 22.

70 *CECBA*, above note 1, s 36.

71 *McCormack*, above note 38 at paras 16–17.

72 *Ontario (Management Board of Cabinet)*, [2002] OLRD No 1170 (McKee) at para 3 [*Psychiatric Hospitals No 2*].

73 Adell et al, above note 7 at 204.

74 *McCormack*, above note 38 at para 49.

aware that its decisions will have such ramifications, but it does not have the mandate to balance bargaining strength.

In the course of negotiating essential services agreements, the parties have, on occasion, tried to include additional matters for resolution by the board, but the OLRB has ruled that it should only exercise its decision-making power to deal with matters related to essential services. It has declined to finalize a comprehensive strike and lockout protocol, including being unwilling to extend the contracts of all unclassified employees by the length of the strike.[75] The OLRB will not decide the terms and conditions of employment for employees not providing essential services.[76] The board may rule on some peripheral matters if needed to finalize the essential services agreement.[77]

When resolving essential services agreements, the OLRB has general broad procedural power, and the specific power to conduct a consultation or an inquiry or both.[78]

The OLRB and the Divisional Court have denied the requests of third-party intervenors to participate in essential services agreement negotiations.

The Ontario Provincial Police Association (OPPA), which at the relevant time provided collective bargaining representation for OPP officers, but not OPP civilians, sought to make submissions on the level of essential services provided by OPSEU-represented civilian employees working as communications dispatchers for the OPP.[79] The OLRB dismissed the request on the basis that the OPPA "had other avenues or forums in which it may pursue its concerns."[80]

The Divisional Court has dealt with one case of persons adversely affected by the lack of essential services. Meat packing businesses affected by the 1996 strike challenged a board decision that meat slaughter

---

75 *Ibid* at paras 39–45.

76 *OPSEU v The Crown in Right of Ontario*, [1999] OLRD No 259 (Alternate Chair Herman) at para 10 [*Herman*].

77 *Misra*, above note 37 at para 29.

78 *CECBA*, above note 1, s 36(2).

79 OPP civilians have since become represented by the OPPA. See Chapter 4 for more on the OPP.

80 *Crown in Right of Ontario v OPSEU (Institutional and Health Care Bargaining Unit)*, [1995] OLRD No 4443 at para 2.

inspection was not an essential service.[81] Because meat inspection was a legal prerequisite to animal slaughter, that decision had the effect of shutting down slaughtering operations at provincially licensed premises. The meat packers argued that they were entitled, as a matter of natural justice, to receive notice of the OLRB proceeding because it affected their interests. The court accepted that the cessation of inspections would cause financial loss to the meat packing industry but found that the *CECBA* does not require notice to such adversely affected persons. The court further noted that "it is perhaps not the [essential services agreement] or the [board's] decision itself which has caused the financial hardship to the applicants but rather the strike."[82] The issue arose again in 2005 with the same result.[83]

3) Essential Services Agreement Contents

a) Content Prescribed by the *CECBA*

An essential services agreement is to have an essential services part and an emergency services part.[84] The essential services part must include identification of the essential services, the number of employees from specified positions who are necessary "to enable the employer to provide the essential services," and the identification of the employees who would be required to work "to the extent necessary to enable the employer to provide the essential services."[85] The content of the emergency services part is not specified. When reference is made to an "essential services agreement," it usually includes both the essential and emergency services parts. The term "essential services" will mean both essential and emergency services, unless emergency services are specifically referred to separately.

b) Which Services Are Essential?

Under the *CECBA*, essential services are defined to mean "services that are necessary to enable the employer to prevent (a) danger to life, health

81 The original OLRB decision is discussed below. The meat packers challenge is addressed in *Weston Abattoir Ltd v Ontario Public Service Employees Union*, [1996] OJ No 5379 [*Weston Abattoir*].

82 *Ibid.*

83 *Ontario Independent Meat Processors, Re*, 2005 CanLII 17821 (ON LRB) (Chauvin).

84 *CECBA*, above note 1, s 30.

85 *Ibid*, s 32.

or safety, (b) the destruction or serious deterioration of machinery, equipment or premises, (c) serious environmental damage, or (d) disruption of the administration of the courts or of legislative drafting."[86] There are relatively few OLRB cases determining whether particular services are essential because, for the most part, the issue of determining which services are essential has been settled between the parties themselves or through the agreed means of private mediator/arbitrators. The focus in litigation has been on what amount or level of essential service needs to be provided.[87]

It is notable that the *CECBA* definition of essential services is different from the definition of "emergency" in the *Emergency Management and Civil Protection Act*,[88] which is "a situation or an impending situation that constitutes a danger of major proportions that could result in serious harm to persons or substantial damage to property"[89] and, as such, determinations under the emergency management legislation, including "essential service" determinations, are not directly relevant to the *CECBA*.

i) Burden of Proof

The burden of proof that services are essential or that circumstances constitute an emergency lies upon the party so alleging.[90] That burden will not be satisfied simply by relying on a prior essential services agreement designating the service as essential, nor will a party be prevented from establishing that a service is essential by its absence from a prior essential services agreement.[91] At the same time, where there is

---

86 *Ibid*, s 30.

87 The most relevant cases on what public services are essential are early federal rulings. Many are summarized in Jacob Finkelman & Shirley B. Goldenberg, *Collective Bargaining in the Public Service: The Federal Experience in Canada* (Montreal: IRPP, 1983) at Vol 2, 492–507 [Finkelman & Goldenberg].

88 RSO 1990, c E.9.

89 *Ibid*, s 1.

90 *CECBA*, above note 1, s 39.

91 *The Crown in Right of Ontario and Ontario Public Service Employees Union, Co-Applicants*, [2005] OLRD No 1784 at para 15 [*Walkerton Jail*]. See also *The Crown in Right of Ontario v OPSEU*, 2005 CanLII 16183 (ON LRB) (Freedman) [*Occupational Health and Safety Inspectors*], finding that the parties must negotiate an essential services agreement for occupational health and safety inspectors, even though they had not negotiated agreements for inspectors in previous rounds; and *The Crown in Right of Ontario v OPSEU*, [2005] OLRD No 2470 (Albertyn) [*Huronia Regional Centre*], finding that an increase in essential

a pre-existing essential services agreement dealing with the same issues, the party seeking a variation in a subsequent round of bargaining will bear the burden of persuasion.[92] Just as in interest arbitration or free collective bargaining, the normal conventions of interest arbitration adjudication should apply where possible. The parties are expected to start from their former status quo and seek to persuade each other to change positions. However, where the issue is the central one of the essentiality of the service itself, the statutory burden of proof—which is on the party alleging that services are essential[93]—is the overriding consideration.

The burden of proof that services are essential is not met by speculation about human behaviour. In 1996, it was agreed that meat slaughter inspection was not an essential service, and that agreement effectively shut down meat packing at provincially inspected abattoirs for the duration of the 1996 OPSEU strike.[94] The MBS then applied to alter the agreement so that there would be limited inspection of meat processing operations, which would allow some meat packing. The MBS claimed this step would take economic pressure off meat packers, thereby removing the temptation to slaughter illegally. In 1996, the OLRB viewed this claim as too speculative to warrant a change to the original agreement[95] and reached a similar conclusion in 2005.[96]

ii) Danger to Life, Health, and Safety

The leading case on what constitutes "danger to life, health, and safety" concerned the Wolfe Island Ferry, which is the provincially operated transportation link between Wolfe Island and the City of Kingston.[97]

---

services at institutions for persons with developmental disabilities was justified by showing that the levels of service in the prior agreement were insufficient to protect the health of the clientele.

92 *Crown v OPSEU, 2004*, above note 50 at para 18; *R v Ontario Public Service Employees Union*, 2015 CanLII 30261 (ON LRB).

93 *CECBA*, above note 1, s 39.

94 See *OPSEU v Management Board of Cabinet, Administrative Unit*, [1995] OLRD No 1802 at para 2, judicial review dismissed; *Weston Abattoir*, above note 81.

95 *The Crown in Right of Ontario, as represented by Management Board of Cabinet*, [1996] OLRD No 914 at para 13 [*Meat Inspectors*]. That decision, at paras 17–19, directed a negotiation of an emergency-services protocol for meat inspectors to ensure that there were sufficient inspectors available to investigate the possibility of illegal slaughter.

96 *The Crown in Right of Ontario v OPSEU*, [2005] OLRD No 1196 (Chauvin).

97 *MBC v OPSEU*, [2002] OLRD No 1091 (Chair Whitaker) [*Wolfe Island Ferry*].

The relevant essential services agreement reduced the number of daily ferry runs for the duration of any strike or lockout. During the OPSEU 2002 strike, the employer applied to increase the number of daily ferry runs to address complaints from island residents. The OLRB accepted that the reduction in ferry service had caused "considerable grief and hardship." An example cited was delay in getting to chemotherapy appointments. However, the reduction was left in place because there was no proof of actual danger to life, health, or safety. Even "serious and real hardship" will be insufficient justification for the provision of essential services.

The broad definition of "health" includes the provision of counseling and recreation, but not vocational training, for the clientele at a psychiatric hospital for the criminally insane[98] and at institutions for individuals with developmental disabilities.[99] The health of residents is maintained through activities and therapy, and, in the absence of such services, they may revert to inappropriate behaviour.

A more complicated determination was made in cases concerning the provincial schools for students who are deaf or blind, and those with severe learning disabilities.[100] During the course of the 2002 strike, the board found that deaf students are put at a significant mental health risk when removed from the supportive environment of the schools. In the short term, the loss of teaching did not endanger health, but, if the strike lasted as long as the summer vacation, that could change. This ruling was refined in 2005. It was determined that the health of all students would be adversely affected if they were deprived of education for more than four weeks.[101]

Services that are needed to support essential services are also essential. Investigation of work refusals by an occupational health and safety inspector is a function that determines whether the refused work is likely to endanger the refusing worker and other workers. The OLRB

---

98 *The Crown in Right of Ontario v OPSEU*, [2005] OLRD No 2226 (Freedman) at paras 5–13 [*Oak Ridge*].

99 *Huronia Regional Centre*, above note 91. It is noted as irrelevant that the employer was intending to close the institutions and place clients in the community, even though that would have the consequence of making the clientele subject to a labour relations regime involving strikes and lockouts without essential services.

100 *Ontario (Management Board of Cabinet) v OPSEU*, [2002] OLRD No 1293 (Chair Whitaker) at paras 10 and 16.

101 *Ontario (Management Board of Cabinet) v OPSEU*, [2005] OLRD No 3522 (Albertyn).

found that "[i]f work refusal investigations are not essential, then other workers might well be engaged in performing unsafe work, and indeed, the refusing worker might well be compelled to engage in that work as a result of peer pressure or economic pressure."[102]

During the lead up to the computer programming crisis of Y2K, caused by the effect of the new millennium on computers' date tracking, the government claimed that the scheduled overhauling of the public service computer system had to continue through the end of the year 1999 to ensure that the computer system would be ready to support the delivery of essential services thereafter. The board ruled:

> In order to be an "essential service" in this context, the primary service itself must be essential, the computer component involved in the delivery of that service must be essential, and the Y2K preparation services must also be essential. It is only if all three conditions are met that the Y2K preparation service will itself be found to be "essential."[103]

It does not matter whether or not the service that is supported is supplied directly by the OPS. For example, public service technical officers supporting telecommunications equipment for municipal ambulance dispatchers provide an essential service.[104]

Further guidance is available from the parties. In 2014, it was understood between them that the following duties are not generally included in essential services: "task force work, policy development, financial planning, budgeting, program planning, training or routine administrative tasks."[105]

In assessing the prevention of danger, it is important to recall that this is to be done without having regard for the availability of non-bargaining unit employees to do the work.[106]

---

102 *Occupational Health and Safety Inspectors*, above note 91 at para 10.

103 *Ontario (Management Board Secretariat)*, [1999] OLRD No 260 (Herman) at para 17 [*Y2K and Courts*].

104 *The Crown in Right of Ontario v OPSEU*, OLRB File 2697-04-M, 21 February 2005 (Albertyn).

105 OPSEU 2014 Essential/Emergency Service Rationale form.

106 See the discussion immediately below about the number of employees necessary to provide essential services.

iii) Specific Sub-definitions – Administration of the Courts

Although the definition of essential services contains three specific sub-definitions—destruction of property, environmental damage, and "disruption of the administration of the courts or of legislative drafting"[107]—only the disruption of the administration of the courts has been the subject of a decision by the OLRB.

Any services which enable the administration of the courts to continue on the same basis as prior to any strike or lockout are essential.[108] Delays or inconvenience amount to disruption of the administration of the courts.

The phrase "administration of the courts" means all the services needed for the day-to-day operation of the courts but does not include other services involved in the administration of justice. The administration of the courts includes courtroom personnel, court officers, and judicial support, including judge's secretaries, law clerks, and library services being used by the judiciary or other court officers.[109] Some aspects of the role of the Crown are also within the administration of the courts. The Crown's "prosecutorial role" and the role of children's lawyer are essential services.[110] However, the role of the Crown "as litigant" or in its role in seeking to "execute upon judgments" does not fall within the administration of the courts. That means personnel involved in civil enforcement and those employed in the legal services branches of government ministries, save and except those personnel involved in prosecution, are not essential.

c) Number of Employees Necessary to Provide Essential Services

It is appropriate to minimize the number of essential services employees and, where it is necessary to have employees available without being active, the "emergency" services designation, discussed below, which

107 *CECBA*, above note 1, s 30.

108 *Y2K and Courts*, above note 103 at para 7.

109 *Ibid* at para 10. In *Ontario (Attorney General) v Ontario Public Service Employees Union*, 2000 CanLII 17008 (ON CA) at para 16, the Ontario Court of Appeal addressed whether the OLRB had properly included judges' secretaries in the OPSEU bargaining unit: "The most serious potential for interference with judicial independence alleged was in the event of a strike or lockout However, [*Y2K and Courts*, above note 103] protects judges' secretaries as essential in the event of a strike or lockout It is highly unlikely that OPSEU and the Crown would negotiate a future 'essential services agreement' in violation of that ruling."

110 *Y2K and Courts*, above note 103 at para 11.

permits flexibility to react by calling in employees should be used as much as possible.[111] Staffing levels are to be "just sufficient for the purpose of providing the essential services. The agreements are designed so that as many members of OPSEU as possible—short of danger to life, health or property—can exercise their right to strike."[112] The OLRB has noted that

> [t]he dilemma inherent in this legislation is that the concept of essential services carries with it the seed for subverting collective bargaining significantly. Removing essential services from the ambit of a strike may eliminate the most potent part of the strike weapon, leaving it an empty shell. And while such sanctions are not frequently resorted to in the overall landscape of collective bargaining, it is axiomatic that the underlying threat of economic conflict is what drives the vast majority of uneventful negotiations and contract settlements. To the extent that the designation of essential services renders the strike sanction relatively toothless, the salutary effect of economic pressure is likely to be correspondingly impaired. Moreover, there is some irony in the parties being required to, in essence, negotiate their own bargaining strength through the essential service agreement process. In addition, it is also fair to say that substantial dilution of that strength may unduly protract a labour dispute.[113]

The number of employees declared essential should come as close as reasonably possible to a "gold standard" of the re-creation of true collective bargaining conditions where all bargaining unit labour would strike or be locked out, thus permitting the parties to use all their economic power.[114] For example, the number of essential occupational

---

111 *McCormack*, above note 38 at para 25; and see *Herman*, above note 76 at para 45; *The Crown in Right of Ontario v OPSEU*, [2005] OLRD No 616, 10 February 2005 (Chair Whitaker) at para 21 [*Crown v OPSEU, 2005*]. It has been noted, at the federal level, that managers will suggest designation with "zeal," not necessarily because they wish to weaken any strike, but because they want to ensure the continuation of the public services for which they are responsible: Finkelman & Goldenberg, above note 87 at 485.

112 *OPSEU v MBC*, [2002] OLRB Rep March/April 15 (Albertyn) at para 12 [*Lauzon*].

113 *McCormack*, above note 38 at paras 13–14.

114 *Crown v OPSEU, 2004*, above note 50 at para 36, where, in response to a management claim that no corrections staff were essential to operate jails, the union made the claim that correctional officers and probation and parole officers were essential. The union also advanced the claim the occupational health and

health and safety inspectors was reduced as the proximity of inspectors' offices to each other permitted "the necessary coverage" to be provided by fewer inspectors.[115]

At the same time, section 32(2) of the *CECBA* requires the parties to identify how many bargaining unit employees are required to perform the essential services part of the agreement *without regard* to the availability of other persons.[116] Where the employer planned to use non-bargaining unit staff to carry out the duties of correctional officers and probation and parole officers, an essential services agreement should still be finalized without regard for the availability of those other employees. Finalizing an essential services agreement on the basis of using bargaining unit workers only would ensure the availability of all possible necessary bargaining unit employees to act as a "safety net."[117]

The OLRB has reserved on the issue of whether the employer has the discretion to make no use of the bargaining unit essential employees contemplated by the essential services part of an essential services agreement.[118] That issue apparently arose because management found the presence of essential services workers in jails to be disruptive and was contemplating operating the correctional facilities with augmented management staff only.

The OPSEU/MBS *Conditions for Essential Services* document permits the employer to unilaterally reduce the required number of essential and emergency services workers *prior* to a work stoppage.[119] The number of employees is then to be fixed at the new, reduced number until the end of the labour dispute unless further reduced by an order of the OLRB. The employer is to notify OPSEU of the reduction by

---

safety officers were essential, which was upheld in *Occupational Health and Safety Inspectors*, above note 91.

115 *Occupational Health and Safety Inspectors*, above note 91 at paras 12–13.

116 *Crown v OPSEU, 2005*, above note 111. It is to be noted that between 1993 and 1995 the *CECBA* did contain a "management offset" provision requiring the employer to first use eligible non-bargaining unit employees to provide essential services before being able to require unionized employees to provide the service": *Public Service and Labour Relations Statute Law Amendment Act*, SO 1993, c 38, s 32(2).

117 *Crown v OPSEU, 2005*, above note 111 at para 23.

118 *Ibid* at para 26.

119 *Conditions for Essential Services*, above note 55 at B9. It seems this right was sought by management to give themselves flexibility as they continued to assess operational needs.

the end of the eighth day following a strike vote or, in the case of its seasonal services, at the end of the eighth working day prior to the start of the season. OPSEU sought to remove the unilateral reduction clause on the grounds that unilateral determinations of essential services levels are contrary to the *CECBA*, that the provision could be used selectively for reprisal, and that the employer may set unsafe levels of service.[120] The OLRB noted that management had not previously invoked the clause and held that management has the ultimate responsibility for the provision of essential services. The board declined to change the clause, noting that any inappropriate management use of the clause could be addressed.

d) Work to Be Performed: Whole Job Versus Essential Duties

Since "the thrust of the statute is to prohibit employees from striking, *to the extent necessary to provide essential services*," there is to be an assessment of what specific work functions are "essential."[121] Hence, the union is able to negotiate that its members will only do essential duties and need not agree that they will perform their entire job unless, of course, it is "essential" that all of the duties of the job be performed. The union is entitled to have an essential services agreement set out which duties are essential and which are non-essential.[122]

This has contrasted with the federal situation. In 1982, the Supreme Court dealt with the meaning of the then-*Public Service Staff Relations Act*[123] and found that the only role for the Public Service Staff Relations Board was to determine whether the employees designated by the employer actually performed any essential services and *not* to determine what job functions were essential.[124]

Union and management representatives negotiate essential services agreements before any strike or lockout, but individual workers and managers must implement the agreements in the workplace during the work stoppage. It can be expected that, during the "charged and

---

120 *Crown v OPSEU, 2004*, above note 50 at paras 31–39.

121 *Herman*, above note 76 at para 21 [emphasis in the original].

122 *Walkerton Jail*, above note 91 at paras 16–17; *Oak Ridge*, above note 98 at para 17.

123 RSC 1985, c P-35, s 79(1).

124 *Canadian Air Traffic Control Association v The Queen in Right of Canada et al*, [1982] 1 SCR 696, as discussed in Finkelman & Goldenberg, above note 87 at 507–12.

difficult circumstances"[125] of any strike or lockout, there will be argument about what functions must be performed. The wording of the essential services agreement itself is to resolve this issue. "There is no further role for individual employees or managers to then unilaterally alter the agreement of the parties by deciding for themselves on a task-by-task basis that certain work assignments are or are not essential."[126]

Where the essential services agreement does simply specify a position, it is to be assumed all of the duties of that job are required to be performed during a strike or lockout,[127] subject only to any agreed restrictions on the range of duties.[128] Where a group of court clerks, with areas of specialization who also occasionally helped out in each other's areas of specialization, declined during a strike to help out in that fashion, the clerks were not entitled to "unilaterally carve out" their primary function and refuse to do other work that they normally performed.[129]

More specifically, where the entire position is designated essential, then:

1) The issue is not whether the tasks were or were not contained in a job description or whether they were or were not within the possible ambit of the duties of a position. The only question is whether an employee actually performed these tasks and duties before the strike commenced. If he or she did so before the strike commenced, then the services have been defined by the parties as essential services . . .
2) If a supervisor chooses to prioritize tasks in the order that they are to be done, that is her or his prerogative, and the essential services worker must follow those instructions.
3) If the supervisor chooses to assign more than one task to the essential services worker to be accomplished in a given time, then the essential services worker will prioritize the tasks. If the

---

125 *Johnston Deferral*, above note 65 at para 18.

126 *Ontario (Management Board of Cabinet)*, [2002] OLRD No 926 at paras 6–7 and 9–11 (Chair Whitaker) [*Forensic Sciences*]. To the same effect, see *Ontario (Management Board of Cabinet)*, [2002] OLRD No 1064 (Chair Whitaker) at para 6; and *Psychiatric Hospitals No 1*, above note 42 at para 7.

127 *Y2K and Courts*, above note 103.

128 *Ontario (Management Board of Cabinet)*, [2002] OLRD No 929 (Chair Whitaker) at para 3 [*Court Houses*].

129 *Ontario (Management Board of Cabinet)*, [2002] OLRD No 1300 (Brown) at para 2.

supervisor chooses to change that order in the midst of those duties, he or she may do so.

4) Since it is unlikely that the same volume of work can be done by fewer people during the strike, it will be necessary to communicate about work volumes, priorities and the order in which tasks are to be performed.[130]

Where the essential services agreement only requires that particular duties be performed, there will inevitably be ambiguities and unresolved details about what is actually required. The OLRB has issued a number of decisions dealing with that issue, including whether it was necessary to turn the lights on and off to maintain the security and supervision of offenders and institutions;[131] whether essential services workers at a jail must collect and account for any clothing and personal effects removed during the admission and strip search of inmates;[132] whether a patient in crisis who had been transported to a hospital needed to be transported home when the emergency had passed, where the essential services agreement included the phrase "calls will be repatriated if necessary";[133] whether probation and parole officers need to identify all sex offender and partner-abuse cases on case registries;[134] whether it was required to load fire-crew equipment onto vehicles in circumstances where the essential services agreement said the essential and emergency work would be limited to the duties listed in a handbook, which made no reference to the loading of equipment onto the vehicles;[135] and whether the employer can use bailiffs assigned to the northern region of the province to move inmates between institutions entirely in the southern region of the province.[136] In the course of resolving these cases, the OLRB developed principles for the interpretation of essential services agreements where specific duties are referenced.

130 *Ontario (Management Board of Cabinet)*, [2002] OLRD No 957 (McKee) at paras 4–5 [*Ottawa Crown Attorneys*]; and, to the same effect, *Ontario (Management Board of Cabinet)*, [2002] OLRD No 1134 (McKellar) at para 9 [*Quantitative Analysis Clerk*].

131 *MBC v OPSEU*, [2002] OLRD No 961 (Trachuk) at para 11 [*Kenora Jail*].

132 *Ibid* at para 11.

133 *Ontario (Management Board of Cabinet)*, [2002] OLRD No 971 (McKee) at para 10 [*CACC No 1*].

134 *Ontario (Management Board of Cabinet)*, [2002] OLRD No 942 (Freedman) at para 7 [*Probation and Parole No 1*].

135 *OPSEU v MBC*, [2002] OLRD No 1143 (Kelly) at para 12 [*Fire Crews*].

136 *OPSEU v MBC*, [2002] OLRD No 1167 (McKellar).

Where the list of duties is not intended to be exhaustive, the duties will be interpreted so as to include both the tasks specifically enumerated and those tasks necessary to carry out the enumerated duty. For example, where the essential services agreement requires a certain process to be performed and then, under the heading "which includes," sets out certain specific duties, a necessary, but unlisted, aspect of the process has to be performed.[137]

If the essential services agreement says a function is to be done in accordance with "current operating practices and procedures," then all current practices and procedures are to be followed as long as they are connected with that function.[138] This applies even if some of those practices may not be essential. On the other hand, if the performance of certain functions is supported by another employee performing an ancillary function, the requirement to carry out the central function will not be taken to mean that the person carrying out the central function must assume the other person's ancillary function.[139]

Another formulation is to use a job description's listed duties "except for the following [specifically set out] non-essential duties" with the addition that "[i]f other duties are assigned, they must be consistent with and relate directly to the essential services duties contained in the job description."[140]

e) Manner in Which Duties Are to Be Performed

In addition to issues about which duties are to be performed, questions have arisen about how those duties are to be performed, beginning with the rate of productivity. It can be expected that the essential services agreement will contemplate a decrease in staff complement during a strike. The essential services staff do not have to work harder to cover the workload of those who are absent.[141] By the same token, essential services staff are not permitted to decrease the volume of work that

---

137 *Ontario (Management Board of Cabinet)*, [2002] OLRD No 950 (Lewis) at para 6 [*Fish Stocking*].

138 *Ontario Management Board of Cabinet*, [2002] OLRD 973 (McKee) at paras 11–13 [CACC No 2].

139 *Ontario (Management Board of Cabinet)*, [2002] OLRD No 1135 (McKellar) at paras 4–6.

140 *Ontario v Ontario Public Service Employees Union*, 2005 CanLII 21364 (ON LRB) (Freedman).

141 *Psychiatric Hospitals No 1*, above note 42 at para 13.

they personally perform, absent specific indications to that effect in the essential services agreement. It would be a violation of the essential services agreement, and the *CECBA*, if decisions about the volume of work were made for any strike-related reason.[142]

The requirement to provide essential services does not mean legislated politeness.[143] "Inappropriate comments (from either side) when everyone is feeling the strain" are not violations of the essential services agreement.

f) Pre-strike Selection of Essential Services Workers

As the number of essential services workers is likely to be less than the number of bargaining unit employees who normally perform the work in question, there is a need to select which specific workers will be required to provide essential services. In addition to ensuring that the persons selected are actually capable of providing the essential services, both parties have an additional interest in the selection criteria. Each party may wish to pick the workers that it believes are most likely to be of assistance during a strike situation. An issue may be whether the workers picked would be likely to perform more work than the required essential services. Essential services work is also a source of income for employees during a strike, so there will be an interest in the fair distribution of the opportunity to perform essential services.

The selection of the bargaining unit employees who will be essential services workers has been found to involve two issues: eligibility and final selection.[144] Bargaining unit employees have been found to be eligible if they are currently performing the work in question and possess any required qualification. If no eligible person is available, the parties are to attempt to negotiate how to fill that position, failing which the employer can fill it as long as the person chosen is able to perform the work after having received up to five days of orientation. Final selection is to be done by a draw that selects as randomly as possible from amongst the eligible staff.

---

142 *Ontario (Management Board of Cabinet)*, [2002] OLRD No 1082 (McKee) at para 17 [*Transportation Enforcement Officers*].

143 *Psychiatric Hospitals No 1*, above note 42 at para 14.

144 *Herman*, above note 76 at para 33.

i) Example of the 2004–2005 OPSEU/MBS Essential Services Agreement

In the OPSEU/MBS *Conditions for Essential Services 2004–2005* document, detailed appendices were established for the selection of employees at each worksite.[145] These appendices provided for local and central meetings to review lists and, failing resolution, referral of disputes to agreed arbitrators. Where there was no qualified employee and the employer exercised its prerogative to pick the employee, the choice could be challenged by the union through recourse to the agreed mediator/arbitrators. The proportion of classified and unclassified employees on the eligibility list was to be matched with the proportion of such employees at the worksite. Various exemptions from providing essential/emergency services were agreed to. Local OPSEU officers, bargaining team members, and OPSEU executive board members were able to choose not to be designated as essential or emergency service employees. Similarly, part-time employees could request not to be designated. In both cases, the employer could refuse the request if there was no one else available to do the work. A virtually identical procedure was established for emergency services.[146] For seasonal services, a selection protocol was established that was to commence four weeks prior to the start of the season.[147]

Essential employees were to be rotated between working and being on strike in a two-week cycle in jails[148] and a four-week cycle elsewhere.[149] This balances the employer interest in continuity with the employee interest in sharing the provision of essential services and getting paid.

g) Obligation to Provide Essential Services During a Strike or Lockout

During a strike or lockout, the employer is entitled to use such agreed essential services employees "as are necessary."[150] There is a requirement that those employees be notified, and then they cannot strike and

145 *Conditions for Essential Services*, above note 55 at A3 and Appendix A.

146 *Ibid*, Appendix B.

147 *Ibid* at B(2)(B) and Appendix D.

148 *Corrections Table Master Agreement for Essential Services*, as ordered by *The Crown in Right of Ontario and OPSEU*, OLRB File 2697-04-M, 7 March 2005 (Freedman) at para 19b.

149 *The Crown in Right of Ontario v OPSEU*, [2005] OLRD No 649 (Albertyn).

150 *CECBA*, above note 1, s 40.

may not be locked out.[151] Emergency services employees are dealt with similarly.[152]

i) Parties' Obligation of Cooperation

There is a statutory obligation to deal with essential services issues in good faith.[153] An essential services agreement is to acknowledge the joint responsibility to try to ensure that sufficient bargaining unit employees are available, and that the union is to cooperate with the employer to obtain a replacement employee when one is required due to the temporary or permanent absence of another employee.[154] The 2004–2005 essential services agreement between OPSEU and the MBS did contain such a statement. Replacements were to be drawn from the pools of classified and unclassified employees.

The employer has been required to provide a list of all bargaining unit employees to OPSEU with respect to all worksites, and not only at those sites at which it is expected that essential services will take place. The union needs this information to find any needed additional eligible employees.[155]

There is a recognized limit to the union's responsibility. In a case where OPSEU had tried to contact workers, with the same lack of success as the employer, it was recognized that the union cannot compel workers to comply with their obligation to perform the work.[156] Where there was an ongoing absence of essential workers, the OLRB directed further staffing protocols be put into place. The protocols set out an order for calling in various groups of employees and stipulated that in the event an essential worker was still not identified, the union was to make its best efforts to cooperate in obtaining workers.[157]

ii) Obligation of Individual Workers (and Employer Notification to Them)

Essential agreements are to contain provision for the notification of employees about their obligation to perform the work. "Those employees to whom notice has been given may not strike. Those to whom no

151 *Ibid*, s 40(2) & (3).
152 *Ibid*, s 42(2).
153 *Herman*, above note 76 at para 31; *Lauzon*, above note 112 at para 12.
154 *Herman*, above note 76.
155 *Ibid* at para 41.
156 *Kenora Jail*, above note 131 at para 5.
157 *Psychiatric Hospitals No 2*, above note 72.

notice has been given may strike. It is critical that any employee knows which it is."[158]

OPSEU/MBS essential services agreements have included an emergency list, or pool, of workers who will be available to replace essential services workers who are absent from their shifts. When the parties neglected to negotiate an emergency list for a particular workplace, the staff at that location had no obligation to provide emergency services.[159]

Individual employees on the emergency list must advise the employer and the union about their availability and make reasonable efforts to be able to receive notice from the employer of a need to report for work.[160] Emergency list workers are required to respond to, and return, telephone calls from managers requesting them to come to work.[161]

The use of the standby and on-call articles of the collective agreement for emergency list workers has been contentious. The OLRB can order the use of those articles if needed for the provision of essential services.[162] It is not clear whether the employer can unilaterally place employees on such status during a strike or lockout if the right to do so is not confirmed in the essential services agreement. The employer is not required to use the standby and on-call pay provisions in the collective agreement to ensure that employees are generally available.[163] However, in the absence of being scheduled to work or otherwise required to stand by, emergency services workers need not wait by the phone. They are "free to make plans or engage in activities which make it impossible for them to report for unscheduled work, especially at short notice."[164]

h) In Addition to Essential Services Workers, Who Else Can Perform Essential Services Work During a Strike or Lockout?

As discussed above, under the *CECBA* the number of employees necessary to provide the services set out in the essential services part (as

---

158 *CACC No 1*, above note 133 at para 5.

159 *Ibid* at para 8.

160 *Ontario (Management Board of Cabinet)*, [2002] OLRD No 1136 (McKee) [*Chatham and Lindsay Jail*]. See, also, the protocol ordered in *Psychiatric Hospitals No 2*, above note 72.

161 *Chatham and Lindsay Jail*, *ibid*, Notice to Employees.

162 *Crown and OPSEU*, [2005] OLRD No 947 (Chauvin) at paras 19–22 [*Crown and OPSEU, 2005*].

163 *Kenora Jail*, above note 131 at para 8.

164 *Chatham and Lindsay Jail*, above note 160 at para 9. To the same effect, see *OPSEU (Union) and Management Board Secretariat*, GSB#2427/02, 26 January 2004 (Brown) at 14.

opposed to the emergency services part) of the agreement is to be negotiated "without regard to the availability of other persons to provide essential services."[165] This does not resolve the extent of the authority of the employer to actually deploy workers during a strike. The issue is addressed ambiguously in the *CECBA*. Section 41.1 states that an essential services agreement "shall not directly or indirectly prevent the employer from using a person to perform any work during a strike or lockout" and any provision in an essential services agreement that does so is "void." What limitations, if any, are there on the employer's ability to assign work covered by the essential services agreement to other bargaining unit employees, managers, or to outside replacement workers?

Concerning the government using its own non-essential workers to do essential services work, this has been the subject of inconclusive litigation. The issue first arose before the OLRB in 1998 when OPSEU and the MBS litigated how an essential services agreement should address what happens if a person, who has been designated as essential pursuant to an essential services agreement, does not show up for work.[166] OPSEU's position was that OPSEU would have to supply another worker to cover that position. The employer argued that it had the right to use any person to perform the work and was of the view that section 41.1 permitted the employer to use managers, OPSEU members who crossed the picket line, or replacement workers. The OLRB only ruled that the essential services workers in question were, by definition, vital to the provision of essential services and that there must be a protocol in place that provides for quick access to another bargaining unit member.

This issue was next addressed during the 2002 strike. At issue was the interpretation of essential services agreement provisions about acting assignments, which the OLRB interpreted to preserve the rights of employees who wished to return to their home position, but not to limit the right of the employer to assign acting employees who chose to cross the picket line.[167]

During the negotiation of the 2004–2005 essential services agreements, the employer argued it had the discretion to decide to decline to use bargaining unit essential services workers and instead to use persons

165 *CECBA*, above note 1, s 32(2).
166 *Misra*, above note 37 at paras 34–40.
167 *Superior Court Registrar*, above note 57 at paras 17–18.

not in the bargaining unit to perform essential services.[168] The OLRB expressly declined to determine the issue.[169] In summary, there is no clear resolution of the extent to which the government can use its own non-essential workers to do essential services agreement work.

The *LRA* certainly permits an employer to redeploy staff in the event of a strike. It would seem that a *CECBA* employer should also be able to do so, provided that the use of such staff is not a danger to life, health, and safety. However, any such redeployment to perform essential services would be a clear indication that it was not actually essential for the employer to use an essential services worker to perform the service. In that case, perhaps there should be no requirement for the essential services worker.

Concerning outside replacement workers, it has been decided that the employer can require essential services workers to attend work and can simultaneously use replacement workers to perform non-essential work.[170] The British Columbia Labour Relations Board concluded differently in finding that the appropriate balance in a "designated" strike regime is to prohibit the use of replacement workers in addition to essential services workers.[171] In 1998, the OLRB stated that the BC Board's analysis made "labour relations sense," but could not be followed because the OLRB was not subject to the same statutory framework.[172] The issue of using replacement workers to do non-essential work was revisited in the 2004–2005 OPSEU/MBS essential services negotiations, and the OLRB expressly declined to deal with the issue.[173] The OLRB did note that the employer had not in the past used outside replacement workers and that, in the 2004–2005 round of bargaining, the employer had expressed its intention to not use them.

The issue of using replacement workers to do essential work has not been litigated. Presumably the justification for the use of replacement workers in the public service would be based on the claim that

168 *Crown v OPSEU, 2005*, above note 111 at para 20. The OLRB did determine that the essential services agreement had to be negotiated without regard to the availability of non-bargaining unit personnel.

169 The OLRB also declined to rule on the issue in *Crown v OPSEU, 2004*, above note 50.

170 *Misra*, above note 37 at para 17.

171 *Beacon Hill Lodge v BCNU and HEU*, (1986) No 2/86 (BCLRB).

172 *Misra*, above note 37 at para 24.

173 *Crown v OPSEU, 2004*, above note 50.

the scheme of the *LRA* permits the use of replacement workers and there is no reason for the OPS to be any different. However, in the *LRA* scheme there is no requirement for any employee in a striking bargaining unit to work during the strike. When the requirement to work is placed on an essential services worker it would seem justified only if that worker is actually needed to do the essential service work. If a replacement worker is already performing that work, there would appear to be no justification for limiting the right of the essential services worker to strike.

i) Emergencies

The *CECBA* does not define an "emergency." It does prescribe that an essential services agreement must include a part that provides for the use of employees in emergencies, but the content of that part is not prescribed.[174] In further contrast to the provisions dealing with the essential services part of the agreement, it appears that the determination of the number of emergency employees does *not* need to be arrived at "without regard to the availability of other persons,"[175] and that the employer has more flexibility to decide whether it "wishes" to deploy emergency workers during a strike or lockout.[176]

Where employees had been designated as emergency workers in a prior essential services agreement, the employer sought to have them designated as essential to ensure that they were readily available. The concern was that the workers might unlawfully avoid being called in for emergency work and that it would be better to have them regularly attending for essential services work. However, the employer did not establish the ongoing need for the performance of the essential work. The OLRB was not prepared to designate emergency workers as essential workers simply because of a concern that they might engage in unlawful behaviour.[177] Instead, such behaviour should be dealt with if it arises.

Where the emergency services part of the agreement includes provision for employer declaration of an emergency, the specific wording

---

174 *CECBA*, above note 1, s 30. The lack of guidance is discussed in *Crown and OPSEU, 2005*, above note 162 at paras 14–15.

175 *CECBA*, above note 1, s 32(1) & (2).

176 Compare *CECBA* s 40(2) with s 41(2).

177 *The Crown in Right of Ontario v OPSEU*, [2005] OLRD No 1885 (Waddingham), dealing with an employer request that fire-fighting services be changed from emergency services to essential services.

of the emergency services "trigger" will govern the obligation of emergency workers to report to work. Where that wording is ambiguous, the employer will only be able to call in workers for a claimed emergency where there is an "objectively legitimate reason" for doing so.[178] Where the union receives notice of an emergency, that notice should include enough information to permit the union to decide whether an emergency exists.

Some emergencies are anticipated and described in the essential services agreement. In the event of an unspecified emergency, employees are to perform the emergency work, subject to the right of the union to file an application that the power to assign that work was abused.[179]

In the 2004–2005 OPSEU/MBS essential services agreement, the parties included the emergency services provisions in the main essential services agreement. They defined emergencies, in a general fashion, as "unforeseen circumstances which call for immediate action," listed specific types of foreseeable emergencies, and included specific details about what would trigger the obligation to provide emergency services work.[180] In the case of any unanticipated emergency, the worksite manager was to immediately inform the union representative. The information was to include the description of the emergency, the employees needed, and the anticipated duration of the emergency. A declaration of a major emergency could be made by the secretary of the Management Board of Cabinet, who was to immediately inform the president of OPSEU about the declaration. Employees called in for specified or designated emergencies were to be required to perform only the emergency work.

j) Terms and Conditions of Employment of Essential (and Emergency) Services Workers

During a strike under the *LRA* regime, the employer can unilaterally set the terms and conditions of employment of any unionized employees, subject only to their statutory employment rights. The lack of negotiated employment entitlements for employees who work during a strike is explained by the fact that those employees are voluntarily choosing to work under the conditions imposed by the employer during a strike of their bargaining unit. The terms and conditions of employment of

---

178 *Fire Crews*, above note 135 at para 8.

179 *Herman*, above note 76 at para 46.

180 *Conditions for Essential Services*, above note 55 at C(9) and site-specific agreements.

essential services workers under the *CECBA* are a different matter, as those workers are required to work during a strike. What principles should govern the setting of their terms and conditions of employment?

During the 1998 OPSEU/MBS essential services agreement negotiations, the position of the union was that the terms and conditions of essential services workers should be bargained and, if necessary, set by the OLRB. The position of the employer was that, while it had the "unilateral right" to set the terms and conditions of employment, it would voluntarily adhere to any agreement that it chose to make with the union.[181] The OLRB held that the bargaining agent retained the right to negotiate for its members and that it was important for the orderly provision of essential services that the terms and conditions of employment be established before essential employees were required to work through a work stoppage.[182]

When the parties were unable to agree on the terms and conditions of employment of essential services workers, the board decided that the collective agreement would normally apply "without interruption" *except for* dues and surplus provisions (discussed below).[183] The subsequent attempt of both parties to alter the application of the collective agreement to essential services workers was rejected by the OLRB on the basis that those issues should be dealt with in collective bargaining.[184]

OPSEU's ability to set the dues of essential services workers has been capped at 31.25 percent,[185] which was the pre-strike dues level plus 30 percent. OPSEU had requested that essential services workers pay 100 percent of their salary as dues, subject to OPSEU then paying those workers the same strike pay given to striking workers. The intent was to put essential services workers in the same financial position as striking employees. The employer's position was that OPSEU's proposal would be unduly disruptive to the smooth provision of workplace services during the strike. The balance struck in 1999 by the OLRB was to adopt the 31.25 percent level of dues that was actually previously negotiated between the parties in the 1996 OPSEU/MBC strike.

---

181 *Misra*, above note 37 at para 28.

182 *Ibid* at para 32.

183 *Ontario (Management Board Secretariat)*, [1999] OLRD No 409 (Herman) at para 2 [*Ontario (Management Board Secretariat)*].

184 *Crown v OPSEU, 2004*, above note 50 at para 30.

185 *Ontario (Management Board Secretariat)*, above note 183 at para 2.

The second exception to the application of the collective agreement concerned employee rights in the event of layoff/surplussing. The OLRB held that those rights should not apply to essential services workers because "there are risks associated with any strike" and it would be unfair to provide surplussing rights to those providing essential services, while excluding those on strike.[186]

As a collective agreement obviously normally permits the performance of essential services, and contains workable negotiated limits on management discretion, it is the logical starting point for negotiation of the terms and conditions of employment of essential services workers and there should be strong reasons for departing from it.

One such reason, demonstrated by the dues determination described above, is that discretionary power permitted under the collective agreement should be capped where its use might otherwise be detrimental to the provision of essential services. Another reason, demonstrated by the ruling on the surplus provisions, is that the continued application of the collective agreement to essential services workers should not provide those workers with any ongoing employment advantage over employees on strike. Accomplishing this latter goal requires more than limiting the application of the surplus provisions. For example, the collective agreement provides for the accumulation of seniority while working. If the seniority accumulation provisions of the collective agreement applied to essential services workers and not to strikers, then essential services workers would, at the end of the strike, have accumulated seniority relative to the employees who were on strike. While the OLRB's jurisprudence does not address that issue, the OPSEU/MBS parties have dealt with it in return-to-work protocols entered into at the end of both of the 1996 and 2002 strikes. In each case, accumulation of seniority during the strike was accorded equally to essential services workers and other employees in the bargaining unit.

i) Management Rights

A union request for a general freeze on the exercise of management rights in respect of the employment of essential services workers during the strike was declined by the OLRB.[187] The employer must continue to comply with its obligations under the collective agreement. When the

---

186 *Herman*, above note 76 at para 13.

187 *Ibid* at para 16.

employer sought to impose a strike-related policy of requiring additional medical certification for sick leave claims by essential services workers, the provision in the collective agreement that the employer was only able to request a medical certificate in respect of an absence of less than five days where it suspected there may be a specific abuse of sick leave continued to apply.[188]

A request for a so-called justice and dignity clause, under which employees discharged for any reason during the strike would be entitled to adjudicative determination on the legitimacy of that discharge prior to it taking effect, was dismissed without reasons.[189]

The management right to make reasonable rules governing essential services employees during a strike has been upheld. The failure to comply with a reasonable rule, in one case the requirement for essential services correctional officers to wear uniforms on duty, is culpable conduct.[190]

However, where the reduction of levels of service during a strike or lockout involved the closure of offices, the OLRB declined to permit the closure of some offices partly because some employees would have been required to travel much longer distances to their new office.[191]

The employer's management right to require overtime under the collective agreement has been limited. Overtime was only to be used to ensure the provision of essential work, unless OPSEU consented.[192] OPSEU was also entitled to complain to the OLRB if it seemed that the employer was undermining the agreed levels of essential service by abusing the right to require overtime. Obviously, the employer's ability to require overtime is also subject to any specifically negotiated term in any essential services agreement limiting the amount of overtime to be worked.[193] Where "mutual agreement" was required for employees to receive compensating leave in lieu of overtime pay, and there had been

---

188 *Ontario (Management Board of Cabinet)*, [2002] OLRD No 1341 (McKellar) at paras 19–23.

189 *Herman*, above note 76 at para 34.

190 *Ontario (Management Board of Cabinet)*, [2002] OLRD No 1165 (McKellar) at para 7.

191 *The Crown in Right of Ontario and OPSEU*, [2005] OLRD No 1775 (Freedman) at para 7.

192 *Herman*, above note 76 at para 15.

193 See for example, *Kenora Jail*, above note 131 at para 10.

a pre-strike practice of granting such leave, the employer was found to be entitled to withhold such agreement during a strike.[194]

There is no private sector jurisprudence with which to compare the OLRB's determinations under the *CECBA* about management rights and essential services workers. Perhaps the most analogous circumstance is the *LRA* "freeze" of management rights that applies where negotiations for a new contract continue after the expiry of the collective agreement and requires that those rights only be used in a status quo or "business as before" manner.[195] It would not be consistent with the *CECBA* essential services scheme for such a "freeze" to prevent the provision of essential services. A possible approach is found to some extent in the board's ruling on overtime assignments. The OLRB limited the power to assign overtime so that it could not be used to facilitate non-essential work. The same possibility of facilitating non-essential work does exist in respect of other issues. Management rights that could be used to encourage employees to perform non-essential work include setting schedules for shifts, breaks, meals, days off, and vacations; regulating employee parking and the use of onsite places to eat meals and take breaks; reassigning employee duties within job classifications; and so on. It is noteworthy that under the 1993–1995 *CECBA* a "freeze" was applied to the exercise of management rights in respect of essential services workers, save and except for changes that were demonstrably necessary to provide essential services.[196]

ii) Employer Discipline

As essential services workers continue to be covered by the collective agreement, which includes the right not to be disciplined without just cause, unjustified discipline is a breach of the essential services agreement. The OLRB's jurisdiction over breaches of the collective agreement gives it direct jurisdiction over discipline of essential services workers.

The starting point in relation to essential services worker discipline is "it is inappropriate to discipline for a refusal to do non-essential

---

194 *OPSEU (Union) and Ministry of Community Safety and Correctional Services*, GSB#3774/03, 18 March 2004 (Briggs) at 5.

195 See Jeffrey Sack, Michael Mitchell & Sandy Price, *Ontario Labour Relations Board Law and Practice* (Markham, ON: LexisNexis Canada, 1997) at paras 8.218–8.239 [Sack et al].

196 For a discussion of how it applied to hours of work provisions, see *McCormack*, above note 38 at paras 30–35.

work."[197] Conversely, refusal to do essential work is culpable conduct, even in circumstances where the employee was of the view that the work was non-essential. Where an employee refused an assignment on the basis of their subjective and mistaken belief that acceptance of the assignment would require them to perform non-essential work, their refusal to comply with the direction to perform the work was found to be culpable conduct.[198] The degree of discipline that such conduct warranted was not decided in the case.

Whether genuine objective doubt about the essentiality of the duty excuses an employee refusal was canvassed in the case of Wendy Molloy. She refused to perform certain duties on a night shift in a correctional institution. The OLRB found that the work was essential, but it was OPSEU's assertion that the characterization of the work in question at the time of Ms. Molloy's refusal was a true "grey area."[199] OPSEU argued that there should be an exception to the normal "obey now, grieve later rule" for arguably non-essential work on the grounds that, if the work proved to be non-essential, there would be no effective means to change the fact that the non-essential work was performed during the strike. OPSEU asserted that, in such circumstances, it was appropriate to refer the question of the work's characterization to dispute resolution and not impose discipline in the meantime. The OLRB agreed that this approach was preferable but that the employer is entitled to enforce its right to manage through the imposition of proportionate discipline. Any harm to the employee was found to be outweighed by the employer's interest in maintaining essential services.

While Ms. Molloy's conduct was found to be culpable, the board also found the one-day suspension to be excessive and reduced it to a written warning, due to a number of factors:

- there was an ongoing dispute between the union and the employer concerning the characterization of the work in question
- there was a dispute resolution process in place, but not engaged, to deal with the dispute

---

197 *Ontario (Management Board of Cabinet)*, [2002] OLRD No 1131 (McLean) at para 8(f) [*Corrections, 9 April 2002*].

198 *Ontario (Management Board of Cabinet)*, [2002] OLRD No 1168 (McKellar) at paras 4 and 5.

199 *OPSEU v Management Board of Cabinet*, [2002] OLRD No 1355 (Kelly) at para 8.

- the employee's refusal appeared to have been motivated by the advice she received from the local union concerning the characterization of the work in question
- other ministries had engaged the dispute resolution process to determine the correctness of the characterization of work as essential/emergency work before resorting to any form of discipline
- the employer made no assessment of Ms. Molloy's employment background before reaching its decision to suspend her[200]

A different resolution was arrived at in an OLRB-ordered consent agreement relating to the OPSEU strike, which incorporated early dispute resolution, as follows:

> (i) The parties agree to abide by the decisions of a Local Dispute Resolution Mechanism (LDRM);
> (ii) The employer is not to discipline for refusal to perform non-essential duties but, is to defer any such action until the decision of the LDRM;
> (iii) For an order identified by the employer to be essential *and* an emergency, the employee is to comply, and the dispute is referred to the LDRM for resolution within 8 hours;
> (iv) For an order identified by the employer to be essential but not an emergency, the employee may choose not to comply, and the dispute will be resolved by the LDRM within one hour;
> (v) If the employer misidentifies an order as either essential or an emergency, the LDRM will provide the appropriate remedy.[201]

At a minimum, this approach would require well-organized workplace parties with a functioning LDRM.

Before there can be discipline, there must be a deliberate refusal to do the work. Where the employee is discussing the order given and has not yet refused to carry it out, failure to perform work for a short period of time is not a culpable refusal.[202]

200 *Ibid* at para 19.
201 *Ontario (Management Board of Cabinet)*, [2002] OLRD No 1125 (McLean) [*Corrections, 18 April 2002*] at para 1.
202 *Ontario (Management Board of Cabinet)*, [2002] OLRD No 1137 (McKellar) at para 6.

iii) Commencement and Cessation of Application of Collective Agreement to Essential Services Employees

The OPSEU/MBS essential services agreements have stated that the collective agreement applies to essential services employees who are "designated and used."[203] The collective agreement applies to employees used to perform emergency services after the employer determines that "an employee is to be used" to perform such work. While it was agreed that essential services employees only receive salary for the days and hours they actually work,[204] the meaning of the "designated" and "used" triggers for the application of other collective agreement entitlements was extensively litigated following both the 1996 and 2002 OPSEU/MBC strikes.

Concerning essential, but not emergency, services workers, they were entitled to the full benefit of collective agreement coverage throughout the strike provided only that, at some point, they were both designated to work and then actually worked.[205] Holiday pay was ordered paid to all classified essential services workers who were designated *and* used subject to an essential services agreement during the 2002 strike.[206] Where a grievor was designated to provide essential services and did provide such services, and then was called in for a shift, they were found to be entitled to call-back pay.[207]

Concerning the duration of collective agreement coverage for emergency workers, their entitlement starts when they are scheduled to work and continues until the last day they actually work.[208] As a result, a worker and their family were entitled to dental benefits incurred after the schedule was set, but prior to their first day of work. The determin-

---

203 *Conditions for Essential Services*, above note 55 at C(3)(a). The same provisions were included in the 1996 essential services agreement.

204 *Ontario Public Service Employees Union (Union) v Ontario (Management Board Secretariat)*, 2003 CanLII 52975 (ON GSB) (Stewart).

205 *OPSEU (Union Grievance) and Management Board Secretariat*, GSB#1510/02, 4 December 2002 (Brown). This essential services worker status also applies to correctional employees who are simultaneously emergency services workers as well: *OPSEU (Union Grievance) and Management Board Secretariat*, GSB#1510/02, 8 March 2004 (Brown) [*Union Grievance*].

206 *Ibid*, 4 December 2002 at 17, 8 March 2004 at 4; and *OPSEU (Ducette) and Ministry of Transportation and Management Board Secretariat*, GSB#1702/02, 5 June 2003 and 20 October 2003 (Brown) [*Ducette*].

207 *Ducette*, *ibid*, 5 June 2003.

208 *OPSEU (Cousins) and Ministry of the Solicitor General and Correctional Services*, GSB#822/96, 23 July 1996 (Roberts) at 4.

ation that the employee "is to be used" occurred when the employee was scheduled to work. Once that determination had been made, the collective agreement applied until the completion of the work. The determination to use an employee to do emergency services work can be made by either posting the shift or by calling in the person.[209] Similarly, emergency services workers were entitled to holiday pay for any holiday that fell between the work being assigned and completion of the work,[210] but only until the completion of their scheduled work.[211]

Employees on emergency status are placed on standby, on-call, or call-back status to the extent authorized in advance by the employer during the selection process[212] or by virtue of the employer making the triggering request of the employee. For example, an emergency services employee gets call-back pay if called back to work between the initial call-in and the completion of the emergency assignment.[213]

Both essential and emergency workers could have call-back pay triggered by the rescheduling required at the beginning or end of a strike. However, such entitlement only arises if the notice of the requirement to report for work is less than the maximum notice that the worker could have received a call-back before the strike started.[214]

k) Worksite Representatives

During a work stoppage, a union continues to represent all employees and has an interest in determining whether the essential services agreement was being complied with, with the result that the union has a right of access to worksites for that purpose.[215] Accordingly, OPSEU was awarded access to the workplace on the first day of the strike and unscheduled visits thereafter. The visits were to be undertaken by two union worksite contacts who could be accompanied by up to an equal number of employer contacts. The OLRB issued a fairly detailed series of decisions delineating the extent of the workplace visit entitlement.

---

209 *Ducette*, above note 206, 20 October 2003 at 2.

210 *Union Grievance*, above note 205.

211 *Ibid.*

212 *The Crown in Right of Ontario and Ontario Public Service Employees Union*, OLRB File 2697-04-M, 10 March 2005 (Chauvin).

213 *Ducette*, above note 206, 5 June 2003 at 5.

214 *OPSEU (Union) and Management Board Secretariat*, GSB#2427/02, 17 October 2003 (Brown) at 12.

215 *Herman*, above note 76 at para 35.

Worksite representatives are entitled to access to any worksite where essential or emergency work is being done or where employees in the bargaining unit who are on strike or who are locked out would ordinarily perform their work. However, union worksite representatives have no entitlement to enter managers' offices or other portions of a bargaining unit site where bargaining unit work is not normally done.[216] Staff washrooms and staff lunchrooms are to be treated as areas where bargaining unit work is usually done, which means that there is the right to access. Similarly, there is to be access to boardrooms, meeting rooms, and IT rooms, provided that bargaining unit work is usually done there.[217] The employer is not entitled to deny access to a location even where there is an ongoing work refusal in respect of that location.[218]

The union must inform management of its intention to exercise access to worksites so that the employer contact can arrange to accompany the union worksite representatives. Similarly, the employer is to provide the union with a list of contacts who will be responsible for promptly arranging the availability of employer worksite contacts.[219]

The union is not required to make an appointment for a worksite visit. However, absent exceptional circumstances, the union is to notify the assigned ministry contact of the intention to conduct a visit. The convenience of the employer will not normally justify delaying or denying a worksite visit. Save in "unusual circumstances," the union is not to conduct more than two worksite visits within any period of twenty-four hours.[220] The visits may be up to forty-five minutes in duration or any reasonably necessary longer period.[221]

A union is entitled to police the essential services agreement through worksite visits, and this may involve disagreement with management, but any such dispute is not to detract from the obligation on both parties to cooperate to ensure compliance with essential services agreements.[222]

---

216 *Ontario (Management Board Secretariat)*, [2002] OLRD No 930 (Albertyn) at para 3 [*Worksite Visits No 1*].

217 *Ontario (Management Board Secretariat)*, [2002] OLRD No 1066 (Albertyn) at para 5 [*Worksite Visits No 2*].

218 *Ontario (Management Board Secretariat)*, [2002] OLRD No 1337 at para 3 (Albertyn) [*Worksite Visits No 3*].

219 *Worksite Visits No 1*, above note 216 at para 3.

220 *Ibid.*

221 *Conditions for Essential Services*, above note 55 at C1.

222 *Lauzon*, above note 112 at para 12.

The parties are not to use "self-help remedies" to resolve disputes over access. Any disputes should be dealt with in accordance with the established dispute resolution processes.[223]

Anyone identified by the union as a worksite representative is entitled to be treated as such by the employer unless and until the employer has made a successful application to the OLRB for a suspension of that person's status. A person's employment status is not determinative of the right to be a worksite representative. Persons who have never been essential services workers are entitled to be union worksite representatives.[224] Alleged picket line difficulties do not justify denying, or even delaying, someone worksite access.[225] Similarly, where a court order prevented an individual from attending at the premises, the employer sought an order that the individual could not be named as a worksite representative.[226] The board noted that under the agreement between OPSEU and the MBS, worksite representatives could have a number of responsibilities away from the worksite, including being a contact person, advising the employer that a worksite visit would occur, and otherwise discussing worksite visits with the employer. It was inappropriate to prevent the individual in question from being a worksite representative, so long as it was understood that performing this function did not release them from any obligations they might have under the court order, including non-attendance at the premises.

During a worksite visit, the union worksite representatives may initiate discussion with bargaining unit employees performing essential or emergency services or bargaining unit work, but only about the nature of the work they are performing and issues of health and safety.[227] Included would be the right to ask employees whether they were bargaining unit employees and, if so, to initiate a conversation regarding the nature of the work they were performing, including determining whether or not they were performing essential or emergency services work. This appears to permit union communication with bargaining unit members about non-essential duties they have voluntarily chosen to perform.

By agreement, OPSEU worksite representatives were able to request information on the hours being worked by employees performing

223 *Worksite Visits No 1*, above note 216 at para 3.

224 *Ontario (MBS)*, [2002] OLRD No 1296 (McKellar) at paras 8–9 [*Duchesne*].

225 *Ontario (MBS)*, [2002] OLRD No 1301 (Brown) at para 11 [*OMAFRA*].

226 *Duchesne*, above note 224 at paras 8–12.

227 *Worksite Visits No 2*, above note 217 at para 6.

essential or emergency services. This information was to be provided within four days of request and up to once per pay period.[228]

Worksite visit rights are not to interfere with the delivery of essential services[229] and, in particular, are not to be used to harass managers or employees.[230] When it is alleged that a particular worksite representative has engaged in harassing conduct, the standard of proof will be "clear, cogent and convincing evidence."[231] The general law of collective agreement administration requires that union representatives are protected from discipline for assertive conduct in meetings with management, particularly in relation to a labour dispute. However, when conduct is so disruptive that it prevents effective communication, it becomes legitimate to demand significant improvement. If improvement does not occur, the employer can seek leave of the OLRB to remove the individual and, where such leave has been granted and in an exceptional case, can be given the power to remove the individual immediately.[232]

l) Occupational Health and Safety Rights and Essential Services

Essential services agreements do not impinge on the rights of the parties or individual employees under the *Occupational Health and Safety Act* (*OHSA*) as "[t]hose rights continue in full force and effect."[233]

In the OPSEU/MBS *Conditions for Essential Services 2004–2005* document, the parties acknowledged that the agreed staffing levels were not themselves a violation of the health and safety provisions of the collective agreement, even though they "do not reflect desirable or required staffing levels for normal operations."[234] However, the *Corrections Agreement* did not contain a similar agreement about the staffing levels.[235]

228 *Conditions for Essential Services*, above note 55 at C1.

229 *Ibid* at C1.

230 *Herman*, above note 76 at para 36.

231 *Lauzon*, above note 112 at para 15.

232 *Ibid* at para 46.

233 RSO 1990, c O.1 [*OHSA*], discussed in *Herman*, above note 76 at para 11.

234 *Conditions for Essential Services*, above note 55 at B(3)(a).

235 The *Corrections Bargaining Unit Master Agreement for Essential Services*, 30 October 2001, and accompanying memorandum "Re: Institutions" state: "This Memorandum of Agreement is not based on a 'business as usual' scenario and shall not be interpreted as what would be advocated by either party in a normal situation with a fully operating service" (*Master Agreement* at para 3), and "[t]he Parties agree, that in order to safely provide the listed Level of Essential Services as negotiated/ordered, they shall co-operate to the fullest extent possible in the

During a strike, the condition of certain workplaces can give rise to health and safety concerns. During the 2002 OPSEU strike, the OLRB found that "a volatile and difficult situation does exist in the [correctional institutions] and the correctional officers who have to work in them do not want to assume unwarranted risks."[236] The board also cautioned that it would ensure *OHSA* rights were not used to "camouflage" illegal strikes or as a "convenient pretext" to shelter protests that did not really involve personal safety.[237] In the end, it is "more appropriate to focus on the actual work refusals and what gave rise to them in determining these appeals rather than assessing what ulterior motives, if any, are behind them."[238] In any event, the right to refuse to work is only to be used in urgent circumstances.[239] In particular, it is inappropriate to refuse to work because of a perceived violation of the essential services agreement, except where such violation actually creates a situation which is likely to endanger.[240]

The right to refuse work was exercised on many occasions during the 2002 OPSEU strike, but there are relatively few OLRB decisions on the issues that triggered those refusals to work. In three cases, the board found that the right to refuse was not justifiably exercised. Where it was disputed whether standard latex gloves were adequate for use during a search of a jail or whether the employer should be providing "FM200 Frisk Master Gloves" with a Kevlar lining that could protect against sharp objects, which might otherwise cut through latex gloves, the board was not persuaded that the latex gloves were so dangerous as to put the correctional officer in such imminent jeopardy that a work refusal was warranted.[241] The employer was not required to bolt down the furnishings in a jail,[242] even although it had been alleged that a correctional

reasonable promotion of safety and health of all employees and offenders" ("Re: Institutions" preamble).

236 *Ontario Public Service Employees Union v Ministry of Correctional Services (Brookside Youth Centre)*, [2002] OOHSAD No 43 at paras 21–23 [*Brookside Youth Centre*].

237 *Corrections, 18 April 2002*, above note 201, citing *City of Toronto*, [1986] OLRB Rep Dec 1834 at para 64.

238 *Brookside Youth Centre*, above note 236 at para 3.

239 *Ibid* at para 8, referring to *OPSEU Local 359 and Local 608 and Ontario (Ministry of the Solicitor General and Correctional Services—Sault Ste Marie Jail)*, [1997] OOHSAD No 319 (Ont Adj Cummings).

240 *Corrections, 9 April 2002*, above note 197 at para 8(f).

241 *Brookside Youth Centre*, above note 236 at para 20.

242 *Ibid* at para 21.

officer previously suffered a concussion when an inmate threw a chair at the officer. Where a search of a facility for inmate contraband and weapons was ordered before correctional officers returned to work, and the officers asserted that canteen containers were not properly searched by the management filling in for the absent correctional officers, the distrust of management's search conduct was not an appropriate basis for a work refusal.[243] On the other hand, inadequate search protocols could give rise to a real safety issue, and management and the union were ordered to jointly develop a search protocol for the institution.

During the 2002 OPSEU strike, nurses working in correctional centres were found to have engaged in a legitimate work refusal. The nurses claimed that, during the strike and in the absence of the normal staffing of correctional officers, they could not be adequately assured of their safety. The employer application for an order to enforce the essential services agreement against them, and for an order that they were engaged in an illegal strike, was declined.[244] The OLRB noted that there had been no discussions between the parties, and no occupational health and safety inspector had been contacted. The nurses' concern about the adequacy of training undertaken by the replacement managers was borne out to some extent when a manager failed to remain as a backup to a nurse while they were on rounds within the jail. Correctional officers were trained for six weeks while the replacement managers received a half-day orientation session. The board found that there was an employer obligation to provide competent and adequately trained supervisors and upheld the nurses' work refusal.[245] The matter was resolved by a subsequent decision that, during a strike, nurses needed to be accompanied by an experienced corrections manager.[246]

Where essential services workers were denied pay for the period of a work refusal, and the OLRB had not ruled on the legitimacy of the refusal, the GSB considered its legitimacy.[247] The reduced staffing that existed in the facility during the strike was a risk found not to be inherent in the grievors' work, and the employer's failure to adequately

---

243 *Ontario (Ministry of Correctional Services)*, [2002] OOHSAD No 42.

244 *Ontario (MBC)*, [2002] OLRD No 931 (Trachuk) at para 3.

245 *Ministry of Correctional Services*, OLRB File 3736-01-HS, 8 April 2002 (Freedman) at paras 15–17.

246 *Ibid*, 10 April 2002.

247 *OPSEU (Metcalf/Mercer) and Ministry of the Solicitor General and Correctional Services*, GSB#926/96, 7 July 1997 (Dissanayake).

adjust operations to compensate for reduced staffing levels created unsafe conditions. The right to refuse unsafe work was not limited to refusing to perform a particular task and the grievors were entitled to refuse work generally. The inspection of the facility by a Ministry of Labour inspector did not comply with the requirements of the *OHSA* and, as a consequence, the grievors were justified in continuing their refusal and should have been paid for the entire period of the refusal, including that portion of it following the inspector's decision.

Where the right to refuse work is exercised because the essential services staffing levels make the workplace unsafe, keeping staffing levels "frozen" at the agreed levels could pressure employees not to exercise their refusal right and might prevent the employer from being able to correct the unsafe situation. Consequently, the employer can unilaterally increase the numbers, but only to the level necessary to restore safe staffing levels.[248] The employer's power to unilaterally alter the staffing level was made subject to the ability of the union to argue that the employer was abusing that power.

The employee who refuses to do work because of health and safety concerns is required to perform any other essential work ordered by the employer. If the replacement work assigned by the employer is non-essential, then it is still to be offered to the employee, but the employee can decide whether to do that work or engage in the strike.[249] Concerning which employees can be asked to perform the essential work refused by an essential services employee, the employer stated it would seek a replacement from employees on the designated list.[250]

4) OLRB Remedies Concerning Essential Services Disputes Arising During a Strike or Lockout

During any strike or lockout under the *CECBA*, the OLRB retains its ongoing *LRA* jurisdiction to hear complaints of anti-union unfair labour practices and allegations of illegal strike and lockout, as well as its *OHSA* jurisdiction to hear occupational health and safety matters. In addition, the OLRB has the power to enforce or amend essential

248 *Herman*, above note 76 at paras 26–27.

249 *Ibid* at para 30.

250 *Ibid* at para 29. This accords with the parameters set in *Misra*, above note 37 at para 43.

services agreements or make such other orders as it considers appropriate.[251] Pursuant to that statutory power, the OLRB has dealt with applications to amend and enforce essential services agreements, either separately or in combined applications.

a) Order to Amend

The OLRB is reluctant to amend an essential services agreement.[252] Making it easy to obtain a variance would undermine the importance of the initial negotiation process and create uncertainty during the work stoppage. At the same time, circumstances may change or new factors may come to light. The party requesting an amendment will face a substantial burden of proof, but the board will carefully review the application to ensure the interests of the public are protected.

Under the *CECBA*, a party may apply for an amendment of an essential services agreement[253] when the essential services agreement fails to provide for essential services, provides service levels that are greater or less than required, or provides for either too many or too few employees. The OLRB's power to amend is limited to altering the level of service.[254] This raises a question about the extent of the OLRB's jurisdiction to alter or prescribe the manner of provision of those services.

There have been very few contested orders requiring amendment of an essential services agreement. The board directed the negotiation of an emergency protocol for meat inspectors to ensure that there were sufficient inspectors available to investigate the possibility of illegal slaughter.[255] Where the employer brought an amendment application to deal with the issue of the alleged lack of safety caused by unlocked inmates when staffing was below normal levels,[256] it was ordered that inmates receive one-third of the unlocked time they received prior to the strike and that the time was to be given in a manner that allowed one-third of the inmates to be unlocked at any one time.

---

251 *CECBA*, above note 1, s 38(3).

252 *Wolfe Island Ferry*, above note 97 at paras 9–10.

253 *Transportation Enforcement Officers*, above note 142 at para 10, followed in *Quantitative Analysis Clerk*, above note 130 at para 10.

254 *Transportation Enforcement Officers*, above note 142.

255 *Meat Inspectors*, above note 95 at paras 17–19.

256 *Ontario (Management Board of Cabinet)*, [1986] OLRD No 4799 (Herman).

Aerial flood-plain surveillance was added to the essential services agreement.[257] The danger was the flooding of small northern communities by ice-jammed rivers. The necessary preventative aerial surveillance had not been included in the essential services agreement, perhaps because no one had contemplated that the strike would still be continuing during flood season.

Provisions to ensure emergency replacements for essential services workers have been added where none were negotiated originally.[258]

If satisfied that an amendment is required, the OLRB has directed the parties to meet to attempt to negotiate the amendment.[259]

b) Enforcement Order

When the OLRB is asked to enforce an essential services agreement, it will not focus on whether the work function in question is essential but on whether it is covered by the essential services agreement.[260] An enforcement application, under section 38 of the *CECBA*, is not to be used to rewrite the essential services agreement. The task before the board is solely to interpret the parties' own agreement.[261] An application to enforce the essential services agreement is often accompanied by a simultaneous application by the employer that the alleged failure of the employees to adhere to the essential services agreement is also an illegal strike.

The OLRB's power to enforce can be employed without a finding that the *CECBA*, or an essential services agreement, has been violated.[262]

The board can enforce an essential services agreement by means of an amendment or augmentation. Where it was alleged that OPSEU failed to comply with an essential services agreement requirement to ensure sufficient bargaining unit employees were available to perform the work, the essential services agreement was amended to add an

---

257 *Ontario (Management Board of Cabinet)*, [2002] OLRD No 1561 (Trachuk).

258 *Ottawa Crown Attorneys*, above note 130 at para 12; *Ontario (Management Board of Cabinet)*, [2002] OLRD No 962 (McKee) at para 8 [*CACC No 3*] .

259 *CACC No 1*, above note 133 at para 9; *Ontario (Management Board of Cabinet)*, [2002] OLRD No 1147 (Chair Whitaker) at para 4.

260 *Psychiatric Hospitals No 1*, above note 42 at para 7.

261 *Ontario (Management Board of Cabinet)*, [2002] OLRD No 1116 (McKellar) at para 7.

262 *Chatham and Lindsay Jail*, above note 160 at para 25.

additional protocol concerning the order in which replacement staff were to be called in and how they were to be reached.[263]

It can be premature to enforce an essential services agreement by amending it. Following alleged difficulties in operating jails, the employer requested that the essential services agreement be amended by deleting correctional officer as an essential position.[264] In effect, the employer argued that correctional officers were systematically failing to provide essential services, that they should no longer have the opportunity to do so, and that the employer would operate the jail without them. OPSEU argued that it was inappropriate for the OLRB to grant such a remedy because it ought only to be considered in the context of an amendment application and not in an enforcement application. Also, the correctional officers never had a chance to perform their duties since the commencement of the labour dispute, presumably because of management's actions and an unsafe workplace. Finally, it was argued that an order deleting the correctional officer position would be contrary to the entire scheme of the essential services provisions of the Act, which envisaged that essential services are to be performed by bargaining unit employees. The OLRB declined the employer's suggestion to delete the position as premature and found that the correctional officers and management ought to be given "one full chance" to demonstrate that they could abide by the *CECBA*. The board then issued orders enforcing the existing essential services agreement.

i) Discretion re Whether to Enforce

The OLRB will exercise discretion in deciding whether to enforce an essential services agreement; there are a range of factors that will be taken into account.

An enforcement order will not be issued unless it serves a useful labour relations purpose. Where the employer acknowledged that it had inappropriately refused to allow a worksite visit and gave an undertaking not to refuse in the future, the OLRB declined to make an enforcement order.[265]

The OLRB has given some limited weight to the presence of the following alternate forums:

---

263 *Psychiatric Hospitals No 2*, above note 72 at paras 2, 3, and Sch A.

264 *Ontario (Management Board of Cabinet)*, [2002] OLRD No 952 (McLean) at para 3 [*Corrections, 28 March 2002*].

265 *Ontario (Management Board of Cabinet)*, [2002] OLRD No 1198 at para 10.

- a local dispute resolution mechanism
- the parties' mediation/arbitration protocol process designed to deal with essential services disputes during the course of the strike

The parties should use any agreed local dispute resolution procedures,[266] and should certainly refrain from using "self-help remedies."[267] Where the parties failed to use the local dispute resolution process, the OLRB has declined to deal further with the matter.[268] Deferral back to the parties has also occurred where there was a factual dispute that could have been resolved "infinitely more easily" by the local parties than by the board at a hearing.[269] "If nothing else, once this [local dispute] process has been carried out, the parties would have a clearer idea about what they were really saying, or perhaps more precisely which statements they were prepared to defend, and what the real factual disputes are."

On a number of other occasions, the OLRB has refused to defer to the parties' dispute resolution process. It has taken jurisdiction where the parties have completely different views of the essential services agreement and there is no reason to think the parties could have productive discussions.[270] There will be no deferral where the matter has already been dealt with by the board on several occasions.[271]

In the OPSEU/MBS *Conditions for Essential Services 2004–2005* document, the parties agreed to a local dispute resolution mechanism, but further agreed that failure to use it would not be raised as an objection to the OLRB hearing any complaint.

The parties can agree that disputes not settled locally will be privately arbitrated. During the 1996 OPSEU strike, the parties agreed that essential services disputes would, for the most part, be resolved by private arbitrators whom the parties themselves had selected to ensure that these individuals were familiar with the issues and readily available. Both parties filed disputes in that arbitration forum and generally abided by the results which took the form of many extremely brief,

266 *Court Houses*, above note 128 at para 4.
267 *Worksite Visits No 1*, above note 216 at para 3.
268 *Ontario (Management Board of Cabinet)*, [2002] OLRD No 1084 (Freedman) at paras 17–18 [*Probation and Parole No 2*].
269 *Ottawa Crown Attorneys*, above note 130 at para 6.
270 *Psychiatric Hospitals No 1*, above note 42 at para 3; *Transportation Enforcement Officers*, above note 142 at para 4.
271 *CACC No 3*, above note 258 at para 5.

informal, and unreported decisions. There was relatively little essential services litigation before the OLRB during the 1996 strike. For the 2002 OPSEU strike, the parties agreed to a *Mediation Arbitration Protocol*, known as the "2002 MAP" process, to be used for the rapid resolution of disputes concerning essential services. The OLRB was prepared to defer to it for factually unique matters that were not of general importance, and the board was also prepared to set up a rapid adjudication process if the private process proved slow or cumbersome.[272] Indeed, such an OLRB process was ultimately established, as discussed below.[273]

ii) Manner of Enforcement

A range of enforcement mechanisms have been used by the OLRB.

The OLRB will first consider means by which the parties can be encouraged to settle their differences, including directing the parties to "communicate forthwith with a view to resolving the issues," requiring the relevant persons to appear at the board, and to only be excused if they file a "signed agreement which ensures and *actually has ensured* that Corrections essential services employees are at work,"[274] appointing a labour relations officer to "interrogate" persons involved in the dispute and to inquire into the dispute,[275] and requiring the relevant staff at the local level to meet with the labour relations officer.[276] The board will decline to appoint a labour relations officer to deal with a dispute where it becomes apparent that neither of the parties has the desire or ability to resolve the situation.[277]

The central remedy employed by the OLRB in enforcement applications has been to direct the parties, or just particular employees, to

---

272 *Ontario (Management Board of Cabinet)*, [2002] OLRD No 939 (Chair Whitaker) at paras 4–7; *Ontario (Management Board of Cabinet)*, [2002] OLRD No 1058 (Chair Whitaker) at paras 3–6. The approach is similar to the OLRB's jurisprudence on deferring to arbitration; see Sack et al, above note 195 at para 8.69.

273 See "Procedure for OLRB Litigation of Disputes Related to Essential Services During a Strike" later in this chapter.

274 This direction was accompanied by the statement that "the Board can virtually guarantee that the workplace parties will like any agreement that they make more than a Board imposed solution": *Ontario (Management Board of Cabinet)*, [2002] OLRD No 944 (McLean) at para 10 [*Corrections, 23 March 2004*] [emphasis in original].

275 *MBC v OPSEU*, OLRB Files 3556-01-M and 3567-01-U, 18 March 2002 (McLean) at para (a).

276 *Corrections, 28 March 2002*, above note 264 at para 13.

277 *Corrections, 9 April 2002*, above note 197 at para 9.

provide essential services in accordance with the guidelines or parameters established by the board's decision.[278] The OLRB has commented that a general direction requiring compliance with the essential services agreement is often effective, and that, once such directions are issued, there is a general absence of requests for clarification, probably due to the parties' good faith.[279] A general direction is a practical solution that does not involve blaming any party.[280]

Compliance has been supported or encouraged with the following directions:

- the filing of a status report about compliance[281]
- requiring "all reasonable efforts" to bring the decision to the attention of the workplace[282]
- OPSEU to assist the employer in expeditiously delivering such a notice to the employees[283]
- the employer to provide copies of a decision to all essential services workers at the start of their next shifts,[284] to provide a copy to each branch office so that it will be seen by affected persons,[285] and to post copies of the decision in the workplaces[286]
- sending the decision and notice by mail to all employees[287]

The OLRB ordered that no one is to impede the implementation of the decision[288] and that any party who has a concern should file a dispute and await the result rather than withdraw essential services.[289]

---

278 *Forensic Sciences*, above note 126 at para 11; *Chatham and Lindsay Jail*, above note 160 at paras 25–27.

279 *Probation and Parole No 2*, above note 268 at para 6.

280 *Ontario (Management Board of Cabinet)*, [2002] OLRD No 1145 (McLean) at para 18 [*Corrections, 22 April 2002*].

281 *MBC v OPSEU*, [2002] OLRD No 636 (McLean) at para 17 [*Corrections, 17 March 2002*].

282 *Worksite Visits No 1*, above note 216 at paras 3 and 8.

283 *Chatham and Lindsay Jail*, above note 160 at para 27.

284 *Court Houses*, above note 128 at para 6.

285 *Probation and Parole No 1*, above note 134 at para 10.

286 *Fish Stocking*, above note 137 at para 9, which decision also required "both the employer and the Union will make reasonable efforts to bring this decision to the attention of the affected employees."

287 *Psychiatric Hospitals No 2*, above note 72 at para 5.

288 *Quantitative Analysis Clerk*, above note 130 at para 11(d).

289 *Ontario (Management Board of Cabinet)*, [2002] OLRD No 1090 (Chair Whitaker) at para 4 [*Oshawa Court House*].

Where there was a heightened concern about the possibility of continued non-compliance on the part of certain employees, the board stated that a continuing violation of an essential services agreement could expose employees to discipline and/or lead to further orders being made against the OPSEU and employees.[290]

In the rare instance of clearly deliberate breaches of the essential services agreement, the OLRB ordered that "employees will not withdraw essential services and OPSEU and its representatives will not counsel, direct or authorize employees to withdraw their essential services."[291] A withdrawal of services could amount to an unlawful strike under section 100 of the *LRA*.[292]

Where an individual played a lead role in deliberate breaches of the essential services agreement, that individual was personally required to not counsel a breach of the essential services agreement and to cooperate with the employer to obtain replacement workers.[293]

A compliance order can be directed to both management and employees. Where the OLRB found widespread violation of correctional essential services agreements, it ordered all correctional essential services employees back to work and ordered the employer to allow them to return.[294]

When enforcing essential services agreements, the OLRB has sometimes found it appropriate to make more specific orders against management.

After a mass *OHSA* work refusal at a jail, the recommencement of essential services work was facilitated by board ordered searches of the entire institution to deal with the risk that inmates had secreted dangerous contraband while correctional officers were absent.[295] In some correctional institutions, the employer said it could not bring correctional officers back to work because managers would refuse to work with them.[296] (The board has stated its willingness to expedite an

290 *Chatham and Lindsay Jail*, above note 160 at para 27 and *Corrections, 22 April 2002*, above note 280, "Notice to Employees."

291 *Oshawa Court House*, above note 289 at para 4.

292 See the "Illegal Strike Declaration" section below.

293 *Ontario (Management Board of Cabinet)*, [2002] OLRD No 1119 (Lewis) at para 4.

294 *Corrections, 17 March 2002*, above note 281 at para 6.

295 *Ontario (Management Board of Cabinet)*, OLRB File 3556-01-M, 14 March 2002 (McLean) at paras 4–7 and Search Orders.

296 *Corrections, 23 March 2004*, above 274 at para 7.

employer appeal concerning an occupational health and safety refusal by front-line managers.) The board noted that the absence of essential services workers from the workplace was by definition unsafe,[297] and so the issue needed to be resolved quickly but effectively. Time has been granted for the parties to negotiate necessary arrangements, and, where the employer assured the board that the facility could be operated in a safe manner prior to the return of the correctional officers,[298] the OLRB has been prepared to allow several days for compliance.

Management has been ordered to pay wages to essential services workers where the lack of payment of wages to essential services workers was, understandably, causing unrest.[299] Where management claimed it could not allow worksite visits because it did not have the keys, it was ordered to have the keys available.[300] The right to workplace access for worksite visits was ordered to be brought to the attention of a particular superintendent, and the employer was to provide access to the union's designated worksite representatives.[301]

Management has been ordered to reinstate persons serving a disciplinary suspension in circumstances where there was continuing disagreement about whether a certain work function was essential.[302] Employees were being disciplined for refusal to perform that function, and the board noted that a continued work refusal would eventually result in the discharge of all the employees. This would nullify the essential services agreement, but "both parties were willing to let that happen for their own strategic and tactical reasons."[303] The OLRB intervened to ensure the provision of essential services. The suspended employees were to be permitted to work without affecting the length of the disciplinary suspension.

Where a party seeks a precise order against specific individuals, the OLRB gives close attention to the nature of the order because such an order can be filed in court and form the basis of a contempt

---

297 *Ibid* at paras 6–7.

298 *Ontario (Management Board of Cabinet)*, [2002] OLRD No 945 (McLean) at para 13.

299 *Oshawa Court House*, above note 289 at para 4.

300 *OMAFRA*, above note 225 at para 12.

301 *Worksite Visits No 3*, above note 218 at para 4.

302 *Corrections, 22 April 2002*, above note 280 at paras 14–16.

303 *Ibid* at para 14.

proceeding.[304] A court will only act to enforce a "clear direction" about "what must be specifically be done and by whom."[305]

The leading discussion of the possibility of a contempt proceeding in connection with essential services arose as a result of a general board direction that all essential probation and parole officers were to provide essential services, and a specific direction to those employees to identify all sex offenders and partner-abuse cases on their respective case register by a certain date.[306] The MBS registered the entire order with the court and subsequently moved for contempt. The court ruled the contempt application was void for procedural reasons dealing with court filings, but also held that the general direction was "ambiguous" and so not enforceable. The specific direction was found to be sufficiently clear and specific to be enforceable by contempt proceedings.

The OLRB has rejected an employer request to incorporate the actual text of the essential services agreement into a decision to make it more readily enforceable by a contempt proceeding. The board was concerned that doing so might have led to judges, rather than the parties and the OLRB, resolving essential services disputes.[307]

c) Enforcement of the *OHSA* — Reprisal Complaints and Appeals of Inspectors Orders

During the 2002 OPSEU strike, there were a number of mass work refusals on the claimed ground of imminent danger to the workers' health and safety. The board encouraged return to work protocols that involved the acknowledgment of the right to refuse, coupled with better mechanisms to address the situation.[308] For example, the parties reached agreement, incorporated into an OLRB order, that the employer would address health and safety concerns before a further work refusal was initiated. Complaints and refusals would be investigated forthwith in accordance with *OHSA* procedures. The parties agreed to provide a safe and healthy work environment for all workers.

The board found jurisdiction to hear an *OHSA* complaint against managers personally, permitted OPSEU to bring the application, acting

---

304 *Corrections, 28 March 2002*, above note 264 at para 14.

305 *MBC v OPSEU*, unreported, 5 April 2002 (ON SCJ), McFarland J, as set out in *Probation and Parole No 2*, above 268 at para 3.

306 *Probation and Parole No 1*, above note 134 at para 7.

307 *Probation and Parole No 2*, above note 268 at para 6.

308 *Corrections, 22 April 2002*, above note 280 at para 1.

as agent for affected employees, and reiterated that the board has the power to make interim orders in respect of substantive matters under the *OHSA*.[309]

Interim relief has been ordered requiring the employer to pay wages that were denied because of the employer's contention that a work refusal was not bona fide.[310] The possible difficulty in recovering overpayments was not a basis for refusing to grant an interim order directing payment where there was a strong *prima facie* case established for entitlement to the payment. The employer was to forthwith pay the wages the employees would have earned, provided the employees signed written authorizations permitting the employer to recover the amounts if there was any further board determination that the employees had not been entitled to the wages.

d) Illegal Strike Declaration

Where the OLRB finds that a union, or some of its members, has breached an essential services agreement, the board may also be asked to rule that the breach is an illegal strike. It will exercise discretion. Even if the employer makes out all its allegations of an illegal strike, it may not be an appropriate case in which to grant relief.[311] One factor may be that, even where the union clearly breached the essential services agreement, it acknowledges having done so and agrees to adhere to the agreements in the future.[312]

Where dealing with a widespread and flagrant violation of essential services agreements, the OLRB made an illegal strike declaration concerning OPSEU, ordered the union to cease and desist, stated that illegal strikers could face significant personal liability, and ordered that "no person is to counsel, aid or assist any other person in the contravention of this Order."[313]

---

309 *Ontario (Management Board of Cabinet)*, [2002] OLRD No 1338 (Freedman) at para 5 [*Ottawa Carleton Detention Centre*]; *LRA*, above note 3, s 96.

310 *Ottawa Carleton Detention Centre*, *ibid* at para 7.

311 *Forensic Sciences*, above note 126 at para 12 and, to the same effect, *Fish Stocking*, above note 137 at para 8.

312 See a settlement to that effect made an OLRB order: *Crown as represented by the Ministry of Health v Ontario Public Service Employees Union*, OLRB File 4184/96, 21 March 1996.

313 *Ontario (Management Board of Cabinet)*, [2002] OLRD No 1345 (Chair Whitaker) at paras 5–8.

In essential services cases, and in its general jurisprudence, the board has stated that the consequence of an illegal strike declaration is that further remedies are available to the employer, including (1) seeking a cease and desist order enforceable in court, with disobedience resulting in fine or imprisonment; (2) seeking damages at arbitration for any lost profits or economic loss;[314] (3) disciplining employees on the basis that engaging in a strike is a breach of their employment obligations; and (4) seeking consent to prosecute, and subsequently prosecuting, employees or the trade union under the *LRA*, with fines against both the union and individuals being a possible consequence.[315]

The requirement in the *CECBA* that essential services workers cannot strike applies only to employees and not to the union,[316] so the union cannot be found to have breached the *CECBA* requirement to perform essential services. However, there is no such limitation in the illegal strike section of the *LRA*,[317] so a union that fails to provide essential services can be found to be engaged in an illegal strike.

When an employer is seeking an illegal strike declaration against a union, sufficient notice is given by setting out the request in the pleadings.[318] Before an illegal strike declaration is made against an individual, that person must receive notice that such a finding of fact may be made.[319] The requisite notice has been held to be twenty-four hours' notification that the employer intends to ask the OLRB to make such a finding, along with provision to the individual of a copy of the necessary pleadings and background decisions.[320]

The board will not require an employee to appear in response to an illegal strike notice unless there is some degree of *prima facie* proof of an illegal strike by that individual. In one application, the employer alleged that the president of OPSEU had engaged in illegal strike activity. The application was dismissed without a hearing because there was

---

314 The *LRA*, above note 3, s 103, sets out the procedure for such a claim, which, under the *CECBA*, above note 1, s 17, would be heard by the GSB.

315 *Ontario (Management Board of Cabinet)*, [2002] OLRD No 1106 (Lewis) at para 4. See also *Monarch Foods Limited*, [1986] OLRB Rep May 661.

316 *CACC No 3*, above note 258 at paras 3–4.

317 *LRA*, above note 3, s 100.

318 *Chatham and Lindsay Jail*, above note 160 at para 25.

319 *CACC No 3*, above note 258 at para 4; *Chatham and Lindsay Jail*, above note 160 at para 24.

320 *CACC No 2*, above note 138 at para 21.

no allegation that she had personally done anything with respect to alleged non-compliance with an essential services agreement.[321]

e) Unfair Labour Practice Complaints Against the Employer

The OLRB may grant remedies against the employer for breaches of the *LRA* occurring in the course of management's administration of essential services agreements. The government employer has argued that the OLRB does not have the jurisdiction to make such findings against government managers personally,[322] as the *LRA* does not bind the Crown,[323] and the *CECBA* does not apply to "employees exercising managerial functions."[324] This argument has not been resolved by the board. In the private sector, the unfair labour practice provisions apply to managers. There is no apparent policy reason for treating government managers differently.

f) Procedure for OLRB Litigation of Disputes Related to Essential Services During a Strike

When hearing essential services matters during a strike, the OLRB has the power to proceed with a single adjudicator and to make rules to expedite the proceedings.[325] The board's rules for expedited proceedings, which apply to *CECBA* essential services litigation, provide for broad, procedural discretion including dispensing with an oral hearing, changing time periods and filing requirements, and limiting evidence and submissions.[326]

The OLRB has very rapidly scheduled many hearings related to essential services. Parties have been ordered to proceed the day after pleadings were filed[327] and, once orders are issued, matters could be

---

321 *Ontario (Management Board of Cabinet)*, [2002] OLRD No 948 (Freedman) at para 4.

322 Employer pleadings, 11 April 2002, application to OLRB.

323 *LRA*, above note 3, s 4.

324 *CECBA*, above note 1, s 1.1(3)9.

325 *Ibid*, s 18.

326 *Rules of Procedure of the Ontario Labour Relations Board*, Rule 41—Expedited Proceedings.

327 *Psychiatric Hospitals No 1*, above note 42 at para 15.

returned to be heard on five hours' notice to the other party.[328] The same approach has been taken for *OHSA* litigation.[329]

Essential services litigation has commonly proceeded by way of consultation. This involves hearing the submissions of counsel and determining matters to the extent possible on the basis of the uncontested facts. The rules of natural justice ensure the parties will be allowed to contest factual differences, at times with cross-examination of a witness.[330] Where the board has determined that such evidence was necessary, it has shown a willingness to arrange for such evidence to be heard in an extremely expedited and time limited fashion.[331]

During the 2002 OPSEU strike, the OLRB established specific, expedited administrative practices that waived formal filing requirements. The parties' private dispute resolution mechanism, known as the 2002 MAP, failed, and the board was required to deal with a significant number of individual cases. The resultant protocol[332] provided that vice-chairs would be made available every day during the strike, including weekends, to hear cases submitted the previous day. The parties retained the right to continue to file applications with the board in the conventional manner.

This expedited procedure was used to resolve worksite visit issues. An OLRB vice-chair rendered a decision setting out general principles about worksite visits and was then asked to hear a number of cases concerning individual disputes about worksite visit difficulties. They ruled they would deal with disputes raising issues of general application, and that the expedited process would deal with site-specific issues.[333]

In the latter stages of the 2002 OPSEU strike, the employer attempted to obtain an order that discipline cases not involving ongoing liability or significant issues of collective agreement or statutory interpretation should be deferred from the OLRB's expedited adjudication process to be heard by the GSB. However, the GSB was not in operation during

328 *Psychiatric Hospitals No 2*, above note 72 at para 4.

329 *Ministry of Correctional Services*, OLRB File 3597-01-HS, 4 April 2002 (Freedman) at para 6.

330 *Chatham and Lindsay Jail*, above note 160 at para 24.

331 *Ontario (Management Board of Cabinet)*, [2002] OLRD No 933 (McLean) at para 4.

332 *Ontario (Management Board of Cabinet)*, [2002] OLRD No 1171 (Chair Whitaker) at para 2.

333 *Ontario (Management Board Secretariat)*, [2002] OLRD No 1152 (Albertyn) at para 4.

the strike, as its clerical staff was represented by OPSEU, and it was not agreed to be an essential service. Had the employer's request for deferral to the GSB been granted, it would have meant that many discipline issues could not have been litigated by OPSEU during the strike. The OLRB ruled that the employer's request was premature.[334]

Different procedural considerations seem to apply where there is a request that a serious finding of wrongdoing be made against an individual. Where the allegation was that an individual had conducted themselves in a harassing fashion such that they were not entitled to be a worksite representative, the OLRB determined that it would proceed to deal with the matter by way of a traditional hearing.[335]

The scheduling of disputes related to essential services during a strike is a challenge for the OLRB. First, the board itself has unionized staff and has not been the subject of any essential services agreement. As a result, during the two OPSEU strikes, the board has functioned without its striking employees. Second, as there have been picketers in front of its offices, it has not held hearings at the board premises. Finally, the OLRB must provide not only substantive but also procedural neutrality. The board may be asked to schedule applications brought by the employer (such as essential services enforcement requiring the performance of essential services and illegal strike declarations), as well as applications brought by the union (such as challenges to discipline, enforcement of the right to workplace visits, and claims of reprisal under the *LRA* and the *OHSA*). It is important that the speed of scheduling of different types of applications supports the rights and obligations of the parties under the legislative schemes in a fashion that does not favour one party.

5) Lack of Meaningful Collective Bargaining

The *CECBA* provides that, where a strike or lockout has lasted at least ten days, a party to an essential services agreement may apply to the OLRB for a declaration that the agreement "has prevented meaningful collective bargaining."[336] On receipt of such an application, the

334 *Ontario (Management Board of Cabinet)*, [2002] OLRD No 1086 (Chair Whitaker) at para 1.

335 *Ontario (Management Board Secretariat)*, [2002] OLRD No 941 (Albertyn) at paras 3–4.

336 *CECBA*, above note 1, s 42.

board is to consider whether enough time has gone by to permit such a determination. It is then only to consider whether the number of essential services workers has prevented meaningful bargaining. Meaningful bargaining takes place when the parties are actually negotiating and are subject to the "threat of effective economic sanctions."[337]

If the OLRB issues the declaration that meaningful collective bargaining has been prevented, it has the power to amend the essential services agreement to change the number of positions or number of employees that are designated.[338] Does this limit the board's power to grant other remedies? *CECBA 1993* specifically included the power to order interest arbitration in this circumstance, but this was removed in the 1995 amendments. The *CECBA* expressly gives the OLRB the power to make other directions or orders that it considers appropriate when finalizing, enforcing, or amending an essential services agreement, but no such general power is stated to exist following a board declaration that meaningful collective bargaining has been prevented.

6) Court Enforcement of Essential Services Agreements

Courts have been prepared to enforce duly registered board orders, as discussed above in the OLRB enforcement section. This section deals with the courts' original jurisdiction over essential services matters. The exercise of this jurisdiction has generally been characterized by a desire to leave the matter with the OLRB.

During the 1996 OPSEU strike, picket line injunctions issued by the court occasionally dealt with the provision of essential services. In several brief endorsements, the court ordered the union to allow essential services workers to report to institutions and ordered those workers to report as required by the essential services agreement, subject only to genuine incapacity.[339] The court has also ordered the employer

337 *McCormack*, above note 38 at para 12.

338 *CECBA*, above note 1, s 42(6).

339 *Her Majesty the Queen v Ontario Public Service Employees Union Local 234 and 530 et al*, unreported, 25 March 1996 (Ont Gen Div, Toronto) (Adams J) at paras 3–4; *Her Majesty the Queen in Right of Ontario v Ontario Public Service Employees Union (Niagara Detention Centre)*, unreported, 27 March 1996 (Ont Gen Div, Toronto) (Adams J); *Her Majesty the Queen in Right of Ontario v Ontario Public Service Employees Union (Elgin Middlesex Detention Centre)*, unreported, 27 March 1996 (Ont Gen Div, Toronto) (Adams J).

to recognize that the collective agreement applies to essential services workers and not to assign bargaining unit work to a non-bargaining unit employee.[340]

The court also issued specific orders against management, prohibiting TV dinners to be served at the Queen Street Mental Health Centre as long as food delivery trucks had access and all cooks were able to perform their shifts;[341] requiring interim on-call payments as may be provided for in the collective agreement "without prejudice to an arbitration to rule to the contrary by declaration but without requiring repayment of any monies paid pursuant to this order";[342] requiring management to facilitate a search of an institution and to request Ministry of Labour occupational health and safety inspectors to investigate the site;[343] distributing paycheques;[344] and taking "all reasonable steps forthwith" to fix allegedly unsafe equipment.[345]

An employer request for an injunction extending a specific order requiring the performance of essential services work in an institution was denied on the basis that the matter was properly before the OLRB.[346] Justice Adams held, "this court is not the primary body responsible for these matters. It is a backstop where peril is present." Pending an ongoing case at the OLRB dealing with a possible amendment of the essential services agreement to deal with inmate movement, the court

---

340 *Her Majesty the Queen in Right of Ontario v Ontario Public Service Employees Union et al*, unreported, 25 March 1996 (Ont Gen Div, Toronto) (Adams J) at para 8.

341 *Her Majesty the Queen in Right of Ontario v Ontario Public Service Employees Union, Local 531 et al*, unreported, 26 March 1996 (Ont Gen Div, Toronto) (Adams J) at para 3.

342 *Her Majesty the Queen in Right of Ontario v Ontario Public Service Employees Union, Local 639 and Gisele Jansen, Steve Gauvin et al*, unreported, 29 March 1996 (Ont Gen Div, Toronto) (Adams J) at para 5.

343 *Her Majesty the Queen in Right of Ontario v Ontario Public Service Employees Union, Local 608 and Darryl Pitfield et al*, unreported, 29 March 1996 (Ont Gen Div, Toronto) (Adams J) at para 4.

344 *Her Majesty the Queen in Right of Ontario v Ontario Public Service Employees Union, Local 617 and Larry McGregor et al*, unreported, 28 March 1996 (Ont Gen Div, Toronto) (Adams J) at para 5.

345 *Her Majesty the Queen in Right of Ontario v Ontario Public Service Employees Union, Local 255 and Randall Monk et al*, unreported, 28 March1996 (Ont Gen Div, Toronto), (Adams J) at para 5.

346 *Her Majesty the Queen in Right of Ontario v Ontario Public Service Employees Union et al*, unreported, 4 March 1996 (Ont Gen Div, Toronto) (Adams J).

issued a five-day injunction dealing with how frequently and under what circumstances inmates were to be allowed out of their cells.[347]

During the 2002 OPSEU strike, the issue of whether a court should deal with essential services issues received more studied attention. When the attorney general brought a motion requiring correctional officers to transfer inmates from correctional institutions to criminal courts, the motion was dealt with by Winkler J, who declined the motion and made the following oral observations during an exchange with counsel for the Crown:

> *The Court:* What jurisdiction do I have to do that?
>
> *Ms. McIntosh*: It's the same jurisdiction that Justice Adams exercised in 1996 when there was a lag time between the effectiveness of the Labour Board and being able to deal with situations and he said that he had this jurisdiction until the Labour Board could deal with a particular situation. It's the same jurisdiction.
>
> *The Court*: But if the problems are due to all sorts of different causes, I have no way of knowing what the causes are. The Labour Board, to the best of my knowledge, is dealing with the matters in a timely fashion and they are dealing with them as they come up and sitting at all odd hours to deal with them. I don't see how there is any basis for me trampling on their jurisdiction. They are pretty good at what they are doing.
>
> . . . These are essential service issues. They are to be dealt with by the Labour Board and dealt with at the ADR process and it is all set up that way and that's the way it has to be dealt with.
>
> . . . There's a serious labour dispute here. I didn't start it. We are trying. There are going to be consequences that people don't like on all 3 sides. Some things are going to impact on the court. I have power to resolve those, but I am not going to do that. There's fall out. We will live with it as best we can. Everybody has to live with it. It impacts on me personally. I don't like it either, but I am not going to do anything that will correct it. I have to live with the consequences. It's part of the reality of the situation, but the Court can't run the labour relations for the government. What you are asking me for—and you can put various spins on—but put an end to the strike, take over the

347 *Ontario (Attorney General) v Ontario Public Service Employees Union et al*, unreported, 29 February 1996 (Ont Gen Div, Toronto) (Adams J).

Labour Board's jurisdiction, all under the guise of the administration of justice. [348]

The court also dealt with an order issued by a family court judge to enforce certain services.[349] That judge's order, issued on the judge's own motion and *ex parte* (without hearing submissions from any party), required the family courtroom clerk to perform a listed set of duties, including, for example, maintaining and updating the judge's library. The ruling of the reviewing judge was that "it is for the Ontario Labour Relations Board to define what the essential services are that the Family Courtroom Clerk is to perform, not the Ontario Court of Justice." Similarly, the civil court refused an urgent motion to enforce the essential services agreement requirement to issue Ontario Disability Support Program cheques on the ground that the OLRB is the appropriate forum and had indicated it would hear urgent matters.[350]

Notwithstanding such reasoning, some attempts to require compliance with essential services agreements were made in 2002 by judges presiding in criminal courts. Where inmates failed to appear in court, and the court was informed that the reason related to the non-provision of essential services by correctional officers, one judge did find, *ex parte* and on his own motion, that correctional officers were in criminal contempt of court and ordered OPSEU to instruct its members assigned to work in the correctional facility to process the inmates.[351] On appeal, the Crown took the position that as no person was identified, there was no conviction for contempt from which to appeal, and OPSEU advised that it would instead move to set aside the mandatory order.[352] The superintendent of the institution, who had provided some of the information on which the motion for contempt was based, was themself the subject of a motion by OPSEU for an order that they were in contempt

348 *Her Majesty the Queen in Right of Ontario v Ontario Public Service Employees Union*, unreported, 26 March 2002 (SCJ) (Winkler J) at paras 8–9, 19, and 46–48.

349 *Ontario Public Service Employees Union v Attorney General of Ontario*, unreported, 29 April 2002 (SCJ) (McFarland J).

350 *Her Majesty the Queen in Right of Ontario v Ontario Public Service Employees Union*, unreported, 28 March 2002 (SCJ).

351 *In the Matter of the Hamilton-Wentworth Detention Centre and Ontario Public Service Employees Union*, unreported, 15 March 2002 (SCJ, Hamilton).

352 *In the matter of the Hamilton-Wentworth Detention Centre and Ontario Public Service Employees Union*, unreported, 22 March 2002 (ON CA). The strike ended before the motion to set aside the order was heard.

of court for misrepresenting facts and/or withholding information. That motion was dismissed on the basis that the superintendent was under no obligation to provide information as an "uninvolved and neutral observer" and under no obligation to present all sides of the various issues.[353] Their comments could not be taken as a *prima facie* indication of deliberate misrepresentation.

In another case, a judge ordered that the president of OPSEU be brought before them to show cause why the president should not be cited for contempt for their alleged role as correctional strike leader in the failure of inmates to appear in court,[354] and, on return of the motion, another judge dismissed the matter in light of an admission by counsel for the ministry that the reason for the failure of inmates to appear in court was a decision by the ministry that it would not transport the inmates on that day. Thereafter, one of the same judges responded to a further failure of an accused prisoner to appear before them as a result of the strike by citing both the minister of correctional services and the president of OPSEU for contempt.[355] The Ontario Court of Appeal heard an aspect of that matter, the question of the appropriate hourly fee for counsel retained to prosecute the case, and in so doing noted that the passage of time may have rendered "the blunt tool of contempt proceedings" no longer necessary.[356] The proceeding was subsequently abandoned.

C. *AMBULANCE SERVICES COLLECTIVE BARGAINING ACT*

The only other essential services regime in Ontario is the *Ambulance Services Collective Bargaining Act*, applicable to municipal ambulance services. The *ASCBA* regime is similar to *CECBA* essential services, including the requirement that an essential ambulance service agreement be in place before any strike or lockout, but with the important difference that, if the essential services agreement deprives the parties of a meaningful right to strike or lockout, the OLRB does have broad powers including the ordering of binding interest arbitration for ambulance workers to the exclusion of any other workers even if part of the

353 *Ontario Public Service Employees Union v Thomas*, unreported, 30 April 2002 (ON SCJ, Hamilton) at para 3.

354 *R v Vincent*, unreported, 15 March 2002 (ON SCJ, Newmarket) (McIsaac J).

355 *Her Majesty the Queen v Wong et al*, unreported, 9 October 2002 (ON SCJ) (McIsaac J).

356 *Her Majesty the Queen v Wong et al*, unreported, 13 May 2003 (ON CA) at para 35.

same bargaining unit.[357] As discussed below, other important differences are:

- covered employees and services are specifically delineated
- unanticipated emergencies give rise to a unilateral employer power to increase the number of workers for a brief period
- the terms and conditions of essential services workers are to be status quo, rather than bargained

Numerous orders have been issued by the OLRB ordering interest arbitration, often with the consent of both parties, following a finding that the essential services agreement deprives the parties of a meaningful right to strike or lockout. The board has considered whether the scheme is vulnerable to being overturned for violation of the *Charter* section 2(d) right and generally concluded that the *ASCBA* is *Charter* compliant.[358]

1) Legislative History

The government introduced the *ASCBA* because some ambulance services had been transferred from oversight by the province[359] to municipalities, which moved them from the *CECBA* essential services regime to the *LRA* with an unfettered right to strike.[360] The bill was supported by the municipalities.[361] The opposition, trade unions, and paramedics opposed the legislation on the ground that paramedics are part of a health care system which is largely under interest arbitration.[362] The

357 The presence of ambulance workers in municipal units that include other employees can produce labour relations tensions. See *Douglas Hamilton and 35 others v CUPE Local 1764*, 2015 CanLII 6939 (ON LRB), where a group of ambulance workers unsuccessfully challenged the unions handling of a strike where ambulance workers were declared 100 percent essential and required to pay higher dues (33 ⅓ percent) in the event of a strike.

358 See the discussion about *Charter* compliance and the *CECBA* earlier in this chapter.

359 Some ambulance services had been designated Crown agencies under *CECBA*, O Reg 181/90.

360 *ASCBA* discussed in Ontario Legislative Assembly, *Hansard*, 17 May 2001, First Reading at 1350 (Chris Stockwell, Minister of Labour).

361 According to the Minister of Transportation: Ontario Legislative Assembly, *Hansard*, 11 June 2001 at 1620 (Brad Clark, Minister of Transportation).

362 Ontario Legislative Assembly, *Hansard*, 7 June 2001 at 1750 (Gerry Phillips, Liberal); 11 June 2001 at 1600 (Marilyn Churley, NDP); 13 June 2001 at 1600 (Bruce Crozier, Liberal) quoting a letter from the Ontario Paramedics Association advocating that binding interest arbitration was appropriate for this essential service.

government did not favour an automatic interest arbitration regime in every case because

> we have to have in mind, at some point in our lives in this place, that every time you make somebody go to an arbitrator and every time that award is significantly more than they would get in a collective bargaining process, somebody pays. Who pays? The taxpayer pays.[363]

Nonetheless, the government agreed that bargaining units composed only of paramedics—stand-alone units—would have very extensive essential services, with only a few paramedics able to go on strike, and such circumstances, where there was a lack of a meaningful right to strike or lockout, warranted interest arbitration.[364] The government estimated there were about forty stand-alone units and about ten units where paramedics are combined with other employees. It was only in the comparatively few combined units, where the presence of large numbers of non-essential employees meant there would be a meaningful right to strike, that a strike or lockout could realistically occur.

2) Scope

The *ASCBA* only covers "ambulance workers"[365] (defined to mean paramedic, dispatcher, and employees as prescribed by regulation,[366] including air ambulance services) engaged in "essential ambulance services"(which are provided to "persons who have suffered a trauma or an acute onset of illness, either of which could endanger their life, limb or functioning"; or to persons judged to be in "unstable medical condition" and requiring the care of a health care provider and the use of a stretcher[367]) plus call taking, dispatching, and incidental services.

---

363 Ontario Legislative Assembly, *Hansard*, 13 June 2001 at 1720 (Chris Stockwell, Minister of Labour).

364 Ontario Legislative Assembly, *Hansard*, 19 June 2001 at 1110 and 1600 (Chris Stockwell, Minister of Labour).

365 *ASCBA*, above note 2, s 1(1).

366 O Reg 633/05.

367 *ASCBA*, above note 2, s 1(1)a.

3) Negotiation of an Essential Services Agreement, and Board Authority

Similar to the *CECBA*, the employer and union are required to negotiate an essential ambulance services agreement and to bargain in good faith to make one.[368] The agreement is to set out the number of ambulance workers required, specify the work they need to do to provide the essential services, identify which workers will work regularly and which are to be called in for unanticipated emergencies, and set out the order of being called in.[369] The agreement remains in effect until terminated.[370] Ambulance workers who are essential under such an agreement are prevented from striking or being locked out when they are part of a larger bargaining unit that is legally able to strike or lockout.[371] There are provisions[372] designed to ensure that there is no identification of particular employees as essential services until the strike occurs.[373] The OLRB has broad discretion to determine the contents of the agreement, give any directions, and modify any determination if there is a change in circumstances.[374] A party can apply for an amendment, which the board can provide.

Expired essential services agreements may be instructive but they do not establish a presumptive baseline. Either party is entitled to have the board take "a fresh look" at the facts.[375]

4) Substantive Content

There is no equivalent in the *ASCBA* to the *CECBA* provision[376] that places the legal burden on the party who wishes to establish that any particular service is "essential."

---

368 *Ibid*, s 3.

369 *Ibid*, s 4.

370 *Ibid*, s 8.

371 *Ibid*, s 14.

372 *Ibid*, s 4(6) & (7).

373 As explained by Chris Stockwell, minister of labour, this is intended to prevent individual knowledge of essential status from influencing strike votes: Ontario Legislative Assembly, *Hansard*, 19 June 2001 at 1100.

374 *ASCBA*, above note 2, s 9.

375 *Corporation of the City of Toronto v Toronto Civic Employees Union, Local 416*, 2012 CanLII 974 (ON LRB) at para 96 [*Toronto, 2012*].

376 *CECBA*, above note 1, s 39.

Response to urgent calls is essential.[377] It has also been agreed that paramedics are to respond when delayed or missed treatment can adversely affect the patient's condition or well-being. Examples of calls which will be responded to include, but will not be limited to, oncology treatments, cardiac diagnostic procedures, dialysis treatment, hospice care, air ambulance, or commercial aircraft departures or arrivals. Routine deferrable transfer requests have been agreed to be non-essential. It is not acceptable for the employer to leave to paramedics the decision about whether to perform a call, as the paramedic certification standards provide that no paramedic shall refuse dispatcher direction.[378] This means the employer must make arrangements with dispatchers to avoid dispatching non-essential calls.

The most contentious issue is the staffing level. While the *ASCBA* is clear that ambulance workers must provide ambulance services to a person who has suffered "a trauma that endangers their life," it is not established by the *ASCBA* whether an ambulance arriving in the shortest time possible is an essential service or whether the Act permits ambulances to arrive later. The board has found that adequate response times are "part and parcel" of providing an essential ambulance service because very reduced services would mean "[p]atients would just have to wait their turn with obvious consequences."[379] However, adequate does not necessarily mean pre-existing:

> Public safety must always be a prominent, perhaps the dominant, consideration. But the Act also dictates that the public interest in free collective bargaining be protected. It is not a question of giving timid tepid lip service to labour relations considerations. Free collective bargaining assumes that there will be negative repercussions in strike or lockout situations.[380]

The *ASCBA* definition of essential ambulance services must mean less than business as usual or the Act would be rendered redundant. It is necessary for the board to consider which ambulance services are

377 *The Corporation of the City of Sault Ste Marie v Unifor Local 1359*, 2018 CanLII 30607 (ON LRB); *Sault Ste Marie*, above note 31.

378 *Ontario Public Service Employees Union v Corporation of the County of Frontenac*, 2014 CanLII 75973 (ON LRB) [*Frontenac, 2014*].

379 *Ibid* at para 15.

380 *Toronto, 2012* above note 375 at para 90.

"genuinely" essential.[381] This is to be done by using existing standards as a "guidepost," particularly as the OLRB recognizes it has no particular paramedical expertise.[382]

There are other elements of regular ambulance servicing that have been found to be essential, or not. Deep sanitizing is essential as it is unacceptable for an ambulance to go out to patients in an unsanitized state.[383] It is also essential to restock ambulances after calls and ensure that medications are current and not expired, as well as to do regular vehicle checks and fuelling of vehicles.[384] It has been agreed that it is not essential to

- move vehicles and equipment for preventative maintenance
- place stock orders
- perform special projects
- host third-party observers
- provide non-essential education
- perform cleaning of exterior surfaces that do not have a direct impact on conspicuity of the vehicle,[385] (or to put it the other way, clean the exterior beyond what is needed to ensure the vehicle is "clearly observable" as an ambulance)[386]
- relieve management staff[387]

It has also been agreed that all vehicles and employees reporting to or leaving work shall be allowed to pass through any picket lines without

381 *Ibid* at para 102.

382 *Ibid* at para 109. The board was influenced by the history of between the parties. While the union said that far less than the normal complement was sufficient, it had for years lobbied that more paramedics were required to meet appropriate standards and "decries the normal paramedic complement as grossly inadequate." At the same time, the city budget indicated a preparedness to manage with further degradation of performance below target standards. In the result, the board ordered the maintenance of 85 percent of complement based on a data driven assessment of the amount of increased demand since the last essential services agreement: *ibid* at para 140.

383 *Frontenac, 2014*, above note 378.

384 *Sault Ste Marie*, above note 31.

385 *Unifor Local 2002 v Ornge*, 2021 CanLII 64720 (ON LRB) (Mitchell).

386 *Frontenac, 2014*, above note 378.

387 *Sault Ste Marie*, above note 31, Appendix A.

delay.[388] Staffing levels have been adjusted upward to take into account specific events, including Toronto's Pride parade.[389]

"The number of ambulance workers that are required to provide essential ambulance services shall be determined without considering whether other persons are available to provide the essential ambulance services."[390] This means the number of essential ambulance workers is to be determined without regard to supervisory personnel, even if they are duly qualified ambulance workers,[391] and even though it is recognized that the exclusion of such personnel from the definition of "ambulance worker" weakens the union's bargaining power by leaving those staff available to perform struck duties. Although it is not required by the Act, this has led to one agreement including a provision that no supervisory or management personnel will operate an ambulance or act as a paramedic during a strike or lockout except (1) in accordance with current superintendent coverage practices or (2) in the case of a "disaster which overwhelms the available resources."[392]

If, as a result of unanticipated emergencies, the agreed number of workers is not adequate to enable the provision of essential services, the employer may increase that number for a period not to exceed seventy-two hours,[393] which time may be exceeded by the agreement of the parties or by order of the board.[394] The OLRB has dealt with employer concerns that an unanticipated catastrophic event might require more than the agreed number, and union concerns that the extra staff might be used for "business as usual."[395] The board noted that unanticipated emergencies must be beyond the anticipated emergencies that are part of business as usual. They must be emergencies that would not normally arise—for example, "emergencies which seasoned professionals would not anticipate in the day to day management" of the service. To

388 *Ibid.*

389 *Toronto (City) v Toronto Civic Employees Union, Local 416*, 2009 CanLII 33904 (ON LRB).

390 *ASCBA*, above note 2, s 4.

391 *The Corporation of the City of Sault Ste Marie v Unifor Local 1359*, 2018 CanLII 30607 (ON LRB).

392 *Canadian Union of Public Employees, Local 1764 v Durham (Regional Municipality)*, 2014 CanLII 33504 (ON LRB).

393 *ASCBA*, above note 2, s 5.

394 *Ibid*, s 6.

395 *Toronto Civic Employees' Union Local 416 v Toronto (City of)*, 2002 CanLII 40418 (ON LRB).

ensure the right oversight, while not frustrating the employer's ability to respond to an unanticipated emergency, the OLRB has ordered that any such deployment of additional staff will be immediately communicated to the union and the union shall have 24/7 access to the board to arrange a consultation on an expedited basis.

The terms and conditions of employment of ambulance workers under an essential services agreement shall be the same as those in effect under the expired collective agreement unless the parties agreed otherwise.[396] This may leave open how work will be distributed during the strike or lockout. Within the limits of the *ASCBA*, the OLRB will support a proposal that will enhance the severity of the economic consequences of a lockout or strike as it will increase the likelihood that meaningful collective bargaining will occur.[397] On this basis, the board ordered the employer's proposal to schedule assignments for the needed 50 percent of the bargaining unit through full-time work assigned by seniority, rather than the union's proposal to distribute work equally among the entire unit. This has not been the consistent approach of the OLRB, which has ordered, without reasons, that shifts be distributed as equitably as possible amongst all workers in the relevant classifications.[398]

The board will not order that the essential services agreement provide for binding interest arbitration.[399] The Act requires the negotiation of an essential services agreement and "[t]he whole point of an ESA is to provide for what is to occur during a strike or lockout." Once an agreement is finalized, it is open to a party to apply for a determination that the *ASCBA* does not provide for a meaningful right to strike or lockout.

5) OLRB Remedies Where the Agreement Prevents Meaningful Strike or Lockout

Under the *ASCBA* section 18, a party to an essential services agreement can apply to the board for a declaration that the agreement has

---

396 *ASCBA*, above note 2, s 15.

397 *Leeds (United Counties) v Canadian Union of Public Employees, Local 4440*, 2008 CanLII 20643 (ON LRB).

398 *City of Toronto v Canadian Union of Public Employees*, 2020 CanLII 18400 (ON LRB).

399 *Frontenac (County) v Ontario Public Service Employees Union*, 2011 CanLII 11508 (ON LRB).

the effect of depriving employees of a meaningful right to strike or the employer of a meaningful right to lock out.[400] The OLRB is to consider if sufficient time has elapsed in the dispute to permit it to make the declaration. In making the decision, the board may amend the agreement and order binding interest arbitration for ambulance workers, even if part of a larger unit, or give any other directions seen as appropriate. The board has stated that "the purpose behind section 18 is to permit the board to intervene and assist the parties where the content of a particular ESA [essential services agreement] deprives the parties' access to the cornerstones of free collective bargaining—the threat of economic sanction through strike or lockout."[401]

Where, under the *ASCBA*, 100 percent of the employees are prevented from striking or being locked out, the board ordered interest arbitration.[402] Also, the essential services agreement will be found to have deprived the employer of a meaningful right to lock out when its terms require that, during a strike or lockout, paramedics are to work their normal shift hours, at normal complement performing all primary and significant duties.[403] In those circumstances, no employees are actually "locked out," as all their hours, conditions of work, and paycheque remain the same.

Concerning interest arbitration as a remedy, the board has broad remedial discretion and has found that, where the employer requests it and the union does not oppose it, it will be appropriate to grant.[404]

Numerous orders have been issued by the OLRB ordering interest arbitration, often with the consent of both parties, following a finding that the essential services agreement deprives the parties of a meaningful right to strike or lockout.[405] The board has noted that the union may be

---

400 *ASCBA*, above note 2, s 18. The board shall not issue such a declaration if at least 75 percent of the employees may strike or be locked out: *ASCBA*, s 18(5). This has never arisen.

401 *Sun Parlour Emergency Services Incorporated (Essex Division) v Service Employees' International Union, Local 1*, 2007 CanLII 14303 (ON LRB) at para 22 [*Sun Parlour*].

402 *Ontario Public Service Employees Union v Royal City Ambulance Service Ltd*, 2004 CanLII 10039 (ON LRB).

403 *Sun Parlour*, above note 401, at para 26.

404 *Ibid* at para 34.

405 *Oneida Nation of the Thames Emergency Medical Services v Ontario Public Service Employees' Union, Local 147*, 2013 CanLII 8709 (ON LRB); *Canadian Union of Public Employees, Local 2974.2 v Corporation of the County of Essex*,

content to have the collective agreement settled by interest arbitration while the employer may seek to avoid such a result. In one such case, the union argued that a full complement of staff was needed to provide essential services while the employer argued that only 50 percent of the staffing complement was essential.[406]

D. PICKETING ISSUES UNIQUE TO GOVERNMENT STRIKES AND LOCKOUTS

In the event of picketing during a *CECBA* strike or lockout, the normal common law and statutory provisions apply, but with three exceptions unique to the OPS and the *CECBA*. The first exception is ensuring essential services are not impeded by picket line activity. The second and third exceptions are limitations on picketing courthouses, which are workplaces for unionized staff, and the Legislative Assembly, which can be seen as the employer of direct employees of government.

1) Picket Line Activity: Ten-Minute Delay and Maintenance of Essential Services

Picketing of the employer's premises by strikers is constitutionally protected expressive activity[407] intended to communicate to those planning to enter the premises the union's messages concerning the labour dispute, including that the union is asking those wishing to enter the premises that they not do so. Picketing is also intended to put economic pressure on the employer by delaying entry. Courts have accepted that a limited delay balances the parties' interests, provided the picketing

---

2015 CanLII 65511 (ON LRB); *Canadian Union of Public Employees, Local 2974.2 v The Corporation of the County of Essex*, 2017 CanLII 61260 (ON LRB); *Halton/Mississauga Ambulance Service, Ltd v Ontario Public Service Employees' Union, Local 277*, 2004 CanLII 47566; *Regional Municipality of Peel (Peel Regional Paramedic Service) v Ontario Public Service Employees Union, Local 277*, 2012 CanLII 75633; *Ontario Public Service Employees Union v Grey (County)*, 2008 CanLII 26553; *Corporation of the County of Lambton (Lambton Emergency Medical Services) v Service Employees' International Union*, 2021 CanLII 58482 (ON LRB).

406 *Frontenac, 2014*, above note 378 at para 9.

407 *Retail, Wholesale and Department Store Union, Local 558 v Pepsi-Cola Canada Beverages (West) Ltd*, 2002 SCC 8 at para 32.

is otherwise lawful.[408] Although sanctioned picket line delays are not unique to public service strikes,[409] judicial standards related to such delays are perhaps most thoroughly developed in the public service strike context, and the extensive jurisprudence from the OPSEU strikes in 1996 and 2002 is a leading, if not the leading, example in Canada.

In the two OPS strikes to date, courts have permitted picketers to impose delays of varying lengths of time on persons seeking to cross picket lines, with a general standard of ten minutes' delay being clarified in 2002.[410]

The vast majority of picket line injunction orders made during the 1996 and 2002 public service strikes were issued by a few judges in Toronto who heard motions for injunctions on short notice, following discussion between counsel for the government and OPSEU. It has been noted that this procedure ensures expeditious hearings that ease picket line tensions.[411]

The orders were almost invariably "bottom line" rulings, issued without reasons. Service of orders was deemed effective on delivery of a copy of the order to counsel for the union, and all motions to vary

---

408 *Sobeys v UFCW, Local 175*, 2013 ONSC 1207, Gray J, and discussion in Kate Hughes & Daniel Wilband, "The Blunt Instrument of Labour Injunctions: the Law and Practice in Ontario," Law Society of Upper Canada (2014), online: www.cavalluzzo.com/docs/default-source/publications/the-law-and-practice-regarding-pickets-(c1261777xa0e3a).pdf?sfvrsn=fc955d5_2; *Bank-Strox Renovation Inc v Laborers' International Union of North America, Local 183*, 2020 ONSC 4911; *Unifor Canada Local 594 v Consumers' Co-Operative Refineries Limited*, 2021 SKCA 34.

409 *Industrial Hardwood Products (1996) Ltd v Industrial Wood and Allied Workers of Canada, Local 2693*, 2001 CanLII 24071 (ON CA).

410 The 2002 rulings are discussed below. The allowable delays in 1996 ranged generally from zero to five minutes. See, for example, *Her Majesty the Queen in Right of Ontario v Ontario Public Service Employees Union and Local 230, P Hugo, J Rathwell, R Barber, D MacArthur, B Scanlon*, unreported, 7 March 1988 (Ont Ct Gen Div, Waterloo) at para 1, ordering no delay of access or egress; *Her Majesty the Queen v Ontario Public Service Employees Union et al*, unreported, 12 March 1996 (Ont Ct Gen Div), ordering that "[s]ubject to any protocol negotiated between the parties, persons wishing to enter into or exit from the building at 2195 Yonge Street will be permitted to do so within five minutes of their intended arrival or departure."

411 Ontario, *Report of the Commission of Inquiry into Events of March 18, 1996, at Queen's Park* (Willard Z. Estey, QC, Commissioner) (Toronto: Ministry of the Attorney General, 1996) [*Estey Report*], Appendix B(1), detailed chronology at para 29.

or amend the order were returnable on two hours' telephone notice to counsel, supported by written material.[412]

a) Ten-Minute Delay Terms and Conditions

During the 2002 strike, the first interim injunction order was issued by Winkler J and concerned the Queen's Park complex. It stated that picketers "shall not impede, obstruct or delay the access or egress of any person for more than 10 minutes."[413] The same term also appears in most of the other orders discussed in this section. Subsequently it was clarified that the ten-minute delay normally applied to entering the struck premises and that exiting was not to be delayed.[414] To facilitate non-contentious compliance with the ten-minute delay period, and to avoid disputes arising from persons trying to circumvent picket lines, orders required certain doors of workplaces to remain locked;[415] parking lot gates to remain closed, except for emergency vehicles;[416] persons to be required to use one particular entrance;[417] all visitors and staff to use only one entrance;[418] and the employer being required to instruct visiting contractors and medical staff to use a particular entrance.[419]

---

412 For example, see *Her Majesty the Queen in Right of Ontario v Ontario Public Service Employees Union*, unreported, 13 March 2002 (SCJ) at para 3.

413 *Ibid* at para 1. To the same effect, see *Her Majesty the Queen in Right of Ontario v Ontario Public Service Employees Union*, unreported, 20 March 2002 (SCJ) at para 1(a) (re 25 Grosvenor St, Toronto).

414 See, for example, *Her Majesty the Queen in Right of Ontario v Ontario Public Service Employees Union*, unreported, 14 March 2002 (SCJ) at para 1(d) (re 33 King St W, Oshawa); *Her Majesty the Queen in Right of Ontario v Ontario Public Service Employees Union*, unreported, 1 May 2002 (SCJ) (re 119 King St W, Hamilton).

415 *Her Majesty the Queen in Right of Ontario v Ontario Public Service Employees Union*, unreported, 20 March 2002 (SCJ) at para 1(c) (re 99 Wellesley St W, Toronto).

416 *Her Majesty the Queen in Right of Ontario v Ontario Public Service Employees Union*, unreported, 22 March 2002 (SCJ) at para 1(b) (re Ministry of Transportation, 1201 Wilson Avenue, Toronto).

417 *Her Majesty the Queen in Right of Ontario v Ontario Public Service Employees Union*, unreported, 5 April 2002 (SCJ), Guelph at para 2 (re Ontario Ministry of Agriculture, Food and Rural Affairs, County Road 18, Fergus).

418 *Her Majesty the Queen in Right of Ontario v Ontario Public Service Employees Union*, unreported, 14 April 2002 (SCJ) at para 1(g) (re 1 Stone Road, Guelph).

419 *Her Majesty the Queen in Right of Ontario v Ontario Public Service Employees Union*, unreported, 27 April 2002 (SCJ) at para 4 (re Vanier Centre for Women).

Persons attending at a Land Registry Office several times in one day only had to engage in one ten-minute delay and thereafter could cross the picket line without delay, provided they identified themselves to the picket captain.[420]

As an alternative to the picketing of all the pedestrian entrances to office buildings shared by the government and other tenants, OPS employees were required to use only one of several entrances and picketing was only permitted at that entrance.[421] In a similar case, picket captains could be stationed in the lobby to "administer" the ten-minute delay to government employees, and government employees were required to report to them for that purpose.[422]

As an alternative to picketing all the entrances to a parking garage shared by government employees and others, picketing was limited to one entrance and all government employees' vehicles were required to use that one entrance where they would be subject to the ten-minute delay.[423]

Where lines of vehicles were blocking traffic on arterial roads as a result of being delayed for ten minutes, a 1996 injunction simply required that the blockage of traffic not occur,[424] with the result that cars were to be "let through" the picket line early if necessary. In 2002, provision was made for vehicles to identify themselves to a picketer and then wait in sight, but off of the arterial road, for the ten minutes.[425]

---

420 *Her Majesty the Queen in Right of Ontario v Ontario Public Service Employees Union*, unreported, 28 March 2002 (SCJ) at para 1(d) (re 300 Water Street, Peterborough).

421 *Her Majesty the Queen in Right of Ontario v Ontario Public Service Employees Union*, unreported, 1 May 2002 (SCJ) at para 1(a) (re 119 King St W Hamilton).

422 *The Manufacturer's Life Insurance and OMERS Realty Corporation and Her Majesty the Queen in Right of Ontario v Ontario Public Service Employees Union*, unreported, 10 April 2002 (SCJ) at para 1(e) (re 5700 Yonge Street, Toronto).

423 *Her Majesty the Queen in Right of Ontario v Ontario Public Service Employees Union*, unreported, 14 April 2002 (SCJ) at para 1(d)(iii) (re 55 Athol St, Oshawa); *Her Majesty the Queen in Right of Ontario v Ontario Public Service Employees Union*, unreported, 16 April 2002 (SCJ) (re 1400 Blair Place, Gloucester).

424 *Her Majesty the Queen in Right of Ontario v Ontario Public Service Employees Union et al*, unreported, 29 February 1996 (SCJ) (re Vanier Centre for Women).

425 *Her Majesty the Queen in Right of Ontario v Ontario Public Service Employees Union*, unreported, 13 March 2002 (SCJ) at para 1(a) (re Ontario Correctional Institute, 109 McLaughlin Rd S, Brampton).

In other situations, persons and vehicles were allowed to enter the site without delay but were subject to the ten-minute delay on leaving.[426]

The ten-minute delay is the total amount of delay for each person. Those waiting in a line need not wait for the ten-minute delay of each person or vehicle in front of them.[427]

Where management staff refused to wait ten minutes before crossing the picket line, the court ordered that they be informed of the relevant ten-minute delay order, and confirmed that the order applied to them.[428]

b) Variations Related to the Receipt or Provision of Essential Services

Courts have varied the usual standard of the ten-minute delay (and related orders) for the benefit of persons receiving or providing essential services. There was to be no delay of

- inmates or inmate vehicles moving in and out of jails[429]
- vehicles containing children and parents at schools for deaf and blind children[430]
- Ontario Disability Support Program (ODSP) clients, as management and the OPSEU were to endeavour to identify the clients

---

426 *Her Majesty the Queen in Right of Ontario v Ontario Public Service Employees Union*, unreported, 3 April 2002 (SCJ), Toronto. at para 1(a) (re 255 Ontario Street South, Milton); *Her Majesty the Queen in Right of Ontario v Ontario Public Service Employees Union*, unreported, 15 April 2002 (SCJ) at para 1(b) (re Ontario Clean Water Agency, 200 Water St, Cambridge).

427 *Her Majesty the Queen in Right of Ontario v Ontario Public Service Employees Union*, unreported, 19 April 2002 (SCJ) at para 1(d) (re Ministries of Environment and Health, Resources Road, Toronto); *Her Majesty the Queen in Right of Ontario v Ontario Public Service Employees Union*, unreported, 23 April 2002 (SCJ) at para 2 (re 77 City Centre Drive, Mississauga).

428 *Her Majesty the Queen in Right of Ontario v Ontario Public Service Employees Union*, unreported, 3 April 2002 (SCJ) at para 1(a) (re Toronto Jails).

429 *Her Majesty the Queen in Right of Ontario v Ontario Public Service Employees Union*, unreported, 16 March 2002 (SCJ), Toronto at para 1(a) (re Toronto Jails); *Her Majesty the Queen in Right of Ontario v Ontario Public Service Employees Union*, unreported, 17 March 2002 (SCJ) at para 1(a) (re Quinte Detention Centre); *Her Majesty the Queen in Right of Ontario v Ontario Public Service Employees Union*, unreported, 26 March 2002 (SCJ) at para 1 (re Maplehurst Correctional Centre).

430 *Her Majesty the Queen in Right of Ontario v Ontario Public Service Employees Union*, unreported, 3 April 2002 (SCJ) at para 1 (re 255 Ontario Street South, Milton).

among those waiting ten minutes at ODSP locations,[431] and persons attending at ODSP locations were not to be falsely told that there was no service inside

- clients of the Ministry of Community, Family and Children's Services[432]
- vehicles identified by management as carrying time-sensitive samples for testing at the Central Public Health Laboratory[433]
- operations at the fish-stocking sites related to the Dorion Fish Culture Station[434]
- the main doors of Ontario Rental Housing Tribunal, except that the government staff working in the building were to use another door where they were made subject to the ten-minute delay[435]
- emergency vehicles (police, fire, ambulance)[436]

The movement of the mailed tax remittance and bank deposit delivery van to and from the Ministry of Finance in Oshawa was ordered, in 1996, to be unobstructed,[437] and in 2002 was initially ordered to be subject to one ten-minute delay daily.[438]

---

431 *Her Majesty the Queen in Right of Ontario v Ontario Public Service Employees Union*, unreported, 9 April 2002 (SCJ) at para 1(a) (re 2195 Yonge Street, Toronto).

432 *Her Majesty the Queen in Right of Ontario v Ontario Public Service Employees Union*, unreported, 1 May 2002 (SCJ) at para 1(b) (re 465 Davis Dr, Newmarket).

433 *Her Majesty the Queen in Right of Ontario v Ontario Public Service Employees Union*, unreported, 19 April 2002 (SCJ) at para 1(a) (re Ministries of Environment and Health, Resources Road, Toronto).

434 *Her Majesty the Queen in Right of Ontario v Ontario Public Service Employees Union*, unreported, 26 April 2002 (SCJ) at para 1(c) (re Dorion Fish Culture Station).

435 *Her Majesty the Queen in Right of Ontario v Ontario Public Service Employees Union*, unreported, 27 March 2002 (SCJ) at paras 1(a)–(b) (re Ontario Rental Housing Tribunal, 2275 Midland Avenue, Scarborough).

436 *Her Majesty the Queen in Right of Ontario v Ontario Public Service Employees Union*, unreported, 15 March 2002 (SCJ), North Bay at para 1(c) (re 447 McKeown Ave, North Bay).

437 *Her Majesty the Queen in Right of Ontario v Ontario Public Service Employees Union and Sally Rudka*, unreported, 17 February 1996 (SCJ) at para (b)(iii) (re 33 King St W, Oshawa).

438 *Her Majesty the Queen in Right of Ontario v Ontario Public Service Employees Union*, unreported, 14 March 2002 (SCJ) at para 1(b) (re 33 King St W, Oshawa). This order was subsequently changed in response to a breach of the earlier order; see the "Consequences of Breach of Injunction Orders" section, below.

There was a permissible two-minute delay of emergency snowplows and ice control equipment, and of employees assigned to that service,[439] and there were orders against obstruction of employees within the five minutes before the commencement of their work shifts.[440]

In 2002, ten minutes' delay of persons attending at a probation and parole office was permissible[441] provided picketers did not otherwise "order, deter, counsel or prevent" the government's clients from reporting to the location;[442] tell persons attending that services were not available or that they did not need to attend;[443] or ask persons about the nature and purpose of their visit.[444]

Five-minute delay of persons visiting incarcerated patients was permitted.[445]

In order to assure picketers that only essential services were being provided in correctional facilities, picketers were to receive reasonable notice of service and supply vehicles that would be seeking access to the site and the reason for the access, along with the right to inspect the vehicles to confirm the information provided by the employer, provided there was no more than a ten-minute delay.[446] Disputes about the

439 *Her Majesty the Queen in Right of Ontario v Ontario Public Service Employees Union*, unreported, 8 March 1996 (SCJ) at para 1 (re Ministry of Transportation).

440 For example, see *Her Majesty the Queen in Right of Ontario v Ontario Public Service Employees Union*, unreported, 1 March 1996 (SCJ) (re Hamilton-Wentworth Detention Centre).

441 *Her Majesty the Queen in Right of Ontario v Ontario Public Service Employees Union*, unreported, 25 April 2002 (SCJ) at para 1(a) (re 155 Clark Boulevard, Unit 15, Brampton).

442 *Her Majesty the Queen in Right of Ontario v Ontario Public Service Employees Union*, unreported, 1 May 2002 (SCJ) at para 1(f) (re 119 King St W, Hamilton).

443 *Her Majesty the Queen in Right of Ontario v Ontario Public Service Employees Union*, unreported, 25 April 2002 (SCJ) at para 1(b) (re 155 Clark Boulevard, Unit 15, Brampton).

444 *Her Majesty the Queen in Right of Ontario v Ontario Public Service Employees Union*, unreported, 26 April 2002 (SCJ) at para 1(e) (re 1916 Dundas St, Unit 1, Whitby).

445 *Her Majesty the Queen in Right of Ontario v Ontario Public Service Employees Union*, unreported, 12 April 2002 (SCJ), Sch A at para 3 (re Mental Health Centre, Penetanguishene).

446 *Her Majesty the Queen in Right of Ontario v Ontario Public Service Employees Union*, unreported, 15 March 2002 (SCJ) at para 1(e) (re Toronto Jails).

contents of vehicles or the reasons for their access to the site were to be referred to the court and did not justify any additional delay.[447]

c) Other Terms of Picket Line Injunctions

The conduct of persons on the picket line was regulated responsively. Picketers were not allowed to demand or request identification, make persons go through more than one picket line,[448] or require those being delayed to wait in a particular location.[449] There were to be no acts of intimidation, including the swarming or jostling of vehicles[450] and, in particular, no acts of intimidation based on bargaining unit membership.[451] Entrances were to remain free of objects.[452] Picketers were not to wear masks or otherwise disguise their faces.[453] Dogs, other than seeing-eye dogs, were barred from the picketed area.[454] Devices that make loud

---

447 *Her Majesty the Queen in Right of Ontario v Ontario Public Service Employees Union*, unreported, 23 March 2002 (SCJ) at para 1(c) (re Toronto East Detention Centre, 55 Civic Road, Scarborough).

448 *Her Majesty the Queen in Right of Ontario v Ontario Public Service Employees Union*, unreported, 14 April 2002 (SCJ) at paras 1(d)–(e) (re 1 Stone Road, Guelph).

449 *Her Majesty the Queen in Right of Ontario v Ontario Public Service Employees Union*, unreported, 19 April 2002 (SCJ) at para b(iii) (re 1201 Wilson Avenue, Downsview).

450 *Her Majesty the Queen in Right of Ontario v Ontario Public Service Employees Union*, unreported, 30 March 2002 (SCJ) at para 1(a)(iii) (re Quinte Detention Centre); *Her Majesty the Queen in Right of Ontario v Ontario Public Service Employees Union*, unreported, 3 April 2002 (SCJ), para 1(a) (re Ottawa-Carleton Detention Centre).

451 *Her Majesty the Queen in Right of Ontario v Ontario Public Service Employees Union*, unreported, 19 April 2002 (SCJ) at para 6(ii) (re 1201 Wilson Avenue, Downsview).

452 *Her Majesty the Queen in Right of Ontario v Ontario Public Service Employees Union*, unreported, 30 March 2002 (SCJ) at para 1(a)(i) (re Quinte Detention Centre); *Her Majesty the Queen in Right of Ontario v Ontario Public Service Employees Union*, unreported, 9 April 2002 (SCJ), Thunder Bay at para 2 (re Thunder Bay Correctional Centre).

453 *Her Majesty the Queen in Right of Ontario v Ontario Public Service Employees Union*, unreported, 3 April 2002 (SCJ), Guelph at para 1(d) (re Ontario Ministry of Agriculture, Food and Rural Affairs, County Road 18, Fergus); *Her Majesty the Queen in Right of Ontario v Ontario Public Service Employees Union*, unreported, 8 April 2002 (SCJ) at para 1(d) (re Quinte Detention Centre).

454 *Her Majesty the Queen in Right of Ontario v Ontario Public Service Employees Union*, unreported, 14 April 2002 (SCJ), Toronto at para (b) (re 55 Athol St, Oshawa).

noises, like bullhorns, were not to be used between 11:00 p.m. and 7:00 a.m., and never to be used to "commit acts of harassment,"[455] or within five feet of persons.[456]

Issues related to the organization of picket lines were resolved by the courts:

- parties were to adhere to any agreed picket line protocol[457]
- picket captains were ordered to be identified,[458] and an identifiable picket captain was ordered to be present at all times[459]
- vehicles were required to approach a picket line at a slow rate of speed and come to a full stop before proceeding through the picket line[460]
- picketers were not to trespass on government property, but were able to cross government property to access their strike headquarters[461]
- picketers who went into picketed buildings at the Queen's Park complex were ordered to not enter without approval from government picket line monitors, which approval was not to be unreasonably denied[462]

---

455 *Her Majesty the Queen in Right of Ontario v Ontario Public Service Employees Union*, unreported, 15 April 2002 (SCJ) at para 3 (re Quinte Detention Centre).

456 *Her Majesty the Queen in Right of Ontario v Ontario Public Service Employees Union*, unreported, 18 April 2002 (SCJ) at para (u)(vi) (re 55 Athol St, Oshawa).

457 *Her Majesty the Queen in Right of Ontario v Ontario Public Service Employees Union*, unreported, 9 April 2002 (SCJ) at para 1 (re Mental Health Centre, Penetanguishene), attaching an extensive protocol agreed to between the parties; *Her Majesty the Queen in Right of Ontario v Ontario Public Service Employees Union*, unreported, 18 April 2002 (SCJ) at para 3 (re 301 St Paul St, St Catharines).

458 *Her Majesty the Queen in Right of Ontario v Ontario Public Service Employees Union*, unreported, 16 April 2002 (SCJ) at para (c)(iv), Toronto (re Ministry of Transportation, 1201 Wilson Avenue, Toronto).

459 *Her Majesty the Queen in Right of Ontario v Ontario Public Service Employees Union* unreported, 16 April 2002 (SCJ) at para 2 (re Ontario Ministry of Agriculture, Food and Rural Affairs, County Road 18, Fergus).

460 *Her Majesty the Queen in Right of Ontario v Ontario Public Service Employees Union*, unreported, 24 April 2002 (SCJ) at para 1(c) (re Quinte Detention Centre).

461 *Her Majesty the Queen in Right of Ontario v Ontario Public Service Employees Union*, unreported, 25 April 2002 (SCJ) at para 1(e) (re 700 Gordon St, Whitby).

462 *Her Majesty the Queen in Right of Ontario v Ontario Public Service Employees Union*, unreported, 17 April 2002 (SCJ) (re Queen's Park Precinct).

- picketers were allowed to use an institution's parking lot rather than parking their cars on grassy areas near the entrance to the institution[463]

Concerning the tunnel connecting the Queen's Park complex directly to a Toronto Transit Commission (TTC) subway station, picketing was permitted during the hours of tunnel operation, with up to eight picketers allowed to be on TTC property, provided they stayed within ten feet of the tunnel door and did not interfere with the ability of TTC patrons to use the station (eventually these orders were extended to all TTC stations).[464] The Divisional Court found this was not secondary picketing because the object of the picketing was the Ontario government and its employees, and not the TTC;[465] and the court further found that the interests of the property owner, union, and public all had to be balanced when informational activity was taking place on quasi-public property.[466]

To avoid safety risks on highways, Ministry of Transportation inspection staff were barred from picketing on the entrances and exits of truck inspection centres on Highway 401,[467] although picketing was permitted on grass-covered medians adjacent to those centres and picketer access to the median was permitted through the paved inspection area, provided the number of picketers was limited to twenty at any one time and one was a transportation enforcement officer familiar with the site.[468]

---

463 *Her Majesty the Queen in Right of Ontario v Ontario Public Service Employees Union*, unreported, 19 April 2002 (SCJ) at para (a)(i) (re Ontario Correctional Institute).

464 *Toronto Transit Commission v Ontario Public Service Employees Union et al*, [1996] OJ No 868 (Gen Div) at paras 3–4, and *Toronto Transit Commission v Ontario Public Service Employees Union et al*, unreported, 15 March 1996 (Gen Div). Both decisions were affirmed on appeal in *Toronto Transit Commission v Ontario Public Service Employees Union et al*, [1996] OJ No 959 (Div Ct).

465 *Ibid* at paras 4 and 5 (Div Ct).

466 *Ibid* at 5. The Divisional Court relied on the Supreme Court decision in *Committee for the Commonwealth of Canada v Canada*, [1991] 1 SCR 139.

467 *Her Majesty the Queen in Right of Ontario v Ontario Public Service Employees Union*, unreported, 27 March 2002 (SCJ) at para 1 (re Ministry of Transportation Truck Inspection Stations on Highway 401).

468 *Her Majesty the Queen in Right of Ontario v Ontario Public Service Employees Union*, unreported, 8 April 2002 (SCJ) (re Trafalgar (Milton) South 401 Inspection Station). This order also provided that the picketers would have access to a public washroom.

To avoid blocking traffic when picketing the construction of a bridge, picketers were not permitted in the travelled lane of traffic, but instead were required to picket in a certain delineated area near the construction.[469]

The private home of an employee, who allegedly worked during the strike even when not an essential services worker, could not be the subject of picketing, interruption of "quiet enjoyment," intimidation, trespassing, or communication with the employee, family, or neighbours.[470]

d) Consequences of Breach of Injunction Orders

Where picketers disobeyed the terms of injunction orders, and especially when this was done repeatedly at the same location, the courts imposed a graduated range of consequences, either individually or in combination.

Individual picketers have been barred from the picket line for four days,[471] or until allowed to return,[472] or for the duration of the strike.[473] A picketer was barred from coming within a kilometre of the institution "until the parties [had] signed a collective agreement,"[474] and in one case from coming within five kilometres of the institution.[475] A group

---

469 *Her Majesty the Queen in Right of Ontario v Ontario Public Service Employees Union*, unreported, 26 April 2002 (SCJ) at para 102 (re Kabinakagami River Bridge, near Hearst).

470 *Her Majesty the Queen in Right of Ontario and Nicole Burley v Ontario Public Service Employees Union*, unreported, 18 April 2002 (SCJ) at para 1; *Her Majesty the Queen and Cecile Lavigne v Ontario Public Service Employees Union*, unreported, 30 April 2002 (SCJ).

471 *Her Majesty the Queen in Right of Ontario v Ontario Public Service Employees Union*, unreported, 23 March 2002 (SCJ) at para 2 (re Toronto East Detention Centre, 55 Civic Road, Scarborough), barring a person, one Mark Dewar, from picketing for four days; *Her Majesty the Queen in Right of Ontario v Ontario Public Service Employees Union*, unreported, 8 April 2002 (SCJ) at para 2 (re Quinte Detention Centre).

472 *Her Majesty the Queen in Right of Ontario v Ontario Public Service Employees Union*, unreported, 26 March 2002 (SCJ) at para 1 (re Mimico Correctional Centre).

473 *Her Majesty the Queen in Right of Ontario v Ontario Public Service Employees Union*, unreported, 22 April 2002 (SCJ) at para 1 (re Ottawa-Carleton Detention Centre).

474 *Her Majesty the Queen in Right of Ontario v Ontario Public Service Employees Union*, unreported, 10 April 2002 (SCJ) at para 2 (re Quinte Detention Centre).

475 *Her Majesty the Queen in Right of Ontario v Ontario Public Service Employees Union*, unreported, 1 May 2002 (SCJ) at para 3 (re Guelph Correctional Centre).

of individually named picketers was barred from the picket line for several days.[476]

Where a picketer was particularly disruptive, they were barred from multiple locations.[477] A barred picketer may nonetheless be entitled to visit the OPSEU office that is onsite.[478] When a picketer is barred from the picket line, they could still pass through it on the way to, and from, performing their scheduled essential service duties.[479]

All picketers and picket captains were directed to ensure that delays did not exceed ten minutes.[480] Where longer delays occurred, the period of delay was reduced from ten minutes to five minutes for four days,[481] for a week,[482] or for the duration of the strike;[483] or to four minutes,[484] then two minutes,[485] including a matching reduction in the delay times agreed to in a protocol.[486] Permissible delay was suspended for a period

---

476 *Her Majesty the Queen in Right of Ontario v Ontario Public Service Employees Union*, unreported, 24 April 2002 (SCJ) at para 2 (re Whitby Jail).

477 *Her Majesty the Queen in Right of Ontario v Ontario Public Service Employees Union*, unreported, 15 April 2002 (SCJ) at para 2 (re 40 St Clair Ave W, Toronto): barring Patricia Ahlberg from 2, 40, and 135 St Clair Ave W.

478 *Her Majesty the Queen in Right of Ontario v Ontario Public Service Employees Union*, unreported, 18 April 2002 (SCJ) at para 3 (re 40 King St W, Oshawa).

479 *Her Majesty the Queen in Right of Ontario v Ontario Public Service Employees Union*, unreported, 15 April 2002 (SCJ) at para 2 (re Whitby Jail).

480 *Her Majesty the Queen in Right of Ontario v Ontario Public Service Employees Union*, unreported, 3 April 2002 (SCJ) at para 3 (re 300 Water Street, Peterborough).

481 *Her Majesty the Queen in Right of Ontario v Ontario Public Service Employees Union*, unreported, 29 March 2002 (SCJ) at para 1(b) (re Toronto West Detention Centre).

482 *Her Majesty the Queen in Right of Ontario v Ontario Public Service Employees Union*, unreported, 17 April 2002 (SCJ) (re Toronto West Detention Centre).

483 *Her Majesty the Queen in Right of Ontario v Ontario Public Service Employees Union*, unreported, 10 April 2002 (SCJ) at para 2(b) (re 33 King St W, Oshawa); *Her Majesty the Queen in Right of Ontario v Ontario Public Service Employees Union*, unreported, 12 April 2002 (SCJ) at para 1(ii) (re Mental Health Centre, Penetanguishene).

484 *Her Majesty the Queen in Right of Ontario v Ontario Public Service Employees Union*, unreported, 10 April 2002 (SCJ) at para 1(a) (re Quinte Detention Centre).

485 *Her Majesty the Queen in Right of Ontario v Ontario Public Service Employees Union*, unreported, 15 April 2002 (SCJ) at para 1(a) (re Quinte Detention Centre).

486 *Her Majesty the Queen in Right of Ontario v Ontario Public Service Employees Union*, unreported, 19 April 2002 (SCJ) at para 1(i) (re Mental Health Centre, Penetanguishene).

of several days before being restored to five minutes.[487] Delay was eliminated,[488] although non-obstructive picketing could still occur.

Picketers were limited to thirty in number for the busy arrival time of 7:30 a.m. to 9:30 a.m.,[489] to twenty-two picketers for four days,[490] to fifteen for seven days,[491] to seven in total,[492] and to five in total.[493] The permissible number of picketers was reduced to three at an entire large facility (increasing to seven after several days).[494]

A pre-existing right to inspect vehicles entering correctional institutions was taken away for several days.[495] Picketers, other than the picket captain, were not to approach within fifteen feet of the sides or rear of vehicles.[496] Striking employees at a correctional institution were

---

487 *Her Majesty the Queen in Right of Ontario v Ontario Public Service Employees Union*, unreported, 24 April 2002 (SCJ) at para 1(a) and (d) (re Ontario Ministry of Agriculture, Food and Rural Affairs, County Road 18, Fergus).

488 *Her Majesty the Queen in Right of Ontario v Ontario Public Service Employees Union*, unreported, 23 April 2002 (SCJ) at para 2(b) (re 33 King St W, Oshawa); *Her Majesty the Queen in Right of Ontario v Ontario Public Service Employees Union*, unreported, 1 May 2002 (SCJ) at para 1(i) (re Guelph Correctional Centre); *Her Majesty the Queen in Right of Ontario v Ontario Public Service Employees Union*, unreported, 26 April 2002 (SCJ) at para 1(i) (re Ontario Correctional Institute).

489 *Her Majesty the Queen in Right of Ontario v Ontario Public Service Employees Union*, unreported, 23 April 2002 (SCJ) at para 2 (re Ontario Ministry of Agriculture Food and Rural Affairs, 1 Stone Road, Guelph).

490 *Her Majesty the Queen in Right of Ontario v Ontario Public Service Employees Union*, unreported, 29 March 2002 (SCJ) at para 1(c) (re Toronto West Detention Centre).

491 *Her Majesty the Queen in Right of Ontario v Ontario Public Service Employees Union*, unreported, 9 April 2002 (SCJ) at para 4 (re Toronto West Detention Centre).

492 *Her Majesty the Queen in Right of Ontario v Ontario Public Service Employees Union*, unreported, 26 April 2002 (SCJ) at para 2 (re Ontario Correctional Institute).

493 *Her Majesty the Queen in Right of Ontario v Ontario Public Service Employees Union*, unreported, 5 April 2002 (SCJ) at para 1(a) (re 300 Water Street, Peterborough); *Her Majesty the Queen in Right of Ontario v Ontario Public Service Employees Union*, unreported, 1 May 2002 (SCJ) at para 2 (re Guelph Correctional Centre).

494 *Her Majesty the Queen in Right of Ontario v Ontario Public Service Employees Union*, unreported, 23 April 2002 (SCJ), at para 3 (re 33 King St W, Oshawa).

495 *Her Majesty the Queen in Right of Ontario v Ontario Public Service Employees Union*, unreported, 24 April 2002 (SCJ) at para A(b) (re Quinte Detention Centre).

496 *Her Majesty the Queen in Right of Ontario v Ontario Public Service Employees Union*, unreported, 8 April 2002 (SCJ) at para 2(c) (re Quinte Detention Centre);

barred from attending at the picket line of a nearby non-correctional workplace for one week.[497]

Picketing was banned at several jails.[498] Picketing was banned from all the streets immediately adjoining a government building, and a motion for contempt of court was brought in response to persistent obstruction of access.[499] The motion for contempt was discontinued as part of the 2002 *Return to Work Protocol*.

Although picketing injunction orders are normally without costs, repeated non-compliance could result in costs being fixed and made payable immediately.[500]

2) Limitations on Picketing Courthouses

A courthouse is a workplace for unionized public servants employed in occupations such as court reporter, court clerk, and court registrar,[501] and picketing at one's own workplace is normally allowable primary picketing.

In accordance with the Supreme Court case prohibiting all picketing in front of courthouses in British Columbia, *BCGEU v British Columbia (Attorney-General)*,[502] the Ontario Court of Appeal ruled, during the 2002 OPSEU strike, that picketing of courthouses in Ontario was not to

---

Her Majesty the Queen in Right of Ontario v Ontario Public Service Employees Union, unreported, 12 April 2002 (SCJ) at para 3 (re Ontario Correctional Institute).

497 *Her Majesty the Queen in Right of Ontario v Ontario Public Service Employees Union*, unreported, 19 April 2002 (SCJ) at para (e) (re 1400 Blair Place, Gloucester).

498 *Her Majesty the Queen in Right of Ontario v Ontario Public Service Employees Union*, unreported, 27 April 2002 (SCJ) at para 1(a)(i) (re Hamilton-Wentworth Detention Centre); *Her Majesty the Queen in Right of Ontario v Ontario Public Service Employees Union*, unreported, 29 April 2002 (SCJ) at para 1(a) (re Toronto area jails).

499 *Her Majesty the Queen in Right of Ontario v Ontario Public Service Employees Union*, unreported, 24 April 2002 (SCJ) (re 33 King St W, Oshawa).

500 *Her Majesty the Queen in Right of Ontario v Ontario Public Service Employees Union*, unreported, 5 April 2002 (SCJ) at para 1(c) (re 300 Water Street, Peterborough); *Her Majesty the Queen in Right of Ontario v Ontario Public Service Employees Union*, unreported, 15 April 2002 (SCJ) at para 5 (re Quinte Detention Centre).

501 *OPSEU/MBC Unified Bargaining Unit Collective Agreement, 2022–2024*, online: https://opseu.org/information/general/find-your-collective-agreement, Wage Schedules.

502 [1988] 2 SCR 214 [*BCGEU v British Columbia*].

be permitted.[503] The ban on picketing applied whether or not the picketing had the effect of actually impeding or obstructing any individual. The court of appeal refused to follow the model of some injunctions that had been issued in the 1996 OPSEU strike, which had only enjoined obstruction and delay by picketers at courthouses.[504] The court also rejected the argument that certain types of picketing, such as informational picketing, may not impede access. There was no consideration given to whether the essential services context of the strike might make a remedial difference given that, in such a strike, employees who attend at work to perform essential services routinely and generally reliably cross their own union's picket lines. An additional order that persons were not to engage in any non-picketing activities calculated to interfere with the court was deleted on the grounds that there was no evidence of any such activities.[505]

The geographic scope of the restriction on picketing was, in some cases, expanded to bar picketing within 100 metres of a courthouse.[506] This was justified on the grounds that it was necessary to keep parking lot entrances open.[507]

---

503 *Ontario Public Service Employees Union v Ontario (Attorney General)*, unreported, 22 March 2002 (ON CA) at para 25, stay pending appeal to Supreme Court denied by the Court of Appeal, [2002] OJ No 1375 (CA).

504 See *ibid* at para 15 with reference to *Attorney General (Ontario) v Ontario Public Service Employees Union*, unreported, 29 March 1996 (SCJ), where it was ordered that picketers were not to "impede[,] obstruct or delay the access of any person or vehicle into or from the Courthouse located at 161 Elgin Street, Ottawa, Ontario," and other injunctions issued in virtually identical terms: *Ontario (Attorney General) v Ontario Public Service Employees Union et al*, unreported, 5 March 1996 (SCJ); *Ontario (Attorney General) v Ontario Public Service Employees Union*, unreported, 12 March 1996 (SCJ), Hamilton; *Ontario (Attorney General) and the Ontario Realty Corporation v Ontario Public Service Employees Union, Local 133 and Local 134 et al*, unreported, 19 March 1996 (SCJ), Windsor.

505 *Ontario Public Service Employees Union v Ontario (Attorney General)*, unreported, 22 March 2002 (ON CA) at para 29.

506 *Ontario Public Service Employees Union v Courthouse for the Superior and Ontario Courts of Justice*, unreported, 25 March 2002 (SCJ), Brockville at para (a); *Ontario Public Service Employees Union v Courthouse for the Superior and the Ontario Courts of Justice*, unreported, 25 March 2002 (SCJ), Cornwall at para (a).

507 *Ontario Public Service Employees Union v Courthouse for the Superior and Ontario Courts of Justice*, unreported, 28 March 2002 (SCJ) at paras 10 and 13, refusing to vary Orders at *ibid*.

Where the courthouse shared a building with other operations, picketing was not permitted at the shared entrance, although it was permitted on a nearby sidewalk;[508] or, if entrances were not shared, picketing was permitted at other entrances[509] and only those persons with business in the courts were able to pass from the other part of the building into the courthouse.[510] Government employees, save court employees and the judiciary, working in a shared building were barred from using the doors to the courthouse, so as to be subject to a ten-minute delay at another door.[511]

3) Limitations on Picketing the Legislative Assembly

The Ontario Court (General Division) has held that "[d]elay and obstruction of entry and egress of members and essential staff of the Legislative Assembly strikes a blow at the very heart of our society and is unacceptable."[512] It is a violation of parliamentary privilege at common law,[513] and a breach of the *Legislative Assembly Act*,[514] which states that it is a punishable breach of privilege to obstruct a member of the assembly. During the 1996 OPSEU strike, an order was issued that picketers could not impede the access of members of provincial parliament (MPPs) and essential staff of the Legislative Assembly through

---

508 *Her Majesty the Queen in Right of Ontario v Ontario Public Service Employees Union*, unreported, 25 April 2002 (SCJ) at para 2 (re Courthouse and Government Building, Highway 11, Kapuskasing).

509 *Her Majesty the Queen in Right of Ontario v Ontario Public Service Employees Union*, unreported, 12 April 2002 (SCJ) at para 1(a) (re 114 Worsley St, Barrie); *Her Majesty the Queen in Right of Ontario v Ontario Public Service Employees Union*, unreported, 29 April 2002 (SCJ) at para 1(a) (re Courthouse, 80 Dundas St W London).

510 *Her Majesty the Queen in Right of Ontario v Ontario Public Service Employees Union*, unreported, 14 March 2002 (SCJ) (re 33 King St Oshawa).

511 *Her Majesty the Queen in Right of Ontario v Ontario Public Service Employees Union*, unreported, 21 March 2002 (SCJ) at para 1(d) (re Small Claims Court, 7765 Hurontario St, Brampton).

512 *Ontario (Speaker of the Legislative Assembly) v Casselman*, [1996] OJ No 5343 (Gen Div), Winkler J at para 23 [*Speaker of the Legislative Assembly*].

513 *Ibid* at para 15; *New Brunswick Broadcasting Co v Nova Scotia (Speaker of the House of Assembly)*, [1993] 1 SCR 319 at 384: "Canadian legislative bodies possess such inherent privileges as may be necessary to their proper functioning These privileges are part of the fundamental law of our land, and hence are constitutional."

514 RSO 1990, c L.10, s 46.

the east door of the main legislative building, and the north door of the neighbouring Whitney Block.

During an OPS strike, the Legislative Assembly is involved in a labour dispute. Where the Speaker took the position that the legislature was "a separate, neutral entity from the Ontario government" and not involved in a "labour dispute," the court disagreed and found the legislature is the "headquarters of the Government of Ontario" and "for the purposes of the province-wide strike of [OPSEU] members, this location may be said to provide the central focus for the picketing and demonstration."[515]

Ontario courts have not, at least to date, ruled that picketing is unacceptable at the legislature. In part, this is because the submissions of the Speaker, in the only injunction proceeding to date dealing with the issue, did not seek to restrain picketing but only to restrain obstruction of ingress and egress. It is notable that, in cases dealing with courthouses, the courts have stated that picketing is an unacceptable interference with the administration of justice because the picket line signals a desire to impede access. Yet this was not the position taken by the Ontario court in respect of the legislature.

There is some additional discussion of these issues in the *Report of the Commission of Inquiry into the Events of March 18, 1996 at Queen's Park*, chaired by Willard Z. Estey, QC, Commissioner.[516] The report dealt with a large demonstration at the legislature that day, which involved obstruction of MPPs' access to the legislature, and the Crowd Management Unit of the OPP using shields, batons, and pepper spray on demonstrators.[517] The report reiterates that "the operation of the legislature cannot be interfered with for, without the Legislature, there is no law, no rule of law, and no democracy."[518] At the same time, the report noted that "[t]here is a long standing practice in Ontario, which might almost be described as a tradition, of demonstrating at Queen's Park,"[519] and that, from OPSEU's point of view, the 1995 election of the Progressive Conservative government meant "a new bar-

---

515 *Speaker of the Legislative Assembly*, above note 512 at paras 9 and 11.

516 *Estey Report*, above note 411.

517 *Ibid*, summary at para 25. For a less dispassionate account, see also Rapaport, above note 4.

518 *Estey Report*, above note 411, Appendix E (1), Parliamentary Privilege and Labour Law, (B) Aspects of Labour Law at 174, para 11.

519 *Ibid*, General Overview of Events at 12 at para 12.

gaining adversary was in control of the Legislature."[520] The legislature tolerated picket lines throughout the strike.[521] The report concludes the legislative precinct is a place where OPSEU can set up a picket line and conduct peaceful demonstrations as long as access to the legislature for MPPs is not hindered.[522]

E. RETURN TO WORK PROTOCOL

At the end of the 1996 and 2002 strikes, OPSEU and the MBS negotiated return to work protocols.[523] There was no legal requirement for such protocols, and they are by no means unique to *CECBA* collective bargaining. Nonetheless, a discussion of the 2002 protocol casts additional light on how the *CECBA* labour relations scheme functions generally, and in respect of the designated bargaining units particularly.

The protocol applied to all of the employees in the OPSEU bargaining units, including seasonal employees on hiatus, and it was enforceable through the grievance and arbitration procedures under the collective agreement.[524]

The protocols have dealt with the following issues:

- seniority and service
- surplus periods
- length of unclassified contracts
- timelines
- "no reprisals"
- discipline
- outstanding proceedings
- recall procedure

All of these issues are discussed in more detail below.

---

520 *Ibid*, at para 36.

521 *Ibid*, Appendix E (1), Parliamentary Privilege and Labour Law, (B) Aspects of Labour Law at 174, para 12.

522 *Ibid*, at 149, para 55.

523 *OPSEU/MBS Return to Work Protocol*, 2 May 2002 [*2002 Return to Work Protocol*]; *OPSEU/MBS Return to Work Protocol*, 29 March 1996 [*1996 Return to Work Protocol*].

524 *2002 Return to Work Protocol*, *ibid*, "Preamble."

1) Seniority and Service

Seniority continued to accrue for all employees during the 2002 strike,[525] but this would not produce seniority credit for unclassified employees who would not otherwise receive it.[526]

While time spent on strike did not generally interrupt continuous service accumulation for purposes of benefits,[527] service credits for some benefits under the collective agreement, including vacation credits, were to accrue only during a pregnancy leave, parental leave, or when absent from duty by reason of injury or illness or long-term disability,[528] and otherwise did not accumulate during a strike. For purposes of consecutive weeks of service requirements for sickness protection, the last day worked before the strike and the first day back after the strike were considered consecutive.[529] Any employees who lost workers' compensation or pregnancy or parental leave payments as a result of the strike were to have those payments retroactively reinstated.[530]

Where the protocol provided that "[t]ime spent on strike shall not interrupt continuous service of an employee for the purpose of . . . [c]alculation of probation periods and appointment to classified service . . . for essential and emergency services workers," the GSB held that the time on strike would be treated as uninterrupted service for all probationers and not just those who were essential services workers.[531]

2) Surplus Periods

For employees who were surplussed before or during the strike, the period of the strike was not to be counted for surplus notice periods, regardless of whether or not employees were essential or emergency workers.[532]

---

525 *Ibid*, Art 33.

526 *OPSEU (Malpage and Walker) and Ministry of the Attorney General*, GSB#0533/96, 12 March 2002 (Briggs).

527 2002 *Return to Work Protocol*, above note 523, Art 10.

528 *Ibid*, Art 31.

529 *Ibid*, Art 25.

530 *Ibid*, Arts 5 & 6.

531 *OPSEU (Barker) and Ministry of Transportation*, GSB#2239/02, 1 December 2003 (Dissanayake) at 10–11.

532 2002 *Return to Work Protocol*, above note 523, Art 4. See also *OPSEU (Barichello) and Ministry of Consumer and Commercial Relations*, GSB#954/96, 7 August 1996 (Roberts).

3) Length of Unclassified Contracts

Both the 1996 and 2002 return to work protocols contained a provision that unclassified contracts would not be terminated because the affected employees engaged in a strike.[533] Following the 1996 strike, the parties supplemented the *Return to Work Protocol* with a settlement that established a process for dealing with the grievances of unclassified employees who alleged that they received differential treatment concerning renewal or extension of their contracts as a result of the strike. The parties agreed that the employer bore the onus of proving that any differential treatment was for legitimate reasons.[534]

After the 1996 strike, the employer counted the five weeks of the strike as part of the unclassified contract period, regardless of whether the employee worked during the strike providing essential services or otherwise. OPSEU argued that the protocol should be interpreted so that time away from work because of the strike would not be counted in the grievors' contract period, and that the contract should continue correspondingly longer in the post-strike period.[535] The GSB accepted the employer argument that the provision was intended only to protect unclassified employees from reprisals for their participation in the strike, but not to benefit them with effective contract extensions.

4) Timelines

For timelines specified under the grievance procedure, the last day before the strike and the first day back after the strike were considered to be consecutive. More specifically, time limits under the referral to arbitration provisions were deemed to have been frozen effective on the first day of the strike and to have remained frozen until seventy-two hours after a new agreement was ratified.[536] Compensation for lost wages during the period of the strike was waived, except where

533 *1996 Return to Work Protocol*, above note 523 and *2002 Return to Work Protocol*, above note 523, Art 13. The *2002 Return to Work Protocol*, Art 14, added "will not be terminated *solely* because" [emphasis added].

534 *Memorandum of Settlement*, 13 June 1996, discussed in *OPSEU (Maxwell) and Ministry of Citizenship, Culture and Recreation*, GSB#951/96, 25 July 1996 (Roberts) at 2 [*Maxwell*].

535 *OPSEU (Radley) and Ministry of Community and Social Services*, GSB#953/96, 12 August 1996 (Roberts) at 2–3.

536 *2002 Return to Work Protocol*, above note 523, Art 28.

grievors were designated essential or emergency and, in those cases, there was no waiver for the period they were engaged in essential or emergency work.[537]

5) "No Reprisals"

Both parties agreed that "all efforts should be made to ensure there is no harassment of managers and bargaining unit employees" and that all persons were to "treat each other with courtesy and respect" consistent with the *Human Rights Code*[538] and discrimination and harassment policies.[539] There were to be no reprisals, discrimination, or retaliation in the workplace for any act or inaction by any employee in relation to the strike.[540] The "no reprisal" language also appeared in the *1996 Return to Work Protocol* and has been the subject of litigation. The GSB has broadly interpreted the type of activity protected by the "no reprisal" clause to include activity for which the employer would otherwise be entitled to discipline the employee. The protocol prevented discipline of an essential services worker engaged in strike activity who left the workplace during work and also disclosed information found in a confidential memo.[541] Similarly, grievances complaining about managerial indiscretions during a strike were dismissed.[542] The GSB found that "[i]t is not uncommon for tempers to flare and for normally civilized individuals to become somewhat short tempered or overtly rude during labour disputes." Since "the parties [had] agreed to move forward," it was not appropriate to hear the grievances.

The GSB examined employer changes to the conditions of employment of certain employees, where the changes occurred shortly after the strike, to determine whether the actions were a reprisal. Reprisal grievances have been dismissed where the GSB was satisfied that the grounds for the employer action arose before the strike,[543] or that the

---

537 *Ibid*, Art 29, specifically (b).

538 RSO 1990, c H.19.

539 *2002 Return to Work Protocol*, above note 523, *ibid*, Art 91.

540 *Ibid*, Art 92.

541 *OPSEU (Ross) and Ministry of the Attorney General*, GSB#356/96, 3 April 1997 (Verity), aff'd *OPSEU v Ontario (Attorney General)*, [1998] OJ No 4303 (Div Ct) [*Ross*].

542 *Ontario Public Service Employees Union (Union) and Ministry of Community Safety and Correctional Services*, GSB# 2003-3774, 30 March 2004 (Briggs).

543 *Ross*, above note 541.

employer was completing changes it had begun pre-strike[544] or during the strike, but for legitimate reasons.[545]

The GSB has also dealt with alleged reprisals by OPSEU members. In one case, the issue was the appropriateness of a lengthy disciplinary suspension of a union local president for telephoning a fellow employee who had chosen to be a replacement worker during a strike and addressing her in a derogatory manner.[546] The GSB found that the grievor's action was work related and constituted just cause for discipline because such violations of the protocol did not "allow the parties to begin the journey back to their normal relationship."[547] However, the GSB also found that the discipline imposed by the employer was so disproportionate that it was also a violation of the protocol. The twenty-day suspension of the employee was reduced to a written warning.

Where OPSEU posted a notice on the union bulletin board identifying employees who crossed the picket line to work and stating that "we will be thinking of you in the days to come,"[548] the employer argued that the notices constituted a breach of the "no reprisals" provision of the *Return to Work Protocol* and removed them. The union grieved that this was interference in union activity. The GSB found the notice was a violation of the protocol and promoted disharmony within the workforce.

The Ontario court has also had occasion to consider the effect of the *Return to Work Protocol*. In *Burley v OPSEU*,[549] a non-essential bargaining unit employee had chosen to work during the strike and fellow employees allegedly picketed her residence and otherwise harassed her. Her civil action, alleging tortious conduct by OPSEU members, was dismissed on the basis that all such complainants were to be addressed

---

544 *Ibid*; *OPSEU (Cushing) and Ministry of Labour*, GSB#590/96, 15 November 1996 (Mikus), dealing with the post-strike cancellation of a compressed work-week agreement where the decision to do so had apparently been made weeks before the strike, but was delayed in implementation.

545 *OPSEU (Humphreys) and Ontario Science Centre*, GSB#803/96, 4 January 1997 (Roberts), dealing with the post-strike replacement of striker with another teacher who did not have the right to strike.

546 *OPSEU (Smythe) and Ministry of the Solicitor General and Correctional Services*, GSB#354/96, 17 June 1996 (Briggs).

547 *Ibid* at 16.

548 *OPSEU (Union Grievance) and Ministry of Finance*, GSB#596/96, 23 July 1996 (Dissanayake) at 3.

549 *Burley v Ontario Public Service Employees Union*, 2004 CanLII 34769 (ON SC) [*Burley*].

by grievances alleging a violation of the *Return to Work Protocol*. The conflict of interest for the union in determining whether to bring such a grievance was viewed as addressable by the employer bringing a grievance. In any event, the entire matter was found to be outside the court's jurisdiction as it was a collective bargaining matter falling within the purview of the GSB and OLRB.

6) Discipline

The issue of discipline for employee actions during the strike was resolved in the *2002 Return to Work Protocol* on the basis that, save in instances where criminal charges were laid, there would be no discipline taken against any employee for any act done during the strike. The result was a removal of all discipline arising from the strike, save and except for those who were criminally charged in respect of incidents during the strike. The parties subsequently agreed that this meant removal of any reference to disciplinary action from employee's files and reimbursement to the employee for any loss of wages or credits.[550]

The *1996 Return to Work Protocol* dealt with discipline somewhat differently. The parties agreed discipline that was a reprisal for strike activity would be removed but that all other discipline would proceed to arbitration on its merits.[551] Then, in a related grievance settlement,[552] all grievances concerning letters of warning and reprimands were withdrawn, save and except for grievances against discipline that was a reprisal for strike activity.[553] All suspension and discharge grievances still proceeded to arbitration.

Removal of discipline is not the same as allowing claimed entitlements to collective agreement benefits. In one GSB case arising out of the 1996 OPSEU strike,[554] essential service workers claimed sick pay for essential service shifts they missed over the course of two days dur-

550 *Memorandum of Settlement*, 19 December 2002 at para 3, as recorded in *OPSEU (Union) and Ministry of Community Safety and Correctional Services*, GSB#3774/03, 22 March 2004 (Briggs) at 4.

551 *1996 Return to Work Protocol*, above note 523, Art 10.

552 *Memorandum of Settlement*, dated 13 June 1996, discussed in *Maxwell*, above note 534.

553 *OPSEU (Addorisio) and Ministry of the Solicitor General and Correctional Services*, GSB#824/96, 25 July 1996 (Roberts) at 4 [*Addorisio*].

554 *OPSEU (Barnes et al) and Ministry of the Solicitor General and Correctional Services*, GSB#1914/96, 18 December 1996 (Roberts).

ing the strike that coincided exactly with a widespread withdrawal of essential services. In a memorandum of settlement ordered into effect by the GSB at the time, OPSEU acknowledged it had breached the essential services and emergency services protocol of the essential services agreement by failing to provide services on the two days in question. The coincidence of the grievors' time off with that of the job action led to the inference that the grievors were not sick as claimed and, consequently, the grievors were not entitled to sick pay. This disentitlement was subject to being reconsidered if the claimed illness was proven to be bona fide.[555]

7) Outstanding Proceedings

The *2002 Return to Work Protocol* provided that outstanding proceedings before any court, including any applications for injunctions, private prosecutions, or contempt, and any applications before the OLRB were to be withdrawn.[556] The protocol applied to prevent individuals from continuing or commencing private actions concerning strike activity and was applied to prevent an individual from suing the union for strike activity.[557]

The protocol also became an issue in the context of OLRB proceedings challenging certain discharges, which proceedings were ongoing at the time of the signing of the *Return to Work Protocol*.[558] The OLRB ruled that the application before it to set the discharges aside would continue as if it had been completed on the day it started and hence it was not subject to the withdrawal of outstanding proceedings.

Concerning grievances, the *2002 Return to Work Protocol* did not require their withdrawal. Article 10.02 (b) of the *1996 Return to Work Protocol* included a more broadly worded withdrawal of "any grievance … for any matter arising during the strike." However, that provision was in a section of the protocol headed "No Reprisals" and was found to refer only to the requirement to withdraw proceedings that were themselves a form of reprisal[559] and was held not to be an

---

555 *Ibid.*

556 *2002 Return to Work Protocol*, above note 523, Art 11.

557 *Burley*, above note 549.

558 *OPSEU v The Crown in Right of Ontario*, *OLRB File*, 0006-02-U, 26 April 2002 (Albertyn).

559 *Addorisio*, above note 553 at 3.

abandonment by the union of the right to grieve other strike issues.[560] The employer violated the protocol's requirement to withdraw tribunal complaints by reporting employees to the College of Nurses for alleged professional misconduct during the strike.[561]

In both 1996 and 2002, the parties agreed to various expedited procedures for the resolution of strike grievances.[562]

8) Recall Procedure

Return to work protocols also included provision for the actual return to work of striking employees. The *2002 Return to Work Protocol* established that all OPSEU members, including all essential and emergency services workers, were to be recalled to work on their first working day following the date of ratification of the settlement. Normal shift rotation was to commence then, and shift workers were to return on their next scheduled shift. Provisions in the bargaining unit collective agreements dealing with days off and advance notification of shift schedules were to be waived to avoid unintended start-up costs.[563] Employees working on compressed workweek schedules did not return to the same point on the schedule that they left it at the beginning of the strike. This meant some employees received extra hours and some got fewer hours. In the 1996 protocol, and in a 2002 post-protocol settlement, the parties agreed to balance hours.[564]

560 *OPSEU (Metcalf/Mercer) and Ministry of the Solicitor General and Correctional Services*, GSB#926/96, 9 April 1997 (Dissanayake) at 10.

561 *OPSEU (Bartley/Peeters) and Ministry of Health*, GSB#588/96, 16 July 1996 (Roberts).

562 As an example, see the arrangements concerning 2002 grievances arising at correctional institutions as outlined in *OPSEU (Balazs) and Ministry of Community Safety and Correctional Services*, GSB#1227/02, 4 March 2004 (Briggs) [*Balazs*].

563 The articles waived were Arts 31, 51, and 55 of the *OPSEU/MBS Collective Agreement*.

564 *Balazs*, above note 562.

F. ILLEGAL STRIKES

The OLRB has dealt with illegal strike allegations in the context of alleged breaches of essential services agreements[565] and in the context of health and safety work refusals.[566]

The courts have jurisdiction in respect of strike activity, both legal and illegal, when their processes are effected.[567] Where the court found illegal strike activity by correctional officers produced delays in in-custody accused persons being brought to court, it was concluded that the *Charter* rights of the accused were breached.[568] The court stated a willingness to address the activity even in the absence of a motion from the attorney general, but determined not to do so because of the expedition of the OLRB in dealing with an unlawful strike application, including the board's finding that the activity of the correctional officers was an illegal strike and the issuing of orders that the employees and union not engage "in a concerted slow down relating to the movement of inmates within the [correctional] institution for the purpose of facilitating their court appearance."

The courts have dealt directly with one illegal OPS strike. As a result of leading the 1979 OPSEU correctional officers' illegal strike that resulted in a separate corrections bargaining category,[569] the President of OPSEU, Sean O'Flynn, pleaded guilty to contempt of the injunction that required the officers to return to work, and was sentenced to thirty-five days in jail. The judge's sentencing reasons included the following:

> [A]nd you felt unreasonable restrictions were placed upon you by the laws of the province ... At some point you determined that you would rise above that law, defy it, and more importantly take 3,000 law-abiding citizens with you ... you must realize that nobody can change the law simply by defying it in the course of their duty ...

---

565 See the "Illegal Strike Declaration" section, above.

566 *Ontario (Community Safety and Correctional Services) v Ontario Public Service Employees Union*, 2009 CanLII 33833 (ON LRB) and the discussion in Chapter 6 re the *OHSA* right to refuse unsafe work.

567 *BCGEU v British Columbia*, above note 502.

568 *Ontario (Inquiry Into Delays in the Delivery of Prisoners to the Peel Courthouse) (Re)*, 2009 CanLII 25143 (ON SC).

569 See the discussions in Chapter 7 about OPSEU, and the "Corrections Interest Arbitration" section below.

> Where would we be if everybody with a cause took this position? We would be faced with chaos. Our society . . . would be a shambles.[570]

The GSB has also had occasion to deal with illegal strike issues. Following the illegal strike in the correctional services category in 1979, the parties entered into a settlement that contained the following terms:

> (5) The government intends to bring to the attention of each employee who has withdrawn his services that it cannot condone illegal work stoppages and that any repetition of such conduct by employees, individually or collectively, will not be tolerated.
>
> (6) There shall be no dismissal, release from employment, or suspension of any employee as a result of his participating in the cessation of work.
>
> (7) The employer may send to all employees who participated in the work stoppage a uniform letter which may be retained in the employee's personnel file.[571]

When the employer issued letters of reprimand to all participating employees, OPSEU grieved that the letters were a violation of the settlement. The GSB found that it was actually the one form of discipline permitted by the settlement.[572]

The GSB was not prepared to remove the letter of discipline for the illegal 1979 strike where the grievor was off duty but still picketed.[573] The picket line interfered with jail operations and, by picketing, the grievor was publicly indicating his support for an illegal strike. This was disciplinable, in part because he was a peace officer, sworn to uphold the law, and his conduct brought the law into disrespect.[574]

When suspensions were levied against persons who engaged in a 1983 correctional services category illegal strike, the GSB rejected the claim that the claimed "provocation" of return to work legislation

---

570 Unreported, 6 December 1979 (ONSC Carruthers J), reported in *The Globe and Mail*, 7 December 1979 at 5.

571 *OPSEU and Civil Service Commission*, GSB#33/80, 8 December 1981 (Chair Weatherill) at 3–4.

572 *Ibid* at 7–8.

573 *OPSEU (Leach) and Ministry of Correctional Services*, GSB#401/84, 5 November 1985 (Samuels).

574 *Ibid* at 5.

justified a reduction of suspensions.[575] The claim that the 1983 suspensions should be reduced because the more serious and widespread 1979 correctional services illegal strike only attracted a letter of reprimand was dismissed on the basis that the earlier discipline was based on an agreement between the parties. The GSB further found that it was appropriate for the employer to vary the penalty depending on whether the grievor's files contained a letter of reprimand for having engaged in the previous 1979 illegal strike. Overall, the employer's discipline was found to be within the reasonable range.

Where all the correctional officers on the day shift at the Windsor Jail claimed sick leave to attend a demonstration to protest the *Inflation Restraint Act*,[576] which capped public service salary increases, the employees were suspended for varying lengths of time. "Employer provocation" was considered. The GSB understood the union to be arguing that its direct employer was also the enactor of the legislation and that this was a special circumstance to be taken into account when evaluating employee conduct. The GSB did note that the separation between the employer and the government of Ontario was somewhat "fuzzy."[577]

In another illegal strike discipline case, the GSB showed greater willingness to adjust the penalty, albeit in unusual circumstances. In *Ontario Public Service Employees Union (Wilson) and Ministry of Correctional Services*,[578] the OPSEU local president at a jail was the only one of his members who went to a demonstration during work hours without leave. He also helped make arrangements to ensure that the attendance of others at the rally had no impact on the operations of the jail. His five-day suspension was reduced to one day.

Where a grievor is disciplined for illegally striking but is able to demonstrate that he was actually off sick, the discipline will be revoked.[579] A similar result was arrived at in relation to incidents in 1999 of allegedly illegal strike activity in the form of feigned illness. The employer ultimately determined not to discipline employees but did refuse to pay those who were not genuinely sick. After a lengthy hearing process, involv-

575 *OPSEU (Gagnon et al) and Ministry of Correctional Services*, GSB#142/83, 20 January 1984 (Brent) [*Gagnon et al*].

576 SO 1982, c 55.

577 *Gagnon et al*, above note 575 at 21–22.

578 GSB#172/83, 29 June 1983 (Samuels).

579 *OPSEU (Baldwin) and Ministry of Correctional Services*, GSB#160/83, 23 January 1984 (Weatherill).

ing statements of evidence and supporting documentation from any employee wishing to maintain a claim of illness at arbitration,[580] the GSB found most employees did not establish the legitimacy of their illness, but those that did were entitled to paid sick leave.[581]

G. INTEREST ARBITRATION FOR RIGHT TO STRIKE UNITS

For right to strike units, there are two forms of interest arbitration set out in the *LRA*: voluntary interest arbitration and first contract arbitration. Modified versions of both are available for *CECBA* collective bargaining.

The *CECBA* incorporates the *LRA* provisions facilitating mutual agreement to voluntary interest arbitration as an alternative to proceeding toward a strike or lockout,[582] with modifications. First, while the *LRA* provisions contemplate the referral of "all matters remaining in dispute" to interest arbitration, the *CECBA* contemplates party agreement to refer "matters" to arbitration. This suggests that *CECBA* voluntary interest arbitration is available for all or only some of the matters in dispute. Where it is used for some of the matters in dispute, it appears that the unresolved matters not referred to interest arbitration can only be the subject of a strike or lockout once the partial interest arbitration has been completed.

The *CECBA* spells out some additional requirements for the establishment of the interest arbitration and the conduct of the hearing. There is a seven-day deadline for the appointment of a single arbitrator or, in the case of an arbitration board, for the appointment of nominees, followed by a five-day limit for the appointment of the chair, and, failing agreement, the minister may appoint the chair. Some procedural provisions of the *Hospital Labour Disputes Arbitration Act*[583] are made applicable.[584]

---

580 *OPSEU (Fogal) and Ministry of the Attorney General*, GSB#0413/99, 28 November 2000 (Briggs).

581 *Ibid.*

582 *LRA*, above note 3, s 40; *CECBA*, above note 1, s 4.

583 RSO 1990, c H14, s 6(8)–(14), (17), and (18).

584 *CECBA*, above note 1, s 4(5).

The *CECBA* prohibits an interest arbitrator from making orders concerning classification.[585] The arbitrator is further prohibited from including "any term that would require either directly or indirectly for its implementation the enactment or amendment of legislation except for the purpose of appropriating money for its implementation."[586]

The first contract arbitration provisions of the *LRA* apply to bargaining units covered by the *CECBA*, with modifications[587] similar to those applied to voluntary arbitration. Given the likely stability of government bargaining units and their representation, the first contract provisions likely have little practical application. A difference from the voluntary arbitration provisions is that the first contract arbitration award cannot include a term guaranteeing "an offer of a job for employees whose positions have been or may be eliminated or that otherwise compels the employer to continue to employ them," although this limitation does not apply to a designated Crown agency.[588] Introduced in 1995 by the Progressive Conservative government at the same time as planned government downsizing,[589] this would appear to be a holdover of the sovereignty concept that reserved certain rights to management under the pre-1993 *CECBA*.

H. CORRECTIONS INTEREST ARBITRATION

OPSEU staff working in corrections have long sought to bargain separately from other direct employees of government on as many issues as possible. Particular concerns have included wage premiums for the dangerous nature of the work based on comparisons with federal corrections and Ontario police salaries,[590] shift premiums for long overnight shifts, mobility between facilities as they were reorganized, and preferential pension treatment. Since the 1970s, OPSEU and the government have been negotiating over how to best accommodate the Corrections

585 *Ibid*, s 52 (1). See discussion in *OPSEU (Union) and Management Board Secretariat*, GSB#0196/00, 4 April 2001 (Gray).

586 *CECBA*, above note 1, s 4(11).

587 *Ibid*, s 5.

588 *Ibid*, s 5(5) & (6).

589 See the discussion in Chapter 9 on job security.

590 See, on wages, the first *CECBA* interest arbitration between OPSEU Corrections and the MBC: *Ontario v Ontario Public Service Employees Union Correctional Services Bargaining Unit*, 2016 CanLII 58971 and 58972 (ON LA) (Burkett) [*Correctional Services, Burkett*].

Bargaining Unit's agenda and its activism through bargaining mechanisms that provided for ever more autonomous bargaining.[591]

The Corrections Bargaining Unit has a history of militancy in support of its own bargaining demands and its occupational health and safety concerns.[592] During the OPSEU strikes of 1996 and 2002, the correctional bargaining unit strike activity was particularly acrimonious and raised concerns about inmate safety and the reduced ability of criminal courts to process and sentence offenders.[593] Strike and lockout preparations for those and other rounds was time consuming and costly.[594]

In 2015–2016, OPSEU and the MBC agreed on their shared intention to create an entirely separate correctional bargaining unit, subject to interest arbitration and covering all employees employed in correctional facilities, with its own collective agreement that was the successor to the agreements previously applicable to corrections.[595] It was further agreed that there would be no requirement for the rebargaining of existing terms and that the separate agreement would not be considered a first agreement for *LRA* purposes. The agreement was implemented by *CECBA* amendments.[596]

---

591 See the history of OPSEU in Chapter 7.

592 This history includes a 1979 illegal strike by correctional officers for greater bargaining autonomy. See the illegal strikes section above, and Chapter 6 on *OHSA* work refusals.

593 See the "Court Enforcement of Essential Services Agreements" section, above.

594 The NDP critic noted the ongoing multimillion dollar cost of strike preparations and stated "imagine how much better off this system would be if that kind of money was spent on making things safer or better resourced, but I digress": Ontario Legislative Assembly, *Hansard*, 28 November 2016 at 1400 (Jennifer French, New Democrat).

595 *Memorandum of Agreement between the Crown and OPSEU in the matter of Development of a Standalone Collective Agreement for the Correctional Bargaining Unit*, 23 November 2015. For discussion of the prior agreements, see Chapter 7. And now see the *OPSEU/MBC Correctional Bargaining Unit Collective Agreement, 2018-2021*, online: https://opseu.org/information/general/find-your-collective-agreement.

596 *Building Ontario Up for Everyone Act, (Budget Measures), 2016*, SO 2016 c 37, Sch 6, Bill 70, *An Act To Implement Budget Measures And To Enact And Amend Various Statutes, Sch 6, Crown Employees Collective Bargaining Act, 1993*. There was no statement of legislative intent by the government other than a prior commitment in the House that the recent tentative collective agreement would provide the "framework" for a standalone correctional bargaining unit: Ontario Legislative Assembly, *Hansard*, 3 December 2015 at 1120 (Yasir Naqvi, Minister of Community Safety and Correctional Services).

Despite the separateness of the Corrections Bargaining Unit, it is required to be represented by the same union as represents the Unified Unit.[597] Furthermore, it has been agreed by that bargaining agent, OPSEU, and the MBC, that seniority (and continuous service) in one unit will be recognized in the other unit and that "employment mobility between the Unified and Correctional Bargaining Units shall be maintained for posting and filling of vacancies, employment stability, health reassignment, pay administration and accommodation."[598] This is crystallized in an agreed "permeability" agreement between the employer and each of the two units.[599]

Since the Corrections Bargaining Unit became subject to interest arbitration, there have been interest arbitration awards. In 2016, while the implementing legislation was pending, the parties agreed to voluntary interest arbitration to conclude the matters remaining outstanding between them.[600] The main issue arbitrated was how to apply the central principle that interest arbitration in the public sector should replicate the settlement the parties would have reached if the dispute had run its otherwise normal course, in combination with the interest arbitrator's additional focus on gradual change and requiring demonstrated need for change. Concerning the correctional officer classification and the claim that a special wage adjustment was warranted, there was an assessment of whether the classification was underpaid relative to comparators. The arbitrator found there had been "deterioration" of Ontario correctional salaries, relative to the comparator federal correctional and Ontario police salaries, which warranted an incremental "catch-up" increase. An interest arbitration was also used to resolve economic issues in 2019.[601]

The *CECBA* interest arbitration provisions are essentially the same as under the *Hospital Labour Disputes Arbitration Act* (*HLDAA*),[602]

---

597 See the discussion of statutory treatment of representation of trade unions in Chapter 7.

598 OPSEU/MBS, *Memorandum of Agreement*, signed 24 January 2020.

599 OPSEU/MBS, *Unified Memorandum of Settlement 2021*, 21 December 2021, Item 26. This agreement is incorporated into the *OPSEU/MBC Unified Bargaining Unit Collective Agreement*, above note 501 and the *OPSEU/MBC Correctional Bargaining Unit Collective Agreement*, above note 595 at Appendix 64.

600 *Correctional Services, Burkett*, above note 590.

601 *Ontario (Treasury Board Secretariat) v OPSEU (Correctional Bargaining Unit)*, 2019 CanLII 24936 (ON LA) (Kaplan).

602 RSO 1990, c H.14 [*HLDAA*].

including providing for either a single arbitrator or a board of arbitration. A procedural difference is that, under the *CECBA*, if a party applies within ten days of a decision, the arbitration board may change a decision if they failed to deal with a matter referred to them or made an error "apparent on the face of the decision."[603] As is the case under the *HLDAA*, the board of arbitration is to "take into consideration all factors it considers relevant, including ability to pay, the economic situation, comparables, the ability to attract and retain employees" and "the extent to which services may have to be reduced, in light of the decision or award, if current funding and taxation levels are not increased."[604] In contrast to the *HLDAA*, but in keeping with the limits on the authority of *CECBA* voluntary interest arbitrators and first agreement arbitrators,[605] the board cannot make an order requiring legislation, except for appropriating money.[606]

I. "RETURN TO WORK" AND WAGE RESTRAINT LEGISLATION

It is "one of the realities of the public service: the employer has access to the legislative machinery and can change the ground rules for labour disputes through legislation."[607] In any strike involving the public sector, let alone the public service, the government may legislate an end to the conflict and prescribe all or part of the contents of the new collective agreement, or the process by which the collective agreement is to be finalized. This mechanism has not been used in response to an OPS strike but the possibility is always present in the collective bargaining considerations of the parties.[608] Governments argue that intervention

603 *CECBA*, above note 1, s 29.8.

604 *Ibid*, s 29.7(2).

605 See sections above.

606 *CECBA*, above note 1, s 29.8(4).

607 *Estey Report*, above note 411, General Overview of Events at 19, para 36. In *Ontario Pipe Trades Council v Ontario (Premier)*, [2001] OLRD No 3040 at para 174, the OLRB rejected the assertion that the legislative removal of certain collective bargaining rights could be an unfair labour practice and affirmed the right of a "sovereign" legislature to change the law for political purposes.

608 An observer of federal collective bargaining has said "public employees understandably believe that a system is biased against them when the employer can resort to Parliament or to legislature to impose a settlement and can call on the courts to give sanction to the law that is passed," Finkelman & Goldenberg, above note 87 at Vol 1, xx. For an academic discussion of how the possibility of

can be a necessary response to public service disruptions that put the public at short-term risk, and that such legislation responds to the pressing need for more cost-effective public services. Critics respond that ad hoc interventions are continually used because they "maintain the façade of equity" of the standing legislation while the state reasserts its power on an ad hoc basis "through the back door."[609] The *Charter* now enables judicial scrutiny of such legislation unless the legislature uses the notwithstanding clause.

The current provisions of the *CECBA* support an argument that it would be inappropriate for the government employer to use its legislative powers to end a *CECBA* union strike by imposing a collective agreement. The existence of a voluntary interest arbitration provision indicates that third-party resolution of a strike is to be consensual. Further, the *CECBA 1995* amendments deleted the explicit authority for the OLRB to order interest arbitration on the grounds that meaningful collective bargaining has been prevented by the essential services regime.[610] Given that the *CECBA* unions have been denied the ability to obtain an order imposing a settlement, it seems more questionable for the employer to retain the right to impose a settlement.

In the event that the legislature was to introduce back to work legislation to end a strike, the *CECBA* provides two mechanisms for guidance. First, it could be a prerequisite for the government employer to successfully apply, under section 42 of the *CECBA*, for an order that the provision of essential services has prevented meaningful collective bargaining. Second, the provisions for settlement of the contract could an interest arbitration modeled on the first agreement arbitration provisions of the *CECBA*. Imposition of interest arbitration has been the long standing means in Ontario for ending a public sector strike.[611] The

---

"return to work" legislation factors into collective bargaining considerations, see Paul Philips, "Theoretical Problems of Public Interest Sector Industrial Relations" (1976) 31:4 *Relations Industrielles/Industrial Relations* 566 at 582. There are numerous examples of legislation ending public sector strikes in Ontario.

609 Claire Mummé, "The State Giveth and Taketh Away: Public Sector Labour Law, the Legitimacy of the Legislative Override Power and Constitutional Freedom of Association in Canada" (2020) 36:4 *International Journal of Comparative Labour Law and Industrial Relations* 495 at 519 [Mummé].

610 See the "Lack of Meaningful Collective Bargaining" section, above.

611 As but two examples, see *Back to School Act (Simcoe Muskoka Catholic District School Board), 2002*, SO 2002, c 20 and *Protecting the School Year Act, 2015*, SO 2015, c 11.

use of this mechanism would rebut any assertions that the government had used its legislative power not only to end the strike, but also to set terms to favour itself in the finalization of the new collective agreement.

The government may also preemptively legislate compensation restraint or other collective bargaining outcomes for public sector collective parties. This has happened fairly frequently in Canada and in Ontario.[612]

Over time, the Ontario governments composed of each of the three major parties have made attempts to reduce government costs by means, in part, of limiting or stopping increases in employee compensation. Government employees were included within the *Inflation Restraint Act, 1982*,[613] which capped increases under collective agreements to 5 percent, and the *Public Sector Prices and Compensation Review Act, 1983*,[614] which required interest arbitrators to report on the financial consequences of their awards. Similarly, the *Social Contract Act, 1993*[615] included the government in a statutory scheme where a failure of parties to arrive at a local expenditure reduction agreement resulted in the imposition of a three-year wage freeze and up to twelve unpaid days of absence per year. There was no modification on account of the specialized government labour and employment legislation already in place. Notably, *CECBA 1993*, which allowed strikes in the public service, and the *Social Contract Act*, which froze contracts, including public service contracts, for three years, were both given first reading in the legislature on the same day.[616]

Since some degree of *Charter* protection for collective bargaining was judicially recognized in 2007,[617] the Ontario government has twice brought in compensation restraint legislation, with quite differential application to the *CECBA* unions. That legislation is reviewed below followed by an assessment of the application of the *Charter*.

---

612 See Joseph B. Rose, "Constraints on Public Sector Bargaining in Canada" (2016) 58:1 *Journal of Industrial Relations* at 93; Thompson & Slinn, above note 8; and Mummé, above note 609.

613 SO 1982, c 55, s 6.

614 SO 1983, c 70, s 3(1).

615 SO 1993, c 5.

616 Ontario Legislative Assembly, *Hansard*, 14 June 1993, No 31 at 1353–54 (Floyd Laughren, Treasurer introducing the *Social Contract Act*; Bob McKenzie, Minister of Labour introducing *CECBA 1993*).

617 See *Health Services and Support-Facilities Subsector Bargaining Assn v British Columbia*, 2007 SCC 27 [*Health Services*].

In 2010, the Liberal government passed the *Public Sector Compensation Restraint to Protect Public Services Act, 2010*,[618] which applied to the Crown and Crown agencies and the public sector but *did not apply* to employees represented by a union or other collective bargaining organization. As a result, it did not raise the issue of violating the right to freedom of association. Under the legislation, from March 2010 to March 2012, pay ranges for non-unionized staff were frozen and there was to be no increase in benefits or payments. The rationale as set out in the 2010 budget was that "[p]rotecting services requires limiting compensation growth to direct scarce resources to service delivery." This was accompanied by the following statement:

> Going forward, the fiscal plan provides no funding for incremental compensation increases for any future collective agreements.
>
> All existing collective agreements in the public sector will be honoured. As agreements are renegotiated, the government will work with transfer payment partners and bargaining agents to seek agreements of at least two years' duration. These agreements should help manage spending pressures, protect public services that Ontarians rely on, and provide no net increase in compensation.[619]

The honouring of existing collective agreements and the negotiation, rather than imposition, of "net zero" agreements meant the Act did not raise *Charter* issues. Of particular interest is that government did actively negotiate with the unions and bargaining agents of the direct employees of government and did reach agreement with the lawyers' associations—the Association of Law Officers of the Crown (ALOC) and the Ontario Crown Attorneys' Association (OCAA)— to a two-year contract with net zero increases in return for future bargaining framework assurances.[620]

In 2019, the Progressive Conservative government legislated public sector wage restraint, which was made applicable to non-unionized and unionized employees, with the *Protecting a Sustainable Public Sector for Future Generations Act, 2019* (Bill 124).[621] At time of writing, and

618 SO 2010, c 1, Sch 24.

619 Ministry of Finance, *2010 Ontario Budget, Section B: Managing Responsibly, Expenditure Management Measures, Compensation Measures*, online: www.fin.govon.ca/en/budget/ontariobudgets/2010.

620 See Chapter 4 on Crown lawyers.

621 SO 2019, c 12 [Bill 124].

subject to appeal, the bill has been struck down as an unjustifiable violation of the section 2(d) *Charter* right to freedom of association.[622]

Bill 124's preamble states that Ontario has a large debt and that the government "seeks to ensure the sustainability of public services by restoring fiscal balance." In the legislature, the minister noted that public sector compensation is roughly half of all government expenditures.[623]

The Act applies to trade unions and organizations that collectively bargain for employees, in addition to non-unionized employees.[624] Neither the OLRB nor an arbitrator or tribunal is permitted to determine whether the Act is constitutionally valid or is in conflict with the *Human Rights Code*.[625] Accordingly, arbitrators declined union requests to consider setting the legislation aside.[626]

The legislation imposes a cap of 1 percent on any increases to each salary rate during each twelve-month period in a three-year "moderation period."[627] This does not prevent an employee's salary rate from increasing in recognition of the following, if authorized under the agreement:

1) The employee's length of time in employment
2) An assessment of performance
3) The employee's successful completion of a program or course of professional or technical education[628]

These permitted increases do not allow for the addition of a new step to the grid.[629] Temporary COVID-19 payments for health care employees have been exempted by regulation.[630] An employer cannot provide compensation before or after the moderation period to make up for compensation not received during the moderation period.[631]

622 *OECTA*, above note 14.
623 Ontario Legislative Assembly, *Hansard*, 28 October 2019 at 1400 (Peter Bethlenfalvy, Minister of Finance).
624 Bill 124, above note 621, s 8.
625 *Ibid*, s 29(1) & (2).
626 *Residence Saint-Louis v ONA*, 2020 CanLII 79382 (ON LA) (Kaplan) [*Residence (Kaplan)*].
627 Bill 124, above note 621, s 10. The timing of the moderation period is different for represented employees (s 9) and non-represented employees (s 17).
628 *Ibid*, s 10(2).
629 *Participating Hospitals (Ontario Hospital Association) v Ontario Nurses' Association*, 2020 CanLII 38651 (ON LA) (Stout) at para 25 [*ONA (Stout)*].
630 O Reg 195/20.
631 Bill 124, above note 621, s 24. After the moderation period, additional compensation can be provided for other reasons: *Knollcrest Lodge v United Food and*

There is also a 1 percent average annual cap on any incremental increases to existing or new compensation entitlements including all forms of payments and benefits.[632] The legislation makes clear that any salary increase applicable to a position or class of positions is an increase in compensation entitlements.[633] In effect,

> wages are limited to an annual increase of 1%. Where the wage increase results in a total compensation increase of less than 1% per year, the amount of compensation available to bring the total cost increase to 1% may be applied to non-wage compensation items.[634]

The increased cost for the employer of providing a benefit "as it existed on the day before the beginning of the moderation period" is not an increase in compensation entitlements.[635] However, this does not exempt the costs of improving benefits,[636] whether that happens by increasing the benefit (e.g., six to seven weeks' vacation) or by the increased cost of providing the benefit stemming from the increase in the base salary. The cost increases of pre-existing benefits are "out of the control of the parties," whereas the cost increases for benefits that flow from a 1 percent increase in wages—the "roll up costs"—are to be included in the 1 percent.[637]

Non-wage changes have been awarded to take effect toward the end of the moderation period so that the "in-period" effect is under

---

Commercial Workers Canada, Local 175, 2022 CanLII 57477 (ON LA) (Stout) at paras 22–28.

632 Bill 124, above note 621, ss 2 and 11. The scope of "compensation" has been found to include employer contributions to a union education fund: *Tabor Manor v Christian Labour Association of Canada*, 2020 CanLII 66104 (ON LA) (Kaplan).

633 Bill 124, above note 621, s 11(2).

634 *Canadian Union of Public Employees, Local 1263 v Niagara Ina Grafton Village*, 2021 CanLII 61467 (ON LA) (Jesin) [*Grafton (Jesin)*]. And see *ONA (Stout)*, above note 629 at para 35; *Mon Sheong Home for the Aged v Ontario Nurses' Association*, 2020 CanLII 8770 (ON LA) (Gedalof); *Michael Garron Hospital v Service Employees International Union, Local 1 Canada*, 2022 CanLII 58195 (ON LA) (White) [*Garron (White)*].

635 Bill 124, above note 621, s 11(3).

636 *Residence (Kaplan)*, above note 626; *Ryerson University v Ryerson University Faculty Association*, 2021 CanLII 49703 (ON LA) (Kaplan).

637 *Hospital for Sick Children v CUPE, Local 281601*, 2020 CanLII 77150 (ON LA) (Kaplan) [*Sick Children (Kaplan)*], rejecting the contrary approach as set out in *Groves Memorial Hospital v OPSEU*, 2021 CanLII 34386 (ON LA) (McNamee).

1 percent, including delayed uniform allowance; employer contribution to an extended health plan; increases to vision, dental, paramedical, weekend, and other premiums; the sick leave accrual formula; increase in pay in lieu for benefits for part-time employees; an increase in early retiree benefits; as well as increases effective after the expiry of the agreement.[638] Is this compliant with the statutory requirement that an employer shall not provide compensation deferred because of the Act?[639]

One arbitrator has taken the view that this "staggering" is the appropriate response to the legislation, holding that the questions to be asked are whether what is proposed by the parties would normally have been agreed to, whether it is justified pursuant to the normal interest arbitration criteria, and then setting the date of implementation of the improvement to comply with the constraints in the Act.[640] This was coupled with carrying over the costing of the amounts not expended in each year to subsequent years, with costing done for the entirety of the term, and leaving the total of any extra amounts available to fund increases in the last year.

This last element of the approach has been the subject of direct comment by the responsible deputy minister to the effect that Bill 124 is specific that the 1 percent maximum on incremental increases to compensation entitlements cannot be moved between twelve-month periods and the provision does not contemplate averaging between years.[641] Context for a letter by the government to an arbitrator is found in the legislative provision that the minister may make an order declaring that a collective agreement or arbitration award is inconsistent with the Act.[642] The arbitrator notes that this Treasury Board approach is contrary to the normal averaging across years in collective bargaining; can be an incentive to award costs earlier in the term, thereby increasing

---

638 See the list of awards summarized in *Foyer Richelieu Welland v CUPE, Local 3606*, 2020 CanLII 97972 (ON LA) (Keller) [*Foyer (Keller)*] plus *FJ Davey Home v Canadian Union of Public Employees, Local 4685-00*, 2021 CanLII 10816 (ON LA) (Stout) at para 26; *St Joseph's Villa, Dundas, Ontario v Canadian Union of Public Employees, Local 1404*, 2021 CanLII 3249 (ON LA) (Nyman); *Shared Hospital Laboratory Inc v Ontario Public Service Employees Union, Local 5113*, 2021 CanLII 49713 (ON LA) (Schmidt).

639 Bill 124, above note 621, s 24.

640 *Foyer (Keller)*, above note 638.

641 Reported in *Glebe Centre v Canadian Union of Public Employees, local 3302–00*, 2021 CanLII 36600 (ON LA) (Keller).

642 Bill 124, above note 621, s 26.

their net effect; and prevents the awarding of items that are consistent with the normal approach to bargaining simply because they cannot be afforded on a single-year overage. Nonetheless, the arbitrator proceeded to implement the direction by granting an identical increase to a weekend premium in each year but not compounding it through incorporating the increase into the base rate for the following year.

It has also been found that staging all increases to occur later than would otherwise be normal "would not replicate free collective bargaining" and would be "completely contrary" to the statutory scheme.[643]

Consideration has been given to the effect of Bill 124 on the bargaining of non-monetary proposals. The argument that a union must be "compensated" for the loss of monetary improvements by the awarding of additional non-monetary proposals has been rejected. Non-monetary proposals are to be evaluated on the basis of normal arbitral principles.[644] A possible, but not actually awarded, example is the awarding of enhanced job security provisions to address challenges in recruitment or retention of employees.[645]

As mentioned, the minister may make an order declaring that a collective agreement or arbitration award is inconsistent with the Act.[646] Where such an order is made, the collective agreement or arbitration award is void and deemed never to have had effect. The MBC can issue directives requiring the provision of information by employers.[647] Non-compliance with a directive can be addressed by the MBC requiring the withholding of funds.[648]

Arbitrators remained seized in the event:

1. the union is granted an exemption to Bill 124, or
2. Bill 124 is amended or withdrawn by the Ontario legislature to provide for increases above 1 percent, or
3. Bill 124 is overturned by the courts and is either
   i) not replaced by similar legislation or

---

643 *Sick Children* (Kaplan), above note 637; and also *Benevolent Society "Heidehof" For the Care of the Aged v Niagara Health Care and Service Workers Union, CLAC Local 302*, 2021 CanLII 49687 (ON LA) (Wilson).

644 *Independent Electricity System Operator v Society of United Professionals*, 2021 CanLII 137444 (ON LA) (Stout) at para 47.

645 *Ibid* at para 46.

646 Bill 124, above note 621, s 26.

647 *Ibid*, s 25.

648 *Ibid*, s 25.1.

ii) replaced by legislation with provisions that might potentially impact the decision-making process undertaken in the issuance of the award.[649]

In *Ontario English Catholic Teachers Assoc v His Majesty* (*OECTA*),[650] released in late 2022, the Superior Court ruled Bill 124 to be void and of no effect. Consideration of any remedy was deferred. As of time of writing, the case is under appeal.

The discussion about the applicability of the *Charter* to Ontario's wage restraint legislation begins with the leading Supreme Court case, *Meredith v Canada (Attorney General)*.[651] That case dealt with federal wage restraint legislation following the 2008 financial crisis. In such circumstances, legislation that was not targeted at particular bargaining and precluded negotiations on wages for a limited period of time by establishing outcomes that were consistent with the "going rate,"[652] while still allowing bargaining on other issues, was found not to infringe freedom of association under section 2(d) of the *Charter*. The case was followed by the Ontario Court of Appeal decision in *Gordon v Canada (Attorney General)*,[653] also upholding the federal wage restraint legislation for similar reasons.

The court in *OECTA* distinguished the federal wage restraint cases on the bases that there was no financial crisis at the time of Bill 124; that wage caps under the bill were less than the "going rate" in either the Ontario public or private sector; and that the federal restraint legislation allowed bargaining on non-monetary issues that had a financial effect while Bill 124 "monetizes" many such benefits and includes them in the salary cap.[654]

The court in *OECTA* also dealt briefly with the most recent prior restraint case, *Manitoba Federation of Labour et al v The Government*

649 *Grafton (Jesin)*, above note 634; *Residence (Kaplan)* above note 626; *Hawkesbury and District General Hospital v United Steel, Paper and Forestry, Rubber, Manufacturing, Energy, Allied Industrial and Service Workers International Union (United Steelworkers)*, 2020 CanLII 47271 (ON LA) (Albertyn); *Garron (White)*, above note 634.

650 *OECTA*, above note 14.

651 2015 SCC 2.

652 *Ibid* at para 28.

653 2016 ONCA 625.

654 *OECTA*, above note 14 at para 206.

of Manitoba.[655] It addressed Manitoba's *Public Services Sustainability Act*,[656] which provides for a broadly applicable four-year restraint, or "sustainability," period beginning on the expiry of collective agreements or arbitration awards in effect on the day the legislation took effect, with compensation limited to specific percentages in each year of 0 percent, 0 percent, 0.75 percent, and 1 percent. This legislation is similar in design to Ontario Bill 124, although the amount of restraint in Manitoba was greater. The Manitoba Court of Appeal found that the Manitoba legislation did not violate freedom of association as guaranteed under the *Charter* because the legislation preserves "a process of consultation and good faith negotiation."[657] Leave to appeal to the Supreme Court was denied. In *OECTA*, the Manitoba case was distinguished on the basis that each case is contextual and fact specific and the Supreme Court not granting leave was of limited significance.

The court in *OECTA* noted that the government had an alternative to wage restraint, which was a "hard line approach in collective bargaining,"[658] and stated:

> If governments are permitted to infringe on Charter rights in times of relative growth and prosperity, in the absence of any present or imminent fiscal urgency without explaining the need to breach Charter rights or the need to pursue inconsistent policies, it would be far too easy for governments to infringe on Charter rights merely by asserting the need for fiscal prudence.
>
> While it might be appropriate to infringe on a Charter right when faced with a serious fiscal challenge, it is not appropriate to do so as part of the day-to-day management of government affairs.
>
> Ontario responds that allowing the government leeway to do that is the essence of democracy. If the government made election promises to cut taxes, it should be permitted to do so. I fully agree. But an election promise to cut taxes does not necessarily give the government the right to breach Charter rights to achieve what appeared to be routine policy preferences rather than urgent societal needs.

---

655 2021 MBCA 85, overruling 2020 MBQB 92 [*Manitoba*], leave to appeal to the Supreme Court refused.

656 SM 2017, c 24.

657 *Manitoba*, above note 655 at para 128, quoting from *Health Services*, above note 617 at para 94.

658 *OECTA*, above note 14 at paras 350 and 353–55.

The Ontario government stated that, while it would appeal the *OECTA* ruling, it would not use the notwithstanding clause to uphold Bill 124.[659]

It is now necessary, when setting the legal context for collective bargaining restraint legislation, to reference section 33 of the *Charter*, the "notwithstanding" clause, usable by a provincial legislature to declare that legislation will operate notwithstanding sections 2 and 7 to 15. For the first time in Ontario, the Progressive Conservative government under Premier Ford has demonstrated its readiness to employ it. In 2018, the government introduced a bill containing such a clause in order to override a Superior Court decision striking down a reduction to the size of Toronto City Council,[660] and it has passed an override bill in response to a Superior Court decision striking down provisions of the *Election Finances Act* dealing with third-party spending on political advertising as a violation of the *Charter* section 2(b) right of expression.[661] At that time, there were no statements by the government delineating when the clause would be used. In introducing the legislation concerning Toronto City Council, the attorney general said that

> section 33 is included as a safety valve, so that Legislatures can have the final say on important matters of public policy.... Some have suggested that section 33 should only be used in non-controversial

659 See CBC News, "Ford Says He Won't Use Notwithstanding Clause for Bill 124 After Court Ruled It Unconstitutional" (1 December 2022), online: www.cbc.ca/news/canada/toronto/ford-jones-flu-season-1.6670423.

660 *Better Local Government Act, 2018*, SO 2018, c 11, legislation reducing the size of Toronto City Council, was struck down by the Superior Court as a breach of the *Charter* right to freedom of expression. The government then introduced the *Efficient Local Government Act, 2018*, which reintroduced substantially the same legislation and added, in s 10 that, pursuant to the *Charter* s 33(1), the relevant provisions were declared to operate notwithstanding the rights in the *Charter*. The Superior Court decision was stayed by the Court of Appeal in *Toronto (City) v Ontario (Attorney General)*, 2018 ONCA 761, with the result that the provincial government did not proceed with the override legislation. The *Better Local Government Act* was ultimately upheld by the Supreme Court in *Toronto (City) v Ontario (Attorney General)*, 2021 SCC 34.

661 *Working Families Coalition (Canada) Inc v Ontario*, 2021 ONSC 7697 [*Working Families*] deals with the original decision and with the overriding legislation, the *Protecting Elections and Defending Democracy Act, 2021*, SO 2021, c 31, s 4, which added a provision to the *Election Finances Act*, RSO 1990, c E.7, s 53.1, stating the Act is declared to operate not withstanding sections 2 and 7 to 15 of the *Charter*.

circumstances, but the definition of "controversial" depends on how one feels about the policy question at the heart of the matter.[662]

Section 33 has been used in Ontario wage restraint legislation to pre-emptively negate a *Charter* section 2(d) challenge. In 2022, the government pre-empted a strike by Ontario public education workers, represented by the Canadian Union of Public Employees, through the *Keeping Students in Class Act, 2022*.[663] The Act required a four-year collective agreement, with no access to interest arbitration, and included the notwithstanding clause.[664] There was no particular explanation provided to the legislature about why the clause was included. There was public controversy, and a diverse union coalition stated that a general strike would take place soon after the legislation passed.[665] The government and CUPE then agreed that the parties would recommence bargaining and the government would repeal the legislation, which it did in the *Keeping Students in Class Repeal Act, 2022* (Bill 35).

The use of the notwithstanding clause has long been politically contentious[666] and, as events in Ontario have shown, it is not readily predictable. Whether it is used in the future in Ontario to uphold "back to work" or compensation restraint legislation rests on its political acceptability.

---

662 Ontario Legislative Assembly, *Hansard*, 17 September 2018 at 100 (Caroline Mulroney, Attorney General) speaking to the *Better Local Government Act*, above note 660. To essentially the same effect, see the speaking to the *Protecting Elections and Defending Democracy Act*, *ibid*: Ontario Legislative Assembly, *Hansard*, 12 June 2021 at 20 (Doug Downey, Attorney General).

663 SO 2022, c 19.

664 *Ibid*, s 13.

665 Tanzim Rashid, "The CUPE Cause Célèbre: Provinces Spend beyond what Canada's Constitutional Drafters Budgeted For" *The Court.ca* (12 December 2022) online: www.thecourt.ca/the-cupe-cause-celebre-provinces-spend-beyond-what-canadas-constitutional-drafters-budgeted-for.

666 *Ibid*; *Working Families*, above note 661, Morgan J, citing Peter Russell, "Standing Up for Notwithstanding" (1991) 29:2 *Alberta Law Review* 293 at 299; and Peter W. Hogg & Allison A. Bushell, "The *Charter* Dialogue Between Courts and Legislatures" (1997) 35:1 *Osgoode Hall Law Journal* 75 at 101.

CHAPTER NINE

Transfers and Downsizing

A. CONTEXT

Following the 1995 election of a new Progressive Conservative government, the structure of Ontario's public service and the broader public sector was rapidly rationalized.[1] Municipalities, school boards, and hospitals were consolidated.[2] Consistent with the tenets of the "new public management" philosophy popular at the time,[3] the government divested a wide range of programs and operations involved in direct service to the public over to municipalities, public hospitals, and other public institutions or agencies or contractors that could, in its view, more appropriately manage these activities. This left ministries to focus more on policy development, supervision, and regulation rather than direct service delivery. As functions were transferred out of government, and government downsized, involved employees transferred with their work, moved to new employment in government, or were laid off in large numbers.[4]

---

1 See the discussion of the labour relations impacts in *Service Employees International Union, Local 204 v Humber/Northwestern/York-Finch Hospital*, 1997 CanLII 15494 (ON LRB) at para 27 and following.

2 Health Services Restructuring Commission, *Looking Back, Looking Forward: The Ontario Health Services Restructuring Commission. A Legacy Report* (2000), online: www.hhr-rhs.ca/en/?option=com_mtree&task=att_download&link_id=5214&cf_id=68; *Fewer School Boards Act, 1997*, SO 1997, c 3.

3 See the brief discussion of "new public management" in Chapter 1.

4 Graham White, "Revolutionary Change in the Ontario Public Service" in Evert A. Lindquist ed, *Government Restructuring and Career Public Service in Canada, 2000* (Toronto: Institute of Public Administration of Canada, 2000), ch 12, 310–45

These changes were unprecedented in Ontario and raised a number of employment and labour relations concerns. First, when functions transfer out of government, will the employees move with their work and what impact will there be on bargaining rights and key terms of employment, wages, seniority, pension, and benefits? Second, if an employee's job in government disappears or is divested and the employee is unable or unwilling to move to a new employer what are the rights of the surplus employee? The legal framework developed to address these questions form the basis of the current job security provisions applicable to the Ontario Public Service (OPS). The current statutory and collective agreement terms that answer those questions are addressed in this chapter in the following order:

- Absence of the statutory right to treat the Crown and any other employer as related or common employers
- Statutory successorship under:
  1) *Crown Employees Collective Bargaining Act, 1993* (*CECBA*)[5]
  2) *Public Sector Labour Relations Transition Act, 1997* (*PSLRTA*)[6]
  3) A special purpose statute
- Negotiated transfer agreements:
  1) Individual agreements between unions and receiving employers
  2) the requirements for government to make "reasonable efforts" on divestment of jobs to obtain offers of substantially similar employment with the new employer, contained in the Ontario Public Service Employees Union (OPSEU), Association of Management, Administrative and Professional Crown Employees of Ontario (AMAPCEO), and Professional Engineers of the Government of Ontario (PEGO) collective agreement
- Surplus employee rights, known in the Ontario government as "job security" entitlements, to separation payments and redeployment within government.

---

at 315. See *OPSEU/MBC Unified Bargaining Unit Collective Agreement, 2022–2024* and *OPSEU/MBC Correctional Bargaining Unit Collective Agreement, 2018–2021*, online: https://opseu.org/information/general/find-your-collective-agreement, Appendix 18 [*OPSEU/MBC Unified and Correctional Collective Agreements*], listing transfers planned or underway at the end of 1998.

5 SO 1993, c 38 [*CECBA*].

6 SO 1997, c 21, Sch B [*PSLRTA*].

Transfers of employees into government have also occurred occasionally. Those have tended to be handled through individual negotiated transfer agreements.[7]

B. LEGISLATIVE AND COLLECTIVE BARGAINING HISTORY

A successor rights provision, providing for the transfer of bargaining rights along with the transfer of ownership of a business, has formed part of the *Labour Relations Act, 1995* (*LRA*) since 1963.[8] Substantially the same provision was applied to the Crown by the *Successor Rights (Crown Transfers) Act, 1977*,[9] and briefly under the *CECBA 1993*. In 1995, as the government began to implement its divestment agenda, the successor rights provisions in *CECBA 1993* were repealed.[10]

Not surprisingly, employee transfer and surplus rights were a dominant issue in collective bargaining, leading to the 1996 OPSEU strike.[11] The resultant changes to the OPSEU/MBC collective agreement featured the requirement for the government to at least make "reasonable efforts" to transfer public servants with their work on similar terms of employment, and significantly changed surplus or "job security" rights for laid-off employees.[12] Similar terms were subsequently included in the

7 For example, see the *Memorandum of Agreement Between the Ministry of Community Safety and Correctional Services and OPSEU*, 18 September 2006, online: http://opseu.org/wpcontent/uploads/2014/04/cnccmoa_2006.pdf for the transfer of employees from the private Central North Correctional Centre (CNCC) to the ministry, which provided that the posting of Ontario Public Service (OPS) vacancies would be waived and that service with CNCC would be treated as OPS continuous service. The agreement was entered into by the Liberal government following a Progressive Conservative five-year pilot project to determine if there was any advantage to private operations to correctional services in Ontario: "Central North Correctional Centre Transferring to Public Sector Operation," *Ontario News Release*, 27 April 2006, online: http://news.ontario.ca/en/release/83436/central-north-correctional-centre-transferring-to-public-sector-operation.

8 SO 1995, c 1, Sch A, s 69 [*LRA*].

9 SO 1977, c 30 [*SR(CT)A*].

10 *Labour Relations and Employment Statute Law Amendment Act, 1995*, SO 1995, c 1, s 23(2).

11 *OPSEU (Union) and Ministry of Agriculture, Food and Rural Affairs*, GSB#1747/96, 8 May 1997 (Gray) at 6 [*Agriculture*]. See the discussion of the 1996 OPSEU strike in Chapter 8.

12 The pre-existing job offer guarantee for employees made surplus by the contracting out or transfer out of the OPS of their work as contained in the *OPSEU/MBC Collective Agreement 1992-1993*, Article 24.17.3, was deleted in the 1996

government's collective agreements with its other unions, AMAPCEO and PEGO.

In 1997, the *PSLRTA* was enacted to facilitate the restructuring of bargaining rights and terms of employment in key broader public subsectors. The Act provides for the more efficient and, in some respects, fairer application of successor rights, and may be applied to new initiatives by regulation. As discussed below, it has limited applicability to the government itself but does provide successor rights protections to OPS unions and employees in divestments where it is applied.

Divestments and enforcement of the protection offered by the reasonable efforts and job security provisions remained a constant concern for public servants and their unions from 1995 to 2006. In the 1998 round of bargaining all parties renegotiated the "reasonable efforts" provisions to set out more specific expectations. By 2006 the pace of divestments had slowed, even reversed.[13] Successor rights were restored to government employees and their unions as part of the new Liberal government's reform of the *Public Service of Ontario Act, 2006 (PSOA)*.[14]

While the reasonable efforts provisions remain in the OPS collective agreements, their purpose was to address the absence of statutory successor rights provisions. With the return of statutory successor rights, the continued significance of the reasonable efforts provisions is now limited, by agreement of the parties, to transactions where successor rights do not apply.[15]

The government has since 2006 facilitated some transfers by passing legislation authorizing the responsible minister to issue an order transfering an undertaking from one public employer to another public employer together with the employees employed in the undertaking The option of a statutorily mandated transfer by minister's order is, for example, currently provided for in the *Connecting Care Act, 2019*.[16]

---

settlement. Now see the *OPSEU/MBC Unified and Correctional Collective Agreements*, above note 4, Art 20 and Appendix 18.

13 See note 7 above re the transfer of the Central North Correctional Centre into government. An aspect of the transfer agreement is addressed in *Ontario Public Service Employees Union v Ontario (Community Safety and Correctional Services)*, 2007 CanLII 24188 (ON GSB) (Gray).

14 SO 2006, c 35, Sch A [*PSOA*]. See the discussion of successor rights below.

15 *OPSEU/MBC Unified and Correctional Collective Agreements*, above note 4, Appendix 14, Successor Rights.

16 SO 2019, c 5, Sch 1, s 40.

Transfers have also been facilitated by negotiated transfer agreements between affected unions and employers.

While the transfer of work or businesses into or out of the public sector is now much less frequent, the continuing evolution of government and the broader public sector means that transfers remain a periodic occurrence.

C. ABSENCE OF A RELATED EMPLOYER PROVISION

The *CECBA* applies only to the Crown and Crown agents designated by regulation as employers of Crown employees.[17] Agencies that are not designated as employers of Crown employees are subject to the *LRA*, including the related employer provision in that Act. The Crown has only been subject to a related employer provision when the *CECBA* briefly incorporated the *LRA* related employer provision between 1993 and 1995.[18]

The *LRA* related employer provision provides that where "related activities or businesses" are "under common control or direction," the board may order that they are to be treated as "constituting one employer" for labour relations purposes.[19] Although there is no statement of legislative intent for the non-inclusion of this provision in the *CECBA*, there is a clear rationale. The related employer provisions common in labour legislation address the need to determine the appropriate employer in the context of modern corporate structures or business arrangements that may not appropriately align a single corporate entity with a business for labour relations purposes.[20] The Crown creates agencies, boards, and commissions for the purpose of setting up the appropriate vehicle for delivering a particular program or undertaking with a planned degree of independence and separation from the direct control of the Crown. The determination of the relationship between the Crown and agencies designated as agents of the Crown for purposes of their labour relations is a political policy choice by the elected executive concerning matters that may have an impact on the government's budget and policy agenda. These are not choices to be second

17 See the discussion of the applicability of *CECBA* in Chapter 7.

18 *CECBA*, above note 5, s 3.

19 *LRA*, above note 8, s 1(4).

20 George W. Adams, *Canadian Labour Law*, 2d ed (Aurora, ON: Canada Law Book, 2004), s 8.6.

guessed from time to time in litigation before an administrative board. The employers for purposes of the *CECBA* can only be the Crown and certain of its separate agencies determined by regulation.

D. STATUTORY SUCCESSORSHIP

1) Successor Rights Under the *CECBA*

In 1977, the legislature enacted the *Successor Rights (Crown Transfers) Act* (*SR(CT)A*), which provided for successor rights when an undertaking is transferred from the Crown, and parallel provisions addressing the transfer of "an undertaking" from an employer to the Crown. The Ontario Labour Relations Board (OLRB) had jurisdiction, consistent with its jurisdiction under the successor rights provisions of the *LRA*, to determine the appropriate bargaining unit, to amend certificates, collective agreements, and/or bargaining units as it deemed necessary, and to address any questions arising from intermingling of employees.

Initially, the OLRB interpreted a transfer of an undertaking under the *SR(CT)A* as analogous to the transfer of a business under the *LRA* sale of business (successor rights) section. Then in 1986 it decided that contracting out the operation and maintenance of Fitzroy Provincial Park was a "transfer" of an "undertaking" within the meaning of the *SR(CT)A*.[21] Under the *LRA*, the contracting out of a particular function was not by itself normally found to be a transfer of a business triggering successor rights.[22] *KBM Forestry Consultants Inc*[23] confirmed the departure from the *LRA* jurisprudence by holding that the continuity of the work was especially significant and that union job protections were not to be threatened by the government transferring a program to a private entity.

In *United Food and Commercial Workers International Union v Parnell Foods Limited*,[24] a case involving the contracting out of onsite food services at four correctional facilities, the OLRB revisited the *KBM* approach and decided to revert to the approach to successor rights provisions applied under the *LRA* and similar provisions in other Canadian

---

21 *Ministry of Natural Resources*, [1986] OLRB Rep March 331 at para 16.

22 See, for example, *Metropolitan Parking Inc*, [1979] OLRB Rep December 1193.

23 [1987] OLRB Rep March 399, aff'd Ontario High Court of Justice, 25 April 1988 at para 11.

24 1992 CanLII 6792 (ON LRB) [*Parnell Foods Limited*].

jurisdictions. The focus returned to whether there was the transfer of an organizational structure, "a business," to use the sale of business language, rather than the mere transfer of work. The board found that a purposive view of the *SR(CT)A* led to the conclusion it was not intended to preserve work opportunities for employees represented by OPSEU, but rather to preserve the bargaining rights attaching to a transferred undertaking.[25] In subsequent cases, the rationale in *Parnell Foods Limited* was applied where contractors took over work, but used their own organization, to hold that no undertaking had been transferred within the meaning of the *SR(CT)A*.[26]

The legislature repealed the *SR(CT)A* as part of the package of legislation that included *CECBA 1993*, which contained provisions that applied the sale of business provisions of the *LRA* to the Crown.[27] Those provisions were repealed in 1995 before any decisions were made interpreting them. Bargaining rights under the *CECBA 1993* had no successor rights protections between 1995 and 2006, when the successor rights provisions of the *LRA* were again incorporated into the *CECBA*.[28] There do not seem to have been policy justifications for the arbitrary decisions to first project Ontario Public Service (OPS) bargaining rights onto OPS contractors or then to deprive public servants of successor rights protection altogether.

The 2006 language incorporating the *LRA* "sale of business" section into the *CECBA* does modify the *LRA* definition of transfer and sale to use the same terminology as the *SR(CT)A* successor rights provision. The original *SR(CT)A* language differed from the *LRA* language to reflect the unique nature of the Crown. One must assume the legislature was aware of the OLRB jurisprudence and would have used different words if a different result was intended. In any event, the *Parnell Foods Limited* reasoning has been applied by the OLRB to the current *CECBA* successor rights provision.[29]

---

25 *Ibid* at para 202.

26 *St Leonard's Society of Metropolitan Toronto*, [1993] OLRB Rep January 56 at para 211; *Mil-Dom-Ex Packaging*, [1992] OLRB Rep December 1155 at para 170.

27 *CECBA*, above note 5, s 10.

28 *Public Service of Ontario Statute Law Amendment Act, 2006*, SO 2006, c 35, Sch D, s 2 amending *CECBA*, above note 5, s 10.

29 *Association of Management, Administrative and Professional Crown Employees of Ontario v Ontario*, 2008 CanLII 60007 (ON LRB) at paras 36–37; *Ontario Public Service Employees Union v Ontario (Children and Youth Services)*, 2010 CanLII 49183 (ON LRB) at para 33 [*York Detention Centre*]; *Ontario Public*

Parnell Foods Limited concerned the purchase by the Crown of services through a commercial procurement process in a competitive market and found that such a transaction was not a transfer of an undertaking. A decision under the current successor rights provision in the *CECBA* found that even in the likely rare situation where a Crown agency provides a service as a successful competitor in a commercial procurement the transaction is similarly not a transfer of an undertaking.[30] This is the same result one would expect under the *LRA* involving private sector employers. However, the OLRB has also noted that

> [w]hile the purpose of successor rights, which is to ensure that bargaining rights are preserved in the event of a transfer of the operation or a part thereof, remains the same in both the public and private sector, the essential elements of the particular operation to which bargaining rights attach may differ depending on the context within which it operates.[31]

In the long-term care home (formerly nursing home) sector, the transfer of a business is linked to the licence to operate a home. The licence is not merely a permission to operate a business. The licence is tied to a specific building and a process that determines the residents that will be cared for in the home. It is in effect an allocation of a particular part of the long-term care home business administered by the Crown.[32] In a post-*Parnell* decision the use by the Crown of a competitive process for transferring beds being operated by the Crown after the revocation of a nursing home licence was found to be a transfer of an undertaking under the *SR(CT)A*.[33]

In the *York Detention Centre* decision,[34] the OLRB applied similar reasoning to the termination of a contract for the operation of a youth detention centre. The York Detention Centre was closed, and the youths detained there moved to other ministry-operated facilities. Arguably

---

Service Employees Union v Ontario Clean Water Agency and American Water Canada Corp, 2013 CanLII 50558 (ON LRB) at para 17.

30 *York Detention Centre, ibid.*

31 *Ibid* at para 38.

32 *Service Employees' Union, Local 183 v Riverview Manor*, 1983 CanLII 979 (ON LRB) and cases cited therein; *Service Employees' International Union, Local 532 v Saint Elizabeth Home Society*, 1992 CanLII 6339 (ON LRB).

33 *Service Employees' International Union, Local 532 v Saint Elizabeth Home Society*, 1994 CanLII 9907 (ON LRB).

34 *York Detention Centre*, above note 29.

nothing but the work of providing secure custody passed to the government. However, the board noted that secure custody services are an "exclusive public service."[35] The right to operate a secure custody business is wholly dependent on a contract with the Crown. The contract to operate York Detention Centre was not a licence but was for an indefinite period. While it was subject to termination on relatively short notice the intention was clearly that the contract continue for a long time. The termination of the contract terminated the contractor's business or undertaking and transferred it to the Crown triggering successor rights.

Even when the Crown or its agencies directly manage and largely fund a sector, the existence of a competitive private sector style market for limited-term contracts may lead to the conclusion that services are simply being purchased so the successor rights provisions do not apply.[36] The OLRB has noted that the particular business context is important:

> Factors which may be sufficient to support a "sale of a business" finding in one sector of the economy may be insufficient in another. In some industries, a particular configuration of assets—physical plant machinery and equipment—may be of paramount importance; while in others it may be patents, "know-how," technological expertise, or managerial skills which will be significant. Some businesses will rely heavily on the goodwill associated with a particular location, company name, product name or logo; while for other businesses, these factors will be insignificant . . . a licence to run a nursing home business was a critical part of that business, to which bargaining rights could attach . . . In that highly-regulated business, the licence was viewed by the board in that case as the key asset.[37]

The determination of whether an undertaking, as opposed to work, is being transferred will depend on the combination of factors considered in applications under the *LRA* having regard for the role of the Crown in the sector involved.

---

35 *Ibid* at para 39.

36 *Ontario Public Service Employees Union v Multi-Professional Support Services Inc*, 2000 CanLII 13394 (ON LRB).

37 *Hotel Employees Restaurant Employees Union, Local 75 v Accomodex Franchise Management Inc*, 1993 CanLII 8023 (ON LRB) at para 70; quoted in *Canadian Airport Workers Union v Goodwill Industries*, 2022 CanLII 17636 (ON LRB) at para 115.

2) *Public Sector Labour Relations Transition Act*

The *PSLRTA* was passed in 1997 to provide a more efficient alternative to the application of the *LRA* successor rights provisions for resolving labour relations issues arising out of the planned amalgamations in the municipal, school, and hospital sectors that involved multiple bargaining units and unions, and potentially other circumstances. The transactions it was originally intended to address have long since been completed. However, the Act has been found by both employers and unions to be preferrable to the successor rights provisions of the *LRA* in certain transfers and has been applied by regulation or amendment to transactions not contemplated when it was first passed.

The application of *PSLRTA* to a proposed transfer has the immediate benefit of resolving any doubt that successor rights apply. The Act:

- protects the seniority of non-union staff swept into a bargaining unit and dovetails the unions' seniority lists;[38] the *LRA* does not
- provides a structured approach to determining post transfer bargaining units and union representation, including mandatory votes unless one union represented 80 percent or more of the employees in the unit prior to transfer[39]
- requires the negotiation of harmonization of employment terms rather than imposing the winning union's collective agreement on new bargaining units
- requires new units to be appropriate to the new employer rather than focusing on preservation of pre-transfer bargaining rights

The *PSLRTA* binds the Crown, but the Crown cannot be a successor employer under the Act,[40] so the bargaining unit reconfiguration and mandatory vote provisions cannot apply to the OPS. In the event the Crown would be a successor, the *LRA* successor rights provisions apply.[41] The Act can be made to apply to prescribed circumstances "upon the occurrence of a prescribed event" and the Crown can be designated as a predecessor employer.[42]

38 *PSLRTA*, above note 6, ss 33 & 34.
39 *Ibid*, s 23(11.1); O Reg 136/16.
40 *Ibid*, s 11.
41 *Ibid*, s 13(2).
42 *Ibid*, s 10.

The application of the Act by statute or regulation remains a potentially useful option in circumstances involving transfers out of the OPS affecting multiple bargaining units and unions similar to the transactions for which the *PSLRTA* was originally designed.

3) Special Purpose Statutes: Transfers by Minister's Order

Transferring an employee with their position to a new employer involves the employee leaving the employ of the predecessor employer and being hired by the successor. An employee may not wish to leave the predecessor or may prefer termination benefits in preference to transferring. The successor employer may be subject to collective agreement terms that require new positions to be posted and offered to its own employees with seniority prior to accepting a transferring employee. Even where these difficulties can be worked out, until that occurs employees are placed in an uncomfortable state of doubt about their future with adverse impacts on employee health, productivity, and retention.

In the broader public sector, the *Connecting Care Act, 2019*[43] currently provides authority to, by minister order, transfer health care employees together with their jobs to a new employer. Similar statutory provisions have been used before.[44] They have real advantages. When a transfer is announced employees are normally concerned about their job so an order that specifies that they will move with their work without any change in the terms of employment is welcomed. An order of this type will normally be issued in circumstances that also give rise to successor rights, providing unionized employees with some assurance that any future changes in their terms will continue to be subject to collective bargaining.

The use of minister's orders or any form of legislation to change the employer of an employee without their consent is legislative interference with an individual's contractual rights. This type of legislation is justified by the role of the Crown as responsible for the conduct of agencies delivering public services and the funding of their employment obligations. Such orders have been and should remain limited to the facilitation of restructuring operations that are and will continue to be

43 Above note 16, ss 40 and 42.

44 For example, the *Community Care Access Corporations Act, 2001*, SO 2001, c 33, s 17.

delivered by or on behalf of the Crown and ensure that the transferred employees' contractual entitlements are preserved.

E. NEGOTIATED TRANSFER AGREEMENTS

Whether employees will move with their work, and the nature of their terms of employment following a transfer are largely dictated by the circumstances. A psychiatric hospital with hundreds of patients suffering from serious mental illnesses is not going to be transferred without the staff also moving. In other cases, transfers may be possible without moving the staff but that may be expensive and risky. Transfers to large contractors interested in taking over operations with their own staff are inconsistent with employees transferring with their work. Employees transferred to large employers, such as municipalities, hospitals, the federal government, and universities, will be integrated into the new employer's compensation and labour relations structure. Employers in sectors or businesses with less favourable compensation levels than the OPS will not readily pay newly hired transferring staff more than their existing staff or more than their collective agreements dictate.

From the union's perspective, seniority-based "bumping" is not desirable, as ultimately a junior member is laid off, but it is normally better than the alternative of laying off a senior employee. However, where a union is faced, as OPSEU was in the 1990s, with large-scale transfers and potentially successive rounds of large-scale bumping, the situation is much more challenging. Rounds of bumping where relatively senior members are displaced spreads uncertainty about job security across the entire bargaining unit with not much benefit. The best result then becomes moving employees with their work on comparable terms of employment. The second-best option is for employees whose work has moved to receive a reasonable termination package or acceptable job offer. In the case of AMAPCEO and PEGO, which faced a much lower number of potential layoffs, moving employees with their work on comparable terms was still the best option but, failing that, allowing them full access to their displacement rights, including bumping junior employees was the next best option.

While retaining the successor rights provisions in the *CECBA 1993* would have facilitated certain important divestments they would have frustrated others. Agreements between the parties to a transfer and the unions affected offer the possibility of addressing the interests of the parties more effectively than a blunt application of a statutory or general collective agreement provision.

1) Individual Transfer Agreements

Regardless of the applicable statutory provisions, the parties to a transfer may choose to negotiate a transfer agreement. A negotiated transfer agreement will limit uncertainty for the employees, avoid potential litigation, and minimize disruption to services.

In the event of a transfer into the OPS, the size of the OPSEU and AMAPCEO bargaining units makes it highly unlikely that the OLRB would use its authority under the successor rights provisions to order a vote under the successor rights provisions. Similarly, a transfer of a relatively small program out of the OPS may not give the OPS union concerned a realistic chance to establish a bargaining unit with the successor employer. In these cases, an early agreement determining how job offers will be made, as well as protecting seniority and other key employment terms of the transferring employees, may be of considerable benefit to all parties.

Negotiations can focus on resolving the actual concerns of the employees, the receiving union, and the new employer rather than the application of a statutory or collective agreement provisions that may not suit the unique facts of the particular transfer. Such an agreement may be the best opportunity for the transferring employees' union to negotiate the protection of its members' seniority. Receiving unions usually recognize that the day after the transfer the transferring employees will be their members so are often willing to recognize their seniority to facilitate a smooth transfer and avoid future complaints.

2) "Reasonable Efforts" Provisions

a) Context

The OPSEU, AMAPCEO, and PEGO collective agreements with Management Board of Cabinet (MBC) all require the employer to make "reasonable efforts" to ensure that, where there is a "disposition or any other transfer" of bargaining unit functions or jobs to the private or broader public sectors, affected employees are offered positions with the new employer on terms and conditions "as close as possible" to their existing terms.[45] These date from the 1996 settlement of the first OPSEU strike under the *CECBA 1993*. In 1995, the new Progressive Conservative government's divestment agenda was implemented in part by the repeal of the successor rights provisions in *CECBA 1993*.[46] A key part of the settlement of the five-week OPSEU strike was the negotiation of Appendix 9 to the MBC/OPSEU agreement that required the Crown to make reasonable efforts to move employees out of the OPS with their work in the event of transfers of functions or job.[47] The settlements of the AMAPCEO and PEGO agreements that followed included terms substantially the same as Appendix 9.

Initially Appendix 9 appeared to work well. For example, the Ministry of Agriculture moved about half its staff out to various employers in the broader public sector (BPS) on the same or comparable terms of employment.[48] However, transferring staff is much more difficult when the new BPS employer is in a sector where pay and conditions are less favourable than in the OPS, or where the new employer is a private sector contractor. The employer addressed these concerns by taking the position that the reasonable efforts provisions should be interpreted to impose only limited process or procedural obligations. At the same time, OPSEU sought to prevent or delay divestments. Over time, neither party proved particularly interested in making Appendix 9 work, except as a last resort. OPSEU spent several years in litigation successfully obtaining interim relief[49] requiring the employer to make an

---

45 *OPSEU/MBC Unified and Correctional Collective Agreements*, above note 4, Appendices 9 and 18; *AMAPCEO/MBC Collective Agreement, 2018–2022*, Art 27.18 [*AMAPCEO/MBC Collective Agreement*], and 2022–2025 Memorandum of Settlement, Item 3, Job Security, online: https://amapceo.on.ca/ops; *PEGO/MBC Collective Agreement, 2019–2022*, Appendix A, Employment Stability, online: https://pego.on.ca/pego-collective-agreements [*PEGO/MBC Collective Agreement*].

46 *Labour Relations and Employment Statute Law Amendment Act, 1995*, SO 1995, c 1. The history of Crown successor rights is discussed above.

47 In *OPSEU (Union) and Management Board Secretariat/Ministry of Transportation*, GSB#498/97, 16 February 1998 (Roberts) at 21 [*Transportation, February 1998 (Roberts)*], the GSB links the resolution of the 1996 strike with the negotiation of the reasonable efforts provisions. See also *Agriculture*, above note 11 at 6.

48 Private interviews.

49 Interim relief from the GSB is discussed in Chapter 11.

increasing list of arguably reasonable, largely futile efforts before divestments could proceed, significantly delaying the government's agenda.[50]

In 1998, with OPSEU's delaying litigation becoming less successful, and another round of bargaining approaching, OPSEU and the government negotiated Appendix 18, which created a complete code of what was required of the employer to satisfy its reasonable efforts obligations under Appendix 9.[51] It effectively replaced Appendix 9 with much more specific reasonable efforts terms that the parties intended to implement. Later AMAPCEO and PEGO also retained the original reasonable efforts language with qualifications similar to those in Appendix 18 that largely but not wholly restrict the significance of Appendix 9.[52]

In 2006, successor rights were restored as part of the Liberal government's *PSOA* reform. While the original reason for the reasonable efforts provisions disappeared with the restoration of successor rights the provisions did not. The OPSEU, AMAPCEO, and PEGO agreements now provide that the reasonable efforts provisions do not apply if the employer determines a transfer is a sale of business. The ultimate authority to determine whether a sale of business has occurred rests with the Ontario Labour Relations Board, not the government.[53] However, where a transfer is the subject of a negotiation process or a competitive procurement the government can require the successor to treat the transfer as a sale of business. By doing so the Crown forecloses any litigation on the issue and all parties can proceed with orderly planning of the transfer.

---

50 See *OPSEU (Union) and Ministry of Transportation*, GSB#320/98, 12 October 1999 (Mikus) at 13 [*Transportation, October 1999 (Mikus)*], where the GSB refers to costly delays and extended negotiations associated with opposition to a contracting out initiative. See also the historical discussion in *OPSEU (Union) and Ministry of Community & Social Services*, GSB#1785/98, 24 February 1999 (Brown) at 2 [*Community, 1999 (Brown)*].

51 *Community, 1999 (Brown)*, above note 50; *Ontario Public Service Employees Union v Ontario (Ministry of Community and Social Services)*, 2003 CanLII 52872 (ON GSB), application for judicial review dismissed, 2005 CanLII 4848 (ON SCDC).

52 *PEGO v Ontario (Ministry of Municipal Affairs and Housing)*, 2003 CanLII 52932 (ON GSB).

53 *Association of Management, Administrative and Professional Crown Employees of Ontario v Ontario*, 2008 CanLII 60007 (ON LRB).

b) "Reasonable Efforts" Litigation Under Appendix 9

The precedents set in the litigation under Appendix 9 were superseded by Appendix 18 but the litigation conducted under Appendix 9 formed the framework for the negotiation of Appendix 18 and helps explain some of the features of Appendix 18 and the current AMAPCEO and PEGO reasonable efforts provisions.

The obligation to make reasonable efforts was held to provide "extremely important"[54] protection for bargaining unit members[55] and was not to be taken lightly.[56] The words "a disposition or any other transfer of bargaining-unit functions or jobs" were broadly construed to include transfers that would be seen as contracting out, in addition to those transfers in the form of a sale of business.[57]

The obligation to make reasonable efforts commences "as soon as the decision to divest is made."[58] This ruling continues to be reflected in the AMAPCEO collective agreement provision requiring decisions to transfer work or jobs to be brought to the Central Employee Relations Committee when they are made.[59]

Failure to offer financial incentives equal to the enhanced severance payable as an encouragement to bidders to provide and/or improve job offers was a breach of the collective agreement.[60] This offer of a small one-time cash amount is clearly unlikely ever to achieve anything but it

54 *OPSEU (Union) and Ministry of Transportation*, GSB#1344/96, 9 June 1997 (Kaplan) at 29, upheld on judicial review, [1997] OJ No 4822 (Div Ct) [*Transportation, June 1997 (Kaplan)*].

55 *Transportation, February 1998 (Roberts)*, above note 47 at 24.

56 *Transportation, June 1997 (Kaplan)*, above note 54 at 29.

57 *OPSEU (Union) and Ministry of Transportation*, GSB#1344A/96, 8 May 1997 (Gray) at 12 [*Transportation, May 1997 (Gray)*], where the GSB held that the external purchase of services formerly provided by government employees fell within definition of "a disposition or any other transfer of bargaining-unit functions or jobs."

58 *OPSEU (Union) and Ministry of Community and Social Services*, GSB#2779/96, 141/97, 2 June 1997 (Kaplan) [*Community, 1997 (Kaplan)*] at 19. See also *OPSEU (Union) and Management Board Secretariat*, GSB#1712/97, 30 January 1998 (Dissanayake) at 15 [*MBS, January 1998 (Dissanayake)*]; *OPSEU (Union) and Ministry of Community and Social Services*, GSB #1859/97, 4 August 1998 (Brown) [*Community, August 1998 (Brown)*] at 12–14; and *Transportation, February 1998 (Roberts)*, above note 47.

59 *AMAPCEO/MBC Collective Agreement*, above note 45, Art 27.18.2.9.

60 *Community, 1997 (Kaplan)*, above note 58 at 20; *Community, August 1998 (Brown)*, above note 58 at 22; *OPSEU (Union) and Ministry of Consumer and Commercial Relations*, GSB#559/97, 26 May 1998 (Roberts) at 28.

has been retained in the AMAPCEO and PEGO collective agreements as the sole requirement necessary for the employer to satisfy its reasonable efforts obligations in respect of transfers that are not done by request for proposal (RFP) or tender.[61] It also appears in Appendix 18.

Employer bi-weekly meetings with the local union in respect of negotiated transfers were required.[62] Both Appendix 18 and the AMAPCEO reasonable efforts terms include provisions for disclosure to the bargaining agents and regular discussions with a labour management committee.[63]

Making reasonable efforts does not require that "every" or "all" efforts be made;[64] nor will it be a breach of the provision if, in the particular circumstances, no job offers are obtainable.[65] In the first decision involving a divestment via a tender, the GSB held that reasonable efforts are "efforts that are reasonable in the circumstances all things considered."[66]

The GSB ultimately determined that, to satisfy the obligation to make reasonable efforts in tendering situations, bidders must be required to offer to hire all affected employees at salaries of at least 85 percent of their OPS salary, recognize their OPS service for purposes of vacation and benefits, and not impose a probationary period; bidders would be awarded additional points to the extent that their proposed terms and conditions of employment reflected what existed in the OPS; and a fund would be established to be used to negotiate improved terms

61 *AMAPCEO/MBC Collective Agreement*, above note 45, Art 27.18.2.5.2; *PEGO/MBC Collective Agreement*, above note 45, Appendix A, Art 2.5(b).

62 *Community, 1997 (Kaplan)*, above note 58 at 21; see also *MBS, January 1998 (Dissanayake)*, above note 58 and *Ontario Public Service Employees Union v Ontario (Ministry of Municipal Affairs and Housing)*, 2003 CanLII 52933 (ON GSB). In the latter case involving PEGO, the employer was required to give PEGO the same information about available jobs as was being given to OPSEU.

63 *OPSEU/MBC Unified and Correctional Collective Agreements*, above note 4, Appendix 18, Art 4.1; *AMAPCEO/MBC Collective Agreement*, above note 45, Art 27.18.2.9.

64 *Community, 1997 (Kaplan)*, above note 58 at 18–19.

65 *Transportation, May 1997 (Gray)*, above note 57; *OPSEU (Union) and Ministry of Community & Social Services*, GSB#2779/96, 24 November 1998 (Stewart) [*Community, November 1998 (Stewart)*].

66 *Transportation, June 1997 (Kaplan)*, above note 54 at 30. See also *Community, November 1998 (Stewart)*, above note 65 at 12; *Community, 1997 (Kaplan)*, above note 58 at 19; *MBS, January 1998 (Dissanayake)*, above note 58 at 10.

and conditions of employment with the successful bidder(s).[67] With some exceptions, these provisions formed the basis for the provisions in Appendix 18 and the AMAPCEO and PEGO collective agreements dealing with reasonable efforts in transfers by tender or RFP.

c) Appendix 18

The reasonable efforts provisions do not apply to transactions that are sales of business for purposes of successor rights under the *LRA*.[68] Appendix 18 and the AMAPCEO and PEGO agreements do provide that where a transfer is undertaken by tender or RFP the employer's reasonable efforts obligations require that proponents be required to offer jobs to affected employees with a rate at least 85 percent of their OPS rate and recognize their OPS service for purpose of vacation, benefits, and other terms, except pension, offered in the proponent's workplace. The MBC must in negotiating a transfer offer an amount equivalent to the amount affected employees would get in enhanced severance (one week's pay per year of service) as an incentive for the receiving employer to make enhanced offers of employment to affected employees.

AMAPCEO and PEGO members may refuse job offers from the receiving employer without penalty and exercise their rights as surplus employees. The OPSEU provisions are more elaborate. Appendix 18 provides for transfers to be placed on one of four Schedules A to D. Each schedule contains a different set of obligations that, if complied with, fully satisfy the employer's reasonable efforts obligations.[69] The extent of the employer's obligations varies substantially across the schedules and there are varying degrees of specificity about what terms and conditions of employment must be offered by new service providers.[70] Access to specific entitlements is determined by the terms of the schedules.[71]

Under Appendix 18, transfers that are not "sales of businesses" are added, by the employer, to Schedule A or C (if the transfer is to be by tender or RFP), B (if the transfer is by negotiated agreement), or D

67 *OPSEU (Union) and Ministry of Transportation*, GSB#320/98, 25 August 1998 (Dissanayake).

68 *OPSEU/MBC Unified and Correctional Collective Agreements*, above note 4, Appendix 14, Successor Rights, above note 15.

69 *Ibid*, Appendix 18, ss 1.1.2, 5.7, 6.7, 6 C.7, and 7.2.

70 *OPSEU (Union) and Ministry of Community and Social Services*, GSB#447/00, 6 December 2000 (Leighton) at 2 [*Community, December 2000 (Leighton)*].

71 For example, see *OPSEU and Ministry of Health and Long-Term Care*, GSB#1723/99, 9 November 2000 (Brown).

(if the transfer will result in the receiving employer creating less than eleven OPSEU bargaining unit level positions in any one municipality). The specific transfers originally listed in each schedule have long since been concluded.

OPSEU may dispute the employer's choice of schedule. The term that a "receiving employer" be "designated in legislation" contained in Article 1.0 of Appendix 18 was found to include legislation that only established a designation process.[72] The inclusion of specific individuals in a tender can also be challenged, although the standard of review has not been determined.[73]

Management or other non-OPSEU bargaining unit positions do not count for the purposes of determining whether the threshold of less than eleven jobs is exceeded for placement under Schedule D.[74] The analysis should focus on the number of jobs required to perform the entire body of work that is transferred from the provincial government, rather than on the number of vacancies created as a result of the transfer of the body of work.[75]

Schedule D is held to be an exception to the "comprehensive arrangement designed to enhance job security"[76] set out in Appendix 18. Transfers under Schedule D do not require the employer to make any efforts to obtain jobs for the affected employees. The GSB has held that any ambiguous language in Schedule D should be interpreted in the way that is most favourable to job security. The GSB drew an analogy between job security and seniority and relied on the well-known arbitral *Tung-Sol*[77] principle that the fundamentally important entitlement of seniority should be upheld to the full extent permitted by the provisions in the collective agreement. Where two plausible inter-

---

72 *OPSEU (Union) and Ministry of Health*, 2000 CanLII 20543 (ON GSB) (Brown) at 6.

73 *OPSEU (Union) and Ministry of the Solicitor General and Correctional Services*, GSB#1252/00, 12 February 2001 (Brown). See also *Transportation, October 1999 (Mikus)*, above note 50 at 9–11.

74 *Community, 1999 (Brown)*, above note 50 at 7–8; *Ontario Public Service Employees Union (Union) v Canada (Ministry of Government Services)*, 2014 CanLII 64820 (ON GSB) (Briggs) at para 42 [*Canada, 2014 (Briggs)*]

75 *Community, 1999 (Brown)*, above note 50 at 12.

76 *Ibid*.

77 *Ibid*, citing *Re United Electrical Workers, Local 512, and Tung-Sol of Canada Ltd*, 1964 CanLII 1021 (ON LA) (Reville). See the discussion of seniority rights in Chapter 1.

pretations of Schedule D exist, the interpretation that avoids placement on Schedule D is to be preferred.

Employees that fall under Schedule D are entitled to all job security rights available to surplus employees including targeted direct assignment, displacement rights and pay in lieu, severance pay, and enhanced severance pay.

Seniority-based job competition and layoff entitlements have been found to constitute "core protections" that the parties intended to preserve in Appendix 18.[78] In transfers effected under either Schedule A[79] or Schedule C,[80] such seniority rights are to be carried over to the new employer. Transfers under Schedule A must ensure that the new employer agrees to a "relative equality" clause for job competitions and a "last-in, first-out" layoff clause as long as the more senior person is able to do the job.[81] Presumably, the same extent of seniority protection is required for transfers under Schedule C.[82] The "end-tailing" of seniority lists is not permissible under a Schedule C transfer.[83] "End-tailing" occurs when two groups of employees are combined by adding the seniority list of one group to the bottom of the seniority list of the other group. It contrasts with "dove-tailing," where the seniority of all employees is on a combined basis.

On the other hand, Appendix 18 does not oblige a new service provider to provide a seniority and layoff system equivalent to that which exists in the OPS. What is required, at least for the purposes of a transfer under Schedule B, is that the affected employees be able to use their OPS seniority within the new service provider's existing layoff provisions.[84]

There are specific time limits for some Appendix 18 grievances.[85] Grievances filed pursuant to Appendix 18, Article 8 are subject to

---

78 *Community and Social Services*, GSB#0447/00, 21 March 2001 (Leighton) at 8 [*Community, March 2001 (Leighton)*].

79 *Community, December 2000 (Leighton)*, above note 70.

80 *OPSEU (Union) and Ministry of the Solicitor General and Correctional Services*, GSB#1252/00, 28 March 2001 (Brown).

81 *Community, March 2001 (Leighton)*, above note 78 at 8.

82 *OPSEU (Union) and Ministry of Health*, GSB#1615/99, 31 January 2000 (Brown).

83 *Ibid* at 18.

84 *Ibid.*

85 *OPSEU (Union) and Ministry of Health and Long-Term Care*, GSB#337/03, 8 March 2004 (Petryshen) at 4 [*Health, March 2004 (Petryshen)*]; *OPSEU (Union) and Ministry of Energy*, GSB#4112/03, 3 May 2004 (Brown) at 5 [*OPSEU (Union) and Ministry of Energy*].

extremely tight time frames;[86] while Appendix 18, Article 4.2 grievances are subject to the collective agreement's standard time frames.[87] Where the essence of a grievance relates to the schedule to which the transfer has been assigned, the sufficiency of a transfer agreement or an RFP and/or the adequacy of the efforts made by the employer in negotiating a transfer agreement, then the more restrictive time limits under Article 8 are applicable.[88] This reflects the employer's desire to avoid having transfers delayed by interim relief orders. However, these time limits are arguably impossibly short and may require practical adjustment by the parties.[89] Where a grievance relates to the contents of job offers made by a new service provider, the standard longer time limits in Article 4.2 are applicable.[90] The authority granted to the GSB under the *LRA*[91] to extend the time "for taking any step in the grievance procedure" is applicable to the time limits in Article 8 and the GSB possesses the authority to extend the time limits in appropriate circumstances.[92]

Turning to severance and termination pay entitlements, employees who accept job offers under the Appendix 18 or refuse "good job offers," which are offers at wages of at least 85 percent of their OPS wage, with recognition of their OPS seniority, are limited to getting only the severance pay they would be entitled to under Article 53 or 78.[93] For purposes of Article 53 or 78, a deemed resignation under the reasonable efforts provisions is not a "voluntary resignation."[94]

---

86 The *OPSEU/MBC Unified and Correctional Collective Agreements*, above note 4, Appendix 18, Art 8.2, requires that grievances relating to Art 5.0 or Art 6C.0 "must be *resolved* 15 days prior to the closing of the tender" [emphasis added]. Article 8.3 and Art 8.4.2 also require that grievances filed thereunder must be fully resolved within a seven-day time frame. See *OPSEU (Union) and Ministry of Health and Long-Term Care*, GSB#1495/00, 24 January 2002 (Brown) at 13 [*Health, January 2002 (Brown)*].

87 *Health, March 2004 (Petryshen)*, above note 85 at 4.

88 *Health, January 2002 (Brown)*, above note 86 at 5–11; *OPSEU (Union) and Ministry of Energy*, above note 85 at 10–11.

89 *Canada, 2014 (Briggs)*, above note 74 at 42.

90 *OPSEU (Union) and Ministry of Energy*, above note 85 at 13.

91 *LRA*, above note 8, s 48(16).

92 *Health, January 2002 (Brown)*, above note 86 at 10 and 14.

93 *Ontario Public Service Employees Union (Bye et al) v Ontario (Ministry of Health and Long-Term Care)*, 2003 CanLII 52882 (ON GSB).

94 *Ontario Public Service Employees Union v Ontario (Ministry of Revenue)*, 2010 CanLII 72682 (ON GSB).

Employees who opt out of tenders or RFPs under Schedules A and C get pay in lieu, severance pay, and enhanced severance pay, but not displacement rights. Employees who do not get a good job offer under Schedule B are entitled to the normal surplus options available under the collective agreement. As mentioned, employees under Schedule D are entitled to all severance and termination entitlements available to surplus employees.

Employees who are deemed to have resigned under Appendix 18 for purposes of the collective agreement are not, as a result of that deeming, considered to have resigned for purposes of the termination and severance provisions of the *Employment Standards Act*.[95]

Under Appendix 18 and the analogous provisions in the AMAPCEO and PEGO collective agreements, the employees displaced by a transfer made by tender or RFP have the right to submit bids to be the new service provider on the same basis as other bidders.[96]

F. SURPLUS EMPLOYEE RIGHTS, AKA "JOB SECURITY": SEPARATION PAYMENTS AND REDEPLOYMENT WITHIN GOVERNMENT

1) Introduction

In the OPS, the employer has the right to eliminate positions. The *PSOA* permits such an action, and the OPS collective agreements do not include any provision that prevents it. The two OPSEU bargaining units, Unified and Correctional, are treated as a single unit for purposes of redeployment and displacement.[97]

All three unions' collective agreements provide that an employee proposed to be laid off is entitled to notice and the opportunity to elect compensated separation from employment, or access to collective agreement rights to a reskilling opportunity, or, within the same or similar

95 *Ontario Public Service Employees Union v Ontario (Ministry of Health and Long-Term Care)*, 2003 CanLII 52878 (ON GSB). See also SO 2000, c 41, Part XV [*ESA*].

96 *OPSEU/MBC Unified and Correctional Collective Agreements*, above note 4, Appendix 18, Art 2.2.2; *AMAPCEO/MBC Collective Agreement*, above note 45, Art 27.18.2.5(3); *PEGO/MBC Collective Agreement*, above note 45, Appendix A, Art 2.4.

97 The unique nature of the OPSEU units, and their "permeability" for purposes of job security, is discussed in Chapter 8.

classification, to redeploy into a vacant position or to displace a junior employee. These rights, colloquially known as "job security" rights, provide a degree of employee protection against non-disciplinary job loss.

The position being abolished may or may not have an incumbent, or person "assigned" to the job. When the position does not have an incumbent, neither the *PSOA* nor the relevant collective agreements contain any specific rights to challenge any aspect of the employer's decision to eliminate the position. If an employee occupies the abolished position, the first question is whether the layoff is bona fide for one of the permitted reasons under the *PSOA* and not an unreasonable exercise of management rights,[98] disguised discipline, discrimination, or creates a health and safety violation.[99] The *PSOA* only permits layoffs for listed reasons.[100] Those reasons, and the less extensive layoff process for non-unionized public servants, which does not include seniority-based entitlements, are discussed in Chapter 3. The remainder of this section deals with the bona fide layoff of unionized public servants and, more specifically, with the layoff entitlements found in the OPSEU/MBC collective agreements and related entitlements, which have been the subject of significant litigation at the GSB. The AMAPCEO provisions have been subject to very limited litigation but are well explained in AMAPCEO Fact Sheets.[101]

These redeployment provisions are complicated and challenging to understand and apply. The complexity of the provisions is further compounded for laid-off OPSEU employees because time frames for making major decisions are limited, and the impact of those decisions can be significant.[102] To assist the employees with the decisions they must make, the employer has prepared interpretive bulletins and a standardized redeployment package, which is provided at least six working days[103]

---

98 The limited ability of unionized employees to contest the bona fides of a layoff is discussed in the Chapter 10 section on the reasonable exercise of management rights.

99 *OPSEU (Union) and Ministry of Community and Social Services*, GSB#588/01, 9 January 2005 (Johnson).

100 *PSOA*, above note 14, s 39.

101 AMAPCEO, online: http://www.amapceo.on.ca/OPS/surplussing. See also fact sheets on Reskilling, Targeted Direct Assignment and Bumping, Transition Exit Initiative, Voluntary Exit Option, Voluntary Exit Registry.

102 See "Pre-surplus Notice" section below.

103 As required by *OPSEU/MBC Unified and Correctional Collective Agreements*, above note 4, Art 20.1.2.1.

prior to the issuance of an individual's surplus notice. In addition, the parties can meet locally and at the ministry level to plan and develop supports in advance of the pending surplussing. There is also a subcommittee of the Central Employee Relations Committee (CERC) and the Joint Employment Stability Subcommittee with the mandate to review layoffs of fifty or more employees in a ministry.

2) Basic Entitlements of Different Types of Public Servants

For full-time OPSEU-represented regular employees, the layoff process and entitlements are set out in the OPSEU/MBC collective agreements, Articles 20 and 53, as modified by Appendices 9, 10, 13, 17, and 18, and Article 19. For part-time regular employees, Article 62 further modifies these provisions. For fixed-term employees, the termination payment and limited redeployment entitlements are found in Articles 31 through 34. For probationary regular employees, Article 20.12 applies.

The focus of this section is on full-time regular employees.

3) History of OPSEU/MBC "Job Security" Provisions

Most of the current provisions were put into place in 1996 following the first OPSEU strike, in which job security was a central issue due to downsizing and divestment agenda of the then recently elected Progressive Conservative government.[104] The former entitlement of an employee whose position was abolished to receive a guaranteed job offer in the OPS was replaced with enhanced severance and redeployment rights plus the obligation of the employer under Appendix 9 section 1 to make "reasonable efforts" to have employees divested from the OPS receive comparable terms of employment with the new employer.[105] When the 1 January 1994 to 31 December 1998 collective agreement took effect, Article 20, titled "Employment Stability," replaced the former Article 24, titled "Job Security." The Article 20 rights described below are those still in effect as of date of writing.

---

104 For a partisan account see David Rapaport, *No Justice, No Peace: The 1996 OPSEU Strike Against the Harris Government in Ontario* (Montreal and Kingston: McGill-Queen's University Press, 1999).

105 See the discussion of reasonable efforts above.

The current agreement states that "[f]or purposes of Article 20, lay-off means the same as release per Section 39 of the *Public Service of Ontario Act, 2006*."[106] This reinforces the entitlement to only be released or laid off for the reasons set out in *PSOA* section 39. The agreement also states that "[w]here a lay-off may occur *for any reason*" the identification of a surplus employee shall be by seniority,[107] but this does not mean that OPSEU-represented employees have forfeited the protection of the *PSOA* section 39 limitation on the allowable reasons for layoff. The broader language is intended to address the introduction of the additional job security protections into the collective agreement, as they may result in the consequential layoff of an employee other than the surplussed employee.

4) Relocation or Divestment/Contracting Out or Elimination of Position: Whether Appendix 13 or Appendices 9 or 18 Apply

In determining which provisions of the collective agreement apply when a position occupied by a regular incumbent ceases to exist in the OPS, it is useful to first determine if the position is being relocated, divested/contracted out, or eliminated. Appendix 13 addresses the relocation of positions within the public service. In the event of divestment/contracting out, Appendix 18 applies, as dealt with in the "reasonable efforts" section of this chapter. Article 20 applies if a position is being eliminated.

5) Appendix 13: Relocation of an Operation Beyond a Forty-Kilometre Radius

Appendix 13 applies "when a ministry decides to change the operation's headquarters to a location outside a forty (40) kilometer radius of that operation's current headquarters." The Appendix sets out the extent of the employee right to relocate with their position and be eligible for relocation expenses. It also provides that employees who reject the change in headquarters will have full access to the redeployment provisions.[108] However, the employer is not required to accept more

106 *OPSEU/MBC Unified and Correctional Collective Agreements*, above note 4, Art 20.17.2.

107 *Ibid*, Art 20.1.1 [emphasis added].

108 *OPSEU/MBC Unified and Correctional Collective Agreements*, above note 4, Appendix 13, Art 2(b). The change in an operation's headquarters does not trigger

employees at the new headquarters than there are positions available. The positions will be offered first to the most senior employees.

In order for an employee to have Appendix 13 rights, both of the following criteria need to be met. First, the operation's headquarters must be relocating to a new OPS headquarters. Second, the position(s) at the new location must be similar enough in content to be deemed to be the employee's position.

The "headquarters" of an operation is the headquarters of the employees employed in or in respect of that operation.[109] This suggests that the move that triggers the application of Appendix 13 is the movement of the place of work of a number of employees, rather than the relocation or rearrangement of the management structure. A change in "the location for productive activity" will trigger the article.[110] However, the work at the new location must be a continuation of the work previously done. This requires a close, although not absolutely identical, match. There must be an "identity or continuity" of "purposes and work methods."[111]

Once the transfer triggers the right, the application of the Appendix is not negated by a subsequent discontinuance of the work at the new location. The question is not how long the work will last at the new location, but only whether the necessary work is being done at the new location after the move occurs.[112]

The work must be within the OPS at the new location at the time the transfer occurs in order for Appendix 13 to apply. Appendix 13

---

redeployment provisions for the affected employees or the new positions where, in accordance with Art 3 of Appendix 13, affected employees are offered and accept the opportunity to go to the new headquarters location. Decisions of the GSB determining the number of positions at the new headquarters to be offered do not take into account the redeployment rights of other employees: *OPSEU (Union) Ministry of Solicitor General and Correctional Services*, GSB#1154/98, 18 May 2000 and 24 January 2001 (Leighton); *OPSEU (Kerhanovich/Behrsin) and Ministry of Transportation*, GSB#2776/96, 18 May 2000 (Gray) [*Kerhanovich/Behrsin*]. Positions which are vacant after the application of Appendix 13 are available for Art 20.5 redeployment.

109 *Kerhanovich/Behrsin*, *ibid* at 17.

110 In *OPSEU (Union) and the Ministry of the Solicitor General and Correctional Services*, GSB#1154/98, 18 May 2000 (Leighton) at 8 and 10, an award dealing with the closure of three jails and transfer of work to other jails, the GSB found that the employer was required to apply the provisions of Appendix 13.

111 *Kerhanovich/Behrsin*, above note 108 at 18.

112 *Ibid* at 20.

has been found not to apply to employees whose work is privatized.[113] This means that employees claiming divested jobs must bear any cost of relocating. Where the union argued that the lack of relocation allowances for divested employees resulted in a gap in protection, the GSB held that the decision whether to fill the gap was a matter for the parties to negotiate.[114]

Appendix 13 does not set out a minimum number of affected employees needed to meet the definition of an operation, and it has been applied to a single incumbent.[115] Where more employees elect to be relocated than there are available positions in the new headquarters, the least senior employees will be laid off[116] and have full access to the redeployment provisions. It is not necessary that all of the work being done at one location move to another location in order for Appendix 13 to apply.

6) Whether the Application of Article 20, the Job Security Article, Is Triggered

a) Required Degree of Change to a Position

Once it has been determined that the surplussing is not covered by Appendices 13 or 9 and 18, it is still not certain that Article 20 will apply. In addition to the previously discussed obligation that the layoff itself be bona fide and not a disguised dismissal, there is the requirement that the degree of change to the position be sufficient to constitute a layoff. The dynamic nature of work in the OPS produces the consistent challenge of deciding if, in fact, the workplace change amounts to the abolition of the current position. Obviously, the complete elimination of the job in question will trigger the application of Article 20. More contentious circumstances arise when some aspects of the work continue to be performed in the OPS, but there are significant changes in either duties or location. A sufficiently significant change in either may trigger the application of Article 20.

There is no language in Article 20, or elsewhere in the collective agreement, that defines when a change in duties warrants reclassification

---

113 *OPSEU (Union) and Ministry of the Solicitor General and Correctional Services*, GSB#1252/00, 8 February 2001 (Brown).

114 *Ibid*.

115 *Kerbanovich/Behrsin*, above note 108.

116 *OPSEU/MBC Unified and Correctional Collective Agreements*, above note 4, Appendix 13, Art (3).

of a position rather than its deemed abolition.[117] The practice in the OPS is that, if the purpose of the position remains unchanged, changes made to the duties and responsibilities normally result in the evolution and possible reclassification of the position rather than its abolition. An early decision of the GSB found that a reassignment of 30 percent of the duties warranted the abolition of the position.[118] This remains the common approach of the parties. The parties have generally been successful, when addressing duty changes, in avoiding disputes about the applicability of Article 20. The reassignment of a position to another ministry does not activate the layoff provisions, whether or not the employees would prefer to decline transfer to that other ministry in favour of accessing the redeployment provisions.[119] An organizational change in the reporting relationship does not, by itself, warrant the abolition of a position.[120]

There is a fact-specific and somewhat vague determination that must be made about whether the change in location is sufficiently great to constitute the abolition, versus relocation, of the position. According to the current leading case, *Kerhanovich/Behrsin*, the determination is dependent on whether the employee is required to move out of the position's functional "work area."[121]

b) Likelihood of Layoff: Whether It "May Occur"

There can be uncertainty about when plans are firm enough to warrant the commencement of the application of Article 20.[122] The term "may occur" in Article 20.1.1 determines the degree of certainty needed to require the employer to identify the surplus employee and commence the application of the employment stability provisions of Article 20 and/or the applicable Appendices. Given the extensive procedure involved in

---

117 The other article in the *OPSEU/MBC Unified and Correctional Collective Agreements*, above note 4, concerned with the degree of change required to trigger an entitlement is Art 7, Pay Administration. Article 7.1 covers pay treatment for employee movement to a higher classification.

118 *OPSEU (Skinner) and Ministry of Industry and Tourism*, GSB#226/79, 10 November 1981 (Ellis) at 6, aff'd, *Ontario v Ontario Public Service Employees Union*, [1983] OJ No 1068 (Div Ct).

119 *OPSEU (Babb et al) and Ministry of Community and Social Services*, GSB#1173/88, 8 August 1990 at 18–19.

120 *Kerhanovich/Behrsin*, above note 108.

121 *Ibid* at 16.

122 There have been announced, but unimplemented, plans that would have resulted in layoffs. For example, annual Ministry Business Plans have contained divestments that have not materialized.

applying Article 20, the application of the article will only be triggered by a "clear likelihood" that the layoff will occur, the mere possibility being insufficient.[123] It is not in the interests of either employees or the employer to have individuals surplussed, only to subsequently learn that the work of a unit would continue, or that, after a reorganization, there was a continuing need for more incumbents than originally anticipated.

Employer surplussing decisions have been left intact even when it was subsequently shown that an excessive number of employees were surplussed,[124] or that the layoff was somewhat premature.[125] Employees will be able to exercise all their seniority-based rights up to the point when the surplus assignment actually takes effect.[126] If an employee, having been surplussed in a bona fide release, is assigned or alternatively accepts a severance package and exits the OPS, there is no right to be reassigned back into their former position, even if it should subsequently be found to still exist. However, if a surplussed employee is still available for Article 20.5 assignment into a vacancy, they should perhaps have the first opportunity to be reassigned into the former position once it is recognized as not being truly redundant.

The parties have met to establish redeployment protocols for numerous circumstances where operations were downsized over extended periods of time. Leading examples are the protocols dealing with the multiple closures of correctional facilities[127] and the 2005 agreement to

---

123 *OPSEU (Union) and Ministry of Community and Social Services*, GSB#2507/86, 26 August 1988 (Samuels) at 8, followed in *OPSEU (Barnes/Forsythe/Mercer) and Ministry of Community and Social Services*, GSB#1259/89, 28 February 1991 (Dissanayake) at 7–8 [*Barnes/Forsythe/Mercer*].

124 *OPSEU (Whiteside/Stewart et al) and the Ministry of Health*, GSB#330/92, 1 June 1993 (Kaplan) [*Whiteside/Stewart*]; *OPSEU (Beatty et al) and the Ministry of Transportation*, GSB#1135/93, 8 March 1996 (Kaplan) [*Beatty*]; *OPSEU (Radford) and the Ministry of Natural Resources*, GSB#1426/96, 12 June 1997 (Knopf) [*Radford*]; *OPSEU (Pilon et al) and Ministry of Community and Social Services*, GSB#1254/99, 5 November 2001, and 2 June 2003 (Brown).

125 *OPSEU (Tran) and Ministry of Consumer and Commercial Relations*, GSB #1860/96, 25 February 1998 (Kaufman).

126 *Whiteside/Stewart*, above note 124 at 32–33.

127 As discussed in *OPSEU (Union) and Ministry of Community Safety and Correctional Services*, GSB#2002-2095, 24 February 2004 (Briggs) at 2. See *OPSEU (O'Toole et al) and Ministry of Correctional Services*, GSB#1790/00, 26 March 2003 (Briggs). More than forty decisions about these agreements were issued by Vice-Chair Briggs. See the discussion in Chapter 11 re the GSB and corrections mediation.

establish a reasonable efforts committee with respect to the expected closure of three developmental services facilities.[128] The main purpose of these protocols was to allow the ministry to continue staffing during the transition to a smaller workforce while providing the affected employees with staged access to the redeployment benefits.

c) Selection of Employees: By Seniority Within "Administrative District or Unit . . . or Other Such Work Area"

Article 20.1.2.1 of the OPSEU/MBC collective agreements defines the boundary or area of search within which seniority is compared for purposes of selecting which employee is to be laid off when a position is abolished. The phrase "in an administrative district or unit, and other such work area" is used. The employer has significant discretion in defining an administrative unit so that it goes beyond the physical location of a work site to include such units as a region[129] or a branch.[130] A ministry is permitted to look beyond the confines of a particular workplace even where the workplaces of the appropriate organizational unit are more than forty kilometres apart. At the same time, management has been permitted to define an administrative unit more narrowly as one of three offices, despite the common supervision and near proximity of the three offices.[131] The employer must only reach a reasonable determination about organizational structure when determining the administrative district or work area to use when identifying the least senior employee to be surplussed.

7) Reskilling Appendix

In the OPSEU/MBC Collective Agreements, the parties enhanced the job security provisions by providing the opportunity for an employee to accept an employer identified job outside their classification prior to the

---

128 *OPSEU/MBC Collective Agreement, 2005–2008*, Appendix 36, removed from the current *OPSEU/MBC Unified and Correctional Collective Agreements*, above note 4.

129 *OPSEU (Parayankuzhiyil) and Management Board Secretariat*, GSB#2385/95, 28 October 1997 (Verity).

130 *OPSEU (Paul) and Ministry of Natural Resources*, GSB#2295/92, 6 October 1995 (Stewart).

131 *OPSEU (Laurin/Joly) and Ministry Tourism & Recreation*, GSB#1759/90, 30 October 1991 (Verity).

employee activating their rights under Article 20.[132] Appendix 66 provides that "during organizational transformation" it is in the interests of both parties for opportunities across the OPS to be created for the purposes of reskilling employees since this leads to increased employment stability as well as expanded opportunities for reassignment with the OPS and job retention" and recognizes that "employees who face job loss due to organizational transformation shall be given priority over employees who do not." A Joint Transition and Reskilling Committee is created which may include representatives from the applicable ministry. The *AMAPCEO/Treasury Board Secretariat Memorandum of Agreement on Reskilling* is similar to OPSEU's agreement with regard to committee mandates and intent to initiate retraining activities prior to deciding if actual surplussing is required.[133]

For employees "affected" by the organizational transformation, where the employer can identify a direct assignment including reskilling and training, the employee has six days to respond. If the employee takes the assignment, there is a three-month period in the job, which may include any retraining, "during or following the employment-related retraining, to allow for an assessment to be made regarding the qualifications and suitability of the employee for the assigned position."[134] If the employee is not qualified to perform the work, they are entitled to commence their Article 20 rights.

8) Pre-surplus Notice (Article 20.1.2.1)

The OPSEU/MBC Collective Agreements include a requirement for written pre-notice of surplus by the employer and an election by the about-to-be-surplussed employee. Article 20.1.2.1 provides that not less than six working days prior to receiving the notice of layoff an employee will be provided with the opportunity either to elect compensated separation from employment, or to access the full collective agreement rights to be redeployed into a vacant position, or to displace a junior employee.

---

132 *Memorandum of Agreement re Employee Reskilling and Transition*, signed on ratification, and incorporated in *OPSEU/MBC Unified and Correctional Collective Agreements*, above note 4, appended to Appendix 66 [*OPSEU MoA Reskilling*].

133 *AMAPCEO/Treasury Board Secretariat, Memorandum of Agreement—Reskilling (OPS)*, 13 July 2020, online: https://amapceo.on.ca/ops.

134 *OPSEU MoA Reskilling*, above note 132, Article 5.1.

Pre-surplus employees who fail to make an election are included in the full redeployment process excluding displacement. (The employee who receives a pre-surplus notice but does not initially elect compensated separation may request the remaining pay in lieu and the separation allowance at any time during the subsequent six-month notice period, provided only that the redeployment assignment match has not been made.)

Removing employees who prefer to exit the OPS with a monetary package from the redeployment process during the pre-surplus period increases the likelihood of matching the remaining surplus employees to vacancies or displacement opportunities. The same benefit exists for the remaining employees if, during the pre-surplus period, an employee elects to take advantage of a pension option.

It is particularly important to maximize the range of opportunities for those who choose redeployment within the OPS because their relative seniority is of limited use. The employer only has to match the surplussed senior employee to one less senior non-surplussed employee.[135] If the matched senior employee then elects not to displace the junior employee, and instead picks a severance option, the matched junior potential displacee is not subject to displacement by any other more senior surplus employee during the round of displacement matching. This results in job retention of junior employees while more senior employees may be laid off due to the absence of a junior employee to match with them during the original matching process. Further, junior employees keep their current jobs while more senior employees working in the same workplace may have to relocate at their own expense to retain employment because their one displacement or vacancy match was located in another workplace.

An employee who is displaced, in accordance with Article 20.4, in the first or second matching round,[136] can in turn displace a junior employee because, for each of these rounds, the pool of potential displacees is re-established.

---

135 *OPSEU (Union) and the Ministry of Natural Resources and Management Board Secretariat*, GSB#318/96, 17 June 1996 (Briggs) [*Natural Resources, June 1996 (Briggs)*], interpreting the *OPSEU/MBC Unified and Correctional Collective Agreements*, above note 4, Art 20.4.1.8, which state: "No later than one (1) week following commencement of the notice period, the employer will advise the surplus employee of the position into which he or she is eligible to displace."

136 *OPSEU/MBC Unified and Correctional Collective Agreements*, above note 4, Art 20.4.1.2.

a) Employee Portfolio

Before the six-working-day pre-election window, the employee is provided with a document titled "Employee Portfolio." The portfolio is to be completed and returned to the ministry if the employee wishes to access the employment or redeployment provisions. Employees are to identify their skills and experience, and the employer uses this information to match employees to positions. The employer can do the matching because each vacant position has a job information package, provided by the ministry, that identifies what skills/qualifications are necessary and which of two established levels (functional or advanced) are required for the position. The employee is requested to identify, in the employee portfolio, geographic locations to which they are prepared to be assigned (in accordance with Article 20.3.2), and the employer is obliged to give consideration to the vacancies within forty kilometres. The employee can amend the requested search area of the portfolio, along with the other sections at any time including during the notice period. No later than five days after it is amended and submitted, the revised employee portfolio is deemed to be effective. Appendix 40 of the collective agreement provides that, where fifty or more employees are threatened to be surplussed, the employer will provide ministry-level training on completing the portfolios.

If the employer identifies a vacant position that matches the employee requirements in an identified area, the employee cannot decline the match in favour of further vacancy searching or in favour of the Article 20.2 and Appendix 9, paragraph 4 exit monies. The rejection of a vacancy match to a location identified in the employee portfolio after the ten-day notice period is treated the same, for purposes of further redeployment disentitlement, as a match to a vacancy within forty kilometres after the pre-notice period.

9) Entitlements Following Pre-notice: Separation Payments or Redeployment

By virtue of Article 20.1.2. of the *OPSEU/MBC Collective Agreement*, the two choices of the employee in receipt of pre-notice are compensated separation from employment or redeployment (which may include displacement of another employee).

a) Separation Payment: Notice and Pay in Lieu (Article 20.2) and Severance Allowance (Appendix 9, Paragraph 4)

Article 20.2.1.3 of the collective agreement stipulates that the employee receives the six months' notice contemplated by the *Public Service Commission, Employment Policy*,[137] or "with mutual consent" the employee may resign immediately and receive the equivalent pay in lieu of notice. By electing to request pay in lieu during the ten-day notice period, the employee is forfeiting their right to access the redeployment provisions. An employee who makes this choice also receives a severance allowance under Appendix 9, paragraph 4. The only employment right that remains during the six months, for an employee who elects to receive these payments, is the limited right to apply for vacant positions, including those otherwise restricted to current employees of the OPS.

This initial right to exit exists notwithstanding that there may be a comparable and immediately available position to which the employer would want to assign the employee. An employee who accepts pay in lieu of notice at the beginning of the notice period receives the whole six months' pay in one payment, but forfeits the six months' benefits and pensionable service.

An employee can elect to work out the six months' notice. It is accepted by the parties that the employee can be assigned reasonable alternate work for all or part of the six months, and/or remain away from work for the balance while drawing pensionable wages and benefits. An employee in that position may also accept the remaining pay in lieu at any time during the six-month notice period.[138] This means that the employee can elect to have the employer do the search for a vacancy or displacement match, then subsequently request pay in lieu if not initially successful in being matched.

As noted previously, an employee who elects to be redeployed and is matched to a vacancy within forty kilometres, or to a vacancy in a location identified in the employee portfolio, then loses, along with further redeployment rights, all entitlement to the pay in lieu and Appendix 9, paragraph 4. The loss of further Article 20 entitlements occurs whether

---

137 Public Service Commission, *Employment Policy* (2012), effective 6 November 2020, discussed in Chapter 2.

138 *OPSEU/MBC Unified and Correctional Collective Agreements*, above note 4, Art 20.2.1.3 read, in part, "Pay in lieu *for the balance of the notice period* shall only be granted where the Employer determines that operational requirements permit an employee's exit from the workplace prior to the expiration of six (6) months notice" [emphasis added].

or not the employee accepts the redeployment offered. If the assignment is refused, the employee is deemed to have quit, and only the regular Article 53 resignation payment is available. A displacement match can be declined without affecting the surplus employee's severance entitlements or assignment to a vacancy right, but acceptance of such a match ends these rights.

Article 20.2 does not appear to provide for a notice period longer than six months. However, the employer may decide on layoffs that will occur more than six months in the future and, since the GSB has decided that the employer is required to initiate Article 20 provisions when there is "a real likelihood"[139] that positions would be abolished, a question arises: what rights do ministries and surplus employees have when it is reasonably clear that a layoff will occur, but it is projected that the effective date is more than six months away?

As noted previously in this section, the parties have negotiated protocols for situations where workplaces are acknowledged to be winding down over a period of time. Surplus employees are given temporary assignments to, and may be recalled to, the positions from which they were surplussed. However, there is no obligation or right to provide a notice period of greater than six months. Even if the work continues, and remains characterized as temporary, such that there is access to the Article 20.8 "temporary vacancy" provisions,[140] there is no other collective agreement provision that permits a surplussed employee to continue in their previous position beyond the six-month time frame.

Employees who access the pay in lieu and separation payment provisions have a limited right to apply for internal vacancies that would otherwise be restricted to individuals actively employed in the OPS;[141] but this right is truncated. The GSB's standard of review of a job competition for a surplus employee who applies to a restricted job competition is only "good faith," and not correctness, and so is similar to that of a fixed-term employee exercising job competition rights.[142]

139 *Barnes/Forsythe/Mercer*, above note 123 at 9.

140 *OPSEU/MBC Unified and Correctional Collective Agreements*, above note 4, Art 20.8 (Temporary Vacancies).

141 Part of Art 20.2.3 reads: "The employee will be eligible to apply for restricted competitions from the last day of work until twenty-four (24) months from the date on which lay-off would otherwise have occurred."

142 See *OPSEU (Union) and Management Board Secretariat*, GSB#0405/99, 8 May 2001 (Abramsky) at 18 and the discussion about job competitions rights for surplus and fixed-term employees in Chapter 10.

Where an employee has accepted pay in lieu, and is subsequently reappointed to the OPS, Articles 20.2.4 and 20.2.5 establish the extent of the obligation to repay pay in lieu, separation allowance, and severance money. The employer reserves the right to require that repayments be gross, pre-deduction amounts and paid in full before the former employee can return to work. To date, there have been no GSB decisions on whether this position is unreasonable for the individual seeking re-employment. The repayment obligation applies even if the reappointment is to fixed-term service.[143]

i) Employment Standards Act, 2000 *Rights*

The *Employment Standards Act, 2000* (*ESA*) severance pay and termination pay provisions[144] apply to all employees, including those covered by collective agreements, and, where the *ESA* provides a greater entitlement than the collective agreement, the *ESA* governs.[145] While the general application of the *ESA* is discussed elsewhere in this book, one aspect is addressed here. The termination and severance pay contained in the redeployment provisions of Article 53 of the *OPSEU/MBC Collective Agreement* provides termination and severance pay that generally exceed those of the *ESA* for full-time and part-time regular OPSEU employees,[146] and, accordingly, the collective agreement normally applies. However, in rare instances, the *ESA*'s severance pay provisions, as distinguished from the termination pay provisions, exceed those of the collective agreement. This anomaly occurs in the severance pay of regular employees who have accumulated significant prior service as fixed-term employees. The collective agreement's seniority article does not use a calendar-based calculation of seniority, and instead employs an hours-based formula that compresses the length of service of former fixed-term employees in calculating the regular seniority date used for

143 *OPSEU (Union) and Management Board Secretariat*, GSB#459/96, 15 July 1996 (Briggs). *Ontario Public Service Employees Union (Pereira) v Ontario (Ministry of Community and Social Services)*, 2005 CanLII 55139 (ON GSB) (Leighton) reiterates the earlier decision.

144 *ESA*, above note 95.

145 *OPSEU v Ontario (Ministry of Health and Long-Term Care) (Severance Pay Grievance)*, [2003] OGSBA No 40 (Brown) at paras 10–12, where the GSB found, relying on s 5 of the *ESA*, that in the absence of a greater benefit, the deemed resignation provisions in the collective agreement cannot prevail over the employment standard governing termination and severance.

146 *ESA*, above note 144, Part XV, Termination and Severance of Employment.

determining severance pay.[147] By contrast, the *ESA* severance entitlement provisions are based on commencement of employment, which is generally the initial date of hire into the fixed-term service.[148]

b) Redeployment

i) Overview

There is a precise and mandatory order in which the steps of the redeployment articles are to be implemented. As discussed above, the initial entitlement of an employee on the abolition of their position is to take a severance package and exit. The right to immediate exit with a full severance package ceases to exist upon the offer of viable vacancy or upon the acceptance of a displacement opportunity.

If the employee elects to remain available for redeployment or does not provide a written election, the employer's initial search will be for placement through a voluntary exit match. This involves identifying an employee who wishes to voluntarily exit in return for separation payments, and then placing the surplussed employee in that position. If there is no voluntary exit match available, the next possibility to be canvassed will be a vacancy match. The employee is to be offered one placement in a vacancy.[149] Surplus employees who decide, in accordance with Article 20.1.3.2 or 20.1.3.3, to remain employed during the six-month notice period and who elected during the pre-surplus notice period to be considered for displacement, have the right at the beginning of the sixth month of the notice period to be offered no more than one opportunity to displace a junior employee. The displacement match will be identified in accordance with Article 20.4. The employer will advise the employee of the match and the employee has one week to accept.

If a displacement match is declined or no displacement offer can be made, the search for a vacancy placement will continue until either one offer is made or the employee resigns with a severance package or is laid off at the end of the notice period.

The right to displacement is primarily within the home ministry, first to positions within forty kilometres and if none are available then

147 *OPSEU/MBC Unified and Correctional Collective Agreements*, above note 4, Art 18.1.1 (b).

148 *ESA*, above note 144, s 65(2).

149 *OPSEU/MBC Unified and Correctional Collective Agreements*, above note 4, Art 20.3.1.1.

to positions beyond forty kilometres. Thereafter, the search extends to other ministries within forty kilometres. The employee can elect to forgo the search for displacement or placement opportunities beyond forty kilometres. There is no right to be assigned a displacement in another ministry that is beyond forty kilometres. Following lack of placement or displacement, the employee is eligible for conditional assignment to a vacancy for which the employee is likely to become qualified by retraining. This defined sequence of steps for redeployment applies even where it is clearly the employee's preference, or to the employee's advantage, to forgo a particular placement or displacement.[150]

During the notice period, the employee also retains the right under Article 6 to apply for positions that are outside of the redeployment parameters of Article 20. Finally, if no other redeployment occurs, the employee will have either recall rights for twenty-four months under Article 20.6 or the right to apply to restricted competitions for more than twenty-four months under Article 20.2.3.

Within each redeployment step, there is no collective agreement provision that determines the sequence of determining which surplus employee will get which of a number of the potential viable matches. However, where there is more than one match in a particular step for more than one surplus employee, the matching is done sequentially starting with the most senior employee.

The GSB has noted that the application and interaction of the various redeployment provisions of the collective agreement is complicated[151] and mandatory,[152] and that

> [t]here is an aspect of the "luck of the draw" as is patently evident on the facts of the instant Grievance . . . The wording of that Article does

---

150 *OPSEU (Read et al) and Ministry of Health*, GSB#1548/89, 14 December 1990 (Gorsky) [*Read*]; *OPSEU (Weeman) and Ontario Realty Corporation/Management Board Secretariat*, GSB#1963/95, 7 July 1999 (Finley) [*Weeman*].

151 *OPSEU (Becker) and Ministry of Transportation and Communications*, GSB#511/82, 16 May 1983 (Samuels) at 13. This case dealt with a grievor disputing her re-assignment following a surplussing. The grievor was seeking to be assigned to a vacancy in another ministry at her current classification level instead of being assigned to a vacancy within her home ministry at a lower classification level. The section of the award is quoted in *Read*, *ibid* at 17–18, and also in *OPSEU (Palangio) and Ministry of Transportation and Communications*, GSB#227/83, 7 March 1983 (Verity) at 9 [*Palangio*].

152 *Read*, above note 150 at 19, finding that the grievor had to decide whether to accept a matched vacancy and could not exercise a displacement right.

> not permit an employee to shop around for assignments . . . Simply stated, if an assignment is offered and refused, the employee is then subject to lay-off . . . The assignment provisions of surplus employees under that Article is not designed to provide an employee with a preferred job, or a choice among jobs, or even the same job. It is designed however, to provide a job with an element of salary protection through the device of the assignment and the red circling provisions.[153]

Where the ministry, acting in good faith, mistakenly surpluses the wrong employees, the placement or displacement process need not necessarily be undone.[154] The situations where specific employees are mistakenly surplussed incorrectly may occur when the ministry underestimates the volume of work that will be performed after the downsizing. However, the parties may agree to undo a mistaken placement or displacement.

Generally, in order to be reassigned to a job in the OPS, two conditions must be met:

1) the job must be deemed a viable and available position for placement or displacement purposes
2) the position must be one for which the surplus employee has the requisite level of qualification

The two following subsections contain more detailed descriptions of the order of the search for placement opportunities and the steps used to implement displacement rights. There is discussion of what will be deemed to be a viable position for inclusion in the process and what standard will be applied to the assessment of the individual surplus employee's qualifications and ability to take up a position.

ii) Placement Rights

As noted in the overview, the placement provisions are in place before and after the displacement rights.

A surplus employee is only entitled to be offered one permanent appointment. Seniority is given fullest effect when implementing the

153 *Palangio*, above note 151 at 9, ruling against an employee's claimed right to choose between placement assignments.

154 *Beatty*, above note 124; *Radford*, above note 124; *Whiteside*/Stewart, above note 124 where the grievors' positions or similar positions continued to receive long-term funding after the grievors were surplussed.

assignments within forty kilometres (home ministry first, then other ministry) in that the most senior employee is assigned to the closest vacancy. This pattern of correlating vacancy distance to seniority then continues for the assignments outside forty kilometres (home ministry first, then another ministry).

Under Article 20.4.1.6, the employee has the right to elect whether or not to be considered for vacancies beyond forty kilometres. Further, in the employee portfolio, the employee can identify in order of preference the locations outside of the forty-kilometre radius for which they would like to be considered. Although there is no collective agreement provision enshrining the order of preference, the employer has operationalized the order of consideration of employee preferences by starting with the employee portfolio of the most senior employee. If the employee has not indicated a preference, then the closest location of those selected will be used. Once the search has been exhausted for the most senior employee, the process is repeated for the second most senior, and so on. If there is more than one match to the preferred municipality, the location closest to the employee's current workplace will be selected.

iii) Displacement Rights

Article 20 provides that the displacement process is used only if a placement into a vacancy does not take place within the first five months.

During the displacement process, the surplus employee has the right to elect whether or not to bypass the displacement rights of Article 20.4.1.6 in favour of the sequential right to be considered for a match to a displacement in accordance with Article 20.4.1.7. The employee also retains the right to decline any proffered match in favour of placement rights or an exit package. The decision to accept or decline the displacement match has to be made within one week of being advised of the match and in the absence of any certainty as to what, if any, placement opportunity will subsequently be available.

The steps of the search for a viable displacement match involve, in the following order: the home ministry within a forty-kilometre radius; the home ministry beyond a forty-kilometre radius; and a former ministry within a forty-kilometre radius. Unlike the steps in the placement process, there is no final displacement sequence that includes a non-home ministry beyond a forty-kilometre radius. The surplus employee who elects to have the employer search for a displacement match in the home ministry outside of forty kilometres cannot then refuse an identified match in favour of a search for a displacement match in another ministry within forty kilometres.[155]

Although there is no collective agreement provision that sets out the mechanism for matching senior to less senior employees in the displacement process, the parties follow a GSB-sanctioned matching process that has come to be known as "the best bump of the day."[156] For surplussing exercises where there is more than one employee being laid off, the most senior displacer is matched with the most junior displacee. The second most senior displacer is then matched to the second most junior displacee and so on. This is the only displacement entitlement. This process of matching the most senior to the most junior is followed in each step of the displacement process. Accordingly, the most senior displacer displacing outside of forty kilometres is entitled to be assigned only to the position, including location, of the most junior displacee. This is the one match offered, even if the displacee works hundreds of kilometres away and there is a displacee being matched to a less senior displacer who works much closer. The impact of the process can be somewhat mitigated by the job-trading provisions of Article 10.3, which allow displaced employees, and other employees, to register with the ministry human resources branch to locate a job trade of mutual benefit between two employees. Portfolios are also used for matching job trades. There are no relocation expenses paid to displacing employees.

During the ranked displacement process, the point is arrived at where the next possible displacement is a less senior employee in the class with the maximum salary closest to, but not greater than, the maximum salary of the surplus employee's current classification. In interpreting the relevant article, the GSB has ruled that the employer is obliged to only consider *that one* classification.[157] This rule will apply even if there is no incumbent in the identified classification who could be displaced. The GSB has rejected the union's assertion that the employer should continue its review through descending classifications in the series, until a classification was found that had an incumbent

155 *OPSEU/MBC Unified and Correctional Collective Agreements*, above note 4, Art 20.4.1.7; *OPSEU (Union) and Management Board Secretariat*, GSB#484/96, 14 July 1996 (Briggs).

156 In *Natural Resources, June 1996 (Briggs)*, above note 135, the arbitrator found this method to be an acceptable part of the redeployment exercise.

157 *OPSEU (Penney) and Ministry of Natural Resources*, GSB#697/96, 13 March 1997 (Verity) at 11.

with less seniority than the surplus employee. In the GSB's view, that would add "an additional step not actually contained in the language of the provision."[158]

The employees who are displaced in the first or second round of a displacement exercise have full redeployment rights, including the rights to displace. Employees who are displaced in the third round of a displacement exercise have full redeployment rights, except for the right to displace. Where the displacing employee subsequently does not physically attend at the workplace to assume the position of the displaced employee, the displaced employee remains surplussed. Junior employees, who were tentatively matched, but not displaced, in a particular round of displacement, are available for matching in subsequent rounds of displacement.

iv) Viable Positions

Surplussed employees can be denied assignment into a position that is itself likely to be abolished. The GSB ruled that making such "job threatened" positions unavailable for displacement purposes is reasonable where surplus employees would use up bumping rights to take up positions that were immediately surplussed.[159] The GSB further determined that the word "position" can be taken to refer to a position of "reasonable permanence or stability." A six-month wait until abolition is too long to justify deeming the position as "job threatened" and the GSB recommended that the parties meet to set a more appropriate standard. The parties were subsequently unable to agree on precise criteria for deeming a position to be "job threatened," although they did agree that ministries are to advise if a position identified for displacement is expected to exist for less than six months.

Where the position in question is a term position, it is not "viable" or available for displacement. This can be so even where there is a

158 *Ibid* at 12. This ruling was confirmed in determining a group of identical, individual, Art 20 grievances filed against the Ministry of Transportation, which had limited its search to the Technician 1 Construction classification: *OPSEU (Selby) and Ministry of Transportation*, GSB#2600/96, 2 June 1999 (Abramsky); *OPSEU (Fink) and Ministry of Transportation*, GSB#2601/96, 2 June 1999 (Abramsky); *OPSEU (Furness) and Ministry of Transportation*, GSB#2683/96, 2 June 1999 (Abramsky).

159 *OPSEU (Union) and the Ministry of Transportation and Management Board Secretariat*, GSB #2670/96, 14 May 1997 (Roberts).

reasonable expectation that the position will become a regular position. The leading case concerns newly created multi-ministry information kiosks known as "common counters."[160] While initially a trial, they became permanent and, at the time of the grievance, had existed for more than one year, staffed by fixed-term employees. The union raised the concern that these permanent positions were not available to surplussed regular employees and instead could be offered to fixed-term staff. The GSB found that, absent any allegations of bad faith, there was no requirement to convert a fixed-term position to a regular position before the expiry of the conversion period.

v) *Qualifications and Ability*

The qualifications and ability of the laid-off employee are compared with the requirements of the position being assessed as a potential match for placement or displacement. This standard of "requisite" or needed ability does not involve a comparison of the "relative" qualifications and ability of the two individuals and is quite different from the process of comparing skill and ability that occurs in job competition grievances. The most senior surplus employees are entitled to exercise certain entitlements, provided they possess the following degrees of requisite ability in the following circumstances:

- For displacement, the ability to perform the work of the identified employee
- For redeployment and recall, being "qualified" to perform the required duties
- For the voluntary exit option, being able to perform the normal requirements of the position without training
- For conditional assignment, retraining will likely qualify the employee for the position

In the leading case of *OPSEU (Loebel) and Ministry of Municipal Affairs and Housing*,[161] "qualified" was interpreted to mean possessing the minimal qualifications needed to do the job. This remains the standard even though the collective agreement provision no longer uses the

160 *OPSEU (Union) and Management Board Secretariat*, GSB#0105/99, 27 September 2000 (Mikus) [*MBS, September 2000 (Mikus)*].

161 GSB#331/82, 15 February 1983 (Verity) [*Loebel*], followed in *OPSEU (Smith) and Ministry of Northern Development and Mines*, GSB#1625/93, 8 February 1995 (Kaplan).

word "minimal." It was reasoned that this low threshold is appropriate to make it easier for employees to successfully exercise their redeployment rights. While the required standard of competence is not high, the person must possess all the qualifications without the necessity of more than a few days' orientation[162] and without extensive training.[163] The requirement to be qualified may, in some cases legitimately require immediate ministry specific qualifications:

> In circumstances where the Employer is going to raise this kind of requirement as an essential qualification, it must demonstrate, on the balance of probabilities, that this "fully-functional" or "virtually-fully-functional" qualification is integral to the core duties and responsibilities of the particular position, and therefore the position cannot be expected to provide a familiarization period.[164]

It has also been found that "[i]n order to respect the jurisprudence of this Board, it is important not to define the core components in a manner that effectively elevates the minimal qualifications required to do the job to the level of proficiency demonstrated by an experienced person currently performing in that role."[165]

The *Loebel* standard of minimum competence has been applied to recall. OPSEU argued that, because recall represents the last chance of an employee already on layoff, the requirements for recall should be more liberal than those for displacement or redeployment.[166] The union further argued that the duties the laid-off employee should be required to perform should only be the portion of the job that would actually have to be done on return to work, and not all the work of the identified employee.

---

162 *OPSEU (Henderson) and Ministry of Citizenship*, GSB#1097/91 and 1269/91, 31 March 1992 (Barrett).

163 *Ontario Public Service Employees Union (Halsall) v Ontario (Agriculture, Food, and Rural Affairs)*, 2009 CanLII 15420 (ON GSB) (Briggs); *Ontario Public Service Employees Union (Sessions) v Ontario (Health and Long-Term Care)*, 2015 CanLII 89911 (ON GSB) (Williamson).

164 *Ontario Public Service Employees Union (Nucci) v Ontario (Health and Long-Term Care)*, 2011 CanLII 86400 (ON GSB) (Lynk) at para 49.

165 *Ontario Public Service Employees Union (Falco) v Ontario (Labour)*, 2013 CanLII 50387 (ON GSB) (Devins) at 22; *Ontario Public Service Employees Union (Ramlogan) v Ontario (Treasury Board Secretariat)*, 2016 CanLII 7449 (ON GSB) (Williamson).

166 *OPSEU (Bouchard) and Ministry of Environment*, GSB#1587/98, 30 October 2002 (Brown) at 9 [*Bouchard*].

The GSB held that, because recall involves filling the vacant position in all respects, the employee had to be able to do the whole job.[167] Thus, the qualifications required for recall under Article 20.6.1 will be the same as those required to be eligible to displace under Article 20.4.1.1.

There is a distinction between placement, whether through redeployment or recall, into a vacant position and displacement of an existing employee. There is a compelling rationale for recognizing an exception to the requirement of having the ability to do the whole job in the context of a vacancy in a position for which training is mandatory or routinely undertaken.[168] When a position that requires employee training is vacant, whoever is appointed to fill it will be trained. If every new employee in the position receives training, then the surplus employee should also be entitled to that training and should be evaluated on the basis of their suitability to receive that training.[169] When there is no vacancy, the situation is different. As the incumbent has completed the mandatory training, there is no need to train anyone, unless the incumbent is displaced by the surplus employee. In the context of a displacement, the employer can successfully argue the surplus employee is unqualified because they require training already possessed by the incumbent.[170]

10) Interrelationship of Article 20 with Other Articles

a) Job Competitions

Job security entitlements prevail over the job competition process. (Article 6.6.2 provides that Article 20 is one of several articles that have priority over Article 6, "Posting and Filling of Vacancies or New Positions," and Article 20.18 also stipulates that a vacancy filled in accordance with Article 20 need not be posted.) This means that a position in the job competition process is available for the placement of a surplussed employee up until the time the job is offered to the successful applicant.[171]

---

167 *Ibid* at 10.

168 *OPSEU (Bouchard) and the Ministry of Environment*, GSB#1587/98, 16 July 2004 (Brown).

169 *OPSEU (Hill and Campbell) and Ministry of Labour*, GSB#492/83 and GSB#493/83, 12 October 1984 (Roberts), followed in *OPSEU (Bazinet) and the Ministry of Environment*, GSB#1298/96, 14 April 1998 (Mikus) at 44 [*Bazinet*].

170 *Bouchard*, above note 166 at 9, overruling *Bazinet*, *ibid* at 44.

171 In order for a position to be posted it must "clear" the redeployment unit of the ministry and the corporate redeployment unit. The posting ministry and the corporate redeployment unit keep track of what positions have cleared and will

b) Pregnancy and Parental Leave

The positions of employees on pregnancy and parental leave can be surplussed during the leave. The employee has the option of returning immediately to the home position to accept the notice and begin the surplus process or wait until the end of the leave.[172] If the employee is returning to a comparable position, their position is not as clear. If the return is to a comparable position because, for example, the employee's duties, which constituted the home position, were restructured/reassigned as part of a workplace reorganization, it appears the assignment would have priority over an Article 20 assignment. However, if the return is to a comparable position because the home position was abolished while the employee was on leave, the returnee would, at the time of the return, be surplussed in accordance with the provisions of Article 20.

c) Article 25 (Special Leave)

Generally, the positions of employees who are on special leave are not deemed to be vacant because the employee is on leave. However, the position remains available for surplussing and displacement notwithstanding that the employee is on leave.[173]

d) Article 42 (Long-Term Income Protection)

The provisions of Article 20 apply to employees who are eligible to receive long-term insurance plan (LTIP) benefits and who are eventually able to return to full-time employment. Once an employee is eligible to receive LTIP benefits, the home regular position is to be deemed a vacancy and made available for redeployment purposes. Once the employee is able to return to full-time employment, they have full access to the Article 20 redeployment provisions.

In addition to the full redeployment entitlements under Article 20, returnees from LTIP may also seek to have their current health circumstances accommodated with an assignment outside of the assignment parameters of Article 20. The collective agreement sets out the salary

---

rescind clearance if there appears to be a pending surplus exercise that would benefit from having the vacancy available. One of the roles of the Joint Employment Stability Subcommittee under Art 19.2 is to review the generated reports and make recommendations as to the appropriateness of clearances and denials.

172 Management Board Secretariat, *OPS Interpretive Bulletin* 25 (26 August 1997).

173 *Ibid.*

treatment of employees who are assigned for health reasons to a position in a classification having a lower maximum salary than their previous salary and states that the only special redeployment treatment in such situations is that the provisions of Article 6 (posting and filling of vacancies or new positions) do not apply. The rights of non-LTIP employees assigned for health reasons may be inferior to the more extensive entitlements of surplussed LTIP returnee employees with regard to the severance pay and displacement entitlements of Article 20. At the same time, human rights jurisprudence requiring that workplace rules provide equality of treatment[174] may prevent any inferiority of treatment between persons with Article 20 rights versus employees being reassigned for health reasons. Accordingly, LTIP returnees gaining access to Article 20 redeployment would also have access to the broader options of placement that appear to exist for other health reassignments.

Article 20 does not apply to the position of a person on the short-term sick leave plan.[175]

e) Fixed-Term Positions

For the purposes of redeployment, positions occupied by term incumbents are considered to be vacant,[176] notwithstanding that the fixed-term incumbent is "displaced" by the assigned surplussed regular employee. This is subject to the pre-emptive conversion of the fixed-term position to a regular position. Positions converted to regular status are no longer considered vacant for Article 20.3 placement purposes if there is an incumbent whose status is also converted to regular.[177] Instead, the incumbent is recognized as being subject to the full displacement matching process. As a result, in periods of government "downsizing," fixed-term employees may be reluctant to self-identify themselves and their positions for conversion to regular status, as it may make them liable to displacement by more senior, regular employees.

However, an initially deemed temporary position that is later determined to be regular is available for Article 20.3 placement

---

174 See, for example, *British Columbia (Public Service Employee Relations Commission) v BCGSEU*, [1999] 3 SCR 3.

175 As there is no Art 42.10 equivalent in Art 44 (Short-Term Sickness Plan).

176 Art 20.5, and see *MBS, September 2000 (Mikus)*, above note 160.

177 Art 31A.15.1.2 reads that the incumbent "*will*" [emphasis added] be converted to regular status if the prerequisite eighteen-month condition is met; but there is no Art 6.6.2 equivalent that provides for Art 20 supremacy.

notwithstanding that the position has been occupied by an incumbent who would otherwise meet the Temporary Assignments Article eighteen-month criteria set out in Article 8.6.3. Under Article 8.6.3, the employer may have discretion to decide whether to confer regular status upon fixed-term incumbents who have successfully competed for a job but do not meet the requisite "full-time" hours criteria for conversion in Article 31A.15.1.2. However, the GSB has not yet determined that issue.

11) Technological Change

Under Article 20.13, where "the introduction of technological change in equipment or methods of operation" results in the surplussing of employees, the employer must give both the employees and the union at least three months' notice of the change. Such notice does not extend any other notice given under the collective agreement. It runs concurrently with any other such notice. Once notice of technological change is given under this provision, the matter is then referred to the CERC to attempt to resolve issues relating to the reallocation and retraining of the affected employees that arise out of the impending change/release.

The application of the technological change provisions has only been considered once. OPSEU argued that the closure of an older correctional facility and subsequent opening of a state-of-the-art "super jail" was a technological change in the "method of operation."[178] The GSB found the closure of the facility constituted a "cessation of operation" rather than a change.

12) Attrition

Article 20.9.1 states that, "wherever possible," the employer will "utilize attrition as a means of reducing the workforce." The word "workforce" is restricted in scope to members of OPSEU, and so the GSB does not have jurisdiction under Article 20.9.1 of the agreement to determine the merits of a claim that a position occupied by a non-bargaining unit

---

178 *OPSEU (Sostar et al) and Ministry of Public Safety and Security*, GSB#2819/02, 17 July 2003 (Briggs) at 8–9.

member should have been eliminated by attrition before the grievor's position was declared surplus.[179]

13) Accommodation

At times, the appropriate human rights accommodation may be to rescind the initial match and continue the redeployment search. To date, the GSB has found in one case that there was insufficient evidence to support the assertion that the appropriate accommodation was to modify the normal application of the redeployment process.[180] The employer's position is that any accommodation process is undertaken *after* an employee is matched to a position and, to this end, the employer invites employees who are being surplussed to identify, in their employee portfolios, any accommodation needs.

If a vacancy is identified for both an employee under notice of release ("surplus notice") or recall entitlements, and a non-surplussed employee in need of accommodation who is eligible for a health reassignment,[181] the assignment priority will be determined by the parties on a case-by-case basis.

---

179 *OPSEU (Robertson) and Ministry of Northern Development and Mines*, GSB#2167/96, 23 November 1997 (Roberts) at 10.

180 *Weeman*, above note 150 at 20.

181 See the discussion of the *MGS Reassignment Program Guide* (Revised 2019) in Chapter 6.

CHAPTER TEN

Key Aspects of the OPSEU/MBC Collective Agreements, as Interpreted by the GSB

Statutory and collectively bargained rights together make up the full range of the employment entitlements of unionized employees. The key aspects of the Ontario Public Service Employees Union (OPSEU)/ Management Board of Cabinet (MBC) collective agreement selected for discussion in this chapter form a major part of the distinct employment regime governing OPSEU represented *Public Service of Ontario Act, 2006* (*PSOA*)[1] Part III appointed government employees working in the Ontario Public Service (OPS). Those provisions:

- require management rights to be exercised reasonably if they have an impact on collective agreement rights
- limit assigning bargaining unit work to non-bargaining unit employees
- require that, in job competitions "where qualifications and ability are relatively equal, seniority shall be the deciding factor"
- require ongoing work to be staffed permanently rather than with term contracts
- provide ongoing seniority to seasonal employees
- require just cause for discipline and dismissal, as discussed in particular detail concerning conduct expectations and correctional officers

1 SO 2006, c 35, Sch A [*PSOA*].

Other important collective agreement rights, those applying in the event of divestment and layoff, are discussed under "reasonable efforts" and "job security" in Chapter 9.

Security of employment and giving effect to seniority are key union bargaining priorities. The resultant collective agreement provisions represent perhaps the fundamental difference between the rights of unionized and non-unionized employees in the OPS.

All these collective agreement rights supplement

- rights and obligations under the *PSOA*, as discussed in chapters 2 and 3
- rights under general employment related legislation and the closely related collective agreement provisions discussed in Chapter 6

Similar collective agreement rights to those discussed in this chapter are contained in the MBC collective agreement with the Association of Management, Administrative and Professional Crown Employees of Ontario (AMAPCEO), the bargaining agent for government employees most similar to those represented by OPSEU.[2] However, those rights have not been the subject of the same body of caselaw as the OPSEU entitlements discussed below.

A. REASONABLE EXERCISE OF MANAGEMENT RIGHTS

Prior to the *Crown Employees Collective Bargaining Act, 1993* (*CECBA)*, bargaining about an extensive range of management rights was prohibited by statute, including provisions dealing with promotions, demotions, transfers, and layoffs.[3] Now, the only remaining prohibitions are on bargaining the arbitrability of classifications[4] and the prohibition against an interest arbitrator ordering a "job offer guarantee."[5] Otherwise, management rights are now fully bargainable by the parties.

OPSEU and the MBC have bargained a fairly standard management rights clause stating that the "right and authority to manage the business and direct the workforce . . . shall be vested exclusively in the

---

2 For a discussion of the bargaining agents of the employees of government, see Chapter 7.

3 In *CECBA 1972*, s 17(1), which preceded the *Crown Employees Collective Bargaining Act, 1993*, SO 1993, c 38 [*CECBA*].

4 See *ibid*, s 52(1), as discussed in Chapter 11.

5 See *ibid*, s 5(5), as discussed in Chapter 9.

Employer," with the addition of the statement that management has the right to make "reasonable rules and regulations," all "subject only to the provisions" of the collective agreement.[6] Under this clause, management has the right to determine the "timing and manner in which it opts to get its work done,"[7] subject to the contractual limits on management rights as articulated by the Grievance Settlement Board (GSB).

1) Avoidance of Bad Faith

Where the exercise of a management right will have an impact on a collective agreement right, the management action must be carried out in pursuit of a legitimate government objective and must be rational.

OPSEU (Bousquet) and Ministry of Natural Resources,[8] the leading GSB case on management rights, sets out the basis for limiting the exercise of a management right. There must be a provision in the collective agreement that would be undermined or affected. If the exercise of the management right has such an effect, then it must meet two interrelated tests. First, it must be carried out in good faith, which requires that an employer have "a genuine intention to carry out a legitimate government objective."[9] The decision cannot be a "disguised means of achieving impermissible ends based on discrimination or other grounds

6 *OPSEU/MBC Unified Bargaining Unit Collective Agreement, 2022–2024* and *OPSEU/MBC Correctional Bargaining Unit Collective Agreement, 2018–2021*, online: https://opseu.org/information/general/find-your-collective-agreement, Art 2.1 [*OPSEU/MBC Unified and Correctional Collective Agreements*]. The MBC collective agreements with AMAPCEO and PEGO have similar language.

7 *OPSEU (Balanchandran) and Ministry of Consumer and Business Services*, GSB#0884/01, 18 April 2003 (Herlich) at 10.

8 GSB#541/90, 1 March 1991 (Gorsky) at 35–36 and 64 [*Bousquet*]. The case occurred under the pre-1993 *CECBA*, when the statute itself reserved certain rights to management, but the case concludes the statutory provision makes no difference when determining the implied limits on the exercise of management rights.

9 *Ibid* at 61. For an example of alleged bad faith, namely reprisal for union activity, see *OPSEU (Dobroff) and Ministry of the Environment*, GSB#905/03, 31 January 2005 (Dissanayake) at 15 [*Dobroff, 2005*]. It is recognized that it is bad faith to "deliberately tilt the field with a view to preferring one employee over another," but it is acceptable to "tilt the field" for the genuine government purpose of utilizing a keen, good, and trained employee for a temporary assignment: *Ontario Public Service Employees Union (Fitzpatrick et al) v Ontario (Community Safety and Correctional Services)*, 2016 CanLII 7450 (ON GSB) (Anderson) at 4–5, citing *Ontario Public Service Employees Union (Perez) v Ontario (Ministry of Community and Social Services)*, 2003 CanLII 52894 (ON GSB) (Abramsky) [*Perez*].

unrelated to the making of genuine management decisions."[10] Second, it must meet the test of reasonableness, which only requires that there be "a rational relationship between the facts leading to the making of the decision and the decision itself." Where it can be seen that the decision follows logically from the facts, the reasonableness test will be met. The GSB has stressed that it "will hesitate to substitute its view for that of the employer as long as [these] minimum tests are met . . . Management . . . need not be correct."[11]

While it has been observed by the GSB that the *Bousquet* test is not different in substance from the private sector jurisprudence,[12] the GSB has shown a particular willingness to review the exercise of management rights.[13]

The requirement for a collective agreement impact can be met without showing that a provision was violated but only that it will be affected. "It is clear that the collective agreement need not provide for the subject matter of the dispute explicitly."[14] It can be "a derivative

10 *Dobroff, 2005, ibid* at 15.

11 This paragraph has been endorsed in *Ontario Public Service Employees Union (Osborne) v Ontario (Natural Resources)*, 2013 CanLII 31979 (ON GSB) (Petryshen) at para 15.

12 *OPSEU (Boulet) and Ministry of Community and Social Services*, GSB#1189/99, 8 August 2000 (Brown) at 10 [*Boulet*].

13 The leading GSB cases are *OPSEU (McIntosh) and Ministry of Government Services*, GSB#3027/92, 15 December 1993 (Dissanayake); *Boulet*, above note 12; *OPSEU (Pilon et al) and Ministry of Community and Social Services*, GSB#1254/99, 5 November 2001 at 21–25 [*Pilon, 2001*] and 2 June 2003 (Brown); *OPSEU (Young et al) and Ministry of the Attorney General*, GSB#1455/00, 10 July 2002 (Abramsky) [*Young, 2002*]; *OPSEU (Emmett et al) and Ministry of Health and Long-Term Care*, GSB#0147/01, 19 August 2002 (Johnston) at 14 [*Emmett*]. See also *OPSEU (Ashley) and Ministry of Community, Family and Children's Services*, GSB#1700/01, 5 November 2003 (Abramsky); *Ontario Public Service Employees Union (Dufour et al) v Ontario (Community and Social Services)*, 2015 CanLII 89914 (ON GSB) (Briggs) at 33; *Ontario Public Service Employees Union (Cote et al) v Ontario (Natural Resources and Forestry)*, 2020 CanLII 63603 (ON GSB) (Wacyk) at 18. For a similar approach dealing with a disability insurer's decisions about the rehabilitation plan for a grievor, see *Ontario Public Service Employees Union v Ontario (Treasury Board Secretariat)*, 2017 CanLII 90156 (ON GSB) (Parmar) at 7–8.

14 *Ontario Public Service Employees Union (Beek et al) v Ontario (Community Safety and Correctional Services)*, 2007 CanLII 30453 (ON GSB) (Petryshen) at 8, citing *Regina Police Assn Inc v Regina (City) Board of Police Commissioners*, 2000 SCC 14 at para 25.

right, not an independent one."[15] An example is that, in the absence of a collective agreement right to contest temporary assignments, the denial of a temporary assignment was evaluated against the *Bousquet* test because the denial affected the grievor's rights to subsequently compete for permanent vacancies. There needs to be the demonstration of a "sufficient link."[16]

The GSB has found that employer decisions had no impact on a collective agreement right. Management has "unfettered discretion" when it is acting "on its own initiative and in its own interest within its exclusive sphere."[17] The GSB has declined to take jurisdiction over grievances that simply allege unequal treatment in the exercise of management rights.[18] When management so acts, employees should seek their remedy at the bargaining table, not at the GSB. Instances where management rights have been found by the GSB to be non-reviewable include:

- the granting of merit increases[19]
- the inconsistent enforcement of scheduled hours of work resulting in comparatively negative impacts on employees who work all their hours, but without discrimination on a prohibited ground[20]
- the allocation of overtime, where the relevant article of the collective agreement did not mention the distribution of overtime, but merely provided for overtime pay once overtime was awarded and performed[21]
- the authorization of travel expenses[22]

---

15 *Perez*, above note 9.

16 *Ontario Public Service Employees Union (Dobroff et al) v Ontario (Environment)*, 2008 CanLII 19779 (ON GSB) (Dissanayake) at 25–26.

17 *OPSEU (Drew) and Ministry of Correctional Services*, GSB#331/89, 19 December 1989 (Slone) at 8. To the same effect, see *Ontario Public Service Employees Union (Halsall) v Ontario (Agriculture, Food, and Rural Affairs)*, 2009 CanLII 15420 (ON GSB) (Briggs); *Ontario Public Service Employees Union (Seguin et al) v Ontario (Ontario Science Centre)*, 2012 CanLII 6203 (ON GSB) (Briggs).

18 *Ontario Public Service Employees Union (Santangelo et al) v Ontario (Transportation)*, 2015 CanLII 36171 (ON GSB) (Dissanayake).

19 *OPSEU (Anthony) and Ministry of Labour*, GSB#1977/99, 28 April 2004 (Abramsky).

20 *Ontario Public Service Employees Union (Pletikos) v Ontario (Community and Social Services)*, 2013 CanLII 72578 (ON GSB) (Dissanayake) at 4 and 7.

21 *OPSEU (Carter et al) and Ministry of Correctional Services*, GSB#2291/86, 25 July 1988 (Knopf).

22 *OPSEU (Bott/Prosser) and Ministry of Revenue*, GSB#1525/89, 14 June 1991 (Dissanayake).

- the indemnification of legal fees incurred by a grievor in the course of defending themself against allegations relating to the workplace, although the GSB left open the question of whether it would take jurisdiction concerning an allegation that the indemnification policy had been administered in a bad faith manner[23]
- the payment of professional fees[24]
- most obviously, there is no jurisdiction to review management decisions regarding positions outside the bargaining unit, whether or not those decisions were made in good faith[25]

There has been some caution expressed about dismissing violations of the management rights clause simply because no other collective agreement right is "involved."[26] A vice-chair has noted: "It remains unclear to me, however, that this necessarily means the employer can conduct itself in an arbitrary, discriminatory or bad faith manner without fear of any possible review by this Board" and flagged that there needs to be consideration of the circumstances where the conduct is unacceptable for other reasons.[27]

The GSB has never actually found that a general reorganization, budgetary, or staffing measure was an unreasonable exercise of management rights. Some management decisions that have been reviewed using

---

23 *OPSEU (Sindall) and Ministry of Solicitor General and Correctional Services*, GSB#589/98, 14 February 2000 (Fisher).

24 *OPSEU (Cherwonogrodzky et al) and Ministry of Finance*, GSB#0994/02, 14 April 2004 (Gray); *Ontario Public Service Employees Union (Lesieur et al) v Ontario (Ministry of the Environment)*, 2005 CanLII 54831 (ON GSB) (Briggs).

25 *Ontario Public Service Employees Union (Schnoflak) v Ontario (Solicitor General)*, 2019 CanLII 118584 (ON GSB) (Petryshen). There is no right for an employee in one unit to contest the failure to be screened in to a job competition in another unit: *Ontario Public Service Employees Union (Heath) v Ontario (Children and Youth Services)*, 2016 CanLII 41669 (ON GSB).

26 *Ontario Public Service Employees Union (Rouatt) v Ontario (Ministry of Labour)*, 2013 CanLII 26531 (ON GSB) (Herlich) at 8. For non-unionized employees within the jurisdiction of the PSGB, management will be constrained from acting in an arbitrary, discriminatory, or bad faith manner, as discussed in Chapter 12.

27 This approach finds some support in the iconic phrase of Rand J that, in certain public regulation forums, "there is no such thing as absolute and untrammelled discretion": *Roncarelli v Duplessis*, [1959] SCR 121 at 140, discussed in Lorne Sossin, "The Unfinished Project of Roncarelli v Duplessis: Justiciability, Discretion, and the Limits of the Rule of Law" (2010) 55:3 *McGill Law Journal* 661, which posits it is often appropriate to determine if the authority was exercised in good faith and for proper purposes.

the *Bousquet* test, but not overturned, include the establishment of new workload levels;[28] the use of temporary, rather than permanent, positions for staffing;[29] the denial of training and developmental opportunities to unclassified/term staff;[30] a refusal on the part of management to meet and negotiate a compressed workweek agreement;[31] the reassignment of duties and backlogging of work;[32] and the conduct of a voluntary competition for temporary assignments.[33]

2) Employer Responsibility to Adhere to Own Policies and Directives

"Nonadherence" to an employer policy is not to be the basis for a griev ance by itself, and a violation of the contract or a statute must also be established.[34] This jurisprudence has not always been consistently applied. *OPSEU (Howes) and Ministry of Transportation and Communications*[35] concerned the statement in a management directive that the designated starting point for calculation of mileage allowances would be "equitable." The GSB found that the ministry had violated its own standards by an inequitable designation, and, on judicial review, the Divisional Court upheld the GSB's ruling and found there was no need to imply a term of fairness because that obligation had been voluntarily assumed by management in its own directive.[36]

An issue that arises concerning employer rules that affect collective agreement rights is whether management can defend its policy as reasonable. Ontario arbitral jurisprudence addresses this by assessing, in accordance with the classic *KVP Co* case, whether it is a "reasonable

28 *Boulet*, above note 12.

29 *OPSEU (Lonsdale) and Ministry of Correctional Services*, GSB#746/89, 31 March 1992 (Fisher) at 9.

30 *Young, 2002*, above note 13.

31 *Emmett*, above note 13 at 14; *Ontario Public Service Employees Union (Sutherland) v Ontario (Labour)*, 2008 CanLII 70535 (ON GSB) (Dissanayake) at 7.

32 *Pilon, 2001*, above note 13 at 24.

33 *Perez*, above note 9 at 9.

34 *Ontario Public Service Employees Union v Ontario (Community Safety and Correctional Services)*, 2017 CanLII 65618 (ON GSB) (Tims) at para 238. For the standard of review applied for non-unionized employees by the PSGB, see Chapter 12.

35 GSB#356/82, 25 November 1982 (Verity) at 11–12.

36 *Queen in Right of Ontario and Ontario Public Service Employees Union* (1984), 45 OR (2d) 361 (Div Ct) at 366. See also *OPSEU (Ruper) and Ministry of Correctional Services*, GSB#372/84, 8 October 1985 (Gorsky) at 18.

rule."[37] *KVP* sets out factors—including clarity, notice, and consistent enforcement—that have been applied by the GSB.[38] The board has also held that, while the union has the onus of proving lack of reasonableness, it may not take much evidence to shift the evidentiary burden to the employer to address those factors.[39]

3) Procedural Fairness Requirements

The common law right of procedural fairness does not normally extend to employees in the OPS who are covered by the provisions of a collective agreement. The procedural and substantive protections available to grievors facing discipline under the collective agreement ultimately far exceed the common law's basic procedural fairness entitlements because the GSB is able to hold a full hearing and completely review the question of just cause.[40] There is some limited authority that elements of common law procedural fairness may apply to depending on the circumstances.[41] Where the employer conceded that unionized employees

---

37 See *KVP Co* (1965), 16 LAC 73 (Robinson); Donald J.M. Brown & David M. Beatty, *Canadian Labour Arbitration*, 3d ed (Aurora, ON: Canada Law Book, 1988) at para 4:1520.

38 See, for example, a review of an attendance management plan, in part to determine if it is a reasonable policy: *Ontario Public Service Employees Union (Union Grievance) v Ontario (Ministry of the Solicitor General and Correctional Services/Management Board Secretariat)*, GSB#1925/96, 31 May 1999 (Abramsky) at 57–73.

39 *Amalgamated Transit Union—Local 1587 v Ontario (Metrolinx)*, 2022 CanLII 70871 (ON GSB) (Nairn) at para 39.

40 *OPSEU (Thompson et al) and Ministry of Correctional Services*, GSB#128/78, 14 May 1979 (Swan) at 19–20. A subsequent case, much to the same effect, which does not mention *Thompson*, is *OPSEU (Tanevsky) and Ministry of Consumer and Commercial Relations*, GSB#0763/88, 13 July 1989 (Dissanayake) at 10–11, where the vice-chair follows the private sector jurisprudence, notably *Re Board of Education for the City of London and Ontario Secondary School Teachers' Federation District 4*, 1984 CanLII 5145 (ON LA) (Brandt) at 36, which held that

> where there is an employment relationship whose terms and conditions are governed at least in part by a collective agreement which contains mechanisms by which decisions taken by the employer can be challenged, there is no need for the articulation of a general duty of fairness. The mechanism already exists within the grievance and arbitration process for ensuring a form of procedural protection.

41 *Ontario Public Service Employees Union (Vojto-Ioannidis) v Ontario (Ministry of Community Safety and Correctional Services)*, 2005 CanLII 55168 (ON GSB) (Abramsky).

were entitled to pre-dismissal procedural fairness, the GSB held that a unionized employee has the right to know the reasons for the termination and get an opportunity to respond, regardless of the terms of the collective agreement.[42] The common law duty of fairness was found to require that the employee be given an opportunity to respond at a time when there was still a possibility of altering the discipline. Perhaps the best view is that the lack of a pre-disciplinary opportunity to respond to allegations is a factor to consider in assessing whether the employer's actions were justified.[43]

One unresolved issue is the appropriate consequence of any employer failure to provide the procedural fairness actually required by the grievance procedure. The GSB has stated that, in the appropriate case, failure to disclose evidence in keeping with grievance procedure requirements may result in its non-admissibility.[44]

Management issuance of a formal pre-grievance report may trigger an enforceable procedural fairness obligation. The employer was found to have breached its duty of procedural fairness where an investigation report concerning the investigator's findings of sexual harassment had the following flaws:

- failure to put allegations to the grievor for response
- bias
- lack of thoroughness
- lack of documentation[45]

The GSB ordered the report to be destroyed but, as the final decision maker had reached his own separate factual finding, supported by the evidence before the GSB, that the sexual harassment had occurred, no other relief was granted, and the discharge was upheld.

42 *OPSEU (Grummett) and Ministry of Financial Institutions*, GSB#1656/90, 27 June 1991 (Keller) at 10. The reasoning is also applied in *OPSEU (Chircop) and Ministry of Transportation*, GSB#3039/92, 20 December 1995 (Kaufman) at 89–90.

43 For a brief discussion to that effect, see *OPSEU (Rose) and Ministry of Community and Social Services*, GSB#864/94, 28 August 1995 (Backhouse) at 10.

44 *OPSEU (Lewis) and Ministry of Education and Training*, GSB#1222/99, 10 April 2000 (Abramsky) at 13.

45 *OPSEU (Hurge) and Ministry of Attorney General*, GSB#348/92, 24 April 1995 (Kaplan) at 165–72.

4) Discretionary Management Decisions

Discretionary management decisions referenced in the collective agreement, such as granting or refusing discretionary leaves, must be made reasonably. Building on private sector jurisprudence, the GSB held, in the seminal case of *Re Young and the Crown in Right of Ontario (Ministry of Community and Social Services)*, that where an article in the collective agreement explicitly gives discretion to management about granting leave, that discretion must be exercised in a non-discriminatory and reasonable manner.[46] The GSB established the following principles:

- The employer, in deciding whether to grant or deny a leave of absence, must consider the merits of the individual application. It cannot rely on "floodgates" arguments.
- The employer must turn its mind to the particular request, and consider both the harm to management's objectives in granting the request and the importance of the request to the employee and the hardship caused by the denial.
- An arbitration board's role is limited to determining whether the employer has acted reasonably and without discrimination and has turned its mind to the merits of the particular request. The board's concern is the reasonableness of the decision, not its "correctness."

The type of consideration that management must give was elaborated upon in *OPSEU (Kuyntjes) and Ministry of Transportation and Communications*,[47] where the GSB stated a willingness to enforce the following standards in relation to the exercise of discretion:

- The decision must be made in good faith and without discrimination.
- The decision must be a genuine exercise of discretionary power, as opposed to rigid policy adherence.
- Consideration must be given to the merits of the individual application under review.
- All relevant facts must be considered and, conversely, irrelevant considerations must be rejected.[48]

---

46 *Re Young and the Crown in Right of Ontario (Ministry of Community and Social Services)*, 1979 CanLII 3955 (ON LA) (Swinton) at 5–6, quoting private sector awards.

47 GSB#513/84, 9 April 1985 (Verity) at 16 [*Kuyntjes*].

48 For an example of a consideration being found irrelevant, see *OPSEU (Senese) and Ministry of Community and Social Services*, GSB#363/89, 14 February 1990 (Fraser) at 6.

The same principles have been applied to other decisions referenced to be discretionary like whether to approve a lateral transfer,[49] and grant a request for access to temporary exit initiative severance. Where there was no contractual limit on which severances the employer should approve, the employer was able to decide the timing, and limit access to circumstances where the position could be eliminated, rather than providing those severances to senior employees at the end of their career,[50] and do so subject only to the principles set out in *Kuyntjes*.

In assessing a request for a leave to undertake a course of study, it is reasonable for the employer to consider:

- other vacancies
- work requirements
- that the employee is unlikely to return to work
- that the leave created costs for the employer to train and pay a replacement
- its complement of employees and whether the granting of a leave would result in staffing obligations due to the operation of the collective agreement[51]

It is "hard to conceive of any other expectation by the parties except that discretion would be exercised in a reasonable fashion."[52] A focus is the reasonableness of the procedure followed in the exercise of the discretion and, so long as procedural reasonableness has occurred, the

---

49 *Ontario Public Service Employees Union (Magee) v Ontario (Natural Resources)*, 2009 CanLII 15419 (ON GSB) (Dissanayake).

50 *Ontario Public Service Employees Union (Kimmel-Union) v Ontario (Treasury Board Secretariat)*, 2018 CanLII 119569 (ON GSB) (Devins) at paras 38–40; *Ontario Public Service Employees Union (Klonowski et al-Union) v Ontario (Treasury Board Secretariat)*, 2019 CanLII 118489 (ON GSB) (Devins); *Ontario Public Service Employees Union (Union-Heath et al) v Ontario (Treasury Board Secretariat)*, 2021 CanLII 26602 (ON GSB) (Devins); *Ontario Public Service Employees Union (Union-Uetz et al) v Ontario (Treasury Board Secretariat)*, 2022 CanLII 35397 (ON GSB) (Devins); *Ontario Public Service Employees Union (Union-Johnston et al) v Ontario (Treasury Board Secretariat)*, 2022 CanLII 35384 (ON GSB) (Devins).

51 *Ontario Public Service Employees Union (Sookdeosingh) v Ontario (Solicitor General)*, 2022 CanLII 31338 (ON GSB) (Petryshen); *Ontario Public Service Employees Union (Botosh) v Ontario (Attorney General)*, 2018 CanLII 45308 (ON GSB) (Abramsky) at paras 62–69 and cases cited therein.

52 *OPSEU (O'Brien) and Ministry of Correctional Services*, GSB#1157/86, 26 June 1987 (Gandz) at 9–10 [*O'Brien*].

GSB should generally defer to management's judgment.[53] Even if the GSB disagrees with the resultant management decision, it should not interfere unless it finds the decision to be unreasonable.[54]

The employer's procedural responsibility includes making reasonable efforts to gather the relevant facts.[55] An employee should not be limited to the written reasons initially submitted to the employer, but rather be allowed to clarify and expand.[56] However, it is the grievor's responsibility to bring the relevant facts to the attention of the managerial decision maker,[57] and the employer is entitled to rely on the facts as presented by the grievor.[58] There is an obligation to investigate further if the employer initially disbelieves the reasons given, but no such obligation exists when finding that the reasons given did not warrant the granting of the leave.

Supervisors may rely on subordinates for advice or recommendations and for the transmitting of information about the request, but the decision maker must make the decision themself,[59] and the employer must ensure that the decision maker understands all the facts correctly and takes the degree of distress experienced by the employee into

---

53 *Ibid* at 10. See also *OPSEU (Thurman) v Ontario (Ministry of Health and Long-Term Care)*, 2003 CanLII 52897 (ON GSB) (Johnston) at 9 [*Thurman*], stating that the reasonableness standard of review is to be applied to the employer's decision-making process, and that the GSB's role is not to assess the correctness of the employer's decision, and see *Ontario Public Service Employees Union (Duret) v Ontario (Attorney General)*, 2015 CanLII 47656 (ON GSB) (Dissanayake).

54 *OPSEU (Donnon) and Ministry of Health*, GSB#2136/91, 26 June 1992 (Barrett) at 7; *Ontario Public Service Employees Union (Williams) v Ontario (Attorney General)*, 2015 CanLII 47772 (ON GSB) (Dissanayake).

55 *O'Brien*, above note 52 at 16; *OPSEU (Leger and Legacy) and Ministry of Correctional Services*, GSB#506/87, 21 July 1988 (Dissanayake) at 9–12; *OPSEU (Sahota) and Ministry of Correctional Services*, GSB#2454/87, 23 August 1988 (Verity) at 9–12 [*Sahota*]; *OPSEU (Carvalho) and Ministry of Attorney General*, GSB#821/88, 6 April 1989 (Kirkwood) at 8–9.

56 *OPSEU (Montgomery et al) and Ministry of Health*, GSB#605/92, 25 June 1993 (Finley) at 14.

57 *OPSEU (Mailloux) and Ministry of Correctional Services*, GSB#87/88, 27 February 1989 (M. Picher) at 18 [*Mailloux, 1989*]; *Ontario Public Service Employees Union (Maxwell) v Ontario (Community and Social Services)*, 2018 CanLII 33077 (ON GSB) (Dissanayake).

58 *OPSEU (McNally) and Ministry of Health*, GSB#2176/91, 7 July 1992 (Gray).

59 *OPSEU (Sandham) and Ministry of Health*, GSB#802/92, 3 March 1993 (Dissanayake) at 4–5 [*Sandham*].

account.[60] Demonstrating that the procedural obligation was fulfilled will oblige the employer to lead evidence explaining how any decision to deny the leave was made.[61]

The employer must establish reasonable criteria for determining whether or not to grant leave so that like cases will be treated alike.[62] Seemingly "differential treatment" of leave requests will be scrutinized.[63] However, there is no absolute requirement that the employer give reasons for denying a leave request, although it may be preferable that it do so.[64]

The burden of proof is not to be shifted to the employer but remains with the union. In the GSB's view, putting the burden on the employer to establish that it has conducted a full investigation, considered all relevant material, and exercised its discretion in keeping with the standards that govern the decisions of persons exercising statutory powers of decision, risks "judicializing" decision making in the day-to-day management of the employer's operations.[65]

The GSB's most common remedial approach to the inappropriate denial of leaves has been to determine, on the merits, whether the leave is to be granted, rather than remitting the issue to the employer for reconsideration.[66] Often, the full canvassing of the evidence during the hearing has put the GSB in a reasonable position to determine what is usually a factually specific issue of limited ongoing relevance. In such circumstances, the GSB has stated a willingness to deal with the merits of the leave, given that the *CECBA* and the collective agreement

---

60 *OPSEU (Elesie) and Ministry of Health*, GSB#24/79, 1 October 1980 (Swinton) at 6–7 [*Elesie*]; *OPSEU (Constable) and Ministry of the Solicitor General*, GSB#207/89, 3 May 1990 (Emrich) at 13 [*Constable*].

61 *Sandham*, above note 59 at 4.

62 *Elesie*, above note 60 at 5.

63 *Sahota*, above note 55 at 12.

64 *OPSEU (Neeb) and Ministry of Finance*, GSB#1438/02, 31 January 2003 (Abramsky) at 5.

65 *Mailloux, 1989*, above note 57 at 17, followed in *Constable*, above note 60. To the same effect, see *Thurman*, above note 53 at 11.

66 Most cases cited above are resolved in this way, but they do not contain much explicit comment on why this approach is taken. For a rare, direct, but still very brief, discussion of the remedial issue, see *OPSEU (Latulippe) and Ministry of Correctional Services*, GSB#1000/86, 16 December 1987 (Samuels) at 6. For a case in which the employer was ordered to reconsider, see *Constable*, above note 60.

contemplate final resolution at the GSB.[67] The matter may also be remitted to the decision maker for determination, where the decision should be made in the fully informed exercise of their discretion,[68] or by the intended decision maker.[69]

B. LIMITATIONS ON ASSIGNING BARGAINING UNIT WORK TO NON-BARGAINING UNIT EMPLOYEES, KNOWN AS "CONTRACTING IN"

Following the private sector "contracting in" jurisprudence, the GSB has found that the OPSEU/MBC collective agreements limit the employer's assignment of bargaining unit work to non-bargaining unit employees. In *Pilon, 2001*,[70] the GSB held that collective agreements contain "an implied restriction on the performance of bargaining unit work by all employees outside the bargaining unit, regardless of whether they have managerial responsibilities." This implied restriction addresses the potential use of more precarious workers in government, a matter not addressed by the *PSOA*.

The extent of that restriction will be determined by all relevant factors, which will include the quantity of work in dispute, and whether the duties regularly assigned to members of the bargaining unit overlap the regular duties of the other employees concerned.[71] The volume of work transferred to non-bargaining unit employees must be "close to

---

67 *OPSEU (Arora) and Ministry of the Environment*, GSB#1099/89, 3 July 1990 (Stewart) at 15–16.

68 *Constable*, above note 60, and *Ontario Public Service Employees Union (Taylor et al) v Ontario (Community Safety and Correctional Services)*, 2014 CanLII 30090 (ON GSB) (Petryshen), where the decision maker was not aware of key facts, followed in *Ontario Public Service Employees Union (White) v Ontario (Solicitor General)*, 2019 CanLII 118593 (ON GSB) (Mikus) [*White*].

69 See *White, ibid* at para 12, noting the initial decision maker was not the "Deputy Minister or designee" referenced in the collective agreement article and so the matter was remitted to the employer "in order that it may exercise its discretion properly."

70 Above note 13 at 20.

71 AMAPCEO has obtained a broad-ranging disclosure order dealing with "the identification of people performing bargaining-unit work who are not members of the unit even though they would be characterized properly as employees of the provincial government": *AMAPCEO (Policy) and Management Board Secretariat*, GSB#1928/02, 14 July 2003 and 23 September 2003 (Brown) at 8 (14 July 2003).

a full shift."[72] Where the work at issue has not always been assigned to bargaining unit members, it is not likely to be work over which the union can claim exclusive jurisdiction.[73] The GSB has determined that the restriction prevents the government from using temporary agency-staff for its "core" and "predictable seasonal" staffing needs.[74]

To provide some additional flexibility, the parties have agreed to the employer using IT consultants unless that "directly results in the lay-off of a bargaining unit employee."[75]

The implied restriction does not apply where the employer validly "contracts out" the relevant work by hiring a third-party employer to direct and control employees, even where the employer has ensured that the third-party employer is to meet a contracted performance standard.[76]

In remedying the inappropriate assignment of bargaining unit work to non-bargaining unit employees,[77] the GSB noted that the then *Public Service Act (PSA)* prevented the GSB from providing for appointment of employees to the public service. (The current *PSOA* operates in the same fashion because a worker needs to be a Crown employee in order to be a member of a government bargaining unit, which requires explicit appointment by the Crown and cannot be inferred from their work.[78]) The GSB rejected the argument that this makes the *Pilon* rule inapplicable, holding that

> [t]he labour relations rationale behind this rule is that without such an implied restriction, the employer could undermine the union's collective agreement rights by assigning most or all of the work performed by its members to other employees. The same labour relations mischief can also be achieved through the process of using agency employees to perform bargaining unit work. Taking the Ministry's argument to

72 *Ontario Public Service Employees Union (Union) v Ontario (Ministry of Government Services)*, 2013 CanLII 4663 (ON GSB) (Petryshen).

73 *Ontario Public Service Employees Union (Union) v Ontario (Solicitor General)*, 2019 CanLII 126477 (ON GSB) (Petryshen) dealing with cleaning work at a correctional institution that had previously been performed by inmates.

74 *OPSEU (Union) and Ministry of Health and Long-Term Care*, GSB#1942/94, 20 February 2002 (Fisher) at 4 [*Health, 2002*].

75 As discussed in *Ontario Public Service Employees Union (Union) v Ontario (Government Services)*, 2012 CanLII 49877 (ON GSB) (Petryshen).

76 *Ontario Public Service Employees Union (Union) v Ontario (Treasury Board Secretariat)*, 2015 CanLII 14195 (ON GSB) (Petryshen) at para 18.

77 *Health, 2002*, above note 74 at 4.

78 See *PSOA*, above note 1, s 52, discussed in Chapter 2 and Chapter 7.

> its natural extreme, the Ministry, indeed the entire Provincial Government, could staff most or all of its OPSEU job functions through the use of private sector staffing agencies.[79]

The GSB cannot change the employment status of individual agency-staff, but it can require the employer to not use such staff for its core staffing.

C. JOB COMPETITIONS

Seniority-based preference in job competitions, while commonplace in broader public sector collective agreements, takes on additional significance in the public service where advancement is intended to be merit based.[80] Since 1992, the OPSEU/MBC collective agreement has contained the following term:

> In filling a vacancy, the Employer shall give primary consideration to qualifications and ability to perform the required duties. Where qualifications and ability are relatively equal, seniority shall be the deciding factor.[81]

Compared to the public sector arbitral law, the GSB jurisprudence is especially extensive.

The Public Service Grievance Board (PSGB) job competition jurisprudence, discussed in Chapter 12, is significantly different from that of the GSB. The key difference is that, for non-bargaining unit employees, there is no collective agreement entitlement at issue, and therefore no basis for asserting any type of claim based on seniority. The PSGB is concerned about compliance with employer policies and whether the competition was generally fair.

The discussion below is ordered by dealing with remedy first, then the order of proceeding, and finally the factors that the GSB will consider in assessing the competition process.

---

79 *Health, 2002*, above note 74 at 6–7.

80 See the discussion of seniority in Chapter 1.

81 *OPSEU/MBC Collective Agreement, 1992–1993*, Art 4.3.1. The same article is now Art 6.3 of *OPSEU/MBC Unified and Correctional Collective Agreements*, above note 6. The clause now applies to fixed-term employees: Art 31A.16.1. Note the limited application to surplussed employees discussed below.

1) Remedy

The two main remedial choices have been summarized as follows:

> [T]here are two standards—one for ordering the grievor into the position and one for ordering a re-run. If the Board is to order the grievor placed into the position, the Union must prove, on the balance of probabilities, that the flaws *would* have affected the outcome. In other words, the grievor must show, on the balance of probabilities, that he or she would demonstrate relative equality if a proper selection procedure had been done. In a re-run situation, the Union must establish, on the balance of probabilities, that the flaws *could* have affected the outcome. If neither onus is met, the grievance must be dismissed.[82]

a) Awarding the Position to the Grievor

To be awarded the position through a grievance, a *senior* unsuccessful candidate must demonstrate qualifications and ability that are *relatively equal* to those of the successful candidate, but while a *junior* unsuccessful candidate must demonstrate qualifications and ability that are *superior* to those of the incumbent.[83]

The GSB will only appoint the grievor to the position where it has sufficient information to assess the respective qualifications and abilities of the candidates and where, on the basis of this information, it can determine that the grievor with greater seniority is at least relatively equal to the successful candidate,[84] or that the junior grievor is more

82 *Ontario Public Service Employees Union (Naczynski) v Ontario (Ministry of Economic Development and Trade)*, 2006 CanLII 17523 (ON GSB) at 22–23 (Abramsky) [*Naczynski*].

83 *OPSEU (Remark) and Ministry of Revenue*, GSB#149/77, 29 January 1979 (Swinton) at 2 [*Remark*], cited in *OPSEU (Labonte) and Ministry of Transportation*, GSB#35/89, 8 September 1989 (Watters) at 5 [*Labonte*]. The GSB first determined that it had jurisdiction to direct that a grievor be appointed to a job as a remedy under the pre-1977 wording of the relevant article, which then included the phrase, "in the opinion of the employer." In *OPSEU (Zuibrycki) and Ministry of Industry and Tourism*, GSB#100/76, 16 February 1981 (Pritchard), the GSB held that, in spite of the wording of the article, it had jurisdiction to appoint the grievor to the position. The board's decision was upheld by the Divisional Court: *Regina v OPSEU* (1982), 35 OR (2d) 670 (Div Ct).

84 *OPSEU (Sauve) and Ministry of Transportation*, GSB#1695/91, 3 May 1993 (Gray) at 31–39 [*Sauve*], as opposed to the contrary, but less convincing, view in *OPSEU (Coulter and Charleau) and Ministry of Correctional Services*, GSB#1395/88, 2 April 1991 (Watters) at 19, and cases cited therein [*Coulter and Charleau*].

qualified. Such information may not have been before the employer's job competition panel, but can come to the attention of the board at the arbitration, which gives the grievor the opportunity to address any claimed deficiencies in information gathering by the selection committee, and then the information can warrant awarding the job to the grievor.[85] It is not sufficient for the grievor to assert such information exists as it must be submitted to the GSB.[86]

Where the GSB finds that the grievor was superior to the incumbent, or relatively equal with greater seniority, the grievance will not be defeated because the employer demonstrates that another candidate (who did not grieve) was more deserving.[87] That other candidate's failure to grieve means that their claim to the position is forfeited.

b) Ordering the Competition to Be Rerun

Where the union has not established that the position should be awarded to the grievor, the GSB may still order the competition to be rerun.

There is a lack of consensus about when the GSB should order a rerun of a job competition. In one case, a panel of the GSB required the union to show, on a balance of probabilities, that the grievor would have won the competition but for the defects.[88] In contrast, another panel has held that where the GSB finds defects in a competition, it will order the competition rerun unless satisfied that the deficiencies could not have prejudiced the grievor.[89] The most common and the most logical view is that the union needs to show that the selection process was flawed and that the flaw may have affected, or casts doubt, on the result of the competition.[90] To put the matter another way, the GSB will order the competition rerun

---

85 *Ontario Public Service Employees Union (Andraychak) v Ontario (Children and Youth Services)*, 2010 CanLII 68791 (ON GSB) (Abramsky) at 12.

86 *Ibid; Naczynski*, above note 82 at para 65.

87 *OPSEU (Frisken) and Ministry of Labour*, GSB#2034/94, 5 June 1997 (Gray) at 10–11 [*Frisken*], and cases cited therein.

88 *OPSEU (Bent) and Ministry of Transportation*, GSB#1733/86, 23 January 1989 (Fisher) at 12 [*Bent*].

89 *OPSEU (Laforest) and Ministry of Community and Social Services*, GSB#1983/87, 28 April 1989 (Roberts) at 13 [*Laforest*].

90 *OPSEU (Skagen and Glemnitz) and Ministry of the Attorney General*, GSB#1934/87, 24 October 1988 (Springate) at 13–14; *OPSEU (Palatino/Ragos/Patterson) and Ministry of Health*, GSB#1968/89, 5 December 1990 (Kaplan) at 50–51 [*Palatino*]; and see also *OPSEU (Sedore) and Ministry of Transportation and Communications*, GSB#250/83, 17 January 1985 (Delisle) at 9.

when a flaw or combination of flaws in the process used by the selection panel make it impossible to determine if the right result was reached.[91] Where there are flaws that the GSB finds to be immaterial, because it has been able to determine a fair result was nonetheless arrived at, there will be no order requiring the competition to be rerun.[92]

When ordering that a competition be rerun, the GSB will generally attach conditions.[93] The conditions may include that

- the competition be limited to the grievor and the incumbent
- the interview panel be newly constituted
- the interview panel discount any of the experience that the incumbent obtained in the position since their appointment to the position as the successful candidate in the competition (the experience prior to the competition remaining relevant)
- competition flaws be corrected
- the GSB's requirements for competitions be followed[94]

In a case where the incumbent had been in the position for two years, the GSB added two further conditions.[95] First, the panel was to refrain from asking questions focusing on specific tasks that are required to be performed in the job. Second, where the job had changed significantly since the incumbent took up the position, this was not

---

91 *Coulter and Charleau*, above note 84 at 19; *OPSEU (Anderson) and Ministry of Finance*, GSB#1677/93, 2 March 1999 (Dissanayake) at 22 [*Anderson, 1999*].

92 *OPSEU (Kai) and Ministry of Solicitor General and Correctional Services*, GSB#3289/92, 23 April 1997 (Abramsky) [*Kai*], and cases cited therein; *OPSEU (Wright/Wasky) and Ministry of Health*, GSB#1832-33/91, 16 February 1994 (Watters) at 45; *OPSEU (Peters) and Ministry of Revenue*, GSB#1423/90, 27 November 1991 (Kaplan) at 31; *OPSEU (Vaillancourt) and Ministry of Health*, GSB#1620/87, 1 February 1990 (Wilson) [*Vaillancourt*]; *Association of Management, Administrative and Professional Crown Employees of Ontario (Gomes) v Ontario (Seniors and Accessibility)*, 2022 CanLII 80255 (ON GSB) (Gee) at paras 8–9 [*Gomes*].

93 *OPSEU (Alam) and Ministry of Community and Social Services*, GSB#735/85, 31 August 1987 (Brandt) at 18–19 [*Alam, 1987*]; *Coulter/Charleau*, above note 84 at 19–20; *Laforest*, above note 89 at 16–17; *Palatino*, above note 90 at 53; *OPSEU (Esmail) and Ministry of Revenue*, GSB#1186/87, 5 September 1990 (Dissanayake) at 22–23 [*Esmail*]; *Ontario Public Service Employees Union (Brimicombe et al) v Ontario (Labour)*, 2010 CanLII 42117 (ON GSB) (Dissanayake) at 8 [*Brimicombe*].

94 *Brimicombe*, *ibid*, as followed in *Ontario Public Service Employees Union (Hamada) v Ontario (Solicitor General)*, 2020 CanLII 105721 (ON GSB) (Williamson) at para 30 [*Hamada*].

95 *Alam, 1987*, above note 93 at 19–20.

to prejudice the grievor. If the grievor was qualified for the original position, then the grievor could have learned the new duties. Hence, it is reasonable to have regard for the duties of the job at the time of the posting of the job competition because, otherwise, the incumbent would have an unfair advantage.

If the grievor is successful in the rerun, they should be compensated for all lost wages and benefits that resulted from the flawed selection process.[96]

c) Awarding Compensation Only

In one case, where a rerun of the competition would otherwise have been ordered, the GSB noted a multi-year delay and awarded damages of one or two years' salary differential to the grievors.[97] After the passage of several years, it was time for a final resolution of the staffing of the positions. In another case where a rerun would have been readily ordered, but for a delay of five years, the GSB was nonetheless inclined to rerun the competition, because the incumbents had no right to positions that had been awarded through a process that did not comply with the collective agreement.[98] The board indicated it was "ready to make difficult decisions," but asked the parties to try to resolve the case.

Where the competition was not ordered rerun, but the employer deliberately provided false information and, under oath, an employer representative gave false evidence, general and punitive damages were awarded.[99]

---

96 See *Brimicombe*, above note 93 at paras 97 and 99; *Ontario Public Service Employees Union (Askarzada et al) v Ontario (Community and Social Services)*, 2018 CanLII 7261 (ON GSB) (Harris). See also *Esmail*, above note 93. In that case, the incumbent did not participate in the rerun and so the GSB was not in a position to know if the grievor would have been successful in the competition. Nonetheless, the GSB ordered full retroactive compensation for the grievor, reasoning at 12: "If someone has to suffer the risk of a loss in these circumstances, it must be the party at fault rather than the innocent party."

97 *OPSEU (Weir/Taylor) and Ministry of Revenue*, GSB#1311/92, 17 July 1993 (Backhouse) at 7.

98 *Anderson, 1999*, above note 91 at 37–38.

99 *Gomes*, above note 92 at paras 18–31.

2) Order of Proceeding and Non-suit Motions

As the union bears the onus of proving the competition was flawed, it will be expected to proceed first, even though the employer knows the reasons for the selection of the successful candidate. The union is to be provided with full disclosure and be allowed to cross-examine the incumbent.[100]

In response to a non-suit motion, the grievor need only show significant support for the claim that they are qualified, or demonstrate a significant defect in the conduct of the competition.[101] The rationale for this low threshold is again that the content of a job competition, particularly the evaluation of candidates other than the grievor, is within the knowledge of the employer. Once the grievor proves a *prima facie* case, the evidentiary burden shifts to the employer. In so ruling, the GSB dealt with two pre-existing lines of cases by declining to follow the decisions that had required the grievor to show a *prima facie* case of superiority, or at least relative equality, and instead following the cases that stressed the employer could reasonably be required to explain its own reasoning.

Where a union survives a non-suit motion, and the employer calls no evidence, the remedy may very well still be a rerunning of the competition rather than the awarding of the job,[102] as the GSB may not have the evidence on which to determine that the grievor was the best candidate. However, where the union is able to establish a *prima facie* case for the relative equality of the senior grievor with greater seniority, and that case is not rebutted, the GSB may award the position to the grievor.[103]

---

100 *OPSEU (Eaton) and Ministry of Transportation and Communications*, GSB#0629/85, 24 April 1987 (Knopf) at 2 [*Eaton*].

101 *OLBEU (Cooke) and Liquor Control Board of Ontario*, GSB#2474/87, 18 July 1991 (McCamus) at 30 [*Cooke*].

102 *Ibid* at 31–33, and union nominee dissent; *OPSEU (Watkin) and Ministry of Health*, GSB#902/89, 9 January 1992 (Samuels) at 5.

103 *Sauve*, above note 84 at 34.

3) Factors Considered in Deciding Whether to Award the Position to the Grievor or Rerun the Competition

a) Specific Terms of the Article

i) "Qualifications and Ability to Perform the Required Duties"

The employer is not to act unreasonably or in bad faith when either establishing the qualifications or applying them to the job. [104] The *qualifications* and *ability* on which the employer focuses the competition must relate to the job in question, and not to the applicants' ability and qualifications in the abstract.[105] While the employer is entitled to establish the qualifications required, the qualifications must reasonably relate to the work to be performed.[106]

The use of the conjunctive "and" in the OPSEU/MBC article is to be interpreted as meaning that the employer is to give separate and full consideration to both the qualifications and ability of each person interviewed.[107]

Once the field has been narrowed to those applicants who have the minimum required qualifications and abilities, the weight that the employer thereafter gives to each applicant's strength in each relevant qualification or ability should correspond (at least roughly) with the degree to which the duties of the job require that qualification or ability.[108]

Past job performance, particularly of similar job functions, must be considered and given appropriate weight.[109] However, the competition must be designed so that it does not give an unfair advantage to someone who is performing the job in question on a temporary basis.[110]

---

104 *Remark*, above note 83.

105 *OPSEU (Buller) and Ministry of Transportation and Communications*, GSB#113/82, 3 August 1983 (Samuels) at 11 [*Buller*]; *Doherty*, GSB#43/76, 13 May 1977 (Beatty) at 12 [*Doherty*]; *Sauve*, above note 84 at 18.

106 *OPSEU (Beck) and Ministry of Government Services*, GSB#196/89, 3 November 1989 (Watters); *OPSEU (Maclean) and Ministry of Transportation*, GSB#782/89, 4 January 1991 (Gorsky), where the GSB found that a bilingual designation was reasonably related to the requirements of the position; *OPSEU (Booth) and Ministry of Solicitor General*, GSB#386/91, 4 December 1992 (Gorsky) at 26 and following, where the GSB found that the bilingual designation was not reasonably related to the requirements of the position.

107 *Doherty*, above note 105 at 10.

108 *Sauve*, above note 84 at 20, and cases cited therein.

109 *Ibid* at 19.

110 *Esmail*, above note 93 at 18–19.

ii) "Relatively Equal"

After establishing that they have the requisite qualifications and ability for the job, a senior grievor still needs to prove that they are at least relatively equal in the relevant areas to the junior incumbent.[111] A junior grievor needs to be more than relatively equal. Where the junior grievor's credentials were more impressive, but the senior candidate was at least relatively equal for purposes of the given position, the GSB noted that "[w]e cannot accept the theory that 'the best man must always win,' because that is not the complete meaning of Article 4.3. The proper tests must always be related to the requirements of the position."[112]

In determining whether two candidates are "relatively equal," the GSB has noted that the private sector jurisprudence test of "relative equality"[113] is really about determining if one employee is more qualified by a "substantial and demonstrable margin."[114] This is a somewhat flexible standard, as the required degree of difference between the applicants may change depending on the nature of the job. It is seen as impractical to determine if candidates are exactly equal.[115] GSB panels have always been reluctant to provide an abstract statement about the required degree of equality and instead have emphasized the need to focus on the specific attributes of the applicants and the job in question.[116]

Putting the job competition score differences in percentage terms is seen as helpful but not conclusive.[117] While not stating so definitively, the GSB has suggested that a difference of 8 or 9 percent could be enough to find candidates were not equal[118] and that 15 to 18 percent

---

111 *Doherty*, above note 105 at 9.

112 *OPSEU (Saras) and Ministry of Solicitor General*, GSB#139/79, 5 November 1980 (Jolliffe) at 15.

113 As set out in *Re Textile Workers Union and Lady Galt Towels Ltd* (1969), 20 LAC 382 (Christie), and expanded upon in *Great Atlantic & Pacific Tea Co of Canada Ltd and Canadian Food and Allied Workers Union* (1979), 21 LAC (2d) 444 (Weatherill).

114 *OPSEU (Anderson) and Ministry of Environment*, GSB#105/86, 15 January 1988 (Wright) at 10–11.

115 *OPSEU (Worsley) and Ministry of Government Services*, GSB#347/81 (Draper) at 5–6, cited in *Vaillancourt*, above note 92 at 10.

116 *Labonte*, above note 83 at 6. See also *OPSEU (Vandevalk) and Ministry of the Environment*, GSB#1957/89, 8 May 1991 (Low) at 5; *CUPE (Jeffrey) and Workers' Compensation Board*, GSB#554/88, 6 November 1992 (McCamus) at 18–19; *Sauve*, above note 84 at 18.

117 *Frisken*, above note 87 at 7.

118 *OPSEU (Lake) and Ministry of Health*, GSB#226/90, 24 July 1991 (Kaplan) at 24.

would likely result in such a finding.[119] Parties have agreed and the GSB has accepted that candidates within a differential of 10 percent are relatively equal.[120]

b) Selection Procedure

During the information gathering part of the process

> the employer must employ a process of decision-making designed to consider the relative qualifications and ability of the candidates in a competition, which will ensure that sufficient relevant information is adduced before the decision-makers in order that they may make their comparisons in the confidence that they are able to thoroughly and properly compare the qualifications and abilities of the competing applicants.[121]

Candidates' qualifications and abilities must be assessed objectively. Subjective, or "gut level," determinations cannot be substituted for objective criteria.[122]

Perfection is not required as "it is possible to pick holes in almost any process run by mere mortal human beings."[123] There is also a

---

119 *OPSEU (Nixon) and Ministry of Transportation*, GSB#2418/87, 16 November 1988 (Fisher) at 3 [*Nixon*], where the GSB also dealt with the question of whether a difference in scores, which measure qualifications and ability, should be expressed as a percentage of a "perfect" score, or as a percentage of one of the actual scores being compared, and decided the latter approach should be used. This approach is endorsed in *Frisken*, above note 87 at 7. See also Leonard Marvy, "Making Sense of the Use of Numerical Calculations in the Application of Relative Equality Provisions" (2000) 8 *Canadian Labour and Employment Law Journal* 373.

120 *OPSEU (Difederico) and The Crown in Right of Ontario (MAG)*, GSB#1992-0827, decision of Vice-Chair Petryshen, 9 February 2007; *Ontario Public Service Employees Union (Leung) v Ontario (Finance)*, 2014 CanLII 63516 (ON GSB) at para 41.

121 *OPSEU (Quinn) and Ministry of Transportation and Communications*, GSB#9/78, 13 December 1979 (Prichard) at 7–8 [*Quinn*], quoted in *OPSEU (Hall/Powers) and Ministry of Correctional Services*, GSB#716/89, 7 December 1990 (Gorsky) at 26–28 [*Hall/Powers*], and followed in *Buller*, above note 105 at 8 and *Anderson, 1999*, above note 91 at 22.

122 *OPSEU (Thirumalai) and Ministry of Industry, Trade and Technology*, GSB#979/86, 1 November 1989 (Slone) at 18 [*Thirumalai*], followed in *Anderson, 1999*, above note 91 at 31.

123 *OPSEU (Saras) and Ministry of Labour*, GSB#457/85, 29 April 1988 at 9, as quoted in *Anderson, 1999*, above note 91 at 21.

recognition that the employer must be able to adjust the process to respond to practical realities. Different methods can be used in different circumstances, so long as the methods are reasonable.[124] However, the GSB's flexible approach will not prevent the board from assessing the entire process to determine if it was well-enough conducted to make the result defensible.[125]

OPSEU (MacLellan and DeGrandis) and Ministry of Government Services[126] established a full set of criteria by which to judge whether the selection procedure used by an employer generated adequate information:

1) The candidates must be evaluated on all the relevant qualifications for the job as set out in the position specification.
2) The various methods used to assess the candidates should address these relevant qualifications insofar as is possible; for example, interview questions and evaluation forms should cover all the qualifications.
3) Irrelevant factors should not be considered.
4) All members of a selection committee should review the personnel files of all the applicants.
5) The applicants' supervisors should be asked for their evaluations of the applicants.
6) The information concerning all the applicants should be accumulated in a systematic way.

The GSB has repeatedly stressed that interview and/or test results should not be relied upon to the exclusion of other evidence of the qualifications and abilities of the applicants. It has been noted ministries have a "slavish devotion" to interview scores and "it is simply mind-boggling that the selection panel in this case received specific advice to adopt

124 *OPSEU (Ruby and Budnark) and Ministry of Transportation and Communications*, GSB#505/82, 27 February 1987 (Palmer) at 10–11, who quotes the English saying that "there are horses for courses"; *OPSEU (Alam) and Ministry of Community and Social Services*, GSB#140/84, 9 October 1990 (Roberts) at 29; *OPSEU (Group-Stewart) and Ministry of Solicitor General and Correctional Services*, GSB#1999/98, 25 September 2000 (Harris) at 8.

125 *OPSEU (Group) and Ministry of Solicitor General and Correctional Services*, GSB#1999/98, 1 March 2002 (Harris) at 11–12 [*Group, 2002*].

126 GSB#506/81, 18 May 1982 (Samuels) at 25–26 [*MacLellan and DeGrandis*]; followed in *OPSEU (Poole) and Ministry of Health*, GSB#2508/87, 27 September 1988 (Samuels) [*Poole*], and, more recently, in *Group, 2002*, above note 125 at 9.

the very process that had been repeatedly disapproved in a long line of Board decisions."[127] The board has repeatedly stated that the employer needs to consider information from outside the formal interview/test process,[128] including supervisors' assessments of past job performance in identical or relevant positions (it is not enough for the selection committee to seek supervisors' assessments only after it has chosen the successful candidate),[129] personnel files,[130] résumés, and other information included in applications.[131] Failure to consider the above-mentioned material will readily cause a panel to decide that there was a real possibility that the material would have made a difference and hence overturn the competition;[132] although the competition will be upheld where the GSB is able to consider the material and determine that the results of the competition would have been the same.[133] It is particularly important that actual performance be given "serious consideration" where some candidates have actual experience in the position being competed.[134]

Even where past related experience is used as a basis for pre-interview screening, it must still also be given weight in assessing the relative qualifications and abilities of the final candidates.[135]

---

127 *Brimicombe*, above note 93 at 8; *Ontario Public Service Employees Union (Hogan/Paul/Montgomery) v Ontario (Community and Social Services)*, 2011 CanLII 83715 (ON GSB) (Dissanayake) at 12 [*Hogan*].

128 *Group, 2002*, above note 125 at 11–12, and cases cited therein.

129 *Naczynski*, above note 82 at 20; *Ontario Public Service Employees Union (Boucher) v Ontario (Northern Development, Mines and Forestry)*, 2011 CanLII 78576 (ON GSB) (Dissanayake) [*Boucher*]; *Nixon*, above note 119 at 3; *Anderson, 1999*, above note 91 at 32.

130 *Quinn*, above note 121; *OPSEU (Hoffman et al) and Ministry of Transportation and Communications*, GSB#22/79, 29 May 1981 (Barton) at 8; and concerning performance appraisals, see *OPSEU (Ellsworth et al) and Ministry of Community and Social Services*, GSB#361/80, 26 June 1981 (Jolliffe) at 20 and 23 [*Ellsworth*].

131 See also *Ellsworth*, *ibid* at 23–24; *Poole*, above note 126.

132 *Boucher*, above note 129; *Palatino*, above note 90 at 48.

133 *Kai*, above note 92 at 36–40.

134 *Re Liblik/Scipnek*, GSB#2525/91 (Dissanayake) at 19–20, referenced in *Hamada*, above note 94 at para 22.

135 *Sauve*, above note 84 at 19; *Nixon*, above note 119 at 4–5.

Attendance history has been held to be a proper consideration in a job competition "if regular attendance is reasonably required to discharge the responsibilities of the position."[136]

Building on the list in *MacLellan and DeGrandis*, the GSB has provided additional guidance, which is discussed below.

i) Minimum Qualifications

The employer may establish minimum requirements for each desired required qualification and may refuse to give any further consideration to those applicants who are found not to have all of these minimum qualifications or abilities. However, such minimums must be reasonable.[137] The focus can be on the qualifications and ability to perform the actual duties as opposed to qualifications or abilities "in the abstract."[138] A level of French proficiency that bears a reasonable relationship to the work can be made a requirement.[139]

ii) Pre-interview Screening

There is no employee right to an interview for a position, but pre-interview screening must be done in a fair and comprehensive manner.[140] The screening process may screen out candidates who meet the qualifications for the position.[141]

The employee's résumé needs to set out all the information they want to have considered by the screening panel:[142]

---

136 *OPSEU (Riddock) and Ministry of Correctional Services*, GSB#1206/89, 25 October 1990 (Emrich) at 7 [*Riddock*].

137 *Ontario Public Service Employees Union (Lewis) v Ontario (Finance)*, 2007 CanLII 51778 (ON GSB) (Jackson); *Sauve*, above note 84 at 19, and cases cited therein; *OPSEU (Borecki) and Ministry of Natural Resources*, GSB#256/82, 18 October 1982 (Swinton) at 8 [*Borecki*].

138 *Ontario Public Service Employees Union (O'Brien/Lepage) v Ontario (Northern Development, Mines and Forestry)*, 2011 CanLII 83713 (ON GSB) (Dissanayake) at 12–13 [*O'Brien/Lepage*].

139 *Ontario Public Service Employees Union (Robinson) v Ontario (Tourism Marketing Partnership Corporation)*, 2014 CanLII 80979 (ON GSB) (Anderson).

140 *OPSEU (Kuyntjes/Larman) and Ministry of Transportation and Communications*, GSB#920/85, 21 December 1987 (Gandz) at 5–6, and cases cited therein.

141 *Ontario Public Service Employees Union (Breton) v Ontario (Northern Development, Mines, Natural Resources and Forestry)*, 2022 CanLII 35392 (ON GSB) (Gee) at para 6 [*Breton*].

142 *Borecki*, above note 137 as referenced in *Breton*, *ibid* at para 7.

> When reading the applications, it is appropriate for the [job competition] panel to use its knowledge of the details of educational programs completed or positions held by the candidate, but it is not appropriate for the panel to consider knowledge of the candidates as individuals as, to do so for some, but not others, would be unfair.[143]

A pre-interview screen need not cover every required skill and ability.[144] However, the GSB must be satisfied that the screening mechanism fairly screens out the applicant without requiring review of additional information[145] and will decline to review additional information, as the board's role "ought not to be one of sitting in the position of the employer" and repeating the screening but rather ensuring the original screening was in good faith, "fair, reasonable and consistent."[146] Factors will be whether the process and scoring were consistently done, and whether relevant, and not irrelevant, information was considered.

If there is a flaw in the screening process, the union must still show that the flaw caused the grievor to not reach the threshold for being screened in.[147] If the grievor was improperly screened out, then the remedy needs to be determined. It has been suggested that the grievor be granted an interview following which the selection panel would reconsider its decision.

iii) *Use of Tests*

"The use of tests to screen out applicants should not be relied on to the exclusion of other evidence of the qualifications and abilities which the test is designed to measure."[148] Each question on any test must be weighted to ensure that the weighting is in "rough proportion" to the requirements of the job.[149] The scoring of the answers will be scrutinized.[150] Tests based on the requirements of the job will be given

---

143 *Breton*, above note 141 at para 8.

144 *OPSEU (Weekes) and Ministry of Correctional Services*, GSB#53/89, 5 July 1991 (Gorsky) at 64.

145 *Ibid.*

146 *O'Brien/Lepage*, above note 138 at 9–10.

147 *Breton*, above note 141 at paras 11 and 15.

148 See *Sauve*, above note 84, followed in *Ontario Public Service Employees Union (Myles) v Ontario (Finance)*, 2007 CanLII 30450 (ON GSB) (Carrier).

149 *Group, 2002*, above note 125 at 21.

150 *Ontario Public Service Employees Union (Smith) v Ontario (Northern Development and Mines)*, 2007 CanLII 59345 (ON GSB) (Mikus).

considerable weight, but more weight will usually be given to prior successful performance of the job duties.[151]

iv) Interviews

In *Esmail*, the GSB held that

> [a] job interview . . . must not be approached as a means of judging a performance. The purpose is not to determine who can better handle an interview. It is a process of information gathering for the purpose of ascertaining the true abilities and qualifications of the candidates.[152]

Care needs to be taken to ensure the questions test job skills, not other skills. It is unfair for a competition for a cook position to involve an unclear question, to the detriment of an experienced cook whose English was a second language.[153] It is also unfair to require power point presentations when such a presentation is not a skill related to the position.[154]

In order for interview questions to be marked in a meaningful fashion, panel members should agree in advance on "correct" or acceptable answers. The weight to be given to each part of a multi-part question should also be pre-determined.[155]

v) Consensus Scoring

The use of "consensus scoring," marking candidates based on discussion among members of the selection panel, has been contentious. It has been suggested that it is inappropriate and should not be allowed, because it can lead to "horse-trading" amongst selection committee members and undue influence being exerted on a dissenting member of the selection panel.[156] However, the GSB has more frequently held that consensus scoring can be acceptable.[157] The board's conclusion

151 *Hall/Powers*, above note 121 at 18. See also *Sauve*, above note 84 at 19.

152 *Esmail*, above note 93 at 19–20.

153 *Hamada*, above note 94 at para 29.

154 *Hogan*, above note 127 at 9–10.

155 *Ibid* at 20; *Thirumalai*, above note 122 at 15–16.

156 *Bent*, above note 88 at 1–3.

157 *Palatino*, above note 90 at 51, quoting *OPSEU (Eadie) and Ministry of Correctional Services*, GSB#766/88, 14 June 1989 (Devlin) at 13, and holding that, by itself, the practice of group discussion of scoring is at most a marginal defect. See also *OPSEU (Alam) and Ministry of Community and Social Services*, above note 124 at 25–26; *Riddock*, above note 136 at 9–10.

about the practice will depend on whether the selection panel simply attempted to arrive at consensus or whether individual members of the selection panel were required to agree on the score. If panelists do not exercise their own judgment, this is a defect that could warrant granting a remedy.[158] In other words, group discussion must not prevent each selection panel member's assessment of the candidates from having its weighted influence on the final scores.

vi) Bias

A supervisor of one of the applicants can serve on a job competition panel.[159] Nor does the GSB require that there be a human-resources professional or an "outsider" (someone from another division) on the panel. However, where selection panel members personally know the work of only one or some of the applicants, the GSB will closely examine the evidence to determine if this gave rise to any bias.[160] A panel member familiar with the candidate cannot give points for knowledge or experience they "know" the candidate has if that knowledge was not demonstrated during the interview.[161]

Job competition panels are not permitted to be biased against one of the candidates, and there are cases where bias has, in effect, been found.[162] In other cases, the GSB concluded that the personal knowledge of panel members did not interfere with the proper conduct of the competition.[163]

---

158 *Bent*, above note 88 at 3.

159 *Anderson, 1999*, above note 91 at 23; *Palatino*, above note 90 at 52.

160 *Anderson, 1999*, above note 91; *OPSEU (Loconte) and Ministry of Culture and Communications*, GSB#2573/87, 27 February 1989 (Fraser) at 29. *Cooke*, above note 101 at 27, puts the proposition more strongly: "where one supervisor is present, efforts must be made to ensure that other candidates are not handicapped by this fact."

161 *Naczynski*, above note 82 at 26.

162 *Anderson, 1999*, above note 91 at 32–33; *Eaton*, above note 100 at 14.

163 *Ontario Liquor Board Employees Union (Netta et al) and Liquor Control Board of Ontario*, GSB#1404/97, 20 December 1999 (Mikus) at 47; *Vaillancourt*, above note 92; *OPSEU (Woods) and Ministry of Transportation*, GSB#2253/87, 25 January 1989 (Watters) at 9.

4) Surplussed Employees

Under the OPSEU/MBC collective agreements, surplussed employees who receive pay in lieu of notice have a contractual right to apply to restricted competitions.[164] Where the employer argued that this meant only the right to apply, but not the right to compete or to have disputes arbitrated, the GSB has reasoned that such a narrow interpretation would make the right to apply almost meaningless.[165] Surplussed employees are protected against bad faith decisions and have the right to have their applications considered in good faith, in the same manner as the applications of unclassified, now fixed-term, employees.

D. CONVERSION OF FIXED-TERM TO REGULAR EMPLOYMENT

Under the *PSOA*, fixed-term employees may be appointed for "one or more" terms.[166] This raises the concern that the employer could use fixed-term employees to fill continuing positions.[167] The OPSEU/MBC collective agreements contain provisions for the "Conversion of Fixed-Term Positions to Positions in the Regular Service" after eighteen months in agreed circumstances. The purpose of the articles has been stated to be to redress the "mischief" of indiscriminate use of fixed-term employees to do continuing full-time work that should be done by regular employees.[168] A balance is struck by allowing the employer to make long-term fixed-term appointments, while also requiring recognition of the existence of ongoing positions.[169]

---

164 *OPSEU/MBC Unified and Correctional Collective Agreements*, above note 6, Art 20.2.3.

165 *OPSEU (Union) and Management Board Secretariat*, GSB#0405/99, 8 May 2001 (Abramsky) at 17.

166 *PSOA*, above note 1, s 32(4).

167 There were previously limits in the predecessor *PSA* regulation, and when those were removed, in the OPSEU/OPS collective agreement since 1989: *OPSEU/MBC Unified and Correctional Collective Agreements*, above note 6, Art 31A.15.

168 *OPSEU (Mistry) and Ontario Human Rights Commission*, GSB#569/96, 10 February 1998 (Verity) at 7 [*Mistry*]. In the 2005–2008 *OPSEU/MBC Collective Agreement*, the parties also agreed to a letter of understanding requiring a year over year percentage reduction in the number of unclassified employees.

169 *OPSEU (Justus) and Ministry of Revenue*, GSB#879/91, 16 March 1992 (Knopf) at 20 [*Justus*].

Article 31A.15.1.1 states:

> Where the same work has been performed by an employee in the Fixed-Term Service for a period of at least eighteen (18) consecutive months, except for situations where the fixed-term employee is replacing a regular employee on a leave of absence authorized by the Employer or as provided for under the Central Collective Agreement, and where the ministry has determined that there is a continuing need for that work to be performed on a full-time basis, the ministry shall establish a position within the Regular Service to perform that work.

Article 31A.15.1.2 provides that where a fixed-term position is "converted" to regular full-time, the incumbent will be made a regular term employee provided they have been in the position for eighteen months and provided there are no potential claims to the position by laid off employees.

The key terms in Article 31A.15.1.1 have been dealt with by the GSB:

Employee: Where there is an incumbent who has been in the position for eighteen months, that person will be appointed to the position without the need for a posting.[170] Where the necessary work remains present, but there is no incumbent at the time of the board order, the position will be posted.

When there is no ongoing incumbent, must the eighteen-month total have been accrued by a single employee in the position or can the position have been occupied by more than one employee? In a case decided under somewhat different provisions, the GSB held that "an employee" did not mean "the same employee," but "any employee."[171] The article is seen as converting positions, not individuals, to regular status, and so there is no need for the position to have been occupied by just one person. However, there must be a recognizable position staffed for eighteen consecutive months, not simply a total of eighteen months.

---

170 See, for example, *OPSEU (Conversion Grievance) and Ministry of Attorney General*, GSB#461/96, 10 February 1997 (Briggs) at 9.

171 *OPSEU (Union) and Ministry of Correctional Services*, GSB#803/91, 19 December 1994 (Dissanayake) at 6–7 [*Correctional, 1994*]. See also the inconclusive discussion in *OPSEU (Union) and Ministry of Transportation*, GSB#211/02, 9 April 2003 (Brown) [*Transportation, 2003*].

Hours worked collectively by a group of fixed-term employees cannot simply be pooled.[172]

Same Work: Where there is a single employee who works for the requisite period of time, the article only requires that the "same work" be done by that employee. That work need not be done in a single position or in the same geographical location.[173] As long as the work as a whole is the same, then the article will apply even if the employee also does an incidental or limited amount of different work.[174] Performing the work of different classifications will, in most instances, mean that the work is not the same.[175]

Has Been Performed: Since striking employees are not performing work, a period during which a fixed-term employee is on strike will not count toward the accumulation of the eighteen-month period.[176]

Except for Situations Where the Fixed-Term Employee Is Replacing a Regular Employee on a Leave of Absence: Where the fixed-term employee is assigned to replace a regular employee on a leave, there is a cessation of the accumulation of the eighteen-month period of time, but that cessation only applies where the fixed-term employee is temporarily doing the actual duties of a regular employee on leave. If the fixed-term employee is really continuing to perform the prior duties of a fixed-term position, the assignment to "backfill" the person on leave will not be seen as a legitimate replacement,[177] and the time nominally worked in the replacement position will still count toward the eighteen-month total. The replacement exception does not apply at all when the regular employee is away on secondment, rather than a leave of absence.[178] In that circumstance, the time spent by the fixed-term employee in the position does count toward the accumulation of the total needed for conversion to regular status.

---

172 *OPSEU (McPhail et al) and Ministry of Attorney General*, GSB#1873/97, 5 May 2003 (Briggs) at 6 [*McPhail*], dealing with freelance court reporters.

173 *Ibid* at 7–9; *Mistry*, above note 168 at 10.

174 *Mistry*, above note 168 at 12.

175 *McPhail*, above note 172 at 9.

176 *Transportation, 2003*, above note 171.

177 *Mistry*, above note 168 at 10.

178 *OPSEU (Adamo et al) and Ministry of Correctional Services*, GSB#1234/93, 22 November 1995 (Kaplan) at 10–11 [*Adamo*].

Where the Ministry Has Determined That There Is a Continuing Need: The mere fact that the work has been assigned to a fixed-term employee (or employees) for a period of more than eighteen months produces a "rebuttable presumption" that the ministry has determined there is a continuing need.[179] Management could decide to stop having the work performed or have it done on a basis other than full-time, but if management continues to have full-time work performed, the position is subject to conversion.[180]

In deciding whether the presumption of continuing need is rebutted, the GSB will look at the events after the filing of the grievance. Where fixed-term contracts had continued for several years, and a conversion grievance might very well have succeeded if filed earlier, the GSB will still look to see if the employer is *continuing to have the work done* at the time of the grievance and thereafter.[181] It will certainly not be sufficient for the grievor to be simply working out their notice after being been released from employment.[182]

Where management decides to dispense with the position, then the presumption of continuing need will be rebutted. Where the grievor's position was only extended past the (then) required two-year period because the employer was actively reviewing whether to continue the position, and the employer shortly thereafter determined that it would not have the work done any more, the GSB declined to convert the position, holding that the employer had actually determined that there was no ongoing need for the work to be performed.[183] Whether the discontinuance of work is a wise decision from the point of view of the efficient operation of the service was not for the board to decide. However the decision made by the employer about the "continuing need for that work" must be made in a bona fide manner and with reasonable regard for the facts.[184]

---

179 *OPSEU (Lynch-Burrus) and Ministry of Community and Social Services*, GSB#1078/92, 8 February 1995 (Dissanayake) at 13 [*Lynch-Burrus*]; *Correctional, 1994*, above note 171 at 10.

180 *Transportation, 2003*, above note 171 and cases cited therein.

181 *OPSEU (Sinnathurai) and Ministry of the Attorney General*, GSB#749/96, 9 February 1997 (Briggs) at 11–12 [*Sinnathurai*]; *OPSEU (Sopha) and Ministry of Attorney General*, GSB#748/96, 8 February 1997 (Briggs) [*Sopha*].

182 *Sopha*, *ibid* at 10–11.

183 *Lynch-Burrus*, above note 179 at 11–12.

184 *Mistry*, above note 168 at 16.

The question of whether the conversion obligation exists where the employer is going to continue to have employees perform the work for more than eighteen months, but not indefinitely, has been examined in the context of an announced government intention to privatize particular work. The continuing need must be that of the government and not of a private sector employer to whom work is being transferred.[185] "Continuing need" cannot relate to an entity that is not a party to the collective agreement; so the issue becomes whether the remaining duration of employment by the government is sufficient to support a finding of "continuing need." Where there was an anticipated, but not certain, privatization to take place six months or more in the future, the GSB has found that that length of time constitutes a "continuing need" for the work.[186] Even where the board accepted the certainty of the end of the work, ongoing employment of only twelve months has been found to be sufficient to establish continuing need.[187] However, the continuation of government employment for some additional months was not found to be sufficient to prove continuing need where a ministry could demonstrate that it told unclassified employees almost from the beginning of their employment that their work was temporary and would be transferred to the private sector.[188]

The employer is also free to continue to have the work done by means other than a full-time position. The employer can assign the work to other staff or decide to have the work done on a part-time basis, even if this means that the job of a long-term fixed-term employee is ended;[189] but, if full-time work is ongoing, the employer is to convert the position.[190]

---

185 *OPSEU (Union) and Ministry of Finance*, GSB#1237/98, 11 December 1998 (Briggs) at 12 [*Finance, 1998*].

186 *Transportation, 2003*, above note 171 at 17.

187 *OPSEU (Burditt) and Ministry of Health*, GSB#1179/96, 16 May 1997 (Briggs) at 13.

188 *Finance, 1998*, above note 185 at 11.

189 *Mistry*, above note 168 at 18; *OPSEU (Jennings) and Ministry of Revenue*, GSB#2228/91, 29 March 1993 (Stewart) at 18 [*Jennings*]; *Adamo*, above note 178. See also *Sinnathurai*, above note 181 at 8, where, in the context of a massive reduction of work on province-wide basis, the work of the unclassified grievor was absorbed by existing staff at the receiving ministry.

190 *Mistry*, above note 168 at 18.

A "mere hiatus," or pause, in full-time staffing of the position, due to delayed funding, will not remove the conversion obligation.[191]

An administrative directive imposing a freeze on filling vacancies cannot override the conversion requirement.[192]

On a Full-Time Basis: A "full-time" basis means that the stipulated minimum number of hours is being worked on a "straight time" basis, without including overtime and many leaves.[193]

E. RIGHTS OF SEASONAL EMPLOYEES

"Seasonal" employees are appointed for at least eight consecutive weeks but less than twelve consecutive months, to an annually recurring full-time position.[194] Article 32 of the OPSEU/MBC collective agreements provides for a range of entitlements for such employees, including, most notably, the right to be recalled on the basis of seniority to the "same position" in the following season.[195] This provision is intended to give priority and a measure of seniority based job security to senior seasonal employees.[196] This supports a broad inquiry whether, on comparison of the job in successive seasons, the substance of the job and the nature of the duties are "substantially similar" and so considered the same position.[197] It is recognized that duties and responsibilities may change somewhat from year to year in the "same position." Job title and position classification, and even work location, are not determinative.

The probationary period of seasonal employees is two full periods of seasonal employment (of at least eight consecutive weeks each), worked

191 *Jennings*, above note 189 at 19; *OPSEU (Hamilton) and Management Board Secretariat*, GSB#493/01, 2 July 2003 (Leighton) at 10.

192 *Correctional, 1994*, above note 171 at 9.

193 *Ontario Public Service Employees Union (Jacobs et al) v Ontario (Solicitor General)*, 2020 CanLII 97349 (ON GSB) (Hewat) at paras 48–53 and cases cited.

194 *OPSEU/MBC Unified and Correctional Collective Agreements*, above note 6, Art 32.2.1

195 *Ibid*, Art 32.5.1.1.

196 *Ontario Public Service Employees Union (Union) v Ontario (Natural Resources and Forestry)*, 2022 CanLII 106480 (ON GSB) (Dissanayake) [*Forestry, 2022*] referencing the history of the provision in detail; *Re Anderson*, GSB#471/86 (Roberts) at 13–14.

197 *Forestry, 2022*, *ibid* at para 10; *Ontario Public Service Employees Union (Union) v Ontario (Natural Resources and Forestry)*, 2019 CanLII 97253 (ON GSB) (Dissanayake) at 11–12.

in consecutive years in the same position in the same ministry.[198] The right of recall is lost if the employee is unavailable for or declines an offer of re-employment.[199]

1) Seasonal Employment

The threshold issue is whether the individual's employment meets the definition of seasonal employment.

The weeks of employment must total eight, be consecutive, and occur without interruption, for qualification as a seasonal employee.[200] The requirement for the weeks to be consecutive means that contracts of shorter than eight weeks' duration that are separated by "an interval of time" cannot be combined to meet the threshold of eight weeks.[201] However, *the eight-week period* of time need not be worked entirely in the same position, as the mandated consecutive weeks are the minimum term for appointments of *employees*, but do not relate to the duration of any particular *position*. As a result, an employee can accumulate the eight weeks by working consecutively in more than one position with a shorter term.[202]

For a position to be eligible to be treated as seasonal employment, it must recur annually. This means there must be a "foreseeable regularity and repetitiveness"[203] involved in the employee's appointments in successive years. Where the work was seasonal, but there was no guarantee that the work would be undertaken in a subsequent year, the GSB held that the positions were not "annually recurring."[204] In any event, the "core duties" of the position need to remain the same from one year to

198 *OPSEU/MBC Unified and Correctional Collective Agreements*, above note 6, Art 32.3.1.

199 *Ibid*, Art 32.4.2.1(d).

200 *OPSEU (Union) and Ministry of Natural Resources*, GSB#2181/90, 25 February 1993 (Barrett) at 5.

201 *OPSEU (Hall et al) and Ministry of Natural Resources*, GSB#1282/88, 26 June 1990 (Epstein) at 5 [*Hall*], followed in *OPSEU (Millar) and Ministry of Natural Resources*, GSB#675/89, 7 May 1992 (Verity) at 9 [*Millar*].

202 *Hall*, *ibid*, and *Millar*, *ibid*.

203 *OPSEU (Union) and Ministry of Transportation*, GSB#1623/87, 14 June 1989 (Samuels) at 4.

204 *Ibid*.

another, and "some overlap" is not sufficient.[205] Where the seasonal employee has been appointed to another type of unclassified appointment (for example, as a student), but can show that the employment nonetheless continues to meet the definition of seasonal employee, the board will order that the employee be treated accordingly.[206]

A prerequisite for a seasonal employee to be able to exercise a right to recall is the completion of the probationary period (the termination of probationary seasonal employees is subject to the same legal tests and issues as the termination of other probationers). A minimum period of eight weeks' probation is required, but it can be longer because the probationary period that must be completed is of whatever duration the employer sets in a given season.[207]

The position to which the recall right attaches is a position actually formally occupied, and not a position that the employee may have casually done in part.[208] Seasonal employees can hold more than one position. Where an employee accepts a *seasonal* position and then, as a result of being employed in that position, they are unable to accept another offer of employment, the declining of the second offer of employment does not trigger a loss of all seasonal employment seniority,[209] although it will presumably mean the loss of the recall right for the position not accepted.

Concerning employment status between seasonal contracts, the GSB in *OPSEU (Ballak) and Ministry of Natural Resources*[210] concluded that their employment actually comes to an end at the end of each season and then recommences. The board noted: (1) the former *PSA* provision that, where the employment of a public servant is for a

205 *Forestry, 2022*, above note 196 at paras 97–98; *OPSEU (Wiltshire) and Ministry of Natural Resources*, GSB#1041/93, 20 July 1995 (Kaplan) at 10, where the grievance was dismissed in part because, although the grievor was employed in subsequent seasons for the same ministry at the same office, the positions had significantly different duties.

206 *OPSEU (McConnell) and Ministry of Natural Resources*, GSB#587/94, 19 June 1995 (Dissanayake).

207 *OPSEU (Lobraico) and Ministry of Natural Resources*, GSB#1905/87, 25 May 1989 (Forbes-Roberts) at 13–14, citing *OPSEU (Bean) and Ministry of Natural Resources*, GSB#612/86, 15 March 1988 (Verity) at 11.

208 *OPSEU (Beacock) and Ministry of Transportation and Communications*, GSB#1249/85, 30 November 1987 (Forbes-Roberts) at 4.

209 *OPSEU (Goldberg) and Ministry of Natural Resources*, GSB# 840/94, 19 June 1995 (Backhouse) at 4.

210 GSB#1869/92, 2 November 1993 (Knopf) at 12–13 [*Ballak*].

specified period, the status of public servant ceases at the expiry of that period (which provision is found in the current *PSOA*[211]); and (2) the entirely consistent collective agreement treatment of seasonal employees, in that they are offered "employment" at the start of each season and lose carry-over seniority on declining an offer of "re-employment." The result is that only the specifically bargained between season employment entitlements will apply, and further rights will not be implied. Article 32 functions like a collective agreement within a collective agreement,[212] giving seasonal employees rights to job security, bridged seniority, ongoing benefits, and attendance credit accumulation. However, given the extensive statement of expressly stated rights, other rights are not to be implied.[213] Seasonal employees *do not* have the between season right to apply as employees for vacant positions, as there is no specific provision to that effect.

Where the provisions of the collective agreement that relate to seasonal employees do not specifically apply, the GSB has declined to bridge employee entitlements from one season to another. Employees who were full-time, as opposed to seasonal, but who received regular, seasonal reassignment to a higher classification, were found not to be entitled to have annual merit increases applied to the salary of that annually recurring temporary classification.[214] The union referenced that seasonal employees received annual merit increases. The full-time employees were found not covered by the seasonal employee provisions, but rather by the collective agreement provision dealing with temporary assignment pay.[215]

It is notable that the ongoing relationship between the employer and the seasonal employee has been found sufficient to bridge *Employment Standards Act, 2000* (*ESA*)[216] entitlements. According to an employment standards adjudicator, the provisions of the collective agreement and the practices of the parties indicate a clear intention to structure and protect an ongoing relationship, and so seasonal workers remain

211 *PSOA*, above note 1, s 54.

212 *OPSEU (Union) and Management Board of Cabinet*, GSB#915/88, 4 July 1990 (Wilson) at 9.

213 *Ballak*, above note 210 at 12–13.

214 *OPSEU (Brousseau et al) and Ministry of Transportation*, GSB#2448/96, 17 November 1999 (Petryshen).

215 *Ibid* at 8.

216 SO 2000, c 41 [*ESA*].

employees during their hiatus for severance-pay entitlement purposes under the *ESA*, notwithstanding the then-*PSA* and current *PSOA* provision stating that status as a public servant only continues for the specified period.[217]

Conversion of unclassified seasonal employees to classified or full-time status has been claimed where the employment is virtually continual. The GSB has responded by noting the statutory entitlement of the employer to have ongoing unclassified contracts,[218] although it would be ready to review the potential applicability of the collective agreement provisions for conversion of unclassified positions to classified ones.

F. JUST CAUSE FOR DISCIPLINE AND DISMISSAL RE GENERAL CONDUCT EXPECTATIONS

1) Context

The OPSEU/MBC Collective Agreements state, "It is understood that the right of the Employer to discipline or dismiss employees shall be for just cause" and set out the right to grieve any disciplinary action by the employer.[219] This is a standard clause for collective agreements, and it has been applied so as to *not* hold unionized direct employees of government to particularly high standards of conduct, save as required by specific ethical obligations unique to public service or by the obligations appropriate to specific positions of trust, such as correctional officers.

Certain aspects of public servants' ethical conduct obligations—confidentiality, discretion in speech, conflict of interest, public comment, and political activity—have been addressed specifically in the *PSOA* and common law, and they are discussed in Chapter 3. Otherwise, there are good reasons to avoid broader generalizations about the ethical uniqueness of public service employment.

First, a substantial ethical obligation forms part of every employment relationship. It has been found by courts that there is a "general duty of good faith owed by an employee to his employer during the

217 *Re Ontario Ministry of Natural Resources*, [1992] OESAD No 218 (Adj Randall).

218 *Justus*, above note 169; *OPSEU (Bennett) and Ministry of Tourism and Recreation*, GSB#2884/91, 13 May 1997 (Leighton).

219 *OPSEU/MBC Unified and Correctional Collective Agreements*, above note 6, Art 21.1.

currency of his employment."[220] The same general expectation forms part of the arbitral jurisprudence concerning unionized employees:

> It is an established principle of the common law governing an employer/employee relationship that "an employee is under a duty to serve his employer with good faith and fidelity and not deliberately do something which may harm his employer's business." This has been held to be an implied term of any collective agreement unless it is explicitly excluded.[221]

So, a general employment duty of good faith conduct applies to public servants, and other public and private sector employees alike.

Second, the employment consequences of the duty of good faith conduct are to be determined by a job-specific analysis. The Supreme Court has held there must be a balanced "proportionality" between management's rights and recognition of the crucial importance of employment for the employee.[222] There is not to be any presumptive acceptance of general standards set by management without regard for the actual requirements of the given employment relationship. Justice Iacobucci stated:

> I favour an analytical framework that examines each case on its own particular facts and circumstances, and considers the nature and seriousness of the dishonesty in order to assess whether it is reconcilable

---

220 *Faccenda Chicken Ltd v Fowler*, [1986] 1 All ER 617 (CA), as cited in *57134 Manitoba Ltd v Palmer* (1989), 37 BCLR (2d) 50 (BC CA) at 56. A more recent formulation is that "parties generally must perform their contractual duties honestly and reasonably and not capriciously or arbitrarily": *Bhasin v Hrynew*, 2014 SCC 71 at para 63, which extends to employment contracts: *Matthews v Ocean Nutrition Canada Ltd*, 2020 SCC 26 at para 40.

221 *Re Regional Municipality of Hamilton-Wentworth and CUPE, Local 167*, 1978 CanLII 3420 (ON LA) (Kennedy) at 53–54, citing *R v Fuller et al, Ex parte Earles and McKee*, 1968 CanLII 326 (ON CA), cited in turn in *Re Ministry of Attorney General, Corrections Branch and British Columbia Government Employees' Union* (1982), 3 LAC (3d) 140 at 158 [*BCGEU*], and *Serco Facilities Management and PSAC (Baggs)* (2000), 91 LAC (4th) 289 (Oakley) at 299.

222 *Reference Re Public Service Employee Relations Act (Alta)*, [1987] 1 SCR 313, Dickson J at 368, endorsed in *McKinley v BC Tel*, 2001 SCC 38 at para 38 [*McKinley*]. See also *Slaight Communications Inc v Davidson*, [1989] 1 SCR 1038, where Dickson CJC discusses that it is consistent with the values of the *Canadian Charter of Rights and Freedoms*, Part I of the *Constitution Act, 1982*, being Schedule B to the *Canada Act 1982* (UK), 1982, c 11 [*Charter*] to address the unequal nature of the employment relationship.

> with sustaining the employment relationship. Such an approach mitigates the possibility that an employee will be unduly punished by the strict application of an unequivocal rule that equates all forms of dishonest behaviour with just cause for dismissal. At the same time, it would properly emphasize that dishonesty going to the core of the employment relationship carries the potential to warrant dismissal for just cause, but also points to the general importance of an assessment of employee obligations that is based on the actual requirements of the position in question.[223]

There has been no interest in exempting public service employment from this kind of approach. Indeed, the leading Supreme Court decision in *Fraser v PSSRB* applies exactly this kind of approach to the central public service issue of public criticism of the government employer,[224] and the GSB has explicitly applied the *McKinley* proportionality approach to assessing the impact of dishonesty on the employment relationship.[225]

2) On-Duty Conduct

The seminal GSB case of *Maw and Ministry of Transportation and Communications*,[226] decided by the first chair of the GSB, established that in the public service, just as in the private sector, the discharge of employees is a last resort, to be used only where it is clear that corrective measures would not be successful. In other words, discharge is only appropriate when the employee-employer relationship is no longer viable.

In that case and subsequent cases, the GSB also adopted the well-known private sector lists of factors[227] for determining the propriety of

---

223 *McKinley*, above note 222 at para 57, Iacobucci J delivering the judgment of the Court.

224 *Fraser v PSSRB*, [1985] 2 SCR 455, discussed at length in Chapter 3. See also *BCGEU*, above note 221 at 161, as followed in *Alberta and AUPE, Loc 6 (Smith), Re*, 1996 CanLII 20357 (AB GAA) (Moreau) at 415.

225 *Ontario Public Service Employees Union (Lunario) v Ontario (Community Safety and Correctional Services)*, 2015 CanLII 60425 (ON GSB) (Luborsky) at paras 39–42 [*Lunario*].

226 *OPSEU (Maw) and Ministry of Transportation and Communications*, GSB#1/75, 15 December 1975 (Beatty) [*Maw*].

227 *Re USWA, Local 3257 and The Steel Equipment Co Ltd*, 1964 CanLII 984 (ON LA) (Reville) applied in *Maw*, *ibid* at 13, and see *OPSEU (Bradley) and Ministry of Education and Training*, GSB#1050/94, 8 March 1996 (Finley) at 25–26; *OPSEU (Lewis) and Ministry of Education and Training*, GSB#1222/99,

disciplinary sanctions, including discharge. These factors centre on the rehabilitative potential of the grievor as a reasonably good and trusted employee, which includes the following considerations:

- the seriousness of the offence in terms of company policy and company obligations
- whether company rules have been consistently enforced
- the grievor's state of mind and motivations at the time
- degree of remorse
- past record
- the impact of the discipline

In labour relations, it can be viewed as suspect to subject similarly situated employees to different levels of discipline. The GSB has noted that the feasibility of being consistent "declines when one attempts to apply it across disparate ministries throughout the public service or even across disparate institutions within the same ministry."[228] Ultimately, the need for consistency and "the exercise of discretion to modify a penalty must both be applied and assessed in the particular circumstances of each given case."

The GSB has certainly not accepted that it should hold all public servants to especially high standards. In a 1979 decision, *Bernardi and Liquor Control Board of Ontario*,[229] the grievor was the manager of a Liquor Control Board of Ontario outlet dismissed for falsifying records. In upholding his discharge, the GSB vice-chair did state that "our decisions should not compromise the principle that all members of the public service of Ontario, both bargaining unit employees and supervisory personnel, should be held to a high standard of integrity in

---

15 February 2001 (Abramsky) at 19–20; *OPSEU (Adam) and Ministry of Community Safety and Correctional Services*, GSB#2003-0892, 24 February 2005 (Herlich) at 23–28; *Canadian Broadcasting Corporation and CUPE* (1979), 23 LAC (2d) 227 (Arthurs) at 230–31, applied by the GSB in *OPSEU (Martin) and Ministry of Health*, GSB#346/92, 13 September 1995 (Verity) at 9–10, and *Ontario Liquor Control Boards' Employees Union (Huvos) and Liquor Control Board of Ontario*, GSB#2003-0710, 31 October 2003 (Abramsky) at 11–12. See also *OPSEU (Menzies) and Ministry of Transportation*, GSB#751/91, 18 October 1991 (Waisglass).

228 *OPSEU (Horan) and Ministry of Public Safety and Security*, 23 October 2002 (Herlich) at 21–22.

229 GSB#102/79, 17 December 1979 (Prichard) at 19 [*Bernardi*].

all their actions." This view was only cited in two subsequent cases[230] and was not given any particular weight in either case. Instead, the GSB has engaged in weighing all the factors that would be generally applicable, in the public or private sector, when deciding on discipline. In the early leading case of *OPSEU (Rice) and Ministry of Transportation and Communications*, the GSB applied the trend in private sector jurisprudence away from automatic discharge for theft and toward a contextual inquiry, recognizing that while public servants are to "be held to high standards of integrity in all their actions," disciplinary matters come down to the "grievor's prospects for acceptable conduct in the future."[231]

When applying general arbitral principles to the question of whether to reduce disciplinary penalties, the GSB has had regard for higher standards of conduct required for particular types of trusted positions. Welfare workers are responsible for making benefits decisions on the basis of program eligibility requirements, supported by confidentially held highly sensitive personal information[232] and to do otherwise is a breach of public trust.[233] All employees with access to computerized records containing confidential information about members of the public have a "high duty" to maintain that confidentiality.[234] Employees at the Family Responsibility Office work to ensure women receive the support to which they are entitled, and female clients will share their most personal family circumstances, which may involve family violence. Clients would lose confidence in staff that were viewing vile pornography at work.[235] Inspectors can expect to have any information about their previous

---

230 *Penner and Liquor Control Board of Ontario*, GSB#307/80, 9 March 1981 (Barton) at 6–8; *OPSEU (Rice) and Ministry of Transportation and Communications*, GSB#754/85, 16 April 1986 (Samuels) at 5 [*Rice*].

231 *Rice*, *ibid* at 5 citing *Bernardi*, above note 229 at 19. See also *OPSEU (Tyler) and Ministry of Community and Social Services*, GSB#601/82, 23 January 1984 (McLaren) at 17.

232 *Ontario Public Service Employees Union v Association of Management, Administrative and Professional Crown Employees of Ontario*, 2010 CanLII 52649 (ON GSB) (Stewart) discussing what security checks are appropriate.

233 *Ontario Public Service Employees Union (Chabanova) v Ontario (Community and Social Services)*, 2011 CanLII 23159 (ON GSB) (Devins) at 92–93.

234 *Ontario Public Service Employees Union (Fortin) v Ontario*, 2017 CanLII 16719 (ON GSB) (Luborsky) at para 25.

235 *Ontario Public Service Employees Union (Aboutaeib/Carletti) v Ontario (Community and Social Services)*, 2011 CanLII 83707 (ON GSB) (Johnston) at 51.

misconduct disclosed by the prosecution to the accused.[236] Driver examiners are trusted not to compromise the integrity of the driver's licence system.[237] Courthouse workers need to maintain courthouse decorum and avoid swearing and yelling at a co-worker who behaved in a manner found to be offensive and irritating.[238] Institutional health professionals must maintain a high standard of propriety when dealing with patients in their care.[239] The same is true of correctional officers in their care of inmates, discussed in detail below. The expectation of propriety for persons engaged in the institutional care of vulnerable persons is reinforced by statutory provisions in the *PSOA* and the *CECBA* that limit the PSGB's and GSB's remedial power to reinstate staff found to have used excessive force on, or to have sexually assaulted, residents of facilities.[240]

a) On-Duty Conduct of Correctional Officers

Inmates admitted to a correctional facility "lose their ability to care and protect themselves. It is the correctional staff that must provide that care and protection and to not do so creates many risks to the inmates, to other staff and to the institution."[241] Correctional officers hold a position of power over vulnerable inmates that can be easily abused and so their overall conduct should be "beyond reproach."[242] Force is not to be used against an inmate unless required to prevent harm and

---

236 *Ontario Public Service Employees Union (Union) v Ontario (Government Services)*, 2011 CanLII 23158 (ON GSB) (Stewart).

237 *OPSEU (Dyer/Papple/Smeltzer) and Ministry of Transportation and Communications*, GSB#1129/94, 11 December 1996 (Dissanayake) at 7, dealing with driver examiners who gave themselves motorcycle licences without taking the necessary road test.

238 *Ontario Public Service Employees Union (Ryan) v Ontario (Attorney General)*, 2017 CanLII 47140 (ON GSB) (Dissanayake) at para 78.

239 *OPSEU (Chan) and Ministry of Health*, GSB#911/86, 22 September 1988 (Brandt) at 8, concerning the dismissal of a Psychiatric Nursing Assistant at the Queen Street Mental Health Centre for the sexual abuse of a patient.

240 Re the GSB, see *CECBA*, above note 3, s 7(4), discussed in Chapter 11; re the PSGB, see *PSOA*, above note 1, s 24(1), discussed in Chapter 12.

241 *Ontario Public Service Employees Union (Fitzgerald et al) v Ontario (Solicitor General)*, 2020 CanLII 39020 (ON GSB) (Gee).

242 *OPSEU (Mailloux) and Ministry of Correctional Services*, GSB#1064/90, 8 June 1995 (Kirkwood) at 70, concerning dismissal of a correctional officer for alleged sexual assaults on former female inmates. To the same effect see *OPSEU (Campbell)*, GSB#1876/91, 3 November 1994 (Charney) at 15. There is also a specific statutory obligation to cooperate in investigations, which is found in s 22 of the *Ministry of Correctional Services Act*, RSO 1990, c. M.22, as discussed below.

maintain order.[243] Use of force can be necessary in the correctional officer role and is by no means always excessive.[244] Excessive use of force is "a breach of trust of the highest order," only compounded when the correctional officer fails to tell the truth about the incident.[245]

Excessive use of force cases have come before the GSB "with a concerning frequency."[246] However, it has been identified that a hopefully real and sustained raising of management standards has produced a reduced toleration of excessive use of force. This managerial "change in attitude" has resulted more consistently in discharge as the penalty, which means older cases resulting in more limited discipline are of little value,[247] as "the level of abuse of inmates that may at one time have been tolerated, and that may not have led to termination, is simply no longer acceptable."[248] It has been noted that there is also more training on de-escalation techniques, defensive tactics, and report writing.[249]

An important part of the evolving treatment of excessive use of force has been identifying and addressing a persistent and sometimes condoned "code of silence"[250] operating as follows:

---

243 See *Ministry of Correctional Services Act*, *ibid*, O Reg 778, s 7(1) and an early discussion in *OPSEU (Thompson et al) and Ministry of Correctional Services*, GSB#128/78, 14 May 1979 (Swan) at 26.

244 For a discussion of use of force found to not be excessive, see *Ontario Public Service Employees Union (Pratt) v Ontario (Community Safety and Correctional Services)*, 2018 CanLII 109257 (ON GSB) (Sheehan) at paras 82–87.

245 *OPSEU (Beltrano et al) and Ministry of Community Safety and Correctional Services*, GSB#2003-3597, 11 August 2008 (Petryshen) [*Beltrano*], quoted in *Ontario Public Service Employees Union (Esser) v Ontario (Community Safety and Correctional Services)*, 2015 CanLII 90136 (ON GSB) (Watters) at para 423 [*Esser*].

246 *Ontario Public Service Employees Union (Wild) v Ontario (Community Safety and Correctional Services)*, 2016 CanLII 18941 (ON GSB) (Harris) at para 21.

247 *Ontario Public Service Employees Union (Maude) v Ontario (Community Safety and Correctional Services)*, 2016 CanLII 18935 (ON GSB) (Petryshen) at para 37 [*Maude*].

248 *Ontario Public Service Employees Union (Gour) v Ontario (Community Safety and Correctional Services)*, 2016 CanLII 18733 (ON GSB) (Misra) at para 97.

249 *Ibid*. The *Ministry of Correctional Services Act*, above note 242, Reg 778, ss 1.2–1.3, as amended by O Reg 574/21, requires biennial use of force and de-escalation training.

250 *Beltrano*, above note 245 quoted and expanded upon in *Ontario Public Service Employees Union (Zolnierczyk) v Ontario (Community Safety and Correctional Services)*, 2011 CanLII 17011 (ON GSB) (Herlich) at 22 [*Zolnierczyk*]. See also *Ontario Public Service Employees Union (Gillis et al) v Ontario (Community Safety and Correctional Services)*, 2008 CanLII 26249 (ON GSB) (Abramsky) [*Gillis*].

> As the summary of the evidence discloses and as a number of decisions have referenced, there is a code of silence in correctional institutions which places considerable pressure on a CO [correctional officer] to refrain from disclosing the misconduct of fellow officers to management. In a setting where COs rely on each other to a considerable degree for safety, it is perhaps not entirely surprising that the code of silence is a part of the reality of the jail. Another aspect of this reality is that a CO who breaches this unwritten rule is likely to face serious adverse consequences. The code of silence operates to protect COs who engage in misconduct and to some extent it condones and encourages misconduct. The code of silence also operates to turn those COs who elect not to remain silent into victims. They will likely be labeled a rat and generally ostracized. They will often be harassed in various ways, inside and outside of their institution. They may find that the only way to address the stress associated with being labeled a rat is to change institutions or give up correctional duties.

As an example of the "code of silence" in operation, the GSB in 2013 found that when a witness correctional officer (CO) described a slap of an inmate, two other witness COs lied about the incident.[251] The arbitral result for those who lied was effectively three-year suspensions, with only their long service preventing the discharge of the employees.[252] It is to be hoped that lengthy suspensions for proven lying will encourage honesty. The GSB has noted that "the code of silence is so pervasive that it would take a concerted and sustained effort by management and the Union to address it."[253]

Discharges for excessive use of force are more likely to be upheld where the grievor continues denying the unreasonable use of force in reports filed, disciplinary interviews, and in testimony before the GSB, as the continued denial leaves the GSB unpersuaded that misconduct of this nature will not recur in the future,[254] and also where the grievor minimizes the incident and their responsibility, and produces unsatisfactory excuses.[255] Discharges are less likely to be upheld where the

251 *Ontario Public Service Employees Union (Marshall et al) v Ontario (Community Safety and Correctional Services)*, 2013 CanLII 72584 (ON GSB) (Abramsky).

252 *Esser*, above note 245

253 *Gillis*, above note 250 at 64.

254 *Ontario Public Service Employees Union (Goden) v Ontario (Community Safety and Correctional Services)*, 2018 CanLII 64393 (ON GSB) (Watters) at para 104.

255 *Zolnierczyk*, above note 250.

grievor recognizes the seriousness of their misconduct and is genuinely apologetic, particularly when combined with significant years of service free of any significant discipline.[256]

There are common law and legislative provisions supporting serious consequences for excessive use of force. A conviction for committing a criminal act can amount to a finding of fact binding on the GSB.[257] There is the above-mentioned statutory limit on the ability to order reinstatement to the same position in which the grievor engaged in unreasonable use of force.[258] Criminal courts have found that deliberate beatings of inmates by correctional or police officers normally warrant custodial sentences, partly due to the breach of public trust.[259]

There are a range of other functions crucial to the safety of inmates, including the timing and quality of tours or inspections of cells, escorting, counts of ward populations, and safeguarding of keys, that must be performed according to institutional policy in order to ensure the security and safety of the institution,[260] and failure to fulfill these obligations can be cause for serious discipline and discharge; for example, where a fight between inmates is not stopped and causes serious injury to an inmate in the grievor's custody.[261]

b) Section 22 of the *Ministry of Correctional Services Act*

Section 22 of the *Ministry of Correctional Services Act* states that the ministry can dismiss any employee of that ministry who obstructs an inspection or investigation or withholds any information required by an inspector for an inspection or investigation. "Section 22 drives home the expectation for honesty and integrity on the part of those engaged in correctional service in the express requirement to take responsibility and be accountable for one's actions and trust that those actions will

256 *Maude*, above note 247 at para 48.

257 See the discussion in Chapter 11.

258 *Ibid.*

259 See, as an example, *R v Rosa*, 2011 ONCJ 348.

260 *Ontario Public Service Employees Union (Langford et al) v Ontario (Community Safety and Correctional Services)*, 2017 CanLII 30327 (ON GSB) (Stephens); *Ontario Public Service Employees Union (Paplinskie) v Ontario (Community Safety and Correctional Services)*, 2018 CanLII 14309 (ON GSB) (Watters).

261 *Ontario Public Service Employees Union (Miller) v Ontario (Solicitor General)*, 2019 CanLII 118279 (ON GSB) (Devins).

be assessed according to the appropriate standard."[262] The threat of dismissal does not violate the *Charter* as there is no "right to remain silent" in an administrative investigation.[263]

The obligation to provide information has been found not to extend to giving a sworn statement.[264] Further, where the grievor is facing a criminal charge and has already given a full statement to the employer, the employee is justified in asking what further information is actually required before answering the employers' further questions. In order for a breach of the obligation under section 22 to be its own violation, there must be a clear failure to cooperate with an investigator, best supported by advising the employee of the requirement to cooperate.[265]

Where the employer argued that the provision establishes a non-reviewable penalty of dismissal for any proven withholding of information from an inspector, the GSB affirmed its general remedial jurisdiction to substitute a lesser penalty.[266] Failures to disclose information that were clear violations of section 22 of the Act were not found by themselves to warrant dismissal, and the GSB and PSGB have substituted delayed reinstatements amounting to one-year suspensions.[267]

The ministry's internal policy on employee representation at a section 22 investigation meeting permits such a representative to be present if the employee is likely to be disciplined, the representative is readily available so there will be no unreasonable delay, and the employee asks to have a representative present.[268] The representative may attend only as an observer and may not "coach, direct or actively participate in the review process, but may raise concerns for the record about the

262 *Jurkus v Ontario (Solicitor General)*, 2022 CanLII 31358 (ON PSGB) at para 156 [*Jurkus*].

263 *Keating v Ontario (Community Safety and Correctional Services)*, 2009 CanLII 15648 (ON PSGB) at paras 30–31 [*Keating*], citing *R* v *March*, [2006] OJ No 664 (CJ).

264 *OPSEU (Hyland) and Ministry of Correctional Services*, GSB#1062/89, 8 May 1991 (Ratushny) at 25

265 *Keating*, above note 263 at para 42.

266 *OPSEU (Dvorak et al) and Ministry of Correctional Services*, GSB#113/83, 16 August 1984 (Saltman) at 11.

267 *OPSEU (Bedeau et al) and Ministry of Correctional Services*, GSB#52/83, 5 December 1983 (Jolliffe) at 124; *Jurkus*, above note 262 at paras 173–78.

268 As set out in a Ministry of Correctional Services policy, updated to October 2003. The essentially identical 1985 version of the policy is discussed in *OPSEU (Kent) and Ministry of Correctional Services*, GSB#549/87, 7 November 1989 (Roberts) at 4–5.

application of these procedures." Clearly, the role of a representative, as contemplated by the ministry, is limited. The GSB has not commented on the acceptability of such limitations.

3) Off-Duty Conduct

In reviewing discipline for off-duty conduct, the GSB has followed the well-known private sector case *Millhaven Fibres Ltd v Oil, Chemical & Atomic Workers Int'l Union, Local 9-670 (Mattis Grievance)*,[269] which requires, for discipline to be sustained, that the off-duty conduct "harms the company's reputation or product"; "renders [the employee] unable to perform his duties satisfactorily"; "leads to refusal, reluctance or inability of the other employees to work with him"; shows "guilt of a serious breach of the Criminal Code, thus rendering his conduct injurious to the reputation of the company and its employees"; or "places difficulty in the way of the company properly carrying out its function of efficiently managing its work and efficiently directing its work forces." In addition to consideration of all the factors, the decision is to be approached "as an organic whole."[270]

Failing to report a criminal charge to the employer and resisting arrest while bragging about long service as a correctional officer were found to "demonstrate a disrespect of and for the law" that is incompatible with being a correctional officer and an officer of the peace, while the correctional officer's incarceration made it difficult to imagine the ability to effectively manage inmates.[271]

---

269 [1967] OLAA No 4 [*Millhaven Fibres*], cited by the GSB in *OPSEU (Clinton) and Ministry of Community and Social Services*, GSB#2201/93, 27 October 1994 (Briggs) at 19 and 25–27 [*Clinton*] and *Lunario*, above note 225 at paras 43–44. See also *OPSEU (Thompson) and Ministry of Transportation and Communications*, GSB#29/76, 20 May 1976 (Beatty).

270 *Ontario (Transportation) v OPSEU, 2013 ONSC 7227*, where the Divisional Court judicially reviewed a GSB decision reinstating a transportation enforcement officer named Richard and found that the Millhaven Fibres factors had been unreasonably applied as reinstatement was inappropriate for a short service transportation enforcement officer who publicly masturbated before women on more than a dozen occasions, as he was least of moderate risk to re-offend over the long term, his ability to testify as a law enforcement officer would be compromised, and other workers would be reluctant to work with him or trust him.

271 *Ontario Public Service Employees Union (Williams) v Ontario (Community Safety and Correctional Services)*, 2011 CanLII 83721 (ON GSB) (Abramsky) at paras 15–16.

The GSB has applied the *Millhaven Fibres* tests in reviewing discipline or discharge for off-duty sexual assault, particularly of victims connected to the workplace and minors. For example, the GSB upheld a discharge where the grievor was dismissed from his position at a Child Parent Resource Institute for sexually assaulting his babysitter.[272] The babysitter was a student on a work placement at the grievor's workplace at the time of the incident. Discharge of a long service employee has been upheld for off-duty sexual assault of minors and accessing and storing pornography on a ministry computer.[273]

In the 1994 case of *Ontario Public Service Employees Union (Mandar) and Ministry of Correctional Services*,[274] the grievor, a correctional officer working with male adult offenders, was dismissed when the employer was notified that the grievor had been convicted of sexually touching his eleven-year-old goddaughter. The GSB determined that discharge was not appropriate in the grievor's case. The grievor had a praiseworthy work record with no discipline, he was not in a "sensitive and highly visible position" representing his employer to the public, and there was no evidence to suggest that he was untrustworthy or a danger or threat to the public, to inmates, or to fellow employees. The most troublesome issue for the GSB was the employer argument relating to expected workplace difficulty. The GSB heard evidence that there is a stigma attached to sexual offences against minors, which could result in workplace reprisals from inmates and staff, but concluded that this was not a just basis for upholding a dismissal.

Where the conduct is not connected with the workplace and does not compromise its reputation, discipline may be inappropriate even where an employee is convicted of an offence. The GSB has considered counterbalancing factors, including (1) the ministry had not been compromised by the grievor's misconduct, (2) the crimes were relatively insignificant, (3) the criminal penalty did not affect the grievor's ability to do their job, (4) the grievor's job did not involve contact with

---

272 *Clinton*, above note 269. In *OPSEU (Kiviloo) and Ministry of Correctional Services*, GSB#433/82, 11 January 1983 (Verity), the GSB upheld the reprimand of a probation officer for inappropriate conduct toward a young female volunteer with the ministry.

273 *Ontario Public Service Employees Union (Grievor) v Ontario (Natural Resources)*, 2008 CanLII 32797 (ON GSB) (Jackson) at 77–79.

274 GSB#87/93, 15 March 1994 (Waisglass).

the public or the police, (5) the nature of the grievor's work did not present them with the opportunity to commit similar offences at work, and (6) the grievor was a good employee who was well liked by their co-workers and supervisor.[275]

275 *OPSEU (Gutierrez) and Ministry of Attorney General*, GSB#419/80, 15 May 1981 (Roberts) at 14. For cases where evidence was led that a number of correctional officers had been convicted of off-duty criminal offences but not disciplined, see *OPSEU (Gardiner) and Ministry of Correctional Services (#1)*, GSB#1113/89, 5 February 1991 (Fisher) and *OPSEU (Gardiner) and Ministry of Correctional Services (#2)*, GSB#160/92, 15 March 1994 (Gray).

CHAPTER ELEVEN

Grievance Settlement Board: Jurisdiction, Administration, Procedure, and Remedies

The *Crown Employees Collective Bargaining Act, 1993* (*CECBA*) provides that all differences arising from a collective agreement covering Crown employees will be arbitrated by the Grievance Settlement Board (GSB).[1] This makes the GSB responsible for providing expeditious dispute resolution, through mediation and arbitration, of a large volume of grievances between the Ontario government and designated Crown agencies, and their unions.

The GSB has a unique tribunal structure centred on the agreement of these institutional parties about governance, administration, and adjudicative composition. The board has developed a distinct set of expedited arbitration procedures, and approaches to disclosure, particulars, non-suits, and interim relief.

The *CECBA* does impose specific restrictions on the GSB's remedial authority when dealing with criminal convictions after a finding of either unnecessary force or sexual assault and with classification disputes.

A. JURISDICTION

The GSB's jurisdiction over all differences arising from a collective agreement covering Crown employees has at least three effects. First, the jurisdiction of the GSB is confined to dealing with grievances concerning

1 SO 1993, c 38 as amended [*CECBA*], s 7(1)–(3). The GSB website is www.psab.gov.on.ca.

a specific group of employees consisting of the direct employees of government and of designated Crown agencies.[2] Second, individual unionized employees must resolve their disputes with the employer through the GSB, or tribunals with overlapping jurisdiction. The courts generally lack jurisdiction. Third, the Crown and trade unions cannot use private arbitrators for the adjudication of their differences, because the Act renders inapplicable the provisions in the *Labour Relations Act, 1995* (*LRA*), which would otherwise impose a deemed private rights arbitration clause and ministerial appointment of rights arbitrators.[3]

Within these parameters, the GSB's jurisdiction is broad. It is "a creature of statute" empowered to deal with grievances under expired contracts,[4] although time limits for the filing of grievances may still apply to limit retroactivity.[5] The board has rejected the argument that it has no jurisdiction over an alleged breach of minutes of settlement. The minutes themselves came within the definition of a collective agreement, in that the document set out an agreement in writing between the employer and an employee organization, and covered terms and conditions of employment.[6] Accordingly, the GSB determined that the *CECBA* deemed the memorandum to contain a provision for resolution of differences by the board and took jurisdiction over a breach of the memorandum of settlement even when the settlement did not expressly confer jurisdiction. Even if parties intend to exclude the grievance procedure from any minutes of settlement, their intentions cannot

---

2 The scope of that group of employees and employers is discussed in Chapter 7.

3 *CECBA*, above note 1, s 7(2) makes the *Labour Relations Act, 1995*, SO 1995, c 1, Sch A [*LRA*], s 48(1)–(6) inapplicable. The potential use of private mediators is discussed below.

4 *Re OPSEU and The Queen in the Right of Ontario* (1985), 51 OR (2d) 474 (Div Ct) at 9–10 [*OPSEU and Ontario, 1985*], overturning *OPSEU (Clerk Six General) and Management Board of Cabinet*, GSB#564/82, 4 September 1984 (Weatherill) in which the GSB had determined that it did not have jurisdiction over grievances filed in respect of expired collective agreements. See *OPSEU (Northcott/Ostman) and Ministry of Natural Resources*, GSB#734/94, 13 October 1995 (Dissanayake).

5 Following *OPSEU and Ontario, 1985*, above note 4, the extent of retroactivity was dealt with in *OPSEU (Clerk Six General) and Management Board of Cabinet*, GSB#564/82, 8 September 1992 (Kennedy).

6 *Ontario Public Service Employees Union and Civil Service Commission*, GSB#33/80, 28 July 1980 (Chair Weatherill) at 6. See also *OPSEU (Pietrobon) and Ministry of Health*, GSB#2257/95, 4 April 1997 (Mikus) at 7–8.

supersede the Act. The *CECBA*,[7] combined with collective agreement just cause protection, gives the GSB jurisdiction to review the release of a probationary employee, even in the face of a more specific provision in the collective agreement that explicitly denied probationers the right to grieve their dismissal or release.[8]

1) Recognized Expertise

As a specialized tribunal, the GSB has "the added advantage" of continuously dealing with the same parties and the same collective agreements, with the result that there is "a highly developed understanding of the parties, the issues and the jurisprudence."[9] On this basis the GSB has taken jurisdiction over disputes between bargaining agents about representation of employees[10] that could also have been addressed by the Ontario Labour Relations Board (OLRB). The *CECBA* also gives the GSB authority over any claim for illegal strike damages.[11]

In deferring to the GSB, the Divisional Court has noted the expertise that the tribunal exercises in the course of fulfilling its "over-arching responsibilities in the field of union-government labour relations."[12] Curial deference has been shown to the board's findings of fact[13] and its remedial orders.[14] The same deference was paid to its interpretation of an employment-related statute, which is a task that "lies at the core of the work of labour arbitrators."[15] In the context of an injunction

---

7 *CECBA*, above note 1, s 7(3).

8 *Ontario Public Service Employees Union (Niyonkuru) v Ontario (Ministry of Transportation)*, 2013 CanLII 88092 (ON GSB) (Devins) at paras 27–28 and the cases cited therein. For discussion of probationary release, see Chapter 3.

9 *OPSEU (Union) and Management Board Secretariat*, GSB#2003–2386, 17 January 2005 (Briggs) at 8, where the GSB rejected a motion asserting that the familiarity might bias the decision.

10 See *Ontario Public Service Employees Union (Union) v Ontario (Revenue)*, 2008 CanLII 70536 (ON GSB) (Herlich) at para 30, discussed in Chapter 7 re exclusions.

11 *CECBA*, above note 1, s 17 as discussed in Chapter 8.

12 *Professional Association of Compensation Employees v Ontario (Workers Compensation Board)*, [1997] OJ No 4115 (Div Ct) at para 41.

13 *OPSEU v Ontario Ministry of Correctional Services*, [1986] OJ No 292 (Div Ct).

14 See *OPSEU (Union) and Ministry of Community, Family and Children's Services*, GSB#447/00, 19 July 2004 (Leighton), upheld on judicial review, *Ontario (Ministry of Community and Social Services) v Ontario (Grievance Settlement Board)*, 2005 CanLII 4848 (ON SCDC).

15 *OPSEU v Ontario et al*, 2012 ONSC 2348 at para 24.

proceeding in which a party was seeking to have the court take jurisdiction over a collective agreement right, the court affirmed the jurisdiction of the board, noted its resolution of contentious matters, and held the board "has the expertise and has been able fairly and competently to address issues comparable to those in dispute."[16]

At the same time, the courts have intervened when satisfied the GSB has not properly fulfilled its responsibilities. In rejecting the proposition that the GSB had to follow private arbitral jurisprudence and did not "have the leeway to dispense equity by ignoring the law," the Divisional Court held that the GSB was not bound by any such jurisprudence and that the GSB should have fully considered whether or not to follow the jurisprudence in question.[17] When the GSB granted a grievance due to the employer losing evidence, the Court of Appeal found natural justice required a hearing on the merits, during which the effect of the lost evidence could be addressed.[18]

2) Jurisdiction over Employment-Related Statutes and Civil Liability

The GSB has the same express jurisdiction and responsibility as private labour arbitrators under the *LRA* to "interpret and apply human rights and employment related statutes regardless of any conflict with the collective agreement."[19] For example, the scope of the GSB's jurisdiction includes disputes over the *Public Service of Ontario Act, 2006* (*PSOA*)[20] entitlements of unionized employees.[21] The jurisdictional overlap with

16 *Ontario Public Service Employees Union Local 439 v Royal Ottawa Health Care Group*, [2001] OJ No 446 (Div Ct) at para 27.

17 *OPSEU v Ontario Ministry of Community and Social Services*, [1995] OJ No 3869 (Div Ct) at para 11, Adams J.

18 *Ontario (Ministry of Community, Family and Children Services) v Crown Employees Grievance Settlement Board*, 2006 CanLII 21173 (ON CA), Goudge JA dissenting [*Ontario v GSB (CA)*].

19 *CECBA*, above note 1, s 7 makes the *LRA*, above note 3, s 48(12)(j) applicable to the GSB. See *Parry Sound (District) Social Services Administration Board v OPSEU Local 324*, 2003 SCC 42.

20 SO 2006, c 35, Sch A [*PSOA*].

21 In *Smith v OPSEU and the Ministry of the Environment*, unreported endorsement of the Divisional Court, 5 May 2003, leave to appeal to the Court of Appeal denied, 29 August 2003, a grievor brought an individual application for judicial review to set aside a settlement of his layoff grievance. When his individual standing was challenged, he argued that he had personal rights as a public servant under the predecessor to the *PSOA*, including the right not to be

other tribunals responsible for Ontario's employment statutes of general application is discussed in Chapter 6.[22] Like other arbitrators, the GSB is also subject to the broad Supreme Court ruling in *Weber v Ontario Hydro*[23] that where the "essential character" of the dispute is one that arises from the collective agreement then the issues are to be dealt with by grievance arbitration and not by the courts. Chapter 13 deals with the very limited remaining circumstances in which unionized employees can access the courts to assert a claim.

When the Crown has a statutory or common law obligation that affects employee interests, the GSB's authority is not to determine the extent of the obligation, but "to interpret the collective agreement so as to address the Crown's obligation qua employer."[24] Where the Crown determined that it needed to disclose serious misconduct information about Ministry of Labour inspectors to an accused facing prosecution for violations of the *Occupational Health and Safety Act* (*OHSA*)[25] and the *Employment Standards Act, 2000*,[26] the GSB determined Crown disclosure obligations did not oblige the Crown to request a police record check of Ministry of Labour inspectors, and that such inquiries, in the absence of the inspector's consent, did not take account of the inspector's privacy interest. The police records check, absent the employee's permission, was found by the board not to be an appropriate exercise of management rights under the collective agreement. On judicial review, the GSB was found to have exceeded its jurisdiction in purporting to interpret and limit the Crown's disclosure obligations in conducting prosecutions.

---

dismissed by a manager who allegedly lacked the necessary delegated authority. The Divisional Court held that the dispute arose out of the exercise of the management right to lay off employees under the collective agreement and consequently was under the exclusive jurisdiction of the GSB.

22 See the discussion of the Supreme Court decision of *Northern Regional Health Authority v Horrocks*, 2021 SCC 42 about the overlap with the Human Rights Tribunal of Ontario.

23 [1995] 2 SCR 929 [*Weber*].

24 *Ontario v OPSEU*, 2012 ONSC 2078 at para 35, on judicial review overturning *Ontario Public Service Employees Union (Union) v Ontario (Government Services)*, 2011 CanLII 23158 (ON GSB).

25 RSO 1990, c O.1 [*OHSA*].

26 SO 2000, c 41.

B. GOVERNANCE, FUNDING, ADMINISTRATION, AND COMPOSITION OF ADJUDICATORS

In 1974, the *CECBA* was amended to remove the grievances of unionized employees from the Public Service Grievance Board (PSGB) and place that jurisdiction in a newly created GSB, operating with three-person panels consisting of a vice-chair and union and management members.[27] The GSB's administration has since evolved to be ever more based on the consensus of the parties, and to use single arbitrators only.

The present GSB's structure uniquely combines governance by the institutional parties with attributes of a "statutory institutional labour relations tribunal" like the OLRB and characteristics of ad hoc rights arbitration.[28] There is a shared management and union responsibility for oversight of a unified funding and administrative structure that facilitates the parties being able to select specific mediator/arbitrators for individual cases.

The composition and administration of the GSB is determined by agreement of the parties and, "failing such," by the chair,[29] subject to any specific legislative requirements. Before the chair exercises any power without agreement of the parties, the chair must "request and consider the views of those who failed to agree."[30]

The GSB is formally composed of the chair and alternate chair,[31] who are selected by agreement of the Crown and the *CECBA* trade unions, and then appointed by the Lieutenant Governor in Council (LGIC).[32] (Presumably, the Crown acting as employer will not agree to an appointment that would be unacceptable to the LGIC.) If the parties fail to agree, the chair will be selected and appointed by the LGIC. The parties are no doubt motivated to reach agreement by the fact that any unilateral appointment by the LGIC is in effect unilateral appointment

---

27 *An Act to amend the Crown Employees Collective Bargaining Act, 1972*, SO 1974, c 135. This was stated to have been done in response to the reform agenda of the Civil Service Association of Ontario, OPSEU's predecessor: Ontario Legislative Assembly, *Hansard*, 30 January 1975, No 157 at 7089–90 (Eric Winkler, Chair, Management Board of Cabinet).

28 See the commentary in *OPSEU (Ross) and Ministry of the Solicitor General and Correctional Services*, GSB#2690/96, 25 August 2003 (Herlich) at 8 [*Ross*].

29 *CECBA*, above note 1, s 47(6).

30 *Ibid*, s 47(8).

31 *Ibid*, s 47(1).

32 *Ibid*, s 47(2).

by the government employer, which would compromise the neutrality of the GSB.

The GSB is not subject to a general power of the LGIC to make regulations such as applies to the OLRB.[33]

1) Partnership Agreement

The employer and union parties to the GSB have entered into a partnership agreement,[34] which establishes a Governance Council with the responsibility, in conjunction with the chair, for discussing and determining "all matters necessary for the fair, effective, and expeditious resolution of disputes," including appointments, general administration of the GSB, and the inclusion of new participants into the partnership agreement. The Governance Council is to be composed of an equal number of representatives from the unions and the employers.

There is also provision for a financial advisory committee to meet and then make recommendations on financial matters to the Governance Council.

The Governance Council is scheduled to meet quarterly, with the meetings presided over by the chair. There is an agreed system for weighted voting on contentious matters. In order for a non-financial motion to pass, it must have the support of a majority of the union vote and a majority of the employer vote. In order for a financial motion to pass, it must have two-thirds support in both groups. Although the largest members, the Management Board of Cabinet (MBC) and the Ontario Public Service Employees Union (OPSEU), have many more votes than the smaller unions and employers,[35] there is a general tradition of consensus amongst management and amongst unions. In the event of a tied vote, the chair casts the deciding vote.

---

33 *LRA*, above note 3, s 125.

34 *Partnership Agreement to Facilitate the Governance of the Grievance Settlement Board*, as of August 2019, which is substantially the same as the version in the Grievance Settlement Board, *Annual Report 2003–2004*, available from the GSB [*GSB, Annual Report 2003–2004*], Appendix F at 20–22.

35 For example, out of the 178 votes for management, the MBC has eighty-nine on account of OPSEU, combined with twenty-eight on account of AMAPCEO, while the next largest employer is the Liquor Control Board of Ontario at twenty-four.

2) Costs and Funding

The GSB is funded as a budget item of the Ministry of Labour, Immigration, Training and Skills Development (referred to as the Ministry of Labour).[36] The costs of the GSB are operating expenditures (premises, IT, staff) and per diem arbitrator fees. Those costs are to be shared between the Crown and the other parties as follows:[37]

- The parties to an individual mediation/arbitration equally share its costs.[38] The GSB has noted this "user pays" system affects the users' approach to dispute resolution before and after the grievance is filed with the board because of the impact on their internal budgets.[39]
- Other GSB costs are to be shared 50/50 between the Crown employers and the trade unions.[40]
- If the unions fail to agree amongst themselves, the chair, after consulting, is to determine a method of cost sharing that is proportionate to the use of the resources of the GSB by each union.[41]

The GSB bills each of the Crown employers and unions for their share of the costs. The GSB has consistently recovered all of its expenditures since 1996. Those revenues are deposited in the Consolidated Revenue Fund (CRF).

The board receives its funding from the CRF through the Ministry of Labour's Expenditure Estimates pursuant to an appropriation authorized by the legislature.[42] It has been noted that the GSB is not permitted to retain funds and use them to improve its administrative systems.[43] The result is that, although the GSB collects enough revenue to cover all its costs, at times "the financial pressures faced by the

---

36 GSB, *Business Plan 2022–2023 to 2023–2025*, online: www.psab.gov.on.ca/en/gsb/publications.html [GSB, *Business Plan 2022–2023 to 2023–2025*].

37 *CECBA*, above note 1, s 47(7).

38 *Ibid*, s 47(7)1.

39 GSB, *Business Plan 2022–2023 to 2023–2025*, above note 36 at 10.

40 *CECBA*, above note 1, s 47(7)2.

41 *Ibid*, s 47(7)3.

42 Minister of Labour and Chair, GSB, *Memorandum of Understanding*, 21 May 2008, affirmed in 2013, 2018, and 2019, online: www.psab.gov.on.ca/english/gsb/publications.htm, Art 5.1.2 [*MOU*].

43 Leslie MacLeod, *Grievance Administration Project, Final Report*, unpublished (Management Board Secretariat, 2000) at 46 [*MacLeod Report*].

Ministry of Labour have prevented it from making necessary investments in the GSB."[44]

The GSB staff provide services to the PSGB, and expenditures made on behalf of the PSGB are recovered and refunded to the GSB.[45]

3) Administration

The GSB has a full-time registrar, deputy registrar, several other staff, permanent offices, and hearing rooms. The registrar is responsible for all administrative matters and shares responsibility for all policy matters with the chair.[46] The staff are public servants employed by the Ministry of Labour, appointed under Part III of the *PSOA*. The non-managerial staff are represented by OPSEU and covered by its Unified Bargaining Unit collective agreement with the MBC.[47] (During both the 1996 and 2002 OPSEU strikes, the GSB staff were not proposed to be or designated essential and the GSB did not operate.) Pursuant to the *PSOA*, the Public Service Commission (PSC) has delegated human resources authority to the registrar, who is responsible to the commission for carrying out that function in accordance with government directives.[48] In summary:

> The [Grievance Settlement] Board has the advantage of the administrative and personnel resources of the Ontario Public Service, while at the same time it is able to obtain the services of neutrals in the private sector. Thus, the Board is in the position of being able to avail itself of the best of both sectors, uniquely positioning it to respond effectively and innovatively to the challenges which have presented themselves.[49]

4) Memorandum of Understanding with Government

Under the *Adjudicative Tribunals Accountability, Governance and Appointments Act, 2009*,[50] the government has a responsibility to "ensure that adjudicative tribunals are accountable, transparent and

---

44 *Ibid.*

45 GSB, *Business Plan 2022–2023 to 2023–2025*, above note 36 at 2.

46 GSB, *Annual Report 2003–2004*, above note 34 at 4.

47 *MOU*, above note 42, Art 5.1.3.

48 *Ibid*, Arts 5.5.2 and 5.5.9.

49 GSB, *2000–2001 Annual Report*, available from the GSB.

50 SO 2009, c 33, Sch 5 [with the GSB listed in Sch 1, s 12], s 1.

efficient in their operations while remaining independent in their decision-making." Like other adjudicative tribunals, the GSB is subject to a range of requirements, including a *Memorandum of Understanding*, mandate and mission statement, accountability framework, and the preparation and publishing of annual business plans and annual reports, all to be approved by its "responsible minister," the minister of labour, and an ethics plan to be approved by the integrity commissioner.

The 2008 *Memorandum of Understanding* between the chair and minister of labour[51] is relatively standard for adjudicative agencies in setting out a careful balance of adjudicative independence and systemic accountability:

- The minister acknowledges the independence of the board in the conduct of the proceedings before it and in the rendering of its adjudicative decisions.
- The minister is responsible for assessing that the GSB is fulfilling its legislative mandate and business.
- The chair is responsible to the minister for fulfilling the legislative mandate and business plan and all directives such as financial, administrative, human resources, and other corporate policies, including ethics and conflict of interest, and disclosure of wrong-doing, as well as policies in respect of French language services, freedom of information, workplace harassment, and equal opportunity. (Note that the GSB's process for selecting individual mediator/arbitrators is specifically exempted by the *CECBA*[52] from the application of the MBC *Procurement Directive*.)
- The chair shall ensure that there is a timely, effective, and efficient caseload management system to resolve disputes, including appropriate alternative dispute resolution mechanisms.
- The chair shall evaluate the performance of board arbitrators based on performance measures.

The *Member Framework*[53] sets out position descriptions for the chair and arbitrators. The chair position description sets out key responsibilities:

51 *MOU*, above note 42.

52 *CECBA*, above note 1, s 51.1.

53 GSB, *Member Framework and Code of Ethics*, online: www.psab.gov.on.ca/en/gsb/pdf/gsb_accountability_and_ethics_framework_.pdf.

- *Law and procedure:* Promotes clarity and predictability in the exercise of independent decision making.
- *Strategic leadership:*
  - » Mentors and develops arbitrators by providing oversight and advice.
  - » Ensures independence in adjudicative functions by setting standards of interaction and acts as the liaison to the stakeholder and government.
- *Agency governance:* With the Governance Council, determines appointments or reappointments that respect and promote the principles of equity, diversity, quality, merit, and regional representation.

The part-time arbitrator position description sets the expectation that an arbitrator:

- issues clear, well-written, soundly reasoned decisions that are understandable and can be implemented by the parties to a dispute
- acts as a mediator by listening to the parties' positions, assisting the parties in defining underlying issues and interests, focusing the parties' attention on what a workable settlement would be, and facilitating a resolution between the parties

The included Code of Ethics states "[a]rbitrators must at all times uphold the integrity of the office, exhibiting the highest standards of honesty, impartiality and dignity as well as competence in labour relations matters and the law relating thereto."

5) Proposals for Legislative Change

During the Progressive Conservative government of 1995–2003, there were two discussion papers on administrative tribunals, which contained specific recommendations about the GSB. The 1997 *Wood Report* found no public interest rationale for a public arbitration service and advocated use of private arbitrators unless the government service was more cost effective.[54] Later in 1997, a Ministry of Labour review

54 Government Task Force on Agencies Boards and Commissions (Bob Wood, MPP, Chair), *Report on Restructuring Regulatory and Adjudicative Agencies* (Toronto: The Task Force, 1997) at 15.

found that the GSB cost essentially the same as private sector arbitration, and that privatization of the GSB could result in a cost increase because of higher private sector arbitrator fees.[55]

In 2001, a Ministry of Labour consultation paper proposed a "unified workplace tribunal" for multiple workplace issues (labour relations, occupational health and safety, workers' compensation, rights arbitration) to ease jurisdictional challenges and centralize many appointments.[56] The paper also stated that removing the constraints of government agency status from the GSB would "give the parties the flexibility to adopt a structure and process that meet their needs for providing efficient and timely resolution of disputes." The nature of the new "structure" was not fully specified. Ultimately, the "unified workplace tribunal" approach was not implemented.

In 2017, under a Liberal government, the *CECBA* was amended to provide increased flexibility to the parties in selecting and paying mediator/arbitrators, within the existing governance and funding structure.[57]

6) Mediator/Arbitrator Selection and Remuneration

Prior to *CECBA* amendments in 2017, arbitrators were appointed as vice-chairs and then paid rates determined by the government.[58] Now, and similar to how ad hoc rights arbitration panels operate, the parties, on agreement, establish a roster of mediator/arbitrators,[59] who can then be selected by the parties to mediate specific matters. The amounts paid to the mediator/arbitrators shall be determined by the parties subject to any limits set by the LGIC.[60] No such limits have been set. The LGIC continues to set the remuneration for the chair and vice-chair.[61] The chair contracts with the mediator/arbitrators for their services and

---

55 Ministry of Labour, *Review of the Grievance Settlement Board, Report on Consultations*, 17 October 1997 at 5.

56 Ministry of Labour, *Looking Forward: A New Tribunal for Ontario's Workplaces, 2001* at 12–13, 33.

57 *Stronger, Healthier Ontario Act (Budget Measures)*, SO 2017, c 8, Sch 6—Bill 127, and *Stronger, Fairer Ontario Act (Budget Measures)*, SO 2017, c 34, Sch 11—Bill 177.

58 *CECBA*, above note 1, prior to Bill 127, s 47(2) and (9).

59 *Ibid*, s 47.1(3) with the chair selecting if the parties fail to agree.

60 *Ibid*, s 47.1(8)–(9).

61 *Ibid*, s 47(4).

maintains the roster.[62] The parties also pick the sequence for addressing outstanding matters.[63]

The GSB advises these changes have facilitated the improvement of the arbitrator retention and compensation practices, resulting in more dates offered by a larger roster of arbitrators and "significantly enhanced" service to the parties.[64]

There is no provision for sidespeople. In an exceptional case, a three-person panel can be established, composed of one of the panel of mediator/arbitrators chosen by the Crown, one chosen by the trade unions, and one jointly selected or the chair if the chair agrees.[65]

The individual retainer model has the advantage of only incurring arbitral costs when there are cases to adjudicate. The GSB tracks the number of grievance files that it opens annually.[66] From 1999 to 2021, 76,745 files were opened, for an annual average of 3,655. The greatest annual increase was 67 percent in 2002–2003, following the 2002 OPSEU strike, and the greatest decrease was 25 percent in 2019–2020. The highest volume year was 2003–2004 at 4,034. The lowest volume was in 2000–2001 at 1,838. In 2021, the volume was 2,924. Although no further breakdown is available, a review of GSB cases over the years indicates the single largest percentage of arbitrations by a significant margin deal with the OPSEU/Ministry of Correctional Services relationship.

Note that, for mediation only, the parties can also pick "any other person,"[67] and it appears in that case that they make their own arrangements. As only a mediator/arbitrator or the chair can "determine a matter"[68] (that is, decide), the parties cannot give a private mediator any decision-making authority, nor do the practices and procedures or rules or statutory restrictions on the powers of the board apply to any such private process.[69]

---

62 *Ibid*, s 47.1(5).

63 *Ibid*, s 50(1.1).

64 *GSB Annual Reports 2017–2018* and *2018–2019*, online: www.psab.gov.on.ca/en/gsb/publications.html.

65 *CECBA*, above note 1 s 49(2).

66 The following data was obtained on request from the GSB in the fall of 2021.

67 *CECBA*, above note 1, s 47.2.

68 *Ibid*, s 49(1).

69 *Ibid*, s 47.1(7).

C. FOSTERING ADJUDICATIVE CONSISTENCY

While the selection of mediator/arbitrators for specific cases carries with it the risk of a less consistent approach to matters, the GSB structure fosters adjudicative consistency. Four main measures are employed for that purpose: consistency of adjudicators; mandatory tribunal practices, procedures, and rules; a statutory standard that the arbitrators of the GSB are "one board"; and a jurisprudential commitment to following precedents (the *Blake* principle).

At the GSB, there has been consistency and stability of adjudicators. The majority of the GSB mediator/arbitrator roster have been arbitrators for at least twenty years and at least one-third have been arbitrators at the GSB for that long. In addition, the relatively new appointment process described above is described as allowing "the Board to retain the services of experienced third party neutrals who have the confidence and respect of the parties."[70]

1) Practice and Procedure

The GSB has the power to determine its own practice and procedure,[71] which is to be followed by the mediator/arbitrators.[72] That power is subject to two statutory limitations. First, the GSB must give parties a full opportunity to present evidence and submissions.[73] Second, this power is made subject to the *CECBA* provisions dealing with the GSB, and to "any requirements under the *Labour Relations Act*."[74] The meaning of this latter phrase is not clear. One applicable requirement may be for the GSB to render a decision within thirty days, or such longer time as the parties agree, with the Minister of Labour retaining the ability to make orders concerning delayed decisions.[75] However,

70 GSB *Annual Report 2021–2022*, online: www.psab.gov.on.ca/en/gsb/publications.html at 1.

71 *CECBA*, above note 1, s 48(1).

72 *Ibid*, s 47.1(7). The practice and procedure and rules do not expressly apply to the chair when the chair hears the matter, but it is to be expected that the chair will adhere to the *GSB Rules of Procedure* (below note 77).

73 *CECBA*, above note 1, s 48(1).

74 *Ibid*.

75 These matters are dealt with in *LRA*, above note 3, s 48(7)–(11), which are made applicable to the GSB through *CECBA*, *ibid*, s 7(1) & (2).

this appears inconsistent with the more specific power of the GSB, as a statutory tribunal, to determine its own practice and procedure.

2) Rules

Pursuant to its rule-making power,[76] the GSB has established a short set of rules[77] to be followed by the mediator/arbitrators.[78] The rules include the following:

- *Location of hearings:* Hearings are to be held where the parties agree, and in the event of disagreement, as determined by the GSB. While most hearings are held in Toronto, the GSB will exercise its discretion having regard to the balance of convenience for the parties.[79]
- *Written or electronic hearings:* Where the parties agree, the hearing can be held, in whole or in part, in written or electronic format or any combination and, if they disagree, the GSB can decide. (As with many adjudicative tribunals, the COVID-19 pandemic led to a large increase in video hearings at the GSB, which is likely to continue.)
- *French/English:* Hearings are to be held in French at the request of either party.
- *Notice of constitutional question:* Proper notices of a challenge to the constitutional validity of a legal provision or a claim for a remedy under the *Canadian Charter of Rights and Freedoms*[80] must be given at least fifteen calendar days in advance to the GSB, the other parties, and the attorneys general of Ontario and Canada.
- *Days:* Days means Monday to Friday.

---

76 *CECBA*, above note 1, s 48(2). The rules made under the power given by the section are not regulations within the meaning of the *Regulations Act*, RSO 1990, c R.21, s 1. The GSB can also establish forms, but has not done so.

77 GSB, *Rules of Procedure*, online: www.psab.gov.on.ca/en/gsb/board_rules.html [*GSB Rules of Procedure*].

78 *CECBA*, above note 1, s 47.1(7).

79 *Association of Management, Administrative and Professional Crown Employees of Ontario (Sergeant) v Ontario (Health and Long-Term Care)*, 2011 CanLII 86399 (ON GSB) (Petryshen).

80 Part I of the *Constitution Act, 1982*, being Schedule B to the *Canada Act 1982* (UK), 1982, c 11 [*Charter*].

- *Case management:* Where a grievance referred to the GSB is left unscheduled or adjourned for more than twelve months, the GSB may peremptorily schedule the grievance and make an appropriate order.

The rules governing three frequently litigated matters—consolidation of cases, disclosure, and interim relief—are discussed below.

3) "One Board"

Any determination of a mediator/arbitrator on the roster of the board is "a determination . . . of the Board,"[81] and the GSB has long held that

> the Grievance Settlement Board is one entity—it is not a series of separately constituted boards of arbitration. Under the *Crown Employees Collective Bargaining Act*, there is a "Grievance Settlement Board"—that is, one Board.[82]

This means that a mediator/arbitrator can exercise the authority of the board, including the jurisdiction to consolidate a case before them with a case for which the parties have selected another mediator/arbitrator. (For discussion of when to consolidate matters, see the "Consolidation" section below.)

4) The *Blake* Principle

As stated by the Supreme Court in *Weber v Ontario Hydro*:

> The first significant difference between courts and tribunals relates to the difference in the manner in which decisions are rendered by each type of adjudicating body. Courts must decide cases according to the law and are bound by stare decisis. By contrast, tribunals are not so constrained. When acting within their jurisdiction, they may solve the conflict before them in the way judged to be most appropriate. In

---

81 *CECBA*, above note 1, s 47.1(6).

82 *Ontario Public Service Employees Union (Cody et al) v Ontario (Community Safety and Correctional Services)*, 2018 CanLII 109248 (ON GSB) (Parmar) at paras 34–35 [*Cody*], quoting *Blake et al and Amalgamated Transit Union*, GSB#1276/87, 3 May 1988 (Shime) [*Blake*].

> labour arbitration, the arbitrator is not bound to follow the decisions of other arbitrators, even when similar circumstances arise.[83]

This does not mean tolerance for arbitrariness. As the Supreme Court stressed in *Canada (Minister of Citizenship and Immigration) v Vavilov*,[84] tribunals are to foster a "harmonized decision making culture" and decisions that depart from previous decisions must be justified:[85]

> Those affected by administrative decisions are entitled to expect that like cases will generally be treated alike and that outcomes will not depend merely on the identity of the individual decision maker—expectations that do not evaporate simply because the parties are not before a judge.[86]

The GSB has fostered consistency through an expectation that earlier rulings will be followed unless there are "exceptional circumstances." The central case is *Blake et al and Amalgamated Transit Union*[87] in which Owen Shime, a long-serving chair of the GSB, ruled that the private sector standard of "manifest error" for departing from earlier decisions of other arbitrators is too lax a standard for the GSB. On the basis that the GSB is "one entity," he found "there is no right for one panel to overrule or sit on review of another." Hence the GSB determined that "exceptional circumstances" must exist before the board is justified in not following an earlier ruling. There was no identification or delineation of what constitutes exceptional circumstances, although the party seeking review of an earlier decision bears the onus of establishing the existence of such circumstances.

The intention of the *Blake* principle is that the GSB will produce findings of fact and law that are binding in subsequent proceedings where the issue is identical.[88] However, the scope of the principle should not be overstated. There needs to be close attention to what the earlier case actually decided, and the GSB is not required to follow an earlier

---

83 *Weber*, above note 23 at para 14.

84 2019 SCC 65.

85 *Ibid* at paras 130–31.

86 *Ibid* at para 129.

87 *Blake*, above note 82.

88 *OPSEU (Pickett) and Ministry of Community Safety and Correctional Services*, GSB#1999-1224, 5 February 2004 (Harris) at 5.

case that is distinguishable from the extant case in front of the panel on material and relevant grounds.[89]

The Divisional Court in *Ontario (Ministry of Correctional Services) v Ontario Public Service Employees Union (OPSEU)* (the *Dupuis* decision)[90] agreed with a manifest error policy and, in *obiter*, stated "some concern" with the exceptional circumstances test. In *OPSEU (Carson/French) and Ministry of Correctional Services*,[91] a GSB panel noted that the role of the Divisional Court, on a judicial review, was limited to deciding whether a decision is patently unreasonable and, as the court in *Dupuis* did not so find, the original *Blake* test remained intact. However, the GSB in *Carson/French* went on to construe the *Blake* principle as being that previous decisions are to be followed unless those decisions are manifestly wrong *or* unless there are exceptional circumstances. This does not seem to be a justifiable reading of *Blake*, given that *Blake* found the manifestly wrong standard to be too lax a standard. It has since been pointed out that the effect of the *Carson/French* decision was to make the whole issue "somewhat obscure."[92]

Several cases then created even more uncertainty by putting forward different suggestions for the test to be used. In one case, it was suggested that the test is whether "good reasons can be shown as to why the previous decision is wrong"[93] and, in another case, whether the prior award was "rationally defensible."[94]

---

89 *Ontario Public Service Employees Union (Haist) v Ontario (Solicitor General)*, 2022 CanLII 122326 (ON GSB) (McLean) at paras 18–21; *OPSEU (Aubin) and Ministry of Correctional Services*, GSB#390/91, 24 September 1991 (Brandt) at 10.

90 [1990] OJ No 729 (Div Ct).

91 GSB#582/89, 7 August 1990 (Kirkwood).

92 *OPSEU (Rohrer) and Ministry of Correctional Services*, GSB#0001/89, 5 October 1990 (Wilson) at 8.

93 *OPSEU (Rigglesworth) and Ministry of Transportation*, GSB#637/90, 30 March 1992 (Fisher) at 6.

94 *OPSEU (Weaver and Warsi) and Ministry of Finance*, GSB#1087/99, 18 May 2001 (Gray) at 10. While this case is outside the mainstream of the GSB's rulings on the *Blake* principle, it does contain an interesting argument in favour of consistency generally, when it points out, at 10, that the parties need not be stuck with a bad decision forever:

> The parties have the opportunity to renegotiate their collective agreement periodically. They can change the language on which a "bad" decision was based, to make it clear that they intend a different result. When the parties have had that opportunity and no such change is made, consistency with the earlier decision is an even more compelling consideration when interpreting the unchanged language.

A more direct reappraisal of the *Blake* principle, after *Dupuis*, is found in *OPSEU (McInnis) and Ministry of Community and Social Services*,[95] where it was suggested the Divisional Court's decision in *Dupuis* cast real doubt on the validity of the exceptional circumstances test set out in *Blake*. The GSB found that, while continuity in decisions is critical, the GSB cannot fulfill its obligation to deal with the matter before it by following manifestly wrong decisions. In *McInnis* a modest "exceptional circumstance" was found in an obviously untenable interpretation of the collective agreement. The GSB arbitrator was clearly trying to uphold the *Blake* principle in a way that did not require the perpetuation of a "manifest error."

The original *Blake* principle has been reaffirmed in a decision by Susan Stewart, the next long-serving chair of the GSB, which states that the board "speaks in one voice, providing the parties with consistent direction and discouraging the relitigation of issues that have been ruled upon. It is only in exceptional circumstances, circumstances that extend beyond manifest error, that the Grievance Settlement Board would depart from the path established in a previous decision."[96] *Blake* applies to all parties under the GSB's jurisdiction, and not just to the cases of any one union.[97]

The net effect of the GSB's ongoing consideration of the "exceptional circumstances" test in *Blake* is to retain it, but to apply it carefully so that it is not a barrier to achieving a just result. Decisions have found that, in addition to manifest error, there need be exceptional circumstances that justify a fresh determination of the issue[98] or circumstances that "truly, clearly and unambiguously merit the description of exceptional."[99]

Concerning new evidence, the party seeking to rely on new evidence as an exceptional circumstance must demonstrate that the new

---

95 GSB#2967/92, 5 October 1993 (Kaplan) [*McInnis*].

96 *OPSEU (Fox et al) and Ontario Human Rights Commission*, GSB#0507/01, 5 September 2001 (Stewart) at 7 [*Fox #1*].

97 *AMAPCEO (Shiv Sud) and Ministry of the Environment*, GSB#0888/00, 1 March 2001 (Abramsky) at 8. See also *AMAPCEO (Policy) and Management Board Secretariat*, GSB#1357/00, 22 April 2002 (Knopf) at 17–18.

98 *OPSEU (Union) and Ministry of the Solicitor General and Correctional Services*, GSB#1252/00, 28 March 2001 (Brown) at 7.

99 *OPSEU (Pinazza et al) and Ministry of Community Safety and Correctional Services* and *Keating*, GSB#2002-0840, 9 August 2004 at 13.

evidence could not previously have been obtained through reasonable diligence and that it would be practically conclusive of the issue.[100]

There are two points of view on the issue of new argument. Where a new, extremely persuasive argument was brought forward, the GSB has determined this can amount to "exceptional circumstances" that allow a departure from previous decisions, depending on the significance of the issue in dispute and the argument presented.[101] The contrary view was reached when the GSB was faced with two conflicting lines of decisions. The board noted that, in such circumstances, a decision maker must choose, but when the choice had been made in an earlier decision, that choice should be respected; and the board further commented that matters must remain settled, "notwithstanding fancy new arguments," if there is to be some measure of predictability.[102]

Previously overlooked authority of real relevance has been viewed an exceptional circumstance, as the board in *Blake* "did not intend the perpetuation of a result which is reached in the absence of a consideration of relevant legal authorities."[103]

D. ALTERNATIVE DISPUTE RESOLUTION: MEDIATION AND EXPEDITED HEARINGS

In addition to standard rights arbitrations, the GSB has extensively employed mediation and expedited hearings to deal with large numbers of grievances. The "clients" expect the board to be more of a dispute

100 *OPSEU (Gould and Field) and Ministry of Transportation*, GSB#674/88, 8 February 1990 (Knopf) at 6–7 [*Gould*].

101 *OPSEU (Arnold) and Ministry of Correctional Services*, GSB#255/91, 28 April 1993 (Dissanayake) at 16; *Ontario Public Service Employees Union (Johnston) v Ontario (Attorney General)*, 2011 CanLII 60319 (ON GSB) (Dissanayake) at para 18 [*Johnston (Dissanayake)*]. See also *OPSEU (Watts) and Ministry of Community and Social Services*, GSB#1340/90, 21 May 1991 (Stewart) at 10 and *Ontario Public Service Employees Union (Lariviere) v Ontario (Ministry of Community Safety and Correctional Services)*, 2005 CanLII 55163 (ON GSB) (Dissanayake) at 27–28.

102 *OPSEU (Blondin et al) and Ministry of Community and Social Services*, GSB#78/89, 31 August 1989 (Slone) at 7–8. See also *Gould*, above note 100 at 7, where the vice-chair held that "the party should have to demonstrate that it wishes to make a new argument that there had been no prior opportunity to make."

103 *Johnston (Dissanayake)* above note 101 at para 15, applied in *Ontario Public Service Employees Union v Ontario (Solicitor General)*, 2021 CanLII 71640 (ON GSB) (Carrier) at paras 55 and 64.

resolution agency rather than simply an adjudicative agency.[104] Different and flexible methods of alternative dispute resolution are continually explored to maintain and increase efficiency, effectiveness, and economy.[105] The GSB has stated it will try to "ensure that the best practices of innovative and efficient dispute resolution processes are extended to all workplaces" by encouraging constructive problem solving in the workplaces where the problems occur.[106] The GSB has been commended by the parties for being willing to react to the parties' needs.[107]

1) Mediation

The board continues to resolve more than 80 percent of the grievances brought before it through mediation, rather than arbitration.[108] Particular workplaces have developed their own mediation protocols, utilizing mediator/arbitrators who have developed in depth knowledge about the workplaces, enhancing their effectiveness. "Accordingly, the parties are able to reach resolutions that meet their needs and are acceptable to them."[109]

2) Mediation/Arbitration

OPSEU and MBC have a combined mediation/arbitration procedure set out in the OPSEU/MBC collective agreements.[110] Mediation is to be used first and then, if there is no settlement, arbitration. The mediator/arbitrator may limit the evidence. A "succinct decision" is to be given within five days unless the parties agree otherwise. The cases are to have no precedential value. Grievances concerning dismissal, sexual harassment and/or human rights, and union grievances with corporate

---

104 GSB, *Business Plan 2022–2023 to 2023–2025*, above note 36 at 10.

105 *Ibid* at 9.

106 GSB, *Annual Report 2000–2001*, available from GSB at 2–3.

107 Comments of OPSEU and MBC representatives as contained in *MacLeod Report*, above note 43 at 46.

108 GSB, *Business Plan 2022–2023 to 2023–2025*, above note 36 at 5.

109 GSB, *Annual Report 2018–2019*, online: http://www.psab.gov.on.ca/english/gsb/publications.htm at 2 and 20.

110 *OPSEU/MBC Unified Bargaining Unit Collective Agreement, 2022– 2024* and *OPSEU/MBC Correctional Bargaining Unit Collective Agreement, 2018–2021*, online: https://opseu.org/information/general/find-your-collective-agreement, Art 22.16 [*OPSEU/MBC Unified and Correctional Collective Agreements*].

policy implications, are to proceed through the regular arbitration procedure. The mediation/arbitration process has been augmented with process orders directing the exchange of particulars and production prior to the hearing and time allocations for evidence so the hearing can be completed in one day.[111] Oral evidence has been time limited.[112] Evidence has been ordered to be given through written declarations from each intended witness supported by a readiness to testify if directed to do so by the arbitrator.[113] This has been extended to agreeing that relevant facts each party wishes to rely upon would be presented by counsel orally, including what its witnesses "will say" if called to testify.[114] It was further agreed that, only on certain narrow areas where facts were in dispute, could the parties call viva voce evidence.

Other parties, like OPSEU and the Liquor Control Board of Ontario, have also agreed to mediation/arbitration with reasons, with agreement that the arbitrator make any findings of disputed facts in an informal and summary fashion, and that the expedited decision is not intended to have any precedential value.[115]

The *GSB Rules of Procedure*[116] also include a mediation/arbitration procedure for the OPSEU and MBC parties, setting out the following additional refinements: the mediation of "a reasonable number" of grievances on each day of hearing, the advance exchange of information and documents, an "endeavour" not to use "external counsel" (that is, external to the Ontario government or OPSEU), and quick, oral decisions whenever possible.

Commenting on this procedure, the former chair of the GSB has remarked: "Moving immediately to arbitration upon the failure of the mediation process allowed the parties to capture the time investment

111 *Ontario Public Service Employees Union (Burns) v Ontario (Labour)*, 2017 CanLII 47078 (ON GSB) (Anderson).

112 *Ontario Public Service Employees Union (McGann et al) v Ontario (Attorney General)*, 2022 CanLII 31354 (ON GSB) (Anderson).

113 *Ontario Public Service Employees Union (Baumgartner et al) v Ontario (Attorney General)*, 2020 CanLII 97353 (ON GSB) (Anderson).

114 *Ontario Public Service Employees Union (Union) v Ontario (Attorney General)*, 2015 CanLII 14196 (ON GSB) (Dissanayake).

115 *Ontario Public Service Employees Union (Anderson) v Ontario (Liquor Control Board of Ontario)*, 2015 CanLII 9052 (ON GSB) (Luborsky).

116 Above note 77, Appendix A, OPSEU/Treasury Board Secretariat—Mediation/Arbitration Procedure.

that they had just expended, as there was no duplication of preparation time."[117]

3) High-Volume Hearings

The OLRB has noted that the parties often develop alternative dispute resolution processes to resolve large numbers of grievances arising in specific settings or dealing with specific issues, and that the experience has not only been efficient, but also "without the legalisms often constraining the litigation process, a mediated resolution of a dispute frequently deals more realistically with the substantive issues underlying the conflict."[118] The practice of not having grievors present has been found to not violate the duty of fair representation as the practice is "rooted in the labour relations purposes of the process,"[119] particularly where the union informs itself of the relevant facts and the grievor has an opportunity to provide relevant information.

a) Mediation at Correctional Facilities/Warehouses

The GSB's particularly active caseload at jails and warehouses[120] is routinely managed by a mediation/arbitration process with the following rules:

- Scheduling is done a year in advance using dedicated mediators/arbitrators.
- Multiple locations are selected for each month.
- Two days of mediation per location are scheduled.
- Mediations are long days, typically ten to twelve hours.
- Multiple grievances are dealt with each day.[121]

---

117 Susan Stewart, GSB Chair, "The OPSEU and MCSS Protocol—Expediting Dispute Resolution," unpublished paper at 5 [Stewart, *Expediting*].

118 *Rajko Seat v Ontario Public Service Employees Union*, 2017 CanLII 41405 (ON LRB) at para 22.

119 *Ibid* at para 43.

120 Although most frequently used in response to the large caseload for OPSEU/Corrections, referenced in GSB, *Business Plan 2022–2023 to 2023–2025*, above note 36 at 14, a similar process has been put in place for many Liquor Control Board of Ontario warehouse grievances: *Ontario Public Service Employees Union (LeClair) v Ontario (Liquor Control Board)*, 2014 CanLII 74780 (ON GSB) (Devins).

121 GSB, *Business Plan 2022–2023 to 2023–2025*, above note 36, Environmental Scan: Internal Factors at 9.

In these expedited circumstances, the GSB has been reluctant to allow parties to request production orders or to put grievances over to later dates, as it would be "contrary to the intention of the parties that they have a quick process."[122]

This process is pioneering and maximizes "field sensitivity," which can be a key asset of administrative tribunals.[123] There is a continuing opportunity for increased use of hybrid mediation/arbitration rather than mediation then arbitration.

b) Corrections Central Med/Arb Protocol

The current expedited processes build on the evolving experience with resolving large numbers of grievances arising in jails between OPSEU and the Ministry of Correctional Services, originally due to the "transition" of employees caused by a major re-organization of correctional facilities. That led to an agreement in 2000 on streamlining the litigation process, with all such grievances referred to a single GSB mediator/arbitrator.[124] The expectation was that all decisions would be consistent, but without precedent and prejudice, and that the arbitrator would determine the expedited process to be followed. In 2005, a new collective agreement provision caused a change in status for a number of employees from fixed term to a new category of "flexible part time," which led to a further volume of grievances, for which the same process was used. This was the origin of the existing mediation/arbitration practice, language in the OPSEU/MBC collective agreements and GSB rule. The mediator/arbitrator had the following additional comments:

> I recognize that some grievors and managerial employees may wish to attend and provide oral evidence. However, given the task at hand and the time by which to do it, I order only the committee members from each party will attend.

---

122 *Ontario Public Service Employees Union (McLaughlin) v Ontario (Community Safety and Correctional Services)*, 2019 CanLII 35316 (ON GSB) (Misra) at para 13.

123 Cristie L. Ford, "Dogs and Tails: Remedies in Administrative Law" in Colleen M. Flood & Lorne Sossin, eds, *Administrative Law in Context* (Toronto: Emond Montgomery Ltd, 2008) at 49–51.

124 The arbitrator was Felicity Briggs, one of the GSB's longest-serving adjudicators, who has passed away. The arbitrators meeting room at the GSB offices has been named the Mikus-Briggs Room, for Ms. Briggs and another deceased arbitrator, Loretta Mikus: Message from the Chair, *GSB Annual Report 2018–2019*, above note 109.

> It may be that in a few instances some confusion might arise regarding certain facts. It might also happen that I will find that insufficient evidence has been provided. In those instances, should they arise, I will direct the parties to speak again with their principles to ascertain the facts or the rationale behind the particular outstanding matter. In the event I find there is still uncertainty regarding facts, I reserve the right to ask for viva voce evidence. It is my hope that this need shall never arise.
>
> My decisions will contain brief reasons and sufficient rationale so as to provide the parties with an interpretation thereby allowing them to move forward.[125]

It is recognized that there will be cases where "the only way to get to the bottom of the matter" will be testimony and cross-examination.[126]

In 2011, the OPSEU/MBC parties formalized this approach in a "Corrections Med-Arb Protocol."[127] The parties agreed to prioritize the scheduling of sessions at institutions based on the number of relevant grievances and the state of local institutional labour relations. The session is to be held at the institution if practical. One joint preparation day and two mediation days are to be scheduled six months in advance. A list was to be agreed locally thirty days in advance. If a grievance appears to be too complex, or other issues are identified, the grievance is to be rescheduled. Positions are to be exchanged in advance with two members of the local receiving preparation time. Not included are grievances about

- overtime (agreed to be addressed at separate "Local Overtime Days"[128] and, if not resolved, at provincial overtime med-arb days with only provincial representatives in attendance with the vice-chair)
- attendance management
- grievances with corporate-wide implications (including strike related grievances, transition, and human rights)

---

125 *Ontario Public Service Employees Union (Hollingsworth et al) v Ontario (Attorney General)*, 2011 CanLII 10246 (ON GSB) (Briggs).

126 *Ontario Public Service Employees Union (Butsch) v Ontario (Community Safety and Correctional Services)*, 2010 CanLII 18880 (ON GSB) (Stephens).

127 OPSEU/MBC, *Corrections Med-Arb Protocol*, signed 8 April 2011.

128 The process is reviewed in *Ontario Public Service Employees Union (Gregoire et al) v Ontario (Solicitor General)*, 2021 CanLII 26598 (ON GSB) (Sheehan).

If the mediation does not settle the matter, the mediator/arbitrator, based on the evidence provided at the mediation session, shall immediately or within fifteen days decide the matter without reasons and without precedent and prejudice.[129] This process has been used even when the grievor does not agree.[130] The GSB can decide the grievance is not suitable for med-arb because the evidence is insufficient, there are conflicting legal interpretations, "the decision may impact on the institution's ongoing business practices," or for any other reason.

The process was extended to cover the litigation arising from the "roll-over" of fixed-term staff to regular (classified status), and to probation and parole recruitment.[131]

This process has continued for more than twenty years, accompanied by an ongoing joint Ministry Employment Relations Committee of the parties that works to resolve policy issues.[132] The entire process has been highly effective and positively viewed by all parties.[133]

c) Expedited Protocols for Other Major Events

There was a central precedent for expeditiously resolving large numbers of grievances. In the summer of 1998, OPSEU and the MBC, in conjunction with the GSB, began to deal with an accumulation of approximately 20,000 backlogged grievances. The exercise involved the creation of ministry-specific protocols for simultaneous mediation/arbitration of many grievances, often with similar facts/issues. Most of the grievances were resolved within a two-year period.[134] A similar

---

129 *Ontario Public Service Employees Union (Smith) v Ontario (Community Safety and Correctional Services)*, 2015 CanLII 14193 (ON GSB) (Johnston).

130 *Ontario Public Service Employees Union (Kennett) v Ontario (Community Safety and Correctional Services)*, 2015 CanLII 20922 (ON GSB) (Briggs).

131 *Ontario Public Service Employees Union (Messner) v Ontario (Community Safety and Correctional Services)*, 2015 CanLII 8796 (ON GSB) (Briggs); *Ontario Public Service Employees Union (Brar) v Ontario (Solicitor General)*, 2021 CanLII 119109 (ON GSB) (Misra).

132 *Ontario Public Service Employees Union (Mathison) v Ontario (Solicitor General)*, 2021 CanLII 26594 (ON GSB) (Misra). See the review of the career with both the MBC and OPSEU of the long-time union co-chair of the Ministry Employee Relations Committee, Barry Scanlon, in *Ontario Public Service Employees Union v Ontario (Community Safety and Correctional Services)*, 2010 CanLII 64238 (ON GSB) (Herlich).

133 Stewart, *Expediting*, above note 117 at 5.

134 See the discussion in *Ontario Public Service Employees Union (Union) v Ontario (Ministry of Community Safety and Correctional Services)*, 2005 CanLII 54837

process was put in place to deal with disputes arising from the 2002 OPSEU strike. Expedited grievance protocols were also established to deal with "bargaining unit integrity" grievances about the scope of work covered by the collective agreement.[135] The parties have also established an expedited hearing of security screening clearance cases by selected GSB arbitrators on a rotating basis.[136]

As a high-water mark of efficiency, the GSB facilitated an agreement between OPSEU and the MBC that a large volume of grievances dealing with privatization of government work and collective agreement job security-rights would be mediated or arbitrated to completion within seven days of the filing of the grievance.[137] The speed of such adjudication has been properly characterized as "rather remarkable."[138]

d) Grievance Clusters

In cases not heard under the mediation/arbitration process, similar techniques have been employed where a single set of circumstances gives rise to many grievances. In what was expected to be a lengthy multi-grievance review of the occupational health and safety issues needed to ensure a safe working environment, the parties were required to develop a litigation "plan" dealing with the likely ordering of evidence, documents admissible on consent and requiring proof, agreed statements of fact, and "will say" statements, leading to a litigation timetable and the basis for scheduling hearing days.[139] When evidence was required from a large number of grievors, evidence was to be by written declarations, subject to any needed cross-examination.[140] In a potentially very lengthy case, the arbitrator proposed and the parties

---

(ON GSB) (Briggs), and in Robin Gordon & Timothy G.M. Hadwen, "Strategies to Resolve a Grievance Backlog: The OPSEU/MBS Case Study" (2003) 10 *Canadian Labour and Employment Law Journal* 417.

135 *Ontario Public Service Employees Union (Union) v Ontario (Government Services)*, 2011 CanLII 60313 (ON GSB) (Petryshen).

136 *Ontario Public Service Employees Union v Ontario (Government Services)*, 2014 CanLII 20591 (ON GSB) (Stewart).

137 See *OPSEU/MBC Unified and Correctional Collective Agreements*, above note 110, Appendix 18, Art 8.4.2 (i). The substantive issues are discussed in Chapter 9.

138 GSB *Annual Report, 2000–2001*, available from the GSB.

139 *Ontario Public Service Employees Union (O'Flaherty) v Ontario (Solicitor General)*, 2020 CanLII 105703 (ON GSB) (Luborsky) at paras 25–26.

140 *Ontario Public Service Employees Union (Wellwood et al) v Ontario (Education)*, 2016 CanLII 90000 (ON GSB) (Anderson).

accepted that the central issue be dealt with first, with the facts proposed by the union assumed to be true, and afterwards that evidence be restricted to proximate events.[141]

In addition to mediation/arbitration, it is worth considering if the OLRB practice of a consultation format, directed by the adjudicator, would also be a useful process for the OPS parties.[142]

4) Communication with Just One Party

In the course of mediation, mediation/arbitration, or settlement discussions, the GSB will have communications with only one party at a time. This is typically done with the agreement or implicit consent of the other party.

Different considerations arise when a formal hearing is underway and there is communication between the arbitrator and only one party without the consent or agreement of the other party. Such contact is still fairly commonplace because the GSB is a tribunal that serves a select group of parties, and so panel members and representatives develop social relationships.[143] Such contact does not, in itself, raise any reasonable apprehension of bias. In *OPSEU (Kowal) and Ministry of Health*, the GSB heard and accepted testimony from a former vice-chair of the GSB and president of the Ontario Labour Management Arbitrators' Association, Kenneth Swan, that he had social contacts with one counsel without the knowledge or consent of the opposite counsel, and that such contacts are "entirely proper in the absence of any discourtesy or attempt to conceal or any impropriety as, for example, any discussion of a case in progress."[144]

---

141 *Ontario Public Service Employees Union (Cusack) v Ontario (Community Safety and Correctional Services)*, 2016 CanLII 7452 (ON GSB) (Petryshen) at para 4.

142 The OLRB uses an expedited, informal adjudicator directed process of consultation to deal with duty of fair representation complaints, as described in OLRB *Information Bulletin* 11, online: www.olrb.gov.on.ca/InformationBulletins-EN.asp.

143 *OPSEU (Kowal) and Ministry of Health*, GSB#813/88, 21 December 1989 (Verity) at 19.

144 *Ibid* at 12.

E. STANDARD HEARING PROCEDURE

1) Public Interest

The GSB is a public statutory tribunal, with a mandate to adjudicate grievances between the provincial government and its employees, which can raise statutory issues, and genuine public interest in the government's actions. An "open court" policy applies.[145]

a) Access to Hearings

The GSB has consistently held that there is a significant public interest in full, public access to its hearings, and that any concerns about the privacy or other interests of participants in those hearings should be dealt with by measures other than an *in camera* hearing. The seminal case on this issue is *OPSEU (Ralph) and Ministry of Correctional Services*.[146] A correctional officer had used a fire hose on inmates and the case had attracted media attention. The employer asked that the hearing be closed to the public and the press, because of risks to institutional security and inmate privacy. The GSB held that a "heavy onus" lay on the party seeking to close a hearing as "the best safeguard against the arbitrary use of power or merely careless injustice is the full light of public scrutiny." The board refused to exclude the press and public from the hearing, but asked the press not to reveal the names of inmates who might testify and told the parties that it would consider applications from either party that certain evidence be received *in camera*.

Subsequently, the public interest in the subject matter of GSB cases has been emphasized as "serious, even overriding."[147] The GSB refused to exclude the public from a hearing where the grievor had been fired for sexual misconduct with a client, noting that the clients of the ministry were disadvantaged individuals who were vulnerable to ministry employees upon whom they rely. In order to protect the client's dignity, the GSB asked that the media not publish the client's name. In another case, the union asked that the hearings about alleged sexual harassment at correctional institutions be held *in camera* to protect the grievor from

---

145 *Ontario Public Service Employees Union (Cull) v Ontario (Health and Long-Term Care)*, 2017 CanLII 71798 (ON GSB) (Abramsky) at 6 [*Cull*].

146 GSB#212/78, 4 July 1979 (Swan).

147 *OPSEU (Tyler) and Ministry of Community and Social Services*, GSB#428/84, 31 May 1985 (Swan) at 10.

reprisals.[148] It was asserted that the subculture of correctional officers led to a very negative view of "ratting." The GSB refused, noting that the workplace in question was a public institution, and held that "a closed, secret proceeding is less likely to enhance the aims of the parties that workplaces be free from discrimination and harassment."[149] Where a request was made to keep a hearing *in camera* because the testimony might be used in a concurrent civil proceeding, the GSB refused on the grounds that its concern is labour relations, and the courts would regulate their own process.[150]

The GSB is subject to the *Freedom of Information and Protection of Privacy Act*.[151]

b) Anonymity of an Individual

The onus is on the party requesting anonymization of the identity of an individual referenced in a decision to establish exceptional or compelling circumstances. The normal sensitivity of medical or career information will not be sufficient.[152] Exceptional circumstances that warrant anonymity may be found to include avoiding the continuation of a poisoned work environment, the agreement of the parties that it is appropriate, and a lack of dispute about the facts, meaning that the "mischief of accusations being made 'behind a veil of anonymity'" does not arise.[153] The GSB has noted that the focus on the benefits of an "open courts" policy is being lost as there is more societal focus on privacy and anonymization requests become more frequent.[154]

---

148 *OPSEU (Glover-McCarthy/McCarthy) and Ministry of Correctional Services*, GSB#1489/93, 16 June 1994 (Tacon).

149 *Ibid* at 8–9. See the discussion of the "code of silence" in the section on conduct expectations in Chapter 10.

150 *OPSEU (Sammy et al) and Ministry of Correctional Services*, GSB#0224/01, 6 March 2002 (Harris) at 8.

151 RSO 1990, c F.31, Reg 460: General, Item 36. The Minister of Labour is designated as the head. For discussion of *FIPPA*, see Chapter 6.

152 *Cull*, above note 145 at paras 42–43.

153 *Ontario Public Service Employees Union (Grievor) v Ontario (Community Safety and Correctional Services)*, 2017 CanLII 92683 (ON GSB) (Carrier) at 2.

154 *Association of Management, Administrative and Professional Crown Employees of Ontario v Ontario (Attorney General)*, 2021 CanLII 58440 (ON GSB) (McLean) at para 75.

2) Hearing Process

For a tribunal that prizes expedition and flexibility of process, the GSB has also developed an extensive procedural jurisprudence, particularly when dealing with individual grievances. The board seems to have concluded that, in such cases, significant advance process requirements support fairness and efficient use of hearing days.[155]

a) Adjournments

The board has been willing to adjourn grievances in the absence of the grievor. The board has stressed the importance of the grievor having the opportunity to explain non-attendance, but also noted that it "scrutinizes explanations rigorously."[156] There may be instructions to the grievor to request relevant information from the grievor's doctor.[157]

Two factors are given weight in determining whether the extreme response of dismissal of a discharge grievance becomes appropriate:[158] first, apparent lack of interest on the part of the grievor, shown by ignoring attempts by the union to communicate, or by ignoring a board order; and second, whether the grievor has actually been made aware that their grievance may be dismissed if they fail to attend scheduled hearings. Where the grievor has been given a chance to explain their non- attendance and has been non-responsive, the grievance will be dismissed and the GSB has held "it would not be reasonable or appropriate to adjourn the proceeding indefinitely on sheer speculation that [their] silence is due to some health reasons."[159]

---

155 Possible factors involving the parties are an OPS workplace "culture" of many rules, and that OPSEU does not always exercise the degree of control over, or screening of, grievances normally expected of a union due to deference to grievor wishes, as discussed in the carriage rights section in Chapter 7.

156 *Association of Management, Administrative and Professional Crown Employees of Ontario (JM) v Ontario (Community Safety and Correctional Services)*, 2017 CanLII 85185 (ON GSB) (Parmar) at para 46; *Ontario Public Service Employees Union (Khan) v Ontario (Government and Consumer Services)*, 2019 CanLII 109990 (ON GSB) (McLean).

157 *Ontario Public Service Employees Union (Cupskey) v Ontario (Liquor Control Board of Ontario)*, 2019 CanLII 118224 (ON GSB) and 2020 CanLII 32550 (ON GSB) (Parmar).

158 *Ontario Public Service Employees Union (Byabagamba) v Ontario (Government & Consumer Services)*, 2016 CanLII 51068 (ON GSB) (Dissanayake) at para 18.

159 *Ontario Public Service Employees Union (Slaght) v Ontario (Liquor Control Board of Ontario)*, 2019 CanLII 126471 (ON GSB) (Dissanayake) at para 8;

The GSB has declined to adjourn grievances *sine die* absent evidence that there is a reasonable likelihood the grievor will be able to participate at some later date.[160]

In non-discharge cases, the grievor has been required to explain the reasons for non-attendance prior to rescheduling and at risk of dismissal of the grievance.[161] Where the grievor, after being informed of the hearing particulars, failed to attend without communication, the grievance was dismissed subject only to the grievor having two weeks to fully explain their non-attendance.[162]

b) Consolidation

A GSB rule empowers the consolidation of grievances where "two or more proceedings have a question of law or fact in common, the relief claimed arises out of the same transaction . . . or for any other reason an order ought to be made."[163] The GSB may abridge the time for placing a grievance on the hearing list and order that the proceedings be heard at the same time or one immediately after the other, or order that any of the proceedings be stayed until after the determination of any other of them.

The GSB's authority to consolidate matters is not precluded by the moving party's failure to turn its mind to the matter during the parties' agreed joint file review process. As "[t]he GSB is the master of its own proceedings," there are consolidation matters that will be decided by the board during the course of a proceeding.[164] While it was initially held the power to consolidate is limited when the two matters are being heard before different arbitrators,[165] the better view is that, as "one board"

Ontario Public Service Employees Union (Claer) v Ontario (Government and Consumer Services), 2022 CanLII 31330 (ON GSB) (Petryshen).

160 *Ontario Public Service Employees Union (Bremner) v Ontario (Attorney General)*, 2021 CanLII 26645 (ON GSB) (Misra); *Ontario Public Service Employees Union (Toman) v Ontario (Government and Consumer Services)*, 2019 CanLII 126488 (ON GSB) (Devins), citing *OPSEU (Sitek) v Ministry of Community Safety and Correctional Services* (2013) GSB #2012-0579 (Devins).

161 *Ontario Public Service Employees Union (Wojtkun) v Ontario (Solicitor General)*, 2020 CanLII 97347 (ON GSB) (Anderson).

162 *Ontario Public Service Employees Union (Labiris) v Ontario (Liquor Control Board of Ontario)*, 2020 CanLII 97358 (ON GSB) (Herlich).

163 *GSB Rules of Procedure*, above note 77, r 3.

164 *Association of Management, Administrative and Professional Crown Employees of Ontario (Chiba/Argyropoulos) v Ontario (Attorney General)*, 2017 CanLII 7061 (ON GSB) (Misra) at para 56.

165 *Ibid* at paras 34–35.

rather than sole arbitrators, the GSB and each of its adjudicators has the authority to consolidate grievances at any stage, including after another arbitrator has been appointed by the parties to determine certain of the grievances.[166] The fact that another arbitrator has been appointed to certain grievances is relevant to how to exercise jurisdiction, and the board has considered whether the other arbitrator has commenced the arbitration and whether the motion for consolidation is motivated by an attempt to avoid adjudication by a particular arbitrator.[167]

The GSB has often ordered that grievances be heard together. The key factor for "consolidation" is a closely related series of occurrences involving the same, or a small group of, people. The GSB has identified that consolidation will save time and remove the need for persons to testify more than once,[168] reduce the "risk of inconsistent findings,"[169] and make the best use of resources.[170] The GSB has decided to hear grievances together in the following circumstances:

- Grievances contesting discipline and the communication about the discipline[171]
- Several grievors disciplined for the same incident[172]
- Two union policy grievances about important seniority calculation issues involving "the same set of facts" and "the same group of employees"[173]
- Health and safety grievances from different parts of a facility for the developmentally handicapped, where an employer "downsizing" led to common concerns about the adequacy of staffing levels and training[174]

---

166 *Cody*, above note 82 at paras 28–46.

167 *Ibid* at para 47.

168 *OPSEU (Palazzo) and St Lawrence & District Ambulance Service Ltd*, GSB#1455/97, 8 July 1988 (Abramsky) at 22 [*Palazzo*].

169 *OPSEU (Latimer) and Ministry of the Solicitor General and Correctional Services*, GSB#0131/95, 22 June 1999 (Kaufman) at 5 [*Latimer, 1999*].

170 *OPSEU (Union Grievance) and Management Board of Cabinet*, GSB#1526/91, 18 March 1993 (Kaplan) at 15 [*Union, 1993*].

171 *Ontario Public Service Employees Union (Kennett) v Ontario (Ministry of Community Safety and Correctional Services)*, 2014 CanLII 64819 (ON GSB) (Misra).

172 *Ontario Public Service Employees Union (Moore) v Ontario (Community Safety and Correctional Services)*, 2014 CanLII 48017 (ON GSB) (Nairn) at 5–6.

173 *Ibid* at 14–15.

174 *OPSEU (Hardeman et al) and Ministry of Community and Social Services*, GSB#1206/90, 9 April 1991 (Verity).

- One job competition giving rise to grievances from different employees[175]
- Further examples of continuing "discrimination and harassment" involving the same personnel (with consolidation being ordered even though the hearing on earlier incidents was well under way)[176]
- An asserted "pattern" of discrimination culminating in dismissal[177]
- Multiple instances of alleged discrimination on the basis of union activity, including a job competition grievance;[178] and, in another case, a grievance about the installation of video cameras and suspension of the local president, where both management actions were alleged to be discrimination against the union activity of the local president[179]
- Separate incidents giving rise to the grievor's disciplinary suspension and their discharge respectively, where the grievor and a particular manager were the common, main witnesses[180]
- An overtime pay grievance and a second grievance, filed more than two years later, claiming the work was bargaining unit work, when the work in question for both grievances was the same[181]
- Alleged violations of an attendance management policy and related *Human Rights Code (HRC)* violations were heard together with a policy grievance concerning the same attendance management policy[182]

---

175 *OPSEU (Piva) and Ministry of Finance*, GSB#1284/94, 23 January 1996 (Gorsky).

176 *OPSEU (Fournier) and Ministry of Transportation*, GSB#1530/93, 22 September 1995 (Kaplan) [*Fournier*]; *Latimer, 1999*, above note 169.

177 *Ontario Public Service Employees Union (Frater) v (Solicitor General)*, 2021 CanLII 7233 (ON GSB) (Wacyk) [*Frater*].

178 *OPSEU (Dale et al) and Ministry of Health and Long-Term Care*, GSB#783/00, 14 November 2001 (Abramsky) [*Dale*].

179 *Ontario Public Service Employees Union v Ontario (Natural Resources and Forestry)*, 2019 CanLII 109983 (ON GSB) (Petryshen).

180 *Palazzo*, above note 168.

181 *OPSEU (Hunt et al) and Ministry of the Attorney General*, GSB#0534/01, 23 January 2004 (Abramsky).

182 *Human Rights Code*, RSO 1990, c H.19 [*HRC*], discussed in *OLBEU (Policy) and Liquor Control Board of Ontario*, GSB#0557/01, 2 January 2004 (Dissanayake) at 3–7. The case notes agreement that the same authority would exist under the *LRA*.

- Two grievors claiming they were harassed by each other, with one grievor discharged for assaulting the other[183] (this can produce the challenge of conflicting grievors, which the GSB was aware of, but opined could be managed)
- Grievances ordered to be heard together with grievances that have not been referred to arbitration[184]

Although it is rare, the GSB has declined to order consolidations. Consolidation of two accommodation grievances involving the same grievor was rejected when the grievances arose two-and-a-half years apart and dealt with different accommodation issues.[185] A spectrum of interconnected issues about cannabis use addressed in multiple grievances was divided into separate impairment and testing groupings to avoid an unwieldy and delayed hearing.[186] Where a grievance was not ready to proceed and involved different managers and a broader range of issues, it was not consolidated with an existing discharge grievance involving the same grievor.[187] Health and safety grievances were not consolidated with a grievance about the employer's right to reorganize work, about which there had already been four days of hearing.[188]

Evidence concerning an incident not yet grieved was admitted at a hearing for the purposes of determining whether there was a continuing course of conduct and to assist in determining the appropriate remedy, but there was no assumption of jurisdiction of that incident as a grievance.[189]

While it is clear that the GSB has the power to order that separate grievances be heard together, the next question is how. The different arrangements can theoretically include:

---

183 *Ontario Public Service Employees Union (Upson) v Ontario (Community Safety and Correctional Services)*, 2013 CanLII 56967 (ON GSB) (Harris) [*Upson*].

184 *Dale*, above note 178; *Ontario Public Service Employees Union (Cartier) v Ontario (Ministry of Health and Long-Term Care)*, 2006 CanLII 17525 (ON GSB) (Stephens) [*Cartier*].

185 *Ontario Public Service Employees Union v Ontario (Solicitor General)*, 2022 CanLII 31336 (ON GSB) (Williamson).

186 *Amalgamated Transit Union—Local 1587 (Policy) v Ontario (Metrolinx)*, 2021 CanLII 127112 (ON GSB) (Nairn).

187 *Frater*, above note 177 at 19–20.

188 *OPSEU (Ferraro) and Ministry of Community, Family and Children's Services*, GSB#1200/00, 17 July 2002 (Mikus).

189 *Latimer, 1999*, above note 169 at 6.

- the claims/grievances are merged or blended into one
- the evidence and argument regarding *all* the claims or grievances are heard together in one hearing concurrently
- the evidence and argument regarding each claim or grievance is heard serially, one after the other[190]

The history of the consolidation rule assists in addressing the extent of the power of a GSB arbitrator to order different kinds of consolidation. Prior to the rule, there were GSB decisions involving multiple virtually identical classification grievances, in which the GSB found that the *CECBA* only gave authority over practice and procedure and not over the substantive issue of consolidated grievances being determined on the basis of a representative or test case.[191] The "technically correct sense" of consolidation results in "the melding of several grievances into one"; and the creation of such a "group grievance" was viewed as a substantive ruling beyond the GSB's powers under the collective agreement or the Act.[192] The GSB held it could not order determination of consolidated grievances on the basis of a test case, but did have the power to decline to hear repetitive evidence. Then the consolidation rule was promulgated, giving the GSB the power to "consolidate" grievances with each other in all senses of that word, including merging them into one. Despite this, there is no apparent example of the GSB actually merging grievances so that they become one, or fewer. It has been found that "to fuse two proceedings into one" requires "an identity of interest."[193]

The presumptive starting point for the hearing of consolidated grievances is that all the evidence for all the grievances will be heard at once followed by all of the argument.[194] Concurrent hearings are preferred, as they can be efficient and allow all of the common process issues, including production and particulars, to be resolved at the begin-

---

190 *OPSEU (Vassallo et al) and Ministry of the Solicitor General and Correctional Services*, GSB#3042/92, 14 August 1996 (Kaufman) at 6–7 [*Vassallo*].

191 *OPSEU (Clerks 3 General) and Ministry of Health*, GSB#240/84, 4 February 1985 (Verity) at 7.

192 *OPSEU (Neamtz et al) and Ministry of the Environment*, GSB#516/84, 30 April 1985 (Gorsky) at 4 and 13.

193 *Upson*, above note 183 at 8–9, adopting *CAW—Canada and Dresser Canada Inc*, [1987] OLRB Rep October 1234 (Surdykowski) at para 8.

194 *Ontario Public Service Employees Union (Lupiani) v Ontario (Transportation)*, 2018 CanLII 33074 (ON GSB) (Dissanayake) at para 14.

ning. Only one case has deviated from that procedure and required a separate mini-hearing for each case, which was to deal with natural justice concerns arising because the first case was already under way when the cases were consolidated.[195]

The GSB has addressed concerns about the risk of cases being prejudiced through consolidation by reassuring parties that each grievance will be addressed on its own merits.[196] The likelihood that a party may have to make alternative, presumably potentially conflicting, submissions is not a bar to consolidation.[197] Where a party resisted consolidating two grievances, as the opposite party's evidence had started on one grievance but was not yet complete, the GSB noted that the party resisting consolidation had not yet commenced calling its evidence and so would not be prejudiced by the consolidation.[198] Where the parties had agreed to having cases heard together, one party sought a ruling to disallow evidence that could only be of assistance to certain grievors. The grievors were employees working in the same position and who filed classification grievances at different times. Arguably, the grievors who filed at an earlier point were only entitled to rely on facts that occurred prior to the filing of their grievances and could not rely on facts arising from consideration of grievances filed later. The GSB declined to make the order, but acknowledged that it would have to be vigilant and only apply specific evidence to those grievors' cases where the evidence would be relevant and admissible.[199]

Mechanisms to address the possibility of procedural prejudice to the party resisting consolidation have included orders for written particulars[200] and disclosure of all supporting documents prior to the next day of hearing.[201] The consolidation of grievances not yet referred to the GSB with grievances already referred was addressed by ordering all the grievances to be mediated together and if unsuccessful to hear the grievances in related groupings.[202]

---

195 See *Union, 1993*, above note 170 at 15.

196 *Palazzo*, above note 168 at 22.

197 *Union, 1993*, above note 170 at 15.

198 *Latimer, 1999*, above note 169 at 5.

199 *OPSEU (Kalimootoo/Bourne et al) and Ministry of Citizenship*, GSB#884/91, 22 May 1992 (Low) at 4.

200 *Fournier*, above note 176 at 5.

201 *Dale*, above note 178 at 11–12.

202 *Cartier*, above note 184.

Although there is no specific rule on the topic, the GSB also has authority to bifurcate proceedings, including preliminary objections, in appropriate cases, having regard for distinctness and efficiency.[203]

c) Particulars

Particulars are important to the fair and expeditious resolution of grievances.[204] However, "a grievance is not the equivalent of a statement of claim, and particulars are not meant to be formal pleadings."[205] Employers should not be required to comb through their records to determine whether there is any factual basis for the grievor's complaints, guess at the basis for the complaint, or wait for evidence to be tendered at a hearing to be provided with the basis for a claim against them.[206] But, "nor should parties expect to be provided with every detailed fact of a case through particulars. The purpose of particulars in labour arbitration is the identification and understanding of the issues involved, not the complete revelation of the expected evidence. The arbitration hearing itself is the proper place for the full airing of the evidence."[207]

Particulars are to include not merely legal conclusions, but also the facts which the union and the grievor assert support any such conclusion and demonstrate the discrimination or breach of the collective agreement alleged. With respect to each act or omission alleged, the particulars shall indicate what was done or not done, when, where, by what means, and by whom, and, to the extent that motivation may be a relevant fact,

---

203 *Amalgamated Transit Union—Local 1587 (Union) v Ontario (Metrolinx—GO Transit)*, 2015 CanLII 76839 (ON GSB) (Dissanayake) at 4–8; *Ontario Public Service Employees Union (Union) v Ontario (Government and Consumer Services)*, 2016 CanLII 76527 (ON GSB) (Dissanayake); *Association of Management, Administrative and Professional Crown Employees of Ontario (Jackson et al) v Ontario (Finance)*, 2017 CanLII 65774 (ON GSB) (Dissanayake).

204 *Ontario Public Service Employees Union (Ryall) v Ontario (Ministry of the Solicitor General)*, 2022 CanLII 106478 (ON GSB) (Lynk) [*Ryall*]; *Ontario Public Service Employees Union (Kanellos) v Ontario (Health and Long-Term Care)*, 2015 CanLII 14199 (ON GSB) (Williamson); *Ontario Public Service Employees Union (Gates et al) and the Crown in Right of Ontario (Ministry of Health and Long-Term Care)*, GSB#2005-3003, 2007 CarswellOnt 10726 (Dissanayake) at paras 5 & 6 [*Gates et al*].

205 *Ryall*, above note 204 at para 11.

206 *Re Ontario (Ministry of Community Safety and Correctional Services) and OPSEU (Singh)*, 2005 CarswellOnt 11501 (Abramsky) at paras 17, 18, 22, and 30.

207 *Ryall*, above note 204 at para 11.

with what motivation.[208] To put it another way, a party must provide the "who, what, where, when, and how" of the allegations.[209]

Parties "must set out their case with sufficient detail that the opposing party will know the case they must meet."[210] Minor gaps may be permitted if they "do not impair the ability of the employer to respond to the grievance."[211]

Particulars can be general when the allegation is that some practice is general, but any specific incidents to be relied on must be particularized.[212] "What the Union is not entitled to do is to allege in its particulars normal or general condonation and then later adduce evidence with respect to specific incidents of condonation which it has not particularized."

Particulars will be used as needed to clarify the issues in a grievance alleging discrimination.[213] To particularize discrimination, there is a need to set out the claim that a protected characteristic was a factor in decisions to engage in discriminatory treatment and set out specific examples of differential treatment.[214] It is not sufficient to allege the prohibited grounds and the actions complained of, as there must be

---

208 *Ontario Public Service Employees Union (Jackson) v Ontario (Children, Community and Social Services)*, 2021 CanLII 37030 (ON GSB) (Banks) at 6 [*Jackson*], quoting from *Gates et al*, above note 204, quoting *Ross*, above note 28.

209 *Ryall*, above note 204 at para 11; *Ontario Public Service Employees Union v Ontario (Ministry of Community Safety and Correctional Services)*, 2006 CanLII 37571 (ON GSB), citing *OPSEU (Union) and Ministry of Community Safety and Correctional Services* (2006), GSB#2003-5766 (Briggs).

210 *Ontario Public Service Employees Union (Grievor) v Ontario (Community Safety and Correctional Services)*, 2017 CanLII 52711 (ON GSB) (Devins) at para 7.

211 *Ontario Public Service Employees Union (Baker et al) v Ontario (Liquor Control Board of Ontario)*, 2021 CanLII 95724 (ON GSB) (Dissanayake) [*Baker, 2021*].

212 *Ontario Public Service Employees Union (Dartch) v Ontario (Solicitor General)*, 2021 CanLII 26593 (ON GSB) (Anderson) at para 19.

213 *Ontario Public Service Employees Union (Hagopian) v Ontario (Finance)*, 2019 CanLII 35306 (ON GSB) (Gee). See the discussion of human rights cases in Chapter 6.

214 *Jackson*, above note 208 at para 30; *Ontario Public Service Employees Union (Pickett/McCormick/Holden) v Ontario (Ministry of Correctional Services)*, 2003 CanLII 52866 (ON GSB) (Harris) at para 9 [*Pickett/McCormick/Holden*] and cases cited therein.

support for an inference that the grievor was targeted due to the prohibited grounds.[215]

It is recognized that such allegations "require a broad scope of evidence" but at the same time claims of discrimination should not be developed as the case proceeds and should be particularized in a "crisp and clear fashion."[216]

Particulars that "on their face" do not demonstrate a breach of the collective agreement can be struck, but as the effect of doing so is the same as excluding evidence, determinations of relevance should be made cautiously prior to hearing the full context needed to assess relevance.[217] "Out of scope events may be made relevant because they explain, characterize, or contextualize the events within scope." The provision of particulars should not preclude the leading of the contextual evidence needed to fully understand subtle problems like systemic racism. It is to be questioned whether it is in keeping with the informality of the grievance procedure to have motions to strike particulars.

Using disclosure to find a basis for an unparticularized claim "places the cart before the horse."[218] The GSB has consistently held that there is an onus on the union to provide sufficient particulars prior to the triggering of the employer's obligation to disclose information.[219]

Where, despite particulars being requested and provided, there is an attempt to call unparticularized evidence, the board will decline to hear it as it is prejudicial to timely adjudication. The alternative of adjourning to permit the employer to investigate the new allegations

---

215 *Ontario Public Service Employees Union (Jackson) v Ontario (Children, Community and Social Services)*, 2021 CanLII 82489 (ON GSB) (Banks) at paras 65–67.

216 *Pickett/McCormick/Holden*, above note 214 at 9, quoting *Klonowski et al and Ministry of Finance*, 2002, GSB#1799/99. See also the discussion of the "three-year" principle referenced in Chapter 6 governing the retroactivity of permissible evidence of an alleged course of discriminatory conduct.

217 *Jackson*, above note 208 at paras 40–42, citing *OPSEU (Louis) v Ministry of Training, Colleges, and Universities* (2019) GSB#2016-0806 (Gee) and setting out further considerations about whether to hear disputes about the relevance of particulars and weighing the risk of delaying proceedings.

218 *Jackson*, above note 208 at para 32.

219 *Ontario Public Service Employees Union v Ontario (Ministry of Community Safety and Correctional Services)*, 2006 CanLII 31463 (ON GSB) (Briggs) [*Union, 2006 (Briggs)*]; *Ontario Public Service Employees Union (Bhandari) v Ontario (Education)*, 2007 CanLII 46155 (ON GSB) (Briggs).

and potentially to call additional evidence should only be allowed in "very exceptional circumstances."[220]

Failure to provide particulars, when unexplained and sustained, can result in dismissal of the grievance.[221]

The GSB has frequently ordered quite extensive particulars accompanied by a detailed litigation timetable.[222]

d) Disclosure

The GSB rule on disclosure sets out a broad power to order production at any time "for inspection of documents arguably relevant to the grievance that are not privileged and that are in the possession, control or power of a party or any other person."[223] This authority includes ordering pre-hearing production without the necessity of a *subpoena duces tecum* returnable on the day of the relevant hearing.[224] The GSB has opined that the parties should resolve disclosure matters between themselves and not require an order of any kind unless one is truly necessary.

But, where desirable, detailed orders are made requiring production of documents relating to particular matters.[225]

220 *Ontario Public Service Employees Union v Ontario (Labour)*, 2010 CanLII 64226 (ON GSB) (Dissanayake).

221 *Baker, 2021*, above note 211; *Ontario Public Service Employees Union (Mochama) v Ontario (Municipal Affairs and Housing)*, 2022 CanLII 106486 (ON GSB) (Carrier).

222 *Ontario Public Service Employees Union (Assenov) v Ontario (Solicitor General)*, 2020 CanLII 39013 (ON GSB) (Gee) and cases cited therein; *Ontario Public Service Employees Union (Sparkes) v Ontario (Solicitor General)*, 2019 CanLII 126461 (ON GSB) (Misra) and cases cited therein; *Ontario Public Service Employees Union (Troost) v Ontario (Community Safety and Correctional Services)*, 2018 CanLII 64400 (ON GSB) (Anderson); *Ontario Public Service Employees Union (Frost) v Ontario (Community Safety and Correctional Services)*, 2014 CanLII 74775 (ON GSB) (Harris); *Ontario Public Service Employees Union (Morgan) v Ontario (Community Safety and Correctional Services)*, 2011 CanLII 100933 (ON GSB).

223 *GSB Rules of Procedure*, above note 77, r 4.

224 *OPSEU (Samaroo) and Ministry of Correctional Services*, GSB#0491/94, 16 June 1999 (Gray).

225 For example, see *OPSEU (Cherwonogrodzky et al) v Ontario (Ministry of Finance)*, 2003 CanLII 52927 (ON GSB) (Gray); *Ontario Public Service Employees Union (Brosseau et al, Union) v Ontario (Revenue and Government Services)*, 2011 CanLII 83723 (ON GSB) (Gray).

Disclosure need only be made in response to adequately particularized claims,[226] and so, if necessary, the fulfillment of both particularization and disclosure obligations will be timetabled.[227]

The GSB has generally adopted the standard arbitral jurisprudence on disclosure, focusing on whether the documents requested are "arguably relevant," considering whether the production of the material in question would cause undue prejudice, and refusing to permit a "fishing expedition."[228] Employer internal discussions about grievances (save if the discussions involve legal advice or preparation for litigation) are subject to disclosure.[229] Where the discipline decision maker may have been influenced by the personnel file, the entire file has been ordered produced.[230] Safeguards may be applicable when individual privacy interests are involved, as discussed in Chapter 6.

The employer is not normally required to disclose how similar cases were handled,[231] absent particulars that offer "a reasonable foundation or link" to the allegation of differential treatment.[232]

Inability to disclose due to inadvertently losing documents is to be addressed by means other than simply allowing a grievance.[233]

---

226 Where a party's case has not been adequately particularized, disclosure may be delayed until particulars have been provided: *OPSEU (Union) and Ministry of Community Safety and Correctional Services*, GSB#2260/99, 31 March 2004 (Mikus) and *Union, 2006 (Briggs)*, above note 219.

227 See discussion of litigation timetables above in the "Particulars" section.

228 *OPSEU (McQueen) and Ministry of the Solicitor General and Correctional Services*, GSB#0383/97, 5 October 1998 (Briggs) at 8–10, citing *West Park Hospital and Ontario Nurses' Association* (1993), 37 LAC (4th) 160 (Knopf); *OPSEU (Hunt) and Ministry of the Attorney General*, GSB#0534/01, 4 November 2004 (Abramsky); *Union, 2006 (Briggs)*, above note 219 at 20 and cases cited.

229 *Ontario Public Service Employees Union (McCormick) v Ontario (Transportation)*, 2006 CanLII 42762 (ON GSB) (Stephens) at 9–10.

230 *OPSEU (Tefoglou) and Ministry of Correctional Services*, GSB#1378/97, 2 April 1998 (Abramsky) at 4–5; *OPSEU (Kumor) and Ministry of the Solicitor General and Correctional Services*, GSB#1698/96, 27 March 1998 (Finley) at 4–5, making an exception because the file was voluminous.

231 *Ontario Public Service Employees Union (Union) v Ontario (Community Safety and Correctional Services)*, 2007 CanLII 51780 (ON GSB) (Briggs).

232 *Ontario Public Service Employees Union (Morsi) v Ontario (Finance and Revenue)*, 2008 CanLII 70538 (ON GSB) (Devins).

233 *Ontario v GSB (CA)*, above note 18, applied in *Ontario Public Service Employees Union (Phagau) v Ontario (Liquor Control Board of Ontario)*, 2016 CanLII 7445 (ON GSB) (Harris).

e) No *Prima Facie* Case

At the beginning of the hearing, and prior to the calling of the evidence by the party with the onus, there is an opportunity for the responding party to bring a motion that the grievance does not make out a *prima facie* case and need not be responded to. The question for the GSB is whether the asserted facts, if taken as true, are "capable of supporting" the alleged violation of the collective agreement.[234] If the theory of the case is reasonable, and the particularized facts would, if true, result in a finding of a breach of the collective agreement on that theory, the motion should be dismissed. If the asserted facts are not capable of establishing the elements necessary to substantiate the violation, then the motion will succeed, and, for purposes of making that decision, the board will interpret the collective agreement and decide legal issues.[235]

In respect of allegations of bad faith, the "sincere belief" that the allegation is well founded is not sufficient to defeat the motion, as there must be alleged objective facts which could lead to a bad faith finding.[236]

Concerning a motion that there is no *prima facie* case of discrimination, the fundamental principle is the same (e.g., whether the facts, if accepted as true, are capable of establishing the elements necessary to substantiate the prohibited discrimination claimed by the union).[237] The grievor must show there is a *prima facie* case that the grievor has

---

234 *Ontario Public Service Employees Union (Martin et al) v Ontario (Community and Social Services)*, 2015 CanLII 60449 (ON GSB) (Anderson) at para 6 [*Martin (Anderson)*]. And see *Ontario Public Service Employees Union (Couture) v Ontario (Government Services)*, 2011 CanLII 100922 (Dissanayake); *Ontario Public Service Employees Union (Roy) v Ontario (Solicitor General)*, 2021 CanLII 138271 (ON GSB) (Dissanayake) at paras 20–21.

235 *Ontario Public Service Employees Union (Brydges et al) v Ontario (Transportation)*, 2014 CanLII 74778 (ON GSB) (Dissanayake) at 9–10, paras 19–22 [*Brydges*].

236 *Ontario Public Service Employees Union (Wong) v Ontario (Government Services)*, 2012 CanLII 24021 (Dissayanake) at para 19.

237 *Ontario Public Service Employees Union (Morgan) v Ontario (Children and Youth Services)*, 2014 CanLII 30274 (ON GSB) (Tims) and cases cited therein; *Brydges*, above note 235 at paras 23–43; *Ontario Public Service Employees Union (Bilardo) v Ontario (Labour)*, 2014 CanLII 74774 (ON GSB) (Herlich) at 3; *Ontario Public Service Employees Union (Zingel) v Ontario (Finance)*, 2017 CanLII 30342 (ON GSB) (Dissanayake); *Ontario Public Service Employees Union (Poblete) v Ontario (Government and Consumer Services)*, 2019 CanLII 21745 (ON GSB) (Herlich) at paras 7–28; *Ontario Public Service Employees Union (Solomon Smith et al) v Ontario (Children, Community and Social Services)*, 2019 CanLII 126475 (ON GSB) (Anderson) at para 8; *Ontario Public Service Employees Union (Mohamed) v Ontario (Attorney General)*, 2022 CanLII 122355 (ON GSB) (Mohamed).

a characteristic protected from discrimination, that an adverse impact was experienced, and that the protected characteristic was a factor in that adverse impact.[238]

A *prima facie* case of alleged breach of the employer's occupational health and safety obligations is made out by asserting facts that, objectively assessed, would establish existing precautions were not reasonable.[239]

f) Non-suit Motion and the Lack of Need to Elect Whether to Call Evidence

At the conclusion of one party's case, the other party can bring a motion for non-suit. The GSB, as a tribunal with its own responsibility to streamline the proceedings, has said it may invite a non-suit motion and the parties should be ready to be asked, "perhaps at any appropriate point in any particular proceedings, what useful purpose is to be served by continuing those proceedings."[240]

The legal principles that govern the determination of a non-suit motion were originally summarized in *Ontario (Ministry of Transportation) and OPSEU (Whan et al)*:[241]

1) In a non-suit motion, the standard of proof expected from a responding party is that of a *prima facie* case, which is significantly lower than the standard of proof on a balance of probabilities.
2) In determining whether a *prima facie* case has been made out, the test is whether some evidence exists to support the claim, which requires an answer or explanation from the other side.
3) In applying the standard of a *prima facie* case, any conflicts in or doubts about the facts must be determined in favour of the party responding to the motion.

---

238 As summarized in *Ontario Public Service Employees Union (Martin) v Ontario (Transportation)*, 2022 CanLII 35398 (ON GSB) (Dissanayake) at para 22 [*Martin (Dissanayake)*].

239 *Martin (Anderson)*, above note 234; *Ontario Public Service Employees Union (Laderoute) v Ontario (Community Safety and Correctional Services)*, 2018 CanLII 55847 (ON GSB) (Gee); *Martin (Dissanayake)*, *ibid* at para 15.

240 *Ross*, above note 28 at 8.

241 2007 CanLII 6889 (ON GSB) (Dissanayake); *OPSEU (Gareh) and Ministry of the Attorney General*, GSB#1665/98, 16 September 2002 (Brown) [*Gareh*].

4) In assessing the existence of a *prima facie* case, *viva voce* evidence as well as all documentary evidence before the board must be considered.
5) In examining the evidence before it, the board will not assess the quality, reliability, or the credibility of the evidence.
6) Where a non-suit motion is granted, a written decision with reasons will follow. However, where a motion is denied, no reasons, oral or written, will be issued.[242] (This is the practice in order to reduce any unfairness that could result from the moving party having the benefit of a "half-time score" about the strengths and weaknesses of their case.)[243]

This list has since been amended to add to point 3 that the test of whether there is some evidence to support the claim assumes that the evidence meets a minimum threshold of credibility.[244] The sufficiency of evidence required is "whether the evidence presented 'could be sufficient to lead' to a ruling in favour of the grievance" if the arbitrator "assumed its witnesses to be credible and drew in its favour all inferences reasonably supported by direct evidence."[245] More recent elaboration is that no weight should be given to any contradictory evidence of a witness on a specific matter, or to evidence that is "patently ridiculous." Further, unsupported conclusions of fact have "no probative value."[246]

---

242 Followed in *Ontario Public Service Employees Union (O'Connor) v Ontario (Finance)*, 2008 CanLII 9600 (ON GSB) (Lynk); *Ontario Public Service Employees Union (Vingar) v Ontario (Health and Long-Term Care)*, 2014 CanLII 30275 (ON GSB) (Lynk).

243 *Ross*, above note 28 at 11.

244 *Ontario Public Service Employees Union (Pacheco) v Ontario (Solicitor General)*, 2020 CanLII 38998 (ON GSB) (Petryshen).

245 *Ontario Public Service Employees Union (Allin et al) v Ontario (Ministry of Revenue)*, 2010 CanLII 38781 (ON GSB) (Dissanayake), followed in *Ontario Public Service Employees Union (Deprophetis) v Ontario (Ministry of Labour)*, 2010 CanLII 72683 (ON GSB) (Dissanayake); *Ontario Public Service Employees Union (Gauntlett) v Ontario (Finance)*, 2008 CanLII 70504 (ON GSB) (Gray) at 6–14; *Ontario Public Service Employees Union (Thompson) v Ontario (Liquor Control Board of Ontario)*, 2012 CanLII 67531 (ON GSB) (Brown) at paras 31–32. As an example of insufficiency of the evidence of province-wide practices required to succeed, see *Ontario Public Service Employees Union (Spicer/Union) v Ontario (Labour)*, 2012 CanLII 29899 (ON GSB) (Herlich) at 6–7.

246 *Ontario Public Service Employees Union (Bharti) v Ontario (Natural Resources and Forestry)*, 2015 CanLII 19330 (ON GSB) (Anderson) at 3–4, applied in *Martin (Anderson)*, above note 234; *Ontario Public Service Employees Union*

The GSB has routinely exercised the discretion to permit a motion for non-suit without requiring the moving party to elect whether to call evidence.[247] This deviation from the common legal approach of requiring an election[248] stems from the 1990 decision in *OPSEU (Faler) and Ministry of Correctional Services*.[249] The GSB noted that if the motion was allowed, the length of the hearing would be substantially reduced and if the motion was denied, it would not have added much to the overall length of the case. The traditional rationales for forcing the party moving the non-suit motion to make an election were reviewed. It had been thought that the requirement to elect would discourage weak and time-wasting motions. It also avoided the possible perception of unfairness that could develop if an arbitrator heard only part of a case, issued a substantive ruling, and thereafter proceeded to hear the rest of the case and issued a potentially conflicting ruling. The GSB concluded, in *Faler*, that these reasons no longer justified an absolute requirement for an election. With multi-day arbitrations, the extra time for a non-suit motion was minimal and a non-suit motion had the potential to significantly shorten the proceedings. The concern about unfairness resulting from the moving party obtaining early information about the GSB's views, if the motion was not successful, could be dealt with by the GSB not providing any reasons for the dismissal of a non-suit motion.[250]

(Asztemborski et al) v Ontario (Treasury Board Secretariat), 2017 CanLII 92686 (ON GSB) (Briggs); *Ontario Public Service Employees Union (Brown et al) v Ontario (Labour, Training and Skills Development)*, 2020 CanLII 14818 (ON GSB) (Gee).

247 The seminal case on this issue is *OPSEU (Faler) and Ministry of Correctional Services*, GSB#218/89, 27 February 1990 (Fisher) [*Faler*]. *Faler* has been followed in *OPSEU (Gibson/Patterson) and Ministry of Community and Social Services*, GSB#319/93, 27 July 1994 (Barrett); *OPSEU (Toplin) and Ministry of Correctional Services*, GSB#2690/92, 5 July 1995 (Waisglass), and cases cited therein at 4; *OPSEU (Kolman) and Ministry of the Solicitor General & Correctional Services*, GSB#1372/92, 21 October 1997 (Mikus); *OPSEU (Holmes) and Ministry of the Solicitor General and Correctional Services*, GSB#157/98, 16 October 2000 (Saltman).

248 For the common approach, and its advantages, see, as an example: *Masonry Council of Unions Toronto and Vicinity and Its Members Bricklayers, Masons Independent Union of Canada, Local 1 v Emarosa Group Inc*, 2021 CanLII 140450 (ON LA) (Slaughter) at para 19.

249 *Faler*, above note 247.

250 *Ibid* at 7.

The *Faler* approach to non-suits was soon the subject of direct criticism by the Divisional Court. In *OPSEU (Cahoon) and Ontario Development Corporation*,[251] the GSB granted a motion for non-suit, overturning the discharge of an employee, without requiring the union to elect to call evidence. The GSB ruled that the employer had made a fatal error in failing to call a witness to testify about the reasons for the discipline, even though the grievor was proved to have engaged in very serious misconduct. On judicial review, the Divisional Court described the GSB's decision as "riddled with errors." These errors included several relating to the non-suit motion. First, civil courts always require the moving party to elect whether to call evidence and there was no reason to apply a different approach before an administrative tribunal. Second, in dealing with the merits of the motion, the GSB had mistakenly applied a balance of probabilities test rather than the appropriate "some evidence" or "*prima facie* case" test. Third, the GSB was apparently "unaware of its duty to lean in favour of a respondent to a non-suit motion and of its discretion to permit evidence omitted through inadvertence to be adduced."

Nonetheless, the GSB has continued to follow *Faler*, rather than *Cahoon*. It must be the GSB's view that *Faler* does set out reasons why an administrative tribunal could have different procedural approaches from a court.

It is not clear what weight the GSB should give to the strength or weakness of the case being challenged. In one case, the board stated that it will be more likely to not require election where it has real "although perhaps unspecified or unparticularized concerns" about the case that is being challenged.[252] More recently, the GSB has held that it should not use the strength of the case as an important criterion for assessing the argument about whether to require an election.[253] Instead, an election will not be required *unless* the party responding to the motion can meet

251 GSB#773/85, 4 November 1987 (Verity), quashed in *Ontario v OPSEU*, [1990] OJ No 635 (Div Ct).

252 *Ross*, above note 28 at 9. The moving party was not put to its election, although the motion was dismissed.

253 *Ontario Public Service Employees Union v Ontario (Ministry of Community, Family and Children's Services)*, 2004 CanLII 55322 (ON GSB) (Dissanayake) [*Barillari*]; *Ontario Public Service Employees Union (Anthony et al) v Ontario (Community Safety and Correctional Services)*, 2007 CanLII 14608 (ON GSB) (Harris).

the onus of convincing the GSB that the particular circumstances of the case do require an election.[254] The GSB's concern is that use of the "strength of the case" criterion will cause the parties to include a full argument on whether a *prima facie* case has been made out as part of their argument on whether there should be a requirement to elect. Then, if the moving party is put to its election, and elects not to call evidence, that party would have to protract the case by making the same *prima facie* case argument again on the non-suit motion itself. The approach of not weighing the strength of the case on the motion to elect is based, in part, on the belief that the limited number of parties that appear in front of the GSB would not abuse the non-suit motion for tactical advantage simply because an election is not required.[255]

A party responding to a non-suit motion asked to reopen its case and this request was refused, with the GSB noting that the evidence sought to be admitted "was not merely an oversight or a procedural matter" and had been available throughout.[256]

Where multiple grievances are being heard at the same hearing, some can be non-suited and others allowed to proceed. In such a case the GSB may reserve its reasons for upholding the motion, in part, until its final decision on the merits of the remaining grievances.[257] To rule on a grievance-by-grievance basis could give the moving party the advantage of insight into the board's thinking. On the other hand, the GSB has, in a lengthy and complicated case, issued a decision on a non-suit motion dismissing some, but not all grievances, with quite extensive reasons.[258]

3) Reconsideration and OLRB Jurisdiction

The GSB, like other arbitration boards, does not have jurisdiction to reconsider and change a finding or decision it has already made on the merits of an issue in dispute.[259] This does not prevent correcting errors

254 *Barillari*, *ibid* at 8.

255 *Ibid* at 7.

256 *OPSEU (Reid) and Ministry of Community & Social Services*, GSB#2098/96, 17 August 1998 (Leighton) at 5. Also note the comment of the Divisional Court in *Ontario v OPSEU*, [1990] OJ No 635 (Div Ct) about permitting the parties to remedy a mistake.

257 *Vassallo*, above note 190 at 11–12.

258 *Gareb*, above note 241.

259 *Ontario Public Service Employees Union v Ontario (Municipal Affairs and Housing)*, 2010 CanLII 42763 (ON GSB) at paras 37–43.

or dealing with matters on which it has remained seized in order to implement the decision.

The OLRB "has the jurisdiction, in the course of making a decision with respect to an issue before it, to arrive at different conclusions on questions of fact and law than those arrived at by the GSB, but the Board lacks jurisdiction to make a decision with respect to matters settled by the decision of the GSB."[260] The OLRB does have jurisdiction to deal with allegations of a breach of the duty of fair representation allegedly committed in connection with GSB hearings.

F. REMEDIAL AUTHORITY

1) General Approach

Apart from the unusual *CECBA* specific restrictions on remedial authority discussed at the end of this section, the GSB has much the same statutory remedial authority and limitations as the *LRA* provides for rights arbitrators.[261] The GSB's decisions are binding on the parties to the collective agreement and on "the employees covered by the agreement who are affected by the decision."[262]

A liberal approach to the exercise of the GSB's remedial authority was set out in *OPSEU (Carol Berry) v Ontario (Ministry of Community and Social Services)*,[263] where the Divisional Court held that the resolution of differences was the object of arbitration boards, both in the public and private sectors, and, accordingly, the GSB's remedial power should be interpreted to ensure that it can effectively bring about a final and binding settlement. The board's jurisdiction is "unrestricted" and "its mandate is remedial."[264]

---

260 *Ontario Public Service Employees Union v Ontario (Community Safety and Correctional Services)*, 2009 CanLII 27447 (ON LRB) (Anderson) at para 62.

261 *CECBA*, above note 1, s 7 makes *LRA*, above note 3, s 48(12), (13), and (15)–(17) applicable to the GSB.

262 *LRA*, *ibid*, s 48(18), which remains applicable to the GSB, by virtue of not being expressly excluded under *CECBA*, *ibid*, s 7(2).

263 *OPSEU (Carol Berry et al) v Ontario (Ministry of Community and Social Services)*, [1986] OJ No 152 (Div Ct) [*Berry*], following *Regina v OPSEU et al* (1982), 35 OR (2d) 670 (Div Ct).

264 *Berry*, *ibid* at 15.

Further to the GSB's jurisdiction to interpret and apply human rights and employment-related statutes,[265] the GSB has exercised wide-ranging remedial authority in making extensive rulings, orders, and damage awards to address human rights and occupational health and safety violations. See the *HRC* and *OHSA* sections of Chapter 6. This same range of remedies has also been applied to address employer anti-union actions that are a breach of the *LRA*.[266]

It is interesting to note that *CECBA* limits the remedial authority of any voluntary interest arbitrator and of the OLRB so that, in both cases, "[n]o order of the board shall include any term that would require either directly or indirectly for its implementation the enactment or amendment of legislation except for the purpose of appropriating money for its implementation," but that no such limitation applies to the GSB.[267]

The GSB has said that

> [t]he instant bargaining relationship (i.e., that between OPSEU and the Crown) is a mature one. And as a Vice-Chair of this Board, I can take notice that the parties' bargaining relationship, while it can be as adversarial as any other one might encounter, is typically characterized by good faith and professionalism on both sides. These parties consistently exhibit an impressive ability to resolve the labour relations issues which separate them.[268]

This observation led the GSB to view bad behaviour by the employer as an aberration and to refrain from issuing a cease and desist order.

The GSB has demonstrated a willingness to issue broad decisions clarifying OPS policies.[269] For example, the board had this to say concerning the use of health information:

---

265 See the brief discussion in the "Jurisdiction" section at the beginning of this chapter.

266 *Ontario Public Service Employees Union v Ontario (Community Safety and Correctional Services)*, 2016 CanLII 48167 (ON GSB) (Herlich) at paras 97–99 and 145–61 [*Community Safety, 2016 (Herlich)*]. Since no issue was raised about the GSB's authority to declare a violation of the *LRA*, that issue was not argued although there is no apparent reason to question that authority.

267 For the limitation on interest arbitration, see *CECBA*, above note 1, s 4(11), and on the OLRB, s 16(2). It is likely an unnecessary limitation as legislative authority is not delegable.

268 *Community Safety, 2016 (Herlich)*], above note 266 at para 146.

269 Topics have included attendance management and security checks. OPSEU filed an OPS-wide grievance about the introduction of an attendance management program: *Ontario Public Service Employees Union (Union Grievance) v Ontario*

> By way of remedy, the employer is directed to change its practices and processes to be in compliance with this decision as necessary. In addition, the relevant documents used including the Guide, the consent form, the cover letter etc. should be amended to be consistent with the actual practices, so that the employee would clearly be aware of what exactly he/she is consenting to and how the employer would be sharing the information. This would also assist to achieve consistency in the implementation of policy and practice by managers and HR Specialists throughout the province.[270]

At the same time, the GSB has maintained the distinction between policy and individual grievances whereunder individual grievances can give rise to recourse for the grievor(s) limited in scope to the individual; while union policy grievances can result in broader relief having an impact on the bargaining unit as a whole.[271] Where a policy grievance is filed, and raises a genuine interpretive issue of practical relevance, there will be a willingness to deal with the issue(s) it raises even if there is no claim that a specific individual employee has been denied a collective agreement right.[272] The GSB has held that "where the parties are clearly able to identify interpretive disputes, the collective bargaining system and the parties themselves are far better served by having those interpretive disputes resolved sooner rather than later."

(Ministry of the Solicitor General and Correctional Services/Management Board Secretariat), GSB#1925/96, 31 May 1996 (Abramsky) required changes; and the litigation continued in *Ontario Public Service Employees Union (Pilger et al) v Ontario (Ministry of Community Safety and Correctional Services)*, 2011 CanLII 67953 (ON GSB) (Abramsky). The union also grieved the introduction of a new process for employee security checks: *Ontario Public Service Employees Union (Union) v Ontario (Management Board Secretariat)*, 2003 CanLII 52975 (ON GSB) (Stewart) [*OPSEU v MBS, 2003 (Stewart)*] resulted in a new policy; litigated in *Ontario Public Service Employees Union v Association of Management, Administrative and Professional Crown Employees of Ontario*, 2010 CanLII 52649 (ON GSB) (Stewart).

270 *Ontario Public Service Employees Union (Union) v Ontario (Treasury Board Secretariat)*, 2017 CanLII 52709 (ON GSB) (Dissanayake) at 26.

271 *Ontario Public Service Employees Union (O'Flaherty) v Ontario (Community Safety and Correctional Services)*, 2018 CanLII 109253 (ON GSB) (Luborsky) at 19.

272 *Ontario Public Service Employees Union (Union) v Ontario (Government Services)*, 2012 CanLII 49878 (ON GSB) (Herlich) at 4–5.

2) Interim Relief

a) Context

The GSB has the power "to make interim orders concerning procedural matters," due to the *CECBA*'s incorporation of arbitrators' powers under the *LRA*.[273] Although the GSB relies upon the same provision available to the OLRB and private arbitrators, its interim relief jurisprudence gives a more expansive, and substantive interpretation to the words "concerning procedural matters."[274] It is not clear why. The problems of remedial delay, including the difficulty of crafting a true "make whole" remedy, apply to both the private sector and the public sector. There is now reason to question this GSB jurisprudence.

In the seminal interim relief decision, *OPSEU (Nield) and Ministry of Labour (Neild #1)*,[275] the grievor had been directed to divest himself of his ownership share of an automotive body shop because of a perceived conflict of interest. The GSB held that allowing the grievor to retain his interest in the business until his grievance was determined was a "procedural matter," thereby coming within the power granted in the *LRA*. On judicial review, the Divisional Court agreed. The court held that the central issue of whether the grievor had a conflict of interest was not decided by that interim order. The interim order simply removed "the urgency of a decision of the central issue by permitting Mr. Nield to retain his investment in his body shop until determination of the merits of the grievance."[276] In *OPSEU (Belanger et al) and Ministry of Health*, the GSB later held that

---

273 *LRA*, above note 3, s 48(12)(i).

274 In *Ontario (Management Board of Cabinet)*, [1996] OLRD No 3477 at 787, the OLRB held that its power to grant "interim orders concerning procedural matters" was limited to regulating the conduct of the proceeding and related matters. See Jeffrey Sack, Michael Mitchell & Sandy Price, *Ontario Labour Relations Board Law and Practice* (Markham, ON: Butterworths, 1997) at paras 8.28–8.31. Similarly, a private board of arbitration has held that the jurisdiction granted by the identical legislative provision relied on in *OPSEU (Nield) and Ministry of Labour*, GSB#1471/96, 21 October 1996 (Roberts) [*Nield #1*] was "restricted to matters of procedure primarily in the conduct of the hearing." However, neither the OLRB nor private arbitration cases were judicially reviewed.

275 *Nield #1*, *ibid*, upheld *Ontario v Ontario Public Service Employees' Union*, [1997] OJ No 427 (Div Ct) [*Ontario v OPSEU, 1997*].

276 *Ibid*.

> [t]he Divisional Court's ruling indicates that this board retains broad residual powers to issue interim orders pertaining to the conduct of the parties in the workplace, provided that the relief is not dispositive of the issue or issues in the grievance . . . and provided the evidence presented meets the appropriate tests.[277]

The relief sought in *Nield* was described as "pertain[ing] to the manner in which the parties will proceed with respect to one another in the interim."[278] The upshot is that, at the GSB, the phrase "to make interim orders concerning procedural matters" has been held to include quite expansive regulation of the manner in which the parties can act pending the final decision in a case.

Following *Nield* and *Belanger*, the jurisdiction of the GSB to grant broad interim relief was challenged, and confirmed by the board, on at least two further occasions.[279] The GSB noted, relying in part on the principle of adjudicative consistency set out in the *Blake* case, that there was a consistent body of caselaw about interim relief.[280]

More recent caselaw from the Divisional Court raises a real question about this approach. In *Ontario Power Generation v Society of Energy Professionals* (*OPG*),[281] the court read down its earlier *Nield* decision, finding that the legal meaning of "procedural matters" does not include substantive relief.[282] Argument based on the *OPG* case has been made to the GSB, but the board has declined to decide the issue, and has instead resolved interim relief applications on other grounds.[283]

---

277 *OPSEU (Belanger et al) and Ministry of Health*, GSB#976/93, 11 March 1997 (Kaufman) at 4 [*Belanger*].

278 *Ibid* at 4. See also *OPSEU (Latimer) and Ministry of the Solicitor General and Correctional Services*, GSB#0131/95, 13 March 2000 (Kaufman) at 31 [*Latimer, 2000*], where the GSB states that an interim order can help the parties to "maintain a reasonable relationship pending the final resolution of the grievances."

279 *Fox #1*, above note 96; *OPSEU (Union) and Management Board Secretariat*, GSB#0001/03, 17 April 2003 (Stewart) [*Union #1*].

280 *Union #1*, above note 279 at 5.

281 2007 CanLII 342 (ON SCDC).

282 See also *International Electrical Workers, Local 636 v Power Stream Inc* (2008), 180 LAC (4th) 87 (Jesin).

283 *Ontario Public Service Employees Union v Ontario (Community Safety and Correctional Services)*, 2009 CanLII 59458 (ON GSB) (Albertyn); *Association of Management, Administrative and Professional Crown Employees of Ontario (Union) v Ontario (Government Services)*, 2012 CanLII 24030 (ON GSB) (Herlich) at para 11 [*AMAPCEO (Herlich)*].

Note that since the *Statutory Powers Procedure Act* does not apply to grievance arbitration, the interim relief power available under that Act to administrative tribunals is not available to the GSB.[284] Collective agreements can grant interim relief powers to arbitrators, but no such provisions have been negotiated in the OPS.

The most high-profile use of the authority to grant interim relief has been in grievances by OPSEU, in which the union has sought enforcement of a collective agreement provision that "reasonable efforts" would be made to obtain comparable employment for persons whose OPS jobs were eliminated due to the disposition or transfer of bargaining unit functions to the private sector or the broader public sector. The GSB issued several orders enjoining the employer from proceeding with a disposition or transfer of bargaining unit functions until it had obtained significantly improved job offers for affected employees from the new employers.[285] The result of the interim orders delaying the transfers was that affected employees transferred to a new employer on better terms and conditions of employment.[286] In the absence of the GSB's jurisdiction to grant interim relief, it is unlikely that anything other than damages would have been available for the affected persons.[287]

The GSB has taken jurisdiction to grant interim relief even when the impugned action was directed or mandated by statute.[288] This meant that, in the circumstances of divestment of the provision of social assistance to municipalities from the province, the GSB could, if the

---

284 *Statutory Powers Procedure Act*, RSO 1990, c S.22; inapplicable due to s 2(d); interim relief power s 16.

285 *OPSEU (Union) and Management Board Secretariat*, GSB#1196/97, 29 October 1997 (Dissanakaye) [*Union #2*]; *OPSEU (Union) and Ministry of Natural Resources*, GSB#0252/98, 18 June 1998 (Petryshen) [*Union, 1998 (Petryshen)*]; *OPSEU (Union) and Ministry of Transportation*, GSB#180/98, 3 June 1998 (Stewart) [*Union #3*].

286 *Union, 1998 (Petryshen)*, *ibid* at 7–8. For a discussion of OPSEU's use of interim relief applications and other legal strategies to enforce the "reasonable efforts" provision in the collective agreement, see Gavin Leeb, "A Global Experience Up Close and Personal: Ontario Government Workers Resist Privatization" (2002) 9 *Canadian Labour and Employment Law Journal* 1.

287 However, in *OPSEU (Union) and Ministry of Community and Social Services*, GSB#0447/00, 21 March 2003 (Leighton), the GSB did hold, at 14, that its remedial authority enabled it to issue a cease-and-desist order in respect to bargaining unit functions that had been contracted out.

288 *OPSEU (Union) and Ministry of Community & Social Services*, GSB#1859/97, 15 May 1998 (Kaplan) [*Union #4*].

appropriate tests were met, grant a stay of the transfer of the existing caseload pending the resolution of the grievance.

Arbitrators including the GSB are precluded from granting interim reinstatement of an employee.[289] Note that substantive interim relief, including the interim reinstatement of the complainant, is available from the OLRB in *OHSA* matters.[290]

b) Procedure and Evidence for Interim Relief Applications

The GSB rule requires the following:

1. An application for interim relief must be made in writing to the registrar with a copy to the other party. The request must
   a. clearly identify the grievance to which it relates and include a copy of same;
   b. include a signed declaration of a person having first-hand knowledge particularizing all of the facts on which the applicant relies in its request for interim relief. The signed declaration may set out statements of the declarant's information and belief if both the source of the information and the fact of the belief are specified in the declaration;
   c. set out why the applicant party submits that interim relief is necessary on an urgent basis as well as the specific relief sought; and
   d. address whether there is an arguable case on the merits in the grievance and the balance of harm or inconvenience to the respective parties.[291]

The rule also deals with the need to give notice of any additional facts to be relied on. The board has declined to permit such facts in the absence of notice, a statement of those facts, or reasons for not providing same.[292]

By its very nature, an application for interim relief does not involve extensive evidence on the merits of the grievance as it is only necessary to show an arguable case. How much evidence is required? The GSB will order the provision of particulars, including particulars of the harm

289 *LRA*, above note 3 at s 48(13).

290 *Ray Martin v Tricin Electric Ltd*, [2004] OLRD No 5259 (McLean).

291 *GSB Rules of Procedure*, above note 77, Appendix A.

292 *Ontario Public Service Employees Union (Bharti) v Canada (Ministry of Natural Resources and Forestry)*, 2014 CanLII 64818 (ON GSB) (Anderson) at 3–4 [*Bharti*].

that each party alleges will occur if interim relief is, or is not, granted.[293] The grievor will normally be expected to provide evidence, which can be by affidavit for purposes of expedition, and can be subject to cross-examination.[294] The absence of direct evidence is not necessarily fatal, as the GSB has, on occasion, accepted counsel's submissions as a reasonable and logical prediction of what could occur.[295]

The unavailability of a witness is not a reason to deny interim relief, although it may affect the length of time for which the interim relief order continues.[296]

c) Substantive Test

The GSB has determined that the following principles are among those that should inform consideration of an application for an interim order:

- It is not the time to examine the merits of the case.
- It is not limited to rare and exceptional circumstances.
- It must be assessed in its labour relations context.
- There can be no "boilerplate" or "one-size-fits-all" approach.
- Consideration needs to be given to what harm may occur if an interim order is not granted, and what harm may occur if it is.
- A "balancing of harm" test should be used.
- Delay in making the application may be a factor in denying it.[297]

---

293 *OPSEU (Union) and Ministry of Public Safety and Security*, GSB#2113/02, 13 March 2003 (Dissanayake).

294 *Ontario Public Service Employees Union (McCormick) v Ontario (Ministry of Transportation)*, 2006 CanLII 17517 (ON GSB) (Abramsky) at 8–9 [*McCormick (Abramsky)*].

295 *Union #2*, above note 285 at 8–9; see also *OPSEU (Union) and Ministry of Community and Social Services*, GSB#893/98, 9 October 1998 (Mikus) [*Union #5*] at 4; *OPSEU (Nield) and Ministry of Labour*, GSB#1471/96, 28 November 1996 (McKechnie) at 11–15.

296 See *Nield #1*, above note 274; *OPSEU (Clarke) and Ministry of the Attorney General*, GSB#2004-3263, 26 January 2005 (Abramsky) [*Clarke*].

297 *OPSEU (Stewart) and Ministry of Correctional Services*, GSB#1000/94, 23 May 1995 (Gorsky) at 4–6 [*Stewart (Gorsky)*]. Although the above list was first developed under a prior version of the *LRA*, the GSB has confirmed that it remains applicable: *OPSEU (Union) and Ministry of Community & Social Services*, GSB#2779/96, 4 April 1997 (Kaplan) at 11 [*Union #6*]; *OPSEU (Fox et al) and Ontario Human Rights Commission*, GSB#0507/01, 27 September 2001 at 6 [*Fox #2*].

In the judicial review of the *Nield* decision discussed above, the Divisional Court was careful to observe that the interim orders issued by the GSB did not decide the central issue in the grievance, nor did the interim orders make a finding "relevant to its determination."[298] The court's caution that an order for interim relief not decide the central issue in dispute has been often acknowledged by the board.[299] The GSB has declined to order interim accommodation of a Metrolinx coach technician who needed to operate vehicles after he was removed from work due to the suspension of his driver's licence, finding that the requested order would decide the central accommodation issue in dispute.[300]

In general terms, the interim relief orders granted by the GSB fall into one of two categories: (1) orders preventing or enjoining the employer from taking certain actions; or (2) orders partially reversing an action already taken in order to restore the pre-existing state of affairs. Examples of employer actions that were halted include a direction to divest oneself of an interest in a business;[301] the issuance of a tender to privatize certain bargaining unit work;[302] the imposition of a policy requiring personal security checks;[303] the termination of a secondment;[304] a plan to transfer residents from provincial residential facilities;[305] and the transfer of bargaining unit work to municipalities pursuant to legislative direction.[306] Examples of the reversal category include the return of furniture used by ambulance officers when at their base;[307] the provision of short-term sick benefits;[308] the return of dismissed employees

---

298 *Ontario v OPSEU, 1997*, above note 275.

299 *Belanger*, above note 277; *Latimer, 2000* above note 278; *OLBEU (McIlwain) and Liquor Control Board of Ontario*, GSB#2077/02, 25 June 2003 (Watters) [*McIlwain*]; *Amalgamated Transit Union—Local 1587 (Janczak) v Ontario (Metrolinx—GO Transit)*, 2017 CanLII 7059 (ON GSB) (Misra) [*Janczak*] and cases cited therein including *Canadian Union of Public Employees Local 1750 v Ontario (Workplace Safety and Insurance Board)*, 2013 CanLII 18483 (ON GSB) (Briggs).

300 *Janczak*, above note 299.

301 *Nield #1*, above note 274.

302 *Union #2*, above note 285; *Union #3*, above note 285.

303 *Union #1*, above note 279.

304 *Clarke*, above note 296.

305 *Union #6*, above note 297.

306 *Union #4*, above note 288.

307 *Belanger*, above note 277.

308 *Latimer, 2000*, above note 278.

to the payroll, but not to their jobs;[309] the reinstatement of employees following discharge;[310] and, in circumstances where the larger issue was ongoing discrimination, the grievor whose long-term disability benefits were about to expire was ordered returned to the payroll even if suitable employment was not found for them.[311]

When considering an application for interim relief, the GSB will apply a twofold test originally developed by the OLRB.[312] The party bringing the application for interim relief must satisfy the board that

1) the applicant union has an arguable case on the merits of the grievance; and
2) the balance of harm or inconvenience favours granting interim relief.

A request for a new test has been rejected,[313] and the GSB has reaffirmed the appropriateness of the twofold test on a number of occasions.[314]

i) *Arguable Case*

The first branch of the test is met by establishing there is an arguable case for the merits of the grievance. This entails setting out assertions which constitute at least an arguable breach of the collective agreement or an arguable case for a remedy within the parameters of the GSB's remedial jurisdiction.[315] Guidance may be taken from the test used by the courts for granting interlocutory injunctions. There, one must show

---

309 *OPSEU (Group Grievance, Sammy et al) and Ministry of Correctional Services*, GSB#0224/01, 9 October 2001 (Harris) [*Group Grievance, Sammy*].

310 *OPSEU (Leeder) and Ministry of Health*, GSB #2498/93, 30 January 1995 (Finley) [*Leeder #1*]; *OPSEU (Montgomery/Rankin) and Ministry of Health—Ottawa Carleton Regional Ambulance)*, GSB#2624/94, 21 August 1995 (Finley) [*Montgomery/Rankin*]; *Stewart (Gorsky)*, above note 297.

311 *OPSEU (Ranger) and Ministry of Community Safety and Correctional Services*, GSB#2002-2375, 6 October 2004 (Leighton).

312 *Leeder #1*, above note 310 at 2, applying *Loeb Highland*, [1993] OLRB Rep March 197 (McCormack). See also *Stewart (Gorsky)*, above note 297 at 4.

313 *Union #6*, above note 297 at 11.

314 *Fox #2*, above note 297; *Union #1*, above note 279; *Ontario Public Service Employees Union (Moon) v Ontario (Ministry of Education)*, 2003 CanLII 52995 (ON GSB) (Mikus) [*Moon*].

315 *Moon*, above note 314 at 3, where the GSB dismissed an application for interim relief on the basis that there was not an arguable case that the grievor would succeed at arbitration.

that "there is a serious question to be tried."[316] Before the GSB, the parties have agreed that an arguable case existed where the grievor denied the employer's allegation that their work performance was substandard.[317] A denial of the employer's allegations is sufficient because it is inappropriate on an interim relief application to make evidentiary determinations relating to the merits.[318] It is not necessary to establish that the grievance is likely to succeed; rather, what does need to be established at the first stage is that the grievance does raise a real issue.[319] An application for an interim order was dismissed because there was not enough information to determine whether there was an arguable case on the merits.[320]

ii) Balance of Harm or Inconvenience

In most cases, the decision to grant or deny interim relief will turn on the GSB's finding on the second branch of the test, namely, which party will bear the most harm or inconvenience if the order is or is not granted.[321]

This determination involves consideration of a number of factors: labour relations considerations, "the risk of usurping existing processes,"[322] whether the party could be compensated in damages, whether the application for interim relief was brought expeditiously, and the length of time required to obtain a ruling on the merits.[323] Unlike court interlocutory injunctions, the existence of irreparable harm is not a mandatory requirement.[324] The GSB has rejected the proposition that a showing of irreparable harm is determinative of the second branch of the test.[325]

---

316 *American Cyanamid Co v Ethicon Ltd*, [1975] AC 396 (HL) at 407.

317 *OPSEU (Leeder) and Ministry of Health*, GSB#2498/93, 21 August 1997 at 2 [*Leeder #2*].

318 *Stewart (Gorsky)*, above note 297 at 7.

319 *Bharti*, above note 292.

320 *Moon*, above note 314.

321 *Union #5*, above note 295; *Union #1*, above note 279; *McIlwain*, above note 299.

322 *McCormick (Abramsky)*, above note 294.

323 *OPSEU (Union) and Management Board Secretariat*, GSB#0610/02, 4 September 2002 (Petryshen) at 5 [*Union #7*].

324 *Stewart (Gorsky)*, above note 297 at 5.

325 *Leeder #2*, above note 317 at 13–15.

Yet, it is evident that the existence of irreparable harm, or at least the potential thereof, is given considerable weight by the GSB. Aside from early cases,[326] very few orders granting interim relief have been issued in the absence of a finding that irreparable harm to the grievor(s) and/or the union[327] either will, or is likely to, occur if the order is not granted. Potential harm is insufficient especially if remedying it is within the remedial capacity of the board.[328] Additionally, a finding that the impact on the employer will be limited and that there are no concrete immediate concerns has been a factor favouring the grant of interim relief,[329] sometimes on terms that balance the parties' interests.[330]

There is no basis to grant interim relief where the alleged harm can be fully remedied if the grievance is upheld at the conclusion of the hearing.[331]

The presence of some specific inconvenience being suffered by the grievor, apart from normal inconvenience, is influential.[332] In *OPSEU (Fox et al) and Ontario Human Rights Commission*,[333] the union sought an interim order enjoining the employer from carrying through with its threat to discipline or discharge the grievors if they did not meet a deadline to satisfy certain performance standards. The union argued that the grievors would experience irreparable emotional and psychological harm if they were fired. In denying the application for interim relief, the GSB held that the union had failed to satisfy the requirement to show a specific inconvenience. The board was balancing the employer's stated "extremely important and fundamental interest" in setting and

326 For example, see *Montgomery/Rankin*, above note 310 at 17.

327 While the cases from *Nield #1*, above note 274, onwards deal with the harm to grievors, in *Union #5*, above note 295, the GSB acknowledged that harm to the union was also relevant and/or could be basis for the grant of interim relief.

328 *AMAPCEO (Herlich)*, above note 283 at para 29.

329 *Stewart (Gorsky)*, above note 297 at 11–12; *Group Grievance, Sammy*, above note 309; *OPSEU v MBS, 2003 (Stewart)*, above note 269.

330 As was done in cases on security checks: *Association of Management, Administrative and Professional Crown Employees of Ontario and Ontario Public Service Employees Union v Ontario (Government Services)*, 2010 CanLII 18838 (ON GSB) (Stewart); *Ontario Public Service Employees Union v Ontario (Government Services)*, 2010 CanLII 38793 (ON GSB) (Stewart).

331 *Union #6*, above note 297; *Union #7*, above note 323; *AMAPCEO (Herlich)*, above note 283 at 6–7.

332 *Stewart (Gorsky)*, above note 297 above at 6.

333 *Fox #2*, above note 297 at 7.

enforcing performance standards. Where the employer can assert the potential for a crucial interest to be undermined, the union may need to show a degree of harm beyond that which would normally be expected to follow from loss of employment.

d) Jurisdiction Confined to Grievance

The interim relief jurisdiction of the GSB is limited to the subject matter of the proceeding, which in turn is defined by the grievance.[334] In *Nield*, the grievance before the GSB was the employee's complaint that the employer had directed the grievor to divest himself of his interest in a body shop, and the GSB ruled it was without jurisdiction to enjoin against discipline or discharge.[335]

e) Prematurity

The application will not be premature because the impugned action has yet to occur. The GSB has observed that the courts have held that a grievance may be filed about the mere introduction of a policy.[336] The board has held that it does not make sense to wait until the harm is done, when the very purpose of interim relief is to prevent it from occurring.[337]

3) *CECBA* Specific Restrictions on Remedial Authority

The *CECBA* imposes three specific restrictions on the remedial authority of the GSB. The first two restrictions relate to discipline and discharge cases:

- A criminal finding of guilt concerning the incident in question must be accepted by the GSB as conclusive evidence that the employee committed the act or omission.
- A GSB finding that the employee applied unnecessary force to, or sexually molested, a resident or a client means the GSB cannot

334 *Nield #1*, above note 274 at 10.

335 *Ibid* at 9. See also *Fox #1*, above note 96, where the GSB relied upon *Nield #1*, to hold that, because the grievances before it referenced the potential for discipline or discharge, it had the jurisdiction to provide interim relief enjoining against the grievors being disciplined or discharged. See also *Union #1*, above note 279 at 5–6.

336 *Union #2*, above note 285 at 3.

337 *Ibid* at 3–4.

provide for the employment of that employee in a position that involves direct responsibility for, or provides an opportunity for contact with, residents or clients.

The third restriction is that the GSB cannot create, alter, or change an employee's classification.

No such limitations apply to the remedial authority of arbitrators under the *LRA*. The provisions relating to discipline were enacted due to the government's disagreement with particular decisions by the GSB, and it is worth considering the principled justifications for this differential treatment of Crown employees. Due to the evolution of the *Charter*-based right to freedom of association, the constitutionality of some of these types of restrictions might be open to question.[338]

a) Criminal Conviction or Discharge Considered Conclusive Evidence

Where a grievance concerning the discipline or discharge of a unionized Crown employee comes before the GSB, and the act or omission giving rise to the discipline or discharge had resulted in a conviction or discharge for an offence under the *Criminal Code*, then, after any appeal, the conviction or discharge must be taken by the GSB as "conclusive evidence that the employee committed the act or omission."[339]

The background is the events involving a discharged grievor, Jack White, who had been convicted of sexual assault of a person in his care, but was found by the GSB not to have engaged in the alleged conduct, thereby rebutting the *Evidence Act* presumption of the commission of the crime resulting from a conviction[340] and leading to reinstatement

---

338 Although it is not dealing with the same type of restriction, see *Procureur general du Canada c Union of Canadian Correctional Officers—Syndicat des agents correctionnels du Canada—CSN (UCCO-SACC-CSN)*, 2019 QCCA 979, where the Quebec Court of Appeal upheld the *Federal Public Sector Labour Relations Act*, SC 2003, c 22, s 113(b) under which neither staffing nor the pension plan can be the subject of provisions in the collective agreement. The court accepted that the negotiation bans were within the "range of reasonable solutions" available to legislators (para 65) in light of the impact on public finances represented by changing the pension and the risk to the independence of the work of the Public Service Commission in policing the merit function.

339 *CECBA*, above note 1, s 48.1(1).

340 *Evidence Act*, RSO 1990, c E.23, s 22.1, which states that a conviction is proof, "in the absence of evidence to the contrary, that the crime was committed by the person."

and compensation for all lost wages.[341] The GSB stated: "I would not lightly reach a conclusion which is directly opposite to the verdict reached in the criminal courts. However, this is an extreme case, where the evidence is overwhelming and drives me to the conclusion that the presumed fact does not exist."[342] This decision led to the *CECBA* amendment.[343] In the meantime, the original decision was appealed to the Supreme Court, which held it was an "abuse of process" for an arbitrator to relitigate a criminal conviction, absent limited exceptional circumstances including "when fairness dictates the original result should not be binding."[344] Such exceptional circumstances were later proven to exist in White's case when his criminal conviction was quashed as a miscarriage of justice due to the shortcomings of the defence put forward at the criminal trial.[345] Nonetheless, the current *CECBA* provision, which does not provide for exceptional circumstances, remains in effect.

The application of this provision is triggered by a certain degree of commonality between the circumstances giving rise to the criminal charge and those giving rise to the discipline or discharge. The criminal charge must be "in respect of" an act or omission "that results" in discipline. If the criminal prosecution results in a withdrawal of the charge or an acquittal, there is no automatic consequence for the remedial jurisdiction of the GSB.[346] The remedial consequence only occurs if there is a conviction or a discharge.[347] The time for an appeal must have expired or, if an appeal was taken, it must have been dismissed and no further appeal be available. The GSB is statutorily required to grant any

341 *OPSEU (White) v Ministry of Community and Social Services*, GSB#0810/95, 25 May 1999 (Dissanayake).

342 *Ibid* at 93.

343 *Public Service Statute Law Amendment Act*, SO 2001, c 7, s 18 (Bill 25).

344 See *Ontario v OPSEU*, 2003 SCC 64 [*Ontario v OPSEU*], and the more extensive reasons in *Toronto (City) v CUPE, Local 79*, 2003 SCC 63 at para 52 [*Toronto v CUPE*].

345 *R v White*, 2010 ONCA 474.

346 *Ontario Public Service Employees Union (Wild) v Ontario (Community Safety and Correctional Services)*, 2015 CanLII 36169 (ON GSB) (Harris).

347 A "discharge" is a finding of guilt, but not a conviction, and can occur without conditions, which is then known as an unconditional discharge, or with conditions, then being known as a conditional discharge. The applicability of the provision is triggered by a discharge following a guilty plea and there need not be a trial: *OPSEU (Hachey et al) and Ministry of the Solicitor General*, 2022 CanLII 60109 (ON GSB) (Hewat) [*Hachey*].

requested adjournment pending an appeal.[348] Once the issue of appeal is resolved, the employer is entitled to prove the fact of the conviction or discharge at the arbitration. Once proven, the conviction or discharge must be taken as "conclusive evidence that the employee committed the act or omission." The board cannot reach its own determination about whether the incident occurred.

The finding that the act occurred does not prevent consideration of mitigating circumstances that warrant a reduction in the discipline imposed by the employer.[349]

Where the arbitration is scheduled prior to the conclusion of the criminal trial, the GSB will exercise its scheduling discretion, with the key factor being the length of delay that would be caused by the adjournment.[350]

How the circumstances of Crown employees under this *CECBA* provision compare with the circumstances of other employees bears consideration. The Supreme Court has decided that, generally, any arbitrator including the GSB may not "revisit" a criminal conviction,[351] so the difference may not be important in many cases. However, the Supreme Court has left open the possibility of an arbitrator not following a criminal conviction in certain limited circumstances:

> There may be instances where relitigation will enhance, rather than impeach, the integrity of the judicial system, for example: (1) when the first proceeding is tainted by fraud or dishonesty; (2) when fresh, new evidence, previously unavailable, conclusively impeaches the original results; or (3) when fairness dictates that the original result should not be binding in the new context.[352]

---

348 *CECBA*, above note 1, s 48.1(2).

349 *OPSEU (Timmerman) and Ministry of Natural Resources*, GSB#2000-0092, 25 May 2004 (Harris); *OPSEU (Sammy et al) and Ministry of Community Safety and Correctional Services*, GSB#2001-0224, 17 December 2004 (Harris); *Ontario Public Service Employees Union (Collin) v Ontario (Community Safety and Correctional Services)*, 2007 CanLII 11300 (ON GSB) (Harris). For a more detailed discussion of remaining scope available for arbitral decision making, see *Newfoundland and Labrador Housing Corporation and Canadian Union of Public Employees*, 2004 CanLII 94706 (NL LA) (Oakley) dealing with a similar clause.

350 *Ontario Public Service Employees Union (Barbro) v Ontario (Community Safety and Correctional Services)*, 2012 CanLII 76563 (ON GSB) (Mikus).

351 See *Ontario v OPSEU*, above note 344, and the more extensive reasons in *Toronto v CUPE*, above note 344.

352 *Toronto v CUPE*, *ibid* at 52.

This limited possibility of re-litigation available at arbitration for unionized employees in other sectors does not seem to be available for Crown employees under the current *CECBA* provision. However, it is unclear just how much the *CECBA* provision limits the jurisdiction of the GSB to apply the Supreme Court's criteria for re-litigation. A criminal offence comprises two elements: the physical act, known as the *actus reus*, and the criminal state of mind, known as the *mens rea*. The Supreme Court's ruling is to be taken as determining that a criminal conviction is proof of both elements.[353] The GSB's jurisdiction is limited by the statutory requirement to accept that the grievor "committed the act or omission," which may not be the same as the requirement to accept for all purposes that the grievor "committed the offence." It may be that the *CECBA* section determines what the GSB must conclude in respect of the *actus reus*, but not the *mens rea*.[354] Such an interpretation could leave it open for the GSB to apply the Supreme Court's re-litigation criteria to findings about the grievor's state of mind.

b) Restriction on Reinstatement After Finding of Unnecessary Force or Sexual Assault

Since 1978, the *CECBA* has required that, where the GSB finds that an employee has applied force to, except for the minimum necessary force, or sexually molested a defined person, the GSB's remedial authority to order reinstatement of the dismissed employee must not result in the employment of the grievor in a position that involves responsibility for, or possible contact with, defined persons.[355]

The background is the GSB's reinstatement of a residential counsellor who kicked a resident in the face but ultimately expressed remorse for this isolated incident.[356] The GSB said that it had an obligation to both employees and patients; that a genuine effort must be made to accommodate both interests; and only when that could not reasonably be done should the employee's interest give way. The case and reasoning were contentious. When amending legislation limiting the remedial jurisdiction of the GSB was introduced, it had the general support

353 *Registrar, Motor Vehicle Act v Jacob*, 2004 CanLII 9450 (ON SCDC).

354 For a case that indirectly raises this possibility, but does not rule on it, see *Hachey*, above note 347 at para 23.

355 *CECBA*, above note 1, s 7(4).

356 See *OPSEU (Johnston) and Ministry of Community and Social Services*, GSB#7/78, 17 March 1978 (Chair Adams) [*Johnston*].

of both opposition parties. The government's stated objective was to ensure that residents of provincially operated facilities were given the protection they needed and deserved and to reassure the public that such protection would be provided.[357]

The restriction on the GSB's remedial authority applies in respect of two types of victims. The first is a "client," who is defined as a person to whom services are provided in a designated community resource centre.[358] The second is a "resident" in a "facility." A resident is defined as "a person who is an inmate, patient, pupil, or resident in or is detained or cared for in a facility." A series of specific workplaces is listed in defining "facility," but those specifics are made largely redundant by the last definition in the list, which defines a "facility" as "any other workplace where the employee works in carrying out the duties of his or her position."[359] In other words, a resident is someone who meets the personal definition at the place where the grievor works. The relevance of the specifically listed facilities would appear to be to list the locations that the section would apply to if the employee were to engage in unnecessary force or sexual assault while on an off-duty visit to a facility other than their own workplace.

The next issue is the nature of the wrongful conduct in question and, again, there are two categories. The first category involves the application of force. All applications of force are covered, except "the minimum force necessary for self-defence or the defence of another person or necessary to restrain the resident or client." This does not depend on the employer proving the specific allegations on which it acted when discharging the grievor, rather the section applies if the employer persuades the arbitrator that any amount of unnecessary force was used.[360]

The second category is to have "sexually molested a resident or a client." This wording is not precisely defined and does not appear to

---

357 Ontario Legislative Assembly, *Hansard*, 9 November 1978, No 115 at 472 and 28 November 1978, No 128 at 5402 (George McCague, Chair of the Management Board of Cabinet).

358 *CECBA*, above note 1, s 7(5) referring to centres designated under s 15 of the *Ministry of Correctional Services Act*, RSO 1990, c M.22.

359 *Ibid*, s 7(5)(h).

360 *OPSEU (Sindall/Talbot) and Ministry of the Solicitor General and Correctional Services*, GSB#164/96, 23 October 1997 (Gray) at 30 [*Sindall/Talbot*].

exactly match an offence in the *Criminal Code*.[361] The GSB will need to determine whether the grievor engaged in such conduct.

Where one of the enumerated types of wrongful conduct has been committed against one of the defined types of victims, the consequence is a limitation on the remedial power of the GSB concerning the employment of the employee who was involved in the conduct in question. The board cannot provide for employment of that employee in a position that involves direct responsibility for or provides the "opportunity for contact with" any resident or client.

This "limitation's potential for unfairness is apparent" in that, while the GSB cannot order it, the employer can still choose to continue to employ someone in duties involving resident contact even after that employee has engaged in excessive force.[362] In a case where the relevant finding was made, grievors had used excessive force in restraining an inmate and were discharged. However, it became obvious that the grievors' actions were not nearly as serious as alleged, and no worse than the actions of another correctional officer at the same institution who, several years earlier, had only received a fifteen-day suspension for their actions and been allowed to remain in their position involving inmate contact. The board directed that the discharged grievors be restored to employment in a substantially equivalent position and that they receive a fifteen-day suspension, and added that, although it could not be ordered, it would be appropriate for the employer to restore the grievors to their former positions.[363]

This limitation on the GSB's remedial authority has been ignored.[364] In addition, where the board found that the grievor assaulted an inmate but discharge was excessive in part due to the unlikelihood of recurrence,

---

361 See, for example, *Criminal Code*, RSC 1985, c C-46, s 153.1: "Sexual Exploitation of person with a disability" as an example of an offence that would need to be considered for being in scope.

362 *Sindall/Talbot*, above note 360 at 30.

363 The same observation is made in *Ontario Public Service Employees Union (Maude) v Ontario (Community Safety and Correctional Services)*, 2016 CanLII 18935 (ON GSB) (Petryshen) [*Maude*] with the same result, noting at paras 55–56 that it is in the discretion of the arbitrator to specify the equivalent position.

364 For example, see *Ontario Public Service Employees Union (Gour) v Ontario (Community Safety and Correctional Services)*, 2016 CanLII 18733 (ON GSB) (Misra).

the board noted that reinstatement to the former position could not be ordered, but the employer could do so.[365]

There is "no temporal restriction" on the applicability of the section and so the passage of time does not affect the GSB's inability to reinstate the grievor to the type of position in question.[366] The GSB cannot use a lengthy suspension to circumvent the section as the intent is to deny the offender all future contact with the types of individuals listed.[367]

The GSB has noted that the remedial discretion to provide for the employment of the employee in another "substantially equivalent" position limits the board's discretion, but it also constitutes legislative recognition that the board can order the employer to find "substantially equivalent" positions to which employees can be assigned.[368]

In determining whether to order that an employee be placed in an equivalent position, the GSB will consider a range of factors, including the general public interest in safeguarding residents from abuse; traditional criteria borrowed from general arbitration cases, such as the severity of the conduct, the record of the grievor, whether there is an acknowledgement of wrongdoing and remorse, whether the grievor can learn from the penalty and perform acceptably, whether there is an unnecessary risk or cost to the employer if the grievor is reinstated, and whether unnecessary hardship to the grievor occurs without reinstatement.[369]

Remedial issues may also arise after an order reinstating a grievor to a "substantially equivalent" position. The employer has the initial right to choose the position for reinstatement purposes, but the position must be "substantially equivalent."[370] The net penalty imposed

---

365 *Maude*, above note 363 at para 55.

366 *OPSEU (Tucker) and Ministry of Community and Social Services*, GSB#2395/87, 15 April 1992 (Fisher) at 7–8.

367 *OPSEU (Gaston) and Ministry of Correctional Services*, GSB#0117/83, 8 January 1988 (Jolliffe) at 8.

368 *OPSEU (Thompson) and Ministry of Community and Social Services*, GSB#149/89, 24 May 1990 (Wilson) at 19 [*Thompson (Wilson)*].

369 *OPSEU (Foy) and Ministry of Community and Social Services*, GSB#99/79, 19 June 1980 (Swinton) at 13–14 [*Foy*]; *OPSEU (Landry-King) and Ministry of Community and Social Services*, GSB#1593/84, 17 September 1985 (Knopf) [*Landry-King*].

370 *OPSEU (Thibert, McGill and Jung) and Ministry of Correctional Services*, GSB#556/81, 1 October 1985 (Verity) at 11 [*Thibert*], although it need not be "exactly" equivalent: *OPSEU (Travers) and Ministry of Correctional Services*, GSB#79/79, 18 June 1981 (Swinton) at 10 [*Travers, 1981*].

on the employee must remain just and cannot become "disproportionate" because of implementation problems in the ministry.[371] It has been suggested that it may be appropriate to consider positions outside the original ministry. The bar on contact with residents should be subject to a practical interpretation that incidental contact would be permissible. "The concern would seem to be contact which might lead to further confrontation."[372] The employer may be required to fashion a new position for the grievor, but triggering such a remedy would require a very strong claim and a grievor not found guilty of serious misconduct. The grievor may, in some cases, have the right to displace a junior employee, but that is also a discretionary remedy. The prohibition on having "direct responsibility" for inmates means that the grievor cannot be required to be reinstated to a position in "control," which controls security grilles and inmate movement.[373]

Pay level, job content, geographic location, and level of skill and responsibility will all be considered in determining the equivalence of a position.[374] There is no automatic formula and there may be a need to tailor the "substantial equivalency" to fit each individual's circumstances. Even if salary is maintained, that will not be sufficient equivalency by itself. Where it was proposed that a correctional officer be reinstated to a receptionist position, the GSB noted that administrative duties are very different from custodial duties, that the officer position has a higher status, and, even with salary maintained, there is a loss of correctional officer negotiated increases and overtime.[375] Where the new position of electronic supervision officer and the former correctional officer position are "substantially equivalent" in that they require a similar level of skill and responsibility, have a similar hourly rate of pay, are at a similar level of base pay, and both have opportunities for overtime work, then the specific amount of income is not to be included in the equivalency comparison as the grievor cannot claim a certain set quantum of overtime as their entitlement.[376]

---

371 *Travers, 1981*, *ibid* at 7.

372 *Ibid.*

373 *Ontario Public Service Employees Union (Maude) v Ontario (Community Safety and Correctional Services)*, 2017 CanLII 7050 (ON GSB) (Petryshen) at paras 34–35.

374 *Ibid* at 10–11.

375 *Ibid* at para 29.

376 *Ontario Public Service Employees Union (Conry) v Ontario (Community Safety and Correctional Services)*, 2018 CanLII 55863 (ON GSB) (Williamson) at para 31.

The level of pay is recognized as centrally important from the employee's point of view.[377] Where a position with the same normal rate of pay is not available, there is authority to adjust a rate of pay, but that it is to be exercised with discretion.[378] When it was proposed that the grievor simply be given their old rate of pay with all ongoing adjustments in their new normally lower-paid position, the board did an analysis of the net compensation comparability of the two positions and concluded that the new position had some benefits (less danger, less shift work) and that it would be disruptive for an employee guilty of serious misconduct to be paid more than others doing the same work as in the new position.[379] The compromise ordered was freezing, or "red circling," the individual's salary so that it remained at the level of their former position until salary increases for the new position reached that salary level. The grievor was left with a penalty in the form of a long-term negative effect on their salary. The GSB suggested that a different result might be appropriate for an employee with longer service.

When determining the salary of the former position for comparison purposes, credit has been given for a change in classification that would have automatically occurred if the employee had remained in the former position.[380]

Payment of salary for the period between the discharge and the arbitration award has been dealt with as an exercise of remedial discretion. One award has implied that the power to reinstate to a substantially equivalent position is not retroactive,[381] but this reasoning has not been otherwise adopted. A number of reinstatements have been

---

377 *Ibid* at 12; *Thibert*, above note 370 at 9.

378 *Travers, 1981*, above note 370 at 12–13 and *Thibert*, above note 370 at 10–11. *Thibert* was judicially reviewed, in part on this point, and was found by the Divisional Court not to be patently unreasonable: "The Board was not purporting to alter wages within a classification when it required the applicant to pay the grievors at the higher rate mentioned. On the contrary, it was a decision made in an effort to give effect to substantial equivalence": *Re Queen in Right of Ontario and Ontario Public Service Employees Union et al* (1986), 57 OR (2d) 641 (Div Ct) at 650.

379 *Travers*, 1981 above note 370 at 13–14.

380 *OPSEU (Gaston) and Ministry of Correctional Services*, GSB#0117/83, 29 June 1989 at 7–9. The change was the progression from probationary Correctional Officer I to permanent Correctional Officer II.

381 *OPSEU (McGowan) and Ministry of Community and Social Services*, GSB#0888/85, 24 February 1987 (Draper) at 13.

made without retroactive compensation,[382] but grievors have also been reinstated with periods of suspension shorter than the length of time between the discharge and the final award, resulting in some retroactive compensation.[383]

After the decision ordering the reinstatement of the employee to the "substantially equivalent" position, there may be a dispute about whether the position eventually offered is appropriate. The GSB has found that the employer is obliged to pay compensation from the date of the initial reinstatement order onwards,[384] as the employer was liable to take immediate action to find a suitable position. Any other conclusion would mean that delays in the search increased the penalty. Reinstatement to an equivalent position has been ordered to be implemented as soon as possible, with the grievor to be paid within two weeks.[385]

The statutory limitation on the authority of the GSB applies only to the hearing of disciplinary matters. In a job competition grievance for a correctional officer position, the employer refused to consider the application of a grievor who had previously been found to have engaged in resident abuse but was reinstated to a substantially equivalent position.[386] The grievor claimed a violation of the employer obligation to fairly consider all applicants for a vacant position. The board took jurisdiction over the matter, and ruled that the employer should have considered the application. The employer would be able to take the earlier discipline into account when assessing the candidate for the position and could indeed reasonably consider that the prior incident made the grievor unsuitable for the position. The GSB would have the jurisdiction to determine that the previously disciplined grievor was the successful candidate for a position with resident contact, but would by no means automatically conclude that it was appropriate to do so.

---

382 *Johnston*, above note 356 at 12; *Oldendorp*, GSB#135/77, 28 December 1977 at 16; *Landry-King*, above note 369 at 11–12; *OPSEU (Serrao) and Ministry of Health*, GSB#1759/86, 31 August 1988 (M. Picher) at 11.

383 *Foy*, above note 369 at 18–19; *Sindall/Talbot*, above note 360 at 32.

384 *OPSEU (Travers) and Ministry of Correctional Services*, GSB#213/78, 79/79, 11 February 1982 (Swinton) at 6.

385 *Thompson (Wilson)*, above note 368 at 23.

386 *OPSEU (Van't Hullenaar) and Ministry of Correctional Services*, GSB#1390/86, 2 May 1989 (Ratushny).

c) No Creation, Alteration, or Change of Classification

The *CECBA* section 51 prohibits the GSB from requiring the creation of a new classification, or the alteration of an existing classification and from requiring a change to be made in the classification of an employee.[387] This has not prevented the parties from agreeing that the job evaluation system was outdated and needed to be replaced, and to a joint working group involved in a classification reform process, including mediation, but there was no waiver of the management right to manage the system.[388]

To further ensure there can be no binding adjudication of classification grievances, section 52 of the *CECBA* renders void any provision in a collective agreement under the Act that authorizes an arbitrator or board of arbitration or another tribunal to determine disputes regarding a classification system or the classification of an employee. It has been found that section 52 does not apply to the GSB, as that section is in "Part IV—Miscellaneous" and not in "Part III—Grievance Settlement Board."[389] An internal committee, set up under a memorandum of settlement appended to the collective agreement to hear classification complaints, but without binding authority, has been found not to be a tribunal within the meaning of section 52.[390]

i) Background

The pre-1993 *CECBA* entitlement of an individual to grieve that "his position has been improperly classified"[391] was extensively enforced. The GSB jurisprudence at the time permitted claims of improper classification to be advanced on two independent bases, the "standards approach" (whether the job fits within the class standard) and the "usage approach" (whether it could be shown that the grievor was

---

387 *CECBA*, above note 1, s 51. Discussed in *Ontario Public Service Employees Union (Metcalfe et al) v Ontario (Government Services)*, 2012 CanLII 6212 (ON GSB) (Stephens) and *Ontario Public Service Employees Union (Union) v Ontario (Training, Colleges and Universities)*, 2013 CanLII 42613 (ON GSB) (Carrier), which references s 52, discussed below, although the issue is addressed by s 51.

388 *OPSEU/MBC Unified and Correctional Collective Agreements*, above note 110, Appendix 34.

389 *OPSEU (Union) and Management Board Secretariat*, GSB#0196/00, 4 April 2001 (Gray) [*Union #8*] at 17–18.

390 *OPSEU (Union) and Management Board Secretariat*, GSB#2695/96, 1 May 1997 (Briggs) [*Union #9*] at 16.

391 *CECBA*, above note 1, prior version s 18(2).

doing the same job as someone in a higher classification).[392] The "usage" approach was justified, in the leading case of *OPSEU (Beals and Cain) and Ministry of Community and Social Services*, as follows:

> It may be assumed that among the objectives of the employer's classification system are the achievement of uniformity in policy and consistency in practice throughout the public service, and equitable treatment of individual employees. It follows that it is an abuse of the system and unfair to employees where the positions of employees who are performing substantially similar work are placed in different classifications. By intervening where that condition is found to exist, the Board, rather than frustrating the intent or undermining the operation of the classification system, is preserving the legitimacy and the credibility of that system.[393]

This reasoning was questionable, as the result is that a single misclassification could be copied and perpetuated. An approach that was more supportive of classification system integrity was taken by the Classification Rating Committee which heard management classification grievances until 1993. Generally speaking, that tribunal would not reclassify on the basis of a single comparison, but required proof that the employer had engaged in a more widespread practice of giving a higher classification to employees whose jobs were similar to the grievor.[394]

In the pre-1993 versions of the OPSEU/MBC collective agreement, the parties agreed that the authority of the GSB was limited to confirming the existing classification or awarding the claimed classification.[395] In *Ontario Public Service Employees Union (Berry and Alcampo) and Ministry of Community and Social Services*,[396] the GSB found that

---

392 *OPSEU (Braund et al) and Ministry of Correctional Services*, GSB#39/89, 18 June 1990 (Slone) at 15–16, and the cases cited therein.

393 *OPSEU (Beals and Cain) and Ministry of Community and Social Services*, GSB#29/79, 20 May 1981 (Draper) at 11. As for the argument that the comparator (in the higher classification) was wrongly classified, see *OPSEU (Taylor) and Ministry of Health*, GSB#478/85, 21 October 1987 (Brent).

394 *Young et al and Ministry of Revenue*, C/0011/91, 20 July 1992 (Jackson) at 3–4, followed in *Marcolin and Ministry of Transportation*, C/0013/91, last hearing 7 June 1994 (Jackson). See also *McGillivray and Ministry of Natural Resources*, C/0003/92, 1993, last hearing 25 November 1993 (Jackson) at 2–3.

395 *OPSEU/MBC Collective Agreement 1992–1993*, Art 27.1.12.

396 GSB#217/83, 21 June 1988 (Verity).

certain income maintenance officers were improperly classified, but the classification claimed was also improper and so, in accordance with the collective agreement limitation, the GSB dismissed the grievance. On judicial review, the Divisional Court held that the GSB had the power to order the employer to find or create a classification for grievors. The GSB's authority was "untrammeled" since it was required to "decide the matter."[397] When the matter was returned to the GSB, the GSB ordered the employer to create a new classification. The GSB's remedial jurisdiction was subsequently clarified to include deciding whether the content of a new classification adequately captured the grievors' work.[398] This remedial approach was extended to permitting grievors to claim reclassification into the classification scheme that the employer had reserved for management employees.[399]

When the very broad GSB jurisprudence was combined both with a classification system that consisted to a large extent of classifications based on specific descriptions of work, and with the many changes in government work that occurred during the 1970s and 1980s and continued, the result was a large number of cases in which reclassification was ordered.[400] There is no public justification for the 1993 introduction of the limitation on the GSB's authority to address classification grievances, but it appears that the government was concerned about its continuing and uncontrollable liability and the union did not object for two reasons. First, ad hoc classification grievance awards were using up some of the funds available for bargaining wage increases addressing union membership priorities. Second, the 1993 legislation was generally

397 *Berry*, above note 263 at 12–15.

398 *OPSEU (Anderson et al) and Ministry of Natural Resources*, GSB#0497/85, 26 August 1986 (Roberts), upheld in *OPSEU v Ontario (Ministry of Natural Resources)* (1990), 75 OR (2d) 212 (Div Ct), where the Divisional Court reinforced the finding in *Berry* and held that the GSB's "unrestricted remedial jurisdiction" included the power to "instruct management to alter or amend the class standards to reflect properly the duties and responsibilities of the grievors."

399 *OPSEU (Canning et al) and Ministry of Government Services*, GSB#558/84, 23 September 1987 (Samuels) at 4–5 describes the history of the litigation on this issue.

400 See any of the leading cases cited above. As a single example of the elaborate jurisprudence that developed on many points, see the discussion of whether to grant retroactivity earlier than twenty days prior to the filing of the grievance in *OPSEU (Letourneau) and Ministry of Health*, GSB#1158/92, 17 August 1995 (Stewart).

very positive for OPSEU, with management rights being reduced and the right to strike coming into effect.[401]

In considering the vulnerability of this limitation to a *Charter* challenge for infringing on freedom of association, it is notable that there is no restriction on the bargaining of classification salary adjustments and, indeed, they are an ongoing feature of OPSEU/MBC bargaining.[402]

ii) Defining the Scope of the Restriction

While the *CECBA* section 51 generally prohibits the GSB from reclassifying employees, some of the GSB's relevant jurisprudence does not actually deal with section 51. A number of the relevant cases arose under a specific earlier agreement between OPSEU and the MBC that stipulated that all classification grievances were withdrawn.[403] In other cases, the employer incorrectly relied on section 52 of the *CECBA* without objection from the union. In any event, all the cases discussed below deal with the scope of limitations on classification grievances.

Any grievance that involves the reclassification of the grievor "at some point in time" is a classification grievance,[404] including the following:

- a dispute about proper placement on the salary grid that required resolution of the grievor's correct classification in a former position[405]
- in respect of a job evaluation system, resolving the weight to be given to certain sub-factors, which in turn determined the salary grade or classification[406]

---

401 See legislative history in Chapter 1 re the *CECBA 1993* amendments.

402 See *OPSEU/MBC Unified and Correctional Collective Agreements*, above note 110, General Notes and Allowances.

403 Section 8 of the Local Appendix to the *Sectoral Framework Agreement*, 1 August 1993, between the parties, which was executed pursuant to the *Social Contract Act, 1993*, SO 1993, c 5. See the outline of the history in *Union #9*, above note 390.

404 *OPSEU (Aitken) and Ministry of Health*, GSB#678/87, 21 December 1993 (Gorsky) at 22 [*Aitken*]. To the same effect, see *Re Ontario Public Service Employees Union and the Crown in Right of Ontario et al* (1983), 44 OR (2d) 51 (Div Ct) holding that "the issue of the 'time when' can be just as much a classification grievance as a simple claim for reclassification."

405 *Aitken, ibid* at 22. The employer's objection was based on the prohibition against "classification grievances" set out in the "Local Appendix" referred to above.

406 *Canadian Union of Public Employees—Local 1750 v Ontario (Workplace Safety and Insurance Board)*, 2006 CanLII 26390 (ON GSB) (Nairn) at 20.

- a requested adjustment of the date of an employer reclassification of employees, where the GSB was being asked to engage in a prohibited comparison of the duties and responsibilities of different classifications for classification purposes[407] (it appears the GSB will maintain that position even when there is no real dispute about the comparison)
- adjusting the date on which the employer chooses to move an employee from an "under fill," or entry-level classification, to the normal classification, even though the grievor had finished the entry-level training and orientation and the employer agreed that the work being done by the grievor was the same as that of the higher-rated classification[408]
- addressing the grievor's bumping rights after being surplussed:[409] where the grievor wanted to return to a prior position, but their classification had been downgraded and the collective agreement did not permit bumping up a classification, resulting in a claim that the position had been wrongly downgraded, which would entail a comparison of their work against their classification
- where there was a dispute about whether the grievor was entitled to acting pay for temporarily performing the duties of a higher paid classification and the issue was the comparison between the grievor's acting duties and the higher classification[410]
- where grievors do not seek reclassification, but only acting assignment pay based on a claim of a management bad faith refusal to maintain an historical equivalency with another classification[411]

---

407 *OPSEU (Wilson/Anastasakos et al) and Ministry of Transportation*, GSB#0147/95, 28 March 2001 (Dissanayake) at 18–19 [*Wilson/Anastasakos*].

408 *OPSEU (Knaap) and Ministry of the Solicitor General and Correctional Services*, GSB#3164/92, 8 November 2000 (Dissanayake) at 10–11, and the cases cited therein, dismissing grievances challenging the timing of the reclassification of grievors from correctional officer I "under fill" position to correctional officer II.

409 *OPSEU (Rosamond) and Ministry of Citizenship, Culture and Recreation*, GSB#2086/96, 16 December 1998 (Leighton).

410 *OPSEU (Collins) and Ministry of the Solicitor General*, GSB#807/85, 26 November 1987 (Kirkwood) at 4; *OPSEU (Decarie) and Ministry of Consumer and Commercial Relations*, GSB#910/93, 29 November 1994 (Gray) at 22; *OPSEU (Boyer) and Ministry of the Environment*, GSB#0742/00, 24 October 2001 (Abramsky), and cases cited therein.

411 *OPSEU (Dobroff) and Ministry of Environment*, GSB#2003-0905, 31 January 2005 (Dissanayake) at 15–17.

The prohibition on reclassification only applies to the reclassification of a position, not to deciding whether a grievor should be in the position.[412] In a job competition grievance, the remedy of assigning the grievor to a new position that had a higher classification did not involve classifying a position and the *CECBA* did not preclude requiring that the employer put a grievor in a particular position.

If the position has already been reclassified, and the grievor is simply seeking to have that determination applied for a retroactive period, jurisdiction has been taken on the basis that it was not required to determine the proper classification of the grievor's position "at some point in time" because that had already been done.[413]

Where the collective agreement states that unclassified employees are to be paid at a rate "equivalent" to classified employees, there is jurisdiction over disputes concerning the appropriate rate of pay for unclassified public servants. Management's selection of an "equivalent" classification can be challenged when unclassified employees are doing the same work as classified employees in a different classification or where there is no equivalent civil service position.[414] Where unclassified employees are in the same classification as the comparable classified employees, neither type of employee can grieve that they are misclassified.[415]

iii) Discrimination and Health and Safety Claims

The GSB has considered claims that employees have been classified in violation of their rights under the *HRC*. In a case prior to *CECBA* section 51, but dealing with a somewhat similar jurisdictional issue, individuals with disabilities hired under an affirmative-action program as radio operators at the Ontario Provincial Police (OPP) detachment at Queen's

412 *OPSEU (Frisken) and Ministry of Labour*, GSB#2034/94, 5 June 1997 (Gray) at 13.

413 *OPSEU (Gaffar et al) and Ministry of Transportation*, GSB#434/95, 28 March 2001 (Dissanayake); see also *Wilson/Anastasakos*, above note 407 at 25–28 concerning grievor Levere; and *Service Employees Union (Burns et al) v Ontario (Transportation)*, 2010 CanLII 7281 (ON GSB) (Abramsky).

414 *OPSEU (Barker et al) and Ministry of the Attorney General*, GSB#2476/92, 12 July 1993 (Kaplan) at 11, followed in *OPSEU (Yole) and Ministry of the Solicitor General and Correctional Services*, GSB#1004/95, 23 August 2002 (Briggs) at 16. See also *Ontario Public Service Employees Union (Carson) v Ontario (Community Safety and Correctional Services)*, 2009 CanLII 43623 (ON GSB) (Herlich) at 13.

415 *OPSEU (Foreman) and Ministry of Education*, GSB#2002-1806, 31 March 2005 (Abramsky).

Park grieved that they were paid at lower rates than other OPP radio operators.[416] The grievances were found to be "discrimination grievances," not "classification grievances," giving the GSB authority to issue a classification remedy if the grievors were in the wrong classification by reason of *HRC* prohibited discrimination. Similar reasoning was applied to the effect of a pregnancy leave on the "on the job" training requirement for the progression from one classification to another.[417] The GSB has held the steps necessary can be taken to ensure the proper accommodation of the grievor's disability and, for that purpose, the GSB has jurisdiction under the *HRC* to alter an employee's existing classification in order to properly remedy a breach.[418]

The GSB held that the health and safety provisions in the collective agreement cannot be used to correct a pay discrepancy, even where satisfied that a pay difference caused tension between two groups of employees and stress for the lower-paid group.[419]

iv) Upholding Agreement Concerning Classification System

A union–management agreement concerning the classification system is enforceable because "[t]he employer's assertion that the statute permits it to unilaterally alter the classification system with total impunity is certain to have adversely affected the parties' labour relations and unnecessarily so if it is untrue."[420] Where the parties had agreed to the creation of a new class-series and the issue was whether the grievors'

416 *OPSEU (Courte/MacGregor et al) and Ministry of Solicitor General*, GSB#1946/93, 7 November 1994 (Roberts); *OPSEU (MacGregor et al) and Ministry of Solicitor General*, GSB#1946/93, 5 November 1996 at 1. Note that, while the case arose prior to section 51, similar restrictions had already been agreed to by the parties.

417 *OPSEU (Theoret) and Ministry of Finance*, GSB#1674/93, 2 May 1995 (Roberts) at 8.

418 *OPSEU (Alcock) and Ministry of Public Safety and Security*, GSB#1998/1368, 7 October 2003 (Petryshen) at 17, upheld on judicial review, unreported decision of Divisional Court, 21 December 2004.

419 *OPSEU (Lyons) and Ministry of Health*, GSB#2289/93, 10 November 1999 (Petryshen) at 13–14, concerning a claim by registered nurses for the forensic allowance paid to another classification. The GSB also stated that "[l]ike other employees who believe they deserve more pay or additional benefits, they will have to rely on the bargaining process to achieve their objective."

420 *Union #8*, above note 389 at 17.

classifications were to be included, the board can "properly determine if they were part of the deal."[421] After the parties agreed to an internal process for addressing classification concerns, their procedural agreement was enforced.[422]

---

421 *OPSEU (Group) and Ministry of Finance*, GSB#1773/99, 2 April 2001 (Watters) at 57.

422 See cases dealing with the Joint System Subcommittee (JSSC), continued under the *OPSEU/MBC Unified and Correctional Collective Agreements*, above note 110, Art 22.12.2 and Appendices 7 and 8: *OPSEU (Union) and Management Board Secretariat*, GSB#1834/99, 27 September 2000, and 1 March 2001 (Petryshen).

CHAPTER TWELVE

Public Service Grievance Board

A. PURPOSE AND FUNCTION

The Public Service Grievance Board (PSGB) allows non-union public servants in ministries and commission public bodies to require specific performance of their employment terms. This ensures the rule of law within the lower and middle management ranks of the Ontario Public Service. The terms of employment in the public service are established by the elected executive either by negotiating collective agreements covering unionized public servants or by directives and policies covering non-unionized employees. As a practical matter, the elected executive cannot directly supervise the administration of the terms it has established. Several mechanisms are in place to ensure the terms established by the government are properly implemented. The ability of unions to grieve alleged failures under their collective agreements and the ability of non-union employees to similarly complain to the PSGB continued by the *Public Service of Ontario Act, 2006* (*PSOA*)[1] are important vehicles for ensuring the elected executive's decisions and agreements are properly implemented.

The PSGB was originally created in 1960 when the increase in the size of government following the Second World War and the increase in the number and complexity of issues facing the elected executive made the traditional supervision of the public service by ministers impossible. At the time the public service was not unionized but the Civil Service

1 SO 2006, c 35, Sch A [*PSOA*]. For a broader discussion of this point see Chapter 2.

Association of Ontario that would become the Ontario Public Service Employees Union was beginning to assert itself as bargaining agent for public servants.[2] When formal collective bargaining was legislated in the 1970s and the Grievance Settlement Board (GSB) was created, the PSGB continued as the dispute settlement vehicle for public servants excluded from collective bargaining.

Employment relationships, including those of public servants, are essentially contractual, though the terms of public servants' contracts include statutory components and are determined within a statutory context. The business of the Ontario government depends on a vast array of contractual relationships of which employment contracts are a modest part. The courts are the usual place to go to enforce contracts, but courts do not specifically enforce employment contracts.[3] Typically courts only become involved in enforcement of employment contracts when the employment is terminated and only damages are in issue. The PSGB is designed to be the vehicle to provide management and excluded employees with the assurance that their employment contracts will be honoured and remedies provided for failures to do so.

The public service does, as a matter of course, comply with legislation, the directions of the elected executive, and its contractual commitments, but an effective legal system requires some meaningful avenue of appeal for those who feel they have been treated improperly or unfairly. The elected executive and the public should be able to look to a process that examines, exposes, and corrects deficiencies in compliance with the terms of employment in the public service.

The public service depends upon the long-term commitment of its front-line and middle management. Correctional officers, inspectors, and other staff need the support of experienced front-line managers when they are confronted with difficult potentially dangerous situations. Not providing front-line managers with some of the same job security and right to enforce their employment terms as they had as a union member does not encourage people to seek advancement. The institutional knowledge and expertise of the public service resides to a large degree with middle management. The loyalty of those employees to public service is critical to the effectiveness of the public service.

---

2 See Chapter 7 for the history of OPSEU.

3 *Atomic Energy of Canada Ltd v Sheikholeslami*, [1998] 3 FC 349 at para 11; *Dunsmuir v New Brunswick*, 2008 SCC 9 at para 108. See also Chapter 13.

Ensuring that these managers are treated fairly and are confident they will be treated fairly is essential to the purposes of the *PSOA*.

The PSGB has three broad functions: contractual dispute resolution, regulation of delegated managerial authority, and protection against reprisal for acting in compliance with the political activity and disclosure of wrongdoing parts of the *PSOA*.

When a matter reaches the PSGB for determination on the merits, the PSGB provides mediation and adjudication in a manner and at a standard consistent with the GSB, labour boards, and arbitrators. Indeed, the PSGB draws its members from the same pool of arbitrators and labour and employment law practitioners. Unfortunately, the PSGB is not currently permitted to properly fill its role under the *PSOA*. As will be discussed below, the lack of a grievance process and short rigid time limits mean preliminary motions foreclosing adjudication on the merits are far too numerous. The jurisdiction limiting nature of the time limits on complaints regarding terms of employment and discipline circumscribes the PSGB's ability to provide effective dispute resolution and review of disciplinary decisions.

The PSGB is intended to redress the imbalance in power between non-union employees and the employer,[4] but it is not a forum for reviewing the government's employment policies. Its function is to provide rulings on personal grievances about the application of the government's policies, not to make policy decisions in the abstract.[5]

B. JURISDICTION

As a statutory tribunal the PSGB's jurisdiction is limited to matters over which it is given authority by legislation.[6] Regulation 378/07 gives it authority over complaints regarding dismissal, discipline, and terms and conditions of employment made by employees appointed by the Public Service Commission (PSC) under Part III of the *PSOA* (employees in ministries, excluding the minister's office, and commission public bodies) that are not members of a collective bargaining unit.[7] The PSGB

4 *Morrison v Ontario (Human Rights Commission)*, 1997 CanLII 10282 (ON PSGB) [*Morrison*].

5 *Brown and Ministry of Correctional Services*, PSGB#P/0898/80, 25 April 1980 at 15.

6 *Kutchaw v Ontario*, 2017 CanLII 16731 (ON PSGB) at para 6.

7 O Reg 378/07, s 5(1) subject to exceptions in s 5(2) and, concerning a complaint about working conditions or terms of employment, the exceptions in s 7(2) discussed below.

is also given authority to hear complaints of reprisal under the political activity and disclosure of wrongdoing parts of the *PSOA* by employees employed in ministries, including ministers' offices, and commission public bodies but not in a collective bargaining unit.[8]

Authority is also provided under the *Election Act* and *Auditor General Act* for the PSGB to hear discipline and dismissal grievances of employees of the Office of the Chief Electoral Officer and the Provincial Auditor.[9] Regulation 378/07 applies to these grievances with necessary modifications.

The statute makes a decision of the PSGB final but does not include any stronger privative language.[10]

The scope of the PSGB's jurisdiction differs depending on the class of employee and type of complaint. The parties to a PSGB complaint are the individual complainant(s) and the employer. In the case of a complaint against the outcome of a competition there may properly be a third party, the successful incumbent, over whom the PSGB would also have jurisdiction. The PSGB has no jurisdiction over positions or employees covered by a collective agreement.[11] In the event of a conflict between the terms the PSGB enforces and a collective agreement term enforced by the GSB, the collective agreement prevails.[12]

Individual employees may move or be moved in or out of a bargaining unit. The PSGB has no jurisdiction over matters arising under a collective agreement since the GSB has exclusive jurisdiction over those matters. A complaint may only be brought by an employee who is not represented by a union or the Ontario Crown Attorneys' Association or the Association of Law Officers of the Crown.[13] Bargaining unit members who take temporary assignments in excluded positions currently remain members of their bargaining unit during their temporary assignment under the terms of the various collective agreements covering public servants. As long as an employee on assignment to an excluded position remains a dues-paying member of a bargaining unit,

---

8 *PSOA*, above note 1, ss 104(3) and 140(3).

9 *Election Act*, RSO 1990, c E.6, s 117(3) & (4); *Auditor General Act*, RSO 1990, c A.35, s 26(4) & (5).

10 *PSOA*, above note 1, s 26.

11 *Burt v Ontario (Ministry of Correctional Services)*, 1993 CanLII 3344 (ON PSGB) [*Burt*].

12 *PSOA*, above note 1, s 152.

13 O Reg 378/07, s 5(2)1 & 2.

they are not entitled to file a complaint with the PSGB.[14] The PSGB has authority to continue to hear a complaint by a member of a bargaining unit that was filed before they moved into a bargaining unit, including a complaint about failure to comply with a settlement of a PSGB complaint.[15] An employee whose permanent (commonly called "home") position is excluded but takes a temporary assignment to a bargaining unit position will normally become subject to the applicable collective agreement and consequently will not be entitled to make a complaint to the PSGB.[16]

The right to bring complaints concerning dismissal, discipline, and terms and conditions of employment is further limited to permanent full-time employees, fixed-term employees working in classified positions, and part-time employees working at least fourteen hours a week and at least nine days every four weeks.[17] Employees working in a term classified position,[18] fixed-term position on a non-recurring project, professional or special capacity, irregular or on-call basis, temporary help program, or a student position during a school vacation at the time of the alleged contract violation cannot make a complaint.[19] In the event a fixed-term contract has lapsed at the relevant time but the employee has continued to work, in the absence of evidence to the contrary, the employee will be subject to the same terms as the lapsed contract.[20]

---

14 *Wilson v Ontario (Community Safety and Correctional Services)*, 2019 CanLII 21765 (ON PSGB) at para 47 [*Wilson*]; *Cartwright v Ontario (Ministry of Community Safety and Correctional Services)*, 2005 CanLII 53197 (ON PSGB) [*Cartwright*]; *Ireland v Ontario (Ministry of Community and Correctional Services)*, 2006 CanLII 30739 (ON PSGB) [*Ireland*]; *Lafreniere v Ontario (Community Safety and Correctional Services)*, 2008 CanLII 70542 (ON PSGB) [*Lafreniere*]; and *Roknic v Ontario (Community Safety and Correctional Services)*, 2009 CanLII 15650 (ON PSGB) [*Roknic*].

15 *Lafreniere*, *ibid*.

16 *Ireland*, above note 14.

17 O Reg 378/07, s 5; *Roselle v Ontario (Solicitor General)*, 2021 CanLII 95128 (ON PSGB) at para 3 [*Roselle*].

18 A "term classified" position is a type of fixed-term position separate from other fixed-term positions to which applies particular terms in Part VI of the Management Board of Cabinet, *Compensation Directive*, 20 August 2007, provided to the authors [*MBC Compensation Directive*].

19 *MacKinnon v Ontario (Community Safety and Correctional Services)*, 2016 CanLII 68794 (ON PSGB) at para 18.

20 *Ibid*.

The process, including time limits, for bringing dismissal, discipline, and working condition complaints to the PSGB is set out in regulation[21] and is a mandatory precondition for the PSGB to have jurisdiction to hear the complaint.[22] The PSGB has no jurisdiction to waive a step in the process or extend the restrictive and confusing time limits.[23]

Except for a grievance against a dismissal by the dismissed employee,[24] only employees can complain to the PSGB. Former employees such as retirees cannot bring a complaint to the PSGB.[25]

C. COMPLAINT PROCESS AND TIME LIMITS

1) Complaint Process for Dismissal, Discipline, and Terms and Conditions Grievances

Compliance with the process for filing a complaint with the PSGB concerning dismissal, discipline, or terms of employment or working conditions, and the time limits for each step are set out in Regulation 378/07 and are mandatory preconditions to the PSGB's jurisdiction to hear such complaints. The PSGB has no power to amend or waive the steps or time limits established by the regulation. The filing of a complaint with the PSGB is also subject to rules made by the PSGB pursuant to the *Statutory Powers and Procedures Act* (*SPPA*).[26] The PSGB has authority to relieve against failures to comply with those rules. A different and more generous process applies to complaints of reprisal under the political activity and disclosure of wrongdoing provisions.

There is no grievance process. Employees have a very limited fourteen-day period to file a notice of their intention to complain with their deputy minister or the chair of the PSC if they work in a commission public body.[27] Following the giving of notice there is a dispute resolution period when the employer may meet with the complainant

---

21 O Reg 378/07, ss 8–10.

22 *Jackson v Ontario (Community Safety and Correctional Services)*, 2011 CanLII 36564 (ON PSGB) at para 38 [*Jackson*].

23 *Breslin v Ontario (Solicitor General)*, 2021 CanLII 37121 (ON PSGB).

24 The words in O Reg 378/07, s 5(1) "or other person" refer to persons grieving after dismissal as a public servant.

25 *Kettle v Ontario (Transportation)*, 2015 CanLII 89903 (ON PSGB); *Burt v Ontario (Community Safety and Correctional Services)*, 2011 CanLII 23300 (ON PSGB).

26 RSO 1990, c S.22 [*SPPA*]; see *PSOA*, above note 1, s 23(1)1.

27 O Reg 378/07, s 8(1).

to try to resolve the matter or not as it chooses. Following the end of the dispute resolution period the complainant has fourteen days to file their complaint with the PSGB.

Delivery of a notice of intention to complain to the complainant's deputy minister means delivery directly to the deputy minister's email, fax line, or office. Delivery to a senior official of the ministry or counsel for the ministry is not satisfactory unless they are acting as a delegate of the deputy minister for the purpose of accepting service of the notice.[28] The same is true for delivery to the chair of the PSC.

2) Complaint Process for Reprisal Complaints

There is no legislated complaint process for reprisal complaints. Complainants file their applications directly with the PSGB by email using the form provided for in the PSGB's rules.[29] The form is available on the PSGB's website.[30] The board will deliver a copy to the employer. The employer is required to file a response on the appropriate PSGB form within sixty days of receiving a copy of the complaint. The time for reply may be extended after consultation with the parties.[31]

3) Time Limits for Dismissal, Discipline, and Terms and Conditions Grievances

a) What Are the Time Limits?

An employee's fourteen-day period to file notice of intention to complain begins on receiving notice of the dismissal or discipline or becoming aware of the alleged violation of their terms and conditions of employment.[32] The notice must set out the reason for the complaint.[33]

Before a complaint may be made to the PSGB, the dispute resolution period following the initial giving of notice must expire.[34] A filing made before the dispute resolution period ends will not give the PSGB jurisdiction to hear the matter. The actual length of the dispute resolution

28 *Thomas v Ontario (Solicitor General)*, 2022 CanLII 31381 (ON PSGB).

29 *PSGB Rules*, effective 7 September 2021, r 5, form 1a [*PSGB Rules*]. The *PSGB Rules* and practice notes are publicly available on its website.

30 PSGB, online: www.psab.gov.on.ca.

31 *PSGB Rules*, above note 29, r 7, form 2a.

32 O Reg 378/07, s 8(4).

33 *Ibid*, s 8(3).

34 *Ibid*, s 9(1).

period will vary. If the deputy minister or PSC chair (or their representative) meet with the complainant within thirty days of receiving the notice, the dispute period will end on the earlier of the date the deputy or chair gives notice to the complainant of their decision or thirty days after the meeting.[35] If there is no meeting between the complainant and the deputy minister or the chair within thirty days of the notice being given, the resolution period ends thirty days after the notice was given to the deputy minister or chair.[36]

Once the dispute resolution period ends the complainant must file their complaint with the PSGB within fourteen days.[37] The filing with the board must include a copy of the notice given to the deputy minister or the PSC chair.[38] The PSGB rules require that complaints be filed using a board form and that a copy of the complaint be delivered to the deputy minister or chair.[39]

The time limits in Regulation 378/07 are stated in calendar days.[40] The regulation is interpretated in accordance with the *Legislation Act, 2006*,[41] which treats "days" in the context of limitation periods as calendar days.[42] Since the 2021 revision of the PSGB's rules, the time limits in the rules are also expressed in calendar days.

The time limits are so strict and rigid that complainants are best to file their notice and complaint in a way that ensures they know the date of receipt by the deputy minister or PSC chair and the PSGB. Normally this would be by email. The PSGB deems email communications received when they reach the recipient's inbox.[43] This would appear to

35 *Ibid*, s 9(3) & (4).

36 *Ibid*, s 9(5).

37 *Ibid*, s 10(1).

38 *Ibid*, s 10(2).

39 *PSGB Rules*, above note 29, r 5.

40 *Laforest v Ontario (Solicitor General)*, 2020 CanLII 10543 (ON PSGB) at paras 45 and 49; *Doyle v Ontario (Ministry of Municipal Affairs)*, 2017 CanLII 52705 (ON PSGB) at paras 21–23 [*Doyle 2017*]; *Morris et al v Ontario (Community Safety and Correctional Services)*, 2018 CanLII 109220 (ON PSGB) at para 13; *Hamilton v Ontario (Community Safety and Correctional Services)*, 2019 CanLII 42439 (ON PSGB) [*Hamilton*]; and *Stricko v Ontario (Community Safety and Correctional Services)*, 2018 CanLII 88984 (ON PSGB) at paras 20–22, 41 [*Stricko*].

41 SO 2006, c 21, Sch F, ss 88 & 89.

42 *Fan v Hamilton (City)*, 2015 CanLIl 47123 (ON CONRB) at para 80.

43 *Beach v Ontario (Solicitor General)*, 2020 CanLII 74281 (ON PSGB) at paras 18 and 24; *Dixon v Ontario (Solicitor General)*, 2020 CanLII 74279 (ON PSGB) at para 27 [*Dixon*].

include notices of discipline, notices of intent to file a complaint, deputy ministers' decisions, and the filing of a complaint with the PSGB.

b) Mandatory and Jurisdictional Nature of Time Limits

The current regulations made under the *PSOA* have been held to be written in mandatory language and in the absence of legislative authority to extend time the PSGB cannot extend time.[44] Previously, the PSGB had express authority to extend time limits in the regulations under the former *Public Service Act* (*PSA*).[45] That authority was taken away in 1996, but the time limits were written in directory rather than mandatory language, so the PSGB was still able to extend time.[46] The use of mandatory language in the 2007 regulation resulted in very short, unforgiving time limits that cannot be extended.

The PSGB's decisions regarding the limits on its jurisdiction are consistent with the wider jurisprudence. The *Labour Relations Act, 1995* (*LRA*)[47] includes a provision allowing an arbitrator to extend collective agreement time limits during the grievance process but, unlike the prior Act, not a time limit for referral of a grievance to arbitration. A 1995 decision of an arbitrator that the arbitrator had no jurisdiction to hear a grievance that was referred to arbitration after the time limit had expired was affirmed on judicial review by the Divisional Court and the Court of Appeal.[48] The Ontario Labour Relations Board (OLRB) has jurisdiction over construction labour arbitrations. It ruled it had jurisdiction to extend time for filing a grievance for arbitration. The arbitration clause in question required "notice in writing given to the other party within fourteen (14) regular working days" but had no language specifying an explicit consequence for failure to give timely notice so the OLRB

---

44 *St Amant v Ontario (Ministry of Community Safety and Correctional Services)*, 2013 CanLII 4673 (ON PSGB) at para 10 [*St Amant*]; *Bourgeault v Ontario (Community Safety and Correctional Services)*, 2013 CanLII 84294 (ON PSGB) at para 28 [*Bourgeault*]; *Hamilton*, above note 40 at paras 68–75.

45 Reg 977, RRO 1990, s 54.

46 *Burkholder v Ontario (Government Services)*, 2013 CanLII 84293 (ON PSGB) at para 10 [*Burkholder*]; *St Amant*, above note 44 at para 10.

47 SO 1995, c 1, Sch A [*LRA*].

48 *Employees International Union, Local 204 v Leisureworld Nursing Homes Ltd*, [1997] OJ No 4815 (CA), aff'g [1997] OJ No 1469 (Div Ct), aff'g 21 November 1995 (Arb).

found it to be directory not mandatory.[49] That decision was reversed on judicial review and that reversal was affirmed by the Court of Appeal.[50]

No case more clearly illustrates the mandatory and draconian nature of the time limits for filing complaints at the PSGB than *Telford v Ontario (Finance)*.[51] The complainant filed timely notice with the chair of the PSC and retained a lawyer to handle his complaint. The lawyer attended with the complainant at the meeting with the chair's delegate. When the complainant tried to contact his lawyer after receiving the chair's decision, he was advised the lawyer had died and the Law Society was moving his files to another lawyer who would contact him. Unfortunately, by the time the file was transferred, and the new lawyer contacted him, the time for filing a complaint with the PSGB had passed. When the PSGB was asked to accept the late filing the PSGB responded:

> This lack of power to relieve against the time limits means that the reasons for not meeting the time lines, however reasonable or sympathetic, are not matters that the Board can rely on to extend the time lines.

This is merely a particularly egregious example of a long line of cases where complainants have been denied a hearing of the merits of their claim by the Byzantine nature of the process. As the PSGB has noted:

> The time lines are written in complicated language, with a dispute resolution period of variable length, which can make it difficult to know when it is too late, or even too early, to forward a complaint to the PSGB. This, together with the lack of legislative provision for the extension of time lines in appropriate cases, can lead to unnecessary frustration of parties seeking to solve serious workplace problems, leaving a problem unaddressed, to the detriment of the morale of all concerned. The lack of "user-friendliness" leads to the extensive use of time and resources, including those of the parties and the Board's administrative staff and adjudicators, in explaining and dealing

49 *United Association of Journeymen and Apprentices of the Plumbing and Pipefitting Industry of the United States and Canada, Local 552 v Greater Essex County District School Board*, 2009 CanLII 266 (ON LRB) at paras 53–54.

50 *Greater Essex County District School Board v United Association of Journeymen and Apprentices of the Plumbing and Pipefitting Industry of the United States and Canada, Local 552*, 2012 ONCA 482 (SCC denied leave to appeal, 2013 CanLII 6707 (SCC)), aff'g 2011 ONSC 5554.

51 2016 CanLII 36364 (ON PSGB).

> with technical objections which might be better used for other purposes, including solving the underlying problem that gave rise to the complaint.[52]

Filing a complaint with the PSGB before the end of the dispute resolution period will not give the board jurisdiction to hear the complaint. "A complaint will be untimely in the sense of being too early if it is filed before that dispute resolution period has expired, and too late if it is filed more than fourteen days after the dispute resolution period has expired."[53] Even if the employer indicated verbally that they were not interested in dispute resolution before the end of the dispute resolution period, early filing would not give the PSGB jurisdiction to hear the matter. "The time lines that govern the Board's jurisdiction run based on the parameters set out in the Regulation and are not affected by other communications between the parties. The Regulation does not provide the Board with any discretion to treat verbal representations made by the Employer as changing the regulatory framework."[54]

As the *Telford* case illustrates, the fourteen-day limitation period for filing a complaint with the PSGB following the end of the dispute resolution period is just as rigid as the period for initiating the process. Even if the delay could be attributed to a stress related illness the PSGB has no jurisdiction to extend the time for filing and cannot hear the complaint.[55]

Complaints of violations of the *Human Rights Code* (*HRC*) or the *Canadian Charter of Rights and Freedoms* are complaints regarding terms and conditions of employment and are subject to the process and time limits under the regulation.[56]

In the *Telford* case it was argued that the employer was estopped from objecting to the timeliness of the application. The argument was rejected on the basis that no express or implied representation was made. The question of whether the employer can by an estoppel give the PSGB jurisdiction that the statute does not give was not addressed,

52 *Dixon*, above note 43 at para 43.

53 *Doyle 2017*, above note 40 at para 21.

54 *Morris et al v Ontario (Community Safety and Correctional Services)*, 2018 CanLII 64318 (ON PSGB) at para 14.

55 *Burkholder*, above note 46.

56 *Jackson*, above note 22 discussing the *Human Rights Code*, RSO 1990, c H.19 [*HRC*]; *Gregory v Ontario (Solicitor General)*, 2022 CanLII 70878 (ON PSGB) at paras 36–43, discussing Part I of the *Constitution Act, 1982*, being Schedule B to the *Canada Act 1982* (UK), 1982, c 11.

but as the OLRB has noted, there can be no estoppel of a statutory requirement.[57]

c) When Does the Fourteen-Day Period to Give Notice Begin?

The fourteen-day window for filing the notice of intention to complain to the PSGB begins the date the employee receives notice of the discipline or dismissal about which they wish to complain. An employee cannot wait until they return from suspension.[58] The fourteen-day window to file notice of complaints about working conditions and terms of employment begins on the date the complainant has all the facts relevant for formulating their complaint sometimes referred to as the date the complaint "crystalized."[59]

A decision on one aspect of an accommodation request may crystalize the matter for purposes of that decision but not for purposes of another aspect of the accommodation request where there remained live issues.[60]

The window for giving notice of a complaint concerning the failure of the employer to respond to a request for a leave to take an assignment with the Yukon government, began when the complainant advised the Yukon government she could not take the assignment because she did not have a leave approved.[61] When complainants were given notice of the implementation of a management job evaluation project that resulted in the elimination of the complainants' salary allowance, the board found that the window for filing notice of a complaint began at the time they were informed about the impact on their wages specifically rather than when they were advised of the general terms of the initiative.[62] Time runs from when the complainant has knowledge of all the

---

57 *Universal Workers Union, Labourers' International Union of North America, Local 183 v Saddlebrook Construction Inc*, 2013 CanLII 23211 (ON LRB) at para 22.

58 *Strong v Ontario (Children and Youth Services)*, 2016 CanLII 89880 (ON PSGB).

59 *Barker v Ontario (Natural Resources and Forestry)*, 2021 CanLII 16291 (ON PSGB) at para 80; *Wallace v Ontario (Solicitor General)*, 2022 CanLII 106487 (ON PSGB) at para 20.

60 *Wallace, ibid* at para 39.

61 *St Amant*, above note 44.

62 *Tremblay et al v Ontario (Ministry of Natural Resources and Forestry)*, 2020 CanLII 20407 (ON PSGB); see also *Gauvin v Ontario (Community Safety and Correctional Services)*, 2017 CanLII 89956 (ON PSGB) at paras 28 & 29.

facts necessary to know they have a claim. Not having the evidence to prove those facts does not extend time for giving notice.[63]

In *Paul v Ontario (Solicitor General)*,[64] the complainant commenced a grievance two years after the completion of a competition when he became aware that he had the top score but was not given any of the three positions filled through that competition. His complaint was of unfair, arbitrary, and bad faith treatment, as well as discrimination under the *HRC*. While time for complaining about a job competition normally runs from the time the complainant becomes aware of the results of the competition, this was not essentially a competition grievance. The complainant did not know the facts necessary to ground the complaint until he knew both the result and the fact he had the highest score. The window for a complaint began when he became aware he had the top score. The complaint was timely. This case is distinct from one where a complainant is aware of the facts but is concerned they will not be believed, waits, and finds additional evidence after the window for giving notice has passed.[65]

The PSGB applies the concept of "continuing grievances" found in the labour arbitration cases that treats each instance of an ongoing violation of a term or condition of employment as a new violation that triggers the fourteen-day window to file a notice of intent to complain.[66] Where managers were complaining against employer inaction over a blog alleged to be creating a poisoned workplace, the continued existence of the blog created a continuing grievance.[67] The failure to provide expenses or wages or on-call pay in accordance with the applicable policy may create a continuing grievance.[68]

---

63 *Mroz v Ontario (Community Safety and Correctional Services)*, 2012 CanLII 17222 (ON PSGB) at para 31 [*Mroz*].

64 2021 CanLII 26625 (ON PSGB) [*Paul*].

65 *Mroz*, above note 63 at para 33.

66 *Bourgeault*, above note 44 at para 29; *Lee v Ontario (Ministry of Community Safety and Correctional Services)*, 2011 CanLII 49517 (ON PSGB) at para 31; *Courchesne-Godin et al v Ontario (Children and Youth Services)*, 2017 CanLII 89957 (ON PSGB) at paras 17 and 19 [*Courchesne-Godin et al*].

67 *Hasted v Ontario (Community Safety and Correctional Services)*, 2016 CanLII 7473 (ON PSGB) [*Hasted #1*].

68 *Melville v Ontario (Ministry of Community Safety and Correctional Services)*, 2006 CanLII 17925 (ON PSGB); *Laird v Ontario (Ministry of Community Safety and Correctional Services)*, 2005 CanLII 53192 (ON PSGB) [*Laird #1*]; *Huppmann v Ontario*, 2017 CanLII 16729 (ON PSGB) [*Huppmann*].

The concept of a continuing grievance has no relevance to time for filling a complaint to the board after the dispute resolution period.[69] A continuing grievance ends when the complainant ceases to be subject to the term or condition and the time limit runs from that time.[70]

In the case of a continuing grievance, the remedial claim is normally limited to damages arising during the fourteen days prior to the date of giving notice of proposal to file the complaint, or later.[71]

d) Complainant's Potential Options When a Complaint Is Dismissed as Untimely

As the chair of the PSGB has noted, the dismissal of a complaint as untimely by the PSGB does not necessarily end the matter. While a settlement or decision of the PSGB on the merits will preclude litigation in another forum, dismissal on a preliminary motion for timeliness will not. The PSGB's jurisdiction over many matters is not exclusive. Dismissals may be challenged in court and human rights complaints can be pursued at the Human Rights Tribunal of Ontario (HRTO), for example.[72]

Litigating a case in an alternate forum is likely to take more than a year. Most employment disputes end in a settlement eventually. An early settlement before expenses in money, loss of time, and aggravation are incurred is normally the best result for all concerned. The PSGB provides mediation more quickly than most tribunals, and its vice-chairs are not only experienced employment mediators but are familiar with the eccentricities of public service employment. An early mediation at the PSGB is usually the best option both parties will have to get a satisfactory final resolution at a limited cost.

e) Time Limits for Reprisal Complaints

Reprisal complaints for disclosure of wrongdoing and political activity are not subject to the time limits in the regulations. They are not subject to any statutory time limit. The PSGB has not confronted a reprisal complaint made after a substantial delay. There are no legislated time limits for reprisal complaints under the *Occupational Health and Safety*

69 *Bourgeault*, above note 44 at para 29.

70 *Marshall v Ontario (Ministry of Community Safety and Correctional Services)*, 2006 CanLII 30742 (ON PSGB); *Hasted #1*, above note 67 at para 25.

71 *Huppmann*, above note 68 at para 17; *Laird #1*, above note 68.

72 *Preston v Ontario (Education)*, 2021 CanLII 71622 (ON PSGB) at paras 36–37.

Act (*OHSA*)[73] or unfair labour practice complaints under the *LRA*.[74] The OLRB has made a rule that requires applicants to make complaints promptly.[75] The OLRB has a practice of insisting on an explanation of any delay longer than a year before allowing a complaint to proceed.[76] The PSGB has indicated that it will dismiss complaints under the doctrine of laches or excessive delay.[77] Absent extenuating circumstances, an alleged reprisal serious enough to complain about should be complained about promptly and certainly within a year.

Where a reprisal complaint made outside the time limits specified for complaints under the regulation proceeds, only the alleged reprisal will be addressed on the merits. Consideration of any related discipline or terms and conditions complaints will remain time barred.[78]

D. COMPLAINTS (GRIEVANCES)

1) Discipline and Dismissal

a) Dismissal for Cause

Complaints concerning dismissal for cause may be brought to the PSGB by employees who are otherwise entitled under Regulation 378/07 to complain to the PSGB who have completed their probation period, or if they are on a fixed-term contract have completed twelve months of continuous service on one or more successive contracts.[79]

The PSGB is expressly prevented from reviewing a dismissal without cause on reasonable notice.[80] However, where such a dismissal is alleged to have been a reprisal contrary to the political activity or disclosure of

73 RSO 1990, c O.1 [*OHSA*].

74 *Yaniv Froehlich v City of Toronto*, 2021 CanLII 70140 (ON LRB) at para 11 [*Yaniv Froehlich*].

75 OLRB, *Rules of Procedure*, online: /www.olrb.gov.on.ca/Documents/Rules_of_Procedure-EN.pdf, s 5-1.

76 *Yaniv Froehlich*, above note 74 at para 13.

77 *Laird #1*, above note 68; *Chyczij v Ontario (Ministry of Labour)*, 2005 CanLII 53190 (ON PSGB).

78 *Binda v Ontario (Environment)*, 2011 CanLII 93306 (ON PSGB) at para 33.

79 O Reg 378/07, s 6.

80 *PSOA*, above note 1, s 38(2); O Reg 378/07, s 4(2)3. For discussion of *PSOA* s 38, see Chapter 3.

wrongdoing provisions the PSGB would appear to have jurisdiction to hear the complaint.[81]

Dismissal (layoff) under section 39 is not subject to substantive review but may be reviewed to ensure that it was made in good faith. The Court of Appeal in *Burgess v Ontario* held that the PSGB had jurisdiction to hear a complaint under a similarly worded provision of the predecessor *PSA* where the complainant alleges that a layoff was made for disciplinary reasons.[82] The PSGB has held that it has the jurisdiction to review a layoff, pursuant to the predecessor provision in the *PSA* to section 39, when the complainant alleges bad faith in the decision to dismiss.[83] The complainant has the onus to prove bad faith.[84]

The board will not substitute its decision for a business decision of the employer, but when a decision is made to reduce staff in a multi-incumbent position for business reasons the choice of the persons to be laid off "cannot be done in an arbitrary and capricious manner."[85] Under the PSC's *Employment Policy*, the determination of the employees to be laid off in a downsizing of multi-incumbent positions is determined by competition among incumbents for the remaining positions.[86] A job competition or alternative process based on merit for selecting those in a multi-incumbent position to be declared surplus is reviewable for procedural fairness.[87]

b) Discipline

Employees who are entitled under Regulation 378/07 to file complaints with the PSGB may complain to the PSGB about discipline imposed on them.[88]

81 O Reg 378/07, s 4(3); *PSOA*, above note 1, s 104(3) and (9); *Nason v Ontario (Government and Consumer Services)*, 2016 CanLII 68795 (ON PSGB).

82 *Burgess v Ontario*, 2001 CanLII 24073 (ON CA) at paras 25 and 28–30.

83 *Trudell and Ministry of Agriculture and Food* (unreported), PSGB#P/6/90 at 13; *Handlarski v Ontario (Ministry of Finance)*, 1996 CanLII 5648 (ON PSGB); *Roy v Ontario (Ministry of Labour)*, 1996 CanLII 5649 (ON PSGB) [*Roy*]; *Reinholz v Ontario (Ministry of Environment and Energy)*, 1999 CanLII 13878 (ON PSGB) [*Reinholz*].

84 *Handlarski*, above note 83.

85 *McGrath v Ontario (Ministry of Labour)*, 1995 CanLII 4583 (ON PSGB) [*McGrath*].

86 Public Service Commission, *Employment Policy, 2012*, 6 November 2020, provided to the authors, s 10.6 [*PSC Employment Policy*]. That policy is discussed in Chapter 2.

87 *McGrath*, above note 85; *Roy*, above note 83.

88 O Reg 378/07, s 3(1).

A poor performance appraisal based on a letter of reprimand cannot be complained against at the PSGB as discipline.[89] Placement on a tracking protocol agreed to with a union recording findings under an employer harassment prevention policy that is not considered part of a disciplinary record cannot be complained against as discipline.[90] However, the board has said "an action may be properly found to be disciplinary even though it is not initiated or seen by the employer in that light."[91]

The denial of "benefits such as promotion and training as a result of being a respondent in unproven complaints" under the *Workplace Discrimination and Harassment Policy* (now the Management Board of Cabinet (MBC) *Respectful Workplace Policy (RWP))* may be the basis for a discipline complaint.[92] A transfer, if it can be shown to have been made for a punitive purpose, may be complained against as discipline.[93]

Warnings that form part of a disciplinary record for purposes of progressive discipline may be complained against. Once a letter of discipline is removed from an employee's file and ceases to be part of the discipline record of the employee, an outstanding complaint against the discipline is moot and may be dismissed.[94]

c) Standard of Proof in Disciplinary Matters

When hearing discipline and dismissal complaints, the PSGB applies the same standards of proof and considerations in determining the

---

89 *MacLennan v Ontario (Community Safety and Correctional Services)*, 2011 CanLII 24754 (ON PSGB).

90 *Medeiros v Ontario (Community Safety and Correctional Services)*, 2010 CanLII 15649 (ON PSGB).

91 *Cardoza v Ontario (Community Safety and Correctional Services)*, 2011 CanLII 86404 (ON PSGB) at para 106 [*Cardoza*].

92 Management Board of Cabinet, *Respectful Workplace Policy (Policy to Support a Respectful Workplace and Prevent Workplace Harassment and Discrimination)*, 1 October 2017, copy made available to authors [*MBC RWP*], discussed in *Mously v Ontario (Community Safety and Correctional Services)*, 2010 CanLII 81436 (ON PSGB) [*Mously*].

93 *Aspiotis v Ontario (Community Safety and Correctional Services)*, 2019 CanLII 21767 (ON PSGB) at para 123 [*Aspiotis*]; *Doyle v Ontario (Municipal Affairs and Housing)*, 2018 CanLII 109219 (ON PSGB) at para 42 [*Doyle 2018*].

94 *Alemu v Ontario (Children, Community and Social Services)*, 2019 CanLII 35319 (ON PSGB) [*Alemu*].

appropriate level of discipline as labour arbitrators and the GSB.[95] Issues of managerial conduct are viewed in the context of the job requirements, managerial responsibilities, and the employer's reasonable expectations of a manager.[96] The standard for upholding discipline or dismissal for cause requires "the disciplinary action has to be established on the balance of probabilities, on clear and cogent evidence, and viewed in the context of the job requirements and expectations of a manager, which are legitimately higher than those of the average bargaining unit employee."[97] However, this does not mean managers can be held to strict adherence to policies when the employer has allowed "known practices to exist and continue in the workplace, those practices come to reflect the contractual standard."[98]

d) Criminal Convictions

If an employee is convicted or discharged of an offence under the *Criminal Code* in respect of an act or omission that results in discipline or dismissal, proof of the conviction is conclusive evidence before the PSGB that the employee committed the act or omission.[99] This same provision applies to the GSB, which has extensive jurisprudence on the topic (as discussed in Chapter 9).

e) Remedies in Dismissal and Discipline Complaints

The PSGB's approach to upholding or mitigating employer discipline or dismissals is typical of labour arbitrators and is inherently fact specific. It may reverse, reduce, or modify disciplinary dismissals and suspensions or other discipline and provide for full or partial compensation for lost wages and benefits based on the board's determination of what

---

95 See, for example, *Huppmann v Ontario (Solicitor General)*, 2019 CanLII 86415 (ON PSGB); *Roselle*, above note 17; *Gronski v Ontario (Community Safety and Correctional Services)*, 2015 CanLII 67988 (ON PSGB) [*Gronski*]; *Potter v Ontario (Community Safety and Correctional Services)*, 2018 CanLII 102749 (ON PSGB); *Jones v Ontario (Community Safety and Correctional Services)*, 2013 CanLII 74166 (ON PSGB).

96 *Dyson v Ontario (Community Safety and Correctional Services)*, 2014 CanLII 8245 (ON PSGB) at para 13 [*Dyson*]; *Gronski*, above note 95 at para 121. See the discussion in Chapter 3 of general standards of conduct.

97 *Keating v Ontario (Community Safety and Correctional Services)*, 2009 CanLII 15648 (ON PSGB) at para 9; *Gronski*, above note 95 at para 90.

98 *Jurkus v Ontario (Solicitor General)*, 2022 CanLII 31358 (ON PSGB) at para 117.

99 *PSOA*, above note 1, s 25.

if any discipline is appropriate in the circumstances including any discipline record. Compensation for lost wages is subject to mitigation. The board will not award amounts for legal costs or reduce amounts earned in mitigation to offset a successful complainant's legal costs.[100] However, the PSGB is under two legislative constraints.

The PSGB is prevented from reinstating an employee it finds has sexually molested or applied excessive force to a vulnerable person to a position with responsibility for, or contact with, vulnerable persons as defined by regulation.[101] The definition of vulnerable person includes adult inmates in correctional facilities.[102] The restriction applies to persons who apply force or molest but not to a supervisor who fails to stop them.[103] The board may reinstate a person to an equivalent position without responsibility for or contact with vulnerable persons. Very similar provisions apply to the GSB, which has extensive jurisprudence on the topic, as discussed in Chapter 9. In the event the PSGB determines reinstatement to an equivalent position is not warranted, compensation in lieu of reinstatement may be ordered.[104] Unlike labour arbitrators dealing with employees under a collective agreement, the PSGB will not include compensation for loss of collective bargaining rights in the calculation of damages. The employer has the power to dismiss on reasonable notice, so damages will be based on considerations similar to the calculation of common law reasonable notice of termination.

The PSGB will substitute a suspension where it finds dismissal is excessive. It may substitute a suspension greater than the one month provided for in the legislation.[105] The authority to provide a suspension of longer than twenty days appears to flow from the PSGB's discretion to determine the appropriate level of compensation for time not worked while a dismissal grievance was being litigated.[106] Compensation for lost wages is a damage award that is calculated on the basis of the employee's lost opportunity to earn income. Determination of the amount of

---

100 *Potter v Ontario (Community Safety and Correctional Services)*, 2019 CanLII 35320 (ON PSGB) at para 5 [*Potter*]. See the discussion of legal costs below.

101 *PSOA*, above note 1, s 24.

102 O Reg 378, s 15.

103 *Bazger v Ontario (Community Safety and Correctional Services)*, 2017 CanLII 25423 (ON PSGB) at para 129 [*Bazger #1*].

104 *Dyson*, above note 96 at paras 15 & 16.

105 *PSOA*, above note 1, ss 34–35. This issue is also addressed by the GSB, as discussed in Chapter 3.

106 *Potter*, above note 100 at para 1.

such an award is at the discretion of the PSGB. Alternatively, since the statutory restriction applies to the PSC, authority for lengthy suspensions may be seen as implicit in the PSGB's broad, remedial jurisdiction to resolve dismissal grievances.

The PSGB has no jurisdiction to amend or override a collective agreement provision. Consequently, any potential disciplinary remedy involving a demotion or other return to a bargaining unit position is subject to the limits on the employer's right under the applicable collective agreement to return the employee to the bargaining unit. The jurisdiction of the PSGB to order such a remedy has not been litigated but the uncertainty should be sufficient to convince the PSGB not to consider such a remedy.[107]

2) Working Conditions and Terms of Employment

a) Exclusions

Members of the Senior Management Group, Branch Directors, public servants headquartered outside Ontario, and lawyers are excluded by section 7(2) of Regulation 378/07 from grieving terms and conditions of employment.

The PSGB's jurisdiction over working conditions is also subject to the legislative exclusion of five topics of complaint:

1. The term or duration of the public servant's appointment to employment by the Crown
2. The assignment of the public servant to a particular class of position
3. A dismissal without cause under subsection 38(1) of the Act or a matter relating to such a dismissal
4. The evaluation of a public servant's performance or the method of evaluating his or her performance
5. The compensation provided or denied to a public servant as a result of the evaluation of his or her performance[108]

i) Exclusion of Classification Complaints

The exclusion of "assignment" to "class of position" have been found to mean "the class, or classification, assigned by the employer, which determines its pay range, among other things. Section 4(2) has been

107 *Bazger #1*, above note 103 at para 130.

108 O Reg 378/07, s 4(2).

seen as aimed at removing classification complaints from the board's jurisdiction, rather than prohibiting all disputes over a transfer or reassignment, disciplinary or otherwise."[109]

Historically the PSGB has never had this jurisdiction. Another board, the Classification Rating Committee, had that responsibility until 1993 when its operation was frozen under the *Social Contract Act, 1993*[110] and never restored.

The PSGB has ruled that complaints seeking parity with employees in another classification are essentially about classification and outside the board's jurisdiction.[111] Complaints by managers frustrated by eroded pay differentials are also not within the PSGB's jurisdiction. The PSGB's jurisdiction is limited to enforcing compensation levels fixed by the body authorized to set levels of compensation, not to set new compensation levels.[112]

Disputing one aspect of a complainant's compensation (removal of a salary allowance or on-call pay, for example) does not make the complaint about "the assignment to a particular class of position."[113] Allegations that a complainant is being assigned work of another classification are not outside the board's jurisdiction, though the complainant would need to establish that the assignment was unsafe or contrary to a term of employment to obtain a remedy.[114]

ii) Exclusion of Performance Evaluation Complaints

The exclusion of the "evaluation of . . . or the method of evaluating performance" or "compensation . . . as a result of the evaluation" includes

---

109 *Doyle 2018*, above note 93 at para 42; *Tremblay et al v Ontario (Natural Resources and Forestry)*, 2020 CanLII 52544 (ON PSGB) [*Tremblay et al*].

110 SO 1993, c 5.

111 *Ilika v Ontario (Community Safety and Correctional Services)*, 2014 CanLII 76834 (ON PSGB) at para 21.

112 *Garratt et al v Ontario (Health and Long-Term Care)*, 2005 CanLII 53194 (ON PSGB) at 7 [*Garratt #1*]. At the time of that decision the Civil Service Commission set compensation levels. For discussion of current authority to set compensation, see Chapter 2.

113 *Hasted #1*, above note 67 at para 34; *Johnston et al v Ontario (Community Safety and Correctional Services)*, 2019 CanLII 65197 (ON PSGB) at para 36 [*Johnston et al*]; *Tremblay et al*, above note 109.

114 *Boucher v Ontario (Community Safety and Correctional Services)*, 2018 CanLII 119631 (ON PSGB) at para 20 [*Boucher*].

policies related to these matters,[115] alleged violations of such policies,[116] instructions, directions, performance plans, training, or threats related to performance evaluations.[117]

Alleged unfair, unequal, and inequitable treatment by the employer as a result of the impact of a pay freeze on pay-for-performance payments is beyond the PSGB's jurisdiction.[118] A complaint or part of a complaint that relates to pay for performance is beyond the board's jurisdiction even if the employer can be proven to have made an error in calculating the complainant's pay.[119]

The board in *Bowmaster v Ontario (Solicitor General)*[120] held that it did not have jurisdiction to hear a complaint that a performance evaluation was made in an arbitrary, discriminatory, or in bad faith manner but did have jurisdiction to hear an allegation that an evaluation was discriminatory contrary to the *HRC*. The board noted that *Aspiotis v Ontario (Community Safety and Correctional Services)*[121] was the only decision that appeared to suggest a performance evaluation could be reviewed on a complaint that it was made in an arbitrary, discriminatory, or in bad faith manner but was properly read not as a complaint about a performance appraisal but as a case of an alleged disciplinary transfer over which the PSGB clearly has jurisdiction.

b) What Are Working Conditions and Terms of Employment?

The PSGB enforces working conditions and terms of employment as the terms of employees' contracts of employment. Since the PSGB decision in *Kanga v Ontario (Ministry of Health)*,[122] the words "working

115 *Szewczuk v Ontario (Community Safety and Correctional Services)*, 2008 CanLII 70544 (ON PSGB).

116 *Tyrrell v Ontario (Ministry of Community Safety and Correctional Services*, 2004 CanLII 55241 (ON PSGB); *Schmohl v Ontario (Community Safety and Correctional Services)*, 2015 CanLII 89902 (ON PSGB).

117 *Allen v Ontario (Community Safety and Correctional Services)*, 2009 CanLII 43639 (ON PSGB) at para 11 [*Allen*].

118 *Smith et al v Ontario (Ministry of Community Safety and Correctional Services)*, 2014 CanLII 48098 (ON PSGB).

119 *Berenbaum v Ontario (Ministry of Labour)*, 2011 CanLII 23299 (ON PSGB).

120 2020 CanLII 105698 (ON PSGB) [*Bowmaster*]; subsequently cited in *Berezowsky v Ontario (Solicitor General)*, 2021 CanLII 82509 (ON PSGB) [*Berezowsky*]; *Paul*, above note 64 at para 31; *Seales v Ontario (Solicitor General)*, 2022 CanLII 31378 (ON PSGB).

121 *Aspiotis*, above note 93.

122 1986 CanLII 95 (ON PSGB) [*Kanga #1*].

condition" or "a term of his or her employment" have been read expansively, and given a "broad and liberal interpretation" in accordance with the *Legislation Act, 2006* and in keeping with the broad interpretations typical in labour relations matters before the courts and tribunals.[123] The *MBC Compensation Directive*, the *PSC Employment Policy*, and related directives and policies set out the contractual terms of employment of employees not subject to a collective agreement.[124] Employment-related legislation, notably the *HRC* and the *OHSA*, also form part of employees' terms of employment enforceable by the PSGB.[125]

In *Scott et al v Ministry of Transportation*,[126] the board held that "an employment policy introduced by the employer became a 'working condition or term of employment' when it was intended as an employment commitment and is generally applied as such." In that case a commitment not to do certain things had been applied and not formally withdrawn so it continued to be a term of employment of the complainants. However, a program such as a voluntary exit program that solicited interest in the nature of a pre-contractual representation without a policy or directive with a specific process for determining entitlement does not create an enforceable contractual term.[127] The PSGB would only have jurisdiction to review a complaint over a refusal of a voluntary exit under such a program if it involved an allegation of a violation of the *HRC*.[128]

A policy will become enforceable where it is introduced by the employer as an employment commitment and is generally applied in such a manner,[129] but the fact a policy has become an enforceable commitment does not prevent the employer from changing the practice on appropriate notice.[130] Terms of employment may include a term created

---

123 SO 2006, c 21, Sch F, s 64. *Bazger v Ontario (Solicitor General)*, 2021 CanLII 37123 (ON PSGB) at paras 10–15 [*Bazger #2*] referencing the *MBC Compensation Directive*, above note 18. See reference to the *PSC Employment Policy*, above note 86.

124 *Ibid.*

125 *Tighe v Ontario (Solicitor General)*, 2020 CanLII 45594 (ON PSGB) at para 10 [*Tighe*].

126 PSGB#P-0001/96, 7 July 1998 at 2 [*Scott*], cited in *Tighe*, above note 125 at para 39.

127 *Tighe*, above note 125; *Berezowsky et al v Ontario (Solicitor General)*, 2021 CanLII 37122 (ON PSGB).

128 *Tighe*, above note 125 at para 55.

129 *Scott*, above note 126 at 24.

130 *Ibid.*

by past practice.[131] However, the practice would have to be of a type that indicated a consistent policy or commitment was in place.[132] Previous more favourable discretionary decisions do not create a term of employment allowing the board to require similar favourable decisions in the future.[133] Past practice is more likely to be a significant consideration when a departure may suggest arbitrary or discriminatory conduct toward a particular individual.[134]

If the employer makes a promise to pay a benefit beyond or outside the established terms of employment set by MBC or PSC directive or policy and an employee works in reliance on such a promise the PSGB will enforce the promise.[135] The PSGB will apply the doctrine of promissory estoppel where an employee is given an assurance, acts on it, and then the assurance or promise is not fulfilled.[136]

In *Tremblay et al v Ontario (Natural Resources and Forestry)*,[137] the board addressed the introduction of a directive that resulted in a group of highly skilled senior staff in the Ministry of Natural Resources' Aviation Unit losing their salary allowances. These allowances had been in place for years to recruit and retain people with skills essential to the operation of Ontario's water bombers and other aircraft. The salary allowance was removed by a new MBC directive. The PSGB found that the issue was not a classification matter but an entitlement to a contractual benefit that had been promised to the complainants on hiring. While the Crown continued to employ them, it was required to meet its original contractual commitment. This is clearly a better result than having key staff quit and sue or find other jobs and quit but it stretches the PSGB's jurisdiction.

The *PSOA* gives the employer broad management rights limited by legislation and the contractual terms of an employee's employment.[138] "The only constraint in the exercise of managerial rights is that the

---

131 *Hasted #1*, above note 67 at para 35; *Scott*, above note 126 at 26.

132 *Courchesne-Godin et al*, above note 66 at para 34.

133 *Joncas v Ontario (Solicitor General)*, 2021 CanLII 26622 (ON PSGB) at para 28.

134 *Harris et al v Ontario (Ministry of Community Safety and Correctional Services)*, 2005 CanLII 53193 (ON PSGB).

135 *Johnston v Ontario (Ministry of Community and Social Services)*, 1999 CanLII 13882 (ON PSGB).

136 *Maiwand v Ontario (Solicitor General)*, 2021 CanLII 57993 (ON PSGB) [*Maiwand*].

137 2020 CanLII 52533 (ON PSGB).

138 *Bazger #2*, above note 123 at para 11; *Wickham-Johnson v Ontario (Solicitor General)*, 2021 CanLII 37119 (ON PSGB) at para 21.

employer not act in a manner that is arbitrary, discriminatory, or in bad faith."[139] In *Drakos v Ontario (Community Safety and Correctional Services)* the board stated that

> [t]he board's jurisprudence has long recognized its jurisdiction to deal with allegations that treatment by the employer is arbitrary, discriminatory or in bad faith, or a breach of policy such as a Statement of Ethical Principles. . . . An employer may be found to have acted arbitrarily where the action that is taken is unreasonable or unsupported by a valid business purpose.[140]

The PSC *Employment Policy* provides that public service employment practices are to "apply the principles of merit," be "fair, objective, reasonable and transparent," and "balance organizational and individual interests."[141] Employees are to be "treated with fairness and dignity throughout the employment relationship."[142] Unreasonable exercises of managerial discretion in, for example, designating an employee's headquarters for travel expense purposes could be challenged as contrary to these provisions.[143] Employees are entitled to be advised of potentially material changes in a new position when it is offered to an employee.[144]

The PSGB is concerned with the enforcement of the existing terms and conditions of a complainant's employment contract, including the requirement that those terms and conditions be administered and applied fairly, reasonably in good faith, and not arbitrarily.[145] "An allegation of arbitrary, discriminatory or bad faith conduct . . . must relate to an existing term or condition of employment which the board has jurisdiction to enforce."[146]

139 *Wickham-Johnson, ibid* at para 10.

140 2013 CanLII 88258 (ON PSGB) at para 43.

141 *PSC Employment Policy*, above note 86, Principle 6-2.

142 *Ibid*, Principle 6-6.

143 *Re The Queen in right of Ontario and Ontario Public Service Employees' Union et al*, 1984 CanLII 2148 (ON SC), cited with approval in *Kanga #1*, above note 122 at 14; *Shilman v Ontario (Ministry of Community and Social Services)*, 1989 CanLII 167 (ON PSGB) [*Shilman*].

144 *Shilman, ibid.*

145 *Berezowsky*, above note 120 at para 27.

146 *Ibid* at para 27.

The board requires "something more than a belief that something is unfair, no matter how deeply held."[147] The requirement is fairness in process. The substantive content will vary with the circumstances.[148]

The employer owes a duty of fairness in any investigation of alleged violations of the *RWP*,[149] the *HRC*, or in connection with a grievance under a collective agreement.[150] A manager who is the subject of a serious allegation in either a grievance, or *RWP* complaint or other complaint of misconduct is entitled to expeditious notice of the details of the allegation and an opportunity to respond to it before the employer makes commitments that might compromise the manager's interests.[151] Similarly, an employee accused of conflict of interest is entitled to be treated fairly in the sense of being allowed to know and respond to the allegations against them.[152]

In *Garratt v Ontario (Health and Long-Term Care)*,[153] a complaint asking for a process for setting and communicating wages was held to be seeking a new term rather than enforcement of an existing one and beyond the board's jurisdiction. The board noted that

> [e]specially in the managerial setting, where contracts of employment are not collective, but individual, it is not enough to say that it is fair or would be more fair if a grievor was paid more, or not less, than some other employee. In order to succeed, a grievance must show that the difference is improper, either because it offends a specific term or condition of employment, or *some more general principle of law.*[154]

A sense of unfairness or unhappiness is not a basis for a complaint.[155] The board will not interfere with a discretionary decision by manage-

---

147 *Hugh MacDonald et al v Ontario (Community Safety and Correctional Services)*, 2014 CanLII 76836 (ON PSGB) at para 17 [*Hugh MacDonald et al*].

148 *Cardoza*, above note 91 para 15.

149 The *MBC RWP*, above note 92, is further discussed in Chapter 6.

150 *Masters v Ontario*, 1994 CanLII 10571 (ONSC); *Cardoza*, above note 91; *DaSilva v Ontario (Ministry of Health)*, 1997 CanLII 10281 (ON PSGB) [*DaSilva*]. The investigation of human rights complaints is addressed in Chapter 6, Section C.

151 *Cardoza*, above note 91 at para 92; *Gaetano v Ontario (Ministry of Municipal Affairs and Housing)*, 2000 CanLII 20352 (ON PSGB) [*Gaetano*].

152 *Doyle 2018*, above note 93 at para 51.

153 *Garratt #1*, above note 112.

154 *Maiwand*, above note 136 at para 35, quoting *Ransome v Ontario (Health and Long-Term Care)*, 2006 CanLII 4278 (ON PSGB).

155 *Maiwand*, above note 136.

ment unless the complainant establishes that the decision was made on an arbitrary or discriminatory basis or in bad faith.[156]

c) Constructive Dismissal

Complainants occasionally claim to be constructively dismissed. No such claim is possible before the PSGB.[157] Constructive dismissal is a common law doctrine allowing an employee, faced with an employer's refusal to follow their employment contract, to cease employment, and claim the without cause termination benefit of damages in lieu of reasonable notice.[158] To bring a complaint before the PSGB the complainant must be either employed as a public servant or dismissed for cause. An employee who quits and alleges constructive dismissal is no longer an employee and the PSGB has no jurisdiction to hear the complaint. Such a complaint is essentially a claim for damages for a not for cause dismissal. Under the *PSOA*, not for cause dismissals fall under section 38, a section that is outside the PSGB's jurisdiction.[159] More fundamentally, the purpose of the PSGB is to provide for specific enforcement of employees' employment terms. If an employee's concerns fall within the PSGB's jurisdiction, the job of the PSGB is to order the employer to comply with its contractual obligations not to allow an employee to repudiate their contract of employment and claim damages. If the concern relates to matters not within the PSGB's jurisdiction, the PSGB does not gain jurisdiction by characterizing the issue as constructive dismissal.

The doctrine of constructive dismissal exists at common law because at common law the courts do not specifically enforce employment contracts so employees must accept a change imposed by the employer or quit and sue for damages. If a fundamental change in an employee's employment terms occurs that falls outside the jurisdiction of the PSGB, the employee may quit and take their chances making a claim for constructive dismissal damages in the courts.[160]

---

156 *Chyczij v Ontario (Labour)*, 2009 CanLII 59147 (ON PSGB) at para 106.

157 *Reinholz*, above note 83.

158 *Farber v Royal Trust Co*, [1997] 1 SCR 846 at paras 33–34; *Potter v New Brunswick Legal Aid Services Commission*, 2015 SCC 10 at para 30.

159 O Reg 378/07, s 4(2)3.

160 *Benedict v Ontario*, 2000 CanLII 22713 (ON SC).

d) Salary Compression

The terms salary "compression" and "inversion" refer to situations where there is a narrowing or even the reversal of the difference in salary between managers and their direct subordinates, typically members of a bargaining unit. It may also capture situations where bargaining unit employees get a benefit not available to their supervisors. While these circumstances cause considerable discontent among the managers concerned, salary compression or inversion, or the fact the bargaining unit has a benefit not available to their supervisors, is not a basis for a successful complaint to the PSGB.[161] As the board noted in *Laird v Ontario (Community Safety and Correctional Services)*,[162] "there is nothing this board can do to remedy salary grievances, unless there has been a clear breach of a term and condition of employment or a policy, or discriminatory or bad faith reasons for the decision."

e) Transfers

The employer has the right to transfer or assign employees, provided that it is not done in an arbitrary manner or is discriminatory or made in bad faith.[163] Where a transfer is a response to misconduct, it is disciplinary and the PSGB will require the employer to prove the alleged misconduct and establish that the transfer is an appropriate disciplinary response. When the employer disputes the disciplinary nature of a transfer, the onus falls on the grievor to show that it was disciplinary. A transfer in response to voluntary conduct without agreement is punitive and disciplinary.[164] The employer's characterization of a transfer as non-disciplinary is not necessarily determinative.[165] In the event of a non-disciplinary transfer, the onus falls on the grievor to show it was arbitrary, discriminatory, or done in bad faith.[166]

---

161 *Garratt et al v The Crown in Right of Ontario (Ministry of Health and Long-Term Care)*, 2005 CanLII 53195 (ON PSGB) [*Garratt #2*]; *Ransome v Ontario (Health and Long-Term Care)*, 2006 CanLII 42782 (ON PSGB); *Laird v Ontario (Community Safety and Correctional Services)*, 2009 CanLII 43638 (ON PSGB) [*Laird #2*] and cases cited therein.

162 *Laird #2*, *ibid* at para 18.

163 *Murphy v Ontario (Ministry of Transportation)*, 1999 CanLII 13876 (ON PSGB) [*Murphy*].

164 *Kanga and Ministry of Health*, PSGB#P/0007/86, P/0010/86, 13 July 1990 at 38 [*Kanga #2*].

165 *Ibid.*

166 *Murphy*, above note 163; *Boucher*, above note 114 at para 43.

Transfers may be justified where the employer requires the grievor's experience in a different position.[167] Where a manager is having difficulty in their current position they may be transferred and the transfer will not be disciplinary in nature.[168] The employer is not obliged to allow a poor work environment to continue even where the employee does not wish to move.[169] Where a medical condition does not allow an employee to maintain regular attendance sufficient to supervise an operation, they may be moved to a temporary assignment.[170] A transfer may be an appropriate response where an employee's actions have created an actual or potential conflict of interest.[171]

f) Human Rights

Allegations that an employee has been treated contrary to the provisions of the *HRC* fall within the PSGB's jurisdiction to determine grievances regarding working conditions and terms of employment.[172] An employee who is not entitled to file a working conditions and terms of employment complaint has no recourse to the PSGB with respect to a human rights complaint unless it arose in the context of a discipline complaint.[173] The *RWP*[174] issued by the MBC is intended to ensure compliance with the *HRC* and meet the obligation under the *OHSA* to have a harassment policy.[175] This policy, like other MBC directives and policies, are employment terms and conditions the PSGB enforces.[176]

Employees have the option of taking allegations of violations of the *HRC* to the HRTO, so the inability to proceed to the PSGB does not deny a person the ability to have their human rights complaint

---

167 *Murphy*, above note 163.

168 *Ibid.*

169 *Kanga #2*, above note 164.

170 *Bardhan v Ontario (Ministry of Health)*, 2000 CanLII 20351 (ON PSGB) [*Bardhan*].

171 *A Grievor and Ministry of Health*, PSGB#P/0014/90, 13 August 1991; the transfer of a manager who had sexual relations with representatives of organizations that did business with her unit was upheld.

172 *Tighe*, above note 125 at para 10; *Charlton v Ontario (Community Safety and Correctional Services)*, 2007 CanLII 24192 (ON PSGB) (Carter) [*Charlton*]; *Parry Sound (District) Social Services Administration Board v OPSEU, Local 324*, 2003 SCC 42.

173 *Fani v Ontario (Environment, Conservation and Parks)*, 2021 CanLII 26639 (ON PSGB) at para 18.

174 *MBC RWP*, above note 92, s 6.3.

175 The law related to harassment and the *OHSA* is discussed in Chapter 6, Section D.

176 *Gaetano*, above note 151; *DaSilva*, above note 150; *Paul*, above note 64 at para 27.

adjudicated. When similar allegations of human rights violations are made in both a complaint to the PSGB and an application to the HRTO, the tribunal will defer consideration of the application pending the resolution of the PSGB complaint.[177] Similarly, if the parties choose to proceed with a hearing before the tribunal, the PSGB will defer hearing of the complaint before it.[178]

The PSGB's authority to enforce the *HRC* and related directives and policies is confined to matters within its jurisdiction. In *Bowmaster v Ontario (Solicitor General)*,[179] complainants alleged their performance ratings were changed in violation of the *HRC*. Performance ratings are not matters that can be grieved to the PSGB, but the board held it had "jurisdiction to entertain and determine that narrower statutory allegation" that after the performance ratings were made, they were then changed contrary to the *HRC*.

A human rights complaint to the PSGB is subject to dismissal for failure to comply with the time limits on complaints under the regulations. However, the window for filing a complaint runs from the time the complainant became aware of the facts necessary to establish discrimination. In the case of a competition case, this can be long after the date the complainant was told the result of the competition that normally triggers the fourteen-day period to file notice of a complaint concerning a competition.[180] Dismissal of a PSGB complaint about human rights as untimely does not prevent the complainant taking the same allegations to the HRTO where the limitation period is longer

In addressing the human rights issues raised by the grievance of a management employee, the PSGB has no jurisdiction to grant remedies that have an impact directly on collective agreement rights.[181] The PSGB's authority is to hear complaints by non-bargaining unit employees against the employer. If a non-bargaining unit employee seeks a remedy against a union or bargaining unit member, or another non-bargaining unit employee they must take their complaint to the

177 *Bangura v Ontario (Community and Social Services)*, 2011 HRTO 23; *Jackson v Ontario (Labour)*, 2013 HRTO 87; *Taylor v Ontario (Community Safety and Correctional Services)*, 2018 HRTO 1549.

178 *Baccega v Ontario (Solicitor General)*, 2020 CanLII 45593 (ON PSGB) at para 45 [*Baccega*]. Deferrals are addressed at greater length in Chapter 6.

179 *Bowmaster*, above note 120.

180 *Paul*, above note 64.

181 *Burt*, above note 11.

HRTO.[182] However, the failure of the employer to address harassment or discrimination by bargaining unit members would allow a complainant to obtain a remedy against the employer.[183]

g) Job Competitions

Under its authority to hear grievances concerning working conditions and terms of employment, the PSGB has jurisdiction to ensure competitions are conducted in a procedurally fair manner and that management exercises its discretion in good faith without bias in accordance with the applicable policies.[184] The PSGB's authority is limited to ensuring the requirements for competitions established by the PSC under the authority of the *PSOA* are followed as intended.[185] This includes the right to a decision untainted by discriminations or bias[186] following a competition structured in accordance with the applicable policies.[187] In the event the board finds a competition has not been properly conducted and fairly decided, the remedy would normally be limited to ordering a rerunning of the competition.[188] The board's role is to review the fairness of the completion and compliance with binding policy, not to substitute its

182 *Taylor-Baptiste v Ontario Public Service Employees Union*, 2012 HRTO 1393 at para 42 [*Taylor-Baptiste*]; reconsideration denied, 2013 HRTO 180, where the tribunal made the interesting finding that a public blog containing sexist remarks about a manager were not harassment in the workplace unless the posts were made while the posting employee was in the workplace, and that sexist remarks on a public blog by a union official were internal union communication that did not violate the *HRC* but did not preclude blog posts being a violation of the *HRC* in other circumstances; one hopes the decision would be different in the post-#MeToo world.

183 *Taylor-Baptiste*, *ibid* at para 27.

184 *Lacombe v Ontario (Ministry of Colleges and Universities)*, 1990 CanLII 2587 (ON PSGB); *McAdam v Ontario (Ministry of Finance)*, 1996 CanLII 5655 (ON PSGB) [*McAdam*].

185 *PSC Employment Policy*, above note 86, Recruitment and Selection; *Vipari v Ministry of Community and Social Services*, PSGB#P/0033/94, 14 November 1995 at 15–16 [*Vipari*].

186 *Paul*, above note 64 at paras 25–26.

187 *Williams v Ontario (Ministry of Correctional Services)*, 2002 CanLII 45640 (ON PSGB), where the PSGB restricted a competition to employees facing layoff and therefore entitled to priority.

188 *Majkot v Ontario (Ministry of the Attorney General)*, 1999 CanLII 13879 (ON PSGB) [*Majkot*].

decision for that of management.[189] However, where the challenge to a competition is grounded in an allegation of discrimination contrary to the *HRC*, the potential remedy could include placement.[190]

A grievance merely claiming that the employer has made the wrong choice may be dismissed as not disclosing a potential violation.[191] Where a complainant alleges the panel failed to gather relevant information the board, like the GSB, will expect the complainant to identify the relevant information that was not considered and establish that it would or at least could have made a difference to the result.[192]

The PSGB approaches competition grievances in much the same manner as the GSB and labour arbitrators. Successful applicants in competitions that are the subject of a complaint are entitled to notice of the PSGB hearing.[193] Like the GSB the board recognizes that some subjectivity in evaluation is inevitable.[194] The PSGB has not been as specific as the GSB about the review of personnel files, ranking of résumés, and contacting references, but has noted that an assessment would be "more thorough if personnel files had been reviewed, references had been contacted and résumés considered by all members of the panel."[195]

The role of the board is not to judge the questions that were asked, but the board will review the interview questions to determine whether they reflect the job requirements and are capable of evaluating the skill in question.[196] Like the GSB, the failure of all panel members to participate in all interviews, and an overemphasis on interviews, are flaws that might lead to an order to rerun the competition.[197]

When the PSGB determines that a flaw has occurred in a competition process, it then considers whether the flaw is sufficiently serious that it might reasonably be expected to have influenced the result.[198]

---

189 *McAdam*, above note 184; *Brander and Ministry of Correctional Services*, PSGB#P/0006/92, 7 December 1992 [*Brander*].

190 *Paul*, above note 64 at para 53.

191 *McAdam*, above note 184.

192 *Mitta v Ontario (Municipal Affairs and Housing)*, 2013 CanLII 42027 (ON PSGB) at para 103 [*Mitta*]. For a discussion of the GSB jurisprudence, see Chapter 10, Section C.

193 *Oke v Ministry of Energy*, PSGB#P/0002/88, 26 April 1989 at 10–11.

194 *Mitta*, above note 192 at para 89.

195 *Ibid* at para 95.

196 *Ibid* at paras 78 and 85.

197 *McCready v Ontario (Treasury Board Secretariat)*, 2021 CanLII 37124 (ON PSGB).

198 *Ibid*; *Vipari*, above note 185 at 15; *Mitta*, above note 192 at para 103.

The result of a competition will not be disturbed where the flaws that were found did not influence the result.[199]

There is a fundamental difference between competition arbitrations under collective agreements and those before the PSGB. Seniority or length of service is not a consideration in PSGB competition cases. The PSC policy specifies "[e]mployee selection must be based on a thorough assessment of the candidate's ability to demonstrate the qualifications required for effective performance."[200] The policy specifies the principle of merit among others will apply to employment practices but makes no mention of seniority.[201]

Merit is considered by the PSGB to be the central principle governing recruitment and promotion.[202] Procedural fairness is recognized to be fundamental to protecting the merit principle in two respects: first, a selection process must be both fair and seen to be fair to maintain the confidence of employees and the public, both of which are essential to the successful application of the merit principle; second, a fair competition process is viewed as necessary to allow choices based on merit to be made effectively.[203]

While the PSGB has never placed a complainant in a position after finding a competition to be flawed and would be reluctant to do so, it has suggested it has the authority to do so.[204] Where competition has been selected as the means of filling a position the jurisdiction of the PSGB to fill the position having found the competition to be flawed is open to question. In an earlier decision the PSGB said, "[t]his Board has no jurisdiction to second-guess the employer's decision as to the most suitable candidate, nor has it the authority to substitute its views on the candidates for those of the selection committee."[205] Unlike grievances under collective agreements where, upon establishing the more senior employee is qualified or relatively equally qualified, the employee has a right to the position, the final decision in a competition for a non-union position in the public service involves an exercise of management discretion after a properly conducted competition.

199 *Vipari, ibid*; *Mitta, ibid* at paras 64 and 102.
200 *PSC Employment Policy*, above note 86, 8-29.
201 *Ibid*, 6-2.
202 *Vipari*, above note 185 at 15–16; *Mitta*, above note 192 at paras 63–64.
203 *Vipari, ibid*; *Mitta, ibid*.
204 *Majkot*, above note 188.
205 *Brander*, above note 189.

In a 1996 decision, Vice-Chair Willes stated "[t]he Board has no authority to place a civil servant in a position, but only to review the process of selection where an allegation of error or impropriety is made. This board lacks authority to provide the remedy of placement of a successful grievor in a position,"[206] but two years later he remedied a violation of a grievor's right to compete for a position by ordering that the grievor be given the position in issue or an equivalent position. In that case, with the passage of time, the incumbent's experience would not allow the grievor a fair opportunity if a competition was ordered.[207] Directing a competition was not an appropriate remedy in the circumstances. Directing the employer to give the grievor a position, rather than a specific position, avoided usurping the Civil Service Commission's (now the PSC's) jurisdiction, but provided an effective remedy.

A decision to hold a position vacant pending a re-organization or in anticipation of the need to redeploy surplus staff is not subject to review by the PSGB.[208] Management has the right, subject to the requirements of MBC directives (now the PSC *Employment Policy*), to determine the area of search.[209] Employees have no right to an interview.[210] Management may set and apply screening criteria and may fill positions without a competition in accordance with directives or policies providing for the redeployment of surplus staff or staff development programs. However, where a competition is subject to review by the PSGB, the employer will not be allowed to pre-empt the PSGB's decision by filling the position without competition.[211]

In reviewing individual competitions, the PSGB is not bound by, but will consider, the GSB jurisprudence. On the matter of consensus scoring, the practice of having all the members of a competition panel agree on a single score for each question, the PSGB has adopted the GSB's

---

206 *Gayle v Management Board Secretariat*, PSGB#P/0062/93, 1 March 1996.

207 *Itenson and Ministry of Community and Social Services*, PSGB#P/0005/94, 29 October 1998 at 12–13.

208 *Cohen and Ministry of the Environment*, PSGB#P/0015/85, 1 August 1986; *Frawley v Ontario (Ministry of Community and Social Services)*, 1989 CanLII 168 (ON PSGB) [*Frawley*].

209 *Smally et al and Ministry of Correctional Services*, PSGB#P/0019/87, 12 February 1988; *Anthony and Ministry of Community and Social Services*, PSGB#P/0022/94, 14 November 1995.

210 *McAdam*, above note 184; *Colacci and Ministry of Consumer and Commercial Relations*, PSGB#P/0912/82, 10 August 1982.

211 *Vipari*, above note 185 at 12–13.

view that the practice tends to be inappropriate and sufficiently serious to order a competition rerun.[212] Each member of a competition panel should record their individual evaluation of each interview question or item evaluated and the scoring of the competition should be determined on the basis of these scores. Individual flaws may be insufficient to warrant interfering in a competition result, but cumulatively may bring it into question.[213] Using a single reference is a flaw but alone does not bring the result of the competition into question. Having a member of a competition panel give an applicant a reference is not necessarily a flaw. However, where significant weight is given to references, only one reference is used and a panel member gives one applicant a reference, the competition will be fatally flawed.[214]

An employee with the right to grieve terms and conditions of employment may grieve the fairness of their treatment in a competition for a senior management position.[215] A member of a bargaining unit has no right to grieve a management competition before the PSGB,[216] even when they are acting in an excluded position.[217] The PSGB will protect a management employee's right to apply for a bargaining unit position, but it has no jurisdiction to review the selection process.[218] The GSB has exclusive jurisdiction over grievances regarding bargaining unit positions.[219] In effect, bargaining unit staff have no right to grieve competitions for non-bargaining unit positions and excluded employees have no right to challenge the selection process for bargaining unit positions.

E. PRACTICE AND PROCEDURE

The PSGB is subject to the *SPPA*. In the event of conflict between the *SPPA* or rules made under the *SPPA* and regulations made under the

212 *Majkot*, above note 188.
213 *Vipari*, above note 185.
214 *Ibid.*
215 *Simpson and Ministry of the Attorney General*, PSGB#P/0001/89, 13 June 1994.
216 *Lansey and Ministry of Correctional Services*, PSGB#P/0920/83, 28 November 1983 (Little); *Frawley*, above note 208; *DeMers v Consumer and Commercial Relations*, PSGB#P/0019/90, 9 September 1991; *Ihasz and Ministry of Finance*, PSGB#P/0004/01, 12 October 2001 at 3.
217 *Cartwright*, above note 14; *Roknic*, above note 14.
218 *Burt*, above note 11.
219 *Ibid.*

PSOA the regulations prevail.[220] The PSGB has made rules governing practice before the board. The rules authorize the PSGB to issue practice notes.[221] The process and time limits for making a complaint to the PSGB are governed by a *PSOA* regulation,[222] discussed above. The PSGB website added a "frequently asked questions" section in 2022 that gives specific plain language answers that complainants need to know when making a complaint.

When a hearing date is set on agreement of the parties the parties are expected to be available on the date unless extraordinary circumstances have arisen. When seeking an adjournment, a party is expected to seek the agreement of the opposing party. In the absence of extraordinary circumstances or agreement of the parties an adjournment may be denied.[223]

The practices and procedures before the PSGB are in general typical of labour and employment arbitrations and tribunal hearings. The PSGB members are appointed by order in council and are experienced labour arbitrators or practitioners. They sit as single person panels of the board.

While PSGB decisions are not binding on future panels the board will follow previous decisions on points of law and practice unless there is compelling reason not to. PSGB decisions are final,[224] subject to a right to reconsider.[225]

1) Reconsideration

The PSGB has adopted an approach to reconsideration similar to the OLRB for similar reasons.[226] Reconsideration is not an appeal or an opportunity to repair the deficiencies in a party's original case or to relitigate a case. It is available to correct an obvious error or address an important policy issue that was not given adequate attention or consideration in the original decision.[227]

---

220 *PSOA*, above note 1, s 23(1)2; *SPPA*, above note 26.

221 *PSGB Rules*, above note 29, r 4.

222 O Reg 378/07.

223 *Bartlett v Ontario (Solicitor General)*, 2022 CanLII 91066 (ON PSGB).

224 *PSOA*, above note 1, s 26 and *PSGB Rules*, above note 29, r 13.

225 *PSGB Rules*, above note 29, r 26.

226 *Baccega*, above note 178 at para 20.

227 *Ibid* at para 32.

2) Mediation

Mediation at the PSGB is a confidential, voluntary, and normally a mediation/arbitration process.[228] The board member that mediates will conduct a hearing if the mediation is unsuccessful and base any decision only on the evidence and submissions at the hearing.[229] The PSGB schedules in person mediations at its Toronto offices to reduce its costs.[230] Since mediation is voluntary, the employer can insist on proceeding with preliminary motions before considering mediation,[231] though it is common to engage in mediation while reserving the right to make a preliminary object if no settlement is reached.

3) Rules

The PSGB rules include forms for filing complaints with separate forms for complaints under the regulation to the *PSOA* and reprisal complaints under the *PSOA* itself and employer responses.[232] Complaints and responses may be amended with leave of the board.[233]

The rules give the PSGB broad scope for the scheduling, location, and format of hearings or consultations, requiring production of documents, witness statements, expert reports, particulars, and granting adjournments,[234] all of which are subject to the common law duty of administrative fairness. PSGB proceedings are generally not recorded but permission to use recording devices may be requested.[235] The board may also schedule case management meetings and now in virtually every case the board schedules a thirty- to sixty-minute meeting or call usually within a month, in accordance with PSGB Practice Note 2. Whether preliminary objections, if there are any, will be heard before or after a mediation will be decided at this case management meeting together

---

228 *Mously*, above note 92 at para 23.

229 *Barnes v Ontario (Solicitor General)*, 2021 CanLII 37097 (ON PSGB) at paras 25–28.

230 *Allen v Ontario (Community Safety and Correctional Services)*, 2015 CanLII 67821 (ON PSGB).

231 *Wilson*, above note 14 at para 8; *Stricko*, above note 40 at para 9.

232 *PSGB Rules*, above note 29, r 5, 6 & 7.

233 *Ibid*, r 8.

234 *Ibid*, r 12, 20, and 21–24.

235 PSGB *Practice Note* 6.

with whether motions will be argued in writing or in person and other pre-hearing issues.[236]

The board's rules allow consolidation of cases that raise a common issue or arise from a common transaction or other reason.[237] The board often deals with similar complaints by deciding a representative complaint that sets a precedent for the other similar matters. Where this is not acceptable to members of the group the board may consolidate the matters for purposes of hearing the common issue.[238]

The *SPPA* gives the PSGB the power to make interim orders[239] but not orders for interim reinstatement.[240]

4) Particulars

The PSGB may order a complainant to provide particulars of a complaint.[241] Such an order may be made at any time before the hearing is complete but are usually made as preliminary matters. Particulars must specify the "who, what, when, and where" of the factual allegations being asserted but not the actual evidence to be presented at a hearing.[242] They will be the facts that the PSGB will consider in dealing with requests for disclosure from the employer[243] and motions to dismiss a complaint as not disclosing a *prima facie* case, so they must address all the elements necessary to establish a right to a remedy. They must be sufficient and useful so "that the employer knows the case it has to meet."[244]

The PSGB will require complainants who have not provided sufficient particulars in a human rights complaint to the board to provide particulars that include "the identification of the specific prohibited ground(s) relied on under the *Code*, as well as any assertions of fact (the 'who, what, when, where') relied on by the Complainant in asserting

236 PSGB *Practice Note* 3.

237 *PSGB Rules*, above note 29, r 25.

238 *Bowmaster v Ontario (Solicitor General)*, 2020 CanLII 32998 (ON PSGB) at para 8.

239 *SPPA*, above note 26, s 16-1.

240 O Reg 378/07, s 14.

241 *PSGB Rules*, above note 29, r 12.

242 *Boucher v Ontario (Community Safety and Correctional Services)*, 2016 CanLII 7470 (ON PSGB) at para 4.

243 *Gardiner v Ontario (Ministry of Community Safety and Correctional Services)*, 2004 CanLII 55240 (ON PSGB) [*Gardiner*].

244 *Simon v Ontario (Labour)*, 2006 CanLII 42781 (ON PSGB) at motion 3 [*Simon*].

that they were discriminated against in violation of the *Code*."[245] A complaint will not be dismissed as not stating a *prima facie* case even if the allegations are vague, provided that deficiency can be remedied by an order for particulars at a later stage. Complainants are not required, in a systemic discrimination case, to include every element of the "who, what, when, where" formula so long as they provide a useful "synopsis of the factual basis for the case that the party intends to call."[246] The PSGB limits particulars of a course of harassment or discrimination to the three years prior to the incident that is the subject of a timely delivery of a notice of complaint.[247]

Where a complainant fails or refuses to provide adequate particulars the complaint should be dismissed without a hearing.[248]

5) Preliminary Motions to Dismiss: No Jurisdiction/*Prima Facie* Case

The PSGB must have jurisdiction over the complainant, the complaint, and the subject matter of the complaint. The complainant must be an employee entitled to bring a grievance to the PSGB. The complaint must have been filed in accordance with Regulation 378/07 or allege a reprisal under the political activity or disclosure of wrongdoing provisions. Finally, the complaint must allege a violation within the jurisdiction of the PSGB.

A viable case before the PSGB requires the complainant to establish three things:

1) An existing term or condition of employment
2) Facts establishing a breach of that term or condition
3) A connection between the breach and the remedy requested or some remedy within the board's jurisdiction[249]

---

245 *Reay v Ontario (Solicitor General)*, 2021 CanLII 119056 (ON PSGB) at para 4; *Bowmaster v Ontario (Solicitor General)*, 2021 CanLII 119326 (ON PSGB) at para 4.

246 *Simon*, above note 244, at motion 3.

247 *Simon*, *ibid*; see Chapter 6.

248 *Ibid*; *Gardiner*, above note 243; *Lawrence v Ontario (Solicitor General)*, 2021 CanLII 57975 (ON PSGB) [*Lawrence*]; *Dwyer v Ontario (Solicitor General)*, 2021 CanLII 82487 (ON PSGB).

249 *Hasted v Ontario (Solicitor General)*, 2019 CanLII 78782 (ON PSGB) at para 35 [*Hasted #2*]; *Allen*, above note 117; *Maiwand*, above note 136 at para 34.

In order to establish a *prima facie* case for discrimination, a complainant must provide particulars that if proven demonstrate that they (1) are covered by an enumerated ground, (2) were the subject of adverse treatment, and (3) the enumerated ground was a factor in their being subject to the alleged adverse treatment.[250] The mere fact that a non-racialized person was chosen over a racialized person for a job or that a person covered by an enumerated ground failed in a job competition is insufficient to establish a *prima facie* case for discrimination.[251] By contrast, the allegation that a member of an enumerated group got the highest score but lost while a non-racialized person with a much lower score was awarded a job in the competition would establish a *prima facie* case.[252]

The PSGB's rules permit the board to dismiss a complaint on its own motion without a hearing where the board finds that, assuming all the allegations in the complaint are true, the complainant would not be entitled to the orders or remedies requested.[253] The board may seek further particulars, information, or submissions before dismissing a complaint without a hearing and may act without further notice if the requested material is not provided by the date specified.[254]

If "there is no term or condition of employment, or overriding legal principle preventing the action complained of, the board has no basis to find a breach or award a remedy."[255] If the complaint does not allege such a term or condition of employment or legal principle, it may be dismissed on a preliminary motion by the employer.

Assignment to a particular class of position and the evaluation of an employee's performance are ordinarily at the discretion of the employer and not a basis for a PSGB complaint.[256] A complaint by managers that bargaining unit wage increases have narrowed the gap between the wages of supervisors and the people they supervise (commonly called wage compression) may be dismissed on a preliminary motion.[257] A

---

250 *Maiwand*, above note 136 at para 15.

251 *Ibid* at para 17; *Lawrence*, above note 248 at para 28.

252 *Paul*, above note 64. The jurisprudence on making out a *prima facie* case of discrimination is discussed in Chapter 6, Section C.

253 *PSGB Rules*, above note 29, r 15; *Taylor v Ontario (Community Safety and Correctional Services)*, 2015 CanLII 68786 (ON PSGB) at para 16.

254 PSGB *Practice Note* 1.

255 *Hugh MacDonald et al*, above note 147 at para 18; *Garratt #2*, above note 161.

256 *Maiwand*, above note 136 at para 37.

257 *Hugh MacDonald et al*, above note 147.

claim for overtime assignments under a protocol with a union that did not apply to the employee was dismissed as not stating a *prima facie* case.[258] A complaint alleging intensification of on-call duties and claiming standby pay was dismissed on a preliminary motion as not identifying a contractual provision entitling the employees to standby pay even assuming their duties had intensified.[259]

The board will dismiss complaints, except for those alleging reprisal for disclosure of wrongdoing or political activity, without further hearing if the complainant has missed a time limit or failed to give notice to the deputy minister or chair of the PSC when required by the regulations.[260]

In discipline and dismissal matters, the onus is on the employer, so assuming the complaint has been properly filed, the matter will proceed to mediation or a hearing where the employer must justify the discipline or dismissal.

If the particulars do not disclose facts that if proven make out a *prima facie* case, a motion to dismiss the complaint may be made by the employer. Complaints of reprisal without particulars of an allegation of political activity or disclosure of wrongdoing before the alleged reprisal would be subject to dismissal without further hearing.

6) Mootness

Motions to dismiss a matter as moot are addressed on the presumption that grievances referred to the PSGB will be arbitrated but the PSGB has a responsibility to ensure that both its resources and those of the parties are not expended on pointless or unnecessary litigation.[261] Consequently, the PSGB will find a matter to be moot and dismiss it where a decision will have no legal or practical effect.[262]

If the remedy requested has already been given or the PSGB lacks any ability to grant an effective remedy, the matter will be held to be

258 *Bazger #2*, above note 123.

259 *Johnston et al*, above note 113.

260 *Kurczak v Ontario (Solicitor General)*, 2021 CanLII 134967 (ON PSGB).

261 *Gibson v Ontario (Attorney General)*, 1999 CanLII 32153 (ON PSGB) [*Gibson*], citing *OPSEU and Ontario Realty Corp/Management Board Secretariat*, GSB#2024/97, 19 May 1998 at 17.

262 *Jones and Ministry of Correctional Services*, PSGB#P/0009/92, 30 November 1995 [*Jones*].

moot.[263] Where some limited remedy may be in issue, the PSGB will consider exercising its discretion to dismiss by balancing the presumption grievances should be heard on the merits, the nature of the dispute, the impact of the available remedies, and the costs, both monetary and otherwise, of continued litigation.[264] Even in the absence of any monetary loss or a formal characterization of a matter as disciplinary, a matter that may have a continuing impact on a grievor's reputation or their employment relationship will not be considered moot.[265]

The onus to establish mootness rests with the party alleging mootness, invariably the employer. This onus has been met where a grievance regarding a reprimand was not heard by the PSGB before the reprimand was removed from the grievor's file in the normal course after three years.[266] Where events subsequent to filing a grievance render the requested remedy redundant, the grievance becomes moot.[267] When it is clear that a grievor will not be returning to a workplace, their grievances relating to conditions in that workplace become moot.[268]

F. PUBLIC ACCESS TO HEARINGS AND ADJUDICATIVE RECORDS

The open court principle under section 2(b) of the *Canadian Charter of Rights and Freedoms* applies to administrative tribunals such as the PSGB.[269] The board is subject to the *SPPA*,[270] which requires public access to hearings unless the board determines there is an overriding public security or personal privacy interest that requires protection. The power of adjudicative tribunals to control their own processes includes the ability to "fashion their own mechanism for public access

263 *Wallace v Ontario (Community Safety and Correctional Services)*, 2015 CanLII 32427 (ON PSGB).

264 *Simlote and Ministry of Transportation*, PSGB#P/0009/91, P/0023/92, P/0033/92, and P/0032/93, 4 October 1996.

265 *Bardhan*, above note 170; *Hough v Ontario (Ministry of Community and Social Services)*, 1984 CanLII 37 (ON PSGB) [*Hough*]; *Mously*, above note 92; *Doyle 2018*, above note 93 at para 40.

266 *Jones*, above note 262; *Alemu*, above note 94 at para 10.

267 *Gibson*, above note 261; *Marshall v Ontario (Ministry of Health and Long-Term Care)*, 2005 CanLII 53202 (ON PSGB).

268 *Hough*, above note 265.

269 *CBC v Chief of Police*, 2021 ONSC 6935 at paras 27–29.

270 Above note 26, s 9.

to Adjudicative Records, and to make their own fine-tuned determinations of the correct balance between openness and privacy."[271] The process for non-parties to seek access to PSGB records is set out in Practice Note 5. A motion to limit press access would require notice to interested press organizations and would only be considered, if at all, to the extent necessary to protect the public interest at issue.[272]

In *Doyle v Ontario (Ministry of Municipal Affairs)*[273] the PSGB was asked to disclose to the press the submissions of the parties that included material relating to a disclosure of wrongdoing to the integrity commissioner. The board requested submissions from the integrity commissioner who indicated that assuring "whistleblowers" and witnesses in a wrongdoing investigation that their identities will, as far as possible, be kept confidential is of great importance and release of the information would be contrary to the confidentiality provisions in the *PSOA*. The commissioner claimed exclusive jurisdiction to make disclosures.[274] The PSGB held that the openness of hearings is not absolute, and the board had to balance "the open court principle with claims for confidentiality and privacy, according to the relevant legal and factual context . . . and may involve consideration of the provisions of applicable privacy and other statutes."

The PSGB distinguished between factual material common to the PSGB and commissioner processes and the commissioner's investigation and findings that were not made public. The board found the situation analogous to mediation where the process is kept confidential. The board had found there was no *prima facie* case so while disclosure might reveal the identity of participants in the commissioner's process, it was not needed to understand the board's decision. Disclosure was denied.

G. SETTLEMENTS

Minutes of settlement are a contract. They are subject to the normal rules of interpretation, including that the parties are to be held to the plain meaning of the words read in context unless the result would be

---

271 *Toronto Star v AG Ontario*, 2018 ONSC 2586 at para 49, citing *Doyle 2017*, above note 40 at para 71. The PSGB is not currently subject to the *Tribunal Adjudicative Records Act, 2019*, SO 2019, c 7, Sch 60.

272 *R v Toronto Star Newspapers et al*, 2003 CanLII 13331 (ON CA) at 7.

273 *Doyle 2017*, above note 40.

274 *PSOA*, above note 1, ss 112 and 130.

absurd or illegal or there is evidence that establishes that it was not a valid contract.[275] Proof of bad faith, duress, or fraud when a settlement is made would bring the validity of a settlement into question.[276] The PSGB has indicated that settlements signed voluntarily must be upheld, "or workplace parties would not be able to have confidence in the finality of agreements made and their ability to govern their affairs accordingly. The question of finality of agreements is fundamental to the entire legal system and is especially important in the ongoing operation of any workplace."[277] It is the PSGB's duty to enforce valid settlements.[278]

A settlement forecloses "any further dispute concerning the facts put in issue by the settled grievances, or remedy for those facts."[279] Similarly, the PSGB has declined to allow evidence in respect of alleged discrimination and harassment that have been the subject of a settlement in a different forum.[280] A settlement may resolve matters beyond those before the board at the time of the settlement.[281]

H. REMEDIES

The PSGB's "remedial jurisdiction flows from the Board's statutory mandate to provide a final resolution of employment disputes of those members of the Ontario Public Service falling within its jurisdiction."[282] Its role is remedial, so orders must be directed toward ending or compensating violations of a complainant's rights.[283] The PSGB attempts to put a successful complainant in a position as close to what they would have enjoyed had the violation not occurred.

---

275 *Naccarato v Ontario (Attorney General)*, 2015 CanLII 89904 (ON PSGB) at para 15.

276 *Ibid* at para 16.

277 *Ibid* at para 21, quoting *De Boer v Ontario (Ministry of Community Safety and Correctional Services)*, 2006 CanLII 26475 (ON PSGB) and *Younger v Ontario (Environment)*, 2007 CanLII 30471 (ON PSGB).

278 *Ibid.*

279 *Chyczij v Ontario (Labour)*, 2008 CanLII 70543 (ON PSGB).

280 *Simon*, above note 244.

281 *Bingham v Ontario (Government Services)*, 2011 CanLII 10255 (ON PSGB) at para 22; *Antoncic v Ontario (Community Safety and Correctional Services)*, 2009 CanLII 15649 (ON PSGB).

282 *Charlton*, above note 172.

283 *Morrison*, above note 4.

The *PSOA* and regulations put specific limitations on the PSGB's remedial authority. The PSGB has no jurisdiction to make orders altering terms of employment established under a collective agreement.[284] Its authority to reinstate a person who has abused a resident or client is restricted.[285] The PSGB has no authority to determine grievances regarding classification of a position or performance appraisals, and it does not, as a result, have authority to make an order regarding classification of positions, the conducting of performance appraisals, or the alteration of an appraisal.[286] While the PSGB cannot remedy a complaint about the conduct of a performance assessment, where loss of performance pay results from the violation of another term or condition of employment a damage award may compensate for the lost performance pay.[287]

The PSGB may provide declaratory relief[288] and may order the employer to cease and desist,[289] remove documents from files,[290] restore attendance credits,[291] pay out attendance credits,[292] reimburse expenses,[293] and pay interest.[294] The PSGB does not view ordered apologies as a meaningful or appropriate remedy.[295]

Within its jurisdiction the PSGB has taken a broad view of its remedial powers. "After a breach, the focus is on what the aggrieved party lost as a result of the breach, i.e. the difference between what he would have received if the contract had been kept and what he actually received,"[296] including the lost opportunity to earn overtime income.[297]

---

284 *Burt*, above note 11.

285 *PSOA*, above note 1, s 25; see the discussion of discipline and dismissal above.

286 O Reg 378/07, s 4(2)2, 4, and 5.

287 *Cardoza*, above note 91 at paras 121–24.

288 *Hough*, above note 265; *MacDonald v Ontario (Community Safety and Correctional Services)*, 2014 CanLII 8244 (ON PSGB) [*MacDonald*].

289 *Girling v Ontario (Ministry of the Solicitor General and Correctional Services)*, 2002 CanLII 45638 (ON PSGB) [*Girling*].

290 *Kanga and Ministry of Health*, PSGB#P/0007 and 0010/86, 28 October 1991 [*Kanga #3*].

291 *Ibid.*

292 *Ibid.*

293 *Sillman and Ministry of Community and Social Services*, PSGB#P/0003/88, 28 April 1989 (including union dues); *Kanga #3*, *ibid* (travel expenses).

294 *Kanga #3*, *ibid*; *MacDonald*, above note 288.

295 *Girling*, above note 289.

296 *Cardoza*, above note 91 at para 120.

297 *Ibid.*

Where an award includes compensation for lost benefit coverage, the calculation may be based on the cost to the employee of not having coverage, rather than the premium cost.[298] While the PSGB may not appoint a grievor to a specific position where reinstatement is not possible following an improper transfer, it may order the employer to appoint the grievor to a position that is suitable and of interest to the grievor.[299] In response to discrimination the PSGB may issue a "direction that the employer make all reasonable efforts to find a position comparable in responsibility and remuneration to the position held by the grievor but in a work environment free of any threat of racial harassment."[300]

Punitive damages are not available from the PSGB.[301] The regulations provide broad remedial authority, but no indication of authority to punish.[302] The purpose of punitive damages is to express the court's condemnation and punish, not compensate. The PSGB draws its jurisdiction from statute, not common law. The authority to resolve a grievance does not provide authority to express condemnation or impose retribution on the provincial treasury.[303] Punitive damages are viewed as detrimental to ongoing employment relationships.[304] Clear legislative direction would be required to give the PSGB jurisdiction to award punitive damages. No such direction exists. Broad remedial authority is provided in the *PSOA* to remedy reprisals in respect of disclosure of wrongdoing and political activity, but punitive damages are expressly excluded.[305]

The PSGB has authority to and will order aggravated damages.[306] Such damages are compensatory and thus distinct from punitive damages. They recognize extraordinary or non-pecuniary damages, such as the intangible losses associated with mental distress or humiliation or injury to one's dignity. Grievors have the onus of proving both that aggravated damages are warranted and the basis for calculating the

298 *Rackham and Ministry of the Solicitor General and Correctional Services*, PSGB#P/0020/91, 14 August 1996.
299 *Kanga #2*, above note 164.
300 *Charlton*, above note 172.
301 *Bardhan*, above note 170; *Morrison*, above note 4.
302 *A Grievor and Ministry of Health*, PSGB#P/0014/90, 13 August 1991.
303 *Morrison*, above note 4.
304 *Ibid.*
305 *PSOA*, above note 1, ss 104(10) and 140(11).
306 *Morrison*, above note 4.

quantum of damages, which may place their health and emotional status in issue when it would otherwise be irrelevant.[307]

Like courts and other administrative tribunals, the PSGB does not have jurisdiction to award damages for claims that are within the jurisdiction of the Workplace Safety and Insurance Board (WSIB), including compensation for mental distress as a result of workplace harassment.[308] Early cases awarding damages for matters compensable by the WSIB are implicitly overruled. However, the PSGB has jurisdiction to address claims for violation of an employee's dignity interest under the *HRC* that are not compensated for by the WSIB.[309] The PSGB awarded aggravated damages of $1,000 to redress the indignity and distress resulting from the violation of the grievor's privacy interest by an unannounced, unwarranted search of his office,[310] and in a second case awarded $5,000 in damages for "the loss of peace of mind involved in the breach of the fair process provisions" protecting respondents in *Workplace Discrimination and Harassment Policy* investigations.[311]

1) Interim Relief

Proceedings before the PSGB are subject to the *SPPA*.[312] That Act grants the PSGB power to issue interim orders, which includes the power to provide substantive interim relief.[313] This broad power is limited by the regulations under the *PSOA* that prevent the PSGB from ordering interim reinstatement of a person as an employee.[314]

---

307 *Ibid.*

308 This issue is discussed at length in Chapter 6, including detailed discussion of the leading case of *Ontario Public Service Employees Union (Monk et al) v Ontario (Community Safety and Correctional Services and Ministry of Children and Youth Services)*, 2010 CanLII 28621 (ON GSB), aff'd 2012 ONSC 2348, aff'd 2013 ONCA 406. See also *Bardhan*, above note 170; *Parrack v Ontario (Community Safety and Correctional Services)*, 2008 CanLII 70546 (ON PSGB) [*Parrack*]; and *Hasted #2*, above note 249 at para 24.

309 *Parrack*, *ibid*; *Hasted #2*, *ibid* at para 26.

310 *Morrison v Ontario (Human Rights Commission)*, PSGB#P/0037/94, P/0037/95, 8 December 1998.

311 *Cardoza*, above note 91.

312 *PSOA* above note 1, s 23(1).

313 *SPPA*, above note 26, s 16-1, as discussed in *Mueller v Ontario (Community Safety and Correctional Services)*, 2018 CanLII 109218 (ON PSGB) at para 24 [*Mueller*].

314 O Reg 378/07, s 14.

The PSGB has recognized that substantive interim relief is an extraordinary remedy and the person seeking such an order has the onus to establish that it is necessary.[315] The PSGB will not grant interim relief when its broad remedial power will be sufficient to grant appropriate relief in the event of the complainant's success after a hearing on the merits.[316]

2) Costs

The board's policy was that costs would only be awarded in the most egregious cases.[317] There appear to have been only two cases where costs were awarded, both of which were decided under the now repealed *PSA*.[318]

The PSGB does not presently have jurisdiction to award costs. Since the *PSOA* was enacted the PSGB has drawn its authority from that Act and has been subject to the *SPPA* section 17.1, which only permits tribunals to order costs when "a party has been unreasonable, frivolous or vexatious or a party has acted in bad faith; and the tribunal has made rules" governing the ordering of costs.[319] The PSGB has no such rules.

The *PSOA* expressly prohibits the ordering of costs in reprisal complaints under the disclosure of wrongdoing and political activity provisions.[320]

---

315 *Mueller*, above note 313 at para 25.

316 *Ibid* at para 27; *Graham v Ontario (Community Safety and Correctional Services)*, 2013 CanLII 57074 (ON PSGB).

317 *Potter*, above note 100 at para 16; *Cardoza*, above note 91.

318 *Callaghan v Ontario (Ministry of Agriculture and Food)*, 1992 CanLII 2748 (ON PSGB); *Girling*, above note 289.

319 *Becker Milk Company Ltd, Re*, 2005 CanLII 38894 (ON SCDC) at para 9; *MacDonald v Downtown Health Club for Women*, 2009 HRTO 1647; *Barrington v The Institute of Chartered Accountants of Ontario*, 2010 ONSC 338 at para 258; *Registrar REBBA v Jolly*, 2016 ONSC 2338.

320 *PSOA*, above note 1, ss 104 and 140.

CHAPTER THIRTEEN

Access to the Courts

A. SUMMARY

This chapter's primary focus is access by non-unionized public servants and government appointees to the courts to enforce the terms of their employment through actions for breach of employment contracts (wrongful dismissal) and applications for judicial review to enforce statutory rights or the common law duty of fairness. The nature and scope of the exclusion of unionized employees from access to the courts in favour of grievance and arbitration processes are also reviewed.

The Canadian law governing employment by the Crown begins with British common law that gave the Crown essentially unfettered control over almost all its employees and office holders.[1] With the dissolution of the British Empire following the Second World War and the ending of appeals to the Judicial Committee of the British Privy Council in 1950, Canadian courts initially modified the common law to reflect a more balanced approach to the interests of the Crown and its employees. By the dawn of the twenty-first century, the Supreme Court was moving to fundamentally transform the common law governing employment by the state to reflect the needs of a diverse democratic society. At the same time the relationship between Canadian governments and their

---

1 *Shenton v Smith*, [1895] AC 229 (PC) at 234–35: "If any public servant considers that he has been dismissed unjustly, his remedy is not by a lawsuit, but by an appeal of an official or political kind."

employees and appointees was increasingly governed by statute and is of course still evolving.

The right of non-unionized members of the Ontario Public Service (OPS)[2] or government appointees to sue the Crown in contract is a recent development. Employees of the Crown and appointed office holders were considered to hold their employment or office at pleasure, dismissible without notice or compensation, until the late 1990s. Public servants not included in a bargaining unit, and government appointees, now have a contract of employment at common law that may be enforced in court under the regular law of contract.[3] The *Public Service of Ontario Act, 2006* (*PSOA*) and regulations provide for complaints to the Public Service Grievance Board (PSGB) against dismissal for cause by most public servants employed directly by the Crown.[4] The Court of Appeal has held that the courts will exercise concurrent jurisdiction with the PSGB at least in respect of certain dismissals.[5]

Office holders will normally be limited to seeking damages under their employment contract and precluded from seeking judicial review of their termination.[6] In the event an office holder is appointed at pleasure or is appointed on good behaviour or has some statutory procedural protection, they have the right to procedural fairness in the event of termination during the term of their appointment, enforceable on judicial review. Appointees to adjudicative boards do not have constitutional protections analogous to judges.[7] Whether they have administrative law protections will depend on the statutory context.[8]

2 OPS refers to direct employees of the Crown technically persons appointed under the authority of the Public Service Commission under Part III of the *Public Service of Ontario Act, 2006*, SO 2006, c 35, Sch A [*PSOA*], discussed in Chapter 2 section B(1).

3 *Wells v Newfoundland*, [1999] 3 SCR 199 at para 24 [*Wells*]; *Dunsmuir v New Brunswick*, 2008 SCC 9 at para 113 [*Dunsmuir*].

4 *PSOA*, above note 2, as discussed in Chapter 12 section B.

5 *Burgess v Ontario (Ministry of Health)*, 2001 CanLII 24073 (ON CA) at paras 32–34 [*Burgess*]; see also *Benedict v Ontario*, 2000 CanLII 22713 (ON SC) [*Benedict*]; *Preston v Ontario (Education)*, 2021 CanLII 71622 (ON PSGB) at para 37 [*Preston (PSGB)*].

6 *Dunsmuir*, above note 3.

7 *Ocean Port Hotel Ltd v British Columbia (General Manager, Liquor Control and Licensing Branch)*, 2001 SCC 52 at para 23 [*Ocean Port*].

8 *Ibid* at para 24.

The terms of employment of unionized public servants are governed by statute which, with limited exceptions, excludes the courts in favour of grievance and arbitration processes.[9] The employment of non-commissioned Ontario Provincial Police officers is also statutory and similarly excludes access to the courts.[10] Though not subject to collective bargaining legislation, the Crown's lawyers have collectively bargained terms of employment enforceable through private arbitration.[11]

B. CONTEXT

The *Constitution Act, 1867* did not address the employment of public servants in any detail.[12] Ontario, as representative of the Crown within its jurisdiction, had the authority of the Crown to employ public servants and appoint officers.[13] Ontario was part of the British Empire until it dissolved following the Second World War. Appeal from Canadian courts to the Judicial Committee of the British Privy Council was not ended until 1949,[14] so Canadian common law was British common law until then. Canada's judges and lawyers were trained in the common law of the British Empire, so it endured in Canada long after 1950. This was significant for the common law governing public employment, which was designed for a public service that ruled a class-ridden colonial empire. The Crown had largely unfettered control over its employees and office holders. With very few exceptions, Crown employees and office holders were engaged "at pleasure," which conflated the right to dismiss and the terms of a dismissal, granting complete discretion to the Crown. Those few appointments that were on good behaviour attracted

---

9 *Nelson v Ontario*, 2020 ONCA 751, leave to appeal ref'd 2021 CanLII 112316 (SCC) [*Nelson*].

10 *Rivers v Waterloo Regional Police Services Board*, 2019 ONCA 267, leave to appeal ref'd 2019 CanLII 99448 (SCC) [*Rivers*]; *Abbott v Collins*, 2003 CanLII 46127 (ON CA) [*Abbott*].

11 *Nelson et al v Her Majesty the Queen in Right of Ontario et al*, 2019 ONSC 5415 [*Nelson et al*]; see the discussion of the bargaining by associations of Ontario government lawyers in Chapter 4.

12 *Constitution Act, 1867* (UK), 30 & 31 Vict, c 3, reprinted in RSC 1985, App II, No 5, s 134 [*Constitution Act, 1867*]. See the discussion of the constitutional treatment of the employment of public servants in Chapter 1.

13 *Verreault (JE) & Fils Ltée v Attorney General (Quebec)*, [1977] 1 SCR 41 at 47 [*Verreault*].

14 *Supreme Court Act, 1949*, 13 Geo VI, c 37.

the right to natural justice, meaning at the time an entitlement to an almost court-like process, making its application to most administrative decisions impractical if not impossible.

Between 1978 and 2008 the Canadian courts modernized Canadian public sector employment law, first by introducing the variable standard of fairness to judicial review of the termination of office holders, then by applying the normal law of employment contracts to separate the right of the Crown to terminate its employees and office holders from the terms of dismissal. As the courts were moving to modernize the common law, legislatures were increasingly replacing or modifying the common law with statutory provisions. In Ontario the right to appoint at pleasure was expressly preserved.

The growth of the administrative justice system raised the question of the extent to which it was or should be independent from government. The suggestion that appointees to adjudicative boards may have constitutional protections analogous to judges was raised and has been rejected. Express statutory protections such as legislated lengths of appointments on good behaviour have been an option but in practice provisions of this nature are rare in Ontario. However, the courts have been willing to infer that adjudicative appointments for a fixed term are on good behaviour. The extent to which courts will entertain an application for judicial review of the termination of an appointee will rest on the interpretation of the governing statute.

1) Modernizing the Common Law: *Nicholson* to *Dunsmuir* (1978–2008)

Lord Reid, in the often-cited 1963 English House of Lords decision of *Ridge v Baldwin*,[15] divided the possible common law employment relationships with the Crown into three categories:

1) the master and servant relationship, which could be terminated by the Crown without notice, compensation, or reasons
2) the office held at pleasure, where no duty to act fairly exists, since the employer can decide to terminate the employment for no other reason than their displeasure

---

15 [1963] 2 All ER 66 at 71–72 (HL) [*Ridge v Baldwin*], cited in *Nicholson v Haldimand-Norfolk Regional Board of Commissioners of Police*, [1979] 1 SCR 311 [*Nicholson*]; *Knight v Indian Head School Division No 19*, [1990] 1 SCR 653 [*Knight*], among many others.

3) the office from which the employee cannot be removed except for cause, where the office holder was entitled to natural justice before the employer could dismiss for cause

The legal rights of persons employed by the Crown as an employee subject to master and servant law or as an office holder at pleasure were the same though the social status of officers was significantly higher.

Historically, employment in the public service in common law jurisdictions fell into the first or second category.[16] The judicial view was that since employment by the Crown was exclusively for the good of the public, it was essential for the public good that the Crown should be able to end the employment as it saw fit, except in certain exceptional cases.[17] The Crown could not only terminate, but could also reassign, demote, or suspend an employee at pleasure.[18] Even fixed-term contracts were deemed to be terminable at pleasure.[19] In the 1930s, the Privy Council rejected the view that contract formed no part of the relationship between the Crown and its employees, but confirmed the traditional judicial view that an employment relationship with the Crown was at pleasure unless there was clear provision to the contrary in the statute or the appointment document.[20] As a result, Ontario courts did not apply the common law of contract to the dismissal of those serving the Crown until the end of the twentieth century.[21]

The situation began to change in the 1970s when the *Crown Employees Collective Bargaining Act*[22] was passed, making the employment of bargaining unit employees entirely statutory, both removing bargaining unit employees from the jurisdiction of the courts and providing them job security rights never previously available to public

---

16 *Ridge v Baldwin*, *ibid* at 65: "Apart from judges and others whose tenure of office is governed by statute, all servants and officers of the Crown hold office at pleasure."

17 *Dunn v The Queen*, [1896] 1 QB 116 at 120 [*Dunn*].

18 *Mills v Alberta*, [1986] 5 WWR 567 (Alta CA) at 570.

19 *Dunn*, above note 17.

20 *Reilly v The King*, 1933 CanLII 379 (UK JCPC) [*Reilly*].

21 In *Clarke v Ontario (Attorney General)*, [1966] 1 OR 539 (CA), the court held that, notwithstanding the terms of the Ontario *Public Service Act*, SO 1961–62, c 121, the Cabinet retained the power to dismiss members of the public service at pleasure. *Clarke* was still the law in Ontario in the 1990s; see *Malone v The Queen* (1983), 45 OR (2d) 206 (HCJ), leave to appeal ref'd; *Edgecombe v Ontario (Attorney General)*, [1995] OJ No 1761 (Gen Div).

22 SO 1972, c 67.

servants. In *Nicholson*,[23] the Supreme Court criticized the concept of appointment at pleasure as anachronistic but did not overrule the traditional law. The Court decided that Nicholson was entitled to fairness, a more flexible standard than the rigid requirement of natural justice, because he was an office holder subject to dismissal for cause.[24]

In 1980, the Supreme Court began to balance the relationship between the Canadian state and its employees by finding that a casual government employee could sue in contract for unpaid wages but declined to extend this finding to government employees generally.[25] The Court's reasoning is from another time:

> It is also important to note that in Anglo-Canadian law, the relationship between a civil servant and his employer is not, strictly speaking, a relationship with an abstract being, the State: it is a relationship with a relatively more concrete entity, the Crown, which "personifies the state," . . . The Crown is also the Sovereign, a physical person who, in addition to the prerogative, enjoys a general capacity to contract in accordance with the rule of ordinary law.

A year later Laskin CJ in obiter comments called dismissal "at pleasure" an anachronism and suggested it could be displaced by a contrary provision in an "engagement."[26]

In 1990, the new doctrine of a variable concept of fairness allowed the Supreme Court in *Knight v Indian Head School Division No 19*[27] to extend the right to fairness before termination at pleasure to office holders, but not other public servants.[28] The case included a dissent arguing the matter was appropriately addressed as one of employment

---

23 *Nicholson*, above note 15. An "engagement," it would seem, is what Crown employees had before the courts were sure they had an employment contract.

24 The decision in *Ridge v Baldwin*, above note 15, had expanded the requirement of natural justice to certain administrative decision. *Nicholson*, above note 15, by applying a more flexible standard of fairness signaled the end of court like natural justice or nothing.

25 *Attorney General of Quebec v Labrecque et al*, [1980] 2 SCR 1057.

26 *Nova Scotia Government Employees Association et al v Civil Service Commission of Nova Scotia et al*, [1981] 1 SCR 211 at 222–23.

27 *Knight*, above note 15.

28 *Alberta Union of Provincial Employees v Alberta*, 2000 ABQB 600 at para 22. "The fact that one of the parties to the employment contract is a public authority does not *per se* inject any element of public law": *R v Post Office, ex p Byrne*, [1975] ICR 221.

and that there must be some statutory basis for applying the doctrine of fairness to the termination of an employee.

Meanwhile, the Ontario courts continued to wrestle with applying an evolving common law. *Murphy v Ontario (Attorney General)*[29] concerned the termination without cause of four members of the board of Ontario Hydro. The governing legislation specified a fixed term and provided for removal for cause. The court held that those provisions did not permit termination without cause. The employment law doctrine that a court will not order specific performance of a contract for personal service did not apply since the matter was a judicial review of an order in council (OIC), not an action to enforce an employment contract.

The 1998 Ontario Court of Appeal decisions in *Hewat v Ontario*[30] and *Dewar v Ontario*[31] addressed appeals from the successful judicial review of OICs terminating the fixed-term appointments of members of a police commission and the Ontario Labour Relations Board (OLRB) mid-term. The Divisional Court quashed the OICs but ordered damages consistent with a remedy for wrongful dismissal. The Divisional Court followed *Preston v British Columbia*,[32] a decision of the BC Court of Appeal that treated judicial review of the termination of a fixed-term OIC as essentially an action for wrongful dismissal where the employer may terminate the employment but must pay damages for the appointees lost wages to the end of the fixed term.

The applicants in *Hewat* argued that treating the matter as essentially actions for contractual damages failed to address what appeared to be an undermining of the independence and perception of impartiality of the OLRB, an important adjudicative tribunal. The Court of Appeal accepted the argument and simply quashed the OIC terminating the applicants' appointments, presumably entitling them to their lost wages. The court declined to order reinstatement since the appointments had expired, were close to expiry, or had been filled. In *Dewar* the Court of Appeal did not vary the Divisional Court's order but rejected the Crown's appeal on the basis that the Crown was precluded from terminating fixed-term appointments mid-term without cause.

---

29 1996 CanLII 7968 (ON SC).

30 1998 CanLII 3393 (ON CA) [*Hewat*].

31 1998 CanLII 2985 (ON CA).

32 1994 CanLII 877 (BC CA).

Then, in 1999 the Supreme Court in *Wells v Newfoundland*[33] dealt with the case of an appointee on good behaviour whose office was eliminated by statute. Historically an office holder in those circumstances had no right to compensation.[34] *Wells* held that office holders engaged on terms typical of an employment relationship had a contract of employment. The elimination of the office holder's position terminated the contract but did not, unless the legislation provided so expressly, deprive the office holder of the right to damages under their employment contract. In reaching this decision the Supreme Court found that the legal relationship between office holders and the state was contractual, except for judges, ministers of the Crown, and others who fulfill constitutionally defined roles the terms of which are dictated by the terms and conventions of the Constitution. The decision in *Wells* did not preclude office holders from seeking public law remedies for the failure to provide them fairness in making decisions to terminate an appointment. The decision seemed to suggest that contractual, rather than public law remedies, were to be preferred.[35]

In the 2008 decision in *Dunsmuir v New Brunswick*,[36] the Supreme Court revisited the question of the application of public law fairness to decisions to terminate office holders. The case concerned the dismissal without cause, but with pay in lieu of notice, of David Dunsmuir, an employee appointed under the New Brunswick *Civil Service Act*.[37] He was also appointed by OIC to a number of statutory court offices for the Judicial District of Fredericton. The *Civil Service Act* specified that dismissals of employees under that Act were "governed by the ordinary rules of contract."[38] Mr. Dunsmuir grieved his dismissal to arbitration where he was successful in obtaining an order declaring his dismissal void *ab initio*. The arbitrator relied on *Knight* to find that Mr. Dunsmuir's employment was "hybrid in character," both an employee under statute and an office holder "at pleasure," entitling him to fairness prior to dismissal. The arbitrator found that he had not been accorded the

33 *Wells* above note 3.
34 *Reilly*, above note 20.
35 David Mullan, *Administrative Law* (Toronto: Irwin Law, 2001) at 18.
36 *Dunsmuir*, above note 3.
37 SNB 1984, c C-5.1.
38 *Ibid*, s 20.

required fairness.[39] The Crown was successful on judicial review of the arbitrator at both the Court of Queen's Bench and the Court of Appeal.

The Supreme Court took advantage of the case to revise the standard of review generally and, most significantly for our purposes, the common law applicable to the dismissal of office holders.[40] While the Court affirmed that "public decision makers are required to act fairly in coming to decisions that affect the rights, privileges or interests of an individual,"[41] the ordinary law of contract, not the public law duty of fairness, was found to apply to the termination of office holders that have a contract of employment.[42] In the circumstances of the case the Crown was entitled to dismiss Mr. Dunsmuir without giving a reason or having regard for procedural fairness.[43] To the extent that *Knight* had applied the public law doctrine of fairness to employee office holders it was expressly overruled.[44] Mr. Dunsmuir's remedy was limited to ordinary contractual remedies,[45] which did not include reinstatement.[46] He was awarded eight months pay in lieu of notice.

2) Implications for Current Law

The implications for members of the OPS that also hold an appointment to an office is clear: they have no public law entitlement to procedural fairness on dismissal.[47] The application to OIC appointees to boards, agencies, and commissions is more qualified.

Dunsmuir held that the dismissal of a public employee should be viewed as a typical employment law dispute. However, a public law duty of fairness will still apply where a public employee is not protected by a contract of employment. This is the case with judges, ministers of the Crown, and others who "fulfill constitutionally defined state roles"

39 *Dunsmuir*, above note 3 at para 15.

40 *Ibid* at paras 24 & 25.

41 *Ibid at* paras 79 and 82. In *Canada (Attorney General) v Mavi*, 2011 SCC 30 at para 51, *Dunsmuir* was described as creating a "rather narrow *Dunsmuir* employment contract exception from the obligation of procedural fairness" not intended to otherwise diminish the requirements of procedural fairness.

42 *Dunsmuir*, above note 3 at para 112.

43 *Ibid* at para 117.

44 *Ibid* at para 114.

45 *Ibid* at para 113.

46 *Ibid* at para 108.

47 *Redmond v Hamilton (City)*, 2008 CanLII 67892 (ON SCDC).

and may also apply to public office holders expressly appointed to hold office "at pleasure." The Ontario *Legislation Act, 2006*[48] authorizes appointments at pleasure and that power is regularly used in making appointments to non-adjudicative bodies. A duty of fairness may also flow by necessary implication from a statutory provision governing an appointment. The Supreme Court cited as an example a case where an office holder was entitled to be given three weeks' notice of a motion to dismiss them, implying a right to be heard in response to the motion.[49]

Dunsmuir created three types of appointee office holders for purposes of judicial review for fairness: appointees at pleasure with no common law contractual rights on dismissal but some right to fairness, appointees on good behaviour or with a legislated right to fairness on dismissal, and appointees employed on contract express or implied with no access to judicial review. The facts in *Wells* and *Dunsmuir* did not represent the spectrum of positions filled by appointees or the concerns that mid-term dismissal may raise. They addressed cases where the issues were those typical of employment contracts. *Wells* involved the financial impact of the elimination by statute of an appointee's position. *Dunsmuir* involved the termination of an employee that was by statute subject to the common law of employment on dismissal but held "offices" as an incident of his employment. These cases did not address the concerns about the impact of mid-term dismissal of an appointee to an adjudicative or regulatory board or agency where independence will be a practical and possibly a legal concern of not only the appointees but parties before the board or agency and potentially the public.

C. ACTIONS FOR WRONGFUL DISMISSAL

Public servants including appointees have a contract of employment express or implied enforceable by a civil action under the common law of employment unless they fill constitutionally defined roles, are expressly employed at pleasure, or are subject to collective bargaining legislation or other terms that exclude applications to the courts on dismissal. While non-unionized public servants' right to sue for wrongful dismissal seems established, the existence of the right to complain to the PSGB raises the question of whether the courts should defer to that process.

48 SO 2006, c 21, Sch F, s 76(1).

49 *Dunsmuir*, above note 3 at paras 115–16.

1) Non-unionized Members of the OPS

a) Concurrent Jurisdiction of Courts with the PSGB

Wells established that "the general law of contract will apply unless specifically superseded by explicit terms in the statute or the agreement."[50] Persons retained directly by the government outside the scope of the *PSOA* are governed by common law contractual arrangements, which are enforceable through the courts. The terms of employment of non-unionized members of the OPS are largely determined by legislation and Management Board of Cabinet (MBC) and Public Service Commission directives that are subject, in many respects, to enforcement through complaints to the PSGB.

The PSGB may hear complaints regarding dismissal for cause and discipline.[51] With some significant exceptions it may also hear complaints about working conditions. Members of the senior management group (SMG) within the public service can grieve discipline and dismissal for cause but not working conditions or dismissal without cause.

The courts retain residual jurisdiction to enforce employees' contractual rights unless explicitly excluded by legislation.[52] The Supreme Court has favoured what it calls the exclusive jurisdiction model in determining the jurisdiction of tribunals and the courts where an issue appears to fall within the jurisdiction of more than one tribunal or a tribunal and the courts.[53] Even where the courts retain residual concurrent jurisdiction in contract over a matter that can be adequately addressed by an administrative appeal process, the Supreme Court has indicated that the courts should decline to hear the matter and allow it to be addressed by the applicable administrative appeal process.[54]

The *PSOA* does not explicitly exclude the courts' jurisdiction. Thus, residual jurisdiction exists for Ontario courts to enforce non-unionized public servants' contractual rights. Even where the complaint process leading to arbitration at the PSGB applies, the process is not written in terms that necessarily preclude access to the courts, leaving open

---

50 *Wells*, above note 3 at para 30.

51 The jurisdiction of the PSGB is reviewed in detail in Chapter 12.

52 *Vaughan v Canada*, 2005 SCC 11 at paras 2 and 27–29 [*Vaughan*].

53 *Weber v Ontario Hydro*, [1995] 2 SCR 929 [*Weber*]; *Regina Police Assn Inc v Regina (City) Board of Police Commissioners*, 2000 SCC 14 [*Regina Police Assn*]; *Vaughan*, above note 52.

54 *Vaughan*, *ibid* at paras 33–42.

the question of when the courts will choose to exercise their residual jurisdiction.[55]

The caselaw is not straightforward. *Benedict v Ontario*[56] involved a former SMG member employed under the *Public Service Act* (*PSA*) who was not entitled to grieve changes to his working conditions. His position was eliminated during a reorganization, and he opted for early retirement but subsequently sued for damages and declaratory relief alleging constructive dismissal. Since he had resigned for purposes of the *PSA*, he fell outside the jurisdiction of the PSGB to hear a complaint of dismissal under the *PSA*. The court facilitated access to a remedy by finding that a public servant in Mr. Benedict's position could sue, basing their claim on the doctrine of constructive dismissal since they could not otherwise grieve the change to their working conditions.

In *Burgess*, the Court of Appeal allowed a non-unionized public servant who was entitled to grieve dismissal for cause to the PSGB to bring a contractual claim for unjust dismissal in court following his release under section 22(4) of the *PSA* after being declared surplus. The PSGB was given express authority to hear grievances concerning dismissal for cause under section 22(3) of the *PSA*, but there was no similar reference to a release under section 22(4) of the *PSA*. The court found that the PSGB did have jurisdiction to deal with allegations of a disguised dismissal, as was alleged by Mr. Burgess, but the courts were also an appropriate forum to deal with such allegations and ought not to defer to the grievance process.

The court in *Burgess* based its decision on four considerations. Courts have extensive expertise in wrongful dismissal matters. The legislation does not express a clear preference for the PSGB given the failure to grant express authority to review releases without cause on reasonable notice under section 22(4).[57] The use of the word "may" in granting the right to grieve suggests the PSGB process is optional. The decision in *Wells* requires that there be an "explicit term" to abrogate employees' right to challenge court their termination for breach of contract,[58] and it is not present. The court found no such "explicit terms" preventing access to the courts and no explicit terms granting

55 *Burgess*, above note 5; *Vaughan*, *ibid*.

56 *Benedict*, above note 5.

57 The *PSOA*, above note 2, also authorizes dismissal without cause on reasonable notice at s 38 and O Reg 378/07, s 4(2)3 specifically precludes review by the PSGB.

58 *Burgess*, above note 5 at paras 37–45.

jurisdiction to PSGB over terminations not expressly made for cause. Consequently, the court should not defer claims in the nature of Mr. Burgess's to the PSGB.

There is reason to question this reasoning. In dealing with similar questions regarding whether to defer to grievance processes under federal legislation, the Ontario Court of Appeal had asserted in two decisions[59] that the word "entitled" to grieve suggested that the grievance process was optional in the same manner as it focused on the term "may" grieve in the *Burgess* case to suggest that the process was optional. While not questioning the result in these two cases the Supreme Court in *Vaughan* rejected this logic, noting that the term "entitled" meant employees were not required to grieve, not that the process was optional.[60] One would expect "may grieve" to be interpreted similarly.

Benedict and *Burgess* concerned termination of employment where no explicit right to grieve was provided. The cases raised issues concerning changes in working conditions that, as members of the SMG, the employees have no right to grieve. The right to grieve working conditions to the PSGB is, even when it is granted, subject to significant exceptions. Classification decisions, for example, cannot be grieved. In circumstances where a claim for constructive or unjust or disguised dismissal is based on allegations that are not subject to or are only partially subject to a potential complaint before the PSGB a court will not defer to the PSGB complaint process. With respect to matters that are expressly subject to review on a complaint to the PSGB, it has a clear legislative mandate and broad remedial power to respond to employees' concerns, which suggests that the courts would defer such contractual claims to the PSGB process.[61]

However, the PSGB complaint process does not include a formal grievance process and does not provide the comprehensive forum for employment-related matters typically found in labour arbitration schemes that courts have been concerned not to undermine. The *PSOA* provides for dismissal on reasonable notice or compensation in lieu but excludes the PSGB's jurisdiction over disputes arising from such dismissals. Determination of disputes about notice or pay in lieu of notice are left to the courts, suggesting at least concurrent jurisdiction over

59 *Guenette v Canada (Attorney General)*, 2002 CanLII 45012 (ON CA) at para 25; *Danilov v Atomic Energy Control Board*, 1999 CanLII 4480 (ON CA) at para 11.

60 *Vaughan*, above note 52 at para 28.

61 *Ibid.*

dismissals where damages as opposed to reinstatement are in issue.[62] The PSGB itself has recently suggested that a complainant barred by the rigid rather Byzantine time limits for complaints to the PSGB may seek relief through the courts regarding their dismissal based on the rulings in *Burgess* and *Benedict*.[63]

Where a court is prepared to entertain a contractual claim, public servants would also appear to be able to bring class action proceedings alleging violations of their contractual rights.[64]

b) Content of the Contract of Employment

The holding in *Wells*, that the terms of an employment contract with the Crown are now "found in the written and verbal manifestations of the agreement, applicable statutes and regulations, and the common law,"[65] would appear to apply to all employment relationships with the Crown. Relevant provisions of the *PSOA* and regulations are clearly incorporated into public servants' employment contracts. An employee is entitled to rely on the representations of an official with ostensible authority.[66] Express contractual terms are binding.[67] Government policies may also form part of the employment contract.[68] MBC directives and government policies are not regulations, and persons contracting for employment with the Crown cannot be deemed to know of them. Notwithstanding that these directives may be authorized by statute, may be administratively binding on government officials, and may unilaterally amend the terms of an employee's employment, they are not incorporated into a contract of employment and enforceable against the employee until they come to the attention of the employee.[69]

---

62 *PSOA*, above note 2, s 38 and O Reg 378/07, s 4(2)3.

63 *Preston (PSGB)*, above note 5 at para 37.

64 *Kranjcec v Ontario*, 2004 CanLII 17687 (ON SC) [*Kranjcec*].

65 *Wells*, above note 3 at para 33.

66 *Hawkins v Ontario*, [1985] OJ No 1162 (HCJ); *Blais v Canada (Attorney General)*, 2004 FC 1638 at para 25, but they may be amended on notice, at para 27, citing *Verreault*, above note 13.

67 *Klassen v Canada*, [2004] FCJ No 224 (TD) at para 32.

68 *Fitzgerald v Waterford Hospital Board* (1997), 148 Nfld & PEIR 271 (Nfld CA) at para 12.

69 *Turner-Lienaux v Nova Scotia (Attorney General)* (1993), 48 CCEL 128 (NSCA) at 138; *Appleby-Ostroff v Canada (Attorney General)*, 2011 FCA 84 at para 30; *Plumadore v Canada (Attorney General)*, 2016 FC 553 at para 49.

c) Contractual Remedies

The Ontario courts have not yet addressed the assessment of damages in connection with an action by a public servant, but *Wells* and *Dunsmuir* establish that standard remedial principles apply. While damages for termination of an employment contract are normally limited to an amount in lieu of reasonable notice, the fact that the terms of Wells's employment limited the power to dismiss on notice meant that damages were calculated based on the loss of opportunity to earn salary and benefits for the balance of the contract, discounted for the possibility of the employee not working the full term. In any event, the usual rules relating to mitigation of damages apply.[70]

Termination of an employee's contract of employment is, unless there is a contractual provision otherwise, not itself a wrong at law. Damages are based on an implied requirement for reasonable notice.[71] The *PSOA* expressly permits dismissal on reasonable notice.[72] However, where a public servant is declared surplus and denied the benefit of redeployment rights under regulation, policy,[73] or directive, they may have a claim for damages greater than compensation for a period of reasonable notice. In *Leonetti v Hussman Canada Inc*,[74] the Ontario Court of Appeal addressed the issue of damages where a private-sector employment contract included provision for two senior employees to return to the bargaining unit in the event that they lost their management positions. The court found that, had their contractual right to return to the bargaining unit been honoured, they would have worked until retirement. Damages were assessed on that basis, "discounted for contingencies such as lay off, illness, accident, voluntary early retirement and plant closing."

The same principles would seem to apply to the assessment of damages in circumstances where public servants are denied the benefit of redeployment provisions that, by legislation, policy, or express agreement, form part of their terms of employment. The Newfoundland

---

70 *Wells*, above note 3 at para 65.

71 *Finn v St John's (City)* (2002), 220 Nfld & PEIR 245 (Nfld CA) at para 52; *Vorvis v Insurance Corporation of British Columbia*, [1989] 1 SCR 1085 at para 13; *Wallace v United Grain Growers Ltd*, [1997] 3 SCR 701 at para 103.

72 *PSOA*, above note 2, s 38(1), discussed in Chapter 2.

73 For example, the Public Service Commission, *Employment Policy*, 6 November 2020, provided to the authors, Targeted Direct Assignment.

74 1998 CanLII 2213 (ON CA), application for leave to appeal ref'd [1998] SCCA No 344.

and Labrador courts have addressed the assessment of damages where a public employee is denied redeployment rights. The first case involved a public servant who lost his position at age fifty as a result of reorganization.[75] As a consequence of an adverse recommendation by a superior, which he was not allowed to respond to, he was not given a position otherwise available to him under the government's redeployment policy. The court held that, since he was not dismissed for cause, he could not be denied an alternative position for cause. Damages were assessed, subject to mitigation, on the basis of a finding of fact that he would have been employed in an alternative position until retirement had the redeployment policy been properly applied. In addition, non-pecuniary damages were assessed as a result of the impact of the negligent implementation of the redundancy policy.

The second Newfoundland and Labrador case concerned the claim of a public servant whose department was eliminated after a change in government.[76] In a public statement, the new minister said only incompetent employees would be dismissed. By mistake, a long-service employee near retirement was treated as a temporary employee and terminated before his position was formally eliminated. Contrary to government policy, no efforts were made to place him in a new position. The failure to follow the policy was a breach of the employment contract. The court was able to largely ignore the issue of deductions for contingencies in assessing damages since the delay in the legal process allowed the court to know the actual extent of mitigation and determine that the employee would have been able to work to retirement. Aggravated damages were awarded for the humiliation and embarrassment caused by the early termination in the context of the minister's comments. However, punitive damages were denied since the conduct was negligent rather than malicious.

At common law, specific performance of employment contracts or reinstatement is not available,[77] but there have been rare exceptions.[78]

---

75 *Bradbury v Newfoundland (Attorney General)*, 2001 NFCA 63.

76 *Sweetland v Newfoundland (Minister of Development)*, 2002 CanLII 45654 (NL SC).

77 *Atomic Energy of Canada Ltd v Sheikholeslami*, [1998] 3 FC 349 at para 11; *Dunsmuir*, above note 3 at para 108. The court stated: "It is true that the remedy of reinstatement is not available for breach of contract at common law."

78 *Smith v Attorney General (NS)*, 2004 NSCA 106 [*Smith*], leave to appeal ref'd [2004] SCCA No 498 (QL); *Connolly v Attorney General (NS)*, 2004 NSCA 107. Reinstatement is not a remedy available in a common law action for unjust

In the case of the Crown there is a further obstacle to an injunction or order for specific performance since they are prohibited under the *Crown Liability and Proceedings Act, 2019*,[79] with the very narrow exceptions of "a deliberate flouting of established law, or Crown employees are acting beyond their jurisdiction."[80]

A rare example of specific performance being ordered in an employment case is the Nova Scotia case of *Smith*.[81] Two staff members of a Nova Scotia youth centre were accused, and then eventually cleared, of allegations of abuse of residents. They were party to an agreement that provided for their reinstatement. Their deputy minister ended the agreement without a suitable offer of a position. It was held that there was an arguable case that re-employment was necessary to their recovery from the trauma of the false accusations, that the deputy minister had exceeded his statutory authority by acting outside the terms of the agreement and that, in the circumstances, damages would not provide sufficient redress. Interim injunctive relief was granted.

The finding that an injunction is available against a deputy minister where they act outside their statutory authority, the consequence of which is to require the Crown to continue a person's employment, tests the limit of a court's authority under the *Crown Liability and Proceedings Act, 2019*. The Ontario provisions[82] are substantially similar to the Nova Scotia provisions.[83] The statutes each provide that an injunction may not issue against an official of the Crown if the effect is an injunction against the Crown.[84] A declaration is the remedy available in a final decision but is not available as interim relief.[85] A declaration is not enforceable in the manner of an injunction but is normally honoured by the Crown.[86]

---

dismissal, but these matters concerned interim enforcement of a settlement agreement that expressly required reinstatement.

79 SO 2019, c 7, Sch 17, s 22.

80 *Nelson et al*, above note 11 at para 25.

81 *Smith*, above note 78.

82 *Crown Liability and Proceedings Act*, above note 79, s 22.

83 *Proceedings Against the Crown Act*, RSNS 1989, c 360, s 16(2) & (3).

84 *Ibid*, s 14(2).

85 *Crown Liability and Proceedings Act*, above note 79, s 22(4); *Nelson et al*, above note 11 at para 26.

86 *Lount Corporation v Attorney General of Canada*, [1984] 1 FC 332 at 365, aff'd [1985] 2 FC 185.

2) Appointee Office Holders

Unless an appointee is appointed "at pleasure" under a statutory authority that permits or requires appointments to be made "at pleasure," or occupies a constitutionally defined office, the appointee will be entitled to seek contractual remedies on dismissal in a civil action.[87] Their contract of employment will be made up of the applicable legislative provisions, the written and verbal "manifestations" of the terms of employment and the common law.[88]

Damages and mitigation will be assessed in the same manner as dismissals under private employment contracts.[89] Where an appointment for a fixed term, not at pleasure, is terminated prior to the completion of the term the appointee will be entitled to damages based on the remuneration owed for the balance of the contract in the same manner as employees on a fixed-term employment contract terminated in similar circumstances.[90] Office holders retained at pleasure are not protected by contract and are not entitled reasonable notice of termination, or common law damages.[91]

An appointee's terms of employment may include undertakings by the Crown regarding the duties of the appointee.[92] In the absence of an express statutory restriction, appointees would appear to be able to rely on the doctrine of constructive dismissal should their position be altered substantially or they be denied the ability to conduct the responsibilities of their office.[93] Where the actions of the Crown alter the intended functions of an agency so as to fundamentally change the responsibilities of an appointee's position, the appointee may also be able to claim to have been constructively dismissed.[94]

There is the possibility that a legitimate expectation of consideration for renewal could give rise to a claim in damages for breach of an

---

87 *Wells*, above note 3; *Kranjcec*, above note 64 at para 26; *Dunsmuir* above note 3.
88 *Wells*, *ibid* at para 33.
89 *Wells*, *ibid* at paras 63 and 65.
90 *Wells*, *ibid* at para 65.
91 *Dunsmuir*, above note 3 at para 115.
92 *Fiske v Nova Scotia (Attorney General)*, 2001 NSSC 99 at para 160 [*Fiske*].
93 *Potter v New Brunswick Legal Aid Services Commission*, 2015 SCC 10.
94 *Fiske*, above note 92 at para 162.

employment contract if damages could be proven.[95] A claim for negligent misrepresentation may also be possible.[96]

A claim for reinstatement is not a remedy available in a civil action in contract.[97] Reinstatement for a failure to act fairly or follow the legislated procedures in dismissing an office holder is only available, if available at all, on judicial review of the decision to terminate an appointment.[98]

D. JUDICIAL REVIEW

In *Wells* the Court noted that "legislative decision making is not subject to any known duty of fairness." It also noted that terminations that result from a public policy choice are distinct from "instances where an employee's competence or capabilities are at issue."[99] Decisions made on broad grounds of public policy resulting in dismissals will not entitle individual appointees affected to procedural fairness.[100]

> In essence, the majority in *Knight* (which remains applicable to "at pleasure" appointees) found that, where a public body decides to terminate the employment of an individual, there is only a general duty to act fairly if the decision is administrative and specific (as opposed to legislative and general) and final (as opposed to preliminary).[101]

1) Standard of Review

On judicial review the court must determine if in the circumstances the applicant has been accorded procedural fairness. The standard of

95 *Rossmo v Vancouver (City) Police Board*, [2001] BCJ No 2698 (SC) at para 120, upheld on appeal, [2003] BCJ No 2761 (CA).
96 *Matkowski v Saskatchewan*, 2007 SKQB 46.
97 *Dunsmuir*, above note 3 at para 108.
98 *Mourant v Town of Sackville*, 2014 NBCA 56; Paul Daly, "Beware the Artful Pleader: The Public-Private Divide," online: http://canliiconnects.org/en/commentaries/30257.
99 *Wells*, above note 3 at paras 58 & 59.
100 *Martineau v Matsqui Institution*, [1980] 1 SCR 602 at 628.
101 *Martin v Vancouver (City)*, 2008 BCCA 197, leave to appeal ref'd [2008] SCCA No 321 at para 75.

review with respect to whether the requirements of procedural fairness have been satisfied is correctness.[102]

The court may also review both the factual determinations that the alleged misconduct occurred and that they warrant dismissal where an appointee on good behaviour is dismissed. The standard of review in respect of these matters is reasonableness.[103] With respect to the question of whether the alleged misconduct warrants termination of an appointment, considerable deference is owed to the Crown.[104] The Crown has the prerogative to determine when "behaviour" is or is not compatible with a particular office. "Into this field of ultimate prerogative authority, which I venture to suggest has legitimate constitutional roots, the judicial arm must move gingerly and diffidently, and must eschew sweeping declarations."[105]

2) Fairness: Appointees at Pleasure

Appointees will only be treated as being appointed "at pleasure," and therefore subject to dismissal without notice or compensation, if such a term is imposed unambiguously. In Ontario, the *Legislation Act, 2006* authorizes appointments "at pleasure" and appointments are regularly made expressly "at pleasure," though not to adjudicative or regulatory positions.[106]

In finding that appointees at pleasure were entitled to fairness, the majority in *Knight* said "[s]ince the respondent could be dismissed at pleasure, the content of the duty of fairness would be minimal and I would tend to agree that notice of the reasons for the appellant Board's dissatisfaction with the respondent's employment and affording him an opportunity to be heard would be sufficient to meet

102 *Canada (Citizenship and Immigration) v Khosa*, 2009 SCC 12 at para 43; *Shoan v Canada (Attorney General)*, 2018 FC 476 at para 13, aff'd 2020 FCA 174, leave to appeal ref'd 2021 CanLII 37641 (SCC) [*Shoan #2*].

103 *Canada (Minister of Citizenship and Immigration) v Vavilov*, 2019 SCC 65; *Shoan #2*, above note 102 at para 14; *Shoan v Canada (Attorney General)*, 2017 FC 426 [*Shoan #1*] at para 35; *Wedge v Canada (Attorney General)*, 1997 CanLII 5331 (FC) [*Wedge*]. For a recent review of the standard of review jurisprudence see Sara Blake, *Administrative Law in Canada*, 7th ed (Toronto: LexisNexis Canada, 2022).

104 *Shoan #2*, above note 102 at para 143.

105 *Weatherill v Canada (Attorney General)*, 1998 CanLII 7320 (FC) at para 28.

106 See Chapter 5 for a discussion of Ontario appointment policies.

the requirement of fairness."[107] The Federal Court of Appeal in *Pelletier v Canada (Attorney General)* described employment at pleasure as "intrinsically precarious."[108] *Dunsmuir* described the purpose of requiring fairness before dismissing appointees at pleasure as limited to ensuring "public power is not exercised capriciously."[109]

Where the government terminates the appointment of persons named to office at pleasure and proposes to act on the basis of the person's suitability, the duty of procedural fairness requires that the person be informed of the possibility of removal, of the reasons for that removal, and given the opportunity to respond. In hearing the response, the government will be held to a standard of at least having an open mind, in the sense of not having made a final decision before hearing the response.[110] Government is not in any event required to have just cause.[111]

Keen v Canada (Attorney General)[112] concerned a commissioner of the Canadian Nuclear Safety Commission appointed on good behaviour who was also appointed at pleasure as the president of the commission. The government became concerned about her appropriateness as president following a reactor shutdown that caused a dangerous shortage of medical isotopes. She was provided correspondence setting out the government's concerns and provided a written reply. Her appointment as president was then revoked. The court found that the fairness obligation had been satisfied by merely being told the concerns and allowed to make a written response.

3) Adjudicative/Regulatory Tribunals: Requirement for Independence

Adjudicative and regulatory tribunals are part of the administrative state for which the elected government is responsible, and, unlike courts, they do not enjoy a constitutional status separate from the elected executive. In *Ocean Port*,[113] a litigant unsuccessfully challenged a decision maker appointed "at the pleasure of the Lieutenant Governor in Council" for

107 *Knight*, above note 15, L'Heureux-Dubé J at 683.
108 *Pelletier v Canada (Attorney General)*, 2008 FCA 1 at para 61 [*Pelletier*].
109 *Dunsmuir*, above note 3 at para 115.
110 *Pelletier*, above note 108.
111 *Ibid* at para 44.
112 2009 FC 353 [*Keen*].
113 *Ocean Port*, above note 7 at para 24.

a one-year part-time term as having insufficient security of tenure to be able to provide a fair and independent hearing. The Supreme Court confirmed administrative tribunals "are, in fact, created precisely for the purpose of implementing government policy. Implementation of that policy may require them to make quasi-judicial decisions."[114] The decision noted that

> [i]t is well established that, absent constitutional constraints, the degree of independence required of a particular government decision maker or tribunal is determined by its enabling statute. It is the legislature or Parliament that determines the degree of independence required of tribunal members. The statute must be construed as a whole to determine the degree of independence the legislature intended.[115]

This point was reiterated strongly in *CUPE v Ontario (Minister of Labour)*,[116] where the unions asserted that the ad hoc interest arbitration boards were flawed because they lacked indices of institutional independence such as security of tenure, financial security, and administrative independence. The Court reaffirmed that in the face of clear statutory direction, there are no grounds to import common law doctrines of independence and stated that "the Court cannot substitute a tribunal for the one designed by the legislature."[117] The ad hoc tribunals at issue in that case were intended to exist for one hearing. There was no ongoing question of security of tenure or financial security.

Institutional independence has implications for the employment conditions of appointees to adjudicative agencies, but independence is for the benefit of the public and the litigants.[118] The institutional independence of courts is grounded in the Constitution. The administrative tribunals, adjudicative or otherwise, are creatures of statute. Adjudicative independence as a legal principle is a requirement of natural justice that is an aspect of common law and is subordinate to statutory provisions. As a matter of public policy, the Ontario Court of

---

114 *Ibid* at para 24.

115 *Ibid* at para 20.

116 2003 SCC 29 [*CUPE*].

117 *Ibid* at para 190.

118 *Ref re Remuneration of Judges of the Provincial Court of Prince Edward Island*; *Ref re Independence and Impartiality of Judges of the Provincial Court of Prince Edward Island*, [1997] 3 SCR 3 at para 193 [*Ref re Remuneration of Judges*]; *R v Lippé*, [1991] 2 SCR 114 at 139.

Appeal in *Hewat* was correct that in practice tribunal members need to have some real independence to maintain the appearance of integrity,[119] but the extent of a tribunal's independence is a matter for the legislature. The decision in *Ocean Port* makes that clear:

> It is well established that, absent constitutional constraints, the degree of independence required of a particular government decision maker or tribunal is determined by its enabling statute. It is the legislature or Parliament that determines the degree of independence required of tribunal members. The statute must be construed as a whole to determine the degree of independence the legislature intended.[120]

The argument was raised in a number of cases that at least some adjudicative tribunals had sufficiently court-like authority that the guarantees of independence implied in the Constitution for judges should also apply to appointees to such tribunals. The argument drew some strength from the application of these protections to justices of the peace.[121] In *Saskatchewan Federation of Labour v Government of Saskatchewan*,[122] the Saskatchewan Court of Appeal held that the constitutional guarantees of judicial independence did not extend to members of the Saskatchewan Labour Relations Board.

Any doubt about the question of administrative boards being accorded institutional independence of the kind enjoyed by the courts has been removed by the decision in *Walter v British Columbia*.[123] The appeal concerned an application by the chair of the BC Review Board seeking the application of the principles of judicial independence to his position. The board, and the equivalent review boards in each province, including Ontario's Review Board, exist to determine whether persons

---

119 *Hewat*, above note 30 at para 163. The judgment references some of the many academic and other commentaries on the importance of appointment processes and appointment terms that support adjudicative independence; see, for example, S. Ronald Ellis, "Appointments Policies in the Administrative Justice System: Lessons from Ontario: Four Speeches" (1997) 11 *Canadian Journal of Administrative Law and Practice* 205.

120 *Ocean Port*, above note 7 at para 20.

121 *Ell v Alberta*, 2003 SCC 35.

122 2013 SKCA 61, leave to appeal ref'd 2013 CanLII 83789 (SCC).

123 2019 BCCA 221, leave to appeal ref'd 2019 CanLII 117835 (SCC) [*Walter*]; *Hokhold v Canada (Attorney General)*, 2019 BCSC 1106 at para 70, stating "constitutional principle of judicial independence, which animates judicial immunity, does not extend to administrative decision-makers."

found not criminally responsible should be released from custody.[124] The chair's position is to be filled by a judge, a retired judge, or a person qualified to be appointed as a judge. There was no question that section 7 of the *Canadian Charter of Rights and Freedoms* (the *Charter*)[125] is engaged and that the work of a review board is at the judicial end of the spectrum of administrative tribunals. The court summarized the law:

> A high degree of judicial independence must be afforded to all courts and judicial officers as a natural outgrowth of the commitment to the separation of powers between and among the legislative, executive, and judicial branches of government. . . . Administrative tribunals that must be independent for the purpose of adjudicating specific *Charter* claims do not require judicial independence for the same purpose and to the same extent. The guarantee of their independence is context specific.[126]

Although the decision went on to say: "[w]hile the appellant should enjoy a measure of constitutionally protected independence," the appeal was dismissed without any specific comment about the appropriate manner of providing appropriate financial independence.[127] The court expressed concern that a strong argument could be made that the absence of a limit on the downward discretion the minister had in setting the Review Board chair's remuneration may afford inadequate protection for the chair's financial independence. The chair's salary had been increased and no declaration had been requested so no order was made. The court noted that the process had resulted in "inappropriate" direct negotiations between the chair and attorney general, suggesting the need for an appropriate process for establishing an appropriate level of remuneration.[128]

The principle of judicial independence arises from the structure of Canada's Constitution that is based on the institutional separation of the three branches of government: the judicial, the executive, and the legislative. Judicial independence concerns the maintenance of the

---

124 *Criminal Code*, RSC 1985, c C-46, s 672.38; the review boards are to be treated as if established under each province's laws, so they operate as provincial agencies.

125 Part I of the *Constitution Act, 1982*, being Schedule B to the *Canada Act 1982* (UK), 1982, c 11 [*Charter*].

126 *Walter*, above note 123 at para 109.

127 *Ibid* at para 113.

128 *Ibid* at para 115.

institutional separation of the judiciary and the executive.[129] Administrative boards and agencies are creatures of statute that are created to implement government policy. They will be granted a degree of independence by statute, but they remain part of the administrative apparatus of government. The requirements for independence of administrative boards and agencies arises from the "principles of fundamental justice which call for the independence of a decision-maker as an essential part of procedural fairness."[130] In the rare cases of administrative tribunals, such as review boards, that adjudicate matters involving individual liberty and consequently section 7 *Charter* rights, the tribunals must be independent for that purpose but the required extent of independence is "context specific."[131]

4) Appointees on Good Behaviour/Legislated Requirements for Fairness

The federal Parliament has provided for appointments to certain federal adjudicative and regulatory boards to be on good behaviour for a statutorily fixed term.[132] Currently Ontario has only provided this level of security to certain legislative officers.[133] In those cases, Ontario also established a statutory process for removal by the legislature.

Fairness will be required for the removal of appointees with a contract of employment if a measure of fairness is required explicitly or implicitly by the governing statute. *Dunsmuir* expressly approved a decision that held, when a statute provided that dismissal of a teacher could only take place if the teacher was given three weeks' notice of the motion to dismiss, the teacher was entitled an opportunity to respond.[134] The New Brunswick Court of Appeal held that a provision requiring

---

129 *Ref re Remuneration of Judges*, above note 118 at para 125; *Walter* above note 123 at para 70.

130 *Walter*, above note 123 at para 69.

131 *Ibid* at para 109.

132 For example, *Canadian Radio-television and Telecommunications Commission Act*, RSC 1985, c C-22, s 3(2): Directors; *Bank of Canada Act*, RSC 1985, c B-2, s 6(3) and 9(1): Governor and Directors; *Broadcasting Act*, SC 1991, c 11, s 36(3): CBC Board of Directors.

133 *Auditor General Act*, RSO 1990, c A.35, ss 4 & 5; *Ombudsman Act*, RSO 1990, c O.6, ss 3 & 4; *Members' Integrity Act, 1994*, SO 1994, c 38, ss 23-1 & 23-2; *Freedom of Information and Protection of Privacy Act*, RSO 1990, c F31, ss 5 & 6; *Financial Accountability Officer Act, 2013*, SO 2013, c 4, ss 3–4.

134 *Dunsmuir*, above note 3 at para 116.

that, prior to termination by a municipal council, the office holder was to get notice of their possible termination implies a level of fairness that at least allows the appointee to respond to concerns about their suitability.[135] This type of provision is not found in current statutes respecting OIC appointees in Ontario. However, the case confirmed that post-*Dunsmuir* the governing statute provides the context for determining whether a duty of fairness exists.

The degree of independence and the consequent impact on the employment terms of appointees is essentially a matter of statutory interpretation. In the case of adjudicative boards, the process of statutory interpretation will be influenced by the presumption that, absent express statutory provisions to the contrary, the legislature expects adjudication to be conducted fairly by an independent, impartial adjudicator.[136]

Administrative tribunals and boards have varying functions on a spectrum from the essentially executive functions of policy development and implementation to the essentially judicial function of dispute resolution through a formal hearing process. Tribunals at the executive or policy end of the spectrum may require minimal procedural protections whereas those engaged in hearing and deciding disputes may have court-like powers calling for a high standard of procedural fairness "including a higher requirement of independence."[137]

Administrative tribunals and boards are creatures of statute, and it is the legislature that is responsible for defining the rules governing their operation. The common law doctrines of procedural fairness and natural justice are subject to amendment or exclusion by statute. While the courts are not going to substitute common law provisions for statutory ones, different considerations apply when the legislation is silent or ambiguous about the nature of an appointment.[138] Courts may infer that the legislature intended an adjudicative tribunal's processes would comport with the principles of natural justice,[139] which include

---

135 *Ouellette v Saint-André, an incorporated rural community*, 2013 NBCA 21 at para 17 [*Ouellette*].

136 *Ocean Port*, above note 7 at para 21.

137 *Bell Canada v Canadian Telephone Employees Association*, 2003 SCC 36 at para 21 [*Bell Canada*].

138 *Ocean Port*, above note 7 at para 21.

139 *Ibid*.

a decision maker of "impartiality and independence."[140] Although the precise standard of independence required will depend on all the circumstances,[141] the more adjudicative or court-like the tribunal is, the more independence may be required.[142]

There are good policy reasons for government to give up the comparatively rarely used convenience of dismissing appointees at pleasure[143] or merely with notice or pay in lieu of notice. There is the human resource benefit of the ability to offer secure employment to good candidates for important positions. More importantly, this security would serve to ensure office holders feel confident to advise elected officials, based on their own opinion, rather than what elected officials may wish to hear; and ensure public office holders carry out their duties without fear of reprisals from elected officials.[144] A tribunal must maintain a public perception of independence to be respected as the place where final decisions are made fairly and finally,[145] which is one of the government's purposes in having regulatory and adjudicative tribunals.

The requirements of fairness to litigants and the need to protect the integrity of the adjudicative process will not allow a court to ignore clear legislative authority for what it might view as violation of the appropriate independence of a tribunal.[146] However, courts will resolve ambiguity in the statutory language against finding an appointment can be terminated at pleasure.[147] Where a statutory power to appoint or remunerate adjudicative appointees is exercised in a manner inconsistent with the purpose of a statute to establish a credible adjudicative tribunal there may be scope for review.[148] The three essential conditions of judicial independence, security of tenure, financial security, and

---

140 *2747-3174 Québec Inc v Quebec (Régie des permis d'alcool)*, [1996] 3 SCR 919 at para 39 [*2747-3174 Québec Inc*]; *Canadian Pacific Ltd v Matsqui Indian Band*, [1995] 1 SCR 3, Lamer CJ and Cory J [*Canadian Pacific*]; *Katz v Vancouver Stock Exchange*, [1996] 3 SCR 405.

141 *2747-3174 Québec Inc*, above note 140 at para 39. See also *Baker v Canada (Minister of Citizenship and Immigration)*, [1999] 2 SCR 817 [*Baker*] at paras 21–22, L'Heureux-Dubé J.

142 *Bell Canada*, above note 137 at para 24.

143 *Ouellette*, above note 135 at para 17.

144 *Ibid*.

145 *Hewat*, above note 30.

146 *Ocean Port*, above note 7; *Saskatchewan Federation of Labour v Saskatchewan*, 2010 SKCA 27 [*Saskatchewan, 2010*].

147 *Saskatchewan, 2010*, *ibid* at paras 42–48.

148 *CUPE*, above note 116.

institutional independence, are considerations in determining whether a tribunal is sufficiently independent to avoid the appearance of bias, but their significance must be weighed in the specific administrative context.[149] The absence of one or even two conditions may not be fatal in an administrative tribunal.[150] OIC appointments requiring a high degree of independence would appear to require fixed remuneration, whether salary or per diem, which is not subject to variation based on performance.[151] While the *Legislation Act, 2006* authorizes appointments at pleasure, exercising that discretion when appointing members of an adjudicative tribunal, particularly one at the judicial end of the procedural fairness spectrum, might be regarded as inappropriate and potentially expose the appointment process to judicial review.

The holding by the Ontario Court of Appeal in *Hewat* that an appointment on a fixed term necessarily implies an appointment on good behaviour subject to judicial review has been implicitly overruled by the decision in *Dunsmuir*. The remedy for most such appointees is now an action in contract for damages. However, the statutory context of appointments to an adjudicative tribunal, such as the OLRB, under review in *Hewat*, imply a level of independence for the board that requires that fixed-term appointments are on good behaviour. In deciding on the remedy in *Hewat*, the Court found that quasi-judicial tribunals required some degree of independence and that the image of independence was undermined by breaching fixed-term appointments. In *Saskatchewan Federation of Labour*, the Saskatchewan Court of Appeal addressed this issue in respect of appointees to the Saskatchewan Labour Relations Board and concluded that appointments on a fixed term were on good behaviour.[152]

The legislation considered by the Saskatchewan Court of Appeal differed from the Ontario legislation in several potentially significant aspects. The Saskatchewan appointments were made expressly at pleasure. However, the Saskatchewan legislation provided that appointees held "office during pleasure only, unless a contrary intention is expressed in . . . the enactment by or pursuant to which he or she is appointed."[153]

149 *Valente v The Queen*, [1985] 2 SCR 673; *Canadian Pacific*, above note 140 at para 83.

150 *CUPE*, above note 116 at paras 190–91.

151 *Bell Canada*, above note 137 at para 24.

152 *Saskatchewan, 2010*, above note 146.

153 *Ibid* at para 33.

There was no other legislative authority for the Saskatchewan Crown to appoint at pleasure. By contrast, sections 76 and 47 of the Ontario *Legislation Act, 2006* grant the Crown authority to appoint at pleasure "unless, (a) a contrary intention appears; or (b) its application would give to a term or provision a meaning that is inconsistent with the context." The Saskatchewan Court of Appeal found that a deeming provision does not grant authority and that, in any event, the nature of the language creating the Saskatchewan Labour Relations Board expressed by implication a contrary intention foreclosing the presumption of an appointment at pleasure.[154] An explicit expression of a contrary intention was not necessary.[155] The finding that a "contrary intention" can be implied from the adjudicative nature of a tribunal would, in the Ontario context, preclude the Crown from expressly appointing members of adjudicative tribunals at pleasure.

With respect to adjudicative or regulatory tribunals where the purpose of the tribunal calls for a measure of independence and the statutory provisions support the implication that independence is intended, a fixed-term appointment may be taken as implying an appointment on good behaviour. This would be particularly so if the Crown may be a litigant before the tribunal. Very explicit statutory language would be required to permit the Crown to litigate before an adjudicator it could remove at will.

The authority of Ontario to make appointments at pleasure is not treated as extending to appointing members of adjudicative boards such as the OLRB. The *Agencies and Appointments Directive* provides that appointees to adjudicative and regulatory boards are for a fixed term and are not specified to be at pleasure in contrast to other appointments that are normally at pleasure.[156]

5) Appointees on Good Behaviour/Content of Fairness Requirement

The Supreme Court in *Baker v Canada (Minister of Citizenship and Immigration)*[157] described the duty of procedural fairness generally as "eminently variable and its content is to be decided in the specific

154 *Ibid* at paras 33–35.

155 *Ibid* at para 47.

156 Management Board of Cabinet, *Agencies and Appointments Directive*, 9 February 2018, online: www.ontario.ca/page/agencies-and-appointments-directive, s 3(2)2.

157 *Baker*, above note 141 at para 21.

context of each case,"[158] with the underlying purpose of ensuring "a fair and open procedure, appropriate to the decision being made and its statutory, institutional, and social context, with an opportunity for those affected by the decision to put forward their views and evidence fully and have them considered by the decision-maker."[159] The requirements of fairness before a decision to dismiss an appointee is made will vary depending on the context including the nature of the alleged misconduct, the supporting evidence, the statutory mandate of the tribunal, and the response of the appointee to the allegations.

The decision to terminate an appointment rests with the appointing body, in the case of OIC appointees, Cabinet. The courts recognize that Cabinet as "a collective body of Ministers, is required to rely on the advice of staff and of individual Ministers to assist in reaching decisions on the wide range of issues for which it is responsible."[160] Cabinet is entitled to rely on investigation reports, other material prepared by staff and the recommendations of the responsible minister.[161] While an appointee will be entitled to have their response to an investigation forwarded to Cabinet they are not entitled to appear before Cabinet. There is no entitlement to a meeting with the responsible minister, though, if the context and the nature of the investigative process was such that a meeting appeared necessary to properly respond to the allegation, one could be required or at least a summary explanation why it was not considered necessary to provide it to the appointee.[162]

Cabinet or the responsible minister is entitled to establish the process for investigating alleged impropriety by an appointee. The process must ensure the appointee is advised of the allegations in detail, the evidence against them, and then allowed to present a full response. An investigation is not a judicial process and does not entitle an appointee to a hearing or to cross-examine persons interviewed by an investigator. Even where allegations are of disputed serious personal misconduct such as sexual harassment a hearing process is not required. However, an investigation must accord the appointee procedural fairness.[163]

---

158 *Ibid* at para 21, quoting *Knight*, above note 15.

159 *Baker*, above note 141 at para 22.

160 *Attorney General of Canada v Inuit Tapirisat et al*, [1980] 2 SCR 735 at 753; *Wedge*, above note 103.

161 *Wedge*, *ibid*.

162 *Shoan #1*, above note 103 at paras 123–24.

163 *Shoan v Canada (Attorney General)*, 2016 FC 1003 at para 35 [*Shoan #3*].

Where an investigation is ordered the investigation may be subject to judicial review for procedural fairness.[164]

Vennat v Canada (Attorney General)[165] quashed the decision of the Governor in Council to dismiss the president and chief executive officer of the Business Development Bank of Canada, appointed on good behaviour, for a failure to provide procedural fairness. The decision held that the investigative process should be non-judicial and non-formalistic but must give the affected party a "real opportunity" to respond to the reasons for the employer's dissatisfaction.[166] Mr. Vennat's reputation was at issue, and he strenuously contested the truthfulness of certain facts, raising the level of fairness required. He was entitled to an inquiry where he could present evidence by "affidavit, interviews or counterevidence."[167]

The allegations arose from adverse comments about Mr. Vennat by a judge hearing a complex case where Mr. Vennat was a witness but not a party. Cabinet relied largely on those comments. The decision held that, when the dismissal of an appointee on good behaviour is being considered, "procedural fairness required that a personalized inquiry be conducted before proceeding with the applicant's removal." *Vennat* also held that appointees on good behaviour are entitled to reasons for their dismissal.[168] In addition to identifying the misconduct relied upon, the reasons must summarily explain why the appointee's arguments were dismissed.[169] These reasons will not be as detailed as a judicial or quasi-judicial decision. The *Vennat* case was unusual in that the Governor in Council relied on the comments of a trial judge rather than an investigation report. In the normal course an investigation report should include and address the appointee's responses.

In considering a Cabinet decision, courts are not entitled to go behind the Cabinet's stated reasons, normally recitals in the OIC terminating an appointment.[170] Failure to provide reasons or adequate

---

164 *Masters v Ontario*, 1993 CanLII 8530 (ON SC), aff'd 1994 CanLII 10571 (ON SC); *Shoan #3*, *ibid*.

165 2006 FC 1008 [*Vennat*].

166 *Ibid* at para 214.

167 *Ibid* at para 170 [translation].

168 *Ibid* at para 87.

169 *Ibid* at paras 92–93 and 95.

170 *Keen*, above note 112 at para 55, citing Dickson J in *Thornes's Hardware Limited v The Queen*, [1983] 1 SCR 106 at 115 [*Thornes's*].

reasons is not a standalone basis for quashing a decision.[171] Where reasons are not given expressly, but a decision is made in accordance with an investigation report or recommendation, the report or recommendation may be considered in determining the reasonableness of the decision.[172] Where a Cabinet decision is based on grounds set out in a minister's report, and there is no other evidence, the reasons for the Cabinet decision "are those of the Minister."[173] Inadequate reasons may not allow a court to be satisfied that an appointee has been accorded fairness or that a decision is reasonable.[174]

In contrast to the fairness owed to appointees on good behaviour, the decision in *Ouellette v Saint-André* held, where a municipal clerk treasurer was entitled to notice of a municipal council meeting to determine by a supermajority whether he should be dismissed for cause, fairness in the circumstances was required to

> be minimal, yet reasonable and efficient. Those minimal features consist of an opportunity to know the concerns about one's performance that could lead to termination, and an opportunity to explain them or demonstrate why they have no merit. Obviously, an appropriate opportunity should be afforded to the office holder to make the necessary enquiries and prepare a response. Whether that response is in writing or in person, would no doubt be a matter to be determined by the Council.[175]

6) Standard of Review

A discussion of the ever-evolving standard of judicial review is beyond the scope of this book. However, Cabinet has broad discretion in deciding what constitutes cause to dismiss a senior official, so its decision will be approached with deference on a standard of reasonableness.[176] Judicial review of the revocation of an OIC by Cabinet may require consideration of Cabinet's reasons, which may be provided in the recitals in the OIC revoking the appointment. The Supreme Court has stated

171 *Newfoundland and Labrador Nurses' Union v Newfoundland and Labrador (Treasury Board)*, 2011 SCC 62 at paras 14 and 16.

172 *Ibid* at para 20.

173 *Oberlander v Canada (Attorney General)*, 2004 FCA 213 at para 35.

174 *Shoan #1*, above note 103 at para 142.

175 *Ouellette*, above note 135 at para 24.

176 *CUPE*, above note 116 at para 154.

that a court normally has neither the duty nor right to investigate the motives behind an OIC.[177] Review of an OIC for reasonableness is limited to "whether the OIC is inconsistent with the statutory purpose of the *Act*, failed to comply with a legislative requirement or was enacted in the context of egregious circumstances."[178]

7) Remedies on Judicial Review

Public law remedies are discretionary but, where a court finds a decision has been made unfairly, the usual remedy is to declare the dismissal void *ab initio*.[179] This means the office holder will be returned to their position and be entitled to unpaid wages.[180] While arguably the payment of wages owing should not be subject to mitigation, the courts have distinguished between quashing a dismissal and a tailored order regarding remedy.[181] In the case of appointments that have expired the appointee will be limited to compensation for the part of the term following the dismissal. Where a position has been filled by a new appointee a court will be reluctant to order reinstatement.[182] Courts have on occasion been reluctant to require the elected executive to continue the services of an executive they do not wish to employ.[183] An order quashing a dismissal on public law grounds does not prevent the appointee from being dismissed successfully a second time for the same reasons using a revised fair process.[184]

In *Shoan v Canada (Attorney General)*,[185] judicial review of an OIC revoking Shoan's appointment on good behaviour was granted where an investigation report supporting one of the grounds for dismissal mentioned in the OIC had been successfully reviewed for the investigator's failure to act fairly. Shoan's appointment was then revoked by

177 *Consortium Developments (Clearwater) Ltd v Sarnia (City)*, [1998] 3 SCR 3 at paras 44–45, citing *Thornes's*, above note 170 at 112; *References re Greenhouse Gas Pollution Pricing Act*, 2021 SCC 11 at para 606.

178 *Ecojustice Canada Society v Alberta*, 2021 ABQB 397 at para 35.

179 *Dunsmuir*, above note 3 at para 108.

180 *Ibid.*

181 *Emms v Canada*, [1979] 2 SCR 1148; *Re Nicholson and Haldimand-Norfolk Regional Board of Commissioners of Police*, 1980 CanLII 1660 (ON CA).

182 *Hewat*, above note 30.

183 *Carol Roberts v Commissioner of the Northwest Territories*, 2002 NWTSC 68.

184 *Dunsmuir*, above note 3 at para 108; *Shoan #2*, above note 102.

185 *Shoan #1*, above note 103.

a second OIC expressly relying only on the grounds not brought into question by the decision. Judicial review of the second revocation of Shoan's appointment was denied.[186]

E. UNIONIZED PUBLIC SERVANTS

In the mid-1980s the Supreme Court held that the grievance arbitration provisions typical of Canadian labour legislation gave labour arbitrators exclusive jurisdiction over the enforcement of collective agreements and matters arising out of the law of master and servant in respect of bargaining unit members.[187] In 1995, the Supreme Court determined that labour arbitrators had exclusive jurisdiction over all matters arising under a collective agreement, including tort claims, subject only to the residual discretionary jurisdiction of courts to grant relief not available at arbitration.[188] The *Crown Employees Collective Bargaining Act, 1993*[189] gives the Grievance Settlement Board (GSB), like other labour arbitrators, exclusive jurisdiction over the "interpretation, application, administration or alleged violation" of the collective agreement.[190] The exclusive jurisdiction model has been applied to police officers whose terms of employment are determined by a typical collective bargaining scheme and a statutory discipline process.[191] The employment of non-commissioned Ontario Provincial Police officers is subject to a similar statutory scheme that similarly limits the jurisdiction of a court.[192]

Not all disputes arising in the workplace or arising between an employer and bargaining unit member fall within arbitrators' exclusive jurisdiction. Unionized employees still have access to the courts in the relatively rare case of matters falling outside the scope of arbitrators'

---

186 *Shoan #2*, above note 102.

187 *St Anne Nackawic Pulp & Paper v CPU*, [1986] 1 SCR 704.

188 *Weber*, above note 53; *New Brunswick v O'Leary*, [1995] 2 SCR 967.

189 SO 1993, c 38, s 7(3).

190 *Nelson*, above note 9; *Giorno v Pappas*, 1999 CanLII 1161 (ON CA) [*Giorno*]; *Northern Regional Health Authority v Horrocks*, 2021 SCC 42 at paras 21–23 [*Horrocks*], discussed in Chapter 11.

191 *Regina Police Assn*, above note 53. The issue in the case was the division of jurisdiction between arbitration and the police disciplinary process, which is discussed in Chapter 4.

192 *Rivers*, above note 10; *Abbott*, above note 10; *Ontario Provincial Police Collective Bargaining Act, 2006*, SO 2006, c 35, Sch B, s 4(1).

exclusive jurisdiction. When a bargaining unit employee is involved in a civil matter, the court must determine whether the dispute falls within the ambit of an arbitrator's exclusive jurisdiction under the applicable legislation and collective agreement.[193]

The application of the exclusive jurisdiction model as opposed to concurrent or overlapping jurisdiction models is based on two considerations. First, that jurisdiction should be based on the essential nature of a matter based on the facts, not on mere legal characterization.[194] Second, that concurrent or overlapping jurisdiction between labour arbitrators and the courts may undermine the legislative purpose.[195] Consequently, arbitrators have been found to have exclusive jurisdiction over matters within the scope of the collective bargaining relationship whether or not they are expressly addressed in the collective agreement. For example, wrongful dismissal or constructive dismissal,[196] conspiracy to deprive an employee of their employment,[197] denial of job advancement or employment benefits,[198] interference with contractual relations,[199] infliction of mental distress where the "infliction" is closely associated with the employment relationship and is captured by the collective agreement,[200] and tort claims against supervisors[201] have all been found to fall in arbitrators' exclusive jurisdiction. Crossclaims, based on varied types of alleged tortious conduct by a public servant against co-workers joined in a claim against Ontario are within the exclusive jurisdiction of the GSB.[202]

A dispute over an agreement between employer and union that is not a part of the collective agreement falls within the jurisdiction of an arbitrator, not the courts.[203] A dispute regarding a statutory rather than

193 *Weber*, above note 53 at para 51.
194 *Ibid* at para 43.
195 *Ibid* at para 58.
196 *Bouchard v Canada (Minister of National Defence)*, 1999 CanLII 9105 (FCA).
197 *Bhaduria v Toronto Board of Education*, 1999 CanLII 4745 (ON CA), leave to appeal ref'd [1999] SCCA No 212 [*Bhaduria*]; *Jadwani v Canada (Attorney General)* (2001), 2001 CanLII 24157 (ON CA), leave to appeal ref'd [2001] SCCA No 200 [*Jadwani*].
198 *Ruscetta v Graham*, 1998 CanLII 2118 (ON CA), leave to appeal ref'd [1998] SCCA No 220.
199 *Jadwani*, above note 197
200 *Bhaduria*, above note 197.
201 *Dwyer v Canada Post Corp*, 1997 CanLII 1110 (ON CA)
202 *Rheaume v Ontario*, 2018 ONSC 5116 at para 40.
203 *Allen v Alberta*, 2003 SCC 13.

a collective agreement term may fall within an arbitrator's exclusive jurisdiction if "there is a real contextual connection between the statute and the collective agreement such that a violation of the statute gives rise, in the context, to a violation of the provisions of the collective agreement."[204]

A defamation action by a bargaining unit employee against a fellow public servant that was a non-bargaining unit, non-managerial board member was found by the Ontario Court of Appeal to be within the exclusive jurisdiction of an arbitrator.[205] In that case, the plaintiff had filed a grievance that had been settled in regard to the facts alleged in the action. However, the Ontario Court of Appeal has found that allegations of defamation leading to criminal investigation and charges are beyond the exclusive jurisdiction of arbitrators since initiating criminal proceedings is beyond discipline processes contemplated by collective agreements.[206]

In *Northern Regional Health Authority v Horrocks*,[207] the Supreme Court reiterated that "an arbitrator's exclusive jurisdiction extends only to disputes which expressly or inferentially arise out of the collective agreement." The Court went on to cite with approval several decisions where courts entertained damage claims arising out of pre-employment contracts.[208] The Court also approved a Quebec Court of Appeal decision that allowed a bargaining unit member's defamation action against a member of management to proceed.[209] The allegation in the case was that a management member of a joint labour management committee had described the plaintiff as making sexist remarks about a female member of the committee. The Quebec Court of Appeal recently

---

204 *Brown v University of Windsor*, 2016 ONCA 431 at para 45; *British Columbia Teachers' Federation v British Columbia Public School Employers' Association*, 2005 BCCA 92.

205 *Giorno*, above note 190.

206 *Rukavina v Ottawa (Police Services Board)*, 2020 ONCA 533, leave to appeal ref'd 2021 CanLII 22781 (SCC); *Piko v Hudson's Bay Co*, 1998 CanLII 6874 (ON CA).

207 *Horrocks*, above note 190 at para 22. The issue in *Horrocks* is whether or not human rights tribunals have concurrent jurisdiction with labour arbitrators, discussed in Chapter 6.

208 *Goudie v Ottawa (City)*, 2003 SCC 14; *Wainwright v Vancouver Shipyards Co Ltd*, 1987 CanLII 166 (BC CA); *Johnston v Dresser Industries Canada Ltd (CA)*, 1990 CanLII 6808 (ON CA).

209 *Côté v Saiano*, 1998 CanLII 12963 (QC CA).

distinguished its earlier decision on the basis that while in both cases the plaintiff was described as having engaged in sexist conduct, in the latter case, the alleged defamation was made in the course of the defendant carrying out their duties as a representative of the employer, giving arbitrators exclusive jurisdiction.[210]

An action by the Crown was allowed to proceed against a former bargaining unit employee of Ontario Realty concerning allegations that the public servant had participated in a scheme with a second employer to defraud the agency.[211] The court concluded that since the action intertwined with allegations against non-public servants, the conduct complained of was not in relation to his job duties as a public servant but was done as an employee of another employer and he was no longer a public servant, the essential nature of the action did not arise under the collective agreement.

Retired BC public servants, most of whom were former bargaining unit members, were allowed to proceed with a class action over changes to their post-retirement benefits.[212] The post-retirement benefits had been provided under statute. The court concluded "the benefits were never the subject of collective bargaining. They were made available to union and non-union employees alike even before collective bargaining became the norm in the province's civil service" and "will involve arguments as to contract formation, Crown obligation, and statutory interpretation," which do not require the expertise of labour arbitrators.[213] In contrast, a class action regarding administration of a pension plan that covered members of nine bargaining units and some non-union employees was found to fall within the exclusive jurisdiction of labour arbitrators.[214] The pension plan was mentioned in the collective agreements so fell within an arbitrator's jurisdiction notwithstanding the potential procedural problems associated with multiple bargaining units. The dissent focused on the risk of conflicting decisions and the fact the pension plan represented a single fund covering all nine units and unrepresented staff and would have held the matter did not arise out of the individual collective agreements.

---

210 *Pinard v Laplante*, 2022 QCCA 1119.

211 *Ontario Realty Corp v P Gabriele & Sons Ltd*, 2002 CanLII 10638 (ON SC).

212 *Bennett v British Columbia*, 2007 BCCA 5, leave to appeal ref'd 2007 CanLII 67864 (SCC).

213 *Ibid* at para 47.

214 *Bisaillon v Concordia University*, 2006 SCC 19.

Though not subject to collective bargaining legislation, the Crown's lawyers have collectively bargained terms of employment enforceable through private arbitration under the *Arbitrations Act, 1991*.[215] The lawyers' agreements provide for arbitration in language similar to the statutory language in labour legislation. The *Arbitration Act, 1991* at section 6 expressly limits judicial jurisdiction in matters that have been referred to arbitration. Courts should not intervene in matters where there is a remedy available under the lawyers' collective agreements.[216]

215 SO 1991, c 17. See the discussion about Crown lawyers in Chapter 4.
216 *Nelson et al*, above note 11 at para 21.

Bibliography

Books and Articles

AAGAARD, LINSAY. "Fiduciary Duty and Members of Parliament" (2008) 31:2 *Canadian Parliamentary Review* 31.

ADAMS, GEORGE. *Canadian Labour Law*, 2d ed (Aurora, ON: Canada Law Book, 2004).

ADELL, BERNARD, MICHEL GRANT & ALLEN PONAK. *Strikes in Essential Services* (Kingston, ON: IRC Press, Queen's University, 2001).

ALLEN, SIR CARLETON K. *Laws and Orders*, 3d ed (London: Stevens, 1965).

ARNOTT, BRUCE & DEANNA EXNER. *Annotated Occupational Health and Safety Act* (Aurora, ON: Canada Law Book, 2003).

ARTHURS, HARRY W. *Collective Bargaining by Public Employees in Canada: Five Models* (Ann Arbour: University of Michigan, Institute of Labour and Industrial Relations, 1971).

ARULANANTHAN, NIROJA. *An Evaluation of the Ethic of Neutrality in the Ontario Public Service: A Thesis on the Conflict of Interest Process and Its Impact on Public Servants* (2019) Master of Arts Thesis, University of Toronto.

ASSOCIATION OF MANAGEMENT, ADMINISTRATIVE AND PROFESSIONAL CROWN EMPLOYEES OF ONTARIO. *OPS Inclusive Workplace Policy and Program Review*, November 2020, online: amapceo.on.ca/publications.

AUCOIN, PETER. "New Political Governance in Westminster Systems: Impartial Public Administration and Management Performance at Risk" (2012) 25:2 *Governance* 177.

AXWORTHY, THOMAS S. & JULIE BURCH. *Closing the Implementation Gap: Improving Capacity, Accountability, Performance and Human Resource*

Quality in the Canadian and Ontario Public Service (Kingston, ON: Queen's University, Centre for the Study of Democracy, 2010).

BACH, STEPHEN & LORENZO BORDOGNA. *Public Service Management and Employment Relations in Europe: Emerging from the Crisis* (London: Routledge, 2018).

BACH, STEPHEN, ET AL, EDS. *Public Service Employment Relations in Europe: Transformation, Modernization or Inertia?* (London: Routledge, 1999).

BALL, STACEY R. *Canadian Employment Law* (Aurora, ON: Canada Law Book, 1996).

BARNES, LESLIE W.C.S. *Consult and Advise: A History of the National Joint Council of the Public Service of Canada* (Kingston, ON: IRC Press, Queen's University, 1975).

BELL, GEORGE G. & ANDREW D. PASCOE. *The Ontario Government-Structure and Functions* (Toronto: Wall & Thompson, 1988).

BLAKE, SARA. *Administrative Law in Canada*, 7th ed (Toronto: LexisNexis Canada, 2022).

BOROWY, JAN B. "Essential but Precarious: Changing Employment Relationships and Resistance in the Ontario Public Service" in Leah Vosko ed, *Precarious Employment: Understanding Labour Market Insecurity in Canada* (Montreal: McGill-Queen's University Press, 2006) ch 7.

BOURGON, JOCELYNE. *A New Synthesis of Public Administration: Serving in the 21st Century* (Montreal: McGill-Queen's University Press, 2011).

BOYD, BRENDAN, JARED J. WESLEY & ANDREA BOUNCE, ET AL. "The Public Servant's Role in Democracy" (2021) 64:3 *Canadian Public Administration* 423.

BRADLEY, ANTHONY W. & KEITH D. EWING. *Constitutional and Administrative Law* (London: Longman, 1997).

BREDT, CHRISTOPHER D. & CARA F. ZWIBEL. "Public Service of Ontario Act: Sword or Shield?" in Janet E. Minor & J.G. Cowan, eds, *The Six-Minute Administrative Lawyer* (Toronto: Law Society of Upper Canada, 2009).

BROCK, JONATHAN. "United States Public Sector Employment" in Carlo Dell'Aringa et al, eds, *Strategic Choices in Reforming Public Service Employment: An International Handbook* (New York: Palgrave, 2001).

BRODSKY, GWEN, SHELAGH DAY & FRANCES M. KELLY. "The Authority of Human Rights Tribunals to Grant Systemic Remedies" (2017) 6:1 *Canadian Journal of Human Rights* 1.

BROWN, DONALD J.M. & DAVID M. BEATTY. *Canadian Labour Arbitration*, 5th ed (Toronto: Carswell, 2019).

BROWN, DONALD J.M. & JOHN M. EVANS. *Judicial Review of Administrative Action in Canada* (Toronto Carswell, 2009).

BRYANT, MICHAEL J. & LORNE SOSSIN. *Public Law* (Toronto: Carswell, 2002).

CAMERON, DAVID R. & GRAHAM WHITE. *Cycling into Saigon: The Conservative Transition in Ontario* (Vancouver: UBC Press, 2000).

CAMPBELL, ENID. "Oaths and Affirmations of Public Office under English Law: An Historical Retrospect" (2000) 21 *Journal of Legal History* 1.

CAMPOLIETI, MICHELE & CHRIS RIDDELL. "Interest Arbitration and the Narcotic Effect: Evidence from Three Decades of Collective Bargaining in Ontario" (2019) 57:3 *British Journal of Industrial Relations* 421.

CAMPOLIETI, MICHELE, ROBERT HEBDON & BENJAMIN DACHIS. "Collective Bargaining in the Canadian Public Sector, 1978–2008: The Consequences of Restraint and Structural Change" (2016) 54:1 *British Journal of Industrial Relations* 192.

CANADIAN JUDICIAL COUNCIL. *Ethical Principles for Judges (2021)*, 2021 CanLIIDocs 2336.

———. *Why Is Judicial Independence Important to You?* 2016 CanLIIDocs 4688.

CARON, RENÉE. "Merit in Staffing: The Principle and the System" (2000) 9 *Canadian Labour and Employment Law Journal* 459.

CARON, RENÉE. *Employment in the Federal Public Service* (Aurora, ON: Canada Law Book, 2001).

CARSON, JONATHAN. "Two Steps Forward, One Step Back: Legislating Labour Relations in the Ontario Public Service" (2011) *Meetings of the Canadian Political Science Association*, online: www.cpsa-acsp.ca/papers-2009/Carson.pdf.

CARTER, DONALD. "Legal Regulation of Collective Bargaining in the Ontario Public Sector" (1974) 29 *Relations Industrielle/Industrial Relations* 776.

CAVALLUZZO, PAUL J.J. "Strikes in the Public Sector in the Second Millennium—Employee Right or Government Policy?" Cambridge Lecture, 1999, unpublished.

CEYSSENS, PAUL. *Legal Aspects of Policing* (Toronto: Earlscourt Legal Press, 1994).

CEYSSENS, PAUL & SCOTT CHILDS. *Ontario Police Services Act, Fully Annotated* (Toronto: Earlscourt Legal Press, 2017).

CHARIH, MOHAMED & ARTHUR DANIELS. *New Public Management and Public Administration in Canada* (Toronto: IPAC, 1997).

CHAYKOWSKI, RICHARD P. "Labour Relations Policy and Practice, and Regulation of the Right to Strike in the Broader Public Sector: The Implications of Saskatchewan Federation of Labour" (2016) 19:2 *Canadian Labour and Employment Law Journal* 483.

———. *Time to Tweak or Re-boot? Assessing the Interest Arbitration Process in Canadian Industrial Relations*. CD Howe Institute, Commentary 539 (2019), online: www.cdhowe.org/sites/default/files/attachments/research_papers/mixed/Commentary_539pdf.

CHAYKOWSKI, RICHARD P. & ROBERT S. HICKEY. *Reform of the Conduct and Structure of Labour Relations in the Ontario Broader Public Service: Report to the Commission on the Reform of Ontario's Public Service* (Kingston, ON: Queen's University, School of Policy Studies, 2012).

———. "Principles for Labour Relations Policy Reform in the Wake of the Drummond Report on Ontario's Public Services" (2013) 17 *Canadian Labour and Employment Law Journal* 379.

CHITTY, JOSEPH. *Prerogatives of the Crown* (London: Butterworths, 1820).

CLARKE, AMANDA & BENJAMIN PIPER. "A Legal Framework to Govern Online Political Expression by Public Servants" (2018) 22 *Canadian Labour and Employment Law Journal* 21 1.

COLLINS, STEPHANIE B. "The Space in the Rules: Bureaucratic Discretion in the Administration of Ontario Works" *Social Policy and Society* (2015), online: www.cambridge.org/core/journals/social-policy-and-society/article/abs/space-in-the-rules-bureaucratic-discretion-in-the-administration-of-ontario-works/3C5F69180606A693B7DE378704060FF1.

COOPER, CHRISTOPHER A. *At the Pleasure of the Crown: The Politics of Bureaucratic Appointments* (Vancouver: University of British Columbia Press, 2020).

D'ANDREA, JAMES A. *Employee Obligations in Canada* (Aurora, ON: Canada Law Book, 2003).

DAINTITH, TERENCE & ALAN PAGE. *The Executive in the Constitution: Structure, Autonomy and Internal Control* (Oxford: Oxford University Press, 1999).

DALYS, BEVERLY. *No Longer a "Two-Bit" Union: The History of the Ontario Liquor Boards Employees' Union* (OLBEU, 1990).

DAWSON, ROBERT M. *The Civil Service of Canada* (London: Oxford University Press, 1929).

———. *The Government of Canada* (Toronto: University of Toronto Press, 1970).

DELL'ARINGA, CARLO, ET AL, EDS. *Strategic Choices in Reforming Public Service Employment: An International Handbook* (New York: Palgrave, 2001).

DELLER, DEBORAH. "Selection and Appointment of Clerks in Canadian Jurisdictions" (2018) 41:3 *Canadian Parliamentary Review* 2.

DONOVAN, RONALD. *Administering the Taylor Law* (Ithaca: ILR Press, 1990).

DOOREY, DAVID. "The Stubborn Persistence of the Lawyer Exemption in Canadian Collective Bargaining Legislation" (2022) 45:1 *Dalhousie Law Journal* 65.

———. *The Law of Work*, 2d ed (Toronto: Emond Publishing, 2020).

DUSSAULT, RENE & LOUIS BORGEAT. *Administrative Law: A Treatise*, 2d ed, Vol 1 (Toronto: Carswell, 1985).

DUTIL, PATRICE A. *Searching for Leadership: Secretaries to Cabinet in Canada* (Toronto: University of Toronto Press, 2008).

DYZENHAUS, DAVID. "Constituting the Rule of Law: Fundamental Values in Administrative Law" (2002) 27 *Queen's Law Journal* 445.

ELLIOTT, CHERYL. *Ontario's Equity Laws: A Complete Guide to Pay and Employment Equity* (Toronto: Thomson Reuters, 2017).

ELLIS, MARK. *Fiduciary Duties in Canada* (Toronto: Carswell, 2004).

ELLIS, S. RONALD. "Appointments Policies in The Administrative Justice System: Lessons from Ontario: Four Speeches" (1997) 11 *Canadian Journal of Administrative Law and Practice* 205.

———. *Unjust by Design: Canada's Administrative Justice System* (Vancouver: UBC Press, 2013).

ENGLAND, GEOFFREY, PETER BARNACLE & INNIS M. CHRISTIE. *Employment Law in Canada*, 4th ed (Toronto: LexisNexis Canada, 2005).

EVANS, BRYAN. "Capacity, Complexity, and Leadership: Secretaries to Cabinet and Ontario's Project of Modernization at the Centre" in Patrice Dutil, ed, *Searching for Leadership: Secretaries to Cabinet in Canada* (Toronto: University of Toronto Press, 2008) ch 4.

EVANS, BRYAN M. & CARLO FANELLI, EDS. *The Public Sector in an Age of Austerity: Perspectives from Canada's Provinces and Territories* (Montreal: McGill-Queen's University Press, 2018)

FAIRBROTHER, PETER. *Politics and the State as Employer* (London: Mansell, 1994).

FINKELMAN, JACOB, QC. "Public Sector Bargaining: Some Basic Considerations" (1976) 16 *Queen's Law Journal* 14.

FINKELMAN, JACOB & SHIRLEY B. GOLDENBERG. *Collective Bargaining in the Public Service: The Federal Experience in Canada* (Montreal: IRPP, 1983).

FLINDERS, MATTHEW. *The Politics of Accountability in the Modern State* (London: Routledge, 2017).

———. *The Politics of Accountability in the Modern State* (Aldershot: Ashgate, 2001).

FORCESE, CRAIG & AARON FREEMAN. *The Laws of Government: The Legal Foundations of Canadian Democracy* (Toronto: Irwin Law, 2011).

FORD, ROBIN & DAVID ZUSSMAN, ET AL. *Alternative Service Delivery: Sharing Governance in Canada* (Ottawa: KPMG/IPAC, 1997).

FRANKEL, SAUL J. "Staff Relations in the Public Service: The Ghost of Sovereignty" (1959) 2 *Canadian Public Administration* 65.

———. *Staff Relations in the Civil Service: The Canadian Experience* (Montreal: McGill University Press, 1962).

FREDMAN, SANDRA & GILLIAN S. MORRIS. *The State as Employer: Labour Law in the Public Service* (London: Thomson Learning, 1990).

FRIEMAN, MARK. "Convergence of Law and Policy and the Role of the Attorney General" (2002) 16 *Supreme Court Law Review* (2d) 335.

FRYER, JOHN L. "Provincial Public Service Labour Relations" in Gene Swimmer & Mark Thompson, eds, *Public Sector Collective Bargaining in Canada* (Kingston: IRC Press, Queen's University, 1995).

GALL, PETER A., ANDREA L. ZWACK & KATIE BAYNE. "Determining Human Rights Issues in the Unionized Workplace: The Case for Exclusive Arbitral Jurisdiction" (2005) 12 *Canadian Labour and Employment Law Journal* 381.

GILBERT, DOUGLAS & LES LIVERSIDGE. *Workers' Compensation in Ontario: A Guide to the Workplace Safety and Insurance Act* (Aurora, ON: Canada Law Book, 2001).

GOLDENBERG, SHIRLEY. "Collective Bargaining in the Provincial Public Services" in *Collective Bargaining in the Public Service* (Toronto: IPAC, 1973) 11.

GOODSELL, CHARLES. *The New Case for Bureaucracy* (New York: Sage Publications, 2015).

GRUBE, DENNIS. "Responsibility to Be Enthusiastic? Public Servants and the Public Face of Promiscuous Partisanship" (2014) 28:3 *Governance* 305.

GUNDERSON, MORLEY, ED. *Collective Bargaining in the Essential and Public Service Sectors: Proceedings of a Conference* (Toronto: University of Toronto Press, 1975).

GUNDERSON, MORLEY & FRANK REID. "Public Sector Strikes in Canada" in Gene Swimmer & Mark Thompson, eds, *Public Sector Collective Bargaining in Canada* (Kingston, ON: IRC Press, 1995).

HADWEN, TIMOTHY G.M. & ROBIN GORDON. "Strategies to Resolve a Grievance Backlog: The OPSEU/MBS Case Study" (2002) 10 *Canadian Labour and Employment Law Journal* 417.

HAIVEN, LARRY. "Industrial Relations in Health Care: Regulation, Conflict and Transition to the 'Wellness Model'" in Gene Swimmer & Mark Thompson, eds, *Public Sector Collective Bargaining in Canada* (Kingston, ON: IRC Press, 1995) 236.

HANBIDGE, JOHN F. "The History of Labour Relations between the Ontario Crown Attorneys and the Government of Ontario" (1996) 3 *Ontario Crown Attorneys' Association Newsletter* 10.

HEARD, ANDREA. *Canadian Constitutional Conventions: The Marriage of Law and Politics* (Toronto: Oxford University Press, 1991).

HEATH, JOSEPH. *The Machinery of Government: Public Administration and the Liberal State* (New York: Oxford University Press, 2020).

HEBDON, ROBERT. "The Freezing Effect of Public Sector Bargaining: The Case of Ontario Crown Employees" (1995) 24 *Journal of Collective Negotiations in the Public Sector* 233.

HEBDON, ROBERT & MAURICE MAZEROLLE. "Regulating Conflict in Public Sector Labour Relations: The Ontario Experience 1984–1993" (2003) 58 *Relations industrielles/Industrial Relations* 667.

HEBDON, ROBERT & ROBERT STERN. "Tradeoffs Among Expressions of Industrial Conflict: Public Sector Strike Bans and Grievance Arbitrations" (1998) 51:2 *Industrial and Labor Relations Review* 204.

HODGETTS, JOHN E. *From Arms Length to Hands On: The Formative Years of Ontario's Public Service 1867–1940*, Ontario History Series (Toronto: University of Toronto Press, 1995).

———. *Pioneer Public Service: An Administrative History of the United Canadas, 1841–1867* (Toronto: University of Toronto Press, 1956).

———. *The Canadian Public Service: A Physiology of Government: 1867–1970* (Toronto: University of Toronto Press, 1973).

HODGETTS, JOHN E. & ONKAR P. DWIVEDI. *Provincial Governments as Employers: A Survey of Public Personnel Administration in Canada's Provinces* (Toronto: IPAC, 1974).

HOGG, PETER W. *Constitutional Law of Canada* (Toronto: Thomson Carswell, 2007).

HOGG, PETER W. & ALLISON BUSHELL. "The Charter Dialogue Between Courts and Legislatures" (1997) 35 *Osgoode Hall Law Journal* 75.

HOGG, PETER W. & PATRICK MONAHAN. *Liability of the Crown*, 4th ed (Toronto: Carswell, 2011).

HUGHES, KATE & DANIEL WILBAND. "The Blunt Instrument of Labour Injunctions: The Law and Practice in Ontario" Law Society of Upper Canada (2014), online: www.cavalluzzo.com/docs/default-source/publications/the-law-and-practice-regarding-pickets-(c1261777xa0e3a).pdf?sfvrsn=fc955d5_2.

HUNTER, JOSH & SARAH KRAICER. "Keeping the Scales of Justice Balanced—Québec Justices of the Peace and Judicial Independence" (2017) 81 *Supreme Court Law Review* 149.

JONES, DAVID & ANNE S. DE VILLARS. *Principles of Administrative Law*, 4th ed (Toronto: Carswell, 2004).

JUILLET, LUC & KEN RASMUSSEN. *Defending a Contested Ideal: Merit and the PSC of Canada 1908–2008* (University of Ottawa Press, 2008).

KEITH, NORMAN A. *Ontario Health and Safety Law* (Aurora, ON: Canada Law Book, 2004).

KERNAGHAN, KENNETH. "Getting Engaged: Public-Service Merit and Motivation Revisited" (2011) 54:1 *Canadian Public Administration.*

———. "Shaking the Foundation: New Versus Traditional Public Service Values" in Mohamed Charih & Arthur Daniels, eds, *The New Public Management and Public Administration in Canada* (Toronto: IPAC, 1997).

KERNAGHAN, KENNETH & JOHN LANGFORD. *The Responsible Public Servant: Second Edition* (Toronto: IPAC, 2014).

KERNAGHAN, KENNETH & DAVID SIEGEL. "Power, Politics and Bureaucracy" in R.S. Blair & J.T. Mcleod, eds, *The Canadian Political Tradition, Basic Readings*, 2d ed (Scarborough, ON: Nelson Canada, 1993).

KEYES, JOHN M. "Loyalty, Legality and Public Sector Lawyers" (2019) 97:1 *Canadian Bar Review* 129.

KOCHAN, THOMAS, DAVID B. LIPSKY, MARY NEWHART & ALAN BENSON. "The Long Haul Effects of Interest Arbitration: The Case of New York State's Taylor Law" (2010) 63:4 *Industrial and Labour Relations Review* 565.

LEEB, GAVIN. "A Global Experience Up Close and Personal: Ontario Government Workers Resist Privatization" (2002) 9 *Canadian Labour and Employment Law Journal* 1.

LINDQUIST, EVERT A. & GRAHAM WHITE. "Streams, Springs, and Stones: Ontario Public Service Reform in the 1980s and the 1990s" 37:2 *Canadian Public Administration* 267.

LIPSKY, MARTIN. *Street-Level Bureaucracy* (Russell Sage, 1980).

LODGE, GUY & BEN M. ROGERS. *Whitehall's Black Box—Accountability and Performance in the Senior Civil Service* (London: Institute for Public Policy Research, 2006).

MACNEIL, MICHAEL, MICHAEL LYNK & PETER ENGELMANN. *Trade Union Law in Canada* (Toronto: Canada Law Book, Thomson Reuters Canada, 2017).

MAINGOT, JOSEPH P. *Parliamentary Privilege in Canada*, 2d ed (Montreal: McGill-Queen's University Press, 1997).

MALLORY, JAMES R. *The Structure of Canadian Government* (Toronto: MacMillan of Canada, 1971).

MARSHALL, GEOFFREY. *Constitutional Conventions: The Rules and Forms of Political Accountability* (Oxford: Clarendon Press, 2001).

MARTIN, ANDREW F. "The Immunity of the Attorney General to Law Society Discipline" (2016) 94:2 *Canadian Bar Review* 413.

———. "Where Are We Going? The Past and Future of Canadian Scholarship on Legal Ethics for Government Lawyers" (2021) 99:2 *Canadian Bar Review* 322.

MARVY, LEN. "Making Sense of the Numerical Calculations in the Application of Relative Equality Provisions" (2000) 8 *Canadian Labour and Employment Law Journal* 373.

MATTHEWS, KATE. "Neither Fish nor Fowl: The Evolution of the Ontario Crown Attorneys' Association" *Crown's Newsletter*, Vol 8, December 2017.

MCCAULEY, JOCELYN. *Officers of the Assembly and the Ontario Legislature: Reconsidering the Relationship* (July 2020) Master's Research Paper, York University, online: http://yorkspace.library.yorku.ca/xmlui/bitstream/handle/10315/37805/Jocelyn%20McCauley%20-MRP.pdf?sequence=1&isAllowed=y.

MCELLIGOT, GREG. *Beyond Service: State Workers, Public Policy and the Prospects for Democratic Administration* (Toronto: University of Toronto Press, 2001).

MOLOT, HENRY L. "Employment During Good Behaviour and at Pleasure" (1989) 2 *Canadian Journal of Administrative Law and Practice* 238.

———. "Governor in Council Appointees: Employment Based on Statute or Contract" (1999) 13 *Canadian Journal of Administrative Law and Practice* 265.

MULGAN, RICHARD. "Truth in Government and the Politicization of Public Service Advice" (2007) 85:3 *Public Administration* 569.

MULLAN, DAVID. *Administrative Law* (Toronto: Irwin Law, 2001).

MUMMÉ, CLAIRE. "The State Giveth and Taketh Away: Public Sector Labour Law, the Legitimacy of the Legislative Override Power and Constitutional Freedom of Association in Canada" (2020) 36:4 *International Journal of Comparative Labour Law and Industrial Relations* 495.

———. "Unifying the Field: Mapping the Relationship Between Work Law Regimes in Ontario" (2020) 43:2 *Dalhousie Law Journal* 543.

NORTHCOTE, STAFFORD H. & C.E. TREVELYAN. *Report on the Organization of the Permanent Civil Service* (House of Commons, London, 1854).

ONTARIO LIQUOR BOARDS EMPLOYEES UNION. *Celebrating 50 Years* (Toronto: Ontario Liquor Boards Employees Union, 2003).

ORGANISATION FOR ECONOMIC CO-OPERATION AND DEVELOPMENT. *Committing to Effective Whistleblower Protection* (Paris: OECD Publishing, Paris, 2016).

OSBORNE, DAVID & TED GAEBLER. *Reinventing Government: How the Entrepreneurial Spirit is Transforming the Public Sector* (Reading, MA: Addison-Wesley, 1992).

PEIRCE, JON & KAREN J. BENTHAM. *Canadian Industrial Relations,* 3d ed (Toronto: Pearson Education Canada, 2006).

PETERS, B. GUY & JON PIERRE, EDS. *Politicization of the Civil Service in Comparative Perspective* (London, Routledge, 2004).

PETERS, B. GUY & DONALD J. SAVOIE, EDS. *Revitalizing the Public Service: Governance in the 21st Century* (Montreal: McGill-Queen's University Press, 2001).

PHILIPS, PAUL. "Theoretical Problems of Public Interest Sector Industrial Relations" (1976) 31 *Relations industrielles/Industrial Relations* 566.

POND, DAVID. "Legislative Control of Cabinet Appointments to the Public Service: A Canadian Case-Study in the Political Limits to Parliamentary Reform" (2008) 61:1 *Parliamentary Affairs* 52.

RAPAPORT, DAVID. *No Justice, No Peace: The 1996 Ontario Public Service Employees Union Strike Against the Harris Government in Ontario* (Montreal: McGill-Queen's University Press, 1999).

RESHEF, YONATAN & SANDRA RASTIN. *Unions in the Time of Revolution: Government Restructuring in Alberta and Ontario* (Toronto: University of Toronto Press, 2003).

ROBERTS, WAYNE. *Don't Call Me Servant* (Toronto: OPSEU, 1994).

ROSE, JOSEPH B. "Constraints on Public Sector Bargaining in Canada" (2016) 58:1 *Journal of Industrial Relations* 93.

———. "From Softball to Hardball: The Transition in Labour-Management Relations in the Ontario Public Service" in Gene Swimmer, ed, *Public Sector Labour Relations in an Era of Restraint and Restructuring* (Don Mills, ON: Oxford University Press, 2000).

———. "Regulating and Resolving Public Sector Disputes in Canada" (2008) 50:4 *Journal of Industrial Relations* 545.

———. "Regulating Essential Service Disputes in Canada: The Designation Model" (2018) 69:4 *Labor Law Journal* 194.

———. "The Complaining Game: How Effective Is Compulsory Interest Arbitration?" (1994) 23 *Journal of Collective Negotiations in the Public Sector* 187.

RUSSELL, PETER. "Standing Up for Notwithstanding" (1991) 29 *Alberta Law Review* 293.

———. *The Judiciary in Canada: The Third Branch of Government* (Toronto: McGraw-Hill Ryerson, 1987).

SACK, JEFFREY. "Ability to Pay in the Public Sector: A Critical Appraisal" (1991) *Labour Arbitration Yearbook* 277.

SACK, JEFFREY, MICHAEL MITCHELL & SANDRA PRICE. *Ontario Labour Relations Board Law and Practice* (Markham, ON: LexisNexis Canada, 1997).

SAVOIE, DONALD J. "The Canadian Public Service Has a Personality" (2006) 49:3 *Canadian Public Administration* 261.

———. *Breaking the Bargain: Public Servants, Ministers and Parliament* (Toronto: University of Toronto Press, 2003).

SAYWELL, JOHN T. *The Office of the Lieutenant-Governor: A Study in Canadian Government and Politics* (Toronto: University of Toronto Press, 1957).

SCHINDLER, F.F. *Responsible Government in Ontario* (Toronto: University of Toronto Press, 1969).

SHILTON, ELIZABETH. "'Everybody's Business': Human Rights Enforcement and the Union's Duty to Accommodate" (2014) 18 *Canadian Labour and Employment Law Journal* 209.

SOSSIN, LORNE. "Speaking Truth to Power? The Search for Bureaucratic Independence in Canada" (2005) 55 *University of Toronto Law Journal* 1.

———. "The Unfinished Project of Roncarelli v Duplessis: Justiciability, Discretion, and the Limits of the Rule of Law" (2010) 55:3 *McGill Law Journal* 661.

STEWART, SUSAN. "The OPSEU and MCSS Protocol—Expediting Dispute Resolution," unpublished paper.

SULEIMAN, EZRA. *Dismantling Democratic States* (Princeton, NJ: Princeton University Press, 2003).

SUNKIN, MAURICE & SEBASTIAN PAYNE, EDS. *The Nature of the Crown* (New York: Oxford University Press, 1999).

SWAN, KENNETH P. "Safety Belt or Straightjacket? Restrictions on the Scope of Public Sector Bargaining" in Geoffrey England, ed, *Essays on Collective Bargaining and Industrial Democracy* (Don Mills, ON: CCH Canada, 1983).

———. "Whistleblowing, Employee Loyalty and the Right to Criticize: An Arbitrator's Viewpoint" in William Kaplan, ed, *Labour Arbitration Yearbook, Vol 2* (1991).

SWIMMER, GENE, ED. *Public Sector Labour Relations in an Era of Restraint and Restructuring* (Don Mills, ON: Oxford University Press, 2001).

SWIMMER, GENE & MARK THOMPSON, EDS. *Public Sector Collective Bargaining in Canada* (Kingston, ON: IRC Press, 1995).

THOMPSON, MARK & SARA SLINN. "Public Sector Industrial Relations in Canada: Does It Threaten or Sustain Democracy?" (2013) 34 *Comparative Labor Law and Policy Journal* 393.

TODRES, ELAINE M. "Women's Work in Ontario: Pay Equity and the Wage Gap" (1990) 22:3 *Ottawa Law Review* 555.

TUCKER, ERIC. "Regulating Strikes in Essential Services: Canada" in Moti Mironi & Monika Schlachter, eds, *Regulating Strikes in Essential Services: A Comparative 'Law in Action' Perspective* (2019), online: http://ssrn.com/abstract=3277648.

TWEEDSMUIR, LORD (JOHN BUCHAN). "The Civil Service" (Speech to the Civil Service Dinner, Ottawa, 7 October 1937) in *Canadian Occasions, Addresses by Lord Tweedsmuir* (Toronto: Musson, 1941).

WARRIAN, PETER. *Hard Bargain: Transforming Public Sector Labour-Management Relations* (Toronto: McGillian, 1996).

WARSKETT, ROSEMARY. "Law, Regulation, and Becoming 'Uncivil': Contestation and Reconstruction within the Federal Administrative State" in Michael MacNeil et al, eds, *Law, Regulation and Governance* (New York: Oxford University Press, 2002).

WATT, R.A. "The Crown and Its Employees" in Maurice Sunkin & Sandra Payne, eds, *The Nature of the Crown* (Oxford: Oxford University Press, 1999).

WEEKS, PHILLIPA. "The Reshaping of Australian Public Service Employment Law" in Marilyn Pittard & Phillipa Weeks, eds, *Public Sector Employment in the Twenty First Century* (Australian National University E Press, 2007).

WELLINGTON, HARRY H. & RALPH K. WINTER JR. *The Limits of Collective Bargaining in Public Employment* (1969) Faculty Scholarship Series, Yale Law School.

WHEARE, SIR KENNETH. *Modern Constitutions* (Oxford: Oxford University Press, 1951).

WHITE, GRAHAM. "Revolutionary Change in the Ontario Public Service" in Evert A. Lindquist, ed, *Government Restructuring and Career Public Service* (Toronto: IPAC, 2000).

WILSON, HALL T. *Civil Servants and the Future of Capitalist Democracies* (Leiden: Brill, 2001).

WILSON, R. PAUL. "Trust but Verify: Ministerial Policy Advisors and Public Servants in the Government of Canada" (2016) 59:3 *Canadian Public Administration* 337.

ZACKA, BERNARDO. *When the State Meets the Street* (Cambridge, MA: Harvard University Press, 2017).

Ontario Reports and Studies

CIVIL SERVICE COMMISSION. *1996–1997 Annual Report* (Toronto: Management Board of Cabinet, 1997), online: www.gov.on.ca/mbs/english/mbs/civil.

CIVIL SERVICE COMMISSION. *2002–2003 Annual Report* (Toronto: Management Board of Cabinet, 2003).

COMMISSION OF INQUIRY INTO EVENTS OF MARCH 18, 1996 AT QUEEN'S PARK (Willard Z. Estey, QC, Commissioner, Ontario). *Report of the Commission of Inquiry into Events of March 18, 1996 at Queen's Park* (Toronto: Ministry of the Attorney General, 1996).

COMMISSION ON FREEDOM OF INFORMATION AND INDIVIDUAL PRIVACY. *Report of the Commission on Freedom of Information and Individual Privacy: Public Government for Private People* (1980), Vol 2 (Toronto: Ministry of Government Services: J.C. Thatcher, Queen's Printer, 1980).

COMMITTEE ON GOVERNMENT PRODUCTIVITY (COGP). *Interim Report No. 1* (Toronto: Queen's Printer, 1970).

DRUMMOND, DONALD. *Report of the Commission on The Reform of Ontario's Public Service* (Queen's Printer for Ontario, 2012).

GOVERNMENT TASK FORCE ON AGENCIES BOARDS AND COMMISSIONS (Bob Wood, MPP, Chair). *Report on Restructuring Regulatory and Adjudicative Agencies, 1997* (Toronto: The Task Force, 1997).

GRIEVANCE SETTLEMENT BOARD. *Annual Report 2000–2001* (Toronto: The Board, 2002).

———. *Annual Report 2003–2004* (Toronto: The Board, 2005).

———. *Annual Reports 2017–2018* and *2018–2019, 2021–2022*, online: www.psab.gov.on.ca/en/gsb/publications.html.

———. *Business Plan 2022–2023 to 2023–2025*, online: www.psab.gov.on.ca/en/gsb/publications.html.

HEALTH SERVICES RESTRUCTURING COMMISSION. *Looking Back, Looking Forward: The Ontario Health Services Restructuring Commission. A Legacy Report* (2000), online: www.hhr-rhs.ca/en/?option=com_mtree&task=att_download&link_id=5214&cf_id=68.

HUGGINS, ARLENE. "Independent External Review of Complex WDHP Cases" (23 November 2018), online: www.ontario.ca/page/independent-external-review-complex-wdhp-cases#section-2.

KERNAGHAN, KENNETH. *The Future Role of a Professional Non-Partisan Public Service in Ontario* (Toronto: The Panel on the Role of Government in Ontario, Research Paper No 13, 2003), online: www.law-lib.utoronto.ca/investing.

LITTLE, JUDGE WALTER. *Report of the Special Advisor, His Honour Judge Walter Little, on Collective Bargaining in the Ontario Government Service* (Toronto: Queen's Printer, May 1969).

MACLEOD, LESLIE. *Grievance Administration Project, Final Report*, unpublished (Management Board Secretariat, 2000).

MANAGEMENT BOARD SECRETARIAT. *The Ontario Public Service in the 21st Century: Discussion Paper on the Public Service Act* (March 2000).

———. *Updating the Public Service Act: An Overview of Proposed Legislative Amendments* (April 2001).

MARTIN, DIANNE. *Legal Sites of Executive-Police Relations: Core Principles in a Canadian Context* (Toronto: Ipperwash Inquiry/Osgoode Hall Law School Symposium on Police and Government Relations, 28–29 June 2004), online: www.ipperwashinquiry.ca/policy_part/conference.html.

MEWETT, ALAN W. *Report to the Attorney General of Ontario on the Office and Function of the Justices of the Peace in Ontario* (Toronto: Ministry of Attorney General, 1981).

MOHER, W.P. *Managing Human Resources in the Ontario Public Service* (Toronto: Queen's Printer for Ontario, 1986).

OFFICE OF THE INTEGRITY COMMISSIONER OF ONTARIO. *Annual Report 2017–2018*, Commissioner's Message.

———. *Guidance on Political Activity for Ministers' Office Staff.*

ONTARIO. Report of The Commissioners Appointed to Inquire Concerning the Mode of Appointing and Remunerating Certain Provincial Officials Now Paid by Fees and The Extent of The Remuneration They Should Receive, *Ontario Sessional Papers*, 1895, No 081/032 (Toronto: Warwick Bros. and Rutter, 1895).

ONTARIO LAW REFORM COMMISSION. *Report on Political Activity, Public Comment and Disclosure by Crown Employees* (Toronto: Ministry of Attorney General, 1986).

ONTARIO PENSION BOARD. *2020 Annual Report*, online: http://reports.opb.ca/2020/assets/pdf/OPB-2020-Annual-Report.pdf.

ONTARIO PUBLIC SERVICE RESTRUCTURING SECRETARIAT. *Transforming Public Service for the 21st Century: An Ontario Perspective* (Toronto: Queen's Printer, April 2000).

REVIEW INTO THE MEAT REGULATORY AND INSPECTION REGIMES IN ONTARIO (THE HONOURABLE ROLAND J. HAINES, REVIEWER). *Report of the Review into the Meat Regulatory and Inspection Regimes in Ontario* (Toronto: Ministry of the Attorney General, 2004).

ROACH, KENT. *Four Models of Police-Government Relationships* (Ipperwash Inquiry/Osgoode Hall Law School Symposium on Police and Government Relations, 28–29 June 2004), online: http://wayback.archiveit.org/16312/20211208072648/http://www.attorneygeneral.jus.gov.on.ca/inquiries/ipperwash/report/vol_3/index.html.

ROYAL COMMISSION OF INQUIRY INTO LABOUR DISPUTES (COMMISSIONER: IVAN C. RAND), *Report of the Royal Commission of Inquiry into Labour Disputes* (Toronto: Queen's Printer, 1968).

SARS COMMISSION (THE HONOURABLE ARCHIE CAMPBELL, COMMISSIONER). *Second Interim Report—SARS and Public Health Legislation* (Toronto: The Commission, 5 April 2005).

SOSSIN, LORNE. *The Oversight of Executive Police Relations in Canada: The Constitution, the Courts, Administrative Processes and Democratic Governance* (Ipperwash Inquiry/Osgoode Hall Law School Symposium on Police and Government Relations, 28–29 June 2004), online: www.ipperwashinquiry.ca/policy_part/conference.html.

WEILER, PAUL C. *The Professional Employee in Government: A Report to the Honourable Murray Elston Chairman, Management Board of Cabinet, Government of Ontario, on the Appropriate Methods for Establishing Conditions for Professional Employees of the Government of Ontario*, unpublished (January 1988).

Ontario Government Directives and Policies

MANAGEMENT BOARD OF CABINET. *Agencies and Appointments Directive*, 9 February 2018, online: www.ontario.ca/page/agencies-and-appointments-directive.

———. *Compensation Directive*, 20 August 2007, provided to the authors.

———. *Continuation of Existing Classes and Salaries Directive*, 12 May 2017, online: www.ontario.ca/page/continuation-existing-classes-and-salaries-directive.

———. *Disclosure of Wrongdoing Directive—Employees/Appointees of Public Bodies (i.e., Agencies)*, 12 May 2017, online: www.ontario.ca/page/disclosure-wrong-doing-directive-employees-appointees-public-bodies-ie-agencies.

———. *Human Resources Management Directive*, 12 May 2017, online: www.ontario.ca/page/human-resources-management-directive.

———. *Merit Increases Directive*, 12 May 2017, online: www.ontario.ca/page/merit-increases-directive.

———. *Perquisites Directive*, 12 May 2017, online: www.ontario.ca/page/perquisites-directive.

———. *Respectful Workplace Policy (Policy to Support a Respectful Workplace and Prevent Workplace Harassment and Discrimination)*, 1 October 2017, copy made available to authors.

———. *Salary Rates/Ranges Directive*, 12 May 2017, online: www.ontario.ca/page/salary-rates-ranges-directive.

———. *Hours of Work Directive*, 12 May 2017, online: www.ontario.ca/page/hours-work-directive.

———. *Travel, Meal, and Hospitality Expenses Directive*, November 2004, online: www.ontario.ca/page/travel-meal-and-hospitality-expenses-directive-2020.

———. *Recruitment and Selection for Senior Management Group Employees Operating Policy*, June 1999.

ONTARIO PUBLIC SERVICE. *OPS Anti-Racism Policy*, 2 April 2018, online: www.ontario.ca/page/ontario-public-service-anti-racism-policy#antiracismpolicy.

PUBLIC SERVICE COMMISSION. *Employment Policy*, effective 6 November 2020, provided to the authors.

———. *Classification and Position Administration Directive*, effective 1 November 2012, provided to the authors.

———. *Disclosure of Wrongdoing Directive—Employees in Ministries / Ministers' Offices*, 12 May 2017, online: www.ontario.ca/page/disclosure-wrongdoing-directive-employees-ministries-ministers-offices.

———. *Human Resources Management Delegation of Authority Directive*, 12 May 2017, online: www.ontario.ca/page/human-resources-managment-delegation-authority-directive.

Federal Reports and Studies

ADVISORY COMMITTEE ON LABOUR MANAGEMENT RELATIONS IN THE FEDERAL PUBLIC SERVICE. *Identifying the Issues: First Report* (Ottawa: The Committee, May 2000).

———. *Working Together in the Public Interest, Final Report* (Ottawa: The Committee, June 2001).

ARTHURS, HARRY W. *Labour Disputes in Essential Services* (Ottawa: Privy Council Office, 1968).

CANADA LAW REFORM COMMISSION. *Legal Status of the Police, Study Paper* (Ottawa: The Commission, 1981).

COMMISSION OF INQUIRY INTO THE SPONSORSHIP PROGRAM & ADVERTISING ACTIVITIES (JOHN H. GOMERY, COMMISSIONER). (Ottawa: Privy Council, 2005), Vol. 1, *Who Is Responsible?*

———. (Ottawa: Privy Council, 2006), Vol 2, *Restoring Accountability.*

GOW, IAIN. *A Canadian Model of Public Administration* (Ottawa: Canada School of Public Service, 2004).

PRIVY COUNCIL OFFICE. *Guidelines for Deputy Ministers* (Ottawa: Queen's Printer, 2001).

ROYAL COMMISSION OF INQUIRY ON FINANCIAL MANAGEMENT AND ACCOUNTABILITY (LAMBERT COMMISSION). *Final Report* (Ottawa: Supply and Services Canada, 1979).

SOSSIN, LORNE. "Defining Boundaries: The Constitutional Argument for Bureaucratic Independence and Its Implications for the Accountability of the Public Service," in Commission of Inquiry into The Sponsorship Program & Advertising Activities (John H. Gomery, Commissioner), (Ottawa: Privy Council, 2005), *Research Studies, Vol 2* (2006).

TASK FORCE ON PUBLIC SERVICE VALUES AND ETHICS (JOHN TAIT, CHAIR). *A Strong Foundation: Report of the Task Force on Public Service Values and Ethics* (Ottawa: Canadian Centre for Management Development, February 2000).

WORKING GROUP ON DISCLOSURE OF WRONGDOING. *Report of the Working Group on Disclosure of Wrongdoing* (Ottawa: Public Service Human Resources Management Agency, 2003), online: www.hrma-agrh.gc.ca/reports-rapports/wgdw-gtdaf_e.asp.

Table of Cases

Index

Note: Page numbers followed by "n" with numbers refer to footnotes.

About the Authors

Tim Hadwen is a retired public servant and labour lawyer. He held a range of senior management positions in the Ontario Ministries of Education, Health, Government Services, and the Attorney General. His public service responsibilities included managing the government's involvement in broader public sector labour relations. He led the implementation of the *School Boards' Collective Bargaining Act, 2014*, the merger of the staff of the Community Care Access Centres with the Local Health Integration Networks, and several compensation restraint initiatives.

Prior to joining government, Tim was General Counsel for the Ontario Public Service Employees Union and Assistant Director, Arbitration at the Ontario Nurses' Association. Formerly, he was a partner at Cavalluzzo, Hayes and Shilton, a leading union-side labour law firm.

David Strang, BA, LLB, LLM, was called to the Bar in 1981 after articling with the union-side firm of Maclean Chercover. He began his career as Ontario coordinator and counsel with the Upholsterers International Union then moved to the Laborers International Union of America Provincial District Council as counsel and assistant manager. In 1989 he joined the Legal Branch of the Ontario Ministry of Labour. In 1993 he transferred to the Labour Practice Group seconded by the Attorney General to provide advice and represent the Crown in its role as employer of the Ontario Public Service. He has regularly represented the Crown in grievance arbitrations and other labour and employment litigation and negotiations, including those leading to AMAPCEO's original voluntary recognition agreement and OPSEU's Appendix 18. He frequently advised on labour and employment issues raised by proposed policy initiatives and was seconded to the Ministry of Education to advise on the development and implementation of the *School Boards Collective Bargaining Act*. Since retirement in 2016, he has engaged in a part-time labour and employment practice representing Crown agencies in the community health sector.

FSC
www.fsc.org
MIX
Papier | Fördert gute Waldnutzung
FSC® C083411

Kolibri 360 GmbH
Ferdinand-Jühlke-Straße 7
99095 Erfurt, Deutschland
produktsicherheit@kolibri360.de